Fodor's up CLOSE

SPAIN

the complete guide, thoroughly up-to-date

SAVVY TRAVELING: WHERE TO SPEND, HOW TO SAVE

packed with details that will make your trip

CULTURAL TIPS: ESSENTIAL LOCAL DO'S AND TABOOS

must-see sights, on and off the beaten path

INSIDER SECRETS: WHAT'S HIP AND WHAT TO SKIP

the buzz on restaurants, the lowdown on lodgings

FIND YOUR WAY WITH CLEAR AND EASY-TO-USE MAPS

FODOR'S TRAVEL PUBLICATIONS

NEW YORK • TORONTO • LONDON • SYDNEY • AUCKLAND

www.fodors.com

First Edition

ISBN 0–679–00667–2

ISSN: 1531—3395

FODOR'S UPCLOSE™ SPAIN

EDITOR: Christine Cipriani

Editorial Contributors: Shane Christensen, Michael de Zayas, Nikko Hinderstein, Edward Owen, AnneLise Sorensen, Robert I.C. Fisher, Rebecca Miller Ffrench, Conrad Paulus

Editorial Production: Tom Holton

Maps: David Lindroth, *cartographer*; Rebecca Baer, *map editor*

Design: Fabrizio La Rocca, *creative director*; Tigist Getachew, *cover and text design*; Jolie Novak, *senior picture editor*; Melanie Marin, *photo editor*

Production/Manufacturing: Angela L. McLean

Cover Art: Dimitri Cleek/Masterfile (La Sagrada Familia, Barcelona)

SPECIAL SALES

Fodor's upCLOSE™ Guides and all Fodor's Travel Publications are available at special discounts for bulk purchases for sales promotions or premiums. Special editions, including personalized covers, excerpts of existing guides, and corporate imprints, can be created in large quantities for special needs. For more information, contact your local bookseller or write to Special Markets, Fodor's Travel Publications, 280 Park Avenue, New York, NY 10017. Inquiries from Canada should be directed to your local Canadian bookseller or sent to Random House of Canada, Ltd., Marketing Department, 1265 Aerowood Drive, Mississauga, Ontario L4W 1B9. Inquiries from the United Kingdom should be sent to Fodor's Travel Publications, 20 Vauxhall Bridge Road, London SW1V 2SA, England.

PRINTED IN THE UNITED STATES OF AMERICA

10 9 8 7 6 5 4 3 2 1

CONTENTS

I. BASICS *1*

2. MADRID 24

3. OLD AND NEW CASTILE 75

4. THE BASQUE COUNTRY 114

5. CANTABRIA AND ASTURIAS 155

6. GALICIA 184

7. EXTREMADURA 214

8. ANDALUSIA 239

9. THE CANARY ISLANDS 308

10. VALENCIA AND MURCIA 341

11. THE BALEARIC ISLANDS 368

12. BARCELONA 386

13. CATALONIA 439

14. ARAGÓN 479

15. NAVARRE AND LA RIOJA 498

INDEX 518

TRAVELING UPCLOSE

ave dinner at 10 PM. Pad through a quiet cathedral. Hike the Pyrenees. Plunge into a fiesta. Climb a medieval fortress and survey the plains below. Memorize the symphony of the streets—then get lost. And if you want to experience the heart and soul of Spain, whatever you do, don't spend too much money.

The deep, rich experience of Spain for which your traveler's heart yearns is something money can't buy. Going lavish is the surest way to keep yourself on the sidelines. Three-star restaurants are great, but they don't serve tapas. Deluxe hotels have their place, but not when your beige room could be anywhere from San Sebastián to Seattle. Better to hang your hat in a place with the atmosphere you've come so far to experience.

In short, if you want to see Spain up close and savor the essence of its people and culture, this book is for you. We'll show you the offbeat sights, the bars and cafés where locals hang out, and the *hostales* and pensions where you'll meet fellow travelers. And because you probably want to see the famous places, too, we give you tips on losing the crowds, not to mention quirky and obscure background facts.

OUR GANG

Who are we? We're a bunch of writers who share a certain footloose spirit and a passion for all things Spanish. Some of us live in Spain, while others never turn down the chance to venture back to the plains and *palacios*, valleys and villages, beaches and bars. We've revealed all of our favorite places *and* made it clear where we made wrong turns, so you can learn from our mistakes and experience Spain to the fullest. If you can't take your best friend on the road, or if your best friend is hopeless with directions, stick with us.

Fodor's veteran **Shane Christensen** has covered parts of Argentina, Brazil, Ecuador, and Paraguay. No sooner did he finish writing up the Balearic Islands than the U.S. State Department called and appointed Shane to the Foreign Service. He is now back in Washington, D.C., feverishly studying Farsi in preparation for his posting in Dubai.

Editor **Christine Cipriani** put on reporter's boots for this book and fell in love with all things Galician, especially Santiago de Compostela, the amazing sun showers, the green, hilly countryside, and Albariño wine.

After graduating from Sarah Lawrence College with a master's degree in poetry, **Michael de Zayas** moved to Barcelona, where he heard rumors of wild parties going on elsewhere in Spain. He strapped on a backpack and set off on a yearlong odyssey of *sevillanas* (flamenco-style dancing), *encierros* (bull runs), and *calimocho* wine of dubious quality—raw material towards his own book on Spanish fiestas. Having subsequently authored four chapters of *upCLOSE Spain*, Michael is recovering, and writing, in New York.

Nikko Hinderstein first traveled to Spain in 1989 and has yet to be captivated by another European country—she returns each year to see old friends and "new" hidden treasures. A background in cooking and studio art inspires her to climb castles, taste local wines, discover unknown museums in the hinterlands, stay up too late at fiestas, and take note when, on rare occasion, her Spanish food is served with a garnish.

Raised in Cornwall, England, journalist **Edward Owen** has worked in London, Toronto, Sydney, and, since 1980, Madrid. Long a foreign correspondent for London's *Times, Sunday Times*, and *Daily Express*, he now specializes in travel, wine, and gastronomy. Extolling the Spanish climate and the Spaniards' vim and vigor, Ed leads a mean, drink-till-you-drop tapas crawl that doubles as a cure for jet lag.

It was only a matter of time before **AnneLise Sorensen,** half Danish and half Catalan, went to live in her ancestral region, surrounded by aunts, uncles, cousins, and *la Avia* (Grandma)—she now splits her year between San Francisco and Barcelona. Fortified by *tallat* (coffee with a dash of cream) and *pan amb tomaquet* (bread smothered with tomato and olive oil), AnneLise covered all of northeastern Spain for us. In past lives she wrote about San Francisco, Ireland, and Northern Ireland for various Fodor's guides; future plans include holing herself up in a riverside *hostal* to write a travel novella.

A SEND-OFF

Always call ahead. We knock ourselves out to check all the facts, but things change constantly in ways that no one can fully anticipate. Especially if you're making a once-in-a-lifetime trip, call, call ahead. Trust us on this one.

And if something still doesn't go quite right, as inevitably happens with even the best-laid plans, stay cool. Missed your bus? Stuck in the airport? Use the time to study the people. Chat with a stranger. Study the newsstands or flip through a local publication. Take a walk. Find the silver lining in the clouds, whatever it is. And do send us a postcard to tell us what went wrong and what went right. You can e-mail us at: editors@fodors.com (specify *upCLOSE Spain* on the subject line) or write the *upCLOSE Spain* editor at Fodor's upCLOSE, 280 Park Ave., New York, NY 10017. We'll put your ideas to good use and let other travelers benefit from your experiences. In the meantime, *buen viaje*!

INTRODUCTION

Spain and its exuberant way of life have much to teach the astute traveler. Listen up and loosen up: These Mediterranean peoples are direct descendants of the ancient Greeks and Romans, born to *carpe diem*. *A vivir que son dos dias* (live it up; life is short) is Spanish for Horace's "Seize the day," and indeed Spaniards often seem intent on seizing two at a time. Pleasure and passion are at least as key as profession here—people work to live rather than live to work. Aesthetic values tend to eclipse practical ones, dinners and conversations last as long as they need to, and sleep is just a chance to gather strength for a new assault on living life to its fullest. Why are dinner and bedtime so late? There's too much to do! Don't fight it— take a leisurely walk with no destination in mind, linger over dinner until midnight, and dance until dawn.

In imagining the Spanish landscape, you may picture the scorched, orange plains of La Mancha, where Don Quixote tilted, or the softly rolling hills of Andalusia, or even the overdeveloped beaches of the Costa del Sol. But after Switzerland, Spain is the most mountainous country in Europe, and also one of the most geographically diverse, ranging from the soggy northwest (wetter than Ireland) to the haunting plains of the central *meseta*, from the cascading trout streams of the Pyrenees to the marshes and dunes of Doñana National Park, on the Costa de la Luz. There are deep caves, lonely coves, rock canyons, mountain meadows, coastal rice paddies, volcanic island peaks . . . and, of course, the great, snowy wall of the Pyrenees, separating Spain from France and northern Europe.

More than almost any other country its size—it's the second largest in Europe, after France—Spain is characterized by the distinctness of its parts and peoples. The Galicians of the northwest are descended from the same Celtic tribes that colonized the British Isles. Bagpipes are a local instrument, and kilts not unknown; and the local language, Gallego, is a mixture of Spanish and Portuguese. The Basque country, whose eastern end abuts the French border, also has its own language, Euskera, a tongue so mysterious that linguists have never agreed where it began. Local pride is fierce here; the Basque language and culture are purposefully celebrated, and independentist sentiment is strong. Outright separatism is embodied in the terrorist group ETA (Euskadi Ta Askatasuna), which has killed almost 900 Spaniards over the past three decades. (The violence is extremely unlikely to affect travelers.) The Catalans, who populate northeastern Spain around Barcelona, speak the country's most substantial regional language, Catalan, which is closer to Provençal French than to Castilian (Spanish); residents of the province of Valencia and the Balearic islands speak and study in their own local versions of Catalan. All of these areas suffered systematic cultural and linguistic repression under the totalitarian centralist pressure of the Franco regime.

The story of this land, a romance-tinged tale of counts, caliphs, crusaders, and kings, begins long before written history. The Basques were among the first here, huddling in the cold mountain valleys of the north. The Iberians came next, apparently crossing the Mediterranean from North Africa around 3,000 BC. The Celts arrived from the north about a thousand years later. The seafaring Phoenicians founded Gadir (now Cádiz) and several coastal cities in the south. The parade continued with the Greeks, who settled parts of the east coast, and then the Carthaginians, who founded Cartagena around 225 BC—and who dubbed the then-wild, forested country Spania.

Modern civilization really began with the Romans, who expelled the Carthaginians and turned the peninsula into three imperial provinces. It took the Romans 200 years to subdue the fiercely resisting Celts, Iberians, and Basques—ending shortly before the birth of Christ—but their influence was lasting. Evidence of the Roman epoch is left today in the great ruins at Mérida, Segovia, Tarragona, and other cities; in the peninsula's legal system; and in the Latin base of its three Romance languages. In the early 5th century, various invading barbarians crossed the Pyrenees to attack the weakening Roman empire. The Visigoths became the dominant force in northern Spain by 419, establishing their kingdom at Toledo and eventually adopting Christianity.

But they, too, were to fall before a wave of invaders, this time that of the Moors, a Berber-led Arab force that crossed the Strait of Gibraltar from North Africa. The Moors swept through Spain in an astonishingly short time, meeting only token resistance and launching almost eight centuries of Muslim rule—a period that in many respects was the pinnacle of Spanish civilization. Unlike the semibarbaric Visigoths, the Moors were extremely cultured. Arabs, Jews, and Christians lived together in peace during their reign, although many Christians did convert to Islam.

The Moors never managed to subdue northwestern Galicia and Asturias, and it was in the latter that a minor Christian king, Pelayo, began the long crusade that came to be known as the Reconquista (Reconquest). By 1085, Alfonso VI of Castile had captured Toledo, giving the Christians a firm grip on the north. In the 13th century, Valencia, Seville, and finally Córdoba—the capital of the Muslim caliphate in Spain—fell to Christian forces, leaving only Granada in Moorish hands. Two hundred years later, two Catholic monarchs, Ferdinand of Aragón and Isabella of Castile, were joined in a marriage that would change the world.

The year 1492 is a watershed in Spanish history, the beginning of the nation's political golden age and the moment of some of its worst excesses of intolerance. That year, the 23rd of Ferdinand and Isabella's marriage, Christian forces conquered Granada and unified all of current-day Spain as a single kingdom. Jews and Muslims who did not convert to Christianity were expelled from the country en masse. Christopher Columbus, under the sponsorship of Isabella, landed in the Americas, initiating the Age of Exploration; but the departure of educated Muslims and Jews was a blow to the nation's economy from which it would never recover. The Inquisition, which had been established in 1478, further persecuted those who chose to stay. The colonies of the New World greatly enriched Spain at first, but massive shipments of Peruvian and Mexican gold later produced terrible inflation. The so-called Catholic Monarchs and their centralizing successors maintained Spain's unity, but they sacrificed the spirit of international free trade that was beginning to bring capitalist prosperity to other parts of Europe.

Ferdinand and Isabella were succeeded by their grandson Carlos, who became the first Spanish Habsburg and one of the most powerful rulers in history. Cortés reached Mexico and Pizarro conquered Peru under his rule. Carlos also inherited Austria and the Netherlands and in 1519, three years into his reign, was elected Holy Roman Emperor (as Charles V), wasting little time in annexing Naples and Milan. He championed the Counter-Reformation and saw the Jesuit order created to help defend Catholicism against European Protestantism. But Charles cost the nation with his penchant for waging war, particularly against the Ottomans and German Lutherans. His son, Philip II, followed in the same expensive path, ultimately defeating the Turks and ordering the construction of the somber Escorial monastery, outside Madrid. It was here that Philip died, 10 years after losing the Spanish Armada in an attack on Protestant England.

The War of the Spanish Succession was ignited by the death, without issue, in 1700 of Charles II, the last Spanish Habsburg. Philip of Anjou was crowned Philip V and inaugurated the Bourbon line in Spain (a representative of which sits on the throne today). The Bourbons of that era, a Frenchified lot, copied many of the attitudes and fashions of their northern neighbors, but the infatuation ended with Napoleon's 1808 installation of his brother, José Bonaparte. Mocked bitterly as "Pepe Botella" for his fondness for drink (*botella* means "bottle"), Bonaparte was widely despised, and an 1808 uprising against him in Madrid—chronicled harrowingly by the great painter Francisco de Goya y Lucientes (1746–1828)—began the War of Independence, known to foreigners as the Peninsular War. Britain, siding with Spain, sent the Duke of Wellington to the rescue. With the aid of Spanish guerrillas, the French were finally expelled, but not before they had looted Spain's major churches and cathedrals. Most of Spain's American colonies took advantage of the war to claim their independence.

The rest of the century was not a happy one for Spain, as conservative regimes grappled with civil wars and revolts inspired by currents of European republicanism. The final blow came with the loss of Cuba, Puerto Rico, and the Philippines in 1898, a military disaster that ironically sparked a remarkable literary renaissance—the so-called Generation of '98, whose members included writers Miguel de Unamuno and Pío Baroja and poet Antonio Machado. In 1902 Alfonso XIII came to the throne, but rising civil strife got the better of him and ended in his self-imposed exile in 1931. A fledgling republic followed, to the delight of most Spaniards, but the 1936 election of a left-wing Popular Front government ignited bitter opposition from the right. In the end, a young general named Francisco Franco used the assassination of a monarchist leader as an excuse for a military revolt.

The Spanish Civil War (1936–39) was the single most tragic episode in Spanish history. More than half a million people died in the conflict. Intellectuals and leftists the world over sympathized with the elected government, and the International Brigades (with many American, British, and Canadian volunteers) took part in some of the worst fighting, including the storied defense of Madrid. But Franco, backed by the Catholic Church, got far more help from Nazi Germany, whose Condor legions destroyed the Basque town of Guerníca (in a horror made infamous by Picasso's monumental painting), and from Fascist Italy. For three years, European governments stood quietly by as Franco's armies vanquished Barcelona, Madrid, and the last capital of the Republic, Valencia.

Unofficially sympathetic to the Axis powers during World War II, Spain was largely shunned by the world until the United States agreed in 1953 to provide aid in exchange for land on which to build NATO bases. Gradually, the shattered economy began to pick up, especially with the surge of tourism that gathered steam in the late 1960s. But when Franco announced in 1969 that his successor would be Juan Carlos, the grandson of Alfonso XIII and a prince whose militaristic education had been strictly overseen by the aging general, the hopes of a nation longing for freedom sagged.

Imagine the Spaniards' surprise when, six years later, Franco died and the young monarch revealed himself to be a closet democrat. Under his nurturing, a new constitution restoring civil liberties and freedom of expression was adopted in 1978. On February 23, 1981, the king proved his mettle once and for all, when a nostalgic Civil Guard colonel with visions of a return to Franco's authoritarian regime held the Spanish parliament captive for some 24 hours. Only the heroism of King Juan Carlos, who personally called military commanders across the country to ensure their loyalty to the elected government, quelled the coup attempt. The Socialists ruled Spain from 1982 until early 1996, when conservative José María Aznar was elected prime minister.

The post-Franco renaissance has been not just political and economic (Spain joined the European Union in 1986) but also creative. Whereas the first third of the century—before the 40-year cultural silence of the Franco regime—produced such towering figures as poet Federico García Lorca, filmmaker Luis Buñuel, and painters Pablo Picasso, Joan Miró, and Salvador Dalí, the last quarter will be known for novelist Camilo José Cela's 1989 Nobel Prize, filmmaker Pedro Almodóvar's postmodern Spanish films, Basque sculptor Eduardo Chillida's blocky forms, and the conceptual works of Catalan painter Antoni Tapiès, not to mention the international performing artists Plácido Domingo and José Carreras.

When you get here, take the country as the Spanish do, piece by piece. Spain at the turn of the 21st century is a patchwork of cultures and nationalities: Andalusia and Catalonia are as different as France and England, maybe more so. The miracle is that a common language and a central government have managed to bring these "Autonomous Communities" as close together as they are. Castilians, Basques, Galicians, Asturians, Catalans, and Andalusians all contribute separately and equally to a Spain that begins the new millennium as one of the most vibrant nations in Europe.

SPAIN

Bay of Biscay

Ferrol
A Coruña
Vilalba
Ribadeo
Luarca
Gijón
Ribadesella
Santander
Oviedo
Cangas
de Onís
PICOS DE
EUROPA
Bilbao
Santiago de
Compostela
Lugo
Mieres
Muros
C A N T A B R I A N
M T S .
Pontevedra
Ponferrada
León
Burgos
Logro
Vigo
Ourense
Astorga
Tui
Benavente
Palencia
Valladolid
Zamora
Tordesillas
Duero
Salamanca
Adanero
Segovia
SIERRA DE GUADARRAM
Avila
Guadalajar
Ciudad
Rodrigo
El Escorial
MADRID
P O R T U G A L
SIERRA DE GREDOS
Toledo
Tara
Plasencia
Talavera
de la Reina
Aranjuez
Tajo
Guadalupe
Alcázar de
San Juan
Trujillo
Guadiana
Ciudad
Real
Abenójar
Valdepeñas
Badajoz
Almadén
Jerez de los
Caballeros
Zafra
SIERRA MORENA
Fregenal
de la Sierra
Bailén
Linares
Ubed
Córdoba
Baeza
Ca
Aroche
Jaén
Guadalquivir
Ecija
Baena
Seville
Carmona
Guadix
Lucena
Granada
Huelva
Antequera
Loja
SIERRA
*Gulf of
Cadiz*
Sanlúcar de
Barrameda
Ronda
Nerja
COSTA DE LA LUZ
Jerez de
la Frontera
Torremolinos
Motril
*ATLANTIC
OCEAN*
Estepona
Fuengirola
Marbella
COSTA DEL SOL
Algeciras
Gibraltar
TO CANARY
ISLANDS
Strait of Gibraltar

SPAIN

FRANCE

San Sebastián
Hondarribia
Roncesvalles
Vitoria
Pamplona
Jaca
PYRENEES
ANDORRA
ogroño
Huesca
La Seu d'Urgell
Figueres
Tudela
Barbastro
Vic
Gerona
Soria
Ebro
Zaragoza
Manresa
COSTA BRAVA
RRAMA
Calatayud
Lleida
Montserrat
Medinaceli
Daroca
Alcañiz
Barcelona
ajara
Tajo
Caminreal
Tarragona
COSTA DORADA
Monreal del Campo
Tortosa
Teruel
La Jana
Vinaròs
Balearic Sea
TO MINORCA →
Tarancón
Cuenca
Castellón de la Plana
COSTA DEL AZAHAR
Palma
de
ñ
Jucar
Sagunto
Majorca
Requena
Valencia
Ibiza
BALEARIC ISLANDS
Albacete
Eivissa
Alcaraz
Hellín
Alicante
Formentera
Segura
Elche
COSTA BLANCA
Minorca
eda
Orihuela
Ciutadella
Cazorla
Murcia
Mahón
Lorca
Manga del Mar Menor
NEVADA
Cartagena
Mediterranean Sea
A
Almería
COSTA DE ALMERIA
ALGERIA
N
0   100 miles
0   150 km

XIII

Bay of Biscay

A Coruña
A CORUÑA
LUGO
Gijón
Oviedo
Santander
VIZCAYA
Santiago de Compostela
ASTURIAS
CANTABRIA
Bilbao
Lugo
León
BURGOS
LA R
Pontevedra
GALICIA
LEON
PALENCIA
Palencia
Burgos
PONTEVEDRA
Ourense
OURENSE
ZAMORA
Valladolid
VALLADOLID
Duero
S
Zamora
CASTILE-LEON
Salamanca
SEGOVIA
GUAI
SALAMANCA
Segovia
PORTUGAL
AVILA
Ávila
Guadalajara
MADRID
R
MADRID
Toledo
CACERES
Tajo
TOLEDO
Aranjuez
Trujillo
CASTILE-LA MANCH
EXTREMADURA
Alcázar
Guadiana
CIUDAD REAL
Badajoz
Ciudad Real
BADAJOZ
Valdepeñas
CORDOBA
Córdoba
JAEN
HUELVA
Guadalquivir
Jaén
ANDALUSIA
SEVILLE
Granada
Huelva
Seville
Antequera
GRANADA
COSTA DE LA LUZ
Jerez
MALAGA
ATLANTIC OCEAN
CADIZ
COSTA DEL SOL
Gibraltar

EUSKADI (BASQUE COUNTRY)

San Sebastián

YA

GUIPUZCOA

Vitoria
ALAVA   Pamplona

TREVIÑO   **NAVARRE**

Logroño

A RIOJA

Soria

SORIA

GUADALAJARA

ra   Tajo

FRANCE

ANDORRA

HUESCA
Huesca   LLEIDA   GIRONA

CATALONIA

Zaragoza   Lleida   Girona

ARAGON   BARCELONA   COSTA BRAVA

ZARAGOZA   Barcelona

TARRAGONA   Tarragona

TERUEL   Tortosa   COSTA DORADA

Teruel   CASTELLON

Cuenca   Balearic Sea   TO MINORCA →

CUENCA

ICHA   Castellón de la Plana

Valencia

Requena   COSTA DEL AZAHAR

VALENCIA   Ibiza   Palma

Albacete   Mallorca

ALBACETE   ALICANTE   BALEARIC ISLANDS

Alicante   Eivissa

COSTA BLANCA   Formentera

MURCIA   Minorca

Murcia   Ciutadella   Mahón

Lorca

Cartagena

Mediterranean Sea

ALMERIA

Almería

COSTA DE ALMERIA

N

ALGERIA

KEY

—·—·— Regions
——— Provinces
⊙ Provincial capitals

0   50 miles
0   75 km

BASICS

BY EDWARD OWEN

AIR TRAVEL

Regular nonstop flights serve Spain from the eastern United States; flying time from New York is seven hours. Flying from other North American cities usually involves a stop.

Flights from the United Kingdom to Spain are more frequent, serve small cities as well as large ones, and are priced very competitively. Flying time from London is just over two hours. If you're coming from North America and would like to land in a city other than Madrid or Barcelona, consider flying a British or other European carrier (just know that you may have to stay overnight in London or another European city on your way home). There are no direct flights to Spain from Australia or New Zealand.

Major carriers, including American, Delta, US Airways, Iberia, and United, provide regular service from the United States. Most flights from the U.S. go through New York, Washington, or Miami, but American has daily direct flights from Dallas–Fort Worth, and US Airways flies from Philadelphia (reserve well in advance). Many carriers serve London and other European capitals daily, but if you shop among Madrid travel agencies, you'll probably find better deals than those available abroad, especially to and from Great Britain.

There are numerous daily flights *within* Spain.

AIRLINES

FROM THE U.S. • **Air Europa** (tel. 888/238–7672, www.air-europa.com). **American** (tel. 800/433–7300, www.aa.com). **Continental** (tel. 800/231–0856, www.continental.com). **Delta** (tel. 800/221–1212, www.delta-air.com). **Iberia** (tel. 800/772–4642, www.iberia.com). **Spanair** (tel. 888/545–5757, www.spanair.com). **TWA** (tel. 800/892–4141, www.twa.com). **US Airways** (tel. 800/622–1015, www.usairways.com).

FROM THE U.K. • **Air Europa** (tel. 902/401501, www.air-europa.com) to Madrid. **British Airways** (tel. 0345/222111, www.britishairways.com) to Alicante, Barcelona, Bilbao, Madrid, Málaga, Murcia, Seville, and Valencia. **British Midland** (tel. 0870/607–0555, www.britishmidland.com) to Madrid. **Easy-Jet** (tel. 902/299992, www.easyJet.com) to Barcelona, Madrid, and Palma de Mallorca. **Go** (tel. 901/333500, www.go-fly.com) to Alicante, Barcelona, Bilbao, Ibiza, Madrid, Málaga, and Palma de Mallorca. **Iberia** (tel. 0207/830–0011, www.iberia.com) to Alicante, Barcelona, Bilbao, La Coruña, Madrid, Málaga, Santiago de Compostela, Seville, and Valencia.

OFFICES IN SPAIN • **Air Europa** (tel. 902/401501, www.air-europa.com). **American Airlines** (tel. 91/598–2068, www.aa.com). **British Airways** (tel. 902/111333, www.british airways.com). **Continental** (tel. 91/559–2520, wwwcontinental.com). **British Midland** (tel., shared with Lufthansa, 902/220101, www.britishmidland.com) to Madrid. **Delta** (tel. 91/577–650, www.delta-air.com). **EasyJet** (tel. 902/299992, www.easJet.com). **Go** (tel. 901/333500, www.go-fly.com). **Iberia** (tel. 902/400-500, www.iberia.com). **Spanair** (tel. 902/131415, www.spanair.com). **TWA** (tel. 91/310–3094, www.twa.com). **US Airways** (tel. 91/444–4700, www.usairways.com).

WITHIN SPAIN • **Air Europa** (tel. 902/401501, www.air-europa.com). **Iberia** (tel. 902/400500, www.iberia.com). **Spanair** (tel. 902/131415, www.spanair.com).

AIRPORTS

Most flights from the U.S. and Canada land in, or pass through, Madrid's Barajas (MAD). The other major gateway is Barcelona's El Prat de Llobregat (BCN). From the U.K. and elsewhere in Europe, regular flights also land in Málaga (AGP), Alicante (ALC), Palma de Mallorca (PMI), and on Gran Canaria (LPA) and Tenerife (TFN).

INFORMATION • Madrid: **Barajas** (tel. 91/305–8343). Barcelona: **El Prat de Llobregat** (tel. 93/298–3838).

CHECK-IN AND BOARDING

Airlines routinely overbook planes, on the assumption that not everyone with a ticket will show up. When everyone does, airlines ask for volunteers to give up their seats; these volunteers usually get a certificate for a free flight and are rebooked on the next flight out. If there are not enough volunteers, the airline must choose who will be denied boarding. The first to get bumped are passengers who checked in late and those flying on discounted tickets—so **get to the gate and check in as early as possible,** especially during peak periods.

Always **bring a passport and government-issued photo I.D. to the airport**, as it will likely be required for check-in.

CUTTING COSTS

The cheapest airfares to Spain must usually be purchased in advance and are nonrefundable. **When you're quoted a good price, book it on the spot**—the same fare may not be available the next day. Budget airlines really only have a few seats at their advertised bargain prices, so book as early as possible. Always **check different routings** or look into using different airports. Travel agents, especially low-fare specialists (*see* Discounts & Deals, *below*), can be helpful.

Consolidators are another good source: they buy tickets for scheduled international flights at reduced rates from the airlines, then sell them at prices that beat the best fare available directly from the airlines, usually without restrictions. Sometimes you can even get your money back if you need to return the ticket. Carefully read the fine print detailing penalties for changes and cancellations, and **confirm your consolidator reservation with the airline.**

CONSOLIDATORS • **Cheap Tickets** (tel. 800/377–1000). **Discount Airline Ticket Service** (tel. 800/576–1600). **Unitravel** (tel. 800/325–2222). **Up & Away Travel** (tel. 212/889–2345). **World Travel Network** (tel. 800/409–6753).

DISCOUNT PASSES

If you buy a round-trip transatlantic ticket from Iberia (*see above*), you might want to purchase a **Visit Spain pass,** good for four domestic flights during your stay. You must purchase the pass before you arrive in Spain, and book all flights in advance; the cost is $260 ($350 if you include flights to the Canary Islands), less $20–$50 if you travel between October 1 and June 14.

On certain days of the week, Iberia also offers *minitarifas* (minifares), which can save you 40% on domestic flights. You must buy tickets in advance and stay over Saturday night.

DUTY-FREE SHOPPING

Duty-free shopping is no longer possible within the European Union, but if you're flying out of the E.U., you can often reclaim the V.A.T. (I.V.A. in Spain) tax that you paid on goods worth more than 15,000 ptas. See Taxes, *below*.

ENJOYING THE FLIGHT

For more legroom, **request a seat in the emergency aisle** (as long as you don't mind being responsible for handling the door in an emergency). Try not to sit just in front of the emergency aisle or in front of a bulkhead, as seats may not recline. If you have special dietary needs, such as vegetarian, low-cholesterol, or kosher meals, **ask for special meals when you reserve**. To fight jet lag on long flights, try to maintain a normal routine: **get some sleep at night**. By day, **eat light meals, drink water** (not alcohol), and **move around the cabin** to stretch your legs.

The Spanish predilection for cigarettes notwithstanding, most airlines serving the country, including Iberia, do not allow smoking on either international or domestic flights.

HOW TO COMPLAIN

If your baggage goes astray or your flight goes awry, complain right away. Most carriers require that you **file a claim immediately. Iberia** has a special number in Spain for lost property (tel. 91/305–4598).

AIRLINE COMPLAINTS • U.S. Department of Transportation **Aviation Consumer Protection Division** (C-75, Room 4107, Washington, DC 20590, tel. 202/366–2220, airconsumer@ost.dot.gov, www.dot.gov/airconsumer). **Federal Aviation Administration Consumer Hotline** (tel. 800/322–7873).

BIKE TRAVEL

Long distances, an abundance of hilly terrain, and climate (hot summers, rainy winters) make touring Spain by bike less than ideal. That said, Spain's numerous nature reserves are perfect for mountain biking, especially in spring and fall, and many have specially marked bike paths.

Throughout Spain, it's generally better to **rent a bike locally** than deal with the logistics of bringing your own, as bikes are not usually allowed on long-distance trains; to bring one on, you need to reserve a sleeping berth, pack your bike up, and check it as luggage. On regional trains, you can only lug the bike at certain times of the day. To find out which regional trains accept bikes, ask for the RENFE leaflet "Transporte de bicicletas" in Madrid or consult RENFE's Web site (www.renfe.es).

BIKES IN FLIGHT

Most airlines accommodate bikes as luggage, provided they're dismantled and boxed. You'll pay about U.S.$5 for a bike box (often free at bike shops), and at least $100 for a bike bag. You can sometimes substitute a bike for a piece of checked luggage at no charge; otherwise, the cost is about $100.

BOAT AND FERRY TRAVEL

Regular car ferries connect the U.K. with northern Spain. Brittany Ferries sails from Portsmouth to Santander; P&O European Ferries sails from Plymouth to Bilbao. Spain's major car-ferry line, Trasmediterránea, connects mainland Spain to the Balearic and Canary Islands. If you want to drive from Spain to Morocco, you can take a Trasmediterránea or Buquebus car ferry from Málaga, Algeciras, or Tarifa; both lines also offer a catamaran service that takes half the time of the standard ferry.

INFORMATION • In the U.K.: **Brittany Ferries** (tel. 0990–360360). **P&O European Ferries** (tel. 0990/980555).

In Spain: **Brittany Ferries** (tel. 942/220000). **Buquebus** (tel. 902/414242). **P&O European** Ferries (tel. 94/423–4477). **Trasmediterránea** (tel. 902/454645).

BUS TRAVEL

Within Spain, a vast array of private companies provides bus service that ranges from knee-crunchingly basic to fairly luxurious. (See the appropriate chapters for the names of the companies serving each region.) Fares are lower than the corresponding train fares, and service is more extensive: if you want to reach a town not served by train, you can be sure a bus will go there. Smaller towns don't usually have a central bus depot, so ask the tourist office where to wait for the bus to your destination. Note that service is less frequent on weekends.

It's a long journey to Spain by bus from London or Paris, but the buses are modern, and the fares are a fraction of what you'd pay to fly.

FROM THE U.K. • **Eurolines/National Express** (tel. 01582/404511 or 0990/143219).

BUSINESS HOURS

BANKS & OFFICES

Banks are generally open weekdays from 9 to 2 and Saturday from 8:30 or 9 to 1. In the summer, most banks close at 1 PM on weekdays and stay closed on Saturday. Currency exchanges at airports and train stations stay open later; you can also cash traveler's checks at El Corte Inglés department stores until 9 PM. Most government offices, including post offices, are open weekdays from 9 to 2 only. Office hours are usually 9–2 and 4–7 except from June to August, when the heat dictates *horas intensivas* (intensive hours): 8 to 3 only.

MUSEUMS AND SIGHTS

Most museums are open from 9:30 to 2 and 4 to 7 every day but Monday. Schedules vary, of course, and change for the high and low seasons, so **confirm opening hours** before you plan your day. A few large museums, such as Madrid's Prado and Reina Sofía and Barcelona's Picasso Museum, stay open all day.

PHARMACIES

Pharmacies keep normal business hours (9–1:30 and 5–8), but every town, or city neighborhood, has a duty pharmacy that stays open 24 hours.

SHOPS

When planning a shopping trip, remember that **almost all stores in Spain close for at least three hours midday.** The only exceptions are large supermarkets and the department-store chain El Corte Inglés. Stores are generally open from 9 or 10 to 1:30 and from 5 to 8. Most shops are closed on Sunday, and in Madrid and several other places they're also closed Saturday afternoon. That said, larger shops in tourist areas may stay open Sunday in summer and during the Christmas holiday.

CAMERAS & PHOTOGRAPHY

Spain's multifarious landscapes lend themselves to memorable snapshots. Short of leaving the lens cap on, or hitting Galicia on a particularly dark day, it's hard to take bad pictures here. You'll probably get the best outdoor pictures in the early morning and evening, as harsh midday sun can make contrasts excessive. On the beach, remember that reflected glare can confuse your light meter.

Note that some museums and monuments prohibit photography; others ban the use of flash or a tripod. You are not allowed to take photographs of military installations, nor should you take pictures of police.

EQUIPMENT / PRECAUTIONS

All major brands of film are readily available in Spain, and at reasonable prices. Try to buy film in large stores or photography shops such as the chain **Aquí**, as film sold in smaller outlets may be out of date or stored in poor conditions.

To have film developed, **look for shops displaying the Kodak Q-Lab sign,** a guarantee of quality. If you're in a hurry and happen to be in a large town or resort, you will, of course, find shops that will process film in a few hours. Always **keep your film out of the sun,** and once you've exposed it, develop it immediately or keep it as cool as possible. X-ray machines in Spanish airports are said to be film-safe.

VIDEO

Video systems in Spain are on the PAL system, used in Britain and much of continental Europe (though not France). Tapes for other systems are hard to come by, so take a good supply with you. In airports, **keep videotapes away from metal detectors.**

INFORMATION • Kodak Information Center (tel. 800/242–2424). The *Kodak Guide to Shooting Great Travel Pictures* is available in bookstores or from Fodor's Travel Publications (tel. 800/533–6478; $16.50 plus $5.50 shipping).

CAR RENTAL

Avis, Hertz, Budget, and National (the latter partnered in Spain with the Spanish agency Atesa) all have branches at major Spanish airports and in Spain's larger cities. Smaller, regional companies offer lower rates. All agencies have a wide range of models, but virtually all cars in Spain have a manual transmission—**if you don't want to drive a stick shift, reserve weeks in advance and specify automatic transmission,** then **call again to confirm** your automatic car before you leave for Spain. Rates in Madrid begin at the equivalents of U.S.$55 a day and $240 a week for an economy car with air-conditioning, manual transmission, and unlimited mileage. Add to this a 16% tax on car rentals.

For cheap deals, **look into wholesalers,** companies that do not own fleets but rent in bulk from those that do. These firms often have better rates than traditional agencies, though you must pay said rates before you leave home.

INTERNATIONAL AGENCIES • Alamo (tel. 800/522–9696; 0208/759–6200 in the U.K.). **Avis** (tel. 800/331–1084; 800/879–2847 in Canada; 02/9353–9000 in Australia; 09-525-1982 in New Zealand). **Budget** (tel. 800/527–0700; 0144/227–6266 in the U.K.). **Dollar** (tel. 800/800–6000; 0208/897–0811 in the U.K., where it is known as **Eurodollar**; 02/9223–1444 in Australia). **Hertz** (tel. 800/654–3001; 800/263–0600 in Canada; 0208/897–2072 in the U.K.; 02/9669–2444 in Australia; 03/358–6777 in New Zealand. **National** (tel. 800/227–3876; 0208/750–2800 or 0845/722–2525 in the U.K.).

IN SPAIN • National/Atesa (tel. 902/100101).

WHOLESALERS • Auto Europe (tel. 207/842–2000 or 800/223–5555, fax 800/235–6321, www.autoeurope.com). **Europe by Car** (tel. 212/581–3040 or 800/223–1516, fax 212/246–1458, www.europebycar.com). **DER Travel Services** (9501 W. Devon Ave, Rosemont, IL 60018, tel. 800/782–2424, fax 800/282–7474 for information; 800/860-9944 for brochures, www.dertravel.com). **Kemwel Holiday Autos** (tel. 800/678–0678, fax 914/825–3160, www.kemwel.com).

INSURANCE

When driving a rental car, you are generally responsible for any damage to or loss of the vehicle. The collision policies sold with European rentals usually do not cover theft; before you buy insurance from the rental agency, see what coverage your personal auto-insurance policy and credit cards provide.

REQUIREMENTS AND RESTRICTIONS

Your own driver's license is valid in Spain, but you may want to get an International Driver's Permit for extra assurance. Permits are available from the American or Canadian automobile association, or, in the United Kingdom, from the Automobile Association or Royal Automobile Club. Note that while anyone over 18 with a valid license can drive in Spain, some rental agencies will not rent cars to drivers under 21.

SURCHARGES

Before you pick up a car in one city and leave it in another, **ask about drop-off charges or one-way service fees,** which can be substantial. Note, too, that some rental agencies charge extra if you return the car *before* the time specified in your contract. To avoid a hefty refueling fee, **fill the tank just before you return the car,** remembering that gas stations near the rental outlet are likely to overcharge.

CHILDREN IN SPAIN

Children are greatly indulged in Spain. You'll see kids accompanying their parents everywhere, including bars and restaurants, so bringing yours along should not be a problem. Shopkeepers will shower visiting children with *caramelos* (sweets), and even the coldest waiters tend to be friendlier when you have a youngster with you. And although you won't be shunted into a far corner if you bring kids into a Spanish restaurant, **you won't find high chairs or special children's menus.** Children are expected to eat what their parents do, so it's perfectly acceptable to ask for an extra plate and share your food. Be prepared for late bedtimes, especially in summer—it's common to see toddlers playing cheerfully outdoors until midnight. Hotels can often refer you to an independent baby-sitter (*canguro*). If you decide to rent a car, **arrange for a car seat when you reserve.**

FLYING

If your kids are two or older, **ask about children's airfares.** As a general rule, infants under two who will not occupy a seat fly at greatly reduced fares, or even free. If you're traveling with infants, **confirm carry-on allowances when you reserve**. In general, for babies charged 10% of the adult fare you are allowed one carry-on bag and a collapsible stroller; if the flight is full, the stroller may have to be checked or you may be limited to less.

Experts agree that it's a good idea to use safety seats aloft for children weighing less than 40 pounds. Airlines set their own policies; U.S. carriers usually require that the child be ticketed, even if he or she is young enough to ride free, because the seats must be strapped into regular seats. **Check your air-**

line's policy on using safety seats during takeoff and landing. And since safety seats are not allowed everywhere in the plane, get your seat assignments early.

FOOD

Visiting children may turn up their noses at some of Spain's regional specialties. Although kids seldom get their own menus, most restaurants are happy to provide simple dishes, such as plain grilled chicken, steak, or fried potatoes, for the little ones. *Pescadito frito* (batter-fried fish) is one Spanish dish that most kids do seem to enjoy. If all else fails, familiar fast-food chains such as McDonald's, Burger King, and Pizza Hut are well represented in the major cities and popular resorts.

LODGING

Most hotels in Spain allow children under a certain age to stay in their parents' room at no extra charge, but others charge them as extra adults. **Find out the cutoff age for children's discounts.**

COMPUTERS ON THE ROAD

Virtually every Spanish town with at least one traffic light has at least one cybercafé, most with hourly rates under 500 ptas. If you need to bring your computer, bring an adapter and junction plug for use with Spanish phone sockets, and also an adapter and transformer, if necessary for Spain's 220v sockets (*see* Electricity, *below*). Only a few high-end hotels, mainly in the major cities, provide data ports for Internet access in guest rooms.

CONSUMER PROTECTION

Whenever shopping or buying travel services in Spain, **pay with a major credit card** so you can cancel payment or get reimbursed if there's a problem. If you're doing business with a travel company for the first time, **contact your local Better Business Bureau and the attorney general's office** in your own state and the company's home state—have any complaints been filed? Finally, if you're buying a package or tour, always **consider travel insurance** that includes default coverage (*see* Insurance, *below*).

Council of Better Business Bureaus (4200 Wilson Blvd., Suite 800, Arlington, VA 22203, tel. 703/276–0100, fax 703/525–8277, www.bbb.org).

CUSTOMS & DUTIES

Keep receipts for all purchases. Upon reentering your home country, **be ready to show customs officials what you've bought.** If you feel a duty is incorrect, or you object to the way your clearance was handled, note the inspector's badge number and ask to see a supervisor. If the problem isn't resolved, write to the appropriate authorities, beginning with the port director at your point of entry.

From countries that are not part of the European Union, visitors age 15 and over may enter Spain duty-free with up to 200 cigarettes or 50 cigars, up to one liter of alcohol over 22 proof, and up to two liters of wine. Dogs and cats are admitted as long as they have up-to-date vaccination records from their home country.

AUSTRALIA

Australian residents 18 or older may bring home $A400 worth of souvenirs and gifts (including jewelry), 250 cigarettes or 250 grams of tobacco, and 1,125 ml of alcohol (including wine, beer, and spirits). Residents under 18 may bring back $A200 worth of goods. Prohibited items include meat products. Seeds, plants, and fruits need to be declared upon arrival.

INFORMATION • Australian Customs Service (Regional Director, Box 8, Sydney, NSW 2001, tel. 02/9213–2000, fax 02/9213–4000).

CANADA

Residents who have been out of Canada for at least 7 days may bring home C$500 worth of goods duty-free. If you've been away less than 7 days but more than 48 hours, the duty-free allowance drops to C$200; if your trip lasts 24–48 hours, the allowance is C$50. You may not pool allowances with family members. Goods claimed under the C$500 exemption may follow you by mail; those claimed under the lesser exemptions must accompany you. Alcohol and tobacco products may be included in the 7-day and 48-hour exemptions but not in the 24-hour exemption. If you meet the age requirements of the province or territory through which you reenter Canada, you may bring in, duty-free, 1.14 liters (40 imperial ounces) of wine or liquor *or* 24 12-ounce cans or bottles of beer or ale. If you are 16 or older you may bring in, duty-free, 200 cigarettes and 50 cigars. Check ahead of time with Revenue Canada or the Department of Agriculture for policies regarding meat products, seeds, plants, and fruits.

You may send an unlimited number of gifts worth up to C$60 each duty-free to Canada. Label the package **unsolicited gift—value under $60.** Alcohol and tobacco are excluded.

INFORMATION • Revenue Canada (2265 St. Laurent Blvd., Ottawa, Ontario K1G 4K3, tel. 613/993–0534; 800/461–9999 in Canada, fax 613/957–8911, www.ccra-adrc.gc.ca).

NEW ZEALAND

Homeward-bound residents 17 or older may bring back $700 worth of souvenirs and gifts. Your duty-free allowance also includes 4.5 liters of wine or beer; one 1,125-ml bottle of spirits; and either 200 cigarettes, 250 grams of tobacco, 50 cigars, or a combination of the three up to 250 grams. Prohibited items include meat products, seeds, plants, and fruit.

INFORMATION • New Zealand Customs (Custom House, 50 Anzac Ave., Box 29, Auckland, tel. 09/359–6655, fax 09/359–6732).

UNITED KINGDOM

Residents who have traveled only within the European Union need not pass through customs upon returning to the U.K. If you plan to come home with large quantities of alcohol or tobacco, check EU limits beforehand.

INFORMATION • HM Customs and Excise (Dorset House, Stamford St., Bromley, Kent, tel. 0207/202–4227).

UNITED STATES

Residents who have been out of the country for at least 48 hours (and who have not used the $400 allowance or any part of it in the past 30 days) may bring home $400 worth of foreign goods duty-free.

U.S. residents 21 and older may bring back 1 liter of alcohol duty-free. In addition, regardless of your age, you are allowed 200 cigarettes and 100 non-Cuban cigars. Antiques, which the U.S. Customs Service defines as objects more than 100 years old, enter duty-free, as do original works of art done entirely by hand, including paintings, drawings, and sculptures.

You may also send packages home duty-free: up to $200 worth of goods for personal use, with a limit of one parcel per addressee per day (except alcohol or tobacco products or perfume worth more than $5); label the package **personal use** and attach a list of its contents and their retail value. Do not label the package **unsolicited gift** or your duty-free exemption will drop to $100. Mailed items do not affect your duty-free allowance on your return.

U.S. Customs Service (1300 Pennsylvania Ave. NW, Washington, DC 20229, www.customs.gov; inquiries: tel. 202/354–1000).

DINING

Spaniards love to eat out, and restaurants in Spain have evolved dramatically thanks to a favorable economic climate and burgeoning tourism. A new generation of Spanish chefs—some with international reputations—has transformed classic dishes to suit contemporary tastes, drawing on some of the freshest ingredients in Europe.

The restaurants in this book have been chosen because they offer great value. Most offer a fixed-price meal menu—the *menú del día*, or menu of the day—at lunchtime, and occasionally at dinnertime as well. Because the entrée selections are usually classic regional dishes, these menus are a wonderfully economic way to sample Spain's awesome gastronomic variety.

MEALS

Most restaurants in Spain do not serve breakfast (*desayuno*). For a morning jolt of coffee and toast, or perhaps a croissant, head to a bar or a so-called cafeteria between 6 and 11:30 AM. Lunch (*almuerzo* or *comida*), usually served between 1:30 and 3:30, traditionally consists of an appetizer (soup, salad, or vegetable), a main course (usually without vegetables but perhaps with potatoes), and dessert, followed by coffee. On many *menús del día,* coffee—which is the real thing in Spain, no kidding around—is an alternative to dessert, and alcohol costs extra. *Tapas* (appetizers, finger food) are taken at a bar early in the evening. The best bars give you a free tapa with a drink; you can then order a larger portions, or *ración*, of the same treat. Usually the choices and prices are well displayed; sometimes the tapas themselves are arrayed on the counter, in which case you need only point at the ones you want. Dinner (*cena*) is usually served between 9 and 11 PM and can be rather light, with perhaps only one course. If you can't hold out till 9, make the most of the tapas hour.

PAYING

Credit cards are widely accepted in Spanish restaurants. If you pay by credit card, **tip your server in cash.** Restaurant checks almost always include service, but this is *not* the same as a voluntary tip. The maximum tip is about 10%; many Spaniards leave less.

RESERVATIONS

We mention these only when they're essential. For popular restaurants, call as early as you can.

REGIONAL CUISINE

Spain does not have a single cuisine, but rather various cuisines representing its distinct regional cultures. Spain's most famous dish, paella, originated in Valencia and is not actually prevalent throughout the country. Basque and Catalan cooking are considered the finest in Spain—Basque cuisine centers on fresh fish and meat dishes, while Catalan cooking revolves around vegetables and interesting sauces. Galician cuisine is a bit simpler, but centers on equally fresh fish and shellfish. The roasts of central Castile are renowned, as are the fried fish and the cold soups—*gazpacho* and the almond-based *ajo blanco*—of Andalusia. The classic winter dish in Madrid and many other parts of Spain is the *cocido*, a hearty stew eaten in two parts: the soup, then the meat.

BOOZE

Unbeknownst to many, Spain is the world's largest vineyard, and now produces better-value wines (*vinos*) than its neighbors, including good full-bodied reds (*tintos*) from Ribera del Duero, lighter reds from La Rioja, rosés (*rosados*) from Navarre and Catalonia, and whites—*blancos*—from Rueda, Catalonia, Galicia, and La Mancha. Galicia's fresh, fruity white *Albariño* is pricey but deluxe with local seafood. In Asturias, hard cider (*sidra*) is king, and has a grainier, more apple-y texture than its British counterpart. The Basque Country makes a light, slightly fizzy white wine called *txakoli*. Many set menus include wine, which in summer can be a table red mixed with carbonated lemonade (*gaseosa*) to make a poor man's sangria. Sangria itself, served in jugs, can be surreptitiously strong; it's made with red wine, lemonade, sliced fruit, ice, cinnamon, and shots of spirits and liqueurs. (Don't touch the sangria left sitting around in some bars.)

Jerez de la Frontera, the home of sherry, is Europe's largest producer of brandy (*coñac*), and Catalonia the world's major source of *cava* (white sparkling wine). Spain produces many brands of lager (*cerveza*), the most popular of which are San Miguel, Cruzcampo, Aguila, and Mahou.

The drinking age is 16.

DISABILITIES & ACCESSIBILITY

Unfortunately, Spain has done little to make traveling easy for people with disabilities. In Madrid only the Prado and some newer museums, such as the Reina Sofia and Thyssen-Bornemisza, have wheelchair-accessible entrances or elevators. Most of the churches, castles, and monasteries on a sightseer's itinerary involve quite a bit of walking, often on uneven terrain.

RESERVATIONS

When discussing accessibility with an operator or reservations agent, **ask hard questions.** Are there any stairs, inside *or* out? Are there grab bars next to the toilet *and* in the shower/tub? How wide is the doorway to the room? To the bathroom? For the most extensive facilities, **opt for newer accommodations.**

In the United States, the Americans with Disabilities Act requires that travel agencies serve the needs of all travelers. Some firms specialize in working with people with disabilities.

TRAVEL AGENCIES

Access Adventures (206 Chestnut Ridge Rd., Rochester, NY 14624, 716/889–9096, dltravel@prodigy. net), run by a former physical-rehabilitation counselor. **CareVacations** (5-5110 50th Ave., Leduc, Alberta, Canada T9E 6V4, tel. 780/986–6404 or 877/478–7827, fax 780/986–8332, www.carevacations.com), for group tours and cruise vacations. **Flying Wheels Travel** (143 W. Bridge St., Box 382, Owatonna, MN 55060, tel. 507/451–5005 or 800/535–6790, fax 507/451–1685, thq@ll.net, www.flyingwheels.com). **Hinsdale Travel Service** (201 E. Ogden Ave., Suite 100, Hinsdale, IL 60521, tel. 630/325–1335, fax 630/325–1342, hinstrvl@interaccess.com).

COMPLAINTS • **Disability Rights Section** (U.S. Department of Justice, Civil Rights Division, Box 66738, Washington, DC 20035-6738, tel. 202/514–0301 or 800/514-0301); **TTY** (tel. 202/514–0301 or 800/514–0301, fax 202/307–1198 for general complaints). **Aviation Consumer Protection Division,** (see Air Travel, above) for airline-related problems. **Civil Rights Office** (U.S. Department of Transportation, Departmental Office of Civil Rights, S-30, 400 7th St. SW, Room 10215, Washington, DC 20590, tel. 202/366–4648, fax 202/366–9371), for problems with surface transportation.

DISCOUNTS & DEALS

Be a smart shopper: compare all your options before making decisions. A plane ticket bought with a promotional coupon from a travel club, coupon book, or direct-mail offer may not be cheaper than the least expensive fare from a discount-ticket agency. What you get is as important as what you save.

AIRLINE TICKETS

Try **800/FLY–4–LESS** and **800/FLY–ASAP**.

PACKAGE DEALS

Don't confuse package vacations with guided tours. When you buy a package—say, a plane ticket and several days' lodging—you travel on your own, just as though you had planned the trip yourself. Fly-and-drive packages combine airfare and car rental. If you **buy a rail/drive pass**, you might save on train tickets and car rentals. All Eurail- and Europass holders get a discount on Eurostar fares through the Channel Tunnel.

DRIVING

Driving is the best way to see Spain's rural areas and get off the beaten track. The main cities are connected by a network of excellent four-lane *autovías* (freeways) and *autopistas* (toll freeways; "toll" is *peaje*), which are designated with the letter A and have speed limits of up to 120 km (74 mph). The letter N indicates a *carretera nacional* (basic national route), which may have two or four lanes. Smaller towns and villages are connected by a network of secondary roads maintained to varying standards by the regional, provincial, and local governments.

Spain's major routes bear heavy traffic, especially during holiday periods. Drive with care, and don't get intimidated: the roads are shared by a potentially perilous mixture of Spanish drivers, slow-moving trucks and farm vehicles, suicidal bicyclists (even on freeways), Moroccans en route between France and North Africa, and, of course, tourists, some of whom are accustomed to driving on the left side of the road. In the summer, be prepared, too, for extremely heavy traffic on national coastal routes—when they're only two lanes wide, you can creep along for hours.

AUTO CLUBS

IN SPAIN • **Real Automobile Club de España** (C. José Abascal 10, Madrid, tel. 91/594–7400 office, 900/112222 for breakdown assistance).

OVERSEAS • **American Automobile Association** (AAA, tel. 800/564–6222).

Australian Automobile Association (AAA, tel. 02/6247–7311).

Automobile Association (U.K.) (AA, tel. 0990/500600).

Canadian Automobile Association (CAA, tel. 613/247–0117).

New Zealand Automobile Association (NZAA, tel. 09/377–4660).

Royal Automobile Club (U.K.) (RAC, tel. 0990/722722 for membership; tel. 0345/121345 for insurance).

EMERGENCIES

The rental agencies Hertz and Avis have 24-hour breakdown service. If you belong to AAA, CAA, or AA, you're eligible for emergency assistance from their Spanish counterpart, RACE (tel. 900/112222).

FUEL

In cities, it can be difficult to locate gas stations, but outside town they're plentiful. Some stations on major routes are open 24 hours. Most stations require self-service, though prices are the same as those at full-service pumps. You punch in the amount of gas you want (in pesetas, not liters), unhook the nozzle, pump the poison, then pay—only at night must you pay before you fill up. Most pumps give you a choice of gas, including leaded, unleaded, and diesel, so **be careful to pump the right kind of fuel** for your car. All newer cars in Spain use *gasolina sin plomo* (unleaded gas), which is available in 95 and 98 octane. *Super,* or regular 97-octane leaded gas, is being phased out. Prices vary little between stations; at press time they averaged 138 ptas. a liter for *sin plomo* (unleaded, 95 octane), 148 ptas. a liter for super, and 152 ptas. a liter for unleaded, 98 octane. Credit cards are widely accepted.

MAPS

Detailed road maps are readily available at bookstores and gas stations. The annual *Guía Campsa* atlas lists hotels, restaurants, and gas stations.

ROADS

Spain's highway system includes some 6,000 km (3,600 mi) of beautifully maintained superhighways. Still, you'll find stretches of major national highways that are only two lanes wide, where traffic often backs up behind slooooooow, heavy trucks that you'll find difficult to pass. *Autopista* tolls are steep.

The morning and evening rush hours are notoriously long and congested in and around Madrid and Barcelona. If possible, **avoid rush hour,** which can last until 11 AM (hey, this is Spain) and, in the evening, from 7 to 9.

RULES OF THE ROAD

Always carry your driver's license, passport or I.D. card, and insurance when driving. Spaniards drive on the right side of the road and **yield to the right when in doubt,** except on traffic circles or roundabouts. Horns are banned in cities, but that doesn't keep Spaniards from blasting away. Speed limits are 50 kph (31 mph) in cities, 100 kph (62 mph) on N roads, 120 kph (74 mph) on the *autopista* or *autovía,* and, unless otherwise signposted, 90 kph (56 mph) on other roads. Seat belts are compulsory, and children under 10 may not ride in the front seat.

The Spanish highway police are particularly vigilant about speeding and illegal passing. Fines start at 15,000 ptas. and go up according to your speed—and the police can legally demand payment from non-Spanish drivers on the spot. While it's true that local drivers, especially in cities like Madrid, will park their cars just about anywhere, you should **park only in legal spots.** Parking fines are steep—from 15,000 to over 30,000 ptas. if your car is towed away, resulting in fines, hassle, and wasted time.

SAFETY

Important: Never leave *anything* of value in your car, not even in the trunk. Thieves can spot a rental car a mile away, and seem to be able to smell what's inside it. Especially around airports, cities, and coastal freeways, **be extremely wary if someone tries to flag you down or offers to help with an alleged tire puncture**—he has distraction and theft in mind. Women passengers occasionally have their bags snatched through car windows at traffic lights.

ELECTRICITY

To use electric equipment from the United States, **bring a converter and adapter.** Spain's electrical current is 220 volts, 50 cycles alternating current (AC); the wall outlets take Continental plugs, with two round prongs.

If your appliances are dual-voltage, you'll need only an adapter. Do not use 110-volt outlets, marked FOR SHAVERS ONLY, for high-wattage appliances such as hair dryers. Most laptop computers operate equally well on 110 and 220 volts, so they require only an adapter; but modem use also requires a special adapter for Spanish phone sockets. *See* Computers on the Road, *above.*

EMBASSIES

For national embassies in Spain, *see* Basics *in* Chapter 2. The consular-services department in your embassy can help if your passport gets lost or stolen; they cannot provide money or airline tickets.

EMERGENCIES

The pan-European **emergency phone number 112** is operative in most of Spain. If it doesn't work, dial the emergency numbers below for the national police, local police, fire department, or urgent medical care. On the road, there are emergency phones marked **SOS** at regular intervals on *autovías* (freeways) and *autopistas* (toll highways).

If your documents are stolen, contact both the local police and your embassy in Madrid (*see* Basics *in* Chapter 2). If you lose a credit card, phone the issuer immediately (*see* Money, *below*).

IN DIRE STRAITS • **National police** (*policía nacional*; 091). **Local police** (*policía municipal*; 092). **Fire department** (*bomberos*, 080). **Urgent medical care** (*servicio médico*; 061).

ENGLISH-LANGUAGE PUBLICATIONS

In cities and major resorts, you'll have no trouble finding newspapers and magazines in English. U.K. newspapers are available on the day of publication. The most readily available U.S. publications are *Time*, the *International Herald-Tribune*, and *USA Today*.

BOOKS

The major airports sell books in English, including the latest paperback bestsellers. Bookshops in Madrid, Barcelona, Alicante, and some other large cities, plus the Costa del Sol towns and the Balearic and Canary Islands, also sell English-language books.

LOCAL MEDIA

Several major cities and resorts have their own English-language publications aimed primarily at resident expats, including Madrid, Barcelona, Alicante, Málaga, Mallorca, and the Canary Islands.

RADIO AND TELEVISION

Spain is served by two state-owned national channels, two private networks, regional channels in some areas, and local channels. Many hotels have satellite service, which usually includes at least one news channel in English (CNN, BBC World, or Sky News).

ETIQUETTE & BEHAVIOR

Spaniards are very tolerant of foreigners and their strange ways, but you should always behave with courtesy. Be respectful when visiting churches: casual dress is fine if it's not gaudy or unkempt. Spaniards object to men going bare-chested anywhere other than the beach or poolside, and they generally don't look kindly on public displays of drunkenness.

When addressing Spaniards with whom you are not well acquainted, use the formal *usted* rather than the familiar *tu*. For more on conversation, *see* Language, *below*.

GAY & LESBIAN TRAVEL

In summer, some beaches on the Balearic Islands (especially Ibiza), the Costa del Sol (Torremolinos and Benidorm), and the Costa Brava (Sitges and Lloret del Mar) become gay and lesbian hot spots. In winter, on the Canary Islands, Playa del Inglés and the nudist part of Maspalomas are popular.

Generally speaking, the situation for gays and lesbians in Spain has improved dramatically since the end of Franco's dictatorship: The paragraph in the Spanish civil code that made homosexuality a crime was repealed in 1978. Violence against gays does rarely occur, but it's generally restricted to the rougher areas of very large cities.

LOCAL RESOURCES • **Gai Inform** (Fuencarral 37, Madrid, tel. 91/523–0070 evening). Teléfono Rosa (Finlandía 45, Barcelona, tel. 900/601601).

TRAVEL AGENCIES • **Different Roads Travel** (8383 Wilshire Blvd., Suite 902, Beverly Hills, CA 90211, tel. 323/651–5557 or 800/429–8747, leigh@west.tzell.com). **Kennedy Travel** (314 Jericho Turnpike, Floral Park, NY 11001, tel. 516/352–4888 or 800/237–7433, main@kennedytravel.com, www.kennedytravel.com. **Now Voyager** (4406 18th St., San Francisco, CA 94114, tel. 415/626–1169 or 800/255–6951, www.nowvoyager.com). **Skylink Travel and Tour** (1006 Mendocino Ave., Santa Rosa, CA 95401, tel. 707/546–9888 or 800/225–5759, skylinktvl@aol.com, www.skylinktravel.com) serves lesbian travelers.

HEALTH

Sunburn and sunstroke are real risks in summertime Spain. On the hottest of sunny days, even those who are not normally bothered by strong sun should cover themselves up, apply sunblock lotion, drink plenty of fluids, and limit sun time for the first few days.

If you require medical attention, ask your hotel's front desk for assistance or **go to the nearest public Centro de Salud** (day hospital); in serious cases, you'll be referred to the regional hospital. Medical care is good in Spain, but nursing is perfunctory, as relatives are expected to stop by and look after inpatients' needs. In some popular destinations, such as the Costa del Sol, there are volunteer English interpreters on hand.

Spain was recently documented as having the highest number of AIDS cases in Europe. Those applying for work permits may be asked for proof of HIV-negative status.

OVER-THE-COUNTER REMEDIES

Over-the-counter remedies are available at any *farmacia* (pharmacy). Spanish pharmacists are trained to know exactly how each medicine works, and thus often act as unofficial GPs. Patent medicines, even aspirin and indigestion tablets, are only sold in pharmacies. The names of some medicines will look familiar, such as *aspirina*, while others are sold under various brand names. If you regularly take a non-prescription medicine, bring a sample box or bottle with you to aid the Spanish pharmacist in giving you its local equivalent.

HOLIDAYS

Spain's national holidays are: New Year's Day (January 1), Epiphany (January 6), Good Friday (April 13 in 2001; March 29 in 2002), May Day/Labor Day (May 1), Assumption (August 15), National Day (October 12), All Saints' Day (November 1), Constitution Day (December 6), Immaculate Conception (December 8), and Christmas (December 25). If you want to see—or avoid—some of Spain's biggest fiestas, note that Carnival precedes Ash Wednesday (February 28 in 2001); and Semana Santa, or Holy Week, begins on Palm Sunday (April 8 in 2001; March 24 in 2002), leading up to Easter (April 15 in 2001; March 31 in 2002).

In addition, each region, city, and town has its own holidays honoring patron saints, local harvests, political events, you name it.

If a public holiday falls on a Tuesday or Thursday, remember that **some businesses close on the nearest Monday or Friday** for a long holiday weekend called a *puente* (bridge).

INSURANCE

The most useful travel-insurance plan is a comprehensive policy that includes coverage for trip cancellation and interruption, default, trip delay, and medical expenses (with a waiver for preexisting conditions). Without insurance you will lose all or most of your money if you cancel your trip, regardless of the reason. Default insurance covers you if your airline or tour operator goes out of business. Trip-delay insurance covers expenses that arise because of bad weather or mechanical delays. Study the fine print when comparing policies.

A key component of travel insurance is coverage for medical bills incurred if you get sick on the road. Such expenses are not generally covered by Medicare or private policies. U.K. residents can buy a travel-insurance policy valid for most vacations taken that year, but check the rules concerning preexisting conditions. British and Australian citizens need extra medical coverage when traveling overseas.

Always **buy a travel policy directly from the insurance company.** If you buy it from an airline, or tour operator that goes out of business, you will probably not be covered for the agency or operator's default, a major risk. Before making any purchase, **review your existing health and homeowner's policies** to find what they cover away from home.

TRAVEL INSURERS • In the U.S.: **Access America** (6600 W. Broad St., Richmond, VA 23230, tel. 804/285–3300 or 800/284–8300, fax 804/673–1583, www.previewtravel.com), **Travel Guard International** (1145 Clark St., Stevens Point, WI 54481, tel. 715/345–0505 or 800/826–1300, fax 800/955–8785, www.noelgroup.com). In Canada: **Voyager Insurance** (44 Peel Center Dr., Brampton, Ontario L6T 4M8, tel. 905/791–8700; 800/668–4342).

INFORMATION • In the U.K.: **Association of British Insurers** (51-55 Gresham St., London EC2V 7HQ, tel. 0207/600–3333, fax 0207/696–8999, info@abi.org.uk, www.abi.org.uk). In Australia: **Insurance Council of Australia** (tel. 03/9614–1077, fax 03/9614–7924).

LANGUAGE

Although Spaniards exported their language to all of Central and South America—indeed, it's the third most widely spoken language in the world, after Mandarin and Hindi—you may be surprised to find that Spanish is not the principal language in all of Spain. The Basques speak Euskera; in Catalonia, you'll hear Catalan; in Galicia, Gallego; and in Valencia, Valenciano. While almost everyone in these regions also speaks and understands Spanish, local radio and television stations may broadcast in these languages, and road signs may be printed (or spray-painted over) in the preferred regional language. Spanish is referred to as Castellano (Castilian).

Fortunately, **Spanish is fairly easy to pick up, and your efforts to speak it will be graciously received.** Learn at least the following basic phrases: *buenos días* (hello—until 2 PM), *buenas tardes* (good afternoon—until 8 PM), *buenas noches* (hello—after dark), *por favor* (please), *gracias* (thank you), *adiós* (good-bye), *sí* (yes), *no* (no), *los servicios* (the toilets), *la cuenta* (the bill/check), *habla inglés?* (do you speak English?), *no comprendo* (I don't understand). For more helpful expressions, pick up a copy of *Fodor's Spanish for Travelers*.

If your Spanish breaks down, you should have no trouble finding people who speak English in major cities and coastal resorts, but you won't necessarily be able to count on the bus driver or the passerby on the street. Those who do speak English may speak the British variety, so don't be surprised if you're told to queue (line up) or take the lift (elevator) to the loo (toilet). Many guided tours offered at museums and historic sites are in Spanish; ask about the language that will be spoken before you sign up.

PHRASE BOOK & CASSETTES • *Fodor's Spanish for Travelers* (tel. 800/733–3000 in the U.S.; 800/668–4247 in Canada; $7 for phrasebook, $16.95 for audio set).

LANGUAGE STUDY

A number of private schools in Spain offer Spanish-language courses of various durations for foreigners. **Don Quijote** is one network with schools in several locations around Spain. The international network **Inlingua** has 30 schools in Spain. Some Spanish universities, including Barcelona, Salamanca and Málaga, have longer-term Spanish programs, usually covering two months or more.

Back home, the state-run **Instituto Cervantes**, devoted to promoting Spanish language and culture, teaches both in their offices worldwide, and can advise you on other courses in Spain.

PROGRAMS • **Instituto Cervantes** (122 E. 42nd St., Suite 807, New York, NY 10168, tel. 212/689–4232). **Don Quijote** (Placentinos 2, 37998 Salamanca, tel. 923/268860). **Inlingua International** (Belpstrasse 11, Berne, CH-3007, Switzerland, tel. 4131/388–7777).

LODGING

By law, room prices must be posted at the reception desk and should indicate whether or not the value-added tax (IVA; 7%) is included. Breakfast is normally *not* included. Note that high-season rates prevail not only in summer but also during Holy Week and local fiestas.

The lodgings we review represent great values—comfortable digs for less, and usually far less, than 10,000 ptas. a night—with a few splurges thrown in.

APARTMENT & VILLA RENTALS

If you want a home base that's roomy enough for a group and comes with cooking facilities, **consider a furnished rental**. These can save you money, especially if you're traveling with a group. Home-exchange directories sometimes list rentals as well as exchanges.

INTERNATIONAL AGENTS • **Hometours International** (Box 11503, Knoxville, TN 37939, tel. 865/690–8484 or 800/367–4668, hometours@aol.com, http://thor.he.net/~hometour/). **Interhome** (1990 N.E. 163rd St., Suite 110, N. Miami Beach, FL 33162, tel. 305/940–2299 or 800/882–6864, interhome@aol.com, www.interhome.com). **Vacation Home Rentals Worldwide** (235 Kensington Ave., Norwood, NJ 07648, 201/767–9393 or 800/633–3284, vhrww@juno.com, www.vhrww.com). **Villas and Apartments**

Abroad (1270 Avenue of the Americas, 15th floor, New York, NY 10020, tel. 212/897–5045 or 800/433–3020, vaa@altour.com, www.vaanyc.com). **Villas International** (950 Northgate Dr., Suite 206, San Rafael, CA 94903, tel. 415/499–9490 or 800/221–2260, villas@best.com, www.villasintl.com).

CAMPING

Camping in Spain is not a wilderness experience. The country has more than 500 campgrounds, and many have excellent facilities, including hot showers, restaurants, swimming pools, tennis courts, and even nightclubs. But in summer, especially in August, be aware that **the best campgrounds fill with Spanish families, who move in with their entire households**—pets, grandparents, even sofas and the kitchen sink and stove. You can pick up an official list of all Spanish campgrounds at the tourist office.

It can be hard to find a site for independent camping outside established campgrounds. For safety reasons, you cannot camp next to roads, on riverbanks, or on the beach, nor can you set up house in urban areas, nature parks (outside designated camping areas), or within one kilometer of any established campsite. To camp on a private farm, seek the owner's permission.

YOUTH HOSTELS

No matter what your age, you can **cut lodging costs by staying in hostels.** In some 5,000 locations in more than 70 countries around the world, Hostelling International (HI), the umbrella group for a number of national youth-hostel associations, offers single-sex, dorm-style beds and, in many hostels, rooms for couples and family accommodations. Membership in any HI national hostel association, open to travelers of all ages, allows you to stay in HI-affiliated hostels at member rates; one-year membership is about U.S. $25 for adults (C$26.75 in Canada, £9.30 in the U.K., $30 in Australia, and $30 in New Zealand). Members have priority if the hostel is full, and they're eligible for discounts around the world—even on rail and bus travel in some countries.

ORGANIZATIONS • Hostelling International—American Youth Hostels (733 15th St. NW, Suite 840, Washington, DC 20005, tel. 202/783–6161, www.hiayh.org). **Hostelling International—Canada** (400-205 Catherine St., Ottawa, Ontario K2P 1C3, tel. 613/237–7884, www.hostellingintl.ca). **Youth Hostel Association of England and Wales** (Trevelyan House, 8 St. Stephen's Hill, St Albans, Hertfordshire AL1 2DY, tel. 01727/855215 or 01727–845047, www.yha.uk). **Australian Youth Hostel Association** (10 Mallett St., Camperdown, NSW 2050, tel. 02/9565–1699, www.yha.com.au). **Youth Hostels Association of New Zealand** (Box 436, Christchurch, New Zealand, tel. 03/379–9970, www.yha.org.nz).

In Spain: for everyone under 26 and students under 30, the budget travel agency **TIVE** can help make affordable hotel and transport arrangements (Fernando el Católico 88, Madrid, tel. 91/543–7412, fax 91/544–0062).

HOTELS

All hotel entrances are marked with a blue plaque bearing the letter H and the number of stars. The letter R (standing for *residencia*) after the letter H indicates an establishment with no meal service. The designations *fonda* (F), *pensión* (P), *hostal* (Hs), and *casa de huéspedes* (CH) indicate budget accommodations. In most cases, especially in smaller villages, rooms in such buildings will be basic but clean; in large cities, they can be downright dreary.

The Spanish government rates hotels with one to five stars. While quality is a factor, **the rating is technically only an indication of how many facilities the hotel offers.** For example, a three-star hotel may be just as comfortable as a four-star hotel but lack a swimming pool.

The state-run chain of paradors operates about 80 luxury hotels with good restaurants serving regional food, mainly in old castles, monasteries, and convents in scenic—rather than urban—parts of Spain. If you have a little extra cash, consider spending it on a night in one of these relaxing havens.

There is a growing trend in Spain toward small country hotels. Estancias de España is an association of more than 40 independently owned hotels in restored palaces, monasteries, mills, and farms, generally in rural Spain; contact them for a free directory. Similar associations serve individual regions.

Although a single room (*habitación sencilla*) is usually available, singles are often on the small side. Solo travelers might prefer to pay a bit extra for single occupancy of a double room (*habitación doble uso individual*). We always indicate whether or not a hotel's rooms have private bathrooms.

ORGANIZATIONS • AHRA (Andalusian Association of Rural Hotels; Cristo Rey 2, Úbeda, Jaén, tel. 953/755867, fax 953/756099). **Estancias de España** (Menéndez Pidal 31-bajo izq., 28036 Madrid, tel. 91/345–4141, fax 91/345–5174). **Hosterías y Hospederías Reales** (hotels in Castile–La Mancha; Frailes 1, Villanueva de los Infantes, Ciudad Real, tel. 902/202010, fax 926/361788).

MAIL & SHIPPING

Spain's postal system, the *correos,* works, but delivery times can vary widely. An airmail letter to the United States may take anywhere from four days to two weeks, and delivery to other destinations is equally unpredictable. Sending your letters by priority mail (*urgente*) ensures speedier arrival. Beware that many post offices are only open in the morning, usually 9–2, and there can be long lines. You can buy cartons in various sizes for sending stuff home.

OVERNIGHT SERVICE

When time is of the essence, or when you're sending valuable items or documents overseas, you may want to use an overnight courier (*mensajero*). The major international firms, such as Federal Express and UPS, have representatives in Spain; the biggest Spanish courier service is Seur.

MAJOR AGENCIES • DHL (tel. 902/122424). **Federal Express** (tel. 900/100871). **MRW** (tel. 900/300400). **Postal Express—Correos** (tel. 902/197197). **Seur** (tel. 902/101010). **UPS** (tel. 900/102410).

POSTAL RATES

Standard-size airmail letters to the United States and Canada cost 115 ptas. up to 20 grams. Letters to the United Kingdom and other EU countries cost 70 ptas. up to 20 grams. Letters within Spain are 35 ptas. Postcards are charged the same rates as letters. You can buy stamps at any post office (Correos) or at a licensed tobacco shops (*estanco* or *tabacalera*). If you are sending envelopes which are not a standard size (the post office has a list)—greetings cards' envelopes often aren't—mail them from a post office if you don't want them sent back, since there is a surcharge. Always put a return address on whatever you are sending—apart from postcards.

RECEIVING MAIL

Because mail delivery in Spain can often be slow and unreliable, it's best to have your mail sent to American Express. Mail can also be held at a Spanish post office; have it addressed to your name c/o Lista de Correos (the equivalent of poste restante) in the town you'll be visiting. Postal addresses should include the name of the province in parentheses, e.g., Marbella (Málaga).

INFORMATION • In the U.S., call **American Express** (tel. 800/528–4800) for a list of offices overseas. In Spain, call the **Correos** (tel. 902/197197).

MONEY

Spain is no longer a budget destination, but prices still compare slightly favorably to those elsewhere in Europe. A three-course *menú del día* with bread and wine normally costs around 1,500 ptas. Coffee in a bar generally costs 125 ptas. (standing) or 150 ptas. (seated). Beer in a bar: 125 ptas. standing, 150 ptas. seated. Small glass of wine in a bar: 100 ptas. Soft drink: 150–200 ptas. a bottle. Ham-and-cheese sandwich: 300–450 ptas. Two-kilometer (1-mile) taxi ride: 400 ptas., but the meter keeps ticking in traffic jams. Local bus or subway ride: 135–150 ptas. Movie ticket: 500–800 ptas. Foreign newspaper: 300 ptas. In this book we quote admission prices for adults only, but note that **children, students, and senior citizens almost always pay reduced fees.** For information on taxes in Spain, *see* Taxes, *below.*

CREDIT CARDS

We do not mention credit cards unless a hotel or restaurant does not accept them ("Cash only"). With a major credit card or an E.U. Eurocard, you can get a cash advance—usually up to 25,000 ptas. in one day—from any of Spain's numerous ATMs, as long as you remember your four-digit personal identification number. Needless to say, do not carry the number and the card in the same place.

REPORTING LOST CARDS • In Spain: **American Express** (tel. 900/941413). **Diners Club** (tel. 901/101011). **Master Card** (tel. 900/974445). **Visa** (tel. 900/971231).

CURRENCY

As of January 1, 1999, Spain's official currency is the European monetary unit, the Euro. Prices are often quoted in both pesetas and Euros—convenient for Americans, as the Euro is similar in value to a U.S. dollar—but until January 2002 the Euro will be used only on the level of trade and banking, so the peseta (pta.) continues to be legal tender. You can, however, purchase traveler's checks in Euros, convenient if you'll be traveling to more than one Euro-denominated country (Austria, Belgium, Finland, France, Germany, Ireland, Italy, Luxembourg, the Netherlands, Portugal, and Spain).

The peseta will theoretically be withdrawn from general circulation in July 2002. Until then, Spanish bills are worth 10,000, 5,000, 2,000, and 1,000 ptas.; coins are 500, 200, 100, 50, 25, 10, 5, and 1 pta. Be careful not to confuse the 100- and 500-pta. coins—they're the same color and almost the same size. At press time exchange rates were extremely favorable for English-speaking travelers: 194 ptas. to the U.S. dollar, 128 ptas. to the Canadian dollar, 283 ptas. to the pound sterling, 101 ptas. to the Australian dollar, and 77 ptas. to the New Zealand dollar. One Euro was worth U.S. 85¢.

CURRENCY EXCHANGE

For the most favorable exchange rates, **change money in banks.** Although ATM transaction fees may be higher abroad than at home, ATM rates are excellent because they're based on the wholesale rates offered only by major banks. You won't do as well at exchange booths in airports or train and bus stations, in hotels, in restaurants, or in stores. To avoid standing in line at an airport exchange booth, **get some Spanish currency before you leave home.**

EXCHANGE SERVICES • International Currency Express (tel. 888/278–6628 for orders in the U.S., www.foreignmoney.com). **Thomas Cook Currency Services** (tel. 800/287–7362 in the U.S. for phone orders and retail locations, www.us.thomascook.com).

TRAVELER'S CHECKS

Traveler's checks are widely accepted in cities. If you'll be staying in small towns or rural areas, bring extra cash. Lost or stolen checks can usually be replaced within 24 hours. To ensure a speedy refund, buy your own traveler's checks—don't let someone else pay for them—and make the call yourself if you need to request a refund. Irregularities can cause delays.

OUTDOOR ACTIVITIES

Spain's fair weather is ideally suited to outdoor sports virtually year-round, though in summer you should restrict physical activity to early morning or late afternoon. Spain is particularly kind to hikers, watersports enthusiasts, and, believe it or not, skiers. The country's sports federations have the best information; local tourist offices (see Visitor Information, below) can also be helpful.

HIKING

The national parks and regional nature reserves are perfect for hiking and rock climbing, especially the Pyrenees and the Picos de Europa. The parks' visitor centers and outing clubs usually have plenty of information. Spain's most famous walk is the centuries-old Camino de Santiago (Way of St. James) pilgrimage across northern Spain, trod since the Middle Ages and currently rather popular (see Box: The Beaten Path in Chapter 6).

INFORMATION • Federación Española de Montañismo (Alberto Aguilera 3, Madrid, tel. 91/445–1382).

SKIING

Not everyone thinks of sunny Spain as a skier's destination, but it's the second most mountainous country in Europe (after Switzerland) and has an impressive 28 ski centers. The best slopes are in the Pyrenees; there's also good skiing in the Sierra Nevada, near Granada.

INFORMATION • Federación Española de Deportes de Invierno (Winter Sports Federation, Arroyo Fresno 3A, Madrid, tel. 91/376–9930). **Recorded ski report** in Spanish (tel. 91/350–2020).

WATER SPORTS

With 1,200 miles of coastline, Spain has no shortage of water sports. Yacht marinas dot the Mediterranean coast. The coast near Tarifa, on Spain's southernmost tip, constitutes the windsurfing capital of mainland Europe, and surfing is good on the northern coast and, especially, the shores of the Canary Islands. Spain's best dive sites are Granada province and the Cabo de Gata (near Almería); regional tourist offices can direct you to the local diving clubs.

INFORMATION • Federación Española de Vela (Spanish Sailing Federation, Luís de Salazar 12, Madrid, tel. 91/519–5008). **Federación de Actividades Subacuáticas** (Underwater Activities Federation, Santaló 15, Barcelona, tel. 93/200–6769).

PACKING

Pack light. Although baggage carts are free and plentiful in most Spanish airports, they're rare in train and bus stations. Summer is hot nearly everywhere; visits in winter, fall, and spring call for warm clothing and, in winter, boots.

On the whole, Spaniards dress more stylishly than Americans or the British. It makes sense to wear casual, comfortable clothing and shoes for sightseeing, but you'll want to **dress up a bit in big cities, especially for decent restaurants and nightclubs.** American tourists are easily identified by their sneakers and bright clothing—to blend in, wear dark, subdued colors and leather shoes or boots. Note that this is more than a mere fashion issue: crime against tourists is presently *rife* in Madrid and Barcelona, so **colorful tourist wear puts you at greater personal risk.**

On the beach, anything goes. It's common to see females of all ages wearing only bikini bottoms, and many of the more remote beaches allow nude sunbathing. Regardless of your style, **bring a cover-up** to wear over your bathing suit when you leave the beach. For men, bathing shorts with zippered pockets can double as daytime resort wear.

In your carry-on luggage, **pack an extra pair of eyeglasses or contact lenses** and **enough of any medication you take** to last the entire trip. To avoid delays in customs, carry medications in their original packaging. You may want to ask your doctor to write a spare prescription using the drug's generic name, since brand names may vary from country to country. **Never pack prescription drugs or valuables** in luggage to be checked. A can of spray-on stain remover can be helpful if you've brought dry-cleanables, and a Swiss-style pocket knife is always handy. Finally, don't forget to carry the addresses of offices that handle refunds of lost traveler's checks.

CHECKING LUGGAGE

Your airline decides how many bags you can carry onto the plane. Most allow two, but not all, so make sure that everything you carry aboard will fit under your seat or in the overhead bin, and line up for boarding early for the best dibs on bin space. If you have a seat at the back of the plane, you'll probably board first, while the overhead bins are still empty.

Note that baggage allowances on overseas flights might be determined not by piece but by weight— generally 88 pounds (40 kilograms) in first class, 66 pounds (30 kilograms) in business class, and 44 pounds (20 kilograms) in economy. Airline liability for baggage on international flights amounts to $9.07 per pound or $20 per kilogram for checked baggage (roughly $640 per 70-pound bag) and $400 per passenger for unchecked baggage. You can buy additional coverage at check-in for about $10 per $1,000 of coverage, but it excludes a rather extensive list of items, shown on your airline ticket.

Label each of your bags with your name, address, and phone number (if you use your home address, cover it so potential thieves can't see it readily). **Pack a copy of your itinerary** inside each piece of luggage. When you check in, **make sure that each bag is correctly tagged** with the destination airport's three-letter code. If your bags arrive damaged or fail to arrive at all, file a written report with the airline *before* leaving the airport.

PASSPORTS & VISAS

Make two photocopies of your passport's data page—one for someone at home and another for you, carried separately from your passport. If you lose your passport, promptly call the nearest embassy or consulate *and* the local police, who will fill out a report (*denuncia*) for you to sign.

ENTERING SPAIN

Visitors from the U.S., Australia, Canada, New Zealand, and the U.K. need a valid passport to enter Spain. Australians who wish to stay longer than a month also need a visa, available from the Spanish Embassy in Canberra.

PASSPORT OFFICES

The best time to apply for a passport, or to renew your old one, is in fall or winter. Before any trip, check your passport's expiration date, and, if necessary, renew it as soon as possible.

AUSTRALIA • Passport Office (tel. 131232, www.dfat.gov.au/passports).

CANADA • Passport Office Information Service (tel.819/994–3500 or 800/567–6868, www.dfait-maeci.gc.ca/passport).

NEW ZEALAND • Passport Office (tel. 04/494–0700, www.passports.govt.nz).

UNITED KINGDOM • Passport Agency (tel. 0990/210410, http://www.ukpa.gov.uk/ukpass.htm).

UNITED STATES • National Passport Information Center (tel. 900/225–5674; 35¢ per minute for automated service, $1.05 per minute for operator service; http://travel.state.gov/passport_services.html).

SAFETY

Unfortunately, petty crime is a huge and growing problem in Spain's most popular tourist destinations. The main offenses are pickpocketing and mugging in Madrid and Barcelona, and theft from cars all over the country. Tourists are the prime targets for all three. **Be on your guard as you wander, and make an effort to blend in:** wear dark clothes (*see* Packing, *above*), try to keep your camera concealed, and avoid flamboyant map reading. The Japanese Embassy has complained to Spanish authorities that tourists who appear East Asian seem to be at particular risk.

We cannot overemphasize that you should **never, ever leave anything valuable in a parked car,** no matter how quickly you'll return, how friendly the area feels, or how invisible the item seems once you lock it in the trunk. Even when you're *present*, thieves work very efficiently, often puncturing a tire and then offering to help change it, thus distracting you while a companion loots your stuff. In airports—indeed, everywhere—laptop computers are choice prey. And reporting a theft can be just as agonizing, with lines waiting three hours or more at some central Madrid police stations.

WOMEN IN SPAIN

The traditional Spanish custom of the *piropo* (a shouted "compliment" to women walking down the street) is more or less defunct, though women traveling alone may still encounter it on occasion. The piropo is harmless, if annoying, and should simply be ignored. Always hold your bag close, and never carry all your worldly possessions in it. Late at night, phone a taxi if your destination is a long walk away, especially in Madrid.

SENIOR CITIZEN TRAVEL

Senior citizens, known politely as the *tercera edad* (third age) in Spain, can usually get discounted admission to museums and exhibitions. Spaniards take pride in looking after everyone in their families, so it's quite common to see extended families dining or drinking together. When buying medicine, reserving a hotel room or renting a car, inquire about age-related discounts.

SHOPPING

Spain has plenty to tempt the shopper, from fashionable clothing to high-quality regional crafts. Shoes and leather accessories are as chic as you'll find. Many of the best buys are food items; just check customs restrictions in your home country before purchasing edibles (*see* Customs & Duties, *above*). Spanish guitars, flamenco and classical guitar CDs, capes, wines, olive oil, saffron, and vacuum-packed ham all make great souvenirs, albeit some more permanent than others.

Spain's major department store is **El Corte Inglés,** with branches in all good-size cities.

STUDENT TRAVEL

Students can often get discounts on admission to museums and other sights, as well rail passes.

Student I.D.s & Services: In the U.S.: **Council Travel** (CIEE; 205 E. 42nd St., 14th floor, New York, NY 10017, tel. 212/822–2700 or 888/268–6245, info@councilexchanges.org, www.councilexchanges.org). In Canada: **Travel Cuts** (187 College St., Toronto, Ontario M5T 1P7, tel. 416/979–2406 or 800/667–2887, www.travelcuts.com).

In Spain: for everyone under 26 and students under 30, the budget travel agency **TIVE** can help make affordable hotel and transport arrangements (Fernando el Católico 88, Madrid, tel. 91/543–7412, fax 91/544–0062).

TAXES

Value-added tax, similar to sales tax, is called IVA in Spain (pronounced "*ee*-vah " for *impuesto sobre el valor anadido*). It is levied on both products and services such as hotel rooms and restaurant meals. When in doubt about whether tax is included, ask, "Está incluido el IVA ? "

The IVA rate for hotels and restaurants is 7%, regardless of their number of stars or forks. A special tax law for the Canary Islands allows hotels and restaurants there to charge 4% IVA. Menus will generally say at the bottom whether tax is included (*IVA incluido*) or not (*más 7% IVA*).

While food, pharmaceuticals, and household items are taxed at the lowest rate, most consumer goods are taxed at 16%. A number of shops, particularly large stores and boutiques in holiday resorts, participate in Global Refund (formerly Europe Tax-Free Shopping), a V.A.T. refund service that makes getting your money back relatively hassle-free. On purchases of more than 15,000 ptas., you're entitled to a refund of the 16% tax. **Ask for the Global Refund form** (called a Shopping Cheque) in participating stores. You show your passport and fill out the form; the vendor then mails you the refund, or—often more convenient—you **present your original receipt to the IVA office at the airport when you leave Spain.** (In both Madrid and Barcelona, the office is near the duty-free shops. **Prepare to wait at least an hour for this airport process, as lines can be long**.) Customs signs the original and refunds your money on the spot in cash (pesetas), or sends it to their central office to process a credit-card refund. Credit-card refunds take a few weeks.

VAT REFUNDS • Global Refund (707 Summer St., Stamford, CT 06901, tel. 800/566–9828, taxfree@us.globalrefund.com, www.globalrefund.com).

TELEPHONES

Spain's main phone system, Telefónica, is generally efficient. Direct dialing is the norm. Note that only cell phones conforming to the European GSM standard will work in Spain. WAP mobile phones with Internet connectability also function.

COUNTRY CODES

The country code for Spain is 34. Phoning home: dial 00 for an international line, then country code 1 for the United States and Canada, 44 for the United Kingdom, 61 for Australia, or 64 for New Zealand.

DIRECTORY ASSISTANCE

For information in Spain, dial 1003. International operators, who generally speak English, are at 025. Many resorts have light-blue operator-assistance Telefónica cabins right by the beach.

INTERNATIONAL CALLS

International calls are awkward from coin-operated pay phones because of the enormous number of coins needed; and they can be expensive from hotels, as the hotel usually adds a hefty surcharge. The best way to phone home is to use a public phone that accepts phone cards (*see* Phone Cards, *below*) or go to the local telephone office, the *locutorio:* Every town has one, and major cities have several, usually packed with immigrants wiring money home. You converse in a quiet, private booth, and you're charged according to the meter. If the call ends up costing 500 ptas. or more, you can pay with Visa or MasterCard.

To make an international call yourself, dial 00, then the country code, then the area code and number. Before you leave home, **find out your long-distance company's access code in Spain.** Many bars will let you make a metered call on their phone without a huge markup—but check the *paso* (charge per digit) rate first.

LOCAL CALLS

All area codes begin with a 9. To call within Spain—even locally—dial the area code first. Numbers preceded by any kind of 900 code are toll-free; those starting with a 6 denote a cellular phone. Remember that **calls to cell phones are significantly more expensive than calls to regular phones;** you'll need to deposit at least 100 ptas. into a coin-operated pay phone.

LONG-DISTANCE SERVICES

AT&T, MCI WorldCom, and Sprint access codes make calling long-distance relatively convenient, but you may find the local access code blocked in many hotel rooms. First ask the hotel operator to connect you. If the hotel operator can't comply, ask for an international operator, or dial the international operator yourself.

One way to improve your odds of getting connected to your carrier is to travel with more than one company's calling card (a hotel may block Sprint, for example, but not MCI). If all else fails, call from a pay phone.

ACCESS CODES • In the U.S., **AT&T/USADirect** (tel. 800/874–4000). **MCI WorldCom** (tel. 800/444–4444). **Sprint Express** (tel. 800/793–1153). In Spain, **AT&T** (tel. 900/990011). **MCI** (tel. 900/990014). **Sprint** (tel. 900/990013).

PHONE CARDS

To use a newer pay phone, you need a special phone card (*tarjeta telefónica*), which you can buy at any tobacco shop or newsstand, in denominations of 1,000 or 2,000 ptas. Some such phones also accept credit cards, but phone cards are far more reliable for this purpose.

PUBLIC PHONES

You'll find pay phones in individual booths, in special telephone offices (*locutorios*), and in many bars and restaurants. Most have a digital readout so you can see your money ticking away. If you're calling with coins, you need at least 25 ptas. to call locally, 75 ptas. to call another province, and 100 ptas. to call a mobile. Simply insert the coins and wait for a dial tone. (At older models, you line coins up in a groove on top of the dial and they drop down as needed.)

TIME

Spain is on Central European Time, one hour ahead of Greenwich Mean Time and six hours ahead of Eastern Standard Time. Like the rest of the European Union, Spain switches to daylight saving time on the last weekend in March, and switches back on the last weekend in October. The Canary Islands are one hour behind the rest of Spanish time.

TIPPING

Waiters and other service staff expect to be tipped, and you can be sure that your contribution will be appreciated. If, on the other hand, you experience bad or surly service, don't feel obligated to leave a tip.

Restaurant checks almost always include service, but this is *not* the same as a voluntary tip. **Do not tip more than 10% of the bill**, and leave less if you eat tapas or sandwiches at a bar—just enough to round out the bill to the nearest 100. Tip cocktail servers 50–75 ptas. a drink, depending on the bar.

Tip taxi drivers about 10% of the total fare; add more for long rides or extra help with luggage. Note that rides from airports carry an official surcharge to the metered fare plus a small handling fee for each piece of luggage.

If you stay in a hotel for more than two nights, tip the maid about 100 ptas. per night.

TOURS & PACKAGES

Because everything is prearranged on a package tour, you'll spend less time planning—and often get it all for a reasonable price.

BOOKING WITH AN AGENT

Travel agents are excellent resources. Do collect brochures from several agencies, however, as some agents' suggestions may be influenced by relationships with tour and package firms that reward them for volume sales. If you have a special interest, **find an agent with expertise in that area.** ASTA (*see* Travel Agencies, *below*) has a database of specialists worldwide.

Make sure your travel agent is familiar with the rooms and other services in any hotel he or she recommends. Ask about the hotel's location, room size, beds, and whether the hotel has any specific amenities you need. Has your agent been there in person or sent others whom you can contact?

BUYER BEWARE

Every year consumers are stranded or lose their money when tour operators—even large ones with excellent reputations—go out of business. **Check out the operator.** Ask several travel agents about its reputation, and try to **go with a company that has a consumer-protection program**. (Look for information in the company's brochure.) In the United States, members of the National Tour Association and the United States Tour Operators Association are required to set aside funds to cover your payments and travel arrangements in the event that the company defaults. It's also a good idea to choose a company that participates in the American Society of Travel Agents' Tour Operator Program (TOP); ASTA will act as mediator in any disputes between you and your tour operator.

Remember that the more your package or tour includes, the better you can predict the ultimate cost of your vacation. Make sure you know exactly what is covered, and **beware of hidden costs.** Are taxes, tips, and transfers included? Entertainment and excursions? These can add up.

REFERRALS • American Society of Travel Agents (see Travel Agencies, below). **National Tour Association** (NTA; 546 E. Main St., Lexington, KY 40508, tel. 606/226-4444 or 800/682-8886, www.ntaonline.com). **United States Tour Operators Association** (USTOA; 342 Madison Ave., Suite 1522, New York, NY 10173, 212/599-6599 or 800/468-7862, ustoa@aol.com, www.ustoa.com).

TRAIN TRAVEL

On routes with convenient schedules (not the rule in rural areas), trains are the most economical way to go. First- and second-class seats are reasonably priced, and you can get a bunk in a compartment with five other people for a supplement of about U.S.$25. Spain's wonderful high-speed train, the 180-mph AVE, travels between Madrid and Seville (with a stop in Córdoba) in less than three hours. The fast intercity Talgo service is also efficient. The rest of the state-run rail system, however—known as RENFE—remains below par by European standards. Local train travel can be tediously slow, and most long-distance trips run at night. While overnight trains have comfortable sleeper cars, first-class fares that include a sleeping compartment are comparable to airfares. RENFE's Web site (*see below*) can be invaluable in making sense of all this, and charting your itinerary; it shows exact schedules and fares for every train in the country.

International overnight trains run from Madrid to Lisbon, Madrid to Paris, and Barcelona to Paris. A 10-hour daytime train runs from Barcelona to Grenoble and Geneva. If you purchase a same-day round-trip ticket for a journey within Spain, you get a 20% discount; if you purchase a different-day round-trip ticket, a 10% discount applies. Most Spaniards buy train tickets in advance by standing in long lines at the station. The overworked clerks rarely speak English, however, so if you don't speak Spanish, you're better off going to a travel agency that displays the blue-and-yellow RENFE sign. The price is the same.

Commuter trains and most long-distance trains forbid smoking, though some long-distance trains have smoking cars.

SCHEDULES AND FARES • RENFE (tel. 902/240202, www.renfe.es/ingles).

CUTTING COSTS

If you're coming from the United States or Canada and planning extensive train travel, **look into rail passes.** If Spain is your only destination, consider a **Spain Flexipass**. Prices begin at U.S.$150 for three days of second-class travel within a two-month period and $190 for first class. Other passes, such as **Inter Rail (**22 days second-class travel in Spain, Portugal, and Morocco from 31,565 ptas., depending on age) cover more days and longer periods.

Spain is one of 17 European countries in which you can use the **Eurailpass,** which buys you unlimited first-class rail travel in all participating countries for the duration of the pass. If you plan to rack up the miles, get a standard pass. These are available for 15 days ($544), 21 days ($718), one month ($890), two months ($1,260), and three months ($1,558). If your needs are more limited, look into a **Europass**, which costs less than a Eurailpass and buys you a limited number of travel days, in a limited number of countries (France, Germany, Italy, Spain, and Switzerland), during a specified time period.

In addition to the Eurailpass and Europass, Rail Europe sells the Eurail Youthpass (for those under age 26), the Eurail Saverpass (which gives a discount for two or more people traveling together), a Eurail Flexipass (which allows a certain number of travel days within a set period), the Euraildrive Pass, and the Europass Drive (which combines travel by train and rental car). Whichever you choose, remember that you must **buy your pass before you leave for Europe.**

Many travelers assume that rail passes guarantee them seats on the trains they wish to ride: not so. You need to **reserve seats in advance** even if you're using a rail pass. Seat reservations are required on some trains, particularly high-speed trains, and are wise on any train that might be crowded. You'll also need a reservation if you want a sleeping berth.

RAIL PASSES • Rail Europe (226–230 Westchester Ave., White Plains, NY 10604, tel. 914/682–5172 or 800/438–7245; 2087 Dundas E, Suite 105, Mississauga, Ontario, Canada L4X 1M2, tel. 416/602–4195; www.raileurope.com). **DER Tours** (Box 1606, Des Plaines, IL 60017, tel. 800/782–2424,

CLIMATE: HARD DATA

Average daily temps (in degrees Fahrenheit) stack up as follows. Note that in summer, Madrid gets very hot during the day and rather cool at night, while Barcelona holds steady in the 70s.

	Jan. Feb.	Mar. Apr.	May June	July Aug.	Sept. Oct.	Nov. Dec.
MADRID	43	52	65	75	63	45
BARCELONA	50	56	67	76	68	54
SEVILLE	53	61	72	83	73	56
GRANADA	46	54	67	78	67	51

800/282–7474). **CIT Tours Corp.** (342 Madison Ave., Suite 207, New York, NY 10173, tel. 212/697–2100; 800/248–8687; 800/248–7245 in western U.S.).

FROM THE UNITED KINGDOM

Train services to Spain from the United Kingdom are not as frequent, fast, or affordable as flights, and you have to change trains (and stations) in Paris. It's worth paying extra for a Talgo express or the Puerta del Sol express to avoid having to change trains again at the Spanish border. Journey time to Paris is around six hours; from Paris to Madrid, it's an additional 13 hours. Allow at least two hours in Paris for changing trains. If you're under 26 years old, Eurotrain has excellent deals.

INFORMATION • British Rail Travel Centers (tel.0207/834–2345). **Eurotrain** (52 Grosvenor Gardens, London SW1W OAG, U.K., tel. 0207/730–3402). **Transalpino** (71–75 Buckingham Palace Rd., London SW1W ORE, U.K., tel.0207/834–9656).

TRANSPORTATION WITHIN SPAIN

After France, Spain is the largest country in Western Europe, so exploring more than a fraction of the country involves considerable domestic travel. If you want the freedom of straying from your fixed itinerary on a whim, driving is the best choice. Spain's roads are generally fine, though traffic can be heavy on major routes, trucks can clog minor routes, and parking is a problem in cities (*see* Driving, *above*).

Spain is well served by domestic flights, though of course these cost more than ground options. Train service between the largest cities is fast, efficient, and punctual, but trains on secondary regional routes can be slow and infrequent, and involve tedious connections (*see* Train Travel, *above*). In such cases, buses are far more convenient (*see* Bus Travel, *above*).

TRAVEL AGENCIES

A good travel agent puts your needs first. Look for an agency that has been in business at least five years, emphasizes customer service, and has someone on staff who specializes in your destination. In addition, **make sure the agency belongs to a professional trade organization.** The American Society of Travel Agents (ASTA), with 27,000 agents in some 170 countries, is the largest and most influential in the field. Operating under the motto "Integrity in Travel," it maintains and enforces a strict code of ethics and will step in to help mediate any agent-client disputes if necessary. ASTA also maintains a Web site that includes a directory of member agents. (If a travel agency is also as your tour operator, *see* Buyer Beware *in* Tours & Packages, above.)

REFERRALS • American Society of Travel Agents (ASTA; tel. 800/965–2782 24-hr hot line, astanet.com). **Association of British Travel Agents** (68–71 Newman St., London W1P 4AH, tel. 0207/ 637–2444, abta.co.uk, www.abtanet.com). **Association of Canadian Travel Agents** (1729 Bank St., Suite 201, Ottawa, Ontario K1V 7Z5, tel. 613/521–0474, acta.ntl@sympatico.ca).

Australian Federation of Travel Agents (Level 3, 309 Pitt St., Sydney 2000, 02/9264–3299, 02/9264–1085, www.afta.com.au). **Travel Agents' Association of New Zealand** (Box 1888, Wellington 10033, tel. 04/499–0104, taanz@tiasnet.co.nz).

VISITOR INFORMATION

TOURIST OFFICE OF SPAIN • Chicago (845 N. Michigan Ave., Chicago, IL 60611, tel. 312/642–1992, fax 312/642–9817). **Los Angeles** (8383 Wilshire Blvd., Suite 960, Beverly Hills, CA 90211, tel. 213/658–7188, fax 213/658–1061). **Miami** (1221 Brickell Ave., Suite 1850, Miami, FL 33131, tel. 305/ 358–1992, fax 305/358–8223). **New York** (666 5th Ave., 35th floor, New York, NY 10103, tel. 212/265–8822, fax 212/265–8864). **Canada** (2 Bloor St. W, 34th floor, Toronto, Ontario M4W 3E2, Canada, tel. 416/961–3131, fax 416/961–1992). **London** (22–23 Manchester Sq., W1M 5AP, tel. 0207/486-8977, fax 0207/486-8034).

TRAVEL ADVISORIES • U.S. Department of State (tel. 202/647–5225; http://travel.state.gov/ travel_warnings.html).

WEB SITES

Check out the World Wide Web when you're planning. You'll find everything from up-to-date weather forecasts to virtual tours of major cities. Fodor's own Web site, www.fodors.com, is a great place to start your online travels. For more information on Spain, visit www.okspain.org, www.tourspain.es, www.cyberspain.com, and www.red2000.spain.

WHEN TO GO

May and October are the optimal times to come to Spain, as the weather is generally warm and dry. May gives you more hours of daylight, while October offers a chance to enjoy the harvest season, which is especially colorful in the wine regions. In April you can see some of Spain's most spectacular fiestas, particularly Semana Santa (Holy Week); and by then the weather in southern Spain is warm enough to make sightseeing comfortable.

Spain is the number-one destination for European travelers, so **if you want to avoid crowds, come before June or after September.** Crowds and prices increase in the summer, especially along the coasts, as the Mediterranean is usually too cold for swimming the rest of the year, and beach season on the Atlantic coast is shorter still. Spaniards themselves vacation in August, and their annual migration to the beach causes huge traffic jams on August 1 and 31. Major cities are relaxed and empty for the duration; small shops and some restaurants shut down for the entire month, but museums remain open.

CLIMATE

Summers in Spain are hot: temperatures frequently hit 100°F (38°C), and air-conditioning is not widespread. Try to **limit summer sightseeing to the morning hours**. That said, warm summer nights are among Spain's quiet pleasures.

Winters in Spain are mild and rainy along the coasts, especially in Galicia. Elsewhere, winter blows bitterly cold. Snow is infrequent except in the mountains, where you can ski from December to March in the Pyrenees and other resorts near Granada, Madrid, and Burgos.

FORECASTS • Weather Channel Connection (tel. 900/932–8437 in the U.S., 95¢ per minute; www.weather.com).

MADRID

BY EDWARD OWEN

O n one side of Madrid's Puerta del Sol—the city's and, in effect, the nation's traffic hub—stands a statue of a large bear gazing up into a strawberry tree. The bear became the symbol of Madrid back when this land was a hunting ground, in the 13th century; and he liked the madrona shrub because its big, strawberry-like berries, taken in quantity, make the forager tipsy.

In many ways the bear is an apt symbol for Madrid's 2.9 million people. Bears can seem cuddly but can also be dangerous. Madrileños are a happy, generous bunch, but get them into cars and they morph into suicidal maniacs. The male bear goes back on the prowl soon after mating; the male Madrileño, surveys show, has probably never made his bed, knows the kitchen only well enough to locate the fridge, and does most of his entertaining in restaurants and bars. In the summer, when his family has decamped to the seaside or their ancestral village, this stereotypical married Romeo is often nicknamed Rodríguez, because he invokes this Spanish equivalent of Smith when making restaurant reservations with his mistress.

Madrid is really a vast collection of the best and the worst of Spain: art, architecture, cuisine, social life, corruption, and anarchy. High on a plain just south of the Sierra de Guadarrama (the city sits at 2,150 ft), the city is seared by cold in the winter and scorched by dry heat in the summer. Established by the Moors in 852, it was named imperial capital of the Habsburg king Felipe II in 1561. The same royals founded the superb Prado art collection. After the Spanish Civil War (1936–39), immigrants poured in from all over Spain, and Madrid remains a national melting pot, with 18 different culinary types of Spanish restaurants alone.

After Franco's death, *La Movida,* or The Movement (to change), set off an explosion of cultural freedom that gave the Spanish capital a new lease on life. A combination of new money and a traditionally incompetent city hall (the state usually appoints a yes-man as mayor) can mean that half the city is under construction at any given time; and the security of citizens and tourists on the streets takes a back seat to the design of underground parking lots. But Madrid's zest for life is unparalleled anywhere else in the world, and Madrileños are justly proud of their unique metropolis. Just as bears hunt for the sweet things in life, Madrileños go to extremes to satisfy their hedonistic urges, even at the risk of self-destruction. A never-ending search for nocturnal highs has endowed Madrid with the most frenetic and sustained nightlife of any capital in Europe. No one ever orders a last drink here; it's always called the second-to-last, *la penúltima.*

In the city center, wide boulevards sweep past distinctive *barrios* (neighborhoods), each crammed with a maze of little streets and alleyways. There are rich rewards for those who poke around. As Madrileños say, "*de Madrid al cielo*"—from Madrid to heaven.

BASICS

AMERICAN EXPRESS

Cardholders can exchange currency or traveler's checks, replace lost or stolen AmEx cards, receive mail, and get tourist information in the AmEx office **at Plaza de las Cortés 2,** next door to Spain's parliament building (tel. 91/322–5440, 900/994426 for traveler's-check refunds; open weekdays 9–5:30, Sat. 9–noon). Take the Metro to Banco de España; from C. de Alcalá, take C. del Marqués de Cubas south.

CURRENCY EXCHANGE

American Express (*see above*) offers reasonable exchange rates and charges no commission. The same goes for the department store **El Corte Inglés,** of which Madrid has 10 branches, most open till 9 PM Monday to Saturday and some open till 8 on Sunday. The most central store is at Calle Preciados 3, on Puerta del Sol. For larger transactions, you're better off at **banks** like Banco Santander Central Hispano (BSCH), Banco Bilbao Vizcaya Argentaria (BBVA), or Caja de Madrid, all of which charge a commission (500 ptas–1,000 ptas.) but offer significantly better rates. **ATM** machines that accept most credit cards and some bank cards (including Cirrus and STAR) are also plentiful. For an in-person transaction after hours, try the smaller *cambios* (exchange outlets) along Gran Vía and Sol—they're a ripoff, but some stay open all night. Whenever you see a sign saying NO COMMISSION, read the exchange rates themselves very carefully.

CYBERSPACE

Just off the Puerta del Sol, in front of McDonald's, **Amiweb Cyber** (C. Mayor 4, 4th floor, tel. 91/532–0821; Metro: Sol; open Mon.–Sat. 10–9) charges 250 ptas. an hour for Web use. Near Atocha station, **Cybermad** (C. Atocha 117; Metro: Atocha), open every day but Sunday 11–11, has 30 computers (300 ptas./hr) plus scanner, printer, and fax service. **X-net** (C. San Bernardo 81, tel. 91/594–0999; Metro: San Bernardo; open Sun.–Thurs. 10 AM–2 AM, Fri.–Sat. 10 AM–3 AM) has a café.

DISCOUNT TRAVEL AGENCIES

Madrid has relatively few discount or "bucket" airfare agents, but some airfare deals are advertised in *The Broadsheet* and *In Madrid* (*see* English-language Publications, *below*). The best-known general agency is **Viajes Zeppelin,** of whose several branches the most convenient is at Plaza Santa Domingo 2 (tel. 91/542–5154; Metro: Santo Domingo). **Britain Travel Service** (Doce de Octubre 26, tel. 91/409–0040; Metro: Sainz de Baranda or Ibiza) sells discount and charter tickets to and from Britain and Ireland. **TIVE** (Fernando el Católica 88, tel. 91/543–7412, fax 91/544–0062, Metro: Moncloa; open weekdays 9–2, Saturday 9–2 for information only) specializes in student (under 30) and youth (under 26) travel and can help book transport and lodging throughout Spain. If you're traveling between Madrid and one other city in Spain, inquire about package deals with the popular nationwide agency **Viajes Halcón** (C. Alcalá 4, tel. 91/523–4138; Metro: Sol, or Gran Vía 39, tel. 91/532–5971; Metro: Gran Vía). **Mundo Amigo** (Clavel 5, tel. 91/524–9210; Metro: Gran Vía) sells cheap guided bus and adventure tours for young people, some in English.

Other firms offering travel deals and discount hotel vouchers are **American Express** (Plaza de las Cortés 2, tel. 91/322–5500; Metro: Banco de España), **Carlson Wagons-Lits** (Paseo de la Castellana 96, tel. 91/563–1202; Metro: Nuevos Ministerios), and **Pullmantur**, across the street from the Royal Palace (Plaza de Oriente 8, tel. 91/541–1807; Metro: Opera).

EMERGENCIES

Dial **112** for all police, ambulance, or fire services. For referrals to **English-speaking doctors** go to Conde de Aranda 7 or call 91/435–1823. **English-speaking dentists:** Eduardo Fernandez Blanco (Avda. América 4, bajo D, tel. 91/725–2172). Ian Daniel (Clínica Dental Cisne, Magallanes 18, tel. 91/446–3221).

The major **hospitals** are **General Gregorio Marañón** (Dr Esquerdo 47, tel. 91/586—8000); Clínico San Carlos (Plaza de Cristo Rey, tel. 91/330–3000); **La Paz** (Paseo de la Castellana 261, tel. 91/358–2600); **Ramón y Cajal** (Carretera de Colmenar, Km 9, tel. 91/336–8000); and **12 de Octubre** (Carretera de Andalucía, Km 5.4, tel. 91/390–8000); and, for children, **Niño Jesús** (Ménendez y Pelayo 65, tel. 91/503–5900).

EMBASSIES

Australia (Paseo de la Castellana 143, tel. 91/579–0428, open Mon.–Thurs. 9–1 and 2–4:30, Fri. 9–2). **Canada** (C. Núñez de Balboa 35, tel. 91/431–4300, open weekdays 9–12:30). **Great Britain** (C. Fernando el Santo 16, tel. 91/319–0200, open weekdays 9–1:30 and 3–6). **Ireland** (C. Claudio Coello 73, tel. 91/576–3500, open weekdays 10–2). **New Zealand** (Plaza de la Lealtad 2, tel.91/523–0226, open weekdays 9–1:30, 2:30–5:30). **United States** (C. Serrano 75, tel. 91/577–4000, open weekdays 9–12:30 and 3–5).

ENGLISH-LANGUAGE PUBLICATIONS

In Madrid, a monthly tabloid for the young at heart, carries entertainment listings and articles of interest to foreigners in Madrid; it's available at some embassies and at expat hangouts, such as Irish pubs. *The Broadsheet* is a monthly English-language magazine. Most newsstands in the city center have some English-language newspapers and magazines (such as *Time* and the *International Herald-Tribune*), as do branches of the department store El Corte Inglés and the book and music store Crisol.

LAUNDRY

You won't find any laundromats in central Madrid, so ask your hotel or *hostal* if you want to wash garments by hand in your sink. Buy some hand-wash (*lavado a mano*) detergent like **Norit** and go to it— Madrid's summer heat makes it easy to dry clothes. **Dry cleaners** (*tintorerías*) tend to be slow and expensive, and they often damage clothes. The most useful item for any traveler is a can of **Cebralin Quitamanchas,** a spray that removes most greasy stains (including the olive oil that drips from many tapas) and can be brushed off when dry.

LOST AND FOUND

Where your *objeto perdido* (lost property) turns up depends on where you lost it. If you drop something in **Barajas Airport,** inquire at an information desk or call 91/393–6000. If you leave something on a **RENFE train,** inquire at the one of the main stations on that line or call 902/240202. For items left on airport or city **buses,** contact EMT (C. Alcántara 24, tel. 91/406–8843). For losses in **taxis** or on the **Metro,** present yourself at Plaza de Legazpi 7 or call 91/588–4364, 91/599–4346, or 91/506–6969. If you lose your **passport,** contact your embassy (*see above*) or the main post office, the Palacio de Comunicaciónes (Plaza Cibeles, tel. 91/537–6494).

MAIL

The main **post office** (Correos) is called El Palacio de Comunicaciones (Plaza Cibeles, tel. 91/536–0110, 902/197197 general information; Metro: Banco de España), open weekdays 8 AM–9:30 or 10 PM, Saturday 8:30–2, Sunday 10–1. Infuriatingly, most of Madrid's other post offices are open only in the morning: weekdays 8:30–2 and Saturday 8:30–1. You can always buy stamps at an *estanco* (tobacconist) and drop your postcards into a yellow **mailbox** on the street.

PHARMACIES

Pharmacies are easily identified by their flashing neon-green crosses. There are permanent 24-hour pharmacies at C. Mayor 59, C. Toledo 46, C. Goya 89, C. Conde de Peñalver 27, and C. Ferraz 13; the daily newspapers list additional pharmacies currently on 24-hour duty (*farmacias de guardia*). Pharmacies that close early usually display in their windows the address of a nearby pharmacy with longer hours.

TELEPHONES

Madrid has two **Telefónica** phone banks, one at Paseo de Recoletos 37–41 (Metro: Colón), the other at Gran Vía 30 (Metro: Gran Vía). Both are open Monday–Saturday 9 AM–midnight and Sunday 10 AM–midnight. Around town, many **pay phones** take credit cards. If you see a LOCUTORIO check out the prices, as these facilities cater to immigrants calling home and wiring money.

VISITOR INFORMATION

Madrid has four **regional tourist offices.** The main office is at **Duque de Medinaceli 2,** near the Westin Palace Hotel (tel. 91/429–4951; open weekdays 9–7 and Sat. 9–1). The others are at **Barajas Airport** (tel. 91/305–8656; open weekdays 9–7, Sat. 9:30–1:30), **Chamartín train station** in northern Madrid (tel. 91/315–9976; open weekdays 8–8, Sat. 9–1), and the remote **Mercado de la Puerta de Toledo** (Glorieta Puerta de Toledo, 3rd floor, tel. 91/364–1876; open weekdays 9–7, Sat. 9–1). The tiny **city tourist office** at Plaza Mayor 3 (tel. 91/366–5477 or 91/588–1636, open weekdays 10–8, Sat. 10–2, Sun. 10–2) has only a few pamphlets but leads English-language tours of Madrid's *casco antiguo* (old quarter) every Saturday, departing from the office at 10 AM. In summer, the *ayuntamiento* (city hall) also sends a few "tourist hosts," identifiable by their bright-yellow clothing, out to the major sights to welcome wanderers and answer questions.

COMING AND GOING

BY PLANE

Barajas Airport is about 12km/7 mi east of Madrid on the N-II road to Barcelona. The drive into town normally takes about 20 minutes, but can be much longer during rush hour. Barajas is the hub for all domestic flights and offers several daily shuttle flights to Barcelona. Partly because a new airport is under construction, air traffic at Barajas can get congested; allow plenty of time to check in for departing flights. For **general information,** including the status of flights in progress, call the airport (tel. 91/305–8343, 91/305–8344, 91/305–8345, or 91/393–6000). For airlines flying into Madrid, *see* Air Travel in Chapter 1.

The airport's three linked terminals include currency-exchange booths, ATMs/cash machines, luggage lockers, car-rental agencies, a tourist office, a RENFE (train) reservation office, and a post office.

By far the cheapest way into town is the **Metro** (open daily 6 AM–1:30 AM), a bargain at 135 ptas. per ticket, even if you do have to change trains to get downtown. For 450 ptas. you can also take a **bus** to the central Plaza Colón, where you can hail a taxi to your hotel; buses leave the airport every 15 minutes between 5:40 AM and 2 AM, slightly less often very early or late in the day. Watch your belongings, as the underground Plaza Colón bus station and its environs are a favorite haunt of purse snatchers and con artists. **Taxis** wait near the clearly marked bus stop outside the international arrivals terminal (do not hire one that touts its services out loud)—expect to pay at least 2,000 ptas. (more in heavy traffic) plus a small surcharge late at night, on national holidays, and for each piece of luggage the driver handles. Make sure the driver turns on the meter; off-the-meter "deals" need only be made for trips beyond city limits.

BY BUS

Madrid has no central bus station; buses are generally less popular than trains (though they can be faster). Most of southern Spain is served by the **Estación del Sur** (Méndez Álvaro, tel. 91/468–4200), while buses for much of the rest of the peninsula, including Cuenca, Extremadura, Salamanca (2½ hours, 2,250 ptas.), and Valencia (4 hours, 5,770 ptas.), depart from **Auto Res station** (Plaza Conde de Casal 6, tel. 91/551–7200). There are several smaller stations, however, so inquire at travel agencies for the one serving your destination.

Bus companies of interest include **La Sepulvedana** (Paseo de la Florida 11, near Estación de Norte, tel. 91/530–4800), serving Segovia (90 minutes, 845 ptas.), Avila (80 minutes, 945 ptas.), and La Granja; **Herranz** (Fernández de los Ríos, tel. 91/543–8167; Metro: Moncloa), for El Escorial (50 minutes, 380 ptas.) and the Valle de los Caídos; **Continental Auto** (Intercambiador de Autobuses, Avenida de América, tel. 91/745–6300; Metro: Avenida de América), serving Cantabria, the Basque region, Logroño, Pamplona, and Soria; **Autobuses Madrid-Granada** (Intercambiador de Autobuses, Avenida de América, tel. 91/745–6300; Metro: Avenida de América), serving Granada (5½ hours, 1,970 ptas.); and **La Veloz** (Mediterraneo 49, tel. 91/409–7602; Metro: Conde de Casal), with service to Chinchón (1 hr., 415 ptas.).

BY CAR

Felipe II made Madrid the capital of Spain because it was at the center of his peninsular domain, and to this day many of the nation's highways radiate from Madrid like the spokes of a wheel. Originating at Kilometer 0—marked by a brass plaque on the sidewalk of the Puerta del Sol—these highways include the A6 (to Segovia, Salamanca, and Galicia), A1 (Burgos, the Basque Country, and France), N-II (Guadalajara, Barcelona, and France), N-III (Cuenca, Valencia, Mediterranean coast), A4 (Aranjuez, La Mancha, Granada, and Seville), N401 (Toledo), and N-V (Talavera de la Reina and Portugal). The capital is surrounded two ring roads, the M30 (inner) and M40 (outer), from which most of these highways are easily picked up.

To **rent** a car, you need a valid driver's license—an International Driving License is best for non-EU citizens—and a credit card. The major international agencies have offices at the airport and downtown: **Avis** (Gran Vía 60, tel. 902/135531), **Budget** (José Abascal 31, tel. 901/201212), **Europcar** (Estación de Atocha, tel. 917/211222), **Hertz** (Edificio de España, Plaza de España, and Estación de Atocha; tel. 902/402405), and **National–Atesa** (Gran Vía 80, tel. 902/100101).

To skip town for the price of a tank of gas, call **Autos Compartidos** (Carretas 33, tel. 91/522–7772; open weekdays 10–2 and 4:30–8)—they'll try to hook you up with someone driving your way.

If your car gets towed away by the **grúa,** the dreaded municipal service for bad parkers, call 91/343–0050 to find out where it is and how much you need to cough up to recover it (roughly 15,000 ptas. a minute).

BY TRAIN

Madrid has three main train stations (*estaciones)*: Estación Chamartín, Estación Atocha, and Estación de Norte (also known as Príncipe Pío), all served by the Metro. Generally speaking, **Chamartín** (tel. 91/315–9976), near the northern tip of Paseo Castellana, sends trains north and west, including Barcelona (7½ hrs, 5,300 ptas.), San Sebastián, Burgos (3½ hrs, 3,000–3,500 ptas.), León, Oviedo, La Coruña, and Salamanca (2½ hrs, 2,150 ptas.), as well as France and Portugal. **Atocha** (tel. 91/328–9020), at the southern end of the Paseo del Prado, anchors the wonderful, high-speed (180 mph) **AVE** train to Córdoba and Seville (2½ hrs to Seville, 8,400 ptas.) and serves other points mainly south and east, including Toledo (1 hr, 760 ptas.), Segovia (2 hrs, 800 ptas.), Seville , Málaga (4½ hrs, 7,000 ptas.), Córdoba, and Valencia (3 hrs, 5,700 ptas.). **Norte** (tel. 91/506–7067 for *cercanías*) is primarily for *cercanías* (commuter trains) and *regional* (local) trains to Madrid's western suburbs, including El Escorial.

For schedules and reservations, contact Spain's national train company, **RENFE** (tel. 902/240202; www.renfe.es/ingles)—there are representatives in all major train stations, and leading travel agents can also sell train tickets. If you purchase tickets with a credit card over the phone, you can even have them delivered to your hotel. In addition to the AVE, RENFE offers high-speed **TALGO express trains** to some cities, interspersed with cheaper, slower trains on the same routes.

RENFE participates in the European InterRail pass, which buys you a month of unlimited rail travel in 29 European countries and Morocco. Holders of InterRail passes must still make seat reservations on most trains, and must note that the pass is *not* valid on AVE and TALGO 200 trains. RENFE also sells **BIJ** (Billete Internacional para la Juventud) passes to those under 26 traveling (with stops) between two determined points in Europe. Rail travelers with bicycles have major and expensive problems, as bikes are not allowed on long-distance trains unless the owner has booked a *litera* (bunk, couchette) or *coche cama* (sleeping compartment), and must still be dismantled and put in a box.

GETTING AROUND

Madrid's main sights—and most of the action in general—are in the city center, the oldest part of town. In most cases, it's ideal to stay here, then plan your travels so you can walk from one sight to another. Central Madrid is roughly bordered by the Palacio Real (to the west), Gran Vía (north), the Parque del Retiro (east), and the Lavapiés area (south). In addition, some sights beckon from the streets on either side of Paseo de la Castellana, north of the Prado. The Bohemian Malasaña barrio, north of the center, is also worth a visit at night—especially on weekends, when it veritably heaves with people—but you're spoiled enough for nocturnal choice in the center of town.

The amount of traffic that normally clogs the streets, resulting in rampant double parking and 4-AM traffic jams, is reduced by about 60% in August. The rest of the year, by far the quickest mode of transport is the Metro.

BY BIKE OR SCOOTER

Rent bicycles at **Karacol Sport** (C. Tortosa 8, tel. 91/539–9633), scooters and motorcycles at **Moto Alquiler** (C. Conde Duque 13, tel. 91/542–0657). For any of the above you'll need your passport, your driver's license, and either a cash deposit or a credit card. If you're *loco* enough to battle Madrid's traffic on a two-wheeler—an extremely dangerous proposition on weekdays—this can be a fast and pleasant way to see the city. It's much safer on weekends, at which time you'll see other cyclists about. (If you've brought your own bike and want to travel by train, *see* Coming and Going–By Train, *above*).

BY BUS

Red city buses and their blue, natural gas–powered brethren, run between 6 AM and midnight and cost 135 ptas. per ride. After midnight, buses called *buhos* (night owls) run out to the suburbs from Plaza de Cibeles. Signs at every stop list all other stops by street name, but these are hard to comprehend if you don't know the city well. For 200 ptas. you can buy a route map from an **EMT** kiosk on the Puerta del Sol or Plaza de Cibeles; there you can also buy a 10-ride Metrobus ticket for 705 ptas., valid for both bus and Metro travel. If you speak Spanish, call 91/406–8810 for bus information.

Exact change is preferred, but drivers will usually make change under protest for a 1,000-pta. note. If you've bought a 10-ride ticket, step just behind the driver and insert it in the ticket-punching machine until the mechanism goes "ding."

A number of **sightseeing buses**, mostly brightly painted double-deckers, link Madrid's main attractions. **Trapsatur** (tel. 91/302–6039) runs the *Madrid Visión* tourist bus, which makes a 1½-hour sightseeing circuit of the city with recorded commentary in English. No advance reservation is needed; just show up at Gran Vía 32. Buses also leave from the front of the Prado Museum every 1½ hours beginning at 12:30 Monday–Saturday, and 10:30 on Sunday. A round-trip ticket costs 1,500 ptas.; a day pass, which allows you to get on and off at various attractions, is 2,000 ptas. A similar hop-on, hop-off service on an open-top double-decker is operated by **Sol Pentours** (Gran Vía 2, tel. 902/303903).

For organized day trips to sites outside Madrid, such as Toledo, El Escorial, and Segovia, contact **Julià Tours** (Gran Vía 68, tel.91/559–9605). Some of the buses are a little dated.

BY CAR

Driving in Madrid is not for the faint of heart. It's virtually impossible to drive and navigate simultaneously, not only because of one-way streets, tunnels, and bridges, but because locals pay scant attention to such niceties as traffic lights and pedestrian crossings. Parking is nightmarish, traffic is always heavy, and the city police are not exactly prominent. The only exception is August, when the streets are largely emptied by the lemminglike exodus to the coast.

BY METRO

Madrid's subway system is quick, frequent, and, at 135 ptas. a ride, cheap. Even cheaper is the *billete de diez* or **Metrobus** (the latter valid on buses as well), which buys you 10 rides for 705 ptas. There are 10 color-coded Metro lines: Just note the final station of the line you need, and follow the signs to the correct corridor. Route maps are posted in every station and distributed in brochure form. Smoking is prohibited. Exits are marked *salida*. Trains run from 6 AM to 1:30 AM; a few entrances close earlier.

BY TAXI

Taxis are among Madrid's truly good deals. Metered fares start at 190 ptas. and rise 95 ptas. per km (½ mi) thereafter (125 ptas. per km at night, on weekends, and beyond city limits). Numerous supplemental charges, however, mean that your total cost often bears little resemblance to what you see on the meter: You pay a 150-pta. supplement on Sunday and between 11 PM and 6 AM; 150 ptas. to go to a sports stadium or the bullring; and 400 ptas. to or from the airport, plus 50 ptas. per suitcase.

Taxi stands are numerous, and taxis are easily hailed in the street (except when it's raining). Available cabs display a green LIBRE sign during the day and a green light, easier to see, at night. Generally, a tip of about 25 ptas. is fine for short rides; you may want to go as high as 10% for a trip to the airport. If you don't see any cabs, you can call one through **Tele-Taxi** (tel. 91/371–2131); **Radioteléfono** (tel. 91/547–8200); or **Radio Taxi Gremial** (tel. 91/447–5180).

BY TRAIN

Cercanías (commuter trains) and RENFE trains operate from the three main stations (Chamartín, Atocha, and Norte/Principe Pío) plus Nuevos Ministerios, beneath Paseo de la Castellana, and Recoletos, under Paseo de Recoletos near Plaza Colón. Get schedules and fares from any one of these stations or from RENFE's information line (tel. 902/240202). Atocha has service to **Toledo, Segovia, El Escorial,** and **Aranjuez,** including the special steam-pulled Tren de las Fresas (Strawberry Train) to Aranjuez in season (*see* Near Madrid *at end of chapter*). Atocha also serves the winter **ski resorts** in the Guadarrama Mountains. You can reach **Sigüenza** from Chamartín.

MADRID METRO

KEY
- **1** Metro Terminals
- ○ Metro Stations
- **■□** Transfer Stations
- ─── Railway Lines
- • Train Stations

Herrera Oria
9
Pitis
7
Lacoma
Avda. Ilustación
Peñagrande
Antonio Machado
Valdezarza
Francos Rodríguez
Ciudad Universitaria **6**
Metropolitano
Guzmán el Bueno
Islas Filipinas
Canal
Quevedo
San Bernardo
Moncloa **3**
Argüelles **4**
Ventura Rodríguez
Pl. de España
Príncipe Pío
Lago
Batán
Campamento
Empalme

Barrio del Pilar
Ventilla
Valdeacederas
Tetuán
Estrecho
Alvarado
Cuatro Caminos
Ríos Rosas
Iglesia
Alonso Cano
Bilbao
Noviciado
Tribunal
Santo Domingo
Callao
Gran Vía
Sol
Ópera
La Latina
Puerta de Ángel
Alto de Extremadura
Lucero
Santa María **4**
San Lorenzo
Campo de las Naciones
Mar de Cristal **8**
Aeropuerto
Barajas 8
Canillas
Esperanza
Arturo Soria
Avda. de la Paz
Alfonso XIII
Canillejas **5**
Torre Arias
Suanzes
Ciudad Lineal
Pueblo Nuevo
Ascao
García Noblejas
Simancas
San Blas
Las Musas **7**

8 Fuencarral
Begoña
Chamartín
Plaza Castilla **1**
Duque de Pastrana
Pío XII
Cuzco
Santiago Bernabéu
Nuevos Ministerios
Rep. Argentina
Colombia
Concha Espina
Cruz del Rayo
Prosperidad
Avda. de América **7 8**
Cartagena
P. Avenidas
B. Concepción
Quintana
El Carmen
Diego de León
Ventas **2**
Manuel Becerra
Gregorio Marañón
Rubén Darío
N. de Balboa
Alonso Martínez
Colón
Serrano
Velázquez
Lista
Goya
Chueca
Sevilla
Banco de España
Retiro
P. de Vergara
O'Donnell
Ibiza
Tirso de Molina
Lavapiés
Antón Martín
Atocha
Atocha Renfe
Sainz de Baranda
Estrella
Vinateros
Artilleros
Pavones
Valdebernardo
Vicálvaro
San Cipriano
Puerta de Arganda
Rivas Urbanizaciones
Rivas Vaciamadrid
La Poveda
Arganda del Rey **9**

Laguna **6**
Carpetana
Oporto
10
Aluche **5**
Vista Alegre
Carabanchel
Marqués de Vadillo
Urgel
Opañel
Plaza Elíptica **11**
Usera
Abrantes
11 Pan Bendito
Acacias
Pirámides
Palos de la Frontera
Embajadores
Méndez Álvaro
Legazpi **3**
Conde de Casal
Menéndez Pelayo
Pacífico
Puente de Vallecas
Nueva Numancia
Portazgo
Alto de Arenal
Miguel Hernández
Sierra de Guadalupe
Villa Vallecas
Congosto 1
Pontones
R. Manzanares

WHERE TO SLEEP

The good news for budget travelers is that Madrid has about 300 *hostales* (budget hotels), most in or near the city center. The bad news is that the best properties are often booked in advance—if you know your travel dates, reserve well before you arrive. Wandering around with your luggage in Madrid's searing summer heat is not much fun, and makes you a tempting target of tourist-related petty crime.

When choosing a room, bear in mind that central Madrid can be noisy almost all night long. Street-side rooms in most *hostales* have charming little wrought-iron balconies, but an inner room might give you more sleep. If you're here in the summer, you might want to ask about air-conditioning as well (*aire acondicionado*). Most *hostales* do not serve food, but bars and cafés are open all hours, and you'd be hard pressed to spend more than 400 ptas. for a light breakfast (a little more if you want for fresh-squeezed Spanish orange juice). Madrid tap water is fine to drink, but do bring soap and shampoo. All *hostales* are in apartment buildings, so their addresses include street number, floor number, and *dcha*. (*derecha*—turn right at the top of the stairs) or *izqda*. (*izquierda*—left at top of stairs).

PLAZA SANTA ANA

Just southeast of the Puerta del Sol, and walking distance from the Prado and Plaza Mayor, this is Madrid's main tapas area. As dusk falls, the myriad restaurants and bars serve early-evening victuals to live jazz, deafening disco, or whatever else they're in the mood for. Lodging here carries a higher-than-usual risk of nighttime noise, especially on weekends.

UNDER 4,000 PTAS. • Pensión Poza. Rooms in this pension are purely basic, devoid of frills and priced to match. A double with sink and shared bath costs 2,400 ptas.; the three with showers (none have toilet; that's down the hall) are 3,800 ptas. Aim for one of the three rooms with balconies. *Nuñez del Arce 9, 1st floor, tel. 91/522—4871. Metro: Sevilla. 14 rooms, none with bath.*

UNDER 5,000 PTAS. • Hostal Lucense. This place is particularly popular with Australians, as friendly owner Micaela García once lived Down Under. The small guest rooms have white walls and tile floors; most have a writing table; and three have balconies. All but one of the rooms share bath facilities. *C. Núñez del Arce 15, 1st floor, tel. 91/522–4888. Metro: Sevilla. 12 rooms, 1 with bath. Cash only.*

Hostal Villar. Because it has 46 rooms on three floors, Villar gives you a decent chance of landing a room. That said, the area is noisy, some rooms are ratty, and reservations are sometimes forgotten. Doubles with full bath (including tub) cost 5,000 ptas., those with toilet and shower 4,200 ptas., and those with only sink 3,500 ptas. The friendly family in charge keeps the place clean—if not exactly spiffy—and airport shuttle service is available. *C. Príncipe 18, tel. 91/531–6600, fax 91/521–5073. Metro: Sevilla. 40 doubles, 30 with bath, 6 singles. In-room safes.*

Hotel Castro. Several of the cozy rooms in this agreeable place have balconies; those in back are quieter. Rooms have tile floors, light-hued decor, writing tables, fans, and modern bathrooms. Doubles with bath are 5,000 ptas. *C. León 13, 1st floor, tel. 91/429–5147. Metro: Sevilla or Antón Martín. 13 rooms. Cash only.*

UNDER 6,000 PTAS. • Hostal San Antonio. This is a really nice *hostal*, with clean, bright, modern, en-suite rooms for 5,500 ptas. The general look is white with parquet floors; some rooms have balconies with flowers. The owners are very friendly. *C. León 13, 2nd floor, tel. 91/429–5137. Metro: Antón Martín or Sevilla. 14 rooms.*

UNDER 8,000 PTAS. • Hostal Alfaro. These bright rooms (doubles: 6,000 ptas.) are clean and well decorated in white and green, with tile floors and modern bathrooms. The owners are welcoming, and there's a public lounge. *Ventura de la Vega 16, 2nd floor izqda., tel. 91/429–6173. Metro: Sevilla. 22 rooms.*

Hostal Sardinero. Calle del Prado is noisy, and rooms with balconies get the brunt of it; but inner rooms are quieter, and Sardinaro is a pleasant place. The white rooms have parquet floors, up-to-date bathrooms, and safes; doubles with bath cost 7,000 ptas. *C. del Prado 16, 3rd floor, tel. and fax 91/429–5756. Metro: Sevilla. In-room safes. 12 rooms.*

Hotel Santander. This old-fashioned hotel is attractive and friendly. The spacious doubles come in various styles—some with carpets—and have old but clean and functional bathrooms. Each costs 8,000 a night. Laundry service is a bonus option. *C. Echegaray 1 (at Carrera de San Jerónimo 26), tel. 91/429–9551, 91/429–6644, or 91/429–4644; fax 91/369–1078. Metro: Sevilla or Sol. 35 rooms.*

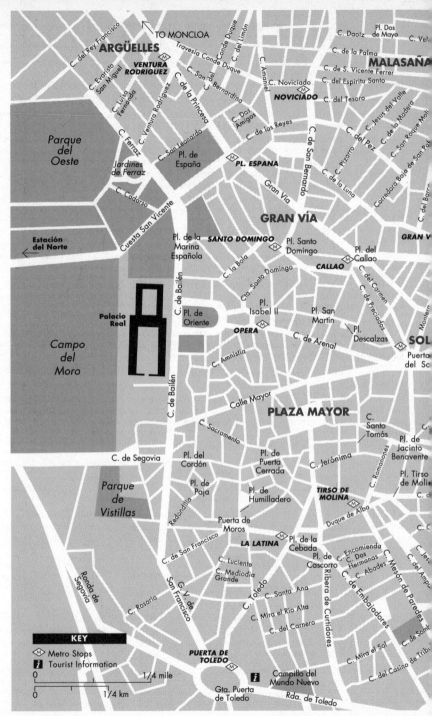

TO MONCLOA

ARGÜELLES

VENTURA RODRIGUEZ

C. del Rey Francisco

C. Evaristo San Miguel

C. Luisa Fernanda

C. Ferraz

C. Ventura Rodriguez

Travesía Conde Duque

Conde Duque

C. del Limón

C. San del Bernardino

C. de la Princesa

C. Amaniel

C. Noviciado

C. Dos Amigos

C. de los Reyes

Parque del Oeste

Jardines de Ferraz

C. de San Leonardo

Pl. de España

C. Cadarso

PL. ESPAÑA

Gran Vía

C. de San Bernardo

Estación del Norte

Cuesta San Vicente

Pl. de la Marina Española

SANTO DOMINGO

C. la Bola

C. de Bailén

Cta. Santo Domingo

GRAN VÍA

Pl. Santo Domingo

Pl. Dos de Maya

C. Daoiz

C. Vel

C. de la Palma

MALASAÑA

C. de S. Vicente Ferrer

C. del Espíritu Santo

NOVICIADO

C. del Tesoro

C. del Pez

C. Jesús del Valle

C. de la Madera

C. San Roque Pat

C. Pizarro

Corredera Baja de San Pab

C. de la Luna

C. del Barc

Pl. del Callao

CALLAO

GRAN V

C. del Carmen

C. de Preciados

Palacio Real

Pl. de Oriente

OPERA

Campo del Moro

C. de Bailén

Pl. Isabel II

Pl. San Martín

C. de Arenal

C. Amnistía

Monter

SOL

Puerta del So

Pl. Descalzas

Calle Mayor

PLAZA MAYOR

C. Sacramento

C. de Segovia

Pl. del Cordón

Pl. de Puerta Cerrada

C. Jerónima

C. Santo Tomás

Pl. de Jacinto Benavente

Pl. Tirso de Moli

C. de

C. Romanones

Parque de Vistillas

Pl. de Paja

Redondilla

Pl. de Humilladero

TIRSO DE MOLINA

Duque de Alba

Puerta de Moros

LA LATINA

Pl. de la Cebada

Pl. de Cascorro

C. Encomienda

C. Dos Hermanas

C. Abades

Ronda de Segovia

C. Rosario

G. V. de San Francisco

C. de San Francisco

C. Luciente

C. Mediodía Grande

C. Toledo

C. Santa Ana

C. Mira el Río Alta

C. del Carnero

Ribera de Curtidores

C. de Embajadores

Mesón de Paredes

C. del Amp

C. Jes

C. de Sant

C. de Tribi

PUERTA DE TOLEDO

C. Mira el Sol

C. del Casino

KEY

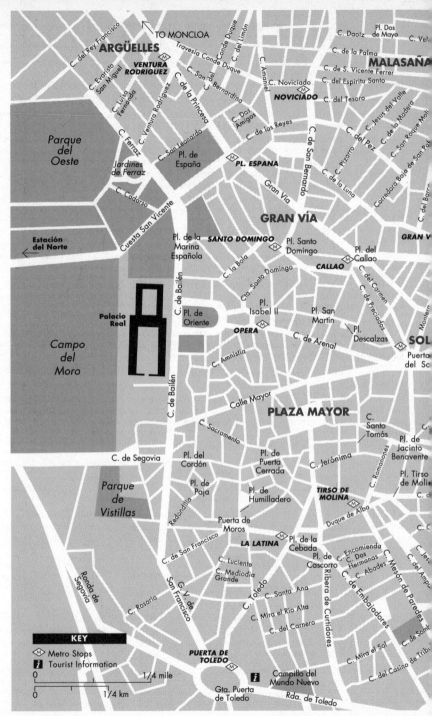 Metro Stops

ℹ️ Tourist Information

0 _____ 1/4 mile

0 _____ 1/4 km

Gta. Puerta de Toledo

Rda. de Toledo

Campillo del Mundo Nuevo

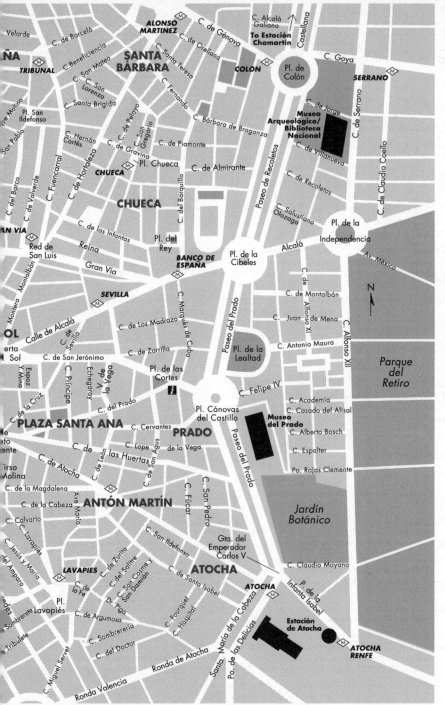

33

PRADO

From anywhere in this pleasant area, it's a short walk to Madrid's three major art museums, botanical gardens, and Parque del Retiro—not to mention the tapas bars of Plaza Santa Ana.

UNDER 7,000 PTAS. • Hostal Armesto. Small and hospitable, the Armesto has just six rooms, each a double priced at 6,500 ptas. Said rooms are pleasant but spartan, with tile floors, fans, clean bathrooms, and various color schemes. Ask for one of the two rooms overlooking the garden. *C. San Agustín 6, 1st floor dcha., tel. 91/429–0940 or 91/429–9031. Metro: Banco de España. 6 rooms. Cash only.*

Hostal Cervantes. Tea and coffee are nice perks here, served by efficient owners in the lounge. Rooms are spacious—indeed, almost luxurious—and decorated in various colors. A double costs 6,500 ptas. *Cervantes 34, 2nd floor, tel. 91/429–8365, fax 91/429–2745. Metro: Banco de España. 22 rooms.*

Hostal Dulcinea. Set on a quiet street near the Prado and some good tapas bars, the friendly Dulcinea has very reasonably priced doubles, at 6,000 ptas. a night. Rooms are clean, bright, and cozy, with tile floors, tables, fans, and modern bathrooms. *C. Cervantes19, 2nd floor dcha., tel. 91/429–9309, fax 91/369–2569. Metro: Banco de España. 13 rooms.*

Hostal Villamañez. In the same building as the Armesto (*see above*), the friendly Villamañez rents doubles with full bath for 6,500 ptas. Rooms are modern and bright-white, with tile floors; three overlook the garden. *C. San Agustín 6, 2nd floor dcha., tel. 91/429–9033, fax 91/429–8197. Metro: Banco de España or Antón Martín. 8 rooms. Cash only.*

Hotel Gonzálo. Steps from the Prado and Thyssen-Bornemisza museums, the Gonzálo is a fresh, bright hotel with quiet rooms and a lounge. Doubles with bath start at 6,400 ptas. a night. Rooms are mostly white, with tile floors and fans. *C. Cervantes 34, 3rd floor, tel. 91/429–2714, fax 91/420–2007. Metro: Banco de España. 12 rooms.*

UNDER 9,000 PTAS. • Hotel Mora. You can't get closer to the Prado (it's across the road), and the price is right (8,875 ptas. for a double with shower-only bathroom)—so reserve well in advance. The friendly, modern, five-floor Mora has a sparkling faux-marble lobby and large rooms with private safes. For breakfast and lunch, the attached café is excellent, affordable, and popular with locals. *Paseo del Prado 32, tel. 91/420–1569, fax 91/420–0564. Café, bar. 61 rooms.*

GRAN VÍA

This central strip used to be Madrid's main shopping and business thoroughfare but now has a sort of passé look, with fast-food outlets and a few theaters. Steer well clear of the red-light district behind the towering Telefónica building (Gran Vía 28).

UNDER 5,000 PTAS. • Hostal Residencia Flores. Doubles cost only 4,000–5,000 ptas. (with shared or private bath) at this eighth-floor *hostal*, which has good views over the surrounding red-tile rooftops. Rooms are clean, fresh, bright, spacious, and decked out in various color schemes. Breakfast is available for 300 ptas. *Gran Vía 30 (enter at Gonález Jiménez Quesada 2), 8th floor dcha., tel. 91/522–8132. Metro: Gran Vía or Callao. Breakfast room. 10 rooms, 4 with bath. Cash only.*

UNDER 7,000 PTAS. • Hostal Andorra. This pleasant, reasonably modern *hostal* has a large lounge and a friendly, helpful owner. The spacious rooms are bright, clean, and well supplied, with white walls, cream-color curtains, carpets, safes, and clean bathrooms with hair dryers; doubles go for 6,000 ptas. Breakfast is served, for 450 ptas., and they'll do your laundry if you like. *Gran Vía 33, 7th floor, tel. 91/532–3116 or 91/531–6603, fax 91/521–7931. Metro: Gran Vía. In-room safes. 20 rooms.*

UNDER 8,000 PTAS. • Hostal Residencia Besaya. Run by a friendly Italian woman, Besaya overlooks Gran Vía and Calle San Bernardo. The cozy rooms have shiny parquet floors and area rugs beneath white walls and pink curtains and bedspreads, and there's a large, attractive sitting area. Doubles with shower-only bathroom cost 8,000 ptas. *C. San Bernardo 13, 8th floor, tel. 91/541–3206, fax 91/541–3207. Metro: Santo Domingo. Phone, laundry. 19 rooms.*

UNDER 11,000 PTAS. • Hotel Regente. If you want to splurge, do it in this large, central, comfy 10-floor hotel. The reception area is all wood paneling, dark leather, and helpful staff. The bright, often spacious rooms (double with bath: 10,700 ptas.) are done in pastels, with polished wooden floors. Breakfast is 600 ptas., a tad expensive, so you may want to pop outside for coffee; the café serves a 1,200-pta. lunch menu. Drop off your laundry if you can't stand it anymore. *Mesonero Romanos 9, tel. 91/521–2941, fax 91/532–3014. Metro: Gran Vía. Breakfast room, cafeteria. 147 rooms.*

SOL AND PLAZA MAYOR

The Puerta del Sol and majestic Plaza Mayor are a five-minute walk from each other. Lodging in this area gives you the perfect base for exploring old Madrid and sampling affordable restaurants and ancient tapas bars, not to mention the Plaza de Orienta and Royal Palace. The Prado museum is two or three Metro stops away.

UNDER 4,000 PTAS. • Hostal Encarnita. You're close to the Plaza Mayor, but this place is pretty basic, with small, spartan doubles with sink for 2,900 ptas. (plus one double with shower for 3,400 ptas.). Use of the shower down the hall costs 200 ptas. a pop; happily, there is no charge for the toilet. At least the owners are friendly, and the TV lounge grants some breathing room. *Marqués de Viuda de Pontejos 7, 4th floor, tel. 91/531–9055. Metro: Sol. 12 rooms, 1 with bath. Cash only.*

Hostal Patria. At press time this small *hostal* was being renovated, and made the impressive promise to rent each of its seven spacious doubles with complete bath for about 3,600 ptas. a night. The location— right next to the Puerta del Sol—could not be more central. *C. Mayor 10, 4th floor, tel. 91/366–2187. Metro: Sol. 7 rooms. Cash only.*

Hostal Rodríguez. Roberto Rodríguez rents out double rooms in his private apartment for 1,800 ptas. (with sink and shared bath) and 3,600 ptas. (with shower-only bathroom). Rooms are spacious but extremely basic, with old furniture and tired-looking showers. Hey, there's satellite TV in the lounge . . . *C. Mayor 14, 4th floor, tel. 91/365–1084. Metro: Sol. 8 rooms, 4 with bath. Cash only.*

UNDER 6,000 PTAS. • Hostal Alicante. This *hostal* is clean and well looked after, featuring simple, white rooms with parquet or tile floors. Doubles with bathtubs are 6,000 ptas., with shower 5,500 ptas. *C. Arenal 16, 2nd floor dcha., tel. 91/531–5178. Metro: Sol. 17 rooms.*

Hostal Residencia Ruano. Here, the four bright double rooms with shower go for 5,800 ptas. a night; the rest share bath facilities but cost a mere 3,500 ptas. The rooms are basic white, the bathrooms old but functional. *C. Mayor 1, 3rd floor dcha., tel. 91/532–1563. Metro: Sol. 22 rooms, 4 with bath. Cash only.*

Hostal Valencia. You walk up four floors to this small, friendly joint, where a double with modern bathroom, fan, and usually a balcony goes for 5,500 ptas. The rooms, painted in pastels, are somewhat worn, but the bathrooms are entirely spiffy. *C. Espoz y Mina 7, 4th floor, tel. 91/521–1845. Metro: Sol. 7 rooms. Cash only.*

UNDER 9,000 PTAS. • Hostal Centro Sol. Bright, smart doubles with bath go for 8,100 ptas. in this unusually elegant *hostal* with a small lounge and laundry service. Some rooms have parquet floors; others have carpets. *Carrera de San Jerónimo 5, 2nd floor, tel. 91/522–1582, fax 91/522–5778. Metro: Sol. 35 rooms. Cash only.*

Hostal La Macarena. Don't worry—no one's doing the macarena here. Friendly, comfortable, and well kept, this place overlooks a quiet square near Plaza Mayor and lots of Old World taverns. Rooms are salmon or yellow, with red curtains, new wood furniture, and immaculate bathrooms with tubs. Doubles cost 8,500 ptas. Only fans and balconies help you with the summer heat, but they'll take your sweaty laundry off your hands. *Cava de San Miguel 8, tel. 91/366–6111, fax 91/364–2757. Metro: Sol or Opera. 25 rooms.*

Hostal Tijcal. A high-class *hostal* seems a contradiction in terms (especially near Plaza Mayor), but the well-decorated Tijcal might be it. These bright, spotless rooms are pink or yellow, with contemporary furniture and private bathrooms; the rate is 7,270 ptas., with a possible discount in July and August. *C. Zaragoza 6, 3rd floor, tel. 91/365–3910 or 91/366–8011, fax 91/364–5260. Fan, laundry, breakfast (500 ptas.), in-room safes. 32 rooms.*

CHUECA

Slightly off the tourist track, this area has a neglected look, but the avant-garde and gay communities have opened cool bars and restaurants.

UNDER 5,000 PTAS. • Hostal Jemasca. Rooms here are small and character-free, but they're clean and cheap: doubles with bath (some with tub, some with shower only) cost a mere 4,500 ptas. *C. Palma 61, 2nd floor, tel. 91/532–7011. Metro: Noviciado. 40 rooms. Cash only.*

UNDER 7,000 PTAS. • Hostal Residenacia Ginebra. It's nothing special—and the owner is somewhat cantankerous—but Ginebra rents clean, modern rooms with private bath for 6,000 ptas. a night. *C. Fuencarral 17, 1st floor izqda, tel. 91/532–1035 or 91/522–3753. Metro: Gran Vía. 16 rooms. Cash only.*

UNDER 11,000 PTAS. • Hotel Monaco. If you've got some extra cash, blow it on a memorable stay in this former brothel. Double rooms with full bath cost 10,700 ptas., and what rooms! They're restored in a quasi–Art Deco style, with fancy ironwork, satin curtains, and mirrors everywhere. This is no secret, so reservations are crucial. Breakfast is 600 ptas. *C. Barbieri 5, tel. 91/522–4630, fax 91/521–1601. Bar, breakfast room. 32 rooms. Cash only.*

MALASAÑA

North of the city center, the Bohemenian Malasaña area is just three Metro stops from the Puerta del Sol, five stops from the Prado.

UNDER 8,000 PTAS. • Hostal Sil. These bright, modern, rooms come in salmon and white, with parquet or tile floors and sparkling bathrooms. Doubles with private bath run 7,900 ptas.; the few with private sink and shared bath are 6,000 ptas. Some rooms have fans. The staff is friendly and efficient. *C. Fuencarral 95, 3rd floor dcha., tel. 91/448–8972 or 91/593–0993, fax 91/447–4829. Metro: Tribunal or Bilbao. 20 rooms.*

SANTA BARBARA

North of Chueca, Santa Bárbara has an oblong plaza with a popular beer-and-shrimp bar (Cervecería Santa Bárbara) and myriad hostelries.

UNDER 5,000 PTAS. • Hostal Castilla. Popular with students and other young 'uns, this simple, friendly hostal rents small, spare but clean doubles with private bath for 4,500 ptas. (bathtub) or 3,700 ptas. (shower). *C. Santa Teresa 9, 3rd floor, tel. 91/310–2176. Metro: Alonso Martínez. 10 rooms, 6 with bath. Cash only.*

ARGÜELLES

Northwest of Plaza de España, Argüelles is a buttoned-up, largely tourist-free residential area with a Corte Inglés department store. You're a short walk from the Parque del Oeste and, in summer, the terrace bars along Paseo del Pintor Rosales.

UNDER 4,000 PTAS. • Pensión Conde de Alba. This little hostal has more singles than doubles, some with private bath (shower only; 3,600 ptas.) and some with private sink and shared bath (3,400 ptas.). The doubles are bright and spacious, but you get what you pay for; furnishings are minimal. *Juan Álvarez Mendizábal 44, 2nd floor dcha., tel. 91/542–2839. Metro: Ventura Rodríguez or Argüelles. 11 rooms. Cash only.*

MONCLOA

Near the university district, this residential area is popular with students.

UNDER 6,000 PTAS. • Hostal Oxford. True, you're several Metro stops from the action, but these quarters are Old World attractive, with antiques and friendly owners. Clean, bright doubles with bathtubs are 5,500 ptas.; those with showers are 4,500 ptas. *Guzmán el Bueno 57, 1st floor, tel. 91/544–8257, fax 91/544–1302. Metro: Argüelles or Moncloa or Islas Filipinas. 6 rooms. Cash only.*

ANTÓN MARTÍN

This lively but somewhat seedy area is near Plaza Santa Ana and the old Lavapiés quarter, and within easy walking distance of the Reina Sofia art museum and Atocha train station.

UNDER 4,000 PTAS. • Pensión Pacios. Here you pay 1,800 ptas. *per person* to stay in a small double or single with private sink and shared bath. Furnishings are relatively basic, but some rooms have balconies. The general vibe is agreeable. *C. Atocha 28, 2nd floor, door A, tel. 91/369–3371. Metro: Antón Martín. 8 rooms, none with bath. Cash only.*

UNDER 9,000 PTAS. • Hostal Residencia Castilla 1. Decor is basic but modern here, in either salmon or beige. Some rooms have balconies. Cozy doubles with full bath cost 8,000 ptas. *C. Atocha 43, 2nd floor dcha., tel. 91/429–0095 or 91/429–3425, fax 91/532–7766. Metro: Antón Martín. 15 rooms.*

ATOCHA

Ultraconvenient to one of Madrid's main long-distance train stations, this site is also good for art lovers: steps from the Reina Sofia museum, a few more steps from the Prado and Thyssen-Bornemisza.

UNDER 6,000 PTAS. • Hostal Alegría. Hard by Atocha station, this pleasant, friendly hostal has a large, public top-floor terrace. Rooms are bright, clean, and well furnished, with modern bathrooms; doubles with private bath are 5,000 ptas. Only two rooms have air-conditioning, so if it's hot, by all means inquire. *Rafael de Riego, tel. 91/528–7682, fax 91/527–7236. Metro: Atocha. 19 rooms, 11 with bath.*

WHERE TO EAT

The Spanish appreciate fresh food, cooked simply to bring out its elemental flavor, then served with a glass of *tinto* (red wine), *blanco* (white wine), *rosado* (rosé), or *cerveza* (beer). For the traveler, having dinner in a series of tapas bars is a great way to get acquainted with Madrid's culinary and human attractions. The word *tapa* means "lid," and may derive from the piece of bread once used to keep the flies out of a glass of wine. Most decent bars give you a free tapa when you order a drink; actual tapas bars are those that specialize in larger portions of tapas called *raciones* (portions) or *pinchos* (skewers), for which they do charge. (You can often request a half ration, a *media ración*.) Price lists are usually well displayed, and you can usually see the food on the counter or in the open kitchen; remember that it's cheaper to eat at the bar than to sit down and be waited on.

Meals here last for hours. Lunch is usually served from 2 to 3:30; dinner starts between 9:30 and 11 and goes on from there. Many of the restaurants listed below are especially popular at lunch, so if that's the meal you're after, get a table around 1:30 to avoid a wait. The same strategy does not work for dinner; the only restaurants open before 9 are either dreadful or aimed expressly at tourists (or both). Note that service is *not* included on the bill in Madrid; a 10% tip is ample.

Spain's booming tourist industry has incited restaurants, cafeterias (cheap eateries), and many bars to provide a *menú del día* (menu of the day) at lunchtime on weekdays. For a low fixed price—usually 1,000–1,500 ptas.—you can choose from several options for each of three courses: say, salad, vegetable, or pasta followed by meat or fish, then fruit, flan, or coffee plus bread and wine, beer, or mineral water. These menus are incredibly good value when you think how much the food and drink would cost at home. In Madrid's less posh restaurants, it's quite common, especially in the summer, for workers to wash down their meals with a mixture of red wine and carbonated lemonade. Some restaurants serve particular dishes, such as paella, on certain days of the week.

In winter, Madrid's hearty, two-course stew, *cocido madrileño*, is usually a filling bargain, consisting of a soup with *fideos* (pasta) followed by a plate of chickpeas, meat, sausages, and cabbage. (In effect, you're served the liquid and solid portions of the stew separately.) Breakfast is usually strong coffee with toast, a croissant, or *churros*—sweet twists of deep-fried batter, a Madrid classic—with butter and jam. Most bars will also make you the ubiquitous *bocadillo* (baguette sandwich), commonly served with ham and cheese. Markets are good places to assemble your own bocadillos for a picnic, with baguettes, *queso* (cheese), and *jamón York* (boiled ham) or pricier *jamón serrano* (air-cured ham).

TAPAS BARS

The best way to experience old Madrid is to go on a tapas crawl between Plaza Santa Ana, the Puerta del Sol, and Plaza Mayor. The rules: casual dress, no handbags, eyes out for muggers and pickpockets, leave small change for each bartender, and treat yourself to a taxi home from the last bar.

Start around 8:30 PM (if you can wait that long) at **La Venencia** (C. Echegaray 7, off San Jerónimo). A *venencia* is the tiny, long-handled sampling tube used to taste sherry blends from the barrel. Several decades' worth of faded Jerez fiesta posters decorate the rusty walls of this venerable institution. Order your aperitivo of *fino* and the chilled dry sherry (150 ptas.) will be served with olives. Tapas include cheese and *cecina* (dried, smoked beef).

Next, look in at **Los Gabrieles** (C. Echegaray 17), once a brothel frequented by matadors and King Alfonso XIII. This may be the finest tiled bar in Madrid, with a panoply of exquisite, multicolor turn-of-the-20th-century advertisements. Drinks are expensive, and tapas are somewhat beside the point.

Continue down the street and duck off to hit **Toscana** (Manuel Fernández y González 10). It may already be packed—the numerous hefty *raciones* go for around 600 ptas.—but you can always squeeze in at the bar. Go back up the alley to the justly famous, family-run, often crowded **La Trucha** (Manuel Fernández y González 3), where you can reserve a table inside and watch the jolly cooks in the little kitchen, or dine outside in nice weather. For 900 ptas., start with La Verbena—canapés of smoked fish and chilled cod-liver paté on toast. La Trucha's *tortilla española* is unique—as light as a soufflé—and the grilled fresh asparagus and *trucha truchanad* (deep-fried trout with ham and garlic) are superb.

Continue up the alleyway and turn left into Plaza Santa Ana. Up on your right is **Taberna Viña P,** which serves shrimp in *alioli* (garlic mayonnaise) on hot toast for 900 ptas., and *tigres,* or stuffed mussels (*mejillones*). Across the square is **Cerveceria Alemana**, hardly changed since Hemingway scribbled at its marble-top tables; it's good for a drink, though the tapas are nothing to write home about. Nearby are the jazz clubs **Café Central** and **Café Jazz Populart** (*see* After Dark, *below*) and the 37 trendy bars of Calle Huertas, behind the Alemana.

At the top of the plaza to the right, take Nuñez del Arce and turn left by the tiled Villa Rosa disco into the alleyway Álvarez Gato. **Las Bravas** (C. Álvarez Gato 3; also C. Espoz y Mina 13, Pasaje de Matheu 5, and C. Cruz 15) is famous for having invented the hot, red *brava* sauce served with roast potatoes (*patatas bravas*, 345 ptas.). Turn right down Calle de la Cruz and leftish into Calle Victoria: On your left is **La Casa del Abuelo** (C. Victoria 12), which has great *gambas a la plancha* (grilled shrimp; 595 ptas.) and *gambas al ajillo* (garlic shrimp; 735 ptas.). Farther down the street is **El Club** (C. Victoria 4), which special-izes in paella and has a cheap bocadillo counter. Continue down to the **Museo de Jamón** (corner of C. Victoria and C. de San Jerónimo), part of a chain that offers great values on Spain's tangy, air-cured hams.

Push on toward the Puerta del Sol and Calle Mayor. Veer left up the pedestrian Calle Postas and then rightish into Calle Sal—suddenly you're in the vast, traffic-free, 17th-century Plaza Mayor, its buskers, artists, and tourists paying outrageous prices to kick back at the outdoor terraces. The best free tapas are at **El Soportal** (Plaza Mayor 33) and the Andalusian **Torre del Oro** (Plaza Mayor 26); in the latter, however, gory photos of bulls winning bullfights may not do wonders for your appetite. Cut across the plaza to Cava de San Miguel, lined with several touristy tapas bars; this eventually leads to Cava Baja, where, down on the right, **La Chata** (Cava Baja 24) offers a good free tapa with a good glass of wine (200 ptas.) and scrambles some mean eggs with asparagus and ham (green eggs and ham!—900 ptas.).

Up in Chueca, **Bocaíto** (C. Libertad 6) has two bars piled with expensive but filling tapas, such as shrimp and garlic on toast. In Salamanca, your excuse for settling into cozy **La Taberna del Buey** (C. General Pardiñas 7) is the mound of tasty Swiss cheese they give away with each drink. (The fancy canapés are more for the well-heeled locals.) If you've visited the Museo Lazaro Galdiano (*see* Worth Seeing–Spanish Culture and History, *below*), cross Calle Serrano to long-established **José Luis** (C. Ser-rano 89), an upmarket tapas bar with beer and wine at decent prices, highly tempting if you're anything but completely destitute. If you attend a bullfight, leave Las Ventas (the bullring), head across Calle Alcalá, and walk one block to **Puerta Grande** (C. Pedro Heredia 23) for the most atmospheric bull-related bar and restaurant in town. Rich *rabo de toro* (bull's-tail stew) for two is 1,250 ptas. Farther up Alcalá on the left, **El Rincón de Jerez** (C. Rufino Blanco 5) is a charming, tiled Andalusian bull bar with *manzanilla*, a strong white wine from the Deep South. At 11 PM after bullfights, the crowd sings to the Virgin Mary, who glows in a niche in the wall here.

RESTAURANTS

CASCO ANTIGUO

Madrid's central old city includes Plaza Mayor and the narrow twisting streets leading to the Latina dis-trict.

UNDER 1,200 PTAS. • Mi Pueblo. English-speaking Ramón Baldellon has served bargain meals in this rustic little bistro near Plaza Mayor for more than 20 years. At lunchtime, his 1,100-pta. menú del día gives you a big old choice of eight appetizers and entrées plus dessert or coffee and a glass of wine. House specialties are regional sausages and kebabs that you grill at your table in funny little earthen-ware barbeques. *Costanilla de Santiago 2, tel. 91/548–2073. Metro: Sol or Opera. Closed Mon. and Aug.1–15. No dinner Sun.*

Taberna de Antonio Sanchéz. A 10-minute walk from Plaza Mayor to the old Lavapiés area (*see* Worth Seeing–Neighborhoods, *below*) and a step back in time brings you to this wood-beamed 1830 tavern. Take tapas by the zinc-topped bar, with its stuffed bull's head and bullfight pics, or Madrileño meals in the somewhat stuffy restaurant in back. The 1,100-pta. lunchtime menu might offer a *menestra* (mix-ture) of vegetables, tuna, potatoes, *rabo de toro* (bulls'-tail stew), *olla gitana* (a bean, vegetable, and meat stew), tortilla with onion and cod, dessert or coffee, and a half carafe of wine. This place is a seri-ous tourist attraction, so if you must carry a purse or pack, grip it tightly on your way in and out. *Mesón de Paredes 13, tel. 91/539–7826. Metro: Tirso de Molina. No dinner Sun.*

UNDER 1,500 PTAS. • El Almendro. This quaint, gaily painted old bar on the corner of an alleyway is especially popular at night. Strong, white manzanilla wine is sold in half bottles for 600 ptas. At lunchtime, it's easier to grab a table or a beer barrel on the ground floor or in the basement, and order a salad for 375–900 ptas., some large *roscas* (bread rings) stuffed with paté, chorizo, or *lomo* (pork loin) for 850–1,225 ptas., or *huevos rotos* (roughly scrambled eggs with potatoes) for 900 ptas. *C. Almendro 13, tel. 91/65–4252. Cash only.*

UNDER 3,000 PTAS. • Palacio de Anglona. This massive (400-seat) restaurant takes up several stories in a modernized old palace. The informal crowd likes the posh setting (painted tables, fuchsia walls), attentive service, relaxing background music, and modern Basque cuisine. Options include grilled vegetables (875 ptas.), sirloin with wine and foie gras (1,550 ptas.), and eggplant stuffed with cod (775 ptas.). A bottle of agreeable red Chivite Feudo *crianza* costs 1,200 ptas., and there's good ice cream for dessert. *C. Segovia 13, tel. 91/366–3753. Metro: Latina or Sol.*

CHUECA

UNDER 1,500 PTAS. • La Bardemcilla. Owned by Monica Bardem, sister of Spanish film actor Javier, this fresh, bright, and comfy restaurant-bar attracts a hip young crowd. The yellow walls are hung with paintings and photographs, and the parquet floors all but gleam. At lunchtime the menu costs a 1,250 ptas., including a beer or glass of wine. On Tuesday the main course is the hearty winter stew *cocido madrileño;* on Thursday it's paella. Doors are open till 3:30 AM. *C. Augusto Figueroa 47, tel. 91/ 521–4256. Metro: Chueca. Closed Sun. and 1st wk in Aug. No lunch Sat.*

Momo. Traditional cuisine gets modern touches in this friendly, quick-service, modern joint with orange walls and yellow-blob ceiling lights. The 1,250-pta. menú del día might get you a crisp lettuce salad with onions, orange chunks, and sesame dressing, followed by turkey with mild curry sauce and french fries, accompanied by bread, two glasses of wine, and dessert. À la carte meals are also very reasonable, with Caesar salad for 600 ptas. *C. Augusto Figueroa 41, tel. 91/532–7162. Metro: Chueca.*

Taberna Carmencita. Opened in 1850, this little Basque restaurant has a faded elegance. (Poets like García Lorca, Pablo Neruda, and Alberti were regulars.) The home cooking appears in a few different set menus (1,500 ptas.), each served with a half carafe of wine. Jolly waitresses fuss around the small tables, set between old, tiled walls, gleaming brass trim, lace curtains, and parquet floors; think about bean salad, chicken wings, meatballs, or good old *cocido madrileño* between October and May. *C. Libertad 16, tel. 91/531–6612. Metro: Chueca or Banco de España. Closed Sun. and Aug. No lunch Sat.*

Tienda de Vinos (Casa Angel). Already saddled with two names, this simple tavern is also known to locals as El Comunista, after a guitarist who used to play here. Opened in 1890 and hardly changed since, the Tienda has marble-top tables, high ceilings, and half-paneled walls hung with photos of bygone stars. Meals are a great value: Starters include lentils (300 ptas.), garlic soup (400 ptas.), and mixed vegetables (400 ptas.); follow them with veal fillet (500 ptas.), innards such as liver, kidneys, or brains (hey, you're not in Kansas anymore; 500 ptas.), or a plate of mixed cheeses or cold sausage (400 ptas.). A half carafe of wine costs 300 ptas. *C. Augusto Figueroa 35, tel. 91/521–7012. Metro: Chueca. Closed Sun. and Aug.–mid-Sept. Cash only.*

UNDER 2,000 PTAS. • Casa Vallejo. Considering the 18 delicious choices you're given for the two main courses, and the charming setting—yellow walls, red linens, prints, paintings, and discreet music—this cozy place offers exceptional value. There's a delicate touch to the tropical salad; the steamed scallops are tender; the lambs' kidneys are grilled to perfection; the *lomo* (pork loin) gets a Cointreau sauce; and desserts include apple strudel. The lunchtime set menu is 1,800 ptas. San Lorenzo is a narrow side street just west of Hortaleza and Chueca. *C. San Lorenzo 9, tel. 91/308–6158. Metro: Alonso Martínez. Reservations essential. Closed Sun. No dinner Mon.*

UNDER 2,500 PTAS. • Restaurante Extremadura. Of these two Extremaduran restaurants, No. 31 is larger and has much more atmosphere, with elegant, pink, half-tiled walls, yellow brocade curtains, nicely set tables, and a small bar. (No. 13 is bright and pleasing but a little on the touristy side.) The menú del día for both lunch and dinner is 2,500 ptas. A typical plan comprises salad or vegetables followed by roast game, perhaps goat, in season plus bread, dessert, and a large carafe of wine. *C. Libertad 13, tel. 91/531–8958. Closed Sun. night, Mon., and Aug.; C. Libertad 31, tel. 91/523–3503. Metro: Banco de España or Chueca. Closed Wed. and July. No dinner Tues.*

GRAN VÍA

This long, wide avenue has seen better days, but part of it still fills up at night with movie- and theatergoers. Fast-food joints proliferate.

UNDER 1,500 PTAS. • Vía 59. This big, modern, bright, split-level café-restaurant near Plaza de España serves surprisingly good food and takes no siesta. Snag some tasty salmon pinchos at the bar on your way in (195 ptas.). The 1,400-pta. menu might include gazpacho, pasta, or spinach and eggs followed by veal escalope with Roquefort sauce or stewed squid, bread, a glass of wine, and coffee or a strawberry tart. À la carte, there's pasta, pizza, and paella; the latter, for one person, is 1,450 ptas. *Gran Vía 59, tel. 91/547–6767. Metro: Plaza de España or Santo Domingo.*

MALASAÑA

Busier at night than during the day—especially on weekends—this arty district around Plaza Dos de Mayo has narrow, cobblestoned, tree-lined streets and a number of relaxed little restaurants.

UNDER 1,200 PTAS. • La Glorieta (formerly Restaurante Castilla). There's a Mediterranean vibe here, with rough white walls, yellow linens, fresh flowers, and some sofa seating. The menu nods toward the sea: The 1,100-pta. lunch menu might offer salad, fish soup, lamb chops, roast bream, half a bottle of wine, and strawberries with cream. *Manuela Malasaña 37, tel. 91/448–4016. Metro: Bilbao or San Bernardo. Closed Sun. and Aug.*

Sandos. In summertime, sit outdoors on this corner of Plaza Dos de Mayo and tuck into clams with rice, veal escalope, grilled hake, dessert, and half a bottle of wine for 1,100 ptas. Regardless of the weather, you can also opt for pasta (from 700 ptas.) or a large pizza (from 1,000 ptas.). *Plaza Dos de Mayo 8, tel. 91/448–8414. Metro: Bilbao, Tribunal, or San Bernardo. Cash only.*

UNDER 1,500 PTAS. • El Txoko. This classy yet friendly little Basque bistro, complete with wood beams, serves a 1,500-pta. menú del día that's popular with locals. House specialties include peppers stuffed with meat, veal escalope in cream sauce, and cod omelet; your choices come with dessert and half a bottle of wine. *Manuela Malasaña 9, tel. 91/448–4688. Metro: Bilbao or Tribunal. Closed Sun.–Mon. No dinner Tues.*

PLAZA DE ESPAÑA

Just east of the plaza there's an eclectic mix of foreign restaurants that, lacking native chefs, are generally substandard. The few exceptions follow.

UNDER 1,500 PTAS. • El Charro. Open since 1957, this old Mexican favorite offers a hefty lunch menu ("El Especial Charro") for 1,300 ptas., perhaps including enchiladas with chili con carne, *arroz con pollo* (chicken with rice), and *frijoles fritos* (refried beans). Nachos and *jalapeños rellenos* (stuffed peppers) are ready side dishes. For 1,600 ptas. you can opt for the menu that adds a selection of starters (*antojitos*) and two glasses of wine to your main courses. À la carte choices are many—a veal taco (780 ptas.), a margarita (525 ptas.). It's a cheerful place; the large outer area has ivy and picture windows. *C. San Leonardo 3, tel. 91/547–6439. Metro: Banco de España. Closed Mon. and Aug. No lunch Tues.*

La Corte. This bright, spacious, Castilian-style tavern is a 10- to 15-minute walk uphill from Plaza de España, across from the Conde Duque complex (a showbiz venue with an art gallery). The menú del día (1,325 ptas.) packs generous portions of pasta or, say, a casserole of kidney beans with clams, followed by steak, fish, or pizza plus bread, dessert, and a bottle of wine. You can splash out here if you want to; the à la carte menu has pizzas, pastas, and steaks, and the pricier menus are still good values at 2,850 and 3,750 ptas. *Conde Duque 30, tel. 91/548–3791. Metro: Plaza de España or San Bernardo. No dinner Sun.*

La Llama. Set in a large wooden cabin with ivy climbing the side windows, this genuine Peruvian restaurant (next to El Charro; *see above*) has a fun 1,200-pta. set lunch menu with your choice of five starters and five entrées. Good bets are *papa rellena* (potato stuffed with meat) and *ropa vieja con frijoles y arroz* (beef with rice and black beans). The tiled tables are handsome, travel posters give some flavor, and the pisco sour cocktail (495 ptas.), served with tacos and hot red sauce, should put you in the mood if nothing else does. *C. San Leonardo 3, tel. 91/542–0889. Metro: Plaza de España. Closed Mon.*

OPERA

This area near the Palacio Real and the Teatro Real opera house is a delight to explore, with large terrace bars and small restaurants opening onto newly recobbled streets.

UNDER 1,500 PTAS. • Kalas. On a side street near Plaza de Oriente, Kalas is a cozy little place serving fresh market produce on its Monday–Saturday 1,500-pta. menú del día, and in winter it does Sunday brunch. Painted in modern pastel colors in need of a second coat, it's still clean and bright and the Cuban-American owners can turn out a salad with cucumber, prawns, and yogurt followed by chicken with apple or scrambled eggs with salmon and cod, or, eggplant stuffed with fish plus coffee or dessert and one glass of wine. *C. Amnistia 6, tel. 91/559–1755. Metro: Opera. Mar.–Sept., closed Sun., no dinner Mon.; Oct.–Feb., closed Mon.*

La Botillería. In a prime position overlooking the Royal Palace, the weekday lunch menu is 1,400 ptas. with, say, salads and paella to start, main courses with fish or meat or fried eggs with potatoes and *morcilla* (black sausage), with ice-cream or fruit to finish as well as bread and a little carafe of wine. This café is another classy addition to the catering empire of Opus Dei priest Jesús Lezama, with lots of brass, dark wood, stained glass, yellow brocade drapes, and even a well-fed resident sparrow. *Plaza de Oriente 4, tel. 91/548–4620. Metro: Opera.*

PASEO DE FLORIDA

Casa is a must for a budget lunch if you come to see the Goya frescoes in the hermitage of San Antonio de la Florida (*see* Worth Seeing–Houses of Worship, *below*) but it's popular with locals for cheap group binges in the evening. The area is pleasant.

UNDER 2,500 PTAS. • Casa Mingo. Styled as an Asturian cider tavern, cheery Casa Mingo is across the street from the hermitage of San Antonio de la Florida, near the Manzanares River. For about 2,000 ptas. you can feast on succulent roast chicken, salad, and sausages plus, of course, hard cider. You dine on long, shared plank tables or, in nice weather, outdoors. Arrive early to avoid a wait (around 1 for lunch, 8:30 for dinner), as crowds are likely. *Paseo de la Florida 2, tel. 91/547–7918. Metro: Príncipe Pío. Cash only.*

PLAZA SANTA ANA

In addition to Madrid's thickest array of tapas bars, Santa Ana is thronged with well-priced, well-decorated restaurants popular with local professionals.

UNDER 1,000 PTAS. • Bar Pizza. Generous portions, a 950-pta. set menu with wine, and a cozy bistro atmosphere make this joint *muy* popular with young backpackers, who, inexplicably sometimes wait an hour or two for a table. Pizzas are complemented by pastas and big salads of apple, celery, and Roquefort cheese. The premises are clean but worn, with nicotine-color ceilings, half-paneled walls, brown marble tables, and a terra-cotta tile floor. *C. León 8, tel. 91/420–1298. Metro: Antón Martín or Sevilla. No lunch Tues.*

La Finca Susana. By 2 PM on weekdays, there's a line for the bargain menú del día (995 ptas.) at this large, trendy, fun place near the Sevilla Metro station. The fresh, Mediterranean meals might start with lasagna or a salad of leeks and anchovies, then move on to stewed rabbit, pork loin in soy sauce, or duck with couscous and prunes. *C. Arlabán 4, tel. 91/369–3557. Metro: Sevilla.*

UNDER 1,350 PTAS. • Artemisa. Healthy vegans pack this bright, no-smoking vegetarian for gazpacho, creamed vegetable soup with Parmesan cheese, and other imaginative dishes including some with chicken for carnivorous companions. The wine is organic. The long, cozy dining area has pink walls, art posters, and new wooden furniture. There's another branch at Tres Cruces 4 (tel. 91/521–8721; Metro: Gran Vía). *C. Ventura de la Vega 4, tel. 91/429–5092. Metro: Sevilla.*

Botafumeiro. This agreeable Galician place in an alley near Plaza Santa Ana has clean, sensible modern decor and good tapas. The menú del día (1,100–1,500 ptas.) includes appetizers like scrambled eggs with blood sausage or carrot soup, and entrées tending toward stewed meat and fish. *C. Álvarez Gato 9, tel. 91/522–0669. Metro: Sol or Sevilla. Closed Tues. and July.*

UNDER 1,500 PTAS. • Isadora. Amid wood-paneled walls and eclectic art, this bistro is packed at lunchtime with office workers tucking into the 1,500-pta. weekday menu— one of the best in Madrid, with pasta or a big salad followed by juicy *pollo asado* (roast chicken) or stuffed *calabacín* (eggplant). The *ensalada de salmon y bacalao* (salmon and cod salad; 1,600 ptas.), is a meal in itself, but desserts are equally generous—apple strudel with ice cream, or *fresas con nata* (strawberries and cream). Chef-owner José Gomèz Esteban, who has lived in London and speaks excellent English, often wanders around making sure everyone is happy. At night the après-theater and -flamenco crowd takes over. *C. Huertas 6, tel. 91/369–4391. Metro: Sevilla and Anton Martín. Closed Sun., holidays, and Aug. Cash only.*

El Club. This ratty glass-and-chrome cafeteria has served Madrid's best cheap paella since 1973. A large shellfish/chicken paella for two is 3,000 ptas.; add a jug of sangria (1,100 ptas.) and perhaps a tossed salad (490 ptas.). Alternately, the hefty set menu (1,500 ptas.) might offer seafood soup, salad, a dollop of paella or steak, roast lamb, suckling pig, or mixed fried fish, and bread, wine, and dessert or coffee. If you're really out of cash, pick up a 300-pta. bocadillo at the counter, open 6:30 AM–2:30 AM. *C. Victoria 4, tel. 91/522–2293. Metro: Sol.*

La Biotika. Welcome to the purists' vegetarian hangout, where a small shop at the entrance sells macrobiotic groceries. Compact and cozy, the restaurant concocts enormous salads, hearty soups, fresh bread, and creative tofu dishes that make healthy, flavorful meals. *C. Amor de Dios 3, 91/429–0780. Metro: Sevilla or Antón Martín. Cash only.*

Matador Parilla. This happy, two-story, wood-beamed tavern is popular with a young set for its good-value grilled meats, pizzas, and pastas. The cheapest set menu (1,400 ptas.) might offer a salad, oxtail stew, and grilled sausages; the "El Juli" bullfight menu (4,000 ptas. for two) includes baked potatoes, a big mixed grill, and a bottle of wine. *C. de la Cruz 13, tel. 91/522–3595. Metro: Sol. Closed Mon.*

Restaurante Gallego Do Salmón. With lots of wood and pink-granite floors, this is a pretty smart Galician. On weekdays, the menú del día holds steady at 1,500 ptas. day and night, and usually buys you a fillet of grilled salmon with tartar sauce or *lacón con grelos* (boiled ham with beet tops) plus a bottle of wine. *C. León 4, tel. 91/429–8997. Metro: Sevilla or Antón Martín. Closed Mon.*

Sanabresa. Classic, sensibly priced Spanish fare attracts crowds who want a filling meal here; just be prepared for the bright lights, plastic plants, and booming TV. The setting is spotless, and service is good. Choice usually include *pechuga villaroy* (fried, breaded chicken breast in béchamel sauce) and, on Thursday, paella. Arrive early—1:30 for lunch, 8:30 for dinner—to avoid having to cool your heels. *C. Amor de Dios 12, 91/429–0338. Metro: Antón Martín and Sevilla. Closd Sun. and Aug.*

UNDER 1,700 PTAS. • Restaurante Pereira. Fish is the thing at this large, bright Galician; opt for the 1,700-pta. menú del día and you get a choice of fruits of the sea. Starters include salads, soups, and vegetables; the entrée is often swordfish or trout, accompanied by bread and half a bottle of white wine, with flan or ice cream for dessert. *C. Cervantes 16, tel. 91/429–8403. Metro: Sevilla or Antón Martín. Closed Mon. and Aug. No dinner Sun.*

PRADO

Avoid that museum cafeteria—take a break from the art to sample just a bit more of Madrid.

UNDER 1,200 PTAS. • El Txoko. Part of Madrid's Euskal-Etxea (Basque Center), this is *the* bargain-basement restaurant and bar, with green and yellow walls, prints by Basque artists, and wooden tables topped with plastic cloths. Helpful, English-speaking Iziar Manzarbeitia runs the casual little den, dishing out generous portions of soup, chicken in sauce, tuna, or battered sole, all with bread, dessert, and a bottle of good *tinto*. On Sunday, it's just great tapas until 3 PM. *C. Jovellanos 3, tel. 91/532–3443. Metro: Banco de España. Closed Mon. and Aug. No dinner Sun. Cash only.*

UNDER 1,500 PTAS. • Al Natural. Festooned with paintings of fruit and vegetables and big wicker-basket lamp shades, this long, arched *salón* has a warm, cavernous glow; indeed, it might be Madrid's most inviting vegetarian restaurant. The 1,450-pta. set menu includes fancy salads, soybean sausages with wild mushrooms, and stuffed eggplant, and each day there's a different chicken or fish dish for companions. *C. Zorrilla 11, tel. 91/369–4709. Metro: Banco de España. No dinner Sun.*

UNDER 2,000 PTAS. • Champagneria Gala. Down toward the Reina Sofía museum and Atocha station, Gala is a good evening choice, with a menú del día for 1,750 ptas. The appetizing choices range from hearty bean stew and paella to *fideus* (noodles) and risotto. The "champagne" thing is a bit of a tease, since the Catalan cava costs extra. While we're at it, the paella could be better; still, reserve ahead or get here really early. The inner dining area is a glassed-in patio with a canopy of trees and plants; the walls of the outer area are painted in a riot of color. *C. Moratín 22, tel. 91/429–2562. Metro: Antón Martín or Atocha. Cash only.*

La Vaca Verónica. A highly efficient all-female crew runs this colorful place, popular for its transatlantic fusion cooking. The menú del día (1,900 ptas.) gives you a big plate of that day's meat—say, a strip of steak with picante sauce—and a choice of potatoes, peppers, or one of many salads, followed by home-made dessert and bottomless coffee, not to mention bread and wine. À la carte you've got pastas, grills, a meaty pie, and cheesy vegetables. *C. Moratín 38, tel. 91/427–9827. Metro: Atocha or Antón Martín. Closed Sun. No lunch Sat.*

CAFÉS

Madrid's traditional cafés have long been meeting sites for the intelligentsia, who may hold *tertulias* (discussion groups) over endless cups of coffee or stronger stuff. Several cafés now serve raciones and full-blown set menus as well as snacks, and most have summer terraces on which refreshment costs a little more.

Café Comercial. The oldest café in Madrid—open since about 1870, and run by the Contreras family since 1909—Comercial now has the newest touch, a bank of computers. A haunt of writers, thespians, and film types, it's mostly tawny marble, with brass fittings, columns, mirrors, and a good view of the traffic circle on the edge of Malasaña. Beer starts at 150 ptas.; a toasted sandwich mixto (ham and cheese sandwich) goes for 400 ptas. *Glorieta de Bilbao 7, tel. 91/521–5655. Metro: Bilbao. Open Mon.– Thurs. 7 AM–1 AM, Fri. and Sat. 8 AM–2 AM, Sun. 1 PM–11 PM.*

Café Gijón. Over a century old, this venerable café is beloved of writers and artists, who often gather at the window tables after lunch. Here, said lunch includes a standard set menu for 1,500 ptas.; at night you can opt for the same or descend to the cavelike restaurant for the works. The terrace bar is good for after-work people-watching. *Paseo de Recoletos 21, tel. 91/531–7037. Metro: Banco de España or Colón.*

El Espejo. This old bar and restaurant have great Belle Epoque tiles and Art Deco furnishings, not to mention enticing tapas on the counter. The new terrace bar, a pleasant pit stop for tapas and cheap meals year-round, is in a splendid iron-framed conservatory; in summer, a pianist serenades the late-evening outdoor crowd as skateboarders clatter by on the wide sidewalk. *Paseo de Recoletos 31, tel. 91/ 308–2347. Metro: Colón.*

MARKETS

Near Plaza Mayor, the **Mercado de San Miguel** (Plaza de San Miguel, tel. 91/548–1214; Metro: Sol) occupies a restored wrought-iron hall. It's basic, but fine for picnic supplies. Better is **Antón Martín** (C. Santa Isabel 5, tel. 91/369–0620; Metro: Antón Martín); still better is **La Paz** (C. Ayala 28, tel. 91/435–0743; Metro: Serrano). Despite its northern origins, **Marks & Spencer** (C. Serrano 52, tel. 91/520–0000; Metro: Serrano) is a real showplace for fresh Spanish foodstuffs, especially cheese.

The easiest place for general grocery shopping is **El Corte Inglés** (*see* Shopping, *below*). For upscale stuff, seek out El Corte Inglés's Gourmet Club department or **González** (C. León 12, tel. 91/429–5618; Metro: Sevilla or Antón Martín), open until late Tuesday–Saturday.

Most bars will wrap a bocadillo for you. **El Club,** near Plaza Santa Ana (*see* Where to Eat, *above*), has cheap takeout food of all kinds.

FIESTAS

Madrid's calendar may pack more holidays than that of any other European capital. For **La Romería de San Blas** (February 3), Madrileños in 17th-century costume hold a mass and picnic by the Observatorio in Parque del Retiro to commemorate St. Blaise. **Semana Santa** (Holy Week) brings evening processions from various churches, especially on Holy Thursday and Good Friday. On Holy Saturday night in the town of Chinchón (*see* Near Madrid, *below*), 200 actors stage a Passion play at 9 PM. For **Las Mayas,** held the first Sunday in May in the Lavapiés district, each street elects a May Queen (*maya*), who sits surrounded by flowers in a sort of spring fertility ritual. Madrid's annual urban blowout takes the form of the **Fiestas de San Isidro** (May 10–26), a flurry of events featuring big-time bullfights and culminating in big-time music and dance on the Día de San Isidro (May 15).

For the **Fiesta de la Hermita de San Antonio de Florida** (June 13), a holiday that should perhaps be celebrated more widely, *señoritas* line up to throw pins in the hermitage's baptismal font, dip their hands, and ask St Anthony for a boyfriend. If any pins in the water stick to their hands, they will successfully snag that number of *novios* in the coming year.

A **Christmas Fair** enlivens the Plaza Mayor from mid-December through January 5, the eve of Epiphany. For **Noche Vieja** (New Year's Eve), crowds pack the Puerta del Sol to witness the clock strike midnight, quaffing cava and eating a grape for each of the 12 chimes. If you don't choke, your wishes come true.

EXPLORING MADRID

FEATURE ATTRACTIONS

ARAB WALL

The city of Madrid was founded on the hill near Calle Cuesta de la Vega beside the ruins of this wall, which protected a fortress built here in the 8th century by Emir Mohammed I. In addition to being an excellent defensive position, the site had plentiful water and was called *Mayrit,* which is Arabic for "water source" and the likely origin of the city's name. All that remains of the *medina*—the old Arab city that was formed within the walls of the fortress—is the neighborhood's crazy quilt of streets and plazas, which probably follow the same layout they had more than 1,100 years ago. *Cuesta de la Vega, near Puente de Segovia. Metro: Opera.*

BANCO DE ESPAÑA

Spain's massive central bank, built in 1884, takes up an entire block. It is said that the nation's gold reserves are held in great vaults that stretch under the Plaza de Cibeles traffic circle all the way to the fountain, surrounded by an underground river. The bank is not open to visitors, but if you can dodge traffic well enough to reach the median strip in front of it, you can take a decent snapshot of the fountain and the palaces with the Puerta de Alcalá arch in the background. *C. Alcalá 50, Plaza de Cibeles. Metro: Banco de España.*

BOLSA DE COMERCIO

Madrid's stock exchange is the dynamo of Spain's recent economic growth, yet—now that stocks are traded electronically—there is no more frenetic human activity around the leafy Plaza de la Lealtad. Fronted by neoclassical columns, the basilica-like building was designed by architect Enrique María Repullés and inaugurated in 1893. A splendid neo-Baroque clock towers from the center of the floor—which was known by traders as the "park" thanks to its proliferation of fine wood—and looky-loos get a grand view of financiers at work from the upper-floor gallery. *Plaza de la Lealtad 1, tel. 91/589–1408. Tours weekdays at noon; bring passport or ID.*

CASA DE AMÉRICA

A cultural center and art gallery focusing on Latin America, the Casa de América is housed in the sumptuously decorated, allegedly haunted Palacio de Linares—built 1873–88 by the Marqués de Linares, whose father had made his fortune in the New World.

The building resonates with mystery; a secret spiral staircase leads up to the marquess's study, from which a discreet window overlooks the front door. But the real mystery concerns the young noble's marriage. His father told him he could marry whomever he wanted, but when the marqués announced his love for the daughter of the nearby tobacconist, Dad's attitude changed dramatically, and he never said why. The marqués—José—assumed the problem was class, and he married his love, Raimunda, after his father died. Later, however, going through his father's papers, he discovered a letter telling him that Raimunda was his half-sister. The couple were horrified, but they obtained permission from Pope León XIII to live together as long as they remained celibate. Legend has them burying their child in a wall, and it is she who allegedly haunts the palace now. *Paseo de Recoletos 2, tel. 91/595–4809. Metro: Banco de España. Admission: 450 ptas. Open by appointment.*

CASÓN DEL BUEN RETIRO

Free with a Prado ticket, this Prado annex is just a five-minute walk from the main museum. The building (once a ballroom), the nearby Army Museum, and the formal gardens in the Retiro are all that remain of the Buen Retiro palace, Madrid's second royal complex, which filled the entire neighborhood until the early 19th century. On display are 19th-century Spanish paintings and sculpture, including works by Sorolla and Rusiñol. At press time the complex was scheduled to reopen in late 2001 after a regal restoration, with brand-new halls devoted to 17th- and 19th-century Spanish art. *C. Alfonso XIII. Metro: Banco de España.*

CAVA DE SAN MIGUEL

The narrow, picturesque streets behind the Plaza de la Villa are well worth exploring. From the Plaza Mayor, turn onto the Plaza de San Miguel, with the glass-and-iron San Miguel market on your right. Proceed down Cava de San Miguel past the row of taverns built right into the retaining wall of the plaza above. Each one specializes in a different food: Mesón de Champiñones, mushrooms; Mesón de Boquerónes, anchovies; Mesón de Tortilla, excellent Spanish omelets; and so on. Madrileños and travelers alike flock here each evening to sample the food and sing along with raucous musicians, who delight in playing foreign tunes for tourists.

As Cava San Miguel becomes Calle Cuchilleros, you'll see **Botín** on the left, a onetime haunt of Ernest Hemingway established in 1725 and proud of its status as Madrid's oldest restaurant (actually the oldest in the world, according to the *Guinness Book of World Records*). Curvy Cuchilleros was once a moat just outside the city walls. *Metro: Sol or Opera.*

CENTRO DE ARTE REINA SOFIA

Named for present-day Queen Sofía, Madrid's museum of modern art is housed in a converted hospital whose classic, granite austerity is somewhat relieved (or ruined, depending on your point of view) by the two glass elevator shafts on the facade. The collection focuses on Spain's three great modern masters: Pablo Picasso, Salvador Dalí, and Joan Miró.

Take the elevator to the second floor to see the permanent collections; the other floors house visiting exhibits. The first rooms are dedicated to the beginnings of Spain's modern movement and contain paintings from around the turn of the 20th century. The focal point is Picasso's 1901 *Woman in Blue*— hardly beautiful, but strikingly representational compared to his later works. Moving on, be sure to see Dalí's splintered, blue-gray *Self-Portrait* in which the artist depicts a few of his favorite things: a morning newspaper and a pack of cigarettes. The other highlight here is Picasso's *Musical Instruments on a Table,* one of many variations on this theme.

The Reina Sofía's showpiece is Picasso's famous *Guernica* which occupies the center hall and is surrounded by dozens of studies for individual figures within it. The huge painting depicts the horror of the Nazi Condor Legion's bombing of the ancient Basque town of Guernica in 1937, an act during the Civil War that brought Spanish dictator Francisco Franco to power. The work—in many ways a 20th-century version of Goya's *The 3rd of May*—is something of a national shrine, as evidenced by the solemnity of Spaniards viewing it. The painting was not brought into Spain until 1981; Picasso, an ardent antifascist, refused to allow it to enter the country until democracy was restored.

The room in front of *Guernica* contains, among other things, six canvases by Miró, known for his childlike graphicism. Opposite is a hall dedicated to Salvador Dalí, with paintings bequeathed to the government in the artist's will. Although Dalí is perhaps best known for works of a somewhat whimsical nature, many of these canvases are dark, haunting, and bursting with symbolism. Among the best known are *The Great Masturbator* (1929) and *The Enigma of Hitler* (1939), with its broken, dripping telephone.

The rest of the museum is devoted to more recent art, including the massive, gravity-defying sculpture *Toki Egin* by Eduardo Chillida, considered Spain's greatest living sculptor, and five textural paintings by Barcelona artist Antoni Tàpies, whose works incorporate such materials as wrinkled sheets and straw. *C. Santa Isabel 52, tel. 91/467–5062, http://museoreinasofia.mcu.es. Admission: 500 ptas., free Sat. after 2:30 and all day Sun. Open Mon. and Wed.–Sat. 10–9, Sun. 10–2:30.*

CONGRESO DE LOS DIPUTADOS

The lower house of Spain's parliament (*cortés*), this 19th-century building leapt to prominence on the evening of February 23, 1981, when gun-toting Colonel Antonio Tejero led a group of guards into the chamber and held Spain's administration at gunpoint in an attempted coup. As cameras captured the drama, shots were fired into the ceiling (and were left here, to remind politicians that they're not immortal). As tanks took to the streets in Valencia and hundreds of Basques and Catalans fled to neighboring France, Madrid was deserted, its denizens parked fearfully indoors. After a tense standoff in and around the Cortés, the new King Juan Carlos got on TV and told the Spanish people that his military commanders would remain loyal to him. The coup collapsed without bloodshed, and Spain's fledgling democracy was set in stone. *Plaza de las Cortes, tel. 91/390–6000. Metro: Banco de España or Sevilla. Open by appointment Mon.–Sat. 10–12:30.*

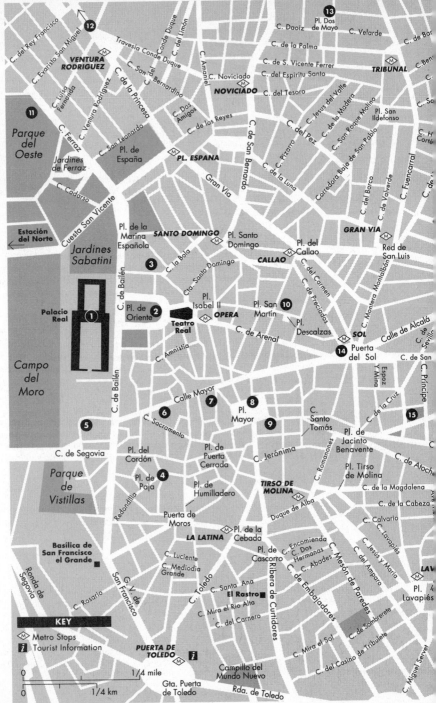

C. del Rey Francisco

VENTURA
RODRIGUEZ

C. Evaristo San Miguel

C. del Limón

Conde Duque

Travesia Conde Duque

C. Amaniel

C. Noviciado

C. de S. Vicente Ferrer
C. del Espiritu Santo

C. del Tesoro

Pl. Dos
de Mayo

C. Daoiz

C. Velarde

C. de Bar

C. de la Palma

TRIBUNAL

C. Ben

C.

C. San Bernardina

C. Luisa
Fernanda

C. Ferraz

C. Ventura Rodriguez

C. de la Princesa

C. San Bernardo

C. Dos
Amigos

C. de los Reyes

NOVICIADO

C. Jesus del Valle

C. de la Madera

C. San Roque Molino

Pl. San
Ildefonso

C. So

C. H
Corte

11

Parque
del
Oeste

Jardines
de Ferraz

C. San Leonardo

Pl. de
España

C. Cadarso

PL. ESPAÑA

Gran Via

C. de San Bernardo

C. del Pez

C. C. Pizarro

C. de la Luna

Corredera Baja de San Pablo

C. del Barco

C. de Valverde

C. Fuencarral

C. de

Estación
del Norte

Cuesta San Vicente

Jardines
Sabatini

Pl. de la
Marina
Española

SANTO DOMINGO

C. la Bola

Cta. Santo Domingo

Pl. Santo
Domingo

CALLAO

Pl. del
Callao

C. del Carmen

GRAN VIA

Red de
San Luis

C. Montera Mantabán

Palacio
Real

C. de Bailén

Pl. de
Oriente

Campo
del
Moro

C. de Bailén

Teatro
Real

Pl.
Isabel II

OPERA

C. de Arenal

C. Amnistia

Pl. San
Martín

Pl.
Descalzas

SOL

Puerta
del Sol

Calle de Alcalá

C. de San

C. de Sevilla

Pl. de
Preciados

3

2

1

10

14

Parque
de
Vistillas

C. de Segovia

Pl. del
Cordón

Pl. de
Paja

Redondilla

C. Sacramento

Calle Mayor

Pl. de
Puerta
Cerrada

C. Jerónima

Pl.
Mayor

C.
Santo
Tomás

Pl. de
Jacinto
Benavente

C. Ramanones

Pl. Tirso
de Molina

C. de la Cruz

C. de Atoch

C. de la Magdalena

C. Príncipe

15

5

6

7

8

9

4

Basílica de
San Francisco
el Grande

Ronda de Segovia

C. Rosario

G. V. de San Francisco

Pl. de
Humilladero

Puerta de
Moros

Pl. de la
Cebada

LA LATINA

C. Luciente

C. Mediodia
Grande

C. Toledo

C. Santa Ana

El Rastro

C. Mira el Río Alta

C. del Carnero

Duque de Alba

TIRSO DE
MOLINA

C. de la Cabeza

C. Calvario

C. Lavapiés

Pl. de
Cascorro

Pl. de
Dos
Hermanas

C. Encomienda

C. Abades

C. Mesón de Paredes

C. de Embajadores

Ribera de Curtidores

C. Jesus y Maria

C. del Amparo

LAV

Pl. L
Lavapiés

KEY

Ⓜ Metro Stops

𝒊 Tourist Information

PUERTA DE
TOLEDO

Campillo del
Mundo Nuevo

C. de Sombrerete

C. Mira el Sol

C. del Casino de Tribulete

C. Miguel Servet

0   1/4 mile

0   1/4 km

Gta. Puerta
de Toledo

Rda. de Toledo

12

13

i

i

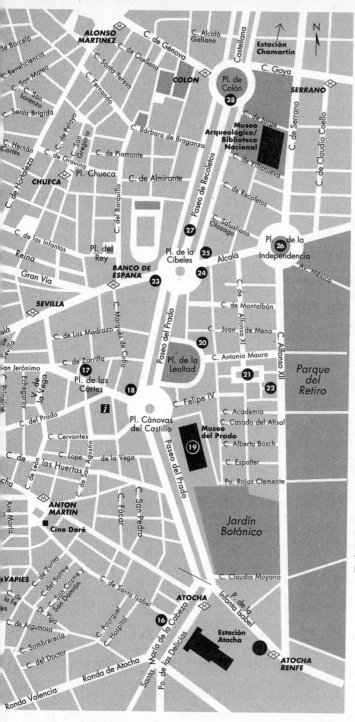

Arab Wall, 5
Banco España, 23
Bolsa de
Comercio, 20
Casa de
America, 25
Casón de
Buen Retiro, 22
Cava de
San Miguel, 7
Centro de Arte
Reina Sofía, 16
Congreso de los
Diputados, 17
Convento de la
Encarnación, 3
Convento de las
Descalzas
Reales, 10
Faro de Madrid, 12
Museo del
Ejército, 21
Museo
del Prado, 19
Museo Thyssen-
Bornemisza, 18
Palacio de
Communi-
caciones, 24
Palacio de
Santa Cruz, 9
Palacio Real, 1
Paseo de
Recoletos/
Paseo del
Prado, 27
Plaza de Colón, 28
Plaza de la Paja, 4
Plaza de la Villa, 6
Plaza de la
Oriente, 2
Plaza Dos
de Mayo, 13
Plaza Mayor, 8
Plaza Santa Ana, 15
Puerta de Acalá, 26
Puerta del Sol, 14
Templo de
Debod, 11

CONVENTO DE LA ENCARNACIÓN

Once connected to the Royal Palace by an underground passageway, the Augustinian Convent of the Incarnation was founded in 1611 by the wife of Felipe III. It holds several artistic treasures, but the main attraction is the reliquary, which holds among sacred bones a vial containing the dried blood of St. Pantaleón, which is said to liquify every year on July 27. You can enter on the same ticket used at Descalzas Reales (*see below*). *Plaza de la Encarnación, tel. 91/547–0510. Metro: Sol. Admission: 425 ptas. Open Tues.–Sat. 10:30–2:45 and 4–5:45, Sun. 11–2.*

CONVENTO DE LAS DESCALZAS REALES

The 16th-century Convent of the Royal Barefoot Nuns was restricted for 200 years to women of royal blood. Its plain, brick-and-stone facade hides a treasure trove, including paintings by Zurbarán, Titian, and Brueghel the Elder, as well as a hall of sumptuous tapestries crafted from drawings by Peter Paul Rubens. The convent was founded in 1559 by Juana of Austria, whose daughter shut herself up here rather than endure marriage to Felipe II. A handful of nuns (not necessarily royal) still live here, cultivating their own vegetables in the convent's garden. You can only visit as part of a guided tour, usually conducted once a day in English and the rest of the day in Spanish. *Plaza de las Descalzas Reales 3, tel. 91/454–8800 info, 91/454–8803 to book visit. Metro: Sol. Admission: 700 ptas. Open Tues.–Thurs. and Sat. 10:30–12:45 and 4–5:45, Fri. 10:30–12:45, Sun. 11–1:45.*

FARO DE MADRID

Looking like a half-finished airport control tower, this landlocked 1992 *faro* (lighthouse) gives you a great view of Madrid and the Guadarrama Mountains. A 12-person glass elevator soars to the observation deck 320 ft above the nearby Arco de la Victoria, a 1956 monument to Franco's victory in the Civil War. *Avda. de los Reyes Católicos s/n, tel. 91/544–8104. Metro: Moncloa. Admission: 200 ptas. Open Tues.–Fri. 10–1:45 and 5–6:45, weekends 10:30–5:15.*

MUSEO DEL EJERCITO

A real treat for arms-and-armor buffs, this army museum is right on the museum mile and was originally the main entrance and reception hall of the Buen Retiro royal palace, mostly destroyed during the Napoleonic wars. Among the 27,000 items on view are a sword that allegedly belonged to the Spanish hero El Cid; suits of armor; bizarre-looking pistols with barrels capable of holding scores of bullets; Moorish tents; and a cross carried by Christopher Columbus. It's an pretty entertaining collection. *C. Mendez Nuñez 1, tel. 91/522–8977. Metro: Banco de España. Admission: 100 ptas. Open Tues.–Sun. 10–2.*

MUSEO DEL PRADO

When the Prado was commissioned by King Carlos III, in 1785, it was meant to be a natural-science museum. The king, popularly remembered as "Madrid's best mayor," wanted the museum, the adjoining botanical gardens, and the elegant Paseo del Prado to serve as a center of scientific enlightenment for his subjects. By the time the building was completed in 1819, its purpose had changed to exhibiting the mind-blowing collection of art gathered by Spanish royalty since the time of Ferdinand and Isabella. The museum is now adding a massive new wing, designed by Rafael Moneo, that will resurrect long-hidden works by Zurbarán and Pereda and more than double the number of paintings on display from the permanent collection.

Painting is one of Spain's greatest contributions to world culture, and the Prado's jewels are its works by the nation's three great masters: Francisco Goya, Diego Velázquez, and El Greco. The museum also holds masterpieces by Flemish and Italian artists, collected when their lands were part of the Spanish Empire. The museum benefited greatly from the anticlerical laws of 1836, which forced monasteries, convents, and churches to forfeit many of their artworks for public display.

Enter the Prado via the Goya entrance, with steps opposite the Ritz Hotel, or the less-crowded Murillo door opposite the Jardín Botánico. The layout changes (pick up a current floor plans), but the first hall on the second floor, starting from the Murillo entrance, is usually dedicated to **Goya.**

You can see the meticulous brushwork of **Velázquez** (1599–1660) in his numerous portraits of kings and queens. Look for the magnificent *Las Hilanderas* (*The Spinners*), evidence of the artist's talent for painting light. The Prado's most famous canvas, Velázquez' s *Las Meninas* (*The Maids of Honor*), combines a self-portrait of the artist at work with a mirror reflection of the king and queen in a revolutionary interplay of space and perspective. Picasso was obsessed with this work and painted several copies of it in his own abstract style, now on display in Barcelona's Picasso Museum.

Bureau de change

Cambio

外国為替

In this city, you can find money on almost any street.

NO-FEE FOREIGN EXCHANGE

The Chase Manhattan Bank has over 80 convenient
locations near New York City destinations such as:

    Times Square
    Rockefeller Center
    Empire State Building
    2 World Trade Center
    United Nations Plaza

Exchange any of 75 foreign currencies

◯ CHASE

THE RIGHT RELATIONSHIP IS EVERYTHING.®

The south ends of the second and top floors are reserved for **Goya** (1746–1828), whose works span a staggering range of tone, from bucolic to horrific. Among his early masterpieces are portraits of the family of King Carlos IV, for whom he was court painter—one glance at their unflattering and imbecilic expressions, especially in *The Family of Carlos IV*, reveals the loathing Goya developed for these self-indulgent, reactionary rulers. His famous side-by-side *Clothed Maja* and *Naked Maja* may represent the young duchess of Alba, whom Goya adored and frequently painted. No one knows whether she ever returned his affection. The adjacent rooms house a series of idyllic scenes of Spaniards at play, painted as designs for tapestries.

Goya's paintings took on political purpose starting in 1808, when the population of Madrid rose up against occupying French troops. *The 2nd of May* portrays the insurrection at the Puerta del Sol, and its even more terrifying companion piece, *The 3rd of May*, depicts the nighttime executions of patriots who had rebelled the day before. The garish light effects in this work typify the romantic style, which favors drama over detail, and make it one of the most powerful indictments of violence ever committed to canvas.

Goya's "black paintings" are dark, disturbing works, completed late in his life, that reflect his inner turmoil after losing his hearing and his deep embitterment over the bloody War of Independence. *Saturn Devouring One of His Sons* may concern the cruel, destructive force of time.

The Prado's ground floor is filled with early Flemish paintings, including the bizarre masterpiece *Garden of Earthly Delights* by **Hieronymus Bosch,** which was recently restored. On the same floor is a hall filled with the passionately spiritual works of **El Greco** (Doménikos Theotokópoulos, 1541–1614), the Greek-born artist who lived and worked in Toledo. El Greco is known for his mystical, elongated faces. His style was quite shocking to a public accustomed to strictly representational images; and because he wanted his art to provoke emotion, El Greco is sometimes called the world's first "modern" painter. Two of his greatest paintings, *The Resurrection* and *The Adoration of the Shepherds*, are on view here. It's also worth stopping for Titian's *Self-portrait* and Raphael's fine *Visitation. Paseo del Prado s/n, tel. 91/420–3768, www.mcs.es/prado. Admission: 500 ptas; free Sat. after 2:30 and all day Sun. Open Tues.–Sat. 9–7, Sun. 9–2.*

MUSEO THYSSEN-BORNEMISZA

Madrid's newest art center occupies the Renaissance-era Villahermosa Palace, stylishly renovated by Rafael Moneo with plenty of natural light and lush, deep-salmon walls. The ambitious collection of 800 paintings traces the history of Western art through examples from every important movement, beginning with 13th-century Italy.

The works were gathered from the 1920s on by industrialist Baron Hans Heinrich Thyssen-Bornemisza and his father. At the urging of his Spanish wife (a former Miss Spain), the baron agreed to donate the collection to Spain. Critics have described the collection as the minor works of major artists and the major works of minor artists, but the museum itself is beautiful, and its Impressionist paintings are the only ones on display in the country.

One of the high points here is Hans Holbein's *Portrait of Henry VIII* (purchased from the late Princess Diana's grandfather, who used the money to buy a new Bugatti sports car). American artists are also well represented; look for the Gilbert Stuart portrait of George Washington's cook, and note how closely the composition and rendering resemble the artist's famous painting of the Founding Father himself. Two halls are devoted to the Impressionists and post-Impressionists, including many works by Pissarro and a few each by Renoir, Monet, Degas, Van Gogh, and Cézanne.

Within 20th-century art, the baron shows a proclivity for terror-filled (albeit dynamic and colorful) German expressionism, but there are also some soothing works by Georgia O'Keeffe and Andrew Wyeth. *Paseo del Prado 8, tel. 91/369–0151. Metro: Banco de España. Admission: 700 ptas. Tues.–Sun. 10–7.*

PALACIO DE COMUNICACIONES

This ornate building on the southeast side of Plaza de Cibeles is Madrid's main post office. Pop in for stamps if you need them, or make use of the phone center. *Plaza Cibeles, tel. 902/197197 for general info. Metro: Banco de España. Open weekdays 9 AM–10 PM, Saturday 9–8, Sunday 10–1.*

PALACIO DE SANTA CRUZ

Near Plaza Mayor, this 17th-century Habsburg palace with four huge courtyards has been used as a prison and a courthouse; since 1901 is has housed Spain's Ministry of Foreign Affairs. In the 19th century, George Borrow—an itinerant English Bible salesman better known for his wonderful travel chronicles—was incarcerated here for three weeks, accused of spreading liberal ideas. A diplomat in one of the garret offices has the depressing task of trying to regain Gibraltar from the British; at least there's a comfortable sofa for siestas. *Plaza de Santa Cruz, tel. 91/379–9550. Metro: Tirso de Molina. Visits by written appointment.*

PALACIO REAL

The Royal Palace was commissioned in the early 18th century by the first of Spain's Bourbon rulers, Felipe V, after Madrid's first Alcázar (a 9th-century Moorish fortress) burned down and the palace was built on the same strategic site. Before you enter, stroll around the graceful Patio de Armas and admire the classical French architecture. King Felipe was obviously inspired by his childhood days at Versailles with his grandfather Louis XIV. Look for the stone statues of Inca prince Atahualpa and Aztec king Montezuma, perhaps the only tributes in Spain to these pre-Columbian American rulers. Notice how the steep bluff drops westward to the Manzanares River—on a clear day, this vantage point also commands a good view of the mountain passes leading into Madrid from Old Castile, and it becomes obvious why the Moors picked this particular spot for a fortress.

Inside, the palace's 2,800 rooms compete with each other for over-the-top opulence. A nearly two-hour guided tour in English of the principal 50 rooms winds a mile-long path through the palace. Highlights include the Salón de Gaspirini, King Carlos III's private apartments—a riot of rococo decoration, with swirling, inlaid floors and curlicued, ceramic wall and ceiling decoration, all glistening in the light of a 2-ton crystal chandelier; the Salón de Trono, an exceedingly grand throne room with the royal seats of King Juan Carlos and Queen Sofía; and the banquet hall, the palace's largest room, which seats up to 140 people for state dinners. No monarch has lived here since 1931, when Alfonso XIII was hounded out of the country by a populace fed up with centuries of royal oppression. The current king and queen live in the far simpler Zarzuela Palace on the outskirts of Madrid, using this palace only for state functions and official occasions such as the first Middle East peace talks, held here in 1991.

You can also visit the Biblioteca Real (Royal Library), which has a first edition of Cervantes's *Don Quixote*; the Museo de Música (Music Museum), where five stringed instruments by Stradivarius form the world's largest collection; the Armería Real (Royal Armory), with Europe's largest array of historic suits of armor and some frightening medieval torture implements; and the Real Oficina de Farmacía (Royal Pharmacy), with an assortment of vials and flasks that were used to mix the king's medicines. *Plaza de Oriente, tel. 91/542–0059. Metro: Opera. Admission: 950 ptas., guided tour 1,000 ptas. Open Tues.– Sat. 9–6 (9–5 in winter), Sun. 9–3 (9–2 in winter). Closed during official receptions.*

PASEO DE RECOLETOS / PASEO DEL PRADO

Traffic notwithstanding, this wide boulevard with tree-lined walks is perfect for a north–south stroll between Plaza de Colón, the Thyssen, the Prado, the Botanical Gardens, and the Reina Sofia. In summertime, café tables line its length. The grand yellow mansion roughly 100 yards north of Plaza Cibeles, now a bank, was once home of the Marqués de Salamanca, who a century ago built the adjoining posh neighborhood that bears his name. The much-photographed Plaza Cibeles is encircled by the Palacio de Comunicaciónes, the Banco de España, the army headquarters and the Casa de América. The splendidly sculpted Fuente de la Cibeles features Cybele, goddess of nature, heading west in a chariot pulled by lions. The diety now has to cope with football fans: Real Madrid supporters celebrate here when their team wins a championship.

The section called Paseo del Prado was built in the late 18th century as a nature walk leading past the Prado (originally conceived as a natural-history museum), the Botanical Gardens, and a hospital, since demolished, devoted to the study of the curative properties of plants. The fountain in Plaza Canovas del Castillo depicts the sculpted god Neptune, overlooked by the Prado and Thyssen museums and the Palace and Ritz hotels. Neptune's fork disappears occasionally; one of the luxury abodes must have cutlery issues. *Metro: Colón or Banco de España.*

PLAZA DE COLÓN

This massive modern square is named for Christopher Columbus, and a statue of the explorer—identical to one in Barcelona's port—looks west from a high tower on one corner. Beneath the plaza is the Centro Cultural de la Villa, a new performing-arts facility, and the airport bus station. Behind Plaza Colón is Calle Serrano, Madrid's premier shopping street (think Gucci, Prada, and Loewe); cruise it in either direction for some serious window shopping. *Metro: Colón.*

PLAZA DE LA PAJA

Laid out at the top of a hill, on Costanilla San Andrés, the Plaza de la Paja was the most important square in medieval Madrid. Although a few upscale restaurants have moved in, the site retains its own atmosphere. The church at the top is that of San Andrés; around the back lived San Isidro himself, Madrid's patron saint.

The plaza's jewel is the **Capilla del Obispo** (Bishop's Chapel), built between 1520 and 1530. This was where peasants deposited their tithes—literally, one-tenth of their crop—as the stacks of wheat on the chapel's ceramic tiles attest. Architecturally, the chapel marks a transition from the Gothic period, which gave the structure its blockish shape, to the Renaissance, source of the decorations. Try to get inside to see the intricately carved polychrome altarpiece by Francisco Giralta, featuring scenes from the life of Christ. Opening hours are erratic; you'll have the best chance of a peek during mass or on a feast day.

PLAZA DOS DE MAYO

This plaza is at the heart of the bohemian Malasaña district, where kids frolic by day and their elders frolic at night, especially on weekends or during a barrio fiesta. The graffiti-scarred neighborhood remains as rebellious as it was on fateful May 2, 1808, when Madrileños made an heroic last stand against Napoléon's occupying troops at the barracks here. In that event, two brave artillery captains, Luis Daoiz and Pedro Velarde, gathered 60 soldiers, armed 150 civilians, and resisted French retaliation for an hour. The plaza's brick arch is all that remains of the barracks; beside it, a memorial by Antonio Solá immortalizes the two "popular heroes." The captains did have drawn swords, but these have long since disappeared. *Metro: Tribunal, Bilbao, or San Bernardo.*

PLAZA DE LA VILLA

Madrid's town council has met in this medieval-looking complex since the Middle Ages, and it remains the **ayuntamiento** (city hall). The oldest building is **Casa de los Lujanes**, on the east side—the one with the Mudéjar tower. Built as a private home in the late 15th century, the house carries the Lujanes crest over the main doorway. Also on the east end is the brick-and-stone **Casa de la Villa** (1629), a classically Madrileño structure with its clean lines and spire-topped towers. Connected by an overhead walkway, the **Casa de Cisneros** (1537) is one of Madrid's rare examples of the flamboyant plateresque style, which has been likened to splashing water—a liquid exuberance wrought in stone. Down Calle de Codo, off the plaza, on the right is a signed convent where nuns sell cookies 9:30–1 and 4–6:30; just ring the bell. *C. Mayor (2 blocks west of Plaza Mayor). Metro: Opera. Ayuntamiento open for free guided tour in Spanish Mon. at 5.*

PLAZA DE ORIENTE

The stately plaza in front of the Royal Palace is surrounded by massive stone statues of various Spanish kings from Ataulfo to Fernando VI. These sculptures were meant to be mounted on the balustrade on top of the palace (where there are now stone urns), but Queen Isabel of Farnesio, one of the first royals to live in the palace, had them removed because she was afraid their enormous weight would bring the roof down. But according to palace insiders, the queen wanted the statues removed because her own likeness had not been placed front and center.

The statue of King Felipe IV in the center of the plaza was the first equestrian bronze ever cast with a rearing horse. The action pose comes from a Velázquez painting of the king with which the monarch was so smitten that in 1641 he commissioned an Italian artist, Pietro de Tacca, to turn it into a sculpture. De Tacca enlisted Galileo's help in configuring the statue's weight such that it wouldn't topple over.

In the minds of most Madrileños, the Plaza de Oriente is forever linked with Francisco Franco. The *generalísimo* liked to speak from the balcony of the Royal Palace to his thousands of followers as they crammed into the plaza below. Even now, on the November anniversary of Franco's death, the plaza fills with supporters, most of whom are old-timers, though in the 1990s the occasion drew some Nazi flag–waving skinheads from other European countries in a chilling fascist tribute. *Metro: Opera.*

PLAZA MAYOR

Austere, grand, and often surprisingly quiet compared to the rest of Madrid, this arcaded square has seen it all: autos-da-fé (trials of faith, i.e., public burnings of heretics); the canonization of saints; criminal executions; royal marriages, such as that of Princess María and the King of Hungary in 1629; bullfights (until 1847); masked balls; fireworks; and all manner of events and celebrations. It still hosts fairs, bazaars, and performances.

Measuring 360 ft by 300 ft, Madrid's Plaza Mayor is one of the largest and grandest public squares in Europe. It was designed by Juan de Herrera, the architect to Felipe II and designer of the El Escorial monastery, northwest of Madrid. Construction of the plaza lasted just two years and was finished in 1620 under Felipe III, whose equestrian statue stands in the center. The inauguration ceremonies included the canonization of four Spanish saints: Teresa of Avila, Ignatius of Loyola, Isidro (Madrid's male patron saint), and Francis Xavier.

This space was once occupied by a city market, and many of the surrounding streets retain the names of the trades and foodstuffs once headquartered there. Nearby are Calle de Cuchilleros (Cutlers' Street), Calle de Lechuga (Lettuce Street), Calle de Fresa (Strawberry Street), and Calle de Botoneros (Button-makers' Street). The plaza's oldest building is the one with the brightly painted murals and the gray spires, called Casa de la Panadería (the Bakery) in honor of the bread shop on top of which it was built. Opposite is the Casa de la Carnicería (Butcher Shop), now a police station.

The plaza is closed to motorized traffic, making it a pleasant place to sit in the sun or while away a warm summer evening at one of the sidewalk cafés, watching alfresco artists, street musicians, and Madrileños from all walks of life. Every Sunday morning, stamp and coin vendors set up shop, and around Christmas the plaza fills with stalls selling trees, ornaments, and nativity scenes, as well as all kinds of practical jokes and tricks for the Día de los Inocentes (December 28)—the Spanish version of April Fool's Day. *Metro: Sol.*

PLAZA SANTA ANA

This somewhat rundown plaza is one of the hubs of Madrid's heaving weekend nightlife, chock-a-block with tapas bars and after-hours nightclubs and dives (*see* Tapas Bars, *above, and* After Dark, *below*). It's also the heart of the more salubriously named Barrio de Las Letras—roughly, Literary Quarter—so called because the **Teatro Español,** a Spanish theatre founded in 1745, stands on the site of the earlier Corral del Príncipe, a 16th-century open-air comedy theater. The Teatro Español only stages plays written by Spaniards, and fortunately two great writers lived nearby: Miguel de Cervantes (1547–1616) and Félix Lope de Vega (1562–1635). Monuments to Pedro Calderón de la Barca (1600–81) and Federico García Lorca (1899–1936) stand at opposite ends of the square. *Metro: Sevilla or Antón Martín.*

PUERTA DE ALCALÁ

This triumphal arch was built by Carlos III in 1778 to mark the site of one of the ancient city gates. You can still see the bomb damage inflicted during the Civil War. *Metro: Retiro.*

PUERTA DEL SOL

The so-called Sun Gate is not just Madrid's central plaza; it's essentially Spain's central plaza, marking Kilometer 0 for the nation's wheel of principal highways. (The mark is on the southern sidewalk, in front of the neoclassical government building.) On New Year's Eve, revelers pack the plaza clutching bottles of cava and by tradition swallow a grape at each of the 12 chimes of the plaza's clock.

It is said that there was a city gate here during the time of Ferdinand and Isabella, backed by a castle bearing a sun motif; but by the 16th century the Puerta del Sol was taking shape as a plaza, bordered by a hospital and two convents. All that remains of the two onetime fountains is a copy of the statue of Mariblanca, Madrid's Venus. Recent additions: the equestrian statue of king-mayor **Carlos III,** who designed the Paseo del Prado and Puerta de Alcalá. A statue of **El Oso y el Madroño** (the bear and the strawberry tree), the symbol of Madrid, stands at the entrance to the main shopping area. *Metro: Sol.*

TEMPLO DE DEBOD

This authentic 4th-century BC Egyptian temple was donated to Spain in gratitude for its technical assistance with the construction of the Aswan Dam. It's near the site of the former Montaña barracks, where Madrileños bloodily crushed the beginnings of a Francoist uprising in 1936. *Hill in Parque de la Montaña, near Estación del Norte, tel. 91/765–1008.. Metro: Plaza de España. Admission: 300 ptas; free Wed. and Sun. Open Tues.–Fri. 10–1:30 and 4:30–6 (Apr.–Sept. 4:30–7:45), weekends 10–8.*

MUSEUMS

CASA DE LA MONEDA

Housed in the granite hulk of the former Spanish mint and stamp factory, this museum tells the story of filthy lucre through the ages, from the first use of stones, salt, shells, and bracelets to the euro.

History suggests that Europe's new single currency will not last forever. Having hosted so many invaders and interlopers over the centuries, Spain has amassed a fine collection of coins from the ancient Greeks, Romans, Visigoths, and Moors, not to mention home-grown change. The history of notes is also well documented, and there's a good display of Spanish stamps. *C. Dr. Esquerdo 36, tel. 91/566–6544. Metro: O'Donnell. Admission free. Open Tues.–Fri. 10–2:30 and 5–7:30; weekends 10–2.*

MUSEO ARQUEOLÓGICO

This palatial museum is a fascinating introduction to Iberia, with some 100,000 exhibits including the *Dama de Elche*, a bust of a wealthy, 4th-century Iberian woman. Note that her headgear is a rough precursor to the mantillas and hair combs still associated with traditional Spanish dress. The ancient Visigothic votive crowns are another highlight, discovered in 1859 near Toledo and believed to date from the 8th century. The biggest attraction, however, is underground, in the garden—a replica of the prehistoric cave paintings in Altamira, Cantabria. (Access to the real thing is highly restricted.) The museum shares its neoclassical building with the **Biblioteca Nacional** (National Library). *C. Serrano 13, tel. 91/577–7912. Metro: Colón or Serrano. Admission: 500 ptas., free Sat. after 2:30 and all day Sun. Museum open Tues.–Sat. 9:30–8:30, Sun. 9:30–2:30; reproduction cave paintings, Tues.–Sat. 11–2:30 and 5:30–6:30, Sun.. 11–2:30.*

MUSEO CERRALBO

This intriguing mansion near Plaza de España was built in 1883 for the wealthy Enrique de Aguilera y Gamboa, 17th marqués of Cerralbo—an intellectual writer, conservative politician, amateur archaeologist, and fanatical collector of art and artifacts. The marqués left the house and doo-dads to the state when he died in 1922; the latter include paintings by Zurbarán, El Greco, Varonés, Tibera, and Cano and thousands of curios from all over the world, from armor to peace pipes. Most notable is El Greco's *The Ecstacy of St. Francis of Assisi*, which survived a trip to Moscow for safekeeping during the Civil War.

The mansion itself is one of three in Madrid (along with the Museo Lázaro Galdiano and Museo Romántico) that really show how the other half, or the other 0.1%, lived during one of Spain's happier periods. Here, the ground-floor mirrored ballroom reflects the owners' busy social life; in the study upstairs, the husband dedicated himself to reading, writing, and charting the course of his collection, knowing he would bequeath it to Spain (he and his wife were childless). *C. Ventura Rodriguez 17, tel. 91/547–3646. Metro: Ventura Rodríguez. Admission: 400 ptas. Open Tues.–Sat. 10–2, Sun. 10:30–1:30.*

MUSEO DE AMÉRICA

Madrid's Museum of America has one of Europe's finest collections of pre-Colombian art and artifacts. The centerpiece is the extremely rare illustrated glyph parchment of the Mayan *Códice Tro-cortesana* (1250–1500), known as the Madrid Codex since it was found in a private collection here in the 19th century. Equally eye-popping is the **Treasure of the Quimbayas**, a bunch of 1,000- to 1,500-year-old gold and silver figures from Colombia.

Two floors of rooms show hoards of old artifacts retrieved by Spanish conquistadors and other adventurers between the 16th and 20th centuries, as well as documents relating to their trips. Some rooms, organized rather confusingly, cover various aspects of Latin American life through the ages. *Avda. Reyes Catolicos 6, tel. 91/549–2641. Admission: 500 ptas. Metro: Moncloa. Open Tues.–Sat. 10 AM–3 PM, Sun. 10–2:30.*

MUSEO DE ANTROPOLÓGIA

Also known as the Museo de Etnología, this three-story building near the Parque del Retiro is Spain's premier anthropological museum, with sections devoted to human evolution in Africa, America, Asia, Europe, and the Pacific. The Pacific area, on the ground floor, is largest, with substantial holdings from the Philippines. Much of this stuff was first displayed in the Palacio de Velázquez (in the park) in 1887, including the 33-ft canoe hewn from a single tree trunk. Items from each ethnic group are divided by religious and ecological criteria.

Ghouls will enjoy the grisly exhibits on the order of deformed female skulls from Bolivia and the Philippines, a mummified male *guanche* from Tenerife, and a tattooed Maori death mask. And don't say Spaniards are short: the skeleton of Don Agustin Luengo y Capilla, a 19th-century Extremaduran, reveals a man 7 ft 4 in tall when he died at age 26. *C. Alfonso XII 68, tel. 91/530–6418. Metro: Atocha–RENFE. Admission: 400 ptas. Open Tues.–Sat. 10 AM–7:30 PM, Sun. 10–2.*

MUSEO DE LA CIUDAD

Adjoining the Auditorio Nacional de Música, this modern facility traces Madrid's development from the earliest times to the present day. Cool models of the city show its growth, as well as individual buildings such as the bullring; costumes and books add some cultural color. And if you've been dying to know how the city's utilities work, settle in and read about everything from the water works to the gas supply. *Príncipe de Vergara 140, tel. 91/588–6599. Metro: Cruz de Rayo. Admission free. Open Mon.–Sat. 10–2 and 4–6 (5–7 in summer), Sun. 10–2.*

MUSEO DE SAN ISIDRO

Just opened in 2000, this museum has a mixture of archaeological items found in the capital—more than 300,000, yikes—and relics pertaining to Madrid's patron, St. Isidro. Born in 1082, Isidro was, according to legend, a farm laborer near the Manzanares River. He actually did very little work, but had the best-tended fields thanks to hours of prayer. When his employer came out to investigate this phenomenon, he saw two angels ploughing along on either side of the man. Because Isidro once saved his son after the boy fell into a well (by willing the water to rise to the top), his remains were, until about 100 years ago, paraded through Madrid in times of drought in the hope that he would bring rain.

The museum occupies a 16th-century palace on the site where the saint supposedly lived in the 11th and 12th centuries. You can see the well from which Isidro's son was allegedly rescued near a small chapel. Sadly, there are no explanations in English and, worse, no indication that the saint's body actually rests elsewhere—in the Catedral de la Almudena. But purists might still enjoy the rest of the finds, which date from Neolithic times through to the present day. *Plaza de San Andrés 2, tel. 91/366–7415. Admission free. Open Tues.–Fri. 9:30–8, weekends 10–2.*

MUSEO NAVAL

An ugly glass facade on the historic Paseo del Prado belies a ship-shape series of displays recounting the history and triumphs of one of the world's greatest navies. The prize exhibit is the map of the Americas made by Juan de la Cosa in 1500—the first one drawn in Europe, probably presented to avid sponsors Ferdinand and Isabella. There are ancient tomes, early globes, details of explorers' routes, navigational gadgetry, weapons, items from Christopher Columbus's expeditions, and old charts; one room displays items recovered in 1991 from the *Nao San Diego*, a galleon sunk off the Philippines by the Dutch in 1600. *Paseo del Prado 5, tel. 91/379–5299. Metro: Banco de España. Admission free. Open Tues.–Sun. 10:30–1:30.*

SPANISH CULTURE AND HISTORY

BIBLIOTECA NACIONAL

Spain's National Library has recently undergone years of renovations and finally has an accessible way of showing off its treasures. An interactive book museum allows visitors to see almost 500 of the most emblematic works, a history of writing from its origins to the CD-ROM. *Paseo de Recoletos 20, tel. 91/580–7759. Metro: Serrano or Colón. Admission free.*

CASA-MUSEO DE LOPE DE VEGA

Félix Lope de Vega (1562–1635), still the most prolific playwright ever, is considered only second to Cervantes in Spanish literature. Perhaps that's why Lope de Vega's house is now on Calle Cervantes; politics, politics. (Cervantes lived just up the street.) Lope de Vega wrote some 1,800 comedies and 400 mystery plays, plus numerous sketches and lyrics. Although he became a priest in 1614, his passionate scribblings reveal that he did not renounce all of life's earthly pleasures.

The playwright bought this house in 1610 and lived here until he died. Reopened as a museum in 1930, it contains only a few pieces of his furniture; the rest came from a convent, a fact that might have amused him. Still, the house looks much as it was when he lived here, lined with 1,500 books; and the garden contains a small well and some trees described in his writing. *C. Cervantes 11, tel. 91/429–9216. Metro: Antón Martin or Sevilla. Admission: 200 ptas., free Wed. Open Tues.–Fri. 9:30–2, Sat. 10–2.*

CENTRO CULTURAL CONDE DUQUE

You're most likely to come across these old barracks during a festival, as jazz, flamenco, and pop concerts are occasionally held in its huge patios. City Hall also tried to stage ballet here, but there was an unseemly uproar when those at the front—in the most expensive seats—could not see the dancers' feet on the raised stage. The barracks are named after Gaspar de Guzmán (1587–1645), Conde Duque de Olivares and a favorite of Felipe IV.

The main door of the *cuartel* (barracks) is a masterpiece of Baroque stone carving by Pedro de Ribera, who built the barracks in the 18th century for King Felipe V's royal guard. In 1869 the barracks suffered a major fire and fell into ruin; the city took over in 1969 and restored the three-story building. One wing contains an art gallery. *C. Conde Duque 9–11, tel. Centro Cultural: 91/588–5824. Metro: Noviciado or San Bernardo. Open Tues.–Sat. 10 –2 and 5:30–9, Sun. 10:30–2:30.*

CINE DORÉ

This hip little gem of an Art Nouveau movie theater was built in 1923 by Críspulo Moro and lovingly restored after its renaissance as La Filmoteca Española, home of the Spanish National Film Archives. A stucco facade with small pillars gives way to a sleek lobby and café-bar trimmed with smart pink neon. Film buffs make good use of the bookshop. The two small, entirely modern theaters show Spanish films and eclectic foreign films in their original languages; periodic festivals feature particular directors or genres. *C. Santa Isabel 3, tel. 91/369–1125. Metro: Antón Martín. Admission: 225 ptas. Box office open daily 4:15–10:30; bookshop open daily 4:15–10.*

CIRCULO DE BELLAS ARTES

Easily recognized from Calle Alcalá for its towering architecture and the huge picture windows on its magnificent lounge-bar, the Círculo is Madrid's official fine-arts club. The six-floor 1926 building, designed by Antonio Palacios (author of the nearby Palacio de Comunicaciones in Plaza Cibeles) contains a theater, concert hall, movie theater, exhibition spaces, workshops, and a library. It's generally a hive of activity; foreign correspondents meet guests here for breakfast or dinner. But the focal point is the bar, which centers around a splendid sculpture of a reclining nude woman, and has great views of the street. In summer there's a relaxed terrace on the broad sidewalk out front. Regular *tertulias* (highfalutin' discussion groups) meet by the side windows, and in February the Carnival Ball is, as it should be, a well-disguised riot. *C. Marqués de Casa Riera 2, tel. 91/360–5400. Metro: Banco de España. Admission: 100 ptas. Open daily 10–midnight. Closed Aug.*

FUNDACIÓN JUAN MARCH

In the heart of the Salamanca district, this dynamic cultural and scientific foundation was established in 1955 by Juan March, a Mallorcan banker and entrepreneur. If you're an arts junkie, pop in to see what's on. Near the main entrance are three large sculptures by Berrocal, Chillida, and Torner. The groundfloor exhibition area holds some major art shows, and the popular basement concert series offers free performances at noon on Monday and Saturday. The foundation library specializes in material on Spanish theater and magicians, and the study centers for biology and the social sciences are internationally respected. *C. Castelló 77, tel. 91/435–4240. Metro: Nuñez de Balboa. Admission free. Open Mon.–Sat. 10–2 and 5:30–9, Sun. 10–2.*

LAS CUEVAS DE LUIS CANDELAS

One of the oldest taverns in town, this cellar joint beneath Plaza Mayor is named after a 19th-century Madrideño version of Robin Hood, Luis Candelas (1804–37)—a carpenter's son famous for his ingenious ways of tricking the rich out of their money and jewels without violence. On one occasion, he entered a drapery shop holding the end of a rope. After he purchased large quantities of fabric, the draper started adding up his bill; Candelas asked him to hold the rope while he loaded the drapes onto his mule. It was some time before the shopkeeper emerged to find the rope tied to a post.

After numerous escapes from prison, Candelas was finally sentenced for committing some 40 house robberies, and garrotted in a public execution near the Puerta de Toledo. The tavern's caves (*cuevas*) are painted with scenes of Madrid, and the huge earthenware *tinajas* of wine in the cellar below the bar are just as richly decorated. *C. Cuchilleros 1, tel.91/366–5428. Metro: Sol.*

MUSEO DE ESCULTURA AL AIRE LIBRE

In 1970 the architects of the Juan Bravo bridge over the Paseo de Castellana decided to fill the space on either side of the boulevard below with resilient abstract sculptures by 20th-century Spanish artists. The dominant work, by noted Basque sculptor Eduardo Chillida, is a concrete piece called *Sirena Varada* (Stranded Mermaid), which hangs on the east side from four rods. Other sculptures include a penguin by Joan Miró, works by Andrés Alfaro, Martín Chirino (whose *Mediterean* sits in the middle of a cooling waterfall), Julio González, Rafael Leoz, Mariel Martí, Alberto Sánchez (*Toros Ibéricos*, or Iberian Bulls), Eusebio Sempere, Francisco Sobrino, and José María Subirachs, the last of whom is responsible for the angular figures on the west side of Barcelona's Sagrada Familia. On the west side of the bridge are two egglike bronzes by Pablo Serrano. *Below Juan Bravo bridge on Paseo de Castellana, just south of Glorieta de Emilio Castelar. Metro: Ruben Dario, Castellana exit.*

MUSEO LAZARO GALDIANO

Set in a walled garden on the corner of Serrano and Maria de Molina, this stylish 1903 palace houses one of the most interesting private art collections in Spain. The ornate decor and layout have hardly changed since the home-museum was bequeathed to the nation in 1948. José Lázaro Galdiano (1862–1948) founded a famous intellectual magazine, *La España Moderna,* but his main passion was collecting fine books, art, furniture, medals, watches, archaeological finds, religious artifacts, Limoges enamels, medieval ivory, jewelry, indeed anything that made his eyes sparkle.

After marrying Paula Florido, an Argentine heiress, in 1903, Galdiano built the palace in celebration, and to house his collection. The central vestibule is surrounded by two floors of galleries and some fine painted ceilings. The collection is displayed in 30 rooms on three floors. In Sala II, look for the exquisite 13th-century Limoges staff; in Sala VII, a 7th-century BC Phoenician jug; in Sala XII, a Gainsborough female portrait; in Sala XVII, an exceptional 1525 portrait of Doña Ana de Austria, one of Felipe II's wives, by Sánchez Coello, and a 17th-century portrait of Doña Inés de Zúniga, Condesa de Monterrey, painted in her voluminous farthingale dress by Juan Carreño de Miranda; in Sala XX, the portrait of St. John the Baptist, c. 1495–1505, by Hieronymous Bosch; in Sala XXIII, El Greco's St Francis of Assisi. Six Goyas culminate the collection in Sala XXX; *The Threshing Field,* 1786, was a sketch for a tapestry cartoon that's now in the Prado. *The Entombment,* 1771–72, was painted for the chapel of the Counts of Sobradiel, Zaragoza, and the two oil sketches of Hermenegild and St Elizabeth were meant for the church of San Fernando de Montetorrero, Zaragoza. *The Witches' Sabbath* (Aquelarre), 1798, was part of a series. *C. Serrano 122, tel. 91/561–6084. Metro: Rubén Dario (Castellana exit) or Nuñez de Balbao (Velázquez exit). Admission: 500 ptas. Open Tues.–Sun. 10–2.*

MUSEO NACIONAL DE ARTES DECORATIVAS

Should it occur to you to wonder where Spain's passion for ornamental tiles, ceramics, leatherwork, carved furniture, and general flair for interior design comes from, don't miss this undersung 19th-century palace overlooking the Parque del Retiro. The 15,000 exhibits include a handsome chapel from a convent in Ávila, complete with a leather altar; various Mudéjar artifacts (created by Moors living under Christian rule); and a complete 18th-century Valencian kitchen with 1,500 tiles forming a domestic scene. *C. Montalbán 12, tel. 91/532–6499. Metro: Retiro or Banco de España. Admission: 400 ptas. Open Tues.–Fri. 9:30–3; weekends 10–2.*

MUSEO MUNICIPAL

The Municipal Museum's huge Baroque doorway, carved in granite and white stone from the Sierra de Guadarrama, centers on the figure of San Fernando surrounded by other figures, flowers, and decorations. The building was erected as a hospice between 1722 and 1799. The displays are a random sampling of Madrid lore, including maps showing how Madrid has grown over the years (one drawn in 1656; a detailed city model from 1830) and the reconstructed dens of two Madrid writers, Mesonero Romanos (1803–92) and Ramón Gómez de la Serna (1888–1963). The shop is great for Madrid-centric books, prints, old photographs, maps, and cards. *C. Fuencarral 78, tel. 91/588–8672. Metro: Tribunal. Admission: 300 ptas., free on Wed. and Sun. Open Tues.–Fri. 9:30–8, weekends 10–2.*

MUSEO ROMÁNTICO

The so-called Romantic Museum owes its name as much to its clever design as the mansion of an intelligent, well-to-do, 19th-century family as to Romanticism in the Spanish arts. It was in fact built in 1776—and is showing its age—for a general, and acquired in 1920 by the Marqués de la Vega-Inclán (1858–1942), who founded Spain's fab network of state-owned parador hotels as well as refurbishing El Greco's house in Toledo and Cervantes' in Valladolid. The marqués's horde of 19th-century paintings, books, and furniture form the nucleus of today's museum. Room 13 is an intimate chapel with a Goya painting of San Gregorio Magno above the altar. The ballroom has a fine Pleyel piano that belonged to Queen Isabella II. The Mariano José de Larra Room (No. 17), dedicated to that great 19th-century satirical journalist and writer, holds some of Larra's furniture and effects, including the dueling pistol with which he killed himself after being rejected by the woman he loved. *C. San Mateo 13, tel. 91/448–1045. Metro: Tribunal or Alonso Martínez. Admission: 400 ptas. Open Tues.–Sat. 10–3, Sun. 10–2.*

MUSEO SOROLLA

The mansion and studio of Joaquín Sorolla, a Valencian impressionist painter, has been lovingly preserved as it was when he died in 1923. Built in 1910 with an Andalusian style garden, it's an oasis of taste and culture. Many of the works on display are Sorolla's well-known beach scenes, but there are also studies of Spanish customs and regions. Many of the pictures are connected with Sorolla's contract to supply paintings of Spanish fiestas to New York's Hispanic Society of America. *General Martínez Campos 37, tel. 91/310–1584. Metro: Iglesia. Admission: 400 ptas. Open Tues.–Sun. 10–3.*

PLAZA DE TOROS LAS VENTAS

Madrid's main bullring has been moved up Calle Alcalá, farther from the city center, at least three times over the centuries. Inaugurated in 1934, the neo-Mudéjar Las Ventas, seating 24,000, is the largest and fairest of them all. Young Spanish matadors are brave to undergo their *alternativa* (qualifying fights) here, and no self-respecting *torero* can make it until he's fought under the critical gaze of Tendido Siete (Section 7), where the most demanding and vociferous crowd sits. The statues outside the main entrance depict two famous bullfighters, Antonio Bienvenida and José Cubrero.

On one side of the bullring is the **Museo Taurino,** where the whole gamut of bullfight paraphernalia sits on display. In case you need a chilling reminder of what it's all about, check out the blood-stained suit of lights (*traje de luces*) that Manolete was wearing when he was killed in Linares, Andalusia, in 1947. *Museo Taurino: C. Alcalá 237, tel. 91/356–2200. Metro: Ventas. Admission free. Open Tues.–Fri. 9:30–2:30, Sun. 10–1.*

REAL FÁBRICA DE TAPICES

Established in 1721 by Felipe V, the Royal Tapestry Factory is probably the only 18th-century factory still working in Madrid. It's kept busy these days repairing the carpets at the Ritz Hotel and making new carpets and tapestries to order for wealthy clients. On display are some of Goya's "cartoon" paintings, executed as studies for tapestries for the royal family (most are in the Prado). *C. Fuenterrabía 2, tel. 91/434–1028. Metro: Menéndez Pelayo. Open weekdays 9–12:30.*

SOCIEDAD GENERAL DE AUTORES

One of Madrid's best examples of Art Nouveau architecture, the two-floor Palacio Longoria was built by the Catalan architect Jose Grassés Riera for a banker, the Marqués de Longoria. The facade is distinctly Gaudí-esque; inside, there's a splendid staircase of marble, iron, and brass. The palace is now headquarters for Spain's intellectual copyright organization. *Fernando VI 8, tel. 91/349–9550. Metro: Alonso Martínez.*

TEATRO REAL

Built in 1850, the neoclassical Royal Theater was long a cultural center for Madrileño society. Plagued by disasters in recent years, including fires, a bombing, and profound structural problems, the house reopened to worldwide fanfare in 1997 after almost a decade of restoration. Replete with golden balconies, plush seats, and state-of-the-art equipment for operas and ballets, the theater is a modern showpiece with its vintage appeal intact. The top-floor bar has good views of the Royal Palace. *Plaza de Oriente 1, tel. 91/516–0660 box office, 91/516–0696 tours. Metro: Opera. Guided tours available Tues.–Sun. 10:30–1:30.*

SCIENCE AND TECHNOLOGY

MUSEO DE CIENCIAS NATURALES

Packing minerals, meteorites, mammals, and birds, the Museum of Natural Science is divided between two buildings at the top of a small park. The area to the left contains interactive displays, including lessons in ecology, and examples of life forms from tiny insects to elephants. An important Spanish excavation site, Atapuerca, is shown in cross-section: Some of Europe's earliest human remains, dated at 780,000 years old, were found near Burgos in 1997.

To the right, near the gift shop, are modern two-story displays concerning the origins of the earth, invertebrate life, the conquest of Earth, reptiles, and mammals. An unusual highlight is the 1.8-million-year-old skeleton of Megatherium Americanum—a bearlike creature from the Pleistocene period, found in Argentina in 1788. Post-Spielberg, the inevitable life-size reproduction model of a dinosaur skeleton found in the United States stands near a giant Glyptodon armadillo (10 ft long and over 4 ft high), also from Argentina. *Paseo de la Castellana 80, tel. 91/411–1328. Metro: Gregorio Marañon or Nuevas Ministerios. Admission: 400 ptas. Open Tues.–Fri. 10–6, Sat. 10–8, Sun. 10–2:30.*

MUSEO NACIONAL DE CIENCIA Y TECNOLOGÍA

Hundreds of inventions are on display in the National Museum of Science and Technology, from astrolabes to pressure cookers. Three main sections focus on measuring the universe, experimental science, and technology in industry. Interactive devices demonstrate acoustics, optics, pressure, hydraulic lift, and visual distortion. *Paseo de las Delicias 61, tel. 91/530–3121. Metro: Delicias. Admission free. Open Sept.–June, Tues.–Sat. 10–2 and 4–6, Sun. 10–2:30; July–Aug., Tues.–Sun. 9–3.*

MUSEO DEL AIRE

Out at the Cuatro Vientos (Four Winds) airfield west of Madrid, this museum tells the story of Spanish aviation with documents, films, videos, models (over 100), photographs, drawings, paintings, flight plans, Air Force regalia, profiles of star aviators, and, of course, aircraft. The weirdest flying machine is the Autogiro, called *La Cierva*—half plane, half helicopter; there are also planes that achieved a particular feat or were flown by famous people. *Carretera de Extremadura, Km 10.5, tel. 91/509–1690. From Atocha station, take train to Cuatro Vientos, then bus to Aeródromo de Cuatro Vientos. By car, take N-V to Km 10.5 and turn off at sign for Museo de Aire; from M-40, turn off at sign for Cuatro Vientos. Admission: 100 ptas., free Wed. Open Tues.–Sun. from 10 AM.*

MUSEO FERROVIARIO

The four tracks of the 1880 Delicias station once conveyed the main line to Portugal. They're now part of a railroad museum with over 30 old locomotives—steam, diesel, and electric—as well as rolling stock and carriages. The museum café is housed in a 1930s dining car. Kids at heart will love the model-train layouts. *Paseo de las Delicias 61, tel. 902/228822. Metro: Delicias. Admission: 500 ptas. Open Tues.–Sun. 10–3.*

REAL OBSERVATORIO ASTRONÓMICO

As part of his grand plan to study nature in the vicinity of his Buen Retiro palace, Carlos III ordered Juan de Villanueva, architect of the nearby Prado, to build this observatory in a corner of the Parque del Retiro. Opened in 1790, it was the third observatory in Europe, after those in Paris and Berlin. There's a small display of 18th- and 19th-century telescopes, and a modern Foucault pendulum that demonstrates the earth's rotation. Apply in writing ahead of time if you want to see the larger telescopes, the English clocks, and the prized 1790 telescope. *C. Alfonso XII 3, tel. 91/527–0107. Metro: Atocha. Admission free. Open Mon.–Thurs. 9–2.*

HOUSES OF WORSHIP

BASILICA DE SAN FRANCISCO EL GRANDE

In 1760, Carlos III built this impressive basilica on the site of a Franciscan convent, allegedly founded by St. Francis of Assisi in 1217. The dome, 108 ft in diameter, is one of the biggest in Spain and larger than that of St. Paul's in London, where its 19 bells were cast in 1882. The seven main doors were carved of American walnut by Juan Guas. On either side of the circular church are three chapels, the most famous being on the left on entering which contains a Goya masterpiece depicting San Bernardino de Siena preaching to King Alfonso V of Aragón. The figure standing on the right, not looking up, is a self-portrait of Goya. The 16th-century Gothic choir stalls came from La Cartuja del Paular in rural Segovia. Scaffolding has thronged the dark church for years to enable the restoration of its frescoes. *Plaza de San Francisco 2, tel. 91/365–3400. Metro: Latina and Puerta de Toledo. Open Tues.–Fri. 11–12:30 and 4–6:30.*

CATEDRAL DE LA ALMUDENA

The first stone of the cathedral (which adjoins the Royal Palace to the south) was laid in 1883 by King Alfonso XII, and the end result was consecrated by Pope John Paul II in 1993. The building was intended to be Gothic in style, with needles and spires, but as time ran long and money ran short, the design was simplified by Fernando Chueca Goitia into the more austere classical form you see today. The cathedral houses the remains of Madrid's patron saint, St. Isidro, and a wooden statue of Madrid's female patron saint, the Virgin of Almudena, which is said to have been discovered following the Christian reconquest of Madrid in 1085. Legend has it that a divinely inspired woman named María led authorities to a secret spot in the old wall of the Alcázar (which in Arabic can also be called *al-mudeyna*), where the statue was found framed by two lighted candles inside a grain storage vault. That wall is part of the cathedral's foundation. *C. Bailén s/n, tel. 91/542–2200. Metro: Opera. Admission free. Open daily 10–1:30 and 6–7:45.*

ERMITA DE SAN ANTONIO DE FLORIDA

Built in 1770 and covered in four months with Madrid murals by Goya, this little hermitage makes a good excuse for a food-and-culture trip. Goya is buried here, and the Asturian food at Casa Mingo (*see*

Where to Eat–Paseo de Florida, *above*) is a great value. *Glorieta de San Antonio de Florida 5, tel. 91/ 542–0722. Metro: Príncipe Pio. Admission: 300 ptas., Wed. and Sun. free for EU citizens. Open Tues.– Fri. 10–2 and 4–8, weekends 10–2.*

SAN JERÓNIMO EL REAL

This church was first built in 1464 because Enrique IV found Madrid's main church by the stinking Manzanares river somewhat unhealthy. It was used by his successors, Ferdinand and Isabella, as a *retiro* (religious retreat), a tradition maintained by Felipe IV after the Buen Retiro palace was constructed nearby; but the building was substantially damaged during the Napoleonic wars. The ruined cloisters are now being incorporated into a much-needed new wing for the neighboring Prado. The door to the left of the altar leads to the royal meditation rooms; above the door on the right is the shield of the Catholic monarchs—minus the pomegranate symbol of Granada, since at that time they had yet to conquer that city and expel the Moors from Spain. *Moreto 4, tel. 91/420–3078. Metro: Banco de España or Atocha. Open July–Sept., daily 9–1:30 and 6–8; Oct.–June, daily 9–1:30 and 5:30–8.*

SAN NICOLÁS DE LAS SERVITAS

The tower of the church of St. Nicholas is one of the oldest buildings in Madrid, and may have once formed part of an Arab mosque. It was more likely built after the Christian reconquest of Madrid in 1085, but the brickwork and the horseshoe arches are clear evidence that it was crafted by either Moorish workers (Mudéjars) or Christians well versed in the style. Inside the church, exhibits detail the Islamic history of early Madrid. *Plaza de San Nicolás s/n, tel. 91/559–4064. Metro: Opera. Donations accepted. Open Tues.–Sun. 6:30 AM–8:30 PM or by appointment.*

SANTA BARBARA

This spiffy 1757 Baroque church was designed by François Carlier and built, along with a large adjoining convent (now the Palacio de Justicia), by the Portuguese queen Bárbara de Braganza, who died a year after it was finished. She and her husband, Ferdinand VI (1713–59), are buried here in magnificent tombs: Fernando's, to the right of the nave, has a neoclassical design, with tiers of angels. The adjoining statues are Charity and Justice. Bárbara's tomb is in a separate chapel to the right of the main altar, and is rarely open to the public. Sculptures of the couple flank the high altar. *C. General Castaños 2. Metro: Alonso Martínez or Colón. Open weekdays 9–1 and 5–9.*

SAN ANTONIO DE LOS ALEMANES

One of Madrid's most beautiful churches sits in a run-down red-light district not far from the Gran Vía. The elliptical interior is covered by frescoes painted by two Madrid artists, Francisco de Ricci and Juan Carreño, and an Italian, Luca Giordano—they portray the life of St. Anthony of Padua (1195–1231), a Franciscan monk who was actually born in Portugal. The roof shows him ascending to heaven. On the right of the altar is *Calvary,* a masterpiece of a painting by Lucas Jordán. The church was designed to adjoin a hospital founded for the Portuguese by Felipe III in 1607. After Portugal obtained independence in 1640, however, the Austrian Queen Mother of Spain, María Ana, dedicated the church and hospital to the Germans (*alemanes*). *C. Puebla 22. Metro: Callao or Gran Vía. Open weekdays 9–1.*

PARKS AND GARDENS

CAMPO DE MORO

Spreading out beneath the Royal Palace to the west, this photogenic formal park—the Moor's Field— has clusters of shady trees, winding paths, and a long lawn leading up to the immense palace, twice as large as Buckingham Palace. *Campo de Moro, Cuesta de San Vicente. Metro: Príncipe Pio. Admission free. Open fall–spring, Mon.–Sat.10–6, Sun. 9–6; summer, Mon.–Sat. 10–8, Sun. 9–8.*

CASA DE CAMPO

Need a break from the baking asphalt and traffic fumes? Pack a picnic and repair to this 4,300-acre park west of the city where you can swim, sunbathe, visit the dolphins in the **Zoo-Aquarium**, or release adrenaline in the fun fair known as **El Parque de Atracciones.** The quickest approach is by Metro, but the Teleférico cable car (*see below*) offers spectacular views. Outdoor cafés line one end of the large boating lake near the Lago Metro station; Lago is also convenient to the swimming-pool complex, **Piscinas Casa de Campo,** which can be crowded on summer weekends but pleasant during the week. From early May to mid-June, you can have lunch at Venta del Batán, overlooking the corrals where bulls are kept for the annual San Isidro festival bullfights in Las Ventas. *Parque de Attracciones, tel. 91/463–*

2900. Metro: Batán. Admission 575 ptas; rides extra. Open Oct.–Dec., weekends noon–11 PM; Jan.–June, weekdays and Sun. noon–11 PM, Sat. noon–1 AM; July–Sept., weekdays and Sun., noon–1 AM, Sat. noon–2 AM. Zoo-Aquarium: tel. 91/512–3770. Metro: Batán. Admission: 1,655 ptas. Open daily 10:30–sunset. Piscinas Casa de Campo, Avda. del Angel s/n, tel. 91/463–0050. Metro: Lago. Admission: 500 ptas. Open May–mid-Sept., daily 10:30–8.

ESTACIÓN ATOCHA

A park in a railroad station? Why not? The old Atocha station, designed by the same architect who built the Palacio Cristal in the Parque del Retiro, has a soaring glass-and-steel canopy, ideal for the tropical palms and plants that now cram the humid plaza alongside bars and restaurants. It's good for a break after the Reina Sofia art museum. *Metro: Atocha.*

JARDINES SABATINI

The formal gardens north of the Royal Palace are crawling with stray cats, but still a pleasant place to rest or watch the sun set. *Metro: Opera or Plaza de España.*

PARQUE DEL OESTE

Enjoy a summer-evening *aperitivo* at one of the numerous terrace bars overlooking Western Park from Paseo del Pintor Rosales. Sloping down toward the Manzanares River, the park features a large rose garden, the Templo de Debod (*see* Feature Attractions, *above*), and the Teleférico cable car (*see below*). *Metro: Argüelles or Plaza de España.*

PARQUE DEL RETIRO

Named after the royal *retiro,* or retreat, that was the church of San Jerónimo, this expanse was the private playground of royalty, with naval battles staged on the lake and animals released for hunting. During the Napoleonic invasion, French troops destroyed the park entirely, leaving only one tree: the huge Mexican ahuehuete, a bald cypress planted in 1633 near the Casón de Buen Retiro. But Isabella II had the park restored in the 19th century, and it now boasts 300 acres of green encompassing formal gardens, fountains, lakes, exhibition halls, a puppet theater, children's play areas, and outdoor cafés. On weekends it fills with street musicians, jugglers, clowns, gypsy fortune-tellers, sidewalk painters, and hundreds of Spanish families out for a walk. The park hosts a month-long book fair in May and occasional flamenco concerts in summer, and you can always tool around the lake in a rowboat beneath the gaze of a stone Alfonso XII. West of the Rosaleda rose garden, look for a statue called the Angel Caido (Fallen Angel)—Madrileños claim it's the only one in the world depicting the Prince of Darkness before (well, during) his fall from grace. *Metro: Retiro, Principe de Vergara, or Ibiza.*

REAL JARDÍN BOTÁNICO

Just south of the Prado, the botanical gardens are a pleasant place to stroll or veg under the trees. True to the wishes of King Carlos III, they hold an array of plants, flowers, and cacti from around the world, not to mention a collection of bonsais donated by Felipe González, prime minister of Spain from 1982 to 1996. *Plaza de Murillo 2, tel. 91/420–3017. Metro: Atocha. Admission: 250 ptas. Open summer, daily 10–9; fall–spring, daily 10–6.*

TELEFÉRICO

Kids love this cable car, which takes you from just above the Rosaleda gardens of the Parque del Oeste to the center of Càsa de Campo. Just be warned that the walk from the cable car dropoff to the zoo and amusement park is at least 2 km (1 mi), and you'll have to ask directions. *Estación Terminal Teleférico, Parque del Oeste, tel. 91/541–7450. Metro: Argüelles. Tickets: 535 ptas. return. Open Apr.–Sept., daily 11 AM–sunset; Oct.–Mar., weekends 12–3 and 4–sunset.*

NEIGHBORHOODS

Although Madrid is officially divided into *barrios*, Madrileños tend to refer to each one by the name of its major street or plaza. For more on the great plaza and monuments in these neighborhoods, flip back to Feature Attractions, *above.*

PLAZA MAYOR

This is the heart of Habsburg Madrid, or Madrid de los Austrias, dominated in the 15th and 16th centuries by the monarchs who then ruled Spain. It was Felipe II, son of Carlos I (a.k.a. Holy Roman Emperor Charles V of Austria) who made Madrid the capital of Spain and ordered the construction of the Plaza Mayor on the site of the old marketplace. Juan de Herrera—architect of the monolithic El Escorial monastery, where Felipe II lived on the slopes of the Guadarrama Mountains nearby—was summoned; he also ended up designing the **Palacio de Santa Cruz,** just outside the plaza's southeast entrance.

As the royal court settled in Madrid, this area prospered from their construction of palaces, support of monasteries, and renovation of churches. City Hall, in the nearby **Plaza de la Villa**, was built at the end of the 17th century. The maze of streets southwest of Plaza Mayor are packed with bars and restaurants; and the area between Cava Baja (thronged with tapas bars) and Calle Segovia comprises old alleys and squares lined with historic apartment buildings, such as **Plaza de la Paja.**

OPERA / PLAZA DE ORIENTE

The gigantic **Palacio Real** (Royal Palace) takes up the whole west side of the spacious half-moon that is Plaza de Oriente. Opposite the palace, in the center of a semicircle of extremely expensive apartments, is the **Teatro Real** (Royal Theater), Madrid's opera house. The plaza *behind* the theater is called Opera (for the Metro stop), or Plaza Isabel II.

Ever since Calle Bailén (*bailén* actually means "they dance") was routed underground in front of the palace, the **Plaza de Oriente** has gotten pretty grand, with some excellent music and book stores and a proliferation of classy bars and restaurants such as Café de Oriente, most of them run by an Opus Dei priest. South of the palace is the **Catedral de la Almudena;** to its north, the Senado (Senate).

LA LATINA / LAVAPIÉS

Madrid's famous Sunday-morning flea market, **El Rastro** (*see* Shopping, *below*), spreads out around Calle de la Ribera de Curtidores, where La Latina and Lavapiés essentially merge. The working-class neighborhood **La Latina**, named after an erstwhile hospital founded by the Latin teacher of Queen Isabella, is considered the heart of **Castizo Madrid,** where dyed-in-the-wool Madrileños live alongside urban gypsies and together have some great summer fiestas. (The word *castizo* means "authentic.")

The narrow streets of **Lavapiés** may have been rebuilt, but the old tenements of Madrid's medieval **Jewish castizo area** are now inhabited by a few struggling artists and large colonies of Chinese and North African immigrants, the latter of whom are not the best of friends. In this area, increasingly violent muggings of tourists—some attracted to the historic **Taberna de Antonio Sanchez**—grew so rife in 2000 that 100 extra police were sent onto patrol here, but the problem continues. If you want to poke around this gritty area, bring nothing of value and be extremely streetwise.

PLAZA SANTA ANA / HUERTAS

Past literary residents of this **Barrio de las Letras** have included Lope de Vega, Cervantes, Quevedo, and Góngora. The **Teatro Español**, a jewel of a theater in **Plaza Santa Ana,** stands on the site of an old Globe-style, open-air venue where comedies were performed starting in 1583. Nearby, at the **Cervecería Alemana,** Ernest Hemingway used to settle down at a marble-top table and down the odd drink or 12. Tapas bars abound, and when they close on weekends, revelers want more—hence the nearly 40 bars on neighboring **Calle Huertas,** which fire up everything from jazz to classical music to disco funk until the dawn chorus. Neighbors' efforts to stem the noise and crowds have thus far failed; you've got to feel for them.

PASEO DEL PRADO / ATOCHA

This stretch is known as the Paseo del Arte (Art Walk), because the wide, leafy boulevard Paseo del Prado links one of the finest concentrations of art in the world: the **Thyssen-Bornemisza** museum, the **Prado,** and the **Reina Sofia** museum of modern art. On the boulevard's eastern side is the Barrio de San Jerónimo, one of the most exclusive districts in central Madrid since it also borders the Parque del Retiro. Halfway along Paseo del Prado is Plaza Cánovas del Castillo, with its fountain of Neptune. Clustered around here is enormous wealth and power: the Bolsa (stock exchange), the Ritz and Palace hotels, the Thyssen-Bornemisza and Prado museums, and the **Congreso de los Diputades**, the lower house of Spain's parliament. Down toward Atocha station, east of the *paseo*, is the **Jardín Botánico** (Botanical Garden), an oasis of flora. The Reina Sofia is across from Atocha train station at the boulevard's southern end; and under the glass canopy in the station itself is a steamy tropical garden with palms

SALAMANCA / RETIRO

The Salamanca district is roughly bordered by the Paseo Recoletos (Paseo de la Castellana), María de Molina, Francisco Silvela, and Alcalá. This is where Madrid's upper crust lives, in six- to eight-floor apartment blocks, wearing mink and Barbour in the winter and silk in the summer—both perhaps picked up in the boutiques that line Salamanca's two major shopping streets, Calle Serrano and Calle Goya. The buildings were put up in 1862–63 by the Marqués de Salamanca, whose own palace stands at Paseo de Recoletos 10, about 100 yards from Cibeles. Sipping a drink on the summer terraces of the two venerable Recoletos café-bars, the Gijón and the Espejo, is a popular pastime for locals and travelers alike.

The beginning of Calle Serrano is marked by the **Puerta de Alcalá** arch, at the corner of the Parque del Retiro.

SOL

The whole Puerta del Sol area got a substantial facelift in the 1990s, its new trees and recobbled streets brightening up previously shabby alleyways. Most of the area north to **Gran Vía** is now a pedestrian precinct, with access to boutiques and the major department stores. The **Puerta del Sol** itself is Ground Zero for sightseeing. To the east, Calle Alcalá leads to Cibeles; Carrera de San Jerónimo leads to the Prado; to the south lies Lavapiés; and to the west, Calle Mayor leads to the Plaza Mayor and Calle Arenal leads down to the Plaza de Oriente, Teatro Real, and Palacio Real.

CHUECA / MALASAÑA

Chueca's maze of narrow, somewhat shabby streets sits between Paseo de Recoletos and Calle Fuencarral. Plaza Chueca is the hub of what has become Madrid's **gay quarter,** where a lot of flair and imagination has infused the local restaurants, bars, and clubs. All are welcome here, but unfortunately, Chueca's longtime drug problem has not been completely expunged. **Calle Almirante** has some exotic boutiques, Calle Barquillo is lined with electronics shops, and the streets around Fuencarral have good-value shoe stores.

Malasaña, northwest of Chueca across Calle Fuencarral, is Madrid's artiest district, best explored for nightlife purposes. For years this area was neglected, even though Madrileños took their last stand here against Napoléon's invading troops on May 2, 1808, as immortalized by Goya's painting in the Prado. The Spanish version of the Alamo tragedy took place on **Plaza del Dos de Mayo.** The neighborhood is named for a local 16-year-old seamstress, Manuela Malasaña, who was executed by the French after their victory for carrying a pair of scissors (they decreed it an offensive weapon). The area has just received the trees-and-cobblestones treatment, but store shutters are still caked in graffiti, and young urban rebels—including squatters—rub shoulders with the newly arrived yuppies.

CASTELLANA / AZCA

This business district began life in 1969 on the west side of Paseo de la Castellana, between the behemoth Nuevos Ministerios government complex and, to the north the **Palacio de Congresos** convention center, with its huge exterior mural by Joan Miró. Some 30,000 people work in Azca, many in the **Torre Picasso,** Madrid's tallest office building (46 floors), designed by the architect of New York's World Trade Center, Minoru Yamasaki.

Across Plaza de Lima from the Moda Centro Comercial shopping mall is the 90,000-seat **Estadio Santiago Bernabeu,** home of FC (*fútbol club*) Real Madrid. Knowing that football was the opium of the masses, Franco always made funds available for Real Madrid, and the team rewarded him by winning the European Championship five times in a row. Around the stadium are several U.S.-style fast-food joints.

CHAMARTÍN

The most useful landmark in this northern district is Estación Chamartín, Madrid's main railway station for the rest of Europe. The surrounding urban sprawl is of no interest, but across the **Plaza de Castilla** transport hub to the southwest (dominated by the twin leaning office towers called the Puerta Europa), bars, shops, and restaurants start in earnest along Bravo Murillo and down Castellana. South of the Colombia Metro station, near **Plaza de República Dominicana,** lives an international crowd, served by a good mix of reasonably priced eclectic eateries and the excellent two-floor food market on Calle Potosi (near Príncipe de Vergara).

GRAN VÍA / PLAZA DE ESPAÑA / ARGÜELLES

Strolling northwest on Gran Vía, you'll realize this grand avenue has seen better days. The movie theaters are still emblazoned with huge, hand-painted posters, but the rest of the pickings are mostly second-rate shops, restaurants, and clubs. Behind the towering **Telefónica** building is a seedy red-light district, stomping ground of drug addicts. The scenery brightens in Plaza de España, if you warm to the convoluted monument to **Cervantes** and Don Quixote, and the 1940s and '50s Modernist efforts in the form of two contrasting "skyscrapers." Around Calle San Leonardo and Calle San Bernardino are some foreign restaurants; between Calle Princesa and Calle Martín de los Heros, several multiplex cinemas show foreign films in their *versión original,* with Spanish subtitles.

Argüelles, northwest of Plaza de España, is a conservative residential area stretching to the Moncloa district and the **Faro de Madrid** observation tower. From near here the **Teleférico** cable car swings over the Manzanares River valley to the **Casa de Campo** park, granting great views of the city.

SHOPPING

Madrid's best buys are chic clothing, shoes, leather goods, jewelry, ceramics, guitars, prints and posters, olive oil, cured ham, saffron, and wine. There are two main shopping areas. The first, in the center of town around the **Puerta del Sol,** includes the major department stores (El Corte Inglés, the French book-and-music chain FNAC, etc.) and mid-range shops in the streets nearby. The second area, far more elegant and expensive, is the **Salamanca** district, bounded roughly by Calles Serrano, Goya, and Conde de Peñalver, all just off the Plaza de Colón. These streets, and Calle Serrano, in particular, have Madrid's widest selection of swank boutiques and designer fashions.

The capital's newest mall is a quadruple-decker: the **Centro Comercial ABC** (Paseo de la Castellana 34 or C. Serrano 61), named for the daily newspaper founded on its premises in the 19th century. The building is a beautifully restored landmark, with an ornate tile facade; inside, a large café is surrounded by shops of all kinds, including the trendy, good-value Zara chain and several leather stores.

DEPARTMENT STORES

Spain's biggest department store, **El Corte Inglés,** has the best selection of just about everything, from auto parts to groceries to fashions and souvenirs (C. Preciados 3, tel. 91/531–9619, Metro: Sol; C. Goya 76 and 87, tel. 91/432–9300, Metro: Goya; C. Princesa 56, tel. 91/454–6000, Metro: Argüelles; C. Serrano 47, tel. 91/432–5490, Metro: Serrano; C. Raimundo Fernández Villaverde 79, tel. 91/418–8800, Metro: Nuevos Ministerios).

The British chain **Marks & Spencer** (C. Serrano 52, tel. 91/520–0000. Metro: Serrano) is best known for its woolens and underwear, but homesick expats head straight for the food shop in the basement, which sells abundant nosh to go.

FLEA MARKETS

On Sunday, Calle de Ribera de Curtidores (Metro: Latina or Puerta Toledo), is closed to traffic and jammed with outdoor stalls selling everything under the sun—its weekly transformation into **El Rastro.** The crowds grow so thick that it takes a while just to advance a few feet amid the hawkers and gawkers. The market sprawls into most of the surrounding streets, with certain areas specializing in particular products. A word of warning: Pickpockets *abound* here. Hang onto your purse or wallet, and if you must bring a camera (strongly discouraged), know that you're likely to attract unseemly attention.

Many of the goods sold here are wildly overpriced. But what goods! The Rastro has everything from antique furniture to exotic parrots and cuddly puppies; from pirated cassette tapes of flamenco music to key chains emblazoned with symbols of the CNT, Spain's old anarchist trade union. Practice your Spanish by bargaining with the vendors over garish paintings, colorful Gypsy oxen yokes, heraldic iron gates, new and used clothing, even hashish pipes. They may not lower their prices, but sometimes they'll throw in a handmade bracelet or a stack of postcards to sweeten the deal. The whole spectacle shuts down around 2 PM.

Off the Ribera are two *galerías,* courtyards where small shops offer higher-quality, higher-priced antiques and other goods. These shops are also open during the week, as are those lining the Sunday market.

SPECIALTY STORES

BOOKS

Casa del Libro (Gran Vía 29, tel. 91/521–2113; Metro: Gran Vía), has an impressive collection of English-language books, including Spanish classics in translation and detailed guides to Madrid. It's also a good source for maps and cookbooks. The French chain **FNAC** (Preciados 28, tel. 91/595–6100; Metro: Callao) has stacks of books (some in English), foreign newspapers and magazines, CDs, videos, and a concert-ticket reservation service. **Booksellers** (José Abascal 48, tel. 91/442–8104; Metro: Gregorio Marañon), also has a large selection of books and magazines in English. **Crisol** (Marqués de Casa Riera 2, basement of Circulo de Bellas Artes, tel.91/522–5100; Metro: Banco de España) carries English-language newspapers and magazines plus Spanish books and CDs. There are branches at C. Goya 14 and C. Serrano 24. The **International Bookshop** (Campomanes 13, tel. 91/541–7291; Metro: Opera or Santo Domingo) sells secondhand books in several languages; you can also prowl for used books on Sunday morning (a few are open all week) in booths on **Calle Claudio Moyano,** near the Jardín Botánico (Metro: Atocha), and in dusty shops near **Plaza Campillo Mundo Nuevo,** the lower part of the Rastro flea market (Metro: Puerta de Toledo). Established in 1950, **La Tienda Verde** (C. Maudes 23 and 38, tel. 91/535–3810; Metro: Nuevos Ministerios)—the Green Store—caters to those planning hikes and other outdoor adventures with detailed maps and guidebooks, albeit in Spanish.

CLOTHING

The **Zara** chain, now international, is an originally Galician phenomenon for those with young tastes and slim wallets. Picture hip clothes that you'll throw away in about six months (Centro Comercial ABC, C. Serrano 61, tel. 91/575–6334. Metro: Rubén Dario, Castellana exit; Gran Vía 32, tel. 91/522–9727, Metro: Gran Vía or Callao; C. Princesa 63, tel. 91/543–2415, Metro: Argüelles; C. Conde de Peñalver 4, tel. 91/435–4135, Metro: Goya).

Cambalache (Victor Hugo 5, tel.91/522–7373; Metro: Gran Vía) was Madrid's first secondhand-clothing store, offering marked-down designer duds from Armani, Escada, and Moschino as well as leather items. For rugged travel wear or skimpy summer tops, browse the bottom half of the Sunday **Rastro** flea market (Metro: Puerta de Toledo).

Century-old **Guantes Luque** (C. Espoz y Mina 3, 91/522–3287; Metro: Sol) sells every kind of glove you can imagine, and then some. Just look in the window. The venerable **Casa Yustas** (Plaza Mayor 30, tel. 91/366–5084; Metro: Sol) is equally well stocked with headgear, from the old tri-corner patent-leather hats of Franco's Guardia Civil to the berets worn by the Guardia's frequent enemy, the Basques. Basque berets are much wider than those worn by the French, and make interesting, unexpected gifts.

If you find yourself window-shopping in Salamanca, have a look at **Seseña** (C. de la Cruz 23, Salamanca tel. 91/531–6840; Metro: Sevilla) even if you don't have 70,000 ptas. handy. These wool and velvet capes—some lined with red satin—have outfitted famous painters, Hollywood stars, and First Ladies since the turn of the 20th century.

FOOD AND WINE

Slabs of *turrón,* a nougat candy made from toasted almonds, sugar, and honey, are Spain's traditional Spanish Christmas sweet. To save expensive dental work, stick (and you will) to the soft (*blando*) variety. Some of the new-fangled flavored *turrones,* like Lacasa's Irish Coffee flavor, are delicious. The "Club Gourmet" sections of El Corte Inglés department stores (*see above*) sell a good choice of Spanish wines, olive oils, and foodstuffs. Handily located near Plaza Santa Ana and Plaza de les Cortés, **González** (C. León 12, tel. 91/429–5618; Metro: Sevilla) gives you the same selection plus the chance to sample the offerings at its wine bar.

Lavinia (C. José Ortega y Gasset 16, tel. 91/426–0604; Metro: Núñez de Balboa) claims to be the largest wine store in Europe.

The violet-flavored boiled sweets of **La Violeta** (Plaza Canelejas 6, tel. 91/522–5522; Metro: Sevilla) are charming and prettily wrapped.

GIFTS

Ceramics are a great buy in Spain, and there are plenty of small ceramic items that are easy to pack, like decorative tiles. The **Antigua Casa Talavera** (C. Isabel la Católica 2, tel. 91/547—3417; Metro: Santo Domingo) is one of the best ceramics shops in Madrid. **El Arco de los Cuchilleros** (Plaza Mayor 9, bajo, tel. 91/365–2680; Metro: Sol) has affordable items as well as a fine display by the best craftspeople in Spain.

Almirante 23 (C. Almirante 23, tel. 91/308–1202; Metro: Banco de España) is an incredible curio shop crammed with miscellany more than 50 years old, from postcards, valve radios, toys, and knick-knacks to posters and theater programs.

MUSIC

For flamenco CDs, English-language books on the art, and such must-haves as castanets, pop into **El Flamenco Vive** (C. Conde de Lemos 7, tel. 91/547–3917; Metro: Opera). Most flamenco guitarists strum a Yamaha, but there's a lovely selection of various Spanish guitars at **Guitarrería F. Manzanero** (C. Santa Ana 12, tel. 91/366–0047; Metro: La Latina). Classical-music lovers will adore **Real Músical,** near the Teatro Real (C. Carlos III 1, at Plaza de Oriente, tel. 91/541–3007; Metro: Opera), which sells CDs, books, sheet music, and musical memorabilia.

SHOES

Cheap, good-quality shoes can be found in the many *zapaterías* (shoe stores) around **Calle de Fuencarral** and **Calle Augusto Figueroa** (Metro: Chueca). Spain's famed *alpargatas* (espadrilles)—rope-soled canvas summer shoes—start at 600 ptas. at **Antigua Casa Crespo,** in offbeat Malasaña (C. Divino Pastor 29, tel. 91/521–5654; Metro: Bilbao or San Bernardo).

AFTER DARK

Deprived of the energy-sapping pleasures of the coast, Madrileños enjoy the most unremitting nightlife of any city in Europe, complete with 4-AM traffic jams. One crank called the post-Franco generation "Eco-Hedonists." The liveliest months are June and July, when, because of the heat, office workers clock "intensive hours" from 8 to 3, take a long siesta, work some more, and, when the air cools down after 10, venture out. In theory, you can dance until daylight, then plunge into a disco for some Latin raving.

The streets best known for *marcha* (action) include Calles **Huertas, Moratín, Segovia, Victoria**, and, heading south, the areas around **Plaza Santa Ana, La Latina,** and **Plaza de Antón Martín.** The adventurous may want to explore the scruffier bars around Malasaña's Plaza Dos de Mayo, where trendy, smoke-filled hangouts line both sides of **Calle San Vicente Ferrer.** Equally brave souls can venture a few blocks east to the notorious haunts of neighboring, gay-toned **Chueca,** where tattoo studios and chic bars break up the narrow streets with techno discos and after-hours clubs.

There's plenty in the way of live music, too, from flamenco to jazz, salsa, and rock. Efforts have been made to restrict bars' hours (particularly near Plaza Santa Ana), as the neighbors and travelers in local *hostales* can't get to sleep, but it will be some time before the lax authorities implement restrictions. Performance tickets for top concerts are best purchased at the hall itself or at **El Corte Inglés** department stores (tel. 902/400222), **FNAC** stores (C. Preciados 28, tel. 91/595–6100), or **Tele-Entradas** (tel.902/101212).

The weekly *Guía del Ocio*—in Spanish, but easy to read—lists film, theater, and music offerings plus restaurants, bars, and clubs.

BARS

Most of the bars listed here are open day and night; some even do breakfast. Remember that it always costs you more to sit down and be waited on. For good drink service, leave a few small coins.

A café can be a cafeteria serving quick snacks, light meals, coffees, and drinks, or it can be a more serious, conversation-oriented place with marble-top tables. In the summer, many bars set up *terrazas* with outdoor tables and chairs. So-called pubs should generally be avoided—yes, even the fun-looking Irish ones—because, proud of their foreign decor, they charge more for drinks and serve slapdash food.

Café Manuela. This old-fashioned café is a Malasaña institution, with an interesting crowd that might be seen thumbing through the numerous magazines lying around, or perusing new works at one of the café's changing art exhibits. *C. San Vicente Ferrer 29, tel. 91/531–7037. Metro: Tribunal.*

Café del Nuncio. Elegant but faded, this café-bar is in one of Madrid's oldest neighborhoods. In summer, tables are set up on the steps leading down to Calle Segovia, giving sippers a pleasant view. *C. Nuncio 12. Metro: La Latina.*

Café de Oriente. Wonderfully ornate inside, with elegant al fresco tables looking toward the Royal Palace in summer, the Café de Oriente is owned by an Opus Dei priest who seems to have taken over the whole area. The snacks are OK, but the restaurant is expensive and overrated. *Plaza de Oriente 2, tel. 91/541–3974. Metro: Opera.*

Café Pepé. Everyone looks like an artist in this offbeat old café near Plaza de Dos de Mayo, good for a relaxed coffee or drink while exploring Malasaña. The ocher walls are hung with mirrors, paintings, and old photographs; coming events are advertised by the door. *San Andrés 12, tel. 91/522–4309. Metro: Tribunal or Noviciado.*

Cervecería Alemana. Over a century old and looking it, this place now fills with tourists searching for Hemingway's ghost, as well as locals meeting up for a chat. The drinks at the marble-top tables are not too costly, but the tapas are. *Plaza Santa Ana 6, tel. 91/429–7033. Metro: Sevilla.*

Círculo de Bellas Artes. It costs 100 ptas. to get into this palatial arts club, but sitting in the enormous bar (by a sculpted female form) and gazing out through picture windows at Calle Alcalá makes it worthwhile. You can even buy English-language newspapers, supplied by Crisol. *Marqués de Casa Riera 2, tel. 91/531–8503. Metro: Banco de España.*

Ducados Café. This place gets packed in the evening for cocktails and snacks, often to live music. Late at night, especially on weekends, the crowd eventually moves downstairs to the disco and bops the night away. *Plaza de Canalejas 3, tel. 91/360–0089. Metro: Sevilla.*

El Ventorillo. Between May and October, this terrace is perfect for taking an evening drink beneath shady trees while watching the sun set behind the Guadarrama Mountains in the distance. El Ventorillo perches on a knoll next to the Bailén viaduct, a five-minute walk from Plaza de Oriente. *C. Bailén 14, tel. 91/366–3578. Metro: Opera.*

Los Gabrieles. You'll pay through the nose to sit in the best tiled bar in Madrid, a brothel in the late 19th and early 20th-centuries. The kaleidoscopically colorful tiles are actually ads for food or drink. In the front side room, elderly women were still plying their trade just a decade ago. *C. Echegaray 17, tel. 91/429–6261. Metro: Sevilla.*

González. In another life, English-speaking owner Vicente spent 11 years in the U.S. as an academic. His smart gourmet shop and wine bar sells good wines and beers at sensible prices, and you can sample the cold cuts, cheeses, and pastries at the bar. *León 12, tel. 91/429–5618. Metro: Sevilla and Antón Martín.*

Hard Rock Café. Rich young kids from adjoining Salamanca no longer line up to get into this American juggernaut, but the ground-floor and basement bars still attract young folk who appear to be looking for more than a burger and french fries. *C. Castellana 2, tel. 91/436–4340. Metro: Colón.*

La Carpanta. The trendy crowd at this old-Madrid late-night venue spills out into the street. Large, warm cheese canapés are 400 ptas.; inside the wood-beam, exposed-brick restaurant, lunch and dinner plates start at 1,000 ptas. *C. Almendro 22, tel. 91/366–5783. Metro: La Latina.*

Larios Café. Despite its status as a new, designer-label hangout, Larios charges excellent prices for its Cuban snacks (from 250 ptas.). The music and dancing go on till 5 AM. *C. Silva 4, tel. 91/547–9394. Metro: Santo Domingo.*

La Negra Tomasa. Live music, Cuban tapas, and lethal cocktails keep this Cuban joint—decorated with palm fronds and fishnets—jumping through the wee hours. *C. Espoz y Mina at Cádiz, tel. 91/523–5830. Metro: Sol.*

Pepé's Kiosko. If, having come all this way, you have a sudden craving for the best BLT sandwich you've ever tasted, these monsters in crispy bread, packed with bacon, lettuce, tomato, and melted cheese, are a bargain at 550 ptas. English-speaking Pepé and his Irish wife, Maria, have long attracted locals and local expats to this outdoor bar in a small Chamartín park, a five-minute walk from the Colombia Metro station. There's Guinness on tap. *C. Puerto Rico 32, tel. 91/350–6015. Metro: Colombia.*

Salón del Prado. If you've got the bucks, the Irish coffees in this fine, old-style café—think high ceilings and lots of wood and brass—are great for recharging your batteries prior to an attack on the club scene. *C. del Prado 4, tel. 91/429–3361. Metro: Sevilla.*

Taberna de Antonio Sanchez. A former hostelry, this 1830 tavern is pretty memorable. Being in Lavapiés, it's now surrounded by communities of immigrants creating a history all their own, but retains its zinc-topped bar, wood paneling, and ancient wine-cellar hoist as well as a stuffed bull or two and lots of photographed matadors. Have tapas at the bar; head to the back for full meals. Be on guard for muggers, and head straight back to the Metro afterward. *Mesón de Paredes 13, tel. 91/539–7826. Metro: Tirso de Molina.*

Viva Madrid. When this old bar, with a great ceiling of plaster figures, reopened in 1980 near the Plaza Santa Ana it set a trend for the whole barrio, attracting a young crowd and a reputation as a pickup place. It's still good for people-watching. *C. Manuel Fernández González 7, tel. 91/429–3640. Metro: Sevilla.*

Yesterday. English-speaking Antonio, a former flamenco dancer, made this the first trendy bar in Huertas—an oasis of calm, with a cozy bar, cane chairs, and poems beneath the tables' glass tops. Antonio's American partner, Nicole, can brief you on other currently cool places to hang out. *Huertas 10, tel. 91/228–4181. Metro: Sevilla or Sol.*

DISCOS / LIVE MUSIC

Entrance to most of Madrid's disco-bars involves the approval of an often surly bouncer. The fee, usually around 1,000 ptas., pays for the first drink. (Street-side touts might also offer two-for-one drink tickets.)

Amadís. Telephones on every table encourage people to call each other with invitations to dance. The scene is sophisticated; teeny-boppers are not welcome. There's often live music. *C. Covarrubias 42 (beneath Luchana Cinema), tel. 91/446–0036. Metro: Bilbao.*

Azúcar. Salsa has become a fixture in Madrid, with its obvious Latin American connections and, more to the point, its growing population of immigrants. Check out the most spectacular moves, and get the best workout, here at Azúcar (Sugar). *Paseo Reina Cristina 7, tel. 91/501–6107. Metro: Atocha.*

But. A highly civilized disco-theater, But gets the best dancers in every genre, from the waltz to the tango. Dance classes are given early each Wednesday night; live shows are cut loose Friday and Saturday. *C. Barceló 11, tel. 91/448–0698. Metro: Tribunal and Alonso Martínez.*

Café Belén. This smooooth café has excellent chill-out and ambient music. Cool down with tasty mint tea or a refreshing mojito. *Belén 5, tel. 91/308–2747. Metro: Chueca or Alonso Martínez.*

Carbones. The small bar becomes more of a disco at night, open till 3:30 AM. Drink prices are sensible, with beers from 300 ptas. and mixed drinks from 800 ptas. *C. Manuel Fernández González 13, tel. 91/369–4665. Metro: Sevilla.*

El Clandestino. Run by a French couple who seem to be Spaniards at heart, this bar-café is a hidden, low-key hot spot with a local following. Think atmosphere without attitude. Impromptu jam sessions are complemented by two floors alternating mellow jazz with house and ambient music. *Barquillo 34, tel. 91/521–5563. Metro: Chueca.*

Joy Eslava. Housed in a converted theater, this large disco is an old standby. Kids take it over in the early evening; their older cousins then keep it going all hours. *Arenal 11, tel. 91/366–3733. Metro: Sol or Opera.*

Kapital. Filling several floors, this mega-disco attracts all kinds but is best described as only for dedicated clubbers. It's open till 6 on weekends. *C. Atocha 125, tel. 91/420–2906. Metro: Atocha.*

La Boca de Lobo. This dark but friendly and colorful place near Santa Ana has two bars on different levels. Live bands and shows often play in the basement. *C. Echegaray 11, tel. 91/429–7013. Metro: Sevilla.*

La Comedia. Just off Plaza Santa Ana, this disco-bar attracts an international crowd, many of whom seem to live here. There's a good mix of music. *C. Príncipe 16, tel. 91/521–5164. Metro: Sevilla.*

Palacio de Gaviria. Located between Puerta del Sol and the Royal Palace, the restored 19th-century Palacio de Gaviria was allegedly built to house one of Queen Isabella II's lovers. An exotic maze, it now serves drinks in a sophisticated setting, with a disco and frequent late-night jazz in the mirrored ballroom. *C. Arenal 9, tel. 91/526–6069. Metro: Sol.*

Siroco. In this well-known disco-bar, groups often play until 12:30 AM Thursday–Saturday, after which time funk and techno reign until 6. *C. San Dimas 3, tel. 91/593–3070. Metro: San Bernardo.*

Soho. Something of a slice of New York in the Salamanca district, Soho is filled with rap and reggae fans. The eclectic menu includes exotic island drinks as well as Spanish variants of Tex-Mex cuisine. *C. Jorge Juan 50, tel. 91/577–8973. Metro: Príncipe de Vergara.*

El Sol. Madrid's oldest *and* coolest disco for wild, all-night dancing is open until 5:30. The music turns live around midnight Thursday, Friday, and Saturday. *C. Jardines 3, tel. 91/532–6490. Metro: Gran Vía or Sol.*

Suristán. This famous disco right near the Puerta del Sol has several bars and distinct atmosphere. From Tuesday to Saturday it's a hip indie spot for rock and pop concerts plus occasional plays and readings. *C. de la Cruz 7, tel. 91/532–3909. Metro: Sol.*

Torero. This neat venue for seasoned smoothies has a circular bar on the ground floor and a small disco in the basement. Think exposed brick and wood beams. *Cruz 26, tel. 91/523–1129. Metro: Sol.*

Villa Rosa. If you like the tiles at nearby Los Gabrieles, you'll be overwhelmed at this onetime flamenco club—one bar looks more like a Seville patio, complete with (sometimes) trickling fountains. Extroverts show their stuff on the slightly raised stage. *Plaza Santa Ana 15, tel. 91/521–3689. Metro: Sol or Sevilla. Open 11–5 AM. Closed Mon.*

CABARET

Berlin Cabaret professes to provide authentic cabaret as it was performed in Berlin in the 1930s (these days the audience is quite different). Combining magic tricks, chorus girls, and ribald comedy, it draws an eccentric crowd for vintage café-theater in an intimate atmosphere. On weekends, the absurd fun lasts until daybreak. *Costanilla de San Pedro 11, tel. 91/366–2034. Metro: La Latina.*

FLAMENCO

Café de Chinitas. The dancing at Chinitas is among the best in Madrid, but it's expensive—reserve only for the late show, not for dinner, and prepare to pay a bundle anyway. Performances start at 10:30 Monday through Saturday. *C. Torrija 7, tel. 91/559–5135. Metro: Santo Domingo.*

Casa Patas. This well-known gypsy hangout offers good, often genuine flamenco and tapas. Prices are more reasonable than elsewhere. Shows are at 10:30 Monday–Thursday, midnight Friday–Sunday. *C. Canizares 10, 91/369–0496. Metro: Antón Martín.*

Corral de la Morería. Again, avoid dinner; sign up to see well-known visiting dance stars work with the resident troupe. Since Morería opened its doors in 1956, celebrities such as Frank Sinatra and Ava Gardner have left their autographed photos for the walls. Shows are daily, from 10:45 PM to 2 AM. *C. Morería 17 (park side of Bailén viaduct), tel. 91/365–8446. Metro: Opera or La Latina.*

La Soleá. This unusual, friendly two-floor space has two tiled rooms with seats around the walls. In the ground-floor bar, flamenco singers drop in to warble with the resident guitarist or perform solo; in the basement, jazz and rock groups play beneath old brick arches. *Cava Baja 34, tel. 91/365–5264. Metro: La Latina.*

JAZZ

Café Central. Madrid's best-known jazz venue is chic and well run, and the musicians are often internationally known. Performances are usually 10 PM–midnight; get here early to avoid sitting behind a pillar. *Plaza de Angel 10, tel. 91/369–4143. Metro: Sol or Antón Martín.*

Cafe del Foro. This funky, friendly club on the edge of Malasaña has live music every night starting at 11:30. The bar is open from 7 to 3. *San Andrés 38, 91/445–3752. Metro: Bilbao.*

Café Jazz Populart. Blues (often from American singers), jazz, Brazilian music, reggae, and salsa start at 11 PM here. The place is crowded, and the walls are festooned with musical instruments. *C. Huertas 22, tel. 91/429–8407. Metro: Antón Martín.*

Clamores. This well-known jazz club serves a wide selection of French and Spanish champagnes as well as the usual bar fare. Seating is better organized then in most such venues. *C. Albuquerque 14, 91/445–7938. Metro: Bilbao.*

La Soleá. The atmospheric brick-vaulted basement of this Old Madrid venue (*see* Flamenco, *above*) hosts frequent live jazz. It's a great, intimate place to listen to music. *Cava Baja 34, tel. 91/365–6264. Metro: La Latina.*

FILM

Nearly a dozen theaters regularly show undubbed foreign films, most in English with Spanish subtitles. These are listed in newspapers and in the *Guía de Ocio* under "V.O." (original version). Your best bet for catching an undubbed new release is **Multicines Ideal** (C. Dr. Cortezo 6, tel. 91/369–2518; Metro: Tirso de Molina or Sol), where several of the nine theaters are usually showing English-language art films. Other leading V.O. theaters include **Alphaville** (C. Martín de los Heros 14, tel. 91/584–4524; Metro: Banco de España) and **Renoir** (C. Martín de los Heros 12, tel.91/559–5760; Metro: Banco de España), both just off Plaza de España. There's a different classic V.O. film every day at **Filmoteca Cine Doré** (C. Santa Isabel 3, tel. 91/369–1125; Metro: Antón Martín), which also has a café and a cinephiliac bookstore.

CLASSICAL MUSIC / DANCE

The glorious **Teatro Real** (Plaza de Oriente, tel. 91/516–0600; Metro: Opera) hosts regular opera and ballet, usually with top international stars and companies. The plush premises include some lovely bars and a posh restaurant. The modern **Auditorio Nacional de Música** (Príncipe de Vergara 146, tel. 91/337–0100; Metro: Cruz de Rayo) is Madrid's main symphonic venue, with two concert halls. Spain's broadcasting service, RTVE, records orchestral, choral, and other concerts in the **Teatro Monumental** (C. Atocha 65, tel. 91/429–8119; Metro: Antón Martín). Tickets are usually cheap. The new, subterranean **Centro Cultural de la Villa** (Plaza de Colón, tel. 91/575–6080 for information, 91/516–0606 for tickets; Metro: Colón) has an eclectic program ranging from gospel and blues to flamenco and Celtic dance.

La Fidula (C. Huertas 57, tel. 91/429–2947; Metro: Antón Martín), near the end of the Huertas bar scene, presents classical musicians and singers an elegant, intimate café setting.

THEATER

English-language plays are rare. When they do come to town, they're staged at any of a dozen venues, so check the newspapers. One theater you won't need Spanish for is the **Teatro de la Zarzuela** (Jovellanos 4, tel. 91/524–5400; Metro: Banco de España), which spotlights the traditional Spanish operettas known as *zarzuela,* roughly described as colorful, bawdy comedy. The internationally renowned **Ballet Nacional de España**—of which superstar Joaquín Cortés was a member—often performs in this theater, and its joyous mix of flamenco, folk, and classical music is not to be missed. The **Teatro Español** (C. Príncipe 25, tel. 91/429–6297; Metro: Seville) keeps the 17th-century Spanish classics alive, in their original tongue.

NEAR MADRID

SAN LORENZO DE EL ESCORIAL

An hour's drive northwest of Madrid, this elegant town on the southern slopes of the Guadarrama Mountains is best known for the gigantic Real Monasterio de San Lorenzo de El Escorial. But Madrileños like to escape here on summer weekends for the fresh mountain air, panoramic views, and cool evenings, not to mention conferences and summer university courses.

BASICS

The helpful **regional tourist office** (C. Floridablanca 10, tel. 91/890–1554, open weekdays 10–2 and 3–5, Sat. 10–2) and the smaller **municipal tourist office** (C. Grimaldi 2, tel. 91/890–5313, open weekdays 10–2 and 3–5, Sat. 10–2) have maps and leaflets.

COMING AND GOING

Trains for El Escorial (1 hr, 370 ptas–430 ptas.) leave hourly from Madrid's Atocha station, some continuing to Ávila. El Escorial's **train station** (tel. 91/890–0413, 902/240202 general info) sits at the bottom of the hill; bus L-1 (10 min, 80 ptas.) will take you to the monastery from here. From Madrid, Herranz **buses** (C. Juan de Toledo, tel. 91/543–3645) leave roughly every half hour from the Intercambiador de Autobuses in Moncloa (Metro: Moncloa), stopping near the monastery. Buy your ticket as you board (50 min, 380 ptas.).

By **car,** take the A-6 out of Madrid and follow signs to the M-505.

WHERE TO SLEEP AND EAT

El Escorial is short on budget lodging, but the rooms available do have phones. Doubles at **Hostal Cristina** (C. Juan de Toledo 6, tel. 91/890–1961) start at 6,000 ptas. Doubles at the cheaper, smaller **Hostal Vasco** (Plaza de Santiago 11, tel. 91/890–1619) start at 4,700 ptas., and there's some good Basque cooking in the restaurant.

There *is* a nice balance of restaurants and tapas bars, many with outdoor terraces. Those on Calle Floridablanca tend to be a rip-off, as tourists show up here by the busload. Walk around the back of Posada de las Cuevas and look for the semi-subterranean bar of 18th-century **Mesón de La Cueva** (C. San Antón 4, tel. 91/890–1517), which offers good tapas and a chance to see the rest of this ancient beamed tavern with an original patio. The peeling mural in the tapas bar commemorates the first arrival of tourists in miniskirts. Nearby **El Colmao** (C. del Rey 26) serves good tapas and a 1,500-pta. set menu. **Barataria** (Plaza de la Constitución 5, tel. 91/896–1915) is an old stone-and-timber landmark *mesón* with a pricey restaurant but cheaper tapas at the bar. The **Cafetín Croche** (C. San Lorenzo 6) is a smart place for drinks or coffee. For cheap drinks and tapas with the locals, swagger into **Bar El Brillante,** in the northwest corner of Plaza de la Constitución.

The municipal **market** is near the Plaza de la Constitución, on Calle del Rey. Assemble a picnic and head up through the pine forests above town for glorious views.

WORTH SEEING

El Escorial, as the **Real Monasterio de San Lorenzo de El Escorial** is normally called, is not only a functioning monastery and church but also a school, library, royal palace, mausoleum, and museum. An austere granite behemoth with 2,673 windows and 1,200 doors, the monastery was built by the monkking Felipe II, primarily as the final resting place for his revered father, Carlos I (a.k.a. Charles V of Austria, the Holy Roman Emperor), whom he succeeded in 1556. It was also envisioned as a palace for Felipe and his entourage during their time on earth, a fitting tomb for future generations of Spanish monarchs, *and* to appease God for the destruction of a French church by Spanish troops in 1557.

At the entrance you can buy a map and make your own way around the huge complex or, better, wait for an English-speaking guide to assemble a group for a 1-hr-45-minute tour of Felipe II's royal apartments and the Pantheon.

The **Palacio de los Austrias**, or royal apartments, surround the basilica, and two of the main bedrooms look straight at the altar—the idea was for Felipe II to partake of mass from his bed while enjoying the view outdoors. The **Sala de Retratos** (Portrait Gallery) holds the folding chair used by the gout-ridden king. The long **Sala de los Paseos** (Walking Gallery) has magnificent German marquetry doors at either end, blue Talavera tiles halfway up the walls, and above, 16th-century maps of the world and paintings of famous Spanish military victories. In 1755, solar adjusters for setting clocks were inlaid into the floor of this space and the adjoining dining room. Felipe's bed stands exactly where it was when he died, at 5 AM on September 13, 1598; the king's last portrait hangs in his study.

You now descend 300 ft below ground to the musty chill of the circular **Royal Pantheon,** finished in 1654 with Spanish black marble and red jasper with Italian gilt bronze decorations. Lighted by a 660-pound chandelier are 26 gray marble coffins, of which 23 are occupied. There are eight other pantheons, of which the one containing Juan de Austria (his image sculpted in Carrara marble) and the **Pantheon of the Royal Children** are most impressive. The latter is known as La Tarta (the Cake) for its polygonal white-marble structure.

Beneath the frescoed, vaulted ceilings of the **chapter houses** are paintings by Titian, Tintoretto, Ribera, Zurbarán, El Greco, and Velázquez as well as several works by the weird and wonderful Hieronymus Bosch, known in Spain as El Bosco.

The **museums,** installed in several rooms at various levels, display art and some of the tools and plans used to build El Escorial. One of Felipe II's favorite paintings was the superb *Calvario* (Calvary) by Roger Van der Weden; another Flemish artist, Michel Coxcie—known as the Flemish Raphael—gets a whole room.

The **library** founded by Felipe II was the first public library in Spain. With written permission, scholars can still thumb through these 40,000 tomes and manuscripts from the 15th and 16th centuries. The 177-ft-long print room is lined with bookcases below a magnificent arched ceiling covered in Tibaldi frescoes depicting the eight major disciplines (Astrology, Dialectics, Geometry, Grammar, Music, Philosophy, Rhetoric, and Theology). The Ptolemaic wooden sphere, made of pine in 1582, puts the earth in the center of the universe.

The **basilica** was completed in 1586, but only the aristocracy were allowed in; plebs were restricted to the *sotocoro* (roughly, "people's church"), at its entrance. The basilica has 45 altars, and the chapel to the left as you enter holds an exquisite 1562 Carrara-marble statue of the crucified Christ by Benvenuto Cellini. On either side of the main altar, above the doors leading to the royal bedrooms, are fine gilded-bronze cenotaphs of Carlos I and Felipe II worshipping with their families. The huge altarpiece, laden with colored marble, jasper, gilt, and bronze sculptures and paintings was designed by Juan de Herrera. It took an Italian silversmith, Jacoppo da Trezzo, seven years to craft the central tabernacle, which is backlit by a window.

The sumptuously furnished **Palacio de los Borbones** within the monastery was created for Carlos IV, who ruled Spain from 1788 to 1808. Some of the framed tapestries were designed by Goya and crafted at Madrid's Royal Tapestry Factory. A china cabinet shows the 1905 china service that was part of the trousseau of Queen Victoria Eugenia, granddaughter of England's Queen Victoria, when she married Alfonso XIII in 1906. *Tel. 91/890–5903. Admission: 850 ptas. Open Tues.–Sun. 10–6. Tours (950 ptas.) 10–1:30 and 4–6.*

La Silla de Felipe II—Felipe II's Chair—is a charming viewpoint on a small wooded hill from which Felipe II could watch his vast folly (it used up most of the gold from the New World) grow during 21 years. To reach it, take the road west past the monastery, go down Paseo de Carlos III , and follow the signs to Herrería-Golf.

VALLE DE LOS CAÍDOS

The left turn for the Valley of the Fallen, one of the most depressing sites in all of Spain, is 8 km (5 mi) east of San Lorenzo de El Escorial on the M-600. From here the road snakes 6 km (4 mi) north to the giant cross, 492 ft high, that towers over a huge **basilica** hewn out of the Guadarrama granite by Franco's prisoners between 1941 and 1960. It was intended as a monument to the half million people killed in the Spanish Civil War (1936–39), but there are only two graves—Franco and José Antonio Primo de Rivera, leader of the fascist Falange that supported him, are buried by the altar. At least there's a good view from the funicular at the base of the cross. Herranz runs a Tuesday–Sunday bus here from El Escorial, leaving at 3:30 PM and returning at 5:30. *Admission to basilica: 700 ptas., funicular from basilica to base of cross 375 ptas. Open daily 10–8; funicular can be erratic.*

CHINCHÓN

The little town of Chinchón, 45 km (28 mi) southeast of Madrid, is one of the most picturesque in all of Spain thanks to its outstanding medieval **Plaza Mayor.** This charming, slightly topsy-turvy square is surrounded by three-floor beamed houses whose interconnecting wooden balconies fill with spectators when the plaza hosts bullfights or pageants. The plaza actually appears in several films, including *Around the World in 80 Days* and two movies by Orson Welles, *Chimes at Midnight* and *The Immortal Story* (Welles loved Chinchón).

Easily accessible from Madrid but delightfully rural in flavor, Chinchón is packed with Madrileños on weekends, rushing to get themselves wedged into the balconies of Plaza Mayor restaurants or, in the winter, invading the parador, which serves an elaborate, and filling version of *cocido Madrileño*. And no meal here is complete without a glass of the local *anís* firewater (anise), known throughout Spain as Chinchón. In a few small bullrings on the edge of town, groups amuse themselves with *capeas*, waving capes at frisky young bulls.

BASICS

The is no tourist office, but you can pick up leaflets at the offices in Madrid. The leaflet on the parador hotel, which you can pick up at reception (just outside the southwest corner of Plaza Mayor), is a good substitute. You won't really need a map, except perhaps to find the cheap lodging uphill from Plaza Mayor.

COMING AND GOING

La Veloz buses (tel. 91/409–7602) run regularly from Avenida del Mediterráneo 49, Madrid (1 hr, 415 ptas.). On weekdays they depart every hour between 7 AM and 11 PM, with the last bus returning to Madrid at 7:30 PM; on Saturday buses run 8 AM–10 PM, with the last bus from Chinchón at 9 PM; on Sunday, they're every 90 minutes from 9 AM to 10:30 PM, with the last bus from Chinchón at 9:30 PM. There is no **train** service.

By **car,** take the A-III southeast out of Madrid and turn off *before* Arganda to the M-311, then follow signs to Chinchón. The road passes the Jarama Valley, where the U.S. Abraham Lincoln Brigade battled Franco's nationalists.

WHERE TO SLEEP

UNDER 7,000 PTAS. • Hostal Chinchón. Double rooms here, near the Plaza Mayor, have wood beams and Castilian furniture. There's a small pool on the roof. Doubles with private bath start at 6,500 ptas. *C. José Antonio 12, tel. 91/894–0108, fax 91/894–0108. Restaurant, pool. 10 rooms.*

UNDER 9,000 PTAS. • Hostal Mesón la Cerca. Rooms here are modern—with thoughtful touches like private safes—but Castilian-cozy, with lots of wood. Double rooms with bath start at 8,000 ptas. *C. Cerca 9, tel. 91/893–5565, fax 91/893–5082. Restaurant, in-room safes. 25 rooms.*

WHERE TO EAT

Castilian cooking shines here, headlined by strong winter stews (often with beans), good beef, game in season, and roast baby lamb and suckling pig. The local red wines are cheap if you fill up a container from one of the bodegas in town, but the best-known local product is *anís*. This clear, sticky, licorice-flavored Chinchón liqueur is popular as a heart-starter with breakfast in the morning, especially for those working in the fields but also for some Madrid taxi drivers, which may explain some terrifying journeys. The most lethal combination—allegedly a hangover cure—is called *sol y sombra* (sun and shade), a mix of Chinchón anise and brandy.

Eating in Chinchón is generally expensive, especially in the Plaza Mayor. If you can part with 2,700 ptas., the *cocido Madrileño* (Madrid stew) at the **parador** (Avda. Generalissimo 1, tel. 91/894–0836) is a memorable binge in historic surroundings, with about 10 courses plus bread and wine. Reservations are essential, as this is a real occasion—the *cocido* is served only at lunchtime Friday–Sunday between mid-September and mid-June.

Three local restaurants offer good-value menús del día year-round. Suitably decorated with cheerful red-and-white-check tablecloths, heavy Castilian furniture, and a great, sloping beamed ceiling, **El Mesón el Duende** (C. José Antonio 8, tel. 91/894–0807) specializes in roasts, bean stews, and suckling pig. **El Mesón la Cerca** (C. Cerca 9, tel. 91/893–5565) is part of an upmarket *hostal* in renovated 200-year-old buildings. Set menus of Castilian fare cost 1,200 ptas. on weekdays, 2,000 ptas. on weekends, both including bread and wine. **El Mesón el Cazador** (C. José Antonio 11, tel. 91/894–0425) is modern, with tiles around the lower half of the walls and antlers and wild boar mounted higher up. The name of the game is game. **El Mesón Cuevas del Vino** (C. Benito Hotelano 13, tel. 91/894–0206) is amusing; strong red wine in the dank cave-cellars costs a mere 100 ptas., while the expensive meals upstairs (at least 3,500 per person) are taken amid rows of giant *tinajas* (huge, Ali Baba–type earthenware vats) and an old olive-oil press.

WORTH SEEING

The first houses were built on what is now **Plaza Mayor** in the 15th century, and the circle was completed by 1683. In the past, some of the square's 234 balconies were owned separately from the houses to which they were attached, so immense was their value during fiestas. Homeowners now profit handsomely by renting out their balconies for these popular events, particularly when a portable ring is erected in the plaza for bullfights. The square buzzes every weekend with its numerous bars and restaurants, as well as shops selling local anís, garlic, and ceramics.

Looming over the plaza is the church of **Nuestra Señora de la Asunción.** Built between 1534 and 1626, it was sacked and burned by the invading French in 1808, then rebuilt. Goya's brother Emilio was a chaplain here, and Goya painted the magnificent *Asunción de la Virgen* (Assumption of the Virgin) that hangs above the altar. *Plaza Mayor, tel. 91/894–1105. Open for mass.*

Chinchón's **parador,** a converted 17th-century Augustinian convent, is well worth a trip for its cloisters and elegant gardens with privet hedges, cypress trees, and roses. The large, squat 15th-century **castle** on the hill overlooking Chinchón (closed to the public) was also burned by the French in 1808; before that, it was home to the *marquéses* of Chinchón, one of whom discovered the properties of quinine in South America and gave his name to the bark, cinchona, that contains this antimalarial medicine. The castle was last used as a distillery.

SHOPPING

The **Alcoholera de Chinchón** in Plaza Mayor sells Chinchón liqueur. If you lean toward aviation fuel, go for the *seco especial* (special dry), which is about 72% proof; the *dulce* (sweet), at 40% proof, is a less dangerous option. Madrileños also buy hefty strings of Chinchón garlic to decorate their kitchens. A number of shops around **Plaza Mayor** sell local ceramics, honey, and wine.

FIESTAS

Chinchón throws several notable parties: Carnival in February; the Fiesta del Anís, Vino, y Ajo (Garlic, Anís, and Wine Festival) in March; Holy Week plays and pageants; bull running and fighting on July 25, and more of the same in mid-August (13–18) and October.

ARANJUEZ

This spacious, neatly laid out town 47 km (29 mi) south of Madrid sprang up around a charming royal palace with formal gardens on the banks of the strangely green Río Tajo. Once the site of a Habsburg hunting lodge, Aranjuez became a favorite summer residence of the Bourbons in the 18th century— they expanded a 16th-century palace and added other buildings, designed extensive gardens, and planted woods. In the 19th century, it became a popular retreat for Madrileños.

Smack in the middle of a fertile plain, the area is known for its fruits and vegetables, especially strawberries and asparagus. The main road from Madrid to Andalusia used to pass through Aranjuez, clogging it with traffic and fumes, but the town's languid atmosphere and former glory have been fully restored. A trip from Atocha station on the Strawberry Train makes a fun excursion.

BASICS

The **tourist office** (Plaza de San Antonio 9, tel. 91/891–0427, open Oct.–June, Tues.–Sun. 10–1 and 3–5; July–Sept., Tues.–Sun. 10–2 and 4–6) is near the colonnade and arches that straddle the roads next to the large Plaza de San Antonio.

COMING AND GOING

There are frequent **trains** (40 min, 395 ptas.) from Madrid's Atocha station. The **train station** in Aranjuez (Carretera de Toledo, tel. 902/240202 general information) is a five-minute walk from the Royal Palace, or a quick hop on Bus 1 or 2. The best-known line is the *Tren de Fresa* (Strawberry Train), a replica of an 1851 steam train that covered this very route. The train runs every Saturday and Sunday from April to October, and the round-trip fare of 3,100 ptas. includes a bus ride to the center of Aranjuez, admission to the sights, and a pint of local strawberries.

AISA buses (bus station: C. Infantas) connect Aranjuez with Madrid's Estación del Sur (40 min, 395 ptas.), with connections to Chinchón and Toledo. By **car,** simply follow the N-IV south from Madrid.

Once here, your inner tourist will exult in the little **tourist train** that trundles around town, charging 600 ptas. a pop.

WHERE TO SLEEP

The cheapest *hostal* is the historic, elegant **Rusiñol** (C. San Antonio 76, 1st floor, tel. and fax 91/891–0155). Painter and writer Santiago Rusiñol (1861–1931), famed for his pictures of the gardens in Aranjuez, once lived in room 14. Some rooms have minibars. Doubles with private bath start at 5,400 ptas.; those with private sink and shared bath, 3,300 ptas.

WHERE TO EAT

Kiosks all over the place sell the main summer fare, strawberries and asparagus. Dining out tends to be pricey because the main trade is only on weekends, so consider a picnic in the palace's lovely gardens. (Classical-music aficionados can hum Joaquín Rodrigo's *Concierto de Aranjuez*, which, despite its Andalusian undertones, was inspired by these gardens. The Miles Davis version is haunting.) The town's **market**, open weekdays and Saturday mornings 9–2, is near the tourist office on the corner of Calle de Abastos and Carretera de Andalucía.

The 40-year-old yet modern **Casa de Comidas Gobernación** (C. Governación 12, tel. 91/891–6576, cash only), adorned with pictures of Aranjuez, serves salads, entrecôte steaks, and swordfish at reasonable prices. The set lunchtime menus costs 1,100 ptas. on weekdays 1,600 ptas. on weekends.

WORTH SEEING

Aranjuez's pink and white **Palacio Real** (Royal Palace) reflects French grandeur. The high point of the opulent interior is a room covered entirely with porcelain; there are also numerous elaborate clocks and a museum of period costumes. The shaded riverside gardens, **El Jardín del Príncipe,** cover 375 acres with exotic trees, many from the New World. Statues and fountains inviting pleasant relaxation after the palace tour. *Tel. 91/891–1344. Admission: palace 500 ptas., gardens free. Open: palace May–Sept., Tues.–Sun. 10–6:15; Oct.–Apr., Tues.–Sun. 10–5:15. Gardens May–Sept., daily 8–6:30; Oct.–Apr., daily 8 AM–8:30 PM.*

Built by Charles IV in 1804, the charming **Casa del Labrador** (Farmer's Cottage), a small palace at the eastern end of the gardens, has a jewel-like interior bursting with color and crowded with delicate objects. Between the Royal Palace and the Casa del Labrador is the **Casa de Marinos** (Sailors' House), with a gondola that belonged to Philip V and other decorated pleasure boats that once plied the river. *Admission: Casa del Labrador 425 ptas., Casa de Marinos 350 ptas. Open May–Sept., Tues.–Sun. 10–6:30; Oct.–Apr., Tues.–Sun. 10–5:30.*

FIESTAS

Aranjuez's main **fiestas** are held the last week of May—bull runs, bullfights, an agricultural show, and a ceramics fair—and the first weekend of September, when similar events are joined by a colorful staging of the Motín de Aranjuez (Aranjuez Rebellion), when the townspeople rose up against the hated royal favorite, Godoy, and caused the abdication of Carlos IV.

OLD AND NEW CASTILE

BY EDWARD OWEN

C entral Spain is an immense land of stark vistas, disparate temperatures, and the haunting marks of a 2,000-year-old history: hundreds of medieval Moorish and Christian castles, soaring golden cathedrals, ancient Roman monuments, and legends such as macho El Cid and his puny successor, Don Quixote.

Hogging the nation's great flat *meseta* (plain), Castile is divided politically into the Autonomous Communities of Castile-León (Castilla y León), to the north, and Castile–La Mancha (Castilla–La Mancha) to the south. Divided by a mountain range called the Central Cordillera, running northeast to southwest, the plain occasionally gives rise to 8,000-ft mountains in the Sierra de Guadarrama, just north of Madrid, and the Sierra de Gredos national park, southwest of Ávila. Castile's few rivers have carved twisting gorges out of the arid soil, but a summertime bird's-eye view of the expanse features miles of scorched red and brown earth, scarred by occasional canyons and dotted with green wherever irrigation systems nurture the parched land.

The Romans had a presence here and built Segovia's great aqueduct in the process. The Visigoths arrived in the 6th century to scrounge around as the empire crumbled. In 711 the Moors invaded, and the Christian battle for reconquest took the next eight centuries to complete. Fine castles from that yo-yo struggle still stand, perched strategically on hills overlooking towns or on outcrops at the crooks of river gorges. Indeed, the architectural legacy of all these groups is stunning. Christians working for the Moors left what are known as Mudéjar buildings; after the Christians took over, Muslim craftsmen working for the Christians established the Mozarabic style. Romanesque and early Gothic churches were built as the Moors were driven south, especially along the Camino de Santiago pilgrimage route in the north. As the Renaissance progressed, fancy Isabelline facades (crafted during Isabella's reign, 1474–1504) were succeeded by the highly decorative style of stonework called plateresque (named for its resemblance to silver, or *plata*), exemplified in Salamanca. Castilian forests were cut down to build the ships that established the Spanish empire, but great tree trunks still shore up ancient *mesónes* (stone taverns). And amid the gray-stone castles of La Mancha, white windmills—used to grind corn and remind people of Don Quixote—crown ridges above the plain.

Just as the Spanish spoken in Valladolid is considered the Queen's English of the Castilian tongue, Castile might be called the cultural backbone of Spain. Fast freeways and good trains link all the major cities, so exploring this country of monarchs, knights, and saints is easy—indeed, potentially addictive. Cervantes asked in *Quixote,* "Can we ever have too much of a good thing?"

GALICIA

Ourense
N120
Sil
Verín
N525
Donado
Puebla
de Sanabria
León
Almanza
N621
N601
La Bañeza
C622
CASTILE-LEON
Benavente
CA20
Mayorga
N630
Río Bernesga
N120
Río Órbigo
Medina de
Rioseco
NVI
N601
Alcañices
N122
Vallado
N601
Río Duero
N630
N122
N620
Tordesilla
El Cubo de
Tierra del
Vino
C605
Medina del
Campo
N620
Salamanca
N501
CASTILE-LEC
Vitigudino
C525
C517
C512
N620
Río Huebra
Vecinos
Peñaranda de
Bracamonte
C605
Ciudad
Rodrigo
C515
El Cabaco
N630
Ávilo
Miranda
del Castañar
C512
El Barco
de Ávila
N110
C501
Sierra
de Gredo
PORTUGAL
Villanueva
de la Sierra
C513
Jarandilla
N110
Plasencia
Coria
C501
C501
EXTREMADURA
Navalmoral
de la Mata
NV
CASTILE
N
Oropesa
Talavera d
la Reina
NV
Casar de
Cáceres
Río Salor
Arroyo
de la Luz
Valdelacasa
de Tajo
Navaherm
San Vicente
de Alcántara
N523
Aliseda
Guadalupe
Trujillo
EXTREMADURA
Montánchez
C90
Albuquerque
La Roca
de la Sierra
Miajadas
Valdecaballeros
Montijo
E90
Puebla de
Alcocer
Badajoz
Don Benito

0   60 miles
0   90 km

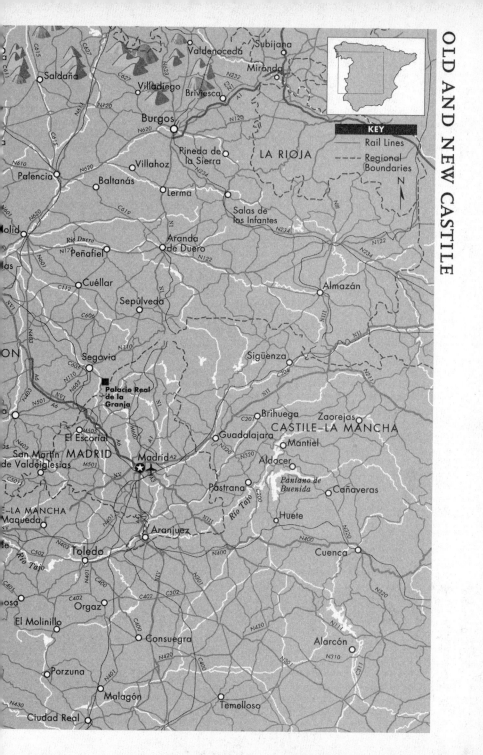

KEY
— Rail Lines
--- Regional Boundaries

N

LA RIOJA

CASTILE-LA MANCHA

Saldaña
Valdenoceda
Subijana
Miranda
Villadiego
Briviesca
Burgos
Pineda de la Sierra
Villahoz
Palencia
Baltanás
Lerma
Salas de los Infantes
olid
Peñafiel
Río Duero
Aranda de Duero
Cuéllar
Almazán
Sepúlveda
Segovia
Sigüenza
Palacio Real de la Granja
Brihuega
Zaorejas
El Escorial
Guadalajara
Mantiel
San Martín de Valdeiglesias
MADRID
Madrid
Aldocer
Pástrana
Pantano de Buenida
Cañaveras
-LA MANCHA
Maqueda
Huete
Aranjuez
Toledo
Río Tajo
Cuenca
Orgaz
El Molinillo
Consuegra
Alarcón
Porzuna
Malagón
Temelloso
Ciudad Real

FOOD

Castilian roasts are the region's calling card. Great earthenware platters of sizzling suckling pig and baby lamb are hauled out of traditional, dome-shape, wood-fired ovens. Game such as partridge, hare, and rabbit augment such fine meats as huge T-bone steaks from one of Europe's oldest breeds of cattle, from Ávila, or roasted goat from hilly terrain. Northern Castile is renowned for its pork-based sausages, red and white beans, and vegetables. León produces superb blue cheese, while La Mancha is known for its Manchego. Guijuelo, south of Salamanca, cures the finest of Spain's unique acorn-fattened, air-dried hams, served in tangy, succulent slithers. Castile–La Mancha boasts the world's largest vineyard— 2,400 square mi of vines producing increasingly palatable wines from areas such as Valdepeñas. Castile-León is better known for quality wine than quantity, with fruity, full-bodied reds from Ribera and fragrant, delicate whites from Rueda.

TOLEDO

Just an hour (71 km/44 mi) from Madrid by anything but foot, Toledo should be the first destination for anyone hoping to soak up Spain's complex history and experience a remarkably unspoiled, compact Spanish city crammed with architectural jewels. Christians, Moors, and Jews once lived together in peace here—it was no coincidence that Spain hosted the first major conference in the Middle East peace process (Madrid, 1991).

Tinged with mysticism and drama, Toledo was long the spiritual and intellectual capital of Spain. If you approach from Madrid, your first glimpse of Toledo will comprise its northern gates and battlements rising up on a massive granite escarpment. The flat countryside comes to an end, and a steep range of ocher-color hills rises on each side of the town.

The rock on which Toledo stands, bounded on three sides by the Río Tajo (River Tagus), was inhabited in prehistoric times, and there was already an important Iberian settlement here when the Romans came in 192 BC. The Romans built a fort on the highest point of the rock—where you now see the huge Alcázar, the dominant building in Toledo's skyline—and this was later remodeled by the Visigoths, who transformed the town into their capital by the middle of the 6th century AD. In the early 8th century the Moors arrived.

The Moors strengthened Toledo's reputation as a great center of religion and learning. Unusual tolerance was extended to those who continued to practice Christianity (the so-called Mozarabs) and to the town's exceptionally large Jewish population. Today the Moorish legacy is evident in Toledo's strong crafts tradition, the mazelike arrangement of the streets, and the predominance of brick rather than stone. For the Moors, beauty was a quality to be savored within rather than displayed on the surface, and it is significant that even Toledo's cathedral—one of the most richly endowed in Spain—is hard to see from the outside, largely obscured by the warren of houses around it. Long after the departure of the Moors, Toledo remained secretive, its lives and treasures hidden behind closed doors and forbidding facades.

Alfonso VI, aided by El Cid, captured Toledo in 1085 and styled himself emperor of Toledo. Under the Christians, the town's strong intellectual life was maintained, and Toledo became famous for its school of translators, who spread to the West a knowledge of Arab medicine, law, culture, and philosophy. Religious tolerance continued, and during the rule of Peter the Cruel (so named because he allegedly had members of his own family murdered to advance himself), a Jewish banker, Samuel Levi, became the royal treasurer and one of the wealthiest and most important men in town. By the early 15th century, however, hostility toward both Jews and Arabs had grown as Toledo developed more and more into a bastion of the Catholic Church.

As Florence had the Medicis and Rome the papacy, so Toledo had its long and distinguished line of cardinals, most notably Mendoza, Tavera, and Cisneros. Under these great patrons of the arts, Renaissance Toledo emerged as a center of humanism. Economically and politically, however, Toledo began to decline in the 16th century. The expulsion of the Jews from Spain in 1492, part of the Spanish Inquisition, had particularly serious economic consequences for Toledo; the decision in 1561 to make Madrid the permanent center of the Spanish court led to the town's loss of political importance; and the expulsion from Spain of the converted Arabs (Moriscos) in 1601 resulted in the departure of most of Toledo's

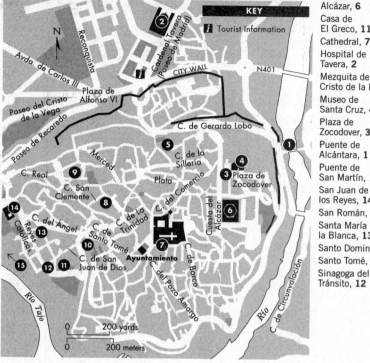

Alcázar, **6**
Casa de
El Greco, **11**
Cathedral, **7**
Hospital de
Tavera, **2**
Mezquita del
Cristo de la Luz, **5**
Museo de
Santa Cruz, **4**
Plaza de
Zocodover, **3**
Puente de
Alcántara, **1**
Puente de
San Martín, **15**
San Juan de
los Reyes, **14**
San Román, **8**
Santa María
la Blanca, **13**
Santo Domingo, **9**
Santo Tomé, **10**
Sinagoga del
Tránsito, **12**

KEY

i Tourist Information

celebrated artisan community. Many descendants of the Sephardic Jews who fled from Toledo still have the old keys to their houses and can speak old Spanish, known as Ladino, handed down from one generation to another. The years the painter El Greco spent in Toledo—from 1572 to his death in 1614—were those of the town's decline. Its transformation into a major tourist center began in the late 19th century, when the works of El Greco came to be widely appreciated after years of neglect. Today Toledo is prosperous and conservative, expensive, silent at night, and closed in atmosphere. Yet Spain has no other town of this size with such a concentration of monuments and works of art.

BASICS

VISITOR INFORMATION

The **tourist office** at Puerta de Bisagra, the city's northern entrance, is a helpful stop before you climb uphill to see the sights (tel. 925/220853). It's open weekdays 9–6, Saturday 9–7, and Sunday 9–3. There's a smaller office at Plaza del Consistorio 1 (tel. 925/254030), open Monday 10–2:30, Tuesday–Sunday 10–2:30 and 4–7.

MAIL

The **post office** is on Calle La Plata (s/n, tel. 925/223611).

COMING AND GOING

Frequent **trains** connect Toledo with Madrid's **Atocha** station (1¼ hrs, 760 ptas.). A few morning trains leave the Chamartín station as well. The **train station** is a 15-minute walk from the tourist office and town entrance at Puerta de Bisagra.

Toledo's **bus station** is on Avenida Castilla La Mancha (tel. 925/215850). Buses run by **Galiano Continental** (1–1¼ hrs, 585 ptas.) leave Madrid's Estación Sur every half hour. From Toledo's bus and train stations, you can catch Bus 5 or Bus 6 to Puerta de Bisagra, site of the tourist office, or charge straight into town and up the hill to Plaza de Zocodover.

By **car** travel time from Madrid is about 50 minutes on the N401. Stop briefly at the tourist office for a map (take the first exit from the Puerta de Bisagra traffic circle); then, if you're so inclined, visit the Hospital de Tavera and church of Santiago del Arrabal, just inside the Bisagra gate; then park behind the Alcázar, at the top of the city.

GETTING AROUND

Walking is the only way to get around Toledo's maze, and you *will* get lost at least once. The endlessly winding streets and steep hills can be exasperating, especially when you're looking for a specific sight in the searing heat of summer; but the best way to appreciate this town is to absorb its medieval atmosphere. Plan to spend the whole day, and a night if possible.

WORTH SEEING

ALCÁZAR

The name means "fortress" in Arabic and alludes to the Moorish citadel that stood here on the highest part of the city from the 10th century to the Reconquest. The building's south facade, its most severe, is the work of Juan de Herrera, of El Escorial fame. The east facade incorporates a large section of battlements. The finest facade is undoubtedly the northern, one of many Toledan works by Alonso de Covarrubias, who did more than any other architect to introduce the Renaissance style here.

Within the building are a military headquarters and a large military museum—one of Spain's few remaining homages to Francoism, hung with tributes from various right-wing military groups and figures from around the world. The Alcázar's architectural highlight is Covarrubias's harmonious Italianate courtyard, which, like most other parts of the building, was largely rebuilt after the Civil War, when the Alcázar was besieged by the Republicans. Though the Nationalists' ranks were depleted, they held on to the building from July 21 to September 28, 1936. Franco later turned the Alcázar into a monument to Nationalist "bravery"; the office of the Nationalist general who defended the building, General Moscardó, has been left exactly as it was after the war, complete with peeling ceiling paper and mortar holes. Here you can hear a reenactment of the telephone conversation between Moscardó and his son, held by the Republicans, when the general told his son they had to do their duty. The gloomy tour can continue with a visit to the dark cellars, which evoke living conditions at the time of the siege.

More cheerful is a ground-floor room full of beautifully crafted swords, a Toledan specialty introduced by Moorish silversmiths. At the top of the grand staircase, which apparently made even Charles V "feel like an emperor," are rooms displaying a vast collection of toy soldiers. *Cuesta Carlos V, tel. 925/223038. Admission 200 ptas. Open fall–spring, Tues.–Sun. 10–2:30 and 4–6; summer, Tues.–Sun. 10–2:30 and 4–7.*

CASA DE EL GRECO

This tourist magnet stands on property that once belonged to Peter the Cruel's Jewish treasurer, Samuel Levi. El Greco did once live in a house owned by this man, but it's pure conjecture that he lived in this particular one. The interior, done up in the late 19th century to resemble a "typical" house of the 16th, is a pure fake, if a pleasant one. The museum next door displays a few of the artist's paintings, including a large panorama of Toledo with the Hospital de Tavera in the foreground. *Samuel Levi 3, tel. 925/224046. Admission 200 ptas., free weekends. Open Tues.–Sat. 10–2 and 4–6, Sun. 10–2.*

CATHEDRAL

Jorge Manuel Theotokópoulos was responsible for the cathedral's Mozarabic chapel, the elongated dome of which crowns the right-hand side of the west facade. The rest of this facade is mainly early 15th century and features a depiction of the Virgin presenting her robe to Toledo's patron saint, the Visigothic Ildefonsus.

Enter the cathedral from the 14th-century cloisters to the left of the west facade. The primarily 13th-century architecture was inspired by the great Gothic cathedrals of France, such as Chartres, but the squat proportions give it a Spanish feel, as do the wealth and weight of the furnishings and the location of the elaborate choir in the center of the nave. Immediately to your right as you enter the building is a beautifully carved plateresque doorway by Covarrubias, marking the entrance to the Treasury. The latter houses a small Crucifixion by the Italian painter Cimabue and an extraordinarily intricate late-15th-century monstrance by Juan del Arfe, a silversmith of German descent; the ceiling is an excellent example of Mudéjar workmanship.

From here walk around to the ambulatory, off the right side of which is a chapter house featuring a strange and quintessentially Spanish mixture of Italianate frescoes by Juan de Borgoña. In the middle of the ambulatory is a dazzling and famous example of Baroque illusionism by Narciso Tomé known as the *Transparente*, a blend of painting, stucco, and sculpture.

Finally, off the northern end of the ambulatory, you'll come to the sacristy, where you'll find a number of El Grecos, most notably the work known as *El Espolio* (Christ Being Stripped of his Raiment). One of El Greco's earliest works in Toledo, it offended the Inquisition, which accused the artist of putting Christ on a lower level than some of the onlookers. El Greco was thrown into prison, and there his career might have ended had he not by this time formed friendships with some of Toledo's more moderate clergy. Before leaving the sacristy, look up at the colorful and spirited late-Baroque ceiling painting by the Italian Luca Giordano. *Arco de Palacio 2, tel. 925/222241. Admission 700 ptas. Cathedral open Mon.–Sat. 10:30–noon and 4–6, Sun. for mass only. Museum open daily 10:30–6, but you must buy tickets in advance for visits between noon and 4.*

HOSPITAL DE TAVERA

The last work of Alonso de Covarrubias (*see* Alcázar, *above*), this hospital stands outside the city walls beyond Toledo's main northern gate, Covarrubias's imposing Puerta de Bisagra. Unlike the former Hospital de Santa Cruz (*see* Museo de Santa Cruz, *below*), this complex is unfinished and slightly dilapidated, but it still has plenty of character and, in its southern wing, the evocatively ramshackle **Museo de Duque de Lerma,** looked after by two exceptionally friendly and eccentric women. The most important work in the museum's miscellaneous collection is a painting by the 17th-century artist José Ribera. The hospital's monumental chapel holds El Greco's *Baptism of Christ* and the exquisitely carved marble tomb of Cardinal Tavera, the last work of Alonso de Berruguete. Descend into the crypt to experience some bizarre acoustical effects. *Duque de Lerma 2, tel. 925/220451. Admission 500 ptas. Open daily 10:30–1:30 and 3:30–6.*

MEZQUITA DEL CRISTO DE LA LUZ

The mosque-turned-chapel of Christ of the Light sits in a small park above the town's northern ramparts. The gardener will open the gate and show you around; if he's not there, inquire at the house opposite. Originally a tiny Visigothic church, the chapel was transformed into a mosque during the Moorish occupation, and the Islamic arches and vaulting survive—making this the most important relic of Moorish Toledo. The chapel got its name when the horse of Alfonso VI, riding into Toledo in triumph in 1085, fell to its knees out front (a white stone marks the spot); it was then discovered that a candle had burned continuously behind the masonry throughout the time the so-called infidels had been in power. The first mass of the Reconquest was said here, and later a Mudéjar apse was added (now shielded by glass). After you've seen the chapel, the gardener will take you across the ramparts to climb to the top of the Puerta del Sol, a 12th-century Mudéjar gatehouse. *Admission: tip gardener. Open any reasonable hr.*

MUSEO DE SANTA CRUZ

One of the joys of this museum is its location in a beautiful Renaissance hospital with a stunning classical-plateresque facade. Unlike Toledo's other sights, the museum is open all day (except Monday) without a break and is wonderfully quiet in the early afternoon. The light and elegant interior has changed little since the 16th century, the main difference being that works of art have replaced the hospital beds; among the displays is El Greco's *Assumption* of 1613, the artist's last known work. A small museum of archaeology has been arranged in and around the hospital's delightful cloister, off which is a beautifully decorated staircase by Alonso de Covarrubias. *Cervantes 3, tel. 925/221036. Admission 200 ptas. Open Mon. 10–2 and 4–6:30, Tues.–Sat. 10–6:30, Sun. 10–2.*

PLAZA DE ZOCODOVER

Toledo's main square was built in the early 17th century as part of an unsuccessful attempt to impose a rigid geometry on the chaotic Moorish ground plan. Nearby **Calle del Comercio** is Toledo's narrow but lively pedestrian thoroughfare, lined with bars and shops and shaded in the summer months by awnings suspended from the roofs of tall houses.

PUENTE DE ALCÁNTARA

Here is the town's oldest bridge, Roman in origin. Next to the bridge is a heavily restored castle built after the Christian capture of 1085, and above this, a vast and depressingly severe military academy, a typical example of Fascist architecture under Franco. The bridge is off the city's eastern peripheral road, just north of the Puente Nuevo.

PUENTE DE SAN MARTÍN

A pedestrian bridge on the western edge of the town, the Puente de San Martín dates from 1203 and features splendid horseshoe arches.

SAN JUAN DE LOS REYES

This convent church in western Toledo was erected by Ferdinand and Isabella to commemorate their victory at the battle of Toro in 1476 and was intended to be their burial place. The building is largely the work of Juan Guas, who considered it his masterpiece and asked to be buried here himself. Guas, one of the greatest exponents of the Isabelline, or Gothic, plateresque, was an architect of prolific imagination and great decorative exuberance. In true plateresque fashion, the white interior is covered with inscriptions and heraldic motifs. *Reyes Católicos 17, tel. 925/223802. Admission 200 ptas. Open daily 10–1:45 and 3:30–5:45 (until 6:45 in summer).*

SAN ROMÁN

A virtually unspoiled part of Toledo hides this early 13th-century Mudéjar church with extensive remains of frescoes inside. It has been deconsecrated and now serves as the Museo de los Concilios y de la Cultura Visigótica (Museum of Visigothic Culture), featuring statuary, manuscript illustrations, and delicate jewelry. *San Clemente s/n, tel. 925/227872. Admission 100 ptas. Open Tues.–Sat. 10–2 and 4–6:15, Sun. 10–2.*

SANTA MARÍA LA BLANCA

Founded in 1203, Toledo's second synagogue is nearly two centuries older than the more elaborate Tránsito. The white interior features a forest of columns supporting capitals of enchanting filigree workmanship. Stormed in the early 15th century by a Christian mob led by St. Vincent Ferrer, the synagogue was later put to a variety of uses—as a carpenter's workshop, a store, a barracks, and a refuge for reformed prostitutes. *Reyes Católicos 4, tel. 925/227257. Admission 200 ptas. Open daily 10–2 and 3:30–5:45 (6:45 in summer).*

SANTO DOMINGO

A few minutes' walk north of San Román is this 16th-century convent church, where you'll find the earliest of El Greco's Toledo paintings as well as the crypt where the artist is believed to be buried. The friendly nuns at the convent will show you around an odd little museum that includes documents bearing El Greco's signature. *Plaza Santo Domingo el Antiguo s/n, tel. 925/222930. Admission 150 ptas. Open spring–fall, Mon.–Sat. 11–1:30 and 4–7, Sun. 4–7; winter, Sat. 11–1:30 and 4–7, Sun. 4–7.*

SANTO TOMÉ

Topped with a Mudéjar tower, this chapel was specially built to house El Greco's most famous painting, *The Burial of Count Orgaz*, and remains devoted to that purpose. The painting—the only El Greco to have been consistently admired over the centuries—portrays the benefactor of the church being buried with the posthumous assistance of St. Augustine and St. Stephen, who have miraculously appeared at the funeral to thank him for all the money he gave to religious institutions named after them. Though the count's burial took place in the 14th century, El Greco painted the onlookers in contemporary costumes and included people he knew; the boy in the foreground is one of El Greco's sons, and the sixth figure on the left is said to be the artist himself. In summer try to come here as soon as the building opens, as you may have to wait in line to get inside later in the day. *Plaza del Conde 4, tel. 925/256098. Admission 200 ptas. Open fall–spring, daily 10–5:45; summer, daily 10–6:45.*

SINAGOGA DEL TRÁNSITO

Financed by Samuel Levi, this 14th-century rectangular synagogue is plain on the outside, but the inside walls are sumptuously covered with intricate Mudéjar decoration, as well as Hebraic inscriptions glorifying God, Peter the Cruel, and Levi himself. It is said that Levi imported cedars from Lebanon for the building's construction, à la Solomon when he built the First Temple in Jerusalem. Adjoining the main hall is the Museo Sefardí (Sephardic Museum), a small museum of Jewish culture in Spain. *Samuel Levi s/n, tel. 925/223665. Admission 400 ptas. Open Tues.–Sat. 10–2 and 4–6, Sun. 10–2.*

WHERE TO SLEEP

A room in Toledo's modern **Parador Conde de Orgaz,** on the edge of town (Cerro del Emperador s/n, tel. 925/221850), is a splurge, at roughly 19,000 ptas. a night. If you have a car, pay a visit regardless—the building has a magnificent view of Toledo, and you're welcome to have a drink on the terrace.

UNDER 8,000 PTAS. • Hostal La Campana. Near the church of Santo Tomé, this small hostal has simple but tasteful rooms. Rooms 103 and 203 have the best views of the church's 13th-century Mudéjar tower. Parking is available nearby. Doubles run 7,500 ptas. including tax. *La Campana 10, 45002, tel. 925/221659, fax 925/221652. 10 rooms.*

Hostal San Tomé. Rooms in this charming, central, newish *hostal* have white walls, tile floors, and well-equipped bathrooms. Rooms 32 and 33, on the top floor (there's an elevator), have small terraces looking down on the busy street, while rooms in back look onto the quiet garden of the Palacio de Fuensalida. There's parking nearby. Rates for a double hover around 7,000 ptas. *Santo Tomé 13, 45002, tel. 925/221712, fax 925/225855. 10 rooms.*

UNDER 7,000 PTAS. • Hostal Centro. Enter this place on Calle Nueva, just off Plaza Zocodover. Owned by the same people who bring you the Nueva Labrador (*see below*), these rooms are spacious and equipped with private bath, but they share their labyrinthine building with offices. Doubles cost 6,500 ptas. *C. Nueva 3, tel. 925/257091, fax 925/252848.*

Hostal Nuevo Labrador. On a quiet street near the Alcázar, this new hostal has modern rooms with tile floors and private bath (6,420 ptas.). The restaurant downstairs, El Rincón de Eloy, has white floors and black-wicker chairs but no windows. Set menus cost 1,500 or 2,000 ptas. *Juan Labrador 10, tel. 925/ 222620. 12 rooms.*

UNDER 5,500 PTAS. • Pensión Santa Ursula. Near the cathedral, these are seven extremely clean, fresh-looking rooms with yellow walls, white-tile floors, and private bath. Doubles cost around 5,300 ptas. *Santa Ursula 14, 45002, tel. 925/213325. 7 rooms.*

WHERE TO EAT

Since Toledo lives off the tourist trade, the souvenir shops alternate with bars and restaurants that can really fill up, especially on weekends and when tour groups invade like lemmings. If you're really intrigued by a particular place, try to reserve. On weekdays and Saturday morning you can shop for picnic food at the small Plaza Mayor outdoor **market,** augmented by an adjoining supermarket. *Panaderías* (bakeries) abound on Calle de las Tormerías, leading up from the market.

If the navigational trials of the sightseeing maze have you parched, unwind at **Palacio Sancara** (Alfonso X El Sabio 6, tel. 925/215972). Around the corner from the church of San Román, off Plaza Juan de Mariana, this Arabian café-bar has plush couches, low tables, soothing classical music, and colorful tapestries. In the afternoon it's perfect for hot tea and sweets, while at night it draws Toledanos for *copas de noche* (evening cocktails). When early evening starvation threatens, seek good tapas and drinks at the big **Gambrinus** tavern (C. Santo Tomé 10, tel. 925/214440) or at nearby **Cafetería Delfín** (Taller del Moro 1).

Toledo's culinary signature is *perdiz* (partridge), usually served as either *estofada* (a stew with steamed potatoes) or *escabeche* (cold and pickled in vinegar), the latter an acquired taste unless you have a thing for vinegar. Another hearty version is partridge in a stew with white beans. *Codorniz* (quail) is also locally reared. Saffron, called *azafrán* in Spanish, comes from crocus flowers grown just south of Toledo, near Consuegra, and its distinctive flavor adds to *cuchifrito,* a local lamb stew made with tomatoes, eggs, and white wine. The local red table wine is dark, strong stuff. If you like cheese, look for the cured 100%-sheep's-milk *oveja,* a variety of Manchego.

UNDER 2,500 PTAS. • Restaurante-Café El Río. Cheerful and bright, this airy two-story place has yellow walls, artificial flowers, and a summer terrace. Entrées include *perdiz* (partridge), *cordonices toledanos* (Toledo quail), *merluza en salsa verde* (hake in parsley sauce), and *carnes a la brasa* (grilled meats). The *menús del día* (menus of the day) cost 1,350 or 2,500 ptas. *C. Nueva 7, tel. 925/220011.*

Restaurante Maravilla. With a quaint atmosphere and modestly priced menus, Maravilla is a great choice. Specialties include Toledan preparations of partridge or quail and a variety of seafood dishes. Set menus range in price from 900 to 2,200 ptas., so take your pick; the 1,600-pta. *menú de la casa* includes drinks. If you're stuck for lodging, note that there's a 14-room hostal upstairs, with en-suite doubles for 6,500 ptas. *Plaza Barrio Rey 5, tel. 925/228582 or 925/228317.*

Restaurante-Mesón Palacios. This popular tavern with tile walls and beamed ceilings has two set menus (1,000 and 1,700 ptas.), each with a dozen dishes to consider for each of the first two courses. Filling starters include paella and *judias blancas con chorizo y rabo* (white beans with cured sausage and oxtail); main courses include *tortilla de salmón ahumado* (Spanish omelet with smoked salmon) and *pollo asado* (roast chicken). *C. Alfonso X El Sabio 3, tel. 925/215972 or 925/22349.*

UNDER 3,500 PTAS. • **El Patio.** Across from the post office, this local favorite invites outdoor dining on a tiled patio with potted plants and a central fountain. The menu is classically Toledan, featuring *cordero* (lamb), *cordonices* (quail), and *solomillo* (sirloin steak). You can choose your level of luxe here: the menús del día carry disparate prices of 1,500 and 3,200 ptas. *C. la Plata 2, tel. 925/220006.*

SHOPPING

If you've got a sweet tooth, sink it into Toledo—the town is known for its superb marzipan, sold worldwide in all shapes and sizes. The sweet almonds are crushed and kneaded raw with sugar, glucose (for preservation), and water before being heated to the boiling point for sterilization, then molded and roasted. Boxes of assorted *mazapán* are sold by the cloistered nuns of the Royal Monastery of **Santa Ursula** (C. Ursula 3) at 1,300 ptas. for half a kilogram (about a pound). The pastry shop **Santo Tomé** has made marzipan since 1956 and sells it in two locations (Santo Tomé 5; Plaza Zocodover).

The province of Toledo is the most renowned crafts center in Castile, if not all of Spain. The Moors established silver work, damascene (metalwork inlaid with gold or silver), embroidery, pottery, and marzipan traditions here, and next to Toledo's church of San Juan de los Reyes, a turn-of-the-20th-century art school keeps these crafts alive. For cheap pottery try to hit one of the large roadside emporiums on the outskirts of town, on the main road to Madrid.

Buying damascene can be a problem, as Toledo's (too) many souvenir shops are manned by silk-tongued vendors schooled in the art of extracting travelers' money. Everything in **Simian** (Santa Ursula 6, tel. 925/250546)—a large, well-run shop founded more than 100 years ago—is made by hand, and you can watch three craftsmen at work on the premises.

SEGOVIA

With a hulking Gothic cathedral and one of the finest Roman aqueducts in the world, Segovia (88 km/55 mi west of Madrid, 67 km/42 mi northeast of Ávila) is the most perfect Castilian—as opposed to Moorish—city within easy reach of Madrid. Appearing just beyond the northern foothills of the Guadarrama Mountains, the city sits dramatically above an undulating plain on a huge boat-shape shelf of rock. The rivers Eresma and Clamores line either side of its precipitous bows; at one end is the fairy-tale Alcázar castle, arguably copied by Disneyland in its dreamy white emblem.

You can spend a glorious day or two wandering Segovia's clean, cobbled streets, marveling at sudden views out toward the snowcapped mountains or the tawny plain, and OD'ing on Romanesque churches. Trouble is, sitting still feels good, too: Segovia serves more than 70,000 plates of its justly celebrated baby lamb and suckling pig—roasted in huge, wood-fired Segovian ovens—to affluent Madrileños escaping the capital on weekends. And the early-evening ritual of sitting outside with an *aperitivo* in the tree-lined Plaza Mayor—amid the chatter of locals and the clacking of storks' beaks as they, too, gossip from the cathedral's funky buttresses—is really quite magical.

An important military town in Roman times, Segovia was later established by the Moors as a major textile center. Captured by the Christians in 1085, it was enriched by a royal residence, and in 1474 the half sister of Henry IV, Isabel the Catholic (married to Ferdinand of Aragón), was crowned queen of Castile here. By that time Segovia was a bustling city of about 60,000 (there are 54,000 today), but its importance soon diminished as a result of its taking the (losing) side of the Comuneros in the popular revolt against the emperor Charles V. Though the construction in the 18th century of a royal palace in nearby La Granja revived the town's fortunes somewhat, it never recovered its former vitality. Early in the 20th century Segovia's sleepy charm came to be appreciated by artists and writers, among them painter Ignacio Zuloaga and poet Antonio Machado.

SEGOVIA

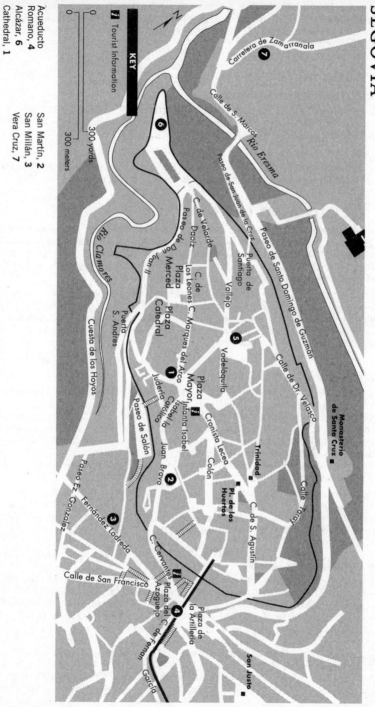

KEY

i Tourist Information

0   300 yards

0   300 meters

N

Carretera de Zamarranala

Calle de S. Marcos

Río Eresma

Paseo de San Juan de la Cruz

Paseo de Santo Domingo de Guzmán

Puerta de Santiago

C. de Velarde

Paseo del Don Juan II

Paseo de Daoiz

C. de los Leones

C. Marques del Arco

Plaza Merced

Plaza Catedral

Puerta S. Andres

Río Clamores

Cuesta de los Hoyos

Juderia Isabel la Católica

Juan Bravo

Paseo de Salón

Vallejo

Vadelaguila

Plaza Mayor, Infanta Isabel

Cronista Lecea

Colón

Trinidad

Pl. de los Huertos

C. de S. Agustín

Calle de Dr. Velasco

Monasterio de Santa Cruz ■

Calle Taray

Paseo Ez. Fernández González

Paseo Ez. Fernández Ladreda

Calle de San Francisco

C. Cervantes

Plaza del Azoguejo

Plaza de la Artillería

C. de Fernan Garcia

San Justo ■

1

2

3

4

5

6

7

i

Today Segovia swarms with tourists and day-trippers from Madrid, and you may want to avoid it in the summer, on holidays, and on good-weather weekends. Still, it feels far less crowded and hemmed-in than Toledo and has nothing like Toledo's glut of souvenir shops. On winter weekdays you can best appreciate the town's haunting peace.

BASICS

VISITOR INFORMATION

Segovia's two tourist offices are easy to find. The **city tourist office,** open daily 10–2 and 5–8, is at Plaza Mayor 10 (tel. 921/460334). The **regional tourist office,** also open daily 10–2 and 5–8, sits in the shadow of the aqueduct (Plaza del Azoguejo 1, tel. 921/462906).

MAIL

The **post office** is at Plaza Huertos 5, east of the Plaza Mayor (tel. 921/461616; open weekdays 10–2 and 5–10). A weekly **market** is held in Plaza Huertos on Thursday morning.

COMING AND GOING

The **train station** (C. Obispo Quesada, tel. 921/436666, 902/240202 for general info) exchanges about eight trains a day with Madrid (2 hrs, 800 ptas.). Buses from the sleazy **bus station** (C. Ezequiel González, tel. 921/443010) also serve Madrid amply (1½ hrs, 765 ptas.). Both stations are in the new town, from which Bus 2, 3, or 4 (85 ptas.) can take you to the Plaza Mayor; otherwise, hoist your pack and follow signs to the CENTRO HISTÓRICO, a 15- to 20-minute walk.

By **car** from Madrid, you can take the A6 freeway (which levies a toll for the tunnel under the Guadarrama Mountains), then exit onto N603 for Segovia; or take the slower but more scenic A6/N601 combination over the scenic Navacerrada pass (6,102 ft). As you head down out of the mountains, you'll pass wooded picnic areas beside a gurgling river; farther on, 11 km (7 mi) before Segovia, you'll pass the Versailles-style palace and gardens of La Granja de San Ildefonso.

GETTING AROUND

If you approach Segovia on N603, the first building you see is the cathedral, as it seems to rise directly from the fields. Between you and Segovia lies, in fact, a steep, narrow valley, which shields the old town from view—only when you descend into the valley do you begin to see the town's spectacular position. To put the city in perspective, turn left onto Paseo Ezequiel González as soon as you reach the modern outskirts, and follow the road marked RUTA PANORÁMICA—you'll soon descend the narrow and winding Cuesta de los Hoyos to the bottom of the wooded valley, south of the old town. Above, you'll see the Romanesque church of San Martín to the right, the cathedral in the middle, and on the far left, where the rock ledge tapers, the turrets, spires, and battlements of the Alcázar.

Approaching on the N601, turn left at a traffic circle to Paseo Ezequiel González, or continue straight for a stunning view of the tiered arches of the aqueduct. Park near here if you're visiting at a peak time (summer; weekends year-round); if not, go around the traffic circle in front of the aqueduct, take the last right before the structure, and drive up into the city.

WHERE TO EAT

Restaurants in the old town cater to tourists with money to burn; it's hard to get a find a menú del día for less than 2,000 ptas. **La Cueva de San Esteban** (C. Valdelaquila 15, tel. 921/460982) serves up tasty menus for 900 ptas., including two glasses of wine. If it's offered, try the paella at **La Catedral** (C. Marqués del Arco 32, tel. 921/460551), where the full menu costs 1,500 ptas. weekdays and 2,500–3,000 ptas. on weekends.

WHERE TO SLEEP

UNDER 9,000 PTAS. • **Hostal Fornos.** Just opened in 1999 off Plaza Mayor, the family-run Fornos rents doubles for 8,500 ptas. a night. Rooms are painted salmon and green, and their modern bathrooms have full tubs. The hallways are hung with mirrors and dappled with handpainted flowers. *Infanta Isabel 13, tel. 921/460198. 10 rooms.*

UNDER 6,000 PTAS. • Hostal Don Jaime. This place occupies a historic building near the Roman aqueduct. The rooms have huge windows, peach or apricot walls, green curtains, and private bathrooms with full tubs. Doubles cost 6,000 ptas. *Ochoa Ondategui 8, tel. 921/444787. 10 rooms.*

Residencia Tagore. A 10-minute walk southeast of Plaza Mayor, Tagore is sometimes flooded with student groups, but it may be the best deal in Segovia, with doubles running 4,000–5,500 ptas. It's a kind of budget resort, with pool, TV room, library, restaurant, and laundry facilities. *C. Santa Isabel 13, tel. 921/420035. Restaurant. 29 rooms.*

WORTH SEEING

ACUEDUCTO ROMANO

Segovia's Roman aqueduct ranks with the Pont du Gard in France as one of the greatest surviving examples of Roman engineering. Spanning the dip that stretches from the walls of the old town to the lower slopes of the Sierra de Guadarrama, it's about 2,388 ft long and rises in two tiers—above what is now the Plaza del Azoguejo, whose name means "highest point"—to a height of 92 ft. The total length of the water channel from the mountains is some 15 km (9 mi). The raised section of stonework in the center originally carried an inscription, of which only the holes for the bronze letters remain. The massive granite blocks were held together by neither mortar nor clamps, but the aqueduct has been standing since the end of the 1st century, and during recent major restoration work some blocks had to be pinned together after damage caused by vibration from traffic that used to go underneath it. The only damage it has suffered is the demolition of 36 of its 166 arches by the Moors, and these were later replaced on the orders of Ferdinand and Isabella. Steps at the side of the aqueduct lead up to the walls of the old town, offering an amazing side view of the structure. *Plaza de Azoguejo.*

ALCÁZAR

Possibly dating from Roman times, this castle was considerably expanded in the 14th century, remodeled in the 15th, altered again toward the end of the 16th, and completely redone after being gutted by a fire in 1862, when it was used as an artillery school. The exterior, especially when seen from the Ruta Panorámica, is certainly imposing, but the castle is little more than a medieval sham—and Disney copied its poetic silhouette for use in an even newer context. The last remnant of the original structure is the keep through which you enter; also real are the medieval strongboxes, coin press, and random artillery. Crowned by crenellated towers that seem to have been carved out of icing, the keep can be climbed for superb views; the rest of the interior is a theatrical mockup of how the palace *may* have looked. *Plaza de la Reina Victoria Eugenia, tel. 921/460759. Admission 400 ptas. Open May–Sept., daily 10–7; Oct.–Apr., daily 10–6.*

PLAZA MAYOR

Segovia's busy, oblong, tree-lined Plaza Mayor is dominated by the 17th-century *ayuntamiento* (town hall) and, on one end, the cathedral. It's a wonderful place to sit at a terrace café and watch the world go by.

CATHEDRAL

Begun in 1525 and completed 65 years later, Segovia's lovely cathedral was intended to replace an earlier one near the Alcázar, destroyed during the revolt of the Comuneros against Charles V. It's one of the most harmonious in Spain and one of the country's last great examples of the Gothic style. The designs were drawn up by the leading late-Gothicist Juan Gil de Hontañon but executed by his son Rodrigo, in whose work can be seen a transition from the Gothic to the Renaissance style. The tall proportions and buttressing are pure Gothic, but much of the detailing—on the crossing tower, for instance—is classical. The golden interior, illuminated by 16th-century Flemish windows, is remarkably light and uncluttered, the one distracting detail being the wooden, neoclassical choir. You enter through the north transept, which is marked MUSEO; turn right, and the first chapel on your right has a Lamentation group in wood by the Baroque sculptor Gregorio Fernández.

Across from the entrance, in the southern transept, is a door opening into the late-Gothic cloister—this and the elaborate door leading into it were transported from the old cathedral and are the work of Juan Guas, architect of the church of San Juan de Los Reyes, in Toledo. Under the pavement immediately inside the cloisters are the tombs of Juan and Rodrigo Gil de Hontañón; that these two lie in a space designed by Guas is appropriate, for the three men together dominated the last phase of the Gothic style in Spain. Off the cloister, a small **museum** of religious art, installed partly in the first-floor chapter house, has a white-and-gold 17th-century ceiling, a late and splendid example of Mudéjar *artesanado* work. *Marqués del Arco 1, tel. 921/435325. Admission to museum 250 ptas. Open June–Sept., daily 9–7; Oct.–May, daily 9:30–6.*

SAN ESTÉBAN

This porticoed church is one of Segovia's major Romanesque monuments. Though the interior has Baroque facing, the exterior has kept some splendid capitals, as well as an exceptionally tall, attractive, postcard-ready tower. Due east of the church square is the **Capilla de San Juan de Dios**, next to which is the former pension where the poet Antonio Machado spent his last years in Spain. The family that looked after Machado still owns the building, and will show you the poet's room on request, with its paraffin stove, iron bed, and round table. The church is open for mass only, normally daily 8–10 and 7–9. *Plaza de San Estéban, no phone.*

SAN MARTÍN

This Romanesque church stands in an attractive little plaza by the same name. *Plaza San Martín, tel. 921/443402. Open for mass, usually weekdays 11:30, 12:30, and 7:30, Sun. 1.*

SAN MILLÁN

A perfect example of the Segovian Romanesque, this 12th-century house of worship is perhaps the finest in town apart from the cathedral. The exterior is notable for its arcaded porch, where church meetings were once held. The virtually untouched Romanesque interior is dominated by massive columns, whose capitals carry such carved scenes as the Flight into Egypt and the Adoration of the Magi. The vaulting on the crossing shows the Moorish influence on Spanish medieval architecture. *Avda. Fernández Ladreda 26 (5-min walk outside town walls), no phone. Open for mass only, daily 8–10 and 7–9.*

VERA CRUZ

Built of local warm-orange stone, this isolated Romanesque church went up in 1208 for the Knights Templar. Like other buildings associated with this order, it has 12 sides, inspired by the Church of the Holy Sepulchre in Jerusalem. Your trip here pays off in full when you climb the bell tower and see all of Segovia profiled against the Sierra de Guadarrama, which is capped with snow in winter. *Carretera de Zamarramala s/n, on northern outskirts of town, off Cuesta de los Hoyos, tel. 921/431475. Admission 150 ptas. Open May–Sept., Tues.–Sun. 10:30–1:30 and 3:30–7; Oct.–Apr., Tues.–Sun. 10:30–1:30 and 3:30–6.*

SHOPPING

Calle Daiza, leading to the Alcázar, overflows with touristy ceramics, textile, and gift shops; you can buy good lace from the Gypsies in Segovia's **Plaza del Alcázar** or by the cathedral, but prepare for some strenuous bargaining and never offer more than half the opening price.

NEAR SEGOVIA: PALACIO REAL DE LA GRANJA

The major attraction in Segovia's immediate vicinity, the Royal Palace of La Granja stands in the town of San Ildefonso de la Granja, on the northern slopes of the Sierra de Guadarrama mountains (*granja* means "farm"). The site was once occupied by a hunting lodge and a shrine to San Ildefonso, administered by Hieronymite monks from the Segovian monastery of El Parral. Commissioned by the Bourbon king Felipe V in 1719, the palace has sometimes been described as the first great building of the Spanish Bourbon dynasty. The 19th-century English writer Richard Ford likened it to "a theatrical French château, the antithesis of the proud, gloomy Escorial, on which it turns its back." The architects who brought it to completion in 1739 and gave it such distinction were, in fact, not French but Italian (Juvarra and Sachetti); they were responsible for the imposing garden facade, a late-Baroque masterpiece anchored throughout its length by a giant order of columns. The interior has been badly gutted by fire, and the few undamaged rooms are heavy and monotonous; the highlight of the interior is the collection of 15th- to 18th-century tapestries, presented in a special museum. It's really the **gardens** that people come to see, with their terraces, ornamental ponds, lakes, classical statuary, woods, and

Baroque fountains backed by the soaring pine-covered mountains. On Wednesday, Saturday, and Sunday evenings in the summer (6–7, May—September), the fountains are turned on, one by one, creating one of the most exciting such spectacles in Europe. The starting time has been known to change on a whim; call to check the time (tel. 921/470020). *11 km (7 mi) southeast of Segovia on N601 toward Navacerrada mountain pass. Admission to palace: 700 ptas., gardens free. Palace open Oct.–May, Tues.–Sat. 10–1:30 and 3–5, Sun. 10–2; Apr.–May, Tues.–Sat. 10–1:30 and 3–5, Sun. 10–6; June–Sept., Tues.–Sun. 10–6. Garden daily 10–sunset.*

ÁVILA

Smack in the middle of a windy plateau littered with giant boulders, Ávila (107 km/66 mi northwest of Madrid) can look wild and sinister. The big deal with this town is the magnificent, well-preserved, ½-mi medieval **wall** that still surrounds it. Begun in 1090, shortly after the town was reclaimed from the Moors, the wall was completed in only nine years—a feat accomplished by the daily employment of almost 2,000 men. It's most striking when viewed from outside the town; for the best view on foot, cross the Adaja River, turn right on the Carretera de Salamanca, and walk uphill about 250 yards to a monument consisting of four pilasters surrounding a cross. Since you can only make so much of a wall, many travelers have a good gawk and move on to, say, Salamanca; this is quite acceptable. If you do pause here to explore the Teresa sights, look back on your way out.

Ávila's walls reflect the town's importance during the Middle Ages. Populated mainly with Christians from Asturias (to balance the encroaching Moors), the town found itself with a high proportion of nobles; decline set in during the 15th century, when the blue bloods decamped to the court of Charles V in Toledo. Later, Ávila's fame centered on St. Teresa, born here in 1515 to a noble family of Jewish origin—Teresa spent much of her life here, leaving a legacy of convents and *yemas* (candied egg yolks), originally distributed free to the poor but now sold for high prices to tourists. The town is well preserved but has a sad, austere, slightly desolate atmosphere. The quietude is dispelled only for the week beginning October 8, when Ávila celebrates the Fiestas de Santa Teresa with lighted decorations, parades, and singing in the streets as well as religious observances.

BASICS

VISITOR INFORMATION
The **tourist office** is at Plaza de la Catedral 4 (tel. 920/211387; open daily 10–2 and 5–8).

MAIL
The **post office** is steps from the tourist office, at Plaza de la Catedral 2 (tel. 920/211354 or 920/211370).

COMING AND GOING

BY BUS
The **bus station** (Avda. de Madrid 2, tel. 920/220154) is 300 yards from the city walls. Ávila-bound **Larrea buses** (tel. 920/226505) leave Madrid three times daily (1½ hrs, 950 ptas.) from the Estación Sur (tel. 91/530–4800).

BY TRAIN
The **train station** (Avda. José Antonio 40, tel. 920//250202, 902/240202 for general info) is ¼ mi from the town center. Local Bus 1 and taxis are available. Numerous trains roll in daily from **Madrid-**Chamartín (1½–2 hrs, 995–1,095 ptas.) and **Salamanca** (1½ hrs, 900 ptas.).

BY CAR
From Madrid take the N-VI northwest, then the A6 toll road with the long tunnel under the Guadarrama Mountains. Turn off at Villacastín (107 km/66 mi) for the N110 to Ávila.

WORTH SEEING

The battlement apse of the **cathedral** forms the most impressive part of the walls. The apse was built mainly in the late 12th century, but the construction of the rest of the cathedral continued until the 18th century. Entering the town gate to the right of the apse, you'll reach the sculpted north portal (originally the west portal, until it was moved in 1455 by the architect Juan Guas) by turning left and walking a few steps. The present west portal, flanked by 18th-century towers, is notable for the crude carvings of hairy male figures on each side; known as "wild men," these figures appear in many Castilian palaces of this period, but their significance is disputed.

The Transitional Gothic interior, with its granite nave, is heavy and severe. The Lisbon earthquake of 1755 deprived the building of its Flemish stained glass, so the main note of color appears in the beautiful mottled stone in the apse, tinted yellow and red. Elaborate, plateresque choir stalls built in 1547 complement the powerful high altar of circa 1504 by painters Juan de Borgoña and Pedro Berruguete. On the wall of the ambulatory, look for the early 16th-century marble sepulchre of Bishop Alonso de Madrigal, a remarkably lifelike representation of the bishop seated at his writing table. Known as "El Tostado" (the Toasted One) for his swarthy complexion, the bishop was a tiny man of enormous intellect, the author of 54 books. When on one occasion Pope Eugenius IV ordered him to stand—mistakenly thinking him to be still on his knees—the bishop indicated the space between his eyebrows and hairline, retorting, "A man's stature is to be measured from here to here!" *Plaza de la Catedral s/n, tel. 920/211641. Admission 250 ptas. Open daily 10–1:30 and 3:30–6:30.*

The 15th-century Mansión de los Deanes (Deans' Mansion) houses the cheerful **Museo de Ávila,** a provincial museum full of local archaeology and folklore. It's a few minutes' walk east of the cathedral apse. *Plaza de Nalvillos 3, tel. 920/211003. Admission 200 ptas., free weekends. Open Tues.–Sat. 10:30–2 and 5–7:30, Sun. 11–2.*

The **Convento de San José** (or de Las Madres), four blocks east of the cathedral on Calle Duque de Alba, houses the **Museo Teresiano,** which displays musical instruments used by St. Teresa and her nuns at Christmas. Teresa herself was a percussionist. *Las Madres 4, tel. 920/222127. Admission 100 ptas. Open fall–spring, daily 10–1:30 and 3–6; summer, daily 9:30–1 and 4–7.*

North of Ávila's cathedral, on Plaza de San Vincente, is the much-venerated Romanesque **Basílica de San Vicente** (St. Vincent's Basilica), founded on the supposed site where St. Vincent was martyred in 303 with his sisters, saints Sabina and Cristeta. The west front, shielded by a narthex, has damaged but expressive Romanesque carvings depicting the death of Lazarus and the parable of the rich man's table. The sarcophagus of St. Vincent, surrounded with delicate carvings from this period, forms the centerpiece of the basilica's Romanesque interior; the extraordinary Asian-looking canopy above the sarcophagus is a 15th-century addition paid for by the Knights of Ávila. *Plaza de San Vicente s/n, tel. 920/255230. Admission 100 ptas. Open daily 10–2 and 4–7:30.*

On Calle de Lopez Nuñez, the elegant chapel of **Mosen Rubi** (circa 1516) is illuminated by Renaissance stained glass by Nicolás de Holanda. Try to persuade the nuns in the adjoining convent to let you inside.

At the west end of the town walls, next to the river in an enchanting farmyard nearly hidden by poplars, is the small, Romanesque **Ermita de San Segundo** (Hermitage of St. Secundus). Founded on the site where the remains of St. Secundus (a follower of St. Peter) were reputedly discovered, the hermitage houses a realistic marble monument to the saint, carved by Juan de Juni. You may have to ask for the key in the adjoining house. *Avda. de Madrid s/n, toward Salamanca. Admission: tip caretaker. Open daily 10–1 and 3:30–6.*

Inside the south wall on Calle Dama, the **Convento de Santa Teresa** was founded in the 17th century on the site of the saint's birthplace. Teresa's famous written account of an ecstatic vision in which an angel pierced her heart would influence many Baroque artists, most famously the Italian sculptor Giovanni Bernini. The convent has a small museum, with relics including one of Teresa's fingers, and you can also see the small, rather gloomy garden where she played as a child. *Plaza de la Santa s/n, tel. 920/211030. Admission 300 ptas. Open daily 10–1 and 3:30–6.*

The **Museo del Convento de la Encarnación** is where St. Teresa first took orders and was then based for more than 30 years. Its museum has an interesting drawing of the crucifixion by her disciple St. John of the Cross, as well as a reconstruction of the cell she used when she was a prioress here. The convent is outside the walls in the north part of town. *Paseo de la Encarnación s/n, tel.920/211212. Admission 150 ptas. Open May–Sept., daily 9:30–1 and 4–7; Oct.—Apr., daily 9:30–1:30 and 3:30–6.*

The main distraction on Ávila's outskirts is the **Monasterio de Santo Tomás.** A good 10-minute walk from the walls among blackened housing projects, it's not where you would expect to find one of the most important religious institutions in Castile. The monastery was founded by Ferdinand and Isabella with the financial assistance of the notorious inquisitor-general Tomás de Torquemada, who is buried in the sacristy. Further funds were provided by the confiscated property of converted Jews who ran afoul of the Inquisition. Three decorated cloisters lead to the church; inside, a masterly high altar (circa 1506) by Pedro Berruguete overlooks a serene marble tomb by the Italian artist Domenico Fancelli. One of the earliest examples of the Italian Renaissance style in Spain, this influential work was built for Prince Juan, the only son of Ferdinand and Isabella, who died at 19 while a student at the University of Salamanca. After Juan's burial here, his heartbroken parents found themselves unable to return to the institution they had founded. In happier times they had often attended mass here, seated in the upper choir behind a balustrade exquisitely carved with their coats of arms; you can reach the choir from the upper part of the Kings' Cloister. The **Museo de Arte Oriental** (Museum of Eastern Art) contains works collected from Dominican missions in Vietnam. *Plaza de Granada 1, tel. 920/220400. Admission: cloister 100 ptas., museum 200 ptas. Cloister open daily 10–1 and 4–8, museum open Tues.–Sun. 11–1 and 4–6.*

WHERE TO SLEEP

UNDER 7,000 PTAS. • **Hostal San Segundo.** This family-run three-floor inn is just beyond the cathedral and city wall, on the eastern edge of the old town. Rooms and common areas are comfortable and elegantly modern, and the amenities (in-room phones and satellite TV; restaurant and bar downstairs) would cost more elsewhere. Double rooms with bath run 5,000–7,000 ptas. depending on the season. *C. San Segundo 30, tel. 920/252590 or 920/252690, fax 920/252790. Restaurant, bar.*

UNDER 6,000 PTAS. • **Hostal Alcántara.** Modest, clean doubles with bath go for 5,300–7,300 ptas. here depending on the season. You're a two-minute walk from the cathedral. *Esteban Domingo 11, 05001, tel. 920/225003 or 920/223804. 9 rooms.*

Casa Felipe. Set in the Mercado Chico tapas area, this small, family-run place rents doubles with bath for 5,500 ptas. a night. *Plaza de la Victoria 12, tel. 920/213924. 11 rooms.*

UNDER 5,000 PTAS. • **Hostal Jardín.** Well situated in the center of town, behind the cathedral, this family-run *hostal* rents rooms starting at 4,500 ptas. a night. *San Segundo 38, 05001, tel. 920/211075. 15 rooms.*

WHERE TO EAT

This is livestock country. Ávila's *ternera* (veal) is nationally famous, especially in the form of enormous T-bone steak (*chuletón de Ávila*) seared on a grill, a dish big enough for two. Roasts are also popular— suckling pig, lamb, goat. Because it's very cold here in winter (Ávila sits at 3,710 ft), there are lots of hearty stews, including an unmistakably Spanish blend of *judías* (white beans), chorizo, and chunky bacon fat. For dessert, *yemas* are ubiquitous; the choice is yours. Good-value local wines come from El Tiemblo and Cebreros.

Plaza de Santa Teresa, just outside the Puerta de Alcázar (Fortress Gate), and the adjoining streets are well stocked with tapas bars, as is **Plaza de la Victoria,** near the town hall.

UNDER 2,500 PTAS. • **Las Canselas.** Locals pack this little tavern full in search of its 2,000-pta. menú del día. Push your way through the loud tapas bar to the dining room, where wooden tables are covered with paper and heaped with combination platters of roast chicken, french fries, sunny-side-up eggs, and chunks of home-baked bread. The chuletón is enormous. Don't be intimidated by the no-nonsense waitstaff or the volume of all the Spanish being shouted back and forth; do as the locals do and knock back a *caña* (small shot of beer usually served with a tapa) while soaking up the ambience. *Cruz Viejo 6, tel. 920/212249. Closed 2nd ½ Jan.*

Mesón del Rastro. This restaurant occupies a wing of the medieval Palacio Abrantes. The worn but attractive Castilian interior features exposed stone walls and beams, low lighting, and dark-wood furniture. Try the lamb and El Barco beans or the *caldereta de cabrito* (goat stew). The place suffers somewhat from its popularity with tour buses, perhaps because the menú del día is so reasonably priced (1,700 ptas.). *Plaza Rastro 1, tel. 920/211218.*

SHOPPING

Buy your loved ones yemas and other sweets at **Pastelerías Muñoz Iselma** (Plaza de Santa Teresa, tel. 920/211170; Plaza de la Victoria 7, tel. 920/213410; Avda. de José Antonio 24, tel. 920/220285). Every Friday (or Wednesday, if Friday is a holiday), two different morning **markets** are held: one in **Plaza de Mercado Chico,** with fruit, vegetables, ceramics, and earthenware, and one in **Plaza San Isidro,** with fabric, clothing, and, strangely, fish.

SALAMANCA

Defined visually and spiritually by one of the world's four oldest universities, Salamanca (205 km/125 mi northwest of Madrid) is "Oxford in the sun" to the thousands of foreign students, diplomats, and businessmen who take intensive Spanish classes here. The university is the dynamo that simultaneously drives Salamanca and helps preserve its treasures. And what treasures—the entire old town is a spectacular display of Renaissance and particularly plateresque architecture—an open-air gallery of carved sandstone facades. The city's 18th-century Plaza Mayor is one of the largest and loveliest in the world, built with the same golden stone used throughout the medieval quarter.

If you approach from Madrid or Ávila, you'll first see the main tower of Salamanca's "new" cathedral rising on the horizon. The best view of the city is perhaps from the northern banks of the wide and winding River Tormes by the sturdy Roman bridge; above this, dominating the view, soar the old and new cathedrals. Piercing the skyline to the right is the Renaissance monastery and church of San Esteban. Behind San Esteban and the cathedrals, and largely out of sight from the river, extends a stunning series of palaces, convents, and university buildings that culminates in the Plaza Mayor.

An important settlement back in Iberian times, Salamanca was captured by Hannibal in 217 BC and flourished as a major Roman station on the north–south road between León and Seville. Converted to Christianity by at least the end of the 6th century, it later passed back and forth between the Christians and Moors and began to stabilize only after the Christian Reconquest of Toledo in 1085. The university grew out of a college founded around 1220 by Alfonso IV of León. Salamanca thrived in the 15th- and early 16th-centuries, and the number of students at the university rose to almost 10,000. The city's greatest royal benefactor was Isabella, who generously financed both the magnificent New Cathedral and the rebuilding of the university. A dual portrait of Ferdinand and Isabella was incorporated into the facade of the main academic building to commemorate her patronage.

Nearly all of Salamanca's other outstanding Renaissance buildings bear the five-star crest of the all-powerful and ostentatious Fonseca family. The most famous Fonseca, Alonso de Fonseca I, was the archbishop of Santiago and then of Seville; he was also a notorious womanizer and one of the patrons of the Spanish Renaissance. Both Salamanca and the university began to decline in the early 17th century, corrupted by ultraclericalism and devastated by a flood in 1626. Some of the town's former glory was recovered in the 18th century, with the construction of the Plaza Mayor by the native Churrigueras, who were among the most influential architects of the Spanish Baroque.

The city suffered in the Peninsular War of the early 19th century and was marred by modern development initiated by Franco after the Civil War; but the university has revived in recent years and is again one of the most prestigious in Europe. Try to stay here on a weekend, as the social atmosphere is something to behold. Fierce competition for the student trade keeps tapas bars, cheap restaurants, pubs, *hostales*, and trendy nightspots jumping—the budget traveler is spoiled for choice.

BASICS

VISITOR INFORMATION

The **city tourist office** is well located, in the Plaza Mayor (tel. 923/279124), open daily 9–2 and 4:30–6:30. For trips farther afield, the **regional tourist office** (Casa de las Conchas, Compania 2, tel. 923/268571) is open weekdays 10–2 and 5–8, Saturday 10–2.

For assistance with travel arrangements, pop into the budget agency **TIVE** (Plaza de la Constitución 1, tel. 923/246129).

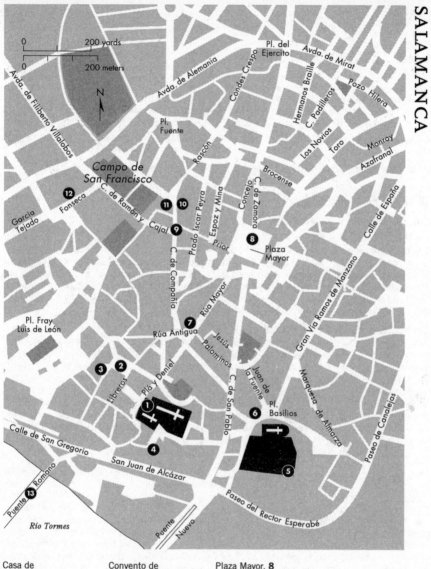

0 | 200 yards
0 | 200 meters

N

Avda. de Filiberto Villalobos

Avda. de Alemania

Pl. del Ejercito

Avda. de Mirat

Condes Crespo

Pozo Hilera

Pl. Fuente

Rascón

Hermanos Braille

C. Padilleros

Los Novias

Toro

Monroy

Azafranal

Campo de San Francisco

Fonseca

C. de Ramón y Cajal

Prado Iscar Peyra

Espoz y Mina

Prior

Brocense

Concejo

C. de Zamora

Calle de España

García Tejado

12

11 **10**

9

8

Plaza Mayor

C. de Compañía

Rúa Mayor

Pl. Fray Luis de León

Rúa Antigua

7

Jesús

Palominos

C. de San Pablo

Juan de la Fuente

Gran Vía Ramos de Manzano

Marquesa de Almarza

Paseo de Canalejas

3 **2**

Libreros

Plá y Deniel

1

4

6

Pl. Basilios

5

Calle de San Gregorio

San Juan de Alcázar

Puente Romano

13

Río Tormes

Puente Nuevo

Paseo del Rector Esperabé

Casa de
Las Conchas, **7**

Casa de
Las Muertes, **10**

Cathedrals, **1**

Colegio Mayor
Arzobispo Fonseca/
Colegio de los
Irlandeses, **12**

Convento de
Las Dueñas, **6**

Convento de
Las Ursulas, **11**

Convento de
San Esteban, **5**

Museo Art Nouveau
y Art Deco, **4**

Museo de
Salamanca/Museo
de Bellas Artes, **3**

Palacio de
Monterrey, **9**

Plaza Mayor, **8**

Puente Romano, **13**

Universidad, **2**

MAIL

The **post office** is at Gran Vía 25 (tel. 923/262000).

COMING AND GOING

Three to four daily **trains** roll into Salamanca from **Madrid**-Chamartín (3 hrs, 2,150 ptas.), all of them stopping in **Ávila** en route (Ávila-Salamanca 1½ hrs, 900 ptas). Salamanca's **train station** is on Plaza de la Estación (tel. 923/225742, 902/240202 for general info), a mile from the Plaza Mayor; if you want to hoof it, head straight southwest down Paseo de la Estación, then down Calle Azafranal. The **RENFE office** in town (Plaza de la Libertad 1, tel. 923/212454) sells tickets.

AutoRes buses (tel. 923/232266) shuttle to and from **Madrid** several times daily (2½ hrs, 1,690–2,250 ptas express).

By **car** from Madrid (205 km/125 mi), take the A6 toll road and exit onto N601 for Salamanca.

WORTH SEEING

CASA DE LAS CONCHAS

The House of Shells was built in 1493 for Dr. Rodrigo Maldonado de Talavera, a professor of medicine at the university and a doctor at the court of Isabella. The scallop motif was a reference to Talavera's status as chancellor of the Order of St. James (Santiago), whose symbol is the shell. Among the playful plateresque details are the lions over the main entrance, engaged in a fearsome tug-of-war with the Talavera crest. The interior has been converted into a public library. Duck into the charming courtyard, which has an upper balustrade carved with virtuoso intricacy in imitation of basketwork. *Compañía 2, tel. 923/269317. Admission free. Open Weekdays 9–9, Sat. 9–2. Closed Sun.*

CASA DE LAS MUERTES

Built in about 1513 for the butler of Alonso de Fonseca II, the House of the Dead takes its name from the four tiny skulls that adorn its top two windows. Alonso de Fonseca II commissioned them to commemorate his deceased uncle, the licentious archbishop who lies in the Convento de Las Ursulas, across the street (*see below*). For the same reason the facade also bears the archbishop's portrait. The small square in front of the house was a favorite haunt of the poet, philosopher, and university rector Miguel de Unamuno, whose statue stands here. Unamuno supported the Nationalists under Franco at the outbreak of the Civil War, but he later turned against them. Placed under virtual house arrest, Unamuno died in the house next door in 1938. During the Franco period students often daubed his statue red to suggest that his heart still bled for Spain. *Las Ursulas s/n.*

CATHEDRALS

For a complete tour of the old and new buildings' exteriors (a 10-minute walk), circle the complex counterclockwise. Nearest the river stands the **Catedral Vieja** (Old Cathedral), built in the late 12th century, one of the most interesting examples of the Spanish Romanesque. Because the dome of the crossing tower features strange, plumelike ribbing, it is known as the Torre del Gallo (Rooster's Tower). The much larger **Catedral Nueva** (New Cathedral) dates mainly from the 16th century, though some parts, including the dome over the crossing and the bell tower attached to the west facade, had to be rebuilt after the Lisbon earthquake of 1755. Work began in 1513 under the direction of the distinguished late-Gothic architect Juan Gil de Hontañón, and as at Segovia's cathedral, Juan's son Rodrigo took over the work after his father's death in 1526. Of the many outstanding architects in 16th-century Salamanca, Rodrigo Gil de Hontañón left the greatest mark, as a leading exponent of the classical plateresque. The New Cathedral's north facade (which contains the main entrance) is ornamental enough, but the west facade is dazzling in its sculptural complexity. Try to come here in late afternoon, when the sun shines directly on it.

The New Cathedral's interior is as light and harmonious as that of Segovia's cathedral, but larger. Here you are treated to a triumphant Baroque effusion designed by the Churrigueras. The wooden choir seems almost alive with anxiously active cherubim and saints. From a door in the south aisle, steps descend into the Old Cathedral, where boldly carved capitals supporting the vaulting feature a range of foliage, strange animals, and touches of pure fantasy. Then comes the dome, which seems to owe much to Byzantine architecture; it's a remarkably light structure raised on two tiers of arcaded openings. Not the least of the Old Cathedral's attractions are its furnishings, including sepulchres from the 12th and 13th centuries and a magnificent curved high altar comprising 53 colorful and delicate scenes by the mid-15th-century artist Nicolás Florentino. In the apse above, Florentino painted an astonishingly fresh Last Judgment fresco.

From the south transept of the Old Cathedral, a door leads into the cloister, begun in 1177. From about 1230 until the construction of the main university building in the early 15th century, the chapels around the cloister served as classrooms for the university students. In the Chapel of St. Barbara, on the eastern side, theology students answered the grueling questions meted out by their doctoral examiners. The chair in which they sat is still there, in front of a recumbent effigy of Bishop Juan Lucero, on whose head the students would place their feet for inspiration. Also attached to the cloister is a small cathedral museum with a 15th-century triptych of St. Catherine by Salamanca's greatest native artist, Fernando Gallego. *Plá y Deniel s/n, tel. 923/217476. New Cathedral admission free, Old Cathedral 300 ptas. Open Oct.–Mar., New Cathedral daily 9–1 and 4–6, Old Cathedral daily 10–12:30 and 4–5:30; Apr.–Sept., New Cathedral daily 9–2 and 4–8, Old Cathedral daily 10–1:30 and 4–7:30.*

COLEGIO MAYOR ARZOBISPO FONSECA / COLEGIO DE LOS IRLANDESES

The little Irish College was founded by Alonso de Fonseca II in 1521 to train young Irish priests. It is now a residence hall for guest lecturers. The surroundings are not attractive; this part of town was the most severely damaged during the Peninsular War of the early 19th century and still has a slightly derelict character. The building's interior, however, is a treat: Immediately inside to the right is a spacious late-Gothic chapel, and beyond it lies one of the most classical and genuinely Italianate of Salamanca's many courtyards. The architect may have been Diego de Siloe, Spain's answer to Michelangelo. *Fonseca 4, tel. 923/294570. Admission 100 ptas., free Mon. Cloisters and chapel open daily 10–2 and 4–6.*

CONVENTO DE LAS DUEÑAS

Founded in 1419, the Convent of the Dames hides a 16th-century cloister that is the most fantastically decorated in Salamanca, if not in the whole of Spain. The capitals of its two superimposed Salamantine arcades are crowded with a baffling profusion of grotesques that can absorb you for hours. There's another good reason to come here: the nuns make and sell excellent sweets and pastries. *Plaza Concilio de Trento, tel. 923/215442. Admission 200 ptas. Open Apr.–Sept. daily 10:30–1 and 4:30–7; Oct.–Mar., daily 4:30–5:30.*

CONVENTO DE LAS URSULAS

Archbishop Alonso de Fonseca I lies here in the Convent of the Ursulines, in a splendid marble tomb created by Diego de Siloe during the first half of the 16th century. *Las Ursulas 2, tel. 923/219877. Admission 100 ptas. Open daily 10–1 and 4:30–7.*

CONVENTO DE SAN ESTABAN

The awesome size of this building is a measure of its importance in Salamanca's history: its monks, among the most enlightened teachers at the university, were the first to take Columbus's ideas seriously and helped him gain his introduction to Isabella (hence his statue in the nearby Plaza de Colón, back toward Calle de San Pablo). The complex was designed by one of St. Stephen's monks, Juan de Alava. The door to the right of the west facade leads you into a gloomy cloister with Gothic arcading, interrupted by tall, spindly columns adorned with classical motifs. From the cloister you enter the church at its eastern end. The interior is unified and uncluttered, but also dark and severe. The one note of color is provided by the sumptuously ornate and gilded high altar of 1692, a Baroque masterpiece by José Churriguera. The most exciting feature of San Esteban, though, is the massive west facade, a thrilling plateresque work in which sculpted figures and ornamentation are piled up to a height of more than 98 ft. *Plaza Concilio de Trento, tel. 923/215000. Admission 200 ptas. Open Apr.–Sept., daily 9–1 and 4–8; Oct.–Mar., daily 9–1 and 4–6.*

MUSEO ART NOUVEAU Y ART DECO

The setting for this museum is the Casa Lis, a modernist building from the end of the 19th century. On display are 19th-century paintings and glass, as well as French and German china dolls, Viennese bronze statues, furniture, jewelry, enamels, and jars. *Gibraltar 14, tel. 923/121425. Admission 300 ptas. Open Oct.–Mar., Tues.–Fri. 11–2 and 4–7, weekends 11–8; Apr.–Sept., Tues.–Fri. 11–2 and 5–9, weekends 11–9.*

MUSEO DE SALAMANCA / MUSEO DE BELLAS ARTES

Comprising mainly 17th- and 18th-century paintings, this museum is also interesting for its 15th-century building, which belonged to Isabella's physician, Alvárez Abarca. *Patio de Escuelas Menores 2, tel. 923/212235. Admission 200 ptas., free weekends. Open Mon.–Sat. 10–2 and 4:30–7:30, Sun. 10–2.*

PALACIO DE MONTERREY

Built after 1538 by Rodrigo Gil de Hontañón, the Monterrey Palace was meant for an illegitimate son of Alonso de Fonseca I. Only one of its four wings was completed, but this one alone makes the palace one of the most imposing in Salamanca. As in Rodrigo's other local palaces, the building is flanked on each side by towers and has an open arcaded gallery running the whole length of the upper level. Such galleries—which in Italy you would expect to see on the ground floor—are common in Spanish Renaissance palaces and were intended as areas where the women of the house could exercise unseen and undisturbed. They also helped to cool the floor below during the summer months. The palace is privately owned, but you can stroll around the exterior. *Compañía s/n.*

PLAZA MAYOR

Built in the 1730s by Alberto and Nicolás Churriguera, Salamanca's Plaza Mayor is one of the largest squares (well, it's slightly oblong) in Spain, and many find it the most beautiful. Its northern side is dominated by the lavishly elegant, pinkish **ayuntamiento** (city hall). The square and its arcades are popular gathering spots for most of Salamancan society, and the many surrounding cafés make this the perfect spot for a coffee break. At night, the plaza swarms with students meeting "under the clock" on the plaza's north side. *Tunas* (strolling student musicians in traditional garb) often meander among the cafés and crowds, playing for smiles and applause rather than tips.

PUENTE ROMANO

Next to the Roman bridge is an Iberian stone bull. Opposite the bull is a statue commemorating Lazarillo de Tormes, the young hero of the eponymous (but anonymous) 16th-century work that is one of the masterpieces of Spanish literature.

UNIVERSIDAD

Parts of the university's walls, like those of the cathedral and other structures in Salamanca, are covered with large ocher lettering recording the names of famous university graduates. The earliest names are said to have been written in the blood of the bulls killed to celebrate the successful completion of a doctorate.

The **Escuelas Mayores** (university faculties; literally, Major Schools) dates to 1415, but it was not until more than 100 years later that an unknown architect provided the building with its gloriously elaborate frontispiece, generally acknowledged as one of the finest works of the classical plateresque. Immediately above the main door is the famous double portrait of Ferdinand and Isabella, surrounded by ornamentation that plays on the yoke-and-arrow heraldic motifs of the two monarchs. The double-eagle crest of Charles V, flanked by portraits of the emperor and empress in classical guise, dominates the middle layer of the frontispiece. On the highest layer is a panel recently identified as representing Pope Martin V (one of the university's greatest benefactors), accompanied by cardinals and university rectors. The whole is crowned by a characteristically elaborate plateresque balustrade. Student legend holds that if you're bright enough to spot the tiny frog, you'll pass all your exams here.

The interior of the Escuelas Mayores, drastically restored in parts, comes as a slight disappointment after the splendor of the facade. But the *aula* (lecture hall) of Fray Luis de León, where Cervantes, Calderón de la Barca, and numerous other luminaries of Spain's golden age once sat, is of particular interest. After five years' imprisonment for having translated the *Song of Solomon* into Spanish, Fray Luis returned to this hall and began his lecture, "As I was saying yesterday. . . ."

Your ticket to the Escuelas Mayores also admits you to the nearby **Escuelas Menores** (Minor Schools), built in the early 16th century as a secondary school preparing candidates for the university proper. Passing through a gate crowned with the double-eagle crest of Charles V, you'll come to a green, on the other side of which is a modern building housing a fascinating ceiling fresco of the zodiac, originally in the library of the Escuelas Mayores. A fragment of a much larger whole, this painting is generally attributed to Fernando Gallego. *Tel. 923/294400, ext. 1150. Admission 300 ptas. Open weekdays 9:30–1:30 and 4–7, Sat. 9:30–1:30 and 4–6:30, Sun. 10–1.*

WHERE TO SLEEP

Beloved of budget travelers, Salamanca has plenty of places to crash, especially around Plaza Mayor. If you get stuck, wander Rúa Mayor, Calle Meléndez, and their side streets.

UNDER 4,000 PTAS. • Fonda San José. Clean, newly renovated double rooms go for a song here (2,200 ptas.), and if you stay a while, the owner might cut you a deal. You do have to share bath facilities and pay 100 ptas. per shower. *C. Jesús 24, south of Plaza Mayor, tel. 923/212724.*

Pensión Estefanía. Next to the Casa de las Conchas, these rooms have the works—dresser, desk, even out-of-date movie posters. Doubles are 3,000 ptas. with shared bath, 3,500 ptas. with private bath. *C. Jesús 3–5 (south of Plaza Mayor), tel. 923/217372. 11 rooms, 6 with bath.*

UNDER 6,000 PTAS. • Pensión Las Vegas. A room here is a great deal, but there are only five, and management will only take a reservation if you pay for the first night up front. Spartan doubles with shared bath are 2,400 ptas.; triples with private bath, 4,000 ptas. Use of the washing machine and dryer costs 1,400 ptas. *C. Meléndez 13 (southwest of Plaza Mayor), tel. 923/218749. Coin-operated laundry. 5 rooms, 2 with bath.*

Pensión Los Angeles. Smack in the middle of the action, Los Angeles is a bargain if you don't mind the noise. Some rooms have great views over the square. Doubles run 3,200–4,500 ptas. *Plaza Mayor 10, tel. 923/218166. 10 rooms.*

UNDER 10,000 PTAS. • Hostal Plaza Mayor. You can't beat the location of this great little hostel, just steps from Plaza Mayor. The only drawback is the noise level on weekends, when student *tunas* sing guitar ballads at the plaza's crowded cafés until the wee hours. Small but modern double rooms go for 8,500 ptas. and fill up fast—reserve in advance if possible. *Plaza del Corrillo 20, 37008, tel. 923/ 262020, fax 923/217548. 19 rooms. Restaurant.*

WHERE TO EAT

You may have noticed the undulating farm country around Salamanca, interspersed with fighting-bull ranches. Just south of here, Iberian pigs snuffle fatty acorns in the wild to make themselves the caviar of Spanish ham—the wonderfully juicy, fragrat *jamón ibérico de bellota.* Budget diners will have to settle for Serrano ham, which is still tangy and tastes great nestled in a *bocadillo* (baguette sandwich) or diced with, say, green or broad beans. Salamanca is known for its *farinato* (cured pork sausages) and *lomo* (cured pork loin). *Chanfaina* is a stew of rice and various meats; *picadillo* is usually minced pork with pimiento and eggs; and *calderillo* is a stew of meat and potatoes. Many desserts are made from local almonds.

Salamanca does have cheap food, but you have to search for it. The university cafeterias serve generous portions at student prices—look for the black-iron gate of the Anaya building's **Las Caballerizas** (C. Tostado 1–9, east of Plaza Mayor, tel. 923/294445, closed weekends) to feast on pork-and-egg combos (under 475 ptas.) in a cool brick-and-mortar cellar. **Bocati** (Iscar Peyra 1–5) serves 100 different bocadillos. There's an indoor **market** on weekdays from 9 to 2 in the Plaza del Mercado, just past the eastern arch of Plaza Mayor.

UNDER 1,000 PTAS. • Cafetería Rue. Easily spotted in the middle of Rúa Mayor, this sidewalk eatery has good meat and vegetable combos for 800 ptas., including wine and bread. *Rúa Mayor 46, southeast of Plaza Mayor, tel. 923/217333.*

Mesón de Cervantes. Cozy atmosphere makes this tavern anything but touristy, despite its Plaza Mayor location. Tapas are 125 ptas. each; the menú del día is 1,500 ptas.; and beer is 200 ptas. *Platos combinados* (combo platters) and set menus are also available. Outdoor seating adds about 125 ptas. to your bill. *Plaza Mayor 15, tel. 923/217213.*

Plus Ultra. This Salamancan institution serves up elaborate pinchos (akin to tapas, but generally smaller). Two big pinchos and wine start at 425 ptas.; platos combinados are 800 ptas. *C. del Consejo 4, north of Plaza Mayor, tel. 923/217211.*

UNDER 3,000 PTAS. • Río de la Plata. This tiny, old-fashioned basement restaurant off Calle de San Pablo has a gilded yet quiet decor. It's a pleasant change of scenery, and the fireplace and local crowd lend warmth. The food is simple but carefully prepared, with good-quality fish, seafood, and roast meat; you can also take tapas at the bar up front. There's a menú del día for 2,500 ptas. *Plaza Peso 1, tel. 923/219005. Closed Mon. and July.*

AFTER DARK

Throngs of students keep Salamanca's nightlife hopping. Partying here means loading up at a pub, then heading to a disco. A good central starting point is **Pub Oba-Oba** (Plaza Corrillo 9, just past southeast arch of Plaza Mayor, tel. 923/269979)—pass through its red-and-white Candyland arches to chug beer (250 ptas.) and sink into a beanbag chair. **Mesón Cervantes** (Plaza Mayor 11, tel. 923/217213; *see* Where to Eat, *above*), an upstairs tapas bar with an entrance on the southeast corner of the plaza, draws crowds to its balcony for drinks and unparalleled views of the action. **Abadia** is a good place to spend a mellow few hours (C. Rúa Mayor 40, no phone). Ditch the tourist hordes and join locals at **El Callejón** (Gran Vía 68, northeast of Plaza Mayor, tel. 923/265467) for reasonably priced drinks (rum is 500 ptas.) and infectious Spanish music that may well get you moving. **Submarino** (Plaza de San Justo, northeast of Plaza Mayor, tel. 923/260264), shaped like a submarine and open till 5 AM, has a dance floor on the bottom deck and a gay bar up top. **Camelot** (C. Bordadores 3, south of Plaza Mayor, tel. 923/212182) is also worth a boogie if you don't mind the kitschy medieval facade and faux royal tapestries; beer is only 300 ptas., and the party lasts till 5 AM. **Gran Café Moderno** (Gran Vía 75, tel. 923/260147) stages performances ranging from poetry readings to live rock. This is where after-hours types end the night before tucking into *churros con chocolate* at daybreak, that classic Castilian snack of fried dough and thick, dark hot chocolate.

SHOPPING

Salamanca is known for its leatherwork, but the finest specimens are pricey. For crafts and unusual gifts, including eclectic pottery, ironwork, and paintings, check out **Indiana** (Meléndez 24, tel. 923/264243) or **De Alvaro** (Mayor 68, tel. 923/413218).

CIUDAD RODRIGO

The medieval walled town of Ciudad Rodrigo (88 km/55 mi southwest of Salamanca), built on a promontory above the Río Agueda, is one of the most beautiful in Spain. Called Miróbriga in Roman times, the town was rebuilt by Conde Rodrigo in the 12th century, with massive ramparts, a castle facing Portugal (the border is 29 km/18 mi west of here), and a cathedral—all in golden sandstone. The French seized the town during the Peninsular War, but it was retaken by the duke of Wellington after an 11-day siege and bloody battle in 1808. Wellington was named El Duque de Ciudad Rodrigo for his victory.

BASICS

VISITOR INFORMATION

The **ayuntamiento** (town hall; Plaza Mayor 27, tel. 923/460050) and the **tourist office** (Plaza de Amayuelas 5, near cathedral, tel. 923/460561; open weekdays 9–2 and 5–7 and weekends 10–2 and 5–8) both have free maps and leaflets.

MAIL

The **post office** (Dámaso Ledesma 12, tel. 923/460117) is just off the oblong Plaza Mayor.

COMING AND GOING

There is no **train** service to Ciudad Rodrigo unless you count the Paris–Lisbon express, which pauses here at a groggy 4:40 AM. The **train station** (Paseo de la Estación s/n, 79, tel. 923/236717) is a 10-minute stroll northwest of the city center via Avenida Filiberta Villalobos and Cuesta Ramón y Cajal.

Buses, however, provide regular transport. The **bus station** (Campo de Toledo s/n, tel. 923/461009) offers frequent service to **Salamanca** (1½ hrs, 715 ptas.), **Madrid** (4 hrs, 2,215 ptas.), and **Fuentes de Oñoro** (20 min, 320 ptas.), at the Portuguese border.

By **car** from Madrid or Salamanca, take the busy N620, popular with trucks going in and out of Portugal.

WHERE TO SLEEP

Conde Rodrigo 1. A converted 18th-century palace in the heart of the old town, this cozy hotel has doubles from 7,900 ptas. Rooms have a traditional look but are nicely updated with minibars and modern bathrooms. The common areas have antique furniture and an old-world feel. There's parking nearby, for a fee. *Plaza de San Salvador 9, 37500, tel. 923/461404, fax 923/461408. 34 rooms. Restaurant.*

Hotel Lima. A five-minute walk from the walled town, this modern hotel caters mainly to bus tours but will do in a pinch. At 7,000 ptas. for a double with bath, rooms are plain but comfortable, with white walls and lime-color curtains and bedspreads. Parking is free. *Paseo de la Estación 48, 37500, tel. 923/ 481819, fax 923/482181. 45 rooms. 2 restaurants, cafeteria.*

Pensión Madrid. Right in the center of the town, this pension has doubles with bath from 3,000 ptas. For a bargain price of 5,000 ptas., however, you can opt for one of three apartments with bathroom, TV, and kitchenette. Each apartment sleeps three or four people. *C. Madrid 20, tel. 923/462467. Cash only. 4 rooms, 4 apartments.*

WHERE TO EAT

Ciudad Rodrigo's weekly **market** has taken place every Tuesday in Plaza del Buen Alcalde, not far from the cathedral, since 1475. **Gregoria Etreros** (Dámaso Ledsma 6, tel. 923/460067) has a wide selection of cakes, pastries, and sweets. Consider picnicking in the castle gardens, in view of the plains below.

UNDER 2,000 PTAS. • El Brasa. About 15 minutes' walk from the old town, on the old main road, this *mesón* serves a 1,600-pta. menú del día. The house specialty is *huevos fritos con farinato* (fried eggs with spicy pork sausage). For a splurge, try a bottle from the magnificent wine cellar, which has a great selection of Spanish and foreign wines. *Avda. de Salamanca 32, tel. 923/460793. Closed 15 days in Nov. No dinner Mon.*

El Sanatorio. This wonderful old tavern in the center of one side of Plaza Mayor is plastered with pictures of Carnival antics (the week before Lent), when costumed revelers and running bulls create mayhem. The tapas at the bar are excellent; the modest restaurant in back serves homemade local dishes at bargain prices. *Plaza Mayor 13, tel. 923/460024.*

Estoril. Named for a small town near Lisbon, this cozy restaurant next to Mayton (*see below*) has been in the same family since 1964. The house specialty, *revuelto Estoril*, is scrambled eggs with wild mushrooms, leeks, and shrimp. A menú del día costs 1,500 ptas. *Talavera 1, tel. 923/460550.*

La Artesa. This Plaza Mayor joint is known for its excellent grilled meats. The menú del día costs 1,500 ptas. *Plaza Mayor s/n, tel. 923/481128.*

UNDER 3,000 PTAS.

Mayton. Framed in wood beams, this dining room has a wonderfully eccentric collection of antiques, ranging from mortars and pestles to Portuguese yokes and old typewriters. In contrast to the decor, the cooking is simple; house specialties are fish, seafood, goat, and lamb. *La Colada 9, tel. 923/460720. Closed Mon. and Oct.*

WORTH SEEING

The **cathedral** combines the Romanesque and transitional Gothic styles, though its exterior walls were scarred by cannonballs fired during the Peninsular War. Look closely at the early 16th-century choir stalls, carved with entertaining grotesques by Rodrigo Alemán. The cloister has carved capitals, and the cypresses in its center lend tranquillity. *Plaza de San Salvador, tel. 923/481424. Admission to cathedral free, museum 250 ptas. Open daily 10–1 and 4–6.*

Ciudad Rodrigo's fortified castle, **Castillo de Enrique II**, was built in 1372. Part of it is now an elegant parador, which the British writer W. Somerset Maugham enjoyed in the mid-20th century. Visitors are welcome; from here you can enjoy the view from the gardens down the steep escarpment to the Roman bridge, with the plain beyond. You can also climb onto the battlements. *Plaza Castillo 1, tel. 923/ 460150. Admission free.*

In 2000 the **Centro de Interpretación sobre Fortificaciones** (Center for the Understanding of Fortifications) was built into Ciudad Rodrigo's walls, with video displays explaining how these and other fortifications were constructed. One exhibit shows the history of fortification through the ages, especially along the Portuguese border. *La Muralla, Puerta del Conde, tel. 923/460561 (tourist office). Admission 200 ptas. Open Apr.–Oct., weekends 10:30–2:30 and 4–6; Apr.–Oct., weekends 10:30–2:30 and 5–7.*

SHOPPING

Local crafts include ceramics and filigree metalwork with gold and silver. For wearable souvenirs, try **Concepción Duque** (Reyes Cayolicos 3, tel. 923/461301), **José Luis Nieves Delgado** (Avda. Béjar 141, tel. 923/461411), and **Joyería Los Concellos** (C. San Juan 5, tel. 923/460163). A **flea market** of clothing and shoes is held weekly (Sat. 10–2:30) on Avenida de Sefarat in Bajada Puerta del Sol, just outside the city walls.

FIESTAS

Ciudad Rodrigo's renowned and riotous **Carnaval del Toro,** which involves some running of bulls, coincides with Spain's general pre-Lenten Carnival celebrations in February or early March.

CUENCA

The quaint, old town of Cuenca is one of the strangest in Spain, built on a sloping, curling finger of rock whose precipitous sides plunge down to the gorges of the Huécar and Júcar rivers. Because the town ran out of room to expand, some medieval houses hang right over the abyss and are now a unique architectural attraction: the Casas Colgadas (Hanging Houses). Moreover, one of these old curiosities contains Spain's only museum of abstract art. The old town's dramatic setting grants spectacular gorge views, and its cobbled streets, cathedral, churches, bars, and taverns contrast starkly with the ugly modern town, which sprawls beyond the river gorges. Though somewhat isolated, Cuenca makes a good overnight stop if you're traveling between, say, Madrid and Valencia.

BASICS

VISITOR INFORMATION

The Infotur **tourist office** (Alfonso VIII 2, tel. 969/232119; open weekdays 9:30–2 and 4–7, weekends 9:30–2 and 4–6:30) is in the old town near the arches of the Plaza Mayor. There's also a **TIVE** budget-travel agency in the new town (Diego Jiménez 8, 2nd floor, tel. 969/232119, open weekdays 9:30–2 and 3:30–8, Sat. 10:30–2), halfway between the old town and the bus and train stations.

MAIL

The **post office** (C. del Parque de San Julián at C. Doctor Fleming, tel. 969/224016) is between the Río Huécar and Parque San Julián.

COMING AND GOING

Cuenca's **train station** (C. Mariano Catalina 10, tel. 969/220720, 902/240202 for general info) is connected to **Madrid**-Atocha (2½ hrs, 1,400 ptas.) via Aranjuez.

AutoRes (tel. 969/221184) provides bus service to and from **Madrid** (2½ hrs, 1,325 ptas.). The **bus station** (C. Fermín Caballero 20, tel. 969/221184) is near the train station; from here Buses 1, 2, and 7 zip up to Plaza Mayor for 80 ptas. If you'd rather walk, turn left after exiting either station and walk uphill for 15 to 20 minutes, following signs for the *casco antiguo*.

By **car** southeast from Madrid (167 km/104 mi), take the free N-III to Tarancón, then exit for the N400 to Cuenca. Alternatively, if you have extra time and want a scenic ride on good roads, take the N-II to Guadalajara, turn right toward Sacedón to see its spectacular gorge and dam, then continue to Cuenca.

WHERE TO SLEEP

Rooms in the old town are concentrated north of Plaza Mayor. The only reason to spend more than 15 minutes in the new town is to save a few hundred pesetas on lodging—there are several budget hostales on Calle Ramón y Cajal, which runs north from the train station, then bears right and turns into Calle las Torres. **Pensión Marín** (C. Ramón y Cajal 53, tel.969/221978) has bright, airy double rooms for 2,400 ptas. a night; downstairs at the same address, **Pensión Adela** (C. Ramón y Cajal 53, tel. 969/222533) is not quite as nice but rents doubles for a reasonable 3,000 ptas. **Pensión El Pilar** (C. Ramón y Cajal 29, tel. 211684) will give you a basic double room for 6,000 ptas.

UNDER 5,000 PTAS. • Pensión Tabanqueta. One of the best cheap places to stay in Cuenca's old town (double room: 4,000 ptas.), this is also one of the best places to eat. The attractive rooms share bath facilities; some look out on the Júcar gorge. *Plaza Trabuco 13, 16001, tel. 969/211290. 6 rooms, none with bath. Cash only.*

UNDER 7,000 PTAS. • Hotel Figón de Pedro. Set in the central old town, rooms in this modern hotel feature white wooden furniture against pale pastels. Doubles with bath run 5,500–6,500 ptas. The owners also run the restaurant downstairs and the Mesón Casas Colgadas (*see* Where to Eat, *below*), adjoining the Museum of Abstract Art. You can park nearby for a fee. *C. Cervantes 13, 16004, tel. 969/224511, fax 969/231192. 28 rooms. Restaurant.*

UNDER 10,000 PTAS. • Posada de San José. The only hotel in a hanging house—indeed, tastefully installed in a 16th-century convent—San José has long been the best place to stay in the old town. Furnishings are traditional, the atmosphere is friendly and intimate, and most rooms overlook the Huécar River gorge. Breakfast in the cafeteria-bar is 600 ptas.; a log fire blazes in winter. Reservations are crucial and should be made well in advance; prices for a double zoom from 4,500 to 9,800 ptas. depending on size and view. *Julián Romero 4, 16001, tel. 969/211300. 29 rooms, 21 with bath. Cafeteria, bar. Closed Christmas wk..*

WHERE TO EAT

Cuenca's most unusual food (if that's the right word) is *zarajo*, not for the faint of heart: cleaned lambs' intestines are wound around a vine twig, then deep-fried or barbecued. They actually make good tapas. *Gazpacho manchego* is nothing like Andalusia's tomato soup; it's a stew made from unleavened bread, hare, partridge, chicken, and ham. *Morteruelo* is shepherd's pâté made with minced pigs' liver, hare, partridge, chicken, ham, belly of pork, and spices. *Ajo arriero* is a paste made with pounded salt cod, garlic, potatoes, bread crumbs, boiled eggs, olive oil, and parsley, served with toasted bread. *Alajú* is a traditional Moorish dessert pastry made with walnuts, bread crumbs, and rosemary honey.

The local wines, which include Casa Gualda (red) and Zagarrón (white), are not bad and in any case not expensive. The local liqueur—usually sold in a bottle resembling a hanging house—is *resolí,* made from anisette, coffee, cinnamon, orange-peel essence, and sugar.

UNDER 3,500 PTAS. • El Figón de Pedro. One of the best-known restaurateurs in Spain, owner Pedro Torres Pacheco has done much to promote Cuenca's excellent cuisine. His pleasantly low-key place in the lively heart of the new town serves a 3,500-pta. fixed-price menu and such local specialties as *gazpacho manchego* (also called *gazpacho pastor*), *ajo arriero*, and *alajú*. Wash your meal down with resolí. *C. Cervantes 13, tel. 969/226821. No dinner Sun.*

UNDER 3,300 PTAS. • Mesón Casas Colgadas. Co-managed with El Figón de Pedro (*see above*), this tavern serves much the same fare but in a more pretentious manner, including a set menu for 3,300 ptas. The ultramodern white dining room does have an amazing view from its perch next to the Museum of Abstract Art in the Casas Colgadas. *C. Canónigos s/n, tel. 969/223509. Reservations essential. No dinner Mon.*

Rincón de Paco. This lively, respected Castilian joint in the new town offers a 2,000-pta. menú del día featuring local cuisine. The bar presents a wide choice of tapas. *Juan Hurtado de Mendoza 3, tel. 969/213418. Closed July 25, Aug. 3.*

UNDER 1,500 PTAS. • Mesón-Bar Tabanqueta. Tapas are excellent here, and the menú del día costs only 1,000 ptas. The dining room has an amazing view of the Júcar River. Upstairs, you can rent a very basic room with shared bath for 4,000 ptas. *Plaza Trabuco 13, tel. 969/211290. Cash only.*

WORTH SEEING

Just off Calle San Pedro, clinging to the western edge of Cuenca's old town, is the tiny, pleasingly dilapidated **Plaza San Nicolás.** Nearby, hovering over the Júcar gorge, the unpaved Ronda del Júcar commands remarkable views of the mountainous landscape. Drink in the best views from the square in front of the **castle**, at the very top of Cuenca, where the town tapers out to the narrowest of ledges—here gorges are on either side of you, with old houses sweeping down toward a distant plateau in front. (The castle itself, which served as the town prison for many years, is now the Hotel Leonor de Aquitanía.) The large imposing building in the Huécar gorge to the east, accessible by a vertigo-inducing pedestrian bridge, is a 16th-century convent that has been tastefully converted to a parador.

Cuenca's most famous buildings, the historic yet funky **Casas Colgadas** (Hanging Houses), form one of Spain's finest and most curious museums, the **Museo de Arte Abstracto Español** (Museum of Spanish Abstract Art). Literally projecting over the town's eastern precipice, this joined group of houses originally formed a 15th-century palace and later served as Cuenca's town hall before falling into disuse in the 19th century. In 1927 the cantilevered balconies that had once hung over the gorge were rebuilt, and in 1966 the painter Fernando Zóbel decided to create inside the houses the world's first museum devoted exclusively to abstract art. Most of the works he gathered were created by the remarkable generation of Spanish artists who grew up in the 1950s and were essentially forced to live abroad during Franco's regime: Carlos Saura, Eduardo Chillida, Muñoz, Millares, Antoni Tàpies, and Zóbel, among others. Even if you don't normally adore abstract art, this museum is likely to win you over with its honeycomb of dazzlingly white rooms against vistas of gorge and sky. *Canónigos s/n, tel. 969/212983. Admission 500 ptas. Open Tues.–Fri. 11–2 and 4–6, Sat. 11–2 and 4–8, Sun. 11–2:30.*

Opposite the Casa Colgadas (on land), the **Museo de Cuenca** has an excellent collection of local archaeological finds dating from prehistory to the 17th century. Roman Cuenca is particularly well represented. *Obispo Valero 12, tel. 969/213069. Admission 200 ptas. Open Tues.–Sat. 10–2 and 4–7, Sun. 10–2.*

Puente de San Pablo, an iron footbridge over the Huécar gorge, was built in 1903 for the convenience of the Dominican monks of San Pablo, who live on the other side. If you've no fear of heights, cross the narrow bridge for a vertiginous view of the river below and an equally thrilling panorama of the Casas Colgadas. A path descends from the bridge to the bottom of the gorge.

The **Museo Diocesano de Arte Sacro** (Diocesan Museum of Sacred Art) is housed in the onetime cellars of the Bishop's Palace. The beautifully clear display features a jewel-encrusted Byzantine diptych from the 13th century; a Crucifixion painting by the 15th-century Flemish artist Gerard David; and two small El Grecos. *From the Plaza Mayor take Calle Obispo Valero and follow signs toward the Casas Colgadas. Obispo Valero 2, tel. 969/224210. Admission 300 ptas. Open Tues.–Sat. 11–2 and 5–8, Sun. 11–2 and 4–8.*

SHOPPING

Alfarería de Luis de Castillo (Plaza Mayor 11, tel. 969/211263) sells pottery by top local artists. The kitschy hanging-house bottles of *resolí,* the local liqueur, are on sale everywhere.

SIGÜENZA

Set between the Río Henares and a magnificent hilltop castle, the medieval town of Sigüenza—population 5,500—may seem peaceful and rural now, but it was the scene of numerous battles between Christian Spaniards (including El Cid) and Moors. Originally an Ibero-Celtic settlement, the city was taken by the Moors in 713; when they were driven out around 1130, Sigüenza became an important religious center for both Christians and Jews. Try to come in late May or June, when the undulating green countryside is splashed with blood-red poppies and a kaleidoscope of other wildflowers.

BASICS

The **tourist office** (Ermita del Humilladero s/n, tel. 949/347007, fax 949/393806), open weekdays 10–2 and 4:30–7, weekends 9–2:30 and 4:30–7, is on the corner of Avenida Alfonso VI (which crosses the river) and Paseo de la Alameda. The **post office** (Parque de San Julián 18, tel. 969/221032), open weekdays 9–2:30 and Saturday 9–1, is not far from the tourist office.

COMING AND GOING

Frequent regional **trains** take about 1½ hours from **Madrid** (Atocha, 1,125 ptas.). The **train station** (tel. 949/391494, 902/240202 for general info) is across the river from town, at the end of Avenida de Alfonso VI; from here it's a short, pleasant stroll into Sigüenza proper.

Buses to **Madrid** (2 hrs 995 ptas.) and **Guadalajara** (1 hr, 595 ptas.) leave from a spot near the **bus station** (C. Floravilla, tel. 949/212500).

By **car** from Madrid (130 km/81 mi northeast), take the free N-II Barcelona highway and exit onto the C204 at Kilometer 104.

WORTH SEEING

Begun around 1150 and not completed until the early 16th century, Sigüenza's remarkable **cathedral** is an anthology of Spanish architecture from the Romanesque period to the Renaissance. The sturdy western facade has a forbidding, fortresslike appearance but hides a wealth of ornamental and artistic masterpieces. Present yourself to the sacristan (the sacristy is at the north end of the ambulatory) for an informative guided tour. The sacristy is an outstanding Renaissance structure, covered in a barrel vault designed by the great Alonso de Covarrubias; its coffers are studded with hundreds of sculpted heads, which stare at you rather disarmingly. The tour then takes you into the late-Gothic cloister, off which is a room lined with 17th-century Flemish tapestries. In the north transept, the ornate late-15th-century sepulchre of Dom Fadrique of Portugal, an early example of the classical plateresque, will be illuminated for you. The cathedral's high point, to the right of the sanctuary, is the Chapel of the Doncel, in which you'll see Spain's most celebrated funerary monument—the tomb of Don Martín Vázquez de Arca, commissioned by Isabella, to whom Don Martín served as *doncel* (page) before dying young in defense of Granada in 1486. The reclining Don Martín is lifelike, an open book in his hands and a wistful look in his eyes. More than a memorial to an individual, this tomb, with its surrounding late-Gothic foliage and tiny mourners, is like an epitaph of the Age of Chivalry, a final flowering of the Gothic spirit. *Admission 300 ptas. Open daily 11–1 and 4–6 (4–7 in summer).*

Set in an early 19th-century house next to the cathedral's west facade, the **Museo Diocesano de Arte Sacro** (Diocesan Museum of Sacred Art) displays prehistoric items and copious religious art from the 12th to 18th centuries. *Tel. 949/391023. Admission 300 ptas. Open Tues.–Sun. 11–2 and 4:30–6:30 (4:30–7:30 in summer).*

The south side of the cathedral overlooks the arcaded **Plaza Mayor,** a harmonious Renaissance square commissioned by Cardinal Mendoza in the 15th century. The surrounding small palaces and cobbled alleys mark the virtually intact old quarter. The palace that belonged to the *doncel*'s family is at Travesana Alta, identifiable by its huge arched doorway and heraldic arms.

The enchanting **castle** at the top of Sigüenza, overlooking wild, hilly countryside, is now a parador. Founded by the Romans but rebuilt at various later periods, the present structure dates mainly from the 14th century, when it was transformed into a residence for Doña Blanca de Borbón, queen of Castile—who was banished here by her husband, Peter the Cruel. Walk right in to admire the magnificent baronial halls. *Parador tel. 949/390100, fax 949/391364.*

WHERE TO SLEEP

UNDER 5,000 PTAS. • Hostal Venancio. Sometimes you get what you pay for; this is very basic accommodation near the tourist office. Doubles with shared bath start at 4,000 ptas. *C. San Roque 3, tel. 949/390347. 17 rooms, none with bath. Cash only.*

UNDER 8,000 PTAS. • Hostal El Doncel. This stone-face building near the tourist office has modern rooms with shower-only bathrooms, starting at 7,500 ptas. for a double. The bar-cafeteria offers a menú del día for 1,200 ptas. *Paseo de la Alameda 1, tel. 949/390001, fax 949/391090. 17 rooms.*

Hostal Motor. At the entrance to Sigüenza from Madrid or Guadalajara, this newish hostal in an older building has 18 modern rooms, all with private bath (shower only), each double going for 7,500 ptas. The restaurant cooks up two set menus, one for 1,200 ptas. and the other, featuring regional specialties, for 3,000 ptas. *Avda. De Juan Carlos I 2, tel. 949/390827, fax 949/390007. 18 rooms.*

WHERE TO EAT

There are plenty of tapas bars to get you through the late afternoon. In front of the tourist office, **Alameda** (Paseo de la Alameda 2, tel. 949/390553) has a good selection, including the regional specialty *migas castellanos* (bread crumbs fried with garlic and chopped pork). Other pit stops with good porky specialties: **Cafe Paris** (Cardenal Mendoza 8, tel. 949/390083), **La Esquinita** (Paseo de la Alameda 6, tel. 949/393300), and, near the river, **Julio** (Vicente Moñux 11, tel. 949/390972) and **Kentia** (Vicente Moñux 9, tel. 949/390058).

UNDER 2,000 PTAS. • Restaurante Medieval. Near the castle-parador, this restaurant is appropriately medieval style, with plenty of stone and wood beams. Specializing in roasts from a Segovian wood-fired oven, it serves a variety of hearty local dishes and a 1,200-pta. set menu. *Portal Mayor 2, tel. 949/393233.*

UNDER 3,000 PTAS. • Calle Mayor. On the street leading up to the castle, this elegant restaurant occupies a 16th-century house, complete with exposed stone walls and wrought-iron chairs. House specialties are fresh vegetables from the owner's garden and traditional Castilian roast lamb and goat. The set menu costs 2,800 ptas. *C. Mayor 21, tel. 949/391748.*

SHOPPING

For those who drink the grape, the best Sigüenza souvenir is a handcrafted leather *bota* (wineskin) from **Jesús Blasco** (Cruz Dorada s/n, tel. 949/391497), on the southwest outskirts.

VALLADOLID

From afar the capital of Castile-León looks like a sprawling industrial city on the Castilian plain (193 km/120 mi northwest of Madrid)—yet Valladolid's old quarter, east of the Pisuerga River, is steeped in Spanish history. Ferdinand and Isabella were married here, Felipe II was born and baptized here, and Felipe III made Valladolid the capital of Spain for six years. The major attraction now is the **Museo Nacional de Escultura** (National Museum of Sculpture), but you can also see the houses where Cervantes and Christopher Columbus lived their last days and enjoy superb Renaissance art and architecture in a largely charming setting.

BASICS

The main **tourist office** (Santiago 19, tel. 983/344013; open weekdays 10–2 and 5–8, Sat. 9–2 and 4:30–8:30, Sun. 11–2 and 4:30–8:30) has free maps and leaflets including, in case you have a car, routes to the nearby Rueda and Ribera vineyards. The **post office** is on Plaza la Rinconada (tel. 983/330660).

COMING AND GOING

The **train station** (Estación s/n, tel. 983/200202, 902/240202 general info) is south of the old quarter, beyond the Parque de Campo Grande. **RENFE** also has a more accessible reservations office at Divina Pastora 6 (tel. 983/368368). There is frequent service to and from **Madrid**, both Chamartín and Atocha stations (2½ hrs, 1,900–2,600 ptas.); trains also head north to **Burgos** (1½ hrs, 945–1,700 ptas.), **León** (2 hrs, 1,450–2,100 ptas.), and the major cities of Galicia, Asturias, and the Basque Country.

The **bus station** (Puente Colgante 2, tel. 983/236308), near the train station, sends vehicles all over Spain. **Autocares Alsa** (tel. 983/235094) drives to and from **Madrid** several times daily (2¼ hrs, 1,580 ptas.)

By **car** from Madrid, follow the A6, which is partly a toll road.

Valladolid's **airport** (tel. 983/415400) is 12 km (7½ mi) outside the city on the northbound N601. Alas, there are no buses; you have to take a taxi into or out of town (2,000 ptas.). **Iberia** (tel. 983/560162) and **Air Europa** (tel. 986/373366) have offices here.

WHERE TO SLEEP

Since Valladolid is both a university city and a major commercial center, lodging runs the gamut. The cheapest hostales are near the cathedral, near the train station, and along Generalíssimo and Marina de Escobar.

UNDER 5,000 PTAS. • Hostal Los Arces. Well located in the old quarter, this hostal was recently done up with traditional Castilian furniture. A double with complete bathroom costs a reasonable 4,800 ptas. *San Antonio de Padua 2, tel. 983/353853. 11 rooms.*

UNDER 7,000 PTAS. • Hostal Lima. These modern rooms have minibars and private bathrooms, but they're a 20-minute walk from the center of the old town. Doubles cost 6,100 ptas. *Tudela 4, tel. 983/398224, fax 983/200067. 21 rooms, 20 with bath.*

Hostal Ramón y Cajal. Just north of the cathedral, opposite the hospital, these double rooms have strong Castilian furniture and private bathrooms. Yes, there *is* an elevator to haul you up five flights. Doubles go for 5,500 ptas. *Avda Ramón y Cajal 12, 5th floor, tel. 983/263222. 9 rooms.*

Hostal Vuelta. Usefully situated near the Plaza Mayor, this old-fashioned place has basic doubles with complete bathrooms and phones for 5,200 ptas. *Plaza del Val 2, tel. 983/356066. 11 rooms.*

UNDER 10,000 PTAS. • Hotel Lasa. This modern hotel is in front of the Parque del Campo Grande, roughly halfway between the bus and train stations and the city center. Decked out with modern furniture, perhaps to suit visiting businesspeople, double rooms cost less on weekends (7,500 ptas.) than they do on weekdays (9,400 ptas.)—both a decent value considering the amount of marble under foot. Parking is available for a fee. *Acera Recoletos 21, tel. 983/390255, fax 983/390255. 62 rooms. Bar, cafeteria.*

Hostal Paris. This elegant old hostal in the old town has a friendly staff and comfortable, well appointed rooms with nice bathrooms and minibars. Doubles cost 8,700 ptas. *Especería 2, tel. 983/370625, fax 983/358301. 37 rooms.*

WHERE TO EAT

The countryside around Valladolid has some booming vineyards that have actually bolstered the local cuisine and economy; look for fragrant, dry Rueda whites, powerful, full-bodied Toro and Ribera del Duero reds, and Cigales *rosados* (rosés). The local cuisine features roast baby lamb, game in season, and fresh vegetables. Pork is often on menus as *lomo* (cured loin) and on tapas bars as *torreznos*, chopped meaty ribs.

For evening tapas and crowd-watching, hover around the Plaza Mayor, especially on **Pasaje de Gutierrez.** Alternatively, head to the **Zona Santa María a la Antigua,** just north of the cathedral, and look around the adjacent Calles Marqués del Duero and Paraíso.

UNDER 2,000 PTAS. • La Perla de Castilla. For Castilian fare with some innovative touches, look no further—you don't see *rabo de toro estofada al vino con salsa de cacao* every day (bull's tail stewed in wine with chocolate sauce). For dessert, perhaps *sopa de coco con sorbete de mandarina al vinagre de toffee* (coconut soup with mandarin sorbet and vinegar toffee)? The menú del día goes for 1,600 ptas. *Avda. Ramón Pradera 15–19, tel. 983/371828. Closed Aug. and Holy Week. No dinner Sun.*

UNDER 3,000 PTAS. • Santi. Set in a 16th-century inn, this excellent Castilian restaurant serves a different succulent vegetable dish each day of the week. The wine cellar is extensive, and desserts are homemade. The menú del día is priced at 2,825 ptas. *Correo 1, tel. 983/339355. Closed Sun. and Aug. 15–31.*

SPLURGE • Mesón Panero. This pricey tavern does particularly good stews, such as *lentejas con costillas* (lentils with spare ribs), *cordero con guisantes* (lamb with peas) and *patatas con manitas de cerdo* (pigs' feet with potatoes)—perhaps an acquired taste. *Marina Escobar 1, tel. 983/307019. No dinner Sun.*

WORTH SEEING

MUSEO NACIONAL DE ESCULTURA

Spain's National Museum of Sculpture is at the northernmost point in Valladolid's old town. The setting—the late-15th-century Colegio de San Gregorio—is a masterpiece of the Isabelline, or late Gothic, plateresque, an ornamental style of exceptional intricacy featuring playful, naturalistic detail. The facade is especially fantastic, with ribs in the form of pollarded trees, sprouting branches, and—to polish off the forest motif—a row of wild men bearing mighty clubs. Across the walkway from the main museum is a Renaissance palace that became a new wing of the museum in 1998, primarily for temporary exhibitions.

The main museum is arranged in rooms off an elaborate, arcaded courtyard. Its collections do for Spanish sculpture what those in the Prado do for Spanish painting—the only difference is that most people have heard of Velázquez, El Greco, Goya, and Murillo, whereas few are familiar with Alonso de Berruguete, Juan de Juni, and Gregorio Fernández, the three great names represented here.

Attendants and directional cues encourage you to tour the museum in chronological order. Begin on the ground floor, with Alonso de Berruguete's remarkable sculptures from the dismantled high altar in Valladolid's church of San Benito (1532). Berruguete, who trained in Italy under Michelangelo, is the most widely appreciated of Spain's postmedieval sculptors. He strove for pathos rather than realism, and his works have an extraordinarily expressive quality. The San Benito altar was the most important commission of his life, and the fragments here allow you to scrutinize his powerfully emotional art. In the museum's elegant chapel (which you normally see at the end of the tour) is a Berruguete retable from 1526, his first known work; on either side kneel gilded bronze figures by the Italian-born Pompeo Leoni, whose polished and highly decorative art is diametrically opposed to that of Berruguete.

Many critics of Spanish sculpture feel that decline set in with the late-16th-century artist Juan de Juni, who used glass for eyes and pearls for tears. Juni's many admirers, however, find his works intensely exciting, and they are in any case the highlights of the museum's upper floor. Many of the 16th-, 17th-, and 18th-century sculptures on this floor were originally paraded around the streets during Valladolid's celebrated Easter processions; should you ever attend one of these thrilling pageants, the power of Spanish Baroque sculpture will be instantly clear.

Dominating Castilian sculpture of the 17th century was the Galician-born Gregorio Fernández, in whose works the dividing line between sculpture and theater becomes tenuous. Respect for Fernández has been diminished by the number of vulgar imitators his work has spawned, even up to the present day, but at Valladolid you can see his art at its best. The enormous, dramatic, and moving sculptural groups assembled in the last series of rooms (on the ground floor near the entrance) form a suitably spectacular climax to this fine assembly. *Cadenas San Gregorio 1, tel. 983/250375. Admission 400 ptas., free Sat. 4–6 and Sun. Open Tues.–Sat. 10–2 and 4–6, Sun. 10–2.*

CATHEDRAL

Never built as originally intended, Valladolid's cathedral is disappointing. Though its foundations were laid in late-Gothic times, the building owes much of its appearance to designs executed in the late 16th century by Juan de Herrera, the architect of the Escorial. Further work was carried out by Alberto de Churriguera in the early 18th century, but the building is still only a fraction of its intended size. The Juni altarpiece is the one bit of color and life in an otherwise visually chilly place. *Plaza de la Universidad 1, tel. 983/304362. Admission: cathedral free, museum 250 ptas. Open Tues.–Fri. 10–1:30 and 4:30–7, weekends 10–2.*

UNIVERSIDAD

The main university building sits opposite the garden just south of the cathedral. The exuberant and dynamic late-Baroque frontispiece is by Narciso Tomé, creator of the remarkable *Transparente* in Toledo's cathedral. Calle Librería leads south from the main building to the magnificent **Colegio de Santa Cruz**, a large university college begun in 1487 in the Gothic style and completed in 1491 by Lorenzo Vázquez in a tentative yet pioneering Renaissance mode. Inside is a harmonious courtyard.

CASA MUSEO COLÓN

Inside the house where Christopher Columbus (Cristóbal Colón) died in poverty in 1506, the excellent **Museo de Colón** (Columbus Museum) has a well-arranged collection of objects, models, and explanatory panels on the explorer's life and times. *Colón s/n, tel. 983/291353. Admission free. Open Tues.–Sat. 10–2 and 5–7, Sun. 10:30–2.*

CASA MUSEO DE CERVANTES

More interesting than the Columbus House, this fellow remnant of Spain's golden age is the tiny house where writer Miguel de Cervantes lived from 1603 to 1606. A haven of peace set back from a noisy thoroughfare near the Plaza Mayor. Furnished in the early 20th century in a pseudo-Renaissance style by the Marquis of Valle-Inclan—creator of the El Greco Museum in Toledo—it has a cozy atmosphere. *Rastro s/n, tel. 983/308810. Admission 400 ptas., free Sun. Open Tues.–Sat. 10–3:30, Sun. 10–3.*

SHOPPING

A market, **El Rastrillo,** is held on Sunday morning between Calles José Luis Arresa and Jesús Rivero Meneses (just across the Puente Isabel la Católica, in the Multiples parking lot). There's good window-shopping on **Calle Santiago** between Plaza de Zorrilla and the Plaza Mayor. The **Centro Comercial Las Francesas** shopping center is good for a gasp—it's set in the magnificent cloisters of an old convent. Acquaint yourself with local wine labels at **Pecados Originales** (Original Sins; Pasaje Gutierrez 6, tel. 983/392326). Check the (huge) price on the Vega Sicilia, Sir Winston Churchill's favorite red and the flagship of the Ribera del Duero region.

AFTER DARK

Students tend to head for Plaza de Cantarranas and the disco **Bagur** (C. de la Pasión 13, tel. 983/377673) or to **Calle Francisco Suárez** for a lively night out. Between the cathedral and the university, **La Cárcava** (C. Cascajares s/n, tel. 983/296767) is a tavern for discerning winos—it specializes in regional wines and serves scrumptious canapés. **Sidrería Paca** (Plaza de Portugalete 7, no phone), near the cathedral, pours Asturian cider by the barrel and mitigates its effects with generous tapas. The **Black Rose** (Maria de Molina 7, no phone) is an Irish pub that fills up late.

BURGOS

Set on the banks of the Arlanzón River, Burgos is a small city with some of Spain's most outstanding medieval architecture. The first signs of the city, if you approach on the NI from Madrid (Burgos is 240 km/150 mi north of the capital), are the spiky twin spires of its magnificent cathedral, rising above the main bridge and gate into the old city center. Burgos's second glory is its heritage as the city of El Cid, the part-historical, part-mythical hero of the Christian Reconquest of Spain.

Burgos has been known for centuries as a center of both militarism and religion, and even today you'll see more nuns and military officers on its streets than almost anywhere else in Spain. The city was born as a military camp in 884—a fortress built on the orders of the Christian king Alfonso III, who was having a hard time defending the upper reaches of Old Castile from the constant forays of the Arabs. It quickly became vital in the defense of Christian Spain. The ruins of the castle erected then still overlook Burgos.

The city's identity as an early outpost of Christianity was consolidated with the founding of the Royal Convent of Las Huelgas, in 1187. Burgos also became an important station on the Camino de Santiago and thus a place of rest and sustenance for Christian pilgrims throughout the Middle Ages.

BASICS

The **city tourist office** (Teatro Principal, Paseo del Espolón 1, tel. 947/288874; open Mon.–Sat. 10–2, 4:30–7:30) is near the Puente (Bridge) de Santa María. The helpful **regional tourist office** for Castile-León (Plaza Alonso Martínez 7, tel. 947/203125) is open daily 9–2 and 5–7. **TIVE** (Avda. de la Paz 20, in the business district east of Plaza España, tel. 947/209881), open weekdays 9–2, can help arrange cheap travel.

MAIL

The **post office** (Plaza Conde de Castro, tel. 947/262750), is open weekdays 8:30–8:30, Saturday 9:30–2.

COMING AND GOING

BY TRAIN

The **train station** (Avda. Conde de Guadalhorce s/n, tel. 947/203560, 902/240202 for general info) is a 10-minute walk south of the town center. Trains are generally slower than buses, but they go to **Madrid** (4 hrs, 3,000–3,500 ptas.), **León** (2 hrs, 2,100 ptas.), **Pamplona** (2½ hrs, 2,200 ptas.), **Barcelona** (6–8 hrs, 5,200 ptas.), and **San Sebastián** (3½ hrs, 2,100 ptas.), among other towns. You can buy tickets at the **RENFE office** (Moneda 21, tel. 947/209131) near Plaza Primo de Rivera, open weekdays 9–1 and 4:30–7:30, Saturday 9:30–1:30.

BY BUS

The **bus station** (Miranda 4, tel. 947/288855) is just east of the train station, just off Plaza de Vega. Continental Auto (tel. 91/745–6300) connects Burgos to **Madrid** (2 hrs 40 mins, 2,010 ptas.) and **San Sebastián** (3¼ hrs, 1,800 ptas.). Enatcar (tel. 947/266370) serves **León** (3½ hrs, 1,800 ptas.). Zatrans (tel. 947/266370) heads east to **Barcelona** (8 hrs, 4,800 ptas.).

BY CAR

From Madrid it's at most a 2½-hr drive on the N-I freeway. From Burgos a toll *autopista* (A68) continues north to Bilbao (159 km/100 mi); the direct route, Burgos–Santander (157 km/98 mi), is less speedy but more scenic, with a mountain pass and spectacular valleys.

GETTING AROUND

Historic Burgos is on the north side of the Arlanzón River: from the train station walk straight up Conde de Guadalhorce, turn right into La Merced by the river, and cross the Puente de Santa María. Soon after this bridge you'll see the tourist office. From the bus station take the short walk up Calle Madrid to the same bridge. The ancient Camino de Santiago pilgrimage route passes through Burgos; to follow it through town from north to south, hit Las Calzadas, Plaza Lesmes, Arco de San Juan, San Juan, Avellanos, Fernán González, Plaza Fernando III Santo, cathedral, Doña Jimena, and, exiting the city, the Arco (Arch) de San Martín. You may see some modern-day pilgrims as you wander.

If your backpack has wrecked your endurance, join children and their grandparents on the **road train** Ciudad de Burgos, which picks tourists up on Calle Nuño Rasura, near the cathedral, and carts them past the main attractions. Each of the frequent daytime trips costs 300 ptas.; the 10:30 PM night trip costs 400 ptas.

WHERE TO EAT

Burgos is yet another stronghold of traditional Castilian roasts, particularly *cordero asado* (roast baby lamb), but is especially well known for its delicious *morcilla*—blood sausage—which, despite its morbid appearance, is lighter and more flavorsome than most morcillas because the filling is mixed with rice and onion. Stews, such as *olla podrida,* are enhanced with local red beans. The region is also famous for its bland, fresh white cheese (*queso de Burgos*), normally served with honey. Southern Burgos province makes 80% of the full-bodied Ribera del Duero red wines, some of the finest in Spain.

You pay extra for the Old World atmosphere near the cathedral, so weigh your restaurant options carefully if you're on a budget. For picnic chow head to the **municipal market,** just east of the bus station (open Mon.–Sat. 8–3), or the **Mercado Norte,** in Plaza de España (open Mon.–Sat. 8–3).

UNDER 2,000 PTAS. • Pancho. Family-run since 1958, this friendly two-floor Castilian *mesón* (tavern) has the usual wood beams but adds a twist: it never closes. Tapas at the bar include *morcilla de Burgos* (the local blood sausage, made with rice) for 175 ptas. and a glass of house wine (100 ptas.). The weekday lunch menu (1,600 ptas.) might include eggplant stuffed with seafood, followed by *rabo de buey* (oxtail stew) or *olla podrida* (the local stew), and rounded out with bread, homemade dessert, and a bottle of wine. *San Lorenzo 13–15, tel. 947/203405.*

Prego. If you've overdosed on Spanish food and could really go for some pizza, pop in here. The menú del día is 1,700 ptas., and you can choose from various salads, pastas, and pizzas. *Huerto del Rey 4, tel. 947/260447.*

UNDER 2,500 PTAS. • Don Nuño. Well situated by the cathedral, Don Nuño is popular with locals. The premises comprise a large terrace for summer dining, a tapas bar, and a semi-subterranean restaurant. You can always ponder three different menus, ranging in price from 1,200 to 2,000 ptas. The cheapest might have a filling Castilian soup, half a roast chicken, bread, dessert, and a few glasses of wine or a beer; the priciest will offer soup or salad followed by lamb chops and flan plus bread and wine. *Nuño Rasura 3, tel. 947/200373.*

Taberna Tanín. Here, just across the Puente de Gasset from the old town, this tapas bar and restaurant has a neo-Castilian look—wooden beams, stone brick, tiles, and exposed brick. Weekday lunch centers on a three-course, 1,400-pta. menú del día that might include potatoes with chorizo, rabo de buey, or *cordero al chilindrón* (lamb stew) plus dessert, bread, and a half carafe of wine. Watch out: combining à la carte choices, such as zucchini with cheese sauce and a big T-bone steak and dessert, will set you back 4,000 ptas. *C. Doctor Fleming (previously División Azúl) 5–7, tel. 947/279999. Closed Wed. Oct.–Mar.; Sun. Apr.–Aug.; and Sept.*

UNDER 3,000 PTAS. • El Angel. This spacious, modern restaurant near the cathedral has its own bakery. Fresh market produce is used in traditional dishes with modern touches. The set menu is a pretty good value at 2,700 ptas., considering the cost à la carte. *C. Paloma 24, tel. 947/208608. Closed Feb. No dinner Sun.*

Mesón del Cid. Once a 15th-century printing press, this family-run hotel and restaurant has been hosting travelers and serving up Burgalese food for four generations. If your cash is weighing you down, blow it here on the 2,700-pta. menú del día; à la carte, the *cordero lechal asado* (baby roast lamb) for one is 2,300 ptas. The rooms are magnificent, with hand-hewn wood beams; to stay on a budget, stop in for a drink and a tapa at the bar. In the same neighborhood, another venerable Burgos restaurant where you can peek and have tapas is **Casa Ojeda** (C. Vitoria 5, tel. 947/206440). *Plaza Santa María 8, tel. 947/205971.*

WHERE TO SLEEP

Cheap, basic hostales are clustered around **Calle Victoria** between Calle Condestable and Bernabé Pérez Ortíz. **Hostal Joma** (San Juan 26, tel. 947/203350) has a few bright doubles with shared bath for 3,000 ptas. a night.

UNDER 8,000 PTAS. • Hostal Carrales. A 10-minute walk from the cathedral, José Luis González has redone his rooms with varnished parquet floors and pastel walls in colors such as salmon. Most doubles have full bathrooms and minibars; all rent for 6,750 ptas. Reservations are essential in summer. *Puente Gasset 4, tel. 947/205916. 21 rooms.*

Hostal San Juan. Set in an historic building next to the Monasterio de San Juan, these rooms are modern and comfortable enough, with parquet floors and walls in shades of yellow. Most double rooms have full bathrooms (7,000 ptas.); the others have a sink, private shower, and shared toilet (5,885 ptas.). You're a 10-minute walk from the cathedral; the hostal also has bikes for rent. *Bernabé Pérez Ortíz 1, tel./fax 947/205134. 15 rooms. Cash only.*

WORTH SEEING

Start your walk at the **cathedral**, the city's high point, which contains such a wealth of art and other treasures that jealous burghers actually lynched their civil governor on the morning of January 25, 1869, for trying to take an inventory. The proud Burgalese apparently feared that the poor man was preparing to remove the treasures.

Most of the cathedral's exterior is sculpted in the Flamboyant Gothic style. The cornerstone was laid in 1221, and the twin 275-ft towers were completed by the middle of the 14th century, though the final chapel was not finished until 1731. There are 13 chapels, the most elaborate of which is the hexagonal Condestable Chapel. You'll find the **tomb of El Cid** (1026–99) and his wife, Ximena, under the transept. El Cid (whose real name was Rodrigo Díaz de Vivar) was a mercenary warrior revered for his victories over the Moors; the medieval *Song of My Cid* transformed him into a Spanish national hero.

At the other end of the cathedral, high above the West Door, is the **Reloj de Papamoscas** (Flycatcher Clock), so named for the sculptured bird that opens its mouth as the mechanism marks each hour. The grilles around the choir feature some of the finest wrought-iron work in central Spain, and the choir itself has 103 delicately carved walnut stalls, no two alike. The 13th-century stained-glass windows that once conducted a beautiful filtered light were destroyed in 1813, one of many cultural casualties of Napoléon's retreating troops. *Plaza del Rey San Fernando, tel. 947/204712. Admission: cathedral free, museum and cloister 400 ptas. Open Tues.–Sat. 9:30–1 and 4–7; Sun.–Mon. and holidays 9:30–11:45 and 4–7.*

Across the Plaza del Rey San Fernando from the cathedral is the city's main gate, the **Arco de Santa María.** Walk through the gate beside the tourist office toward the river and look up above the arch—the 16th-century statues depict the first Castilian judges; El Cid; Spain's patron saint, James; and King Charles I.

The Arco de Santa María fronts the city's loveliest promenade, the **Espolón.** The walkway follows the riverbank and is shaded with luxuriant black poplars.

The **Casa del Cordón,** a 15th-century palace on the Plaza de Calvo Sotelo, is where the Catholic Monarchs received Columbus after his second voyage to the New World. It's now a bank.

Three kilometers (2 miles) east of Burgos, at the end of a poplar- and elm-lined drive, is the **Cartuja de Miraflores.** Founded in 1441, this florid Gothic charterhouse has an unusual link to the Americas: its Isabelline church has a Gil de Siloe altarpiece said to be gilded with the first gold brought back from the New World. To get there, follow signs from the city's main gate. *Admission free. Church open for mass Mon.–Sat. 9, Sun. 7:30 and 10:15; main bldg. Mon.–Sat. 10:15–3 and 4–6, Sun. 11:20–12:30, 1–3, and 4–6.*

On the western edge of town—a long walk if you're not driving—is the **Monasterio de Las Huelgas Reales,** still run by nuns, who live in seclusion behind a double iron grille. Founded in 1187 by King Alfonso VIII and his wife, Eleanor (daughter of England's Henry II), this convent for noble ladies was unprecedented for the powers it gave to the women running it. The present building was originally a summer palace for the kings of Castile; in 1988 it underwent renovations for its 800th anniversary. The convent was conceived in the Romanesque style and housed a royal mausoleum, where its founders still lie. All but one of the royal coffins kept here were desecrated by Napoléon's soldiers, but the one that survived intact contained clothes that form the basis of the convent's medieval textile museum. Don't miss the Chapel of St. James, where Castilian noblemen came to be knighted by the articulated (jointed) statue of Spain's patron saint; the figure lowered its sword arm and dubbed the candidates with a tap on the shoulder. *1½ km (1 mi) southwest of town, along Paseo de la Isla, then left across Malatos Bridge, tel. 947/201630. Admission 700 ptas., free Wed. for EU citizens. Open Apr.–Sept., Tues.–Sat. 10:30–1:15, and 3:30–5:45, Sun. 10:30–2:15; Oct.–Mar., Tues.–Sat. 11–1:15 and 4–5:15, Sun. 10:30–2:15.*

SHOPPING

Burgos is known for its cheeses. The cleverly named *queso de Burgos* (Burgos cheese), a fresh, ricotta-like creation, is sold at **Casa Quintanilla** (C. Paloma 17, tel. 947/202535). Another good buy is a few bottles of local Ribera de Duero *tinto* wines, now strong rivals to those of the nearby Rioja Alta.

AFTER DARK

For a coffee, pop into **Café España** (Laín Calvo 12, east of cathedral), which is almost too popular. Later on, head for the bars, pubs, and discos around **Plaza de San Juan, Plaza Huerto del Rey,** and, near the cathedral, **Calle Fernán González.** If it's beer you want, try **Trol** (C. San Lorenzo 25, tel. 947/263394) or nearby **Pils** (C. La Puebla 3, tel. 947/260911). **Mármendi** (C. La Puebla 20, tel. 947/260909) has an arty atmosphere. **La Trastienda** (Martínez del Campo 4, tel. 947/204244) is festooned with antiques, which you can purchase if your senses haven't been dulled, or perhaps if they have. Conservative Burgos has only two discos, **Caché** (C. Victoria 56, tel. 947/202092) and **Dedos** (C. Jordana 2, tel. 947/278836).

LEÓN

León may be on the Camino de Santiago, but it's still off the main tourist trail, so come and soak up the atmosphere of the superb old quarter in this ancient Castilian city before prices go up and developers' foundations go down.

Anchored by a superb Gothic cathedral and freshened by its ongoing nightlife, the ancient capital of Castile-León sits on the banks of the Bernesga River in the high plains of Old Castile. Historians say the name of the city, which was founded as a permanent camp for the Roman legions in 68 AD, has nothing to do with the proud lion that has been its emblem for centuries but is instead a corruption of the Roman word *legion*. The capital of Christian Spain was moved to León from Oviedo in 914 as the Reconquest spread southward, launching the city's richest era. Walls went up around the old Roman town, and you can still see parts of the 6-ft-thick ramparts in the middle of the modern city.

Today León is an affluent provincial capital and prestigious university town. The wide western avenues are lined with boutiques, while the twisting alleys and topsy-turvy plazas of the old town house the tapas bars, bookstores, and *chocolaterías* (hot-chocolate joints) popular with students.

BASICS

The **tourist office** (Plaza de Regla 3, tel. 987/237082; open daily 10–2 and 5–7:30, with shorter hrs off-season) faces the cathedral.

MAIL / PHONES

The **post office** is south of the old town (Plaza de San Francisco, tel. 987/234290, open weekdays 8:30–8:30, Sat. 9:30–2).

COMING AND GOING

RENFE trains (tel. 902/240202) connect León to **Madrid** (4 hrs, 3,500 ptas.), **Oviedo** (2½ hrs, 945–1,700 ptas.), **Burgos** (2 hrs, 2,100 ptas.), and **Barcelona** (10 hrs, 5,800 ptas.). The **train station** is across the river from the old town (C. Astorga 2, tel. 987/270202): When you arrive, follow Avenida de Palencia west across the river and continue up Avenida de Ordoño II, a 15-minute walk.

Several companies pull into the **bus station** (Paseo Ing. Saenz de Miera, s/n, tel. 987/211000), a five-minute walk west of the train station. **Fernández** (tel. 987/260500) serves **Madrid** (4½ hrs, 2,675 ptas.). **ALSA** (tel. 987/204752) heads north to **Oviedo** (1½ hrs, 1,030 ptas.) and south to **Seville** (10½ hrs, 5,225 ptas.).

By **car** León is 333 km (207 mi) northwest of Madrid, 216 km (134 mi) west of Burgos.

WHERE TO SLEEP

Finding a room in León is easy except during the last week of June, when crowds descend for fiestas including the national celebration of San Juan. Cheap sleeps are speckled along **Avenida de Roma** and **Avenida de Ordoño II,** between the train station and the old town. **Hostal España** (C. Carmen 3, off Avda. de Ordoño II, tel. 987/236014) rents double rooms for 3,850 ptas. a night. **Hostal Oviedo** (Avda. de Roma 26, tel. 987/222236) is a small, friendly, family-run place with slightly dark but clean doubles for 3,745 ptas.

WHERE TO EAT

Because it's poised on the northwestern edge of the *meseta* (Spain's great central plain), on the cusp of the Cantabrian and Galician mountains, León enjoys great variety in its local gastronomy. The area is best known for its meats, sausages, fish, vegetables, cheese, and fruit. *Cecina* (dried and smoked beef) is sold sliced. Try chorizo, the local smoked sausage, or *morcilla* (blood sausage), flavored here with onion. River trout are often served with *tocina,* a strip of fatty pork; *bacalao* (salt cod) is the basis for soups. This is also bean country: hearty winter stews are made of *alubias* (large white beans) or garbanzos (chickpeas), augmented by chopped sausage. The local country stew, *cocido maragato,* is a fabulous value, with several parts of this hearty meal served in sequence. Apples, chestnuts, and cherries are grown locally, and pricey, creamy, rich Valdeón blue cheese comes from the nearby Picos de Europa mountains (savor it with some crusty bread). The local red wine, Bierzo, is a good value. A **market** is held each Saturday morning in the Plaza Mayor.

Most of León's liveliest hangouts are clustered on and around Plaza Mayor and Plaza San Martín, with the former drawing couples and families and the latter a student crowd. This area is called the Barrio Humedo (Wet Neighborhood), for the large amount of wine spilled here late at night. On Plaza Mayor you might want to start your crawl at **Universal, Mesón de Don Quijote, Casa Benito,** or **Bar La Plaza Mayor.** On Plaza San Martín, the **Latino Bar** (Plaza de San Martín 10, tel. 987/262109) gives you a glass of house wine *and* an ample tapa for just 65 ptas., a gift. The whistling proprietor at **Bar Chivani** (Plaza San Martín, tel. 987/256061) will set you up with fried calamari or sardine tapas for 250–350 ptas. Other Plaza San Martín haunts are **Rancho Chico, Nuevo Racimo de Oro,** or **La Bicha.** A modern standout on this lovely old square, **Taberna La Piconera** (Plaza Santa María del Camino 2, tel. 987/212607) charges 100 ptas. for a glass of wine and a large tapa and serves reasonably priced meals. Have a *pinchito* (tidbit) at cozy **Prada a Tope** (Alfonso IX 9, tel. 987/257221), which serves Bierzo wine from a big barrel.

UNDER 1,000 PTAS. • Pizzería Rocco. In nice weather Rocco's outdoor tables are great for surveying the plaza scene and scarfing salad, pasta, or a vegetable dish for 600–800 ptas. *Plaza San Martín 3, tel. 987/201327. Closed Mon. No lunch Tues.*

UNDER 2,000 PTAS. • Casa Pozo. Specialties in this longtime favorite, across from City Hall on historic Plaza de San Marcelo, include roast lamb, river crabs with clams, cod with pimiento and olive oil, and deep-fried hake. You can opt for an excellent set menu at both lunch and dinner: You get bread, wine, dessert, coffee, and your choice of an appetizer and entrée from a list of six of each. Past the small bar (where each drink comes with a free tapa), the bright dining rooms are furnished with heavy Castilian furniture. Owner Gabriel del Pozo Alvarez—called Pin—supervises the busy kitchen while his son, also called Pin, is maître d'. *Plaza de San Marcelo 15, tel. 987/237103. No dinner Sun.*

WORTH SEEING

León is proudest of its soaring Gothic **cathedral**, on the Plaza de Regla, whose flying buttresses are built with more windows than stone. The front of the cathedral has three weatherworn, arched doorways, the middle one adorned with slender statues of the apostles.

Begun in 1205, the cathedral contains 125 stained-glass windows plus three giant rose windows. The glass casts bejeweled shafts of light throughout the lofty interior; a clear glass door on the choir gives an unobstructed view of the altar and the apse windows. You'll see little 13th-century faces looking at you amid a kaleidoscope of colors from the lower-level windows. The cathedral also contains the sculpted tomb of King Ordoño II, who moved the capital of Christian Spain to León. In the **museum**, look for the carved-wood Mudéjar archives, with a letter of the alphabet above each door: it's one of the world's oldest file cabinets. *Plaza de Regla, tel. 987/875770. Admission: cathedral free, museum 500 ptas. Cathedral open July.–Sept., daily 8:30–1:30 and 4–8; Oct.–June, daily 8:30–1:30 and 4–7. Museum open Oct.–June, weekdays 9:30–1:30 and 4–7, Sat. 9:30–1:30; July–Sept., weekdays 9:30–2 and 4–7:30, Sat. 9:30–2.*

The **Basílica de San Isidoro el Real**, on Calle Cid, was built into the side of the city wall in 1063 and rebuilt in the 12th century. Adjoining the Romanesque basilica, the **Panteón de los Reyes** (Royal Pantheon) is sometimes called the Sistine Chapel of Romanesque art, as the vibrant 12th-century frescoes on the pillars and ceiling have been remarkably preserved. The pantheon was the first building in Spain to be decorated with scenes from the New Testament. Look for the agricultural calendar painted on one archway, showing which farming task should be performed each month. Twenty-three kings and queens were once buried here, but their tombs were destroyed by French troops during the Napoléonic Wars. Treasures in the adjacent **Museo de San Isidoro** include a jewel-encrusted agate chalice, a richly illustrated handwritten Bible, and a huge collection of polychrome wood statues of the Virgin Mary. *Plaza de San Isidoro 4, tel. 987/876161. Admission: cathedral free, Royal Pantheon and museum 400 ptas. Open: July.–Aug., Mon.–Sat. 9–8, Sun. 9–2; Sept.–June, Mon.–Sat. 10–1:30 and 4–6:30, Sun. 10–1:30.*

The sumptuous **Antiguo Monasterio de San Marcos** is now a luxurious parador, the Parador Hostal San Marcos. Originally a home for knights of the Order of St. James, who patrolled the Camino de Santiago, and a pit stop for weary pilgrims, the monastery you see today was begun in 1513 by the head of the order, King Ferdinand, who felt that knights deserved something better. Finished at the height of the Renaissance, the plateresque facade is a sea of small sculptures, many of knights and lords. Inside are an elegant staircase and a cloister full of medieval statues. Have a drink in the canopied bar, whose tiny windows are the original defensive slits. The building also houses the **Museo Arqueológico**, famous for its 11th-century Cristo del Monasterio de Carrizo, an ivory Christ with haunting eyes and strangely proportioned limbs. *Museum: Plaza de San Marcos s/n, tel. 987/245061 or 987/236405. Admission 200 ptas. Open May–Sept., Tues.–Sat. 10–2 and 5–8:30, Sun. 10–2; Oct.–Apr., Tues.–Sat. 10–2 and 4:30–8, Sun. 10–2.*

The **Farmacia Marino**, opened in 1827, offers a glimpse into a Spanish drugstore of yore—only the medicines have changed. The ceiling and walls are richly carved, and the latter include a niche for each apothecary jar. The pharmacy is down the street from the cathedral, on Avenida Generalísimo Franco (also known as Calle Ancha).

The **Plaza Mayor**, in the heart of the old town, is surrounded by simple half-timber houses. On Saturday the plaza bustles with farmers selling produce and cheeses. Look at their feet: Many still wear wooden shoes called *madreñas*, which are raised on three heels, two in front and one in back. They were designed to walk on mud in this usually wet part of Spain.

Southwest of the Plaza Mayor is the **Plaza de Santa María del Camino**, which, as the plaque there reminds us, used to be called Plaza del Grano (Grain Square) and hosted the local corn and bread market. The plaza's rural charm is accentuated by the grass growing between the cobbles, an old timber-frame building beside an arcaded one, and the church of Santa María del Camino, where pilgrims stop on their way west to Santiago de Compostela. The curious allegorical fountain in the middle depicts two chubby angels clutching a pillar, representing León and its two rivers.

Ruta de Santiago. As you're wandering the old town, look down occasionally, and you just might notice small brass scallop shells set into the street. The scallop being the symbol of St. James, these were installed by the town government to mark the path for modern-day pilgrims.

Jardínes Papalaguinda. If you're traveling with children, León has a long park on the banks of the Bernesga River, with playground equipment every 100 ft or so.

In the center of the modern city is the **Casa de Botines,** a multigable and turreted behemoth designed at the end of the 19th century by that controversial Catalan, Antoni Gaudí. It now houses a bank and is closed to visitors.

SHOPPING

For fine funky gifts, visit **Tricosis** (Calle Mulhacín 3, tel. 987/202953), a gallery opened by art students from the universities of León and Gijón. Colorful papier-mâché and experimental media form outstanding lamps, candleholders, vases, and frames.

You can buy tasty culinary souvenirs in food shops all over León—roasted red peppers, potent brandy-soaked cherries, candied chestnuts. In **Prada a Tope** (Alfonso IX 9, tel. 987/257221), such goodies are packaged by the house. The gourmet shop **Cuesta Castañón** (Castoñones 2, tel. 987/208070), near Plaza San Martín, is a cool place to browse, with a great range of wines, cured meats, cookies, preserves, and bottled delicacies, not to mention cookbooks. Friendly owner José Marí González usually lets you sample the wares.

AFTER DARK

Most of León's bars double as tapas bars (*see* Where to Eat, *above*). After 11 the streets around **Plaza San Martín** fill with bar-hopping youth. **Mesón Cordero** (Travesía de Recoletas off C. del Cid, tel. 987/201836) serves *cortos* (cheap beers; 125 ptas.) and tapas (200 ptas.). The nicest drink-only bars are **El Troqueluz** (C. Varilla 4, tel. 987/216971), **Café Tirola** (C. Torriano 2, tel. 987/250951), and **Casa Conde** (Plaza Mayor 6, 987/256755).

THE BASQUE COUNTRY

BY MICHAEL DE ZAYAS

I n a nation of regional distinctions there may be no place more distinct than the Basque Country. An ancient, mysterious language is spoken here—Euskera—and the Basque culture, with its own sports, gastronomy, and deep roots to the past, is of a different mind. The country wears a small, green coat of mountainous terrain that, in keeping invading Romans and Moors at bay, preserved the Basques' long history of political autonomy.

Geographically and culturally, the Basque Country includes Navarre and part of southern France, but it is in the three provinces of Spain's País Vasco—Alava, Guipúzkoa, and Vizcaya—that issues of identity and self-determination remain a subject of heated debate and, regrettably, a certain amount of violence. The underground terrorist organization known as ETA (Euskadi Ta Askatasuna, or Basque Homeland and Liberty), an extremely small but radical segment of the population, regularly assassinates political opponents and the odd journalist—nearly 800 murders in three decades. Make no mistake: the more headlines it inspires around the world, the more hated ETA grows here at home. Tourists, moreover, are not on the ETA's agenda, so foreigners need not fear for their safety.

Politics is as much a part of the Basque landscape as forests—political graffiti cover the urban terrain—and in some ways it helps make the Basque Country an exciting place to travel. Basque youth are engaged with issues of self-definition, an energy matched (even if its source is different) by the self-imposed makeover of Bilbao, a city whose metropolitan area claims half the Basque Country's 2 million people.

Despite the vibrant cosmopolitanism of its provincial capitals, Bilbao, Vitoria, and San Sebastián, the Basque Country is largely rural. Its wide-bodied white *caseríos* (farmhouses) and open fertile farmland have a charming rusticity, and its many fishing towns along the coast to France are colorful and picturesque. Add to this the ideally mild summer weather, and the Basque Country remains one of Spain's most irresistible destinations.

BILBAO

Five years ago you needed a reason to stop in Bilbao. Perhaps no other city in Spain had been so blearily urbanized, industrialized, and altogether aesthetically spooked as the city and its Nervión River. Bilbao

THE BASQUE COUNTRY

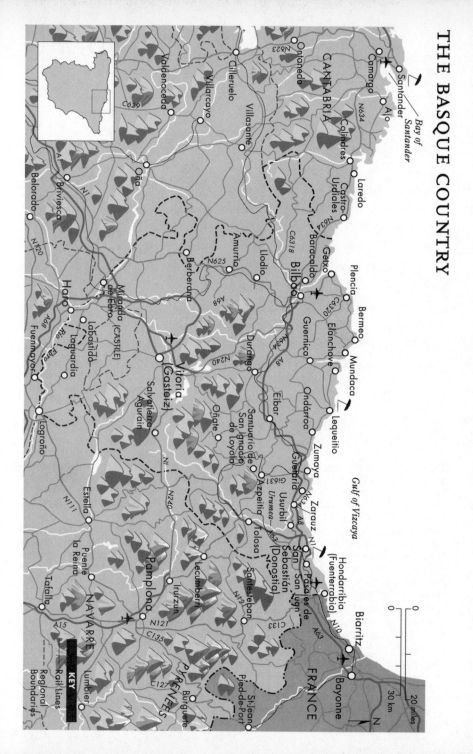

I UNDERSTAND YOU PERFECTLY

The Basque language, Euskera, is the oldest in Europe, and its origins remain stubbornly unknown. Predating the Indo-European language group, Euskera is as closely related to Greek as it is to Castilian Spanish. Written in the Roman alphabet, it traditionally bears a script that appears cartoonish to other Western eyes; Basque signs featuring what looks like a whimsical font are actually in the Basque alphabet.

Cities in this chapter are identified by their Castilian names, which derive from the Basque. In Spanish, the Euskera tx becomes ch (the Basque txuleta, a chop of meat, becomes chuleta); b and i become v and y (Bizkaia becomes Vizcaya); and k becomes c (kalimotxo, the wine-and-Coke cocktail, is calimocho elsewhere).

Agur *(good-bye) is the easiest Basque word to put into use, as it's used even by those Basques—about half—who speak no Euskera. Beyond* Agur, *try* Kaixo *(hello),* Oso ongi? *(How are you?),* bai *(yes),* ez *(no),* mesedez *(please), and* Eskerrik asko *(Thank you). Main Street—Calle Mayor in Castilian—turns into* Nagusia Kalea.

had a soccer team, a good traditional art museum, and some excellent restaurants, but it wasn't somewhere you went on vacation.

And then it happened.

The American architect Frank Gehry took a napkin sketch of what would become the Guggenheim Museum Bilbao and transformed the city into an international tourist destination. Suddenly, a trip to Spain became Barcelona, Madrid, Seville, *and Bilbao,* a development previously inconceivable. Imagine throngs of Europeans, on holiday in the States, skipping Boston, Philadelphia, and Washington and heading straight for Baltimore.

Yet the Guggenheim is actually only one aspect of the city's incredible metamorphosis, part of a massive urban rethinking based on the reclamation of the Nervión. Starting in the early 20th century, heavy industry brought wealth to Bilbao but destroyed its natural beauty; toward the end of the century, industrial decline left the riverbanks with unsightly remains, isolating huge sections of the city. In the late 1980s a coalition of bright Basques determined to turn things around. The Guggenheim, along with the sleek new subway system, were the first fruits of this planning.

Soon, two huge zones of old rail network will be eviscerated, replaced by dazzling new residential areas and green space. The more visible section for travelers—currently a jumble of unused train tracks right next to the Guggenheim—will be called Abandoibarra, with a huge park, a sleek office building, and a river walk linking the Guggenheim to Bilbao's concert hall, the Palacio de la Música.

Also in the works is a tramway that will connect, among other points, the Guggenheim with the old quarter. Major overhauls of Bilbao's port, airport, and other transportation systems, as well as a massive revitalization of its suburbs, will leave Spain's fourth-largest city unrecognizably improved after another five years or so. Bonded by parks, world-class cultural institutions, and clean and efficient transportation, greater Bilbao's million denizens (who constitute the vast majority of the Vizcaya's population) have

BILLBAO

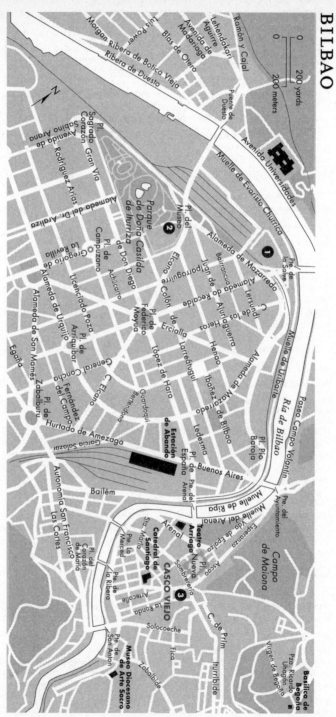

Guggenheim
Museum Bilbao, **1**

Museo de
Arqueológico,
Ethnográfico
e Histórico Vasco, **3**

Museo de
Bellas Artes, **2**

117

more and more reason to whoop it up at their August fiesta, which just happens to be the wildest in all of Spain.

BASICS

VISITOR INFORMATION

The **main tourist office** is extremely helpful, providing free maps and brochures on the city and the rest of País Vasco. Ask for the *Bilbao Guide*, a free bimonthly magazine with complete event listings. *Paseo de Arenal, tel. 944/795770. Open weekdays 9–2 and 4–7:30, weekends 10–2.*

The other tourist office is cleverly located just outside the **Guggenheim.** Inside are a model and computer-generated images of what Bilbao will look like in five or six years if all goes well with the Ría 2000 project. *Avda. Abandoibarra 2, no phone. Open weekdays 11–2 and 4–6, Sat. 11–2 and 5–7, Sun. 11–2.*

There's another information office in the **airport,** open daily 8 AM–11 PM.

CONSULATES

United Kindgom (Urquijo 2, tel. 944/157722). **United States** (Avda. de Ejército 11, tel. 944/758300).

CURRENCY EXCHANGE

Banks are your best bet—you can't miss them on the Gran Vía.

CYBERSPACE

El Señor de la Red (C. Rodriguez Arias 69, tel. 944/277773) is among the best 'Net centers in Spain—cheap (350 ptas. an hour), well stocked (20 fast computers), friendly (free coffee and cookies), and thoughtful (the computers are catercorner from each other for privacy, and each station is supplied with a pad and sharpened pencil). They're open Sunday–Thursday 10–10, Friday–Saturday 10 AM–1 AM; take the Metro to San Mamés.

Closer to the Guggenheim, **Master PC** (Recalde 14, tel. 944/352671), with computers for 600 ptas. an hour, is open weekdays 10–1:30 and 4:30–8 and Saturday 10–1:30.

EMERGENCIES

Police (Luis Briñas 14, tel. 944/205000).

Hospital Civil de Basurto (Avda. Montevideo 18, tel. 944/418800) is west of the action, just past Avenida Sabino Arana.

ENGLISH-LANGUAGE BOOKSTORES

Casa del Libro (Urquijo 9, tel. 944/153200, open Mon.–Sat. 9:30–9), near El Corte Inglés, has a quirky, thoughtful selection of fiction, nonfiction, and poetry, and an excellent stash of travel books. In the *casco viejo,* **Borda** (Somera 45, tel. 944/159465, open Mon.–Sat. 10–1:30 and 4:30–8) stocks obscurer hiking and outdoor-sports guides.

MAIL

The **main post office** is at Urquijo 19 (tel. 944/441004). For regular postal business, there's a **branch** near the tourist office (Viuda Epalza 3, tel. 944/150846). Both are open weekdays 8–2:30 and Saturday 9:30–1.

COMING AND GOING

BY PLANE

Sondika Airport (tel. 944/869300; 944/711210 for Iberia) is 10 km (6 mi) outside the city. A taxi into town costs about 2,500 ptas. Bizkai Bus (140 ptas.) runs to the city every 40 minutes.

BY TRAIN

Bilbao has three train stations, each serving different destinations. RENFE's Estación de Abando (Plaza Circular 2, tel. 902/240202) is a modern facility with a shopping complex, fast food, and a few coin lockers for luggage. There are two trains a day to **Madrid** (4:30 PM—5½ hrs, 4,500 ptas.; 11:30 PM—8½ hrs, 4,200 ptas., 5,700 w/couchette) and **Barcelona** (10 AM—9 hrs, 5,200 ptas.; 10:45 PM—10 hrs, 4,900 ptas., 6,400 w/couchette).

A block away, on the river, is the decorative yellow and powder-blue entrance to the FEVE station (Bailén 2, tel. 944/232266. FEVE trains head west along the coast toward **Santander** (2½ hrs, 925 ptas.).

The local line, EuskoTren (C. Atxuri, 942/008008), departs Atxuri station, on the river in the old town behind the market. One train runs through **Gernika** (50 mins, 315 ptas.) and the Urdaibai Biosphere Reserve to **Bermeo** (1 hr, 400 ptas.); the other terminates at **San Sebastián** (2¾ hrs, 900 ptas.) and is, along with the bus, the best way to get there. Note that EuskoTren does not accept Eurail passes.

BY BUS

The clean and efficient Termibús **bus station** (C. Gutubay 1) is across Bilbao from the old town, just west of Avenida Sabino Arana; the San Mamés Metro stop puts you right there. Present yourself at the appropriate window: PESA (94/424–8899) serves **San Sebastián** (1 hr, 1,120 ptas.). La Unión (tel. 944/240836) runs to **Vitoria** (1 hr, 675 ptas.), **Logroño** (2 hrs, 1,455 ptas.), and **Pamplona** (2 hrs, 1,475 ptas.). ALSA (tel. 902/422242) heads to **Santander** (3½ hrs, 925 ptas.), **Irún** (1¾ hrs, 1,125 ptas.), **Gijón** (5½ hrs, 2,820 ptas.), and **Zaragoza** (4 hrs, 2,450 ptas.). ANSA (tel. 944/274200) takes the big hikes to **Madrid** (5 hrs, 3,300 ptas.) and **Barcelona** (7 hrs, 5,000 ptas.).

GETTING AROUND

If you just want to see the old town and the Guggenheim, you won't need anything but your two feet.

BY METRO

Famous for its sleek, wormlike glass entrance tubes, Bilbao's subway system was designed by Sir Norman Foster. Finished in 1995, it still feels brand-new but isn't much help unless you make use of the San Mamés bus station. Trips are divided into zones; a short trip of up to three stops costs 140 ptas. *Tel. 944/254025. Open Tues.–Thurs. 6 AM–11 PM, Fri. 6 AM–2 AM; Sat. 6 AM–Sun. 11 PM.*

BY TAXI

For a **cab** call 944/448888.

WHERE TO SLEEP

This is where things can get hairy. For all its visitors, Bilbao still has too few nice, affordable lodgings and too many ratty pensions where the sheets haven't changed in 30 years—heck, where *nothing* has changed in 30 years. Reserve a room well in advance. Another reasonable option is to stay in the attractive suburb of Getxo (*see below*), a 20-minute subway ride.

UNDER 7,500 PTAS. • Hostal Mardones. Bilbao's only satisfactory low-budget stay offers 10 rooms with bath, a rarity in the old town; the other eight rooms share three bathrooms. The hyper-friendly (albeit English-free) owner straps on her own rubber gloves each day, and it shows in the positive sheen of the floorboards. An exposed wooden beam or two adds some character to each of the white rooms. Doubles cost 6,000 ptas. with bath, 5,000 ptas. without. *Jardines 4, tel. 944/153105. 18 rooms. Cash only.*

Failing the above, **Pension Mendez** (Santa María 13, tel. 944/16–0364) has 12 sufficiently clean second-floor double rooms with private bath for 7,000 ptas. each. (Avoid the cheaper 12 rooms with shared bath on the fifth floor.) While there's nothing friendly about **Hostal Buenos Aires** (Plaza Venezuela 2, tel. 944/24–0765) and its carpets are disgracefully worn, the rooms (7,500 ptas.) are large, not unclean, and possessed of private bathrooms. The location is good, too—just across the Arenal Bridge from the old town, close to pretty much everything. Neither joint takes credit cards.

UNDER 10,000 PTAS. • Hotel Arriaga. This little hotel lives up to the style of its namesake, the Belle Epoque theater next to the Arenal Bridge. The salons are filled with rugs and plants; guest rooms are similarly comfy, with wooden floors, floral sheets and curtains, private bathrooms, and cute balconies. Aside from paying 9,000 ptas. a night, you'll feel right at home. *Ribera 3, tel. 944/7–0001. 22 rooms.*

Iturriena Ostatua. Set in the heart of the old town and evocatively named ("My Fountain" in Euskera), this is the best small hotel in Bilbao and very possibly the loveliest urban pension in Spain. The owners, both artists, have decorated each room with antique furniture, appealing artwork, clever lamps, and generally a certain flair. Elsewhere, they've exposed the original brick, stone, and wood of the old building and added a courtyard garden. Cheery blue rugs, an abundance of curtains, scents of potpourri, and tasteful bric-a-brac imbue the whole with a homey yet spry air. Doubles range from 9,000 to 10,000 ptas., with breakfast extra. *Santa Maria 14, tel. 944/16–1500, fax 944/158929. 21 rooms.*

WHERE TO EAT

One half-block stretch of Barrenkale Barrena, one of the old town's parallel Siete Calles, holds four good-value eateries serving authentic Basque meals in their upstairs dining rooms. Each day roughly 1,100 diners show up for the *menús del día*, which costs 1,100 ptas. whether you're having lunch or dinner. The four settings are similar; make your choice based on that day's menu, posted outside at each restaurant. The small **Iñaki Taberna** (No. 14) has stained glass and a talkative crowd. Dining rooms in the other three have an identical wood-beam structure and yellow curtains. **Saibigain** (No. 16) is the one with all the hams at the bar downstairs; it has the liveliest atmosphere and the most wood. **Taberna Aitor** (also No. 16) is informal, with a pleasant, somewhat more spacious ground floor. Choose **Kaltzo** (No. 5) for a subdued, more refined experience.

After the **Guggenheim** (which also has a restaurant), you have two sure winners just outside. Across the street and to Puppy's right is the sandwich shop **Heim,** which makes great toasted-French-bread sandwiches to order for 500 ptas. For good pizza (split the 2,000-pta. small), follow your gaze 40 yards farther to the yellow awning at **La Foca Nicanora** (C. Iparraguirre 3).

UNDER 2,000 PTAS. • Kasko. This stylish, attractive restaurant draws crowds of twenty- and thirtysomething kids fitting the same description. You sit beneath a series of hanging metal fish sculptures, part of the lively contemporary decor that may help account for Kasko's success. The 1,175-pta. lunch is always popular (expect a wait), as is dinner—especially for Sunday night's live jam sessions. After dinner the bar continues to swing till late. *Santa María between Nos. 14 and 16, tel. 944/160311.*

Txiriboga Taberna. Across from Kasko, Txiriboga is one of many fine places in the old town to have a tapa and a glass of Rioja wine. It's especially famous for its *croquetas.* The lunchtime menú del día is 1,000 ptas., and the rustic little back room is as fine a setting as any. *Santa María 13, no phone.*

Garibolo. Some vegetarians say this friendly restaurant in the new town is worth a trip to Bilbao in itself; and like any of the few places in Spain that set a pitcher of water before you, it's preceded by a line of people waiting to get in. The large set menu (1,200 ptas.) includes salad or great fresh juice, a terrific soup, and a main dish such as eggplant stuffed with cheese dipped in a chickpea batter and fried, served with a hot carrot sauce. *Fernández del Campo 7, tel. 944/223255. Closed Sun. No dinner Mon.–Thurs.*

Victor Montes. Not to be confused with Bar Victor, across the plaza, Victor Montes is the gathering point for serious, rather expensive *picoteo* (nibbling). Take a look at the well-stocked counter of tapas, which might offer anything from wild mushrooms to *txistorra* (spicy sausages) to *Idiazabal* (Basque smoked cheese) or, for the gastro-fearless, *huevas de merluza* (hake's eggs), all washed down with splashes of cider or wine. For the same prices you can order same tapas outside on the plaza or in the tiny, more elegant dining room upstairs. *Plaza Nueva 8, tel. 944/155603. No dinner Sun.*

Al Jordan. Mihrab-shape mirrors, an Arab chandelier, and a central tiled fountain set the mood for weekend belly dancing (11 PM). The weekday and Sunday lunch menu is 975 ptas.; 1,500-pta. couscous menus are always available. *Elcano 26, tel. 944/104080.*

WORTH SEEING

Run to the Guggenheim, take a day, breathe it in—it's grand—then take another day for the city itself.

GUGGENHEIM MUSEUM BILBAO

No matter how much ink is spilled on the subject, it's hard to overplay the thrill of this breathing phenomenon, this impossibly successful acre of architecture. If you've lived in New York all your life and never visited Frank Lloyd Wright's Guggenheim, so what? For many, that architectural allegro is nothing compared to this ecstasy.

After all, the Guggenheim Museum Bilbao has been hailed as "the greatest building of our time" (architect Philip Johnson), "the best building of the 20th century" (King Juan Carlos), and "a miracle" (Herbert Muschamp, *New York Times*). Frank Gehry's asymmetrical amalgam of limestone, glass, and titanium ingeniously recalls Bilbao's shipbuilding and steel-manufacturing past while using transparency and reflection to create a shimmering luminosity. Inside, the liquidity of the sinuous white "walls" combines with the techno metal and glass forms to speak of the future. Needless to say, this is no easy task, but it's a great deal of fun, as you'll know when you see *Puppy*, Jeff Koons's big, cute floral watchdog, at the entrance. The glass elevator inside conjures up *Charlie and the Chocolate Factory*; and the reptilian titanium scales keep you guessing what the whole conglomeration might be—a fish (Gehry's fond of them), chaos, industrial totem, pancreatic disorder?

That said, leave categories to the art critics: the poetry belongs to you, as you gaze up at each delightedly composed angle and the artwork for which it allows. The lobby atrium is a bit of a space station, flooded with light on bright days, and you'll feel appropriately loony wearing the gray bracelet that serves as your admission ticket. Walk behind Jenny Holzer's vertically scrolling electronic phrase rockets ("I touch your hair") to experience their full streams of consciousness. On weekend evenings a rock band plays here.

In some sense, the Guggenheim's radical design does away with the traditional architectural problem of form and function. People do not come here to see the art. Yet one of the exhilarations of this building is the way in which its wacky shapes are put to use. The long gallery to the right of the atrium, measuring 426 ft long and 98 ft across, is presently the world's largest, making curating as much of an odyssey as viewing. Installation pieces, and large-scale works in general, have a new platform here; indeed, many of the works on display were created specifically for the space they occupy. The *New York Times* called the Guggenheim's 1999 Richard Serra show "the most impressive exhibition of contemporary sculpture in a decade, or maybe more."

On the second floor, you finally think about paintings. The permanent collection, put forth by director Thomas Krens as "a daring history of the art of the 20th century," consists of 200-plus works from New York's Guggenheim and some 50 acquired by the Basque government. The second and third floors exemplify the original Guggenheim collection of abstract expressionist, cubist, surrealist, and geometrical works—artists whose names are synonymous with the 20th century (Kandinsky, Picasso, Ernst, Miró, Calder) and particularly artists of the 1950s and '60s (Pollock, Rothko, De Kooning, Tápies, Iglesias) are joined by contemporary figures (Basquiat, Nauman, Muñoz, Schnabel). And El Guggy," as it's called by some locals, continues to highlight work by established and upcoming Basque artists: in 1999 more than half a million people saw the retrospective of Basque sculptor Eduardo Chillida.

Outside, a long ramp curves gently away from a pond (from which flames erupt every five minutes between 6 PM and 8 PM), a kind of echo to the Nervión river behind it. Exiting the gift shop, you can cross the ramp to the point where the Puente de la Salve highway bridge passes over the long gallery and under the "tail" tower, a brilliant fusion of the museum's life into the city's own. Indeed, one of the main goals of setting the Guggenheim here was to unite the museum and Deusto University, on the hill across the river, with the Museum of Fine Arts, forming an important cerebral triangle (with an angle only slightly obtuse).

In its first two years the Guggenheim attracted 2.6 million visitors, half of them foreigners, and more than what both Guggenheim museums in New York received together in the same period. The museum's economic impact on the Basque Country came to the equivalent of US$400 million, five times the initial investment. People are happy. *Avda. Abandoibarra 2, tel. 944/359080. Admission 1,000 ptas. Free guided tours in English Tues.–Fri. at 1 and 4, weekends at 4; sign up at info desk. Open July 24–Aug. 28, daily 10–8; Aug. 29–July 23, Tues.–Sun. 10–8.*

MUSEO DE BELLAS ARTES

Last year, if you had approached Spain's arguably second-best collection of art (after Madrid's Prado) from the park side, you probably would have passed it by. Only a redbrick wall faced the lovely swath of green; from the road, only a discreet sign and a small statue of Ignacio Zuloaga with his palette cleared things up. In part because of the Guggenheim's success, government cash was freed up for a wonderful Museum of Fine Arts renovation that will open the museum up to the park behind it with a large glass welcome center, a café, a bookstore, and a library. In addition, huge galleries have been cleared for contemporary art on the second floor, and an underground auditorium and restoration workshops have been added.

Don't let the glamorous Guggenheim eclipse this place; depending on your taste, you may find the art here more satisfying. The world-class collection of Flemish, French, Italian, and Spanish paintings includes works by Bruegel, El Greco, Goya, Velázquez, Van Dyck, and Zubarán; featured 20th-century artists include Rivera, Gauguin, Bacon, Cassatt, and Chillida. *Plaza del Museo 2, tel. 944/396060. Admission 400 ptas. Open Tues.–Sat. 10–1:30 and 4–7:30, Sun. 10–2.*

MUSEO DE ARQUEOLÓGICO, ETNOGRÁFICO, E HISTÓRICO VASCO

Housed in a 16th-century convent, the Basque museum covers Basque culture from top to bottom—fishing, whaling, archaeology, pastoral traditions (including a breakdown of various sheep bells)—in

ASTE NAGUSTIA: SEMANA GRANDE

Keep it your little secret, because foreigners, and even most Spaniards, don't know this yet: for pure party punch, Bilbao's annual fiesta blows Pamplona's legendary San Fermín out of the water. This nine-day blowout fills the third week of August, including both weekends. The bullfights are among the most important in Spain, free concerts—pop, flamenco, Celtic, you name it—cover the city from the park to the Plaza Nueva, and there are rural sporting contests (log tossing, woodchopping, jai alai, the usual) and other daytime diversions.

attractive displays with doleful music. If you can read Spanish or Basque you can learn, for instance, about the Basque shepherds who immigrated to the American West in the mid-1800s, and the bark art they left behind on local trees.

Even if you can't read the displays, you'll have no trouble with the massive topographical scale model of Vizcaya province on the fourth floor, its mountains and villages accurate down to individual buildings. You can also walk around the cloisters on the ground floor. Note that the entrance is actually at the back of the convent, on Calle María Muñoz 4. *C. Cruz 4, tel. 944/155423. 300 ptas. Open Tues.–Sat. 10:30–1:30 and 4–7, Sun. 10:30–1:30.*

THE OLD TOWN AND BEYOND

The old town's **Siete Calles** are actually not seven, but nine parallel streets. Chop off the bookends of Calle de la Ronda and Pelota, and there you are: the heart of Bilbao's nightlife. During the day, along narrow Calle Somera, the communicative chirping of caged birds emanates from iron-barred residential balconies.

On Sunday morning the silent streets give way to the hum of the busy **Plaza Nueva market.** Beneath the arches, boys and girls buy goldfish and trade Simpsons cards; men squat over electronic parts set on garbage bags, and foreign travelers marvel at kitschy old postcards, books, and records.

The old town's nerve center is the Gothic cathedral of **Santiago.** At press time the interior was closed for restoration, but the front facade is shiny and white—as if to match the look of the nearby Belle Epoque **Teatro Arriaga,** styled after the Paris Opera House. Walk around the theater to see the stained glass on its back.

Arriaga looks out on the **Plaza Arenal** and **Puente del Arenal** (Arenal Bridge), the latter of which leads you gently out of the old town into the new town's **Plaza Circular.** Here rises a monument to the nobleman and founder of Bilbao Diego López de Haro, after whom the broad central avenue **Gran Vía de Don Diego López de Haro,** lined with shops and boutiques, is named. (If you turn right on Calle Buenos Aires, you'll come to the Puente del Ayuntamiento, across which is the *ayuntamiento,* or city hall, itself—flying a Basque flag that reads NECESITAMOS PAZ—"We need peace.") The Gran Vía is intercepted in the center of the new town by the round, elegant **Plaza de Federico Moyúa,** rimmed by a grand Hotel Carlton, a historic government building, and upscale boutiques including a new DKNY. At the avenue's end, the Monumento al Sagrado Corazón (Sacred Heart Monument) is steps from the proud new **Palacio de Congresos y de la Música,** home of the Bilbao Symphony Orchestra and steps from the cool new **Euskalduna Bridge.** The **Parque de Doña Casilda de Iturrizar,** the only park of note in the city proper, has a pond with 14 species of ducks.

But all these are distractions, as you'll need to conserve some energy to catch the nighttime action. Bars are set up from the Plaza Circular through the Plaza Arenal, and hundreds of thousands of young people fill the streets—down every side alley, to the point where you can barely move—drinking, dancing, and carousing all night, every night. It's a mind-boggling event, suitable for discussion only in tones of hushed reverence and, for the sake of keeping it pure, earnest secrecy.

AFTER DARK

Happily, there is a weekday scene in Bilbao's old town, with drinking and loud chatter until after midnight. On the weekend, which starts on Thursday, that's when things *start* happening. If you want to go out before midnight on a weekend, hit the few bars spilling into the street on Plaza Circular; otherwise, all you need is Siete Calles, particularly Barrenkale and Barrenkale Barrena.

The crowd is largely segregated, though as a newbie you may find the distinction subtle and unimportant. BB gets the *pijo* (yuppie) crowd: well dressed, Chayanne-praising prototypes who party like mad; Barrenkale gets a dustier, dressed-down slacker group that parties like mad. If you ate lunch here during the day, you won't recognize these two streets now; it's as though they've become one united bar. Some doors are for dancing, others for swaying and drink-nursing, but the physical boundaries are otherwise all but indistinguishable. The exceptions are on Barrenkale: **Consorcio** is a serious disco, **Livingstone** is a nice dance bar, and the **Celtic's Tavern** caters to the young Spaniard's fascination with Irish bars and anglophone surroundings.

The best bet after-hours is **Contrato Vacio,** across the river, where a large, well-dressed house grooves to techno. Cross the bridge at the end of either of the Barrenkale streets, where guys are peeing into the river; you can't miss the giant circle-slash logo on the facade.

It looks like a church, and was in fact a convent, but **Bilborock** (Muelle de la Merced 1, tel. 944/15–1306), just across the Puente de la Merced from the old town, now hosts free concerts, plays, and movies as part of a city-run youth initiative.

See those sidewalk tiles with five circles forming a flower? The tourist office makes cufflinks with the pattern; if you're taken with it, get taken at the Gugg, which sells slabs of Bilbao tiles for 3,500 ptas.

SHOPPING

Shoppers can make quite a *paseo* of the Gran Vía, a classic European boulevard lined with Bilbao's chicest boutiques. **El Corte Inglés** is, as usual, in the center of things (Gran Vía 7–9, tel. 944/242211).

OUTDOOR ACTIVITIES

Even from the busy streets of Bilbao, you can see the green of the surrounding hillside. To get out there and hike, bike, kayak, or what-have-you, drop in on **UR 2000** (Viuda de Espalza 10, tel. 944/79–0656).

GETXO

Getxo breathes an air of wealth and despondency worthy of F. Scott Fitzgerald. In the early years of the 19th century, when iron mines brought great prosperity to Bilbao, tycoons built beautiful mansions along the shores and neighborhoods that had lain quiet in Getxo for centuries. Today the mansions and wealth remain, even as the severed joints of the industrial cranes across the beach remind us that all good things must come to an end.

Just a 20-minute subway ride from Bilbao, Getxo must be classified as a suburb, but it's a large place, divided into the residential zones of Algorta and Las Arenas. Algorta, in turn, includes the charming little Puerto Viejo (Old Port) and lavish Neguri, erstwhile winter residence of Spain's well-to-do (*neguri* means "winter city" in Euskera). Dotted with fabulous homes, Neguri's tree-lined streets invite aimless afternoon strolling. A steep climbs takes you up to the tiny, hillside Puerto Viejo, where a charming narrow street packs several excellent fish restaurants. On weekends the bars are abuzz.

BASICS

Across the street from the center of Playa de Ereaga sits the cute, blue **tourist office** (Playa de Ereaga, tel. 944/910800, Metro: Algorta), a relaxed hut you'd more expect to see in Key West or Provincetown. Inside are a number of excellent pamphlets on restaurants, lodging, and outdoor fun; the illustrative map is crucial to understanding Getxo's layout. Grab some free posters while you're there. The office is open mid-June–mid-September, daily 10–8; mid-September–mid-June, weekdays 9–2:30 and 4–7, weekends 10:30–2:30 and 4–8.

WE'RE FINE, THANKS

Recent polls show that only a quarter of Basques support the idea of a Basque nation apart from Spain. In the 2000 presidential elections, in fact, the conservative centralist party Partido Popular, headed by José María Aznar, won majorities in Bilbao, Vitoria, and San Sebastián. In places where economic factors (prosperity-bred indifference, departure of local business due to ETA's negative energy) trump ideology, the difficult stance of Basque nationalist parties may be on its way into history.

COMING AND GOING

The Metro ride from Bilbao to Getxo takes 15 to 20 minutes. There are actually six Metro stops here—for sightseeing purposes, Areeta, the first, is closest to the Puente de Bizkaia; Gobela is the closest to the marina; Neguri is the closest to the tourist office and Ereaga Beach; and Algorta is near the Puerto Viejo.

WHERE TO SLEEP

Getxo has four guest houses with doubles for less than 6,000 ptas., all of which are better than anything of comparable price in Bilbao. Moreover, the trusty tourist office will book rooms for you. If Areeta and Salsidu 21 are full, try **Pensión Basagoiti** (Avda. Basagoiti 72, tel. 944/607975, Metro: Algorta, 4,000 ptas.) or the pink **Pensión Usategi** (Landene 2, tel. 944/603088, Metro: Bidezabal, 6,000 ptas.). Bring cash in both cases.

Pensión Areeta. Start the hunt here: each room is freshly appointed, with wooden floors and en-suite bathrooms, and only 5,500 ptas. The first Metro stop in Getxo leaves you a minute from home, and you're then three blocks from the Puente de Bizkaia. *C. Mayor 13, tel. 944/638136. 13 rooms. Cash only.*

Pensión Salsidu 21. These sunny, spacious rooms with wooden floors are a three-minute walk from the Algorta Metro. Eight doubles share four spotless bathrooms; each goes for 5,800 ptas. a night. Ask the sweet owners for the especially large, desirable bay-window room on the second floor. There's a pleasant salon and a backyard garden for (BYOF) Sunday picnics. *C. Salsidu 21, tel./fax 944/302476. 8 rooms. Cash only.*

WHERE TO EAT

You've come to the right place—beyond what's listed here, Getxo has a slew of pricier restaurants where you can dine like seafood-lovin' royalty. The tourist office's pamphlet "Getxo Restaurants" has an entire page on each worthy establishment, with McDonald's and the marina's other fast-food joints conspicuously absent. In the Puerto Viejo, **Sausalito** serves up good, fresh Mexican in a pinch.

UNDER 2,000 PTAS. • Etxeko Mahaia. The name translates loosely as "the kitchen table," and you can't but feel at home at one of the five tables in this tasteful, intimate upstairs room. As the owners—two wonderful English-speaking women—might tell you, this isn't actually a restaurant, like Karola Etxea across the street, but a quaint place to sample plates of cheese, pâté, and fondue. The *tabla* (wooden serving board) of smoked salmon, trout, codfish, and anchovies is meant to be shared. Some of the Basque treats you'll sample here, as well as jams, fine olive oils, wine, and homemade desserts, are also for sale in the ground-floor shop. *C. Aretxondo 13, tel. 944/607501.*

UNDER 3,000 PTAS. • Karola Etxea. The tourist-office pamphlet reads, "The omnipresent Karola Larrea is a true exponent of matriarchal Basque culture, and she transmits that energy and power into all her dishes." If that's not enticing enough, you have to see the place. Wood beams go crazy on the ceiling and walls, charming you down to the ground of the upstairs dining room. Lanterns and other maritime novelties keep you focused as very soft music plays; otherwise you might swoon, as this is one tastefully cute place. Start off with *chipirones* (cuttlefish) or *gambas a la plancha* (grilled shrimp); fish plates are 2,000–3,000 ptas. *Aretxondo 22, tel. 944/600868.*

WORTH SEEING

Getxo is famous foremost as a haunt of Bilbao's millionaires, and their early-20th-century mansions line a seafront row called **Arriluze.** The most impressive dwelling is the **Lezama Leguizamón Mansion,** built in 1902. Of course, you can't just find good, affordable help these days, and a fortune doesn't buy what it used to. These homes used to have staffs of 50 to 60 full-time workers; today the mansions are divvied by floor among family members.

Playa de Ereaga, popular with surfers, is the town's main beach. The view from here takes in the hundred cranes of industry, skeletons of the very machines that placed these mansions here.

PUERTO VIEJO

Sightseeing in the old port means smelling good food and sitting down to it. From Ereaga Beach, climb up the long stairs: the port town is really one pedestrian street of charming two-story houses, their balconies hung with laundry. A score of wooden tables in a double plaza welcomes you to a lively lunch scene at **Txomin.** At the end of this first street, hang a tiny right and an immediate left for more great restaurants (*see above*).

PUENTE DE BIZKAIA / PUENTE COLGANTE / HANGING BRIDGE

Getxo locals are rightfully proudest of their transporter bridge, the world's only hanging bridge and a light, thin, elegant one at that, preserving the views down the water. Since it opened to traffic in 1893, it has carried more than half a billion people across the river, and you shouldn't miss a chance to add to that figure.

The bridge works like a hanging ferry. Two passenger cars—with room for six autos between them—swing across the river 30 ft above the water, hung by cords that move across the upper trestle. New elevators allow adventurers to walk across the top just for fun. The structure bears an obvious resemblance, in the crisscross metal of its four lean beams, to the Eiffel Tower, and has always inspired stories that it was built by students of Monsieur Eiffel. A more dubious legend (though it would make chronological sense) holds that the bridge was built with materials left over from Eiffel's Parisian erection.

The 72-ft crossing from Getxo takes but 25 seconds. Exit right and climb up the steps to **Miramar,** a diner-style restaurant good for *churros con chocolate*. Welcome to the town of Portugalete, where residents claim the bridge belongs to them: the town is a massing of homes on the river, attractive from a distance. Some of the riverfront residential buildings have colorful facades, but with so many other beautiful places nearby, no guidebook will ever talk about Portugalete, part of the frighteningly industrial left bank of Bilbao's outlet to the sea. It's yours to explore. *Bridge: Admission 35 ptas. per person, 145 ptas. per car. Open 24 hrs. Elevators to top-level walk: Admission 500 ptas. Open daily 10–7:15.*

AFTER DARK

Getxo has—a documented fact—the highest concentration of young people in the Basque Country, which in this case means students attending college in Bilbao. Their night starts at the **Puerto Viejo** (between about 8 PM and 11 PM), then shifts to Cuba Libres (a.k.a. rum-and-Cokes) in the **marina** (about 11 PM–4 AM), followed by road trips to discos out of town. Of course, Bilbao is always 20 minutes away; on weekend nights the Metro runs every half hour.

OUTDOOR ACTIVITIES

Getxo has the largest leisure marina in the Basque Country, and is the sporting center for the western coast of Vizcaya (from Cantabria to the Urdaibai Biosphere Reserve). Renting a bike is easy, as are horseback riding, kayaking, archery, bird-watching, sailing, rock climbing, caving, bungee jumping, and scuba diving.

The tourist office can arrange your heart's desire; alternatively, head to adventure outfitters **KIRIK Monitored** (Konporte 13, Algorta, tel. 944/911746) or **Naturlan** (Villamonte B-13, Algorta, tel. 944/304657), who organize essentially the same activities. For surfboard rental and surfing lessons, the top shop is **Tsunami** (tel. 944/606503), in the marina.

TELL ME NO JAI-ALAI

If you're in Gernika on a Monday, don't miss the 5 PM jai alai action: along with Markina, this town might claim the most important jai alai frontón (court) in the Basque Country. In this game, which has been called the world's fastest, players rocket a hard ball across a long court at speeds of up to 185 mph from a handheld wicker basket that serves as a sort of propulsion glove.

Games are played two against two. One player serves the ball against the front wall, and a point is scored when the ball goes out of bounds or the opponents are unable to return it. Spectators concentrate nearly as assiduously as the players do, as gambling is a fundamental, and official, part of the fun. In fact, jai alai's financial potential carried it across the globe; the game's best players now spend seasons in Miami's frontón.

You'll see a frontón in every Basque town, often hosting handball-like variations such as pelota in addition to jai alai itself. To the uninitiated, the slap of ball on hand sounds painful, but pelota has an earthy appeal.

If you're up for a walk, follow Getxo's coast beyond its bend to the east, toward the high-quality, blue-flag (EU-approved) beaches of Gorrondatxe Aizkorri and Barintxe La Salvaje. Sopelana's beach is right outside the eponymous last stop on Bilbao's Metro. By car, the next town on the coast is **Plentzia**, a very popular summer hangout for Bilbainos, before **Bakio** and the Urdaibai coast begin at Bermeo.

URDAIBAI NATURE RESERVE

Designated a protected area by the Basque government and named a Biosphere Reserve by UNESCO in 1984, Urdaibai is an area of astonishing beauty. Its prime feature is the Ría de Mundaka (Mundaka Estuary), which runs from Gernika to the Bay of Biscay, a fascinating, fickle paella of sand and marshes sinking and rising with the tides. Beaches cover much of the ría's coast, changing dramatically with the tides in size and shape; and a tiny island, Txatxarramendi, houses an oddly located Oceanographic Institute (staff commute by boat).

Much of Urdaibai's land is covered by forest (some of it enchanted—*see* Oma, *below*) and thinly populated. The left bank of the estuary holds a handful of small towns, including Mundaka, which gets some of the best surfing waves on the planet, and Bermeo, an exemplary fishing village. A migratory stop for northern European birds heading to Africa, the reserve is visited by 300 species, including some in danger of extinction, such as the spoonbill. Bird-watching is popular in winter and during migration periods.

If you envision the reserve as forming a V shape around the estuary, Gernika is at the joint, 35 km (22 mi) by road from Bilbao. EuskoTren connects the Vizcayan capital with Bermeo, stopping at many points on the estuary's left bank; the right bank is accessible by car and by Bizkai Bus from Gernika, though service is infrequent. In summer a boat from Mundaka connects the two sides.

GERNIKA

Gernika (Guernica) seems less a fixed place than a spiritual siren, the seat of every Basque soul. During the Spanish Civil War, the planes of the Nazi Luftwaffe were sent with General Franco's blessing to experiment with saturation bombings of civilian targets; Franco appreciated the chance to decimate the traditional seat of Basque autonomy in the bargain. People come to Gernika to honor the memory of that fateful market Monday, April 26, 1937, when more than 1,000 people were killed and the city was destroyed in history's second-ever terror bombing of a civilian population. (The first, much less famous since it inspired no painting, hit neighboring Durango about a month earlier.)

The traditional symbol of Basque independence from Madrid emerged miraculously unscathed: the ancient oak tree of Gernika. It was here that Spanish sovereigns had sworn since the Middle Ages to respect the autonomy of Basque rule, the special local rights (called *fueros*) that so revolted Franco and his centralist movement for Spanish unity.

Today's Gernika is modern and plain, a far cry from the beauty that envelops the rest of the Urdaibai Reserve. But the area around the new Arbol (Tree) de Gernika, planted beside the old one, includes the Vizcayan parliament and makes an interesting historical stop, capped off by the Gernika Museum's documentation of the bombings.

BASICS

VISITOR INFORMATION

Exiting the EuskoTren station, walk straight three blocks to Artekale, and the **tourist office** is on your right (Artekale 8, tel. 946/255892; open summer, Mon.–Sat. 10–7, Sun. 10–2; fall–spring, weekdays 11:30–1:30 and 4–7:30, weekends 10:30–1:30). In front of the tourist office is the Plaza de los Fueros, home of the Gernika Museum and town hall.

Uphill, behind the museum, is the **Urdaibai Information Center** (Palacio Udetxea, tel. 946/257125, open Mon.–Sat. 9:30–1:30), devoted to the biosphere reserve. It's not a tourist office, but it does have videos and models of the reserve, hiking (*senderismo*) maps, and a willingness to explain anything and everything about local flora and fauna. The staff can also help design regional eco-itineraries.

CYBERSPACE

Sysbat Informatica (Juan Kaltzada 5, tel. 946/270014) has an army of computers in a back room, renting each for 700 ptas. an hour with a one-hour minimum charge. They're open weekdays 10–2 and 5–8, Saturday 10–2. The small computer store directly opposite the train station also plans to get wired; have a look.

COMING AND GOING

EuskoTren (*see* Bilbao, *above*) is your best means of public transport. There's a **taxi** stand (946/251002) in front of the train station.

WHERE TO SLEEP

Lodgings in the Urdaibai countryside are more memorable, but there are two reliable stays in town.

UNDER 6,500 PTAS. • **Madariaga Ostatua.** Avoid the other pension on this block, as there's no comparison. Rooms here are impeccably clean, with shiny wooden floors, and come with private bath and a friendly owner. They're as nice as those at Boliña but significantly cheaper, at 5,000–6,000 ptas. per double. *Industria 10, tel. 946/256035. 5 rooms. Cash only.*

UNDER 8,000 PTAS. • **Hotel Boliña.** Handily located on the block behind the tourist office, Boliña offers a basic clean-and-happy situation with fresh pastel-color walls, wooden floors, and clean private baths, all for 6,500–7,500 ptas. a night. The owners run a nice restaurant downstairs. *Barrenkale 3, tel./fax 946/250300. 16 rooms.*

WHERE TO EAT

Across the street from the tourist office, there are two simple choices under the arches. To the left you'll see a red neon sign for **Omago Txiki** (Artekale 3), a small, homey café good for coffee and pastries; to the right is a good pizzeria, **Pizzicatto** (Aktekale 9).

UNDER 2,000 PTAS. • Josu Jatetxea. For seafood within town, Josu's 1,300-pta. menú del día is worth the five-minute walk from the tourist office, past the jai alai frontón. The nine-table restaurant is at the base of an apartment building, so ambience is in short supply; to forget that, start with the excellent *sopa de pescado* (fish soup). If you want fish à la carte, go for the house specialty, *rape al Josu* (angler in a secret sauce). *Carlos Gangoiti 19, tel. 946/254220. Closed Tues.*

SPLURGE • Basseri Maitea. If this is your first peek at the Mundaka Estuary, hold your breath as you approach this 300-year-old farmhouse. Still, the most astounding view may be at close range: you sit under willows and ivy-covered pergolas among lemon trees, all dotted on a mountain clearing decorated with old farm instruments and stone benches. Horses graze nearby. The sculpted gardens alone are worth the trip. All in all, this is one of the top dining experiences in the Basque Country, and costs about 5,000 ptas. a head. Beset by surroundings at once springlike, wild, and romantic, settle down for something sumptuous, like *cordero de leche asado al horno de leña* (milk-fed lamb roasted in a wood-burning oven). If the weather's cold, enjoy the cathedral-like interior, hung with strings of garlic and red peppers. Basseri Maitea is a five-minute drive past Gernika toward Bermeo; take a taxi or even hitchhike if you need to. *Barrio Atxondoa s/n, Forua, tel. 946/253408. No dinner weekdays in winter.*

WORTH SEEING

Gernika's **Casa de Juntas** (Assembly House) is home to the General Assembly, Vizcaya's parliament. For centuries the assembly met outdoors under **El Arbol de Gernika** to discuss matters Vizcayan, a tradition abolished after the last Carlist War, in 1879. Exactly 100 years later, four years after Franco's death, the General Assembly again began meeting on these grounds.

For more than 800 years every lord of Bizkaia took an oath to respect the Basque fueros before claiming his lordship. The present Tree of Gernika was actually planted in 1860. Across the patio is the noble veteran stump, which was moved from the spot next to the neoclassical temple. Now it's nearly overshadowed by the six-column pagoda that shields it. *Tel. 946/251130. Free. Open daily 10–2 and 4–7.*

GERNIKA MUSEOA

Four floors of thorough exhibits document the town's history and the bombings of 1937, supplemented by copies of Picasso sketches that became the painter's internationally famous *Guernica*. *Foru Plaza 1, tel. 946/270213. Admission 350 ptas. Open Mon.–Sat. 10–2 and 4–7, Sun. 10–2.*

EUSKAL HERRIA MUSEOA

The Basque Museum, housed in the Palacio de Alegría (Palace of Joy), displays paintings and a somewhat random selection of artifacts related to Basque culture. The fourth floor, dedicated to temporary exhibits, is notable for its low web of wooden beams. *C. Allende Salazar 5, tel. 946/255451. Free. Open Tues.–Sat. 10–2 and 4–7, Sun. 10–1:30.*

Figures ring the portal on the weathered, 15th-century Gothic church of **Santa María.** Behind the church is the soothing, perfectly maintained **Parque de los Pueblos de Europa,** divided into four parts to represent the Basque Country's four ecosystems: beech, oak, evergreen forests, and brook shrubs. Beyond the park's iron gates, wooden bridges and a pond appear, and you get views of the green Basque countryside in the distance.

To the right across the street, in an attractive, relatively new palace, is an Urdaibai Biosphere Reserve information center. On the lawn in front are two large, abstract sculptures of undoubtedly good intent that may nevertheless lead you to question the aesthetic merits of large, abstract public art. The bronze work is Henry Moore's *Large Figure in a Shelter;* the other, with an interior "window" oriented toward the Tree of Gernika, is Eduardo Chillida's cement *House of Our Father.*

OUTDOOR ACTIVITIES

Bird-watchers will find new thrills in Urdaibai. The naturalists at **Aixerreku** (Tel. 946/87–0244) run eco-logical tours of the biosphere. **Artadi** (tel. 946/73–9199) organizes bird-watching and mountain-biking trips in Urdaibai and other Basque nature parks.

MUNDAKA

Little Mundaka is irresistible. It has an unbeatable corner location on the estuary that takes its name— gazing across, you see sand, mountains, green hills, ocean islands, and thrilling waves that roll by with surfboards clicking under their tongues.

Yes, Mundaka has Europe's best wave—long and powerful, with good tube formations—and the best left-handed entry in the world. At the end of August or beginning of September each year, the World Championship Tour makes its stop here. A small population of surfers lives here year-round, but most come (from the United States, Australia, Britain, Japan, France, you name it) during the peak wave season, from September to December.

WHERE TO SLEEP

UNDER 6,500 PTAS. • Iturbe. Just south of Busturia (2 km/1 mi south of Mundaka, then 3 km/2 mi up a pine-covered mountain), this ranch is a paragon of quiet comfort. The kind owners, who live in the house next door, really let you roam, with full access to the big living room (with couches, fireplace, and TV), the kitchen, and the washing machine. The double rooms are warm, with dark wooden beams, private baths, and welcoming rates (4,500–6,000 ptas.). From Bilbao take EuskoTren toward Bermeo, get off at San Cristóbal, and call the ranch for a pickup. *Barrio Altamira (2 km/1 mi south of Mundaka), tel. 946/178017. 6 rooms. Cash only.*

UNDER 10,000 PTAS. • Hotel El Puerto. Once you see this adorable blue-and-white house on the port, you won't want to stay anywhere else. The owner claims it was the first house built in town, and given this fabulous front-row setting — with views of the Parque Atalaya, the estuary's tip, Laida Beach, across the way, and the surf playing out under your nose—there's little cause to doubt it. Rooms are large and relaxed, with private bath and comfortable cushioned chairs and sofas looking out over balconies to the water. The friendly innkeeping family completes the perfect experience of Mundaka. In summer rates rise to 9,500 ptas. (from 6,500), and rooms are touch and go unless you reserve about five months in advance. *Puerto 1, tel. 946/876725. 11 rooms.*

Hotel Mundaka. The sign above the elevator announces that "Surfers must leave their boards downstairs and clean their feet before going upstairs," but easygoing Hotel Mundaka is known to let the rules slide. Third-floor rooms are the cutest, with slanted wood-paneled ceilings; but all the rooms are spacious, carpeted, thoroughly clean, and equipped with private baths. Look for a green awning and white bay windows. Doubles range from 6,500 to 9,500 ptas., depending on the season. *Florentino Larrinaga 9, tel. 946/876700. 19 rooms.*

WHERE TO EAT

UNDER 1,000 PTAS. • Batzokia. If you're staying on a while to surf, Batzokia's daily 950-pta. *menú* will serve you well. Be ready for tables of locals workers and a no-frills atmosphere, just fresh fish. Three portraits of the founders of the nationalist political party PNV hang on the wall. Go for it. *Calle Olazabal, no phone. Cash.*

UNDER 1,500 PTAS. • Casino. This clean, elegant building in the middle of it all was built in 1818 as an auction house for the local fishermen's guild. But who cares? It has perimeter views of the port and the estuary, and its 1,200-pta. set menu is unbeatable. *Parque Atalaya, tel. 946/876005.*

WORTH SEEING

The **Atalaya** (Lookout) is a lovely park facing the water at the best place to watch the waves. It's dominated by the church of **Santa María**, built over an 11th-century convent. Across the adorable port is another privileged photo position—a fortification left over from one of the Carlist Wars, surrounding the chapel of **Santa Katalina.**

In the summer, a little boat shuttles people across the ría, from the dock by Mundaka Surf to marvelous Laida Beach. Mundaka has a beach of its own, past the same tiny dock.

OUTDOOR ACTIVITIES

There's really only one activity to think about in Mundaka, and ground zero is **Mundaka Surf** (Txorrokopunta 8, tel. 946/876721), where you can rent or buy a surfboard and sign up for lessons in summer. Board rentals are 2,000 ptas. per day, 1,000 ptas. per half day; wet suits are 1,200 ptas. per day, 750 ptas. per half day; and a 10-hour surf class with a rented board is 12,000 ptas. Private classes are also available. All prices include insurance.

BERMEO

Your first glance at Bermeo packs a wallop: long a whaling port, it's the consummate fishing town, with a colorful fishing fleet—the largest on Spain's north coast, and possibly in all of Spain—docked in a harbor backed by attractive hillside houses. It's worth a few hours' exploration, topped by a meal at one of the seafood restaurants overlooking the port.

BASICS

VISITOR INFORMATION
The **tourist office** (Askatasun Bidea 2, tel. 946/179154, open fall–winter, weekdays 9:30–1 and 4:30–7:30, weekends 9:30–1; summer, Tues.–Fri. 9:30–1 and 4:30–7:30, weekends 9:30–1) is on the ground floor of a brick building at the main intersection, across from the casino.

COMING AND GOING
The **EuskoTren** station (*see* Bilbao, *above*) is right down the road from the Bizkai Bus stop at Plaza Lamera Park, which faces the tourist office. Unless you're driving, by all means take the train.

WHERE TO SLEEP

Hostal Zubi Gane. A block behind the port-facing plaza, this friendly little apartment house rents comfortable rooms with peach curtains, freshly painted pastel-color walls, tip-top new sheets, and sunny little balconies: contentment right in town. The five doubles share one bathroom, but it's in perfect condition. A night costs you 5,000 ptas. *Arostegui 25, tel. 946/186944. 5 rooms. Cash only.*

Caserío Artiketxe. Farm implements line the driveway, and vegetables and flowers grow behind this pretty stone house, set in a rural landscape a mile from central Bermeo. Rooms, however, are not rustic but shiny and new, and go for a reasonable 5,000–6,000 ptas., private bath included. *C. Artike Auzoa 16, tel. 946/885629. 6 rooms. Cash only.*

WHERE TO EAT

Bermeo's two best restaurants, Artxanda and Jokin, are next to each other behind the church of Santa Eufeme; to find them, climb the stairs from the port. In town, just behind the Plaza Lamera, **Napolis Pizza** (Prantzisko Deuna [San Francisco] 10, tel. 946/186385) makes pizza to order for 1,000 ptas.

UNDER 2,000 PTAS. • Artxanda. Perched on a cement balcony overlooking the port, Artxanda offers an affordable 1,800-pta. menu for both lunch and dinner on weekdays. The interior has a nautical theme, but if you're here after June, you'll probably want to sit at one of the sunny outdoor tables. *Santa Eufemia 14, tel. 946/880930. No dinner Sun.*

Eneperi Jatetxea. This wonderful 1816 stone *caserío* (farmhouse) has a backyard beer garden with great sea views of the rock island of Aketx. Pleasantly full of diners in summer, the extensive grounds feel like vacation, with festive music, picnic tables under poplar trees, and a wooden hut with wicker chairs. Eat the usual stuff—*lomo* (sirloin), *bonito* (tuna), *croquetas* (usually of ham or fish), chorizo sausage—outside; dining inside is far more expensive. *San Pelaio 89, tel. 946/194065.*

SPLURGE • Jokin. Despite their proximity, Jokin has a view 50% better than that of neighboring Artxanda, so its meal prices are 50% higher. At 3,000 ptas., the weekday menú del día is the most affordable way to enjoy these glassed-in dining rooms above the port. There's a smaller downstairs dining room as well. *Rape Jokin* is angler in a clam and crayfish sauce. *Santa Eufemia 13, tel. 946/884089. No dinner Sun.*

WORTH SEEING

Walk along the docks fronting the **Plaza Lamera**, then ascend into Bermeo itself. The dark, musty dark interior of the church of **Santa Eufemia** (Eupeme Deuna in Euskera), with its wooden floor and cold stone walls, will give you a feel for the real age of the town. Moving on, climb downstairs to the **port** or continue up into town to see the **Museo del Pescador**—the Museum of the Fisherman is housed in the medieval Torre de Ercilla, rare in its urban incorporation (smack in the middle of town, as though it were just another apartment house). The tower's wooden interior houses old boats as well as exhibits on the history of Bermeo's fishing and whaling trades. *Plaza Torrontero s/n, tel. 946/881171. Free. Open Tues.–Sat. 10–1:30 and 4–7:30, Sun. 10–1:30.*

The prominent tower of the 19th-century church of Santa María stands opposite the 1732 *ayuntamiento* (town hall) in the cobblestone **Plaza de Arana Sabino.** Like the Plaza Lamera, this one has a gazebo, used for public festivities.

Near the tourist office (facing it, head right, then turn left) is the Gothic church of **San Francisco,** complete with cloisters. Built in 1357, it's the oldest church in Vizcaya province.

SAN JUAN DE GAZTELUGATXE

At Bermeo's highest point, young couples relax on a field overlooking the sea. Townspeople tend family tombs in the adjoining cemetery at sunset, high above the crashing waves. This site is the starting point for a great hike or drive down the long, green mountain to the medieval island chapel of San Juan de Gaztelugatxe. The chapel is 11 km (7 mi) beyond Bermeo, halfway to the beach town of Bakio: if you're driving, follow the lovely way beyond the lighthouse cape of Matxitxako, which marks the northwestern edge of the Urdaibai preserve, along a rough coastline punctuated by rock islands orbited by mists of seagulls.

You reach the beautiful chapel via a winding isthmus of steps reaching out to the lonely peninsula. The eccentric route will make you think of China's Great Wall. All told, there are 231 steps, which may not sound like much, but they're bloody tiring if you're carrying a heavy pack. The way to the chapel gives you plenty of time to appreciate the peninsula, which is full of caves and channels, rock arches, and columns forged over the years by the surging sea.

There's an incredible picnic spot off Station IX, a grassy path with coastal views extending as far as the popular surfing beach at Bakio. The ocean here is peppered with rock islands, by far the largest of which is Aketx. Sticking straight up from the sea, this crag is impenetrable to humans; seagulls have made it a nesting ground, and they patrol the coastal sky. Though outside Urdaibai, this coast is also protected land.

The chapel itself is small, and open only a few days each year. A rope hangs down from the bell on the roof; tradition dictates that you ring it three times and make three wishes. Tradition also informs us that the English buccaneer Sir Francis Drake took a liking to this spot in the 16th century, flinging the resident chapel warden off the precipice into the sea.

Buses run from Bermeo to Bakio; ask the driver to let you off at San Juan de Gaztelugatxe.

AFTER DARK

If you're in Bermeo on a weekend, check out the bars on **Intxausti Kalea** and **Nardiz Tar Jon Kalea,** across from the church of Santa María, but don't expect much.

OUTDOOR ACTIVITIES

For kayak trips up the ría or other maritime adventures, call **Club Nautico Urdaibai** (Muelle El Martillo, tel. 639/766133).

FIESTA

Once upon a time, there was a mighty rowing contest between Bermeo and Mundaka, a race to the island of Izaro to determine its ownership. Legend has it that Bermeo's boat rowed so fast that it split upon reaching the island, and a sailor drowned; so the town lost a sailor and gained an island.

Every year at noon on July 22, after a morning mass dedicated to Izaro, boats depart from Bermeo to the little island, where the mayor of Bermeo tosses a roof tile into the sea to reassert dominion. The vessels then set off for Elantxobe, the town that judged the original race; and at high tide they cross back over the estuary to Mundaka, to rub things in with their old adversaries over dinner. That night a raucous fiesta is celebrated, with the usual drinking and dancing back in Bermeo.

EAST TO THE OMA VALLEY

With green pastures and pine forests to one side and the fascinating, ever-changing ría to the other, this is one of the most beautiful natural areas on the north coast of Spain.

THE RIGHT BANK

The right bank of the Ría de Mundaka is sparsely populated and connected to the rest of the world only by road and boat, making it perfect for hiking and soaking up gorgeous, unfettered countryside.

WHERE TO SLEEP

A stay in one of the right bank's comfortable farmhouses will redouble your affection for the countryside. Rooms in the two jewels below are worth two or three times what they cost; if both are full, try **Txopebenta** (tel. 946/254923) or **Urresti** (tel. 946/251843), both in the ría-side neighborhood of Gauegiz-Arteaga, both charging roughly 6,000 ptas. for a double.

UNDER 5,500 PTAS. • Bizketxe. If the word *paradise* springs to mind as you drive through the Oma Valley, your impression will only be strengthened by staying in this finely maintained farmhouse. The owners live next door, and the creator of the painted forest (*see below*) a few doors down. It seems a distant afterthought to say that the eight upstairs rooms (four with private bath) are very clean, as this is the perfect rural Basque experience. Spanish travelers start arriving in July; before then, it's all yours. Doubles run 4,000–5,000 ptas. *Valle de Oma 8, tel. 946/254906. 8 rooms, 4 with bath. Cash only.*

UNDER 7,000 PTAS. • Ugalde Barri. In an area full of lodgings to write home about, the best is this adorable wooden cabin with fantastic views of the estuary. The fireplace keeps you snug in winter, while the bright cobalt-blue ceiling bespeaks glorious summer skies; at warmer times, the sunny backyard deck beside the outdoor kitchen makes for relaxed lunches by the backyard pond. The owners, who will pick you up in Gernika if need be, create hiking maps for a living; there may be no better source of information on the Urdaibai Biosphere. Privacy, beauty, space, great furniture (including a desk on which you're bound to start a new novel), and 6,500 ptas. a night for two—you'll want to stay for months. You can also rent one of the attic rooms in the owners' house. *Ugalde Barri, Kanala (follow signs to Playa Laga), tel. 946/256577. 3 rooms. Cash only.*

WHERE TO EAT

UNDER 2,000 PTAS. • Lezika. Set in the narrow Oma Valley, beside the Santimamiñe Caves, Lezika is a real Basque classic. You may not have heard any Euskera in Bilbao beyond *agur*, but travelers are the only ones speaking Spanish in this three-story stone farmhouse. The two huge dining rooms, all stone and wood, are decorated with tools and traps. At 1,500 ptas. the weekday lunchtime menú del día is the way to go; dinner costs twice as much. From Gernika, follow signs to the Santimamiñe Caves and you'll end up on the restaurant's doorstep. *Tel. 946/252975.*

Toki-Alai. This restaurant grants glassed-in, 180-degree views of Playa Laga and makes a nice stop if you're exploring by car. The 1,500-pta. menú del día comes in huge servings; it can be expensive to order à la carte. To get here, follow signs toward the Santimamiñe Caves but keep to the left, on the estuary road. After about 15 minutes you'll curve around to the ocean side and see Playa Laga. *Playa Laga, tel. 946/276163.*

WORTH SEEING

Heading north from Gernika on the east side of the estuary, toward the Laga and Laida beaches, you'll see signs for the **Cuevas de Santimaniné**—but the Spanish has been painted over, so watch for the bison logo. Follow the signs off this main thoroughfare until the road ends at the restaurant Lezika; from here an uphill dirt road to the right leads to the painted forest, a narrower paved road goes straight to the Oma Valley, and 50 yards down to the left, stairs lead the long way up to the caves. Sadly for us, the prehistoric paintings of bison and horses are, for their own protection, closed to the public; but you can still descend into the caves, once inhabited by honest-to-gosh cavemen, with a Spanish-speaking guide. *Free. Guided tours weekdays 10, 11:45, 12:40, 4:30, and 6.*

THE PAINTED FOREST

The fusion of nature and art—nature as subject, meaning, and inspiration—has been the focus of creative exploration since the dawn of known art some 20,000 years ago. But in the pristine Basque countryside, nature and art seem to have achieved a kind of perpetual sacred union, as if the two shared a utopian integrity, or at least an unconscious vigor, unaccustomed to human eyes.

If you're saddened by the hiding of the cave designs, take consolation in the painted forest, *el bosque pintado.* Created by local artist Agustín Ibarrola over several years in the 1980s, the open-air canvas remains a kind of startling secret, making only a rare appearance even in Basque tourist brochures.

In the middle of a pine forest accessible only on foot, you come suddenly across trees painted blue, green, white, yellow, orange, red, turquoise, and lavender. Images on the barks depict anthropomorphic forms—people peeking out from different heights, in different sizes and colors—as well as wide eyes, chunks of fish, stripes, and geometric designs. Ibarrola plays with distance and perspective to create the impression of depth, as when a score of trees with seemingly meaningless strokes of white paint line up to form a herringbone pattern when viewed from a certain angle. (The paint is harmless to the pines.)

In all, there are 42 such designated viewpoints, encompassing the trunks of more than 500 trees. The concept is so simple and natural that it's hard not to be thrilled.

The trail begins at the restaurant Lezika, from which a 3-km (2-mi) dirt road heads through young pines; you can drive this road, too, to its finish. Downhill from this point you'll find the only explanatory placard, a short description by the artist in Spanish and Basque explaining that the time of day, the light, the season, and natural mutable shadings of nature are as much a part of the coloring of the work as the paint itself. Each of the 42 views is given a descriptive name.

Ibarrola's use of space and dimension is not unlike the that of the prehistoric artist who decorated the Santimamiñe Caves, a few miles away: There, the contours of the cave are used to suggest size and add a layer of 3-D reality, as in the hump of a bison's back painted on a curve in the wall. At the far end of the painted forest, a trail leads down to the Oma Valley, where the artist lives.

VALLE DE OMA

Along with a handful of strong, humble stone houses, a single lane winds past sheep alongside a brook idling through verdant pastures to a communal mill. In the pure Oma Valley, you may find yourself filled inexplicably with nostalgia and longing.

The main thoroughfare cuts east though the woods of the Urdaibai Reserve toward the town of Lekeito; stick to the ría on the west instead. On the road overlooking the dazzling estuary, you'll pass the **Castillo de Arteaga**, a simple turreted castle built in 1856. Surrounding the castle is a 16th-century wall with four stumpy towers, which in turn superseded a medieval fort. The whole sits remotely in its landscape, with thoughts and memories it will never share.

SALT OF THE TIERRA

To fall in love with the Basque Country before you come, watch a Spanish-language movie called Tierra *(Earth), by the Basque director Julio Medem, one of the strongest auteurs in contemporary international cinema. You should be able to hunt it down at a video store with a good foreign selection.*

Set in the present-day wine fields of Euskadi, Tierra *infuses traditional Basque life with lyric and erotic energy. Medem's work might be compared with David Lynch's creative distortions of suburban American life, but it assumes strong, unspoken connections between people and the land. Even scenes depicting traditional wood-chopping contests, for instance, manage to be sexy and transfixing.*

The director's mystical vision is consistent. His last film, Los Amantes del Circulo Polar *(Lovers of the Arctic Circle), was well publicized in the United States and elsewhere; his first two films were* Vacas *(Cows) and* La Ardilla Roja *(The Red Squirrel).*

Five minutes past the castle by car, near the end of the right bank, **Playa de Laida** stretches 200 to 400 yards in each direction, depending on the estuary tides. At low tide, the sand extends almost clear across the ría to Mundaka. In summer you can also take a boat from here to Mundaka, though people more often approach this beach from the other side.

The little island of **Izaro** sits just out in the Bay of Biscay. A mile around the corner, another unique beach opens to view, the **Playa de Laga.** A large mountain cliff, Cabo Ogoño, drops gray-faced to the sea, stark amid all the surrounding green. Rough seas make Laga popular for surfing.

Sheltered beyond Cape Ogoño is the tiny fishing village of **Elantxobe**, long a refuge for smugglers. Until a few decades ago, you could only reach Elantxobe by boat; and its few ragged houses, protected by steep cliffs, still have an air of inaccessibility. Everything you discover here, like the lamps and balconies on the cobblestoned Main Street (Kale Nagusia) is yours to keep.

LEKEITIO

If you continue east from Urdaibai along the coast, you'll arrive at the quaint marine town of Lekeitio, where a pretty row of houses backs a small port with big, colorful fishing boats. Right on the beach stands the 15th-century Gothic church of **Nuestra Señora de la Asunción** (Our Lady of the Assumption), complete with flying buttresses. The church faces the Plaza Mayor, where you'll also find the **tourist office** (open Fri.–Sun. 11–2 and 4:30–7:30) and town hall. The beach skirts a hill, then opens wider around the corner, where a large rock-and-pine island nearly brushes the beach. At Avenida Pascual Abaroa 12 (1st floor, tel. 946/840893), you can rent spotless rooms in a **private apartment** for 5,000 ptas., either here or in management's other building, at the port. Each apartment has three private bedrooms and a shared bath. The mauve **Hotel Piñupe** (Avda. Pascal Abaroa 10, tel. 946/842984), next door, rents pert, clean rooms for 7,000–8,000 ptas.

By far the strangest time to visit Lekeitio is September 4—the freaky Fiesta de San Antolín, when men take turns swinging from the necks of dead geese tied to a cable over the port. The winner is he who can hold on the longest before snapping the neck and plunging into the water. Book your room in advance.

Beyond Lekeitio the coastal towns arise peacefully, looking quite a bit like one another, their cute ports skirted by balconied homes and little beaches. After Ondarroa you enter the province of Guipuzkoa, where Mutriku and Deba are followed by the more eventful Zumaia, Getaria, and Zarautz en route to San Sebastián.

THE BASQUE COAST—ZUMAIA, GETARIA, ZARAUTZ

Zumaia may be the best town in the Basque Country for a day of contemplation. Besides a cute fishing port typical of the coastal towns east of Bermeo, Zumaia bears long docks along the fjordlike estuary of the Urola River, which flows with the tides back and forth through town—perfect for an evening constitutional. Yet the best, most curious walk in town is along the acutely triangular pyramidal outcrop that extends half a mile out to sea. Zumaia also has three wonderfully ambient museums, two of them dedicated to local artists.

Zarautz has one of the longest beaches in the Basque Country, and in summer the striped, multicolor canvas tents stretching across its beach are the embodiment of elegant lethargy. From here you can see a giant mouse lying on the water a few miles to the left—that's Getaria, its old town sitting on the tail of the rodentmorphic San Antón Peninsula. It was here that the town waved goodbye to homeboy Juan Sebastián Elcano, who became the first man to sail around the world when he completed the voyage begun by Ferdinand Magellan.

BASICS

VISITOR INFORMATION
The tourist office for **Zarautz** is a block from the beach on Calle Nafarroa (tel. 943/830990; open mid-June to mid-Sept., Mon.–Sat. 9:30–8:30; mid-Sept.–mid-June, weekdays 9–1:30 and 3:30–7:30, Sat. 10–2). In summer there's another information kiosk on the beach.

Getaria and Zumaia have tourist offices only in summer. **Getaria's** (Parque Aldamar, tel. 943/140957) is on the highway, across from the angel monument. **Zumaia's** (Zuloaga Plaza, tel. 943/143396) is on the main road near the gas station in a white edifice shaped like a boat.

COMING AND GOING
EuskoTren (tel. 943/450131) covers this terrain by both train and bus. The **train** can zip you from San Sebastián to Zarautz in 25 minutes for 260 ptas.; Zumaia is eight minutes farther on the same train (125 ptas.). Getaria, between the two Zs, has no train service, but the EuskoTren **bus** from San Sebastián to Zumaia stops in all three towns. You can actually walk the 3½ km (2 mi) to between Zarautz and Getaria, or give up and take a **cab** (tel. 943/131952) for about 1,000 ptas.

WHERE TO SLEEP
With few lodgings to speak of, you'll have to fight off *playa*-flocking Spaniards in the summer. The rest of the year you should have no trouble finding a pleasant, inexpensive room with private bath. Zumaia is the exception, as it has but one hotel; if that one's full, try Bar Tomás in town (they often rent apartments) or just stay in Zarautz.

ZUMAIA
Hotel Zumaia. This fine one-star hotel literally has no competition. Rooms with bath and phone cost 8,000 ptas., 9,500 in summer. *Alai 13, tel. 943/143411, fax 943/860764. 16 rooms.*

GETARIA
Pensión Getariano. Across the street from the old town, this newly refurbished pension is a fair deal, with en-suite doubles from 5,300 to 6,300 ptas. *Herrerieta 1, tel. 943/140567. 16 rooms.*

ZARAUTZ

UNDER 6,000 PTAS. • **Berazadi.** In the summer, when other innkeepers raise their rates, prices at this farmhouse stand firm at 5,500 ptas. The large, clean rooms with private bath do not reflect the rusticity of the house or the setting, but the location allows for short hikes in addition to beach bumming. The house is on the mountainside just past the traffic circle at the end of Zarautz's main street, Calle Nafarroa. *Talai Mendi s/n, tel. 943/833494. 6 rooms. Cash only.*

UNDER 8,000 PTAS. • **Hotel Norte.** Across the street from the tourist office and steps from the beach, this one-star hotel has off-season rates equal to those of the pensions and offers an extra touch of comfort. A clean, modern, spacious double with wooden floor, bath, and phone costs 5,500 ptas., ballooning to 8,000–9,000 ptas. in summer. *Amezti 1, tel. 943/832313. 19 rooms.*

Pension Txiki Polit. A few blocks from the tourist office in Zarautz's main square, Txiki is a hotel-quality lodging with a modern design centered on a circular courtyard. On the top floor some cheaper, not-quite-as-nice rooms share bath facilities. Doubles run 4,000–7,000 ptas. *Plaza Musika, tel. 943/ 835357. 35 rooms.*

WHERE TO EAT

The combination of choice in this tri-town area is grilled fish with *txakolí* wine. In Zarautz, festive tapas bars line the beach.

ZUMAIA

Talai-Pe. If it's spring or summer, you'll probably want to eat on the patio across from the beach beside the Beobide Museum; the only thing between you and the heavens is a blue-and-white-stripe tent, matched by the tablecloths. The indoor rooms are intermittently charming, with curtains and wood ceilings. The menú del día is likely to feature *sopa de pescado* (fish soup) and perhaps *chipirones en su tinta* (cuttlefish in their own ink). *Avda. Julio Beobide s/n, tel. 943/861392.*

GETARIA

Mayflower. Contemplate Elcano's circumnavigation at this restaurant with tables overlooking Getaria's port and beach below. The menú del día packs salad, an entrée (say, delicious grilled sardines), wine, and dessert into 1,275 ptas. *Katrapona 4, tel. 943/140658.*

ZARAUTZ

Karlos Arguiñano. One of the best-known chefs in Spain directs the menu here; indeed, this restaurant may be the best-known site in Zarautz. The small, elegant 15-table dining room looks out over the beach. If it's offered, splash out on the *pasta de tinta de chipirones con crema de garbanzos en escabeche y foie gras* (squid-ink pasta with chickpea cream in pickling brine and foie gras; 2,450 ptas.). *Mendilauta 13, tel. 943/13–0000.*

Txiki Polit. The inexpensive choice for authentic Basque grub is set on the central plaza, with a busy tapas bar preceding the main dining room. *Sopa de pescado* is given away for 375 ptas., *chipirones en su tinta* for 900 ptas. *Plaza Musika, tel. 943/835357.*

WORTH SEEING

ZUMAIA

Zumaia is an extremely pleasant town, with more discrete attractions (museums, old churches) and meditative allures (strolls, picnics) than either of the above. Divided by the tidal flow of the Urola River, it's sewn together by some cute pedestrian bridges.

Do see the beautiful **Museo Zuloaga** (Casa Santiago-Etxea, tel. 943/862341), housed in the lovely gardened estate where painter Ignacio Zuloaga lived in the early 20th century. Besides a large set of Zuloaga's own works, the wonderfully decorated house displays the painter's own collection of works by El Greco, Goya, Zurbarán, and others. In the house across the street—this is countryside now—is the attractive **Museo Laia** (Santiago Auzoa s/n, tel. 943/862512), a museum of Basque crafts, samples of which are sold in the gift shop. Across the river is the studio of another local artist, Julio Beobide; inside the **Museo Beobide** (Avda. Julio Beobide s/n, tel. 943/861608) you'll find sculptures completed on the premises between 1923 and 1969. In front of the museum, a long pier ends in a high stone cul-de-sac with views of the sea. All three museums are open Tuesday–Sunday 10–2 and 4–8.

Up in the old town, two alleys lead to the almost hidden 13th- to 15th-century Gothic church of **San Pedro,** with a dark chamber of an interior. The tiny, secluded plaza out front is walled by stone benches topped with black crosses.

Continue uphill toward the lonely shrine of **San Telmo.** From here fissured cuts in the mountain (resembling corduroy) lead down to the small Itzurun beach; but continue on to the wonderfully strange geological formation that the tourist brochure cryptically calls a "flysch." One half of this long, pointy stretch of rock is green, and horses graze to one side; the other half, gray, drops fantastically to the sea. Walk the unforgettable peak's path above the sapphire waters.

GETARIA

There may be more boats than homes in Getaria; it takes all of about nine seconds to drive past the town on the highway, 3 km (2 mi) from Zarautz. An Art Nouveau **angel** rises atop a small fort at the town's entrance, a symbol of the town's *buenaventura* (good fortune). Climb to the fort's grassy top to survey the scene, from Getaria's port to Zarautz's beach.

The old town—and there's not much more to Getaria—comprises a few cobblestone pedestrian streets leading to a terrific little Gothic church, the 15th-century **San Salvador,** with a wooden floor that slopes up to the altar. The **port** is right behind the church, and it was from here that Juan Sebastián Elcano (1460–1526), prime recipient of the town's good fortune (another is fashion designer Cristóbal Balenciaga), set off to sail the world. When Magellan was killed in the Philippines in 1521, Elcano completed the first circumnavigation of the globe. How come we never learn these details in school? There's a statue of Elcano in a tiny plaza overlooking the port, near the Mayflower restaurant, and another at the entrance to the old town, near the angel. From the port, you can climb out onto the Mouse's back.

ZARAUTZ

You come to Zarautz for the beach, at the end of which the elegant Palacio Narros guards the town's grand past. A sea walk, the **Malecón,** stretches clear across the beach, and in summer the chic sun tents go for a reasonable 1,000 ptas. a day. The town itself is small, centered on the gazebo-laden **Plaza Musika.**

The beach gives you the best perspective on Getaria's jutting peninsula to the left, called **El Ratón de Getaria** (the Mouse of Getaria)—the town rests on the rat's tail. Stare until you laugh out loud with recognition. At the right end of the beach, a series of rocks juts into the sea; make an adventurous hike of it and discover the ruins of an old **chapel.**

OUTDOOR ACTIVITIES

After Santander and Mundaka, Zarautz is the biggest name in mainland Spanish surfing. **Pukas** (Nafarroa 4, tel. 943/835821), near the tourist office, was Spain's first major surf shop and has helped bring major tournaments to Zarautz, still a stop on the world circuit. Rent a board for 1,500 ptas. a day and/or arrange for lessons at the Pukas surf school, open June 15 to September 15.

For mountain climbing, hang gliding, and other adventures of the ilk, talk to **K2 Aventour** (Bañeru 1, tel. 943/130918).

SANTUARIO DE SAN IGNACIO DE LOYOLA

Half an hour south of Zumaia, between the medieval towns of Azkoitia and Azpeitia, is the birthplace of Iñigo Lopez, later St. Ignatius of Loyola—founder of the Society of Jesus, otherwise known as the Jesuits. Canonized in 1622 as Ignatius of Loyola for his defense of the Catholic Church against the tides of Luther's Reformation, Lopez essentially started the movement known as the Counter-Reformation. A group of astounding Baroque buildings—highlighted by the 1738 basilica, with a dome more than 200 ft high—surround the tower house where he was born in 1491. The fortresslike tower contains the room where he experienced conversion while recovering from a wound inflicted in an intra-Basque battle.

Ignatius' reputation as a "soldier of Christ" somewhat belies his teachings, which emphasized mystical union with God, imitation of Christ, human initiative, foreign missionary works, and, especially, the education of youth. His name has been given to five universities in the United States and Canada, and to countless smaller Jesuit schools in North America and around the world. *Open daily 8:30–9.*

SAN SEBASTIÁN

No other place in Spain can prepare you for the romantic splendor of San Sebastián. Belle Epoque architecture exudes refinement onto the tree- and garden-lined streets, stylish denizens pop in and out of chic boutiques and myriad bookstores, and perfect beaches and fine food lure unsuspecting travelers to stay for weeks at a time. The city does everything right.

San Sebastián (Donostia in Euskera) is small enough to leave time for simple pleasures, like reflecting on the weather. It shares a lovely, temperate summer climate with the rest of northern Spain, but San Sebastián is beautiful in the rain, too. It's hard to have a bad day here. In summer and early fall, when international jazz and film festivals add celebrity to what is already one of the most coveted destinations for vacationing Spaniards, San Sebastián can feel somewhat like a flashy club that's hard to get into.

Of course, things haven't always been this good. The city has been nearly wiped out by fire 12 times (13 would be a travesty). After the blaze of 1813—intentionally set by the combined English and Portuguese after they expelled the French—things didn't look so hot. In 1846, however, Queen Isabel II made the city her summer home, seeking a cure for her skin ailments in the Atlantic waters, and the aristocracy followed suit. The city became a favored resort for the wealthy, and to this day San Sebastián is a seaside resort in a class with Nice and Monte Carlo. Rents are higher here than anywhere else in Spain.

Much of the city's charm is a result of the way it was last rebuilt. The 19th-century architecture combines freshness and elegance, and the wide-avenue grid plan is offset by the narrow, pedestrian-only streets of the *parte vieja* (old town) and the graceful arcs of the beaches.

BASICS

VISITOR INFORMATION

The **municipal tourist office** (C. Reina Regente, tel. 943/481166; open June–Oct., Mon.–Sat. 8–8, Sun. 10–2; Nov.–July, Mon.–Sat. 9–2 and 3:30–7, Sun. 10–1) is on the boulevard across from the bridge nearest the sea, behind the Hotel María Cristina. The free maps include a brilliant hotel locator. The **regional tourist office** (Paseo de los Fueros 1, tel. 943/023150; open June–Aug., weekdays 9–1:30 and 3:30–6:30, weekends 9–1; Sept.–May, Mon.–Sat. 9–2 and 3:30–7, Sun. 10–1), a few blocks farther up the river, has pamphlets on the Basque provinces and other parts of Spain as well as San Sebastián city maps. It might be less crowded than the municipal office.

CURRENCY EXCHANGE

Obtain the best rates at banks, which are clustered on Avenida de la Libertad, or at **Change** (Avda. de la Libertad 1, tel. 943/431493), across the street from Citibank.

CYBERSPACE

In the old town, **Donosti-Net** (Embeltrán 2, tel. 943/433306) is a multipurpose tech center with Rothko-inspired wall paint. Internet access costs 350 ptas. for half an hour, 550 ptas. an hour; you can make international calls at amazing rates (less than 10¢ a minute to the U.S.), and they'll rent you a digital camera for 2,000 ptas. a day, then help you send the results e-ward home. Behind the cathedral, **Net Line** (Urdaneta 8, tel. 943/445076; open Mon.–Sat. 10–10) charges 100 ptas. for every 10 minutes on the machine. Closer to the bus station, **Login** (Plaza Ignacio Mercader 7 at C. Illumbe, tel. 943/482750; open weekdays 9 AM–10 PM, weekends 5 PM–10 PM) charges 500 ptas. an hour.

EMERGENCIES

Taxi to **Hospital Nuestra Señora de Aranzazu** (tel. 943/00–7000), just off the city map at Dr. Bergiristain 114.

Police (C. Easo, 41, tel. 092 or 943/450000).

ENGLISH-LANGUAGE BOOKSTORES

San Sebastián is full of great bookstores, most of which carry a token selection of English-language titles. Enjoy a large selection and helpful staff at **Donosti** (Plaza de Bilbao 2, tel. 943/422138). Perched on the circular plaza near the María Cristina bridge, just riverward of the cathedral, it's open every day but Sunday.

LAUNDRY

Lavomatique (Calle Iñigo 14, tel. 943/423871; open weekdays 10–1 and 4–7, Sat. 10–2) is a coin-op facility in the old town. In Gros, the barrio across the river, there's a **laundry** (tel. 943/293150) at Calle Iparraguirre 6, off Miracruz, a couple of blocks past the Santa Catalina Bridge. *700 ptas. per wash, 100 ptas. for 6 mins in dryer. Open 8 AM–10 PM.*

MAIL

The main **post office** (Urdaneta 7, tel. 943/463417) is behind the cathedral, open weekdays 8:30–8:30, Saturday 9:30–2. Are you Griffin or Sabine?

COMING AND GOING

San Sebastián is half an hour from the French border on the N-I.

BY PLANE

The small San Sebastián-Fuenterrabía **airport** (tel. 902/400500; 943/641267 for Iberia) is 20 km (12 mi) outside the city in Hondarribia, known in Castilian as Fuenterrabía. There are daily flights to Madrid and Barcelona. A taxi into town costs about 3,000 ptas.

BY TRAIN

The **train station** (Paseo de Francia, tel. 943/283089) is right across the river from the old town, between the Santa Catalina and María Cristina bridges. Several trains daily serve Madrid (6 hrs, 4,900 ptas.; at night, 9 hrs, 4,600 ptas.) and Barcelona (9 hrs, 4,800 ptas.). In the other direction, head toward Hendaye, at the French border (30 mins, 800 ptas.), and perhaps continue to Paris (8 hrs, 12,000 ptas.; add 2,500 ptas. for a couchette).

Bilbao is accessible by bus (*see below*) or on the commuter train **EuskoTren** (2 hrs, 900 ptas.), head-quartered near the bus station at Plaza Easo. Commuter lines go to Irún and Hendaye every 15 minutes for the negligible price of 200 ptas.

BY BUS

There is no central bus station, but the bus companies serving San Sebastián pull into the same general area. The bus is by far the best way to reach Pamplona, a one-hour, 780-pta. trip on **La Roncalesa** (Paseo de Vizcaya 16, 902/101363). In the same office you can arrange a trip to Barcelona (7 hrs, 2,600 ptas.) on **Vibarsa.**

Within Basqueland, **PESA** (Avda. Sancho el Sabio 33, tel. 902/101210) goes to Bilbao every half hour (75 mins, 1,200 ptas.) and to Vitoria a few times daily (2 hrs, 1,100 ptas.). Franceward, **Interurbanos** runs every 15 minutes to Hondarribia (45 min, 200 ptas.) and Irún (35 min, 165 ptas.).

Heading south into Spain, **Continental Auto** (Avda. Sancho el Sabio 31, tel. 943/469074) runs to Burgos (3 hrs, 2,000 ptas.) and Madrid (6 hrs, 4,000 ptas.).

GETTING AROUND

San Sebastián is small. You can—and will want to—walk everywhere you need to go. For a **taxi** call Donostia (tel. 943/464646), Vallina (tel. 943/404040), or Santa Clara (tel. 943/31–0111). Rent a **bike** for 3,000 ptas. a day at Comet (Avda. de la Libertad 6, tel. 943/42–2351) or Amara Bike (Plaza de los Estudios, tel. 943/45–7367), both open weekdays 10–1 and 4–8, Saturday 10–1.

WHERE TO SLEEP

In a city with 45 *pensiones*, you'd think finding a room would be a cinch. In the old town you can't throw a stick without a three or four *pensión* signs beckoning your bucks. Alackaday, if it's summertime, consider yourself blessed to find anything at all. The very best places to stay, listed below, are often *completos* from April clear to October, and on weekends the rest of the year. Don't even think about getting a room during Pamplona's Feast of San Fermín, the second week of July, or anytime in August, unless you've made reservations well in advance.

UNDER 6,000 PTAS. • Pensión Aussie. The Australian-born Ignacio—call him "Skippy"—hasn't changed the prices on these clean, spacious rooms in 10 years. At peak times the 2,000-a-head pricing and first-come, first-serve reservation system fill the place like a hostel, evidence of Skippy's mag-nanimous disposition. Rooms come in various configurations, but if none are free, the man will hook you up with a stay in someone's home—a priceless piece of info in this popular town. *San Jerónimo 23, tel. 943/42–2874. 14 rooms. Cash only.*

Pensión Aries. These four clean doubles overlook the street from little balconies in the heart of the old city. Priced between 3,500 and 5,000 ptas., they share two bathrooms. *San Jerónimo 22, tel. 943/426855. 4 rooms. Cash only.*

UNDER 8,000 PTAS. • Pensión Amaiur. Before all else, circle the words *Pension Amaiur* and call meticulous, English-speaking Virginia. She and her mother offer delightful rooms that breathe a limpid air, with perfect wallpaper and fresh flowers. The 10 double rooms, which cost 3,500–6,000 ptas., depending on the season, share five immaculate bathrooms (showers only) where you'll find subtle touches like all-natural oat soap. How *do* they stay so pristine? You may find yourself skipping down the carpeted halls. *31 de Agosto, 44, tel. 943/429654. 10 rooms. Cash only.*

Pensión Boulevard. The excellent location of this crisp *pensión*, facing one of the city's most attractive promenades with its back to the old town, matches the state of affairs on the inside. Four spotless, mod-ern doubles with wooden floors share two tidy bathrooms (3,500–6,000 ptas., according to season); the fifth room has a private bath (5,000–8,000 ptas.). The same trustworthy owners run the nearby **Pensión San Lorenzo** (San Lorenzo 2, tel. 943/425516), which has five slightly smaller rooms for 4,000–7,000 ptas. and spanking-new bathrooms. *Avda. Alameda del Boulevard 24, tel. 943/429405. 5 rooms in each bldg. Cash only.*

WHERE TO EAT

Every other Spaniard will tell you that his or her native town has the best food in Spain, but most will agree that San Sebastián has the second-best. Inexpensive seafooderies showcase the best of Basque cuisine, and tapas bars veritably cover the old town. You can't miss at **Martínez** or **La Cepa** (Avda. 31 Agosto 7).

When you're ready for a full meal at 6 but the restaurants aren't, head to the nice mall-like area called **La Brecha** (the Breach, so named because this is where the French fortifications of the old town were finally forced open in the famous 1813 battle), around the intersections of Avenida Alameda del Boule-vard with Calle San Juan and C. Aldamar. Here you'll find reliable, and reliably open, theme-style estab-lishments. For smaller cravings, great homemade potato chips and french fries go for less than 200 ptas. at the little shop on **San Jerónimo 21,** off Calle Puerto. **Iratxo** (San Juan 9) makes good sand-wiches on great bread.

UNDER 2,000 PTAS. • Café Kursaal. As you enter the door on the side of the giant cube, the café is on your left. (To the right is a fancy restaurant run, like the café, by famed Basque chef Martín Berasategui.) On weekdays from 1 to 4:30 a set menu at the stylish and popular café costs 1,500 ptas., a real value considering the ambience, service, and quality of the food, particularly the desserts. *Kur-saal convention center, Avda. de la Zurriola, tel. 943/003000.*

Café Oquendo. The walls are covered with jazz- and film-festival posters and photos of the staff with celebrities, and the crowd has a somewhat intellectual air (to go with your coffee). Of course, tapas are splayed across the bar, and red tables huddle in the back for intimate dining. Fancy cigarettes are avail-able, and sometimes you just need fancy cigarettes. *C. Oquendo 2 (just off Alameda del Boulevard), tel. 943/420736.*

Caravanserai Café. This smart, fashionable eatery is a rare (at this price) combination of pleasant loca-tion, good, inexpensive food, and competent service. The food is not particularly Basque, or even Span-ish, but it'll fill you up—choose from pasta plates, heavy combo dishes (No. 8 brings spaghetti, fries, and chicken breasts), soy burgers, or a variety of salads. In warm weather, eat outdoors, in the shadow of the cathedral. *San Bartolomé 1 (Plaza del Buen Pastor), tel. 943/475418.*

La Cueva. Under a broad-faced brick-and-wood wall in Plaza Trinidad, just off Avenida 31 de Agosto, Cueva sets rustic tables and chairs around wooden barrels on a cobblestone patio, then serves up tra-ditional Basque food in a 1,500-pta. menú del día. *Plaza Trinidad, tel. 943/425437.*

La Mina. Nothing fancy here; you order from the placemat. But the pastas are perfectly prepared and are sold for less than 1,000 ptas. You shan't be saddened by your serving of spaghetti *al funghi*, a sauté with mushrooms, garlic, and parsley. Other simple dining solutions include pizzas and salads. Cheery radio enlivens the downstairs setting. *Urbieta 1, tel. 943/427240.*

Museo del Whisky Taberna. "Can I get a Cuba Libre here?" This place claims the world's largest collection of whiskey; you can get a hell of a Cuba Libre here. The owner used to run a bar at the French border, where truckers proffered samples from their cargo, and a collection grew—today the Museo has more than 2,600 bottles in elegant glass cases. Downstairs, in the piano bar, beside the *Guinness Book of World Records*-cited Smallest Cocktail Shaker (5 cm tall), there's live music nightly from from 11 PM to 3 AM. The classy fun includes trays of complimentary cigarettes. *Alameda del Boulevard 5, tel. 943/426478.*

There are sidrerías throughout the northern Basque Country, but the one closest one to San Sebastián is **Sidrería Kalonje,** up and beyond Monte Igueldo. The dinner dishes are *tortilla de bacalao* (salt-cod omelet), *bacalao frito* (fried cod, served here with green peppers) and *chuletón* (T-bone steak) served with cheese. You're charged by how much you eat (don't ask how they know—they just do); 3,000 ptas. is a typical price. Make reservations (tel. 943/213251) and bring cash, as they take no plastic. To get here, take Bus 16 to the neighborhood of Igueldo, a 20-minute ride, and get off at the jai alai *frontón* (court); Kalonje is 20 yards down on your right.

Koskol. It's barely big enough for three tables, and there's no decor. But to come here hungry and poor is to know a good thing—to wit, half a grilled chicken (that's a lot of chicken) with green peppers and fries for 600 ptas. Two can eat well, with a big salad and a bottle of wine or real cider, for less than 2K; in addition, a diverse selection of fat tortillas is splayed across the bar. *Iñigo 5, no phone. Cash only.*

Real Club de Tenis Ondarreta. This place used to be for tennis-club members only; now it's open to anyone wandering around this end of the beach, at the foot of the Monte Igueldo funicular. Good service accompanies good, standard fare at reasonable prices. Next door is a warm wooden bar, the Wimbledon English Pub. *Paseo Peine de los Vientos (enter between clay and grass courts), tel. 943/314118.*

UNDER 3,000 PTAS. • Café La Perla/Café de la Concha. When you feel you deserve a treat or you're simply too hungry to stumble beyond the beach, step into these Paseo de la Concha neighbors for glassed-in beach views from the dead center of the crescent. Concha, which has a lighter decor, offers a midday menú for 1,450 ptas.—not bad for the real estate—while La Perla starts at 2,250 ptas. Both have popular sunny terraces. Call for dinner reservations on weekends. *La Perla, tel. 943/462484; La Concha, tel. 943/43600.*

Hotel María Cristina. Isn't it worth 1,100 ptas. just to order something called a "Bomba de Castañas"? If you find yourself in a fancy-pants mood, a dessert at the city's ritziest hotel might be in order (though *bombas* must be an acquired taste). Head to the Gritti Bar for sweets or a suave drink, to piano music, under the chandeliers. *C. Oquendo 1, tel. 943/424900.*

WORTH SEEING

For a wonderful two- to three-hour walk incorporating all the sights, follow the city's beaches from one end to the other. Start at the far end of the excellent **Playa de la Zurriola,** across the river in the Gros section of town. As you pull back toward the river you'll find the **Kursaal,** a bold new convention center in what is clearly one of the most important spaces in the city. The translucent glass building has a greenish-gray tint during the day, turning to white when its panels are lighted from within after dark. Architect Rafael Moneo intended the building to look like rocks rising from the sea, which it does if you keep your mind wide open. Stores and a few good restaurants line the street level; contact the tourist office for information on one-hour, 300-pta. tours of the complex.

Pause along the **Puente de la Zurriola,** one of three of the Urumea's late-19th-century French-style bridges, to regard the remarkable sight and sound of waves coming in hard from the sea. At night the black tidal surge sends white foam up to the bridges, and you can feel from a distance a trace of the surf's raw power, linking the whole city to the invisible sea. Across the bridge, the tree-lined commercial **Alameda del Boulevard** marks the southern edge of the old town; it passes the tourist office and, across the boulevard, the old market, newly reborn with boutiques. The Boulevard then stretches past an attractive gazebo and the twin towers of the **Casa Consistorial** (city hall), beyond which Playa La Concha stretches west. If city hall looks like fun, that's because it was designed as a casino in 1887; and its front steps lead down to the formal **Alderi Eder Gardens** and a **carousel.** Few cities have enough romance to inspire unironic carousel rides; San Sebastián may be the finest such place outside Vienna.

The old town centers on the **Plaza de la Constitución.** The apartments surrounding the plaza have starkly numbered doorways, a reminder of the fact that the balconies were once rented for bullfight fies-

LOOK, MA, NO TABLE MAN'NERS

If you're in town between late January and March, don't pass up dinner at a real sidrería, where alcoholic cider is made on the premises. During these months dinner (and only dinner) is served the traditional, unforgettable way— you stand at a long communal table in a bare cider warehouse. Armed with utensils, you pull at the food you want and drink all your heart desires from monstrous 10,000-liter cubas (barrels) of homemade sidra.

tas. City Hall moved from the building marked CASA CONSISTORIAL, now a library, to its current site after gambling was outlawed in the early 20th century.

The ornate church of **Santa María** stands at the north end of Calle Mayor, at the intersection of Calle 31 Agosto. Isn't that a stunningly carved Baroque facade? The interior is strikingly restful, and there's a charming little ship above San Sebastian on the altar. Calle 31 Agosto is named for the battle that took place on that day in 1831, when everything in the wooden old town burned except this street—and the only remaining structures are Santa María and, farther east, the San Telmo Museum and 16th-century Gothic church of **San Vicente.** With your back to Santa María, look straight across town to the front of the neo-Gothic **Catedral del Buen Pastor,** built in 1887. The locals, surrounded by authentic Belle Epoque beauty, don't seem impressed with anything "neo," but Buen Pastor stands proud, and serves as an excellent anchor to the new town.

If you've just been to Bilbao, San Sebastián's beach may win out over a small art museum and cloister. But the city's only major indoor destination is looking sharp after a two-year restoration, and it's still free. The **Museo San Telmo** is housed in one of the few survivors of the 1813 fire, a 16th-century Dominican monastery. Inside, cross the painstakingly cleaned Gothic and Romanesque cloister to the old church: This grand space is draped within by 11 mammoth sepia-color canvases created for the site by the Catalan artist José María Sert, who must have been overjoyed when he learned that the Basque artist Ignacio Zuloaga (one of the museum's administrators) had chosen him to recount the history of the Basque people. It's rare to find such a large, impressive space dedicated to the work of a single artist, and Sert's heroic style fits the bill, even if you can't help feeling that some color (other than tan) might have been nice. The adjoining stone vaults host changing, often very good exhibits of contemporary art. Back in the museum, on the second floor, there's a collection of 19th-century Spanish painting, with one hall dedicated to Zuloaga. The third floor holds a fine collection of 19th- and 20th-century Basque painting. *Plaza Zuloaga 1, tel. 943/424970. Admission free. Open Tues.–Sat. 10:30–1:30 and 4–8, Sun. 10:30–2.*

Walk up from Plaza Zuloaga (between the Museo San Telmo and the movie theater) and around Monte Urgull, the hill that rises from the old quarter. Up on Urgull are a little chapel beneath a huge Sacred Heart statue of Jesus and a little fort, part of the 12th-century Castillo de la Mota, sometimes used for summer exhibitions. Walk around the hill along the water, and the first edifice you'll reach is the **aquarium.** The best part reverses the usual tank experience—the fish are on the outside, you're on the inside. *Carlos Blasco de Imaz, tel. 943/440099. Admission 1,100 ptas. Open July–Aug., daily 10–10; Sept.–June, daily 10–8.*

Amble along past the little **fishing port**, where in summer you can take a boat out to the **Isla de Santa Clara** (300 ptas. round-trip), the small island that protects the city from Bay of Biscay storms. Santa Clara is best for picnics, though some people do swim off its dock.

One of the finest urban beaches in the world, **La Concha** (the Shell) is an crescent of sand stretching between the two hills that flank the city. The Belle Epoque boardwalk is interrupted only by a few waterfront restaurants, not to mention the disco Bataplán. Approaching the far end of the beach, you pass through a tunnel, above which is the **Palacio y Jardines Miramar** (Sea-View Palace and Gardens; grounds open summer, daily 9–9; fall–spring, daily 10–5). From the far side of the tunnel, take the stairs up to the gardens, which can add a slope of green foreground to your panoramic beach photos. Designed in the English-cottage style, the brick-and-limestone palace is used primarily for government receptions. The streets behind the palace form the neighborhood of El Antiguo—the city's original settlement.

Downhill from the palace is **Playa de Ondarreta**, separated from the rest of La Concha by a small outcrop of rocks. Backed by pretty homes, behind it and on Monte Igueldo, Ondarreta Beach retains a smaller, quaint feel.

Before you arrive at the Real Club de Tenis, a sign invites you to the funicular rail, where a cute red car—part of an advertising coup Coca-Cola scored here—can pull you up **Monte Igueldo** for fabulous views of the city and beach below (225 ptas. round-trip; open fall–spring, weekdays 11–6, weekends 11–8; summer, daily 11–10). This is the perspective for San Sebastián's most popular postcards, and absolutely worth the trip. There's also a collection of old-fashioned rides up top (bumper cars, tower from a haunted house) called the **Parque de Atracciones.**

Back on sea level, continuing to the ocean, you'll come to Eduardo Chillida's twisted metal sculpture *Peine de los Vientos* (*Comb of the Winds*), performing its poetic task as the waves crash around it. The platform you're standing on has a few intentional holes, the better to hear the waves rushing beneath you as well as around you. Behind you, at the base of Mt. Igueldo, is a wall of fantastically funky rock in fiery caramel hues—it looks like a wind-worn series of pock-marked layers turned almost completely on its side.

AFTER DARK

The night has two principal zones, but you needn't head farther than the *parte vieja*, where door after door reveals a busy bar crowded with mirthful youngsters. Watering holes are everywhere and similar. **Calle Fermín Calbetón** alone provides a month's worth of barhopping.

Bar Recalde (C. Aldamar 1) may look undistinguished, but it's a bit larger than most and always has interesting people in it. Right around the corner on San Vicente is another cool bar on the odd side, **El Ensanche.** Facing the river, **Be Bop** (Paseo de Salamanca 3) earns high kudos. The two posters of Chet Baker on the wall reveal a predilection for jazz, in addition to world music; equally noteworthy, the bartenders bring the very best out of your drinks. Ask for a *gin kas* (gin with lemon soda). **Altxerri,** on the Alameda del Boulevard off Calle Aldamar, is another winning jazz standard.

The second distinct nightlife zone is behind the cathedral, down **Calle Reyes Católicos** (which has been called Reyes Alcohólicos) and a few side streets, especially Larramedi. These disco-pubs are nicer than those in the old town and draw a more discriminating crowd in their thirties. Just off Reyes Católicos on Larramedi is **El Nido.** If you spend a few hours here bouncing from door to loud door, you're bound to pass through all the good places, including **Udaberri, Azul Cristal,** and **Splash.**

San Sebastián hasn't much of an alternative scene. The best is at bright-red **Bukowski** (C. Egia 18), across the river in the neighborhood called Egia, south of Gros. It's not impossibly far away on foot, but a cab will make the trip more pleasant. Bukowski has frequent live shows, some couches for chilling, and a huge canvas of The Clash.

An excellent, inexpensive film series called *Nosferatu* runs at the **Teatro Principal** (C. Mayor 3, tel. 943/426112); pick up a brochure at the theater or at the tourist office. Besides that, there's usually one movie in town shown in its original language with Spanish subtitles. The **Kursaal** (Avda. de la Zurriola, tel. 943/003000) hosts excellent performing-arts events.

If you find carrying all those peseta coins cumbersome, a small and pleasant **casino** (C. Mayor 1, tel. 943/429214) is open midnight to 5 AM year-round to relieve you of the burden. You need to register your photo ID to enter.

OUTDOOR ACTIVITIES

Surfers should stop by **Pukas** (C. Mayor 5, tel. 943/427228) for boards and equipment year-round and classes in the summer.

FIESTAS

After Epiphany, January 20 marks the first big fiesta of the Spanish year, the Día de San Sebastián, popularly called **La Tamborrada.** For 24 hours starting at midnight, groups dressed in Napoleonic costume parade around, drumming their hearts out.

If you've never been to a Spanish fiesta, the heavy dancing and drinking in the old town during **Semana Grande,** the week beginning August 14, will shock you. Truth is, however, Donostia's fiesta is a dud compared to the goings-on in Bilbao and Vitoria; the number and intensity of nighttime shenanigans don't approach the insane levels of those in the Basque Country's other urban centers. One reason is the very class of the town; vomit doesn't fly here. Another is that tourists have the run of the place in the heart of August. Still, it's another wonderful time in San Sebastián—everyone in the city crowds along La Concha each night for the 10:45 fireworks, followed by a traditional cone of *helado* (ice cream). Then it's off to the old city for the drinking, the drinking, and the drinking. Every weekday night of Semana Grande is like a Saturday any other time of the year, and that's saying something.

San Sebastián's **film festival,** which struts into town for the second half of September, is widely considered fourth in world importance after Cannes, Vienna, and Berlin. Celebrities gallivant, and the usual chichi factor is doubled. Also, in a town with some musical sophistication, the **jazz festival** near the end of July is no slouch.

PASAJES SAN JUAN

Driving by, you wouldn't dare stop at the coastal town just east of San Sebastián—Pasajes, or Pasaia in Euskera—it's an industrial mess. But a closer look reveals three neighborhoods: Puerto (the mess proper), San Pedro, and San Juan. The latter is a charming and fascinating little place, marked in history by a pair of Frenchmen, and dishes up some of the best seafood on the coast.

BASICS
Buses run frequently from San Sebastián to the water at San Pedro, 10½ km (6½ mi) to the east. To get from there to San Juan, just hop on the little skiff that shuttles back and forth (round-trip 70 ptas.).

WORTH SEEING
Call it a town, but **Pasajes San Juan** (Pasaia Donibane) is actually a street—Calle San Juan—and a tight little street at that, flanking one side of the important shipping inlet sidling in from the Atlantic. The only plaza, backed by a jumble of 18th- and 19th-century houses with colorful wooden balconies and varying altitudes and girths, serves as a small parking lot.

If you arrive in San Juan by car, you'll drive very slowly through the single lane, coming inches from the walls of houses on both sides. Villagers will calmly turn sideways into doorways to let you pass. Such is the pace of life. The traffic light changes at each end of the street every 10 minutes. You'll also pass beneath homes built over archways; in one of them, No. 65, Victor Hugo spent the winter of 1846.

Outside Txulotxo, on a wall across from the dock whence boats cross the 50 yards to San Pedro, is a pink-marble dedication to Lafayette on the site where he left for America to aid the revolutionaries. Like the rest of Pasajes, this area is covered with graffiti and propaganda supporting causes no less rebellious. Locals lean left here; no one seems to mind the posters or spray paint, so here they stay.

The tall, 17th-century parish church of **San Juan el Baptista** is farther down San Juan. If the church seems serious, even inscrutable, a few details may reveal its thoughts: the funky white statue above the neoclassical door is St. John himself. Above his head is a tennis ball, origin unknown, improbably lodged in the cracks of the facade. It appears to be a permanent fixture. Inside the church doors to the right is a gold coffin bearing an effigy of a saint, reportedly Santa Faustina, whose sliced throat was her father's doing; he disapproved of her Christian conversion. The Baroque altarpiece is nothing if not golden.

For a scenic trip *out* of town, take the mountain road toward Hondarribia, stopping at hilltop viewpoints with tremendous coastal vistas.

WHERE TO EAT
Victor Hugo notwithstanding, people generally don't come here to write; they mainly want to eat. Each of San Juan's handful of seafood restaurants has a dining room over the water. The best, and most expensive, is **Camara,** with a 3,745-pta. set menu; more reasonable is **Txulotxo,** where *gambas al ajillo* (garlic prawns) and grilled lobster (*langostinos a la plancha*) go for less than half that price.

Money From Home In Minutes.

If you're stuck for cash on your travels, don't panic. Millions of people trust Western Union to transfer money in minutes to 176 countries and over 78,000 locations worldwide. Our record of safety and reliability is second to none. For more information, call Western Union: USA 1-800-325-6000, Canada 1-800-235-0000. Wherever you are, you're never far from home.

www.westernunion.com

The fastest way to send money worldwide.

Find America
WITH A COMPASS

 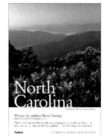 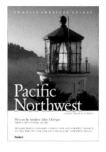

Written by local authors and illustrated throughout with spectacular color images from regional photographers, these companion guides reveal the character and culture of more than 35 of America's most spectacular destinations. Perfect for residents who want to explore their own backyards, and visitors who want an insider's perspective on the history, heritage, and all there is to see and do.

Fodor's COMPASS AMERICAN GUIDES

At bookstores everywhere.

HONDARRIBIA AND
THE FRENCH BORDER

Hondarribia is one of the most charming stops on the Basque coast and perhaps the most memorable of all those places not named San Sebastián. Still, the closest most travelers come is a momentary stop at Hondarribia's sibling border city of Irún. The big trains to France stop at Irún, and while it's not woefully unattractive, it's nothing to spend any time on. Hondarribia, on the other hand (the name was officially adopted in 1979, though the Spanish *Fuenterrabía* persists on a few maps), can make a delightful last—or first—impression of Spain and is well worth an overnight stay. The splendid old town sits on a hill, set off with a medieval noble tower and three small, minaret-like spires; there's also beach and a harbor from which you can cross the river to the French town of Hendaye, which has a longer beach, a nice marina, and, perhaps most important, crepes.

Populated since Roman times, Hondarribia was chartered by King Alfonso VIII in 1203. The town's obvious strategic importance—on the Bidasoa River, which separates it from France—assured the city a checkered history of military triumph and devastation. Today its small population (about 14,000) does quite well via fishing and tourism.

BASICS

VISITOR INFORMATION

Hondarribia shares a **tourist office** with Irún and the French town of Hendaye. At the base of Hondarribia's old town, near the circular fountain (Javier Ugarte 6, tel. 943/645458), it's open July–September, Monday–Saturday 10–8; October–June, weekdays 9–1:30 and 4–6:30, Saturday 10–2.

COMING AND GOING

To visit Hondarribia by **train,** you arrive in Irún. RENFE (tel. 943/616708) and EuskoTren (tel. 943/450131) shuttle frequently between here and San Sebastian.

A **taxi** (tel. 943/633303) from Irún's train station to Hondarribia costs only 600 ptas. The nearest **bus** stop is a five-minute walk from the train station: take Calle Hondarribia up from the station past Plaza San Miguel and Plaza Guipuzkoa. The green bus to Hondarribia (100 ptas.) runs every 15 minutes until 9 PM, making a stop at the airport just before town. Interurbanos buses (tel. 943/641301) connect Irún with San Sebastián for 200 ptas.

Iberia **planes** (airport tel. 902/400500) connect Hondarribia with Madrid and Barcelona.

From Hondarribia's small dock you can take the pleasant five-minute **boat** ride to Hendaye's marina for 200 ptas. In July and August, boats leave every 15 minutes between 10 AM and 1 AM; the rest of the year, they leave every half hour between 3 and 7.

WHERE TO SLEEP

If you get stuck in Irún, know that the train station faces two pensions, **Pension Bidasoa** (C. Estación 14, tel. 943/619913) and **Pension Los Fronterizos** (C. Estación 7, tel. 943/619205), neither of which takes credit cards. Otherwise, taxi to Hondarribia, where the fountain at Plaza San Cristóbal leads you to **Hostal Alvarez Quintero** (tel. 943/642299), open in summer only, with 6,500-pta. doubles with bath. Besides Artzu, listed below, Hondarribia has five gorgeous farmhouses, including **Maidanea** (Barrio Arkoll-Santiago, tel. 943/640855). None of the above take credit cards.

UNDER 6,500 PTAS. • Artzu. Artzu has been in the family since at least 1200 and occupies an isolated spot above the ocean, near the Guadalupe shrine. The views you get just driving up and down each day are simply phenomenal. The premises are calm, clean, and friendly; doubles range from 3,500 to 6,000 ptas. by season. *Barrio Montaña, tel. 943/640530. 6 rooms, 1 with bath. Cash only.*

Pension Txoko Goxua. Facing one of the medieval walls of the old town, Txoko Goxua feels like a small hotel, with clean, efficient rooms for 5,500–6,200 ptas., including private bath. The friendly owner fixes breakfast in the room downstairs, which also serves as a salon. *Murrua 22, tel. 943/644658. 6 rooms. Cash only.*

WHERE TO EAT

For a town its size, Hondarribia has a remarkable number of elegant seafood restaurants. Most stand shoulder to shoulder on Calle San Pedro, but a number hide on the parallel streets.

UNDER 2,000 PTAS. • Mamutzar. Mamutzar reflects the essence of the old town, evoked by the rays of sunshine that occasionally illuminate the dust of its narrow old street. To the strains of classical music, climb the old stairs to the second-floor dining room, its yellow walls intercepted by stone-frame windows, straw chairs, and wooden floorboards. A menú del día is a mere 1,300 ptas., and the food and service are reliably good. *Eguzki 8, tel. 943/645032. Closed Tues. No lunch in summer.*

UNDER 3,000 PTAS. • Hermandad de los Pescadores. The brotherhood under the blue awning serves some of the best seafood in town in a highly pared-down setting. The back room has private tables, but you can also sit at long, wooden communal tables in the main room for a soulful memory of elementary school. Salad and *sopa de pescado* cost 950 ptas. each (do indulge); lobster (*langostino*) is 1,500 ptas. *Zuloaga 12, tel. 943/642738.*

WORTH SEEING

THE OLD TOWN

Hondarribia's wonderful *casco antiguo* offers stone arches, ivied walls, gas lamps, cobblestone streets, coats of arms, daffodils, passageways: all the charm an old town can muster. From the tourist office walk uphill and take the first right onto San Kristobal, which leads into the memorable **Plaza Gipuzkoa.** Across the plaza, climb the old mossy stairs, making a left on **Calle San Nicolás,** a wonderful residential street where the homes have ornamental crested roofs and colored balconies. San Nicolás takes you through the central **Plaza de Armas,** which is dominated by the blank, stone-face stare of the former palace of King Carlos V, now the **Parador El Emperador.** Inside, this 10th-century pile is a romp, a real piece of old Spain. Though only guests can savor the perfect terrace views of the river and France, the bar to the right of the entrance allows you to live out your medieval fantasies. Starting near the bar, climb the railing that clings to the interior stone wall to a second-floor hideout: you'll find low leather seats in a deep windowed recess, true Middle Ages elegance. Huge emblazoned banners drop from a monumental domed and vaulted stone ceiling.

Hondarribia's noble skyline is principally the work of the 15th-century church of **Nuestra Señora del Manzano** (Our Lady of the Apple Tree), which begins Main Street, or Kale Naugusia. Main Street features yet more excellent examples of the traditional northern Basque balconies; at *kale's* end you'll find the **Puerta de Santa María**, the city gate bearing Hondarribia's coat of arms.

BARRIO PESCADOR

Downhill from the old town, the fountained Plaza San Cristóbal begins the marine neighborhood that is the seat of local life. After a plain beginning, **Calle San Pedro** moves to the right and gives way to a precious stretch of traditional fishermen's houses. Plane trees create a pedestrian corridor that passes through a row of homes with colored double balconies and peaked chevron roofs—an extended version of the houses on Calle San Nicolás but more practical, with fruit and flower stands and markets across the street. Most important, house after colorful house has a seafood restaurant on the ground floor. Who can resist the cottage charm of No. 23, Restaurante Zeria Jatetxea, with its stone walls and green, blue, and white trim? (Perhaps someone who's not in the mood to spend more than 3,000 ptas. for dinner.)

SANTUARIO DE GUADALUPE

Hondarribia's shrine to the Virgin of Guadalupe, who has been venerated since the 1500s, is a long way uphill (you can see the steeple from town), but from here the views of Hondarribia, Irún, Hendaye, the river, and the sea are wonderful. Follow the signs to Monte Jaizkibel. Under normal conditions you can see St. Jean de Luz (10 km/6 mi away) and Biarritz, far off on the coast (40 km/25 mi away). *Open daily 10–7.*

If you continue on the road past the shrine, you'll reach the highest viewpoint for miles around, identifiable by the fortlike watchtower. The tower gate is locked, so if you want to get even higher, you'll have to test your wall-climbing skills. A placard points out the sights visible from this height. Heading west, the road follows the ocean past miles of beautiful, sheep-speckled green countryside to Pasajes San Juan.

AFTER DARK

By all means have a drink at the bar in the wonderful **Parador El Emperador** (Plaza de Armas 14, tel. 943/645500).

HENDAYE

The French border is only 100 yards across the Bidasoa River. Take a boat from Hondarribia to Hendaye's sharp, white marina and stroll past the brightly colored apartments and beyond the dunes to the long stretch of sandy beach. Naturally, you'll want a crepe (all right, stick with *churros* if you must) from one of the beachside vendors while you observe the persistent play of surfers. The town itself is a mile inland, new and shiny but nothing of note.

OUTDOOR ACTIVITIES

In Hondarribia you can rent mountain bikes and get bike-trail maps from **Jolaski** (Gabarrai 26, tel. 943/61–6447) to use on the sea-cliff route starting at Mt. Jaizkibel, which makes for equally terrific hikes. Another bike route begins at the town of Andoain and follows an old train line (it's closer to San Sebastián, but you can't rent bikes there). You can also practice *parapente*, the thrilling, vertically oriented version of hang gliding, at Mt. Jaizkibel; Jolaski arranges this and other adventure sports as well.

In Irún, **Club Hípico Jaizubia** (Hiribidea 1, tel. 943/619015) leads horseback-riding trips. For scuba diving talk to **Scuba Du** (Paseo Itsasargi 18, tel. 943/642353), in Hondarribia.

NEAR HONDARRIBIA

France? *Pourquoi pas?* Over the border in Le Pays Basque, things don't change as much as you might expect; Basque signs share space with their French equivalents, pesetas are accepted everywhere, and the architecture is remarkably similar. In fact, red-and-white Basque designs reach their apotheosis in the pretty beach and fishing town of **St. Jean de Luz. Biarritz** is a beach resort (though its beach consists of tiny pebbles) known for surfing, as is **Anglet,** to the north.

A few miles inland, the northern edge of the Basque Country is marked by the city of **Bayonne,** birthplace of the bayonet. It charms with an old French Gothic cathedral; and it, too, has an attractive array of riverside Basque homes.

VITORIA

Vitoria is said to have the highest standard of living in Spain and has served as a model of urban design for several other European cities. Capital of the Basque Country and the second-largest Basque city after Bilbao (with a population of nearly 300,000), it also has the most per-capita green space in Spain and the third-highest such ratio in Europe. The city smiles on public art, most obviously the sculptures *The Walker,* in the Plaza del Aria off Calle Eduardo Dato, and *Seated Bullfighter,* on a bench on Eduardo Dato.

Founded by Navarran king Sancho el Sabio (the Wise) in 1181 as a stronghold against Castile, Vitoria was built largely of gray stone rather than sandstone; so its oldest streets and squares retain a uniquely Vitorian take on the Spanish Middle Ages. The original site was a hamlet called Gasteiz, which remains the city's Basque name. The four prominent steeples on the skyline reflect this well-preserved old town, the best in the Basque Country's major cities.

You can come to Vitoria to uncover its tidy charms, but forget all that when its August fiesta breaks out. The first moments of this yearly party are as frenetic and wildly intense as fun things come.

BASICS

VISITOR INFORMATION

The excellent **regional tourist office** (Parque de la Florida, tel. 945/131321), open weekdays 9–1:30 and 3–7 and weekends 9–1 and 3–7, has information on the entire Basque Country. The **municipal**

tourist office couldn't be better situated (C. Eduardo Dato 11, across from McDonald's, tel. 945/161598) and is generously open Monday through Saturday 10–7 and Sunday 11–2.

CYBERSPACE
Nirv@ana NetCenter (Manuel Iradier 11, tel. 945/154043), a block from the train station, is open Monday through Saturday 10:30–3:30 and 5–10:30, Sunday 5–10:30. The reasonable rate of 400 ptas. an hour is actually reduced in the morning.

MAIL
The main **post office** (Postas 9, tel. 945/140996), near the Plaza de la Virgen Blanca, is open weekdays 8:30–8:30 and Saturday 9:30–2.

CURRENCY EXCHANGE
The main banks, which offer the best exchange rates, are clustered on **Calle Eduardo Dato.**

EMERGENCIES
Hospital General de Santiago (Olaguibel s/n, tel. 945/007600) is a few blocks east of the Plaza de España.

Take a cab to the municipal **police station** (Aguirrelanda 9, tel. 945/161405), as it's outside the city center.

ENGLISH-LANGUAGE BOOKSTORES
Axular (tel. 945/132203) is a fine bookshop with a decent selection of English-language classics for university students. **El Corte Inglés** (tel. 945/266333), at the corner of Paz and Independencia a few blocks east of Dato, has a small selection.

LAUNDRY
Tintoreria 5 A Sec (Independencia 20, tel. 945/282430) charges 1,000 ptas. per load to wash and dry.

COMING AND GOING
Blessed be a city whose train station sits at the base of its main street. Exit RENFE onto Calle Eduardo Dato, the elegant pedestrian commercial avenue that shoots up four clean, stylish blocks to the Plaza de España, gateway to the old town.

BY PLANE
Aeropuerto Vitoria-Foronda (tel. 945/163511; 945/163639 for Iberia Airlines) is 9 km, or 6 mi, outside the city. A taxi from there to town costs about 2,000 ptas.

BY TRAIN
RENFE (Plaza Estación, tel. 945/230202) destinations include **San Sebastián** (1 hr, 40 min; 1,700 ptas.), **Pamplona** (1 hr, 595 ptas. for local train), **Madrid** (4 hrs, 4,200 ptas.), **Burgos** (1½ hrs, 1,900 ptas.), **Oviedo** (7½ hrs, 3,900 ptas.), **Barcelona** (6½ hrs, 4,700 ptas.), and **Zaragoza** (3 hrs, 2,500 ptas.). If you're Bilbao-bound, it's cheaper and faster to take a bus.

BY BUS
From the bus station (Herrán 50, tel. 945/258400) it's a 10-minute walk to the old town. The helpful information desk here will hold your luggage. Destinations vary by company: **Continental Auto** runs to Logroño (take the local bus if you'd rather stop in Laguardia; 1 hr, 805 ptas.), Burgos (90 mins, 920 ptas.), San Sebastián (90 mins, 935 ptas.), and Madrid (5 hrs, 2,870 ptas.). **ALSA** (tel. 945/255509) heads to Pamplona (90 mins, 890 ptas.), Zaragoza (3 hrs, 2,020 ptas.), and **Barcelona** (7 hrs, 4,680 ptas.). La Unión (tel. 945/264626) shoots to **Bilbao** in one hour flat (675 ptas.).

GETTING AROUND
For a **taxi** call 945/273500.

WHERE TO SLEEP

Finding a room is relatively easy outside July and August. If you're coming from the train station, note that the old Hostal Francia, though it retains an attention-getting sign on Eduardo Dato, is defunct; and Pension Zurine, despite another identifiable sign, is better left alone.

Araba 2. There are only four rooms here, and only one has a private bath, but they all cost 5,000 ptas. and are all worth fighting for. The joint is spotless (including the shared bathroom), the wooden floors sparkle, and the owner attends to your needs. You're one block off Eduardo Dato and two blocks from the RENFE station, but drivers can also take advantage of private parking. *C. Florida 25, tel. 945/ 232588. 4 rooms. Cash only.*

Hostal Florida. Rooms here are clean, but it's time for a renovation—the furnishings are antiquated, even if regally so. What Florida does best is professionalism, including a properly manned reception desk. Rooms have little sofas, and half have private baths; doubles cost 4,650 or 5,500 ptas. accordingly. From the train station, take your first right off Eduardo Dato and walk a few blocks down. *Manuel Iradier 33, tel. 945/260675. 15 rooms.*

Hotel Dato. If high-strung gaudiness gets to you, put on your running shoes—Dato was designed for another era. Plastic flowers, a profusion of mirrors and columns, and a cacophony of floral prints mingle beneath the candelabra and—oh, yes—neon. It all seems a ruse to distract from the fact that this is actually an *hostal*, not a hotel. Still, you get a big private bathroom and the best possible location for 5,500 ptas. *Eduardo Dato 28, tel. 945/147230, fax 945/232320. 14 rooms.*

Hotel Desiderio. Here you're guaranteed clean rooms for 5,000 ptas., good-size bathrooms, and fair treatment. Management also runs an older *hostal* on a side street, with doubles for 3,500 ptas. *Colegio San Prudencio 2, tel. 945/251700. 21 rooms.*

Hostal La Paz. With 40 rooms, La Paz is a standby. The small, dormlike chambers are packed with furniture, and most have refrigerators, which you can stock with junk food from the 24-hour reception desk. It seems a touch more costly than it should be (6,000 ptas. per double), but the ship is run tight, and there's a Corte Inglés across the street. *La Paz 3, tel. 945/139696, fax 945/146736.*

WHERE TO EAT

Many of the cafés around the Plaza de España are worth relaxing in, including **Las Tres B.B.B.** (the one with the yellow lamps in the window). Around the Plaza de la Virgen Blanca, **Cafetería Virgen Blanca** has a good atmosphere for *raciones* and *pinchos*. Any outdoor café in the **Parque de la Florida** is the perfect place to enjoy a warm day.

UNDER 1,500 PTAS. • Taberna Al Tulipán de Oro. Next door to the venerable El Portalón (*see below*) is this much humbler but still tasteful and authentic tavern. The small dining room is a cozy mix of brick, stone, and wood. Wonderful smells of Alava meats linger about. House dishes include *chichiquis* (950 ptas.), a chorizo-like pork dish, and for the brave fork, *asadurilla* (900 ptas.), a mixture of pork innards in a tomato sauce. At the bar, locals tackle chorizo *al infierno* flambé, served on a pig-shape terra-cotta dish. *C. Correría 157, tel. 945/142023.*

UNDER 2,000 PTAS. • Hirurak. Run by three stylish thirtysomething women (the Basque name means *Las Tres*), Hirurak is good for a filling, affordable lunch with a friendly, young crowd and soft music in a simple yellow dining room. Homemade desserts are available à la carte. *Cucherilla 26, tel. 945/288147. Closed Mon.*

Museo del Organo. Town sophisticates know about the lithe salad buffet in the suave, green-painted setting of this vegetarian lunch place. The onetime piano shop on this property was called the Organ Museum, so the name stuck, but now the tunes come from Joni Mitchell CDs. Arrive early for the 1,300-pta. lunch or be part of the masses waiting to chow. After salad and vegetable soup, main dishes include *gratinado de berenjas y calabacines* (eggplant and zucchini au gratin), followed by homemade desserts. *C. Manuel Iradier 80, tel. 945/264048. Closed Sun. No dinner.*

SPLURGE • El Portalón. The last word in Vitoria dining is the medieval poem called El Portalón. Even if you're not comfortable with the prices (the menú del día is 2,950 ptas.), you owe yourself a peek inside. Think of it as the city's most important museum—cloaked in dark wood from three-story head to toe, with stone touches, ancient furniture, and stained-glass windows, it's a living piece of pure 15th-century architecture. The restaurant transports you back those 600 years while maintaining an unobstreperous degree of decorum: the linen is monogrammed; the silverware is actually silver. Off the stairs on the third floor is a wonderful chapel from the original house, which was run as an inn. If you're going all the way, try the *lomo de cebón asado en su jugo con puré de manzanas* (filet mignon with apple puree). Have the Ramonísimo for dessert and you'll smile all the way home. *C. Correría 151, tel. 945/ 142755. Closed Sun., Aug. 10–31, and Dec. 23–Jan. 5.*

WORTH SEEING

Completed as we now see it in 1256, Vitoria's medieval **old town** is the best preserved of any in the Basque Country's metropolitan giants. Each of its numerous towers, palaces, and churches has a story to tell. Most of the six principal streets, which curve gracefully in parallel to form the shape of an almond, are named after the workshops and corresponding guilds that formed on each one in the early Middle Ages: Herrería (Blacksmith), Zapatería (Cobbler), Correría (Lacemaker), Cuchillería (Knifemaker), and Pintorería (Painter). Calle Nueva Dentro was the Judería, or Jewish quarter.

Calle Cuchillería is hip, with skateboarders, shops, and youthful boutiques. Calle Correría, which you can take from the top of Plaza Virgen Blanca, is a narrow street of colorful facades and flowered balconies lined by jewelry and antiques stores such as **Unicornio** (No. 13) and bric-a-brac shops such as **Frida Kahlo** (No. 30).

At the back end of Correría, behind the cathedral of Santa María, is the most attractive stretch of Vitoria's old town, highlighted by El Portalón (*see* Where to Eat, *above*). These houses have faded brick-and-blackwood facades and crested roofs supported by beams, trademarks of 15th-century mercantile architecture.

The residential arched passage known as **Los Aquillos,** behind the Plaza de España, was designed as a way to expand from the old city, which is, of course, on a hill. The **Plaza de España** (1791), beneath it, which now holds the Casa Consistorial (city hall), serves as the meeting point between old and new. But if Vitoria has a heart, it's the **Plaza de la Virgen Blanca,** anchored by a flashy monument to the Battle of Vitoria that commemorates the duke of Wellington's defeat of Napoléon's army in 1813. The 14th-century Gothic church of **San Miguel** presides over the large, triangular square; outside, in a jasper niche between the two arches that front the church's terrific stone facade, is the city's patron saint, the Virgen Blanca. The White Virgin smiles graciously with babe, even as she is shielded from the world by mistreated Plexiglas.

The **Plaza de los Fueros,** just southeast of Plaza de España, has a small handball *frontón* and a sculpture by the Basque sculptor Eduardo Chillida.

MUSEO DE NAPIES (FOURNIER PLAYING CARD MUSEUM)

Believe it or not, Vitoria's main attraction is a museum full of playing cards. And, believe it or not, it's fabulous. The three floors of the 1525 Palacio de Bendaría allow a chronological walk through the collection around an arcaded courtyard. In 1868 Don Heraclio Fournier founded a playing-card factory, started amassing cards, and eventually found himself with 15,000 sets, the largest and finest such collection in the world. As you examine room after room of hand-painted cards, the distinction between artwork and game piece quickly gets scrambled. The oldest sets date from the 12th century, making them older than the building, and the story parallels the history of printing. The most unusual and finely painted sets come from India and Japan (the Indian cards are round), as well as the rooms dedicated to tarot. One German set features musical bars that can be combined to form hundreds of different waltzes. By the time you reach the 20th-century rooms, contemporary designs have been debunked as utterly unoriginal. You'll never look at playing cards the same way again. *C. Cuchillería 54, tel. 945/ 255555. Free. Open Tues.–Fri. 10–2 and 4–6:30, Sat. 10–2, Sun. 11–2.*

MUSEO ARQUEOLÓGICO

At the end of Cuchillería you'll find the Museum of Archaeology, housed in the 16th-century Casa Armera de los Gobeo. It's too bad the placards aren't in English (though an English pamphlet is of some assistance) because the stories these artifacts—from prehistory through the Middle Ages—tell about the city and the province of Alava are fascinating. There's a garden at the Cuchillería entrance. *C. Correría 116, tel. 945/181922. Free. Open Tues.–Fri. 10–2 and 4–6:30, Sun. 11–2.*

CATEDRAL DE SANTA MARÍA

Vitoria's 13th- to 16th-century cathedral of St. Mary, renowned for the exquisitely sculpted Gothic doorway on its western facade, might be better described as a 13th- to 21st-century project. It's currently closed for restoration, and due to imploding arches and a floor set at a tricky incline, the reopening is set for 2008—no kidding.

CASA DEL CORDÓN

This 15th-century structure with a 13th-century tower is identifiable by the carved-stone *cordón* (rope) decorating one of the pointed arches of the facade. Have a look inside at one of its changing displays of art, artifacts, or whatever. *C. Cuchillería 24, tel. 945/259673. Free. Open weekdays 6:30 PM–9 PM, Sun. 12–2 and 6:30–9.*

PARQUE DE LA FLORIDA

Vitoria's main park is wonderful in summer, with ducks and trees and whatnot. The New Cathedral is humbly tucked in the side park to the west, beside the Basque parliament. Walking away from the city along Paseo de la Senda (toward the train station), you'll pass the Palacio Zulueta and, passing under the railway bridge, the Ajurianea, home of the president of the Lehendakari (Basque parliament). Paseo Fray Francisco de Vitoria leads past the Museum of Fine Arts and on to the Parque de El Prado. *Southwest of Plaza de la Virgen Blanca.*

MUSEO DE BELLAS ARTES

Not to be outdone by its Basque brethren, Vitoria's Museum of Fine Arts, housed in the elegant Palacio Agustín, has been undergoing a major renovation and is set to reopen in January 2001. The permanent collection focuses on contemporary Spanish painting but also includes works by El Greco, Picasso, and Miró. *Paseo de Fray Francisco 8, tel. 945/181918. Admission free. Open Tues.–Fri. 10–2 and 4–6:30, Sat. 10–2, Sun. 11–2.*

FIESTA • The kickoff to Vitoria's annual fiesta may be the most intense five minutes you will ever experience. It makes the Times Square New Year's countdown—even Madrid's Puerta del Sol New Year's champagne shower—seem almost sad. The date is August 5, Día de la Virgen Blanca. Everyone buys a cigar and a champagne bottle, or two or three, and by 5 PM the Plaza de la Virgen Blanca is all but unrecognizable for all the humanity—except for its central monument, which has been scaled by about 10 brave people.

At precisely 6 PM, a life-size doll named Celedón—a cousin, it would seem, of Mary Poppins—floats magically out of the tower of San Miguel Church on an umbrella and makes a very slow (about five minutes) descent across the plaza on a cable into a first-floor doorway. The descent would be magical enough if it happened in silence, but instead it happens in a serious hail of champagne corks and champagne (wear old clothes), with people screaming and hugging strangers to chants of "Ce-le-*dón,* Ce-le-*dón.*" It is nothing short of madness.

Out of the doorway through which the effigy has disappeared emerges the real life Celedón, looking very much like the apparition that just ferried over the plaza. He makes his way on the ground this time, mobbed and drenched by all, in a kind of walking stage dive back across the plaza to the church, to declare the fiesta officially underway.

Celedón's descent marks not only the start of Semana Grande in Vitoria, which lasts till 1 PM August 9, but the beginning of fiesta season in the Basque Country at large. San Sebastián's Semana Grande begins the weekend after Vitoria's, followed by Bilbao's chaos from August 19 to 27.

AFTER DARK

The old town will give you more than enough material to party with. All you really need to know for a good, long night is that Cuchillería and Pintorería are two streets of required perambulation. But here's the whole story: Things begin early—at, say, 11 or midnight—along the Cuesta de San Vicente, which climbs to Cuchillería from behind Plaza de España. Orient yourself along the Cuesta (on weekends crowds give it away) at **Toloña,** which plays commercial Latin pop.

After this early period—at, say, 1 AM—the real rush begins up the three consecutive streets of Cuchillería, Pintorería, and Nueva Dentro. The *cantónes* (roughly, alleys) between these streets also sway with bodies. The first bar on the left side of Cuchillería, informally called **Bar Rojo** because of its red color, makes a logical first stop. (Most bars have no names or numbered addresses. To a first-timer this neighborhood can seem limitless and mazelike; it's easy to get turned around at first in the curving streets.) A few doors down, at **El 7,** ask for a *copa de Rioja Alaves,* a glass of fancy Basque wine that will run you all of 125 ptas. Nearly all bars in the old town serve sandwiches (usually in the back), but you need not be tipsy to appreciate the selection and high quality of the eats at El 7.

NO LAUGHING MATTER

To see one complication of the "Basque problem" yourself, attend one of the now-ritual Friday-night vigils that take place in Vitoria's Plaza de la Virgen Blanca at 8:00. Citing a Spanish law that calls for the detention of prisoners near their home cities, protestors hold signs calling for the return of jailed Basques—many imprisoned for their ties to the terrorist group ETA—from other points in Spain and France.

Vitoria's rebellious, punk-aesthetic bars are easily recognizable once you're inside. Decor often consists in part of printed pro-ETA propaganda. The thrust is not support for ETA, however, but for the movement to bring Basque prisoners to jails closer to home. Mug-style photos feature prisoners held elsewhere; the phrase to look for, usually posted over an arrowed map of Euskadi, is EUSKAL PRESOAK EUSKAL HERRIA (Basque Prisoners to the Basque Country). These bars can give you a rush of guilty energy, as though you're doing something corrupt just by being there, but they serve some of the cheapest drinks in town.

On the first left turn off Cuchillería, called Cantón de San Francisco Javier, head for the black eagle, that symbol of trouble, hanging in front of the **Herrikoia Taberna.** The name translates into Spanish as Bar del Pueblo—the People's Bar—and serves as hangout for the revolutionary political party EH (Euskal Herria), so here's where you can pick up your stickers, pins, T-shirts, and other insurgent propaganda. There's another such *taberna* with the same name farther along, at Cuchillería 78.

If you can stumble all the way to the end of Cuchillería (stopping off, of course, at tiny **Chimbo** on the left, at No. 57), you've made it to **La Taberna del Tuerto** (C. Correría 151). Designed like the inside of a pirate ship, Tuerto (One-Eye) flies the Jolly Roger and swings like a galley bar: you'll find swords and skulls in addition to the *futbolín* and pool table.

Along Pintorería, look for the blue door and stop at **Extitxu** (No. 3, the second bar on the left) for reliably good music of various kinds. **Four Roses,** on Cantón Santana, between Pintorería and Cuchillería, is currently popular.

Calle Zapatería, on the west side of the old town, is the heavy-metal zone.

After hours, outside the old town, **Odile** (C. Manuel Iradier 58) has a loose crowd dancing to acid jazz and funk. The major *discotecas* are **Maná** (commercial Latin pop), at Calle Florida 39, and **Santa Fé** (techno), on Manuel Iradier just west of Eduardo Dato.

The coolest 60 kids in Vitoria are invariably in **Katanga Factoría Cultural,** a former meat factory converted into a cultural center, recording studio, and rock school (Artapadura 3, tel. 945/12–0113). The large bar and dance hall still show off shiny yellow hooks. Teachers gather for jam sessions Friday at 10:30 PM (free), and DJs usually spin on Saturday. The factory is a few miles outside the old town, and you'll need a cab to find it, but on a good night (Saturday is your best bet), it has an energy few alternative scenes in Spain can match.

OUTDOOR ACTIVITIES

For biking, hiking, rappelling, and other adventures in and around Vitoria and Alava province, contact **Ludoland** (Bekolarra 4, tel. 945/249100). For airborne thrills call **Escuela Alavesa de Parapente** (Cercas Bajas 5, tel. 945/384194).

LAGUARDIA AND THE RIOJA ALAVESA

The wine denomination of La Rioja heads east from the Cantabrian mountains, so while most of it is covered in Chapter 15, it also includes a chunk of the Basque Country—the Rioja Alavesa (that is, relating to the Basque province of Alava). Rioja's red wines are among the best in the world and easily some of the best values in fine wine. The heart of the Rioja Alavesa is the ancient town of Laguardia, a fantastic stopover where you can tour some amazing *bodegas* (wineries) and explore the medieval quarter amid a landscape full of prehistoric tombs and ruins.

Crossing the Sierra de Cantabria south of Vitoria, you enter the dry, southern Mediterranean climate so friendly to the Tempranillo grape. There's nothing subtle about this change; from the Herrera mountain pass, the road quickly plunges almost 5,000 ft to the wine-growing flatlands. Just before descending, you can survey this scene from the impressive gray peaks of the "Rioja Balcony"—looking down at Laguardia, Logroño, Haro, and all the Rioja wine towns.

BASICS

Laguardia's **tourist office** (Sancho Abarca, tel. 941/600845) is at the Puerta de Carnicerías gate into town, open weekdays 10–2 and 4–6:30 and Saturday 10–2, plus Sunday 10–2 in summer.

COMING AND GOING

Laguardia is 10 minutes from Logroño and 15 minutes from Haro, La Rioja's largest cities (*see* Chapter 15). By **car** from Vitoria take the lovely ride down N232 past Peñacerrada. By **bus** take the local toward Logroño, a roughly one-hour trip from Vitoria.

WHERE TO SLEEP

UNDER 5,500 PTAS. • For an intimate Laguardia stay, **Larretxori** (Portal de Páganos, tel. 941/600763) is a large private house with three comfortable en-suite doubles for 5,500 ptas. each. Bring cash.

UNDER 7,500 PTAS. • **Hotel Pachico.** Across from the old town walls near Laguardia's tourist office, these double rooms come with cute beds and good baths for 7,000 ptas. Rooms on the upper floors have balconies with wide views of the vineyards stretching to the Sierra de Cantabria in Navarre. The restaurant downstairs serves breakfast. *Sancho Abarco 20, tel. 941/600009. 14 rooms.*

WORTH SEEING

BODEGAS

If you've never seen a winery before, you'll find the damp, labyrinthine cellars and the sight of hundreds of barrels of aging wine an unforgettable experience. You can hit at least two bodegas in a day, more if you get really drunk. Pick up a complete list at the tourist office or just pop into random bodegas, following the well-marked signs along the road (A3218) that runs past Laguardia and throughout La Rioja.

A visit will usually include a sampling of the bodega's wines and small tapas. Most bodegas sell their wines by the case or in boxes of three or six; a broad price average would be 1,000 ptas. per bottle (yep, great value). Tours are usually available Tuesday through Friday on the hour from 11 to 2, weekends at noon and 1.

Bodegas Heredad Ugarte. A tour of this champion winery guides you through 3 km (2 mi) of underground passageways, where damp niches are actually rented to individuals for the storage of bottles. The temperature is kept at a consistent 16°C (60 °F), and light is minimal so the wines can age properly. Three floors of half-million-liter stainless-steel tanks ferment the grapes before they are stored for aging in oak barrels. Heredad Ugarte shows off 4,000 such *barricas,* each good for about 300 bottles and many inscribed with their future owners' names (one is for Julio Iglesias). At tour's end you taste three wines and chase them with chorizo. All in all, it's a wonderful way to spend 950 ptas. *Carretera N232, Km 61, tel. 945/278833.*

After Heredad Ugarte, two of the very best stops are **Bodegas Palacio** (San Lazaro 1, tel. 941/600057) and **Bodegas Campillo** (Carretera Logroño s/n, tel. 941/600826).

LAGUARDIA

Founded in the 900s by Navarran monarchs as a fortification for protection from the Moors (you can still see the *guard* in its name), Laguardia enjoyed *fueros* (local rights) from 1164.

Just inside the city wall from the tourist office stands the 16th-century former ayuntamiento (town hall), giving way to Calle Santa Engracia, one of the town's three main streets. Note the family coats-of-arms on houses as you walk around. Two churches that were once forts bookend the town at each end of Calle Mayor.

The church of **Santa María de los Reyes** boasts the only surviving polychrome portal in Spain, a late 14th-century door. It's amazing what a little color does. The 14th-century **Casa de la Primicia**, in the middle of Calle de Paganos, is the town's oldest house.

La Vinoteca (Plaza Mayor 1, tel. 941/121213) is a wonderful wine shop with an expert staff eager to help you find the right bottle. They also sell vacuum-packed *complimentos* such as cheese and cured meat.

In Laguardia itself, it can be interesting to see a small bodega, where the grapes are pressed by foot and the machinery is modest. Ángel, the proprietor of **Bodegas Casa-Juan** (Sancho Abarca 22, tel. 941/121241) gives tours, and proffers tastings in a room full of African art collected from a decade of wine work on that continent.

The cellars are part of an incredible underground network of *cuevas* (caves) that exist like a distinct and intricate city beneath Laguardia. Ask the tourist office for a map of this amazing labyrinth, even though, unfortunately, the cellars cannot be visited and are not actually connected; most every house in town once had its own winding cellar.

Should the landscape fascinate you, visit **Labastida**, after Laguardia the finest fortified town in the Rioja Alavesa. The church with the fortlike tower above town has views of the entire Ebro basin. Stay at the comfortable rural inn Zurinea (El Otero, tel. 608/311861).

LA HOYA

A 20-minute walk from Laguardia are the complete ruins of a town that was inhabited from the Bronze Age to the Iron Age (1200–250 BC). Besides the site itself, you can visit a **museum** with displays of artifacts, explications of the town's history, and a life-size replica of one of the old-time dwellings. *Tel 941/121122. Free. Open May.–mid-Oct., weekdays 11–2 and 4–8, Sat. 11–4, Sun. 10–2; mid-Oct.–Apr., Tues.–Sat. 10–4, Sun. 10–2.*

DOLMENS

People have lived and died in the mountainous regions of southern Alava for eons, which means the grounds can be creepy at night. Visit dolmens in the daytime. Spread across the landscape—there are four within the immediate vicinity of Laguardia, and you can reach them by hiking—are ruins of megalithic tombs. Called dolmens in English and Spanish, they consist of what look like huge stone tables—a large slab set atop two or more upright ones. Signs are posted on the A3218 road.

CANTABRIA AND ASTURIAS

BY MICHAEL DE ZAYAS

I f Asturias and Cantabria merged into one body, the result could easily claim to be the most beautiful region in Spain. As it is, pocket-size Cantabria has only the timidity of the very small to keep it from such boasting. Asturias, with almost a third of its land designated park or preserve, might be the country's top retreat for nature lovers. Yet with the exception of Cantabria's capital, Santander, both Autonomous Communities remain largely out of the tourist loop. The landscape offers a contrast between the soaring Cantabrian mountains and the wide, deeply green spaces that roll past colorful fishing towns to the sea.

The name *Cantabria* has a Celtic root meaning "people of the mountain." Called Santander until 1982, the province is sandwiched between the Basque Country, to the east, and Asturias, to the west, on the Bay of Biscay. The population (just over 500,000) is heavily concentrated near the coast, so the vast green expanses of the interior, speckled with tiny hamlets, contain far more cows than humans. The traditional men's costume—a common sight outside the capital—includes the beret.

West of Cantabria lies the Principality of Asturias. The only land west of *here* is far-flung Galicia, and in western Asturias it can be hard to tell the two places apart. The bagpipe, or *gaita*, is more popular than the Spanish guitar, and traditional stilted granaries called *horreos* dot the countryside. The compact urban triangle of Oviedo, Avilés, and Gijón holds most of the region's million-plus population, but mountains cover four-fifths of the Asturian landscape. The heights kept the Moors out of Asturias when the rest of Spain was, to varying degrees, under their thumb; and have always kept Asturias snow-bound for much of each winter. Spring may be the best time to discover the region's incredible natural beauty; even in the celebrated Picos de Europa range, which swarms with activity in summer, human presence is minimal at this time of year. And foreigners almost never venture into Asturias's other parks and preserves.

CANTABRIA

Cantabria has some of the most beautiful postcards in Spain—and the scenery only improves outside the train station. From picturesque coastal towns like San Vicente de la Barquera to the rural hamlets of the prairied countryside to the artistic treasures of medieval Santillana del Mar and the prehistoric caves of Ponte Viesgo and Altamira, Cantabria is a pleasant surprise.

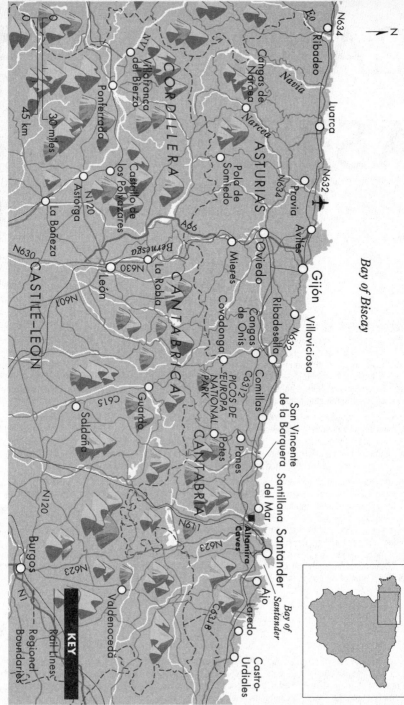

CANTABRIA AND ASTURIAS

N

Bay of Biscay

Ría

Ribadeo
N634
Luarca
N632
Navia
Cangas de Narcea
Narcea
Pravia
Avilés
ASTURIAS
N634
Pola de Someido
A66
Oviedo
Mieres
Gijón
Villaviciosa
N632
Ribadesella
Cangas de Onís
Covadonga
Comillas
PICOS DE EUROPA NATIONAL PARK
C6312
San Vincente de la Barquera
Santillana del Mar

COR DILLERA

Villafranca del Bierzo
NVI
Ponferrada
Castrillo de los Polvazares
Astorga
N120
La Bañeza
N630
N630
León
La Robla
Bernesga
CANTABRICA
N601
CASTILE-LEÓN

Saldaña
C615
Guarda
CANTABRIA
Potes
Panes
Altamira Caves
Santander
Bay of Santander
Ajo
Laredo
Castro-Urdiales
C6318
N611
N623
Valdenoceda
N120
Burgos
N623
N1

45 km
30 miles
30 km

If you've longed for quiet meadows and fairy-tale bridges over gentle streams, you'll explore this region adoringly, filling your journal with the word *green*. Countless towns all but frolic in lush meadows and hills, which eventually give way to long, sandy tracts of beach or the glacial forms of the Picos de Europa Mountains. And no drive within Cantabria takes more than two hours.

Santander is your base for big-city entertainment and long nights of fun, but just a few minutes outside Cantabria's capital, things slow down substantially. The land is still used primarily for crops and livestock. You're sure to run into shepherds, and headlines in a local newspaper might complain of wolf attacks on area cows.

SAN VICENTE DE LA BARQUERA

San Vicente is one of those places that makes you say, "Before I die, I want to go *there*" when you see a picture of it in some obscure book. An ideal tour of northern Spain might well begin with this fishing village, as few places give a more poetic first impression. Even at the bus station you're surrounded by beauty, right on the waterfront avenue. The harbor is half sand, around which maneuver tiny red, green, and blue fishing boats; inland, across two multiarch bridges, rowboats lodge on green shoals midriver. Backed by the Picos de Europa—draped in white half the year—a medieval fortress and a brusque, harmonious church rise on a hill overlooking the town toward the sea.

It can be tempting to drive slowly past the town without stopping—just long enough to affirm its existence, allow its image to form and linger in the mind, and continue on, keeping the ideal intact. Don't. Apartments are going up—you can't blame people for wanting the view—and setting a precedent that's sure to ruin this place in 15 years. Visit little San Vicente while it can still tear at your heart.

BASICS
You can see everything in two hours, easy. Plaza José Antonio is the central square, set in the middle of Avenida de Miramar, which begins at the longer bridge near the bus depot. The avenue follows the water before turning inland, at which point it becomes Avenida Generalísimo. The **tourist office** (Generalísimo 20, tel. 942/710797) is open July–September, daily 10–1:30 and 5–8, and only sporadically the rest of the year. From there turn left a few yards down, just before the second (smaller) bridge and walk uphill on Calle Alta to find the medieval quarter and **police station.**

CYBER SPACE • Magnetron (Padre Ángel 9, tel. 942/710251) is your only choice, so you're in no position to complain about the high prices (800 ptas. for half an hour, 1,500 ptas. for an hour) or limited hours (daily 10–1:30 and 4:30–8).

COMING AND GOING
Arriving by car on N634 will give you the most splendid impression. For the Picos de Europa towns of **Panes, Potes,** and **Fuente Dé, Autobuses Palomera** (tel. 942/880611) makes two trips daily. **ALSA** (tel. 942/221685) heads to the Asturian cities of **Ribadesella, Arriondas** (change here for Asturian Picos de Europa towns like Covadonga), and **Oviedo,** as well as Santander, Bilbao, and France. **La Cantabrica** (tel. 942/720822) serves **Santander, Comillas,** and **Santillana del Mar** plus **Torrelavega,** where you can catch RENFE trains.

FEVE trains (tel. 942/211687) drop you off with a reasonably scenic 20-minute walk into town. Leaving the train station, turn left; when you reach the big bridge, you'll see the small, brick bus depot on your left—in which there's a small tourist office during the summer months.

WHERE TO SLEEP
For the best experience sleep a wee bit outside the urban center to remind yourself of the mountain, prairie, and maritime landscapes around you. The town does have clean and happy rooms, however; so you can't go wrong.

UNDER 6,000 PTAS. • Hostal La Barquera. Attached to a 15th-century hermitage on the water along the edge of town, this place has views of everything: castle, town, bridges. Fishing boats returning from the sea pass by as you lounge beneath the peaceful waterside pergola. At 5,000 ptas. (for a double with bath), it's highly recommended. *Paseo de la Barquera, tel. 942/710075.*

Pensión Liébana. One of several decent pensions in the town's core that rent double rooms for 3,500–5,500 ptas., Liébana pleases with clean rooms in a quaint house behind the main square. There's a restaurant on site. *Ronda 2, tel. 942/710211. Cash only.*

Posada Punta Liñera. It's hard not to get carried away up here. This modern inn is uphill from town, facing the ocean, but you may never want to head back down once you see these vistas of the sea and San Vicente. The view includes centuries-old stone ruins standing in green fields where horses and dogs play above the crashing sea; you'll take great walks. The price doesn't even matter (literally; brand-new doubles run 3,500–5,350 ptas.). Call from the bus or train station, and the owners might pick you up. Reserve in advance for summer stays, and know that August fills up a year in advance. *Barrio Boria 12, tel. 942/711535. Cash only.*

El Molino de Bonaco. You'll be in paradise here if (a) you want to just get away and rent your own little house in the middle of nowhere, 8 wooded km (5 mi) inland from town, or (b) you're traveling in a group of three or four and just want some quiet and a little back-stream fishing or rowing. Three rustic but fully equipped cottages (10,000–12,000 ptas. for two people, 12,000–15,000 ptas. for four), one a former mill with intact innards, sit near each other on this wonderful plot of land. If you're not driving, know that two FEVE trains a day stop right beside the house; request to stop at El Bercenal. *El Bercenal, tel. 942/746270. 3 cottages. Cash only.*

WHERE TO EAT

The local culinary masterpiece is *sorroputún,* a tuna stew to which thin slices of bread are added just before it's served. This might also be your day for oysters; they're cultivated in the *ría* (estuary) around the corner.

UNDER 2,000 PTAS. • Augusto II. There are two Augusto restaurants on parallel streets; the one on Calle Ronda offers four *menús del día.* Fresh seafood is the way to go. The Mercado branch has a more sophisticated, slightly more expensive selection. *C. Ronda 9 and C. Mercado 1, tel. 942/712040.*

Pizzería Ancora. Salads? Pasta? A set menu for 1,000 ptas.? Ancora could save your day, with solid food, cheap. *C. Padre Ángel 17, tel. 942/711523. Cash only.*

UNDER 3,000 PTAS. • Boga-Boga. A garish exhibition of gastronomic medals on the walls is a lot of buildup for simple fish, but Boga-Boga delivers. This is the place for *sorroputún* or a *guiso de bonito* (tuna casserole) for 900 ptas. Afterward, in the tiny anteroom bar, cozy up with a *copa de vino dulce* (glass of sweet wine) and exchange quizzical looks with the fishermen. *Plaza José Antonio 9, tel. 942/710135. Closed Tues. Oct.–May.*

WORTH SEEING

From the Puente de la Barquera, the smaller of the town's two bridges, Calle Alta passes the medieval monuments that make up San Vicente's magnificent skyline. The **castle** and its ramparts date from the 8th century, though modifications along the way have changed its look; it once had, for instance, two towers, which helped fend off Norman and Viking attacks. In the summer the castle is open Tuesday–Sunday 10–1 and 4–7, during which time you can climb the tower.

The *ayuntamiento* (town hall) is housed in the **Palacio de Corro**, built in the 16th century by Antonio del Corro as a hospital for the town's poor. The facade bears the Corro coat of arms. The good deed seems to have paid off, as the man's sepulchre lies at the end of the street in the 13th-century church of **Nuestra Señora de Los Angeles** (Our Lady of the Angels). Modifications in the 15th century made the church look less like a fort; in any case, it looks *old.* Walk around the red-lichened walls for views of the estuary and its attendant birds and rowboats; the mountains; some woods; and a basketball court. The ivy-covered walls of what once was the **Hospital de la Concepción**, a 15th- to 16th-century lodging for pilgrims on the road to Santiago, lie just before the church on the left.

Back down in town, near the foot of the main bridge, the Gothic convent of **San Luís** is open only 48 days a year, usually during the summer. Now on the grounds of a beautiful private estate, it's in ruins, but the dome supports and the cloisters hint at what once was.

The **Santuario de la Barquera,** near the harbor entrance, houses the statue of the Virgin, who gives San Vicente its last name, as it were (*barquera* being the feminine form of "boatman"). According to legend, the Virgin Mary came ashore at the site of this shrine in a small boat after a storm had washed away its fishermen.

PARQUE NATURAL OYAMBRE

Between the estuaries that separate Comillas—beginning with the weird permutations of the Ría de la Rabia—and San Vicente de la Barquera lies the range of coastal ecosystems that make up Oyambre Nature Park, as well as the ría marshlands that form a refuge for water birds. Lacking urbanization entirely, this area makes a great slice of Cantabrian coastline, with cliffs, dunes, grasslands, forest, creeks, and quaint rural *pueblos*. The Picos de Europa loom nearby, watching your every step along the winding, infrequently traveled coastline.

COMILLAS

A small explosion of interesting, relatively recent architecture defines the unusual landscape of little Comillas, led by Antoni Gaudí's green-and-yellow marvel, El Capricho. Comillas saw a surge of creative invention at the end of the 19th century, spurred by the commissions of the first Marqués de Comillas and the summer stay by King Alfonso XII in 1881. In the end all the major players of the Catalan Moderniste movement had left their sign on the town, and Comillas became an aristocratic retreat, a tradition that continues to this day.

So, there's that. And then, the beach—an equally big reason this laid-back town draws, in addition to artists, young *belle*-weather seekers from all over Europe.

BASICS

From the bus stop, walk straight, passing the little gas stand on your right, and you'll reach a main street called Paseo Estrada. The very center of town is ahead, marked by the **Plaza del Ayuntamiento.** El Capricho is uphill to the right, the beach down to the left. From this intersection walk straight ahead one block, turn left, and 20 more yards will bring you to the summer-only **tourist office** (tel. 942/720768), open weekdays 9:30–1 and 4–7.

La Cantabrica (tel. 942/720822) buses connect Comillas with **Santander, Santillana,** and **San Vicente de la Barquera.** The town is not served by train.

WHERE TO SLEEP

Nothing spectacular is available cheaply here, but this little town sees such intense summer tourism that you can't walk far without seeing that reassuring blue square with the white P (for *pensión*). Two affordable pensions with good reputations are **Aldea** (La Aldea 5, tel. 942/720300) and **Villa** (Carlos Díaz de la Campa 23, tel. 942/720217). **Fuente Real** (Sobrellano 19, tel. 942/720155) is ugly, dirty, and best avoided, even if Room 208 does overlook El Capricho from 25 yards away.

UNDER 5,000 PTAS. • Pension Bolingas. For the price, these rooms are fairly clean. If that alone will satisfy you, this is your place: there's nothing cheaper in Comillas. Singles are almost free in the off season; doubles peak at 3,600 ptas. in summer. Bathrooms are shared. The location is central—upstairs from the restaurant-heavy Corro de Campíos. You might be pleasantly surprised; it depends on your mood. *Corro de Campíos s/n, tel. 942/720841. Cash only.*

Pensión Los Abetos. A room in this house, halfway between the cemetery and the university, feels like a room at home. The price for a double—4,500 ptas. year-round—is excellent, though the five rooms share two bathrooms. What you get in return, removed from the center of town, is a great view of Comillas and a bedroom balcony from which to take it in. *C. Manuel Noriega, tel. 942/720727. 5 rooms, none with bath. Cash only.*

UNDER 10,000 PTAS. • Hostal Esmerelda. These spacious rooms have good furniture, phones, modern bathrooms, and a highly central location. The house has a pretty stone facade; like much of Comillas, it was built in the 1880s. There's a restaurant downstairs, with a bar and lounge for guests. Until July 15 double rooms are a good deal at 6,000 ptas.; in August they zoom to 10K. *C. Antonio López 7, tel. 942/720097.*

WHERE TO EAT

In a plazalike area near the town hall called the **Corro del Campíos,** a congregation of restaurants and sweet shops provides a plethora of outdoor seats in summer. There's another restaurant row near the beach parking lot.

UNDER 3,000 PTAS. • **Cafeteria los Castaños.** Although not gastronomically dissimilar from other tapas bars on the Corro de Campíos, Los Castaños provides a modest view of the whole scene from its brown-balconied, glassed-in aerie. *Platos combinados* start at 850 ptas. *C. Carlos Diaz de la Campa, tel. 942/722570.*

Gurea. Comillas's most interesting restaurant serves up a mixture of Basque and Cantabrian cuisine. Make reservations for the outdoor dining room, and try the *buñuelos de bacalao* (codfish fritters). *C. Ignacio Fernández de Castro 11, tel. 942/722446.*

La Caracola. A fair *menú del día*, featuring *cocido montañes*, a filling stew of white beans, meats, and greens, runs 1,300 ptas. here. The food may be less consistent in the summer, when the place gets very busy; it's the only place actually on the beach. You get sandy views from the back dining room. *La Playa, tel. 942/720741.*

WORTH SEEING

Come for Gaudí, but stay for the total effect of the town's odd architecture. The **Casa del Duque del Almodóvar del Río**, that *Psycho*-esque mansion alone in the middle of town, is private; you'll have to chance the dogs. There's a wide-ranging market every Friday near the bus stop.

What Gaudí edifice *isn't* fanciful enough to be called "the Caprice"? One of only three Gaudí whimsies to bless this earth outside Catalonia (the other two are in León and Astorga), the happy green-and-yellow-tile villa called **El Capricho** is now a restaurant, and an expensive one at that. Touring the grounds is free, however. The building is weirdly shaped, with bay curves and chevroned roof peaks, but the most salient detail of this work of young Gaudí is the array of glazed tiles featuring sunflowers in relief, which brighten up the whole. The tower lookout, not to be outdone, is made of Legos; alas, it's closed to the public.

Part of a potent triumvirate, along with El Capricho and the neighboring chapel, the extraordinary **Palacio de Sobrellano** (*sobre llano* literally means "above the plain," as the hills here flatten out toward the sea) once belonged to the Marqués de Comillas. The ornate, neo-Gothic building contains furnishings designed by a young Gaudí. The neo-Gothic chapel next door, complete with flying buttresses, has a steeple that echoes the Capricho's. Viewed from on high, that is, the hill behind town, the chapel seems to communicate with its Gothic brethren, the town cemetery, and the sea, as well as the turreted Casa del Duque. *Tel. 942/720339. Open fall–spring, Wed.–Sun. 10–2 and 4–7; summer, daily 10–2 and 4–7.*

At least El Capricho is a restaurant. Only a small part of the colossal hilltop ex-seminary **Universidad Pontifica,** an ornate turn-of-the-20th-century pile of stone and orange brick, is open to the public, and once inside you see cloisters in ugly disrepair. The colorful church, complete with blue ceiling, is the only treat; designed by the Catalan Moderniste architect Juan Martorell, it's more eye candy with the fascinating Comillas landscape. *Tel. 942/722543. Open Tues.–Sun. 10:30–1:30 and 3:30–6:30. Admission 350 ptas. 40-min tours available.*

Oy, Franco. Rather than change the name of Plaza del Generalísimo Franco, locals just call it **Plaza del Ayuntamiento** and go on their way. The plaza's cobblestone surface, 18th-century houses with wooden bays and balconies, and the strong walls and bell tower of the church of San Cristóbal create a rich atmosphere. The church has a dark stone interior.

Cementerio. There is no better place on the planet to listen to Siouxie and the Banshees. Surrounded by tombstones, the crumbled ruins of an old Gothic monastery look just right on this little hill, with the rough Cantabrian Sea as a backdrop. Ascending from the stone tussle is *The Exterminating Angel,* an unforgettable sculpture by the Moderniste Josep Llimona, whose marble works you may have seen in the Sobrellano Chapel. The Moderniste touches on the surrounding wall are by Lluís Domènech i Montaner, who designed an enlargement of the cemetery. To get here, loop past the beach toward the port and follow the road uphill.

AFTER DARK

In summer Nordic women and local men stir a sinister stew of late-night imbroglio. You, too, should experience the four bars in town. Three huddle together on Victoriano Pérez de la Riva, which branches off the Plaza del Ayuntamiento: **El Chinín** plays what might be called Spanish and British alternative. **El B. J.,** next door, will keep Ricky Martin's hits alive for all time. A few feet away, across the street, **Don Porfírio** parties outdoors (FIESTA FOREVER, reads the sign out front). Up on Calle Antonio López, **Mr. Kiwi Bar** completes the fun (it may be tacky, but it *is* fun), which typically runs from midnight to 4:30 AM. Just past El Capricho's entrance, heading inland, is a small disco called **Pamara.**

OUTDOOR ACTIVITIES

A few good **hiking** trails of various lengths run from Comillas through the gorgeous landscapes hereabouts. The tourist office is your best bet for trail maps.

SANTILLANA DEL MAR

For many, there is no finer Spanish town than Santillana. It will certainly be your favorite if you're into stone. The streets are cobblestoned, and the dwellings, a perfectly preserved collection of 15th-century houses, are made of stone as well—the very brain of Santillana is rock. Sartre called it "a true relic in the life of man." You should blush, therefore, picking up a cheap souvenir: the tiny town is already a memory. Perambulate the streets (there are really just two) with an eye nostalgic for a purer, if less hygienic, life.

The Spanish say the town's name fibs thrice: it's neither *santa*, nor *llana*, nor *del mar*—saintly, on a plain, or on the sea. Perhaps it's phenomenal because of this, with a spiritual simplicity that is in no sense plain.

BASICS

The **tourist office** (tel. 942/818251) is on the Plaza Mayor, at the bison sculpture—modeled on a drawing in the nearby Altamira Caves—atop the mossy stones. The office is open weekdays 9:30–1 and 4–7 plus Saturday 9:30–1 in summer. The town's two **banks** and three ATMs (for currency exchange) and **post office** are also on Plaza Mayor.

COMING AND GOING

Santillana is a wee thing, a road stop easy to miss, even on the slow two-lane highway that passes by. If you've no wheels, the only way into town is by bus. From the bus stop, walk slightly uphill 100 ft (you'll see a bell tower ahead on the right) and cross the road: welcome to Santillana, pedestrian traffic only. Calle Santo Domingo soon splits in two. To the left, Juan Infante runs into the Plaza Mayor, which spits you out to the Colegiata church; to the right, the street changes names three times before reaching the Colegiata—Carrera, Cantón, and Calle del Río.

The bus line **La Cantabrica** (tel. 942/720822) connects Santillana with **Santander, Comillas, San Vicente de la Barquera,** and **Torrelavega,** in the latter of which you can catch RENFE and FEVE trains. La Cantabrica's unmarked bus stop is at the stairs a few yards from the **Autobuses García** (tel. 942/891935) stop, which looks more official, with a bench and whatnot. García also goes to **Torrelavega,** whence FEVE runs to **Santander** every half hour, as well as west into **Asturias.** Buses are much simpler here than trains.

WHERE TO SLEEP

Delightfully, Santillana is full of charming, reasonably priced *posadas*—authentically old inns with quiet, well-maintained rooms. The cheapest options are on the streets surrounding the bus stop in both directions: posada after posada with double rooms for around 4,500 in low season and 7,000 in summer. The pricier posadas and hotels put you in the very center of things, but location matters little in a town this size.

Two of the least expensive are **Posada Revolgo** (Barrio La Robledo, tel. 942/818341) and **Posada Gonzalez** (Barrio La Robleda 8, tel. 942/818178), a stone's throw from each other behind the bus stop. Both rent doubles for 4,000 ptas. off season, 6,000 in summer. **Posada Le Dorat** (Avda. Le Dorat 32, tel. 942/818345), open in summer only, is less attractive but adequate; doubles cost 4,000 ptas. in June and July and jump to 6,000 in August. Le Dorat is clumped with some other inexpensive pensions about 100 yards down the two-lane highway from the posadas. **Posada Santa Juliana** (C. Carrera 19, tel.94/284–0106), open from Easter to November, is a touch more costly (7,500 ptas. in summer), but it's right on the main drag.

Casona Solar de Hidalgos. Do stay in this 16th-century stone *casona* (manor house) if you can. Four of the 12 double rooms rent for 6,000–7,500 ptas.; the prices of the others vary with size of room and level of comfort. Your digs are wonderfully furnished with antiques (including the telephones); the large attic room is especially charming, with wooden floors. Every room has a very large bathroom. Ask to see the library, which might be the best-looking museum in town. The little breakfast room is terrific, *muy* Santillana. You're at the very convergence of the town's main streets. *Santo Domingo 5, tel. 942/818387. 12 rooms.*

WHERE TO EAT

Choices are limited, but they're solidly housed in medieval stone. There's a burger-and-pizza place on the highway (also called Avenida Le Dorat).

UNDER 2,000 PTAS. • Mesón El Castillo. For *picoteo*—cheap tapas snacking—this is your place. Menus are posted outside with (old, unappetizing) photos of *raciones*. For sit-down dining, the cozy back room and upstairs salon provide a complete menu, with combination plates from 950 ptas. *Plaza Mayor 6, tel. 942/840208.*

Casa Cossío. These two venerable, old stone houses in front of the Colegiata form a friendly restaurant (the dining room in the second, across a little patio, is open only in summer). You can't fail by ordering *a la parrilla* (off the grill) from the huge, popular grill in the back—*costillas* (ribs) are 900 ptas., *solomillo* (sirloin) is 1,850 ptas. *Nécora* (crab) and *langosta* (lobster) swim around in a tank. *Plaza Abad Francisco Navarro, tel. 942/818355. Closed Tues. Nov.–March.*

UNDER 3,000 PTAS. • Altamira. When you're ready for dining proper, the main room of this restaurant, next to the hotel of the same name, provides the most authentic experience in town. Decorated in rustic style (a few curtains, copper pots, iron chandeliers), it's exactly what you've come to think a restaurant in Santillana should be. The back dining room and summer patio don't have the same effect, but the food's still good. *C. Cantón 1, tel. 942/818025.*

WORTH SEEING

This town is a gift from the Middle Ages, its private *casonas* and palaces giving a sense of solidity and permanence. A notable example is the **Palacio de los Velarde** (on Plaza de las Arenas, behind the Colegiata), which looks like something from Neptune. For the full effect of life 500 years ago, enter the accessible houses and roam into random hotels and restaurants. The watershed on Calle del Río was used to wash clothes.

A group of monks founded a hermitage and monastery on the site of Santillana's **Colegiata** (Collegiate Church) in the 9th century. After it gained importance, the present church was built in the 12th century in the Romanesque style that predominates in northern Spain, the most recognizable characteristic of which is the series of half-circle arches set back above the door. If you're inspired by this, read the Pamplona chapter of James Michener's *Iberia*; nothing excites him more. The cloister in the rear is considered the church's masterpiece. *Admission: church free, cloister 300 ptas. Open March–Dec. only, daily 10–1 and 4–6:30.*

The **Museo José Otero** begins with a lawn just beyond the plaza outside the Colegiata holding stone (yes, stone) sculptures by native Santillana son José Otero (1908–1994). The collection continues indoors. *Plaza Abad Francisco Navarro s/n, tel. 942/840198. Open daily 9–1 and 4–7:30 (4–10 in summer).*

Casona de los Tagle, private home of the Tagle family, opens its doors on weekends and all summer long for a look around. The house retains all original furnishings, and its huge facade *escudo,* or coat of arms, manifests the pretension inherent in these old manor homes. An exhibition room on the first floor hosts sundry changing displays. *C. Revolvo 23, tel. 942/818141. Admission 500 ptas. Open Oct.–June, weekends 10:30–1:30 and 4:30–8:30; July–Sept., Tues.–Fri. 10:30–1:30 and 4:30–8:30, weekends 10:30–1:30 and 4:30–8:30.*

Housed in the baronial 14th-century Don Borja Tower, which also has a notable coat of arms, the **Fundación Santillana** sponsors free art and historical exhibits. The pleasure is in exploring the house and its interior patio. There's a nice bookstore next door with a couple of English-language titles, both by Tom Clancy. *Plaza Mayor, tel. 942/818203. Free. Open weekdays 10:30–1:30 and 4–5:30, weekends 10:30–2 and 4–8.*

Housed in a former Dominican convent, the **Museo Diocesano** is the premier showcase of Cantabrian religious art, with more than 1,000 works. *Avda. Le Dorat, tel. 942/818004. Admission 300 ptas. Open fall–spring, Thurs.–Tues. 10–1 and 4–6, summer Thurs.–Tues. 9:30–1 and 4–7:30. Closed Feb.*

The **Casas de Águila y La Parra** are two medieval homes that unite for cultural and contemporary-art exhibits. Explore the many floors and be sure to etch your name in the original 17th-century beams. The tourist office is inside. *Open weekdays 9:30–1 and 4–7 plus Saturday 9:30–1 in summer.*

**FIESTAS • ** The night of January 5, before Three Kings Day, a colorful and popular procession brings the gift-tossing Magi and full entourage—camels and all—through the heart of town.

AFTER DARK
Head for Santander.

OUTDOOR ACTIVITIES
Unfortunately, it's not possible to rent a bike here. But a small **hike,** at the very least, is required, if only to catch a glimpse of Santillana from a better vantage point. Facing the two-lane highway from the old town, turn right; to head for the Cantabrian Sea, turn right at the sign for Ubiarco (*see below*).

ALTAMIRA CAVES

For years art students, backpackers, and spelunkers have trekked to the revered site of Altamira—where in 1879 Marcelino Sanz de Sautuola and his daughter Maria discovered a cave filled with 150 Paleolithic paintings—only to find the gift shop closed (or, worse, open). The museum, annotated only in Spanish, is bad. And the last straw: a visit to the caves themselves requires a written request submitted two years in advance.

However, an exact replica of the Altamira Caves is scheduled to open any day now, making Altamira fully accessible for the first time and rendering spray-painting the ceiling a less heinous crime. Anything would be an improvement over that old museum (which is properly called the Altamira Research Center and Museum). If you feel ripped off by the replica and crave authenticity, visit the cave paintings at Puente Viesgo (*see box*) or Ribadesella, Asturias (*see below*).

Altamira is not served by buses, but it's only a mile's walk or drive from Santillana. With your back to the bus stop, go straight, then follow the signs up the hill to the right. *Tel. 942/818005. Admission 400 ptas. Open Tues.–Sun. 9:30–2:30.*

UBIARCO–PLAYA SANTA JUSTA

Reaching this private cove should more than provide one day's exhilaration. An hour's walk from Santillana (or a short García bus ride) brings you to Ubiarco; passing the tiny town, you'll walk under an abandoned building and onto the little Santa Justa Beach. Here a cove of rough rock meets the sea; to the right, an old hermitage is tucked under a rock cliff; and above, on a green pasture, two stone-walled ruins, one with a window (great view), confront the horizon, as at the corner of some old dream. From here cross the green, green sea-swept prairie as far as you like, encountering beaches along the way to Suances.

POTES

Potes has undeniable charms of its own, but its essence is really that of a departure point and lodging center for excursions to Fuente Dé and the Picos de Europa. On Monday it feels more like a community, when the traditional weekly market is held beneath the band shell in the Plaza Capitán Palacios, also called Plaza de Potes.

The road from San Vicente and Unquera in Cantabria (N621) passes through Asturias and the town of Panes, after which the **Desfiladero de la Hermida** pass sends you back into Cantabria. Following the course the Deva River has cut for it, this is one of the deepest chasms in the world. Tell your friends the trip was gorge-ous, and get smacked.

Once you're out of the pass (it takes about 40 minutes), the Picos rise most impressively. From their stony crags the green hills slope down toward you, punctuated by groups of old stone homes with orange-tile roofs, until you reach Potes.

BASICS
Potes's **tourist office** (C. Independencia 30, tel. 942/730787), in the old church of San Vicente, is open daily 10–2 and 4–6 (4–8 in summer).

Only **buses** dare come this far. From Santander or San Vicente de la Barquera, take **Autobuses Palomera** (tel. 942/880611) to Panes or Potes, or to Fuente Dé. From Asturias take **ALSA** (985/848133) to Panes and change to the Palomera line. The bus stop in Potes is in front of the Monumento al Médico

ALTERNATIVE ROCK

You want real prehistoric cave art, but can't sit through Altamira's 700-day cooling-off period? Fear not: Puente Viesgo has your drawings. Two caves were discovered in 1903 in this unspoiled 16th-century hamlet (with a grand hotel) in the pristine Pas Valley, scooped out of a 1,150-ft pyramidal peak called Monte del Castillo (Mt. Castle). One of the caves, Las Monedas, has been closed for two years because of lighting problems, though the real problem is bureaucracy. The other cave, also called Monte del Castillo, is open year-round. In the off season you may be the only one here; in summer the 380-visitor limit is reached every day.

A great number of bison are depicted on these walls, along with some deer, an extinct species of bull with a pointy snout, and even some stick figures—that's us. Some paintings date from as far back as 30,000 years, so are probably about twice as old as those at Altamira. Human remains found here were discovered to have been as much as 120,000 years old.

The cave illustrates some beautiful painting techniques, including that of incorporating the cave's natural surfaces—a raised curve for a bison's hump, a little fissure for an eye. Yet perhaps what speaks most clearly are the paintings of hands: there are 44 in Monte Castillo. They wave to us, reaching out through time. These are self-portraits we recognize, hands like the ones we traced in kindergarten; to create them, painters blew red pigment around their hands through a sort of straw made of hollowed bone, leaving the negative image preserved. There are painted symbols in the cave, too, with unknown meanings but palpable power, as in contemporary paintings by artists who forgo traditional representation.

The countryside here, as most everywhere in Cantabria, is estupendo. A little hike is recommended. You'll find a trail map on the fence of the town park, directly opposite the entrance to the Gran Hotel.

The Continental bus line (tel. 942/225318) connects Puente Viesgo to Santander in one direction, Burgos and Madrid in the other. The only stop, and it is so very unmarked, is in front of the savings bank on the highway, next to the restaurant Casa Sergio. Old men in berets gather here and at La Unión, across the street, for dominos and cards. For a hearty fill try La Unión's local cocido montañes stew.

Puente Viesgo's cave (tel. 942/598425) is open April–Oct., Tuesday–Sunday 9–noon and 3–6:30; November–March, Wed.–Sunday 9–3. Admission is 225 ptas.

Rural park just after the tourist office, where the road heads left. The bus from Potes to **Fuente Dé** stops at every town along the way, and you'll probably want to hop off in San Pelayo—the site, for some reason, of the **Picos de Europa National Park information center** (tel. 942/733201)—as these are the best hiking maps you'll find.

WHERE TO SLEEP

In the event that Casa Cayo is full, ask the tourist office for its list of other stays, complete with prices.

Casa Cayo. For 6,000 ptas. you get a spacious, new double room with private bath and the use of a very nice salon, which has a fireplace for winter nights. A wide terrace overlooks the river. From the main bridge in town, you'll see the Casa's attractive brown balconies. *C. Cántabra 6, tel. 942/730150.*

WHERE TO EAT

Potes forms the heart of the Liébana district, which has a few famous contributions to Cantabrian cuisine. The climate produces two varieties of alcohols, *orujo*, a liqueur, and *tostadillo*, a sweet wine similar to muscatel. *Orujo* comes in four flavors: honey (*miel*); white (*blanco*), which is like *aguardiente*; tea (*té*), picked from the mountain peaks and passes; and cream (*crema*), which tastes exactly like Baileys Irish Cream.

Cocido lebaniego is like *cocido montañes* but uses garbanzos rather than white beans in its stew. Several local cheeses are also recommended. Besides the restaurants listed below, **El Che** (tel. 942/730428) downstairs in the Plaza de Potes has good food and pleasant outdoor service in the summer.

UNDER 2,000 PTAS. • **Asador el Balcón.** To reach this steak house, one of the better values in Potes, go behind the tourist office over a bridge and to the left up the hill. Yeah, if you're tired of walking, it's a drag, but a large interior overlooks the town. The *menú del día* is 1,100 ptas.; *costilla de cerdo* (pork ribs) is 650 ptas. *Epifanio Sánchez Mateo, tel. 942/730464.*

Casa Cayo. Attached to the hotel (*see above*), this traditional favorite has been in business since 1936, its warm dining room overlooking the river from one of the most central positions in Potes. The standard Asturian fare comes in *platos combinados* from 800 to 1,000 ptas. or a *menú del día* (always the best choice if you're hungry) for 1,500 ptas. Tostadillo wine from the house bodega is served from a barrel at the bar. *C. Cántabra 6, tel. 942/730150.*

WORTH SEEING

Some lovely ancient bridges (Potes derives from the old Latin *pontes,* or bridge) cross the rivers Quiviesa and Deva, inviting you to wander the labyrinthine backstreets leading to the **Barrío de la Solana,** the heart of old Potes.

The church of **San Vicente**, in which small exhibitions are held beside the tourist office, is 14th-century Gothic. The **Torre del Infantado**, now the town hall, dates from the 15th century.

AFTER DARK

Downstairs from the Plaza de Potes is a hidden concourse of five or so bars that share the catacomb-like quarters with glassed-in views of the river; the area is commonly called **Los Bajos.** Expect a loud clash of Spanish pop for drinking and dancing.

OUTDOOR ACTIVITIES

Hiking here is do-it-yourself. Get trail maps from the tourist office at Potes and/or the Picos de Europa park office in Los Pelayos. Outfitters will gladly arrange more dangerous activities as well—look for the term *turismo activo*. Two reliable sources are **Europicos** (San Roque 6, tel. 942/730724), beneath the Hostal Picos de Europa, and **Picos Awentura** (Cervantes 3, tel. 942/732161), at the bridge just yards from the tourist office. Both offer a range of activities: three-hour horseback tours are 4,700 ptas.; half-day canoeing *descensos* run from Panes to Unquera for 3,500 ptas.; half-day rappelling trips cost 5,000 ptas.; hang gliding with an instructor, in a different league, will run you 7,000 ptas. for 10 to 15 minutes. SUV tours (called "4 x 4") and four-wheel ATC rentals (called "quad") are also available.

MOGROVEJO

Halfway between Potes and Fuente Dé you'll see one of the most touching things in all of Spain: the view of Mogrovejo with the snowcapped Picos de Europa behind it. You mustn't come this far without stopping to walk among the stone huts and gaze at the vine-covered tower in its breathtaking landscape.

Mogrovejo's old tower, which wears its ivy like a shawl, seems to aspire to become one of the gray peaks that echo its form, and you can't but feel that it achieves a kind of greatness. Amid orange- and black-tile roofs, the intense humility and beauty of the town—where sheep graze in the greenest of pastures and huge birds slowly circle—force you to bless even the ubiquitous scent of manure.

It's just as well there are no accommodations here, but at the foot of the 1-km (½ mi) hill that you walk up to reach the town (remind the bus driver to let you know when he's reached your stop), you can rest at **Mesón Los Llanos** (Carretera Potes, tel. 942/733089), which has good clean rooms with wooden floors and solid bathrooms for 4,000 ptas. They're open weekends year-round, daily from June to September.

FUENTE DÉ

As you approach Fuente Dé by car or foot, you'll see a wall of gray stone rising 2,000 m (6,560 ft) straight into the air. Visible at the top is the tiniest of huts: your destination. To get there, you will soon opt to entrust your life to a little red-and-white funicular—here's to steel cable. A round-trip ride costs 1,300 ptas. Once ascendant, you're hiking along the Ávila Mountain pasturelands, rich in native wildlife, between the central and eastern massifs of the Picos. There's an official entrance to Picos de Europa National Park up here.

Other than one hotel and the remarkably ugly parador, both pricey, there's nowhere to stay in Fuente Dé, as it isn't really a town. The first village over in the direction of Potes—the only direction—is Espinama, a 3-km (2-mi, or half-hour) walk; there you can trust the **Hostal Puente Deva** (Carretera Espinama-Camaleño, tel. 942/736658) for nice double rooms at about 4,500–5,000 ptas.

COMING AND GOING

From Santander or San Vicente de la Barquera, take **Autobuses Palomera** (tel. 942/880611). From Asturias take **ALSA** (985/848133) to Panes and change to the Palomera line. For more on regional transport, *see* Potes, *above*.

SANTANDER

If Santander hadn't lost its old town to a fire in 1941, if it had put its harbor to cosmetic use rather than opt to stare at the machinery of its maritime wealth, if more views had been established to take advantage of the city's natural slopes, which should enable you to look down the rooftops to the wonderful bay, then the capital of this gleaming province might have become one of the world's great resort cities.

As it is, one half is dull, stubborn, and decrepit, while the other is a surprising relief of perfect beaches and gracious manners. Santander cannot compete, as it should, with San Sebastián for north-coast supremacy, but it can provide a great day of exploring the Magdalena Peninsula, including some extraordinary beaches and parks. If only *both* halves were perfect, southern France would weep with envy.

BASICS

VISITOR INFORMATION

Two tourist offices are open all year: the great Cantabrian office at **Plaza de Velarde 5** (usually called Plaza Porticada; tel. 942/310708; open daily 9–1 and 4–7). They will gladly hand you all kinds of pretty pamphlets on the province, usually available in English, including hiking routes on each of the smaller zones within Cantabria. Take advantage, as these are hard to find outside the city. This office even has maps from different cities in Spain. Calling from outside the province, it's cheaper to get Cantabria info by dialing 901/111112 between 9 and 9 daily.

The **city tourist office**, in the gardens near the water (Jardines de Pereda, tel. 942/216120, open weekdays 9–1:30 and 4-7, Sat. 10–1, daily and longer hrs in summer), is also well stocked. During the summer this office offers bus tours three times a day, running from the post office to the lighthouse and back for 500 ptas. Reservations taken here.

In June a second **city tourist office** (tel. 942/740414) opens on El Sardinero Beach, on Avenida de la Reina Victoria opposite the Gran Casino.

Finally, you can usually get a city map from the info desk at the **bus station.**

CONSULATES

The **United Kingdom** consulate is at Paseo de Pereda 27 (tel. 924/220000).

CURRENCY EXCHANGE

In case of emergency, that is, if the banks are closed, El Bar Machichaco (Calderón de la Barca 9, tel. 942/210776), next to the train and bus stations, changes foreign currency and traveler's checks for a good chunk of commission.

CYBERSPACE

The computer and phone shop **InSisTel** (Méndez Núñez 8, tel. 942/318585), open weekdays 10–2 and 4:30–8 and Saturday 10–1, has six computers and charges 300 ptas. for half an hour, 500 ptas. for an hour. Race your addicted brethren one block from the bus station.

Despite the inviting name, there are no books in sight at **El Libro Viejo** (Perines 19, tel. 942/235706), just a bar and two wired computers. Come here when InSisTel is closed; computer use is 500 ptas. for half an hour, 800 ptas. for an hour. Actual hours vary with the owner's whims. Perines runs up from the middle of Calle de San Fernando.

EMERGENCIES

The main **police station** (C. Mercado, tel. 942/200744) is just behind the *ayuntamiento* (town hall).

If you're too sick to leave your room, **Telefarmacia** (tel. 942/634049) will deliver medicines to you for 700 ptas. Otherwise, call 942/220260 to locate the nearest pharmacy. The main hospital is **Marqués de Valdecilla** (Avda. Marqués de Valdecilla, tel. 942/202520).

ENGLISH-LANGUAGE BOOKS

Estudio (C. de Burgos 5 and Calvo Sotelo 21, tel. 942/374950), open daily 9–2:30 and 3:30–9, has the best selection.

MAIL

The main **post office** (Plaza de Alfonso XIII, tel. 902/197197) is across from Plaza Porticada, open weekdays 8:30–8:30 and Saturday 9:30–2.

LAUNDRY

You've got one chance to feel clean: **Lavomatique** (Atalaya 16, tel. 942/313819). They wash and dry for you; you pick your bundle up later and pay 1,100 ptas. per load. Of course, since you have to drag your dirties uphill to get here, you might decide to pay the exorbitant prices of the ubiquitous *tintorerías* lower down, or use the affordable bathroom sink.

Cantabria's first network of roads was laid by the Romans between 30 and 20 BC, and you can still walk a surviving 5-km (3-mi) paved stretch through thick vegetation. About 3 yards wide, the path is covered with smooth, attractive stones, many of which contain wheel ruts from Roman carts. The route officially begins at Pie de Concha and runs uphill to Somaconcha. To get here from Santander, take RENFE Cercanias to Bárcena (610 ptas. round-trip, one hour each way) and follow the pink signs to the trail.

COMING AND GOING

Santander is a quick and easy drive from Bilbao, San Sebastián, or Oviedo along the Autovía del Cantabrico, otherwise known as N634. It's nearly a straight shot south to Burgos (156 km/97 mi) on N623, and from there another 237 km (147 mi) to Madrid on Highway N-I.

The **bus** and **train stations** (both FEVE and RENFE) are, happily, next to each other. Exiting either terminal, turn left and use the walkable tunnel (closed to auto traffic on Sunday for a market) to avoid climbing a ton of stairs. Walk three blocks straight down Calle de Cádiz—or, exiting FEVE, the parallel Calderón de la Barca—to the Pereda gardens. Santander's tourist office is a bit farther on, within the gardens; for the regional Cantabrian office, stocked with great pamphlets on just about everything, turn left and walk two blocks, then cross Calvo Sotelo into the Plaza Porticada.

Taxis line up outside the stations. If you can't find one, call 942/369191.

To get to France, you're best off taking a three-hour bus to the French border town of Hendaye, as trains on the same route take twice as long.

BY BUS

For general bus info call 942/211995. ALSA-Turytrans (tel. 942/221685) goes to the French border at **Irún-Hendaye** (4 hrs, 2,000 ptas.), **Bilbao** (1 hr—less than half the time it would take by train; 1,000 ptas.), **San Sebastián** (3 hrs, 1,800 ptas.), and **Oviedo** (3 hrs, 1,800 ptas.). Continental Auto (tel. 942/225318) heads to **Madrid** (5½ hrs, 3,300 ptas.; the comfort bus, called Supra, also 5½ hrs, costs 4,550 ptas.). Via Carsa heads to **Barcelona** (8 hrs, 5,900 ptas.).

To reach the Cantabrian parts of the Picos de Europa, a splendid idea, hop on a Palomera bus (tel. 942/880611), which goes to **Fuente Dé** (3¾ hrs, 1,500 ptas.) and **Potes** (3 hrs, 1,000 ptas.) along an impressive narrow gorge.

To get to **San Vicente de la Barquera** (1½ hrs, 400 ptas.), **Comillas** (1 hr, 300 ptas.), or **Santillana del Mar** (45 mins, 200 ptas.), use La Cantabrica (tel. 942/720822), especially since trains do not serve Comillas or Santillana.

BY PLANE

There is no bus service to **Aeropuerto de Parayas** (tel. 942/202100), though it's not far outside the city. A taxi will cost 1,500–2,000 ptas.

BY TRAIN

FEVE (tel. 942/211687), which does not take Eurail passes, connects Santander with **Bilbao** (2 hrs, 20 min, 925 ptas.), **Oviedo** (3⅓ hrs, 1,767 ptas.), and **Ribadesella** (2½ hrs, 1,000 ptas.). For most other Cantabrian destinations and for trips east to France, buses are advisable.

RENFE (942/280202) heads to the interior and does not serve Bilbao or the French border. From Santander RENFE's only real specialty is **Madrid** (Talgo 5½ hrs, 4,300 ptas.; overnight Estrella 9 hrs, 4,100 ptas.).

WHERE TO SLEEP

Surrounding the bus and train stations are quite a number of pensions, most with shared bathrooms. Half are antiquated and merciless; the newer ones, for which you'll pay an additional 1,000–2,000 ptas. in high season, generally have private baths and are worth the extra money. These are listed below.

Beach hotels are few and pricey. To stay closer to the water, check into **Hostal Carlos III** (Avda. Reina Victoria 135, tel. 942/271616), open April to November, with doubles for 4,500–6,500 ptas.

UNDER 7,000 PTAS. • Hostal El Carmen. Farther along San Fernando than the eponymous *hostal* (*see below*), beneath the PARKING YUMBO sign, Carmen has big, clean rooms, two of which have balconies. Doubles run 5,000–6,500 ptas. *San Fernando 48, tel. 942/230190. Cash only.*

Hostal San Fernando. Many of these tidy, dependable rooms come with little balconies as well, and start at lower prices off season (doubles 4,000–6,500 ptas.). The location is central to Calle Vargas nightlife, though a long walk from the bus and train stations. *San Fernando 16, tel. 942/371984. Cash only.*

Pensión Plaza. This is the best stay near the bus and train stations, one of very few with phones in each room and hotel-level tidiness. Doubles cost 5,000 ptas. in summer and about 4,000 ptas. off season. *C. Cádiz 13, 942/212967. Cash only.*

Pensión Porticada. Thanks to its bay views from bay windows, this is one of the better station stays. The rooms are spacious and reasonably priced even in high season: 5,000 ptas. for a double with shared (clean) bath, 6,000 ptas. for one with private bath. *Méndez Núñez 6, tel. 942/227817. Cash only.*

UNDER 9,000 PTAS. • Cabo Mayor. Across the street from the bus terminal, these simple, clean rooms range widely in price, from 4,000 to 7,000 ptas. depending on the season. *C. Cádiz 1, tel. 942/211181. Cash only.*

Hotel Romano. This one-star property provides all the comforts of a good, affordable hotel: nice, well-sized rooms, phone, and private bathrooms for 5,000–8,500 ptas. You're just to the side of the FEVE station. *Federico Vial 8, tel. 942/223071.*

WHERE TO EAT

The Barrio Pesquero, on the waterfront near the train station, features great seafood in all price ranges and consistently high quality. You needn't go beyond Marqués de la Ensenada. Five reputable restaurants offer *menús del día* for little more than 1,000 ptas.: **La Gaviota, La Cueva Trasmallos, Los Peñu-cos, Trasmallos,** and **El Vivero.** The seafood paella that a few cook in front of their restaurants as bait is excellent; other affordable dishes include *sardinas asadas* (roast sardines) and fried *calamares romanas* (squid). Elsewhere in town, Santander's best and most expensive restaurants are in the Puerto Chico/Calle Tetuan area and near Playa El Sardinero.

UNDER 2,000 PTAS. • Bodega Antonio. The best *and* cheapest meal in Santander is the 800-pta. weekday *menú del día* served upstairs in this unassuming locale. And if you're in the mood for Mexican, the 1,500-pta. Mex menu (not including drink) delivers plate after plate of filling tacos and other authentic dishes. Reservations are essential—this place is no secret. Look for it one block beyond the pedestrian-tunnel exit on the corner of Calles Cervantes and Rubio. *Rubio 2, tel. 942/ 231115.*

UNDER 3,000 PTAS. • La Cecilia. This fashionable restaurant has a creatively airy, modern look and a young crowd. The *Cecilia al queso,* one of several good salads on offer, comes with shrimp, apple, and three melted cheeses; the sangria is pretty good, too. Reserve ahead for dinner on weekends. *Avda. Pedro San Martin 1 (½ block past Cuatro Caminos intersection at end of C. San Fernando), tel. 942/ 348011.*

Mesón El Castellano. This popular *mesón* has all the signs of such classic taverns: wine barrels, hanging hams, brick, dark wood beams, iron chandeliers. After strolling this pleasant pedestrian street, stop in for a glass of wine and some tapas. *C. Burgos 3, tel. 942/231020.*

As you travel through Cantabria, you might pass the hamlets of Boo (just south of Santander) and Coo (just south of Torrelavega). There's one called Poo in Asturias, just west of Arenas de Cabrales.

Mesón Los Jamones. Cured *jamones* (hams) hang from the bar of this Santander favorite, for which you need reservations to dine in the comfortable back room. Hot fare comes attractively arranged on wooden boards called *tablas,* which come to about 2,000 ptas. a person. Order a tabla of *mar* (surf), *tierra* (turf), or *tierra y mar* (mushrooms, prawns, salmon, french fries, the kitchen sink)—you'll love it. Don't leave out Rioja wine, as the house bottle is excellent and costs only 825 ptas. *Perines 8, tel. 942/371638.*

WORTH SEEING

Viewed from aerial photographs, Santander is divided perfectly in two. On the harbor side it's tightly urban, ending precisely at the summit of its hill. Coming down the other side, urbanization is minimal, and beautiful beaches stretch to the lighthouse.

PASEO DE PEREDA

On a Sunday afternoon everyone heads down to this main ambulatory drag for long walks opposite the elegant (if dirty) apartments leading to the little marina known as **Puerto Chico.** On the water side, the tiny **Palacete del Embarcadero** is worth a peek (admission free; open Tues.–Sun. 11–1:30 and 4–7), a small exhibition space featuring forward-looking contemporary art.

At the start of the *paseo* are the **Jardines de Pereda,** gardens notable mainly for their carousel and other kids' rides. Alas, the greenery is surrounded by traffic. Farther along the Paseo is a **ferry service** (Los Reginos, S.A., tel. 942/216753) with stops at the towns of Pedreño and Somo, across the bay.

PENINSULA DE LA MAGDALENA

A self-contained strolling and sightseeing zone, this peninsular park represents Santander at its best. The vast stretch of green invites frolicking. On the left, overlooking Playa El Sardinero, is a rusty minia-ture **zoo,** where a polar bear and some penguins are caged (go figure). At the top of a hill at the far end is the 19th-century **Palacio de la Magdalena,** or Palacio Real (Royal Palace), which in 1908 was the summer residence of King Alfonso XIII. Beyond this symbol of regal Santander are views of the crash-ing sea and a lighthouse on a small island; to the right is a very green, piney stretch of park. Heading back, you'll pass two smaller beaches, **Playa Bikinis** and **Playa de la Magdalena.** Looking toward the city, the Hotel Real rises elegantly above the fray. Tram rides around the grounds are 350 ptas. *Open daily 8:30–8:30 (8:30 AM–10:30 PM in summer).*

PARQUE DE MATALEÑAS

Continue past the beach, around to the right, for terrific views of the beaches and outer bay. Palm trees provide picnic shade, and the athletic course follows a creek with swans, recalling, in microscopic form,

A SPLASH OF CIDER

Asturias's best waterfalls may be in her nature parks, but your fondest memories may instead feature the 3-ft cascades of sidra that splash around the plazas of every town in the region. Hard Asturian cider—not to be confused with English cider, which is smoother, darker, less flagrantly fruity—is central to every night out here, and a good meal is marked by the dexterous feat of pouring the liquid from the height of your reach to a glass held low in the opposite hand. To get an idea of how tricky this is, take a bottle outside a sidrería and try it yourself.

Here's the procedure: stop into any sidrería and ask for a bottle ("una de sidra"). The bartender will produce a label-free green bottle (each bar stocks just one brand; there's no room for snootiness) and begin to pour. With the bottle raised to heaven and slowly set horizontal, a thin stream of cider wobbles through the air, clashing against the rim of the wide yet paper-thin cider glass, which has been set at a difficult angle to allow splashing, the aim of all these shenanigans being oxidation. The drink is then to be swallowed immediately; if it's not, it begins to change color, the taste goes, and the cider gods are miffed.

Be sure to leave a sip in the glass; its acidity cleans the rim as you empty what's left onto the floor. For obvious reasons, sidrerías have cement floors, often covered lightly with sawdust, but your target should be the gutter at the base of the bar (some sidrerías place wooden buckets around the room). Customarily, the same glass is used by the next person in your group, a practice that both limits alcohol overdose and makes Asturian cider a wonderfully social beverage. Servers work quite hard bouncing back and forth between parties, serving, waiting for the glass to return, and pouring again and again. One bottle of sidra should provide about nine servings, depending on how much is spilled in the process.

Writing about Asturias some 2,000 years ago, the Roman encyclopedist Pliny noted that apple wine was "the typical drink of the territory." And although consumption hasn't always been so complicated, it has never been more popular.

Paris's Bois de Boulogne. Children delight before a score of those rodentlike marsupial wonders, wallabies. *Open daily 9–9.*

EL FARO DE CABO MAYOR

Just beyond Mataleñas Park is Santander's main lighthouse (*faro*). You can stroll the cliffs that stretch past it, watching the turbulent seas crash into rocks below; the lighthouse itself is closed to the public.

AFTER DARK

You can have the time of your life any weekend in Santander knowing just two street names: Vargas and Río de la Pila.

The night starts off at 10 PM on **Calle Vargas.** In summer, clusters of bongo and bagpipe players gather in the promenade separating Vargas from Calle de San Fernando. Drinking places are on the Vargas side: **Bar Gas** (No. 31) and **Campanillas,** a few doors down, are always popular.

At midnight move over a few streets to **Calle San Luis.** Here, at No. 36, is **Casa Teo,** a happy local place where you might actually see old men singing flamenco (amid the swarm of young kids drinking on the street). At **Burgo-Astur** (No. 22) ask for a *cachi,* a liter of wine and Coke that's cheap and surprisingly drinkable. In **El Culebre** (No. 17) a standing-room crowd sings along to punk-pop under a low wooden ceiling.

If this scene strikes you as excessive and uncouth, you belong around the **Plaza de Cañadío,** near the Paseo de Pereda. The streets here are trampled by better-dressed, slightly older folk, and on the whole you'll see less vomit and urine. The **Celtic's Tavern** (Gándara 3) is a more ebullient scene, if less Irish, than you're likely to experience in Dublin, and the **Cervecería Cruz Blanca** (Lope de Vega 5) is always a party. Both bars corner Calle Hernán Cortés.

At 2:30 AM follow the mass migration across town to Río de la Plata. This condensed uphill congregation is the best thing Santander has going for it—flanked by bars and discos, the street positively swarms. **Taberna Cienfuegos,** on the left at No. 13, shows off its dancing clientele through second-floor glass. **La Gramola,** a few blocks up at No. 23, has low wooden beams that create a calmer, hipper atmosphere. Across the street in No. 26, **La Finca** (the Farm), a young crowd crams in for commercial dance action.

In case hunger strikes, the takeout window at **Danas** (No. 16) provides great sandwiches, especially the 375-pta. *carne guisada con mozzarella* (steak-and-mozzarella sandwich). After 5:30 AM or so, ask someone to lead you to a *discoteca,* several of which are scattered about.

For the best view of Santander, take a ferry across the bay to the town of Somo. Otherwise nondescript, Somo has a long, sandy beach that juts far out into the water, and this is the only distance from which to fully appreciate the Magdalena Palace and Santander's fabulous situation. Boats run every half hour between 8:30 and 8:30 daily; 375 ptas. buys you the round-trip.

GRAN CASINO

You came to Spain to roll, right? Picture Bogart here playing poker, roulette, or blackjack. The Spanish casino—slower, smoother, smaller—has only a Spanish name in common with Las Vegas. *Playa El Sardinero at Plaza Italia, tel. 942/276054. Small slots room open daily 5 PM–5 AM; all else, daily 8 PM–5 AM.*

OUTDOOR ACTIVITIES

If you decide to go **skiing** in southern Cantabria—an area known by the charming name of Alto Campoo—any Santander travel agency can arrange transport tickets and ski passes. **Hiking** and **biking** opportunities abound, though it's nigh impossible to rent a bike; you have to get lucky and meet a posada owner who will lend you one.

ASTURIAS

Asturias is immediately lovable, but few outsiders know the serene pleasures of its many protected spaces. Despite its quietude, Asturias is historically resonant as the home of the first Christian kingdom in Spain: it was here, in Covadonga, that resistance to the reigning Muslims began in the 8th century, a campaign that led ultimately (okay, 700 years later) to the Christian Reconquest of Spain. The region has three major cities (the biggest two, Gijón and Oviedo, are wonderful; steer clear of ugly, industrial Avilés) and a number of lovely coastal fishing and beach towns. Indeed, the entire coast is fascinating and well worth exploring via the coastal FEVE train; but Asturias' real strength lies in its nature parks, starring Picos de Europa National Park.

GIJÓN

If Asturias makes the best hard cider in the world, Gijón bears the liquid torch of its stylish imbibing. The largest and liveliest city in Asturias, Gijón has a notably cosmopolitan nightlife. On weekend evenings the whole city is alive with the act of pouring.

Romans lived here in the first century, calling their settlement Gigia, but little is known of Gijón's history between that time and the razing of the city in the 15th century. Later a port was built, and the city grew until Gaspar Melchor de Jovellanos, an intellectual minister of justice under Carlos III in the 18th century, guided it toward heavy industry. Today Gijón's wide, attractive beach is popular with surfers and sunbathers, and along with Santander, it comes in handy as a font of urban entertainment near the Picos de Europa.

BASICS

VISITOR INFORMATION

At the height of summer there are five tourist offices in Gijón. The **main tourist office** (C. Maternidad 2, tel. 985/345561, open daily 10–2 and 4–9), which can help make hotel reservations, is open year-round on the third floor of a building across from the bus station, a block from the train station. The **regional tourist office** (C. Marqués de San Esteban 1, tel. 985/346046, open weekdays 9–2 and 4–6:30, plus Sat. 9–2 in summer), near the marina, has an especially helpful pamphlet called "Alojamientos Turísticos," which lists prices and amenities for lodgings in every town in Asturias.

In the summer, when free walking tours are available, three additional tourist stands open up, one on the large San Lorenzo Beach, another in the lifeguard tower at Poniente Beach, and a third in front of the Teatro Jovellanos, on Paseo Begoña. The city's Web site, www.infogijon.com, features a beach Webcam updated every minute.

CURRENCY EXCHANGE

Banks offer the best rates, followed by **El Corte Inglés** (General de Elorza 75, tel. 985/109000).

CYBERSPACE

Café de los Mundos and **Babilonia** are next door to each other (and co-owned) a block off San Lorenzo Beach at Stair 11 (Canga Arguelles 24, tel. 985/362070). Computer use is 300 ptas. for half an hour, 500 ptas. for an hour.

EMERGENCIES

Police (San José 2, tel. 985/181100).

For 24-hour medical aid, visit **Hospital de Cabueñes** (C. Cabueñes, tel. 985/18–5000).

ENGLISH-LANGUAGE BOOKSTORES

The **English Bookshop** (C. Ezcurdia 58, tel. 985/533–8326), the only exclusively English-language bookstore in Asturias or Cantabria, stocks literature, thrillers, and a few travel guides. Open weekdays 10–2 and 5–8, Saturday 10–2, it's one block behind Playa San Lorenzo, between Calles Caridad and La Playa.

MAIL

The main **post office** (Plaza 6 de Agosto, tel. 985/201306) is open weekdays 8:30–8:30 and Saturday 9:30–2.

COMING AND GOING

Gijón is three hours west of Santander (four and a half hours west of the French border) by car on the Autovía del Cantabrico, which runs along the north coast to A Coruña, Galicia. From Madrid, Gijón is a four-and-a-half-hour drive on Highway N-VI.

Within a block of the train station are hotels, tourist info (exit at C. Pedro Duro; the office is 100 yards down on the right), and the bus station. The old town, the main beach, and everything else are within a 10-minute walk. For a **taxi** call 985/164444.

BY BUS

ALSA (Magnus Blikstad 2, tel. 985/342713) offers the best and quickest service to **Oviedo** (25 mins, 255 ptas.). Other destinations include **Santander** (4 hrs, 2,000 ptas.), **A Coruña** (4–5½ hrs, 3,175 ptas.), and **Madrid** (5½ hrs, 4,000–6,000 ptas.).

BY TRAIN • RENFE (tel. 985/170202) shares a station (Plaza del Humedal) with **FEVE** (tel. 985/342415); just note that night trains depart from the Jovellanos station, on Avenida Juan Carlos I. RENFE also has a ticket office at Calle Asturias 3 (tel. 985/343821). Frequent RENFE trains make the half-hour trip to **Oviedo** (900 ptas.); take FEVE to coastal towns such as **Ribadesella** (730 ptas.).

WHERE TO SLEEP

If you're strapped, there are a number of ratty pensions to choose from, equipped with exposed bulbs and antiquated wall calendars. The next step up is a *hostal,* including **Hostal Maruja** (C. Adaro 4, tel. 985/354980; doubles 5,000 ptas. in summer, 3,000 off season) and **Hostal Plaza** (C. Prendes Pando 2, tel. 985/346562, doubles 6,200 ptas. in summer, 4,000 ptas. off season). If, however, you've got an extra 2,000–3,000 ptas. to spare, the best deal is a double in the new **Hotel Poniente** (Plaza Estación de Langreo, tel. 985/347589), which could not be any closer to the train station and offers a most civilized shoe-shine service. Rooms are 5,000 ptas. in low season, 8,000 ptas. in summer. Roughly the same prices apply to **Hotel Costa Verde** (Fundación 5, tel. 985/354240) and **Hotel Avenida** (Robustiana Armiño 4, tel. 985/352843).

WHERE TO EAT

The first thing you must do in Gijón is sidle up to a sidrería, order a plate of something (if you like shellfish, ask for some delicious sea periwinkles, *bígaros*), and *una de sidra.* A green bottle of cider, the taste of Asturias, will be poured for you personally.

If you're here in the winter and are brave, look for signs saying HAY ORICIOS ("Yes, We Have Sea Urchins"). These purple and green monstrosities, eaten raw (*crudos*) or boiled (*hervidos*), taste just like their source, the bottom of the ocean. They're a delicacy for seafood lovers.

Near the marina, **Café Gijón** (Rodríguez San Pedro 33, tel. 985/346796) is a relaxed, spacious hangout for leisurely reading and snacks. **Blue Sky Café** (San Antonio 6, tel. 985/356141) is stylishly contemporary; chill here after filling up at the nearby **Sidrería El Globo,** a local favorite.

UNDER 3,000 PTAS. • La Galana. This may well be the most attractive and popular sidrería in Gijón. For starters, it's in the Plaza Mayor, the very heart of things. Have a cider at the bar near the giant barrel, or for a meal, head back to the tables beneath the antique wooden crates stocked with empty green bottles. On weekends you'll have to give your name and wait, and even standing room may be minimal; but it's part of the fun. The food is tops—try the plate of local cheeses (*plato de quesos asturianos,* 1,600 ptas.) or classic fish pâté (*pastel de cabracho,* 1,200 ptas.). *Chorizo a la sidra* is the budget filler at 400 ptas. *Plaza Mayor 10, tel. 985/348174.*

WORTH SEEING

The beach walk along the **Paseo del Muro** culminates at the neo-Gothic church of **San Pedro**. From here you can cut across through the attractive **Plaza Mayor** to the **Plaza del Marqués**, identifiable by the statue of Don Pelayo facing the **marina** (*puerto deportivo*). The 18th-century palace facing you is the **Palacio de Revillagigedo**, which houses Gijón's International Art Center (tel. 985/346921). Most of what's worth visiting is near this central biplaza axis.

Everything to the north is in **Cimadevilla**, the old fishermen's quarter, culminating in the Cerro (Hill) de Santa Catalina. Behind Cimadevilla's Plaza Mayor is Plaza Jovellanos, where Gaspar Melchor de Jovellanos was born in 1744. His 16th-century home is the **Museo Casa Natal de Jovellanos** (tel. 985/346313), which, besides exhibits on Jovellanos's life, has a survey of Asturian art. Admission is free; hours parallel those for the Museo Etnográfico (*see below*).

CERRO DE SANTA CATALINA

At the tip of the Cimadevilla Peninsula, St. Catherine's Hill stands bravely out over the Cantabrian Sea, making it a good place for a day's reflection. The grass in this park is an enviable and romantic shade of green; below, the waves tumble onto rock. The gigantic, abstract monolithic sculpture *Elogio del Horizonte* (*Horizon's Elegy*), by Basque artist Eduardo Chillida, has become the city symbol and tourist

SAME OLD, SAME OLD'

Like all Spaniards, Asturians party hard on weekends. Festivities might continue indefinitely if it weren't for those pesky Monday-morning jobs. But the Asturians have found a way to keep things going through Sunday: start early. The last weekend stand takes place in the unremarkable town of Pola de Siero, a small jaunt from Oviedo. Cars converge here from all over the province every Sunday evening.

How this got started is anybody's guess, but young people come to Siero and follow a determined drinking route beginning at 5 or 6 PM in an area called the zona iglesia. The most famous bar here, on a corner by the church (the town is so small that addresses mean little), is called J. B. Once inside, you're unable to move an inch. El Otru is another standard.

Follow Calle Celleruelo—the movement from the church is all in the same direction—to a simple bar called La Petaca. Here everyone drinks the house potion called prubina, available in red or white. At 10 PM head down to Gasoline, a nice two-story bar with a wooden balcony, at the beginning of Calle San Antonio. Continue down San Antonio past a narrow stone-wall path to the perpendicular Calle de Hermanos Felgueroso, along which six larger disco bars help cap off the night. For most, the action ends at midnight, but a final segment of bars stays open till 6 AM for those on vacation.

You need to move slowly down this route (use up the peak six hours), or you'll catch up with a midteen set, which runs an earlier shift down the same path. Follow these instructions any Sunday night and you'll have a pretty good idea what a small-town fiesta is like: intense, dirty, loud, and drunk. The good people of Siero have their priorities.

From Oviedo Economicos Easa runs cheap and frequent buses to Pola de Siero, the last of which returns at 11:15 PM. From Gijón you can take a FEVE train, but here, too, the last return is at 10:15. If you have a car, use it.

motto ("Gijón on the Horizon"). Stand beneath the work and hear how it adventitiously catches the sea winds, humming as though it were about to take off. Quietly, fishing boats do their thing in the water, and behind you the Picos de Europa rise beyond a smaller, protective range.

TERMAS ROMANAS
The remains of Gijón's Roman baths are on display in this attractive subterranean hall. Look for the descent ramp in front of the church of San Pedro, at the end of the beachfront Paseo del Muro. *Campo Valdés, tel. 985/345147. Admission 350 ptas. Open March–June and Sept., Tues.–Sat. 10–1 and 5–8,*

Sun. 11–2; July–Aug., Tues.–Sat. 11–1:30 and 5–9, Sun. 11–2; Oct.–Feb., Tues.–Sat. 10–1 and 5–7, Sun. 11–2.

MUSEO ETNOGRÁFICO DEL PUEBLO DE ASTURIAS

This Asturian folk complex, at the eastern edge of town, across from Parque Isabel La Católica, centers on an incredible *gaita* (bagpipe) museum. *C. La Güelga, 985/532244. Free. Open Sept.–June, Tues.– Sat. 10–1 and 5–8, Sun. 11–2; July–Aug., Tues.–Sat. 11–1:30 and 5–9, Sun. 11–2.*

AFTER DARK

Gijón's nightlife is superb, probably the best on the entire north coast of Spain. It's at least equal to those of the other north stars, A Coruña, Santander, and San Sebastián.

Plays and concerts take place in the elegant 1,200-seat **Teatro Jovellanos** (Paseo de Begoña 11, tel. 985/172409).

For the full nocturnal experience, get some sleep—preferably till 10 PM—then head out for cider and tapas before you dine, or skip dinner altogether and stuff yourself on tapas or *raciones* with cider. The top tapa choice is **La Galana** (*see* Where to Eat, *above*), but sidrerías such as La Rioja and Don Pelayo surround **Plaza Mayor,** and you can hardly go wrong with Sidrería Casa Fernando, on Calle Recoletas. This early scene can already be qualified as nightlife: the sight of young kids pouring their own cider in the plazas is terrific. It's not just a folk tale—they really drink this nectar instead of beer, especially before the bar scenes get going at 1 AM or so.

As for the hardcore partying, that happens in an area called **la ruta de los vinos,** a wonderful, body-jammed drinking-and-dancing zone. The three main parallel streets, branching off Santa Rosa, are Calles Instituto, Begoña, and Buen Suceso, all near the Plaza del Marqués. Ask around for *la ruta* if you have trouble. The same commercial Spanish pop music predominates in these watering holes; one exception, with obvious British leanings, is **Brighton**, which has entrances on Instituto and Begoña. Most bars, in fact, run from one street to the next, so you may enter one bar twice and not (perhaps ever) know it.

Following an innate compass that might merit scientific study, the crowd moves north into Cimadevilla at an unspecified time; for the sake of argument, let's say 3 AM. **Plaza Soledad** has a number of interesting bars, among them the cleverly named **La Plaza** (Julio Fernández 1), which plays an urban *electrónica* sound. Around a corner is another, more independent-minded place for dancing, **Bolaocho.** Look for the eight ball.

Later, when dance fever starts to set in, head for that Gijón classic **El Náutico**, a *discoteca* complex on the boardwalk. If your swing runs Latin, both streets running along the marina have plenty of action; **Cubanísimo** (C. Rodríguez San Pedro 31) leads the four-beat salsa.

OUTDOOR ACTIVITIES

Viesca (San Esteban 16, tel. 985/357369) organizes hiking, biking, and climbing trips to the Picos de Europa. All-day hikes are priced at a group rate of 9,000 ptas.; your portion depends on how many people show up.

Playa San Lorenzo, like many Cantabrian beaches, is a good place to surf. Rent boards at **Tablas** (Paseo del Muro 4, tel. 985/354700), across the street from the beach, near the nightspot El Náutico. Remember that outside summer, Spain's northern beaches are for gentle sunning only; the water is frigid.

FIESTAS

Gijón is a wonderful place to be the night before one of Spain's biggest holidays, August 15 (Assumption, i.e., the ascension of the Virgin Mary into Heaven). For this, the peak of Gijón's **Semana Grande**, the city hosts half a million people, the largest congregation of humanity on Spain's northern coast. At midnight on the riotous 14th, the lights in this area go out and a spectacular half-hour array of fireworks is exploded off the water, easily one of the best such displays in Spain. Immediately after these *fuegos*, concerts kick in on the beach, and the masses party through the night.

The 15th itself is El Día Grande de Gijón. At noon an incredible chain of Asturians links hands across the entire length of San Lorenzo Beach (and curls back along the beachfront *paseo*) for the Danza Prima, a simple, traditional song and dance.

The following weekend brings the **Fiesta de la Cidra**, with free cider tasting and a sidra-pouring contest that sometimes makes headlines.

OVIEDO

Oviedo was the seed of Spain as we know it. The first Christian kingdom was established on this soil, and here the Asturian kings commissioned structures of great beauty and distinction. These buildings are probably the best reason to see Oviedo, capital of the Principality of Asturias.

The legacy of the Asturian era—which began in 722 with the Christians' defeat of the Moorish army in the battle of Covadonga and ended with the death of Alfonso the Great in 910 and the subsequent relocation of the Christian Spanish capital to León—is embodied by 14 exquisite buildings in a style now known as Asturian pre-Romanesque. The best examples are all in Oviedo, and five are UNESCO World Heritage sites: the Cámara Santa (a.k.a. the cathedral), the Foncalada Fountain, the churches of Santullano and San Miguel de Lillo, and the Palace of Santa María del Naranco. The designs of these structures were centuries ahead of their time, and their predominant style remains unique in all the world.

Known for years as a polluted industrial town, Oviedo has done much to literally clean up its image and now presents itself as "the cleanest city in Spain" (with a Golden Broom Award from the European Commission to back it up). Every night of the week the already pothole-free streets are power-washed by cleaning crews. Fancy new lampposts cover the city, imparting a particular elegance to the old town. All that said, the large university population does its best, starting on Thursday night during the school year, to tussle things up.

BASICS

VISITOR INFORMATION

Get all the info you need next to the cathedral, in the heart of the old town, at the **regional tourist office** (Plaza de la Catedral 6, tel. 985/213385), open weekdays 9:30–2 and 4–6:30. Less prepared but well located is the **city tourist office**, at the southeast corner of the Parque de San Francisco, open weekdays 10:30–2 and weekends 11–2 (extended hrs June–Sept.).

CYBER SPACE

Laser (San Francisco 9, tel. 985/200066), off the southeast corner of Parque de San Francisco, may be the first and only 24-hour cybercafé in Spain. What more could you ask for? Surf for 600 ptas. an hour.

EMERGENCIES

Hospital Central de Asturias, Julian Claveria s/n, tel. 985/108000.

MAIL

The main **post office** (Alonso Quintanilla 1, tel. 985/201306) is open weekdays 8:30–8:30 and Saturday 9:30–2.

COMING AND GOING

From the RENFE or FEVE train station, walk straight down Calle de Uría to the end of the Parque de San Francisco. Turn left (by the tourist office), and you'll enter the old town, centered on the cathedral. From the ALSA bus stop, cross the Plaza Primo de Rivera intersection, walk down Fray Ceferino a few blocks to Uría, and follow the directions above. For a **taxi** call 985/250000.

BY TRAIN • RENFE (985/250202) goes to **Gijón** (25 mins, 300 ptas.), **Madrid** (7 hrs, 7,000 ptas.), and **Barcelona** (13 hrs, 8,000 ptas.). **FEVE** (985/289046) laps up the coastal towns west to **Galicia** (A Coruña, 7 hrs, 2,500 ptas.) and east to **Santander** (5 hrs, 1,750 ptas.).

BY BUS • The bus station (Plaza Primo de Rivera) is near the train station but is unmarked, underground, and beneath a tall apartment building. The best locator is a flashing blue-and-yellow sign for the Salesas mall across the street. From here **ALSA** (tel. 985/969696) can take you to **Gijón** (20 mins, 255 ptas.), **Santander** (3½ hrs, 1,710 ptas.), **Madrid** (5½ hrs, 3,825 ptas.) or **A Coruña** (5 hrs, 3,175 ptas.). For local destinations, including Picos de Europa stops like **Cangas de Onís** (40 mins, 700 ptas.), **Covadonga** (45 mins, 805 ptas.), and **Arenas de Cabrales** (1 hr, 995 ptas.), use **Económicos Easa** (C. Jerómino Ibrán, tel. 985/290039), an ALSA subdivision based on a little street outside the main station.

WHERE TO SLEEP

Hostal Oviedo. This is the first possible stop outside the train station. It's satisfactory if you're completely pooped. Doubles with bath run 5,000–6,500 ptas., depending on the season. *C. Uría 43, tel. 985/241000.*

Pension Fidalgo. Well, at least it's across the street from a four-star hotel. Views from the windows also include the Plaza San Juan, where skaters and break dancers gather on weekends. Doubles with bath cost 6,000 ptas. *Jovellanos 5, 3rd floor. tel. 985/213287.*

Hotel Naranco. In the old town on a small cobblestone street, this two-star hotel offers spacious rooms with private bath for 6,000 ptas. and the comforts of a larger, more organized establishment. *C. Carta Puebla 6, tel. 985/220012.*

WHERE TO EAT

Every establishment on Calle Gascona—also known as *el bulevar de la sidra*, Cider Boulevard—is excellent. **Casa Ramón** (Plaza Daoiz y Velarde 1, tel. 985/201415) cooks up traditional fare in a *horno de leña* (wood oven) for under 2,000 ptas.

UNDER 2,000 PTAS. • Yuppi. This is Oviedo's version of Denny's, in case you long for chicken wings and orange vinyl booths. If you're in Spain to escape chicken wings, the *plato del día* (1,195 ptas.) offers pretty good local fare, even by local standards. Meals are served until 12:30 AM Monday through Thursday, 1:30 AM on weekends. *Rosal 13, tel. 985/229429. Closed Sun.*

UNDER 3,000 PTAS. • Sidrería Tierra Astur. The defining difference between Tierra Astur and the other great sidrerías on Calle Gascona is the indoor waterfall, but the long, rich menu doesn't hurt, either. A good sharing plate (in two sizes, for 950 and 1,350 ptas.) is the *tabla de embutidos asturianos*, a sampling of Asturian meats served on a wooden board. At the high end, spring for *merluza a la sidra* (hake in cider; 2,400 ptas.). But if you haven't tried it yet, you can't overlook the humble prince of Asturian cooking, *fabada asturiana*—a powerful stew of white kidney beans, fatback, ham, black sausage, and hard pork sausage. While waiting for your table, browse the Asturian gastronomical goods for sale, including a freeze-dried *fabada* kit, a large selection of local cheeses, and bottles of cider. *C. Gascona 1, tel. 985/215679.*

WORTH SEEING

CATHEDRAL

The Gothic pile at the heart of Oviedo's old town was built from the 14th to the 16th centuries around the city's most cherished monument, the **Cámara Santa** (Holy Chamber), which in turn was built by Alfonso the Chaste (792–842) to hide the Christians' treasures from the Moors. Heavily damaged in the Spanish Civil War, it has since been rebuilt. Inside the chamber is the gold-leaf **Cross of the Angels**, commissioned by Alfonso in 808; the inscription reads, MAY ANYONE WHO DARES TO REMOVE ME FROM THE PLACE I HAVE BEEN WILLINGLY DONATED BE STRUCK DOWN BY A BOLT OF DIVINE LIGHTNING. Try to resist the challenge. *Plaza Alfonso II El Casto, tel. 985/221033. Cathedral free; Cámara Santa 400 ptas. Cathedral open daily 10–1 and 4–7; Cámara Santa open weekdays 10–8, Sat. 10–6:30.*

SAN MIGUEL DE LILLO AND PALACIO DE SANTA MARÍA DEL NARANCO

As you make your way up beyond the city by bus or car, prepare for a shock—the wonderful view of Oviedo in a valley, backed by the Picos de Europa. For the best prospect, walk a little farther uphill past these two 9th-century structures.

The **Palacio de Santa María de Naranco** was designed (for King Ramiro, who knew the value of a good location) to overlook the city from this incredible position. Surrounding the palace are some wonderful trees and a lawn that's an amazing shade of green, creating a striking sense of balance and harmony. Then there's the strange building itself, with delicate, slender columns, multiple arches, upper balconies, and a moss cover setting off what should be a rectangular bore of a building. It's a fascinating pile, with an almost magnetic attraction.

A two-minute walk uphill stands the fabulous pre-Romanesque church of **San Miguel de Lillo,** whose elongated proportions seem a fancy of El Greco's hand, but of course he won't be born for another seven

YOU'RE GOING DOWN WITH ME

Asturias' hardest-core annual fiesta centers on an international kayak race, El Descenso del Sella, which, at noon on the first Saturday in August, starts in Arriondas and finishes 17 km (11 mi) down the river in Ribadesella.

On Friday and Saturday nights both Arriondas and Ribadesella explode in all-night mayhem, with a ridiculous number of bars and outdoor barracas (stalls) blaring music into the streets. Hotels are booked several months in advance, but that's fine; hundreds of people sleep (if they sleep) in tents, cars, or sleeping bags dropped wherever.

Saturday morning in Arriondas presents Asturian traditions both festive and folkloric. Bagpipers roam around playing traditional gaita music, and men and women sport traditional dress including the pointed hunting hat. In a rather wild parade before the race, young people gather in social groups called peñas and drive noisily through the crowds in cars and trucks painted and decorated for the occasion. Cider is poured on every street corner, and the light blue Asturian flag blends into the sky.

Near noon some of the peñas, dressed with tridents and crowns of leaves, storm the waist-high river. On either side of the Sella, thousands crowd in to watch the race begin. The crowd sings "Asturias Patria Querida" and shouts "Viva" as the name of each participating country is announced. When the streetlight on the Puente del Sella turns green, 1,300 kayakers—lined up in thin bands of slick, varied color along the rocky riverbank—dart for the river, filling the water with a blur of vivid color, like an impressionist canvas gone fauve. Oars hit the air, and the race is on.

And they're off: the crowd makes a mad dash to, of all places, the train station, where the special trén fluvial waits for only five minutes. The festival train follows the path of the kayaks, making a few quick stops where people rush out to the riverbank to watch the leaders pass—and so it goes to the finish line.

centuries. A multilevel series of little tiled roofs and another luscious lawn make this one of the most charming churches in Spain. *Tel. 985/257208. Admission 250 ptas. Palace and church open May–Sept., Mon.–Sat. 9:30–1 and 3–7, Sun. 9:30–1; Oct.–Apr., Mon.–Sat. 9:30–1 and 3–5, Sun. 10–1.*

SAN JULIÁN DE LOS PRADOS (SANTULLANO)

Strangely located near the crux of two converging highways (to and from Avilés/Gijón), this church is the best-preserved of Asturias' pre-Romanesque buildings. Having formed part of King Alfonso II's country retreat, the interior is completely covered by wall paintings in the Pompeii tradition. *Highway A66, tel. 607/353999. Free. Open Nov.–April, Tues.–Sun. noon–1 and 4–5; May–June and Oct., Tues.–Sun. 11–1 and 4:30–6; July–Sept., Tues.–Sun. 9:30–1 and 3–6.*

AFTER DARK

In the summer Oviedo loses its party-crazed student crowd; serious night crawlers should repair to Gijón for the evening.

The rest of the year the routine begins with dinner and cider on **Calle Gascona.** Folks then move farther into the old town, where dance action alights at **Kapital** on Thursday (Cimadevilla 15). Any other day, try **El Antiguo** (Peso 10), **Monster** (Sol 9), and **Paraguas** (Plaza de Paraguas), or, for Latin music, **Porsche** (Postigo Alto 5).

To seek out your favorite beer, be it what it may, make for the **Cerveceria Asturianu,** hidden away on a cobblestone street at the edge of the *casco antiguo.* The loving atmosphere here is legendary, especially among foreigners—travelers have literally covered the brick walls with black-marker comments, so Paco, the amicable owner, urges people to sign a guest book. A typical entry reads, "In the Asturianu, wonderful things always happen." The 18-page beer menu may have something to do with it. *Carta Puebla 8, tel. 985/203127.*

RIBADESELLA

Set beside the Ría de Ribadesella, the estuary where the Sella (*say*-ah) River meets the sea, Ribadesella is an attractive fishing town of serious interest to prehistory buffs. Here are some of the finest prehistoric cave paintings in the world and, near the beach, fossilized evidence of still-earlier inhabitants, as in dinosaurs. The town itself is attractive, and the many nearby hiking trails make it a pleasant place to stay.

BASICS

To find the **tourist office** (El Muelle, tel. 985/860038), turn left upon exiting the FEVE station and walk downhill for about 10 minutes until you reach the river. The office (Sept.–June, Tues.–Sat. 10–1 and 4–8, Sun. 11–2; July–Aug., daily 10–10) is in a glass kiosk where the riverside walk begins. The **bus station** is farther along the river from town, a five-minute walk from the tourist office. The Puente del Sella is the long bridge connecting the main town to the beach section.

WHERE TO SLEEP

UNDER 7,000 PTAS. • Hotel Boston. Unremarkable outside but comfortable within, Boston has some nice breakfast salons. The best situated of the inexpensive hotels open year-round, it's directly across the bridge on the beach side, equidistant from town, the beach, and the caves. Doubles with bath cost 4,000 ptas., rising to 6,000 ptas. in summer. *El Pico 7, tel. 985/860966. 15 rooms.*

UNDER 9,000 PTAS. • La Llosona. This 1788 stone-and-wood farmhouse has its own *horreo* (traditional granary on stilts), so you get extra credit for doing your homework on Asturian folk culture. The building has wonderful views of the valley stretching down to Ribadesella, and the scenic hike into town takes but 25 minutes. Double rooms with bath go for 6,000–8,000 ptas. From the caves continue on the road away from town; just before the sidrería La Huertona, turn up the hill and pass a few homes. If you have no car, take a taxi from the bus or train station. *Granda, Ardines, tel. 985/857887. 5 rooms. Cash only.*

WHERE TO EAT

The real restaurants and sidrerías are away from the water, in the back streets of the tiny town. Two of them, Casa Gaspar and Tinin, have outdoor tables on Plaza de la Iglesia; Casa Gaspar serves its local crowd a 1,000-pta. *menú del día* that typically includes fish soup and *pote* (stew) or *trucha con jamón* (trout with ham).

NOTHING NASTY IN THE WOODSHED

If you spend even an hour on the road in Asturias, you'll repeatedly come across rectangular, thatch-roof wooden huts mounted on stone columns. Visible throughout Asturias and Galicia (where they're made of stone rather than wood), these are horreos, *traditional granaries. Not to be confused with the simple stone huts used to shelter livestock in the Picos,* horreos *are used both agriculturally and as architectural accessories.*

UNDER 2,000 PTAS. • Rompeolas. Ribadesella's best restaurant is in the back corner of town, behind the church. Rompeolas is essentially a sidrería, with a warm, dark, stone-walled interior that gives way to a huge back patio in summer; but the dining room next door is equally charming. If you haven't tried fabada yet, order it here; the old wood oven also cooks up delicious meats, and a tank out back holds lobster (*langosta*), crabs (*nécoras*), and clams (*almejas*). For dessert, owner Conchita's *arroz con leche*—rice pudding—is as good as it gets; add cinnamon to taste. *Manuel Fernández Juncos 9, tel. 985/860287.*

WORTH SEEING

Thanks to superb summer weather, the beach here (like those of Llanes to the east and Lastres to the west) makes Ribadesella quite popular for a few months each year. Cross the bridge from town to see some interesting houses along the beachfront avenue at **Playa de la Santa Marina.** At the west end of the beach, an information panel directs you to the shore farther north, where you can step into dinosaur footprints. An English pamphlet called "The Dinosaur Coast," which can be cajoled from the Asturian tourist office, outlines walks along the Jurassic formations between Gijón to Ribadesella.

After crossing the bridge from town, turn left and walk to the white building, visitor center for the fascinating **Cuevas de Tito Bustillo.** Rich prehistoric paintings of horses and deer make these some of the most important caves in Western Europe, on par with those in Altamira (near Santillana del Mar) and in Lascaux, France. Only discovered in 1912 by someone named Tito, the caves were inhabited beginning some 40,000 years ago. If you miss the caves in Altamira and Puente Viesgo, do make time for these, as the contact with ancient man can be quite moving—the paintings are about 20,000 years old.

Only 400 people are allowed into the Cueva de Tito Bustillo each day, and tickets usually sell out early in the morning. A second cave, La Cuevona, welcomes unlimited visitors, however, and is well worth penetrating for its wonderful AV show (ideally, see La Cuevona followed by Tito Bustillo). The entertainment value is similar to that of a long Hollywood-movie trailer. Backed by dripping water, a Spanish voice narrates the history of the cave in moody, almost spooky tones, complete with images of cavemen dancing about the walls. For the full mystical impact, it might actually be more enjoyable *not* to understand the narrative, as you'll pick up the gist solely through mood words like *secretos* and *misterio*. The surprise ending is the show's climax: high above you, a retractable roof slowly opens, allowing sunlight to pour into the cave as through the crater of a volcano, exposing the startling enormity and complexity of the once-inhabited space.

Not nearly as riveting is the museum, or "learning center," next door, with objects under glass. *Tel. 985/861120. Tito Bustillo 330 ptas., La Cuevona and museum free. Open Wed.–Sun. 10–4:15.*

OUTDOOR ACTIVITIES

Ribadesella is a beautiful spot for **kayaking**, whether you just row around in the calm estuary or head back up the river and finish a longer run here. **Canoa La Cuevona** (tel. 985/860331 or 630/350429), run by a former kayaking champ named Canario, leads group trips for all levels of expertise.

SIDE TRIP

If you have a car, be merry, for 7 km (4 mi) outside Ribadesella is a one-of-a-kind driving experience. The road past the Tito Bustillo Caves ends at the tiny town of **Cueva,** which gets its simple name from the fact that you can only drive into it through a natural cave, a somewhat awe-inspiring experience.

The road passes mountain scenery and swaths of countryside green. Just before the final approach to Cueva, the landscape grows particularly lush; suddenly, you turn a corner and a 30-yard-high hole-in-a-mountain devours you: lights out. The cave winds 300 m (185 ft) along the side of a brook, with its natural formations and deeper crevices tastefully spotlighted. On the far side of the cave is a placard with a detailed hiking itinerary. The Ruta de los Molinos (Windmill Route) begins here, a separate countryside expedition.

If you don't have a car, the hike to Cueva from Ribadesella is hard since you need to climb up and down a hill; but the walk is gorgeous from the moment you leave town, and rewarding for serious trekkers. (You can, happily, walk through the cave itself.) Of course, you could just skip on over to see the natural passage and shuttle back on FEVE, which stops in Cueva en route to and from Arriondas.

PICOS DE EUROPA

The history of Spain is tied to the so-called Peaks of Europe, the nearly impenetrable mountain range shared by Asturias, Cantabria, and Castile-León. Originally called the Parque Nacional de la Montaña de Covadonga, this area was declared Spain's first national park in 1918.

The Picos are special for their walkable rocky-mountain paths, their glacial shapes, their deep chasms—some of the deepest in the world—and their eye-pleasing proximity to the sea. Almost anywhere you go in Cantabria and Asturias, you can see these mounds in the distance. The Picos de Europa National Park forms a refuge for some of the Iberian Peninsula's most endangered species, including the brown bear. Vultures and eagles are everywhere. In addition to fauna, the rugged reliefs, abrupt slopes, deep valleys, and towering summits draw humans from all over Spain in the summer; in other seasons the park is relatively quiet, and you can easily get to know its landscapes and towns.

This part of Spain is really about nature, with few man-made creations to distract from the gorgeous setting. Notable exceptions are the shrine and basilica at Covadonga, the ancient redoubt of Christianity from which modern Spain was essentially created, beginning with the push to expel the occupying Moors in the 8th century.

The park has four main entrances. The two in Asturias are Cangas de Onís, from which you can access Covadonga and two gorgeous mountain lakes, and Arenas de Cabrales, which leads to the start of a very popular gorge hike called the Ruta del Cares. The other two are at Posada de Valdeón, in the province of León, from which you can also begin the Ruta del Cares; and at the top of the cable car from Fuente Dé, in Cantabria (*see above*).

BASICS

Perhaps the best reason to stop in Cangas de Onís is the Picos de Europa National Park visitor center, called **Casa Dago** (Avda. Covadonga 43, tel. 985/848614; open Sept.–June, daily 9–2 and 4–6:30; July–Aug., daily 9–9). Outside the center is a large-scale model of the Picos de Europa that's great for orientation; it gives you a sense of the towns' placement beneath the towering mountains. Inside, you can buy extremely detailed guides to the park's most popular hiking routes for 100 ptas., as well as hiking maps and guidebooks. Ask about the free daily trail tours in summer. The small news agent across the street, **El Llagar** (Avda. Covadonga 22), has more literature, some in English. Down the same avenue, in the square next to Hotel Los Lagos, is the **town tourist office** (tel. 985/848005).

COMING AND GOING

ALSA buses run from **Cangas de Onís** (Avda. de Covadonga, tel. 985/848133) to **Covadonga** all year but to the lakes only from June 15 to September 8. To reach the lakes any other time of year, you need a car. From Cangas de Onís you can also reach destinations on the way to **Arenas de Cabrales** (1 hr, 300 ptas.) and **Panes** (2 hrs, 500 ptas.). From Panes **Palomera** (tel. 942/880611) handles the Cantabrian Picos, hitting towns like **Potes** (40 min, 225 ptas.).

WHERE TO SLEEP

If you want to walk the Ruta del Cares, as do most travelers to the Picos de Europa, your best base is Arenas de Cabrales. Turn to the back of the official accommodations brochure—"Alojamientos Turisticos, Guía Official," available from regional tourist offices—where *casas de aldea* are listed. These so-called hamlet homes offer home-style comforts, normally outside large towns, and make unique departure points for exploring the park.

In Covadonga, stay at the **Hospedería del Peregrino** (tel. 985/846047), which looks out at the magnificent church perch.

CANGAS DE ONÍS • Hotel La Plaza. Newly remodeled, La Plaza is still the most affordable thing in Cangas de Onís, with double en-suite rooms for 4,000–6,500 ptas. according to season. Heading away from the Roman bridge, take the second right after the church on Avenida Covadonga. *La Plaza 7, tel. 985/848308.*

ARENAS DE CABRALES • La Casa del Torrejón. Built as a stone fort in 1542, Torrejón has four charming little doubles, each 3,800–5,500 ptas. a night including use of the kitchen. The house, the only peach-color house around, is at the back of town, a few blocks off the main road. *El Torrejón, tel. 985/846411. 4 rooms. Cash only.*

La Naturaleza. Poised at the foot of the Ruta del Cares, La Naturaleza has views of Arenas de Cabrales and the Sella River. Four comfy rooms, none costing more than 4,500 ptas., come with large, clean bathrooms. In summer you can take cheap, home-cooked meals in the large living room; in winter you can thaw by the fire. Technically this is a pension, but it has the cozy feel of a bed-and-breakfast. *La Segada, tel. 985/846487. 4 rooms. Cash only. Closed Dec.–Jan.*

WHERE TO EAT

If you like blue cheese, you must try the park's most famous contribution to Spanish cuisine, called simply *queso de cabrales*.

ARENAS DE CABRALES • Café Cares. This restaurant serves up traditional *cocina asturiana* on the town's main corner, and includes *chuletón* (T-bone steak) and fabada in its 1,300-pta. *menú del día*. The dining room has a wonderful view of the Picos, in case you missed it while walking in. *Arenas de Cabrales, tel. 985/846628.*

COVADONGA • El Repelao. Huge portions make this 1,500-pta. *menú del día* more than worthwhile. If you don't mind pork fat, a key ingredient in the traditional *pote asturiano* (extremely heavy stew made with potatoes, blood sausage, and bacon) make this your first course: a large pot of *pote* is placed on your table to spoon into your bowl, a serving that would easily fill six hungry people. In winter this is the only restaurant in town; look for it on the right when first you enter from Cangas de Onís. *Tel. 985/846022. Cash only.*

WORTH SEEING

Most of the Picos's hotels and restaurants close for the winter, when travelers are few and hiking trails can be obstructed by climactic vicissitudes. Winter is, on the other hand, your only chance to have the park to yourself. The Ruta del Cares is a regular Easter Parade in the summer.

CANGAS DE ONÍS

Most travelers approach the Picos through Cangas de Onís, at the park's northwestern corner. As you enter Cangas from Arriondas, you'll pass an attractive ivy-covered medieval bridge (known as the Puente Romano, or Roman bridge, because of its style) on your right. A cross—the **Cruz de la Victoria,** commemorating Pelayo's victory (as seen on the Asturian flag)—hangs from the peaked bridge, reminding us that this town was the first capital of Christian Spain.

COVADONGA

The terrain grows truly remarkable as you near Covadonga—and then, as if to challenge the increasing beauty of the landscape, the incredible pink, double-spired **Basilica de Covadonga** comes into view, towering high on a rock. On the way there you'll pass a shrine that hovers in rock above a waterfall; this curious spectacle, the **Santa Cueva** (Holy Cave), is considered nothing less than the birthplace of Spain. Here, in 718, a handful of sturdy Asturian Christians led by Don Pelayo (*the* name you need to know to pass history class in Asturias) took refuge here, praying for the strength to turn back the encroaching Moors.

Well, history class tells us they did indeed, and the ensuing Christian kingdom was an early base for the Christian Reconquest of Spain. The approach to Covadonga's cave shrine is magnificent—you pass through a cavernous passage to the little site, perched in the rocks, above the waterfall visible from without. Don Pelayo himself is buried here.

A little farther up the hill is the 19th-century basilica itself and, across the street, a **museum** displaying treasures donated to the Virgin of the Cave over the years, including a gold-and-silver crown studded with more than 1,000 diamonds and 2,000 sapphires. *Explanada de la Basílica, tel. 985/846035. 200 ptas.*

THE LAKES

If you have a car, drive southeast from Covadonga to what are, along with the Naranjo de Bulnes and the Ruta del Cares, the most famous natural features in the Picos de Europa. This wonderful route takes you past sheep, furry cows, and a wild black horse. The lakes, **Lago de la Ercina** and **Lago de Enol,** are frozen and snowed over in winter.

Cars must stop in their tracks here, but the paths leading off each lake make wonderful day hikes.

RUTA DEL CARES AND ENVIRONS

Coming from Cangas de Onís along the northern edge of the park, you'll pass through Poo and other small towns en route to **Arenas de Cabrales.** The wall of mountain that appears as you approach Cabrales is—there's no other way to put it—astounding: the steep, creek-lined canyons, the folds of grass and trees, the omnipresent sheep, the jutting crags of gray rock, staggered and staggering altitudes, winding roads, a panoply of greens . . . they continually astound here.

Heading south to Poncebos, you embark on the most popular path in the Picos, the **Ruta del Cares,** which winds through the deep cleft dividing the central and western massifs. The trek takes 3–4 hours to Caín (9 km/6 mi) and 6–7 hours to Posada de Valdeón, in the province of León (21 km/13 mi). At some points the mountain wall drops 2,000 ft, and your jaw at least 2. You cross bridges looking far below at the Cares and pass through a series of tunnels bored through solid rock. The last 3 km, near Caín, are the most spectacular, with passes, bridges, and winding scenery. Just beyond here is the meadow where legend says Don Pelayo was crowned the first king of Asturias in the 8th century.

Eleven old people (give or take) populate **Bulnes,** and until now neither road or rail has connected this speck of a town with the outside world. Hiking has been the only way in or out, and the walk up—not easy—takes about 45 minutes from the start of the Ruta. A funicular linking Bulnes with Camarmeña was in the works at press time, expected to be up and running sometime in 2001. South of Bulnes is the most famous craggy peak in the Picos, the **Naranjo de Bulnes** (8,264 ft), posing a climb that should only be attempted by experienced mountaineers.

Enveloped in the rich, green folds of the Picos's hills, the hamlet of **Sotres** has no lodging but is still worth a stop; it's probably the purest of the 20 or so towns in this quiet mountain range.

OUTDOOR ACTIVITIES

It's all about hiking and climbing here, with some other rugged adventures thrown in. Trail maps are available at Casa Dago, in Cangas de Onís (*see* Basics, *above*); and the regional tourist offices in Gijón and Oviedo might have extra copies of the English-language pamphlet "Mountain Routes: Hiking, Mountaineering and Mountain Biking," which outlines several itineraries throughout the park and region.

Cangas Aventura (Avda. de Covadonga, tel. 985/849261) is one of a handful of outfitters in Cangas de Onís that specialize in aquatic trips down the Sella River. Canoe (*canoa*) and kayak (*piraguas*) trips are especially popular, but you can easily arrange horseback riding, hiking, canyoning, and bungee jumping at various sites in the park. **Viesca** (Avda. del Puente Romano 1, Cangas de Onís, tel. 985/878200) is another trusty firm.

GALICIA

BY CHRISTINE CIPRIANI

Galicia is the kind of destination you have to explain to friends before and after your trip. People will nod with furrowed brows when you explain that Galicia is in northwestern Spain; they'll pretend to have heard of Santiago de Compostela; and they'll murmur sympathetically at the overcast skies in your photographs. You'll know even as you speak that you're convincing no one else to explore this place—and you'll be glad, as Galicia is a land best kept a traveler's secret.

Green, rainy, and melancholy in all the best ways, Galicia feels like a country all its own, a land beyond Spain both geographically and culturally. Sitting quietly above Portugal on the map, it's a full day's drive from Madrid on slow, tortuous, often foggy mountain roads that eventually make the trip feel like a crusade—which, of course, it is. Galicia's capital, Santiago de Compostela, is one of the most important pilgrimage sites in all of Christendom: its cathedral was built to house the remains of the apostle St. James, and the medieval reverence for relics inspired long-term treks to Santiago from all over Europe. The resulting path, heading west from the French border, became known as the Camino de Santiago (Way of St. James), and to this day, marked by Romanesque churches and the resonance of centuries of footsteps, it imbues much of Galicia with a palpable spirituality.

Settled by the Celts in the 6th and 5th centuries BC, Galicia retains a Celtic flavor that's better compared to France's Brittany than to any other part of Spain, most notably in the form of the *gaita* (Galician bagpipe), stone crosses, and *castros* (fortified villages of round dwellings). The Romans arrived in the 2nd century BC and named the place Gallaecia; they eventually gave way to Christianity and the Visigoths. The Moors did some damage in Santiago, but never managed to extend their Spanish holdings to this relatively inaccessible corner of the peninsula; and by the Middle Ages Galicia was part of the kingdom of Portugal. (The Galician language, Gallego—still very much alive, like Catalan and Basque—is essentially a cross between Castilian Spanish and Portuguese.) In the 15th century the Catholic Monarchs, Ferdinand and Isabella, incorporated Galicia into Spain as we know it, and ever since those imperial days Galician men have been emigrating: mostly to the Americas, where they helped settle Spanish territories, but more recently to other parts of Western Europe. No matter where life takes them, however, most Galicians want to die here: they are by nature prone to *morriña,* a lovely Gallego word referring to a melancholy longing for home, or for something out of reach.

While most of this region is blissfully off the tourist track, Galicia's beaches are well known to Spaniards and other Europeans as a cool escape from summer heat. The coastline consists partly of quiet *rías* (estuaries—low, wide fjords leading out to the Atlantic Ocean) and partly of a poetic rocky stretch called

the Costa da Morte, or Coast of Death, for the threat it poses to ships. Many rías are lined with fishing towns, pine groves, and beaches, a delicious combination; on the Costa da Morte, the wind whips, the surf sizzles, and you stand gloriously alone, or with a lighthouse, on grassy cliff-top mounds. Inland, the region is a spectrum of green, from the dark shadows of pine forests to the yellow, almost fluorescent glow of grapevines (Galicia's white wines are some of Spain's finest, and every other house seems to have its own little vineyard). Scattered across the terrain are traditional stone *horreos* (granaries) on stilts, their sloping roofs usually adorned with a cross at one end and a symbol from ancient Celtic or Galician mythology at the other. Sunsets here are the pinks and blues of baby clothes.

FOOD AND DRINK

Galician seafood is renowned for its freshness and simplicity. Everywhere you go, *mariscos* (shellfish) rule: you'll see *langosta* (lobster), *langostinos, almejas* (clams), *gambas* (shrimp/prawns), *vieiras* (scallops), *mejillones* (mussels), and *cangrejos* (crabs), not to mention *pulpo* (octopus), *anguilas* (eels), *calamares* (squid), and endless other fruits of the sea. Most are served as tapas as well as sit-down meals; a *pulpería* is a bar specializing in octopus. Shellfish and fish alike are prepared elementally: the classic fish dish is *merluza a la gallega,* a slab of hake with a touch of oil and paprika, usually served with potatoes.

Landlubbers' classics are the empanada, a savory meat or fish pie, and *caldo gallego,* a hearty soup of white beans, turnip greens, chickpeas, cabbage, and potatoes. Both are perfect on a cold, damp day. Galicia's best-known cheese, the soft, tart *tetilla,* is shaped like a woman's breast and often beckons *à deux* from shop windows.

Galicia's best wines are the smooth, crisp Albariño and the acidic Ribeiro, both white. Albariño in particular is slowly winning deserved accolades abroad. *Queimada* is a sort of witches' brew, a potent Galician mixture of *aguardiente* (brandy), fruit, and sugar which is set on fire and stirred for several minutes before being consumed, a process that caramelizes the sugar and burns off some of the alcohol. The technique comes from Celtic witches of legend, who on misty nights would stir queimada in Galician forests, chanting over their cauldrons.

DEPARTMENT OF MYSTERY MEAT

One Galician delicacy you've probably never heard of, much less tasted, is percebes—barnacles. Yes, some of those ugly growths are edible, and barnacle fishermen take grave risks to fetch them, clambering up wet rocks as the surf bears down. Small and black with white tips, percebes bear a disconcerting resemblance to monster claws and are covered with a tough tube, which you twist off to uncover the meat. The taste is comparable to that of squid, and the experience enlivens your postcards.

SANTIAGO DE COMPOSTELA

Santiago is one of the most enchanting cities in the Western world. Pilgrimage site, university town, and capital of Galicia, it might be said to combine the best of Spain (joie de vivre, delicious food, exuberant ecclesiastical architecture) with the best of Britain (verdant hills, cozy stone houses, misty days that make you want to curl up with a hot beverage). The streets of Santiago's old quarter are paved with slabs of stone, trafficked only by pedestrians, and lined with arcades, called *soportales,* designed to keep the rain off shoppers' heads. Still, Compostelanos rarely leave home without an umbrella, and you'll find that the stone-swathed streets look entirely picturesque when wet. Even postcards feature rainy scenes, as Santiago is *donde la lluvia es arte*—where the rain is art.

The origin of the Camino de Santiago pilgrimage is the reason for the city's being: one clear night in the year 813, a religious hermit named Pelayo was directed by a mysterious light to a wooded spot on a hill, where a dig revealed a sarcophagus containing the supposed remains of the apostle St. James, who was believed to have preached on the Iberian Peninsula. The Asturian king Alfonso II heard of the discovery, came to see what was up, and ordered a chapel built on the site. So began the cult of St. James, the construction of the nearby cathedral of Santiago, and the long, hard journeys of pilgrims from all over Europe. Not long afterward, in 844, James appeared in a dream to King Ramiro I, promising to help the Spaniards in the Christian Reconquest of Muslim Spain by joining them in battle on a white horse, with sword in hand; and so he did, hence his frequent portrayal as Santiago Matamoros—St. James the Moorslayer. The name Compostela comes from either *campus stellae* (starry field) or *compostium* (burial ground), the latter supported by the relatively recent discovery of Roman and pre-Christian bodies in the same area where James supposedly lies.

What all this means for the average wanderer is that Santiago has one of the most immense and gaze-worthy cathedrals in Spain, an exquisite medieval quarter, and a general sense of buzz, amplified by the town's lively university population. The massive cathedral square and surrounding stone-paved lanes are filled with nattering (or protesting) students, Spanish kids on field trips, happy travelers, and exhausted, ecstatic pilgrims identifiable by their huge backpacks and scallop shells (the symbol of St. James). Food and drink abound in endless eye-pleasing cafés and taverns.

The European Commission named Santiago one of its European Cities of Culture for 2000, along with such heavyweights of heritage as Prague, Bologna, and Reykjavik. The city also experienced a premillennial burst of tourism in 1999, a designated Holy Year (when St. James's Day falls on a Sunday)—an astonishing 5 million people showed up that year, pilgrims and otherwise, overwhelming this city of 100,000. Come here now, when things have calmed down for the moment.

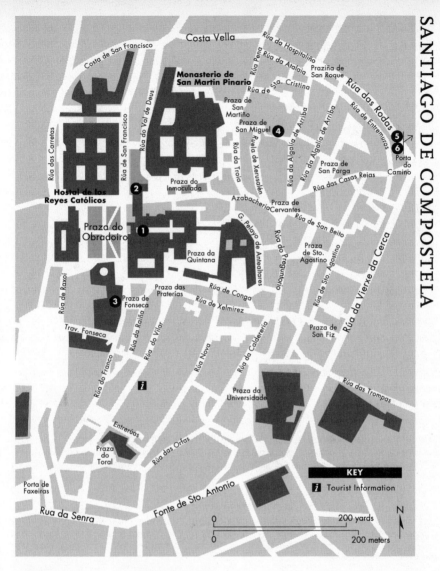

Costa Vella

Costa de San Francisco

Rúa da Hospitaliño

Rúa da Atalaia

Rúa Pena

Costa de San Francisco

**Monasterio de
San Martín Pinario**

Praziña de
San Roque

Sta. Cristina

Rúa de

Rúa das Rodas

Rúa do Val de Deus

Praza de
San
Martiño

Rúa de Entrerruos

Praza de
San Miguel

④

⑤
⑥

Rúa de San Francisco

Rúa das Carretas

Ruela de Xerusalén

Rúa de Algalia de Arriba

Rúa de Algalia de Arriba

Porta
do
Camiño

Rúa do Troia

Praza do
Inmaculada

Praza de
San Parga

**Hostal de las
Reyes Católicos**

②

Rúa das Casas Reias

Azabachería

Praza de
Cervantes

Praza do
Obradoiro

①

Praza de Antealtares

Rúa de San Beito

Praza da
Quintana

G. Pelayo de Antealtares

Praza
de Sto.
Agostino

Rúa da Vierxe da Cerca

Praza de
Fonseca

③

Rúa do Preguntoiro

Rúa de Sto. Agostino

Rúa de Raxoi

Praza das
Praterías

Rúa de Conga

Rúa de Xelmírez

Trav. Fonseca

Rúa da Raiña

Rúa do Vilar

Rúa Nova

Rúa da Caldereria

Praza de
San Fiz

Rúa do Franco

ℹ

Praza da
Universidade

Rúa das Trompas

Entrerúas

Praza
do
Toral

Rúa das Orfas

Porta de
Faxeiras

KEY

ℹ Tourist Information

Fonte de Sto. Antonio

Rúa da Senra

0	200 yards
0	200 meters

N

Cathedral, **1**

Centro Galego
de Arte
Contemporánea, **5**

Colexio de
Fonseco, **3**

Museo de las
Peregrinaciones, **4**

Museo do
Pobo Galego, **6**

Pazo de
Xelmírez, **2**

BASICS

CURRENCY EXCHANGE

Stick to banks, which are all over the town center, as the alternatives (such as the Berenguela photo shop near the cathedral) offer terrible rates. **Banco Bilbao Vizcaya** (Rúa do Vilar 33) is open weekdays 8:30–2. **Caixa Galicia** (Rúa do Franco 58) is open weekdays 8:30–2, plus 4:45–7:15 on Thursday.

CYBERSPACE / PHONES

You can phone, fax, and check your Web-based e-mail at **Cyber Rúa Nova** (Rúa Nova 50). Computer use costs a piddly 200 ptas. an hour; unfortunately, in the case of the Web, it takes about that long to connect. The shop is open Monday to Saturday 9 AM–1 AM, Sunday 10 AM–1 AM.

EMERGENCIES

Police: tel. 092. **Medical aid:** tel. 061. The **Hospital Xeral de Galicia** is closest to the old town (Rúa das Galeras, tel. 981/540000).

LAUNDRY

Venture into the new town to refresh your threads. At **Lavandería Lobato** (Santiago de Chile 7, tel. 981/599954; Avda. de Villagarcía 32, tel. 981/524290), you can do the deed yourself or drop it off and fuhgeddaboudit. **Lavandería la Económica** (Ramon Cabanillas 1, tel. 981/591323) has self-service only.

MAIL

The main **post office** (Travesa de Fonseca at Rúa do Franco, tel. 981/581252), near the cathedral, is open weekdays 8:30–8:30, Saturday 9:30–2.

VISITOR INFORMATION

Santiago's friendly **tourist office** (Rúa do Vilar 43, tel. 981/584081; open weekdays 10–2 and 4–7, Sat. 1–2 and 5–7, Sun. 11–2) is right in the center of the old town. The **regional tourist office** in the middle of Praza de Galicia, just south of the old town (tel. 981/584400), is geared not toward tourist sights but toward cultural events at the University of Santiago and elsewhere. It's open weekdays 10–2 and 5–8.

COMING AND GOING

BY TRAIN

Santiago's **train station** (Praza de Estación, tel. 981/520202, 981/594634 for reservations) is a 15-minute walk south of the old town, along Rúa do Horreo. Trains connect the city with **A Coruña** (1¼ hrs, 595 ptas.), **Vigo** (1½ hrs, 900 ptas.), **Madrid** (9 hrs, 5,900 ptas.), and other destinations in northern Spain and Portugal.

BY BUS

The **bus station** (Rúa de San Caetano, tel. 981/587700) is a half-hour hike east of the town center. To save the walk, take Bus 10 to Praza de Galicia. Leaving town, **Castromil** (tel. 981/589700) serves **A Coruña** (1½ hrs, 825 ptas.), **Pontevedra** (1 hr, 625 ptas.), and the rest of Galicia. **ALSA** (tel. 981/587133) makes the long hauls to **Madrid** (9 hrs, 5,100 ptas.), **Asturias** (Oviedo 6 hrs, 3,740 ptas.), the **Basque Country,** and **Seville.**

GETTING AROUND

Once you've put up for the night, Santiago is entirely walker-friendly. You'll see the sprawling new town, to the south, give way to the largely pedestrianized old town at **Porta de Faxeiras** (if you're driving) or **Praza de Galicia** (if you're coming from the train station). Off the west side of Porta de Faxeiras is the lovely wooded park Carballeira de Santa Susana, also known as La Alameda. Within the old town, three main pedestrian arteries snake south from the cathedral complex: **Rúa do Franco, Rúa do Vilar,** and **Rúa Nova.** (Rúa do Franco was named not for the dictator but for the French workmen who, imported to built the cathedral's Baroque facade, used to sleep in this street.)

For a **taxi** call 981/561028 (Praza de Galicia cab stand) or, in the new town, 981/595964 (Praza Roxa).

WHERE TO SLEEP

UNDER 6,000 PTAS. • Hospedaje Sofia. This place stands firmly in the budget category, with doubles for 4,000–5,000 ptas. and shared baths (rooms have sinks only). The beds are a little saggy, the furniture kind of sad, and the bathrooms not luxe; but all is clean, and Sofia and her mother are so sweet that the tradeoff works if you don't need modern trappings. Room 21 has the nicest street view. You're welcomed by an eclectic jumble of stuff ranging from postcards and potted plants to ceramics and crucifixes. *C. Cardenal Payá 16, 981/585150. 6 rooms, none with bath. Cash only.*

Hospedaje Mera. There's nothing distinctive about these small doubles (4,500–5,200 ptas.), and only a few have gleaming private bathrooms with big showers; but they do have windows you can throw open, some with original stone frames. One room has a terrace with a gorgeous view of the convent of San Francisco. Reserve ahead in winter, as some rooms are used by students (who seem to be well behaved). *Rúa Porta da Pena 15, tel. 981/583867. 12 rooms, 5 with bath. Cash only.*

Hostal Moure. This *hostal* in the lovely northern part of the old town offers inexpensive rooms with parquet floors and shower-only bathrooms. Renovations were in progress when we stopped in, but because Moure is run by the folks who bring you Hotel Residencia Costa Vella (*see below*), we trust in successful results; have a look. It's cheaper than its sibling, with doubles for 4,300–5,500 ptas. *C. de los Laureles (Rúa dos Loureiros) 6, tel. 981/583637 or 981/583364, fax 981/583648. 30 rooms.*

Hostal Pazo de Agra. Apart from the sparkling private bathrooms and ample cabinets, this welcoming little inn has a charming Old World look. The enormous, pretty windows—some with original stone frames—have lace curtains, shutters, and, in some cases, pleasant street views. Peach-color floral bedspreads, white walls, and pale-gray trim keep things soothing, as do the 4,000- to 5,000-pta. rates. Bathrooms have showers only. *Rúa da Calderería 37, tel. 981/589045, 981/583517, or 981/582215. 14 rooms.*

Hostal Suso. Smack in the heart of the old town, this friendly hostal adjoins a bright, equally friendly café-bar that's popular with pilgrims and perfect for breakfast. Double rooms (4,000–5,000 ptas.) have cream-color walls, red bedspreads, smooth wood floors, and clean bathrooms; and there's a small public sitting area for writing postcards. Some rooms look out on the adorable, arcaded Rúa do Vilar—ask for a street view. *Rúa do Vilar 65, tel. 981/586611 or 981/586523. 10 rooms.*

UNDER 8,000 PTAS. • Hotel Avenida. It's all about space here. You're across a busy avenue from the old town, so front rooms might be a touch noisy, but said rooms are gigantic, with smooth, dark-wood floors, old-world sconces, clean white walls (in some cases a stone wall), and smart red-plaid bedspreads. Bathrooms are in bright-white tile, with terra-cotta floors and big mirrors. Even the stone-floor lobby is spacious. For 5,800–7,500 ptas., you're in good shape. *Rúa Fonte de San Antón 4–5, tel. 981/570051 or 981/578007, fax 981/565817. 14 rooms.*

UNDER 10,000 PTAS. • Casa-Hotel As Artes. Steps from the cathedral, this little inn is theoretically overshadowed by the massive Hostal de los Reyes Católicos but in fact has sunnier, lovelier doubles than the parador's pricey caverns. Each room has at least one stone wall, recessed windows with beveled wooden shutters, polished hardwood floors, and a wrought-iron double bed; and each is named after a different artiste and decorated accordingly (the Vivaldi room has tasteful music-manuscript curtains). Robes and slippers are provided, and there's even a tiny sauna. With doubles for 9,500 ptas. (larger ones are 11,000 ptas.), this is not a backpackers' joint, but such warmth and charm are rare at any price. Breakfast is served. *Travesía de Dos Puertas 2 (off Rúa San Francisco), tel. 981/572590 or 981/555254, fax 981/577823. 7 rooms.*

Hostal Pico Sacro. From a nice, quietish street near the cathedral, a small Old World foyer leads to double rooms with smooth wood floors, frilly, baby-blue bedspreads, and immaculate bathrooms with tubs. Prices hover around 7,500–8,500 ptas. *Rúa San Francisco 22, tel. 981/584466, fax 981/583328. 12 rooms.*

Hotel Residencia Costa Vella. Backed by a perfect little garden, this special hotel snuggles right up to Santiago's medieval wall at one of the highest points in the city. The house is classically Galician, but the interior is awash in smooth, blond wood and natural light from floor-to-ceiling windows—the better to behold the garden, stone wall, red-tile rooftops, Baroque convent of San Francisco, and green hills beyond. The decor would look fine in a magazine, from the cheerful yellow wash of the hallways to stylish, mostly red and coral upholsteries to blinding-white bathrooms with primary-color blips. The glass wraps around to an airy breakfast room and reading area. Spend the extra pesetas (doubles range from 7,500–10,000 ptas.) for a perch with a garden view. *Rúa Porta da Pena 17, tel. 981/569530, fax 981/569531. 28 rooms.*

WHERE TO EAT

Presumably because it's so well supplied with tapas bars, Santiago is light on cheap restaurants, but there are several trusty standbys. The lovably scruffy **Casa Manolo** (Rúa Travesa 27, 981/582950, no dinner Sun.), a longtime student and pilgrim hangout, is equally reliable for tapas or a super-cheap *menú del día* (800 ptas.). North of the student district is the Castilian-flavor **Prada a Tope** (Rúa da Troia 10, tel. 981/581909). Yeah, the menu is printed in seven languages, but locals like it, too, and there's a reason—huge tapas and agreeably rustic decor, complete with bare picnic tables.

If you're here on a Thursday, check out the old-fashioned **market** (Praza Abastos, east side of old town) in the morning or early afternoon. Each hall in the 1940s stone building specializes in meat, fish, or produce. For staples hit **Supermercado El Dubres** (Azabachería 8, tel. 981/584304).

UNDER 2,000 PTAS. • El Asesino. Open since 1873, this place looks like a stylized version of your grandmother's house. Coziness incarnate, it has checkered tablecloths, a friendly staff, and walls slathered with tchotchkes, from plates and paintings to an identical pair of photos of a grinning young Julio Iglesias. The *merluza a la gallega* (hake in paprika sauce) is utterly, absolutely authentic and tastes like buttah; the empanadas are also good. *Praza da Universidade 16, tel. 981/581568. Closed Sun.*

UNDER 2,500 PTAS. • Aires Nunes. This three-story arcaded house has a bar, a softly lighted cafeteria (serving *raciones*) with a show kitchen, and a restaurant proper. The last has cream-color walls, bright contemporary lights, and a beautiful blond-wood hutch with painted drawers, a plate rack, and a display of foodstuffs. Most of the fare is basic and forgettable—several different fish in Gallego (paprika) or green sauce—but the *caldo gallego* is delicious. *Rúa do Vilar 17, 981/582516. Closed Sun.*

Carretas. Prices here zoom from minimal to astronomical. As long as you keep an eye on them, Carretas is a good place to plunge into fresh Galician seafood in a classy setting, in this case with upbeat yellow walls. Fish dishes are plenty, but the house specialty is shellfish: for the full experience, order the labor-intensive *variado de mariscos,* a scrumptious platter of langostinos, king prawns, crab, and barnacles, complete with shell cracker. *Salpicón de mariscos* presents the same creatures preshelled. Good old *gambas al ajillo* (shrimp in butter and garlic) are a moderate 1,500 ptas. The Galician wine list is solid. *Rúa de Carretas 21, tel. 981/563111. Closed Sun.*

SPLURGE • A Barrola. Feeling adventurous? The favored tapa here is *oreja con patatas* (pig's ear with potatoes), a Spanish delicacy. With a summer terrace and lots of polished wood, this classy seafood tavern is a favorite with university faculty. The restaurant has a beamed ceiling, original oil paintings, and a niche holding wine and travel books. If you're not up for pigs' ears, the large house salads, mussels *con santiaguiños* (with the meat of a small Atlantic crab), *arroz con bogavante* (rice with squid, lobster, and other shellfish), and thick empanadas of tuna and salt cod are equally tasty. You'll probably drop close to 5,000 ptas. *Rúa do Franco 29, 981/577999. No dinner Sun.*

CAFÉS

Santiago is one of the best cities in Spain for European-style coffee-nursing in warm, historic surroundings. You'll soon encounter the simple, traditional *tarta de santiago,* a dense, almond-flavored cake dusted with confectioner's sugar; A Calderería and Te Iacobus are best for more elaborate desserts.

A Calderería. Gold wallpaper and contemporary art give way to warm stone walls and wood trim; downstairs you get cream-color banquettes with your red semicircular tables. Drinks include coffees, *copas* (libations), and *chocolates,* but it's the desserts and pastries that stand out—"Clip Nougat" is nougat-flavored ice cream with pistachios and toasted almonds. Students keep the vibe unpretentious. *Calderería 26, tel. 981/572045.*

Cafe Bar Literarios. Overlooking Praza da Quintana, with generous windows and tables outside in nice weather, this stone-wall, tile-floor café has dark-wood furniture and a deliberately gaudy mural that incorporates send-ups of classic paintings. Aguardiente rounds out the coffee and drink selections. *Quintana de Vivos 1, no phone.*

Cafe Derby. Once the hangout of Galician poets, this spacious establishment remains a serene place for coffee and pastries. Dark wood and marble keep the Old World aesthetic alive. *Rúa das Orfas 29, tel. 981/596417.*

Cafe Generaciones. The walls are papered with old newspapers in sundry languages, which (along with a blinking game machine) lend a slightly scruffy, vaguely literary aspect to this quietly popular hangout.

The crowd is a cool circa-thirty set focusing on coffee and relaxation. *Praza Cervantes 21, tel. 981/577685.*

Te Iacobus. In the Azabachería branch (the cozier of the two), contemporary wood trim and light fixtures lighten the stone walls. Look down to see a discreet glass cache of coffee beans in the floor. The Calderería store is larger, with clubby wood paneling and a yellow back room. Delicious coffees, teas, coffee drinks, and drink-drinks are served with fruit-based desserts as well as standard sweets. *Azabachería 5, tel. 981/582804; Calderería 42, tel. 981/583415.*

WORTH SEEING

CATHEDRAL
Santiago's historic cathedral is no mere church—it ranks as one of the most significant shrines in the world. Covered with dainty excrescences, the cathedral's twin Baroque towers seem nonetheless utterly anchored, standing firm as they soar. The massive Praza do Obradoiro, out front, is one of the most celebrated squares in Spain, and from here the cathedral entrance is elevated by a zigzag pair of staircases, making the approach that much more heart-stopping for folks who've just spent a month or two crossing Europe to get here.

The cathedral was originally Romanesque, begun in the 11th century and consecrated in 1211. The facade you see before you is, needless to say, Baroque; it was built in the mid-18th century by Galician architect Fernando de Casas y Novoa and a phalanx of Galician sculptors as well as workers (*obreros*) from all over Europe. The highest perch goes to St. James, in his favorite pilgrim costume; beneath him are his two disciples, Theodore and Athenacius, who helped return his remains to Iberia. The bells in the right-hand tower were, according to legend, seized by the Moorish warrior Almanzor in 997 and hauled off to be used as lamps in the great mosque of Córdoba, then grabbed back after the Christian Reconquest.

The cathedral's pièce de résistance is the **Pórtico de la Gloria,** its original entryway. Tucked just inside the present entrance, the Pórtico is one of the finest works of Romanesque art in the world and certainly the most elaborate, with dozens of biblical figures and a surprising feeling of bonhomie. If it's clotted with tourists when you visit, wait until you have space to stand back and admire the sculptures, finished in 1188 by Maestro Mateo. The Pórtico is carved of golden granite and was originally painted, but little color remains—in the 19th century a group of British art students made a plaster mold of this masterpiece for study, and when they removed the plaster, that was the end of the paint. Oops.

To the left is a depiction of the Jewish tribes to whom Jesus was promised as Messiah; to the right, the Last Judgment. The grand central arch depicts the Apocalypse. In the middle is St. James, of course, but above him is Jesus, not otherwise the star of this cathedral. Fanning out above Jesus are the Twenty-Four Elders of the Apocalypse, chatting and playing their instruments, some of which are traditionally Galician, like the two-man *sanfoña* in the center. Immediately surrounding Jesus are the four evangelists—Matthew, Mark, Luke, and John—scribbling away on their Gospels (Mark is the one with the lion). Flanking this arch on the left pillar are the prophets Moses, Daniel, Isaiah, and Jeremiah; on the right pillar, the apostles Peter, Paul, James, and John the Evangelist. Note that the prophets are holding scrolls, while their descendants have books at their disposal (new media). Much is made of the prophet Daniel's fetching smile: what is amusing him? One sly suggestion has him grinning at the woman opposite, one of the few female figures present, possibly the biblical Esther or Queen Lupa, the pagan queen in charge when James's body first washed ashore. Whoever she is, she was originally sculpted with larger breasts and nose, then trimmed down for discretion's sake.

Below St. James, on the pillar itself, are figures from Jesus' human genealogy, from the Virgin Mary on back to David and Jesse. The roots of the Tree of Jesse have been smoothed over the centuries by pilgrims' fingers; it's customary to place one's hand here in thanks for having finished the journey. At the back of the pillar, positioned for worship, is Maestro Mateo himself—here the ritual is to knock one's forehead against his, in the hope of absorbing some of the artist's genius.

The nave itself is not particularly memorable except for the organ pipes, some of which stick out like horizontal flying buttresses. The mega-Baroque **Altar Mayor** (High Altar) may not be to everyone's taste; topped by Santiago Matamoros, it's an explosion of gold and silver that doesn't really bear close scrutiny. Behind the altar, a jeweled effigy of St. James looks down from his perch; pilgrims embrace his metal cloak as the very last ritual of their pilgrimage. Beneath the altar is a **crypt** containing the presumed remains of James himself.

THE BEATEN PATH

The Bible says, "Ye shall be witnesses unto me both in Jerusalem, and in all Judaea, and in Samaria, and unto the uttermost part of the earth" (Acts 1:8), and 8th- and 9th-century sources have the apostle James preaching in northwest Iberia (remember that Fisterra/Finisterre means "end of the earth"). In any case, James was beheaded by Herod in Jerusalem in AD 44 (Acts 12:2), and here the miracle began: his remains were placed in a stone boat and steered by the hand of God to the banks of the Galician river Iría Flavia, near Padrón. As the boat approached, a panicky horse on the beach carried its rider deep into the water; yet instead of drowning, the pair surfaced with a covering of scallop shells. The scallop remains the symbol of St. James and the Camino.

At peak periods in the 12th century, up to 2 million people walked to Santiago each year, putting it in a class with Rome and Jerusalem. Yet the Reformation and even 20th-century secularism did not kill it off: as Nancy Louise Frey reports in Pilgrim Stories: On and Off the Road to Santiago, nearly 30,000 people made the pilgrimage in 1996, 16% declaring no belief in God and only about half of the rest practicing their faith. The pilgrimage has become a mixture of Christian believers, agnostics, and disaffected professionals taking to the hills to hear themselves think. While most medieval pilgrims were poor and infirm, today's average trekker is an educated, middle-class, thirtysomething Western European. Most find the Camino a life-changing experience. Now as then, pilgrims can stay for little or no money in special refuges en route.

The main path is the camino francés, which enters Spain from France at Roncesvalles and hits Santiago 750 km (465 mi) later, a month's walk. The world's first travel guide, the 12th-century Liber Sancti Jacobi, was written for pilgrims by a French cleric and has some interesting advisories: "The Galicians, ahead of the other uncouth nations of Spain, are those who best agree in their habits with our French people; but they are irascible and contentious."

For a whopping Catholic ritual unique to Santiago, hang around the cathedral toward the end of the daily pilgrims' mass, around 12:45, and hope for thundering organ music: if you catch the **botafumeiro** ceremony (held on church holidays but hard to predict otherwise), you'll never forget it. A gargantuan incense burner measuring about 3 ft tall and weighing 160 pounds, the botafumeiro is lighted, hoisted, and swung on an elaborate pulley by eight practiced laymen called *tiraboleiros* (roughly, "ball pullers"). Once they really get it going, the massive, internally flaming vessel is sailing clear across the transept, from rose window to rose window, forming an inverted arc of more than 100 ft as the music reaches a rousing climax. Particularly if you're standing in the transept, it all feels deliciously precarious, but there have only been four accidents over the centuries (one involving an unplanned trip out the rose window), and none caused personal injury. As the burner's momentum winds down, watch the oldest tiraboleiro grab the botafumeiro and spin with it to bring it to a complete stop. The ritual began in the 16th century as an air freshener: by the time pilgrims reached Santiago, many smelled, shall we say, ripe.

Santiago's cathedral is not ideal for quiet contemplation. It's often filled with Spanish middle-school kids on field trips, who ignore the tiny sign requesting SILENCIO; and the unsubtle altar is unlikely to inspire hosannas. But the place is inspiring for its palpable significance: you can sense how thrilling it would be if you had just walked across the whole of northern Spain to get here. *Praza do Obradoiro, tel. 981/ 560527 or 981/583548. Admission free. Open daily 7:30 AM–9 PM.*

Three display spaces augment the cathedral's historic holdings. The **treasury,** off the right side of the nave, has a few paintings and religious objects, including a giant, gilded silver scallop shell. Skip it if you're short on time. The **crypt,** beneath the stairway to the main entrance, reveals the cathedral's Romanesque foundations and displays beautiful wooden reproductions of the instruments played by the Elders of the Apocalypse on the Pórtico de la Gloria (with photos for guidance), including the intriguing *sanfoña,* or *organistrum,* or early hurdy-gurdy, a traditional Galician stringed instrument played by two. The **museum,** which you enter from Praza do Obradoiro to the right of the cathedral itself, has a botafumeiro, several tapestries in imitation of Goya cartoons, a fine sculpture collection, a galleried walkway overlooking Obradoiro, and an entrance to the cathedral's rich cloister. The arguable main attraction, however, is just inside the entrance: a reconstruction of Maestro Mateo's Romanesque choir, which once filled the cathedral's midsection. The sculptures (original) on the singers' stalls (reconstructed) are flat-out gorgeous, and traces of their medieval paint remain. You can almost—almost—hear the music. *Praza do Obradoiro, tel. 981/560527 or 981/583548. Admission 500 ptas. (joint ticket for treasury, crypt, and museum). Treasury, crypt, and museum open July–Oct., Mon.–Sat. 10–1:30 and 4–7:30, Sun. 10–1:30 and 4–7; Nov.–June, Mon.–Sat. 11–1 and 4–6, Sun. 10–1:30.*

AROUND THE CATHEDRAL—LITERALLY

The cathedral is surrounded by plazas, a tour of which gives you a sense of the shrine's complexity. Moving counterclockwise from Praza do Obradoiro, you come first to the **Praza das Praterías,** or Silversmiths' Square, probably named for its traditional place in Santiago retail, though possibly for the plateresque (silverlike) carving on this part of the cathedral. Stone horses spew water from a popular fountain. From here you can enter the cathedral through the only remaining Romanesque part of its facade, the Porta Norte (North Door): Strangely, the sculptures are not part of a unified work but were instead taken from other parts of the cathedral and glommed onto this arch. The effect is kind of amusing. Look closely and you'll see God creating Adam, and King David posing gracefully with his harp. Next, around the cathedral's beautiful clock tower, is the large, graceful **Praza da Quintana,** well populated with travelers and musicians on fine days. Here you'll find the Porta Real (Royal Door), through which cathedral processions pass, and the famous Porta Santa (Holy Door), or Porta del Pardón (Door of Pardon), built in the 17th century but adorned with Romanesque figures of the Twelve Apostles taken from the cathedral's ruined medieval choir. The door—not the black gate, but a few yards behind that— is opened only during Holy Years. Finally, north of the cathedral is the **Praza da Inmaculada** (or Praza da Acibecheria), faced by the imposing monastery of San Martiño Pinario, now a university building. Walk down through the Arco del Arzobispo (Archbishop's Arch) to complete the circle on Praza do Obradoiro.

PAZO DE XELMÍREZ

Despite its convenient entrance between the Arco del Arzobispo and the cathedral stairs—sandwiched to the left of some former lodgings for high-class pilgrims—the mainly 12th- and 13th-century Pazo de Xelmírez, or Palacio de Gelmírez, is pretty much tourist-free. An unusual example of Romanesque civic architecture, the palace was built for the enterprising archbishop of Compostela during the 12th and 13th centuries; and because it was built onto the cathedral, you can see parts of the cathedral's original Romanesque shell from the palace entrance. Many rooms are still under construction as displays, but the palace has one major charmer if you're moved by Romanesque architecture: its cool, clean vaulted dining hall. The little dudes carved on the vault-rib corbels in this graceful, 100-ft-long space are heartwarmingly lifelike, partaking of food, drink, and music with great medieval gusto. Each one is different; stroll around for a tableau of mealtime merriment. *Praza do Obradoiro, tel. 981/572300. Admission 200 ptas. Open Easter–Oct. only, Tues.–Sun. 10–1:30 and 4:30–7:30.*

PRAZA DO OBRADOIRO

Queen Isabella was responsible for the **Hostal de los Reyes Católicos,** on the north side of Praza do Obradoiro, a stark Renaissance box with a cluster of plateresque decoration around its arched doorway. Note the gargoyles along the roof (the sixth from the right is particularly naughty), the chain motif just below them, St. James (with his pilgrim staff) above the doorway, and Adam and Eve near the bottom of the doorjamb. When Isabella paid a visit to Santiago in 1495 and found that most pilgrims slept in the streets, she ordered a hospital built, assigned a guy to round people up every night, and thus improved the lot of many a pilgrim who couldn't walk another step. Said to be the oldest hotel in the world, the building served as a pilgrims' hospital right up to 1954, when it became a parador (state-run luxury hotel). If you can't afford to stay here, don't despair—the rooms are not as impressive as the facade— but the patios are pleasing, the bar is plush and inviting, the restaurants serve delicious food, and there's an art gallery straight past the entrance, with excellent changing exhibits. *Praza do Obradoiro, tel. 981/582200. Admission free. Open daily 10–1 and 4—6.*

Across from the cathedral is Santiago's city hall, the French-influenced 18th-century **Pazo de Raxoi** (Palacio de Rajoy), topped by a vivid depiction of Santiago Matamoros and Spain's Christian army in the Battle of Clavijo. Rounding out the Praza do Obradoiro on its south side is the 16th-century **Colexio de San Xerome,** or Colegio de San Jerónimo, a university building. Neither is open to the public.

COLEXIO DE FONSECA

Just beyond the Colexio de San Xerome, down Rúa do Franco, is this lovely 16th-century structure, named for the illustrious 15th-century bishop Alonso de Fonseca, who gave it to the university. Indeed, the Fonseca family produced several bishops, and once you identify their coat of arms—a simple pattern of five stars—you'll see it all over Santiago, as the Fonsecas were great builders of educational facilities. The college's multi-tier Baroque cloister has a fragrant garden, and the front rooms host changing high-quality exhibits. Recent example: *Cartography of Galicia,* a collection of handsome 16th- and 17th-century maps of Galicia from all over Europe. *Rúa do Franco s/n, tel. 981/563100, ext. 11077. Free. Open weekdays 11–2 and 5–8:30, Sat. 11–2.*

NORTH OF OBRADOIRO

When you've finished exploring the busy commercial streets south of the cathedral, walk north, on and off the **Rúa Porta da Pena.** Students live and wander here as well, but the neighborhood is much quieter, the rows of pretty Galician houses unsullied, and the views out to the surrounding hills inspiring. Don't leave Santiago without seeing this calmer side of the old town.

CENTRO GALEGO DE ARTE CONTEMPORÁNEA

Long open to all cultures and byways, Santiago connects with present-day creativity in the Galician Center of Contemporary Art, northeast of the old town past the Porta do Camino. The permanent collection places contemporary Galician artists in their international context, and the airy white galleries host temporary exhibits as well. Featured artists have included photographers James Casebere and Tracey Moffatt, painter Jürgen Partenheimer, and typographer Luis Seoane. *Rúa Valle Inclán s/n, tel. 981/546629. Free. Open Tues.–Sun. 11–8.*

MUSEO DO POBO GALEGO

Next door to the contemporary-art museum is the excellent Galician Folk Museum, housed in the convent of San Domingos de Bonaval. Here the displays look back in time, conveying traditional Galician country and seaside life through architecture, trades, crafts, dress, music, and art (this is the place to learn more about horreos). One of the star attractions is part of the structure itself: a 13th-century self-supporting granite spiral staircase, which still connects three floors. *Convento de San Domingos de Bonaval, tel. 981/583620. Free. Open Mon.–Sat. 10–1 and 4–7.*

MUSEO DE LAS PEREGRINACIONES

North of Azabachería (follow Ruela de Xerusalén), the Pilgrimage Museum has a rich array of Camino de Santiago iconography. Sculptures, carved panels, *azabache* (jet) items, and other artworks convey the history of the pilgrimage, changing representations of St. James, and the Camino's relation to the city itself. *Rúa de San Miguel 4, tel. 981/581558. Admission 400 ptas. Open Tues.–Fri. 10–8, Sat. 10:30–1:30 and 5–8, Sun. 10:30–1:30.*

SHOPPING

Tired of tacky postcards? Pick up some arty ones in the bookstore **Librería San Pablo** (Rúa do Vilar 37), open daily 10–1 and 4:30–8 (Sat. 10–1 only).

The large craft store **Amboa** (Rúa Nova 44, tel. 981/583359) specializes in ceramics but is also well stocked with funky wall clocks, creative housewares, and cheap silver jewelry. There's a smaller branch at Azabachería 33; both are closed Sunday. On a tiny lane off Azabachería, **Noroeste** (Ruela de Xerusalén 0, tel. 981/577130), open every day but Sunday, sells contemporary handmade jewelry in gold and silver, with several artisans represented. Prices are not minimal, but they're lower than the attractive white-and-blond-wood setting would suggest.

AFTER DARK

NIGHTLIFE

Santiago's nightlife peaks on Thursday night, as many university students spend weekends at home with their families. The streets of the old town, especially **Rúa do Franco, Rúa do Vilar,** and **Rúa do Raiña,** are crammed with bars, restaurants, and wandering crowds for this last hurrah. Santiago's traditional competitive pub crawl is "Paris to Dakar," a 30-bar marathon named for the famous road race. The idea is to knock back a drink at every bar between **Paris** (Rúa dos Bautizados 11, tel. 981/585986) and **Cafetería Dakar** (Rúa do Franco 13, tel. 981/578192). At the end, he or she with the most brain cells wins. Around 5 AM the crowd moves toward the new town, settling into **El Yate** (Rúa da Senra 24, near Praza da Galicia) for *churros con chocolate.*

The most appealing hangout for the paycheck set is **O Beiro** (Rúa do Raiña 3, tel. 981/581370), a rustic wine bar with a stylish, laid-back thirtyish crowd. The ground-floor back room is essentially a wine cellar, with stone walls and floors, a low wood-beam ceiling, picnic tables, and floor-to-ceiling display shelves of *vino.* Empanadas are free and delicious.

Los Caracoles (Rúa do Raiña 14, tel. 981/561498) is a ham shop and reasonably priced restaurant—menus 1,500 and 2,000 ptas.—that turns into a hoppin' bar late at night. It's known for its *queimada,* which serves two or four people for 1,100 or 2,000 ptas. A little farther east, **Pepe Loba** (Rúa do Castro 7, no phone) is an inviting, stone-and-dark-wood café-bar that seems to inspire romance.

THE ARTS

Check the monthly paper *Compostela,* available at either tourist office, for current goings-on.

Players at Santiago's **Teatro Principal** (Rúa Nova 21, tel. 981/581928) apply the Castilian language to Spanish and non-Spanish plays alike: recent productions have included Beckett's *Endgame* and Strindberg's *Miss Julie.* Tickets start at 1,000 ptas.

If you have ample time, see what's going on at the **Auditorio de Galicia** (981/571026 or 981/573979, www.audigal.es), a long walk or short taxi ride north of town. Home of the Royal Galician Philharmonic, this modern complex has a world-class concert program: recent guests have included the Academy of St.-Martin-in-the-Fields, the Leipzig Gewandhaus Orchestra, and the renowned chamber choir from Barcelona's Palau de la Música Catalana. Jazz offerings are equally international. Recent exhibits in the art gallery featured Basque sculptor Eduardo Chillida, antiquities from the Arab world, and American abstract expressionism.

THE RÍAS BAIXAS

If Santiago is the heart of Galicia, the Lower Estuaries are the soul (or maybe it's the other way around). Ambling quietly into the coast lands, these loping tongues of water are lined with some of Galicia's most laid-back towns and soothing countryside. In summer the beaches of the Rías Baixas attract folks from all over Spain and Europe with a combination of sunshine, blue water, and cool breezes that Andalusia can't claim. The provincial capital, Pontevedra, makes a good launch pad, especially if you're not driving; but the essence of these rías lies beyond the scope of civilization.

PONTEVEDRA

Pontevedra is a highly unassuming little city. Preceded by undistinguished prefab suburbs, it has a hilly, intimate old town with the requisite rainy, Old World look and plazas full of roaming teenagers, chatty old women, and dressed-up little kids. Mass is unusually well attended here; of an evening, you'll see people walking en masse in one direction and wonder what's going on, then see them trotting up the church steps.

A night in Pontevedra's old town might suggest that this city has more bars (and shoe stores) per capita than any other place in Spain; and some of the local graffiti has a dark aspect, reflecting opposition to Europe's new waves of immigrants—who, of course, tend to inhabit cities far larger than Pontevedra. The level of tourism is low enough that you may inspire benign "You're not from around here, are you?" looks. Yet the local theater is staging Ben Jonson's *Volpone*, and the presence of boutiques like Adolfo Dominguez suggests a current of sophistication. It's a hard city to figure; give it a whirl.

BASICS

VISITOR INFORMATION
The **tourist office** (Rúa Xeneral Gutierrez Mellado 3/General Mola 3, tel. 986/850814) is just across Rúa Michelena from the old town; it's open weekdays 9:30–2 and 4:30–6:30, Saturday 10–12:30. In summer the little information booth on Praza de España opens on the same schedule.

CURRENCY EXCHANGE
Stop into **Banco Santander** (Michelena 26) or **Banco Simeon** (Michelena 13), the latter open weekdays 9–2 and, in winter only, Saturday 9–1.

EMERGENCIES
Police: 091 (or Joaquín Costa 19, tel. 986/853800). **Medical aid:** 061. The **Hospital Provincial** is in the new town on Benito Corbal (tel. 986/855500).

MAIL
The **post office** is in the new town, just beyond Praza de la Peregrina, at the intersection of Rúa Oliva and Rúa de García Camba (tel. 986/850677).

COMING AND GOING

Pontevedra's **bus station** (tel. 986/852408 or 986/851313) and **train station** (tel. 986/851313) are across the street from each other on Avenida Alféreces Provisionales—which becomes Avenida de Vigo, then Calle Peregrina—roughly 1 km (½ mi) southeast of the old town. Buses are plentiful, connecting the city with **Cambados, O Grove,** and **Cangas** as well as the biggies (**Santiago, A Coruña, Vigo, Lugo, Madrid**), but the system is complicated; ask the tourist office which company serves your destination.

RENFE trains serve only the majors: **Santiago** (1 hr, 595 ptas.), **A Coruña** (2½ hrs, 1,290 ptas.), and **Vigo** (½ hr, 295 ptas.).

To get around town, hail or call a **taxi** at Praza España (tel. 986/851285). Failing that, try the cabs at Praza de Galicia (tel. 986/852066).

WHERE TO SLEEP

UNDER 5,000 PTAS. • Casa Alicia. This pretty old house on the edge of the old town, near the church of Santa María, is quintessentially European, at least visually. Service can be crabby, depending on who's manning the ship. Doubles range by season from 3,000 to 5,000 ptas. *Avda. de Santa María 5, tel. 986/857079. 4 rooms.*

Hospedaje Penelas. Drawbacks first: sea green predominates in the sunny stairwell (where the air is a bit stuffy), there's one bathroom for all, and the half-tub has only a spray attachment, no standup shower. Advantages: the rooms look down on a cute street, over rooftops, and toward the countryside beyond. The low beds are ultrasoft. And doubles start at 3,000 and stop, in the high season, at 4,000. *Rúa Alta 17, tel. 986/855705. 4 rooms.*

UNDER 8,000 PTAS. • Hospedaje Casa Maruja. The basic but clean and cheap (3,500 ptas.) double rooms in this friendly inn have nice views of the pretty Bank of Madrid building and, at an angle, the church of Santa María. The furniture, mostly of smooth wood but catch-as-catch-can, is augmented by floral bedspreads and lace curtains. Bathrooms have showers only. *Avda. Santa María 12, tel. 986/854901. 8 rooms.*

Hotel Rúas. Across from the Museo Provincial, this hotel is short on charm but clean and convenient. Floral fabrics and '70s furniture characterize the decor; doubles range from 6,000 to 8,000 ptas. If you drive here, they'll whisk your car away and park it for you. *Padre Sarmiento 20, tel. 986/846416, fax 986/846411. 22 rooms.*

WHERE TO EAT

Coffee break: **Cafe Gloria** (Avda. Santa María 5, tel. 986/851240) has an industrial look, with a high ceiling and second-floor black-metal walkway, but it's warmed by brick pillars, red-marble tables, and cushioned wicker chairs. Strong java and passable empanadas fuel your system while you people-watch through the two-story windows.

UNDER 1,500 PTAS. • Carabela. For a simple sandwich, settle into this local institution, perched on a corner of the kid- and pigeon-filled Praza da Estrela and Praza da Ferrería. Each of the enormous arched, recessed windows has one big table with red banquettes—boffo window seats. The lack of curtains allows bright light and a pleasant din as folks of all ages sip coffee, read the paper, and catch up on each other's lives. The old waiters are slightly gruff but totally competent. *Praza da Estrela 16, tel. 986/851215.*

UNDER 2,500 PTAS. • La Chata. With a happy, well-fed crowd ranging in age from the twenties on up, this *tapería* is the smartest, liveliest restaurant in town. A free plate of hefty, delicious tapas is served with every drink, but most people park themselves at one of the blond-wood picnic tables and make dinner from *raciones* of these creative little bundles. The cheerful decor is faux Tuscan, with washed orange walls, washed green trim, little trompe l'oeil–type murals, and honeycomb-wire grates for a last rustic touch. *Praza de Curros Enriquez 4, tel. 986/860019.*

O Merlo. Watch out: order a *ración* in this laid-back, old-time tapas joint and you get a full meal. Do not make the mistake of ordering five in the interest of variety. *Albóndigas* (meatballs) provide all the protein two people need; combine them with seafood with the amazing french fries or a platter of *champiñones* (mushrooms) or other veggies. Above the bar hang thousands of key chains, and behind the bar hang the proprietors, a friendly older couple. The TV has been known to blare the Spanish version of *Who Wants to Be a Millionaire? Avda. Santa María 4, tel. 986/844343. Closed Mon.*

WORTH SEEING

THE OLD TOWN

Pontevedra's *zona peatonal*, or largely pedestrianized old town, is the city's main attraction, and large enough to get you pleasantly lost a few times. The most charming square is not Praza da Leña, as is sometimes parroted, but **Praza do Teucro** or the smaller, sloping **Praza da Verdura,** which has a nice neighborhood feel.

Within the old town is a bona fide contemporary art gallery, **Anexo** (Charino 10, tel. 986/896803), open weekdays 12–2 and 7–9. The changing exhibits are pretty funky—perhaps too eager to shock, but worth dropping in to see, in part because the whole gallery feels fascinatingly out of context in this part of town.

BASILICA DE SANTA MARIA A MAJOR

Poised at the northwestern edge of the old town, almost overlooking the Río Lérez, this 16th-century sandstone church was built with contributions from fishermen. The plateresque facade of golden sandstone hides some lovely, sinuous vaulting, a wooden altarpiece, and, at the back, the Romanesque *Imagen de San Pedro,* a portal of active little scenes finished in 1165. *North end of Avda. Santa María, no phone. Free. Open daily 10–1 and 5–9; mass at noon and 8.*

CAPILLA DE LA VIRGEN PEREGRINA

Because Pontevedra was a stop on the *camino portugués,* the pilgrimage route from Portugal to Santiago, the city's postcard landmark is its 18th-century church of the Pilgrim Virgin Mary, a strange neoclassical item facing the old town across the Praza de la Peregrina (Pilgrim's Square). Not only is the church far taller than it is wide, but it has the floor plan of a scallop shell, which means the exterior looks like the front half of a coffee can with two lovely Baroque towers. The interior is not open to visitors, but the building's graceful shape responds beautifully to gentle floodlighting; pass by at night to see it watching benignly over the lively square.

MUSEO PROVINCIAL

Pontevedra's Provincial Museum is a hidden treasure. Housed in two 18th-century *pazos* (manor houses) connected by a second-story stone bridge, it's far larger and more exciting than it looks. Even if you're not normally an antiquity buff, the museum's collection of mint-condition prehistoric artifacts is bound to impress—unlike the usual fragments and shards, these intact items show how startlingly fine were some people's possessions. The time machine then moves forward, only to wander aimlessly between the 12th and 20th centuries. Exhibits are annotated in Gallego or not at all, but an English leaflet is said to be in the works, so do inquire.

You're introduced to **Galician history** from the very beginning, with a fluid succession of Paleolithic, Neolithic, Iron Age, Bronze Age, Iberian, Punic, Celtic, Roman, and Visigothic goods. The incredible **Celtic jewelry** gets a room of its own; check out the strikingly modern-looking finger rings featuring large polished stones of all hues. There's also an interesting (seriously!) collection of **silver** from all over the world, mixing European samples with items from India, Iran, Iraq, China, and the Philippines. Rather than useless Baroque ornaments, these are largely functional objects with a decorative flair—salt-and-pepper shakers, tea infusers, cigarette cases.

Crossing into the other house you encounter a wooden Portuguese sculpture entitled *Que Volva!* ("May You Return!"). Carved in 1928, it depicts a woman placing her hand on the Tree of Jesse in Santiago's cathedral with a look and attitude of clear-eyed love and relief. The wood is somewhat rough-hewn yet highly detailed: note the woman's traditional earrings, not unlike those displayed in the Celtic-jewelry room. Move around to see her face—her eyes are wide open. She is not swooning, contrary to what her pose suggests.

You then pass lots of carved *azabache* (jet) objects and some 17th- and 18th-century **etchings and prints of Santiago,** Matamoros and otherwise. Then the maritime theme kicks in with some large, wooden **model ships,** from Viking vessels to Columbus's *Santa María*.

Upstairs, it's time for **Gallego folk life,** beginning with a ceramic rendition of the Dos de Mayo (2nd of May), 1808, when the Spanish rose up against Napoléon's occupying forces in Madrid and were brutally suppressed. It's a sort of *Guernica* in white glazed porcelain, complete with women in combat. The windows and French doors in this room have unbeatably photogenic views of the neighboring houses and surrounding streets. Farther into this floor, you get **drawings and paintings** of daily life and scenery by a series of 20th-century artists. One series of drawings dates from the 1940s but appears much older, which tells you something—not unappealing, depending on your view—about the Galician countryside. Some of the other series are somber (the Spanish Civil War in black and white), some humorous (caricatures by the famous Galician nationalist Alfonso Castelao).

The mansion's **original kitchen** is done up as a typical country room, complete with stone fireplace. As you come back near the entrance to this building, take the tiny, steep wooden stairs heading down—they deposit you in a reconstruction of the captain's conference room on the battleship *Numancia,* which limped back to Spain after the Dos de Mayo dustup with Peru in 1866. (Admiral Méndez Nuñez was a native Galician.) The entire, beautifully wood-paneled room is skewed, so you actually feel a bit seasick on arrival. The lamp above the table casts wonderfully dark old-world shadows. After some more nauticalia, you lurch back in time to Romanesque religious sculpture, including some **Maestro Mateo** specimens that originally formed part of the Santiago cathedral's Pórtico de la Gloria.

Upstairs in the first building, completing the loop, are mostly **Spanish and Italian paintings** by Ribera, Murillo, Zurbarán, and possibly Tiepolo and El Greco (they're not sure), followed by some **inlay work** that includes amazing engraved ivory in big chests. One novel room contains only a 16th- to 17th-century banquet table and **paintings of Spanish food**—mainly fish and game, graphically depicted. *Praza da Leña s/n, tel. 986/851455. Admission 200 ptas. Open July–Sept., Tues.–Sat. 10–2:15 and 5–8:45, Sun. 11–2; Oct.–June, Tues.–Sat. 10–1:30 and 4:30–8, Sun. 11–2.*

AFTER DARK

On weekends, Pontevedra's streets fill after midnight for a drunken, largely teenage *paseo* that lasts until about 5 AM. A guy—that is, a city employee—wanders the streets the next morning picking up debris. The old town is packed with bars of varying aesthetic stripes, including Goth caverns, rustic taverns, and industrial chambers lighted in red or blue. Most of the action is on the streets radiating from Crucero Cinco Calles; the smartest bars line **Calle Princesa.**

For an infusion of high culture, see what's on at the **Teatro Principal** (Paio Gomez Charino, tel. 986/841862), near the intersection of Charino and Tetuán.

THE PENINSULA DO MORRAZO

South of Pontevedra, the C550 hews close to the shore of the Ría de Pontevedra. Just south of the city, it passes a nasty-smelling paper factory, then the modern towns of Marin, with a naval academy, and Bueu. If you're traveling by bus, get off in Marin and make your way toward the beaches, Praia Porto-celo and Praia Mogor. If you have a car, press south toward Aldán. The road makes hairpin turns through woods, then zooms through villages into little green valleys filled with vegetable gardens and miniature vineyards between clumps of white and rust-color hillside houses. Patches of soft and bright green alternate. Mere feet from the road, in people's backyards, are little stone horreos, some painted white or otherwise personalized. This is a popular summer area, so you'll notice that some homes are new and quite fancy, their windows primly covered off season; plenty of fine dwellings are going up on prime real estate with ría views. Move around with an eye for **views**—you get plenty of great vistas from the road itself. In the distance, peninsulas and the odd little pine-dotted islet pop out one behind the other in fading shades of blue-gray, like a nautical mountain range.

When you itch to get out of the car, start poking around **Aldán** and **O Hío.** Here, at the very crux of this peninsular notch, are endless tiny, quiet (except perhaps in August) **beaches** backed by scrubby pines and enclosed in artful parentheses formed by piles of rocks. The shallows here are turquoise, even in cool weather. Across the little cove, the white and beige houses of the opposite village, capped by red-tile roofs, are terraced down the dark slope of the ría. The foliage is a heady mix of eucalyptus and pine trees, with the odd palm tree thrown in near someone's house. O Hío also has a famous outdoor Baroque stone sculpture, the **Cruceiro de Hío,** depicting Jesus being taken down from the cross. If you can't get enough of this scenery, continue south to the resort town of **Cangas** and start gaping at the Ría de Vigo.

WHERE TO SLEEP

Camping Aldán is a great resource, with campsites for 625 ptas. a day plus 625 ptas. per tent, free hot water, laundry, a three-meal-a-day restaurant, a supermarket, and a playground. Best of all, you get direct access to two small beaches, which you find by walking through a lovely residential area and inspiring a chorus of dogs. The friendly owners, themselves guarded by two huge but friendly German shepherds, can advise you on local hikes. The campground is open from June through October, plus Holy Week. *Signposted on C550; write to Apdo. 127, Aldán, Cangas, Pontevedra, tel./fax 986/329468. No credit cards.*

CAMBADOS

Breezy Cambados is a nice place to cool your heels for a few days. Despite being small and quiet—or perhaps *because* it's so small and quiet—the town hides endless charming nooks and crannies that emerge only with sustained wandering. Gardens are many and luscious. Look around as you stroll: beautiful, fragrant foliage peeks temptingly over the stone walls that surround many old homes. Albariño wine, made right here in the neighborhood, flows freely.

If you drive here, stop in the quiet town of **Combarro** to see its famous long row of horreos facing out to sea.

BASICS

The **tourist office** (Praza do Concello, no phone, usually open Mon.–Sat. 10–1:30 and 4:30–7) is in a booth in front of the bus station. Change money at **Banco Simeon** (Avda. Vilariño 10, tel. 986/543681), open weekdays 8–3 and, in winter, Sat. 8–noon. The **post office** is at Rúa Nova 15.

Despite its one-traffic-light feel, Cambados has its own smoke-filled Internet joint, **Cyber Siglo XXI** (Rúa San Francisco N-8 baso), with computers for 400 ptas. an hour. Doors are open Tuesday–Friday 9–2 and 4–midnight, Monday 4 PM–midnight, and weekends 11 AM till whenever someone locks them.

In an emergency call the **police** (tel. 986/524092), an **ambulance** (tel. 061), or the **fire department** (tel. 085).

COMING AND GOING

Cambados' **bus station** must be one of the most scenic anywhere—buses pull up to the waterfront promenade (Avda. de Galicia s/n, no phone). The easiest connections are **Pontevedra** (1 hr, 315 ptas.) and **Santiago** (2 hrs, 600 ptas.). The town is not served by train.

Hail or call a **taxi** at the Praza do Concello, across from the bus station (tel. 986/542434).

WHERE TO SLEEP

Both these hotels are perfectly adequate. If you're in the mood for any kind of romance, however, consider sleeping in O Grove instead, as its Hostal Montesol is a real treat for the same price.

UNDER 6,000 PTAS. • Hotel El Duende. Bathrooms here have full tubs with shower doors, and the bedrooms gleam with spotless tile floors and dark-wood furniture. Amid the modernity are a few incongruously old-world chairs and sconces. Doubles range by season from 4,300 ptas. to 5,300 ptas. *Rúa Ourense 10, tel. 986/543075 or 986/542900. 17 rooms.*

UNDER 7,000 PTAS. • Hotel Nupe. These rooms are nothing exciting, but they're clean and a block from the water. The best views take in green leaves and rooftops, with the sea off to one side; and two rooms have terraces, albeit on a street with constant car traffic. Bathrooms have half-size tubs. Prices for a double run 5,000–6,000 ptas. *Avda. Vilariño 12, tel. 986/521050 or 986/543713. 28 rooms.*

WHERE TO EAT

Cambados doesn't try too hard for culinary distinction. Cheap eats are best taken at a bar on **Praza de Fefiñáns** or one of the cafés lining the waterfront on **Ribeira de Fefiñáns,** north of the green Paseo da Calzada. That said, O' Arco is one of Spain's lovelier traditional restaurants, well worth the pesetas if you've got 'em.

Amass picnic supplies at the **Moldes** supermarket (Praza Ramón Cavanillas s/n, tel. 986/543805), a biggie open every day but Sunday. They've got more boxed citrus juices than you can shake a branch at.

SPLURGE • O' Arco. Dripping with antiques and charm, the older and smaller of O' Arco's two dining rooms is warmed by a fire on chilly evenings. The list of fish is mouthwatering, and the succulent *lomo de merluza ó Albariño* (fillet of hake in Albariño sauce) fulfills its promise as a Cambados specialty, celebrating the fruit of the local vine. A shellfish feast for two is a reasonable 5,000 ptas.; the fixed-price menu for one is 3,500 ptas. Word to the wise: *especial filloas* are light, decadent, sugared crepes. Reserve one of the tables in the old room if possible, as there aren't many. *Rúa Real 14, 986/542312. No dinner Sun. Nov.–May.*

WORTH SEEING

The obvious place to ground yourself is the **Praza de Fefiñáns,** one of Spain's weirder plazas. It's as large and pretty as any, but there's a thoroughfare running right through it, and part of the square is given over to a parking lot. The 15th-century Romanesque church of **San Benito** is closed to the public but easy on the eyes, with a mottled, aged facade; on its far side, a lovely little garden fronts a small row of traditional Galician houses. Two sides of the plaza are given over to the lovely 17th-century **Pazo de Fefiñáns,** now a working bodega.

From the little plaza in front of San Benito, walk a few steps south on Rúa Fomento and look up on your left, above the stone wall—the house with the red windowpanes has a lovely little **grape arbor.**

If you have the time and inclination, take a little walking tour of charming Cambados houses. (Needless to say, be discreet. . . .) Start at Praza da Leña 10, a stone manor house called **Pazo Torrado,** with unusually small white windowpanes, some carved coats of arms, and—behind a stone wall, of course—a large, luscious garden of pines, palms, and orange trees. Just north of here, turn left at the María José restaurant and walk about 100 ft down to **Rúa as Rodas 6,** on the right. In a grotto on the arch above its inviting front porch, this house has an impressive old pietà sculpture; and there's a tiny gargoyle next to the front door itself. The house opposite, **Rúa Triana 12** (diagonally across the little intersection) is equally cute, with white windowpanes, copious vines, and, above its front door, a painted-tile depiction of the Holy Family, with Jesus as carpenter sawing wood. Backtrack up Rúa as Rodas to the stone cross, where **Praza San Gregorio** has a pretty little patch of garden with benches for a breather. Walk south on either of the two options to a small plaza, where you'll see the house at **Rúa Manuel Morguia 14.** Peek through the gate to a stunningly winsome garden with gracefully curved wrought-iron trellis arches and a central grove of orchids. The garden—indeed, the street—is anchored by what might be the tallest, most majestic, most perfect pine tree on the Iberian Peninsula. Back up for a full view.

Walk east on Rúa San Gregorio and make a momentary U-turn in front of the parador. On your left is A Casa do Albariño (see Shopping, below). Even the Video Club Principe, farther up the street, is housed in an old-style stone beauty of a mansion with giant clam shells, a red-tile roof, a little garden, and an old horreo.

On the left as you enter **Paseo da Calzada,** the tree-lined waterfront promenade, is Cambados' **parador.** If you're long on cash, consider dining here (menú del día 3,500 ptas.), as the sole in Albariño sauce is to die for, and the chef makes an amazing tetilla-cheese ice cream drizzled with honey. The dining room is not nearly as formal as those in most paradors; the breakfast buffet table (present at all hours, if only for effect) is a giant model ship.

In the middle of Paseo da Calzada, in a fountain between the rows of palms, is the **Monumento al Mariscador,** a contemporary sculpture of a shellfisherman in action. Restore yourself here if the sun is out; for refreshment of a different kind, walk north to the cafés on Ribeiro de Fefiñáns or back up Rúa Principe, past the wine shop and Pazo Torrado, to Cafe La Abadia (see After Dark, below).

On the other side of the promenade—past the **Casa Consistorial** (town hall) on Praza do Concello—is another architectural gem, the **Pazo do Salgado** (Praza do Rollo 22). Salamanca has a famous Casa de las Conchas, but here's a lovely unsung version, a stone house livened up with carved stone shells (conchas) and green windowpanes.

Whatever you do in town, by all means make the long walk or short drive to the ruined church of **Santa Mariña,** built in the 15th century and abandoned in the 19th. The ruins are preceded by an astonishingly well-tended cemetery of chock-a-block graves, most covered with marble and capped by pots of robustly fresh flowers in every hue, including spectacular orchids. The church's vaulting remains dramatically intact, the surrounding walls having crumbled. On the altar, Jesus and the cross are covered with cobwebs and other detritus; it seems unfortunate that a site so often visited can't see fit to clean its raison d'être. Just inside the churchyard entrance on the right (as you exit), one grave has a little glass display cabinet with a touching picture of the deceased, a young woman of 25. Follow Avda. da Pastora to end and bear left; ruins are on right.

Above the church, past a cute stone house, is the **Mirador da Pastora.** From here, amid rocks and grass, you have fabulous views of Cambados, the surrounding vineyards, and the adjoining estuary, including scads of fishermen's docks.

If you have a car, check out the ancient **Torre de San Sadorniño,** at the end of a jetty at the southern edge of town, on your way out. The brick ruin is not picturesque enough to warrant a walk, but it's near a sweet old residential neighborhood, and you can see down the coast to O Grove.

AFTER DARK

You'll encounter **Bar Laya** (tel. 986/542436) soon enough—it's the most obvious hangout on the Praza de Fefiñáns, filled with a youngish crowd day and night. Stone walls and close quarters keep the place lively and inviting. **La Abadía** (Praza Francisco Asorei 5, tel. 986/543387) is a laid-back café-bar with an adorable business card on which the abbot himself enjoys a sizable copa. Set in a corner-shape building and amply windowed, it's bright by day, laid-back by night. Coffee is served in handsome speckled crockery.

SHOPPING

Cambados is ground zero for the Albariño wines of the Rias Baixas. Though it's slowly being discovered abroad, this elixir is still hard to find outside Spain. **O Casa do Albariño** (Rúa Principe 3, tel. 986/542236) is a tiny, tasteful emporium of Galician wines and cheeses. One corner of **Bar Laya** (see After Dark, above) is also given over to a substantial wine shop.

Lots of souvenir shops offer traditional Galician witches and schlock, but **Cucadas** (Praza de Fefiñáns, tel. 986/542511; look for sign ARTESANIA DE GALICIA) has a particularly large and amusing selection, some of it quite tasteful, such as baskets, copper items, and Camariñas lace.

WINERY TOUR

A few kilometers south of Cambados toward O Grove, on the right (west) side of the road, is **Bodegas Salnesur,** maker of Condes de Albarei Albariños and aguardientes. You can tour the relatively new, immaculately white bodega year-round, though wine is produced only between roughly September and February. Tours last about 20 minutes. Winemaking is largely automated these days, so you won't catch anyone dancing barefoot in barrels of grapes; still, you inhale some delicious scents along the way. Fax them in advance for a better chance of tasting some actual wine. *C. Bouza 1, tel. 986/543535 or 986/543564 (ask for Marina), fax 986/524251. Admission free. Tours weekdays 9–2 and 3:30–7:30, weekends and holidays 10–2 and 4–8.*

O GROVE AND A TOXA

You approach O Grove (El Grove in Castilian) by driving over an isthmus, which settles you into the proper nautical mood. On the west side of said isthmus is the inviting **Praia da Lanzada,** a sprawling beach with fine sand, a bit of dune grass, and rest rooms. Placards explain the success of past environmental efforts to preserve vegetation and beach sand by moving the road on which you just approached. Wooden walkways invite breezy strolls in any season, though it's often mighty windy here.

O Grove itself is not historic, but the drive out here is gorgeous, past water and a gray-green-brown dunescape, and the surrounding coast has a string of mellow **beaches.** The town's multicolor fishing fleet is charmingly scruffy, in contrast to the uncompelling modern architecture; and some of the sea-facing houses have pretty wrought-iron window grilles. The charming **Monumento al Mariscador,** in the traffic circle at the port, depicts Mr., Mrs., and Junior Shellfisherman, an earnest family of fisherfolk. Just beyond this site, heading out toward the water, the cement wall on the road along the jetty is covered with a nonstop sequence of multifarious painted **murals,** each about 6 ft long. They go on for about ¼ mi; some are actually tile mosaics. Unreconstructed tourists can take a **glass-bottom-boat** (*barco de paseo*) tour, in which groups of gapers descend into the ría to see the creatures, à la Disney World's *20,000 Leagues under the Sea.* Several companies with temptingly campy signs have booths at the port.

From the east end of O Grove, walk or drive across the narrow, white bridge to the pine-covered island of **A Toxa** (La Toja in Castilian), an upscale resort complete with grand hotel and casino. The island is traditionally a spa; legend has it that a man once abandoned an ailing donkey here and upon his return found it up on all fours, bright-eyed and bushy-tailed. The waters are still said to have healing properties, and they're used to make a well-known black soap called Magno. The whole island feels a bit like a country club—you're never sure where you're allowed to walk, what with the tennis courts and golf course—but chunks of it are public.

The west (front) side of the island greets you with vacation homes. The south side has a lovely fat-palmed, manicured garden anchored on one side by the **Capilla de San Sebastián,** a tiny church covered from head to toe in cockle shells; the lower shells are, in turn, covered with graffiti, which look rather hideous and beg the question of who would deface such a shrine. There are no set visiting hours, but the door might be open; inside, against white walls, the vaulting and Stations of the Cross are painted deep periwinkle blue in a nod to the maritime setting.

Of course, there's some serious Atlantic real estate here. A Toxa's eastern edge is the prettiest, its promenade lined on one side with jaw-dropping houses (in styles ranging from red-roof hacienda to white-on-white minimalist), most of them carefully hidden behind pretty stone walls or fluffy gardens. Opposite these lovelies is a straight path rimmed with tall pines and covered with pine needles, a choice place for a short stroll.

O GROVE BASICS

O Grove's **tourist office** is inside the town hall (*ayuntamiento*) at Plaza do Corgo 1 (tel. 986/731415 or 986/732905). In summer there's another booth near the **bus stop** at the port.

For a **taxi** call 986/730161. The **post office** is at Rúa Castelao 58 (tel. 986/731422).

WHERE TO SLEEP

If these prime digs are full, continue up Rúa Castelao for a string of less distinguished but generally adequate budget options.

UNDER 7,000 PTAS. • Hostal Montesol. It's hard to recommend this spic-and-span place too highly in the value-for-money department. Steps from the bridge to A Toxa, you're spitting distance from the gentle waves of the little strait—and, if you're lucky, in full view of this charming scene thanks to your floor-to-ceiling gallery windows. Half the airy rooms have sea views (get one), and the rest behold a garden; some have terraces; and all have tile floors, bathtubs, and sleeper sofas for hangers-on. Natural light prevails throughout. The delightful sea-facing lounge has a wood stove and pine and wicker furniture. Doubles range from 4,500 to 6,000 ptas. Call ahead to reserve, as large groups sometimes fill the rooms. *Rúa Castelao 160, tel. 986/730916. 15 rooms.*

Hotel Tamanaco. Also hard by the bridge to A Toxa, next to Hostal Montesol, this much larger hotel has marble floors and tasteful traditional decor. Only 12 rooms have sea views, so phone ahead for the best digs. Doubles are 4,800, 5,000, or 6,500 ptas., depending on time of year. *Rúa Castelao 162, tel. 986/730446, fax 986/730352. 60 rooms.*

WHERE TO EAT

O Grove's chosen nickname is "Paraiso do Marisco," or Shellfish Paradise. These people know what matters in life: around the second week in October they host a nine-day, come-one-come-all shellfish festival, the Festa do Mariscos. The rest of the year **seafood restaurants** and **tapas bars** dot the streets, none particularly hip but all reasonably trustworthy. Greasy taverns are not the rule here; fresh fruits of the sea are.

VILAGARCÍA DE AROUSA

If you're driving north from Cambados, pass through Vilagarcía de Arousa (follow signs for the city center, then for your next destination) just to experience its waterfront promenade, lined with a decorative, white-painted stone rail. A smattering of cafés offers refreshment, and a road leads out to the **Isla de Arousa.** As you leave town heading north on the C550, there's only a few hundred feet of water and a small fleet of colorful rowboats between you and the pine-covered *isla,* with inviting little sandy beaches and a campground. Beyond the ría, the pastoral peninsula stretches out like a mountain range; at closer range, signs point to a mainland **campground** with stunning ría views.

VIGO AND THE ILLAS CIES

Galicia's largest city, Vigo, is nonetheless one of its least sight-worthy, serving mainly as a fueling and jumping-off point for nearby beaches and the gorgeous Illas Cíes, or Islas Cíes, a tiny trio of islands 35 km (21 mi) west of Vigo in the Atlantic Ocean. Protected as a nature reserve, the islands abound in birds, and the only land transportation is your own two feet: it takes about an hour to cross the main island.

BASICS

There's a **tourist office** on the south side of the port (Estación Marítima, tel. 986/430577), open weekdays 9–2 and 4:30–7:30 and, in summer, Saturday 10–12:30. The staff can steer you toward local beaches, such as Samil and Canido, west of town. Stop into **El Corte Inglés** (Avda. Gran Vía 25–27) for essentials and gourmet picnic supplies.

COMING AND GOING

The **train station** (Praza de la Estación, tel. 986/431114) is southwest of the port; to reach the center of town, follow Rúa Urzáiz to Rúa Principe. **RENFE** (tel. 902/240202) connects this outpost with **Pontevedra** (1½ hrs, 300 ptas.), **Santiago** (1½ hrs, 900 ptas.), **A Coruña** (3 hrs, 1,450 ptas.), and **Madrid** (8 hrs, 5,900 ptas.), and other major cities.

The **bus station** south of town (Avda. Madrid, tel. 986/373411) serves major cities and such worthy beach towns as **Baiona** (40 mins, 300 ptas.); city buses 7 and 12 go to the port.

WHERE TO EAT AND SLEEP

For cheap seafood head down to the waterfront and the **Mercado da Pedra,** where women prepare plates of fresh octopus while you wait (under 1,000 ptas.). Cheap *hostales* line the **Rúa Carral,** which runs from the Monumento al Marqués de Elduayen, on the waterfront, up to the Porta do Sol.

ILLAS CIES

Vapores de Pasaje (Estación Marítima de Ría, tel. 986/437777) runs ferries to the islands for 2,000 ptas. round trip. If one day isn't enough—and it may not be—you can stay over at **Camping Islas Cíes** (tel. 986/438358, open June–Sept.), where sites are 595 ptas. per tent plus 595 ptas. per person, but do reserve, as it's often full.

BAIONA

When Columbus's *Pinta* landed here in 1492, Baiona became the first town to receive news of the discovery of the New World. Once a fortified hilltop castle, Monte Real is now a parador; walk about the **bat-**

tlements for unbelievable harbor and ocean views. On your way into or out of town, check out the graceful **Roman bridge.** Baiona is mainly a summer retreat for affluent Gallegos.

COMING AND GOING

There are no trains to Baiona, but **ATSA buses** (tel. 986/610255) depart Vigo (1 hr, 280 ptas.) every half hour between about 7:30 AM and 8:30 PM, less often on weekends.

TUI

If you have ample time and a car, leave Vigo on the scenic coastal route C555 and drive up the banks of the Miño River, along the Portuguese border. If time is short, jump on the inland A55. Both routes will deliver you directly into the town of Tui (Túy in Castilian). This site was crucial during the medieval wars between Castile and Portugal, which explains why the 13th-century **cathedral** looks like a fortress. The steep, narrow streets are rich with ancient crested mansions, evidence of Tui's past life as one of the seven capitals of the Galician kingdom. Today it's an important border town, and you can see the mountains of Portugal from the cathedral.

COMING AND GOING

ATSA buses (tel. 986/610255) depart Vigo (45 mins, 350 ptas.) every half hour between about 7:30 AM and 8:30 PM, less often on weekends.

In contrast, there are only two **RENFE trains** a day from Vigo to Tui, the last usually in early afternoon (45 mins, 1,000 ptas.).

THE COSTA DA MORTE

It would be misleading to say that the air and water on this wild stretch of Atlantic Spain were in a state of constant tumult. Yet even on a calm day you can feel the latent threat, the history of nautical disasters on these sharp rocks, the damage these waters could do if they suddenly put their minds to it. This is where most of Galicia's barnacle fishermen, *percebeiros*, do their uniquely heroic thing.

Noia and Muros make good transition points from the calm, protected Rías Baixas to the exposed Coast of Death.

NOIA

From Noia's charming old quarter, the Gothic church of **San Martín,** its portal staffed with biblical figures à la Santiago's Pórtico de la Gloria, faces resolutely out to sea. The gravestones in the medieval **cemetery** bear mysterious Celtic inscriptions. Go swimming and sunning at the *praias* **Testal** and **Boa.**

COMING AND GOING

From Santiago de Compostela, **buses** to Noia leave hourly on weekdays, less often on weekends (45 mins, roughly 500 ptas.).

MUROS

The cheerful harbor town of Muros is a popular summer resort with lovely arcaded streets and a Romanesque/Gothic church, **Santa María.** Nearby Louro has some great **beaches**; try Praia de San Francisco or Praia de Area. The bay is dotted with mussel-breeding platforms.

COMING AND GOING

The **bus** from Santiago to Noia (*see above*) continues to Muros, adding about half an hour for a total trip of 1¼ hours.

FISTERRA

There was a time when this lonely, windswept outcrop over raging waters was thought to be the end of the earth—the *finis terrae,* or Finisterre in Castilian. The western world sank into the ocean here with a flourish of rocky beaches. All that's left for today's adventurers is a run-down stone **lighthouse** perched on a cliff (not officially open to the public, though you might find the door ajar). Gazing out at the vast, gray Atlantic from this dilapidated structure can, as George Borrow wrote in the 19th century, "fill the heart with uneasy sensations."

Aside from legends, the only draw in this tiny seaside town is its pleasant (barring storms) main plaza and, just off the plaza's southeast corner, the 12th-century church of **Santa María das Areas.** Romanesque, Gothic, and Baroque elements combine in the impressive but rather gloomy facade. The church is open June–September, daily 9–2 and 3–6; October–May, daily 10–2 and 4–6.

COMING AND GOING

There are several daily **buses** from Santiago (2½ hrs, 1,450 ptas.), but plan carefully if you're making a day trip—the last bus back from Fisterra leaves at 4 on weekdays and 6 on Sunday. On Saturday there's *no* return bus in the afternoon.

A CORUÑA

It's easy to like this windy port city. Shaped like an hourglass, it embraces a charming old-fashioned harbor on one side, a far-reaching bay and surfing beach on the other. Long one of Spain's busiest ports, A Coruña (La Coruña in Castilian) prides itself on being the most progressive city in Galicia, and feels cosmopolitan in a commercial rather than a purely intellectual sense. A Galician adage holds that "while Vigo works, Santiago prays, Pontevedra sleeps, and A Coruña goes out on the town."

You'll also hear a lot more Castilian here than in Santiago, particularly from the young 'uns, though they're taught in Gallego at school. With a population of 250,000 and close ties to the sea, A Coruña turns its gaze outward, earning its keep from fishing, shipping, and retail. In contrast to the University of Santiago's contemplative specialties, medicine and journalism, the University of A Coruña is strongest in business, foreign languages, architecture, and commercial shipping. While many older Coruñesos vacation in their own ancestral villages—which they may have left solely to find employment—young people strap on their backpacks and go abroad.

In the opposite direction, Andalusians (foreigners, really) come to A Coruña in summer to avoid roasting in the southern Spanish sun. With its famous row of glass-galleried harborside homes, a charming old quarter, some little-known medieval churches, an ancient lighthouse, good shopping, and an utter lack of pretension, A Coruña is a widely underrated place.

BASICS

VISITOR INFORMATION

The **tourist office** is right on the harbor, steps from Plaza de María Pita and the old town (Dársena de la Marina, tel. 981/221822; open daily 9–2 and 4:30–6:30).

CURRENCY EXCHANGE

Banks are best, and all of Spain's biggies are clustered behind the obelisk at Cantón Grande/Calle Real and Rúa Nova, on the isthmus. **La Caixa** is open weekdays 8:15–2, plus Thursday 4:30–7:45 between October and May. **Argentaria** is open weekdays 8:30–2:30 (8:30–2 between June and September), plus

Saturday 8:30–1 between June and September. **Banco Atlantico, BBV,** and **Banesto** have similar hours.

CYBERSPACE

The cyberbar **Internet@world** (Juan Flórez 58, tel. 981/143813) is hilariously futuristic, bathed in black light and mottled with planets backlighted in various colors. Each computer is installed in a planet. Surf as long as you like: the elevated chairs are cushioned, and the fee is a negligible 150 ptas. an hour, pre-paid. They're open from 10:30 AM until whenever in the wee hours they feel like closing.

EMERGENCIES

Medical aid: tel. 061. The **Hospital Movello** is in the Ciudad Jardín (tel. 981/147330).

LAUNDRY

There are no self-service laundromats in the old town, but **Folerpas** and **Surf,** both on C. del Hospital near the Museo de Bellas Artes, will do the deed for you.

MAIL

The main **post office** (Aldalde Manuel Casás s/n, tel. 981/208201) is just off the sea side of Avenida de la Marina, north of the Méndez Nuñez Gardens.

COMING AND GOING

BY AIR

Alvedro Airport, south of town, offers daily flights to Madrid and Barcelona plus several flights weekly to Bilbao and Paris. Call Iberia for info (tel. 902/400500).

BY TRAIN

The train station is on the mainland near two key landmarks, the bus station and the department store El Corte Inglés. To reach the old quarter and tourist office, take a bus (No. 1 or 1A), a taxi, or settle into half an hour's walk, keeping the water on your right. **RENFE** (tel. 981/150202) runs several daily trains to **Santiago** (1¼ hrs, 595 ptas.) plus frequent trains to **León** (5–6 hrs, 4,000 ptas.), **Madrid** (8½ hrs, 6,200 ptas.), and **Bilbao** (12 hrs, 5,600 ptas.) as well as other Galician towns.

BY BUS

The **bus station** (tel. 981/239099) is a few blocks southwest of the train station, even closer to El Corte Inglés. IASA makes frequent trips to **Betanzos** (45 mins, 245 ptas.). Castromil serves **Santiago** (1½ hrs, 825 ptas.). ALSA heads east to **Madrid** (8½ hrs, 5,000–7,000 ptas.)

GETTING AROUND

A Coruña's old town is actually on the peninsula, with the new town spreading out and back on the mainland. The old town centers on the **Plaza de María Pita,** with most dining, lodging, and nightlife options clustered nearby. On the east side of the isthmus, just east of María Pita, is the port; on the west side is the **bay** (Ensenada del Orzán), with two surfing beaches. The west knob of the peninsula holds the seaside **Torre de Hercules.** As long as you bed down near the old town, you shouldn't need wheels beyond a taxi ride to the Tower of Hercules.

There are several **taxi** stands around town, including points just west and east of the Paseo Marítimo and old town—Cantón Grande and Puerta Real. If you can't find one, call 981/243333 or 981/287777.

WHERE TO SLEEP

Many historic homes in the old town are cramped and indifferently maintained—thus, most inexpensive lodging is in newer quarters on the streets branching off Calle Real, particularly Rúa Nova. A Coruña is a little short on charming inns, but all the digs listed are convenient to the sights.

UNDER 7,500 PTAS. • Hostal-Residencia Alborán. Ideally located just west of Plaza de María Pita, this place puts you steps from the harbor, old town, and tapas zone. Management is not notably friendly, but that shouldn't mar your stay unless bonding is a priority; the rooms are very clean, and some have gallery views of the quietly bustling street below. Doubles run 5,350–7,000 ptas. *C. Riego de Agua 14, tel. 981/226579, fax 981/222562. 30 rooms.*

Hostal El Parador. These doubles are unusually large, and some have teeny extra rooms in case you're traveling with Junior. Lace curtains soften the large windows; bathrooms, with ⅔-size tubs, are all in white. The super-friendly innkeepers speak excellent English and will cut you a deal (off the usual 5,400–7,500 ptas.) if the inn is not full or if you stay a while. They also run the bar downstairs, but even with the customary sawdust (for catching the tapas mess), all is spic-and-span. *C. Olmos 15, tel. 981/222121 or 981/222268. 6 rooms.*

Hostal La Provinciana. Once past the uninspiring entrance walkway, you're in the throes of a newly designed facility—citrus-orange walls in this room, mint-green in that one, parquet floors and color-tile bathrooms for all. For 4,800–6,995 ptas. it's hard to go wrong; but renovations were still winding down at press time, so have a good look before you move in. *Rúa Nueva 7–9, tel. 981/220400. 20 rooms.*

Hostal Linar. These small, homey rooms have smart-looking furniture, partial wainscoting, and masculine, jewel-tone (largely burgundy) patterned upholstery, finished off by marble-tile bathrooms. The only possible drawback is a heavy load of stair climbing. The large, busy, spiffy café downstairs is perfect for breakfast. Doubles range from 4,000 to 7,000 ptas., depending on season and bed arrangement. *General Mola 7, tel. 981/221092. 18 rooms.*

Hostal Santa Catalina. This place has cheap doubles (4,500–6,500 ptas.) and parking, an unusual combination in a city Coruña's size. Rooms are small and slightly dated, but they have new floors and are generally fine; the bathrooms have cute floral tiles. The reception desk, complete with fresh flowers and a friendly owner, opens onto a nice, airy (if empty) lounge and bar. *Travesía Sta. Catalina 1, tel. 981/228509, 981/226704, or 981/226609, fax 981/228509. 33 rooms.*

WHERE TO EAT

Restaurant dining is not big with Coruñesos, and when they do venture out for a sit-down affair, they often opt to widen their horizons with an Italian meal. Tapas, rather, are the thing, starting on **Plaza de María Pita** and heading west. Calles **Franja, Riego de Agua, Barrera,** and **Galera** and the **Plaza del Humor** are particularly well stocked with bars. A favorite is **El Tequeño** (Plaza de María Pita 21), a casual café-bar specializing in a tangy cheese-filled pastry called, sure enough, the *tequeño*. Miraculously, it's not greasy, and you can order this great snack outside in nice weather.

There comes a time in every trip to Galicia when the earnest traveler, seeking immersion in regional culture, feels a secret flash of revulsion, followed by pangs of guilt, at the thought of another bite of shellfish. When that flash flares, get thee to Coruña's delightful Crêperie Petite Bretagne. You are forgiven. Lean on O Bebedeiro to get you back in the mood.

UNDER 2,000 PTAS. • Adega O Bebedeiro. Despite being steps from the Domus, tiny O Bebedeiro is a find, beloved by locals (who pack it full at night) for its authentic cuisine and low prices. It feels like an old farmhouse, with stone walls, floors, and fireplace; pine tables and stools; and dusty wine bottles and rustic implements everywhere. Bread tumbles out of a big basket on the baker's table. The food is top-notch Gallego: appetizers like *setas rellenas de marisco y salsa holandesa* (wild mushrooms stuffed with seafood and served with Hollandaise sauce) are followed by fruits of the sea at market prices, yanked right off the boat. *Angel Rebollo 34, tel. 981/210609. Closed Mon. No dinner Sun.*

Crêperie Petite Bretagne. This lovely French place serves what must be the freshest, most delicious, most creative salads in all of Spain. The thinking is international—the delicious *ensalada corintia* throws together lettuce, white rice (rice! in Galicia!), apple, pineapple, chicken, and raisins; *ensalada cantonesa* mixes lettuce, avocado, kiwi, Roquefort cheese, and nuts. The salad menu takes ages just to read, and after devouring your selection, you're confronted again with a choice of about 30 dessert crepes, many with fruit. The high-ceiling, cream-color room has dark-wood wainscoting, café curtains, little red table lamps, and country-French accents. Your fellow diners are a mellow crowd of thirtysomething beautiful people. *C. Riego de Agua 13–15, tel. 981/224871.*

WORTH SEEING

If you have a car, drive it around the edge of this maritime town for endlessly changing views: en route to the Tower of Hercules, enjoy the waterfront **Carretera de la Circunvalación,** built in the 1990s with space for bikers, trams, and cars alike. Lining the road are roughly 300 bright-red wrought-iron lampposts, each with a different decoration on its base. Continuing past the lighthouse, and past the Domus museum, you'll round into the bay and rim the beaches, **Playa del Orzán** and **Playa de Riazor.** Between the two beaches is a fabulous roadside monument to, of all things, **surfers**—bright-white and kinetic, the contemporary sculptures breathe new life into the notion of the commemorative sculpture. Just before the football stadium, in Plaza de Portugal, you'll see a similarly fanciful **seagull sculpture.** Behind this plaza is the Ciudad Jardín, or Garden City, home of the upper crust. (Because A Coruña's odd shape precludes new construction, it's actually quite expensive to buy an apartment in the city itself, so today's young folk settle in the 'burbs and commute.) Back in the busy Plaza de Pontevedra (a block inland from the frozen surfers), a sculpted **dove** recalls Pablo Picasso, whose father taught in an art school on this square. The artist lived here from ages 10 to 14 and liked A Coruña very much, though his father didn't; the family left for Barcelona in 1895. Young Pablo exhibited his first paintings in some now-defunct shops at Calle Real 20 and 54.

JARDÍN MÉNDEZ NUÑEZ

Your first trip to the tourist office will probably take you past Méndez Nuñez (on your right), a long sliver of 19th-century garden that grants the entire isthmus a stretch of pleasing green. Running from Plaza de Orense to the post office along Avenida de la Marina, the garden has one unique feature: near the obelisk, across from the Argentaria bank, is a **horticultural clock,** with numbers made of heather, clover, and the flower of the moment, surrounded by a bed of petunias. Only the hands are metal. Right next to it, the same heather spells out the month, and yet another planting indicates the date. The city pays a gardener to dig up and replant the date every day.

CIUDAD DE CRISTAL

To see why sailors from around the world nicknamed A Coruña the Crystal City, stroll Dársena de la Marina—said to be Europe's longest *paseo marítimo,* or seaside promenade. The tourist office makes a handy starting point. While the congregation of boats is charming, the real sight is across the street: a long, gracefully curved row of houses swathed in **glass galleries.** Built by fishermen in the 18th century, the houses actually face *away* from the sea; at the end of a long day these guys were sick of looking at the water. Nets were hung from the porches to dry, and fish was sold right on this street, where the waves once lapped at folks' feet. When Galicia's first glass factory opened nearby, someone got the idea of enclosing these porches in glass, like ship galleons, to keep wind and rain at bay. Some thought the resulting galleries ugly, and until the 19th century it was forbidden to cover entire facades with them; you were only allowed the top floor, hence the facades on the grand Plaza de María Pita—which many of these harbor homes face. People soon discovered the pleasant greenhouse effect, however, and so the glass gallery spread clear across the harbor and eventually throughout Galicia, where it's now an architectural staple.

Each gallery is a bit different; directly opposite the tourist office is one with stained glass. The promenade is lined with cafés and lowbrow seafood restaurants, and the harbor itself is very much alive, luxury liners and all.

PLAZA DE MARÍA PITA

The old town's main square is a beauty, and is gorgeously lighted at night with a soft, subtle glow. Its north side consists of the 1908–12 neoclassical **Palacio Municipal,** or city hall, with three Italianate domes. Beneath the middle dome is the city's coat of arms, showing the Tower of Hercules, a skull and crossbones from the legend of Hercules (*see* Torre de Hércules, *below*), and six scallop shells for the local branch of the Camino de Santiago, the *camino inglés*—Brits would sail down to A Coruña, then walk to Santiago de Compostela (they had it easy). Inside City Hall is a **clock museum** open weekday afternoons, with tickers donated by a private collector.

The monument in the center, built in 1998, depicts the heroine herself, Maior (María) Pita, holding her lance. When Sir Francis Drake came to A Coruña in 1589, the locals were only half finished building the defensive Castillo de San Antón (*see* Ciudad Vieja, *below*), and a three-week battle ensued. The British conquered much of what is now the old town. When María Pita's husband died, she took up his lance and revived the exhausted Coruñesos, inspiring women to join the battle as well; she ended up slaying the man who attempted to plant the Union Jack here, and the British slunk off to try their luck in Portugal.

A Coruña's patron saint is the Virgen del Rosario. When the British arrived in the late 16th century, locals bargained with the Virgin, saying that if she freed them from British rule they'd honor her with a festival each year. They did so, then slacked off; when Napoléon invaded, the locals turned again to the Virgin for help, and she has been fêted on October 7 ever since. On that day the mayor and assorted dignitaries go to the church of San Domenico, retrieve the Virgin's effigy, and parade her around the city. People with glass galleries set out flowers, adding a festive note.

CIUDAD VIEJA

The streets west of Plaza de María Pita are known for their tapas bars, but those to the east hide some lovely, undervisited landmarks. The 12th-century church of **Santiago** (Plaza de la Constitución s/n), the oldest church in A Coruña, was the first stop on the traditional *camino inglés* toward Santiago de Compostela. Originally Romanesque, it's now a bit of a hodgepodge, with Gothic arches, a Baroque altarpiece, and two 18th-century rose windows. Santiago Matamoros is shown with his brother, St. John. There were once two towers above the portal, useful for enemy spotting, but since they were also used to store munitions, they eventually exploded. The bell tower at the back of the church is original. The ledge above the portal, the one with the gargoyles, is a Galician element called a *tornachuvias*, designed to allow for rain erosion. Inside, there were once three naves—you can see where the walls used to be. In the back right corner is a 12th-century granite statue of St. James in pilgrim garb, its original paint still visible. The church smells movingly of age and the sea.

During the Middle Ages, Coruña's town council met on the porch out front, perhaps giving the Plaza de la Constitución its name. Most of the old town, however, was traditionally occupied by the military, and the 18th-century palace opposite Santiago is still used by a naval captain.

A hair northeast, there's beautiful greenery in the **Plaza de la General Escarrada.** Coruñesos successfully fought to keep their military HQ here when Spain suggested moving it to León. It's traditional to drink from the **Fuente del Deseo** (Fountain of the Wish) and make a wish; the water is purportedly safe and delicious.

Walk up **Calle de Damas,** named for the two daughters of the 13th-century king Alfonso IX, who ruled from here for a spell. In a move that seems to owe something to King Lear, Alfonso stipulated that his daughters, Dulce and Sancha, not marry, but they couldn't help themselves; so control of Galicia went to their brother. The yellow mansion on your left was once a noble home; it now belongs to the military. Turn north for the church of Santa María and **Palacio Cornide**—the latter, an 18th-century mansion of pink granite with unusual rounded corners, was used as a summer home by General Franco, whose wife used to stroll onto the balcony to hear mass. The **Colegiata de Santa María** is a Romanesque beauty from the mid-13th century, often called Santa María del Campo (St. Mary of the Field) because it was once outside the city walls but also known as Santa María del Mar (of the Sea) because its construction was funded by fishermen. The facade depicts the Adoration of the Magi, right up to the heads of their horses on the tower; the celestial figures include St. Peter, holding the keys to heaven. The tower is clearly late Romanesque, but the facade was moved forward to expand the church in the 19th century, and you can see the break inside, where the entry expands into the vaulted nave. A quirk of this church is that, thanks to an architectural miscalculation, the roof is too heavy for its supports, so the columns inside lean outward, and the buttresses outside have been thickened. The altar is silver. Couples who want to get married in A Coruña's old town book this poetic church far in advance.

Around the back of the church and to the left is **María Pita's former home** (Herrerías 28), a tight little thing that can only be described as run-down; but hey, it's been lived in for 400 years. Our heroine found three more husbands after losing her first at the hands of the British, but they all managed to die on her, so she eventually expired alone. A few steps east is the arched entrance to the **Convento de Santa Barbara**—at the top a sculpture depicts the Last Judgment, with the sun and moon signifying the beginning and end of life. The archangel Michael weighs souls while pilgrims, saints, and others arrive from the right-hand side. The sculpture is believed to be a former sepulcher. Like many Spanish convent nuns, Santa Barbara's sisters make and sell desserts; in a charming local tradition, friends of a bride-to-be bring the nuns eggs (for their goodies) and ask them to pray for a sunny, auspicious wedding day.

A few steps south is the church of **Santo Domingo,** with a mysterious twisted tower. At the time of Sir Francis Drake and company, Santo Domingo was outside the city wall, but the Brits destroyed it, along with whatever else they could get their hands on; so the church you see was rebuilt inside the city wall at the turn of the 17th century. The military building next door (to the right) was once a mint.

Finally, some air—follow your nose to the **Jardín de San Carlos** (St. Charles's Garden), overlooking the water. The garden centers on the tomb of John Moore, an *inglés* who helped defend the Spanish from bad boy Napoléon in the 1809 Battle of Eviña; and over on the stone lookout structure, Moore is commemorated in poems by Charles Wolfe and Rosalía de Castro. Look down to your right to see the remnants of the old city wall, including two gates (one next to the Hotel Finisterre). The sea used to come right up to this boundary. The cannons just beneath you are original; the sports facilities beneath them belong to a private club. Down to the left is the **Castillo de San Antón** (St. Anthony's Castle), once on an island, where it was preceded, in turn, by a lepers' hospital. Now accessed via landfill, it holds A Coruña's archaeological museum. The building adjoining the garden in which you're standing is an **archive** of the Kingdom of Galicia.

TORRE DE HÉRCULES

Standing guard at the windy, rocky entrance to the Ría de A Coruña is the oldest functioning lighthouse (*faro*) in the world, built by the reigning Romans in the 2nd century. It has since been much restored—the existing structure dates from the 18th century—but the lightning rod on top holds a small sculpture of the original. The slanted "ribbon" around the lighthouse, now merely decorative, was originally a ramp up which oxen hauled supplies for the fire. Inside, you can climb 245 steps for superb views of the city and coastline; in summer the tower opens at night for views of twinkling lights along the Atlantic. The small **museum** at the base contains items dug up during the last restoration.

The lighthouse driveway is surrounded by an informal **sculpture garden** illustrating Celtic and Galician legends—a Celtic warrior here, a boat alluding to St. James there. The most famous legend says that a giant named Gerión once lived here, scaring the wits out of his neighbors—who called on Hercules for help, who promptly vanquished Gerión, buried him here, and built a tower on the spot. Thus the skull on A Coruña's coat of arms, and the name "Tower of Hercules." In reality, the original tower was designed by a obscure Portuguese architect named Lupo under the Roman emperor Trajan (who was born in Spain).

In 1993 an oil tanker tragically hit the rocks here, broke in two, and caught fire. All nearby homes were evacuated for fear of explosion. None occurred, and the crew escaped safely, but the fire burned for days and bits of the wreck were visible for years. Most of the paths you see leading down to the cliff's edge were created by shipwreck voyeurs.

To get here, catch Bus 3 outside the Jardín de San Carlos, or flag a taxi from wherever you happen to be. In summer, there's also a tramway from the Castillo de San Antón. *Carretera de la Torre de Hércules s/n, tel. 981/202759. Admission 400 ptas. Open daily 10–6.*

CASA DEL HOMBRE/DOMUS

Designed by the Japanese architect Arata Isozaki, this dramatic facility is shaped like a ship's sail, faced with tiles of dark-gray slate and sited high over the bay. With a name that translates roughly as the Museum of Mankind, it's essentially an interactive museum of anthropology, with a focus on the human body. The experience can be colored by throngs of screeching children on field trips, but there's some neat stuff in here, including a startling close-up video of a (very fast) human birth. The linguistically inclined will enjoy learning the origin of the Spanish letter *ñ* and seeing how various languages transcribe animal sounds—the pig's snort, rendered in English as "oink," apparently strikes the French as "grj" and the Japanese as "bu bu." Temporary exhibits keep things fresh; a recent display featured gorgeous photographs (by Peter Menzel and others) of families around the world, posed with all their possessions. *Parque de Santa Teresa 1, tel. 981/217000. Admission 300 ptas. Open Sept.–June, daily 10–7; July–Aug., daily 11–9.*

FUNDACIÓN PEDRO BARRIÉ DE LA MAZA

This fascinating, underappreciated cultural institute is perfect for a rainy day (no mere expression in Galicia). The permanent collection centers on paintings and drawings by the Galician artist Francisco Llorens (1874–1948), of which *Sada Desde Sada de Arriba* (roughly, *From Atop the Village of Sada*) is the best-realized Galician landscape, showing a small seaside town backed by hills. Temporary exhibits are much larger, and have featured such luminaries as Roy Lichtenstein and the American-born photographer Alvin Langdon Coburn (1882–1966). Pedro Barrié de la Maza happens to be the count of Fenosa, and one of his projects is the restoration and sponsorship of Galician historic sites, most notably the Romanesque choir at Santiago's cathedral; so one floor is devoted to explaining such efforts. Granted, nothing is in English, but art speaks for itself, right? A bookshop sells the foundation's own titles on Galician arts, culture, and history. Classical concerts and recitals, most featuring Galician artists, are performed almost nightly. *Cantón Grande 9, tel. 981/221525. Admission free. Open Tues.–Sun. 11–2:30 and 5:30–7:30.*

MUSEO PROVINCIAL DE BELAS ARTES

A Coruña's Museum of Fine Arts occupies two lovely old mansions on the edge of the old town. French, Spanish, and Italian paintings are joined by a curious collection of etchings by Goya. *Plaza del Pintor Sotomayor, tel. 981/223723. Admission 450 ptas. Open Tues.–Fri. 10–8, Sat. 10–2 and 4–8, Sun. 10–2.*

AFTER DARK

The bars west of Plaza de María Pita (*see* Where to Eat, *above*) hold crowds till well after midnight. Later, the action moves beachward to clubs on and around **Orzán.** At 6 AM people take *churros con chocolate* in neighboring hangouts.

The **Teatro Rosalía Castro** has a cosmopolitan lineup of Castilian-language plays—such as García Lorca's *A Poet in New York* and Lope de Vega's *Fuente Ovejuna* (*It Serves Them Right*)—and films, such as *Quién Mató a Kurt Cobain?* (*Who Killed Kurt Cobain?*). Don't overlook the opportunity to watch such standbys as *Hamlet* in translation: assuming you read the play when you were supposed to, you'll find that you can follow the action without understanding a word. Theater tickets run 1,000–2,000 ptas. *C. Riego de Agua 21, tel. 981/224775.*

SHOPPING

A Coruña is the most fashionable city in Galicia. **Calle Real** has the best mixture of cool shoes and hot clothing, including an Adolfo Dominguez boutique (at No. 13), Dominguez being a native Galician designer who's known throughout Europe. A stroll down **Calle San Andres,** two blocks inland from Calle Real, or **Avda. Juan Flórez,** leading into the new town, may also yield sartorial treasure.

For more mundane needs, the city has two **El Corte Inglés** stores, one at Juan Flórez 106–108 (tel. 981/273700) and the other in an immense indoor mall a few blocks from the train station (Avda. Ramón y Cajal 57–59, tel. 981/290011).

BETANZOS

A mere 25 km (15 mi) east of A Coruña, this ancient town is worlds away, back in the hilly countryside at the junction of two small rivers. Much of Betanzos is falling apart, yet its houses are stacked so charmingly on the rivers' steep banks that the scenic approach makes a trip worthwhile.

The main square, **Praza de Hermanos García Naveira,** is large and lively, and rimmed by houses covered with white galleries. People here display an unusual level of joie de vivre—they all look happy, and are in any case notably friendly—and you'll know you're in a small town when you start seeing the same faces twice after a few hours. To find the tourist office, go uphill past the statue and turn left on E. Romay, at the Argentaria bank. Several banks on the square itself will change currency.

You can tour Betanzos' trio of medieval churches in quick succession. Armed with a map, walk north on Travesa to the church of **Santa María do Azougue**—in the middle of its Flemish gold-leaf altarpiece, Mary's white robe seems to glow in the dark of the church. Notice the Star of David carved into the left side of the portal, at roughly eye level. A few steps downhill is the stunning early-Gothic church of **San Francisco,** preceded by a small courtyard garden and possessed of a star attraction: possibly the most life-affirming tomb in the world. In the back of this provincial church lies medieval nobleman Fernán Pérez de Andrade, in a 14th-century stone sepulcher on which animals frolic, birds fly, and medieval folk blow horns—and the whole shebang rests on the backs of a stone bear and boar. You have to see it. The church is open daily 9:30–1 and 4–6, with mass from 6 to 7 PM. Back toward the town center, the church of **Santiago** (adjoining Plaza Constitución) bears a nice carved image of the Matamoros himself.

To experience the fabulous topography, walk along **Pescadería** (just southwest of Santa María), stopping to look downhill at each cross street—check out the rooflines, their white galleries backed by the wet green hills across the river. **Ferreiros** is like Lombard Street in San Francisco (California . . .), without the curves. Throughout town the stone planters look like sepulchers, complete with little carved scenes and motifs. At the end of your day, descend to the edge of town and walk all the way around it, a riverside stroll that gives you a slice of daily life and a sense of the town's wonderfully medieval situation.

WHERE TO EAT

Betanzos is actually known for good food, particularly tortillas, readily available in the bars on and around Praza de García Hermanos. Locals frequent the woodsy **Mesón Pulpeiro,** just off the *praza*'s northwest corner (Valdoncel 3, tel. 981/772703), for fish and seafood; meals run 1,000–2,500 ptas. Just downhill from the church of Santiago, where the cute Plaza Constitución becomes Rúa do Castro, the **Banca Café** is a spacious, classy, old-world coffeehouse. Just north of Praza de García Hermanos, **Supermercado Galiz** sells good picnic supplies (Rúa Nueva 8–10, tel. 981/770168) every day but Monday.

WHERE TO SLEEP
UNDER 4,000 PTAS. • Os Arcos (Rúa do Rollo 6, tel. 981/772259 or 981/770057) rents a few rooms above a lo-o-o-o-ng bar and utterly charming restaurant with bright-red tablecloths, yellow lights, and a brown-tone mural of old Betanzos. Basic doubles with shared bath go for 3,000 ptas.

THE RÍAS ALTAS

For reasons that will be pleasingly obvious, this stretch of shore is known as Spain's Costa Verde, or Green Coast. Beaches abound. The **Playa de Area,** just east of Viveiro's old town, is beloved by locals for its clean water and relative calm; if it's crowded, simply continue east on the N634 and poke around for quieter coves.

VIVEIRO

Seagulls cry in this hilly medieval town year-round, recalling its summer-vacation aspect even in the dead of winter. Not much goes on here beyond the Rapa das Bestas (taming of wild horses) in early July, but the views of the Ría de Viveiro from the road east of town are like nothing else in the world: the N642 winds through dark mixed forests high above the islet-speckled water. A charming cultural touch is the local music conservatory, housed in a raspberry-color turn-of-the-20th-century building near the crux of the ría. You might see students poring over scores in one of the nearby café-bars.

COMING AND GOING
Buses and trains pull into the waterfront Travesía de la Marina. **IASA buses** (tel. 982/221760) can carry you along to **Ribadeo** (1½ hrs, 1,250 ptas.). The twice-daily **FEVE train** (tel. 982/550722) between Ferrol and Oviedo stops in Viveiro, connecting it with **Ribadeo** (1 hr, 500 ptas.), **Luarca,** and just about every other hamlet on Spain's northwest coast. Call the station early in the day for details; if you get an answering machine, call FEVE in Ribadeo (see below).

WHERE TO SLEEP
To find these two *hostales*, walk uphill past the Gothic church of San Francisco, then turn right.

UNDER 6,000 PTAS. • Hostal Vila. When was the last time you slept in a carpeted room for 3,300 ptas.? That's the price of a double here in low season; high season sends rates up to a modest 5,500 ptas. The spotless bathrooms have floral tiles, terra-cotta tile floors, and showers with half-size tubs. Breakfast is served. *C. Nicolás Cora Montenegro 57, tel. 982/561331. 12 rooms.*

UNDER 8,000 PTAS. • Hostal-Residencia Mayfre. If the Vila is full, try one of these basic doubles with linoleum-floored bathrooms. Some rooms have extra beds for traveling trios. At 4,000–8,000 ptas., they're competitively priced only in the low season. To find the owners, pop into the café down the street at No. 81. *C. Nicolás Cora Montenegro 68, tel./fax 982/562803. 9 rooms.*

SPLURGE • Hotel Ego. If you have a car, some extra cash and clothes, and a sense of romance, check into this hillside hotel, as the view of the ría is unbeatable—tiny islets and all—and every room enjoys it. The luscious glassed-in breakfast room faces the ría and a cascade of trees. Rooms are carpeted and contemporary, with enormous mirrors and vanity tables; next door you've got a friendly bar and a classy peach-color, ría-view restaurant (dinner 2,000 ptas.). In summer you're ideally situated above the Playa de Area; and on a rainy day you'd much rather be cooped up here than in town, especially off season, when the price won't crush your spirit (doubles cost 10,000–14,000 ptas.). *Playa de Area, off N642, tel. 982/560987, fax 561762. 29 rooms. AE, MC, V.*

RIBADEO

Last stop before Asturias, Ribadeo is an utterly sleepy little town whose delicious (if dilapidated) 19th-century town hall, the **Palacio Municipal,** seems sadly ill-located. The main square has some pretty flower gardens and palm trees, but it's more or less empty. Commercial shipping is the thing here, and you might actually hear some foreign captains' accents.

One look across the ría to Asturias, though, and you might feel like staying a few hours. If the winds are just so, the waves roll *across*, rather than up or down, the estuary. For views that will make a poet out of you, drive or walk the 3 km (2 mi) on the curving, well-maintained road north along the ría—past the ancient **Fuerte de San Damián**, a fort turned exhibition space—to the **Illa Pancha** lighthouse, where the ría meets the sea. This lonely, cliff-lined, usually rainy shore inspires feelings of utter nothingness and total calm. The site is usually deserted, so you can tramp along the grassy mounds to your heart's content, dozens of feet above the salty surf; there are no guardrails. A few short, random paths beckon you back along the cove. If the gate is open, you can cross a small gorge to the lighthouse itself.

COMING AND GOING

IASA buses (tel. 982/221760) pull in from **Viveiro** (1½ hrs, 1,250 ptas.) and **A Coruña** (3 hrs, 1,000 ptas.).

The twice-daily **FEVE** train (tel. 982/130739) between Ferrol and Oviedo stops in Ribadeo, connecting it with **Viveiro** (1 hr, 500 ptas.), **Luarca,** and countless other coastal towns.

WHERE TO EAT AND SLEEP

Grab a coffee and pastry at **El Choyo** (C. Reinante at Villafranca del Bierzo). If you must stay overnight, try the **Mediente** (C. San Francisco), a clean one-star hotel on the main square. Dinner in the restaurant downstairs costs around 2,000 ptas.

EXTREMADURA

BY NIKKO HINDERSTEIN

Spain's long-lost western region is a largely hidden trove of rolling hills, wide valleys, Roman ruins, Moorish arches, Renaissance palaces, fertile orchards of cherries, and windy mountain roads. Running along much of Portugal's border, Extremadura has some of the loveliest scenery and lowest tourist numbers in Spain—a treat as you travel around soaking up Spain's extensive Roman history. On the down side, the area is hard to navigate by bus or train; some towns are too high in the mountains to receive trains comfortably, and the local buses operate on their own gauzy schedule, which could leave you stranded should you be caught up in a hike along a seductive river in the Valle de Jerte or compelled to sample local cuisine at the insistence of your new Extremaduran friends. Renting a car is ideal (reserve before you leave home), allowing you to witness the wide variety of landscapes, ranging from lush green to desert, from wide valleys to rocky peaks. The name *Extremadura* means, roughly, "Land beyond the Duero," referring to the harsh terrain southwest of the River Duero; yet agriculture has prospered here in recent decades, due largely to several new dams. The region's most significant export is liqueur from such prized crops as the *bellota,* a large sweet acorn, and the cherries of the vast northern valleys. The bellota has become Extremadura's symbol, and most locals tote a representative thereof on their key chains.

The Autonomous Community of Extremadura has two provinces, Cáceres, to the north, and Badajoz, to the south. Mérida has been the community's capital since the 1980s. The province of Badajoz hints at the whitewashed towns of Andalusia, with an arid, flat landscape. Northern Extremadura is more mountainous, filled with trees and lakes whose charms are yet hidden from popular tourism. West of all this is Portugal, lending a twist to the border town of Badajoz.

The abundance of Roman ruins here, centered on Mérida's astounding number of immaculately preserved structures, reminds us that present-day Extremadura once had some of the most important cities on the Iberian Peninsula. This region was well established and quite coveted. Though relatively dry, Extremadura produced enough quality exports—including a large number of New World conquistadors—to keep it on the map. The Roman north–south highway known as the Ruta de la Plata, connecting the north country with the port of Seville, was one of the most heavily traveled roads in Iberia. As the Romans left, their cities fell into decline, and to varying degrees Extremadura has been struggling ever since, nestled in a region never fully injected with modern-day prosperity. These days the region is visited mainly by nature enthusiasts, but it should really be on every curious traveler's itinerary—added to the rest of the country, it gives you a more complete sense of Spain and her myriad past lives.

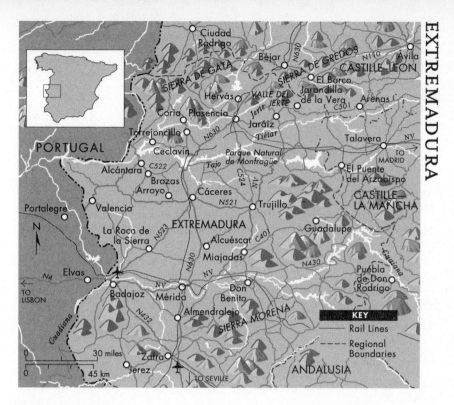

BASICS

GETTING AROUND

Do try to finagle a car, whether you reserve one before leaving home or rent one in, say, Madrid or Seville. A vehicle liberates you from Extremadura's slow, limited trains and constantly changing bus schedules. The roads are well marked, and parking is not too hard to find in the cities. From Madrid the N-V / E90 leads you west to Trujillo or Guadalupe (down the N502); from there you can move on to Mérida and Badajoz. From Mérida you can connect to the N630 going north to Cáceres, Plasencia, and the Valle de Jerte.

That said, plenty of buses zoom around the region, driving less timidly than the few tourists around. Some roads are curvy and steep, so if you're not used to driving a stick shift, you'll get a good workout and perhaps appreciate the added drama.

Only Plasencia, Cáceres, Mérida, and Badajoz are served by train. Of greatest importance is the north–south line between Seville and Plasencia, which leaves Seville at 4:30 PM and hits Zafra at 8, Mérida at 9, Cáceres at 10, and Plasencia at 11:30 PM. The return leaves Plasencia at 7 AM and arrives in Cáceres at 8:20, Mérida at 9:30, Zafra at 10:30, and Seville at 2 PM. The fare for the entire route is 2,945 ptas., with each leg correspondingly cheaper. The train does not run on Sunday.

GASTRONOMY

As elsewhere in Spain, the *jamón* (ham) of the treasured Iberian hog is the locals' favorite food and prized export. Lamb (*cordero*) and goat (*cabra*) or kid (*cabrito*) dishes appear on most Extremaduran menus, prepared in a stew called *caldereta*, named after the cauldron in which it's traditionally cooked.

Cocido extremeño is a sort of chickpea hash with ham and pig fat (tastier than it sounds), and the traditional cold tomato-based Andalusian soup gazpacho is made here with fewer tomatoes, more cucumbers, and sometimes melon. Freshwater creatures from local lakes, such as *trucha* (trout) and *anguilla* (eel), are plentiful. Vegetarians will not revel, but even the pickiest eater will enjoy Extremadura's fresh breads, cheeses, vegetables, and bean dishes; indeed, cheese is a delicacy here, with the creamy *queso de Serena* served for dessert. *Turrón* is a popular nougat candy made with egg. Extremadura produces four wines, but the region's fruit and nut liqueurs are more popular for export.

CÁCERES

The countryside notwithstanding, you'd be missing out if you came to Extremadura without seeing Cáceres, a city in which you can seriously breathe in the history of Spain. Packed into the *casco viejo* (old town), also known as the Ciudad Monumental, are no fewer than 66 historical sites: homes, palaces, monasteries, cathedrals, gates, towers, you name it. Most streets in the old town are pedestrians only (or are so tiny only a few cars dare to squeeze through), adding to the feeling you're literally walking back in time. The effect is so pure that several films have been shot here, including parts of Ridley Scott's *1492: Conquest of Paradise*. Grounded in the typical Spanish history of sieges and takeovers—the Visigoths and Romans left few marks, the Moors built up the old town, and the Christians retouched the buildings with medieval and Renaissance decor—Cáceres is nonetheless most charming for its adaptability to the modern era. Despite the surfeit of 15th-century monuments, the place feels like a real city (which it is—population 68,000). Just outside the maze of shops, restaurants, and historical sites around the old town's Plaza Mayor, you step quickly back into the 21st century, and the rest of Cáceres bustles with commerce and light traffic.

BASICS

Most **banks** and ATMs are on or near Plaza Mayor and Avenida de España. The main **post office,** open weekdays 8–2 and 5–7, Saturday 9–2, is in the new town (Paseo Primo de Rivera 2, at Avda. de España, tel. 927/225071).

CYBERSPACE
Cibercity (Plaza de Bruselas 4, tel. 927/626245) is in a desolate area but is well attended by students. Offering computer use for 400 ptas. an hour and fax service as well, the shop is open Monday–Saturday 10–2:30 and 6–10:30, Sunday 6 PM–10 PM.

VISITOR INFORMATION
The helpful **tourist office** (Plaza Mayor 3, tel. 927/246347), in the old town, is open weekdays 9–2 and 5–7:30, weekends 9:15–2. The modern insert of a building is easy to spot. Handy info includes a list of restaurants featuring local cuisine and some handbooks on Extremaduran fiestas.

COMING AND GOING

The **bus station** (Carretera Gijón/Seville, tel. 927/232550) is on the outskirts of town, a short taxi ride or a long walk up Avenida de Alemania into town. Buses shuttle between here and Trujillo (500 ptas.), Mérida (650 ptas.), Plasencia (1,500 ptas.), Salamanca (2,000 ptas.), and Zafra and Seville (4–6 hrs, 2,200 ptas.) several times a day. Two daily buses serve Badajoz (900 ptas.), and at least six go to Madrid (2,000 ptas.). Vehicles to Córdoba and Barcelona are less frequent. Note that service on most routes is diminished on weekends and holidays.

The **train station** (Avda. de Alemania s/n, tel. 927/235061) is across the street from the bus station. Cáceres is one of Extremadura's few rail-linked cities—there are at least three trains daily to and from Madrid (4,000 ptas.) and several trains daily to and from Mérida, Plasencia, and Badajoz. Within Extremadura, no trip exceeds three hours, and no fare exceeds 1,500 ptas. Other daily trains include one to Barcelona, one to Seville, and one overnight to Lisbon (originating in Madrid) that leaves around midnight.

WORTH SEEING

The main *paseo* (promenade) between the old and new towns is Avenida de España, lined with trees and benches. Enjoy the stroll or take a seat and people-watch with the not-so-shy-about-it Spaniards. Plaza Santa Ana is a bit of an oddity, its tall palm trees swaying in the dry Extremadura breeze. The city is easy to navigate, with signs pointing readily to sights and hotels; just beware of the cobblestone streets, which can twist your ankle if you get too rhapsodically engrossed in the sights.

Most of Cáceres's historic buildings can only be viewed from outside, and anyway the gates and towers make walking through the city an eyeful in itself. The city was once surrounded by 30 **watchtowers,** of which 12 still stand. The outstanding examples are the Torre de la Redonda, Torre del Púlpito, Torre del Horno, Torre de la Hierba, Torre del Portigo, and Torre de Carvajal. The Torre de Bujaco, one of the oldest, dates backs to the 12th century—legend has it that the Moorish soldiers of Abu Yacoub (of whose name "Bujaco" is a corruption) slit the throats of 40 Christian knights here.

PLAZA MAYOR

The Plaza Mayor makes a good launch pad for your excursions, not least because it's endowed with a tourist office and an ample set of steps on which to chill out and plan your attack. Moorish walls still surround the square, protecting the most popular area for craftspeople to exhibit their work. To the right of the tourist office you'll see the **Puerta Nueva** (New Gate), built in the 18th century and topped by the **Arco de la Estrella** (Arch of the Star).

CHURCHES AND PALACES

Built mainly in the 16th century, with Romanesque origins and Gothic and Renaissance elements, the tri-nave church of **Santa María** has been Cáceres's cathedral only since 1957. Many a dignitary of yore is interred here. Next door on the Plaza de Santa María, the **Palacio de Carvajal** was the 16th-century home of a family that would have made the cover of any Renaissance tabloid. After being accused of murdering a town dignitary named Juan Alonso Benevente, the Carvajals summoned King Ferdinand IV and pled their innocence. Thirty days later, after hearings in the Tribunal de Dios (Court of God), two family members were executed, and found to be innocent only after the king's death. Their house was burned down and the site abandoned until the 1960s, when the palace was rebuilt to house the Cáceres Tourist Council and the Handicrafts Board.

Between Plaza de Santa María and Plaza de San Jorge, look for the Jesuit church of **San Francisco Xavier** and the fabulous **Palacio de los Golfines de Abajo,** whose severe but striking facade mixes Gothic, Mudéjar (Arab-influenced), and plateresque (ornate stone carving named for its resemblance to silver work) elements. Ferdinand and Isabella, among other nobles, slept here, and, in the conquistador tradition, Franco was declared head of the Spanish state here in 1936.

The church of **San Mateo** was built mainly in the 14th century and embellished by a 16th-century choir and a Baroque high altar with some heraldic crests. The restored 15th-century **Palacio de las Cigüeñas** (Palace of the Storks) has an intact crenellated tower and walls made of what one brochure calls "rubblework." Most battlements on Cáceres's towers were lopped off by Isabella of Castile in squabbles with her noble subjects, but thanks to its loyal owner, only the Torre de las Cigüeñas made the cut—so to speak.

Along the city's northern walls, just uphill from the Plaza de Santa María, is the 16th-century **Palacio de los Moctezuma-Toledo,** built by Juan Cano de Saavedra with his wife's dowry—his wife being the princess daughter of the Aztec ruler Montezuma. Inside are some interesting frieze paintings combining Roman and Aztec figures. Outside the city wall, through the Socorro Gate and across Calle Zapatería, is the **Palacio de Godoy.** Francisco Godoy was a conquistador who fought with Pizarro and Almagro in Peru and Chile, and the elegance of his beautiful mannerist balcony stands out on this block. A hair east of here is the church of **Santiago de los Caballeros** (St. James of the Knights), its fine 16th-century Gothic architecture courtesy of Rodrigo Gil de Hontañón.

MUSEO DE CÁCERES

Adjoining Plaza San Mateo is the Plaza de las Veletas (Weathervane Square), where the Casa de las Veletas, a 15th-century Moorish mansion built on a 12th-century Almohad fortress now houses the Museo de Cáceres. The collection centers on local archaeological finds from as far back as the Neolithic era, but it's arguably outshined by the building itself, which includes one of the best-preserved *aljibes* (cisterns) in Extremadura. *Plaza de las Veletas 1, tel. 927/247234. 200 ptas. Open Tues.–Sat. 9–2:30, Sun. 10:45–2:30.*

MUSEO PEDRILLA

The 15th-century **Casa de los Sánchez Paredes,** now the town's parador, leads you south out of the old town, via Calle Ancha, to **Plaza de Santa Clara**, with its atypical palm trees. Farther down the steep streets you'll hit Plaza de San Francisco and the city walls—walk through them to find the Museo Pedrilla, looking a bit out of place in its urban surroundings. Once a *lavadero público* (public laundry house), the 16th-century building was later turned into a noble home for the Pedrillas, an art-loving family of dignitaries and politicians. Most works on display, which include paintings, drawings, and sculpture, including some plastic creations, are by Cácereño artists; there's also an exhibit on the history of Extremadura, from prehistoric times to the present day. *Ronda de San Francisco s/n, tel. 927/241633. Free. Open Tues.–Sat. 11–2 and 5–8 (6– 9 in summer), Sun. 11–2*

CASA MUSEO GUAYASAMÍN

Next door to the Museo Pedrilla, this museum has a sister institution by the same name in Quito, Ecuador. Though the collection centers on 20th-century painting and sculpture, one room is dedicated to pre-Columbian art and some colonial religious art in the Baroque style. The featured artist here is Colombian painter Oswaldo Guayasamín, whose works put one in mind of acid-inspired Day-Glo portraits from the 1970s. The benches are something you'd expect on the set of *Mork and Mindy,* and the room colors—yellow, orange, red—make you want to boogie. *Ronda de San Francisco s/n, tel. 927/ 241633. Free. Open Tues.–Sat. 11–2 and 5–8 (6–9 in summer), Sun. 11–2.*

SALA DE EXPOSICIÓN PERMANENTE MUNICIPAL

Attesting to healthy government support for the arts in Extremadura, Cáceres's beautiful, well-maintained Municipal Gallery has a small collection of eclectic goods ranging from painted portraits to the mechanical parts of a clock that occupied a Cáceres tower in the 19th century. The highlights are the haunting, brightly colored *carteles*, or fiesta props, including a gigantic (10-ft-high) king and queen made of wood, cloth, and papier-mâché. *C. Adarve de Santa Ana (just inside city wall, off Plaza Mayor), tel. 927/211152. Free. Open Tues.–Sat. 11–2 and 5–8 (6–9 in summer), Sun. 11–2.*

CUEVA DE MALTRAVIESO

All of Cáceres's museums have information on the Maltravieso Cave, which, in the midst of a modern-day residential neighborhood southwest of town, holds some serious Paleolithic art. Thirty groups of paintings contain 70 stenciled representations of what appear to be human hands—recent studies have shown the hands represent a variety of figures and animals, which explains why some of them appear (as hands) slightly deformed. *Avda. de Cervantes s/n, leading southwest out of town (drive or take a taxi; 10–15 mins). Free with Museo de Cáceres ticket. Open Tues.–Sat. 9–2:30, Sun. 10:45–2:30.*

SANTUARIO DE LA VIRGEN DE LA MONTAÑA

With a car or a taxi you can venture southeast of the city center to the 18th-century Sanctuary of the Virgin of the Mountain, which has a shiny, gold Baroque altar. The statue of the Virgin is paraded through town during the May festival in her honor. On a clear day the view of Cáceres's old town from the front of this building is spectacular. *Follow C. Cervantes until it becomes Carretera Miajadas; sanctuary is a 15-minute drive from central Cáceres, just off the town's tourist map. Donation requested. Open daily 8:30–2 and 4–8.*

WHERE TO SLEEP

UNDER 5,000 PTAS. • Hostal Princesa. A short walk west of the town center, near the cool music store Vehemencia (*see* Shopping, *below*), this place lacks charm, but the rooms are clean, modern, and reasonably priced, with doubles for 4,500 ptas. The jovial owner hopes you'll come down for coffee and toast in the morning. The street outside has plenty of nightlife, and there's a supermarket next door. *Camino Llano 34, tel. 927/227000. 20 rooms, some with bath. Cash only.*

Pension Carretero. This little pension is right on historic Plaza Mayor, albeit with a security camera watching all who enter. The owner keeps the old house in perfect shape, and you'll often see her elder relatives wandering around. Rooms are simple but clean and cost a mere 3,500 or 4,000 ptas. The museumlike lounge is rather formal, with run-of-the-mill antiques, velvet couches, drawn curtains, and polished wood. *Plaza Mayor 22, tel. 927/247482. 13 rooms, none with bath.*

UNDER 8,000 PTAS. • Hotel Goya. Overlooking several popular cafés on the Plaza Mayor, this hotel defends itself against noise with double-pane windows. Rooms vary, but those facing the plaza have little terraces; some have a little lounge as well, and all have modern bathrooms. Doubles with bath go for 7,000 ptas. The staff is helpful, and the optional perks include breakfast, laundry service, and food delivery, all for a fee. *Plaza Mayor 11, tel. 927/249950, fax 927/213758. 38 rooms.*

Hotel Iberia. Also on the Plaza Mayor, across from the tourist office, this remodeled 17th-century palace retains most of its antique charm. The lobby greets you with shiny white marble and comfortable quasi-velvet chairs, and the rooms would be a deal at any price (doubles with bath: 7,000 ptas.), with clean, modern bathrooms, firm beds, and hair dryers. *C. Pintores 2, tel. 927/247634, fax 927/248200. 36 rooms.*

Hotel Los Naranjos. This highly 1970s hotel is dark and smoky, with mirrored walls, red carpets, and hanging gold lamps (think *Dynasty* on the cheap). The building is near the center of town but clear of the busy tourist area; prominent signs make it easy to find. The halls are long and bare, but their white-tile floors are clean to the point of reflection. The rooms, with private bath, have modern fixtures yet somehow send you back an era, with shiny gold-tone paisley comforters. The sweet staff is generous with directions. Doubles run 6,000 ptas. *Alfonso IX 12, tel. 927/243512, fax 927/243508. 36 rooms.*

WHERE TO EAT

Inquire about the city's only vegetarian restaurant, **La Madrogona** (C. General Margallo, across from bullring).

UNDER 2,000 PTAS. • Mesón del Jamón. The front end of this casual deli is a small store selling ham and other local grub. Sit down in back for classic Iberian cooking, including all-meat plates. *Avda. Virgen de Guadalupe 5, tel. 927/221017. Closed Sun.*

Pizza Queen. This place whips up your basic ham-and-pineapple pizzas—California Pizza Kitchen, anyone?—and is a good choice for vegetarians, as you can choose your own toppings. Bonus for the weary: they'll deliver to your hotel. *Plaza Mayor 36 (at C. Ruta de la Plata), tel. 927/225253.*

UNDER 3,500 PTAS. • Florencia. The long list of mainly Italian wines starts dirt cheap and goes right on up. Florencia's menu is a sort of Italian-Spanish fusion, and the food is presented with flair—you'll see actual garnishes and attention to color, both rare in hardscrabble Extremadura. The grilled fish is surprisingly fresh, and the beefsteaks are hearty. You'll probably drop at least 3,000 ptas. *Manuel Pacheo s/n, tel. 927/216868.*

Gran Café. This quaint, slightly divey, extremely smoky place has it all—sit at the popular bar to hang with some locals or settle down to a table (draped with red-check tablecloth) and a view of the busy shopping street below. Don't be scared off by the pictures of food; the menu branches out from typical Spanish fare to croissants and other trendy goodies. *San Pedro de Alcántra 6 (just off Avda. de España), tel. 927/249997.*

SHOPPING

Mansabora Artesania (Plaza de San Juan 4, tel. 927/211884), open every day but Sunday, covers all of life's arty necessities: local craftspeople proudly display their handmade rugs, ceramics, leather goods and, to make it all smell good in your luggage, homemade perfumes and tiny glass bottles.

Vehemencia (Camino Llano 16, tel. 927/215138 or 907/181392), open every day but Sunday, is a record store with mainly Spanish music and a bit of international pop, though mainly from few years ago. The store is west of the old town; you'll see it on the walk up or down to the Museo Pedrilla (next to Bar Mona Lisa, which pumps out more traditional rock and decks its walls with tacky, Andy Warhol-ish art). The store's cool employees know all about upcoming concerts and are a great source of advice on the best local clubs.

AFTER DARK

Cáceres is always hopping around the **Plaza Mayor,** with bars and clubs particularly thick on Calle General Ezponda. On weekends catch live music for a reasonable price (usually circa 500 ptas.) at **Belle Époque,** just off the square (tel. 927/223093). When the bars start closing, around 2 AM, the crowd moves over to the new town's Plaza de Albatros and the surrounding area, called **La Madrila** (far west of the old town, past Avda. Hernán Cortés, south of Parque del Príncipe). If you're a discomane, try **Acuario** (Avda. de España 6)—youngsters call it a *pijos* (yuppies') place, but it's always packed by all

IN FLUX WE TRUST

It's hard to define the 1960s Fluxus movement. Noted practitioners included Yoko Ono, George Brecht, and Nam June Paik; another, Dick Higgins, wrote, "Fluxus is not a moment in history, or an art movement. Fluxus is a way of doing things, a tradition, and a way of life and death." In The Fluxus Reader, *editor and artist Ken Friedman summarizes: "Fluxus... involves more than art history. Literature, music, dance, typography, social sculpture, architecture, mathematics, politics all played a role. Fluxus is an active philosophy of experience that only sometimes takes the form of art.... [It is] a way of... creating social action and life activity." Owen Smith, in* Fluxus: The History of an Attitude, *describes Fluxus art as more frustrating than radical, saying, "Fluxus... does not seek the illumination of some end or fact, but celebrates participation in a non-hierarchal density of experience." In other words, Fluxus art might be vaguely defined as conceptual, with aspects of pop art or Arte Povera; the visual appearance of each piece is not paramount.*

sorts around 3 AM. Other clubs include **Bols** (Plaza de Albatros) and **Kasbah** (C. Profesor Hernández Pacheo), in another bar area near the Plaza de Conquistadores.

FIESTAS

For an extra dash of local excitement, come to Extremadura between April and June. April brings **Semana Santa** processions and the festivals in praise of **San Jorge** (St. George), who helped the Christian troops take control of Cáceres in 1229. In May the town's patron saint, the **Virgen de la Montaña,** is honored with a *romería* (pilgrimage) that fills the streets with fervent expressions of faith. June's medieval festivals offer theatrical reenactments and early classical music. A more contemporary affair, held since 1992, is the **WOMAD** (World of Music and Dance) festival, for which musicians and dancers from all over the world converge in Cáceres over the first half of May. Here in western Spain you might find yourself bopping to the sounds of the Caribbean or swooning to ancient Celtic sounds. Remember that Cáceres is fairly small—book hotel rooms in advance for any of these occasions.

NEAR CÁCERES: MUSEO VOSTELL MALPARTIDA

The obscure town of Malpartida de Cáceres holds a strange and wonderful attraction. The Museo Vostell Malpartida was founded in 1976 by the German expatriate artist Wolf Vostell, an international figure in the postwar art world who first visited Extremadura in 1958 and later declared this particular area (Los Barruecos, or the Baroque Mountains) a "natural monument." He thought its granite boulders, reservoir, and former wool-washing buildings of the previous century were a perfect example of life's interaction with art and nature. Thus, in the spirit of Fluxus art, he founded a museum to allow the public a view of the more solid pieces of this art movement's works. Today the museum combines works from the Vostell collection, the Fluxus collection donated by Gino Di Maggio, and a collection of conceptual art. Some of the newest pieces make use of videos, motorcycles, or cars (no size limitations here) to comment on societal idols. One of the most important works is Vostell's own *El Fin de Parzival* (1988; *The End of Parsifal*, referring to one of the knights of the Holy Grail), a response to some of Dalí's work from 1920s. *Transmigración III* (1958–59) was one of the first works of art anywhere to incorporate video;

another (very) multimedia work is *Por qué el proceso entre Pilato y Jesús duró sólo dos minutos?* (*Why did the trial between Pilate and Jesus last only two minutes?*), which involves the fuselage of an airplane (Mig 21), two cars, three pianos, and nine computer screens. The whole is more than 50 ft tall.

The Fluxus collection was donated by Gino Di Maggio, a late-20th-century curator and director of Milan's Mudima Foundation who edited several Fluxus publications and served as a general supporter of the movement. There are more than 250 pieces here by 31 European, Asiatic, and North American artists. The variety of languages and aesthetics can be a bit confusing; take advantage of the written and video explanations. The conceptual art, represented by 48 artists from around the world, purports to demonstrate how conventional views of art can be shattered, how art can represent ideas beyond the obvious, and how artists relate to their works.

On the same property is an interpretation center for the Barruecos' cattle trails and wool-washing complex. Here Vostell's appreciation for Extremadura and its people is palpable. In 1976 he said, "From the beginning it was my intention to compare, on the same cultural level, the works of contemporary art of the Fluxus-Happening with the rituals of rural life. To establish a dialogue between the peasant and the artist. In this art school in Malpartida everyone is a pupil and everyone a master. Art is life, life is art. It is not necessary to dominate the man who speaks to the stars, who knows about heat; he understands the artist in the same way as the Fluxus artist sanctifies the values of simplicity, the bird songs, the sheep bleating, the language of the stones." We can only wonder what the neighbors thought of this museum when it opened, but it remains an important showcase of 20th-century art and a paragon of Spanish hospitality. *12 km (8 mi) southwest of Cáceres (take N521 west from Cáceres to Malpartida de Cáceres, then head south 3 km/2 mi on Carretera de los Barruecos and follow signs), tel. 927/276492. Admission 200 ptas., free Wed. Open fall–spring, Tues.–Sun. 10:30–1:30 and 4–8:30; summer, Tues.–Sun. 10–1 and 5–7:30. www.museovostell.com.*

PLASENCIA

Nestled between the high mountains of the Sierra de Gredos and spawning valleys, Plasencia is a dichotomy of medieval remains and growing commerce. On approach, you might be startled by so many factories and industrial views after miles of countryside; once you start climbing the narrow streets toward the town center, you'll discern Gothic and Romanesque features on the older buildings. Founded by Alfonso VIII in 1180 after his conquest of this region from the Moors, Plasencia lost most of its old quarter in the Peninsular War of 1808. What remains is impressive enough to spark interest in the town's heritage, and in any case Plasencia makes a good hopping-off point for nearby points of interest.

BASICS
Despite signs pointing you toward hotels and sights, Plasencia's winding streets can be confusing to navigate; and the official city map lacks a lot of street names. The main **tourist office,** in Plaza Mayor, was under construction at press time; its temporary replacement is opposite the cathedral (Plaza de la Catedral, tel. 927/423843, open Mon.–Sat. 9–2 and 5–7:30, Sun. 9–2), in a run-down office with a graffiti-covered door. The staff can help you plan day trips into the countryside and/or point you toward Plasencia's only Internet center, in a computer store on Calle Santa Anna. Beware of the extremely nice guys hanging out in front of the cathedral; they'll open the door for you and expect a handout.

COMING AND GOING
TRAIN • The Monday–Saturday train connecting Plasencia with Seville stops in **Cáceres, Mérida,** and **Zafra;** *see* Coming and Going in the chapter introduction, *above.* Several daily trains connect Plasencia with **Madrid** (3 hrs, 1,965–2,800 ptas.). Call the **train station** for details (Paseo del Estación, tel. 927/410049).

BUSES • Buses are more plentiful than trains but still not easy to figure out. Fortunately, Plasencia's **bus station** (tel. 927/414550) is near the center of town, and the tourist office can always lend a hand. Twice-daily buses serve Madrid and Seville, the latter via Cáceres and Mérida (around 3,000 ptas. to Seville). For sightseeing or bird-watching excursions in the countryside, there are plenty of buses to the small towns around Plasencia and the Parque Natural Monfragüe, well stocked with birds of prey.

WHERE TO SLEEP
There are few hotels and *hostales* in the old quarter, and they're generally overpriced and full. A quick walk around the Plaza Mayor will acquaint you with these. If you have a car, it can be difficult to park

GETS THE ROYAL BLOOD PUMPING

An avid outdoorsman and hunter, the 16th-century Holy Roman Emperor Carlos V frequented the Jerte Valley. One of his favorite hikes is mapped out (stop by the tourist office) so you can follow in his footsteps—the trail starts in Tornavacas and leads down through the Garganta de los Infiernos (Gorge of Hell) to Jarandilla de la Vera, where Carlos V would stay on his way to the Monasterio de Yuste. The whole trip is about 28 km (17 mi) one-way, a long haul; day hikes usually tackle a partial stretch.

near the center, so a hotel on the outskirts might be a better option. Two such options: **Hotel Alpemar** (Avda. de Salamanca s/n, tel. 927/421942, fax 927/421892), which has a garden terrace, a bar, a playground, and double rooms for 6,800 ptas.; and **Hostal Real** (Avda. de Salamanca s/n, tel. 927/412900, fax 927/416824), which offers simple digs, a friendly staff, and doubles for 7,000 ptas.

UNDER 7,000 PTAS. • Rincón Extremeño. Living up to its name, this place is little more than a sparse and simple corner, albeit just off Plaza Mayor, in the heart of the old quarter. The building is small, but some rooms are up four flights of stairs. Most rooms (doubles: 5,900 ptas.) share bath facilities, and most mattresses are lamentably springy. The restaurant downstairs seems to pull in most of the locals for coffee and toast in the morning. *C. Vidrieras 6, tel. 927/411150, fax 927/420627. 24 rooms, 14 with bath.*

SPLURGE • Hotel Alfonso VIII. This heavy, gray century-old building in the center of town conceals a lighter, somewhat frilly decor on the inside, with florals and lush velvets. It's one of the finest lodgings in town, with most rooms updated to a pleasant, modern look and some equipped for wheelchairs. Beds are high and firm. The restaurant has made a real name for itself with Extremaduran delicacies that change seasonally to ensure fresh ingredients. The front desk can change currency, and there's parking around the corner for a fee. Doubles cost 12,000 ptas. *C. Alfonso VIII 32–24, tel. 927/410250, fax 927/418042. 55 rooms, 2 suites.*

WHERE TO EAT

UNDER 2,000 PTAS. • Gredos. This inside of this small, popular Plaza Mayor spot lacks charm, so aim for a seat out on the square. The daily specials tend toward the traditional standards—say, *pescado frito* (fried fish) or *chuleta de cordero* (lamp chop)—and the house gazpacho is made by the matriarch of the family that owns the place. *Plaza Mayor 4, tel. 927/421081.*

Los Monges. Despite the name (The Monks), this place is run by two brothers not of the cloth, but very much the faith of Extremadura: they call their cuisine *nacional*, as in "nation of Extremadura." The *menú del día* is a mere 1,000 ptas. and might include such treats as *bacaloa de los Monges* (cod in a secret spinach sauce) or *cabritos* (kid lamb). The atmosphere is pubby, and there's plenty of beer on tap. *Sor Valentina Mirón 24, tel. 927/420808. Closed Sun. and July–Aug.*

Rigoletto. Homemade pizzas and pastas are on offer at Plasencia's Italian bistro. Most dishes are heavy on the sauce and the cheese, but hey, at least they aren't fried. . . . This is a real family joint, plastic tablecloths and all, but the staff is very accommodating. *Puerto del Sol s/n, tel. 927/421086.*

WORTH SEEING

Plasencia's historic highlight is its **cathedral,** built in 1189 and refinished in 1320. Heavy and Gothic, it looms ominously over the Plaza de la Catedral (tel. 927/414852; admission 150 ptas.; open daily 9–1 and 4–6, later in summer). In 1498 the well-known architect Enrique Egas redesigned the front facade, but the reconstruction never happened; the unfinished wooden doors and marble doorjambs remain at once simple and larger than life. Inside, the cloister leads you to the 13th-century chapter house, notable for its late-Romanesque elements and Moorish-inspired dome. The **museum,** in the truncated nave of the old cathedral, has random archaeological and religious objects.

The **Museo Etnográfico-Textil** (enter on C. Plaza Marqués de la Puebla, tel. 927/421843; open Sept.–June, Wed.–Sat. 11–2 and 5–8, Sun. 11–2; July–Aug., Mon.–Sat. 9:30–2:30) has displays of colorful regional costumes.

At the northwest end of the old quarter is the narrow **Plaza de San Vicente,** at one end of which is the 15th-century church of **San Vicente Ferrer.** The adjoining convent was recently converted to a parador. Lined with orange trees, the carefully preserved square is dominated on its north side by the Renaissance **Palacio de Mirabel** (Palace of the Marquis of Mirabel); go through the arch in its middle, and you'll come to an alley with a back view of the building.

East of the Plaza de San Vicente, at the other end of the Rúa Zapatería, is the **Plaza Mayor,** a cheerful arcaded square where a market has been held every Tuesday morning since the 12th century. The mechanical figure clinging to the town-hall clock tower, on the east side of the square, depicts the clock-maker himself.

PARQUE NATURAL DE MONFRAGÜE

Fauna-rich Monfragüe Nature Park is just 20 km (12 mi) south of Plasencia. Stop into the visitor center in Villareal de San Carlos for hiking maps, and enjoy the greenery that spreads out amid these rocky mountains. Keep your eyes peeled for some of the park's 25 species of vultures as well as black storks, boars, lynx, deer, foxes, and most other animals native to Spain. *Park office: Villareal de San Carlos, on C524 between Plasencia and Trujillo, tel. 927/199134. Open daily 9–2:30 and 5–7; audiovisual show 5 times daily.*

VALLE DEL JERTE

If you were to try to realize your late-winter fantasies of spring, you probably couldn't do better than this: millions of beautiful white cherry blossoms blanketing acres of green valley. Early April is the prime time to come, but the valley's natural bounty is striking at any time of year. This area is untraveled by most Spaniards, let alone tourists, but bird-watchers, hikers, and nature lovers in the know will find it thrilling, well worth the trek. The Spanish imperial eagle, black-eared wheatear, mistle thrush, red kite, and Egyptian vulture are just a few of the birds frequently sighted here.

BASICS

VISITOR INFORMATION • The valley's main **tourist office** (tel. 927/472122) is past (north of) Cabazuela, just off the N110 highway, marked with prominent signs. The staff speaks some English and can be extremely helpful in guiding you around unmarked areas; they can also hook you up with firms that lead hikes and horseback tours or teach hang gliding. Especially helpful are some small hiking maps that describe each hike, detail the route, and give interesting historical background on the area.

COMING AND GOING

You're pretty much on your own in this particular upper reach of Extremadura, as the few trains and buses serving Plasencia do not go much farther north. One **bus** from Plasencia heads up the N110 from Plasencia several times each weekday, stopping at each little town en route—in Jerte it stops in Plaza de las Eras. For details stop in the Valle del Jerte tourist office or call Plasencia's bus station (tel. 927/414550). If you have wheels, drive northeast out of Plasencia on the winding, two-lane N110 and look for signs to the tourist office as soon as you pass Cabezuela.

WHERE TO SLEEP

This is a big camping area, with plenty of places to stop along the road for an open-air experience. The tourist office can also help you find a room in a country inn or a private cabin in one of the valley's *agro-turismos* (rural lodgings).

UNDER 8,000 PTAS. • Los Arenals. These small guest rooms have modern conveniences but have otherwise been around for most of the last century. The sweet staff is eager to tell you about the local cherry orchards. There's a small café downstairs and a playground outside for the kid in you. Doubles go for 7,000 ptas. *Carretera N110, Km 368, tel. 927/470250, fax 927/470386.*

UNDER 10,000 PTAS. • Hospedería Valle de Jerte. Preserved and refurbished, this 16th-century building is now the lap of luxury. The staff will bend over backwards for you, and the rooms will make you want to live here, with great valley views, embroidered white-on-white bedcovers, and velveteen love seats. The simple vibe puts you at ease in the Jerte Valley, as Carlos V and other magistrates felt when they slept here. Each airy room has a new bathroom, a safe, and the all-important minibar, and there's a café on the premises. Doubles are usually 10,000 ptas. in summer, but management is somewhat flexible, so do inquire. *Ramón Cepeda 118, tel. 927/470402, fax 927/470131. 23 rooms, 1 suite.*

WHERE TO EAT

UNDER 2,000 PTAS. • Valle de Jerte. Owned by a sweet local family, this rustic little restaurant-bar just off the highway is the most popular nightspot around. Food and service are both excellent, and the family is very knowledgeable about wine and liquor—ask away. The menu is classically Extremaduran, augmented by daily specials if some fresh trout or vegetables show up. *C. Gargantilla 16, Jerte, tel. 927/470052.*

WORTH SEEING

To get behind the valley's astounding natural scenery and those local liquors you tasted at the restaurant Valle de Jerte, tour one of the hundreds of **cherry orchards** or the several **liqueur factories.** Inquire at the tourist office or just ask a local for advice; people are proud of their local produce and can usually point the way to an informal tour guide.

In the town of Jerte have a peek at the 18th-century parish church of **Nuestra Señora de la Asunción** and the old **Barrio de los Bueyes** (Oxes' Neighborhood), which survived the burning of this area during the Peninsular War in 1809. Jerte also has an **alabaster factory,** known in the region for its intricately designed vases and objets d'art; following a tour, peruse some glowing-white goods in the factory shop. The evocatively named **Reserva Natural Garganta de los Infiernos** (Gorge of Hell Nature Reserve) offers good hiking and swimming nearby.

The town of Tornavacas sits at the head of the Jerte River between two mountain ranges, the Sierra de Bejár and Sierra de Gredos. In the center of the intricate old town sits the 16th-century Baroque church of **La Asunción.** A few kilometers northeast of town on the N110 is the **Puerto de Tornavacas** (Tornavacas Pass; literally, the "point where the cows turn back"), a natural balcony with a magnificent view of the Valle del Jerte. The pass marks the geological boundary between Extremadura and the stark plateau of Castile.

FIESTAS

The springtime **Fiesta del Cerezo en Flor** (Flowering-Cherry Festival) brings drinking, dancing, and traditional dress to a different Jerte Valley city each year. For the festival known as **El Jarramplás,** held in El Piornal during January's feast of San Sebastián, a brightly dressed, ominously masked creature dances down the street beating a drum, and—as the embodiment of evil—is ceremoniously pelted with turnips by the townspeople.

TRUJILLO

For dramatic effect, there may as well be a sign at the entrance to the walled center of Trujillo saying, "Welcome to the Middle Ages." Crooked cobblestone streets wind through whitewashed buildings here, leading you from ancient stone churches to the Moorish castle overlooking the city. This is not the place to break in those fabulous Spanish shoes you bought in Madrid.

The central statue in Trujillo's wide Plaza Mayor depicts the town's favorite son, Francisco Pizarro, riding his horse in full conquistador regalia, with some strange feathers coming out of his hat. (From a distance they look like horns, not altogether inappropriate for someone who single-handedly rubbed out the Incas of South America.) Indeed, a disproportionate number of Spain's 16th-century conquistadors hailed from Trujillo, including Hernando de Alarcón, Francisco de Orellana, Alonso de Monroy, and Diego García de Paredes, who collectively helped seize Venezuela, Chile, California, and the Amazon jungle.

Known as Turgalium to the Romans, Trujillo itself has something of a history of conquest thanks to its strategic location on the main road between Madrid and Lisbon, near Cáceres and Mérida. The city's high point was settled twice by the Romans, once by the Visigoths, once, for a long and prosperous period, by the Moors (who spread the city out beyond the Alcazaba, or fortress), once by King Alfonso VIII in 1186, then again by the persistent Almohad Moors, and finally by the Christians once more—who, legend has it, captured Trujillo with the aid of the Virgin of Victory, now the town's patron saint. Throughout Spain's golden age, the town was affluent and respected, but the 17th century brought illness and decline, leaving Trujillo struggling for its livelihood. The town's ambience still reflects the hard work of craftspeople and those who work off the land.

BASICS

EMERGENCIES
General emergency: 091. **Police:** Plaza Mayor s/n, tel. 927/320108. **Emergency medicine:** Centro de Salud, Paseo Ruiz de Mendoza—continuation of C. de la Encarnación, a few blocks west of post office, tel. 927/320089.

MAIL
The **post office** is on Calle de la Encarnación (tel. 927/320533).

TRAVEL AGENTS
For something a little different, book a tour through **Gárgola** (Plaza Mayor 17, tel. 927/323225, fax 927/323226), which makes travel arrangements for all of Extremadura. Book in advance and indicate—in case they haven't already guessed—that you speak English. The routes vary in theme and length, but most have a historical angle. The Ruta de la Vía de la Plata takes you on bus and horseback through several cities on the ancient north–south Roman road that first populated this region; the Ruta de los Pueblos Blancos gives you photo-ready whitewashed towns. Some tours work medieval dress and props into the mix. Each route is custom-designed, so prices vary; a five-person English-language tour of Trujillo would cost about 9,000 ptas. For help finding a rental car, try **Halcon Viajes** (C. de la Merced, down from Plaza Mayor) or **Turiextremadura** (C. Margarita Iturralde 8, tel. 927/659020, fax 927/659018).

VISITOR INFORMATION
The **tourist office** (Plaza Mayor s/n, tel. 927/322677, open weekdays 9–2:30 and 5–7 [later in summer], Sat. 9:30–3) hides its modern identity next to the stone steps that occupy one whole side of the plaza, holding people-watchers young and old. Inquire about *casa rurales* if you fancy a cabin in the mountains.

COMING AND GOING

There are no trains up into the mountains around Trujillo, so if you don't have a car, stick to the **buses** that shuttle between Madrid, Cáceres, and Badajoz. Express buses leave Madrid for Trujillo four times a day (2½ hrs, 1,200 ptas.); slower buses leave almost every other hour between 8 AM and 9 PM, plus one bus at 1 AM (3¼ hrs, 2,100 ptas.). Service is less frequent on weekends. A few random buses connect Trujillo with Plasencia as well. The **bus station** (tel. 927/321202) is small and unmarked; with patience you'll find it, south of the old city on Calle Marqués de Albayda at the corner of Carretera de Mérida (an industrial block just south of the post office). **Taxis** are always handy, especially in the Plaza Mayor; if you've no luck finding one, call 927/320274.

WHERE TO SLEEP

UNDER 4,000 PTAS. • Hostal Boni Camas. If you don't mind hiking up several flights of stairs to your room, then down the hall to the bathroom, by all means crash here. The very kind owners keep the place spotless, and the bathrooms are at least segregated by sex. Guest rooms are small and sparsely decorated, but they're supremely cheap at 3,000 ptas. a double. *Domingo Ramos 11, tel. 927/321604. 8 rooms. Cash only.*

Hostal Casa Roque. This small, knickknack-cluttered property has basic rooms with basic amenities, that is, most rooms share bath facilities. Your host, the elderly but enterprising Señora Maribel, also runs a trinket shop on nearby Plaza Mayor and is constantly working on sewing projects—embroidery, flamenco dresses, you name it. Double rooms run 3,000–3,500 ptas. *C. Domingo de Ramos (near parador), tel. 927/322313. 8 rooms, 2 with bath. Cash only.*

UNDER 6,000 PTAS. • Hostal Nuria. Smack on Plaza Mayor, Nuria gives you a chance to overlook it from your room. The busy café downstairs can get noisy, but the rooms are clean and reasonably modern—if sometimes tiny—with private bathrooms and wacky Aztec designs on the comforters and curtains. You can't beat the location; if you arrive at night, roll out of bed and into the tourist office for maps the next morning. Doubles cost 5,000 ptas. *Plaza Mayor 27, tel. 927/320907. 22 rooms.*

Hostal Trujillo. A block from the bus station, with garage parking available, this *hostal* is just outside the old city, a short walk from Plaza Mayor. The owner seems to have covered most of the globe in his time, so wall adornments range from old photos of Trujillo and Pizarro conquering Peru to snapshots of the owner with Mickey in Disneyland. An original medieval suit of armor stands guard in the hallway. The rooms (doubles 5,000 ptas.) are nothing special, but they're well kept, and some have little terraces facing the city. A restaurant is in the works. *C. Francisco Pizarro 4–6, tel./fax 927/322274 or 927/322661.*

UNDER 10,000 PTAS. • Hotel Perú. A bit outside town, the Perú appeals to drivers, who can take advantage of its peace, quiet, and huge parking lot. The rooms, painted blue, are modern and clean, with large windows looking off into the sunrise or sunset. A double with bath goes for 9,000 ptas. The staff is very sweet, and the happening bar and restaurant host local family gatherings, right up to wedding receptions. Well-kept flowers and fruit trees soften the terrace. *Carretera de Madrid, Km 251, tel. 927/320745, fax. 927/320779. 60 rooms.*

SPLURGE • Parador Nacional de Trujillo. Set in the former Convento de Santa Clara, the parador adds its modern amenities to Moorish window arches and a Renaissance courtyard, which fills in the spring with colorful, fragrant flowers. Rooms live up to the parador's fine standards, with a medieval air, and most overlook the courtyard. Doubles with bath go for 12,000 ptas., not bad for a parador. The restaurant is one of the best in Trujillo, with hearty Extremaduran and Andalusian dishes; long popular is the *prueba de matanza*—slaughter sampler—a platter of various hams and other forms of pork. *Plaza de Silva 1, tel. 927/321350, fax 927/321366. 45 rooms, 1 suite.*

WHERE TO EAT

UNDER 2,000 PTAS • Chíviri. Decorated in, and representing, the spirit of the conquistadors, this joint just off Plaza Mayor makes you feel like one of the guys, with large portions and big old beer glasses. Meat dishes like stewed lamb and grilled steak are joined by tapas like *migas extremeñas*—fried bread crumbs with peppers, garlic, and belly of pork. The menú del día goes for around 1,400 ptas. *C. Sillerías 7, tel. 927/322919 or 927/323201.*

Pizarro. Compared to Chíviri, Pizarro serves up more elaborate dishes in more normal proportions. The decor is as warm and friendly as the staff, with checkered tablecloths and fresh flowers. Traditional Spanish dishes such as *lomo* (pork tenderloin) and *gambas* (shrimp) are joined by the less common *gallina trufada* (chicken pâté with local truffles), prepared with an ancient, secret Extremaduran recipe. *Plaza Mayor 13, tel. 927/320255. Closed Sun.*

UNDER 3,000 PTAS • Mesón La Troya. Right next to the tourist office, a slew of nice restaurants dish out regional cuisine, their chatty waiters running circles around the premises. Tapas at La Troya feature tasty cuts of Serrano and other locally cured hams; local cheese, a real delicacy (*see* Fiestas, *below*); and seafood salads mixed with wonderful local olive oil. The menú del día costs 2,200 ptas. and is enough to feed several conquistadors, so order it only when famished. At the beginning of the meal you're served a tortilla *de patatas* (potato omelet) whether you want it or not. *Plaza Mayor 10, tel. 927/321364.*

WORTH SEEING

LA VILLA

Trujillo's walled medieval quarter is known as La Villa. Though somewhat restored, it maintains the feel of centuries past, enhanced by the sight of gawky storks nesting in the many towers and high points. The **Alcázar de los Chaves,** along the Calle Almenas wall, represents Trujillo's many reincarnations, having been a fortress, a 15th-century hotel for visiting dignitaries (such as Ferdinand and Isabella), and now a tired-looking college. Continue clockwise around the wall to see four of the original seven gates into town: the **Puerta de San Andrés,** on the west side, was built by the Moors using ancient Roman stones, then amended in the 15th century. The **Puerta de Santiago, Puerta del Triunfo,** and **Puerta de la Coria** are also impressive, albeit somewhat worn after centuries of use. El Triunfo (the Triumphant) gets its name from the Christian soldiers who passed through on January 25, 1232, having finally taken

Trujillo from the Moors. The structure bears the coats of arms of the Orellana, Bejarano, and Añasco families, as well as those of King Ferdinand and Queen Isabella.

Climb up Calle Paloma to see Trujillo's most famous architectural monuments, the church of **Santa María**. Probably built on the site of a 13th-century mosque, the building took shape in the 15th and 16th centuries and has a correspondingly Goth(ic) feel. The highlight is the altar, finished in the late 15th century, adorned with dark, striking oil paintings representing the life of the Virgin Mary. The upper choir is well adorned, complete with coats of arms on the seats Ferdinand and Isabella occupied when they attended mass here. *Plaza de Santa María, 100 ptas.; altar illumination 100 ptas. extra. Daily 10:30–2 and 4:30–7 (5–8 in summer).*

A bit farther up the street (follow signs) is the house in which Francisco Pizarro grew up, the **Casa Museo de Pizarro**, with exhibits on the explorer's life and the links between Spain and Latin America. You enter through a courtyard, where samples of New World plants grow, and you learn from a placard that a surprising number of products now cultivated on a farm near you, such as watermelon, were pilfered from Latin America. The ground floor shows daily life in the Pizarro house; the upper floor addresses the explorer's first years in the Americas, the Incan empire, colonial Peru, and Pizarro's death. Artifacts and etchings embellish the info panels. Among the more interesting items are letters to Pizarro from the king and other dignitaries telling him how fascinating they find his travels and how proud they are of his conquests. *Hike up C. de la Sangre and look for signs to museum; pass church of Santa María. Admission 350 ptas. Open daily 11–2 and 4–6 (4–8 in summer).*

The highest point in Trujillo is occupied by its Moorish **castle**, worth a hike (especially for bird-watchers) for views of the whole city from above, complete with swooping swallows and nesting storks. From here you can compare modern with medieval: to the south are grain silos, warehouses, and residential neighborhoods. To the north are only green fields and flowers, partitioned by a maze of nearly leveled Roman stone walls. The wind carries noise up from town, giving the desolate castle an eerie feel; a lonely fig tree in the main courtyard completes the effect (barring rowdy groups of German or Japanese tourists). *200 ptas. Daily 8–dusk, depending on season.*

Within the city walls, in the far-northern corner of La Villa near the Coria Gateway, is the **Museo de la Coria**, formerly the convent of San Francisco el Real de la Puerta de Coria. As in the Pizarro Museum, the main thrust is the conquest of the Americas, with an emphasis on the troops as well as other (non-Pizarro) conquistadors who led missions over the water. *Tel. 927/321898. Free. Open weekends 11:30–2.*

PLAZA MAYOR

The **Plaza Mayor** sits beneath the walls, formerly part of the expanse known as the Arrabal. Built during the Renaissance, it was the address of choice for wealthy families, and its buildings bear carved representations of people, events, and religious icons of the time. At the north end is a huge bronze statue of Pizarro atop his steed, adorned with feathers and poised for some plundering action; the piece was donated to Trujillo in 1929 by North American sculptor Charles Rumsey. (Rumor says it was intended for a city in South America, and was sent to Pizarro's birthplace because the colonial cousins declined it.) Due mainly to its central location, leading up to the ancient walls, the Plaza Mayor is now where the action is.

Directly behind Pizarro-in-bronze is the church of **San Martín**, probably born in the 14th century but definitely finished in the 16th. Renaissance grilles enclose the side chapels, but the entrance doors represent the change in style, one being classical Renaissance while the other, known as the Puerta de las Limas (Lime Door), has fruity Gothic ornamentation. Many a king of Spain has prayed here, including Charles V, Philip II, and Philip V. Emperor Charles I stopped in on his way west to marry Isabel of Portugal, a move that unified the Iberian Peninsula in 1583. Sometimes you can hear the choir practicing at dusk, completing the time-capsule effect. *Plaza Mayor. Free. Open weekdays for mass (7 PM), weekends roughly 8 AM–10 PM.*

The **Palacio de los Duques de San Carlos** (Palace of the Dukes of St. Charles) is in the northeast corner of Plaza Mayor, opposite the church's Puerta de las Limas. Originally the home to the Vargas and Carvajal families, it was converted to a Hieronymite convent in 1960. Influences are cosmopolitan; the arcaded gallery on the third floor, facing Calle Domingo Ramos, has Corinthian capitals, while the two-story patio inside has Tuscan columns. To enter, summon a nun by pulling the chain in the foyer. The nuns earn part of their living by making traditional local pastries; ask where you might pick some up. *Plaza Mayor. Admission free; donation of at least 100 ptas. requested. Open daily 9–1 and 4:30–6 (until 6:30 in summer).*

Built by Francisco Pizarro's half brother Hernando, the **Palacio de la Conquista,** in the square's south-west corner, has the most elaborate Renaissance decoration in Trujillo. The corner balcony is alive with flowing stone carvings of the Pizarros, their family crest, and Native Americans in shackles, a charming representation of the clan's wealth and accomplishments. The interior is slated to be opened to the public sometime in 2001, with formal stairways, restored antiques, and some 16th-century stables on view. *Plaza Mayor.*

The **Palacio de Orellana-Pizarro** is accessible via the *cañón de la cárcel* (prison passageway) from the courthouse, which sits between the Palacio de la Conquista and Casa del Peso Real. Now the Sacred Heart School, this palace has an impressive courtyard with twin cloisters. Above the doorways are, sure enough, the coats of arms of the Pizarro and Orellana families. It was here that volunteers signed up to enlist in aiding the conquest of Peru. Cervantes stayed here on his way to Guadalupe, where he gave a thank-you speech for his liberation after years in a debtors' prison in what is now Algeria, and he is believed to have written quite a bit on the premises. *Through Cañon de la Cárcel. Open daily 9–2 and 4:30–7.*

SHOPPING

Plenty of tourist shops sell local goods around Plaza Mayor and the surrounding streets. The creatively named Calle Tiendas (Store Street) has clothing stores and smaller shops featuring ceramics, metal pots, and leather. **Calzados Ibañez** (C. Tiendas 15, tel. 927/320410), open weekdays and the first half of Saturday, has some locally made leather boots and shoes. Most mornings **flea-market stands** on the unmarked street behind the parador offer clothing and sundries, and the **Mercado Regional,** on Calle de la Cruces near the bus station, has an array of fresh food.

AFTER DARK

Most of Trujillo's young 'uns hang out in the **Plaza Mayor** drinking a distinctly Spanish concoction, *calimocho*—red wine and Coke—out of large bottles. The town lacks big discos, but you'll find action enough going from bar to bar on the Plaza Mayor and **Calle Garcia de Paredes.** The bars on **Plaza San Judas,** near the parador, have a more traditional local flavor.

FIESTAS

Trujillo's biggest festival is **El Chíviri,** held in the Plaza Mayor on Easter Sunday—thousands of residents and visitors mingle to celebrate the spirit of the city with the usual Spanish-style debauchery. In August and September smaller fiestas honor the town's patron saint, **La Virgen de la Victoria;** starting at the church of San Martín with communal singing and traditional crafts and foods, these fiestas later break into loud music of a different kind.

Cheese lovers of the world, unite—Trujillo is also the proud sponsor of the **Festival de Queso** weekend in late April or early May, for which foodies and chefs come from far and wide. Amid live music and abundant food in the Plaza Mayor, you can sample sheep, cow, and goat cheeses and chat with the farmers who make them. Trujillo is so good at throwing parties, it's often chosen to host the regional festival known as **Día de Extremadura** (early September); ask the tourist office for exact dates. If you miss all of the above, you might still catch a crafts fair, livestock market, or other outdoor event.

GUADALUPE

A scenic and interesting place to begin or end your travels in Extremadura—or take a breather from Madrid—Guadalupe sits high in the mountains, retaining every bit of its 14th-century beauty. The history of this town is more like a fairy tale, stemming from around 1300, when a local shepherd found a statue of the Virgin said to have been carved by St. Luke. It was concluded that the piece had been buried by Christians fleeing a Muslim invasion. As it happened, King Alfonso XI liked to hunt in this area, and when he heard of the statue, he built a church to house it, vowing to build a full-blown monastery should he defeat the Moors in their next run-in. When this indeed transpired, at the battle of Salado in 1340, Alfonso built the **Monasterio de Nuestra Señora de Guadalupe** (Monastery of Our Lady of Guadalupe), then and now the town's biggest attraction. From the 15th to 18th centuries Guadalupe flourished mainly because of the Hieronymites' administration; they turned the monastery into a pilgrimage center rivaling Santiago de Compostela in importance but with an Extremaduran twist, including Moorish architectural elements. The documents that sent Columbus on his first voyage west were signed here, the first Native Americans hauled back to Spain (as servants) were baptized in the fountain in Plaza Mayor, Columbus and Cortés gave thanks here for successful voyages, and the Virgin of Guadalupe became the patroness of the Spanish-speaking world, revered in most New World churches. The monastery enjoyed prosperity for all but about 70 years in the 19th century, not coincidentally the period in which Spain suffered the loss of its overseas territories. After the Spanish Civil War, the Franciscan brothers restored it and turned part of it into the **Hospedería del Real Monasterio**, a wonderful inn with bare rooms but traditional wooden ceiling beams and some serious charm (*see* Where to Stay, *below*).

You enter both the monastery and adjoining **museum** on Plaza Mayor. Obligatory guided tours of the complex leave every half hour. Of interest are the illuminated manuscripts, mainly hymnals, written on large animal-skin pages and bound in metal. Most are so heavy (more than 20 kg/45 lbs each) that they rest on ornate, wheeled book holders resembling large tops, with the ability to spin so that each member of the choir gets a look. The sacristy has several important panels by Zurbarán, his only significant paintings still in the setting for which they were intended. Another room is devoted to fancy clerical vestments; one curiously Goth robe is of black velvet adorned with skulls and crossbones. The tour ends when a monk shows you the famous black Virgin in her Baroque **Camarín**, a little chapel built to house her and tell her life story through painted panels. There's a lot of glitz around the sweet statue, but the sighing Spanish ladies in your group will remind you how important this statue is to the area. *Admission 300 ptas. Open daily 9:30–1 and 3:30–6:30.*

BASICS

The **tourist office** is on Plaza Mayor (tel. 927/154128; open weekdays 9–1:30 and 3–6, Sat. 10–2). These folks are very helpful, but beware that north faces down on the map they give you. Inquire here about horseback rides and rural inns or home stays in the mountains.

The main **post office** (Poeta Ángel Marina 20, tel. 927/367054) is open weekdays 9–2 and 4–6, Saturday 10–2.

COMING AND GOING

Driving into Guadalupe gives you a sight to behold—from a steep, sometimes winding road, you get impressive mountain scenes, dramatic cliffs, and, in the spring, flowering fruit and nut trees. You may well have to stop for a sheep crossing, led by a proper shepherd. Don't expect any trains to climb the mountains.

A few **bus** lines serve the area. To and from Madrid, **La Sepulvedana** buses shuttle twice daily except Sunday, a roughly 5-hr trip; call the Madrid station for details (tel. 91/530–4800). **Mirat** buses (tel. 927/232550) serve Trujillo (1 hr) and Cáceres (2 hrs).

For a **taxi** call 927/367191 or 927/367236.

WHERE TO SLEEP AND EAT

Guadalupe is a small town. Most restaurants are owned by innkeepers, whether they're attached to a hotel or not.

UNDER 5,000 PTAS. • Hostal Cerezo I and II/Restaurant Cerezo. Named after that popular indigenous fruit (*cerezo* means "cherry"), these lodgings typify the best of Extremadura. The staff is young and efficient, most of the clean rooms have little terraces, and the restaurant serves great food in full view of the countryside. This is one of the best deals in Guadalupe, with en-suite doubles for 4,800 ptas. and a menú del día for 1,500. *Gregory López 20 (13 rooms) and Plaza Santa María de Guadalupe 23 (16 rooms), tel. 927/367379, fax 927/367531. 29 rooms.*

Hostal and Restaurant Laguna. One of the newest *hostales* in town (built around the '70s), this place has nice tile floors and firm mattresses. The restaurant serves standard, forgettable *extremeño* fare and is often filled during the day with locals on beer breaks from work. Doubles with bath and piped-in music go for 5,000 ptas., a menú del día for 1,000. *Gregory López 19, tel. 927/367482, fax 927/367170. 11 rooms.*

Hostal and Restaurant Taruta. Around the corner from Plaza Mayor, in the shadow of the monastery's *hospedería*, you see a corner full of restaurants and *hostales*. Taruta is run by a family native to the area and full of helpful directions. The bar can be smoky, but the restaurant upstairs peers quietly at some mountains over the neighbors' rooftops and offers a set menu for 1,400 ptas. Rooms are clean, if simple and a bit dark, but they come with breakfast; a double sets you back 5,500 ptas. a night, 4,500 ptas. with shared bath. *Avda. Alfonso El Once 18, tel. 927/367301, fax 927/367151. 18 rooms, 4 with bath.*

Hostal Polky's. Polky's is a little run-down (and its name plays fast-and-loose with the Spanish language), but the rooms are clean, sturdy, and equipped with private bath. Doubles cost 5,000 ptas. a night. Two doors from the disco of the same name, the *hostal* is run by the same (quirky) family. *Onceno 26, tel. 927/367057. 11 rooms.*

UNDER 8,000 PTAS. • **Hospedería del Real Monasterio de Santa María de Guadalupe.** Quite apart from the delight you'll take in staying in such an amazing historic building, the staff here will treat you like a saint without asking you to pay a king's ransom. Rooms are a bit stark, but the antique furniture and ceiling beams lend character, and the bathrooms are entirely up to date. The restaurant and bar, just off a grand courtyard, offer simple regional cuisine, with a focus on meat stews and a variety of local cheeses for tapas. A double room with bath goes for 7,500 ptas., a set menu for 1,800. *Plaza Juan Carlos I, tel. 927/367070. Closed mid-Jan.–Feb.*

Hostal and Restaurant Alfonso XI. The staff at this welcoming restaurant is extremely friendly, and the food is some of the best in Guadalupe, particularly the pork and white asparagus. The glassed-in dining terrace looks onto the valley and countryside. Some of the simple, modern guest rooms (6,000 ptas.) also have views. *Alfonso Onceno 21, tel. 927/154287, fax 927/154184. 27 rooms.*

SHOPPING

It's nice to support shops in Guadalupe, as most of the locals are artisans and will tell you a story to go with your item of choice. The area is known for its **copperware,** so you'll see beautiful pots and vessels for sale. A surfeit of almond, fig, and hazelnut trees means regional **sweets** abound; look for the local delicacy *higos con chocolate,* dried figs covered with chocolate.

AFTER DARK

Discotecas **Polky, Vértice,** and **H5** are all on the same jammin' corner in Plaza de Juan Carlos I, next to the monastery. The clubs are usually open Thursday through Sunday, with possible expanded schedules during festival weeks. There are a few **bars** as well, but locals who really want to party take off for Mérida or Cáceres.

OUTDOOR ACTIVITIES

The tourist office can hook you up with a horseback tour. Outside the city, in the town of Navalvillar de Pela, **Equiturex** (C. Gabriel y Galán 16, tel. 924/810–0133) runs horseback excursions for groups; a five-hour trip costs around 7,000 ptas. per person.

FIESTAS

The **Fiesta de la Virgen de Guadalupe** is one of the liveliest events in Extremadura. Held September 8, it features processions, dancing, music, and regional food in honor of Hispania's patron saint.

MÉRIDA

With more Roman ruins than any other site in Spain, Mérida is supremely historic and visually stunning. The city dates to 25 BC, when the Roman emperor Octavius Augustus decided to build a settlement on the banks of the Guadiana River, calling it Augustus Emerita (whence "Mérida"). Strategically located for prosperous commerce, military oversight, and political livelihood, the city became capital of the province of Lusitania (one of Iberia's three provinces, the other two being Baetica and Tarragona). Later, in the arms of the Visigoths and Moors, Mérida was less intensely used and cherished. In the 15th century Mérida became a pawn in the feud between the would-be queens Isabella and her niece, Juana la Beltraneja; and territorial battles between the Habsburg and Bourbon families left the city ravaged. It was not until the 20th century that attention turned to the area's archaeological heritage. It's a shame that so many modern buildings were built on top of such a hotbed of history, but excavations do continue, some in major streets.

BASICS

CURRENCY EXCHANGE

Banks and ATMs huddle on and around the Plaza de España.

CYBERSPACE

This ancient town has a new Internet café called **Ware Nostrum** (C. Baños 25, tel. 924/388658), which, in addition to computers in private stalls, has a peppy bar serving coffee cocktails. The walls are decorated with decidedly Old World paraphernalia—Roman busts and such—but rocking music keeps the place up to date. Calle Baños is a very steep street with few other businesses, just down from the Pórtico del Foro. The shop is open daily from 4 PM until *la madrugada* (sunrise); rates are 175 ptas. for half an hour, 300 an hour.

MAIL

The main **post office** is on Plaza de la Constitución, next to the Arco de Trajano (tel. 924/312458), in a grand old building overlooking a quiet square filled with old folk sitting on benches in the shade. Normal hours are weekdays 9–2 and 4–6, Saturday 10–3, but the schedule changes unpredictably in summer.

VISITOR INFORMATION

The municipal **tourist office** is conveniently located at Plaza José Álvarez y Sáenz de Buruaga, next to the Roman theater (tel. 924/315353). The office is open weekdays 9–1:45 and 4–6:15 (5–7:15 in summer), weekends 9:30–1:45. Armed with perfect English, the helpful staff can advise you on hikes in the surrounding mountains.

Friendly **Solis Tours** (Félix Valverde Lillo 8, off northeast corner of Plaza España, tel. 924/316430), run by travel agent Maria Carmen Escudero Lorero, can help you find your way around Extremadura. Book transport and event tickets here, and inquire about rural lodges outside Mérida.

COMING AND GOING

Mérida is easily accessible by **car.** The N630 connects it with Cáceres and Plasencia to the north, and Zafra and eventually Seville to the south; the N-V highway heads toward Badajoz, to the west, and Madrid, to the east. You might picture aridity, but in spring there are green fields and budding trees here.

For a **taxi,** call 924/313309.

BY TRAIN

The **train station** is on the north side of town (C. Cardero s/n, tel. 924/318109). Daily RENFE trains serve **Badajoz** (400–1,200 ptas.), **Cáceres** (3,500 ptas.), **Plasencia** (2 hrs, 1,020–1,800 ptas.), **Seville** (2,000 ptas.), **Ciudad Real** (4 hrs, 2,000 ptas.), and **Madrid** (6 hrs, 4,500 ptas.).

BY BUS

The **bus station** is over the river (Avda. de la Libertad s/n, tel. 924/371404); cross the Puente (Bridge) de Lusitania. **Alsa** (tel. 924/389055) heads north through Cáceres to Asturias and south to Seville (1,550 ptas.) via Zafra. **Auto Res** (tel. 924/371955) goes to Madrid daily (4 hrs., 3,000 ptas.). Use **Leda** (tel. 924/371403) for Badajoz (1 hr, 50 mins) or Seville (3 hrs, 10 min).

WHERE TO SLEEP

UNDER 6,000 PTAS. • Hostal Bueno. It's not the best, but Mérida is not stuffed with commendable lodgings. You're next to the police station, a public parking lot, and a conservatory of music—what more can you ask for? All rooms have private bath and little else; doubles go for 5,000 ptas. For a fee the sweet owner cooks up some mean home-style meals. *Calvario 9, tel. 924/302977 or 696/230075. bath. Doubles 5,000. Cash only.*

Hostal Los Pinos. Across the railroad tracks, a 15-minute walk from Plaza de España, this place has plenty of parking and a view of the Acueducto de los Milagros. A garden terrace and small café give you a place to grab a bite without joining the crowds in the center of town. Rooms are simple, and singles don't have private bathrooms, but all is clean. Doubles are 5,700 ptas. *Avda. Vía de la Plata s/n, tel. 924/311550. 17 rooms, 8 with bath.*

Hostal Nueva España. This relatively modern *hostal* is centrally located yet has parking space, an unusual combination. The staff is helpful. Rooms are decent, and most have private bath; those that don't are equipped with a sink. Doubles with the works cost 5,700 ptas. *Avda. Extremadura 6, tel. 924/ 313356. 31 rooms, 29 with bath. Cash only.*

Hotel Vettonia. Look for this economical modern hotel near the Plaza de Toros. Rooms are rather small, but clean, shiny, and equipped with phones. A double with bath goes for a reasonable 5,000 ptas. *Calderón de la Barca 26, tel. 924/311462 or 924/311063. 27 rooms.*

SPLURGE • Hotel Emperatriz. Set in a 16th-century palace overlooking Mérida's main square, these rooms and halls resonate with tradition and mock-medieval charm. The rooms are simple but well maintained, with far more personality than you can normally ask in this price range (doubles 10,000 ptas.). The restaurant (*see below*) is also worth a visit, and there's a bar in the vaulted basement. *Plaza España 19, tel. 924/313111, fax 924/313305. 40 rooms, 2 suites.*

WHERE TO EAT

Across from the National Museum of Roman Art, plenty of bars and cafés offer snacks, sandwiches to go, or sit-down meals with menus del día not much over 1,200 ptas. There's even a Mexican restaurant—run by a Madrid family of Mexican extraction—with a spicy homemade salsa. The **Mesón Extremeño** (C. José Ramón Mélida 50, tel. 924/303974) serves up exactly what it advertises, typical regional fare.

UNDER 2,000 PTAS. • Cafeteria Via Flavia. Among the many cafés on the Plaza de España, this bar-restaurant is often filled with locals. The bar serves typical tapas, including lunchtime *bocatas* (little sandwiches on rolls) with various hams and cheeses. The restaurant is more traditional, with a garlic-rich gazpacho and, among other entrées, *extremeño* lamb stew. The menú del día costs around 1,200 ptas. *Plaza España s/n (northwest corner), tel. 924/301550.*

Emperatriz. Part of the Hotel Emperatriz (*see above*), this place brings you into a 16th-century palace overlooking the Plaza de España. Look in the lobby and hallways for ceramic plaques explaining bits of local history. Meals are served on classy white linens, yet the menu of the day is a good value (1,700 ptas.), and the dinner menu is full of local goodies like *cabrito* (lamb) and *venado* (venison). *Plaza España 19, tel. 924/313111.*

UNDER 3,000 PTAS. • Victoria. This unassuming restaurant is a block from the Pórtico del Foro. The very small entrance leads to a back room filled with locals enjoying typical cuisine in a welcoming environment. House specialties include *conejo en estilo de Mérida* (Mérida-style rabbit; a secret house recipe) and other Extremaduran meat dishes; for dessert choose from artisan-made sweets or creamy local cheeses. *C. Sagasta 37, tel. 924/303774.*

WORTH SEEING

MUSEO NACIONAL DE ARTE ROMANO

Mérida's collection of Roman art is one of the best in the world, not least because it's presented in a neo-Romanesque building designed by renowned Spanish architect Rafael Moneo. The museum was opened in 1986 by the king and queen of Spain and the president of Italy. The walls are of light-color brick, and the central ceiling is held aloft by nine arches in the same style as the Arco de Trajano, allowing skylights to line the roof and shed natural light on the exhibits. Built on top of some ancient ruins (with an underground tunnel to the amphitheater), the museum displays artifacts from its own site in the crypt on the lower level. (You enter the crypt as part of a counted group, which can get hectic if there are tour groups or schoolkids en masse.) Among the more interesting finds are a bust of Augustus and other sculptures, mosaics, frescoes, jewelry, coins, pottery, and utensils used in a typical Roman house. *José Ramón Mélida 2, tel. 924/311690. Admission 400 ptas., free Sat. afternoon and Sun. Open Tues.– Sat. 10–2 and 4–6 (June–Sept. 5–7), Sun. 10–2.*

TEATRO Y ANFITEATRO ROMANO

Early records of Mérida show a well-conceived (natch) plan aligning the axes of the Roman theater and amphitheater with the city's other key buildings. Designed for full Roman grandeur, these performance venues are a treat to walk through. The steps and seats of the **theater** are large and ponderous, providing excellent seating for any event. You can still see plays here in summer, in the spirit of the ancient Romans. In the gardens behind the main stage, you can view some of the broken columns and mosaics up close, between topiaries. The **amphitheater** is in greater disrepair, with tumbling walls and scant remains of the *vomitorias* (an unseemly word referring to the entrance passageways) or the arches, which originally held the words THE EMPEROR AUGUSTUS, SON OF THE DIVINE CAESAR, SUPREME PONTIFEX, CONSUL FOR THE ELEVENTH TIME, EMPEROR FOR THE FOURTEENTH TIME. Inscribed in 8 BC, when the amphitheater was inaugurated, the inscription indicates that Augustus was either greatly respected or entirely comfortable with self-promotion. In 25 BC you would have come here for your periodic fix of gladiator duels and the founding moments of Spanish interest in bloody fights with beasts. At the close of any local BC festivity, a huge celebration was held in this arena, which, alas, now holds little more than dirt and grass. Still, the few reconstructed arched entryways give an impression of what once was. *Tel. 924/312530. Admission 600 ptas; 800 ptas. for multipurpose ticket including Casa del Anfiteatro and Alcazaba Arabe. Open daily 9–1:45 and 5–7:15 (4–6:15 in summer).*

CASA DEL ANFITEATRO / CASA DE LA TORRE DEL AGUA

Across the parking lot from the Roman theater are the remains of two ancient villas, the Casa de la Torre del Agua (House of the Water Tower) and Casa del Anfiteatro. Not much remains of either, but you can discern the basic structures, built around courtyards. A series of chambers lining the wall of the San Lázaro aqueduct from the Casa de la Torre del were probably used as baths; there is also a kitchen with fireplace and numerous mosaics, including one depicting Venus and Cupid and another showing figures processing grapes for wine. Ongoing excavations uncover utensils and other vestiges of life in the 1st century AD. *Tel. 924/318509. Admission 600 ptas.; free with Teatro Romano ticket. Open daily 9– 1:45 and 5–7:15 (4–6:15 in summer).*

ALCAZABA ARABE

The Arab fortress was probably built mainly in the 9th century under Abd ar-Rahman, emir of Córdoba and founder of that city's great mosque. As you approach from a Roman bridge over the Guadiana River, you can see the structure's Roman and Visigothic origins. Climb the stairs to the battle towers for a great view of the river, which was once more than a muddy stream; it used to flood the Alcazaba on occasion. Excavation and reconstruction of this military site is still under way, leaving the pathways raw, rocky, and crumbling—wear comfortable shoes, not sandals, and step with care. *Tel. 924/317309. Admission 600 ptas.; free with Teatro Romano ticket. Open daily 9–1:45 and 5–7:15 (4–6:15 in summer).*

PLAZA DE ESPAÑA

Mérida's main square is one of the largest in Extremadura, with a huge fountain in the middle. The lively shops and restaurants on the perimeter, some with outdoor seating, are among the city's most popular. The plaza's northwest corner leads to the Alcazaba, the southeast corner to the **Arco de Trajano** (Trajan's Arch), which probably formed part of the city's original Roman gates. Leading down to the arch, Calle Trajano houses some upscale boutiques, a pleasant park with a bench, and, next to the arch itself, the only secondhand-clothing store for miles around. If you didn't pack enough warm clothes, pick up a wool sweater for a few hundred ptas.

COLECCIÓN DE ARTE VISIGODO

Mérida's somewhat crusty collection of Visigothic art and stonework is housed in the 18th-century convent of Santa Clara. *Plaza de Santa Clara (just north of Plaza de España), tel. 924/300106. Free. Open Tues.–Sat. 10–2 and 4–6 (summer 5–7), Sun. 10–2.*

ELSEWHERE IN TOWN

Leaving the theater and central tourist district behind, an easy walk around the city takes you through most of the ruins and museums. Head toward the city center on Calle José Ramón Mélida or Calle Baños, and you'll soon see the amazing ruins of the **Pórtico del Foro** (Forum Portico). Designed around a garden, with a roof over the walkway to keep Romans dry on rainy days, the portico was built in 1 AD of marble rather than granite, possibly to give its sculptures of royals and mythological figures a more noble appearance. A block west you'll see the ruins of Mérida's oldest building, the **Templo de Diana**, and the remains of the Renaissance palace called **Casa de los Milagros** (House of the Miracles). You'll have to use your imagination to block out the surrounding cement boxes. There is no proof positive that this temple is dedicated to the goddess Diana, but it does resemble such a temple in Ephesus, Turkey, and its roofless colonnades are unique on the Iberian Peninsula.

Mérida's patron saint is honored in the **Basílica de Santa Eulalia**, originally built by the Visigoths on a site of a supposed Roman temple and the place where the child martyr Eulalia was burned alive in 340 for spitting in the face of a Roman magistrate. In 1990 excavations revealed layers of other historical settlements, including Paleolithic, Visigothic, and Byzantine. The digging continues daily, but you're still welcome to wander through the crypt and watch the archaeologists from a distance. *Open summer, Mon.–Sat. 10–1:45 and 4–5:45; fall–spring, Mon.–Sat. 10–1:45 and 5–6:45.*

A short drive or long walk downhill over the railroad tracks on the northwest side of town (C. Marquesa de Pinares) takes you past the **Acueducto de los Milagros** (Aqueduct of Miracles), still standing prominently in the field across which it once carried water from the Prosperina Dam, 5 km (3 mi) away. East of there, the **Acueducto de San Lázaro** (Lazarus Aqueduct), which now has but a few pillars and arches left, carried water through two lines to the theater district. Past the ruins is the vast area formerly used as the **Circo** (Circus), otherwise known as the racetrack. Not much remains of this, either, but you can get a feel for its size: 30,000 spectators once gathered here to watch chariot races. Drawn by two (*bigae*) or four (*quadrigae*) horses, the chariots were divided into teams and painted accordingly, usually red, green, blue, or white.

SHOPPING

Remarkably, Roman coins are not scarce, and are therefore not expensive; even some from Augustus's time can be yours for less than 1,000 ptas. These make excellent gifts, as they have high gee-whiz value but take up no space in your luggage. Copies of Roman pottery, mosaics, and bronze sculptures and a few original coins overflow gracefully from the shelves of **Mithra** (C. José Ramón Mélida 35, tel. 924/317379), one of the nicer stores next to the Museum of Roman Art. The front window displays a collection of Roman goods you might expect to find on opening a sealed vault.

The friendly owners of **Garilop** (C. José Ramón Mélida 24, tel. 924/311358), another presentable tourist shop, are happy to chat about Extremadura. The store has a huge selection of ceramic works and a few stunning T-shirts featuring Roman mosaics, as well as some original Roman coins at reasonable prices.

Opposite the Templo de Diana, **Chanquet** (Sagasta 18, tel. 630/714532) is a fine jewelry store with mainly Roman reproductions in silver, bronze, and gold, hand-crafted in-house or elsewhere in Mérida. Bring cash; they don't take plastic.

FIESTAS

Los Festivales de Teatro Clásico (Classical Theater Festival) brings the Roman theater to life in July and August. These performances are internationally renowned, though admittedly it's hard to stage a forgettable show in this space. The tourist office will have details as summer approaches.

Semana Santa (Holy Week) brings illustrious processions, which stop briefly in front of several churches and the Arco de Trajano. As somber music is played, participants carry huge images of saints according to a theme that changes daily .

The **Feria de Septiembre** (September Fair) is Mérida's big civic festival. Travelers flock from far and wide to join the Roman-flavor fun, which includes gladiatorial and theatrical reenactments, music, and, of course, food. Book rooms well in advance if you want to attend. In addition, various **carnivals** throughout the year celebrate Roman history and the general flavor of the town.

AFTER DARK

Don't assume this little town has little nightlife. They can throw down as well as their Roman predecessors, without togas or blood sports. Calle John Lennon lends its rock implication to most of the town's bars and pubs; on the *calle* itself are **Bar John Lennon,** with the biggest dance floor on the block, and **Pub Espuela** (the Spur), styled after the American West but, thankfully, devoid of country music. The latter draws a younger crowd, going down to high-school age.

NEAR MÉRIDA: PREHISTORIC SITES

If you have a car and Mérida has not satisfied your considerable craving for ancient history, rest assured that more pre-Roman evidence lies about. The **Dolmen de Lácara,** a prehistoric tomb, is a prized Extremaduran example of megalithic architecture. The structure is mostly underground; the main chamber was somehow built by sinking blocks of stone into the earth. The dolmen was intended to house collective burials and the deceased folks' belongings, most of which are (so much for that idea) now on display in Badajoz's Museum of Archaeology. To get here, take the N630 out of Mérida; after Aljucén, take the local road northwest to Nava de Santiago and follow signs.

In the village of La Calderita you'll find **El Abrigo de la Calderita**, a cave (*abrigo* means "shelter") with a variety of red-hued paintings. Of particular interest are the images of anthropomorphic beings and idol-type figures gathered around a sun. The cave is a hike up a mountain in the Peñas Blancas Range, so the views from outside are spectacular. A road heading southeast from Mérida deposits you right here, between the villages of Alane and Zarza de Alange.

More than 30 sites with **rock paintings** are scattered throughout the San Serván Mountains, most commonly featuring anthropomorphic beings (including some funny ones with their hands on their hips), quadrupeds (of all sorts), idols (with extremely pronounced eyes), and suns. One questionable painting of a cart suggests this form of art existed through the Chalcolithic era, the Bronze Age, and the beginnings of the Iron Age. Reach the small San Serván range by heading west on the N-IV from Mérida and turning immediately onto the local road to Arroyo de San Serván.

ZAFRA

In his wonderful book *Roads to Santiago,* Dutch traveler Cees Nooteboom writes, "Who gets no snow makes it himself: I have never seen a more dazzling white than the white houses of Zafra...." Just off the N-630 between Seville and Mérida, Zafra is a small town of quaint whitewashed buildings, sprawling plazas, and some disproportionately great hotels, making it an excellent rest stop between Extremadura and Andalusia. Don't be put off by the approach, which features factories from either direction; industry has set up shop here in recent years.

The Lusitanian agitador (chariot driver) Cayo Apuleyo Diocles was the celebrity racer of his time. After winning 1,462 chariot races, he retired at the age of 42 and spent the rest of his days in Mérida, living off his considerable earnings.

Within the town you can see everything in an hour's walk, but do save some time to relax in the unusual Plaza Mayor, which is actually made up of two connected squares, Plaza Grande and Plaza Chica. In the **Plaza Grande**, check out the various coats of arms on the old mansions. **Plaza Chica,** originally a marketplace, is now a classic Spanish plaza, with outdoor seating for several small restaurants. The town seems to be subtly growing, adding a few restaurants and hotels every few years, but the general feel is quiet, and respectful of the Muslim heritage. In the middle of **Plaza de España** are an antiques store and a restaurant with outdoor seating; just off this square is a row of bars, including a nameless dive bar, marked by a Harley-Davidson, that looks like something you'd see in Indiana. All told, Zafra is a good place to kick back if your trip is turning into that of a whirling dervish.

BASICS

The **tourist office** is in Plaza de España, easily found from the only road into town. Official hours are weekdays 11–2 and 5–7, weekends 11–2, but hours seem to fluctuate depending on season, festivals, and perhaps weather. If they're closed, as they often capriciously are, present your inquiries to the kind folks at the parador (*see below*). **Banks** and ATMs cluster around Plaza de España.

COMING AND GOING

You can **drive** from Seville to Zafra in less than three hours. Buses are more frequent than trains. The **bus station** is not far from the center of town (Carretera Badajoz-Granada, tel. 924/553907).

Only the regional (slower) train touches Zafra. The line anchored by Seville passes Zafra en route to Mérida, Cáceres, and Plasencia; the Zafra leg takes 3½ hours and costs 1,265 ptas. Zafra's **train station** is on Avenida de la Estación (tel. 924/550215).

WHERE TO SLEEP AND EAT

Wander around the **plazas** for budget hotels, *hostales*, and pensions.

SPLURGE • Parador Nacional Hernán Cortés. Thanks to the Spanish government and favorable exchange rates, you can splash out in a double room at the 15th-century Alcázar de los Duques de Feria (*see* Worth Seeing, *below*) for a not inconceivable 15,000 ptas. a night. Some of the spacious rooms have wood-beam ceilings, and most overlook the 16th-century marble courtyard. The bathrooms are entirely contemporary, the lounges and hallways are well kept, there's a pool in summer, and the old chapel is now a conference room. The restaurant is by far the best in Zafra, with seasonal variety and perfect service (though not snappy service, this being Spain and all). Desserts are homemade, and worth saving room for. *Plaza María Cristina 7, tel. 924/554540, fax 924/551018. 44 rooms, 1 suite.*

Huerta Honda. Almost in the shadow of the parador, this clean whitewashed hotel has a staff as nice as they come, dedicated to your every need. The central marble patio is softened by orange trees and other flowering plants (*huerta honda* means "deep orchard.") Rooms are fairly modern, with pastel walls and firm mattresses; doubles usually cost 12,000 ptas. Off the lobby is an emblematically Spanish restaurant and bar, complete with locals strumming guitars and singing old tunes on weekends. The owners also run an English bar and Irish pub across the parking lot, which between them have (almost) any beer you might desire. *C. Lopez Asme 30, tel. 924/554100, fax 924/552504. 34 rooms, 1 suite.*

WORTH SEEING

After (or before) enjoying Zafra's essential tranquillity, check out the church of **Nuestra Señora de Candelaria**—nine extraordinary panels on its *retablo* (altarpiece) were painted by Zurbarán, who hailed from Fuente de Cantos, just south of here. The 15th-century **Alcázar de los Duques de Feria** (Fortress of the Dukes of Feria), now the parador, is hard to miss from any direction. Cortés stayed here before his voyage to Mexico as a guest of the dukes; inside you'll find elegant 16th-century decor (*see* Where to Sleep, *above*). The guys at the front desk are very friendly.

BADAJOZ

The modern city of Badajoz looms up from a virtually flat landscape. Most of its buildings are of the dull cement variety, and its streets are usually crowded, but peer a little closer and you'll see a fun, quirky Spanish city in this border town, adequate for a short stay on the way to Portugal. The University of Badajoz is one of the largest in Spain, so a huge percentage of the population consists of students, many from outside Spain; and the average age of the passersby is not much more than 25.

A few miles from the pivotal border with Portugal, Badajoz has a spotty past. There is evidence of settlement here as far back as the Paleolithic era, but some historians argue that the city only came into being in the Visigothic period. Moorish texts proclaim that in 875 Ibn Marwan moved the city from one side of the Guadiana River to the other, anchoring it with the stone gate now called Puerto de San Cristóbal (St. Christopher's Gate). Badajoz was important militarily and politically while the Moors held it, but eventually it suffered the same rise and fall as most other Spanish cities. The Muslims and Christians tossed the place back and forth several times before the conquest by Alfonso IX of León in 1230; battles continued, however, in the form of inter-Castilian rows over church issues, and Badajoz became little more than a military base until the early 20th century, when it finally began to expand beyond its stone walls. These days the city thrives, despite its bedraggled look, on commerce and academe.

BASICS

EMERGENCIES

Police: tel. 092 or 924/210072. **Hospital Provincial:** Plaza Minayo 2, tel. 924/209000. **Hospital Infanta Cristina:** Carretera de Elvas, tel. 924/218100.

MAIL

The main **post office** (Plaza de la Libertad s/n, tel. 924/220204), open weekdays 8–8 and Saturday 9–2, is around the corner from the regional tourist office.

VISITOR INFORMATION

The **municipal tourist office** (Pasaje de San Juan s/n, tel. 924/224981), north of Plaza de España, is open weekdays 8–3 and Saturday 9–1. The helpful staff sings the praises of the city's museums. The equally helpful **regional tourist office** (Plaza de la Libertad 3, next to pale yellow bldg., tel. 924/222763) is open weekdays 9–2 and 5–7:30, weekends 9–2.

A long walk south of the town center on Avenida Maria Auxiladora, you can follow signs to the **Pryca,** a mall open daily, with food, clothes, sporting goods, computers, restaurants, and the only laundromat in town.

COMING AND GOING

For a **taxi** call 924/243101.

BY TRAIN

Several Portugal–Spain trains stop in Badajoz. The Extremadura and Talgo are fastest, leaving Badajoz twice daily for the five-hour trip to Madrid (5,000–6,000 ptas.). The regional train, also twice daily, takes a leisurely approach, hitting all the small towns and arriving in Madrid eight hours later (4,000 ptas.) All of the above stop in Mérida and Cáceres. The **train station** (tel. 924/271170) is on Avenida Carolina Coronado; head across the Puente de Palmas, or just cross the river and follow signs.

BY BUS

The **bus station** is on Calle José Rebollo López (tel. 924/233378. To Madrid, use **Auto Res** (tel. 924/238515). To Mérida, Cáceres, or Trujillo, take the **Ecavisa** (tel. 924/247777) bus to Barcelona. **Elsa** buses (tel. 924/276451) stop in Mérida (after 25 mins) on their way to the Mediterranean coast. **Leda** buses (tel. 924/233334 or 924/233378) run to Zafra (1 hr), Seville (3 hrs), Cáceres (1½ hrs), and Trujillo (2 hrs).

WHERE TO SLEEP

UNDER 7,000 PTAS. • Hostal Niza I. On a quiet street just down from Plaza de España, you'll see signs for the two Niza *hostales*. This was the original, and it looks a bit more used than the newer one down the street. Most of the digs have bathrooms, and all are clean; for 3,200 ptas. a night, you get what you pay for. *C. Arcoagüero 34–35, tel. 924/223173, fax 924/223881. 15 rooms.*

Hostal Niza II. The nicer of the Nizas, this one has been remodeled over the last few years. The hard-working owners are very helpful with directions and seem to know the history of the Alcazaba better than the tourist office does. Doubles with bath are 6,000 ptas. *C. Arcoagüero 34–35, tel. 924/223173, fax 924/223881. 14 rooms.*

Hotel Cervantes. An unsung hero of Badajoz lodging, Cervantes offers great value. The hotel is more than 100 years old, but it's kept in order, with a simple but elegant marble-floor lounge. Rooms are plain but clean, with new bathrooms and reasonable double rates of 5,500 ptas. The adjoining Plaza de Cervantes is quiet, but it conveniently has a bank, grocery store, and pleasant benches where you can sit and behold the orange trees. *C. Trinidad 2 (at southeastern corner of Plaza de Cervantes), tel. 924/223710, fax 924/222935. 28 rooms.*

UNDER 9,000 PTAS. • Hotel Condedu. Just off Plaza de España on a popular street of trendy restaurants and shops, this hotel provides a modern refuge in the center of town. Rooms are simple but have phones and firm beds; doubles with bath go for 7,000 ptas. The restaurant is invariably packed. *Muñoz Torrero 27, tel. 924/207247, fax 924/207248. 34 rooms.*

Hotel Lisboa. A monstrosity of a hotel on the train-station side of the river, this place can be worth its institutional look (think Howard Johnson's) for some air-conditioning and amenities. The front desk can change money, among other things, and rooms are clean and new, some with views over the river. The restaurant and bar keep you fortified in a pinch. A double with bath, including hair dryer, costs 8,000 ptas. *Avda. Díaz Ambrona 13, tel. 924/272900, fax 924/272250. 115 rooms.*

WHERE TO EAT

UNDER 2,000 PTAS. • La Ría. Usually filled with locals watching *fútbol* (soccer) on TV, this place begins with a smoky bar, moving on to a nice, small restaurant in back. The walls are hung with pictures of the food, normally a frightful prospect, but these images are reasonably tasteful. You can usually opt for a 1,200-ptas. menú del día featuring southern Extremaduran specialties, like gazpacho made with melon for a sweeter taste. All desserts are made on the premises, and the flan stands proud. *Plaza de España 7, tel. 924/222005.*

UNDER 2,500 PTAS. • La Buena Pasta. Not only does it have an extensive Italian menu, but La Buena Pasta is one of the few places a vegetarian might enjoy—in the true sense of the word—a meal in these parts. Off Plaza de España in a clump of hip restaurants, this place is cheerfully lighted, the staff is amiable, and the food is blessed with heavenly garlic and fresh tomatoes. Some of the pizza toppings are a little nutty, but the pastas are safely traditional. *Muñoz Torrero 3, tel. 924/261311. No lunch.*

WORTH SEEING

MUSEO DE BELLAS ARTES

You have to look up to see this museum, which hides on a cramped side street in the old town. The collection, with more than 1,000 works of mostly regional art, is classified by movement, such as the Extremaduran realists (1850–1900) and paintings illustrating regional customs (1900–1950). The sections on religious art from earlier periods include paintings by Zurbarán and Luis de Morales. *C. Meléndez Valdés 32, tel. 924/212469. Free. Open Tues.–Fri. 9–2 and 4–6, weekends 10–2.*

MUSEO EXTREMEÑO E IBEROAMERICANO DE ARTE CONTEMPORÁNEO

Keep an eye out for Mr. Spock in the Extremaduran Museum of Contemporary Ibero-American Art (MEIAC) and its outer-planetary setting—the huge, spherical cement building is half-surrounded by crazy metal sculptures. Opened in 1995, it serves as a prime example of Spain's ongoing support for the modern arts. True, it was built from the city's former prison, but it's nicely lighted and more fun than scary. Ranging from the 1980s to present, the many paintings and sculptures highlight artists from Latin America and Portugal as well as Spain. *C. del Museo 2 (south of Plaza de la Constitución), tel. 924/260384. Free. Open Tues.–Sat. 10:30–1:30 and 5–8, Sun. 10:30–1:30.*

ALCAZABA

Badajoz's Moorish fortress represents the city's oldest remaining settlement and holds one of the city's most enduring monuments: the watchtower, called **Torre Espantaperros** (literally, "Dog Scarers' Tower"; figuratively, "Christian Scarers' Tower"). The Alcazaba and tower date from 1169, during the Almohad period, but the bell tower and other additions were built in the 16th century. Within the Alcazaba, in a former duke's mansion, is the **Museo Arqueológico,** with pieces from prehistoric times up to the Moorish period. *Enter via Plaza José Álvarez y Sáez, tel. 924/222314. Admission 200 ptas. Open Tues.–Sun 10–3.*

CATHEDRAL

Towering above the Plaza de España is Badajoz's fortresslike cathedral, standing on the site of a former Visigothic or Mozarabic (Christian under Moorish rule) church. Begun in the 15th century and finished in the 19th, the cathedral is mainly late-Gothic and Baroque, meaning it's intermittently gaudy but still worth a gaze. The **museum** has some guilt-ridden 16th-century panels by Luis de Morales. *Plaza de España, tel. 924/223999. Free; donations accepted. Open Fri.–Sat. 11–1.*

PUERTA DE PALMAS

Perched on the edge of the Guadiana River, this 16th-century gate was one of few original entrances to Badajoz and is now the city's emblem. Between the round, crenellated towers is a Renaissance-style triumphal arch, adding to the favorable landscape in this section of town.

AFTER DARK

The area northwest of **Plaza de España** is hopping at night, with flashy techno bars, popular restaurants, and rustic taverns. Along Calle Meléndez Valdéz, the new teahouse **La Tetería** has a groovy Arabic feel, chess boards, and an entire menu of teas and coffees made with or without alcohol. The bar **Espantaperros,** on Calle Hernan Cortes, is one of the most beloved local hangouts, a good place to ask where else to go if you want a long night.

ANDALUSIA

BY NIKKO HINDERSTEIN

Southern Spain has a rich and colorful history that lends itself to folklore and dazzles travelers by the planeload. The land itself ranges from desert to the tropical Costa del Sol, and from the highest mountains in mainland Spain to low-lying marshes. The great Guadalquivir River is mostly silted over now, but it once carried Spain to international prominence through free-flowing trade and plunder. The creative influence of the Moors—North African Arabs who entered and occupied Spain in the 8th century, calling their kingdom Al-Andalus—is palpable in Andalusian architecture and in open-air markets full of spices, vegetables, and hand-woven textiles. Moorish palaces and fortresses, including Granada's Alhambra, are some of the area's most striking monuments, and many have been turned into charming hotels. In the rural center and along the coast, quaint, emblematic *pueblos blancos* (white villages) reveal a more modest North African heritage, their skinny lanes snaking around whitewashed houses. Even the massive city of Seville, which leads the country in dramatic Easter fiestas, has some distinct *barrios* (neighborhoods) where stores and restaurants are run by descendants of the original owners.

Flamenco music and dance were popularized here by southern Gypsies, and are still performed across Andalusia (Andalucía in Spanish). Nightlife, though compelling throughout Spain, has a particular ease in the temperate zones of the South. Friendly chatter and beverages on tap can captivate through the morning, when it's traditional to go out for breakfast as the sun comes up. A tour of some *bodegas* (wineries) might inspire such behavior—the fast-growing city of Jerez de la Frontera is world headquarters for sherry. Along the Costa del Sol, communities of sun-seeking northern Europeans form a cultural bridge (for better or worse) between ancient fishing villages and the modern *discotecas* on the beach. In recent decades, this blend of cultures has given Andalusia yet another a distinct social identity.

As they did elsewhere in Spain, Romans and Visigoths inhabited this region before the Moors showed up. Several Roman emperors were born here, and the remains of their days are on full view. In 1492, after the Catholics had vanquished the Moors, Christopher Columbus set sail from the southern coast and hauled riches back to Spain's ports. Some of Andalusia's smaller villages exist in a seeming time warp, oblivious to modern technology beyond the exception of the telephone. In these towns you can wake up to the smell of fresh bread being sold on the corner, and fresh-brewed coffee served in a tavern to locals who have never set foot outside their province. This innocence, combined with the excitement of the cities, creates a lure that's hard for most travelers to resist.

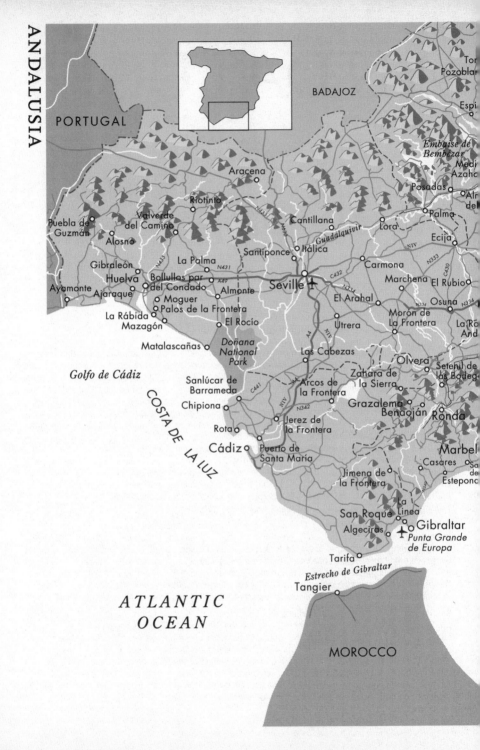

PORTUGAL

BADAJOZ

Tor
Pozoblar

Espi

*Embalse de
Bembézar*

Medi
Azaho

Aracena

Posadas

Alr
del

Ríotinto

Palma

Valverde
del Camino

Cantillana

Lora

Puebla de
Guzmán

Guadalquivir

Ecija

Alosno

Santiponce

Itálica

La Palma

Carmona

Gibraleón

Marchena

El Rubio

Huelva

Bollullos par
del Condado

Almonte

Seville

Osuna

Ayamonte

Ajaraque

Moguer

El Arahal

La Ro
And

Palos de la Frontera

Morón de
La Frontera

La Rábida

Utrera

Mazagón

El Rocío

Matalascañas

*Doñana
National
Park*

Las Cabezas

Olvera

Setenil de
las Bodeg

Golfo de Cádiz

Zahara de
la Sierra

Sanlúcar de
Barrameda

Arcos de
la Frontera

Grazalema

Chipiona

Benaoján

Ronda

Jerez de
la Frontera

Rota

Cádiz

Puerto de
Santa María

Marbel

Casares

Sa
de
Estepon

Jimena de
la Frontera

La
Línea

San Roque

Gibraltar

Algeciras

*Punta Grande
de Europa*

Tarifa

Estrecho de Gibraltar

Tangier

*ATLANTIC
OCEAN*

MOROCCO

COSTA DE LA LUZ

CASTILE–LA MANCHA

recampo
co

el

Cardeña

SIERRA MORENA

Montoro

Córdoba

nodóvar
Río

Espejo

La Carlota

Castro
del Río

Río Guadajoz

Montilla

Baena

Andújar

E. del
Jándula

La Carolina

E. del
Rumblar

Bailén

Linares

Baeza

Jaén

Martos

Alcaudete

Arquillos

Villacarrillo

Úbeda

Torre de
Vinaigre

Cazorla

Jódar

Pozo
Alcón

E. de
Guadalmena

Puente de
Génave

Embalse del
Trance

PARQUE
NATURAL
DE CAZORLA

Huéscar

Cúllar
Baza

Baza

Puente
Genil

La
Subbética

Lucena

Rute

Río Genil

Estepa

da de
alucía

Archidona

Carratraca

Alora

Pizarra

Málaga

Priego de
Córdoba

Embalse
de Iznájar

Loja

Fuentevaqueros

Santa Fe

Granada

Alhama de
Granada

Antequera

SIERRA ALMIJARA

Vélez-Málaga

Frigiliana

Nerja

Almuñécar

Viznar

SIERRA NEVADA

Padul

Las Alpujarras

Salobreña

Guadix

Ádra

Almería

Ojén

Torremolinos

Benalmádena–Costa

Fuengirola

COSTA TROPICAL

Pedro
Alcántara

Mediterranean Sea

N

COSTA DEL SOL
OCCIDENTAL

KEY
— Rail Lines
– – – Regional
　　　Boundaries

0　　　　40 miles

0　　　　60 km

WESTERN ANDALUSIA

Southwestern Spain is one of the country's most historically resonant regions. You *will* see a few tourists on this path, but you'll also be happily blown away by the area's beauty and friendliness. Within Andalusia, the western provinces hold the liveliest flamenco, the birthplace of sherry, and the home of Spain's traditional equestrian sports. That's not even to mention the fresh seafood, dramatic landscapes, or rocky beaches. Doñana National Park, a coastal wetland southwest of Seville, is the largest such park in Spain. Little Sanlúcar de Barrameda, also on the coast, is a top place to enjoy *langostinos* (jumbo shrimp) or another fresh catch of the day in a sunny café on the beach; nearby Jerez de la Frontera, once a battle station on the Christian-Moorish frontier—hence *de la frontera*—is the world's main production site for sherry wine. Running through this part of Andalusia is the mighty Guadalquivir River, conduit for imperial excursions to the Americas back in the 15th and 16th centuries. Today, most towns subsist on tourism, which includes the purchase of local crafts and the joyful consumption of local seafood. Seville, capital of all Andalusia, attracts a wild crowd with its vibrant nightlife and urban atmosphere; the spectacular Alcázar and gonzo fiestas—traditional dress and all—are must-sees for anyone who can handle both a crowd and advance reservations.

SEVILLE

Lying on the banks of the great Guadalquivir, Seville has somehow managed to keep its historical face prominent throughout commercial growth. If you come for one of the famed fiestas of spring and summer, don't be surprised to see locals of all ages getting dolled up in flamenco outfits and clicking castanets in the street. Proud and bustling, Seville is the capital of Andalusia and the fourth-largest city in Spain, yet most residents will greet you with the same smile you see in the *pueblos blancos* (white villages) of the Andalusian countryside.

The history of Seville includes many a name you learned once and filed away in a back folder. The Roman emperors Trajan and Hadrian hailed from the nearby town of Itálica and began their careers here. The city now called Seville was born before the Romans, but it was they who took illustrious hold of it in 205 BC. It was briefly the capital of the Visigothic domain, until the Moors took the reins in 712 and held on for more than 500 years. Historic art and architecture are plentiful here, especially in the form of the tremendous Giralda Tower, formerly a minaret. Next door, the cathedral has an equally stunning presence as the third-largest church in the Christian World.

Seville's many literary and artistic masters have left their mark as well. The University of Seville was once a tobacco factory where Carmen is wooed by Don José in Bizet's opera. Don Juan himself worked his charms throughout 14th-century high society until he was immortalized in Mozart's opera *Don Giovanni* and many other accounts. Rossini's Figaro enjoyed similar stomping grounds in *The Barber of Seville*. Words were written without music, too, not least because Spain's great Miguel de Cervantes killed a fair bit of time in debtor's prison here—it is thought that he began his story of the Man of La Mancha behind bars, placing Don Quixote in a more enviable world of knighthood and gallantry. Less well known to foreigners are Seville's poets, Gustavo Adolfo Bécquer (1836–70), Antonio Machado (1875–1939), and Nobel Prize winner Vicente Aleixandre (1898–1984). Seville native Diego Rodríguez de Silva Velázquez (1599–1660) painted mischievous court scenes complete with sneaky self-portraits and lots of midgets. Bartolomé Estéban Murillo (1617–82), another Sevillano, painted mainly religious scenes.

Because Seville is large (around 700,000 inhabitants) and has high unemployment, not least due to illegal immigration, crime is lamentably common here. Tourists are tempting targets, with their bulky bags, cameras, bright shirts, baggy jeans, and rental cars, not to mention maps. Keep your head up as you wander, and get a sense of your surroundings as quickly as possible. Of course, the hefty population has its pluses; the foreigners now settling here have begun to add their customs to the already rich culture of Spain's most legendarily dreamy town.

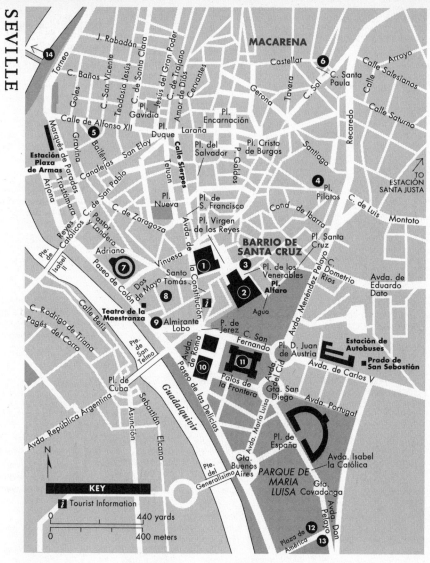

SEVILLE

MACARENA

BASICS

CYBERSPACE

Several Internet joints have flyers at the tourist offices. **Plaza Em@il** (Plaza San Francisco 8, upstairs) is in the heart of town, a block north of the cathedral (take C. Hernán Colón). Internet access costs 500 ptas. an hour; you can also listen to music at each computer. **Cibercenter**, just off Reyes Católicos (Julio César 8, tel. 954/228899, open daily 9–9) gives you service with a smile and access for 500 ptas. an hour. The laid-back, student-run **Cybercafé** (Alameda de Hércules 94, tel. 954/915671, open Mon.– Sat. 11–9) is upstairs from a vegetarian store and small coffee shop. Access costs a mere 400 ptas. an hour, and the staff pitches in if you have any problems. The **Seville Internet Center** (C. Almirantazgo 2, upstairs, room E, tel. 954/500275, open weekdays 9 AM–10 PM, weekends noon–10) is right in the thick of things, steps from the cathedral and post office. In addition to your e-mail and computer needs, they sell prepaid phone cards at decent prices.

Worth a hike from the center of town, just 'cause it's so cool, is the **Tor'net Cyber Café** (C. Torneo 35, on the east side of river, tel. 954/900781, open daily 10–2 and 5–dawn), where the vibe is relaxed and blues or classic rock are usually on the stereo. Drinks are cheap, though access itself is on the pricey side—800 ptas. an hour. **Torredeoro.net** (C. Núñez de Balboa 3, just off Paseo de Colón, near Torre del Oro, tel. 954/502809) is also homey, with coffee and toast for about 200 ptas. in the morning. The computers are coin-operated, which usually means "ripoff," but they only ask 300 ptas. an hour, going down to 200 during Happy Hour (8:30 am–10:30 AM and 11:30 PM–1 AM). **Top City** (C. Cuna 13, upstairs on the left, tel. 954/228050), convenient to Calle Sierpes, has plenty of fab new hardware and charges 600 ptas. an hour.

EMERGENCIES

Police: 092. **Fire:** 080.

In case of medical emergency, **Servicio Andaluz de Salud** (Avda. de la Constitución 18, tel. 955/018000) can help you find the appropriate clinic or hospital. The **Hospital Universitario Virgen Macarena** is at Avenida Doctor Fedriani 3 (tel. 954/557400). The mammoth **Hospital Universitario Virgen del Rocio** (Avda. Manuel Siurot s/n, tel. 954/248181) is near Parque María Luisa.

MAIL

Seville's huge **post office** (Avda. de la Constitución 32, tel. 954/219585; open weekdays 9–8, Sat. 10–2) is right across the street from the cathedral.

VISITOR INFORMATION

There's a huge **tourist office** one block south of the cathedral (Avda. de la Constitución 21, tel. 954/221404, open Mon.–Sat. 9–6, Sun. 10–2). The staff is helpful and multilingual, but usually mobbed by tourists; if you have specific questions, be patient and they'll give you a wealth of information. There are branch offices at the airport (tel. 954/449128) and train station (tel. 954/537626).

There's a smaller **municipal tourist office** at the Puente de Triana—also known as Puente de Isabel II—the bridge nearest the Maestranza bullring (C. Arjona 28, tel. 954/505600, open weekdays 9–8, weekends 9–2).

COMING AND GOING

BY BUS

Seville has two bus stations—ask the tourist office which one handles your route. The **Estación de Autobuses Prado de San Sebastián** (Plaza de San Sebastián, near Parque María Luisa, tel. 957/417111 or 954/417300) handles most Andalusian and western routes. The **Estación Plaza de Armas** (Plaza de Armas, tel. 954/908040) serves most of the northern and eastern routes.

The bus line Alsina Graells Sur (tel. 957/404040 or 957/278100) shuttles between Seville and **Córdoba** (2 hrs, 1,225 ptas.) roughly every two hours between 5:30 AM and 9 PM, and to **Granada** almost as frequently (3 hrs, 2,400 ptas.). Between them, Los Amarillos and Comes cover **Cadíz, Jerez, Arcos, Málaga, Ronda,** and **Sanlúcar de Barrameda.**

BY PLANE

San Pablo Airport (tel. 954/449000) is north of the city on Autopista de San Pablo. There are daily flights to most other airports in Spain, and a few to major cities elsewhere in Europe. Call **Iberia** for information (tel. 913/295767 for reservations, 901/333111 for national flights, 901/333232 for international flights).

BETWEEN THE AIRPORT AND THE CITY • You can catch a **bus** (tel. 902/210317) *to* the airport, a roughly one-hour ride, at Seville's central Puerta de Jerez and a few other spots in town. The bus runs almost every half-hour (Sunday, every hour) between 6:15 AM and 11 PM). The fare is 350 ptas.— a quarter of what a taxi would cost, for a ride more than twice as long. By **car,** getting into and out of the city is easy; just follow the signs.

BY TRAIN

Seville's **Estación de Santa Justa** (tel. 954/540202) is northeast of town on Avenida Kansas City. From Seville to Córdoba and Madrid, **RENFE** (tel. 902/240202) gives you the option of a regular train or the fabulous, high-speed AVE train. The latter doubles the fare but cuts travel time in half, and has quickly become the most popular way to get from Seville to Madrid. Trains from Seville to **Córdoba** depart at least once an hour (45 mins–1½ hrs, 1,100–2,800 ptas.). Trains to **Madrid** leave roughly every half hour (2½–3 hrs, 8,300–9,900 ptas.). Trains to **Jerez de la Frontera** leave roughly once an hour (1 hr, 910 ptas.) and continue to **Cádiz** (1½ hrs, 1,400 ptas.). A few daily trains serve **Granada** (3¼ hrs, 2,700 ptas.) and points farther east.

GETTING AROUND

Three taxi companies are represented in taxi stands at most main plazas and hotels: **Radio-Taxi Giralda** (tel. 954/675555), **Radio-Taxi** (tel. 954/580000), and **Tele-Taxi** (tel. 954/022222).

WHERE TO SLEEP

Even the savviest travelers can find themselves foiled by Seville's high-octane tourism, which sometimes fills every room in town. Lodging is in high demand year-round and ridiculously high demand during the spring fiestas, during which—nota bene—room rates double. The carefree days of traveling by the seat of one's pants are coming to an end, and Seville is the forefront of the reservation revolution: advance phone calls and faxes are highly recommended. Hotels and *hostales* are sprinkled throughout the city but clustered in the center of town (north of the Barrio de Santa Cruz), walking distance from the main sights. Parking is a messy matter—it's often easiest to park in the first presentable spot you see, then take a cab to your hotel.

UNDER 5,000 PTAS. • **Hostal Paco.** Owned by one of the sweetest people you will ever meet, Paco centers on one of the cutest Andalusian patios you will ever see. It's a bit cramped, but flowers and plants overflow onto the marble tiles. The rooms (doubles 4,000 ptas.) are reasonably new, with good mattresses, and most have interior baths. *Pedro del Toro 7, tel. 954/217183. 13 rooms, 3 with bath. Cash only.*

UNDER 7,000 PTAS. • **Hostal Atenas.** Guest rooms here surround a traditional Andalucían patio lined with bright-color tiles and happy plants. The rooms themselves are less exciting, with drab bedspreads, but some look onto the Casa de Pilatos and other ancient buildings next door. Doubles cost 6,500 ptas. *C. Cabellerizas 1, tel. 954/218047, fax 954/227690. 14 rooms, 13 with bath.*

Hostal Capitol. Despite its central location, Capitol is reasonably priced and offers everything you're likely to need *except* an elevator and air-conditioning. The lobby is a friendly place, with caretaker Joaquín occasionally strumming flamenco on his guitar. Rooms are simple, with the occasional antique piece of furniture, and the modern bathrooms have good water pressure. Doubles cost 6,000 ptas. *C. Zaragoza 66, tel. 954/212441. 14 rooms, most with bath.*

Hostal Los Gabrieles. You'll find this older *hostal* across the street from the Plaza de Armas bus station and mall. Rooms facing out front are a bit noisy, but the location works well for morning bus departures, and hey—there's a glow-in-the-dark universe on the ceiling of room 105. Doubles cost 6,000 ptas. *Plaza de la Legión 1, tel. 954/223307. 27 rooms, 12 with bath.*

Hostal Naranjo. Here, the marble lobby is offset by the dark, velvety salon off to the side. Grand stairs lead to the refurbished rooms, most of which have good views of the quiet street below. The olive and nut vending machine in the hall is an interesting touch. Rooms are simple, but they do have phones, safes, and private bathrooms. The pleasant staff speaks a little English. *C. San Roque 11, tel. 954/ 225840, fax 954/216943. 30 rooms. Doubles 6,500 ptas.*

Hostal Nevada. Weary travelers arrive to a lobby of sunny yellow walls and blue tiles in this central *hostal*, located between Plaza Nueva and the bullring. Guest rooms (doubles 6,000 ptas.) have worn antique furniture and large windows overlooking the street. Parking is available for a steep 2,000 ptas. a day. *C. Gamazo 28, tel. 954/225340, fax 954/210016. 13 rooms, 12 with bath.*

Hostal Paris. If you can't get a room at Hostal Paco (*see above*), inquire about the proprietors' other establishments, including the slightly pricier Hostal Paris, installed in a relatively new building. All rooms have private bath and telephone; doubles cost 6,000 ptas. *C. San Pedro Mártir 14 (1 block south of Pedro del Toro), tel. 954/229861, fax 954/219645. 16 rooms.*

Hostal Píno. Expect a warm reception from the family in charge—the sunlit patio is filled with plants and toys—and spotlessly clean rooms with relatively new mattresses. Most rooms also have shiny tile bathrooms. Doubles cost 5,500 ptas. *C. Tarifa 6, tel. 954/212810. 23 rooms. Cash only.*

Hostal Santa Catalina. Across the street from the church of the same name, this *hostal* is a 15-minute northwest of the center of town. Rooms are a tight squeeze, but most have views of the lovely *iglesia*. The hallways enjoy subtle, modern indirect lighting. *C. Alhóndiga 10–12, tel. 954/227192, fax 954/563442. 13 rooms, 12 with bath.*

Pensión Guadalquivir. A block from the cathedral, this tiny place is a treasure. The small rooms have simple beds and private bathrooms. The lobby is just big enough for two people to stand in, but the staff is agreeable and keeps the place clean. Doubles go for 6,500 ptas. *C. García de Vinuese 21, tel. 954/217760, fax 954/214404. 7 rooms.*

UNDER 10,000 PTAS. • Hotel Maestranza. Set near the bullring of the same name, Maestranza is fairly close to all the other attractions and still on a quiet street. The lobby is a blend of styles, largely modern with some attempts at Spanish antiquity. Rooms vary in quality; those upstairs are a bit nicer, with sunny windows. A few rooms have small salons. Doubles run 9,900 ptas. The staff is well versed on local sights and might offer to carry your bags upstairs. *C. Gamazo 12, tel. 954/561070, fax 954/214404. 18 rooms. In-room safes. Doubles 9,900 ptas.*

Hotel Zaida. When light streams down from the lobby skylight onto the white and black tiles below, Zaida's neo-Moorish structure feels bright and open. The building dates from the 18th century, but none of the rooms have recently heard from the ghost that is said to haunt them. Decor is plain, but all rooms have modern facilities and most have a terrace or window onto the quiet street below. You're ideally located around the corner from the Museum of Fine Arts, within walking distance of the cathedral. The staff is extremely helpful, and the cleaning crew is militant. *C. San Roque 26, tel. 954/211138, fax 954/218810. 32 rooms. Doubles 8,000.*

WHERE TO EAT

UNDER 1,500 PTAS. • Cantina Mariachi. To mix things up a little, try one of these authentic Mexican dishes with corn tortillas, tomato salsa, and grilled meats. The roasted vegetable burrito—covered in melted cheddar cheese—is a safe and delicious bet for vegetarians. Meals average 1,200 ptas., and they're open till 2 AM. *Centro Commercial, Plaza de Armas, tel. 954/902917.*

La Mandrágora. If you're tired of fried food and crave some fresh greens, try this vegetarian joint. The chef seems heavily into cheese, so the casseroles (such as zucchini and eggplant topped with hazelnuts) can be pretty hearty; a lighter option could be grilled mushrooms topped with garlic and almonds. Try the house lemonade or other fresh-squeezed juices. The look is plain, with some small colorful artworks on the walls. The menú del día costs around 1,000 ptas. *C. Albuera 11, tel. 954/220184. (call first as their hrs change). Closed Sun.–Tues. Cash only.*

Palacio Imperial Restaurante Chino. A pleasant lunch crowd assembles here daily. Aside from a strange assortment of Spanish/Chinese dishes, the basic Chinese menu offers samplers for two or more people and some strong, interesting ginseng beer. Prices average around 900 ptas. a plate; you can also order take-out. Decor is traditional Chinese. *C. Torneo 20, tel. 954/901336.*

UNDER 2,000 PTAS. • Al'Medina Cocina Marroqui. Experience some of Seville's modern Arabic culture in the form of tasty Moroccan cuisine, across from Hotel Zaida (*see* Lodging, *above*). Carnivores can opt for perfectly grilled or roasted lamb, seafood, or chicken, and vegetarians can have fun with roast-vegetable couscous or veggie *tagine* (stew). The traditional desserts are super-rich, sweetened with honey and centered on nut paste. Details like fluffy red pillows and arched doorways create a light Moroccan atmosphere. *C. San Roque 13, tel. 954/215451. Closed Sun.*

Anima. A new face on the scene, this animated tavern could be classed as a nightspot and gallery as well as a restaurant. Local contemporary art provides decor; indeed, the whole place cries "art school" in a good way, suggesting fresh initiative. The bar serves typical tapas. The full meals are a bit trendy— Spanish, but with a French flair for presentation, in keeping with the art theme. The wine selection is full of delicacies from every region in Spain. *C. Miguel Cid 80, west of Alameda de Hércules, no phone.*

El Buzo. An excellent deal for the price, El Buzo specializes in seafood. The interior is distinctly Mediterranean, mostly white and blue with a tank of live lobsters or crawfish; the outdoor patio is on a triangular street a block from the bullring. The set menu changes between lunch and dinner, but often gives you the option of a time-tested paella with significantly more seafood than any other restaurant in Seville throws in. *C. Antonio Diaz 5, tel. 954/226175 or 954/210231.*

Jalea Real. On the far eastern side of town, near Plaza de la Encarnación, this vegetarian option has a limited selection, but the excellent deli case is filled with new salads every day. Choose one or combine a few in a sampler. *C. Sor Angela de la Cruz 37, tel. 954/216103.*

Las Escobas. Claiming to be the oldest tavern in Spain, Las Escobas dates back to 1386. It has been restored since then, yet maintains an antique feel thanks to heavy wooden furniture and other accoutrements. The delicious meals give a sense of recipes passed down through generations; you might see traditional *cordero al horno* (oven-roasted lamb) and/or beefsteak grilled and topped with a sherry sauce. The ideal location—across from the cathedral—guarantees a crowd and highish prices, but the food is worth the wait. *C. Álvarez Quintero 62, tel. 954/219408, fax 954/227454.*

UNDER 3,000 PTAS. • **Hostería del Laurel.** Hidden in the winding streets of the Barrio de Santa Cruz, near the cathedral and Alcázar, this small restaurant-hotel is a perfect example of the quaint Andalusian inn. The outdoor seating flows into the Plaza de los Venerables, leaving you veritably surrounded by photogenic white and ocher houses. The indoor dining rooms have comfortable wooden chairs, and the tasty regional cuisine runs toward *cordero* (lamb) and simple fried fish. *Plaza de los Venerables 5, tel. 954/220295.*

Modesto. Run by a local family, this modest offering borders the Barrio de Santa Cruz and has terrace dining in season. The tapas bar is usually hopping; upstairs you can sit down to the house specialty, *fritura Modesto,* a variety of small fish fried in tasty local olive oil. Another good choice is *revueltos,* scrambled eggs with your choice of other ingredients. *C. Cano y Cueto 5, tel. 954/416811.*

WORTH SEEING

ALCÁZAR (REALES ALCÁZARES)
Technically called the Reales Alcázares (Royal Fortresses), this is a miraculous conglomeration of a Mudéjar palace—that is, built by Moors under Christian rule—constructed on a former Moorish fortress. Later additions reflect the ruling personalities of the day. The palace was commissioned by Pedro I in 1364, to be designed in Moorish fashion by artisans from Granada and Toledo. The entrance, through the **Puerta del León** (Lion's Gate) is a deep-red wall bearing the coat of arms of the current king and queen of Spain, as this is their official residence when they come to Seville. The Puerta del León leads to the **Patio del León**, a welcoming garden. The huge central patio ahead is the **Patio de la Montería** (Hunting Patio), where royal parties assembled for hunting expeditions.

To the left before you enter the main patio are the Alcázar's oldest sections. The **Sala de Justicia** (Hall of Justice) leads to the tiny **Patio del Yeso** (Patio of Plaster), which retains some original Almohad walls. Across the Patio de la Montería is the **Patio de las Doncellas** (Patio of the Damsels) with more amazing Moorish carving that recalls the fine work in the Alhambra but was actually added by the Renaissance king Carlos V during one of his fits of redecoration. The patio's name is rumored to refer to an annual gift of 100 virgins to the Moorish sultans. Beyond it is the **Salón de Embajadores** (Hall of the Ambassadors), with a carved and gilded wooden dome built in 1427. The wooden balconies were added in 1526 for the wedding of Carlos V to Isabel of Portugal.

The royalty within these walls kept the drama churning through the years, creating stories the Spanish love to tell. The halls of the **Patio de las Muñecas** (Patio of the Dolls), which gets its name from two tiny faces carved on the inside of an arch, lead to the palace bedrooms. Pedro the Cruel supposedly earned his epithet by having his half brother and a Moorish guest, Abu Said of Granada, killed here. The latter was relieved of his jewels after death, and it is said that a large ruby was given to the Black Prince, Edward of Wales, shortly thereafter. The **Patio del Crucero** (Patio of the Crossing) is an almost tropical garden above the old baths. Pedro's mistress, María de Padilla, was quite becoming—legend has it her courtiers lined up to drink her bathwater. Wander through the rest of the gardens and the **Patio de las Banderas** (Patio of the Flags) and think how grateful you are to the dastardly man who made all this beauty possible. *Plaza del Triunfo, tel. 954/502324. Admission: 800 ptas. Open Tues.–Sat. 9:30–5, Sun. 9:30–1:30.*

CATHEDRAL / GIRALDA

Unlike most Gothic cathedrals, Seville's sprawls in all directions. It's a sight to behold, heavy in its Gothic parts yet delicate where it borrows from the mosque on top of which it was built. The mosque was constructed by Yusuf II in 1171, but turned Christian after King Ferdinand III captured Seville in 1248. In 1401 Seville's burgeoning populace tore down all of the mosque except the outer walls and the minaret, in order to build what they considered a more apt symbol of their consequential city. The outcome remains the third-largest church in the world (after St. Peter's in Rome and St. Paul's in London), the largest Gothic structure in the world, and the tallest cathedral in Spain.

The Gothic exterior comes complete with flying buttresses and carved stone facades. You enter through the **Patio de los Naranjos** (Patio of the Oranges), originally part of the mosque. In spring the patio smells sweet enough to erase sins, thanks to the blooming fruit trees; but if that doesn't work, try blessing yourself with fountain water before you enter, a traditional ritual at the mosque. You can enter the central nave through the Puerta de la Granada or Puerta Colorada. The outsize **Capilla Mayor** (Main Chapel) rises to a great height covered with outbursts of detailed gold-leaf carving depicting the life of Jesus and then some.

Despite this lofty talk, the cathedral's interior is surprisingly dark and dreary. Plenty of luminaries are buried here, but the flamboyant south-side memorial to Christopher Columbus—the guy we're arguably most curious about—is a ceremonial empty coffin. (The explorer died alone in Valladolid in 1506.) The **Sacristía de los Cálices** (Sacristy of the Chalices) showcases the mod squad of religious painters: Goya, Zurbáran, Murillo, and Valdés Leal. The **Sacristía Mayor** (Main Sacristy) holds the keys to the city. given by the Moors and Jews to Ferdinand III. The **Capilla Real** (Royal Chapel) is open only to worshippers, and proper attire is required (no short shorts or skirts above the knee). The chapel is lined with tombs of Beatrix of Swabia (wife of Ferdinand III), Alfonso X (the Wise), and, in an urn, the remains of Ferdinand III.

The mosque's old minaret is now one of the cathedral's main attractions, indeed the symbol of Seville: the **Torre de Giralda,** built in the late 12th century. The Christians added a belfry and a lantern in the mid-16th century as well as 24 bells representing Seville's 24 parishes and the 24 knights who fought with King Ferdinand III during the Christian Reconquest. They also added the rotating bronze statue of Faith, which turned as a weather vane—el giraldillo, or "something that turns," thus the name Giralda. Climb to the top for a great view of the city. There are no steps; 35 ramps, wide enough for two horses to pass abreast, wend their way up to the 230-ft-high viewing platform. *Plaza Virgen de los Reyes, tel. 954/563321. Admission: 700 ptas, free on Sun. Open Mon.–Sat. 11–5, Sun. 2–6, plus mass daily at 8:30 AM, 9, 10, noon, and 5 and Sun. 11, noon, and 1.*

TORRE DE ORO

Begun in 1220, the 12-sided Tower of Gold on the Guadalquivir was used by the Moors to extend a chain across the river with the aim of closing the harbor to invading ships. Needless to say, this makeshift maneuver did not work. The large lantern was added in the 18th century as part of an ongoing effort to stay vigilant. The tower earned its name from its original face, honest-to-gosh gold-covered tiles. To this day, sailors swear it looks gold in the afternoon sunlight, though it's now faced entirely in stones. Inside the tower is a **Museo Marítimo,** with a small collection of ship guns and navigational equipment. *Paseo Colón s/n, tel. 954/222419. Admission: 100 ptas. Open Tues.–Fri. 10–4, weekends 11–2.*

MONASTERIO DE SANTA MARÍA DE LAS CUEVAS

Known locally for having housed a ceramics factory between 1841 and 1980 (which produced the famous Cartuja china), this 14th-century building is now the home of the **Centro Andaluz de Arte Contemporáneo** (Andalusian Contemporary Art Center). Most of the works are by Spanish artists, but some represent other Europeans. *Avda. Américo Vespucio 2, Isla de la Cartuja, tel. 954/480611. Admission: 300 ptas. Open Tues.–Sat. 10–8, Sun. and festivals 10–3.*

LA CARTUJA

This river island west of Seville was almost completely refashioned for the 1992 Expo. It takes its name from the Monasterio de Santa María de las Cuevas, which was formerly called the Monasterio de La Cartuja for its Carthusian ancestry. Only bits of the 1992 architecture remain, but if you look over from the city center you'll see some quirky modern structures protruding from the skyline. The **Puerta de Triana** traffic circle, at the entrance to the **Puente del Cachorro** (Puppy Bridge), sends you toward the **Navigation Pavilion,** which offers a thorough look at the history of Spanish ships, including a full-scale reproduction. The city's only **Omnimax Space Theater** shows wide-screen movies. Take an elevator to the top of the **observation tower** for fabulous views of Seville. *Tel. 954/460089. Admission: 1,000 ptas. Observation tower open Tues.–Sun. 10:30–1 and 4:30–7, pavilion Tues.–Sun. 10:30–12:30 and 3:30–6:30.*

HOSPITAL DE LOS VENERABLES

Once a retirement home for priests, this Baroque building in the heart of the Barrio de Santa Cruz has a splendid *azulejo* patio and a small museum of floats from the Cruces de Mayo (Crosses of May) processions. The guided tour is required. *Plaza de las Venerables, behind Teatro de la Maestranza, tel. 954/562696. Admission: 600 ptas. Open daily 10–2 and 4–8.*

HOSPITAL DE LA CARIDAD

This hospital is still used as a home for the elderly and terminally ill, but you're welcome to wander through the patios and the interior church. Don't be grossed out by Juan de Valdés Leal's pieces on the glory of death; the morbid pieces are balanced by comparatively palatable works by Murillo, who was a personal friend of Miguel de Mañara, the hospital's benefactor. Legend has it that Mañara lived a life much like that of Don Juan until he had a premonition of his funeral; after that, he dedicated his life to the Brotherhood of Charity and all his worldly goods and money to the construction of this hospital. Mañara is buried in the chapel, and his sculpted likeness stands opposite the hospital. *C. Temprado 3, tel. 954/223232. Admission: 400 ptas. Open Mon.–Sat. 10–1 and 4:30–6:30, Sun. 9–1.*

CASA DE PILATOS

Between the Santa Cruz and Macarena neighborhoods sits a cluster of churches and convents—walk around for a tour of Mudéjar through Renaissance sacred architecture. The **Casa de Pilatos**, built in the early 16th century by the dukes of Tarifa, got its name from the rumor that the house is modeled after Pontius Pilate's house in Jerusalem (the first owner, Don Fadrique, had just returned from a visit). The central patio is a bright combination of Mudéjar and Renaissance elements; take a guided tour to see some of the well-preserved frescoes and paintings. Surrounding Pilate's House are the church of **San Esteban,** convent of **San Leandro,** church of **San Ildefonso,** church of **Santa Catalina,** and church of **San Pedro.** *Plaza Pilatos, tel. 954/225298. Admission: 1,000 ptas. Open daily 10–1 and 4–6; patio open during siesta.*

CONVENTO DE SANTA PAULA

Like most Andalusian churches, Santa Paula is built on the site of a former mosque. The building is primarily Gothic, with a Mudéjar tower similar to the Giralda. The walls inside hold some interesting tile designs, and there's some ceramic work by Nicolaso Pisano. *C. Santa Paula, tel. 954/536330. Open Tues.–Sun. 10:30–12:30 and 4:30–6:30.*

PALACIO DE SAN TELMO

Possibly one of the most ornate buildings you'll ever see, the Palace of St. Telmo is Churrigueresque, an extremely detailed Baroque style of stone carving named for the exuberant architect and sculptor José Churriguera (1665–1725). The building now holds the office of the president of Andalusia's *junta* (regional government). *Avda. de Roma s/n, tel. 954/597505. Tours by appointment.*

UNIVERSIDAD DE SEVILLA

Prior to the 1950s, Seville's university was the Real Fábrica de Tabacos (Royal Tobacco Factory), Carmen's theoretical place of employ in Bizet's opera. Wander the courtyards for a sense of present-day student life. At one time the factory employed around 3,000 *cigarreras* (women who rolled cigars); stogies are now rolled on the Isla de Cartuja, across the river. *C. San Fernando (facing south walls of the Alcázar), tel. 954/551000. Courtyards open weekdays 9–8:30.*

PARQUE DE MARÍA LUISA

South of the city center on the Guadalquivir River, this is one of the most intricate and beautiful parks in Spain. The traffic circle Glorieta de San Diego, across from a statue of El Cid, marks the entrance to the park and its former casino, now the **Teatro de Lope de Vega** (*see* After Dark, *below*).

The impressive, semicircular **Plaza de España,** the main pavilion for Expo '29, occupies the park's eastern side. Inside the unique arches are brightly colored tiles representing the 50 provinces of Spain; the four bridges over the half moat stand for the four medieval kingdoms of Iberia. In the north end of the park is a sculpture, dedicated to the Sevillian Romantic poet Gustavo Adolfo Bécquer (1836–1870), depicting the different phases of love—worth a ponder, at least in the shade of some nearby trees. The bright flowers and voluptuous plants of the **Plaza de América,** on the far south side of the park, bask in the glow of the surrounding neo-Mudéjar, Gothic, and Renaissance buildings. These are now the **Pabellón Real** (Royal Pavilion), the **Museo de Artes y Costumbres Populares** (*see below*), and the **Museo Arqueológico** (*see below*).

MUSEO DE ARTES Y COSTUMBRES POPULRES

Seville's Museum of Folklore invites you through a series of re-created scenes dating back to the 18th century. There settings include a forge, a winery, a bakery with stone oven, a tanner's shop, and a potter's workshop. The more sophisticated items, such as carriages and musical instruments, are shown as accoutrements of the Spanish courts; costumes on display range from folk to court dress. *Plaza de América s/n (Mudéjar pavilion), tel. 954/232576. Admission: 300 ptas. Open Wed.–Sat. 9–8, Sun. 9–2:30.*

MUSEO ARQUEOLÓGICO

Found in Seville and the surrounding area, the items in the Museum of Archaeology date from prehistoric times to the Middle Ages. The amazing **Carambolo Treasure** includes a whole hoard of 24-karat gold jewelry from the 7th and 6th centuries BC, found outside Seville in 1958. The grounds and reflection pool adjoining the huge Renaissance building are nice for a stroll. *Plaza de América s/n, tel. 954/ 232401. Admission: 250 ptas. Open Tues 3–8 , Wed.–Sat. 9–8, Sun. 9–2.*

MUSEO DE BELLAS ARTES

The high ceilings and wooden beams of a 17th-century convent form the perfect backdrop to Seville's Museum of Fine Arts, one of the best art museums in Spain. The collection moves chronologically from the Middle Ages through the 20th century, with special emphasis on the golden-age School of Seville— Zurbarán, Murillo, and El Greco are well represented, mostly by religious art. (There's a lone painting by Velázquez.) One of Murillo's paintings, *La Servilleta* (*The Napkin*), a depiction of the Madonna and Child, is thought to be painted on a napkin. There are also some fine Baroque wooden sculptures, a quintessentially Andalusian art form. The building's three patios are lined with flowers and trees. *Plaza del Museo, tel. 954/220790. Admission: 250 ptas. Open Tues. 3–8, Wed.–Sat. 9–8, Sun. 9–3.*

BULLFIGHTS

Seville's **Plaza de Toros Real Maestranza** (Royal Maestranza Bullring) is one of the oldest (built 1758) and most famous in Spain, known for its dramatic size and fittingly dramatic bullfights. Starting during Semana Santa (Holy Week)—as if the insanity on the streets weren't enough—the ring, which seats 14,000, comes alive. Fights are traditionally held on Sundays; look for schedules around town the week before the season starts. During Seville's Feria de Abril (April Fair), a week or so after the Semana Santa, Spain's top *toreros* (bullfighters) strut their stuff every day. (Indeed, toreros must pass through Seville at some point to establish their careers.) Tickets can sell out well in advance, so buy in advance from the bullring's **box office** (Paseo de Colón 12, tel. 954/224577)—the ticket offices on Calle Sierpes charge up to 20% commission. The last *corrida* (running of the bulls) is toward the end of October. Inside the Baroque white-and-ocher building is a small **Museo Taurino** with a drawing by Picasso, the stuffed heads of some prize bulls, and sparkly suits worn by toreros past. *Open daily 9:30–2 and 3–7.*

SHOPPING

Seville's main shopping artery is **Calle Sierpes**, in the center of town. If you prefer random alternative goods to trendy boutiques, head north along Calle Sierpes to **Calle Amor de Dios** and check out the skate-n-surf shops (selling mainly overpriced American goods) and the head shops specializing in tie-dyed shirts and hand-blown glass pipes. The secondhand clothes at **Quasi Moda** (C. Amor de Dios 43, tel. 954/900322; closed Sun.) are a treat—clothes range chronologically from bell bottoms to whatever's presently popular, but prices for everything are extremely reasonable. The owner, Bernardo, can point you toward other cool places to shop and will happily find you the perfect jacket if you find Seville unseasonably cold.

For cool shoes, try **Swear** (C. Reyes Católicos 18, 41001, tel. 954/563925; closed Sun.) The staff is extremely hip; ask them what's going on next weekend, or just pick up some of the club flyers distributed here. To match your new shoes, look for a fab new outfit at **Taxi International** (C. la Campaña 2, tel. 954/226477).

La Tienda del Aciete (The Olive Oil Shop; C. García de Vinuesa 31, tel. 954/213030) is a unique little place stuffed with sundry local olive oils and related paraphernalia such as serving vessels, books, and cards. The staff is sweet and knowledgeable. Take home an easy-to-pack sampler set to prove to your skeptical friends that Spanish olive oil really is the tastiest.

AFTER DARK

In keeping with the pan-Spanish virtue of drinking and schmoozing till dawn, Seville packs a huge variety of places to test your endurance. Bars line the riverbanks and practically every street. Some of the poshest nightclubs pump out music—anything from '80s pop to modern techno—until early in the morning. In the heat of summer, crowds move to the bars and benches of the riverbank for a snowball's chance at a breeze. To find out what's on, look in local newspapers or in *ABC Sevilla, Correo de Andalucía, Sudoeste,* or *Nueva Andalucía.* For arts events, consult the monthly leaflet *El Giraldillo.*

For a game of pool, good rock music, and possibly a concert, try **Superpool** (Muñoz León 5), on the north side of town across from the Basilica de la Macarena. Near Calle Reyes Católicos, off Puente de Isabel II, look for the trendy bar **Collage** (C. Julio César, between Reyes Católicos and Marqués de Paradas), a great place to take advantage of air-conditioning when the weather's brutal. A few blocks north and west, almost directly across from Plaza de Armas, is the new and popular **El Otro Sur** (C. Trastamara 29). The name means "The Other South," and this place bills itself as an urban "coffee show"—depending on the night of the week, you might catch a live show or just some decent bar action. The place is usually open Wednesday–Sunday from 4 PM; expect a performance around 11 PM. One of many clubs along the Guadalquivir, the riverside club **Salamandra** (C. Torneo 43; open Fri.–Sat. plus erratic other days) has a lively dance floor with music ranging from the Doors to techno, not to mention occasional flamenco or other ethnic music.

The rest of Seville's nightlife is across the river from the **Puente de San Telmo** (the lighted bridge near the Torre del Oro). The glowing neon area is full of tourists; one of the Irish pubs gets packed with college students, and several restaurants are open late. Following Calle Betis north along the river brings you to more local hangouts such as **Sirocco** (near Plaza de Cuba), which plays alternative music until dawn. A few blocks farther is a cool Arabic teahouse, the **Salón de Thé Salam** (C. Luca de Tena; closed Mon.), where the menu extends from tea to all kinds of coffees, mixed drinks, liquors, and Arabic sweets. On Thursday, there's live traditional lute music. **Luna Park** (Avda. María Luisa s/n) is a small, dark discoteca with nightly drink specials. **Discoteca Milenio** (Puerta de Triana s/n) advertises specials for international students, so the crowd is usually a good mix thereof.

FLAMENCO

Along with Jerez de la Frontera, Seville is alive and kicking with flamenco—indeed, Spain's headquarters for this relatively rare art form. You can have a drink to the sounds of flamenco music in many a tavern, but live shows require advance planning, as tourists crowd them along with locals. If you're interested, dig deep into your pockets and ask your hotel staff if they can make a reservation for you, as they often get deals.

El Arenal. This long-established club near the bullring gives you your own table, rather than installing you on a bench with everyone else. *C. Rodo 7, tel. 954/216492. Admission: 4,100 ptas. (includes 1 drink). Open daily 9:30–11:30 PM.*

El Patio Andaluz. A smaller place with less glitz, El Patio Andaluz packs just as much emotion into each *soleare* (a type of flamenco song). *Avda. María Auxiliadora 18-B, tel. 954/534720. Admissioin: 3,800 ptas. (includes 1 drink). Open daily 8:30–10 PM.*

El Patio Sevillano. These dramatic and traditional shows are aimed at tourists. *Paseo de Colón 11, tel. 954/214120. Admission: 4,000 ptas. (includes 1 drink). Show at 8:30.*

Los Gallos. This place is in the heart of the old quarter, a few blocks east of the Alcázar. The relatively personal environment is a plus. *Plaza de Santa Cruz s/n, tel. 954/216981. Admission: 3,500 ptas. (includes 1 drink). Open daily 9–11:30 PM.*

CLASSICAL MUSIC / OPERA / THEATER

Seville's modern, 1,800-seat **Teatro de la Maestranza** (Paseo de Colón 22; box office in Jardín de la Caridad next door; tel. 954/226573) stages top-notch opera performances. Ballets and concerts are staged year-round at the **Teatro de Lope de Vega** (Avda. de María Luisa s/n, tel. 954/590853 for information, 954/590846 for tickets), in Parque María Luisa.

FLAMENCO

As seductive as the people of Spain, flamenco music and dance are cultural amalgams of ancient traditions. Cave paintings depict similar arm movements, the Phoenicians danced in Cádiz, and southern Iberia was later inhabited by Greeks, whose folk dances involved flamenco-style clapping. The Moors had a strong influence, as evidenced by some dances' Arabic names (zambra, zorongo, fandango). In the 15th century Gypsies began to arrive from northern India, and while they did not "bring" the dance with them—Indian dance remains quite different—they certainly accumulated folk-dance elements on their travels.

Flamenco singing is a bigger mystery. Like Eastern music, it incorporates microtones and repetition, and its interplay with dance involves complex rhythms. Like Latin American ballads, flamenco songs often tell a story.

Flamenco's footwork was only added in the 20th century, as women did not reveal their legs before then. The guitar was not original to the form, either; the strumming and trilling sounds of the flat flamenco guitar are fairly recent additions. Flamenco clubs sprang up in 1840s Seville, where different neighborhoods propounded distinct vocal styles and performers. When competition raised the stakes, women started dancing in seductive dresses. In 1898, a movement called Antiflamenquismo formed to protest the moral breakdown these developments were causing, and public respect for the form plummeted. Clubs closed. Several efforts were made to revive the art, including a 1922 Granada singing contest organized by Federica García Lorca and Manuel de Falla and accompanied by guitarist Andres Segovia; since then flamenco has experienced a long, slow recovery documented in part by Paco de Lucía's guitar recordings. You can now see all kinds of flamenco in Spain, in clubs and on the streets—Gypsies sometimes perform alfresco—but the best flamenco breaks out spontaneously in dive bars or at private parties. Despite its multi-ethnic heritage, flamenco is an art form unique to this senual country.

NEAR SEVILLE

ITÁLICA

Twelve kilometers (7 mi) north of Seville, Itálica is a small town consisting mainly of **Roman ruins.** Founded in 206 BC as a settlement for veteran soldiers, the city had grown important within the Empire by the AD years. The huge amphitheater once held 40,000 spectators. The emperors Hadrian and Trajan were born here, which gave the city extra credence until the Visigoths invaded and turned the place into a quarry. Most of Itálica is still being excavated, but you can take a good look at some of the mosaics and buildings that haven't been moved to Seville's Museum of Archaeology. Practically next door, the tiny town of **Santiponce** has some Roman baths and a Roman theater. *Carretera de Mérida (Ruta de Plata), tel. 955/997376. Admission: 300 ptas. Open Oct.–Mar., Tues.–Sat. 9–5:30, Sun. 10–4; Apr.– Sept., Tues.–Sat. 9–8, Sun. 9–3.*

CARMONA

For the traveler, the walled village of Carmona serves as a bonus to the metropolis of Seville. One of the few still-functioning Spanish cities with roots among the Phoenicians and the Carthaginians, it transforms your environment to something *pre*-Roman within 30 minutes. What remains, more or less in ruins, holds some clues to the Roman settlement here; later additions are in the Moorish, Gothic, Baroque, and Renaissance styles. Generally speaking, the town fits into the whitewashed Moorish category, its center marked by the gate called **Puerta de Sevilla.** Parking is random, but most of it is outside the city walls. A steep but short hike up to the **Alcázar de Arriba** (High Fortress) gives you a sweeping view of the Andalusian countryside.

COMING AND GOING

Carmona is easy to reach by **car**—take the N-IV north and cruise for 32 km (20 mi). You can also take a **bus** from Seville; most buses en route to and from Córdoba and Madrid swing through Carmona. Because the town is so small and has endured so much construction, there is no permanent bus station; call Seville (bus station, tel. 954/417111) or Córdoba (bus line Alsina Graells, tel. 957/236474) for details.

WHERE TO SLEEP

UNDER 7,000 PTAS. • Pensión Comercio. The owners of this pension across the street from the tourist office have run it for several generations. The huge wooden doors bring out the rudimentary charm of the place, and the central patio is a sunny, vibrant spot with terra-cotta tiles, huge plants, and a few cats running around. For a few pesetas you can take breakfast with the family and other guests in the dining room, which looks out to the tower of the Alcázar de Abajo (*see below*). Most rooms have private bath; most doubles cost about 6,000 ptas. *C. Torre del Oro 56, tel. 954/140018. 14 rooms. Cash only.*

Hostal San Pedro. Here, the sweet older-guy proprietor will take you by the hand to show you the rooms. Most rooms are modern—with new mattresses (compensating for the plain decor) and newly tiled bathrooms with tubs—and most have a small terrace, or at least a nice view up to the Puerta de Sevilla. Most of the rooms sleep 3 people, but the price for two hovers around 6,000 ptas. The owner runs a café and beauty parlor downstairs, useful if you're getting shaggy. *C. San Pedro 3, tel. 954/141606. 30 rooms. Doubles 6,000 ptas, Cash only.*

WHERE TO EAT

UNDER 2,000 PTAS. • Almazara Mesón. A quintessential Carmona—nay, Spanish—experience, Almazara serves typical Carmonia cuisine in an old olive-oil mill with wooden beams and white walls and arches.. Seasonal menus feature, among other things, beef stew in the winter and chilled *ajo blanco* (a cold, almond-based cream soup) in the summer; and the homemade desserts are worth the guilt. The staff is unusually attentive, and the bar is fully stocked with local wines. *C. Santa Ana 33, tel. 954/ 190076.*

El Tapeo. Often packed with local families and young couples, this tiny place is known for its tapas and its wide selection of wines. If you sit at the bar, you'll be served a small bowl of spicy olives spiked with half a ton of garlic. Local cheeses are offered as a sampler with fresh, crusty bread. Many of entrées are made with earthy spices, such as mustard seeds and cumin; the *espinaca de Carmona* is fresh spinach and garbanzo beans sautéed in spices and wine. This is one of the few places in Carmona that serve plain old toast and eggs for breakfast. *C. Prim 9, tel. 954/144321.*

Sierra Mayor Carmona. Conveniently located in the Palacio del Marqués de las Torres, this place is part of a relatively new chain that aims to keep its interiors subdued and classic, with wooden ceilings and real plants. The house specialty is the home-cured hams and *embutidos* (hearty stuffed sausages), but the menú del día is usually a good deal, and might come with a fresh green salad topped with white asparagus. *C. San Ildefonso 1, tel. 954/144404. Closed Mon.*

SPLURGE • Parador Alcázar del Rey Don Pedro. A room at Carmona's Moorish parador might break your budget, but a meal at the restaurant doesn't have to. As a reward for hiking up here, the restaurant has a view of the valley below. The fare changes seasonally but always includes typical regional dishes such as gazpacho, sautéed prawns in garlic, and stuffed river trout served over country rice. A menú del día costs 3,700 ptas., so order à la carte if you're on a budget; if nothing else, consider stopping in for *café con leche* and a homemade dessert. *Los Alcázares s/n, tel. 954/141010.*

WORTH SEEING

Just inside the Puerta de Sevilla is the sturdy **Alcázar de Abajo** (Low Fortress), a Roman structure beefed up by the Moors for protection. Within the tower, Carmona's small **tourist office** (tel. 954/ 190955; open weekdays 10–6, Sun. 10–3) hands out maps. Touring the fortress gives you enough height to view the rooftops and surrounding countryside, as well as watch a few educational videos about Carmona (200 ptas.). Hike up a few blocks (any route will do) to **Plaza San Fernando**, a mainly cement square in the midst of 17th-century buildings. The square is filled with frolicking kids and bench-sitting grandparents. A block west of here, a daily **market** offers fresh produce. A little way up Calle Martín, the Gothic church of **Santa María** subtly occupies its street corner, built on the site of Carmona's main mosque. The Mudéjar tower contains part of the original minaret.

Behind the church is the 18th-century **Palacio del Marqués de las Torres**, remodeled to include a small historical museum on Carmona's history and culture. *C. San Ildefonso s/n. Admission free. Open fall– spring, Tues. 11–2, Wed.–Mon.11–7; June–Sept., Tues. 10–2, Wed.–Mon. 10–2 and 6:30–9:30.*

Eventually, at the wall's eastern edge, you'll arrive at the Moorish/Renaissance **Puerta de Córdoba**, originally built by the Romans around 175 AD. At one time, the road into Carmona went through this gate. Dominating this edge of town is the Moorish **Alcázar de Arriba**, built on top of Roman ruins and then converted to a Mudéjar palace by Pedro the Cruel (who did have excellent taste). The original palace was destroyed in 1504 by an earthquake but rebuilt in the 20th century as a parador (state-run luxury hotel).

Just outside the Puerta de Sevilla, down toward the rest of town, is the 1466 church of **San Pedro,** with a façade of delicately sculpted figures and designs. The Baroque tower is nothing but a ripoff of Seville's Giralda, probably commissioned by Pedro the Cruel. The small museum inside displays antique religious bits and a multitude of replicas of Baby Jesus, donated by the faithful on their way through.

Carmona's real treat is the almost intact **Roman necropolis** on the outskirts of town. You must take a guided tour, and it's just as well, for you'd probably miss half of the underground tombs otherwise: Roughly 900 family tombs were carved into these underground chambers between the 4th and 2nd centuries BC. In some, you can still make out some wall paintings of plants and birds. The guide will point out several red-tinted rocks on which cremations took place. Every tomb contains cremated remains, which allowed for efficient use of space. There are two extravagant tombs in the area: The spacious **Elephant Vault** is marked by a weathered sculpture of an earless and tuskless elephant. Not much is known about the inhabitant(s) of the **Servilia Tomb;** it's only certain that one woman was embalmed rather than cremated, she is assumed to have been the daughter of a Roman dignitary. The Servilia tomb is set up like a miniature Roman villa, with vaulted side galleries, remnants of central columns, and colonnaded arches. Across the street is a partially excavated **Roman amphitheater.** *C. Enmedio (follow signs a few blocks out of town), tel. 954/140811. Admission free. Open Sept.–June, Tues.–Fri. 10–2 and 4–6, weekends 10–2; June–Sept., Tues.–Sat. 9–2, Sun. 10–2.*

AFTER DARK

Carmona's *ruta de las tapas* (tapas route) leads through the city from bar to bar. Colorful tiles mark the buildings that have made the tourist office's list of good places to grab a bite. The office has long since run out of guides for this path, but Carmona is small enough that you can find each spot on your own. Lively places proliferate around the Plaza San Fernando, especially down **Calle Prim.**

Just outside the walls, toward the Roman ruins, **Discoteca la Gloria** (C. San Bartolomé 8, tel. 954/140276; open Thurs.–Sat.) is a laid-back club with rock and techno music. Up near the Puerta de Córdoba is a popular hole-in-the-wall called **Piano-Bar Puerta de Córdoba** (C. San Ildefonso 14, tel. 954/142988).

PARQUE NACIONAL DE DOÑANA

Unbeknownst to most of the world, Spain has several illustrious nature parks. Doñana, one of the most ecologically valuable regions in Europe, happens to be an oasis for hundreds of species of birds. Down on the coast in the far-western province of Huelva, bordering the Guadalquivir estuary, the park covers 188,000 acres, of which the public can view only a portion (in fact, only 125 visitors are permitted on the property at a time). Around the five visitor centers, short walking trails invite you to get a feel for the land, and there's rarely a shortage of wildlife even that close to the buildings.

VISITOR INFORMATION

Doñana's wetlands are on the migratory flight path for birds en route between Europe and Africa. In spring, the park becomes a breeding ground for up to 150 species of **rare birds.** When you pull into the parking lot, the wandering peacocks will get you in the mood, at least until they chase you down looking for food. On the A483 road into the park (accessed via the A49 west from Seville), be on guard for sudden movements by motoring bird-watchers; moreover, the occasional miniature sandstorm brews up bad visibility for a few miles.

The Doñana region is named after Doña Ana, wife of a 16th-century duke. Prone to bouts of depression, she crossed the river and wandered into the wetlands one day, never to be seen again.

You'll come first to **El Rocío,** a strange little town with no paved roads and simple white buildings. The tourist office (Avda. de la Canaliega s/n, tel. 959/442684; open daily 10–3 and 4–6) has helpful info on this area, though it's not part of the park.

A few miles farther, on your right, is the park's first visitor center, called **La Rocina** (tel. 959/442340; open daily 9–3 and 4–8). Here you can take a short hike to see some scrubland and stream fauna; there's also a small exhibition on the El Rocío pilgrimage (*see* Sanlúcar de Barrameda, *below*) and an introductory videotape on the history and value of the park.

The main visitor center, called **El Acebuche** (tel. 959/430432 for tour reservations) is almost on the coast, near Matalascañas. Come here for a guided tour, a cup of coffee, or some literature—the gift shop has a few guides in English. Several videos and exhibitions explain the park's ecosystems. The tour—usually 2,500 a person, less if the group is large—consists of a four-hour jeep excursion. Try to call in advance; tours sell out a few hours or days before they depart, depending on the season.

The **José Antonio Valverde** visitor center is in the middle of the park, accessible by three confusing dirt roads. The building has a café-bar, gift shop, and several observation towers—because this center is closer to the river than the others, the surrounding ecosystem attracts more wildlife. Avid birders are rewarded for the lengthy journey it takes to get here.

The Palacio del Acebrón visitor center is accessible from La Rocina, but at press time it was closed indefinitely for reconstruction. The fifth visitor center is accessible only from the eastern side of the Guadalquivir.

WHERE TO SLEEP

There are a few hotels and inns on the highway into the park, useful if you want to spend more than a day trip from Seville. Many close for family holidays toward the end of summer, however, so be sure to call in advance for reservations.

UNDER 6,000 PTAS. • Cabañas de Doñana. Decor in these wooden cabins is simple country, with wooden walls and plenty of blue-check fabric. Twenty minutes from Seville, you're in the middle of nowhere yet close to the park, enjoying your own little patch of nature and a private bathroom. Homemade food is served in the restaurant and café. A cabin for two costs 5,000 ptas. a night; full board costs about 2,000 ptas. additional per person. *Camino de La Palma s/n, Hinojos (A49 to exit 9), tel. 959/506070 or 630/978221. 10 cabins. Restaurant, café.*

UNDER 10,000 PTAS. • Hotel Matalascañas. The beach town of Matalascañas is down on Doñana's coast, and the hotel plays the part with a small pool and a short path to the beach. The staff can set you up with horseback tours, park information, and directions to the nearby commercial center. Rooms are simple, but the mattresses are firm, and each room has a little terrace as well as a private bathroom. Doubles start around 5,900 ptas. and go up steeply from there, particularly on spring and summer weekends. Perks include laundry service, parking, fax service, and a bar. *C. del Pintor Velásquez, sector I, 136, Playa de Matalascañas, Huelva, tel. 959/448438, fax 959/448438. 25 rooms.*

Hotel Toruño. In the middle of the potholes and dirt, there *is* a bit of life in El Rocío. The folks at Hotel Toruño are not so much bird-watchers as bird *appreciators*, well able to tell you about the park and touring options. The rooms, all with bath, are fairly new and well cared for; some have views of the shrubby parkland. Doubles go for 8,000 ptas. *Plaza Acebuchal 22, El Rocío, Huelva, tel. 959/442323, fax 959/442338. 30 rooms with bath. Restaurant, café.*

WHERE TO EAT

UNDER 2,000 PTAS. • El Pastorcito. Just outside El Rocío, this place serves typical tapas and standard (great) seafood. The friendly atmosphere comes in part from the comfortable environment—old wooden tables, handmade baskets on the wall—and in part from the Cabreras family, who will patiently recite the daily specials slowly, if necessary. *Carretera de Almonte, El Rocío, Km 4.5, tel. 959/450205.*

UNDER 3,000 PTAS. • Aires de Doñana. This restaurant has a large outdoor patio overlooking some of Doñana's graceful, spacious marshland. The imaginative kitchen serves traditional Spanish dishes with some French twists, such as creamy sauces and fresh herbs. Specialties include fruits of the local sea—langostinos, jumbo shrimp—and a seared duck breast served over vegetables. The staff is extremely efficient and quite knowledgeable about wines, a pleasant surprise. *Avda. de la Canaliega 1, El Rocío, tel. 959/442719.*

HORSEBACK RIDING

Horses can access a few sites that jeeps can't, such as the fossilized dunes on the beach at Matalascañas, and **Club Hípico–El Pasodoble** (Sector G, parcela 90, Matalascañas, tel. 954/448241 or 629/060545 for reservations, fax 954/406540) is the only company authorized to lead horseback tours through Doñana National Park. The one- and two-day trips are radial, so you see as much as possible, and include a bag lunch. To find the meeting point in Matalascañas, follow the road through the park all the way to the coast.

THE COSTA DE LA LUZ

LA RÁBIDA

This is Columbus country. West of Doñana, northwest along the coast, is La Rábida, featuring the Franciscan **Monasterio de Santa María de La Rábida.** Forgotten by popular American history, this is where Columbus discussed his navigational theories with a group of religious dignitaries, who then spoke to Queen Isabella on his behalf. The Mudéjar building contains a 14th-century sculpture of the Virgen de los Milagros (Virgin of the Miracles) and, in the gatehouse, some detailed early-20th-century frescoes.

About a mile from the monastery, on the coast, is the **Muelle de las Carabelas** (Wharf of the Caravels), sporting replicas of the *Niña, Pinta,* and *Santa María*. Explore the ships and learn the discovery of the Americas from a Spanish point of view in the small museum. *Paraje de La Rábida, tel. 959/530597. Admission: 450 ptas. Open Oct.–Mar., Tues.–Sun. 10–7; Apr.–Sept. 10–2 and 5–9.*

WHERE TO SLEEP AND EAT

Book far in advance if you want to stay at the **Hostería de La Rábida** (tel. 959/350312), next door to the monastery—there are only five rooms, and they're nice, with private bath and old wooden furniture. Doubles cost 7,800 ptas. The restaurant is a good place to grab a simple lunch.

PALOS DE LA FRONTERA

A few miles northeast of La Rábida is the tiny town—poetically named **Palos de la Frontera** (Mast of the Frontier), though for different reasons—from which Columbus's *Niña, Pinta,* and *Santa María* set sail. The royal letter authorizing the expedition was read aloud from the steps of the small church of **San Jorge,** where Columbus and his men took communion before their departure. A block away, in a park, is **La Fontanilla,** the well from which the men drew their water for their journey.

MOGUER

Continuing west from Palos de la Frontera, Moguer is a former port town that now borders on the silted river. Many men came from here to join Columbus's American expeditions; Moguer is now known mainly for strawberries, which grow in fields around the town. The **Convento de Santa Clara,** which dates from 1337, was Columbus's first stop upon his first return from the New World.

In 1956, Moguer lit up on the map when native son Juan Ramón Jiménez won the Nobel Prize for Literature. His tender poem "Platero y Yo" is a youthful recounting of youthful wanderings with his boyhood pet donkey, Platero. The poet's home is now the **Casa-Museo Juan Ramón Jiménez,** where you can take a short guided tour. *C. Juan Ramón Jiménez, tel. 959/372148. Admission: 300 ptas. Open Mon.–Sat. 10–2 and 5–8, Sun. 10–2.*

GETTING AROUND

For a cheese-whiz tour of Columbus's haunts in this area, hop on the little tourist train, **Viztor Turística** (C. Aracena 2, tel. 959/372043 or 959/225795) that runs through these towns, stopping for closer inspection of the sites. The accommodating staff can tailor a route for you and your buds; trips average 1,500 ptas. a person.

ALMONTE

North of El Rocío, the town of Almonte is known for its fruity, sparkling white wine and for the pilgrimage of worshippers crossing the Guadalquivir River to see its sanctuary (*see* Sanlúcar de Barrameda, *below;* the building itself is unremarkable). The wine, a sparkling variety made from indigenous grapes, is called Raígal; there is also a local brand of vermouth, much respected in Spain. You can visit the **bodega** on weekday mornings by appointment (Cooperative Nuestra Señora del Rocío, C. Santiago 69, tel. 959/406103, fax 959/407052).

JEREZ DE LA FRONTERA

Jerez de la Frontera is blessed with some of the kindest people in Andalusia, proud of their heritage and well schooled in the history of their land. Could it be because the sun shines at least 300 days a year here, as on the nearby coast? It's the rare Jerezan who cannot explain to you the precise difference between each local wine and sherry, and some might invite you home to try a glass. English is less widely spoken here than on the Costa del Sol, but the Spanish is slower and more expressive than in northern Spain, so your gestures and facial expressions will go a long way.

And there's much to talk about, not least the many so-called *gitanos* (Gypsies) currently supporting a revival of flamenco in its most traditional forms. Jerez's horses are also world-renowned, trained to perform in historically accurate equestrian feats. The *casco viejo* (old town) is substantial, with several churches, Moorish-style whitewashed walls, winding streets, and a large bullring; indeed, the city as a whole is larger than it looks on the map, with a population of around 180,000 and some entirely modern commercial sections. The town was named by the Moors for its sherry (they called it Scheris, or Xeres); today the bodegas give daily tours and sell wine, sherry, and brandy at generally decent prices.

BASICS

CYBERSPACE

Within the store Jump, on Calle Porvera, look for **CyberPl@ce** (C. Porvera 39, tel. 956/168380), with rates around 600 ptas. an hour. The computer store on the top floor of the **Centro Comercial** (a mall on

Calle Larga just north of the tourist office) has several machines for public use. Several small outfits on the upper floors of office buildings offer Internet access; prowl **Calle Larga** and **Calle Santa María** for signs saying INTERNET. Anything with the @ sign is fair game.

EMERGENCIES

Police: tel. 091 or 956/342172. The **Hospital de Santa Cruz** (Avda. de la Cruz Roja, tel. 956/307454) has an emergency room.

MAIL

The main **post office** is a few blocks from the tourist office, on Calle Cerrón across from the strip of *hostales* on Calle Arcos (tel. 956/342295 or 956/341692, open weekdays 8:30–8:30, Sat. 9–2).

VISITOR INFORMATION

The **tourist office** is on the pedestrian street Calle Larga (C. Larga 39, tel. 956/331150; open weekdays 8–2 and 5–8, Sat. 10–2 and 5–8). Hours can be erratic, but the staff is ever ready with advice on bodegas, excursions, lodgings, and restaurants.

COMING AND GOING

The Andalucía Express **train** between Seville and Cádiz stops in Jerez almost every hour in both directions. From **Seville** to Jerez, the trip takes one hour and costs 910 ptas.; from Jerez to **Cádiz**, it's a 35-minute hop costing 475 ptas. The **train station** is on the east side of town, at the end of Calle Cartuja on Plaza de la Estación—but the main **RENFE office** (C. Larga 34, tel. 956/342319 station, 956/334813 office) has considerably more information.

Buses to nearby towns are frequent. The **bus station** is next door to the train station (C. Cartuja, tel. 956/345207). Star Class and Linesur (both at tel. 956/341063) both go to **Seville** (1½ hrs, 700 ptas.) and **Sanlúcar de Barrameda** (½ hr, 220 ptas.). Secorbus (tel. 902/229292) goes to **Cádiz** (20 mins, 320 ptas.). Los Amarillos (tel. 956/329347) goes slightly farther afield to **Ronda** and **Puerta de Santa María**. Comes (tel. 953/751878) makes long runs to **Seville, Córdoba, Granada,** and **Madrid.**

The **airport** (tel. 956/150000) is a few kilometers northeast of Jerez on the N-IV highway. There are daily flights to most major Spanish cities and a few flights farther afield in Europe. Airlines: **Iberia** (tel. 956/150010), **Aviaco** (tel. 956/150011), and **British Airways** (tel. 956/150093).

GETTING AROUND

Taxis are plentiful, with stands along most major roads; call Tele-Taxi if you can't find one (tel. 956/344860).

WHERE TO SLEEP

UNDER 7,000 PTAS. • Hotel San Andres. The same family has cared for this inn for almost 30 years. The courtyard is a jungle of plants amid beautiful tile walls. Rooms in the newer section are not as homey, but they're clean and well kept; the older section has a few rooms without bath, but the atmosphere makes up for it. Doubles cost 5,000 ptas. The proprietor has a collection of keychains from around the world (accessible on request), and has filled a wall's worth of bookshelves with photo albums documenting the family's world travels. *C. Morenos 12 and 14, tel. 956/340983, fax 956/343196. 18 rooms, most with bath.*

Hotel Torres. The interior patio of this central hotel is of white marble, and most rooms look onto it as well as onto the outside world. Decor is simple and modern, and all rooms have private bath; doubles go for 6,000 ptas. *C. Arcos 29, tel. 956/323400, fax 956/3221816. 30 rooms.*

UNDER 10,000 PTAS. • Hotel Doña Blanca. Just east of the old town, in the more commercial area, this new hotel is well situated for bus-station access and bar-hopping. The clean rooms have firm mattresses, minibars, private safes, and, in most cases, decent views. Most of the staffers speak English, and all are gamely helpful. *C. Bodegas 11, tel. 956/348762, fax 956/348586. 24 rooms, 6 suites. Doubles 10,000.*

Hotel Serit. The lobby of this new building (around the corner from the Doña Blanca) is tackier than the rooms, which are simple and sparkling-clean. Doubles start at 8,000 ptas. Rooms on the ground floor are wheelchair-accessible. The café serves up local specialties. *C. Higueras 7, tel. 956/340700, fax 956/340716. 27 rooms.*

WHERE TO EAT

Touted as the most typical corner of Jerez, the **Plaza Rafael Rivero** area is full of souvenir shops by day, tapas bars by night. For Old-World action and delicious seafood tapas, look for **El Tabanco, Lo Nuestro, Antigua Abacería,** and **Taberna Marinera.**

UNDER 2,000 PTAS. • El Mirador de las Almenas. This place claims to serve food your grandmother would make. Indeed, if you had an Andalusian *abuela* this would be the place to give her the night off. The patio is entirely traditional, with flowers cascading from the windowsills of its 12th-century Moorish wall. Have your seafood grilled or in *paella de mariscos.* The salon upstairs turns into something of a disco on weekend nights; in the summer, you can catch flamenco shows here. The owner is deaf, so the staff speaks a complex and enjoyable blend of Spanish, sign language, and English. *C. Pescaderia Vieja 7 and 9, tel. 956/345279.*

La Almazara. The bar at this central joint serves up local wines and classic tapas made with a variety of local hams, cheeses, and meats. You can dine indoors or out; in the dining room, plants brighten up the corners. The multilingual staff is generous with travel advice. *C. San Pablo 20, tel. 956/321113. Usually closed Aug.*

La Carbona. In addition to some of the best *patatas bravas* (chunky fried potatoes) you'll ever try, La Carbona's house specialties include Andalusian and Extremaduran meat dishes. The room has an antique feel, with wooden ceiling beams, hand-crafted tables and chairs, and a central fireplace for chilly winter evenings. *C. San Francisco de Paula 2 (between C. Arcos and C. Medina), tel. 956/347475.*

UNDER 3,000 PTAS. • Gaitán. This place has earned awards for its exquisite Andalusian cuisine. Between well-schooled Chef Juan Hurtado, the kind staff, and helpful tips on what to order, you'll soon see why. Hotels and the tourist office sometimes have coupons for a free glass of sherry at Gaitán, and there's free parking down Calle Sevilla. *C. Gaitán 3, tel. 956/345859. No lunch in winter.*

La Parra Vieja. Covered with mosaic on the outside, this elegant house has welcomed diners for 120 years. The seafood is fresh, natch, and the meats come from local butchers. *Entrecote de vaca a la parilla* is an impressive beef-tenderloin dish of the restaurant's own devising; *polluelas inglesas con arroz* are English hens baked with spices and served over rice. *C. San Miguel 9, tel. 956/335390. No lunch.*

Tendido 6. Cleverly named for its position opposite Gate 6 of the bullring, this restaurant is filled to the brim with bullfighting gear, not to mention stuffed bulls' heads watching over you. The menu changes seasonally, but you can bet on good ham and other meats. Try an oxtail dish for a far-out but tasty experience. Desserts are homemade; you'll see traditional flan and perhaps an almond tart. *C. Circo 10, tel. 956/344835. No lunch.*

WORTH SEEING

OLD TOWN

The 12th-century **Alcázar,** once home to the Moorish caliph (governor) of Seville, holds its ground on the southern end of the city center. It retains some exquisite details—the baths are some of the best-preserved in Spain, with three sections: a *sala fria* (cold room), *sala temporada* (warm room), and *sala caliente* (hot room). The octagonal mosque has an intricately designed cupola. In the midst of it all, on the site of the original Moorish palace, is the 17th-century **Palacio de Villavicencio.** A *camera obscura,* a lens-and-mirrors device that projects the outdoors onto a large indoor screen, offers a 360-degree view of Jerez from the palace's highest tower—a perfect introduction to the city. *Alameda Vieja, tel. 956/319798. Admission: Alcázar 200 ptas., camera obscura 500 ptas. Open fall–spring, daily 10–6; summer, daily 10–8.*

Next door to the Alcázar, Jerez's 18th-century **cathedral** is a blend of the Gothic, Baroque, and neoclassical styles. Inside, there's a dramatic 15th-century sculpture of *Christo de la Viga* (*Christ of the Beams*). The cupola is octagonal, and the bell tower is, uncharacteristically, separate from the building. *Plaza del Arroyo. Open Mon.–Sat. 6 AM–7 PM, Sun. 11–2.*

The central **Plaza de la Asunción,** known formerly as Plaza de los Escribanos (Writers' Square), is another blend of styles, this time Mudéjar, Renaissance, and neoclassical. The Italian-influenced

Cabildo Viejo (city hall) is a plateresque masterpiece dating from 1575; look for the pious statues of Julius Caesar and Hercules. The 15th-century church of **San Dionisio** is dedicated to Jerez's patron saint. Built in a specifically Jerezan Mudéjar style, it stands on the site of a former mosque.

The unique **Museo de los Relojes** is a museum dedicated to clocks. Show up just before noon to hear an amazing cacophony of chimes. *C. Cervantes 3, tel. 956/182100. Admission: 400 ptas. Open Mon.– Sat. 10–2.*

REAL ESCUELA ANDALUZA DEL ARTE ECUESTRA

A unique highlight of Jerez is the Royal Andalusian School of Equestrian Art, which gives beautiful, thorough demonstrations of the world-famous Andalusian riding tradition. Every Thursday at noon year-round (plus Tuesday at noon between March and October), the school puts on a "Fantasía Ecuestre," in which students execute a variety of moves to period music in 18th-century costume. Between November and February, you can also attend practice sessions and tour the facilities (stables, saddlery, Tack Room Museum, and so forth) Monday, Tuesday, Wednesday, and Friday from 11 to 1. Buy tickets on-site or through any nearby travel agency. *Avda. Duque de Abrantes, tel. 956/ 319635, fax 956/318014.*

BODEGAS

Vineyards and wineries are lush additions to Jerez in more ways than one. If you're interested in seeing one, make reservations—tours do fill up—and indicate that you speak English. You'll be invited to sample pale, dry *fino*, nutty *amontillado*, or rich, deep *oloroso*, and, of course, to spring for a few bottles in the winery shop.

Harvey (C. Arcos 54, tel. 956/346004; open weekdays 9–1, weekends by appt.), maker of Harvey's Bristol Cream, is one of the biggies. The company was founded in Bristol, England, but moved to Jerez in the 19th century to make use of the rich Andalusian soil. The place is designed as a traditional bodega in a pristine environment. Ninety-minute, 450-pta. tours are given Monday–Wednesday and Friday at 10 and noon, Thursday at noon only.

El Maestro Sierra (Plaza de Silos 5, tel. 956/342444; tours Mon.–Thurs. noon and 1:30, Fri. by appt.) has wonderful old wine cellars and several sherries to taste. The feel is down-home, in keeping with the company's "natural" method of winemaking. Tours cost 300 ptas.

Domecq (C. San Ildefonso 3, tel. 956/151500), maker of rich brandies as well as wines, is the area's oldest bodega, founded in 1730. Other local bodegas include **Williams and Humbert** (C. Nuño de Caña 7, tel. 956/346539), **González Byass** (C. Manuel Maria Gonzáles s/n, tel. 956/340000), **Sandeman** (C. Pizarro 10, tel. 956/184306), **Wisdom and Warter** (C. Pizarro 7, tel. 956/184306), and **Diez Merito** (C. Diego Fernandez Herrera s/n, tel. 908/375090). Most are open daily 11–2, with scheduled tours within those hours.

SHOPPING

La Casa del Jerez (C. Divina Pastora 1, across from equestrian school, tel. 956/335184), otherwise known as the Sherry Shop, is a great place to pick up local handicrafts and souvenirs. Wine samples flow freely, and the staff will happily demonstrate the use of the *venecia*, a strange little ladle used to pour sherry. Look especially for interesting local blends of olive oil and for fabric and clothing spun from local wool.

AFTER DARK

Jerez being larger than it looks, Jerez nightlife seems amplified. You can find a nice bar any day of the week; indeed, the tourist office has thoughtfully printed a map with little wine- and martini-glass icons to steer you to the appropriate watering hole. The neighborhood around the **Plaza del Toros** has several English pubs, including the large courtyard of **Canterbury** on Nuño de Cañas (look for the British-style brick building amid the white Moorish walls). Around the **Plaza del Arenal,** several tapas bars stay open late for the drinking crowd. A tourist area by day, **Plaza Asunción** teems with bars and clubs by night. There's even a **salsa club** outside town, best found by hopping in a cab and letting the driver get lost rather than do it yourself. And if you happen to be in town during a fiesta, look no farther than the streets for a good time, as crowds will be diving in and out of the bars 'til morning.

FLAMENCO

Jerez is one of Andalusia's main flamenco centers, with several joints clustered near the Plaza de Santiago. Try to make reservations if you want to see a show. The **Centro Andaluz de Flamenco** (Palacio Pemartín, Plaza de San Juan, tel. 956/344–9265; open daily 10–2) has a library and museum of this great art, as well as a school for those serious about learning the moves. There's a free audiovisual presentation hourly between 10 and 1.

El Laga de Tío Parrilla. This place prides itself on authentic presentations of all the traditional flamenco forms. The audience sits in groups, downing good food and local wines to guitar music, song, and dance. *Plaza del Mercado, tel. 956/338334 or 908/549421. Shows Mon.–Sat. 10:30 PM.*

La Blanca Paloma. In the midst of the bodegas, up the street from the equestrian school, the White Dove offers traditional Andalusian cooking and atmosphere. Flamenco is well presented in this sweet country setting. *Caña del Moro, Carretera de Trebujena, Km 2.5, tel. 956/314750. Shows Fri. and Sat.*

La Taberna Flamenca. Next door to the church of Santiago and a bunch of souvenir shops, this is nonetheless one of Andalusia's most traditional flamenco clubs. The warm environment brims with good food and entertainment. Show up for dinner at 9. *Plaza del Angostillo, tel. 649/383978, fax 956/334217. Admission: free. Shows Tues.–Sat. 10:30 PM.*

Mesón La Bodeguilla. Indulge in regional cuisine here, and enjoy a Barrio San Miguel–style flamenco show. The seafood is impressively well seasoned, especially the fried calamari. The atmosphere is cozy, and prices are not outrageous; the cover includes a free drink. Arrive a little early to snag a good seat. *C. Zarza 4 (off Plaza Cruz Vieja). Admission: 500 ptas. Shows Thurs.–Fri. 9 PM.*

FIESTAS

Semana Santa (Holy Week) is celebrated with as much vigor here as anywhere else. Evening processions involve statues of saints, floats depicting biblical scenes, and candlelight vigils, all to solemn, dramatic sacred music played by (slow) marching bands. Each procession is slightly different, and some involve impressive costumes; pick up a printed schedule just about anywhere.

In early May, Jerez goes wild for its **Feria del Caballo** (Horse Fair), the town's biggest event, with competitions and proud displays of equestrian dancing based on centuries-old traditions. Coming on the heels of Semana Santa, the Feria del Caballo caps a two-week celebration of music, dance, and flamenco called the **Festival de Jerez.**

In the fall, locals celebrate the grape harvest with **Fiestas de Otoño** (Autumn Festivals), a nearly month-long celebration starting in mid-September. Be prepared to dance, eat, watch parades and horse races, and get caught up in historical reenactments.

ARCOS DE LA FRONTERA

This pueblo blanco is at once one of the most picturesque and least visited towns in Spain. If any place in the world can make you feel instantly at home—or at least severely comforted—this is it. Built high on a dramatic cliff overlooking the Guadalete River valley, Arcos de la Frontera has some of the friendliest people you'll meet in Spain. The sole road into town is a treacherous route that climbs into the center of town, arrives at the main square, then winds down the other side of the hill. The streets are so narrow that cars or pedestrians must often wait for the other to pass, as both cannot move through the lanes abreast.

BASICS

CURRENCY EXCHANGE

Most **banks** are on Calle Debajo del Corrall and Calle Corredera.

EMERGENCIES

Police: tel. 956/701652. There's a **health center** (C. Calluvario s/n, tel. 956/700555) in the lower part of town.

MAIL

The **post office** (Paseo de los Boliches, tel. 956/701560; open weekdays 8:30–2:30, Sat. 9:30–1) is west of the old town.

VISITOR INFORMATION

The **tourist office** (Cuesta de Belén, tel. 956/702264; open Mon.–Sat. 9–2 and 5–7, Sun. 11–1:30) is in a niche in the castle on the west side of Plaza del Cabildo. Inquire about 500-pta. walking tours of the old town and some traditional patio courtyards, usually given Tuesday–Saturday at 10:30, noon, and 5.

COMING AND GOING

By **car,** Arcos de la Frontera is easy to find: head east on A342 from Jerez de la Frontera (20 minutes) or the N-IV. The **bus station** is on Calle Corregidores, in the lower part of town; it's best to take a cab up to the center so you don't waste all your energy hiking. **Buses** run to and from **Jerez de la Frontera** (45 min, 225 ptas.) and **Seville** (1½ hrs, 750 ptas.) several times a day; call **Los Amarillos** (tel. 956/342174) for details.

GETTING AROUND

If you're driving, follow the locals' example and pull your side mirrors in as you round corners in the tiniest lanes. The Plaza del Cabildo is filled with parked cars—if you want yours to be among them, give the attendant 100 ptas. and let him take care of it. Spots can be very tight, and if you do your own parking you might need help extracting yourself

WHERE TO SLEEP

UNDER 6,000 PTAS. • Hostal San Marcos. The family that runs this place is well liked in the community, as you'll soon see when the restaurant downstairs fills up. Rooms (5,000 ptas.) are simple and traditional, and each has a bathroom. The large rooftop terrace invites prolonged gazing at the countryside. *C. Marques de Torresoto 6, tel. 956/700721. 4 rooms. Cash only.*

Pensión y Mesón Restaurante El Patio. Proprietor Juan Luis González Oca may as well be your favorite uncle. He's sweet, helpful with travel advice, and, in the unlikely event that you need a haircut, ready with a small barbershop that doubles as an unofficial flamenco museum. Guest rooms (doubles 5,000 ptas.) are basic but clean, and each has a bathroom and a view. The modern restaurant serves traditional dishes, including every form of Iberian ham you can think of. *Dean Espinosa 4 (Callejón de las Monjas, along back wall of monastery), tel 956/702302, fax 956/704388. 8 rooms.*

UNDER 10,000 PTAS. • Hotel Marqués de Torresoto. This 17th-century palace in the heart of the old quarter was once home to the Marqués de Torresoto. Though small, it's well maintained, and snazzy in its own *nuevo*-Moorish way. Rooms have modern bathrooms and, in some cases, relaxing sitting areas; doubles start at 9,100 ptas. and self-inflate to around 11,000 ptas. during fiestas. The building also comprises a Baroque chapel and a porticoed patio, visible on the town's official walking tour. *C. Marques de Torresoto 4, tel. 956/700717, fax 956/704205. 15 rooms. Café. Doubles 9,100 (and 15% during festivals).*

WHERE TO EAT

SPLURGE • Parador Casa del Corregidor. The parador is right on Plaza del Cabildo, possessed of the only parking lot in Arcos's old town. The interior is tastefully designed in a classic Spanish style, and well supplied with quasi-17th-century lounges. Perched next to the overlook, the restaurant is a good place to relax with a view even if you can't afford to stay here (double room: 17,000 ptas.)—the menu features traditional local cuisine (menú del día: 3,500 ptas.). *Plaza del Cabildo s/n, tel. 956/700500, fax 956/701116. 24 rooms. Doubles 17,000.*

Hotel/Restaurante El Convento. This hotel and restaurant are around a tight corner from each other. The restaurant, housed in the 17th-century Palacio del Mayorazgo, has arched marble columns outdoors, wooden ceiling beams indoors. Specialties include partridge in almond sauce, asparagus soup, and Cream of Angels (a light, creamy egg custard) topped with orange-and-carrot jelly and a garnish of fresh cheese. You'll spend around 3,000 ptas. Guest rooms have firm mattresses and modern bathrooms with hair dryers, and most face the valley (those with terrace cost a bit extra). Doubles range from 7,000 to 12,000 ptas. depending on the season. *Restaurant: C. Marqués de Torresoto 7, tel. 956/703233). Hotel: C. Maldonado 2, tel. 956/702333, fax 956/704128. 11 rooms.*

WORTH SEEING

Aside from its general charms, Arcos has several historical sights. Begin your explorations with an ascent to **Plaza del Cabildo,** where you can pick up a map in the tourist office. The plaza's open end serves as a balcony with a wide view of the valley below. Catch a guitarist strumming a traditional flamenco lament and the magic of the moment is complete.

Across from the balcony is the church of **Santa Maria**, a tactful architectural blend of the Romanesque, Gothic, Mudéjar, Renaissance, and Baroque styles. The interior contains a Renaissance altar and a 17th-century choir with a 7th-century Byzantine base. A stroll through the rest of the old town will bring you to the small **Convento de la Encarnación**, with its stark, 14th-century Gothic façade; the church of **Los Jesuitas** (the Jesuits), now a market; the **Convento de las Mercadarias,** with an elaborate Baroque altar; and the angular 15th-century Gothic church of **San Pedro.** The Plaza de San Pedro is often filled with lounging schoolkids. There are also some notable **palaces** in this cramped neighborhood, most with 15th- to 18th-century facades. On the way out of town you'll pass the **Puerta Matrera,** an 11th-century Moorish gate.

SHOPPING

Most people who live in Arcos are artisans, and most craft their creations the same way their ancestors did.

Exposición de Ceramica Artistica (C. Botica 15, tel. 956/704381) is the proud outfit of artist Ramón Carillo Luque, who paints his ceramic pieces in this brightly colored shop. Peruse his decorative tiles, Andalusian dinnerware, and renditions of antique pots and local saints.

The tiny door to the **Galeria de Arte Arx-Arcis** (C. Marqués de Torresoto 11, tel. 956/703951), just down from the Plaza del Cabildo, hides a wonderful collection of local crafts. Some of Spain's nicest handmade wool rugs are made only in Arcos, and you may not even mind squeezing one into your suitcase. Ceramics, prints, baskets, and paintings line the walls and floors with bright colors and intricate designs. Local artist José Manuel Duran Gonzales has a variety of work on display, notably prints of Arcos that accurately capture the town's crooked streets and southern dignity. Part of his studio is in a nearby cave; tours can sometimes be arranged through the owner of Arx-Arcis.

FIESTAS

The pre-Lenten **Carnival**, usuallly in late February, is huge here. March or April is filled with Easter festivities that include Semana Santa processions and a unique running of a bull through the town's tight and winding streets. The Cruces de Mayo (Crosses of May) is akin to May Day. The **Festival de Nuestra Señora de las Nieves** is a procession in honor of Our Lady of Snows, held, strangely enough, in August. (The city rarely gets snow even in winter). The **Feria de San Miguel,** honoring Arcos's patron saint, fills a week at the end of September. **Christmas Eve** excitement centers on a live nativity scene held in the Plaza del Cabildo, in front of the church of Santa María.

CÁDIZ

Cádiz claims to be the oldest continuously inhabited city in the Western world—records indicate that it was founded by Phoenician traders in 1100 BC. Hannibal lived here for a time, and here Julius Caesar first held public office. Jutting into the Atlantic Ocean, the city has a prosperous port that's still used daily for fishing and trading.

After centuries of decline during the Middele Ages and Moorish rule, Cádiz gained commercial prominence after the discovery of the Americas. Columbus set out from here on his second voyage, and Cádiz later became the home base of the Spanish fleet. The city's merchants competed with those in Seville for dominance in transatlantic trade, and when the Guadalquivir River silted in the 18th century, depriving Seville of most of its livelihood, Cádiz became the wealthiest port in western Europe. Most of the city's buildings reflect this wealthy period, including the cathedral, which was garnished with gold and silver from the New World.

BASICS

CURRENCY EXCHANGE

Most banks and currency exchanges are in or near the **Plaza de San Juan de Dios.** Two travel agents also change money: **Gades Tour** (Plaza de España1, tel. 956/224608) and **Socialtour** (Avda. Ramón de Carranza 31, tel. 956/285852).

CYBERSPACE

Students and other travelers frequent the **Informática Café Internet** (Glorieta Ingeniero La Cierva 1, tel. 956/282459, open Mon.–Sat. 11–2 and 5–10, Sun. 5–10), more a bar than a café. The more you drink, the better your deal on Internet access, but the usual fee is 600 ptas. an hour. Look for this place on the long approach to the center of the town, along Playa de la Victoria.

EMERGENCIES

Police: 091 or 092. **Ambulance:** 061. In a minor medical emergency, call the **Red Cross** (C. Santa Maria Soledad 10, tel. 956/222222).

MAIL

The main **post office** is normally on Plaza de Topete, commonly known as the Plaza de las Flores (Plaza of the Flowers). Each day, flower stands are in business until mid-afternoon, adding bright colors and sweet smells to the already plentiful charms of Cádiz. At press time, however, reconstruction had the *correos* temporarily at Avenida Ramón de Carranza 18 (tel. 956/808621).

VISITOR INFORMATION

The city **tourist office** (Plaza de San Juan de Dios 11, tel. 956/241001; open weekdays 9–2 and 5–8, Sat. 9–2) usually hands out maps from a stand in front of the office itself. There's a **regional tourist office** off Plaza de Mina (C. Calderón de la Barca 1, tel. 956/211313; open Mon. and Sat. 9–2, Tues.– Fri. 9–7), at the opposite side of town near a park overlooking the bay.

COMING AND GOING

BY BUS

Estación Autobuses Comes (Plaza de la Hispanidad 1, tel. 956/211763), named for its main company, connects with Seville for about 1,300 ptas. each way, departing roughly every other hour between 7 AM and 11:30 PM. The round-trip is a good deal, at 1,800 ptas. Los Amarillos (tel. 956/285852) also serves **Seville** in addition to neighboring small towns. Secorbus (tel. 956/257415) serves **Jerez de la Frontera** (20 mins, 320 ptas.) and other nearby towns.

BY TRAIN

The **train station** (tel. 956/254301) is along Plaza de Sevilla, steps from Plaza de San Juan de Dios. From **Seville** (1½ hrs, 1,400 ptas.), daily trains leave almost hourly between 6:35 AM and 11:30 PM; in the other direction, trains run 6 AM through 10 PM. The Seville–Cádiz train stops midway in **Jerez de la Frontera;** the leg from Jerez to Cádiz takes 35 minutes and costs 475 ptas.

GETTING AROUND

Taxis are courtesy of Unitaxi (tel. 956/212121).

WHERE TO SLEEP

UNDER 5,000 PTAS. • Hostal Ceuta. This family-run *hostal* is up a few flights of stairs in a quiet residential area near Plaza de Candelaria. The beds, weathered over the years, are a bit springy, and you might also have a bit of a walk to the bathroom, but a double *with* bath costs only 4,500 ptas. There's a neat Arabic-style tearoom across the street. *C. Montanes 7, 1st floor, tel. 956/221654. 7 rooms, 4 with bath.*

UNDER 7,000 PTAS. • Hostal Imar. Quaint Hostal Imar is near the beach rather than the center of town, in a modern area next to the luxury Hotel Playa Victoria and a looming, shiny black condo complex. It's overpriced, especially since most rooms do not have private bath, but the beds are firm and the place is clean. *Glorieta Ingeniero la Cierva 3, tel. 956/260500, fax 956/260307. 30 rooms, some with bath.*

WHERE TO EAT

UNDER 2,000 PTAS. • Cerveceria Marisqueria Baro. One of Cádiz's many beachside eateries, this one has pleasant outdoor seating and plenty of run-of-the-mill but well priced meals (some of the menús del día go for 1,300 ptas.). The ice-cream menu is particularly fulfilling if you've been walking all day, and the view is spectacular. *Edificio Tiempo Libre, Paseo Marítimo, tel. 956/257957*

La Bodeguilla de Cádiz. On a quiet street one block south of the Plaza de Mina, you'll see several of these family-style restaurants. Typical Andalusian gazpacho and *frito gaditano* (fried local fish) are complemented by a decent wine list and a few nonfried foods. *C. San Pedro 22, tel. 956/220594. Closed Mon.*

UNDER 3,000 PTAS. • Arte Serrano. This is one of the nicest places on the playa (beach). Specializing in meat dishes, Serrano offers various kinds of Iberian ham. The seafood is fresh, and plates are well presented; the artistic kebabs dangle from a hook above their platter. On your way out, pick up some local ham, cheese, or wine from the little shop in the lobby. The outdoor tables benefit from a shady roof at lunchtime. Try to make reservations for dinner. *Paseo Marítimo 2, tel. 956/277258, fax 956/288169.*

Grimaldi. Prepare yourself: This may be some of the finest food you'll eat in Spain. Grimaldi is across the street from Cádiz's market, you can bet the chef picks out his own vegetables, fruit, seafood, and meat. A French flair for sauces is in evidence, though the owner swears this is a Cádiz tradition learned from past generations of his family. Either way, you'll swoon for the rich flavors and fine wines. Come with time to spare and order the *arroz marinero* (akin to paella; serves two or three people). *Pimientos del piquillo rellenos de mariscos* make a hearty appetizer: stuffed red peppers filled with seafood in a cream sauce. Dreamy desserts include the regional *tarta del tocino de cielo con almendras* (almond cake topped with a sweet egg custard and whipped cream). You're likely to drop at least 2,000 ptas.; from Monday to Thursday you can opt for a 1,500-pta. menú del día. *C. Libertad 9, tel. 956/228316. Closed Sun.*

La Cava Taberna Flamenca. Dark, dramatic, and intimate, this tavern is a perfect setting for flamenco shows, and indeed they're performed Thursday through Saturday. The long bar leads to a small seating area where you can take tapas. Local old men seem to favor ham; the seafood salad, if available, is fresh and tasty. *C. Antonio Lopez 16, tel. 956/211866. Cash only.*

WORTH SEEING

Cádiz is a multicultural experience, yet you can cover the sights on foot in about an hour. The tourist-office map suggests a sightseeing route, not to mention a tour of the best shopping streets. Upon entering the city you'll pass **Plaza de la Constitución,** through which run some of the remaining Moorish walls. If you continue to the edge of town, you'll see more of these walls; two empty **castles** with battle scars (the practically nonexistent Castillo de San Sebastián and the Castillo Santa Catalina, also in disrepair); and two well-kept **parks** with views of passing ships.

CATHEDRAL

The cathedral is perhaps best viewed from a distance, whence you can admire the gold dome and Baroque façade. It seems to belong in a fantasy landscape, and your thoughts will be supplemented by the rest of the city, which, after all, is a bath of white walls and palm trees *within* a deep blue sea. Begun in 1722, during the city's most illustrious period, it is sometimes called the New Cathedral because it took the place of one built in the 13th century and destroyed in 1592 by the British. (That adjoining structure has been rebuilt, and renamed the church of **Santa Cruz.**) Within the cathedral is a **crypt** containing the remains of Cádiz-born composer Manuel de Falla, who died in 1946. The **museum** displays precious jewels, gold, silver, and various religious items. The cathedral is constantly under renovatioin, but you can usually see the crypt, museum, and church of Santa Cruz. *Plaza de Catedral, tel. 956/ 286154. Admission: museum 500 ptas. Open Tues.–Sat.10–1, mass Sun. noon.*

GRAN TEATRO MANUEL DE FALLA

Follow Calle Virgili west from Plaza de San Felipe Neri to find this interesting, redbrick neo-Mudéjar building. Cádiz's cultural center hosts a full and varied performance program; inquire with the tourist office or box office about current events. *Plaza Manuel de Falla, tel. 956/220828.*

MUSEO HISTÓRICO MUNICIPAL

Next door to the Oratorio de San Felipe Neri is the **Museo Histórico Municipal,** with a 19th-century mural showing the signing of the Constitution in 1812. Well worth a visit in itself is the mahogany-and-ivory model of the city of Cádiz, crafted in 1779 down to the last detail. The little buildings look much as they do today. *Santa Inés, tel. 956/221788. Admission free. Open Tues.–Fri. 9–1 and 4–7, weekends 9–1.*

ORATORIO SANTA CUEVA

This oval-shape 18th-century chapel is a few blocks southeast of the Plaza de Mina. Inside are two smaller *capillas* (chapels), one stark and the other well decorated with Goya frescoes of the Last Supper, the Miracle of the Loaves and Fishes, and the Guest at the Wedding. Next door is the **Iglesia del Rosario.** *C. Rosario (take C. Tinte from Plaza de Mina), tel. 956/287676. Admission: 100 ptas. Open weekdays 10–1.*

ORATORIO DE SAN FELIPE NERI

Southwest of Plaza de Mina, the **Plaza de San Antonio** is similarly well stocked with impressive buildings. A bit farther south along Calle San José is Plaza de San Felipe Neri, home of the Oratorio de San Felipe Neri. Inside this fine church is a dramatic painting of the *Immaculate Conception* by the Sevillian artist Murillo—who fell to his death while working on another painting, the *Mystic Marriage of St. Catherine*, in the nearby chapel of Santa Catalina. Spain's first liberal constitution was declared at this church in 1812, and the Cortes (Parliament) of Cádiz met here in secret while the rest of Spain was under the rule of Joseph Bonaparte, Napoleon's brother, more commonly known as Pepe Botella for his love of the bottle. All visits are guided. *Santa Inés s/n, tel. 956/211612. Admission free. Open daily 8:30–10 AM and 7:30–9:30, Sat. 5:30 PM–6:30 PM.*

PLAZA DE MINAS

This north-side square is one of Cádiz's liveliest both day and night. On its borders, the **Colegio de Arquitectos** (College of Architects) has an interesting ornamental façade; the **Museo de Cádiz** (Provincial Museum) holds a variety of artifacts and paintings, including Zurbarán's *Four Evangelists*. From the Phoenicians, there are white-marble sarcophagi and some jewelry; after that, the archaeological finds run through the Romans and beyond. *Plaza de Mina, tel. 956/212281. Admission: 250 ptas. Open Tues. 2:30–7, Wed.–Sat. 9–8, Sun. 9:30–2:30.*

TORRE TAVIRA

Almost dead in the center of Cádiz, next to the Plaza de las Flores, is one of the city's only remaining medieval towers, 150 ft tall. At the top, you can view the city through a *cámera obscura*, which projects the outdoor panorama onto a screen in a darkened room. *C. Marqués del Real Tesoro 10, tel. 956/212910. Admission: 400 ptas. Open Sept.–June (closed Dec. 25–Jan. 1), daily 10–6; July–Aug., daily 10–8.*

AFTER DARK

The main nightlife surrounds the **Plaza de Mina** and runs through **Calle San Francisco** back toward the **Plaza de San Juan de Dios.** The mix of hangouts includes English-style pubs and a few dance clubs that change names each year. If you end up in the popular Plaza de San Juan de Dios, look for the grand *ayuntamiento* (city hall), beautifully illuminated by night. In the interest of escaping center-city heat, attention shifts in summer to the Playa de la Victoria and the many adjoining clubs and restaurants.

NEAR CÁDIZ

EXPO MARINE AQUARIUM

A quick drive east of Cádiz is an area called San Fernando, where the Expo Marine Aquarium beckons with a day's worth of maritime happiness. Aimed at illustrating local sea life, the facility has 28 aquariums functioning as local and tropical ecosystems. The optional Zoodiac-Safari takes you out on a motorized raft to view coastal wildlife. *Paseo Marítimo la Magdalena, San Fernando, tel. 956/591630, 956/494522 for safari. Admission: adults 600 ptas., children 400 ptas, family of four 1,500 ptas. Open mid-June–mid-Sept. weekdays 10–2 and 6–10, weekends 11–2 and 6–10; mid-Sept.–mid-June, weekdays 9:30–7, weekends 11–8.*

SANLÚCAR DE BARRAMEDA

The quaint fishing village of Sanlúcar de Barrameda, west of Jerez, is dramatically sited at the mouth of the Guadalquivir River. Needless to say, the town was a vigorous participant in the maritime action when the New World was discovered. Columbus sailed out of Sanlúcar on his third voyage to the Americas, in 1498, and in 1508 Ferdinand Magellan launched his circumnavigation of the world from these shores. Now slightly muddy, Sanlúcar's banks look across the river to Doñana National Park (*see above*). Interestingly, roughly half of the town's 61,000 residents are less than 25 years old, making Sanlúcar one of the youngest towns in Spain. (That explains the passels of kids hanging out in the streets.)

The town attracts travelers for its physical appeal, the horse races held on its beach every August since 1845, and the sheer relaxation of what is often a sleepy beach town. South of Sanlúcar proper is the village of Chipiona, with sandy beaches and a stone beacon tower built by the Roman general Scipio Africanus. North of Sanlúcar is a visitor center for Doñana National Park, followed by the little fishing port of Bonanza, whose panoramas of weathered old fishing boats are worthy of a jigsaw puzzle. Peace and quite reign in winter; Sanlúcar comes alive for the Easter fiestas and hums in the summer, when Europeans show up en masse to enjoy the beach, the fresh seafood, and the local *manzanilla* wine. A Sanlúcar prawn with a glass of manzanilla is many a Spanish epicurean's idea of paradise.

BASICS

CYBERSPACE

The **Centro Informatico** (Avda. de la Estación, tel. 956/366006), just off Calzada del Ejercito in a white office building, is a computer store and programming school that throws its computers open to the public whenever class is not in session, usually weekdays 9:30–1:30 and 4–9 plus Saturday 9:30–1:30. Internet access costs 400 ptas. per half hour, with a half-hour minimum.

MAIL

The **post office** is east of the center of town at the corner of Avenida del Cerro Falón and Calle de Correos (Avda. del Cerro Falón 6, tel. 956/360937; open weekdays 8:30–2:30, Sat. 9:30–1). Take Avenida Infanta Beatrix from Calzada del Ejercito and pick up some goodies at the many fruit stands on the way.

VISITOR INFORMATION

The **tourist office** sits in the middle of the Calzada del Ejercito (tel. 956/366110). Note that the map they give you has north at the bottom. Between them, the helpful staff members speak English, French, and German; ask the younger ones to recommend the best clubs and bars, as they insist that some are better than others on each night of the week. It gets complicated.

COMING AND GOING

Linesur **buses** (tel. 956/341063) shuttle almost hourly to and from **Jerez de la Frontera** (½ hr, 220 ptas.) on weekdays starting at 7 AM, less often on weekends. Los Amarillos runs to **Cádiz** (1 hr, 400 ptas.) almost as often, and **Seville** a few times daily (2 hrs, 900 ptas.). You can also catch local buses to **Chipiona** (100 ptas.). Most buses stop in Sanlúcar's Plaza Pradillo, but Linesur stops at Bar La Juana, in the center of town just off Calzada del Ejercito. Ask the tourist office for details.

Sanlúcar is not served by **train.** You must go to Jerez or Cádiz, then catch a bus to Sanlúcar.

By **car,** Sanlúcar is a mere 20-minute drive west from Jerez de la Frontera. Be warned, however, that to get here from Doñana National Park you have to drive up to Seville and back down the eastern side of the Guadalquivir.

If you're in Jerez and ready for a little luxury, consider taking a **taxi** to Sanlúcar (tel. 954/580000; 3,000–4,000 ptas.). For a taxi in Sanlúcar itself, call 956/360004).

WHERE TO SLEEP

UNDER 5,000 PTAS. • Hostal Blanca Paloma. The scent of dinner often flows through this family-run *hostal*. (Alas, you're not invited. . . .) Most rooms lack bath facilities and windows, but you pay only 4,300 ptas. a night. Ask to see your room before you take it—you'll climb up a stairwell surrounding the tiny patio frequented by the owners and their friends. Rooms in back get less street noise. *Plaza de San Roque 9, tel. 956/363644. 10 rooms, some with bath.*

UNDER 10,000 PTAS. • Hotel Los Helechos. Newly remodeled, this place retains all the Andalusian details. The large white patio has colorful tile work and huge potted plants, including a few orange trees; the cafeteria, furnished with wicker, is equally light and airy. Guest rooms are more modern but just as comfortable, with full bathroom and, in most cases, a little terrace overlooking the patio or the street; doubles go for 8,000 ptas. Parking is available nearby, and if you don't have a car, the staff can help arrange local excursions. *Plaza de Madre de Dios 9, tel. 956/361349, fax 956/369650. Cafeteria. 22 rooms.*

Tartaneros Hotel. Pristinely white, this traditional Andalusian building centers on a spiffy patio with zigzag tile patterns. The well-trained staff would probably leap to catch a falling utensil. The lobby is dark, owing to the heavy use of dark wood on its ceilings, but the high windows let in some sun. Guest rooms are clean, newly appointed, and generally assuring of a good night's sleep; each has a full bathroom, minibar, and private safe. Doubles cost 8,000 ptas. The café and bar are open throughout the day. *C. Tartaneros 8, tel. 956/362044, fax 956/360045. 22 rooms, 2 suites.*

Posada de Palacio. A treasure of Andalusian design in itself, this inn is built on top of an antique cistern amid a bevy of palaces and churches dating back to the 15th century. Most of the floors consist of inlaid ceramic tiles; the walls are white plaster; and some of the ceilings have wooden beams. Guest rooms are spacious, with huge windows, and a few have salons with leather couches; doubles run 9,000–10,000 ptas. Subtle pieces of modern art keep the look up to date. The patio has large potted plants and a canopy of vines. You're in the *barrio alto*, up and inland from the center of town. *C. Caballeros 11, tel. 956/364840, fax 956/365060. 13 rooms. Restaurant, bar.*

WHERE TO EAT

UNDER 1,500 PTAS. • Avante Claro. Get your seafood tapas here, amid Sanlúcar's beachfront bars and ice-cream shops. The seafood salad with peppers and olives, lightly tossed in olive oil (make sure it's not the one drowning in mayonnaise), makes a nice light snack on a hot afternoon. The bar is usually filled with old men having a *copa*. The restaurant also serves menús del día for around 1,200 ptas.; one of the entrées is inevitably some sort of fresh seafood. *Bajo de Guía s/n, tel. 956/380915. Closed Sun. Nov.–Apr.*

Mirador Doñana. Set on the beach, with outdoor seating in nice weather, the Mirador specializes in Sanlúcar's renowned jumbo shrimp (*langostinos*), boiled and served with lemon and tartar sauce. On the fried side are lightly battered *soldaditos de pavía* (codfish fritters), great as tapas. *Bajo de Guía s/n, tel. 956/364205. Closed during festivals.*

UNDER 2,000 PTAS. • Bodegón Cultural Mírabrás. Tourists flock here for tapas and Saturday-night flamenco, yet the show is authentic enough to attract locals as well. For dinner only, the food is just average, but it's served with great warmth by the owners themselves. Shows are sometimes held on weekdays in the summer. *C. La Pata 50, tel. 956/381707. No lunch.*

Casa Balbino. The owners of Casa Balbíno pride themselves on running *the* most typical *taberna sanluqueña*, and in 1999 they won an award from Gastrosur, a committee that recognizes excellence in food and tourism.. The white and ocher dining room is suitably post-Moorish. The menu revolves around the catch of the day, and the tapas include such vital Spanish elements as *puntillas* (fried baby squid). Above the bar hang numerous varieties of drying ham and several stuffed bulls' heads (just for fun). *Plaza del Cabildo 11, tel 956/360513. Closed Sun.*

WORTH SEEING

A large avenue—really a huge square—called the Calzada del Ejercito stretches through the center of town, its expanse of grass and benches inviting total vegetation on your part. The town's inland section is known as the *barrio alto* (high quarter), while the section near the water is called the *barrio bajo* (low quarter). In the evening, families buy ice cream on Sanlúcar's beachside promenade and wander slowly back and forth.

The **Fábrica del Hielo** (Ice Factory) is Sanlúcar's visitor center for Doñana National Park, the only such facility on the eastern side of the Guadalquivir. The building was in fact an ice factory, but it now shows audiovisual segments on the park's wildlife and explains Sanlúcar's maritime history. From this side of the river you can take a coastal boat tour on the *Real Fernando,* which gives you two chances to disembark and explore: the **Poblada de la Plancha** is an ancient hut village representing the natural values of early dwellers in the Doñana region, and **Las Salinas** is a marshland known for the variety of bird species that stop here. The on-board gift shop rents binoculars and sells bird guides. The tour lasts about four hours, and you must arrive 15 minutes before departure. Tickets sell out in advance, so call ahead if possible. *Avda. Bajo de Barrameda, tel. 956/363813, fax 956/362196. Boat departures: fall–spring, daily 10 AM; summer, Tues.–Sun. 9:30 AM and 5 PM.*

The center of town has a number of historic sights dating as far back as the 15th century, and all are open daily. The 18th-century **ayuntamiento** (town hall) bears commemorative tiles dedicated to Magellan's pioneering circumnavigation of the world. On the southeast edge of town is the 18th-century **Convento de Las Descalzas** (Convent of the Barefoot Nuns; C. Descalzas), whose archives hold some original letters of St. Teresa of Ávila. To the east, along Calle San Agustín, is the 15th-century **Castillo de Santiago** (C. Cava de Castillo), mostly Gothic but with an 18th-century tower. The 17th-century **Convento de Capuchinos** (Plaza de Capuchinos), once a headquarters for missionaries to the Americas, is filled with portraits of oceangoing evangelists. The altarpiece features the Virgin of the Good Voyage; the little museum has an odd collection of paintings of the patron saints of Spain's provincial capital cities.

BODEGAS

The local wine, manzanilla, is named for its scent of chamomile, which grows along the Guadalquivir. The wine's origins are uncertain, but in the last century manzanilla has established itself as one of Spain's more important white wines. Neophytes may find it hard to distinguish from sherry, but it actually has a tangy, saline flavor thanks to the local Atlantic breezes. With its faint taste of the sea, this wine does not travel well; there are even those who believe it tastes better in the *barrio bajo* than in the *barrio alto.* Acidity is low, and alcohol content is high—up to 20%. Most of Sanlúcar's bodegas are small, housed in historic buildings, and family-run; as in Jerez, they offer morning tours on weekdays by reservation. You can book a tour through a travel agents, sometimes through the tourist office, or by calling the bodega yourself. Prominent winemakers:

Barbadillo (C. Luis de Eguílaz 11, tel. 956/360894). **Herederos De Argüeso** (C. del Mar 8, tel. 956/360112). **La Cigarrera** (Plaza Madre de Dios s/n, tel. 956/381285). **La Guita (**C. Misericordia, tel. 956/361940 or 956/182220). **Pedro Romero** (C. Trasbolsa 60, tel. 956/360736 or 956/361027). **Vinícola Hidalgo** (C. Banda Playa 24, tel. 956/360516).

EQUESTRIAN AFFAIRS

Like Jerez de la Frontera, Sanlúcar de Barrameda knows its horses. Contact any one of these riding clubs for a tour or demonstration: **Centro Hípico Sumariva** (Camino de la Jara s/n, tel. 956/381837). **Club Ecuestre La Garrocha** (Ctra. Chipiona-Rota, Km. 8, tel. 956/374278). **Picadero Las Palmeras** (Barriada El Almendral, tel. 629/282617). **Sociedad de Carreras de Caballo** (Avda. de las Piletas s/n, tel. 956/363202).

AFTER DARK

Most of the action is on and around **Plaza del Cabildo,** one plaza up from the Calzada del Ejercito. Strangely enough, the main cluster of bars is right around the town hall. In summer, the party moves down to the beach. Dance clubs are few but active: For drinks and a good bar atmosphere, try **Aljibe** (C. Bolsa at C. Argueso). On the next street over is **Disco Horus** (C. Santa Ana), the tourist office's pick for the best place to boogie. **Boga** (Entrance on Avda. Infanta Beatriz; open weekends only) is a disco run by the owners of Hotel Guadalquivir; expect a small cover charge. On the square in front of the church of Nuestra Señora de O, look for a cool bar called **Muro,** a good hangout spot with antique metal grates on the wall and good drink prices.

Ask the tourist office for current **theater** and **concert** offerings, sponsored by the town council.

FIESTAS

For **Semana Santa** (Holy Week), Sanlúcar's thirteen brotherhoods take turns leading a procession with their own monstrance (vessel built to hold the Communion host). The town comes alives to honor the fruit of the local vine at the **Feria de la Manzanilla,** held at the end of May—festivities include wine tasting, full-dress horseback parades, and bullfights. Also in May is the **Romería del Rocío** (Ricío Pilgrimage), a dramatic procession of the members of the Rocío brotherhood across the Guadalquivir River to the sanctuary in the village of Almonte and back. Witnessing this is a true Andalusian folk experience. In August, the traditional **Carreras de Caballo** (Horse Races) take place on the beach, and the town council sponsors occasional beachside **antique fairs** and **concerts.**

RONDA

Ronda is one of the prettiest and best maintained of Andalusia's Moorish towns, and it's easy to access from all directions. Nestled in the Serranía de Ronda mountains north of the Costa del Sol, this white-washed settlement rises along a cliff, overhanging a ravine called El Tajo. On either side of the gorge are Ronda's modern, commercial section, El Mercadillo, and historic section, La Ciudad, filled with craft shops and museums. If you drive into town, your only shot at parking is in either of two underground garages in the new town.

Ronda's most stunning feature is the Puente Nuevo (New Bridge), an architectural masterpiece that took almost forty years to build in the mid-1700s. Over the centuries, the bridge has housed a prison and been the unfortunate cause of many deaths, including that of the architect who designed it—he accidentally fell to his demise during an inspection. Hemingway immortalized the bridge in *For Whom the Bell Tolls,* wherein Civil War soldiers threw one another over the edge. (El Tajo spans 210 feet and is 360 feet deep.) Because Ronda attracts crowds of day-trippers from the coast and Andalusia's larger inland cities, the streets are often packed before lunchtime. To experience the placidity of Ronda at rest, stay overnight at one of several friendly hostelries.

BASICS

MAIL
The **post office** (C. Virgen de la Paz 18, across from bullring) is open weekdays 8–2 and 3–5.

VISITOR INFORMATION
Two tourist offices handle the daily influx. Pick up a free map in the office on **Plaza de Blas Infante** (tel. 952/187119). Alternatively: If you drive in from the Costa del Sol, you'll enter the newer part of town on Calle Virgen de la Paz, which takes you past the **Plaza de España** office (tel. 952/871272), a block south of the bullring. Both offices are open weekdays 10–2:30 and 4–7 and Saturday 10–2.

COMING AND GOING

BY BUS
For travel within the area, buses are more plentiful than trains. Portillo (tel. 952/872262) runs to various **Costa del Sol** towns several times daily for around 700 ptas. Comes (tel. 952/871992) heads west a few times daily, hitting **Arcos de la Frontera, Jerez de la Frontera,** and **Cádiz.** Los Amarillos (tel. 956/342174) ranges widely, with destinations including **Seville** (3 hrs, 1,500 ptas.). The **bus station** (Plaza Concepción García Redondo) is two long blocks west of the train station. From here, a quick walk east on Calle Cruz Verde takes you to Ronda's main drag, Carrera del Espinel.

BY TRAIN
Only a few trains wend their way to Ronda each day. From coastal **Málaga** there are two trains daily (2 hrs, 1,200 ptas.). **Granada** and **Córdoba** are on the same route (3 hrs, 1,600 ptas.). **Seville** is also a three-hour trip (2,000 ptas.). The **train station** is on the north side of town (Avda. de Andalucía); call **RENFE** (tel. 902/240202) for more information.

WHERE TO SLEEP

UNDER 8,000 PTAS. • Hotel Virgen de los Reyes. The rooms look a bit tired, but this place is clean and centrally located, and some windows have picture-perfect views of whitewashed buildings. Some rooms share bath facilities; the rest have a small bathroom in which a doorless shower floods the rest of the room, should you wish to use it. Doubles cost 6,000 ptas. a night. The owners can tell you stories about Ronda, so there is an element of charm. *C. Lorenzo Borrego Gómez 13, tel. 952/871140. 30 rooms.*

UNDER 10,000 PTAS. • Hotel Goyesca. Ronda's version of a B&B, this building dates back to the Spanish Civil War and has already had several reincarnations, including quince-jam factory and grain warehouse. The same family has run the hotel for generations, lending a warm, welcoming atmosphere to this Andalusian gem. Styled as various takes on antique Spain, such as La Carretilla (The Wheelbarrow), La Balanza (The Balance), or La Artesa (The Trough), the apartment-style rooms are decorated with their eponymous props, wrought-iron window grates, and locally made ceramic tiles. Beds have high frames and sturdy mattresses. There's a small kitchen off each living room, and a simple breakfast is served in the common dining area. For all this you pay 8,000–10,000 ptas. a night. *C. Infantes 39, tel. 952/219049, fax 952/190657. 4 rooms, each sleeping two.*

Hostel Polo. The central location is only one reason you'll enjoy this three-story hotel. The architecture dates back to the 19th century, but the rooms have all been updated with crisp linens, firm mattresses, and bathtubs. Doubles run 7,000–9,500 ptas. Rumor has it that an Internet café will eventually round out the already homey bar and restaurant. *C. Mariano Soubiron 8, tel. 952/872447, fax 952/872449. 33 rooms. Restaurant, bar.*

WHERE TO EAT

UNDER 2,000 PTAS. • Pizzeria Savoy. Several different cuisines are on offer in this clean, frilly pink restaurant with white table linens; you can order anything from chicken in pineapple sauce to fried calamari to four-cheese pizza. To top off the various stimuli, there's a terrace overlooking the ravine. Service is fairly attentive. *Plaza de la Marced, tel. 952/876936.*

UNDER 3,000 PTAS. • Camelot. As the name suggests, this is a medieval adventure. The stone-floor room is decked out with hanging candelabras, heavy wooden benches and chairs, and coats of arms from Spain and Britain. The dishes, mainly grilled meats and seafood, are served in hearty portions. To get here, head northeast into town from Plaza de la Merced (just west of the bullring) on Calle Puzo and walk two blocks to Calle Sevilla. *C. Sevilla 45, tel. 952/879312. No lunch.*

Pedro Romero. Honoring the big daddy of modern bullfighting, Pedro Romero proffers momentos of the sport, including huge, stuffed bulls' heads. The menu changes seasonally, but you'll always find interesting bites and hearty meals such as *foie gras con salsa de uva y vino Málaga* (pâté with a grape and wine sauce), *migas a la Rondeña* (fried bread crumbs with garlic and salt pork), and *rabo de toro con hierbas* (oxtail stewed in herbs). For dessert, look for the killer cheesecake (*torta del queso*) with lemon-honey sauce. *C. Virgen de la Paz 18 (across from bullring), tel. 952/871110.*

WORTH SEEING

Ronda stretches north and south across the ravine, **El Tajo,** whose name literally means "gash" or "sheer cliff." Several bridges connect the two sides. The **Puente Nuevo** is a good place to start your explorations: Cross to the old town and wander through the artisan shops lining the streets.

You'll encounter the **Casa de Mondragón** along the town's western wall. Appropriated by Ferdinand and Isabella when they seized Ronda in 1485, the palace has two Mudéjar towers, many detailed mosaics, and other Moorish touches. *Tel. 952/878450. Admission: 300 ptas. Open weekdays 10–6 (10–8 June–Aug.), weekends 10–3.*

East of the Casa de Mondaragón is the large church of **Santa María la Mayor.** Ronda's great mosque during the Moorish days, the cathedral mainly reflects additions made during the Gothic, Baroque, and Renaissance periods, including a voluptuous Baroque altar covered in gold leaf. *Plaza Duquesa de Parcent. Admission: 300 ptas. Open daily 10–7.*

Heading farther east, cross the Calle de Armiñan to the **Museo del Bandalero** (Bandit Museum), across from the huge *ayuntamiento* (town hall). a result of Ronda's reputation for banditry in the 19th century. Peruse a collection of bandit garb and read about the "good" bandits who operated much like Robin Hood, and the rest, who were not unlike mobsters, demanding taxes. The museum presents mainly artillery and other bandit artifacts. *C. de Armiñán. Admission: 250 ptas. Open Oct.–May, daily 10–6; June–Sept., daily 10–8.*

North of the Bandit Museum on Calle de Armiñán is the restored **Minarete de San Sebastián,** all that remains of the Moorish mosque destroyed in the Reconquest of 1485. Keep walking north to see the interesting carved facade of the **Palacio del Marqués de Salvatierra,** a unique Renaissance mansion still inhabited by descendants of the original family. You can take a guided tour of part of the house. *Tel. 952/871206. Admission: 300 ptas. Open mid-Sept.–July, Fri.–Mon. 11–2 and 4–6.*

Behind the Palacio del Marqués de Salvatierra, a sneaky little road leads down the ravine to two more bridges: the **Puente Viejo** (Old Bridge), built by the Romans and restored in 1616, and the **Puente Arabe** (Arab Bridge), a restored Moorish construction. Under the Arabic Bridge you'll see signs for the **Baños Arabes** (Arab Baths), whose walls and ceilings are carved with arched and star-shaped vents. The baths are only somewhat excavated and occasionally desolate, so it's wise to approach them in a group. *Admission free. Open Tues.–Sat. 9:30–2 and 4–6, Sun. 10:30–1:30.*

Back up in La Ciudad, head north to Calle Santo Domingo and the **Casa del Rey Moro** (House of the Moorish King), a deceptive name for a Moorish-looking residence that probably never housed a Moorish king. It may stand on top of Moorish ruins; in any case, it was built in 1709 with colorful tiles and beautiful gardens, both alluding to the Mudéjar style. From the garden you can hike down 365 stone steps for a good view of the river. *Cuesta de Santo Domingo 9, tel. 952/187200. Admission: 500 ptas. Open fall–spring, daily 10–7; summer, 10–8 .*

Crossing the Puente Nuevo into the new town, El Mercadillo leads you directly to the **Plaza de Toros** (bullring), one of the oldest, handsomest bullrings in Spain. It was Ronda native Pedro Romero (1954–1839) who founded modern Spanish bullfighting, distinguished by the fact that matadors fight on foot rather than on horseback. Romero's descendants, most of whom are also bullfighters, have perfected his legacy with a cape and distinctive costume. Having killed over 5,000 bulls in his time, Romero helped make Ronda's bullring one of the most heavily used in Spain. Goya painted a picture of Romero in action here, hence the name Goyesca for Ronda's annual bullfighting fiesta (*see* Fiestas, *below*). Inside the bullring is a small museum dedicated to the Romeros and other famed enthusiasts, such as Ernest Hemingway and Orson Welles, who frequented Ronda for the fights. For tickets to an actual fight, call well in advance and expect to pay a pretty penny (3,000 ptas.). *C. Virgen de la Paz, tel. 952/874132. Admission: 300 ptas. Open Oct.–May, daily 10–6; June–Sept., daily 10–8.*

Round off your visit to Ronda with a stroll *around* the Plaza del Toros (there are public rest rooms on the north side!), then relax in the **Alameda del Tajo,** a garden park with benches and a sweeping view over El Tajo. The best shopping street in this part of Ronda is the **Carrera del Espinel.**

OUTDOOR ACTIVITIES

Hot-air ballooning seems popular here, probably due to the vertiginous drop-off. **Lindstrand Balloon School** (tel. 952/875556) takes small groups on relaxing several-hour balloon rides over the mountains and the pueblos blancos; they can also arrange ground tours to view cave paintings or wine cellars. Prices vary widely depending on the time of year and number of people in your group.

AFTER DARK

Open throughout the day and late at night, **Planet Adventure** (C. Molino 5, northwestern part of town, tel. 952/875249) offers food, drink, music, and Internet access. Decor is modern retro, with 1970s hanging lamps, and the kitchen serves cheap pizza, Tex-Mex burritos and chimichangas, and vegetarian items.

There are plenty of bars in the center of town. **El Kalero** (C. Santa Cecilia s/n, no phone) is Ronda's big-screen sports bar, packed during *futbol* (soccer) games. Just west of here is Plaza Carmen Abela, where the late-night café-bar La Farola is a tranquil place for tapas and drinks. **Pub Picasso** (C. Jerez 26, tel. 952/877755) has a purple door and wooden walls with clever inlay patterns. The bar has a huge selection of American and European beers, and the public computer in back is wired. Owned by the same family, **Cotton Club** (C. Artesanos 4, tel. 952/877755) has a similar atmosphere, a wide selection of drinks, Internet access, and an open door till dawn if the crowd warrants. Down the street, **Bolera Café** (C. Jerez 12, tel. 952/190923) has intricately tiled walls and a lounge corner with a huge couch. The bar, specializing in Irish coffee, serves until the sun comes up.

FIESTAS

Ronda goes nuts during festivals. The town's tiny streets are packed with locals and tourists year round, so you can imagine what a fiesta looks like. On the first Saturday of September, the **Feria Goyesca de Pedro Romero,** the good people of Ronda dress up in period wear and head off to watch a bullfight in commemoration of Ronda's 18th- and 19th-century (*goyesca*) bullfighting tradition. Pied Piper–style, a horse-drawn carriage leads a procession through town to the bullring, gathering crowds on its way. You can buy tickets for the fight in advance (tel. 952/876967). Various churches lead processions throughout **Semana Santa** (Holy Week). In May, attention turns quickly back to bullfighting with the **Feria de la Reconquista** (Reconquest Fair), May 20–23, celebrated by daily bullfights and cattle fairs.

NEAR RONDA

BENAOJÁN

West of Ronda toward Seville, the city of Benaoján (population circa 1,700) is known for the prehistoric wall paintings in its **Cueva de la Pileta** (Pileta Cave). Lantern-lighted tours are given to small groups, a relaxed 90-minute experience of ancient renderings of bison, deer, horses (including a pregnant mare). The Cámara del Pescado (Fish Chamber) features a huge painting of a fish said to be about 15,000 years old. *Admission: 850 ptas. Open daily 10–2 and 4–5, sometimes later.*

The nearby **Cueva del Gato** (Cat Cave) holds some prehistoric axes, blacksmithing tools, ceramics, and tools made of bone. The folks at Cueva de la Pileta can direct you.

ACINIPO

This abandoned Roman village thrived in the 1st century AD. Now it is a desolate hillside decorated with **remains of Roman houses** and a **Roman theater.** There's no comparison to the ruins of Mérida, Extremadura (*see* Chapter 7), but the rubble and fallen columns can send your mind wandering back to the days of chariot races and gladiators. If you're driving, head a few miles west toward Seville and turn off at the sign for Acinipo. *Admission free. Open Tues.–Thurs. 10–6, Fri.–Sun. 9–7 (later in summer).*

CENTRAL ANDALUSIA

Central Andalusia is covered with rolling plains, olive orchards, and snow-capped mountain peaks. In this quiet area south of Madrid and north of Granada lie quaint whitewashed villages and artisan workshops selling locally made crafts. First inhabited by the Moors, the pueblos blancos retain a feeling of a tight community: Narrow, winding streets lead to exotic courtyards filled with hanging flowers and creeping vines. Historic churches and homes are well used and respected; many have been turned into charming inns that offer a tangible sense of ancient Spain. Córdoba's great mosque attracts travelers from all over the world, and should not be missed if you're in this part of the country; it's worth every peseta you'll pay in high meal prices and room rates. The small cities of Jaén and Úbeda are known for their unique ceramics and collective support of the arts. The food in this region is worth a sniff as well; local game and meats dominate most restaurant menus.

CÓRDOBA

Capital of its province, the city of Córdoba is unique and well respected since caliph rule in the Middle Ages. Founded around 169 BC by the Romans or Carthaginians, it was the birthplace of such great men as the Roman philosopher Seneca and the poet Lucan. During the Moorish occupation, Córdoba became the most cultivated city in Europe—it's hard to see now, but the city had around 1,000 mosques, 600 baths, street lighting (700 years before London or Paris could say the same), and the constant buzz of creative culture. A multitude of philosophers, doctors, poets, and mystics called Córdoba home, including the philosopher Averroës, who introduced Aristotle's philosophy to Europe, and the Jewish doctor Maimonides. The city gained significant cultural power during the rule of Abderrahman I, who proclaimed himself Emir of Andalusia; under Abderrahman III, the city attained political and military greatness as well. Through all these centuries, Córdoba prospered with an even denser population than Constantinople had. Like the rest of Spain, of course, the city was eventually reconquered by the Christians (in this case in the 13th century) and given churches, convents, hospitals, and Renaissance palaces. Fortunately, while many mosques were destroyed, the principal mosque was mostly preserved. Still something of a cultural center, with around 300,000 residents, the city gets huge tourist crowds in spring and summer.

BASICS

CYBERSPACE

See the Guggenbar (*in* After Dark, *below*) or try Excalabur Café Internet (C. Abogado Enriquez Barrios 9).

VISITOR INFORMATION

The **city tourist office** (Plaza de Judá Leví, tel. 957/472000) is a few blocks from the mosque, in the heart of the old quarter. The **regional tourist office** (Palacio de Congresos, C. Torrijos 10, tel. 957/421535), next to the mosque, has a detailed wooden model of the mosque. There's a **provincial tourist office** in the Plaza de los Tendillas (tel. 957/491677).

COMING AND GOING

BY CAR

Thanks to its central location, Córdoba is extremely easy to access. From Madrid, the N-IV leads straight south to Córdoba en route to Seville. The N432 connects Córdoba with Granada to the east, Badajoz to the west. The N331 heads up from Málaga.

Once you get here, parking can be a problem. Try the parking garage for El Corte Inglés, on Ronda de los Tejares (follow the signs), the garage on the huge Paseo de la Victoria, or the garage across the park on Avenida Republica Argentina. To ensure the safety of your vehicle, tip the uniformed attendant or, at night, the enterprising fellow who appoints himself night watchman.

BY BUS

The new **bus station** (tel. 957/236474) is across the street from the train station. Buses from **Seville** (3 hrs, 1,225 ptas.) and **Granada** (3 hrs, 1,800 ptas.) are run by Alsina Graells Sur (tel. 957/404040 or 957/278100).

BY TRAIN

Trains to and from Madrid and Seville are almost hourly. The wonderful high-speed AVE train zips you down from **Madrid** in less than two hours, and down to **Seville** in an hour. Other easy trains connect Córdoba with **Málaga** (2½ hrs, 2,300 ptas.) and **Cádiz** (2 hrs, 2,500–3,500 ptas.). The **train station** (tel. 957/490202) is just north of town on Avenida de América.

GETTING AROUND

Taxis are always hovering around the main streets and plazas. Call 957/450000 to schedule one in advance.

WHERE TO SLEEP

Córdoba often gets more visitors than it has beds. Do try to reserve a room in advance.

UNDER 5,000 PTAS. • Hotel Granada. On the large, nondescript avenue north of the city itself, this modern hotel blends in with the other buildings. Inside, it's more appealing, and its lets you escape the tourist district without moving beyond walking distance. Rooms are small but clean; doubles cost 3,500 ptas. with shared bath, 4,600 ptas. with private bath. *Avda. de América 17, tel. 957/477000. 30 rooms, 6 with bath.*

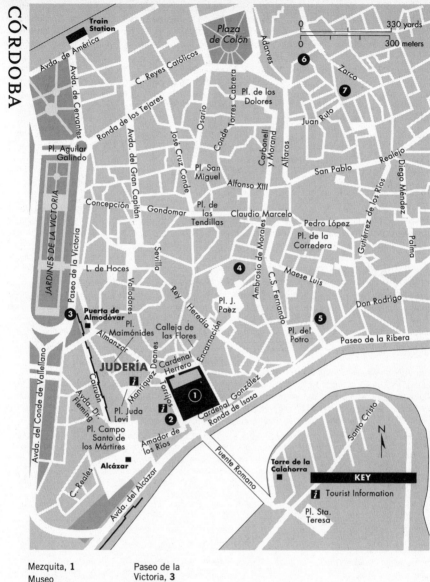

CÓRDOBA

Train Station

Plaza de Colón

JARDINES DE LA VICTORIA

Avda. de América

Avda. de Cervantes

Pl. Aguilar Galindo

C. Reyes Católicos

Ronda de los Tejares

José Cruz Conde

Avda. del Gran Capitán

Concepción

Osorio

Conde Torres Cabrera

Pl. de los Dolores

Adarves

Zarco

Juan Ruto

Carbonell y Morand

Alfaros

San Pablo

Realejo

Diego Méndez

Palma

Gutiérrez de los Ríos

Pl. San Miguel

Alfonso XIII

Pl. de las Tendillas

Gondomar

Claudio Marcelo

Pedro López

Pl. de la Corredera

Paseo de la Victoria

L. de Hoces

Valladares

Sevilla

Rey Heredía

Ambrosio de Morales

C.S. Fernando

Maese Luis

Don Rodrigo

Puerta de Almodóvar

Pl. J. Páez

Pl. del Potro

Paseo de la Ribera

Pl. Maimónides

Calleja de las Flores

Encarnación

JUDERÍA

Manríquez Deanes

Cardenal Herrero

Torrijos

Cairuán

Avda. Dr. Fleming

Pl. Juda Levi

Pl. Campo Santo de los Mártires

Amador de los Ríos

Cardenal González

Ronda de Isasa

Santo Cristo

Avda. del Conde de Vallellano

Alcázar

C. Reales

Avda. del Alcázar

Puente Romano

Torre de la Calahorra

N

Pl. Sta. Teresa

KEY

ℹ️ Tourist Information

0 — 330 yards
0 — 300 meters

Mezquita, **1**

Museo Arqueológico, **4**

Museo de Bellas Artes, **5**

Museo Diocesano, **2**

Palacio de los Marqueses de Viana, **7**

Paseo de la Victoria, **3**

Plaza Santa Marina de las Aguas, **6**

275

UNDER 7,000 PTAS. • Hotel Maestre. This pleasant hotel is in the midst of the museum district, near the Plaza del Potro. Windows guide lots of sunlight into the spacious modern rooms. A double with a clean, tiled bathroom goes for 6,500 ptas.; the nice owners also run the cheaper **Hostal Maestro,** a few doors down. Parking is available for 1,000 ptas. *C. Romero Barros 4–6, tel. 957/472410, fax 957/ 475395. 26 rooms.*

UNDER 10,000 PTAS. • Hotel Mezquita. Next door to the mosque, this newish hotel is actually an updated 16th-century house filled with antiques and grand old atmosphere. Guest rooms are plain and somewhat worn, but most overlook the central patio. Doubles go for 9,000 ptas. The restaurants down the street invite you to dinner with myriad scents. *Plaza Santa Catalina 1, tel. 957/475585, fax 957/ 476219. 21 rooms. Restaurant.*

Omeyas. A central patio lends a comforting, pseudo-Moorish atmosphere to this small hotel. The clean, well-kept guest rooms overlook the patio; doubles cost 10,000 ptas. *C. Encarnación 17, tel. 957/ 492267, fax 957/491659. 29 rooms. Restaurant.*

WHERE TO EAT

Several eating places near the mosque are well established with both locals and travelers. Along Paseo de la Victoria and the other main avenues are plenty of cafés and pastry shops to lighten the load of a sightseeing marathon. Some of the regional cuisine consists of recipes passed down on Moorish and Jewish manuscripts. The local Moriles-Montilla wines come in four main varieties: *finos* (fine), *finos viejos,* or *amontillados* (older fine wines), *olorosos* (aromatic wines), and *olorosos viejos* (older aromatic wines). The alcohol content is usually high—up to 21%—so be careful. Licorice lovers should look for *aguardiente* (anisette), made nearby in Rute, where there's actually a Museo del Anís.

UNDER 2,500 PTAS. • El Rincón de Carmen. Hidden in the winding whitewashed streets of the old Jewish quarter, Carmen's Corner is a somewhat upscale version of Córdoba's typical joints. You get the same food—say, *solomillo* (sirloin) seared and served with saffron rice—but the quality is higher. The menu also features duck and a unique appetizer of crepes filled with sautéed spinach. In deference to non-Spanish travelers, doors open for dinner at 8 PM. *C. Romero 4 (off northwest corner of mosque), tel. 957/291055.*

Los Patios. You won't find a more photogenic patio than the one at this restaurant and small hotel behind the mosque. Potted plants line the dining room, leading you onto the stone-paved patio; from some tables, you can peer out at the mosque's dramatic tower. The food is typical Andalusian, with a nod toward Moorish recipes. The chicken grilled with almond sauce is a hearty meal, and the menú del día often includes a hefty portion of fresh seafood or steak. *C. Cardenal Herrero 14, tel. 957/478340.*

UNDER 3,500 PTAS. • El Caballo Rojo. The Red Horse is both a Córdoba institution and a winner of the National Gastronomy Prize. A leafy passageway leads you away from the mosque's tourist traffic into a typical Andalusian patio. The menu changes seasonally but always offers traditional food with a touch of excitement. Many dishes have a Jewish or Moorish heritage, revealed in honey glazes or saffron-infused sauces. The lamb is highly recommended, as is *alboronia,* a cold salad of roasted vegetables in a spicy sauce. *Cardenal Herrero 28, tel. 957/478001.*

WORTH SEEING

MEZQUITA

Córdoba's absolute must-see is its ancient Moorish **Mezquita** (mosque), nestled between the Guadalquivir River and the whitewashed medieval Jewish quarter. The building's plain stone exterior is deceptively simple: As you enter, some 850 columns rise before you in a forest of jasper, marble, granite, and onyx. The pillars are topped by ornate capitals taken from the Visigothic church that was razed to make way for the mosque. Crowning these, an endless array of red-and-white-stripe arches curves away into the dimness. The mosque was begun in 785 over the foundation of a Roman and then Visigothic house of worship, and you can still see a few of the original columns and capitals. Abderrahman's son, Hixam I, completed the **Patio de los Naranjos** (Orange Court) out front, built eleven naves, and added a minaret, the Torre del Alminar, used to call the faithful to prayer (and later, under the Christians, as a bell tower). The naves were eventually extended over to the river, eight more naves were added, and the oratory was enlarged—and by the time all this happened, the **mihrab** (sacred prayer niche) was thrown off kilter, with the result that it does not face east toward

Mecca, as it must by Muslim law, but in fact faces somewhat south. Agony followed, but it was resolved that the mosque's inspiring architecture made up for this inadvertent glitch. The mihrab and the **qiblah**, the wall in which it nestles, are elaborately carved and decorated; the **maksoureh,** a sort of anteroom for the caliph and his court in front of the mihrab, is covered with breathtaking multicolor mosaic patterns. A discreet passageway allowed the elite to sneak in and out without having to mix with other worshippers.

The mosque commonly moves people to tears—not least, perhaps, because the interior is so dim, enhancing the effect of total transcendence. Natural light enters from only a few small windows. In the mosque's prime, however, its side arches were open to the outdoors, so the space was originally much brighter.

After consecrating the mosque as a house of Christian worship in the 13th century, the Christians hired a Moorish architect to build the **Capilla Villaviciosa** (Villaviciosa Chapel), utilizing arches and details that blend with the existing structure. In the 1520s, however, Charles V undertook to erect an actual **cathedral** smack in the middle of the Moors' masterpiece, and there it still sits, a bubbly Baroque structure among candy-stripe Islamic colums. To the emperor's credit, he was supposedly horrified when he came to inspect the new construction, exclaiming to the architects, "To build something ordinary you have destroyed something that was unique in the world"—not that this sentiment stopped him from tampering with Granada's Alhambra or Seville's Alcázar.

In spring, the orange blossoms in the Patio de los Naranjos are pleasantly fragrant. In a hollow area on the patio's exterior north wall, a small statue called the **Virgen de los Faroles** (Virgin of the Lanterns) stands behind a lantern-hung grille. On the west side (C. Torrijos) is the regional tourist office

JUDERÍA

From the northwest corner of the mosque, a labyrinth of little whitewashed streets makes up the medieval Judería (Jewish quarter), one of Córdoba's unique cultural legacies. Córdoba's Jews lived here until all Jews were expelled from Spain in 1492. Parts of the 'hood are highly commercial, full of souvenir shops hawking ceramics, jewelry, Arabian clothing, crafts, and the usual T-shirts and hats; but other sections are quietly poetic, especially in early evening. The narrow, winding lanes are adorned with hanging flowers—a Córdoba signature—and wrought-iron grates, some barely concealing beautiful Andalusian patios. Note that these delightful stomping grounds are sometimes the province of muggers and pickpockets, especially at night and during the siesta; avoid lingering alone in deserted alleyways.

Near the Plaza de las Bulas you'll find the city's only remaining **synagogue,** one of three medieval synagogues left in Spain (the other two are in Toledo). It's no longer used as a place of worship, but is well visited by people of all faiths. Inside, a detailed Mudéjar motif tops the walls and doorways; one inscription notes the synagogue's founding date, 1315, in Hebrew. Look for the women's gallery and, on the east wall, the arch where the sacred scrolls were stored. *C. Judíos, tel. 957/202928. Admission: 20 ptas. Open Tues.–Sat. 10–2 and 3:30–5:30, Sun. 10–1:30.*

On the Plaza de las Bulas (Bulls' Square) itself is the **Museo Taurino**, Córdoba's Museum of Bullfighting. Two connected mansions make a unique environment for posters and mementos of bullfighting; special attention is paid to fighters who were native to Córdoba. *Plaza Maimónides / Plaza de las Bulas, tel. 957/201056. Admission: 450 ptas, free Tues. Open Tues.–Sat. 9:30–1:30 and 4–7 (5–8 in summer), Sun. 9:30–1:30.*

Just east of the Plaza de las Bulas is a traditional Córdoba flea market, the **Zoco Municipal de Artesanía.** (The word *zoco* is a Spanish rendering of the Arabic word *souk*, or market.) Artisans produce and sell their crafts here daily, creating quite a hotbed of activity. Flamenco is performed here in summer.

Calle Judíos ends at the **Puerto de Almodóvar**, a gate marking the end of the Jewish quarter. Built in the 14th century, the gate was restored in the 19th. Outside the old wall is a statue of the native Roman philosopher Seneca (often covered with graffiti), who committed suicide at his emperor's command.

PASEO DE LA VICTORIA

Modern-day Córdoba's main drag is the wide Paseo de la Victoria, lined with gardens and fountains. Vendors often sell leather bags and clothing from stalls here. At night, families go for walks around the gardens. At the north end, hop over to see the **Gran Teatro** (Avda. del Gran Capitán, box office tel. 957/480237) at the corner of the Paseo and Ronda de los Tejares—many of the city's cultural events are presented here, including ballets and orchestral concerts. The tourist office has a schedule.

MUSEO ARQUEOLÓGICO

Northeast of the mosque, the Museum of Archaeology is another place to soak up the area's past—displays feature objects and mosaics from the prehistoric, Iberian, Roman, Visigothic, Moorish, Mudéjar, and Renaissance periods. The most interesting items are those from the (wealthiest) Roman and Mudéjar eras, including bronze goodies from a panoply of temples and mansions. *Plaza Jerónimo Paez 7, tel. 957/474111. Admission: 250 ptas. Open Tues.–Sat. 10–2 and 5–7 (10–1:30 and 6–8 in summer), Sun. 10–1:30.*

MUSEO DE BELLAS ARTES

Housed in a highly Renaissance building, Córdoba's Museum of Fine Arts was once a charity hospital. The museum was founded by Ferdinand and Isabella, who also received Christopher Columbus here twice. Córdoban artists are favored, but artists from all over Spain are represented, including Valdés Leal, Zurbarán, Murillo, Palomino, Goya, Juan de Mesa, and Mateo Inurria. Portraits of Andalusian beauties by local artist Julio Romero de Torres have their own gallery across from the museum's entrance. *Plaza del Potro 1, tel. 957/471314 or 957/473345. Admission: 250 ptas. Open Tues.–Sat. 10–2 and 5–7 (summer 10–1:30 and 6–8), Sun. 10–1:30.*

MUSEO DIOCESANO

This collection of religious art is housed in a former bishop's palace. The cloister is several stories high, and some of the living and dining rooms are preserved as such. The collection comprises medieval tapestries, prayer books, and paintings as well as wood sculptures. One hall is dedicated to local artists; look for some of Julio Romero de Torres' less provocative works. *C. Torrijos 12, tel. 957/479375. Admission: 200 ptas. Open fall–spring, weekdays 9:30–1:30 and 3:30–5:30, Sat. 9:30–1:30; summer, weekdays 10:30–2 and 4–6:30, Sat. 9:30–1:30. Closed Sun..*

PALACIO DE LOS MARQUESES DE VIANA

One of Córdoba's more unusual mansions, the Palace of the Marquis of Viana consists of several joined houses from around the 17th century. With a total of 12 patios, the complex is also known as the Museum of the Patios, and its sweet-smelling array of flowers and fruit trees are well cared for. The halls and rooms bear rich displays of glazed tiles, china, embossed-leather wall hangings, and firearms. *Plaza Don Glom 2, tel. 957/480134. Open fall–spring, Mon.–Sat. 10–1 and 4–6, Sun. 10–2; summer, Mon.–Tues. and Thurs.–Sat. 9–2, Sun. 10–2. Closed June 1–15.*

PLAZA SANTA MARINA DE LAS AGUAS

Just northwest of the Palacio de las Marqueses de Viana is Plaza Santa Marina de las Aguas, at the edge of the **Barrio de los Toreros** (Bullfighters' Quarter). So named for the disproportionate number of bullfighters who hailed for these streets, the neighborhood features a a statue of the famous bullfighter **Manolete.** Look also for the church of **Santa Marina** and the **Plaza San Miguel,** also known as Plaza de Capuchinos after the 17th-century Capuchin convent that adjoins it. In the center of the square is a statue called **Cristo de los Faroles** (Christ of the Lanterns), featuring eight lanterns hanging from wrought iron.

ALONG THE GUADALQUIVIR

On the river side of the mosque stands a **Puerta Romana** (Roman Gate) and **Puente Romano** (Roman Bridge), built to protect the city from unwanted guests. Cross the Puente Romano to reach the high, 14th-century **Torre de la Calahorra,** which now holds the **Museo Vivo de Al-Andalus** (Museum of Al-Andalus). Here, audiovisual pieces teach you all about Córdoba, with an emphasis on the three-way religious tolerance that obtained in the 10th century, when the Moors ruled. If you have the energy, climb up top for a view of the city and river. *Avda. de la Confederación, tel. 957/293929. Admission: 700 ptas., less without audiovisual presentation. Open fall–spring, daily 10–6; summer, daily 10–2 and 5:30–8:30.*

AFTER DARK

Córdoba is a city of vigor—insomniacs need not worry about keeping themselves busy at night. Around the mosque and **Judería,** most souvenir shops and bars stay open late, keeping the streets well lit for most of the evening (especially Calles Benavente and Buen Pastor). The area north of the Jewish quarter, including **Plaza de las Tendillas,** is often hopping with activity on spring and summer evenings; impromptu flamenco and rock performances are likely sights if you park yourself in one of the surrounding outdoor cafés. Continue north on Avenida del Gran Capitán or José Cruz de Conde and you might be shocked by the Las Vegas feel of the neon lights—but there is, in fact, a huge, 24-hour **casino** (look for bright, flashing lights spelling BINGO) on Calle Gongora, wedged between Gran Capitán and Cruz de Conde. Still farther north, cross the large Ronda de los Tejares into another hotspot of youthful activity based around **Calle Reyes Católicos** (parallel to Ronda de los Tejares, one block north). Virtually every storefront here is a bar or late-night restaurant; look for a brand-new Internet bar, a slew of English-style pubs, and two movie theaters showing recent releases (usually dubbed in Spanish, but occasionally in the original).

For a more alternative—as in music—bar and club scene, cross the wide Paseo de la Victoria to the far western part of the city. Around **Calle Miguel Benzo** and **Calle Marruecos** (both parallel to the Paseo and Avenida Republica Argentina), you'll see tons of graffiti and tons of kids hanging out. The popular restaurant-bar **El Papagayo Verde** (C. Antonio Maura at C. Miguel Benzo) serves up strong mixed drinks to be consumed on cement benches. The **Guggenbar** (C. Marruecos 15, tel. 957/236762) is one of the coolest bars you might ever encounter, at once laid-back—to the tunes of classic jazz or rock—and thoroughly modern, with polished metal curves around the room forming unique seating configurations. There are three computers for Internet use (400 ptas. per hour).

FIESTAS

Semana Santa (Holy Week) brings a procession involving Nazarenes, penitents, *saetas* (ancient solemn laments), and incense. May brings the **Cruces de Mayo** (Crosses of May) festival, for which people decorate crosses and dance around them. The fun continues with patio competitions to see who has the best courtyard tiles, plants, and flowers. There are several **flamenco festivals** each year, and every three years Spain's national flamenco contest is held in Córdoba. In January and September, a **Joyacor** (jewelry fair) comes to Córdoba, and in October you can check out the **Expoalimentación**, a tasty food festival. Pick up some interesting wood products at November's **Expomadera.**

JAÉN

Jaén forms another nexus between Andalusia's Moorish history and the modern struggle for Spain's smaller cities to compete in the modern world. The town center is a commercial mess, full of traffic, shopping centers, and office buildings, while others sections remain quiet whitewashed neighborhoods with Moorish remains and historic churches. Jaén's ancient castle overlooks the city from a few miles away; the huge cathedral takes up a few square blocks downtown; and the restored Moorish baths give you a feel for Jaén in its prime. The Moors called this place Geen—Route of the Caravans—because it formed a crossroads between Castile and Andalusia. Long a frontier between Moorish and Christian land, Jaén is brimming once more, a provincial capital of about 108,000 bordering the autonomous community of Castile–La Mancha.

The city relies on the surrounding countryside to supply its food chain with wild game. Most local restaurants offer typical Spanish cuisine augmented by specials featuring the daily "catch." Interestingly enough, Jaén's main fiesta honors St. Anthony the Abbott, patron saint and protector of animals—neighborhoods compete to build the most spectacular bonfires, around which they perform the traditional *melenchones* dance.

BASICS

CYBERSPACE
Student-run **Ivicus** (C. Maestro Sapena s/n; open daily 10:30–2:30 and 5–midnight) is not terribly convenient, but it exists (*see* After Dark, *below*). Access costs 500 ptas. an hour.

EMERGENCIES
Police: 091. **Red Cross:** 953/251540.

MAIL
The **post office** is in Plaza de los Jardinillos (tel. 952/191112), with a shady, tree-lined park out front.

VISITOR INFORMATION

In 2000, Jaén was enduring the construction of a major underground parking garage, a process that threw tourist facilities into disarray. The large **Patronato de Promoción Provincial y Turismo** (Provincial Tourist Board; Plaza de San Francisco, tel. 953/234411, ext. 127/128) is in the *ayuntamiento* (town hall), a block from the cathedral. The somewhat less informative **city tourist office** (C. Jaén Maestra 18, tel. 953/219116) was closed for most of 2000. The **regional tourist office** (C. Arquitecto Berges 1, tel. 953/222737)—south of Plaza de las Patallas, just west of Paseo de la Estación—can be helpful, but it, too, has an uncertain schedule. All three offices are technically open daily from 8 AM to 3 PM.

COMING AND GOING

Once you're here, there are **taxi** stands in most of the large plazas, especially the one in front of the cathedral.

BY BUS

The **bus station** (tel. 953/250106) is a block off the Paseo de la Estación, on the northern edge of downtown. A local bus line serves nearby towns like Úbeda and Baeza; Alsina Graells heads off to **Granada** (950 ptas, 1½ hrs). Other large companies serve **Madrid** (2,500 ptas, 4½ hrs), **Córdoba, Málaga,** and **Seville.**

BY CAR

Jaén is conveniently situated between Granada and Madrid on the N-IV highway, about 93 km (58 mi) north of Granada. As you approach, you'll see the castle looming high above the city, and then the cathedral poking out from behind the cement blocks.

BY TRAIN

The **train station** (tel. 953/270202) is north of the town center; follow signs on the Paseo de la Estación north. **RENFE** (tel. 902/240202) runs several trains daily to and from **Córdoba** (1,300 ptas.), **Granada** (1,800 ptas.), and **Madrid** (3,000–6,000 ptas.).

WHERE TO SLEEP

Alas, Jaén has too few hotel rooms—if you don't reserve in advance, you may have trouble finding one.

UNDER 6,000 PTAS. • La Española. This spacious, centrally located old house offers both rooms and tasty homemade meals. The rooms are something out of your grandmother's house, with flowery prints and not-so-firm mattresses but with large windows and, well, lots of character. Most rooms have private bath (5,000 ptas.); a double with shared bath is only 4,000 ptas. The menú del día downstairs costs around 1,300 ptas. *C. Bernardo Lopez 9, tel. 953/230254. 16 rooms, 4 with bath. Restaurant.*

Pensión RENFE. Despite its poetic name, this modern pension is closer to the bus station than the train station; should you need it, there's also parking nearby. Guest rooms are spotless, with white linoleum floors and a total lack of art on the walls; doubles run 3,500–5,500 ptas. depending on the season. An elevator facilitates luggage hauls. If you stay a while, you can arrange full board for an additional 2,500 ptas. a day. *Paseo de la Estacíon, tel. 953/274624, fax 953/274624. 39 rooms.*

WHERE TO EAT

The compact neighborhood around the cathedral is filled with restaurants firmly established by years of patronage by locals. Calle Doctor Eduardo Arroyo, a steep street leading down toward the post office, packs all kinds of traditional and ethnic (okay, pizza and Chinese) restaurants.

UNDER 2,000 PTAS. • Casa Vicente. If you've been craving some of Jaén's homemade game dishes, this is the place to dig in. The bar is set up for tapas and hearty drinks, while the friendly dining room is full of families jabbering about the day's events. The kitchen is known for game casseroles, sautéed spinach with earthy herbs, and *cordero* (lamb) preparations. *C. Francisco Martín Mora 1, tel. 953/233333. Closed Sun.*

UNDER 3,000 PTAS. • Parador de Santa Catalina. The food at Jaén's parador hotel is some of the finest in town, and you consume it overlooking the mountains. The parador is built between the ruins and towers of the Moorish castle itself, inviting interesting ambles through the lobby and courtyards.

Order à la carte to keep your personal tab under 3,000 ptas.; the seasonal menú del día (which can be hard to resist) brings you closer to 4,000. *Castillo de Santa Catalina, tel. 953/230000, fax 953/230930.*

WORTH SEEING

CASTILLO DE SANTA CATALINA

Commanding an impressive view, St. Catherine's Castle watches over Jaén, once an invincible fortress—except from its western side. Built by the Nasrid king Ibn el-Ahmar, the castle was conquered by Ferdinand III on Saint Catherine's Day in 1246. After the victory, a chapel was built in her honor, she became the patron saint of Jaén. The ruins make a dramatic setting for the parador in their midst (*see* Where to Eat, *above*). *Follow signs to western edge of town; no phone. Admission free. Open summer, Thurs.–Tues. 10:30–1:30; fall–spring, Thurs.–Tues. 10–2.*

CATHEDRAL

The cathedral is hard to miss, rising as it does above the very center of Jaén. Construction began in 1500, so the detailed Baroque façade consists mainly of lifelike sculptures of King Ferdinand III and his court. In the main chapel, a cloth said to have touched the face of Christ is kept in a silver coffer and exhibited on Good Friday. The small **museum** contains religious paintings by local artists. *Plaza Santa María. Admission: cathedral free, museum 100 ptas. Cathedral open daily 8:30–1 and 4:30–7; museum open weekdays 9–1 and 4–7, Sat. 11–1, Sun. 11–1 and 4–7.*

BAÑOS ÁRABES

Head north down the central Calle Martínez Molina to find the **Palacio de Villadompardo,** which sits on top of Jaén's Arab baths. Villadompardo was a viceroy from Peru; once he had built his mansion on top of these treasures, it was no mean feat to excavate and restore them. Dating back to the 11th century, they're well worth a look. *Plaza Luisa de Marillac, tel. 953/236292. Admission free. Open Tues.–Fri. 9–8, weekends 10–3.*

MUSEO PROVINCIAL

Jaén's delightful little Provincial Museum is housed in a beautiful, ivy-covered stone building with a wonderfully shady rest spot on its entrance stairs. Inside is one of the best collections of Iberian (pre-Roman) artifacts in Spain, and a thorough art collection with Spanish works from all eras. Some of the dramatic religious paintings make impressive use of light and color, and there's a interesting collection of Goya lithographs. In summer the museum takes the afternoon off; call ahead to confirm hours when the mercury rises. *Paseo de la Estación 29, tel. 953/250320. Admission free. Open fall–spring, Tues. 3–8, Wed.–Sat. 8–8, Sun. 9–3; summer, morning only (call for hours).*

AFTER DARK

Most of Jaén's younger partygoers bring their own poison to the cement park along Avenida de Granada, next to the bullring. South and west of that area is the alternative quarter, with tattoo parlors, Internet cafés, and mod bars. Look for more traditional venues around the cathedral and down to the post office. If you're up for a long walk west from Paseo de la Estación to Avenida de Muñoz Grandes, you can follow a crowd into the neighborhood north of here, where you'll find a collection of techno clubs and Internet cafés like the student-run **Ivicus** (*see* Basics, *above*).

BAEZA

Baeza snuggles betwen rolling hills and olive groves 48 km (30 mi) northeast of Jaén. The mammoth **cathedral** in the center of town contains some original details from its days as a mosque—look for these in the Gothic cloisters. In the 16th and 17th centuries, the town's nobility built and reconstructed a great many palaces and civic buildings, giving the town some enduring Renaissance treasures. The **Casa del Pópulo,** on the central *paseo,* has a stunning plateresque façade and houses the town **tourist office** (tel. 953/740444). Poet Antonio Machada taught French at Baeza's **university**, off the Plaza del Pópulo, from 1912 to 1919. All in all, the town's quaint cobblestone squares, whitewashed houses, and scenic natural surroundings well repay a day's visit.

ÚBEDA

Smack in the middle of the province of Jaén, Úbeda enjoys the area's rich supply of olives and olive oil. It tries to be modern, but the city's labyrinth of ancient streets is as confusing as any in Andalusia, and you're sure to pick up a Moorish vibe from the many stone roads and buildings. Signs lead you to the Zona Monumental (old town), full of ornate Renaissance palaces and restored churches. Some parts of the new town, north of the bullring, are a little seedy—be careful with directions, and/or ask a local to direct you around. The people of Úbeda tend to be sweet and helpful.

BASICS

Despite being housed in the large Hospital de Santiago, west of Plaza de Andalucía and north of the bullring, the **tourist office** can be elusive (C. Obispo Cobostel, tel. 953/750897)—it closes during fiestas and conventions, both of which are common in every good-size Spanish city.

COMING AND GOING

BY BUS

The **bus station** (C. San Jose, tel. 953/752157) is on the west side of town; follow C. Obispo Cobos. A few Alsina Graells buses connect Úbeda with **Granada** (2 hrs, 1,300 ptas.), Jaén, and Baeza each day. The company Comes runs long-distance to **Seville, Málaga, Valencia,** and **Madrid.** From the bus station, it's a long walk or a short cab ride to the center of town.

BY TRAIN

Úbeda is not served by train. The closest train station is in **Linares-Baeza,** a few miles west of here; buses (tel. 953/650202) make the connection several times a day.

WHERE TO SLEEP

Because there's a big jump in price between Úbeda's luxury hotels down to the *hostales,* it's important to call ahead to snag a room you can afford. If you can't reserve in advance, hunt for a bed along Calle Ramón y Cajal, just north of the Hospital de Santiago tourist office—look especially for **Hostal El Castillo** (C. Ramón y Cajal 20, tel. 953/751218; doubles around 5,000 ptas.), run by Miss Victoria (*see below*).

UNDER 6,000 PTAS. • Hostal Victoria. Run by a kind matriarchal family, this spotless *hostal* at the end of a narrow street west of the bullring offers the best buy in town. The beds are a little worn, and the log-shape pillows a little disheveled, but the street outside is quiet, and each room has a small bathroom and window. Even traveling businessmen make use of this deal—a centrally located double room for around 5,000 ptas. *C. Alaminos 5, tel. 953/752952. 15 rooms.*

UNDER 8,000 PTAS. • Hotel La Paz. This area, parallel to C. Ramón y Cajal in the new town, is somewhat rundown, but Hotel La Paz keeps its dignity. The building is about a century old, but the interior is entirely modern—the comfy rooms are more than adequate for a weary traveler, with decent mattresses, private safes, and new bathrooms with hair dryers. Doubles go for 7,000 ptas. *C. Andalucía 1, tel. 953/752140. 14 rooms. In-room safes.*

WHERE TO EAT

UNDER 2,000 PTAS. • Mesón Gabino. Specializing in grilled and braised meats, Gabino's chef cooks up a touch more than run-of-the-mill Spanish cuisine. Most dishes have a little flair; the *sopa de andrajos* (tattered soup), for example, is a surprise every night. The cozy dining room is frequented by local families. To get to this eastern locale, follow Calle Losal from Plaza de Marzo to Calle Fuente Seca. *C. Fuente Seca s/n, tel. 953/754207.*

WORTH SEEING

Andrés de Vandelvira, author of Jaén's cathedral, designed Úbeda's Hospital de Santiago (*see* Basics, *above*) and many of the town's other monuments as well, with the result that Úbeda has a pleasingly homogeneous feel. During the 16th century, most of the city's existing palaces were adorned with Renaissance facades.

The town centers on the **Plaza del Ayuntamiento** (Government Square), which in turn centers on an attractive fountain. The **Palacio de los Cobos** sits at the head of the square, its impressive corner balcony holding a central white marble column. Just south of here is the central **Plaza Vázquez de Molina,** the best place to view Úbeda's prize possession: the **Sacra Capilla del Salvador**. Originally designed by Diego de Siloé, who built Granada's cathedral in 1536, the Chapel of the Savior ended up being Vandelvira's first commission here. The chapel remains in good condition after being partially reconstructed after the mad burning of churches during the Civil War; you can take a tour if the caretaker is on duty (make a donation).

Walk around the city for a leisurely look at its many ornate mansions and churches. You can tour a few; inquire at the **Parador Condestable Dávalos** (Plaza Vázquez de Molina 1, tel. 953/750196) about guided city tours, offered twice every day except Monday.

SHOPPING

Úbeda is known locally as a shopping extravaganza. **Calle Valencia,** on the east side of town, is lined with artisans' shops featuring handmade pottery, glass, baskets, and rugs. Úbeda pottery has a distinct green glaze and a woven-lattice pattern on its edges. The streets around **Plaza del Ayuntamiento** are also heavy on cool stores and cafés; if the tourist office is closed when you arrive, look in local shops for tour books with town maps.

PARQUE NATURAL DE CAZORLA

East of Úbeda is the **Parque Natural de Cazorla** (Cazorla Nature Park), a wildlife preserve known for regular sightings of deer and boar, not to mention birds. Within the park is the Cañada de las Fuentes (Gully of the Fountain)—origin of the Guadalquivir River. The mountains reach as high as 6,000 ft here. Hiking, canoeing, and horseback riding are options; if you'd rather not move a muscle, opt for a jeep safari. The **visitor center** at Torre de Vinagre (follow A319 a few miles north from Cazorla; open Tues.–Sun. 11–2 and 4–8) can give you maps and suggest what to do if you happen upon some male bucks clashing antlers over a pretty doe. There's a small hunting museum next door. You can also contact the **Agencia de Medio Ambiente** (Agency of the Environment; C. Tejares Altos, Cazorla, tel. 953/720125) for information on tours and park activities.

EASTERN ANDALUSIA

Eastern Andalusia shines brightest in Granada, one of the most historically resonant *and* physically beautiful cities in the world. Rising from a plain onto three hills, the city is blessed with the remarkable Alhambra fortress-palace—site of the Moors' last stand in Spain—and is not coincidentally the final resting place of the so-called Catholic Monarchs, Ferdinand and Isabella. From several vantage points in the city you can see the snowy peaks of the Sierra Nevada, a heady sight given that the sunny Mediterranean coast is only a few miles beyond them. South of Granada, the Alpujarras mountains within the range are dotted with little villages that earn their keep from fresh cheeses, cured hams, and wool rugs. Down on the coast is Almería, which has a nice beach area and access to a little-known natural park, the Cabo de Gata. Travel through this part of Spain presents you with some of the most variegated landscapes in Spain, ranging from the snowcapped mountains of the Sierra Nevada to the fertile plains around the Darro and Genil rivers to the temperate Mediterranean coast. In a very short time, ski centers give way to windsurfing shops.

GRANADA

If every city were as beautiful as Granada, people would never travel. They would stay home and enjoy their whitewashed alleys, their plazas and parks, their sensual hilltop palace and gardens, and their distant snowcapped mountains, all kissed by bracing alpine air. Along with Seville, Granada is one of the few places in Andalusia that feels like a big city yet retains its Moorish heritage, in part with present-day Arab stores and restaurants. The old and the new thrive in adjacent neighborhoods, separated only by large (new) avenues. Granada has seen more than its share of action—it was the last city in Spain to be captured from the Moors by the Catholic King Ferdinand, who spent seven months at the task. What remained of the Moorish kingdom of Al-Andalus in the late 15th century was run by Boabdil, the Rey Chico (Boy King), called El Zogoybi (The Unlucky) by his subjects. He was defeated at the Alhambra, the beautiful fortress-palace that now draws gawkers from all over the world with its sensual architecture and captivating Arabic carvings. As he fled through the Puerta de los Siete Suelos (Gate of the Seven Sighs), he asked that the gate be sealed forever

The Alhambra sits high on a hill, removed from the hubbub. The city itself consists of the ancient whitewashed Moorish quarter, the Albaicín, climbing up the east side of the river gorge in a tangle of narrow streets that's barely navigable by car. The new town surrounds the city's monstrous cathedral. Apart from an ancient Visigoth settlement on the Alhambra hill, the Moors were Granada's defining inhabitants, having lived here from the 8th to the 15th centuries; and when the caliphate of Córdoba collapsed in the 11th century, Granada became the most important city in Al-Andalus. The Nasrid dynasty, formed in 1238 and based in Granada, became the richest and most powerful kingdom in Iberia. Granada's architecture and archives reveal that during the Moorish era, cultural and intellectual pursuits flourished here.

You could spend a happy few days studying the minutely carved walls and baths of the Alhambra or wandering the surrounding gardens, but don't forget that this is one of the most popular tourist sites in the world—you have to buy a timed ticket in advance, as the number of visitors per hour is limited. Granada is stumbling in its fast-growing commerce, but it stays grounded in its historic neighborhoods and small-scale shops selling locally made jewelry and ceramics. And, interestingly, a new influx of North African immigrants—some legal, some not—is mixing up the town's heritage all over again.

BASICS

CURRENCY EXCHANGE

Conveniently located within view of the sign pointing to the tourist office, a block from the cathedral, **American Express** (Avda. Reyes Católicos 31; open Mar.–Oct., weekdays 9–1:30 and 2–9, weekends 10–2 and 3–7; Nov.–Feb., Mon.–Sat. 9–1:30 and 2–8) changes money at current rates without commission. There are plenty of **banks** and other exchange offices around the major squares and avenues; inspect the rates and aim to veto any place that charges commission. **ATMs** crop up on just about on every post-medieval block.

CYBERSPACE

Madar Internet (C. Caldereria Nueva 12, tel. 958/229429; open Mon.–Sat. 10 AM–midnight, Sun. noon–midnight) is a small but lively student hangout a block west of the Plaza Nueva. The going rate for non-students is 400 ptas. an hour. There's a **no-name** Internet, phone, and fax place next to the Plaza Nueva (C. Joaquín Costa 4, tel. 958/224989, fax 958/221993; open daily 10–2:30 and 5–10:30), with a reasonable Internet rate of 375 ptas. an hour. They advertise the cheapest phone rates to the U.S. and U.K., but these are not in fact anything special. **Internight** (C. Verónica de la Magdalena) stays open till 3 in the morning, packs 40 computers, and has a bar/club atmosphere. A nice, speedy connection costs only 250 ptas. an hour.

The coolest Internet place is off the tourist track, west of the church of San Jerónimo: **Central Perk** (C. Trinidad Morcillo 13, off Avda. Fuente Nueva, open daily 9 AM–2 AM). Yes, they watch *Friends* in Spain, dubbed and repackaged as *Campañeros*. The background is a great selection of pop and alternative music and the bar is fully stocked, as are the 22 computers. One hour at the screen costs 250 ptas.

EMERGENCIES
Police: 092. **Fire:** 080.

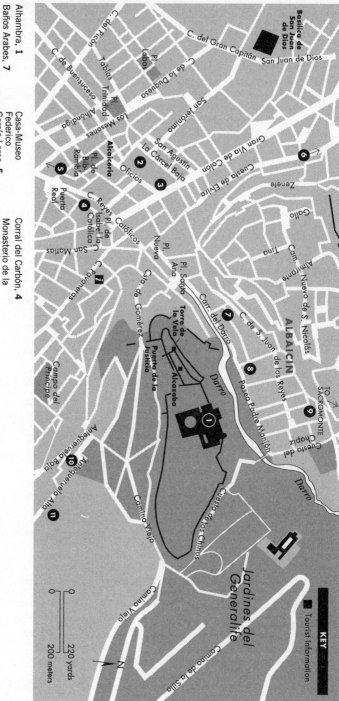

GRANADA

Alhambra, **1**
Baños Árabes, **7**
Capilla Real, **3**
Carmen de los
Mártires, **11**
Casa de Castril, **8**

Casa-Museo
Federico
García Lorca, **5**
Casa-Museo
Manuel de Falla, **10**
Cathedral, **2**

Corral del Carbón, **4**
Monasterio de la
Cartuja, **6**
Sacromonte, **9**

285

In a medical emergency, call 958/282000 for **medical assistance,** 958/284450 for an **ambulance.** Most clinics are on the west side of town, near the Plaza del Toros (hmm).

MAIL

The **post office** (Puerta Real, at corner of C. Acera de Darro and C. Angel Ganinet, tel. 958/224835) is open weekdays 8:30–8:30 PM, Saturday 9:30–2.

VISITOR INFORMATION

The **city tourist office** is in the Corral del Carbón, a former coal house (C. de Mariana Pineda 40, tel. 958/221022). Almost around the corner is the **provincial tourist office** (Plaza Mariana Mineda 10, tel. 958/226688), where you have to pay for maps of places other than Granada but can take enthusiastic advantage of the current bus and train schedules. Both offices are open weekdays 10–7 and Saturday. 10–2.

COMING AND GOING

BY BUS

The **bus station** (Carretera Jaén, tel. 958/185010) sends buses in every direction. Alsina Graells (tel. 958/185480) is the main bus line, with several daily buses to **Jaén** (1½ hrs, 950 ptas.) and **Córdoba** (1½ hrs, 1,800 ptas.), plus two direct afternoon buses that serve **Cádiz** (5 hrs, 3,655 ptas.). To **Seville,** you have a choice of several direct routes (3 hrs, 3,000 ptas.) or a slightly cheaper route that stops in some pueblos blancos (2,355 ptas.). Buses to **Málaga** are almost hourly (1¾ hrs, 1,185 ptas.). Alsina Graells also heads down to **Almería** for around 1,640 ptas. (1½ hrs). Most **Costa del Sol** towns are accessible several times a day for less than 1,500 ptas.; one bus goes directly to **Marbella** four times a day (1¼ hrs, 1,820 ptas.). There's a bus to nearby **Guadix** almost every hour (550 ptas.).

BY CAR

By car, Granada is easy to access from the north or the south. The N323 highway connects Granada to Jaén, Madrid, and, in the other direction, the Costa del Sol. To the west, the N432 reaches Córdoba and Badajoz; to the southwest, the A2 zooms down to Seville; to the southeast, Murcia and Almería are easy trips.

Unfortunately, parking within Granada can be a big headache. Unless you have a reservation at a hotel that offers parking, it's best to leave your car in a secure garage when you arrive and simply take a cab to your hotel. Driving through the Plaza Nueva is an adventure all its own, as giant pegs keep the cars out—an electronic entry system makes you indicate where you're going before the pegs will drop to let you in. Unless you're driving up to the Alhambra, this is not recommended, as there is *nowhere* to park on the streets (the maps lie!). You will be forced to drive through the entire ancient Albaicín before you're deposited once more on a major street, a ridiculous excursion that still might not yield a parking space. Stick to garages.

BY PLANE

Armilla Airport (tel. 958/245237 or –38) is about 17 km (11 mi) southwest of the city center. Iberia has several daily flights to Madrid, Barcelona, Valencia, and certain vacation isles. **Iberia** has an office at Plaza de Isabel la Católica 2 (tel. 958/227592 for information, 901/333222 for reservations). From the airport, an efficient bus (tel. 958/278677) shuttles to Gran Vía Monday–Saturday at 8:15 AM, 9:15 AM, and 5:30 PM and Sunday at 5:30 PM and 7 PM.

BY TRAIN

The **train station** (Avda. de los Andaluces, tel. 958/271272) is useful mainly for long-distance journeys—for travel within eastern Andalusia, you're generally better off taking a bus. There are several daily trains to **Almería** (2 hrs, 1,800 ptas.), **Seville** (3 hrs, 2,700 ptas.), and **Madrid** (6 hrs, 3,600–5,000 ptas.). The ride to **Barcelona** takes 12 hours, so you have a daytime and an overnight option (7,600 ptas.). Call **RENFE** (tel. 902/240202) for information and reservations.

GETTING AROUND

You can usually trip over a **taxi** at any time of day. If they all seem to have disappeared, call 958/132323 or 958/400199.

WHERE TO SLEEP

UNDER 6,000 PTAS. • Hostal Austria / Hostal Viena. The folks in charge of this around-the-corner duo are fairly relaxed and very helpful. Proximity to both Plaza Nueva and the Alhambra are major pluses, not to mention proximity to some good bars. Some rooms overlook the street from little balconies; all are clean, welcoming, and possessed of small private bathrooms and soft mattresses. Doubles go for 5,500 ptas. a night. *Hostal Austria: Hospital Santa Ana 2, tel. 958/227075, 13 rooms; Hostal Viena: Cuesta de Gomerez 4, tel. 958/221859, 10 rooms.*

Hostal Landazuri. Perched on the steep road up to the Alhambra, this is one of Granada's sweetest places to stay. The very entrance makes you feel welcome, and the tiles and Andalusian decor send you back into Spain's past. The rooms are a bit worn, but most of the bathrooms are private and clean. Front rooms have nice street views—watch the international masses march up the hill. Doubles are cheap, at 4,000 ptas. a night, though you must pay cash up front. Parking is available for 1,500 ptas. Breakfast is served downstairs. *Cuesta de Gomerez 24, tel. 958/221406. 15 rooms. Bar, café. Cash only.*

UNDER 10,000 PTAS. • Hotel Alíxares. Don't be dismayed by the tour buses—there's room for everyone in these new, clean rooms, some of which face the Alhambra from right next door. The hotel is a world in itself, with a currency exchange, pool, ATM, hair salon, gift shop, café, bar, garden, and veranda looking across to the Alhambra. (Barbecues are held out here in summer.) The café is a gentle place to chill out in this epicenter of Spanish tourism; a quick ride down the hill on the hotel's shuttle puts you back in the real world. Doubles cost 8,000 ptas. *Avda. de los Alixares s/n, tel. 958/225575 or 958/224102. 168 rooms. Restaurant, bar, pool.*

Hotel Los Tilos. Smack on Plaza Bib-Rambla, this hotel is a bargain considering its central location and sweet staff. Most rooms look out on the plaza, or at least get decent light; an elevator scales high floors with ease. Beds are springy but comparatively firm, and bathrooms are up to date. The plaza is an active one, but is not necessarily a party spot (except during fiestas), so noise shouldn't be a problem. Breakfast is served, and there's parking nearby. Doubles cost 7,600 ptas. *Plaza Bib-Rambla 4, tel. 958/ 266712, fax 958/266801. 30 rooms. Restaurant, laundry service.*

Hotel Juan Miguel. Considering the full-on breakfast buffet, you might enjoy this cheesy spot. The lounge stops just short of singers in red velvet, and the rooms lack a certain je ne sais quoi, but the place is loaded with amenities and ready to serve you. The staff can arrange to whisk you to and from the airport or the Alhambra, or at least help park your car in their garage. You're next to the Puerta Real, near shopping as well as the sights. Rooms are new, with carpets and sanitized bathrooms, and those in front have wonderful views of the snowcapped mountains (beyond a few concrete monstrosities). Doubles average 10,000 ptas.; parking is 1,100 ptas. extra. *Acera del Darro 24, tel. 958/521111, fax 958/ 258916. 66 rooms. Restaurant , café.*

WHERE TO EAT

Next door is to Granero de Abrantes (see below) is **Rincón de Lola**, a new vegetarian restaurant offering stuffed crepes and brown-rice dishes on menús del día for less than 1,600 ptas.

UNDER 2,000 PTAS. • Asirios. Just off the Plaza Nueva, Asirios's good-looking waiters serve up simple Spanish and Mediterranean cuisine. Most entrées come with heaping piles of *papas fritas* (french fries), and the grilled meats come in large servings themselves. The salads, such as *ensalada de aguacate* (avocado salad), are equally voluptuous. Everything is enjoyable, especially if you sit outside and people-watch from the small patio. Doors are open till 2 AM. *Placeta Sillería 3, tel. 958/223928.*

Cafetería Ely. If you find yourself down by the Puerta Real, stop into Ely for some traditional Andalusian food and atmosphere. The hanging bottles of local wine and the hams and sausages lining the bar are a welcome signs to those who enjoy *comida casera* (homemade meals). Tapas include various cheeses, ham, *croquetas*, and gazpacho; the menú del día costs 1,300 ptas. Locals on break from work stop in for lunch, families for dinner. *C. Párrage 3, tel. 958/256058. Closed Sun.*

Granero de Abrantes. Fresh-and-trendy is the thrust of this new restaurant, where the chef wields a juicer with a passion: think fresh carrot juice and *sopa de manzana y zanahorias* (carrot and apple soup). Somebody's scouring the market for exotic ingredients, as in *potage de frijoles, yuca, y platano* (medley of beans, yucca root, and plantains), but they're Spanish enough to offer *solomillo a la pimiento con patatas y ajetas* (fillet of steak with peppers, potatoes, and other goodies) for only 1,450 ptas. *Plaza San Juan, tel. 958/228622. No lunch.*

Naturi Albaicín. After sniffing the wonderful incense and tea smells floating around in the street, help yourself to some delicious vegetarian fare in this dry (Muslim-run) restaurant. The setting is intimate, with seating for only 24, and there's a Moorish stone arch in the center; the Arabic wall decorations emphasize food. The menú del día is usually around 1,300 ptas.; you're likely to spend about 1,700 on dinner. Try the vegetable couscous, *berenjenas rellenos* (stuffed eggplant), or *crepas de espinaches con salsa* (spinach crepes with sauce). The kitchen uses fine ingredients, whole grains, the freshest fruit for dessert. *C. Calderería Nueva 10 (west of Plaza Nueva), tel. 958/220627. No lunch.*

Kirin. Sushi withdrawal? Get your fix at this little Japanese restaurant, where the full sushi menu covers vegetable rolls, *maguro* (tuna), and *unagi* (eel). The regular menu has soups, rice dishes, tempura, and a variety of sautéed meat dishes. The menú del día costs 1,300 ptas. *C. Párraga 9 (next to cinema), tel. 958/260096. Closed Mon.*

UNDER 3,000 PTAS. • Samarcanda Restaurante Libanés. If the sumptuous smell doesn't attract you to this corner of the ancient Albaicín, surely the excellent Mediterranean menu will. Shish kebabs come out sizzling from the grill, and the salads somehow look more exciting than they do just about anywhere else in Spain. Two people can opt for a special taster's menu, course after course of the chef's own showpieces. You'll probably drop 2,500 ptas. and regret not one. *C. Calderería Vieja 3, tel. 958/210004.*

WORTH SEEING

As you wander, be wary of Gypsies who try to give you herbs or flowers. They'll offer to tell your fortune, then demand a fee.

ALHAMBRA

One of the most popular historic sites in the world, and by far the most popular in Spain, the Alhambra is a stunning legacy of the Moors' occupation of Granada and the excellent craftsmanship they sponsored. A walk or ride up Cuesta de Gomerez sends you back into the past before you even enter the **Puerta de las Granadas** (Pomegranate Gate, named for the symbol of Granada, of which the gate sports three)—craftsman still toil away in workshop here, much as they did in the Moors' time.

The Alhambra was begun in 1240 by Ibn el-Ahmar, first king of the Nasrids. At that point it was more like a gated community, protecting houses, schools, baths, and gardens within a defensive wall. The palace itself is an endless, intricate fantasy of patios, arches, and cupolas fashioned of wood, plaster, and ceramic tile—surfaces are lavishly colored, adorned with marquetry and ceramics in geometric patterns, and surmounted by delicate, frothy profusions of lacelike stucco and ornamental statalites. Built of perishable materials, the complex was never intended to last, but to be forever replaced and replenished by succeeding generations. By the 17th century, after they had fallen into several different sets of feuding hands, the buildings were in ruins, used only by vagrants. In 1812, Napoleon's troops took refuge here, but their attempts to blow the place up on their departure were, happily, foiled by a faithful Spaniard. Soon after, the Duke of Wellington used the palace as a respite from the Peninsular War, and gratefully helped restore some of the gardens and buildings. By the time Washington Irving, an American diplomat with a case of wanderlust, moved in and wrote *Tales of the Alhambra* (1832), public interest had been sparked; and in 1862, Granada started the ongoing restoration project that allows a torrent of 8,400 people to walk through the gates each day.

A bit farther uphill, you pass through the **Puerta de Justicia** (Gate of Justice), inscribed with a decree to the effect of "May God make the justice of Islam prosper within her." Different theories surround the carved palm with each finger extended; one holds that the hand symbolizes a peaceful gesture, another that each finger represents one of the five Pillars of Islam (belief in one God, prayer, alms, fasting, and the pilgrimage to Mecca). Past the ticket office, keep to the left and continue through some arched hedges—carefully sculpted to mirror the crenellated fortress walls—down to the **Alcazaba.** The basic structure of the fortress is in decent shape, though the interior Plaza de las Armas is little more than rubble. This is the oldest part of the Alhambra, with 13th-century towers; the bell tower was used by Moors and Christians alike to announce the opening and closing of the local irrigation system. Climb the **Torre de la Vela** (Watchtower), at the far end, for a great view of Granada and the surrounding snowcapped mountains.

Exit the Alcazaba and pass through the **Puerta del Vino** (Wine Gate), whose eastern side is covered with intricate tiles, to face the Renaissance **Palacio de Carlos V.** This incongruous square building, erected in 1526, was the first civic Renaissance building in Spain. The artist who oversaw much of its construction, Pedro Machua, was said to be a disciple of Michealangelo; in any case, he added marble columns for a very Italian look. Bullfights and tournaments were held in the circular courtyard, which takes up much of the building's floor plan and was convenient to the private royal quarters on one side; the space is now exploited for its acoustic qualities during music festivals. At the entrance to the palace is the small but thorough **Museo de la Alhambra**, (tel. 958/226279; admission free; open Tues.–Sat. 9–2:30), where displays of ceramics, wood and plaster sculptures, and metal work highlight Islamic art from the 9th to the 16th centuries. Upstairs, the **Museo de Bellas Artes** (Museum of Fine Arts; tel. 958/224843; admission 250 ptas.; open Tues. 2:30–8, Wed.–Sat. 9–8, Sun. 9–2:30) has sculptures and paintings from the 16th to 18th centuries.

North of the Carlos V behemoth is the Alhambra's main attraction, the **Palacio Nazaries** (Nasrid Royal Palace), where you may want to stop sightseeing and just recline in the shade of intricately carved Arabic walls, reflecting vaguely on the luxurious fountains and smelling fresh roses from the garden. The first section you walk through is the **Mexuar**, formerly used for business and government; from these arched windows you have fabulous views north to the whitewashed Albaicín quarter and the Sacromonte. The oratory and the Cuarto Dorado (Golden Room) filter the sun's rays through latticelike windows; some of the side rooms are still being excavated and restored.

Palace guests would be shown through the Mexuar, then paraded through the central **Patio de los Arrayanes** (Myrtle Court) to admire the long goldfish pond. The huge cedar door at the north end leads to the **Salón de Embajadores** (Ambassadors' Hall), where the Boy King Boabdil signed Granada away and the monarchs later met with Christopher Columbus. This portion of the palace, where sultans entertained their guests while keeping an eye on things from the vantage point of dramatic backlighting, is called the *serallo*. The ceiling is an intricate assemblage of some 8,017 pieces of wood crafted by numerous court carpenters; above one arch is an inscription perhaps aimed at the filibusters of the day—"Few words and you will leave in peace."

To get a feel for the Alhambra and timeless Granada, pick up Washington Irving's Tales of the Alhambra (1832), written with a keen eye and sense of humor during Irving's stay in the palace itself.

Just east of here are the **Baños Árabes** (Arab Baths), their walls covered in bright, sensual ceramic mosaics. Star-shape portholes let in some bathing light. From the balcony, the sultan would peer down into the baths to choose the recipient of his nocturnal affections. Another intimate quarter is that in which the sultan and his family actually lived, along with their servants—the **harem** has some of the most delicate wall carving anywhere in the Alhambra. Much of this work is presently being restored, but you can still get the feel for its sensuality. In the dramatic **Patio de los Leónes** (Lions' Court), where the women of the harem were waited on hand and foot by eunuch servants, twelve lions surrounding a fountain spout water from their mouths, and the streams flow symbolically to the four corners of the earth, literally to the surrounding rooms.

Continue around the court to the **Sala de los Abencerrajes,** possibly the Alhambra's most beautiful gallery, with a stalactite ceiling and a star-shape cupola reflected in the pool below. Boabdil's father is alleged to have massacred 16 members of the Abencerrajes family here upon learning that one of the clan's members had taken a fancy to his favorite woman. The **Sala de las dos Hermanas** (Hall of the Two Sisters), although small, has a unique dome and is covered with metallic glazed tiles. The Arabic inscription running around the room compares its beauty to that of a blooming garden.

The Alhambra's beautifully maintained gardens are called the **Generalife,** after the Arabic term Gennat Alarif (Garden of the Architect). Don't rush through these—allow time to amble slowly through the crenellated shrubs, tropical foliage, charming lily ponds, and hundreds of rose varietals. Up on the **Cerro del Sol** (Hill of the Sun) is a summer palace used by the Nasrid nobility.

Now for logistics: You *must* buy tickets in advance, lest you miss this landmark entirely. To avoid fatal wear and tear on the place, only so many people can enter at one time, so you have to choose a half-hour slot for your entrance to the Palacios Nazaries (once inside, you can spend up to an hour). The rest of the grounds are yours for the day. Nighttime tours offer a different perspective, with dramatic flood-lighting, but nothing beats the sun streaming through the Alhambra's carved skylights. Buy tickets in just about any BBV (Banco Bilbao Vizcaya) bank in Spain, or over the phone with a credit card (tel. 902/224460; from outside Spain, tel. 91/374–5420). To get here from Granada proper, walk up the steep Cuesta de Gomerez, take a taxi, or take the bus from Plaza Nueva (every 15 mins.; 120 ptas). If you're inclined to drive up, be warned that parking is very expensive and there is no shade. *Cuesta de*

Gomeréz, tel. 958/227525 general info. Admission 1,000 ptas. (plus small surcharge on phone purchases). Open Nov.–Feb., daily 9–6; Mar.–Oct., Mon.–Sat. 9–8 and Sun. 9–6. Night tours Nov.–Feb., Sat. 8–10 PM; Mar.–Oct., Tues., Thurs., and Sat. 10–midnight. Ticket office opens ½ hr before opening time (15 mins before opening time for night tours) and closes 1 hr before closing time.

CAPILLA REAL

Next door to the cathedral (but older), the Royal Chapel is where those active Catholic Monarchs, Ferdinand and Isabella, finally lay down their heads for good. After Granada was conquered in 1492, Isabella commissioned this chapel to be built over city's mosque, and the royal couple decreed in their wills that they wished to be buried here. Both of them died before the building was completed, so they were buried in the San Francisco convent, on the Alhambra hill (now a luxury parador), then moved downtown in a huge procession in 1521. The chapel is basically Gothic, though grandson Charles V added some Renaissance details and went so far as to build a huge cathedral next door in the hope of giving the couple an even grander mausoleum (*see below*). The tombs themselves are lavishly decorated with carved marble; the king and queen are depicted at peaceful rest, with a lion and lioness at their feet. Cherubs and saints surround them, exquisitely rendered by the Italian sculptor Domenico Fancelli. The tomb on the left contains Juana la Loca (Joan the Mad), the couple's insane daughter, and Juana's husband, Felipe el Hermoso (Philip the Handsome)—when Felipe met an early death, Juana had his casket toted around with her so that she could kiss his embalmed body each night. Also in the crypt is the small coffin of young Prince Felipe of Asturias, who would have inherited the throne had he lived long enough. The towering altarpiece comprises 34 carved panels depicting religious and historical scenes. The sacristy holds royal swords, Isabella's crown and scepter, and some Flemish paintings owned by the queen; a notable triptych shows the Pietà and Nativity (the third panel, depicting the Resurrection, is in New York's Metropolitan Museum). *C. Oficios, tel. 958/229239. Admission: 350 ptas. Open Mar.–Sept., daily 10:30–1 and 4–7; Oct.–Feb., Mon.–Sat. 10:30–1 and 3:30–6:30, Sun. 11–1 and 3:30–6:30.*

CATHEDRAL

Granada's cathedral was commissioned in 1521 by Charles V, who, finding the Capilla Real "too small for so much glory," envisioned reburying his late grandparents somewhere else. A variety of preeminent architects and artists were involved, yet (or perhaps "so") no particular style was achieved. The portals are plateresque and Baroque; other elements have other Renaissance touches. The interior is filled with stunning marble columns forming arched domes in classical linear styles; the main altarpiece, from 1570, is by the Baroque artist Juan de Aragón. The outcome of Charles's grandiose ambitions is a domineering Renaissance pile in which no royal personage was ever buried. *Gran Vía de Colón, tel. 958/222959. Admission: 350 ptas. Open Tues.–Sat. 10:30–1:30 and 4–7, Sun. 4–7.*

CASA DE CASTRIL

This beautiful 16th-century mansion has an exotic plateresque facade with scallop shells and a fanciful phoenix. Inside you'll find an extravagant staircase and courtyard as well as the **Museo Arqueológico,** which has a preserved Moorish room and some interesting Phoenician finds. *Carrera del Darro 41, tel. 958/225640. Admission: 300 ptas. Open Wed.–Sat. 9–8, Sun. 9–2:30.*

CASA MUSEO DE FEDERICO GARCÍA LORCA

The poet's former summer home is actually called Huerta de San Vincente (St. Vincent's Orchard). The Lorca family only stayed here between 1926 and 1936, but Federico wrote a substantial part of *Así Que Pasen Cinco Años* and *Bodas de Sangre* here. His niece runs the place, so you feel more like you're visiting relatives than touring a museum. The setting reveals a simple life, enhanced by creative touches. On display are some original manuscripts, drawings, photographs, and Lorca's books and piano, all of which are inspiring. To get here, head south from Granada on Calle de Recojidas, past the circle where it turns into Neptuno, and you'll see the Parque García Lorca; the museum overlooks it. Note that you must call in advance on Tuesday, Thursday, and Friday. Buses leave almost every hour for the 20-minute ride to Lorca's birthplace, **Fuentevaqueros,** where his childhood home is also a museum (tel. 958/516453). *C. de la Virgen Blanca s/n, tel. 958/258466. Admission: 300 ptas, free Wed. Open Tues.–Sun. 10–1 and 5–8 (5–7 in winter).*

CASA MUSEO MANUEL DE FALLA

On the hillside south of the Alhambra, near the Hotel Alhambra Palace, is the charming little house where the composer Manuel de Falla (*The Three-Cornered Hat; Nights in the Gardens of Spain; Love, the Magician*) lived and worked. Now a museum, it displays interesting memorabilia and has a fantastic mountain view. *C. Antequeruela Alta, tel. 058229421. Admission: 300 ptas. Open Tues.–Sat. 10–3:30.*

BAÑOS ÁRABES

El Bañuelo (the Little Bathhouse) is reminiscent of the Alhambra's baths but not nearly as well preserved. Light does pierce the ceiling through star-shape vents, but the mosaic wall tiles were probably more inspiring as a backdrop to 11th-century bathers. *Carrera del Darro 31, tel. 958/225640. Admission free. Open Tues.–Sat. 10–2.*

CORRAL DEL CARBÓN

The so-called Coal House is a fine example of how a wonderful Moorish building can stand the test of time if it isn't torn down and built upon. This one was used by Moorish merchants in the 14th century to store goods and lodge traveling salesmen; in the 19th century it stored coal, then was itself restored. Today it houses the tourist office and a small artisan gallery. *C. Mariana Pineda, tel. 958/225990. Admission free. Open Mon.–Sat. 9–7, Sun. 10–2.*

MONASTERIO DE LA CARTUJA

Up on the north side of the city, Granada's Carthusian monastery is a phenomenal Baroque masterpiece. Built over 300 years but mainly in the 17th century, it packs some incredibly elegant Baroque columns and altars, intricate but not gaudy. The walk from the center of town is long, but a taxi can get you here in about 10 minutes. (There's a taxi stand out front for the return trip.) *Paseo de Cartuja, tel. 958/161932. Admission: 350 ptas. Open Mon.–Sat. 10–1 and 4–8, Sun. 10–12.*

Take a break from the shopping circuit at the Bocadilleria in Plaza Bib-Rambla—plenty of seating, quick waiters, and a menu ranging from tapas to hearty sandwiches to fruity cocktails.

MONASTERIO DE SAN JERÓNIMO

For the Renaissance spectrum of Granada, this is your place: Built in the early 16th century, it maintains a Gothic interior with flowing Renaissance elements. The dome and main altar have some amazing stone "drapery." *Rector López Argueta (bordering C. El Gran Capitán), tel. 958/279337. Admission: 350 ptas. Open daily 10–1:30 and 4–7:30.*

SACROMONTE

High in Granada's Sacromonte (Sacred Mountain) district are a number natural caverns. In the 15th century, some bones were found in one of these spaces and believed to be relics of St. Cecilio, the city's patron saint, hence the blessing of the hill. The charming **Abadía de Sacromonte** (Sacromonte Abbey) has some fine religious oil paintings. *Camino del Sacromonte, tel. 958/221445. Admission: 250 ptas. Open Tues.–Sat. 11–1 and 4–6. Sun. 11–12.*

SHOPPING

For classic souvenirs such as tiles, plates, jewelry, *terazea* (wood marquetry), chimes, T-shirts, and so forth, try **Artesanía Gonzáles** (Cuesta de Gomerez 38, tel. 958/220067). Look also for the *puf*, a Moroccon leather pillow sham designed for sitting around the opium pipe. **Pervane** (C. Animas 2, at Cuesta de Gomerez, no phone) specializes in hand-mixed perfumes and small bottles of handblown glass to contain these luscious scents. Farther along Gomerez is a saturation of guitar shops, most around a century old—stick your nose in to watch these instruments take shape. Prices range from 10,000 to 250,000 ptas. **Maestro Luthier** (master guitar maker) **Germán Péraz Barranco** is well known (Cuesta de Gomerez 10, tel. 958/227033). **Casa Ferrer** (Cuesta de Gomerez 26, tel. 958/221832) is a bit more upscale, with professional guitars for up to 400,000 ptas.

Around the Plaza Nueva, **El Zoco Nazari** (C. Imprenta 2 and C. Reyes Católicos 50, tel. 958/225977) has a colorful supply of original mosaic tiles and locally made jewelry. They'll write your name (or someone else's) in Arabic on parchment paper for 1,500 ptas., a great lightweight gift.

For contemporary boutiques and a feel for the Moorish silk markets of yore, prowl the meandering streets around Plaza Bib-Rambla. The gourmet food store **La Alcena** (C. San Jerónimo 3, tel. 958/206890) is a good place to pick up some local olive oil, ham, vinegar from Jerez, natural products from the Sierra Nevada, and even cured venison. They're happy to ship stuff abroad.

Gran Vía de Colon has a more commercial strip of stores mixed with large banks and hotels. **Nectar** (Puerta Real 4, tel. 958/266616; closed Sun.), a homegrown alternative to the Body Shop, provides much of Spain with natural bath products.

AFTER DARK

Granada has an active performing-arts scene. Pick up a *Guía de Ocio* for music and dance listings.

Much of this ancient city stays awake after dark, not least the old Albaicín, where abundant Arabic tea houses serve more than just tea. The bars near Plaza Nueva thump until early morning: The popular **Bodega La Antigualla** serves Mexican food, sandwiches, and drinks to a standing-room-only crowd on the square itself. A few blocks west is an Arab district where falafel is cooked fresh throughout the night. Beaded curtains often lead to the kitchens, filled with fresh mint garnish and homemade pastry desserts (honey-sweetened baklava-type delicacies filled with nuts). **Aquarel Pub,** between Calle Elvira and Gran Vía de Colón, is an artistic environment conducive to having a few *chupitos* (shots).

The area behind the tourist office is filled with cleaner, more upmarket bars serving pricier drinks. **Plaza San Juan de la Cruz** has a few newer bars and pubs with imported beers and finer wines. To the east, the outdoor cafés of **Plaza Bib-Rambla** stay open until 2 or 3 AM to handle the crowds, and the surrounding streets hide several trendy hangouts.

A long walk or short cab ride west toward the bullring (Plaza del Toros) area yields tons of restaurants and some alternative clubs. Across from the bullring itself, near Gate 8, the **Tercer Aviso** (Third Warning; it's a bullfighting thang, tel. 958/206041), claims to be the largest pub in Granada. **Ole y Olé** (tel. 958/800795), near Gate 6, is a modern bar with a glass ceiling.

FLAMENCO

Most of Granada's flamenco clubs are in the Sacromonte, where cave-dwelling Gypsies make a living fleecing tourists. Looking up toward the Alhambra, the old flamenco tavern **Cueva Los Tarantos** (Sacromonte 9, tel. 958/224592) specializes in the Zambra Gitana style. This is a tourist affair; hotels often arrange for groups to be bused here. From Plaza Nueva, head up Carrera del Darro, turn onto Carretera del Chapiz, and look for the neon sign at the end of the first block. Shows are twice nightly. Make reservations, and don't bring more money than you can afford to part with.

Other options: **Cueva La Rocio** (Camino del Sacromonte s/n, tel. 958/227129). **Cueva la Zingara** (Camino del Sacromonte s/n, tel. 958/222271). **Jardines Neptuno (**Arabial s/n, tel. 958/251112). **Peña la Platería** (Placeta de Togieros 7, tel. 958/210650). **Reina Mora** (Mirador de San Cristóbal s/n, tel. 958/401265). **Zambra Maria La Canastera** (Camino del Sacromonte s/n, tel. 958/121183).

FIESTAS

Granada's **International Festival of Music and Dance,** held in late June and early July, brings performances to historic buildings all over town, including the Alhambra (tel. 958/276200 for information, 958/221844 for tickets). The festival office is across from the tourist office in the Corral del Carbón. An **International Flamenco Festival** is held during Corpus Christi in June; locals dress in typical Andalusian costume and parade through town on horseback. During **Semana Santa** (Holy Week), Granada has a unique Procession of Silence at midnight. Bullfights, parades, and public dancing manifest the **Fiesta de la Virgen de las Angustias** the last week of September, in honor of the city's patron saint. January brings the **Feria Nacional de Arte Contemporáneo** (National Contemporary Art Fair).

LAS ALPUJARRAS

The little Alpujarras are some of the most picturesque mountains in Spain. Rising dramatically at the southern edge of the Sierra Nevada, their peaks are usually topped with snow, a refreshing vision when Andalusia's heat sears the rest of the land. The range is known for its tiny white villages, etched into cliffs along steep mountain roads: Each town has its own artisanal specialty. The people of this region are extremely friendly (and a good thing, since tourist offices are few and far between); most appear to be over forty years of age, suggesting that Granada and other large cities lure homegrown kids away. The ski resorts of the Sierra Nevada and proximity to the beach attract vacationers of all ages; in springtime, fresh peaches and figs sweeten the pot. The locals pride themselves on their geographical triangle: *sol, mar, y nieve* (sun, ocean, and snow).

The Alpujarras were first settled when the Moors were expelled from Granada, starting in 1248. When the Alhambra was finally conquered by the Catholics, King Boabdil was given part of this mountainous region to be his fiefdom; but when the Moors refused to convert to Christianity, bloody battles ensued, and they were eventually either converted (and their language and customs forbidden) or exiled to Morocco. To cover the Inquisition's tracks, King Philip II repopulated the Alpujarras with Galician soldiers, and they picked up where the Moors had left off, weaving cloth in red, green, black, and white and maintaining houses with a short, square Berber look.

A handful of towns make good day trips and/or quiet retreats. Roads are generally in good condition, but they're winding and narrow, with nerve-wracking hairpin turns.

LANJARÓN

The melted snow that flows into Lanjarón provides some of the finest mineral water in Spain, sold throughout the country and in other parts of Europe. The bottling company sits right at the town entrance (inquire about tours if you're interested); there are even a few fountains along the street where you can fill your bottle or just have a taste.

BASICS
The **tourist office** is under construction until perhaps 2001; there's a makeshift office in the *ayuntamiento* (town hall) on the north side of the main drag, about a block west of the large water fountain called the Manatial de La Salud (Source of Health). Moving east to west as you enter town, the street changes names in a few short blocks from Queipo de Llano to Cabo Moreno to Avenida de Generalísimo to Avenida de la Constitución. If you get a headache, just stop into any hotel and ask where and whether the tourist office is open—with luck, they'll just give you a map.

COMING AND GOING
BY BUS • Short of driving, this is your best bet for reaching the Alpujarras, as trains can't climb the slopes. Buses from **Granada** serve several Alpujarras towns. Alsina Graells Sur (tel. 958/185480) travels directly to Lanjarón; call Granada's bus station (tel. 958/185010) for details on other destinations. From **Málaga,** there are two daily buses to Lanjarón, but the schedule changes often; it's often easier to take a bus or train to Granada and transfer. The bus stop in each village is usually in front of the largest hotel.

BY CAR • Heading south from Granada on the N232, you'll pass the signposted **Suspiro del Moro** (Moor's Sigh), where Boabdil supposedly took one last look at the city he had surrendered to the Catholics. His supportive mother is said to have barked, "You weep like a boy [some sources say "woman"] for what you could not defend as a man." Give the guy a break—he *was* El Rey Chico, taking the reins in his teens after a miserable childhood with a harsh, jealous father. About 55 km (30 mi) farther, you'll see a turnoff for Lanjarón. The N232 is constantly under construction near the coast, so allow time for delays if you're driving up from the coast; and note that the route is much windier if you turn east at Velez Benaudalla and hit Órgiva before Lanjarón.

Once in Lanjarón, you have to navigate narrow streets and endure the sight of endless NO PARKING signs above rows of parked cars. Whenever a bus or truck comes through, everyone traveling the opposite direction pulls over to let it pass; sometimes a pedestrian hops into the street and starts directing traffic. Resist the signs pointing you toward parking, as they refer to an unpaved lot down several steep roads. Try your luck on the streets.

WHERE TO SLEEP

The main drag is lined with restaurants and lodgings.

UNDER 6,000 PTAS. • Hostal Astoria. The host family will cook up a storm if you opt for the meal plan in their small restaurant. Guest rooms reflect the owners' sweet, cozy nature—the beds are a bit worn, but the bathrooms are fully up to date. A double can be had for 3,800 ptas. *Avda. de la Alpujarra 5, tel. 958/770075. 19 rooms. Restaurant. Cash only.*

Castillo Alcadima. This relatively new apartment-style building is decorated to look old. You can rent by the night (doubles 5,000 ptas.) or by the month, the latter of which you might be inclined to do once you see the old Moorish castle out your window. Rooms are spacious and homey, with handwoven rugs, comfy chairs, and full bathrooms; downstairs you've got parking, an outdoor pool, a garden and terrace, laundry service, a bar, a café, and a restaurant with a sweeping view of the countryside. *C. General Rodrigo 3, tel. 958/770809 or 958/770279. Restaurant, café, bar, pool, laundry service. 28 rooms.*

UNDER 10,000 PTAS. • Hotel Miramar. A modern structure in the center of town, Miramar has a shiny lobby with a hint of 1980s tackiness, but the dramatic spiral staircase swoops you into the spirit if things. In any other city, a room in this building would cost several hundred U.S. dollars a night; here in the hinterlands, you pay 9,000 ptas. for a double with full bath. Dining areas are done in pastels; the spacious guest rooms are also soft in hue, with firm beds and dollhouse-style furniture (white dressers with floral designs). Some rooms have balconies. There's a pool for summer use, and handy parking year-round. *Avda. de Andalucía 10, tel. 958/770161. 60 rooms. Restaurant, pool.*

Hotel Nuevo Palas. One of the fancier places on Lanjarón's main strip, the Nuevo Palas adds a gym and a game room to its outdoor pool. Guest rooms are modern and spacious (and have private safes), though most are on the dark side; pastel touches lighten the mood, as do the small terraces. Doubles go for 7,000 ptas. Breakfast is served in the café. *Avda. 24, tel. 958/770111 or 958/770086. 30 rooms, 2 suites. Café, pool.*

WHERE TO EAT

UNDER 1,500 PTAS. • Bar-Restaurante Palamar. One of Lanjarón's few independent restaurants, Palamar has a covered patio with climbing vines and Moorish arches. Specialties include local favorites like chunky gazpacho and *puchero de hinojos y el remonjón* (fennel stew); the menú del día is usually the best deal, especially when it fresh seafood from the nearby coast. *C. Alpujarra 27, next to park, tel. 908/459704.*

WORTH SEEING

You'll see the large **Parque El Salado** as soon as you enter Lanjarón, on the south side of the main avenue. Salado means either "salted" or "charmed," depending on your feelings about Lanjarón's favorite variety of ham. The park has a nice view of the castle and valley below; park yourself on a shady bench when the heat bears down.

The **Castillo de los Moros** (Moorish Castle) sits high on a lone rocky peak south of town. It's barely been restored, so you can really see the battle scars left by King Ferdinand—*after* the Moors had been exiled out of here. Apparently the Moorish general in charge of the last stand at this castle got so wired as to hurl himself from the high tower as his troops were quashed. To go all the way up, follow the PARKING sign south of town on Calle Alejandro Damas. It's a steep ride or hike past a few shanties and barking dogs, but you end up a few steps from the entrance. There's usually someone here from 10 to 2 and 4 to 6.

ÓRGIVA

A few winding-road miles east of Lanjarón, Órgiva is considered the hub of the Alpujarras thanks to its size. Sitting in a mountain niche, the town is picture-perfect from afar; up close it's a bit run-down. The Thursday-morning **market** is exciting—all of Órgiva comes out to buy and sell local produce, canned goods, ceramics, rugs.

Despite being larger than Lanjarón, Órgiva has fewer lodgings. What is does have is a number of banks and ATMs, should you need some cash. For a hot meal or safe room, try **Taray** (Carretera Tablate-Albuñol, Km 18, tel. 958/784531), a new hotel with neo-Moorish accents in the form of local bedspreads and rugs. Guest rooms are spacious and airy, and most look out onto the estate; doubles with bath cost around 8,000 ptas. The restaurant serves delicious meat and produce, both cultivated mainly on the property.

BEYOND ÓRGIVA

Moving northeast you'll encounter **Bubión**, a small whitewashed town known for a huge resort hotel, the Villa Turística (doubles 14,000 ptas.). From here on, most Alpujarras towns are accessible only by a car and the occasional local bus. **Pitres,** barely a town, has some notable Moorish ruins and is known for its Fuente Agria, a striking natural fountain with flowing water. To find the fountain, climb down the steep stairs from the center of town (ask a local for directions).

If your car can make it, head to the highest village on the Iberian Peninsula, **Trevelez.** Also known for its unique snow-cured hams and its mountain trout, this little town attracts only the most dedicated travelers. On August 5th, the villagers make a pilgrimage to the peak of Mulhacén—technically the highest point in Spain—to celebrate their patroness, the Virgen de las Nieves (Virgin of the Snows).

ALMERÍA

Almería is a rather soulless city on the coast straight south of Granada. There's a patent financial gap between the shacks on the outskirts, the cement blocks closer in, and the new buildings and restored antique structures of the center. Easily approachable, with street signs (yahoo!) and pointers to the tourist office and major hotels, it turns into a beach town in the summer. Reserve in advance if you want to join the hordes of vacationing Europeans.

In ancient eons, Almería was known for its wealth of bronze and silver. The city was ravaged by pirates, from the Phoenicians to the Moors, for its natural riches and strategic location. In the mid-12th century, Alfonso VII gathered the resources of his landside neighbors to vanquish the naval terrorists, but in the 16th century the city was again ransacked by Berber pirates and several earthquakes. Historic sights are few; on the hill south of town is a huge fortress with an impressive stone wall.

Apart from beaches, the province of Almería is now known mainly for its grapes and local wines. As you travel through this easternmost part of Andalusia, you'll see the greenhouses used to raise produce in this arid region. The scenery grows desertlike, and the facilities just plain ugly; avert your eyes to the beautiful ocean opposite.

BASICS

CYBERSPACE

If you need the fix, head north on Rambla de Belén and east on Calle Doctor Carracido to **Factory W** (C. Hermanos Pinzón 57, tel. 950/261096; open weekdays 9–2 and 4–7, Sat. 10–3), where access costs a modest 200 ptas. per half hour. **Ciber Café La India,** north of town (Carretera de Granada, Km. 304, tel. 950/274861; open daily 8–2 and 4–roughly midnight), attracts mostly college kids to its cool atmosphere, bar, and cheap eats.

EMERGENCIES

Police: Avda. Mediterráneo 201, tel. 950/223704 or 091. **Ambulance:** 061. **Hospital Provincial** (tel. 950/235250). **Clínica Torrebermejas** (Avda. de la Estación 25, east side of town, tel. 950/220324).

MAIL

The **post office** (Plaza San Juan Casinello 1, tel. 950/237207), along Paseo de Almería, is open weekdays 8–7, Saturday 9–3.

VISITOR INFORMATION

The friendly, multilingual **tourist office** (tel. 950/272355, open weekdays 9–7, weekends 10–2) is on Parque de Nicolás Salmerón near Calle M. Campos, overlooking the park and the water.

COMING AND GOING

BY BUS

The **bus station** (tel. 950/210029) is on Plaza de Barcelona, a quick walk east of town. Alsina Graells Sur (tel. 950/221888) heads to and from **Madrid** (3,000 ptas.), **Málaga** (2,000 ptas.), **Granada** (1,600 ptas.), and **Seville** (2,800 ptas.) several times daily, and once a day to **Córdoba** (2,800 ptas.). Smaller lines serve Murcia, Barcelona, and the Cabo de Gata nature reserve; call the bus station or Autocares Becerra (tel. 950/224403) for information.

BY PLANE

There's a small domestic **airport** on Carretera Níjar (Km 9, tel. 950/221954 or 950/213700). Call **Iberia** to make plans (tel. 950/213790). For a bus into town, call 950/221422. To get out to the airport, take Bus 14 (every 30 mins.) from the Pizza Hut on Avenida Federico García Lorca.

BY TRAIN

Almería's a bit isolated, really. Trains run to and from **Seville** (2,200 ptas.) four times a day, stopping in Antequera and **Granada** (1,600 ptas.) on the way. Two daily trains serve **Madrid** (2,900 ptas.). The **train station** is on Plaza de la Estación s/n (tel. 950/251135). There's a **RENFE office** at Alcalde Muñoz 1 (tel. 950/231207).

WHERE TO SLEEP

UNDER 10,000 PTAS. • Hotel La Perla. Your hosts, the Rodríguez-García family, claim this is one of Almería's oldest hotels. Fortunately, everything has been restored to contemporary standards, and the family is around daily to keep the place ship-shape. The lobby has lots of mirrors, and the rooms are orderly, with private safes and clean tiled bathrooms. Doubles average 8,000 ptas. in high season, less in the winter. There's parking outside. *Plaza de Carmen 7 (off Puerta Puchena), tel. 950/238877, fax 950/275816. 44 rooms. Snack bar.*

Torreluz II. Don't be confused—on this very plaza are several restaurants and three hotels bearing the name Torreluz. This one offers excellent quality at decent prices. The rooms are soft and cozy, with decent modern prints on the walls, and the bathrooms are pure luxury, with full-size tubs, hair dryers, and extra-soft, extra-large towels. Doubles run 7,500–9,000 ptas. depending on season. *Plaza Flores 1, tel. 950/234399. 74 rooms. Laundry service. Doubles 7,500 ptas. (9,000 ptas. in high season).*

WHERE TO EAT

UNDER 1,500 PTAS. • Taj-Mahal, Templo de Amor. Worth a trek to the Far East (of Almería) is this little love shack serving Indian and Pakistani cuisine. Take a break from fried Spanish food with any of these meat and vegetarian dishes. The delicious lamb couscous with mint sauce adds to the ethnic mix. The menú del día is extremely affordable at around 1,300 ptas. *Avda. Mediterráneo (1 block north of Avda. Cabo de Gata), tel. 950/256557.*

UNDER 2,000 PTAS. • Gerona 12. Around the corner from the tourist office, this clean, modern tea house makes a charming, mellow breakfast spot and has a small gourmet shop to boot. Lunch and dinner consist mainly of tapas. The room is clean and modern, with quiet rock music in the background. *Gerona 12, tel. 950/264036, fax 950/270633. Closed Sun.*

UNDER 3,000 PTAS. • Torreluz Mediterraneo. This thoroughly delightful restaurant is genuinely Mediterranean, its high ceilings leaving plenty of room for decorative trees, flowers, and antique pottery. Dinner starts with a mandatory appetizer—say, salmon pâté—and fresh bread. The attentive staff proffers wine suggestions from the extensive list, and refills your glass the moment your fluid sinks below the lip. The food is highly French in its presentation, with drizzled sauces and carved vegetable garnishes. Look for the *merluza* (hake) in creamy leek sauce or the *solomillo de pata con mostaza* (duck with mustard glaze). The fresh salads, averaging 900 ptas., have leaf lettuce rather than iceberg. The dessert sampler gives you a taste of everything if you can't decide between the elegant after-dinner treats; and every dessert is served with house sherry. You'll spend around 3,000 ptas. for dinner; the lunch menu is usually 1,900 ptas. *Plaza Flores 1, tel. 950/234399.*

WORTH SEEING

Almería is bisected by the **Rambla de Belén**, with the old town to the west and newer developments to the east. Near the coast, the traffic circle Plaza Emilio Pérez meets the commercial **Paseo de Almería,** your first stop for banks, boutiques, and outdoor cafés. West of the tourist office is the neoclassical **Hospital Real** (Royal Hospital); north of here you can navigate some classically tight Andalusian streets to the **cathedral** (tel. 609/575802; admission 300 ptas.; open weekdays 10–5, Sat. 10–1), a fierce Gothic structure designed to withstand attacks from Berber pirates.

Farther north, the **Plaza Vieja** (Old Square), also known as Plaza de la Constitución, has been spruced up, and now sports bright-purple bougainvillea almost year-round. At any point in this area, you can look up to the west and see the towering **Alcazaba** (fortress) hovering over the city; its Moorish walls are still standing despite the earthquakes of 1522 and 1560. The fortress was built by Moorish caliph Abderrahman I starting in 955; Charles III added a bell tower with good views of the city and coast (tel. 950/271617; admission 250 ptas., EU citizens free; open daily 9–8:30).

On the east side of town, Almería's **Centro de Arte** (Art Center) shows contemporary art from local and other European artists. *Plaza Barcelona, tel. 950/269680. Admission free. Open weekdays 11–2 and 6–8, Sat. 6–8, Sun. 11–2.*

AFTER DARK

Nocturnal action centers on **Plaza Flores**, moving down to the beach in summer. In town, try the small **Cajón de Sastre** (Plaza Marques de Heredia 8) for typical *copas*. For a serious rock session, hit **La Caverna** (San Lorenzo 13). For an ancient Greek experience minus the toga, look into **Pub Minerva** (C. Marchales 44, tel. 950/269867). **El Café del Irlandés** (C. General Segura 15, tel. 950/239191) offers darts and hearty beers in an Irish environment. **Alabama** (C. Pablo Picasso 22) plays a blend of country and classic rock.

THE COSTA DEL SOL

The sunny, tropical beaches on Spain's southern coast come as a surprise after miles of arid plains. Just as whitewashed villages dot the Andalusian landscape, the white bodies of northern Europeans dot the coast, reveling in its 320 days of annual sunlight. The coast stretches east from Tarifa—a windsurfing beach looking out toward Morocco—to the province of Granada, where the lusher beaches are known collectively as the Costa Tropical. East of here, the shoreline turns into barren rocky cliffs.

Tourism on the Costa del Sol started in the 1960s with brand-new hotels and the first masses of northern Europeans ("If you build it, they will come"). Gargantuan apartment complexes and luxury hotels were thrown up in haste, lacking what might be called taste. The *costa*'s old fishing villages suddenly found themselves at the forefront of European resorts, catering to crowds of foreigners. Having exhausted the sands, today's developers are building homes in the mountains overlooking the beaches, and golf courses next to the existing resorts.

Beaches and nightlife remain the feature attractions. All along the coast, the outdoors beckons—day cruises to watch dolphins or whales, airy cafés with fresh seafood, beautiful mountains bearing olive orchards and quiet villages, and, of course, the warm gray sands. The most affordable town after dark is Torremolinos, near Málaga, where you can party till dawn and sleep it off on the beach. In contrast, Marbella draws royalty and film stars to its all-night clubs and casinos, which closely approximate the good life. If your tongue is tied after several weeks in Spain, you may be secretly pleased to hear that the Costa del Sol has a massive expatriate British community, to the point where Spanish is largely unnecessary. Many restaurants operate solely in English, and British-owned Gibraltar is, of course, a unique English enclave full of hearty pubs and big, fat breakfasts.

TARIFA

A few miles west of Gibraltar is Tarifa, a lonely spot with commanding views of the Rock and, across the water, Morocco. The town's 10th-century **castle** is famous for its siege of 1292—the Spanish defender, Guzmán el Bueno, refused to surrender even though the attacking Moors threatened to kill his captive son. In defiance, he flung his own dagger down to them, shouting "Here, use this"—or something to that effect. Tarifa became one of the first Moorish settlements on the Iberian Peninsula. The Spanish military turned the castle over to the town in the mid-1990s, and it now contains a museum devoted to Guzmán and his biblical sacrifice (admission 200 ptas.; open Tues.–Sun. 10–2 and 4–6).

ROCK ON

The British colony of Gibraltar is a curiosity, both geographically and politically. The Brits invaded the strategic peninsula in 1704, and today it's the last British colony on mainland Europe. Known locally as "Gib," the tiny town is an English-speaking amalgam of pubs, fish-and-chip shops, and a deteriorating military complex, all dwarfed by the dramatic limestone Rock. A cable car (£4.90 or 1,090 ptas. round trip) can take you up 1,350 ft to the so-called Top of the Rock for spectacular views of Africa, weather permitting. From here you can explore the weird interior of St. Michael's Caves, where stalactites and stalagmites are lit by green and red lights and spooky organ music plays in the background. The cable car also stops at The Ape's Den, home to a bunch of tailless macaques, who wander unfazed among hordes of tourists. Catch the cable car back down or hike the steep, poorly maintained Mediterranean Steps down the east side of the rock, a 45-minute undertaking. For more information on the Rock, visit the main tourist office (6 Kent House, tel. 9567/74950), on Cathedral Square, or the booth just outside Customs.

Gibraltar is not accessible by train, but Comes buses make the trip from most Andalusian cities, including Algeciras (¾ hr, 225 ptas), Málaga (3 hrs, 1,650 ptas), and Cádiz (3 hrs, 1,460 ptas.). You're dropped at the bus terminal (Poligano San Felipe) in the Spanish border town La Linea; from here it's a 15-minute walk south to Gibraltar. The Rock's official currency is the pound sterling, but pesetas are widely accepted, generally at a slightly poorer rate. The airport's exchange bureau is convenient (open daily 9–9) but does not exchange traveler's checks. American Express operates out of Bland Travel (Cloister Bldg., corner of Irish Town Rd. and Market La., tel. 9567/77012).

The Cannon Hotel rents a double with bath for £44.50, including a hearty English breakfast and hearty English proprietors (9 Cannon La., tel./fax 9567/51711). The nearby House of Sacarello (Irish Town at Tuckey's La.) serves affordable sandwiches, wondrous pies, and roasted meats.

The town's windy vantage point has been well exploited—the surrounding mountainsides are covered with windmills, and the beaches are some of the best in Spain for **windsurfing.**

A few miles north of Tarifa are the Roman ruins of **Baelo Claudia,** which may date back to 11 BC. The city was definitely a center of commerce around AD 41–54, known for its salted fish and the resulting paste called *garum* (probably akin to today's anchovy paste). The ruins are still being restored, but antiquity buffs will find them inspiring. All visits are guided. *Carretera de Bolonia (N340), Km 70.2, tel. 956/688530. Tours depart July–mid-Sept., Tues.–Sun. 10, 11, 12, 1, 5, and 6; mid-Sept.–June, Tues.–Sun. 10, 11, 12, 1, 4, and 5. Closed Christmas wk.*

MARBELLA

Spain's headquarters for the international rich and famous, Marbella is the shining star of the Costa del Sol. The whitewashed *casco viejo* (old town) is lined with orange trees and relaxing cafés, and populated year-round by an amiable mixture of Spaniards and Brits. By day, people wander through artisan shops; by night, the action shifts to the beach or to nearby towns with sparkling marinas and discos.

BASICS

CYBERSPACE

American and British students abound here. If you need to check e-mail, they might point you toward the strange little **American Donats and Bagels Cafe** (Travesía Carlos Mackintosh), which has four computers and the same kind of bagel obsession you thought you'd left behind. Just down the block, **Ciber Café 2000** has a whole room of computers and a small tapas bar (C. Galveston near C. Serenate Carretera Ojén, tel. 952/765540); type away for 350 ptas. an hour.

EMERGENCIES

Police: tel. 092. **Ambulance:** tel. 952/774534. **Hospital Comarcal:** tel. 952/862748.

VISITOR INFORMATION

The **tourist office** on the lush Plaza de los Naranjos (tel. 952/823550) has maps and helpful hints. There's another small office at the arched entrance to Marbella (N340, Km 183, tel. 952/822818).

COMING AND GOING

Marbella is right on the N340 between Estepona and Fuengirola. The **bus station** (Avda. Trapiche, tel. 952/764400) serves **Málaga** (1¼ hrs, 650 ptas.) and **Seville** (3 hrs, 2,400 ptas.) as well as the nearby resorts.

If you need a **taxi** once you're here, call 952/774488.

WHERE TO SLEEP

UNDER 8,000 PTAS. • Hotel Linda Marbella. A new addition to Marbella's hotel community, the Linda has already made a name for itself. Most rooms overlook the quiet central patio, which blends pastels with white wicker. Said rooms are clean and sharp, with brand-new bedding and bathrooms; doubles cost 6,000 ptas. The owners, young Spaniards, are happy to help plan your travels. *C. Ancha 21, tel./fax 952/857171. 14 rooms.*

Hostal del Pilar. In a strange twist of promotional instinct, the owner insists this is not a classy joint. It is, however, a relaxed place to hang out—go ahead, have coffee with the other guests in your PJs. Rooms are clean and airy; due to lack of air-conditioning, all those big windows are thrown open in summer. *C. Mesoncillo 4 (off C. Peral), tel. 952/829936. 16 rooms, none with bath.*

UNDER 10,000 PTAS. • Hostal Berlin. Rooms here are small and simple, with a total lack of wall art, but most have nice views. Doubles go for 8,000 ptas. The lobby is *somewhat* decorated with a few mosaic tiles and potted plants. You're east of the *casco viejo*, a few blocks past Avenida Nabeul. *C. San Ramón 21 (just north of Avda. Ramón y Cajal), tel. 952/821310, fax 952/826677. Café. 17 rooms.*

Hotel San Cristóbal. This high-rise in a busy part of town is all about modern amenities. Rooms are slick and clean, with that institutional air-conditioned smell, and most have views. All have private bath. Doubles run 7,800–12,000 ptas. depending on the season. *Avda. Ramon y Cajal 3 (N340), tel. 952/771250, fax 952/862044. 97 rooms.*

WHERE TO EAT

UNDER 2,500 PTAS. • Gulzar. Along with Europeans, many Indian families have relocated to southern Spain. This restaurant has been around for almost eight years, serving homesick Brits (among others) some of the best *naan* bread in the area. The menu appeals to vegetarians and carnivores alike, with hearty spinach dishes as well as grilled meats. Decor is classy, with crisp linens, and meals are served on silver platters individually heated with tea lights. You can even order take-out. *C. Camilo José Cela, one block in from beach, tel. 952/772597.*

UNDER 3,000 PTAS. • **La Comedia.** Local Brits adore this place, not for its English cuisine but for its interesting assortment of flavors—duck eggrolls, Sante Fe grilled swordfish with mango salsa, you name it. The menu changes constantly. You enter from a side street and end up overlooking the square, which is usually filled with a human parade. *Plaza de la Victoria, tel. 952/776478. No lunch.*

La Tricicleta. Almost across the street from La Comedia, this equally spirited restaurant gets a mostly Spanish crowd. A long bar spans most of the dining room, and both are usually bustling. The dinner menu is upscale, featuring traditional Spanish cuisine with an interesting edge—say, steak with port-wine sauce or hazelnut-crusted trout. Prices range widely, from 500-pta. tapas to a 2,500-pta. dinner entrée. Next door, the award-winning café-bar **El Estrecho** (C. San Lazaro 12, tel. 952/770004) serves typical Spanish treats. *San Lázaro s/n, tel. 952/857686.*

WORTH SEEING

Just east of the *casco viejo*, Marbella's **Museo de Bonsai** is a tranquil and unique little treasure—a private bonsai collection hidden in a modern building in a public park. *Parque Arroyo de la Represa, Avda. del Dr. Maiz Viñal, tel. 952/862926. Admission 600 ptas. Open daily 10–2 and 4–6:30.*

The **Museo del Grabado Español Contemporáñeo** (Museum of Contemporary Spanish Engraving) should really be known as one of the best troves of modern art in Iberia. The restored 16th-century building comprises well-lighted galleries filled with unique etchings by such worthies as Picasso, Miró, Dalí, the Basque sculptor Eduardo Chillida (whose work appears all over Spain), and the Catalan painter Antoni Tapiès, creator of challenging abstract works. *C. Hospital Bazán s/n, tel. 952/825035. Admission 300 ptas. Open Nov.–June, weekdays 10–2 and 5:30–8:30, Sun. 10–2; June–Oct., weekdays 10–2 and 6–9.*

MIJAS

Sitting high in the mountains that overlook the coast from a few miles away, the charming town of Mijas is almost picture-perfect. It's not a center of anything (population 7,476) or endowed with a beach, yet Mijas is a prominent city on the Costa del Sol, perhaps due to its well organized local government, golf courses, and fine resorts. If the few budget hotels are booked, Mijas makes a fine day trip.

BASICS

EMERGENCIES
Police: tel. 952/485018. **Hospital Regional:** tel. 952/769952.

VISITOR INFORMATION
The multilingual **tourist office** (Plaza Virgen de la Peña, tel. 952/485900) is open weekdays 9–3. The maps they hand out suggest a touring route. Should you get hooked, they're also ready to help you rent an apartment or buy a house.

COMING AND GOING

Mijas is not served by train. For a **taxi** within town, call 952/476593.

BY BUS
Mijas is served by **Automóviles Portillo** (C. Córdoba 7, tel. 952/380965 in Torremolinos, 952/475066 in Fuengirola). Buses to and from **Fuengirola** (25 mins, 120 ptas.), the nearest beach town, leave almost every 20 minutes. The trip east to **Torremolinos,** which stops in Benalmádena-Pueblo and other towns, takes an hour (185 ptas.); to **Málaga,** an hour and 45 minutes (335 ptas.).

BY CAR
The drive to Mijas from the coast is a curvy, dramatic climb into the mountains. From Fuengirola, simply follow signs to Mijas from the north side of town. (This road was under construction in 2000, the drive didn't get much slower; you might encounter some gravel or dirt patches.)

WHERE TO SLEEP

Believe it or not, there are no hotel rooms in Mijas for less than 14,000 ptas. a night. Within 20 minutes' drive, you can investigate **Rancho La Paz** (Torreblanca, tel.952/486793, fax 952/486355), **Casa Aloha Beach** (Playa El Chaparral, Mijas Costa, tel. 639/576873), and, south along the coast, **Hostal Carmen** (Carretera Cádiz 7, La Cala, tel. 952/493199).

WHERE TO EAT

There are plenty of places to grab a drink and a tapa, but cheap sit-down meals are harder to come by in this scrubbed community. Next to the shrine of the Virgin de la Peña (*see below*), a small café with a view down to the coast serves refreshing drinks (including fresh-squeezed orange juice) and light meals, but it's popular with tourists, so even here the prices are, well, over.

La Alcazaba (Plaza de la Constitución s/n, tel. 952/590253; closed Mon.) is simple and affordable, with a menú del día for around 1,400 ptas. and an excellent view toward the coast. The house specialty is seafood, mainly in its fried or salted forms. Salads are fresh, and the bread is crusty. Next door, **El Mirador** (Plaza de la Constitución s/n, tel. 952/590097; closed Tues.) offers about the same menu for about the same price, with the same view. Okay, the paella is a bit meatier. Eat your heart out for about 1,200 ptas. at **Pizzeria Oscar's,** where pizza and pastas rule the roost (Centro Comercial La Alcazaba, Plaza de la Constitución s/n, tel. 952/590131).

WORTH SEEING

In Plaza Virgen de la Peña, next to the town hall, about 60 donkeys stand around wearing vintage blankets and saddles—these are **burro taxis,** dedicated to showing you the best of Mijas. Their guides give good tours of town for around 1,200 ptas. a head, and they have designated "parking" places throughout the city should you need to pull over for a breather.

The cute shrine of the **Virgen de la Peña** (Virgin of the Rock), the town's patron saint, has an amazing view of the valley below and the coast in the distance. In 1536, the story goes, some local children saw a beautiful dove while playing outside. The dove eventually led them and their reluctant father to a nearby tower, where they saw the Virgin Mary and found several sacred relics. They took these back to the village, and after many tribulations a shrine was erected in the Virgin's honor. Her statue sits amid hundreds of real and fake flowers presented by visiting worshipers. *Open daily 9–7.*

The odd but interesting **Carromato de Max** is a museum of miniatures—the collection of Juan Elegio Miranda, a hypnotist known as Professor Max. Inside an old caravan, you can inspect such curiosities as the Last Supper painted on a grain of rice, the Eiffel Tower on a toothpick, scenes painted on lentils, and even some shrunken heads. The pieces come from all over the world. The museum claims to be one of the most important of its kind, and who can argue? *Avda. del Compas (look for red caravan), no phone. Admission 500 ptas. Open summer, daily 10–10; spring and fall, 10–7 or 10–8; winter, 10–9.*

From the Plaza de la Constitución, walk up the slope beside the Mirlo Blanco restaurant to see one of the smallest **bullrings** in Andalusia. This one wins the charm award. The stuffed bull in the lobby was originally intended for a nightclub in Madrid; it's certainly a rare feeling to be nose to nose with such a creature. You can walk through the well-kept ring when no fight is in session. The bullfighting **museum** down the street, in an alley off Calle Cuesta, contains the collection of bullfighter Antonio José Galán, including posters, more bulls' heads, and velvet costumes. *Tel. 952/485248 for bullring, 952/485548 for museum. Admission 500 ptas. for bullring only, 800 ptas. for bullring and museum. Open summer 10–10, fall–spring 10–6.*

The **Casa Museo** (Folk Museum) is a good introduction to life as it was lived in Mijas a few centuries ago. Different rooms and workshops demonstrate winemaking, baking in a stone oven, weaving, and crafting pottery. Local artisans display their work in the galleries. *Plaza de la Libertad s/n, tel. 952/590380. Admission free. Open weekdays 10–2 and 4–6, weekends 10–2 and 4-8.*

FUENGIROLA

Almost directly south of Mijas on the coast, Fuengirola is a typical beach town, most exciting during the popular summer months. There are no historic sights in the town itself; people come here to get some rays, party along the beach, and perhaps day-trip to a pueblo with a little more substance. That said, the crowds are less excessive here than in Torremolinos—you *can* relax and unwind.

BASICS

Fuengirola has no official **tourist office,** just a town hall that grudgingly hands out maps (Avda. Jesús S. Reina, 6, tel. 952/467457).

Despite the lack of a beautiful old quarter, there is cultural life here—the **Casa Cultural** (Avda. Juan Gómez "Juanito" 12, tel. 952/589349) sponsors concerts, plays, ballets, and other artistic events year-round.

There's a **United States Consulate** at Centro Las Rumpas 1 (tel. 952/474891).

COMING AND GOING

The **bus station** (tel. 952/475066) serves Málaga (45 min, 305 ptas.) and Marbella (1 hr, 315 ptas.). The **train station** (tel. 952/478540) serves mainly Málaga (40 min, 315 ptas.).

WHERE TO SLEEP

UNDER 5,000 PTAS. • Hostal El Cid. The décor is a bit medieval—in the depressing sense—but the rooms are spacious, clean, and equipped with private bath (shower only). An elevator pulls you up. Most look out over the busy street to the beach. The rooftop terrace has a bar, where you'll probably be offered a drink on the house. Doubles go for 5,000 ptas. in high season, less in winter. *Avda. Condes de San Isidro s/n, tel. 952/474844. 46 rooms.*

Hostal Galán. Rooms vary in size, shape, and amenities in this ship-shape British-run *hostal* in the center of town; ask to see yours before you take it. Doubles with bath go for 4,500 ptas. Breakfast is served, and the rooftop terrace has a bar. *C. El Troncón 12, tel. 952/463971. 32 rooms, some with bath.*

UNDER 8,000 PTAS. • Hostal Agur. Rooms in this modern facility a few hundred yards from the beach are cheesy in various ways, including country-knitting and floral-dollhouse motifs. That said, most rooms have new bathrooms and little terraces with beach views. Doubles run 5,000–8,000 ptas. The restaurant serves breakfast. *C. Tostón 2, tel. 952/476666, fax 952/664066. Restaurant. 38 rooms, 2 suites.*

WHERE TO EAT

For dinner, prowl **Avenida Condes de San Isidro** and the streets around **Plaza de la Constitución.** Between here and the beach, restaurants and bars are chock-a-block, none more distinguished than the next in the lower price brackets.

MÁLAGA

Málaga is the unofficial capital of Costa del Sol, mainly because it's so large (population 555,000), yet the city holds its own in culture and history. Dating back to Phoenician and Greek times, Málaga was of some importance to the trading and fishing industries thanks to its proximity to the Guadalmedina River. After the Christian Reconquest, the city prospered, little touched by the drought and earthquakes that ravaged the rest of Spain. Today Málaga is a thriving metropolis and tourist attraction combining sunny beaches, ancient ruins, and contemporary commerce. Art lovers will enjoy hunting down the newly opened birthplace of Pablo Picasso.

The Guadalmedina River runs north through the center of town, crossed by a main drag called (in various sections) Avenida de Andalucía, Alameda Principal, and Paseo del Parque. Most hotels are in the triangular neighborhood west of the port and south of the Alameda Principal; most of the historical sights are just north of this area. Alas, Málaga has endured high unemployment and the attendant crime rate since the 1980s, so be smart about walking alone, and carry your valuables in a tight pocket or a waist belt.

BASICS

CYBERSPACE

The **Instituto Superior de Gestión Empresarial** (C. Alcasabilla 14, tel. 952/602460; open daily 9–2 and 4:30–8:30) imparts all kinds of technical knowledge in a clean, air-conditioned space (in contrast to those where beer and/or cigarettes predominate). Surf the Web for 400 ptas. an hour.

For a few Internet options in bars, *see* After Dark, *below*.

EMERGENCIES

Police: tel. 092 or 952/306091. **State Hospital:** tel. 952/307700.

VISITOR INFORMATION

The extremely helpful **tourist office** (Avda. de Cervantes 1, parallel to Paseo del Parque, tel. 952/604410; open daily 9–6:45) is impressively tolerant of demanding tourists who speak not a word of Spanish.

The **Canadian Consulate** is nearby the tourist office on Avda. de Cervantes (Edificio Horizonte, tel. 952/223346). The **United Kingdom Consulate** is at Duquesa de Parcent 8 (tel. 952/217571).

COMING AND GOING

If you can't find a **taxi**, call 952/327950.

BY BUS

The main **bus station** (Paseo de los Tilos), around the corner from the train station, is home to **Empresa Malagueña de Transportes** (tel. 952/357212). The smaller station, closer to the port and hotel area, is a hub for **Automóviles Portillo** (C. Córdoba 7, tel. 952/214149). Most *incoming* buses stop at both stations. Buses to major Costa del Sol cities such as Marbella, Torremolinos, and Benalmádena Costa depart every 15 minutes throughout the day, usually for less than 1,000 ptas.

BY PLANE

Málaga's **airport,** west of town (tel. 952/048484 for general information, 952/048838 for arrivals, 952/048804 for departures) has grown into the main hub for Costa del Sol air traffic. **Iberia** (tel. 901/333232) has daily flights within Spain, at very high prices compared to train and bus fares. Other airlines touching down in Málaga: **Air Europa** (tel. 952/048247), **Air France** (tel. 952/048192), **British Airways** (tel. 952/048236), and **Swissair** (tel. 952/048180).

BY TRAIN

The **train station** (tel. 952/360202) is on the west side of the river, off the Esplanada de la Estación. **RENFE trains** (tel. 902/240202) run to **Madrid** (4 hrs, 6,600 ptas.), **Seville** (2½ hrs, 2,130 ptas.), and **Córdoba** (2½ hrs, 2,300 ptas.) several times daily. Alas, there is no direct train to Granada; you have to transfer in Bobadilla.

WHERE TO SLEEP

UNDER 10,000 PTAS. • Hostal Pedregalejo. This traditional Andalusian-style house on the west side of the river is painted Mediterranean yellow. The interior is almost as festive, with terra-cotta tile floors and wicker furniture. Each room has a full bathroom and a little lounging area. The same family owns the 12-room **Hostal Elcano** (Avda. Juan Sebastián Elcano 103, tel. 952/204303), a few blocks west. Doubles run 7,000–9,000 ptas. *C. Conde de las Navas 9, tel. 952/293218. 10 rooms.*

Hotel Sur. This modern building is several stories tall, giving some rooms nice views of the city from private balconies. Beds are firm, with crisp linens, and the bathrooms have decent-size showers. That said, rooms are dark, and those on the lower floors can be susceptible to street noise. Doubles cost 8,000 ptas. There's parking nearby. *C. Trinidad Grund, 13. 29001. 37 rooms, tel. 952/224803, fax 952/212416.*

Hotel Lis. One of the older tall buildings in the hotel district, Hotel Lis has strict security. The lobby is nothing but simple; rooms are well kept, and some look toward the water (you're a few minutes' walk from the sea). Doubles with full private bath are 7,600 ptas. in high season, less in winter. Parking is free at night when space allows. *C. Córdoba 7, tel. 952/227300, fax 952/227309. Bar. Doubles for 7,600 in high season.*

WHERE TO EAT

UNDER 1,500 PTAS. • El Vegetariano de la Alcazabilla. Even meat lovers will dig this food. Sure, it's on the healthy side, but the chef makes flavors and colors work together in enticing ways. The menú del día is usually the best bet, as it's only 1,000 ptas. If you're used to patties, the veggie burger is a good choice. Desserts are homemade, and there's nothing healthy about them. *C. Pozo del Rey 5 (in front of Cine Albéniz), tel. 952/214858. Closed Sun.*

Mesón Doña Lola. Ah, paella and local wines—they come alive in this little tavern. The outdoor seating is uninspired, set between two tall buildings; the scenery looks down the block to a park and the port. The staff, however, is full of sunshine, and will gladly help you make a selection. The menú del día costs about 1,000 ptas. *C. Trinidad Grund 4, tel. 952/219358.*

Rincón de Mata. This little dining room is usually packed with local families enjoying traditional Spanish cuisine. The fried and grilled seafood options are especially tasty, as are the sautéed pork and beef fillets. Just off Calle Marqués de Larios, this is also a great place to hang at the bar or grab an afternoon snack during a shopping spree. *C. Esperantos 8, tel 952/213135. No lunch Sun.*

WORTH SEEING

ALCAZABA

Just behind (north of) the tourist office on Avenida de Cervantes are the ruins of a Roman theater, currently being excavated. Look up and you'll see a huge fortress overlooking the city from a small hill— Málaga's Moorish **Alcazaba** was built from the 8th to the 11th centuries and is still being restored to its original 8th-century form. Ferdinand and Isabella lived here for a while after they conquered Málaga in 1487. It's a bit of a hike to the top, but you get excellent views of the park and port. There's a small **archeological museum** inside. *C. Alcazabilla, tel. 952/215917. Open Wed.–Mon. 9:30–6 (9:30–8 in summer).*

BOTANICAL GARDENS

The perenially enjoyable **La Concepción** botanical garden was founded in 1850 by the daughter of the British consul—she married a Spanish shipping magnate, and his fleet captains found themselves with instructions to bring back cuttings from every exotic plant they found. Many of these trees stay green throughout the winter, while others turn shades of autumn in Málaga's mild seasons. In summer, the gardens' jungle aspect takes over, offering more shade and cooler air than you'll find in the heat of the city. Point the cabbie or your car toward Granada; just outside Málaga, follow signs to the garden. *Carretera de las Pedrizas, Km 166, tel. 952/252148. Admission: 400 ptas. Open summer Tues.–Sun. 9:30–9, spring Tues.–Sun. 9:30–8, fall–winter, 9:30–7. Admission: adults 400 ptas.*

Another natural escape is the bird park **El Retiro,** filled with exotic species. Some monks started the collection in the 17th century. Note that admission is on the high side. *Carretera de Coin s/n, tel. 952/621600. Admission 1,300 ptas. Open daily 9–6 (9–8 in summer).*

CASA NATAL DE PICASSO / FUNDACIÓN PICASSO

Málaga's most famous native son, Pablo Picasso, was born here in 1881. The house has been remodeled to contain a library and a collection of the artist's lesser-known works, including drawings, prints, and sculptures. *Plaza de Merced 15, tel. 952/215005. Admission free. Open Mon.–Sat. 11–2 and 5–8, Sun. 11–2.*

CASTILLO DE GIBRALFARO

Farther up the Alcazaba's hill is a magnificent 14th-century castle whose name combines the Arabic word *yabal* (mountain) with the Greek word *faruk* (lighthouse)—at one time there was a lighthouse on this hill, warning of pirates and guiding ships into port. The castle is in surprisingly good shape, its unique well dug more than 130 ft deep into solid rock. The view from here is even better than the view from the Alcazaba; just be prepared for a the steep hike. Treat yourself with a cup of coffee in the stately hilltop **parador.** A **visitor center** displays objects recovered from the castle, including several sets of playing cards that kept soldiers busy in the 16th and 17th centuries. *Admission free. Open daily 9:30–6 (9:30–8 in summer).*

CATHEDRAL

The looming cathedral in the center of Málaga was built between the 16th and 18th centuries on the site of a former mosque. You can tell just by gazing up that something is not quite right; indeed, the building was never finished. The cathedral has been nicknamed La Manquita, the One-Armed Lady, for its lack of a second tower. (One story holds that the money allocated was donated to the American Revolution instead.) Still, it's unique, and the interior holds some intricate wood carvings by Pedro de Mena and a nicely restored choir and altar. There's a small **museum** of religious artifacts next door. *C. de Molina Larios, tel. 952/215917. Admission 200 ptas. Open Mon.–Sat 9–6:45.*

MUSEO DE BELLAS ARTES

Málaga's small but worthy Museum of Fine Arts is right behind the tourist office. One of its more interesting works is an 1890 painting by Enrique Simonet y Lombardo in which a doctor dissects a woman and holds her heart in his hand. The abstract works include some sketches and a sculpture by Picasso. *C. Alcazabilla s/n, no phone. Admission free. Open Tues. 3–8, Wed.–Fri. 9–8, weekends 9–3.*

MUSEO DE ARTES Y COSTUMBRES

The Folk Art Museum has two floors of costumes, religious objects, agricultural tools, and pottery. One style of ceramics from the 18th century, called Barros Malagueños (Bars of Málaga), depicts the costumes and traditions of that era. *Pasillo de Santa Isabel 10, tel. 952/217137. Admission 200 ptas. Open weekdays 10–1:30 and 4–7 (4–8 in summer), Sat. 10–1:30. Admission 200 ptas.*

PALACIO EPISCOPAL

For an about-face experience, walk across the street from the cathedral to the avant-garde expressions on display in the Palacio Episcopal. Sponsored by one of Spain's largest banks, the **Fundación La Caixa** holds an impressive collection of modern art from around the world, most notably pieces by Jean Michel Basquiat, Richard Long, Gerardo del Rivero, and Ferran García Sevilla. *Plaza del Obispo s/n, tel. 952/602722. Admission free. Open Tues.–Sun. 10–2 and 6–9.*

SHOPPING

There are plenty of boutiques and artisan shops in the older quarters, especially on **Calle Marqués de Larios.** A few blocks east, **Los Artesanos** (C. Cister 13, tel. 952/604544) sells crafts and artwork from various Andalusian artists, including stained glass, ceramics, iron work, textiles, leather, baskets, carved wood, even flamenco dresses. There's a Western Union office and currency exchange next door (tel. 902/114189). West of the river, two **El Corte Ingles** stores standy ready to replace whatever you forgot to pack (Avda. de Andalucía 4 and 6, tel. 952/300000).

AFTER DARK

Albénez Multicines, next to the Roman ruins, shows foreign and art films (usually some in English) at 10 PM nightly for 400 ptas. a person.

Most of the cool clubs are on or around **Plaza de la Merced.** The **Art Bar Picasso** (Plaza de la Merced 20, tel. 952/226241) cranks out new music and serves beer all day long. You can use one of several computers in the back for a reasonable 400 ptas. an hour. A few doors down is the very dark, very mod bar **Café Calle de Bruselas** (Plaza de la Merced 16), open 9:30 AM to 4 AM most days. Newly opened at Plaza de la Merced 1, **Sobre Las Mesas Las Tazas** (Over the Table the Cups) is a neat café-bar that often spotlights comedians or short films. West of Merced, Calle Granada is filled with pubs and cybercafés. The mild **Café con Libros** (Coffee with Books) is followed by **Pub Irlandes Morrissey's,** then **Rent@ net** (C. Santiago 8; open Mon.–Sat. noon–midnight, Sun. 4–midnight), where computer use costs 300 ptas. an hour.

TORREMOLINOS

Poised just 4 km (3 mi) from Málaga's airport, Torremolinos will not soon lose its status as one of the Costa del Sol's preeminent party towns. The city's name comes from that of the Arabic tower—Torre de Pimintel—sitting next to one of the many local *molinos* (mills). In the 1930s, an influx of English folk moved to a nearby estate belonging to a respected Englishman, George Langworthy; come the 1950s, hotels, apartments, and resorts went up along the beach, and tourists and expats arrived en masse. You can't entirely blame them—the temperature here averages 72°F (22°C), and the skies are sunny more than 325 days a year. Beach activities and nightlife abound, not to mention fresh *pescaíto frito* (little fried fish) at mealtime.

It says something about this place that two of its annual fiestas are June's Día del Pescaíto—think fresh grilled seafood on the beach—and the Día del Turista, honoring our sort each September (when we finally start to get the heck out).

BASICS

The **tourist office** is at Plaza de Blas Infante 1 (tel. 952/379511. The **post office** is on a main drag through town (C. Palma de Mallorca 23, tel. 952/384518).

WHERE TO SLEEP

UNDER 8,000 PTAS. • Hostal Loreto. The name of the street—Calle Peligro—means Dangerous Street, because it's a steep incline down to the beach. Thus this hotel's primo location, which makes it a good choice for beachgoes and barflies. The lobby is simple and Spanish; rooms are small and comfortable. Prices range depending on season and bath arrangements—doubles without bath go down to 3,500 ptas. in winter, while doubles with bath are 7,000 ptas. in high season. Breakfast is served, though it's a bit pricey at 800 ptas. *C. Peligro 9, tel. 952/370841, fax 952/052398. 25 rooms.*

Hostal Micaela. This homey, family-run place is right around the corner from Loreto. Rooms are older, designed in a forgotten era, but they're clean and have bathrooms. Doubles run 4,000–6,600 ptas. a night depending on season. *C. Bajondillo 4, tel. 952/383310, fax 952/376842. 30 rooms.*

The Red Parrot / El Loro Rojo. There's a pubby atmosphere at this British-run restaurant-hostal, right down to the couches in the bar area. The guest rooms, up a rickety flight of stairs, are not exactly new, but, like the staff, they're warm and friendly. Doubles with bath go for 6,000 ptas. *Avda. Los Manatiales 4, one block north of Plaza Costa del Sol, tel. 952/375445. 14 rooms.*

WHERE TO EAT

UNDER 1,500 PTAS. • Vegetariano Espiga. Hiding in the little neighborhood up Avenida Joan Miró is this rare vegetarian find with fine juices and a general Mediterranean flair. Whole-wheat pizza with mushrooms costs a mere 850 ptas.; Thai spring rolls filled with sautéed cabbage and carrots are just 450 ptas. For dessert, try some berry cobbler or plain old fresh fruit. The menú del día averages around 900 ptas. and includes crusty whole-wheat bread. *Avda. Joan Miró 19, tel. 952/052102. No dinner Sun.*

UNDER 2,500 PTAS. • El Molino de la Torre. One of the oldest seafood restaurants in town, the Tower Mill competes with a slew of others down along the beach. Here, fresh fruits of the sea are served in a series of intimate ocean-view dining rooms at reasonable prices (the menú del día is usually 1,700 ptas.). You're a few minutes' walk from the beach—perfect for an evening stroll. Drivers can park next to the police station on Calle Skal/Iglesia, a block north of the restaurant. If you're stuck for lodging, ask about the owners' apartment building with short-term rentals. *End of C. San Miguel (just past church), tel. 952/387756.*

La Escalera. Set next to the steep stairs down to the beach, "The Staircase" specializes in a suspicious mélange of Italian, French, and German cuisine amid Andalusian decor. The food is hearty and upscale, as in entrées like tenderloin seared with asparagus. Tables fill up fast for dinner, so make a reservation or get here reasonably early. *C. Cuesta del Tajo 12, tel. 952/058024. Closed Sun.*

AFTER DARK

Whether or not you've spent the day shopping in the jam-packed area between Plaza Costa del Sol and the beach, wander back inland to Calle Palma de Mallorca at night to check out the clubs and bars. **Columbus Disco Bar** (C. Palma de Mallorca 27, tel. 952/370831) is straight out of the 1970s, with a red carpet and mirrored walls; it happens to be run by a Finnish family, so the bartenders are suitably blonde. They offer a swank tapas menu and stay open daily from noon until 4 AM. Across the street from the post office is **Palladium** (C. Palma de Mallorca 36–38, tel. 952/384289), which will satisfy even the pickiest of clubbers with several dance floors, a swimming pool (for effect, not for dips), five bars, funky lighting, sound effects, a little pizza restaurant, and parking. The cover, usually around 1,000 ptas., buys you a drink or two; students sometimes get better deals. Around the corner to the south is **Eugenios** (C. Casablanca 14, tel. 952/3811310; open 9 PM–6 AM), a little less ritzy but still pretty exotic, with two dance floors, a tropical terrace, several bars, and a music selection lighter on the techno. The music is live some nights. Entrance is usually free, and females drink free on Tuesday and Thursday.

NERJA

Surrounded by spectacular cliffs and quiet beaches, the pretty town of Nerja sits about 52 km (32 mi) east of Málaga. Mineral deposits in some of the nearby caves date settlement of this area back to the Bronze and Neolithic ages. The first actual record of the city comes from the Arabic poet and geographer Ebn Sadí, who repeatedly rhapsodized Nerja's beauty. The name Nerja comes from the Moorish word *narixa* and the Roman word *naricha*, both meaning "abundant in water." High above the sea on a promontory is Nerja's scenic lookout, the **Balcón de Europa**, site of a fortress in the 9th century. Come here to stand safely on a balcony above a bunch of rocks, listening to the waves crash when the tide rolls in. Alas, the scenery just outside the city involves hideous greenhouses and ongoing construction.

Discovered by children in 1959, the **Cuevas de Nerja** (Caves of Nerja) are filled with stalactites and other natural formations created by thousands of years of dripping water. The 200-ft stalactite is the largest such formation known to man. Some chambers are named for their unique shapes ("the organs," etc.); one bears a painting of a fish that dates back to 12,000 BC. The whole is unlike anything you've ever seen, and well-lighted walkways make it easy to explore—just try to get here early, as tour groups and other travelers form long lines. During July's Nerja Caves Festival, ballets and concerts are performed in this eerie setting. There's plenty of free parking; alternatively, a taxi from Nerja usually costs around 700 ptas. *Carretera Maro (west of Nerja on N340), tel. 952/529520. Admission 650 ptas. Open daily 10–2 and 4–6:30.*

BASICS

The **tourist office** is at the entrance to the Balcón de Europa (tel.952/521531; open weekdays 10–2 and 5–8, later in summer, and Sat. 10–1). The map they hand out is unremarkable, though the staff is cordial.

COMING AND GOING

Nerja is easily accessible on the coastal N340 highway. Alsina Graells (tel. 952/521504) has daily **buses** from **Málaga** (1 hr 20 min, 475 ptas.), **Almuñecar** (½ hr, 300 ptas.), and **Almería** (4 hrs, 1,500 ptas.).

THE CANARY ISLANDS

BY MICHAEL DE ZAYAS

eographically African, culturally European, and spiritually Latin American, Las Islas Canarias are full of contradictions, and thus are they often perceived. Strange, rugged landscapes and rare reservoirs of endemic species are contrasted by balmy, fun-in-the-sun playground beaches. Of course, most come here looking for—and find—the latter.

The best thing about the Canaries (okay, it's true) is their climate, warm in winter and tempered by cool Atlantic breezes in summer. You can swim here year-round. The islands' perfect, springlike weather led Spaniards to coin them Las Islas Afortunadas, the Fortunate Isles. Long considered an earthly paradise, the islands were once thought to be the final remains of lost Atlantis.

A volcanic archipelago 1,280 km (800 mi) southwest of mainland Spain and 112 km (70 mi) off the coast of southern Morocco, the Canaries lie at about the same latitude as central Florida. Each of the seven islands has its own character: La Gomera and La Palma, as well as parts of El Hierro and Gran Canaria, are fertile and overgrown with tropical vegetation, while Lanzarote, Fuerteventura, and stretches of Tenerife are dry as a bone, with lava caves and desert sand dunes. The Canaries' steady winds and perfect waves attract sailboarders and surfers from all over the world; surfers claim the best waves in Europe break on the west coast of Lanzarote, and international windsurfing competitions are held each year on Tenerife and Fuerteventura. The Canaries also have Spain's highest peak, Mt. Teide, which, despite all that sunshine, is capped with snow many months of the year.

Like Spain's other island chain, the Balearics, the Canaries have become a place where Europeans of all stripes—especially northern ones cloyed with cold—cut loose. The islands' first modern-day tourists arrived from England at the turn of the 20th century to spend winter at Puerto de la Cruz, Tenerife; today huge charter flights from Düsseldorf, Stockholm, Zürich, Manchester, and dozens of other northern European cities unload 6 million sun-starved visitors a year. Despite Americans' love for mainland Spain, only a handful of travelers to the Canaries are American. Relegated to the rear of most American guidebooks, the islands have been a tough sell in North America, whence there are no direct flights. The reason: the Caribbean. Only Fuerteventura has beaches that can compare to those east of Mexico. But the Canaries offer natural formations, flora, and fauna that you can't see anywhere else in the world; and the hiking, especially on La Gomera, La Palma, and El Hierro, is terrific.

Heavy tourism mixes strangely with the islands' natural beauty. In the southern resorts of Gran Canaria and Tenerife you'll hear more German than Spanish or English. The endless travel agencies, international eateries, car-rental agencies, water parks, and mini–golf courses attest to a virtual foreign annexation. The core congregation, however, huddles around a few unexciting beaches, leaving the Canaries' purest virtues intact for those who want more than a good tan. An excellent system of natural parks and protected zones preserves one-of-a-kind settings for hiking, biking, and beachcombing. If these appeal to you, avoid Tenerife and Gran Canaria, at least initially. Consider a trip to La Gomera, which many consider the most beautiful island in the chain: it's less than an hour from Tenerife via cheap ferry and remains relatively unexplored.

Unfortunately, arriving in the Canary Islands without a flight/lodging package or other advance planning can lead to real hassles, as finding a last-minute stay is very difficult. Lodgings listed below are the best of the few places that deal directly with individual travelers; the rest are booked most of the year through prepaid package tours. Reserve rooms in advance.

BASICS

COMING AND GOING

Fred Olsen (tel. 922/628200) and **Trasmediterránea** (tel. 902/454645) operate inexpensive ferries among all seven islands. Fred Olsen has newer, more comfortable ships and is the only company to offer helpful brochures with schedules and prices. Most interisland trips last between one and four hours; the few boats departing near midnight are equipped with sleeping cabins.

Tenerife sends boats to all six other islands. Boats to the western isles of La Palma, El Hierro, and La Gomera depart the southern port of Los Cristianos; boats to Gran Canaria (which has two main ports: Agaeta, in the northwest, and Las Palmas, in the northeast) leave from the capital, Santa Cruz.

Gran Canaria has ferry service to Tenerife and to Lanzarote and Fuerteventura, which are mutually connected.

GETTING AROUND

Even if it's not your usual mode of transport, consider renting a car on the Canaries, as driving allows you to see their changing landscapes up close, and the price ultimately equals what two people would spend on bus tickets. Rental agencies are ubiquitous, and you should be able to get a small car with insurance (required) for 3,000–4,000 ptas. a day.

FIESTAS

There may be no greater reason to visit the Canary Islands than to experience the incredible fiesta called Carnaval (Carnival), traditionally the last big fling before Lent kicks in. Although Carnival takes place in most large Canarian towns as well as many cities in mainland Spain—and although Brazilians might scoff at the thought—an argument could be made that humankind knows no greater celebration than the annual blowouts at Las Palmas de Gran Canaria and Santa Cruz de Tenerife. Aiming always to outdo each other in style and intensity, these competing island capitals whip themselves up into 10 ferocious days of 'round-the-clock partying.

In essence, Canary *carnavales* are like drunken Halloween nights set to salsa, a music that sets the islands' celebrations apart. Of the half million people on the streets in each of the two capitals, it would be hard to find one person not in costume. If you don't come prepared, buy a mask from a street vendor, and you'll blend right in.

Although Carnival in Las Palmas is promoted as lasting a month, the serious fun begins in sync with Santa Cruz's celebrations, which start the weekend before Ash Wednesday (usually mid-February) and run at full steam through the following Sunday. If you jetfoil between the two, it's quite possible to experience both cities' mayhem in one night. Don't miss Las Palmas' Drag Queen gala or Santa Cruz's hilarious mock "sardine burial" (*entierro de la sardina*), which marks the end of the fiesta. World-famous salsa bands entertain both cities outdoors from 10 PM to 6 AM.

ATLANTIC

La Palma
Caldera de
Taburiente
San Andres y Sauces
Santa Cruz
de la Palma
El Paso
Breña Alta
Tazacorte
Puerto Naos
Fuencaliente
Punta de
Fuencaliente

Tenerife
La Laguna
San
Andrés
Puerto de
la Cruz
Garachico
La
Orotava
Santa Cruz
de Tenerife
Punta de Teno
Icod de los Vinos
La Gomera
Los Gigantes
Mt. Teide
Alojera
Las Rosas
Playa de las Américas
Valle
Gran Rey
San Sebastián
Playa de Santiago
El Abrigo
Parque Nacional
de Garajonay

Gáldar
Agaete
Cruz
de Tejed
Pozo
las Nie
San Bar
de Tiroj

El Hierro
El
Golfo
Valverde
La Restinga

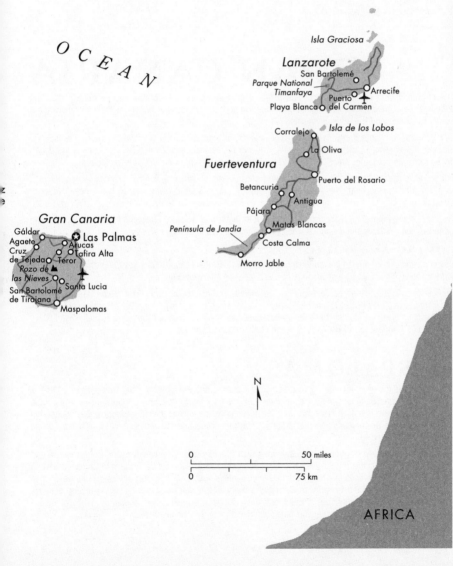

O C E A N

Isla Graciosa

Lanzarote

San Bartolemé

Parque National
Timanfaya

Arrecife

Puerto
del Carmen

Playa Blanca

Corralejo   Isla de los Lobos

La Oliva

Fuerteventura

Puerto del Rosario

Betancuria

Antigua

Pájara

Península de Jandía   Matas Blancas

Costa Calma

Morro Jable

Gran Canaria

Gáldar
Agaete
Cruz
de Tejeda
Pozo de
las Nieves
San Bartolomé
de Tirajana

Las Palmas

Arucas
Tafira Alta

Téror

Santa Lucia

Maspalomas

N

0   50 miles

0   75 km

AFRICA

GRAN CANARIA

The circular island of Gran Canaria has three distinct identities: the capital, Las Palmas (population 370,000), is a thriving business center and shipping port, the white-sand beaches of the south coast are tourist magnets, and the interior is rural.

Las Palmas, the largest city in the Canary Islands, is a multicultural whirlwind, overrun by sailors, tourists, traffic jams, diesel-spewing buses, and hordes of shoppers. One side of the city is lined with docks for huge container ships, while the other harbors the 7-km (4½-mi) Canteras Beach.

The south coast, a boxy 1960s development along wide avenues, is a family resort. At the island's southern tip, the popular Playa del Inglés (roughly, Brits' Beach) gives way to the empty dunes of Maspalomas.

The isle's steep interior highland reaches 6,435 ft at Pico de las Nieves. Though it's green in winter, Gran Canaria does not have the luxurious tropical foliage of the archipelago's western islands.

COMING AND GOING

Gran Canaria's main airport is **Gando** (tel. 928/579094). **Binter** (Alcalde Ramirez de Bethancourt 8, Las Palmas, tel. 928/370877), a subsidiary of Iberia, makes interisland flights.

Ferries from Gran Canaria serve **Tenerife, Lanzarote,** and **Fuerteventura. Fred Olsen** (Luis Morote 4, Las Palmas, tel. 928/495040) reaches Tenerife in under an hour from the northwestern port of Agaete, and supplies free bus service between Agaete and Las Palmas. **Trasmediterránea** (Muelles de León y Castillo, Las Palmas, tel. 928/474439) is the second-largest service.

MASPALOMAS

Maspalomas is the most interesting place on Gran Canaria, but, alas, that doesn't mean it's nice. This is a city—a city of tourists, complete with its own suburbs for tourists. It's easy enough to see why people come here: the sun is hot, the beaches are fine and plenty, the air has a whiff of decadence, the cuisine is varied, and the languages spoken are many. Southern Gran Canaria is an outpost of northern Europe with sunshine mixed in.

Yet there is something terribly, dreadfully wrong with this place. Such a condensation of miniature golf should not exist, and the nightlife is disturbing, almost painful: Avenida de Tirajana, the de facto Main Street, is full of restaurants in which very bad keyboardists sing Neil Diamond in foreign tongues; full of British kids dragging you into restaurants that give them a kickback from your bill; and full of foreigners, segregated by nation, eating the same foods they eat back home. If this is exactly what you need, *Willkommen.* If not, come as an anthropological investigator and be fascinated.

BASICS

CYBERSPACE • On Avenida de Gran Canaria, inside a house beside a furniture store, there's an expensive, nameless **Internet center** (Avda. de Gran Canaria 15, tel. 928/776481) with three computers. It's open daily 9:30–1:30 and 4:30–11 and charges 1,000 ptas. an hour or 20 ptas. a minute.

EMERGENCIES • The clinic **Centro de Salud** (Carretera de Palomita Park, tel. 928/142062) is open 24 hours.

LAUNDRY • To get the sand out, try **Lavacentrum** (Centro Comercial Yumbo Centrum, tel. 928/771382) upstairs in the Yumbo Center. Self-service costs 600 ptas. to wash and 600 ptas. to dry; for a mere 200 ptas. extra, they'll do it for you.

VISITOR INFORMATION • There's a helpful and attractive **tourist office** (Centro Comercial Yumbo Centrum, tel. 928/765332, open weekdays 9–1:30 and 3:30–6) in the Yumbo mall.

GETTING AROUND

Maspalomas is technically split into Playa del Inglés and Maspalomas but only technically; this is one beach area, one state of mind. Generally speaking, Playa del Inglés is older and consists primarily of apartment slabs. The newer, more comfortable bungalow developments are on the west side, in Maspalomas proper. The beach itself has a boardwalk that ends where the Dunes of Maspalomas begin. **Taxis** stop when hailed; if you can't find one, call 928/766767.

BY BUS • Buses cover the island well. On the south side, SALCAI (tel. 902/381110) runs Bus 30 from **Maspalomas** to **Las Palmas** (560 ptas.) every 20 minutes, stopping on the highway in front of the airport. The official airport bus, No. 66, covers the same route every half hour (350 ptas.).

WHERE TO SLEEP

Maspalomas is excessively built-up and continues to grow, even though property near the beach is long gone. Unfortunately, there's still nowhere to stay: everything's prebooked and presold. If you want to vacation here, you need to package a deal in advance with a travel agency. Of course, another solution is to spend each night at La Plaza and the surrounding discos (*see* After Dark, *below*) and simply take off in the morning for some rest on another part of the island.

WHERE TO EAT

However, Maspalomas really isn't Spain, as you'll soon see when you peruse the menus, all of which are printed in English, Spanish, French, German, and Italian.

If you don't know what you feel like, try Chipi-Chipi, on Avenida de Tirajana at the corner of Avenida EE.UU. (United States Avenue), as they have a good variety of international nibbles. Next to Chipi-Chipi is Burger Snack, which is next to Barbados (seafood), which is next to Dallas Chicken and Ribs, which is next to the Oul Triangle Irish Pub, which is next to Dayana Indian Tandoori Restaurant, which is next to La Maison, which is across the street from a handful of Scandinavian places. Farther down Avenida Tirajana you'll find the Hawaiian Bar, La Ligria, Brauhaus, La Paloma, Pancho Villa, Taipei, and Bali. Draw the line at "Benny Hill's Pub–Restaurant–Karaoke–Live Music–Dancing." It's bad for digestion.

This is only one street in Maspalomas, albeit the main one; the same diffusion carpets the city. If Dallas didn't satisfy you, for instance, try the **Harley Rock Diner,** a spin-off on a popular chain mercifully not found here.

UNDER 2,000 PTAS. • **Loopy's Tavern.** A few blocks behind Playa de San Agustín, one of the eastern beaches, Loopy's—an island tradition, dating to 1972—is styled as an American steak house, with friendly waiters, imaginative cocktails, a Western motif, and great meat. Try the shish kebabs, which are served dangling from a hook attached to a wooden serving board. Served with fries and coleslaw, the kebabs cost 1,675 ptas.; a Neapolitan pizza is 810 ptas. *Las Retamas 7, San Agustín Beach, tel. 928/762892.*

WORTH SEEING

The Maspalomas dunes allow you to playact *The English Patient,* groping your way from hill to hill of thirsty sand. Atop a mound, survey the vast sands and hotels stretching far and wide toward mountains of volcanic spew. At sunset the dunes are abandoned: reach beneath the cool surface of sand to feel the day's stored heat, and if you're so inclined, tumble down from the high, soft precipices.

At the end of Avenida de Tirajana, near the beach, is a dunes **information center** and exhibit, run by the island's environmental authority. The question is, how long will this center be here? The dunes can't sur-

Many Canarians have closer blood ties to Cuba and Venezuela than to mainland Spain. The language spoken here is, in both diction and pronunciation, a South American variety of Spanish. (The change most obvious to travelers might be the replacement of the comparatively dull Castilian autobus with guagua, pronounced "wah-wah"). Salsa music—exotic to mainland Spain—is the exclusive music of the islands' wild, pre-Lenten Carnival fiestas.

vive long under the persistent body slam of the frolicking masses. *Hotel Riu Palace lookout point, Avda. de Tirajana, tel. 630/074559. Open Mon.–Sat. 9–1 and 4–9.*

AquaSur. The Canaries' biggest water park has slides, wave pools, and everything else you might expect. *Carretera Palomitas Park, tel. 928/140525. Admission 1,800 ptas. Open daily 10–5.*

At the city tourist office, a German man was overheard asking the receptionist, "Is there anything cultural to do here?"

"Next week," came the answer.

FIESTAS • The Maspalomas **Carnival** takes place within two weeks after the big show at Las Palmas, that is, usually between mid-February and early March.

AFTER DARK

It's weird, very weird. And a little scary. When you arrive in Maspalomas's nightlife districts, you will be descended upon by 1 to 40 people—principally English kids in their twenties or older Moroccan men—offering you drink coupons and enticing you toward certain bars. These people (who call themselves "public relations") work on commission, and the discounts and two-for-one drink specials they offer are real. Most of these people are making an honest living, but others are thieves or drug dealers, so be on guard. If you feel overwhelmed, look around for someone who looks confident, follow him or her into a bar, then slowly familiarize yourself with the scene. Don't linger in indecision.

In the center of town, two *centros comerciales* (CCs)—La Plaza and Kasbah—make up an large, incredible, bizarre center of nightlife. CC Plaza de Maspalomas, called **La Plaza,** consists in essence of a group of downstairs bars, all facing each other. Taking the escalators down into this keyhole-shape, neon-lighted Times Square of the Canaries can be intimidating at first: all the bars look the same, and there's great pressure to choose one quickly. PR people chase you, a great many tables line the entrances (some sit at them, some dance on them), and everyone seems to be looking at you. In one sense it can be easiest to give up and let one of the PR people swoop you into his particular nest. Here's a primer: **Alabama's** plays soul music, **Titanic** plays Latin, and **Scandic, Sunset Blvd, Hippodrome** and **Viking** are indistinguishable.

Upstairs from this orgy are the clubs, where you can dance from midnight to 6 AM: **Pacha,** the legendary Spanish disco chain, **Chic,** which plays hard techno, and, farther along, **Joy.**

Across the street from La Plaza is **Kasbah,** a labyrinthine mall-complex of bars, cheap snack shops, and video arcades. It may be a while before you even discover the mile of loud drinking holes upstairs. **Rock Pub Manhattan** plays Nirvana, **Dady Rock** (sic) plays Bush, and **Turbo Pub** is as "Hard and Heavy" as it advertises. Beyond these are Brazilian music bars and everything else imaginable.

Farther down Avenida Tenerife is an area technically called Centro Comercial (CC) Aguila Roja but known as the **Irish Zone** for its plethora of Irish pubs. Places like **Apilaniitty** and **the Randy Leprechaun** host live sing-alongs.

Yumbo is a large shopping area in the geographical heart of town. At night it's a club zone like Kasbah and La Plaza but with a difference. The names of these clubs—**Buddies, Café Monroe,** and **Bärenhöhle,** to name a few—reveal Yumbo to be openly gay in a way the rest of mainland Spain has never seen. **La Belle** has an open-air drag show.

OUTDOOR ACTIVITIES

Gran Canaria's terrain is ideal for quad (ATC) exploration. **Free Motion** (Hotel Sandy Beach, Avda. de Alfereces Provisionales, tel. 928/777479) offers a variety of quad rental and tour packages starting at 7,900 ptas., as well as hiking and mountain-biking trips. **Canariaventura** (Avda. Francia, in front of CITA complex, tel. 928/766168) guides you through mountain climbing and other, more strenuous outdoor adventures. To scuba dive, contact **Diving Center Nautico** (C. Los Jazmines 2, tel. 928/778168).

The famous **Escuela de Vela de Puerto Rico** sailing school (tel. 928/560772), where Spain's 1984 Olympic gold medalists trained and taught, is in the town of Puerto Rico, about 13 km (8 mi) west of Maspalomas.

LAS PALMAS

There's an indefinable but palpable *something* in the air at Las Palmas, capital of Gran Canaria—a certain rough edge that distinguishes it from its more polite, more compact, slightly more stylish sister, Santa Cruz de Tenerife.

Las Palmas's biggest asset is Playa de las Canteras, the only urban beach in the Canaries that really works. Table after table lines the edge of the sea walk here, looking out over the sands. Made safe for swimming by an artificial reef, the beach can be extremely crowded in summer, but the sand is swept clean every night.

Note the bronze dogs in Las Palmas's old quarter, La Vegueta. The Canaries were named not for yellow songbirds but for a species of dog (canum) found here by ancient explorers. The birds were named after the isles.

BASICS

CONSULATES • **United Kingdom** (Edif. Catalunya, Luís Morote 6, tel. 928/262508). **United States** (Martínez de Escobar 3, tel. 928/222552).

CYBERSPACE • Beneath the Hotel Meliá, on the port side of the narrowest point leading from Playa de las Canteras, **Internet U.S.A.** (Albareda 43, tel. 900/106106, open weekdays 9–9, Sat. 9–2) charges 500 ptas. per hour, 400 ptas. per half hour.

LAUNDRY • **Lavasec** (Joaquín Costa 46, tel. 928/274617) washes and dries a load for 1,050 ptas.

MAIL • The main **post office** (Avda. Primero de Mayo 62, tel. 928/361320) is open weekdays 8:30–2:30 and Saturday 9:30–1.

MEDICAL AID • **Hospital Insular** (Plaza Dr. Pasteur s/n, tel. 928/444000).

VISITOR INFORMATION • The Gran Canaria **tourist office** (tel. 928/264623, open weekdays 9–2) is in a white building in the Parque Santa Catalina.

GETTING AROUND

Las Palmas is strung out for 10 km (6 mi) along a peninsula. Though most of the action centers on the peninsula's northern end, the man-made sights are clustered around the city's southern edge. For a **taxi** call 928/462212.

BY BUS • The **bus station** (tel. 928/368335)—called an *estación de guaguas* in the Canaries—is a 40-minute walk from Playa de las Canteras, across Parque San Telmo. From here, the green SALCAI Buses 5 and 30 (tel. 901/381110) run to Maspalomas (560 ptas.).

WHERE TO SLEEP

If you can get one of the two-person (4,700 ptas.) or three-person (5,500 ptas.) apartments in **Castillo La Playa** (Westerling 18, tel. 928/271112), good luck—you're only a block off the best part of Las Canteras Beach. There are a few old pensions of questionable repute near Canteras; consider staying in the one-star **Hotel Madrid** (tel. 928/360664) for 5,500 ptas. per double or one of a dozen even better establishments for around 8,000 ptas.

Apartamentos Taibe. It may not be new, but it beats the pants off the pensions across the street. Taibe's very large studios, each sleeping two or three, include big sofas and a small kitchen area with a full-size fridge. Two-person studios with bath cost 5,000 ptas. *Luís Morote 42, tel. 928/272312. 25 studios.*

WHERE TO EAT

The long avenue along Playa de las Canteras provides scores of cheap places to eat while basking in the sun and watching the scantily clad frolic. What's missing are some more-elegant restaurants, which might help elevate the aesthetic, which is presently on the tawdry side. One of the few presentable cafés, Bar La Marina, is attached to the Hotel Reina Isabel; its canvas top and potted palms give it a breezy feel.

UNDER 1,000 PTAS. • Buffet Chino País Divino. One block off the beach, this unlimited Chinese buffet proffers soups, rice dishes, meats, vegetables, some seafood, fruit, and eight flavors of ice cream, all for 950 ptas. *Luís Morote 59, tel. 928/223681. Cash only.*

UNDER 3,000 PTAS. • Tapadel. It's easy to fill up at this classic Spanish tapas bar. The various diversions include paella, calamari, and mussels with garlic, and the place stays open until 2 AM. *Plaza de España 5, tel. 928/271640. Cash only.*

WORTH SEEING

CATEDRAL SANTA ANA • Smog-stained St. Anne's Cathedral faces the Plaza Santa Ana. The cathedral took four centuries to complete, so the 19th-century exterior, with its neoclassical Roman columns, contrasts sharply with the Gothic vaulting of the interior. Andalusian-Baroque statues are displayed in the cathedral's **Museo de Arte Sacro,** which is arranged around a peaceful cloister. *Espíritu Santo 20, tel. 928/314989. Admission 300 ptas. Open weekdays 10–2 and 2:45–4:30, Sat. 9–1:30.*

CASA MUSEO COLÓN • The Columbus Museum is housed in a palace where Christopher Columbus may have stayed when he stopped to repair the *Pinta*'s rudder. Nautical instruments, copies of early navigational maps, and models of Columbus's three ships are on display. *C. Colón 1, tel. 928/311255. Admission free. Open Sept.–July, weekdays 9–6, weekends 9–3. Closed Aug.*

CENTRO ATLÁNTICO DE ARTE MODERNO • Opened in 1991, Las Palmas's Center for Modern Art has already earned a name for curating some of the best avant-garde shows in Spain. *Los Balcones 11, tel. 928/311824. Admission free. Open Tues.–Sat. 10–9, Sun. 10–2.*

PUEBLO CANARIO • This model village with typical Canarian architecture is located inside Dorames Park, near the elegant Santa Catalina Hotel and Casino. Regional folk dances are performed here on Thursday (5–7) and Sunday (11:30–1).

AFTER DARK

With the exception of summer, when permanent residents stay in their own bungalows on other parts of the island and the urban evening feels somewhat bare, nightlife begins on the cement **esplanade** near Santa Catalina Park, bordered by Calle Simón Bolivar. Every Friday night crowds line up at the end of this street to buy liquor at the 24-hour store **El Buho**; folks then drink along this park, meeting friends and hanging from about midnight to 2:30 or 3 before hitting the bars. Then, **Parafino** (just off the beach at Calle Nicolas Estevanez) grabs the university crowd. Calle Franchy y Roca is full of people around the dance bars **A+, El Malecón de la Habana, Nova,** and **Abadia.** On Calle Secretario Artiles, **Miau** is a happening, crowded gay bar; **Area** is a big disco. The chief *discotecas* are **Pacha** and **Mogambo,** both on Calle Simón Bolivar. When the weather is warm, people head to the beach after the discos, and the new day dawns.

One of Spain's oldest symphonies, the Orquesta Filarmónica de Gran Canaria, performs between October and May, drawing leading musicians from around the world to its January festival. Buy tix at the orchestra's home, **Teatro Pérez Galdós** (Plaza Mercado, tel. 928/361509).

AGAETE

Leaving Las Palmas by the northern road, you'll pass shantytowns before emerging into the banana plantations of the coastal route. This is the greenest part of Gran Canaria, worth a trip for a seaside lunch in the pleasant village of Agaete.

Agaete is a cluster of white homes set behind an important port. Windmills here harvest the often rough winds. Near the sea, scan the mainland cliff that falls to the water, and you'll notice a cudgel-like rock formation slightly separated from the coast—this is called **El Dedo de Dios** (God's Finger). The ghastly winds have led to unseemly speculation about which finger is being proffered.

WHERE TO EAT

UNDER 1,000 PTAS. • Restaurante El Dedo de Dios. In these two large dining rooms separated by stone arches, scores of long, lazy ferns extend down from the high ceilings to a point just above your head. Views take in the beach and the namesake formation. The hand-painted sign outside adds to the charm; this place is oblivious to how wonderful it really is. Fish and chicken *croquetas* are 500 ptas., as cheap as everything else on the menu. *Puerto de las Nieves, tel. 928/898000.*

THE CENTRAL HIGHLANDS

From Maspalomas take Route GC520 toward Fataga for a nice drive to the center of the island. This is sagebrush country, with interesting rock formations and cacti. A *mirador* (lookout) about 7 km (4 mi) uphill from Maspalomas has views of the coast and mountains.

The area around the village of **Tejeda** is protected as a nature reserve, and you'll find trailheads for hiking everywhere. From Tejeda itself the road begins to ascend through a pine forest dotted with picnic spots to the hotel Parador Cruz de Tejeda. From there continue uphill about 21 km (13 mi) to the **Mirador Pico de las Nieves,** the highest lookout on Gran Canaria—from here you can look out to the surrounding white towns and beyond to the sea. Here, too, is the **Pozo de las Nieves** (Well of the Snows), built by clergymen in 1699 to store snow packed in hay until warmer weather, upon which animals would then carry it down to Las Palmas. Los Pechos (the Breasts) is a military installment, presumably named after its two camouflaged orbs.

From Cruz de Tejeda follow signs to the village of Artenara, roughly 13 km (8 mi) west on the road leading to the parador. The drive gives you great views of the rocky valley and its salient chimneylike formations. You'll see both **Roque Nublo,** the island's most famous natural formation, and **Roque Ventaiga,** which sits like a temple atop a long ridge in the valley. The other mountains seem to bow down in its presence.

The town of **Artenara** itself is unremarkable—except that many of its houses are man-made caves built right into the side of the mountain. You can stay in one, **La Ardeja** (tel. 928/666115), accessed by the main highway into town; it's not too clean, but it's cheap (4,000–5,000 ptas., depending on your bargaining power). Twelve caves nearby—closed to public view, sadly—were used as ritual centers for ancient Canarians. Vulvalike fertility symbols were once found inside.

In town the entrance to the **Mirador de la Silla** takes you through a long mountain tunnel, on the far side of which you can sit in the sun and enjoy a spectacular view—more than worth the trip to Artenara. The lookout area doubles as a restaurant called **Casilli** (tel. 928/666108), where meat dishes run about 1,000 ptas.

LANZAROTE

Lanzarote is mostly solidified lava and dark, disconcerting sand dunes—and the island gets almost no rain—but it's the most user-friendly island in the Canaries. It has made its natural resources available to interlopers in an aesthetically spry, well organized, environmentally friendly way, allowing you a good understanding of Lanzarote's unique natural features in a day or two.

The island was named for the Italian explorer Lancelotto Alocello, who arrived in the 14th century, but Lanzarote may as well be named César Manrique. Born in 1919 in Arrecife, this artist and architect is the unofficial architectural saint of the Canary Islands. Manrique's aesthetic hand is evident throughout Lanzarote, lending the island taste and intelligence: not only did he design most tourist attractions, he convinced the authorities to require that all new buildings be painted white with green trim to suggest coolness and fertility. He also led the fight against overdevelopment, helping to effect a ban on buildings more than four stories high so as to preserve views of the spectacular landscape. Despite its surreal and sometimes intimidating volcanic landscape, Lanzarote has turned itself into an inviting resort through smart planning, with an emphasis on outdoor adventure and conservation of natural beauty. There are

THOSE WERE THE DAYS

Canary Island wine was once prominent on the world stage in more than one sense. Two of Shakespeare's most colorfully named characters joke over a bottle in Twelfth Night *(Act I, Scene 3):*

SIR TOBY BELCH: *O knight, thou lack'st a cup of canary: when did I see thee so put down?*

SIR ANDREW AGUECHEEK: *Never in your life, I think, unless you see canary put me down.*

seven major sights in Lanzarote, designed to set off the island's natural highlights; all except Cueva de los Verdes were designed by César Manrique, who also designed a cute logo for each.

Though still inactive, 100 cones and craters are still present on Lanzarote. Eruptions, which began in 1730 and continued for more than five years in what is now Timanfaya National Park, are among the most important in the history of vulcanology. Though plant and animal life are rare on this barren, largely flat island, lichen paints some of the volcanic hills strange colors. (At the island's northern and southern ends, you'll witness the curious sight of miles of labyrinthine black-stone walls just a few feet high; these are built by farmers to protect pineapple and grape crops from violent winds.) The entire island was declared a UNESCO Biosphere Reserve in 1993, a year after Manrique's death.

COMING AND GOING

Ferries from Fuerteventura pull in at two points: **Arrecife** and **Playa Blanca.** From Arrecife, ferries to **Las Palmas**, Gran Canaria, are run by Trasmediterránea (José Antonio 90, tel. 928/811188) and Naviera Armas (based in Playa Blanca; Muelle Playa Blanca, tel. 928/517912).

From Playa Blanca, **Fred Olsen** (Muelle Playa Blanca, tel. 928/535090) has the only service to **Puerto del Rosario,** Fuerteventura, continuing to Las Palmas, **Gran Canaria.** Naviera Armas also makes the half-hour trip to **Fuerteventura.** Both companies provide free bus service from the ferry to Puerto del Carmen.

There's a small **airport** (tel. 928/823450) in Arrecife, as well as a **Binter** airline office (Avda. Rafael Gonzalez 2, tel. 928/810358).

GETTING AROUND

Outside its capital, Arrecife, the island is divided into three major resort areas: Puerto del Carmen (southeast), Costa Teguise (northeast), and Playa Blanca (south).

Buses cross the island from Arrecife, but you'll spend no more money renting a **car,** and this is by far the best way to explore Lanzarote. There are rental agencies at both ports and in every resort area, and you can usually nab a car without a reservation. Mountain biking has become very popular in the last few years and is actually another practical way to tour the island, as Lanzarote is not particularly hilly.

WHERE TO STAY

It's not easy to find a room in any of the resort areas, as the great majority of lodgings are apartments rented for extended stays. These are very expensive, and generally full, having been reserved through package deals in advance. If you decide you're never going to leave, contact a real-estate office such as **First Choice** (tel. 928/511213) about apartment rentals.

OUTDOOR ACTIVITIES

Some of the best surfing in the world is on Lanzarote's west coast, at Playa de Famara. Take lessons or just rent a board through **La Santa Surf** (928/840279). Diving and windsurfing are available at Costa Teguise (*see below*).

ARRECIFE

Named for its many coral reefs (*arrecife* = reef), Lanzarote's capital is its least-attractive section, but as a major entry point for ferry-borne voyagers, it has the least-expensive accommodation. The local beach isn't bad, either, but Arrecife isn't worth too much time.

Castillo San José and its ocean walk, however, *are* worth your while. This old waterfront fortress was turned into a stunning **Museo de Arte Contemporáneo** (Museum of Contemporary Art) by César Manrique. One of Manrique's paintings is on display along with other 20th-century Spanish works. Go down the space-tunnel staircase for a look at the glass-walled, harbor-view restaurant (*see below*)—here black-and-white furniture, glass walls, and modern art give the remodeled fort an elegant feel. *Avda. de Naos s/n, Arrecife, tel. 928/812321. Admission free. Museum open daily 11–9.*

The bridge behind the tourist office takes you to the squat redoubt **Castillo de San Gabriel,** which houses a museum of archaeology (admission 300 ptas., open Mon.–Sat. 11–6). Returning from the castle, the bridge leads back to Arrecife's main commercial avenue, the pedestrian **Calle Real.** At its southern end, near the beach, is a 13-story monstrosity, a 1970s-era hotel built before the Manrique-influenced height restrictions took effect.

BASICS

The **Hospital General** (tel. 928/801616) is outside the city.

The main **post office** (Avda. Generalísimo Franco 8, tel. 928/800673; open weekdays 8:30–8:30, Sat. 9:30–1) is opposite the tourist office.

The **tourist office** (tel. 928/801517; open Oct.–June, weekdays 9–1 and 4:30–7:30, Sat. 9–1; July–Sept., weekdays 9–1 and 5–7, Sat. 9–noon) is in a black-stone hut in Parque José Ramírez Cerdá, which faces the ocean from Avenida Generalísimo Franco.

GETTING AROUND

From the ferry terminal you must rent a car or take a **taxi** (tel. 928/013023 if none is waiting) into town. The **estación de guaguas** (Vía Medular s/n) is a 25-minute walk from the tourist office on a big avenue skirting town. **Arrecife Bus** (tel. 928/811522) runs the show, with buses to the airport, Playa Blanca (Bus 6, 415 ptas.), Costa Teguise (Bus 1, 160 ptas.), Puerto del Carmen (Bus 2, 200 ptas.), and Playa Honda (Bus 4, 110 ptas.).

WHERE TO SLEEP

Arrecife has the cheapest accommodations on Lanzarote, including a number of pensions; and if you rent a car or bike, the capital's central position makes for easy exploration to the north and south. Besides Cardona (*below*), other budget lodgings include **Hostal San Gines** (Molina 9, tel. 928/812351) and **Pensión España** (Gran Canaria 4, tel. 928/811190).

Hostal Cardona. By far the best budget lodging in Arrecife, this central *hostal* offers hotel quality and a general feeling of sanity. The 4,500-pta. double rooms are large and clean, with new floor tiles. *C. 18 de Julio, tel. 928/811008. 61 rooms. Cash only.*

WHERE TO EAT

Castillo San José. Inside the castle, beneath the art museum, is Arrecife's most stylish restaurant. Well-chosen black tables, chairs, and barstools complement the wooden walls broken by lines of volcanic black rock. Try the cold avocado soup with caviar or the salmon steak wrapped in cured ham. The bar here is open from 11 AM until 1 AM, making it a civilized retreat from noon till night. *C. Puerta de Naos s/n, tel. 928/812321.*

TAHÍCHE

Just outside Tahíche, a 10-minute drive north of Arrecife, the unusual former home of César Manrique has been opened to the public as the **Fundación César Manrique.** Built in 1968 and donated by the artist in 1992, the house is a testament to the power of architecture. A gallery of the artist's abstract, textural paintings, though impressive, raises the question of what (if any) legacy Manrique would have left as solely a painter; by contrast, his home delights with space after intriguing space, and is in many respects the most interesting site on Lanzarote.

Out back, a small pool with a built-in waterfall overlooks the rough remains of a huge, black 1930s lava flow. This contrasts with the whitewashed tunnels that lead past grottoes and terraces to a series of lower-level caves, with palm trees ascending through the roof onto the upper floors. The rooms on the lower level are actual, naturally formed lava bubbles; one resembles a space-age bachelor pad. *Carretera Tahiche–San Bartolome, 2 km (1 mi) west of Tahíche, tel. 928/843138. Admission 1,000 ptas. Open Nov.–June, Mon.–Sat. 10–6, Sun. 10–3; July–Oct., daily 10–7.*

COSTA TEGUISE

Seven kilometers (4 miles) northeast of Arrecife is Costa Teguise, a collection of tasteful green-and-white apartment complexes and a few large hotels. King Juan Carlos owns a villa here, near the Meliá Salinas hotel.

The only place on Lanzarote that's calm enough for windsurfing is Costa Teguise's best beach, Las Cucharas. **Lanzarote Surf Company** (tel. 928/591974) gives lessons and rents boards for 2,500 ptas. an hour or 6,500 ptas. a day. Las Cucharas also has the island's only official diving center, **Diving Lanzarote** (tel. 928/590407), run by a German who rents equipment, leads dives, offers a certification course, and speaks perfect English.

The **Jardín de Cactus** (Cactus Garden), a 10-minute drive north of Costa Teguise between Guatiza and Mala, was Manrique's last project for Lanzarote, opened in 1991. An outdoor amphitheater of volcanic stone, it houses nearly 10,000 cactus plants of more than 1,000 species. Given that cacti can be seen all over the island, however, the appeal here is the aesthetic—you wouldn't expect a collection of spiky protuberances to look so stunning. From the road you can see a windmill overlooking the site, restored by Manrique in 1973; it was once used to grind maize for *gofio,* the island's traditional staple food, a sort of grain hash. Climb inside to inspect the windmill's innards and you get a great view of the garden's layout. *Tel. 928/848020. Admission 500 ptas. Open daily 10–5:45.*

THE NORTH

About 15 km (9 mi) north of Costa Teguise are the **Jameos del Agua** (Water Caverns), opened in 1966 as the island's first Manrique-designed tourist attraction. The *jameos*—an aboriginal, not Spanish, word—are chasms formed when the roof of an underground cave collapsed. You descend long stairs (past an expensive restaurant) to an underground saltwater lagoon, where tiny, blind albino *jameitos* crabs appear as white specks on the rocks and the lagoon floor. These crabs exist nowhere else on earth but in this volcanic tub, and they live on despite the corrosive effects of tossed coins and the persistent mood music piped into the cave. About 40 yards on, you emerge on a second wonderful pool, man-made but similar in aesthetic to the larger one Manrique built in Puerto de la Cruz, Tenerife. Walks along a terrace of rocks and plants lead to the Casa de los Volcanes, a research center. The Jameos host weekend dancing—Manrique called it "the most beautiful nightclub in the world"—in a cool auditorium at the restaurant beneath the rocks. *Tel. 928/848020. Admission 1,000 ptas. days, 1,100 ptas. nights. Open Sun.–Mon. and Wed.–Thurs. 9:30–6:45; Tues. and Fri. –Sat. 9:30–6:45 and 7 PM–3 AM.*

Across the highway from Jameos del Agua, the **Cueva de los Verdes** (Green Caves) is a cave 7 km (4½ mi) long, formed by an incandescent river of lava that erupted more than 4,000 years ago from the Volcán de la Corona in Haría. Locals hid here during 17th-century pirate attacks. Today 1 km of the cave, "embellished" by local artist Jesús Soto in 1964 with lighting and music, is open for guided tours Though it lacks the thrills of water-formed caves, it may be the only cave tour you'll ever experience that has a surprise ending. *Tel. 928/17–3220. Open daily 10–6, last visit at 5 PM.*

Entering the wastelands of Lanzarote's north end, the road to **Mirador del Río** (the River Lookout) passes through Haría and Máguez, valley oasis towns surrounded by palm trees. The green doors and windows of the whitewashed houses, along with old hatted men striking winning poses, may incite you to stop for some photos.

After the stark simplicity of the next town, Yé, the road ends with a view to the tiny islands north of Lanzarote. Designed by Manrique, a glass-and-rock lookout is integrated into the side of a volcano; the huge glassed-in café has attractive mobiles resembling rusted, futuristic versions of the ferns on display throughout the structure's cool, whitewashed, cavernous interior. An outer balcony surveys the river channel that separates the mainland from the Isla Graciosa and the other islands of the Chinijo Archipelago—Montaña Clara, Alegranza, and the Roque del Oeste.

To reach the Isla Graciosa, take the ferry from the nearby town of Orzola. **Lineas Marítimas Romero** (C. García Escámez 11, Orzola, tel. 928/842070) runs the 15-minute ferry, which costs 1,700 ptas. round-trip. Graciosa has only 500 residents and plenty of quiet beaches, and you can sleep here if need and desire be; should you wish to escape the world, try **Enriqueta** (tel. 928/842051), a beachside pension with doubles for 3,000 ptas.

PARQUE NACIONAL TIMANFAYA

Best known as the gateway to the national park, Yaiza is a quiet, whitewashed village with good restaurants. The volcanic Timanfaya National Park, popularly known as Montañas del Fuego (the Fire Mountains), takes up much of southern Lanzarote. As you pass through Yaiza to Uga you'll see the incredible sight of volcanic waste—for 7 km (4 mi), nothing but rocky black spew. Exit this area to an even weirder sight—a caravan of 20 or so camels heading into ruddy-color mountains. A 20-minute bumpy camel ride up nearby hills and back costs 1,500 ptas. per camel. Two people ride on each camel.

The landscape inside Timanfaya is a violent jumble of exploded craters, cinder cones, lava formations, and heat fissures. The park is strictly protected—and you can see it only on a bus tour, which you join after driving past the control gate. Taped commentary in English explains how the parish priest of Yaiza took notes during the 1730 eruption that buried two villages. The restaurant (*see below*) is another curiosity. *Tel. 928/840056. Admission 1,000 ptas. Open daily 9–6; last trip at 5.*

WHERE TO EAT
El Diablo. This must be one of the world's most unusual restaurants—here, in the middle of Timanfaya National Park, chicken, steaks, and spicy sausages are cooked over a volcanic crater using the earth's natural heat. You must pay the 1,000-pta. Fire Mountains tour fee to access the restaurant. *Timanfaya National Park, tel. 928/840057. Open daily noon–3:30.*

PLAYA BLANCA

Playa Blanca is Lanzarote's newest resort. Ferries leave here for Fuerteventura, but there's not much more to the town; tourists come for the exquisite white beaches, reached via hard-packed dirt roads on Punta de Papagayo. The most popular beach is Playa Papagayo, but bring your own picnic, as there's only one bar.

There's a **tourist office** (open weekdays 9–5) inside the ferry terminal. Just up the road is a shopping center with places to rent cars and bikes; **Canauto** (tel. 928/517197) and **UR Rent a Car** (tel. 928/517047) are inexpensive. **España Bike Travel** (tel. 928/518057, closed Sun.) rents mountain bikes for 2,000 ptas. a day, 5,000 ptas. a week.

There's a good **Internet center** (tel. 928/519019) in the deluxe Timanfaya Palace hotel, near Playa Flamingo at the far end of Playa Blanca. While you're here, sneak into the pool. The hotel is wonderful—the graceful sight of its whitewashed Arabic towers backed by the sea and Fuerteventura nearly qualifies it as a tourist attraction. The Internet center is open to the public Monday–Saturday 2:30 PM–10:30 PM and charges 725 ptas. an hour, 450 ptas. for half an hour, and 300 ptas. for 15 minutes.

PUERTO DEL CARMEN

Most beach-bound travelers to Lanzarote head to the sandy strands of Puerto del Carmen. The main beach, **Playa Grande,** is a long strip of yellow sand where you can rent sailboards, Jet Skis, and lounge chairs. The beachfront **tourist office** (Avda. de las Playas, tel. 928/51–3351, open weekdays 10–2 and 6–8) is in a dark volcanic-stone structure; across the street is a 3-km (2-mi) stretch of souvenir shops, car-rental agencies, currency exchanges, and restaurants of every national persuasion, including the fast-food joints you know and love. There's real dining at the little fishing port (*see* Where to Eat, *below*), a 10-minute walk, and just 50 yards uphill from the port is a zone of Irish and British bars, including Victoria Inn, a big nighttime scene for travelers and expats. **Playa de los Pocillos** is slightly north of Puerto del Carmen and the site of most new development; hotels and apartments are restricted, however, to the other side of the highway, leaving the 2-km (1-mi) yellow-sand beach surprisingly pristine. Puerto del Carmen has a **casino** (Avda. de las Playas, Centro Pequeña Europa 12, tel. 928/515000, open nightly 8 PM–5 AM).

WHERE TO SLEEP

Puerto del Carmen's pension **Magec** (Hierro 8, tel. 928/513874) is the only cheap place to stay, but it's *very* cheap, with doubles for 3,700 ptas. a night.

UNDER 10,000 PTAS. / SPLURGE • Lanzarote Sol. If you can afford to treat yourself, the Sol is your cheapest entry to a beachfront Puerto del Carmen resort. The two monster pools, surrounded by palms, are almost worth the price in themselves. Part of one of Spain's best hotel chains, this is a large, quality rest stop with restaurants, shops, currency exchange, bike rentals, and tennis courts; and outside July and August, double rooms here go for about 8,000 ptas., as the hotel happens to lack air-conditioning and king-size beds. In summer you're talking 16,000 ptas. for the same space. *C. Gramma 2, Playa Matagorda, Puerto del Carmen, tel. 928/514888, fax 928/512803. 330 rooms.*

WHERE TO EAT

UNDER 1,000 PTAS. • Freiduría La Lonja. Also at the port, this *freiduría*—purveyor of fried fish—is perfect for smaller appetites. A plate of fish *croquetas* (450 ptas.) allows you to craft perfect sandwiches with the fresh complimentary fresh bread. *Varadero s/n, tel. 928/511377.*

UNDER 3,000 PTAS. • La Casa Roja. La Casa Roja's harborside terrace makes it a travelers' favorite among Puerto del Carmen's side-by-side handful of restaurants, and it is indeed red. The cozy upstairs dining room is decorated with old black-and-white photos of the town and augmented with a dusty wine cellar. Bream baked in salt (1,850 ptas.) is the most popular dish. *Puerto del Carmen, Varadero s/n, tel. 928/596114.*

OUTDOOR ACTIVITIES

Contact **Lanzarote A Caballo** (Carretera Arrecife-Yaiza, Km 17, tel. 928/83–0314) about horseback riding outside Puerto del Carmen. Rent bikes in town at **Renner Bikes** (CC Marítimo 25, 2nd floor, Avda. de las Playas, tel. 629/990775) for 1,500 ptas. a day including lock and helmet.

FUERTEVENTURA

The beaches of Fuerteventura are exponentially better than those of any other Canary Island, yet no one seems to have noticed. Though it's the second-largest hunk of land in the archipelago, Fuerteventura is the least populous, and tourism is relatively new to its population of 20,000.

The Spanish writer and thinker Miguel de Unamuno saw in Fuerteventura's spare, volcanic landscape a virtuous simplicity and noble bluntness. Others might think the blackened fields resemble nothing so much as a construction site. But don't come here for the interior—along the coast are towering sand dunes, blown across the sea from the Sahara (just 96 km [60 mi] away). At times it's not hard to see Fuerteventura as a detached piece of Africa.

The two main resort areas are at the island's far north and south ends. Corralejo, just across the water from Lanzarote, is known for its acres of sand dunes, miles of which are protected and pristine. Endowed with dozens of beaches, including one that's 26 km (16 mi) long, Jandia is experiencing an understandable building craze; but there are miles of virgin coastline left for exploration. You might well do as Unamuno did: "leave roots in the rock."

COMING AND GOING

From Corralejo the ferry ride to Playa Blanca, **Lanzarote,** is quick and cheap (under 2,000 ptas., 35 mins). Contact **Fred Olsen** (Muelle de Corralejo, tel. 928/535090) or **Naviera Armas** (Muelle de Corralejo, tel. 928/867080).

From the port at Puerto del Rosario, **Fred Olsen** (tel. 928/858829) bounces north to Arrecife, **Lanzarote,** and south to Las Palmas, **Gran Canaria. Transmediterránea** (León y Castillo 58, tel. 928/850877) and **Naviera Armas** (tel. 928/851542) head to Las Palmas, **Gran Canaria.**

Fuerteventura's **airport** (tel. 928/860600) is 5 km (3 mi) south of Puerto del Rosario. The interisland airline **Binter** (C. 23 de Mayo 11, tel. 928/852310) has an office in Puerto del Rosario.

WHERE TO SLEEP

As elsewhere on the Canaries, most Fuerteventura hotels do not accept reservations from individual travelers. Many, in fact, deal exclusively with a single tour operator, which may keep them booked solid with German vacationers year-round. We list the few hotels that deal with travelers booking their own trips.

PUERTO DEL ROSARIO

Fuerteventura's capital, Puerto del Rosario (not to be confused with Lanzarote's Puerto del Carmen), has long suffered from an image problem. It used to be called Puerto de Cabra—Goat Port—but the new-and-improved name has not changed the fact that this is a poor city with little of interest to travelers.

BASICS

From the port follow León y Castillo a few blocks and turn left at the largest avenue in town, Calle Constitución. Fuerteventura's **tourist office** (C. Constitución 5, tel. 928/530844, open weekdays 8–2) is on the left. There's no bus station proper, but the main bus stop is in front of the Red Cross, next door to the tourist office. **Tiadhe** buses (tel. 928/852166) can take you about; Bus No. 6 heads to Corralejo every half hour (350 ptas.). To Morro Jable and the south (1,050 ptas.), Bus 10 is direct, Bus 1 is local. For a **taxi** call 928/850059. For medical emergencies call the **Centro de Salud** (tel. 928/531029).

WHERE TO SLEEP

Hostal Tamasite. Rooms here are a little on the dirty side, but they'll do the trick; sad truth is, it's a relief to find something this presentable in town. From the port turn left and walk to the roundabout; Tamasite is a block uphill on the left. Doubles with bath are 5,000 ptas. year-round. *León y Castillo 9, Puerto del Rosario, tel. 928/850280. 18 rooms. Cash only.*

WORTH SEEING

The **Casa Museo Unamuno** retains the bed, desk, and personal effects used by Miguel de Unamuno, Spain's preeminent 20th-century intellectual, during his four-month stay in Fuerteventura during 1924. The museum isn't much, but it solidified the island's place in the annals of Spanish literature. Unamuno came to Puerto de Cabra when a coup d'état cut back on mainland expression, resulting in the 60-year-old's losing his post at the University of Salamanca. During his stay in this building (then the Hotel Fuerteventura) and later in Paris, Unamuno wrote sonnets about the island. In June of that year, seeing the shadow of his own exile in the spare landscape, Unamuno wrote, "*La desnudez, la más noble desnudez, el descarnamiento más bien, es el estilo de esta isla afortunada, en que se gusta toda la hondura del aislamiento. . . . Existe y tiene su estilo, el estilo de la desnudez, el estilo de la sinceridad toda ella. Aquí no hay embustes ni ficción*"—"The bareness, the most noble bareness, emaciation rather, is the style of this fortunate isle, in which all the depths of isolation may be savored . . . It exists and has its own style, a naked style, a sincere style all its own. Here there are no tall tales, no fictions." *C. del Rosario 11, no phone. Open weekdays 9–1 and 5–7, Sat. 10:30–1.*

Examine traditional ovens, furniture, and windmills in the attractive outdoor museum-town of **La Alcogida,** which offers a life-size look at a typical rural island settlement dedicated to the collection of rainwater. Two of the six houses are decked out as homes, and the rest are crafts workshops. Audio guides are available in English. *District of Tefía, 15 km (9 mi) west of Puerto del Carmen, tel. 928/ 175434. Admission 700 ptas. Open Tues.CFri. and Sun. 9:30–5:30.*

CORRALEJO

This small port town 38 km (23 mi) north of Puerto Rosario has a main street (named, wisely enough, Haupstrasse) full of tourist restaurants and some surprisingly charming pedestrian plazas with good seafood. Just out of town, the vast, white sands stretch far and wide, offering incredible bathing, diving, windsurfing, and sandcastle building.

BASICS

The pedestrian areas near the port area make waiting for your ferry pleasant. The **tourist office** (Plaza Grande, tel. 928/866235; open weekdays 9–2 and 4–5, Sat. 9–1) offers a scanty town map and some other bare essentials in a little hut.

Two streets up from Haupstrasse, you'll find all your basic services on the same block: **Mr. Clean** (Juan Sebastián Elcano 11, no phone) will wash and dry your laundry for 1,600 ptas. **Corralejo Bookshop** (JS Elcano 21, tel. 928/535748) has a good selection of used English-language books and will let you trade in your finished novels. The **Internet Saloon** (Falúa 2, tel. 928/535956; open weekdays 9–1 and 6–9, Sat. 9–1:30) lets you log on for 1,000 ptas. an hour, 500 ptas. for half an hour.

Rent a cheap car at **Autos Erika** (Avda. Grandes Playas, tel. 928/866386).

Three companies sell glass-bottom-boat trips to **Lobos Island.** The one with the most frequent daily departures is **El Majorero** (tel. 928/866238), and they sell tickets (1,700 ptas. round trip) at kiosks all around the port.

WHERE TO SLEEP

UNDER 6,000 PTAS. • If Hotel Corralejo doesn't work out, talk to the young, English-speaking staff at **Hostal Manhattan** (Gravina 23, tel. 928/866643).

Hotel Corralejo. Clean, newish rooms are 4,180 ptas., going up to 5,225 ptas. if you want a nice sea view. The entrance is on Calle Delfín, near the attached restaurant. *C. Marina 1, Corralejo, tel. 928/ 535246. 19 rooms. Cash only.*

UNDER 8,000 PTAS. • Corralejo Beach. If you can dispense with a bit more cash in Corralejo—say 7,000–8,000 ptas. for two—try this decent, scaled-down apartment resort with lots of amenities, including a gym, sauna, squash courts, miniature golf, laundry machines, and a restaurant. Most studios face Lanzarote and the Isla de Lobos; all have kitchens and terraces. *Avda. Generalísimo s/n, tel. 928/ 866315, fax. 928/866317. 156 apartments.*

WHERE TO EAT

On Haupstrasse British kids on commission will try to drag you into American Burger and a host of other fast-food joints. Avoid that scene and head a block or two farther to **Plaza Félix Estévez.** Several restaurants jostle for space here, and at night the square is filled with tables, candlelight, and a live band guaranteed to be playing "Guantanamera." The plaza leads to the pedestrian Calle de la Iglesia, which has quieter restaurants, as does the sea walk behind it.

UNDER 2,000 PTAS. • Muelle Chico. The simplest of the restaurants facing the water has a few candlelit tables outdoors and offers quite an affordable and romantic meal. The interior isn't bad either, half stone and half whitewash. The avocado-and-prawn salad (menus in Corralejo come in English, fear not), which comes with a glass of wine, runs 1,175 ptas. *Muelle Chico, Corralejo, tel. 928/535435.*

WORTH SEEING

Playa de Corralejo, about 2 km (1 mi) south of town, is fringed by mountainous sand dunes and faces the Isla de Lobos. The sand stretches from the sea to the feet of volcanoes far inland. Were it not protected as a nature park, this area would surely be the most overdeveloped piece of real estate in the Canaries, but it's pristine and all yours for remote nude sunbathing. Halfway down the beach (it's 9 km/ 6 mi long) is a popular windsurfing spot.

South of Corralejo on the northwest side of the island, **Playa del Aljibe de la Cueva** is overlooked by a castle once used to repel pirates. It's popular with locals.

OUTDOOR ACTIVITIES

The channel between Corralejo and the tiny Isla de Lobos is rich in undersea life and favored by divers as well as sportfishermen. The **Dive Center Corralejo** (C. Nuestra Señora del Pino, tel. 928/535906) is not far from the port. **Puro Nectar** (Juan de Austria 16) is a good local surf shop. **Vulcano Biking** (C. Gravino s/n, tel. 928/535706) rents bikes for a mere 800 ptas. a day.

BETANCURIA

Betancuria, 25 km (15 mi) southwest of Puerto Rosario, was once the capital of Fuerteventura but is now a virtual ghost town, with only 150 residents. Come here for a dose of history.

The weather-worn colonial church of **Santa María de Betancuria** was meant to be the cathedral of the Canary Islands. The **Museo de la Iglesia** (Church Museum) contains a replica of the banner carried by the Norman conqueror Juan de Bethancourt when he seized Fuerteventura in the 15th century. Most of the artwork was salvaged from the nearby convent, now in ruins. The museum is open weekdays 9:30–5 and Saturday 9:30–2; admission is 100 ptas.

The **Museo Arqueológico** (Museum of Archaeology, tel. 928/878241) and a crafts workshop are on the other side of the ravine that cuts through the tiny hamlet.

In **Antigua,** 8 km (5 mi) east, you can visit a restored Don Quixote–style white windmill once used to grind *gofío* (grain hash). The modern metal windmills you see throughout Fuerteventura were imported from the United States and are used to pump water.

WHERE TO EAT
UNDER 2,000PTAS. • El Molino de Antigua. Pull off the highway at the island's trademark white windmill for the most memorable restaurant on Fuerteventura: here you can dine in the shade of the Antigua windmill or in one of two tasteful dining rooms in the structure itself. The food and service are top-notch, and the prices are low. *Carretera de Antigua, Km 20, tel. 928/878220.*

PÁJARA

Pájara, on the booming southern peninsula of Jandia, is home to Fuerteventura's finest beaches. Finals in the Windsurfing World Championships are held along the eastern shores here.

Fuerteventura was once divided into two kingdoms, and a wall was built across the Jandia Peninsula to mark the border. Remnants of that wall are still visible today inland from **Matas Blancas** (White Groves), 42 km (26 mi) south of Pájara on Highway GC640. As you move south along the coast, the beaches get longer, the sand gets whiter, and the water gets bluer. The famous **Playas de Sotavento** begin near the Costa Calma developments and extend gloriously south for 26 km (16 mi). Nude sunning is favored here, except directly in front of hotels.

For windsurfing lessons and board rentals try **Fun Center** (tel. 928/535999) on the Playas de Sotavento.

WHERE TO SLEEP
UNDER 8,000 PTAS. • Apartamentos Caleta del Sol. If you've come to be alone with the white beaches of the southern peninsula, this is your place—there's nothing else around for miles. The best beaches in the Canary Islands stretch out in both directions, and you can have as much privacy as you'd like. A budget family resort, Caleta del Sol is loaded with facilities, including a sauna, Jacuzzi, gym, disco, bar, minimart, and game room. The cheerful two- to four-person apartments, in yellow villas (7,500 ptas. for 2 people Apr.–Sept.; 6,500 ptas. Oct.–Mar.), come with kitchen and living room. *Barranco del Mal Nombre (Tierra Dorada), Pájara, tel. 928/163034, fax 928/549500. 104 apartments.*

WHERE TO EAT
Don Quijote. One of the few Pájara/Costa Calma restaurants outside a hotel, Don Quijote does its best to bring Old Castile to the beach. Shields bearing coats of arms hang between wooden beams, near a suit of armor that would have been too fancy for Quijote himself. Though the food is mainly Castilian, you mustn't leave without a taste of the famous island cheese, *queso de majorero.* Helpful pointer: if you order a large Coke here, you get a large Coke. *Jandia Beach Center 39, Costa Calma, no phone.*

MORRO JABLE

At the very southern tip of Fuerteventura is the old fishing port of Morro Jable. Beyond the town, a dirt roads lead isolated beaches. In fact, beaches along the peninsula's entire windward side remain blissfully untouched.

Inside the CC Shopping Center on Morro Jable's main road (the other malls in town are just called CCs, or "centro comerciales") there's a small **tourist office** (Av. El Saladar s/n, tel. 928/540776, open weekdays 9–1), as well as a kiosk outside. Also in the shopping center is the **Internet Café** (tel. 928/545096, open daily 10–10), which charges the asinine rates of 2,500 ptas. an hour, 1,500 ptas. a half hour. If you must send e-mail, you better have something to say. . . .

WHERE TO SLEEP

Pensión Maxorata. These digs are basic but clean, with tile floors—and they take credit cards, unusual when you're only paying 4,000 ptas. for a double, regardless of season. *C. Maxorata 31, Morro Jable, tel. 928/541087. 8 rooms, 4 with bath.*

EL HIERRO

The smallest and westernmost Canary island, El Hierro is strictly for those who want nature and solitude. There are no great beaches here, and most residents live in mountain villages that to their credit have little in common with the other islands' tropical coast towns. The few travelers who find their way to El Hierro come for the hiking, scuba diving, or relaxing. Once poised at the edge of the Old World map, El Hierro still feels like a forgotten outpost.

COMING AND GOING

Little **Aeropuerto de los Cangrejos** (tel. 922/553700) is 10 km (6 mi) east of the capital, Valverde. **Iberia** has an office here, at the same phone number.

The ferry *Barlavento,* run by **Fred Olsen** (Puerto de la Estaca, tel. 922/551424), connects at San Sebastián, **La Gomera,** and continues to Los Cristianos, **Tenerife. Transmediterránea** (Puerto de la Estaca, tel. 922/550129) shuttles between **El Hierro** and **Los Cristianos.**

VALVERDE

El Hierro's capital sits on a hillside at 2,000 ft. To protect it from pirate raids, the town was built inland in the clouds, and its cobblestone streets always seem to be wet with mist. The church's balconied bell tower was once used to watch the horizon for pirates.

La Sanjora (Av. Dacio Darias s/n, Valverde, tel. 922/551840) organizes diving, hiking, spelunking, hang gliding, mountain biking, and deep-sea fishing trips all around the island.

BASICS

The island's **tourist office** (Doctor Quintero Magdaleno 6, tel. 922/550302) is open weekdays 8:30–2:30 and Saturday 9–1.

WHERE TO SLEEP

If you really need some peace, the **Bungalows Los Roques de Salmor,** on the coast directly west of Valverde, offer five quiet units and a pool 5 km (3 mi) from the town of Tigaday.

Boomerang. Owned by a local islander who once worked in Australia, the Boomerang is right in the middle of town. Rooms for 6,000 ptas. are clean and comfortable, with country pine furniture and tile baths. There's a restaurant and bar. *Dr. Gost 1, Valverde, tel. 922/550200, fax 922/550253. 17 rooms.*

WHERE TO EAT

UNDER 3,000 PTAS. • Mirador de la Peña. One of architect César Manrique's final works (*see* Lanzarote, *above*), the Mirador is El Hierro's most elegant dining spot. In typical fashion, Manrique designed this stone-and-glass restaurant—albeit with an offbeat triangular pavilion—in harmony with its surroundings. The unobstructed panoramic view down to the bay is astounding, and you're welcome to visit the terrace even if you're not hungry. Such a commanding location is kept reasonable by the government-supported restaurant school here, which also keeps the prices low and the service and food exquisite. Note the serpent-dragon in the restaurant's logo, also designed by Manrique. *Carretera de Guarazoca 40, tel. 922/550300.*

WORTH SEEING

Driving around El Hierro, you'll pass terraced farms still plowed with mules. The **Mirador de la Peña,** 8 km (5 mi) west of Valverde at 2,200 ft, offers a spectacular view of El Golfo (the Bay), which juts into the island's northeastern corner.

Edged in rock, El Golfo was formed by what looks like a half-submerged volcanic crater. The part above water is a fertile, steep-sided valley; at the far end is a health spa with salty medicinal waters, called **Pozo de la Salud.** Those who prefer tastier medicine can visit the island's **winery,** housed the big, beige building near the town of Frontera.

The picnic area **Hoya del Morcillo** is in the fragrant pine forest that covers the center of El Hierro. It has barbecue pits, rest rooms, a playground, and campsites, and makes a good starting point for woodsy hikes.

LA RESTINGA

La Restinga is a small, rather ugly fishing port surrounded by lava fields, 54 km (33 mi) south of Valverde at the southern tip of El Hierro. Travelers who come here tend to be scuba fanatics, as some say the diving off this shore is the best in the Canaries.

The best diving center here is **El Meridiano** (Avda. Marítima, La Restinga, tel. 922/557076).

WHERE TO SLEEP

UNDER 6,000 PTAS. • Apartamentos La Marina. These basic but clean two-person apartments occupy a brand-new three-story building on La Restinga harbor, meters from a black-sand beach. All units have kitchens and, better still, balconies with unbeatable sunset views. The price holds steady at 5,000 ptas. year-round. *Avda. Marítima 10, La Restinga, tel. 922/559016, fax 922/559016. 8 apartments. Cash only.*

UNDER 8,000 PTAS. • Punta Grande. Built on an old dock extending into the sea, the four-room Punta Grande is listed in the *Guinness Book of Records* as the world's smallest hotel. It has personality; rooms have exposed stone walls and nautical decor, with erstwhile porthole windows as nightstands. An old diving suit and ships' lanterns hang in the dining room, which serves piping-hot shellfish soups and stews with home-style hunks of bread and goat cheese. Call at least a month ahead, as this little lodging is one of El Hierro's musts. *Las Puntas, Frontera (45 mins from La Restiga), tel./fax 922/559081. 4 rooms. Cash only.*

Pliny called El Hierro Lagartaria— Land of the Lizard—in reference to the giant creatures spotted here in Roman times. A few still pad around the Roques de Salmor, a cluster of rocks off the northwest coast.

WHERE TO EAT

UNDER 2,000 PTAS. • Casa Juan. These two plain dining rooms have large tables to accommodate families, who come to Restinga from all over the island for Casa Juan's delicious seafood soup. The *mojo* sauces (made of lime or orange juice and garlic) served with *papas arrugadas* (literally, "wrinkled potatoes," boiled in seawater) are also outstanding. *Juan Gutierrez Monteverde 23, La Restinga, tel. 922/557102.*

LA PALMA

It's hard not to like an island named the Palm. Even Madonna saw fit to sing the praises of this particular *isla bonita*. Green and prosperous, La Palma managed quite successfully without tourism; now that it's been "discovered," the island is handling its guests with good taste by emphasizing its natural beauty, traditional crafts, and cuisine. The residents, called Palmeros, are especially friendly, and their close links with Cuba (many residents are Cuban, and many Cubans are from La Palma) are evident in La Palma's quality hand-rolled cigars.

Hiking is excellent in the green steeps of Parque Nacional de La Caldera de Taburiente, in the middle of the island. West of the park, banana trees stretch to the edge of the ocean.

COMING AND GOING

The airport at **Santa Cruz** (tel. 922/426100) is 6 km (4 mi) south of the capital. For flights to other islands call Iberia's subsidiary **Binter** (tel. 922/411345).

Fred Olsen (Muelle Santa Cruz, tel. 922/417495) runs a five-hour ferry daily to Los Cristianos, **Tenerife,** and nightly to Valverde, **El Hierro. Transmediterránea** (Avda. Perez de Brito 2, Santa Cruz, tel. 922/411121) runs to Los Cristianos, **Tenerife,** Sunday–Friday and to Santa Cruz, **Tenerife,** on Friday.

Buses are run by **Transporte Insular** (tel. 922/411924), but service is infrequent on weekends. Four or five hundred pesetas will get you anywhere on the island. Schedules are posted at the main bus stop, in front of the Santa Cruz post office.

SANTA CRUZ DE LA PALMA

Finally, a port capital that will bring a smile to your face. In two to three hours you can see everything in this town and actually develop a love for the place.

In naming Santa Cruz (Holy Cross), the town's insidious founders seem to have aimed for maximum confusion: Santa Cruz is also the capital of Tenerife, and Las Palmas is the capital of Gran Canaria. As yet, no cute mnemonic aids in memorizing this mess. Care to dream one up?

This particular Santa Cruz was a major port and bustling shipbuilding center in the early 16th century. Then, in 1533, a band of buccaneers led by French pirate François le Clerc raided the city and burned it to the ground. La Palma was rebuilt with money from the Spanish king, which is why it is now so cutely coherent.

The cobblestoned main street, **Calle O'Daly,** is generally called Calle Real. Peek inside the elegant patio of the early 17th-century Palacio Salazar, which also contains the **tourist office** (C. O'Daly 22, tel. 922/412106; open weekdays 9–1 and 5–7, Sat. 10:30–1). Pick up some of the free glossy booklets on La Palma's lodgings, gastronomy, sports, hiking, history, crafts, and fiestas.

WHERE TO SLEEP
Getting a cheap room in La Palma is probably easier than on any other Canary Island; still, you should always call ahead.

UNDER 5,000 PTAS. • Pensión La Cubana. Young British owners David and Ruth make you feel welcome in this old colonial house, which brings out the best in the qualifier "simple." The wood that predominates is thought to be 200-year-old Canary pine, and random pine cones provide an occasional accent. Interestingly, the rooms, which cost 4,000 ptas. year-round, do not have doors; a curtain gives you privacy from the hall. Bathrooms are shared; each room has only a sink. The balcony of the huge salon overlooks Santa Cruz's cobblestoned main street, the most charming spot in town. *C. O'Daly 24, tel. 922/411354. 6 rooms. Cash only.*

UNDER 8,000 PTAS. • Apartamentos La Fuente. Run by English-speaking owners Rupert, Thomas, and Mona, these apartments are slightly more expensive than those at a pension (4,700 ptas. interior, 5,600 ptas. exterior, 7,750 ptas. larger rooms with sea views), but they have kitchenettes and private bathrooms. There's also a rooftop terrace. *Pérez de Brito 49, Santa Cruz, tel./fax 922/415636. 9 apartments. Cash only.*

WHERE TO EAT
UNDER 2,000 PTAS. • Chipi Chipi. The very existence of this restaurant, tucked away behind dense tropical gardens in the hills above Santa Cruz, affirms humankind's capacity for inspired weirdness. Each party is seated in a private stone hut with a sunroof, and each hut is numbered, giving the general impression of an apartment complex for cavemen. The *menú del día* (1,200 ptas.) combines salad or garbanzo-bean soup, grilled meats, and local red wine. To get here, head northwest of Santa Cruz and continue about 3 km (2 mi) past the church in Las Nieves. Don't be fooled by the ordinary parking lot in front; out back, empty bottles hang from the trees like Spanish question marks. *Carretera de las Nieves 42, tel. 922/411024. Closed Wed. and Sun.*

Los Braseros. From Santa Cruz, follow signs to the Observatorio and you'll go up, up, up to the top of the capital, where an outdoor dining terrace offers wonderful views of the town and sea. The friendly and funny staff serves grilled steaks, pork, and hearty Canarian soups, and all dishes cost less than 2,000 ptas. *Candelaria Mirca, Carretera del Roque 54, Los Alamos, tel. 922/414360. Closed Tues.*

UNDER 3,000 PTAS. • Antica Trattoria. La Palma's best Italian restaurant is in one of its best-known houses. The red-on-yellow balcony stands out even amid the colors of its neighbors on this old seaside row in Santa Cruz's Avenida Marítima (you can enter from Calle O'Daly as well). Sea-view seating choices include a two-table interior and an open-air cobblestone patio. Among the fresh pastas, try *gnocchi alla Sorrentina* (gnocchi in red sauce with mozzarella cheese). *Avda. Maritima 42, Santa Cruz, tel. 922/417116.*

UNDER 3,000 PTAS. • Las Tres Chimineas. An outgoing Palmero and his English wife run this attractive black-stone restaurant in Breña Alta, 6 km (4 mi) west of Santa Cruz. Three decorative chimneys give the building its name; inside are fresh flowers and bright, cheery colors. Local fish are the specialty; *vieja* is the best. You'll have to work a little to keep things under 3,000 ptas. a head, as many consider this the island's best restaurant. *Carretera de Los Llanos de Aridane, Km 8, tel. 922/429470. Closed Tues.*

WORTH SEEING

The triangular **Plaza de España,** in front of the church of El Salvador, is the focus of La Palma's social life and fills with people in the early evening. The church is the only building that survived the pirate fire; it has a handsome Moorish ceiling. Across the street are the four arches of the *ayuntamiento* (city hall).

In nearby Plaza de San Francisco, step inside the church of **San Francisco,** built in 1508 as a Franciscan monastery. It opens within to a wide plaza formed by two large cloisters from the 16th and 18th centuries; here the **Museo Insular** (roughly, Island Museum) traces the navigational and trading history of La Palma and displays Guanche remains. The **Museo de Bellas Artes** (Museum of Fine Arts), upstairs, has a good collection of 19th-century Spanish paintings. *Plaza de San Francisco 3, tel. 922/420558. Admission 300 ptas. Open Oct.–June, weekdays 9:30–1:50 and 4–6:30; July–Sept., weekdays 9–2.*

You can't miss the life-size cement model of Columbus's **Santa María** at the end of Plaza de la Alameda. No, Columbus was never here (that was La Gomera), but the ship is used for a fireworks ritual in a local fiesta. Climb up to the deck for a look at some old maps. *tel. 922/416550. Admission 150 ptas. Open Oct.–June, Mon.–Thurs. 9:30–2 and 4–7, Fri. 9:30–2; July-Sept., Mon.–Thurs. 9:30–2, Fri. 9:30–2.*

The star-shape **Castillo Real** (Royal Castle), on Calle Mendez Cabezola, is a 16th-century fortress. Along nearby **Avenida Marítima,** which faces a splashy seawall, a row of colorful Canarian houses displays typical elements of Portuguese-influenced island architecture: double balconies and shielded posts looking to the sea, evidence of a seafaring vocation. The balconies are actually the backs of the houses; they front Calle Pérez de Brito, a continuation of O'Daly.

Stop into **Tabacos Vargas** (Avda. Marítima 55, tel. 922/412182) to sniff some *palmero* cigars—many with a taste for these items claim that hand-rolled palmeros are better than today's *cubanos.* Follow the nearest street, Balthasar Martín, uphill to No. 83 to see a factory where they're rolled by hand; on the way you'll pass charming single-floor homes with red, green, brown, and blue windows and doors. When you reach the top of the hill, where the factory is, look a few blocks to the right to see cave homes built into a hill.

As nice as Santa Cruz can be, leaving it is even better: you're plunged immediately into thick, green vegetation. The hilltop village of **Las Nieves** (the Snows), 3 km (2 mi) northwest of Santa Cruz, has a beautifully preserved colonial plaza and the opulent **Basilica de Nuestra Señora de las Nieves,** which houses La Palma's patron saint, the Virgin of the Snows. Credited with saving many a ship from disaster, the Virgin sits on a silver altar wearing vestments studded with pearls and emeralds. Chandeliers hang from a carved-wood ceiling.

Don't despair if things get foggy in these hills. Past Las Nieves, a tunnel passes through a mountain and emerges into fabulous sunshine en route to the Taburiente Crater National Park; such are the vicissitudes of La Palma's microclimate.

OUTDOOR ACTIVITIES

The Santa Cruz tourist office and **La Palma Trekking** (San Antonio 92, Breña Baja, tel./fax 922/434540) can advise you on rock climbing and rappelling.

Club Ciclista La Palma (San Antonio 88, Breña Baja, tel./fax 922/434309) has the scoop on mountain biking, which is very popular here.

The newly formed volcanic coast of Fuencaliente is best for scuba diving. Contact **Club La Palma Sub** (Barranco del Carmen 9, Santa Cruz, tel. 922/420355).

PARQUE NACIONAL DE LA CALDERA DE TABURIENTE

The striking Taburiente Crater National Park forms a kind of island in the center of La Palma. The **visitor center** (Carretera General, Km 24, El Paso, tel. 922/497277; open Mon.–Sat. 10–2 and 3–6, Sun. 10–2) is 3 km (2 mi) east of El Paso. Immediately after the visitor center, turn right and drive steeply uphill—mountain bikers zoom fearlessly down and painstakingly up—through thick pine forest. Canarian pine trees are especially adapted to fire and volcanic eruptions, taking only four years to regenerate themselves.

At an altitude of 565 ft, the road ends at the **Mirador Cumbrecita,** a lookout with a wide view of what appears to be—though is not—a huge crater. Modern geologists think the faux crater was formed by a series of small eruptions that pulled the center of the mountain apart. Pine forests edge large escarpments, with small brooks inviting you to take to the trails. A small information center delineates hiking routes; if you obtain a camping permit at the park's main visitor center, then take one of these paths, you can camp on the valley floor. It's often raining or snowing up here, and bright rainbows span the canyon. This is where La Palma's beauty essentially begins.

The white dome and tower across the crater make up the **Observatorio Roque de los Muchachos,** home of Europe's largest telescope. Astronomers say the Canary Islands' peaks have some of the cleanest air and darkest skies in the world.

TAZACORTE

The west side of La Palma is dedicated to banana cultivation, with the result that the coast looks like a conceptual art piece by Cristo—huge tracts of land covered by gray tarp. The trees embody the nourishing power of the sun, asserting themselves over the cheap cement walls that line the roads all the way to the edge of the sea. Drive down through these bursting plantations to **Tazacorte,** the old Guanche capital, or explore **Puerto Naos,** 5 km (3 mi) south, where a sunny black-sand bay created by a 1947 volcanic eruption is now a resort, home to the island's biggest beach.

WHERE TO EAT

The **Puerto de Tazacorte** is a great place for tapas and seafood meals. A run of restaurants, including **Kiosco Teneguia** and **Montecarlo,** front a small black-sand beach with full 1,300-pta. set menus. At the bright yellow **Taberna del Puerto** you can get *media raciones* (small servings) of *gambas al ajillo* (shrimp in garlic sauce), *pulpo a la vinagreta* (octopus vinaigrette), and *chipirones rellenos con queso* (cheese-stuffed cuttlefish) for 300–500 ptas. or *sardinas fritas* (fried sardines) for 900 ptas.

UNDER 3,000 PTAS. • Restaurant Playa Mont. Looking like an upscale beach shack, open on one side to the ocean breezes, the Playa Mont serves some of the best seafood in the Canaries. The secret is in the sauces: traditional *mojos* and a delicious lemon butter. *Puerto de Tazacorte, tel. 922/480443. Closed Thurs.*

OUTDOOR ACTIVITIES

Contact **Club Atlantic 28** (C. del Puerto 10, Puerto del Tazacorte, tel. 922/480911) for diving lessons and equipment rentals. The **Palma Club** (C. Mauricio Duque Camacho 21, Puerto Naos, tel. 922/408172) specializes in paragliding.

LOS LLANOS DE ARIDANE

A few kilometers west of El Paso is **Los Llanos de Aridane,** the island's second-largest town, with nearly 20,000 residents. La Palma's only Internet center, **Ciber,** is here (González del Yerro 1, tel. 922/402361; open Mon.–Thurs. 10–2 and 5–10, Fri.–Sat. 10–2 and 5–midnight), charging 500 ptas. per hour, 250 ptas. per half hour. The **bus station** is on Calle Luis Felipe Gómez.

WHERE TO SLEEP

UNDER 5,000 PTAS. • Pensión Time. On the lively central church square of the town of Los Llanos de Aridane, this is a clean and reliable option for 4,200 ptas. if you're not too picky about sharing a bath.

Ferns pour out over the nice interior courtyard, and wooden floors contribute to the old-Canary-house experience. *Iglesia 3, Los Llanos, tel. 922/460907. 10 rooms. Cash only.*

OUTDOOR ACTIVITIES
For horseback riding contact either of two El Paso outfits: **Cuadra Isla Bonita** (Tacande La Hoya 153, tel. 922/497468) or **Hípico Manivasán** (Camino Cantadores, Los Barros, tel. 922/401265).

FUENCALIENTE

Near Fuencaliente, 28 km (17 mi) south of Santa Cruz, the scenery grows dry as you reach La Palma's volcanic southern tip. Visit the **San Antonio** and **Teneguía volcanoes,** site of the Canaries' most recent eruption: in 1971 Teneguía burst open, sending rivers of lava toward the sea and extending the length of the island by 3 km (2 mi). There are good beaches in the cinders below the volcano, accessible via unpaved roads.

Fuencaliente is the heart of La Palma's wine region. Without paying a peseta, you can visit the modern **Llanovid winery** (C. Los Canarios 8, tel. 922/444078), makers of the islands' most famous label, *Teneguia,* on weekdays 9–2 and 3–6, weekends 10–3.

WHERE TO SLEEP
Should the south draw you, there are three cheap (doubles for less than 5,000 ptas.) stays in Fuencaliente: **Pensión Los Volcanes** (Carretera del Sur 86, tel. 922/444164, fax 922/444062), **Pensión Fuencaliente** (Carretera del Sur s/n, tel. 922/444153), and modern **Pensión Central** (C. Yaiza 4, tel. 922/444018).

WHERE TO EAT
Restaurant Tamanca. A sign on the highway marks the entrance to this restaurant-in-a-cave, 16 km (10 mi) north of Fuencaliente. Inside, traditional meats and fishes are prepared with an island flair. *Carretera General s/n, Montaña Tamanca, Las Manchas, tel. 922/462155.*

OUTDOOR ACTIVITIES
La Palma is considered the highest island in the world in relation to its small area. The resulting wind streams make paragliding an especially attractive thrill. Contact **Parapente Palmasur** (C. La Cruz 2, Barrio de los Quemados, Fuencaliente, tel. 922/444303).

LA GOMERA

This round island looks over its shoulder at the looming Tenerife peak of El Teide, but it is not afraid. Many find La Gomera the most beautiful Canary, for while it's true there are no white-sand beaches, this lack keeps the hordes of package tourists at bay. La Gomera does attract serious, denim-clad backpackers. The mossy, fern-filled central peaks of Garajonay National Park include a rare forest of fragrant laurel trees that's protected as a World Heritage Site, as it preserves tertiary flora that the Ice Age wiped out everywhere else in the world.

The park's mountains fan out into six steep-sided valleys called *barrancos.* Villages in the barrancos are dedicated mainly to small-scale banana growing, and each morning you'll see three or four stalks of bananas awaiting pickup outside each house. The serpentine roads leading in and out of the valleys have so many switchbacks that travel is slow; villages remain isolated. Allow plenty of time—two days if possible—for a drive around La Gomera, as distances are short but take a long time to cover. The roads are not for those afraid of heights.

The best of this sun-blessed island is summed up in the voluptuous name *Beatriz de Bobadillo,* a beautiful, black-haired widow with whom Columbus reportedly had an affair when he stopped at La Gomera to resupply his ships with water. The explorer was apparently in no hurry to get back to the ship and rejoin the boys in their quest west toward India. Even today travelers are surprised by La Gomera's unexpected charms and loathe to return to the world's pressing claims.

COMING AND GOING

Darting off to La Gomera from southern Tenerife is a breeze—any ferry gets you here in less than an hour. **Fred Olsen** (Estación Marítima del Puerto, San Sebastián, tel. 922/871007) runs a state-of-the-art hydrofoil between La Gomera and Los Cristianos, **Tenerife,** as well as ferries to Valverde, **El Hierro. Transmediterránea** (Estación Marítima del Puerto, San Sebastián, tel. 922/871324) also serves Los Cristianos, **Tenerife.**

Aqua-color buses run by Servicio Regular Gomera (tel. 922/873000) depart from the port in **San Sebastián,** with fares no more than 700 ptas. Bus 1 heads west to **Valle Gran Rey** (1 hr) with a popular hiking stop at **Las Paredes;** Bus 2 heads south to **Playa de Santiago** and **Alajero** (45 mins); and Bus 3 goes north to **Hermigua, Agula,** and **Vallehermosa** (45 mins).

Also at the port are two car-rental agencies, including **Rent A Car Piñiero** (tel. 922/141048).

SAN SEBASTIÁN

This busy little port of sailboats and fast ferries is a good place to sleep, but enthusiasm for La Gomera is guaranteed to pick up when you leave town. San Sebastián once had three streets, the middle of which was creatively named Calle Real, and you can find everything you need here. The **tourist office** (C. Real 4, tel. 922/141512; open Mon.–Sat. 9–1:30 and 3:30–6, Sun. 10–1) has great hiking maps. If you get lost, know that the complex housing the tourist office is called the **Casa de la Aguada.**

RP-Shop (C. Real 48, tel. 922/872016) has a wired computer for 18 ptas. a minute or 750 ptas. an hour. The end of Calle Real opens to a relaxed square, **Plaza Constitución,** with bars and cafés leading down to the port.

La Gomera's scraggly capital makes the most of its historical links with Christopher Columbus, for here he made his last charted stop before falling momentarily off the edge of the earth. The **Pozo de la Aguada** (Watering Well), in the interior cobblestone patio of the Casa de la Aguada, is where he stocked up on water, which he later used to anoint the New World. The patio is pleasant, and leads to a small **Museo Colón** with Columbus memorabilia (admission free; open Mon.–Sat. 9–1:30 and 3:30–6, Sun. 9–1:30).

The **Torre del Conde** (Count's Tower) is in a well-maintained park across the street from Plaza Constitución. Built by the Spanish in 1450 for protection from Guanche tribes, the tower sheltered the count's wife, Beatriz de Bobadillo, in 1487 after island chieftains killed her husband. The windows are so small and the whole looks so lonely, it seems hard to blame her for seeking consolation with a sailor man.

Back on Calle Real, the **Casa Colón** (56 Calle Real, open Tues.–Thurs. 4–6) is a simple Canarian house where the explorer supposedly stayed during his time with Beatriz. It's now devoted to exhibits by local artists.

The **Degollada de Peraza,** 15 km (9 mi) south of San Sebastián over a winding road, has a lookout with great views. Guanche chiefs pushed Beatriz's cruel husband, Fernán Peraza, to his death from this cliff.

San Sebastián's clean **black-sand beach,** near the ferry dock, is popular with local families. **Playa de Santiago,** 34 km (20 mi) southwest of town, is a rocky, black-sand affair surrounding a small fishing bay and has the distinction of getting the sunniest weather on the island. Boat excursions leave several times a week from here (and daily from Valle Gran Rey's Puerto de Vueltas) to view **Los Organos,** a cliff visible only from the sea—its hundreds of tall basalt columns resemble organ pipes. The full-day trips double as pilot whale– and dolphin-watching expeditions. For details contact **Tina Tercera** (tel. 922/805699) or **Sirón** (tel. 922/805480); the average price, 5,000 ptas., includes breakfast, lunch, and swimming.

WHERE TO SLEEP

Calle Real (Calle del Medio) has a number of inexpensive pensions, but the houses tend to be very old, with interior patios, creaky wooden planks, and shared baths. If you find this prospect charming—and it usually is—you'll be fine. Try **Pensión Colón** (C. Real 59, tel. 922/870235) or **Pensión Gomera** (C. Real 33, tel. 922/870417), each asking a mere 3,500 ptas. per double; bring cash.

UNDER 6,000 PTAS. • Apartamentos García. If you're on La Gomera for at least three days (a rental precondition), your 5,000 ptas. are well spent on one of these spacious apartments with kitchens and living rooms. Ask for the owner, José—he's a stitch. *Real 27, San Sebastián, tel. 922/870652. 8 apartments. Cash only.*

WHERE TO EAT

A few traditional foods will make you feel closer to the island. *Almogrote* is an orange-hue smoked-cheese pâté with red pepper, served with bread or *papas arrugadas* (wrinkled potatoes). Palm syrup (*miel de palma*) from Alojera is used in local desserts—each local syrup tree, dressed in a metal collar, yields up to 3 gallons of sap a night, and the goo is boiled down into syrup over wood fires the following day.

Besides Casa Efigenia (*below*), visit inexpensive **Gomera Garden** (C. Real 16, no phone), where at night you can dine on the candlelit open-air patio, surrounded by trees. Behind Calle Real, **Cuatro Caminos** (Ruiz de Padrón 38, tel. 922/141260) has a typical fern-bedecked dining room and more-formal second-floor seating.

UNDER 2,000 PTAS. • Casa Efigenia. Efigenia's house is short on decor and big on down-home Gomeran spirit. The food is local, simple, and prepared and served by Doña Efigenia herself—not gourmet but truly authentic. The walls and a dusty case preserve written testaments to Doña Efigenia's role in preserving traditional island cookery. The main course is a vegetable stew; dessert is a heavy cheese-filled cake you smother in miel de palma. The Casa is open daily for breakfast and lunch from 9 to 7. *Las Hallas, tel. 922/804077. Cash only.*

UNDER 3,000 PTAS. • Marqués de Oristano. This is really two restaurants in one. The Canarian patio in the entryway is a tapas bar; the informal open-air grill in back is used for special occasions. Select the cut of beef or lamb you like from a butcher's case. The dining room upstairs serves more sophisticated cuisine at higher prices, such as pork tenderloin in miel de palma or fillet of bass in champagne with saffron and pine nuts. *C. del Medio 24, San Sebastián, tel. 922/141457. Closed Sun.*

NORTH TO AGULO

On the road north from San Sebastián, you'll be immediately struck by the peat-green stone peaks locked in pea-soup clouds. Like much of the island, this region is in the clouds due to the natural mountain barrier that diverts the trade winds, and its mossy trees drip with moisture. There is little traffic on the roads, and you're reminded that, unlike Tenerife, La Gomera is for near-private exploration. The mountain tunnels here are like magic portals, transporting you from a sea of wrinkled greens to gorgeous gorges climbing with palms and cacti.

Hermigua is a terraced town of white houses on the lower end of a green slope that turns to the sea. As you enter, a sign claims Hermigua has "the best weather in the world." When you reach the yellow apartments, turn back for a look at the amazing split rocks known as the **Roques de San Pedro,** with houses practically set within the gap between the two. The sea soon opens to view, and it's easy to mistake the whitish banana-covering tarps for a nice beach. There is a beach here, but the sand is black.

Until very recently the people who lived on the almost vertical slopes of the island's canyons used a mysterious whistling language called *silbo* to communicate across the gorges. Just a little time on La Gomera will convince you that the language sprang from the echolalia of mellifluous birds that fills this island. Though the language is dying out, most older people in rural areas still understand it, and demonstrations are given at a few tourist restaurants, one of which, La Zula, is identifiable by the buses parked in front. Directly in front of the restaurant, a road leads to **Agulo,** a small sea town of narrow stone-paved streets protected by a semicircular mountain ridge; it's the most authentic place on La Gomera. That island you see across the water is Tenerife.

WHERE TO EAT

UNDER 1,500 PTAS. • Bodegón Roque Blanco. If you eat meat, come on home. Serving up tasty fresh steaks (*bistecs*) and chops (*chuletas*) with fries for under 900 ptas., this friendly grill is very popular with trekkers to Vallehermosa, who often stumble on it by accident. The spacious dining room looks out on a rock formation called Roque Blanco (White Rock) in the green valley outside. Order the great homemade bread (*pan casero*) if they have it handy. *Cruz de Tierno, Agulo (between Agulo and Vallehermosa), tel. 922/800483. Closed Mon.*

El Silbo. The rooftop terrace here has views down the Hermigua Valley to the sea. The house specialty is *garbanzas barradas* (500 ptas.), a mixture of meat, garlic, and parsley that's exclusive to the restaurant. For 350 ptas. extra you can mix a little *gofio* (grain hash) into your delicious *potaje de berros* (watercress) soup. Despite the name, silbo whistling is not practiced here. *Carretera General, La Castellana (between San Sebastián and Agulo), tel. 922/880304.*

PARQUE NACIONAL DE GARAJONAY

A few kilometers past Agulo, the road heads south from the central highway to the park's **Juego de Bolas visitor center** (tel. 922/800993; open Tues.–Sun. 9:30–4:30). Along this 9-km (6-mi) track, vibrant flowers tumble over stone terraces. Fog pushed up by the mountains swirls around these rocky roads like vanilla ice cream.

Gardens in front of the center collect flora native to La Gomera. The island has 43 endemic species; if that means nothing to you, consider that the United Kingdom, known for its gardens, has 12 endemic species and Germany, five. Inside, a 20-minute video with English earphone translation gives some entertaining, informative background on park and island history.

Garajonay has 9,845 acres of laurel forest (a variety of evergreen trees that requires precisely this mix of humidity, mild temperatures, and geographic isolation) that date from before the Ice Age. The value of this ancient wilderness lies in its plant species, which disappeared everywhere else during the glacial period. A wilderness of great hikes, the park is as green as can be, with moss carpets and thick, overwhelming canopies.

The **Laguna Grande** is a forest clearing that floods in rainy season; the rest of the year it's not a lagoon at all, but a place to run around. Many hiking trails converge and depart from this point. A circle of rocks in the middle remind us that the clearing was used for witchcraft in times gone by.

VALLE GRAN REY

From the lookout high above this Valley of the Great King, banana-lined roads head down to **Playa de la Calera,** a sandy, black crescent of a beach favored by young people in search of a cheap hideaway. There's a **tourist office** here (Calle Lepanto s/n, tel. 922/805458). Fire-twirling performers add to the color of sunset, as crowds gather along the beach. The funky, red **Discothek Variete Bar** promises nighttime fun. A northern path brings you to **Playa del Inglés,** a quiet nudist beach. **Playa Las Vueltas** is popular with locals and has some more-elegant, but still inexpensive, restaurants and hotels. Full-day sea excursions, including **whale-watching** and swimming trips, depart daily from Las Vueltas port (as well as from Playa de Santiago; *see* San Sebastián, *above*).

WHERE TO SLEEP

Often overlooked, Valle Gran Rey is an attractive option for overnight stays. Consider sleeping here if you plan to stay more than a day in La Gomera (and you should, you should).

UNDER 3,000 PTAS. • Pensión Las Jornadas. For 3,000 ptas. you can bed down in one of these beachfront doubles with bath at one end of Playa del Inglés. The restaurant inside is popular for good fish at low prices; no dish exceeds 1,000 ptas. *Playa de la Calera, Valle Gran Rey, tel. 922/805052. 10 rooms. Cash only.*

UNDER 8,000 PTAS.

Apartamentos Charco del Conde. If you can afford a bit more, these highly comfortable, flower-clad low-rise apartments across the street from Playa Las Vueltas have pine furnishings, kitchens, and private terraces. The pool and general ambience spell *vacation*. Two-person studios are 6,270 ptas., and apartments for three are 7,315; a third of the rooms have sea views. *Avda. Marítima s/n, Valle Gran Rey, tel. 922/805597, fax 922/805502. 50 apartments, 50 studios.*

WHERE TO EAT

La Islita (Playa de la Calera, tel. 922/805000) is an Italian restaurant with pasta dishes for 1,200 ptas. and pizzas for 900 ptas.

UNDER 1,500 PTAS. • Charco del Conde. This attractive, modern beachfront restaurant is effortlessly stylish. Sample good fish, steak, or chicken with *papas arrugadas* and *mojo* sauce from a great backyard patio or a people-watching front porch. Across from Playa del Charco, the restaurant is named for the beach's inlet, which creates a naturally occurring pool (*charco*) that gets refilled with each high tide. This is also where the Guanche chiefs hatched the plot to toss the *conde* (count) of La Gomera off a cliff. Prices are precipitously low: garlic chicken is 850 ptas., avocado salad is 600 ptas., fish soup is 350 ptas. *Carretera Puntilla Vueltas, tel. 922/805403. Closed Sun.*

Mirador de César Manrique. High atop a mountain, this restaurant takes in a powerful view of the entire Gran Rey Valley through floor-to-ceiling windows with nearly 180-degree views. The terrace lookout and the entire complex, which merges with the natural surroundings, were built by Lanzarote artist César Manrique. The service, atmosphere, and food are on par with La Gomera's best at this government-run restaurant school—and the location *is* the best—yet prices are low. One of the most expensive dishes, rabbit cutlets in Oporto sauce, is only 1,250 ptas. The Mirador's aesthetic rush and affordable refinement should not be missed. *Carretera de Arure, tel. 922/805868. Closed Mon.*

TENERIFE

Tenerife is the largest of the Canary Islands, and the only one shaped like a duck. It is towered over by the volcanic peak of Mt. Teide, which, at 12,198 ft, is the highest mountain in Spain. The superlatives continue: the Parque Nacional del Teide, which preserves 21 endemic species, is Spain's most popular national park. The slopes leading up to Mt. Teide from the north are cool and forested with pines; mixed among the tourist attractions are banana plantations and vineyards. To the south of Mt. Teide are dry, barren lava fields and the resort Playa de las Américas, which has sprung up at the edge of the desert over the last 15 years. Its nightlife is crazy.

Tenerife's capital, Santa Cruz, is a giant urban center. Forget whitewashed villas and sleepy streets. Imagine instead the traffic, activity, and crowds of a significant shipping port, and the site of Spain's most raucous fiesta (a title admittedly shared with Las Palmas), the pre-Lenten Carnival.

COMING AND GOING
Tenerife has two airports. **Los Rodeos Airport** (TFN; tel. 922/635998) is 10 km (6 mi) northeast of Santa Cruz. **Binter** (tel. 922/234346) has an office here for flights to other islands. **Reina Sofia Airport** (TFS; tel. 922/759200), in the south of the island, deals primarily with international flights.

There are two ferry ports. Los Cristianos, in the south, is a departure point for **La Gomera** and **La Palma.** Ferries to **Gran Canaria** leave from the northern capital of Santa Cruz. **Fred Olsen** (Muelle Ribera, Santa Cruz, tel. 922/290011) and **Transmediterránea** (Muelle Rivera, Santa Cruz, tel. 922/842246) are the biggest companies.

SANTA CRUZ
Santa Cruz de Tenerife is under construction until 2002 as part of a massive urban-renewal project.

The heart of the capital city is a white cross in the middle of Plaza de España. The cross is a monument to those who died in the Spanish Civil War, which was actually incited from Tenerife while Franco was exiled here. Santa Cruz throbs to salsa emanating from this plaza for two weeks before Lent each year during Carnival, when the plaza is transformed into the center of a network of musical stages.

BASICS
CHANGING MONEY • Quick Change (Plaza La Candelario 1, tel. 922/293812) is on the left immediately after the Plaza de España. They charge a small commission.

CONSULATES • Ireland (C. Castillo 8, 4-A, tel. 922/245671). **United Kingdom** (Plaza Weyler 8, tel. 922/286863).

CYBERSPACE • Ciber Café El Navegante (Callejón del Combate 12, 922/241500), in the middle of the city, charges 800 ptas. per hour of computer use. They don't seem to charge if it's obvious that you have no new mail, but who has no new mail . . . ?

EMERGENCIES • Take a taxi to **Hospital Universitario de Canarias** (Urbanización Ofra, tel. 922/678000), between the capital and La Laguna.

ENGLISH-LANGUAGE BOOKSTORES • Librería La Isla (C. de Robayna 2, tel. 922/285481) has the city's largest selection of *libros en inglés.*

LAUNDRY • **Tintorería de Tenerife** (Mendez Núñez 104, tel. 922/293526) washes, dries, and irons for 600 ptas. a load.

MAIL • The main **post office** (Plaza de España 2, tel. 922/241388) is open weekdays 8:30–8:30, Saturday 9:30–2:30.

VISITOR INFORMATION • The **Tenerife tourist office** (Plaza de España, tel. 922/239–9592; open weekdays 8–6, Sat. 9–1) is on the port-side corner of the Cabildo Insular building. Stocked with information on Tenerife, the Canaries, and really all of Spain, they also provide an incredible, free box set of 22 hiking maps for Tenerife alone (ask for the *caja de mapas de senderos*).

There's a **Santa Cruz tourist office** in a kiosk (tel. 922/248461; open daily 9–1 and 4–7) not far outside the Tenerife office in Plaza de España, but they charge for maps (boo).

COMING AND GOING

The city's heart is the **Plaza de España**. Directly in front of it, heading uphill into town, away from the water, is Plaza de Candelaria. Continuing uphill, the narrow commercial street becomes Calle Castillo, intersected by Calle de Valentin Sanz.

BY BUS • Green TITAS buses (922/531300) are based at the **estación de guaguas** (Avda. Tres de Mayo 47). Bus 111 runs local (90 mins to Las Américas), while Bus 110 runs express (70 mins to Las Américas) to **Las Américas** and **Los Cristianos** for 900 ptas. To **Puerto de la Cruz**, Bus 102 is local, Bus 103 express (30 mins, 500 ptas.). With a 2,000-pta Bono-bus pass, trips longer than 20 km (12 mi) are 50% off, so if you're exploring the island solely by bus, go for it.

WHERE TO SLEEP

The pension situation is a little grubby here; it's best to stick to the cheaper hotels. **Pensión Milema** (Simón Bolivar 3, tel. 922/225879), with doubles for 3,500 ptas., is friendly and nice but a bus ride (No. 906) away from Plaza de España. Steer clear of Pensión Oviedo. If Hotel Océano is full (*see below*), ring **Hotel Anago** (Imeldo Serís 19, tel. 922/245090).

UNDER 4,000 PTAS. • **Pensión Mova.** Double rooms here are tidy, come with private bath, and cost a mere 3,200–3,800 ptas., but the tiles are coming apart. The salon has TV. *San Martín 23 (corner of C. de la Rosa), tel. 922/283261. 21 rooms. Cash only.*

UNDER 7,000 PTAS. • **Hotel Océano.** A big step above everything else in the budget category, Océano gives you a central location, marble floors and walls in your own quarters, a clean bathroom, a little refrigerator, a phone, a TV, and breakfast for 6,000 ptas. If you can afford it, look not elsewhere. *Castillo 6, tel. 922/270800.*

WHERE TO EAT

Callejón del Combate is an extremely pleasant place for a bite. Awnings and umbrellas from both sides of this narrow pedestrian lane touch down above your head, providing shade for the good smells emanating from each direction. The pedestrian streets behind **Calle Castillo** also have good eateries, including Indian and Italian restaurants.

UNDER 1,000 PTAS. • **Pizzería Da Gigi.** This happy yellow-and-blue dining room stretches from Calle Power to the outdoor tables on Callejón del Combate. Pizzas and pastas average around 800 ptas. *C. Power 16, tel. 922/277474.*

UNDER 1,500 PTAS. • **Condal & Peñamil House.** Waitresses dress like the city's early 19th-century *pureras* (cigar rollers) in this civilized tea-and-cigar café: in garb the color of *café con leche*, they bring you inexpensive liqueur and toasted baguettes with jam. An interesting menu option called "Copa, Café y Puro" combines brandy, whiskey, or rum, a specialty coffee, and a select cigar for either 600, 925, or 1,240 ptas. It's the refined choice after you stuff yourself with pizza across the pedestrian street. *Callejón del Combate 9, tel. 922/244976.*

El Hierbita. Under this high, typically Canarian wood ceiling, try El Hierbita's 1,250-pta. *menú del día* for a square meal. Friendly service means you won't have to apologize if you just feel like eggs and fries (400 ptas.). *C. del Clavel 19, tel. 922/244617.*

WORTH SEEING

A plaza on the northern outskirts of town preserves 18th-century cannons on the site of what was the **Paso Alto Fortress.** In 1794 these weapons held off an attack led by Britain's Admiral Nelson; the cannon on the right fired the shot that cost Nelson his right arm.

About 7 km (4 mi) northeast of Santa Cruz, near the town of San Andrés, the **beautiful Playa Las Teresitas** was made from white sand imported from the Sahara desert.

MUSEO DE LA NATURALEZA Y EL HOMBRE • Primitive ceramics and mummies are the stars of Tenerife's Museum of Nature and Man. The ancient Guanches mummified their dead by rubbing the bodies with pine resin and salt and leaving them in the sun to dry for two weeks; check out their handiwork. *Fuentes Morales s/n, tel. 922/209320. Admission 400 ptas., free Sun. Open Tues.–Sun. 10–8.*

IGLESIA DE LA CONCEPCIÓN • A few blocks south of Plaza España, the Church of the Conception is noted for its six-story Moorish bell tower. *Plaza de la Iglesia, no phone. Open daily 10–1 and 4–6.*

PLAZA DEL PRÍNCIPE DE ASTURIAS • The Marquis de Lozoya called this 1857 plaza "the most perfect and beautifully romantic square ever created on Spanish soil." It's okay. On its east end is the **Museo de Bellas Artes** (Museum of Fine Arts), which has paintings by Brueghel and Rivera, a room dedicated to Goya's *Caprichos*—shadowy, satirical etchings—and some contemporary work. *Plaza Príncipe de Asturias. José Murphy 12, 922/244358. Admission free. Open weekdays 10–8.*

PARQUE GARCÍA SANABRIA • The largest park in Santa Cruz by far, this is a green space to get excited about. Bamboo, pine, palm, and bougainvillea mix, toward the back, with peacocks, who shake their blue chests and feathers in an impression of Carnival queens.

AFTER DARK

Outside Carnival time, Santa Cruz is a big disappointment, its nocturnal action relegated to a single street, **Avenida Anaga.** During the academic year all the young people, especially university students, are in La Laguna (*see below*).

Avenida Anaga faces the port. Beginning at Plaza España and running for about seven blocks, this street is crawling with upscale disco-bars, the most prominent of which are **BB+, Mastil, Nooctua,** and the **Camel Bar.** A simple five-minute stroll tells you all you need to know.

LA LAGUNA

La Laguna was the first capital of Tenerife, and although it's known for its nightlife, it's interesting during the daytime as well, having retained many colonial buildings along Calle San Agustín. One of these, the 400-year-old colonial home of a former slave trader, is now the **Tenerife Museo de Historia** (Tenerife History Museum, C. San Agustín 22, tel. 922/825949; admission 400 ptas., free Sun.; open Tues.–Sun. 10–8). Here you can see antique navigational maps and learn the evolution of the island's economy.

Ciber La Laguna (Catedral 33, tel. 922/825120, open Mon.–Sat. 10 AM–2 AM, Sun. 6 PM–2 AM), a purple-walled Internet center on the corner of Calle Trinidad, rents computers for 500 ptas. an hour.

AFTER DARK

If you're hot on the trail of youthful local nightlife on a Thursday, Friday, or Saturday, this is the place to be, and it's just 5 km (3 mi) northwest of Santa Cruz. Calle Catedral has by far the coolest bar of its sort in the Canaries: you access **Galaxia** through an apartment-building entrance on Calle Catedral between Heraclio Sanchez and Doctor Antonio Gonzalez (the unmarked entrance is part of the fun). The interior, separated by low arches, is designed as a series of caves. Alternative music plays over chatter and a table or two of chess.

Along Heraclio Sanchez are a number of classic college hangouts; **7 Islas** is the most famous. Walking down Doctor Antonio Gonzalez in the other direction, you'll reach a plaza swarming with burger joints and crowded bars with names like **Transylvania, El Granjero,** and **La Herradura.** Follow these down to the next street, as **Barrock** is worth the loop around for its indie-rock attitude. To stay out very late, try one of two *discotecas* on Avenida Trinidad, **Barrock I** and **Palco.**

LOS CRISTIANOS

If you've seen one of the most touristy coasts in the Canaries, you've seen them all: hordes of vacationing Europeans packed into prepackaged hotels. Los Cristianos, a former fishing village now forgotten amid the whir of beachfront tourism, extends to Playa de las Américas. The whole is a congregation of fake beaches in small coves.

This is the newest, largest, and sunniest tourist area on Tenerife, its beaches chockablock with high-rise hotels. Sun, beaches, and nightlife are all the attractions. Playa de Las Américas and Los Cristianos are on the southwestern shore, about 1 km (½ mi) from each other but connected by a waterfront sidewalk.

The town of Los Cristianos consists of two small crescents of gray sand surrounded by apartment houses. Around the corner, Playa de las Américas is a series of man-made yellow-sand beaches protected by an artificial reef. For reasons related to political squabbling, Playa de las Américas is now officially referred to as Costa Adeje, after the municipality to which it belongs.

Los Gigantes, about 12 km (7 mi) north of Playa de las Américas, is a smallish gray-sand cove surrounded by rocks and towering cliffs.

VISITOR INFORMATION

The are a few small regional **tourist offices:** one at **Playa de las Americas** (Plaza del City Center, Avda. Rafael Puig, tel. 922/297668; open weekdays 9–9, Sat. 9–5), one in **Los Cristianos** (Centro Cultural, tel. 922/757137; open weekdays 9–3:30, Sat. 9–1), and one at **Playa de Las Visitas** (on the Paseo Marítimo, tel. 922/787011; open weekdays 9–3:30, Sat. 9–1).

WHERE TO SLEEP AND EAT

It's very hard to find rooms on a show-up basis; most hotels are booked in advance through package deals with tour operators. Your best bets are the cheapest places in town, each with doubles for 4,000 ptas.: **Pensión Playa** (tel 922/792264) and **Pensión La Paloma** (tel. 922/790198), both on Calle Paloma, steps from the best Los Cristianos beach and the central promenade of shops and restaurants. Restaurants here consist of American fast food and tacky tourist joints.

AFTER DARK

The nightlife here is as crazy as in Gran Canaria's Maspalomas (*see* that section to save yourself unexpected hassles). The action centers on **Veronica's.**

OUTDOOR ACTIVITIES

AMUSEMENT PARK • The huge and heavily advertised **Aquapark** has tall slides, meandering streams for inner tubes, and swimming pools. *Avda. Austria 15, San Eugenio Alto, tel. 922/715266. Admission 2,100 ptas. Open daily 10–6.*

WINDSURFING • Tenerife's flat eastern coast has the lanky, leery, scraggly, hungry look of undeveloped land. More than 300 days a year, northeasterly winds stir up the side-on waves that make **El Médano,** a rising resort on the beach past the airport, Tenerife's best windsurfing site. **Cabezo** (Edificio Marinela, tel. 922/177378) is the island's biggest store for surfing accessories and rentals of all kinds; they're very helpful in explaining the techniques of fly surfing. **Fun Factory** (tel. 922/176273), beneath the Hotel Calimera Atlantic Playa, rents boards for 6,500 ptas. a day (a cash or Visa deposit of 30,000 ptas. is required). They also rent mountain bikes (1,800–3,000 ptas. per day), body boards (1,200 ptas. per day), and surfboards (3,000 ptas. per day).

PUERTO DE LA CRUZ

Puerto de la Cruz is the oldest resort in the Canaries, but it's still one of the most pleasant. Having retained some of its Spanish charm and island character, the town would live much the same life without its tourists. The old sections have colonial plazas and *paseos* (promenades) for evening strolls, and indeed there's a pleasant garden air to the whole city.

WHERE TO SLEEP

UNDER 5,000 PTAS. • **Pensión Rosa Mary.** Stay here. This pension is right off the town's main square, and the rooftop terrace has views to the sea. Add its price—4,000 ptas. year-round—and these simple, clean rooms with bath are the way to go. *San Felipe 14, tel. 922/383252. 11 rooms. Cash only.*

WHERE TO EAT

The town's main square, **Plaza del Charco,** is surrounded by restaurants offering lively, shaded outdoor dining. People stroll here with ice-cream cones. **Calle Puerto Viejo,** which runs off the main square, is lined with good, cheap restaurants, and the zone around the Lago Martianez pool has lots of international choices.

Casa de Miranda. Just off the central square, this restored house can trace its history to 1730. On the ground floor is an inviting wooden tapas bar strung with hams, gourds, and garlands of red peppers; farther inside is a plant-filled patio. Upstairs, the high-ceilinged dining room serves such favorites as filet mignon in pepper sauce and turbot in shrimp sauce.

El Pescador. This restaurant claims to be in the oldest house in town, and you'll believe it when you feel the wooden floor shake as the waiters walk by. Slatted green shutters, high ceilings, and salsa music create a tropical air. The open interior patio is covered with vines and plants and has old black-and-white photos of the town. Specialties include avocado stuffed with shrimp (900 ptas.). A menú del día is 1,700 ptas. *Puerto Viejo 8, tel. 922/384088.*

Casa Pablo. Dine on huge pizzas (they'll easily feed two) and pasta dishes here. A tasty chicken, olive, and onion pizza is 675 ptas. *Avda. de Venezuela 9, tel. 922/382905.*

WORTH SEEING

Because of the town's uninviting black beaches, its leaders commissioned Lanzarote artist César Manrique to build **Lago Martianez** (tel. 922/385955; admission 350 ptas.; open 10–7, last entry at 5), a forerunner to today's water parks, in 1965. An immense, immensely fun public pool on the waterfront, the Lago has landscaped islands, bridges, and a volcanolike fountain that sprays sky-high. The complex includes a restaurant-nightclub and several smaller pools. If you come to Tenerife, you've undoubtedly packed a swimsuit, so don't leave the island without enjoying this place.

Stroll from Lago Martianez along the coastal walkway to the **Plaza de Europa,** where you can watch the crashing aqua surf. There's a **tourist office** (Plaza de Europa, tel. 922/388777; open weekdays 9–8, Sat. 9–1) beneath the seawall, on top of which is a cannon aimed directly at City Hall.

JARDÍN BOTÁNICO DE LA OROTAVA • It's worth 100 ptas. just to hear the birds here, some of whose whistles sound like TV theme songs. The birds are attracted by thousands of varieties of exotic tropical trees and plants, including the blunt, spiky *palo borracho* (roughly, "drunken club") of Brazil. The grounds are perfectly cared for, and each species is meticulously labeled (the palo borracho is, intriguingly, *chorisia speciosa St. Hil. Bombacaceae*). This is a great place for rest and meditation. *C. Retama 2, tel. 922/383572. Admission 100 ptas. Open Oct.–Mar., daily 9–6; Apr.–Sept., daily 9–7.*

LORO PARQUE • If you're *really* into birds, know that this subtropical garden is home to 1,300 parrots. *Avda. Loro Parque s/n, tel. 922/373841. Admission 2,900 ptas. Open daily 8:30–5.*

OROTAVA

Just a mile uphill from Puerto de la Cruz, the town of Orotava flaunts a row of stately mansions on Calle San Francisco, just north of the Baroque church of **Nuestra Señora de la Concepción.**

Stop into the **Casa de los Balcones** and, across the street, **Casa del Turista** to see a variety of island craftspeople at work: basket makers, cigar rollers, and sand painters. The houses were built in 1632 and 1590, respectively, and have elaborate, Canary-pine balconies and patios. They're absolutely worth a stop. *C. San Francisco 3 and 4, tel. 922/330629. Admission free. Open daily 8:30–6:30.*

WINE COUNTRY

In the quiet town of **Icod de los Vinos,** 26 km (16 mi) west of Puerto de la Cruz, attractive plazas rimmed by unspoiled colonial architecture and Canary-pine balconies form the heart of Tenerife's most historic wine district.

A **dragon tree** towers 57 ft above the coastal highway (C820). After Mt. Teide, this is Tenerife's favorite symbol. Depending on whom you ask, the tree is anywhere from 600 to 3,000 years of age; in any case, an older, more bulbous, doofier-looking tree there never was. The Guanches worshiped dragon trees as symbols of fertility and knowledge, and the sap—which turns red on contact with air—was used in healing rituals.

Five kilometers (3 miles) west of Icod de los Vinos, **Garachico** is one of the most idyllic and best-preserved towns in the Canaries. It was Tenerife's main port until May 5, 1706, when Mt. Teide blew its top, sending twin rivers of lava downhill. One filled Garachico's harbor, and the other destroyed most of the town. Legend has it the eruption was unleashed by an evil monk.

PARQUE NACIONAL DEL TEIDE

Four roads lead to Mt. Teide from various parts of Tenerife, and each takes about an hour to reach the park. The most beautiful approach might be the road from Orotava. As you head out of town to the higher altitudes, banana plantations give way to fruit and almond orchards that bloom in the early months of the year. Higher up is a fragrant pine forest; then all of a sudden the altitude has changed, the pines are gone, and you're on the moon.

The park includes the volcano itself and the **Cañadas del Teide,** a violent jumble of volcanic leftovers from El Teide and its neighboring peak, **Pico Viejo.** Simply put, these stark landscapes suggest another planet. Within the park are blue hills, spiky, knobby protrusions of rock, and different textures and colors of lava.

You enter the national park at El Portillo. Exhibits in the **visitor center** (tel. 922/290129; open daily 9:15–4), which include a video presentation, explain the region's natural history, and the center offers trail maps, guided hikes, and bus tours. A garden outside labels the flora found within the park. There's another info center near Los Roques de García, next to the parador hotel.

A **cable car** (tel. 922/383711; open daily 9–5, last trip up at 4) carries you close to the top of Mt. Teide, after which the final 534 ft to the top take a difficult 40 minutes to climb. You'll notice sulfur steam vents on the way up. The trail to the volcano's rim is closed when it's snowy, usually about four months a year. You can still get a good view of southern Tenerife and Gran Canaria from the top of the cable-car line, but you'll be confined to the tiny terrace of the station's bar (there's a restaurant as well).

Rising several hundred feet above the ground that surrounds them, the bizarre, photogenic rock formations known as the **Roques de García** look from afar like the silhouette of a lost city. These are old volcanic vents that eventually filled with a pasty lava; after several million years of erosion, all you see is the filling of the old chimneys, which now take fantastic shapes. Do walk the two-hour trail around these rocks, one of 21 well-marked hikes inside the park. Nearby, **Los Azulejos** are a series of light blue hills, made so by a neato process called hydrothermal alteration.

VALENCIA AND MURCIA

BY MICHAEL DE ZAYAS

 ogging more than 500 km (300 mi) of Spain's eastern coastline, Valencia and Murcia draw folks from all over Europe in search of the sandy languor of the Mediterranean coast. The province of Valencia has more blue-flag (EU-approved) beaches than any other zone in Europe. Spain's very first tourist resort was Benidorm, and the town's overheated infrastructure still shows no signs of cooling down. Development has since moved north to Denia, following the white sands of the famous Costa Blanca, and south to the serendipitous stretch of Murcia's beach known as La Manga. Beyond the beaches, adventurous travelers can poke around salt lagoons, mountain villages, and Mediterranean port towns.

Geographically, the provinces of Valencia and Murcia unite to mirror the shape of vertical Portugal on the opposite side of Iberia. The Mediterranean Sea, progenitor of Western civilization, has supplied the area with thousands of years of conquest, culture, and, at times, financial prosperity. Though the Romans spent much time here, it was the Moors who first brought wealth and structure and, among other contributions, introduced the now-famous Valencia orange. Rodrigo Díaz de Vivar, nicknamed El Cid (the Master) by the Moors, conquered Valencia in 1093 and turned it into his own feudal estate. Town names in Valencia beginning with *Beni*—Benicássim, Benidorm, Benifalim, Beniloba—testify to centuries of Moorish dominance. *Beni* is Arabic for "son of," derived from the Semitic root *ben* (descendant), like the Gaelic *Mc* in McDonald.

In the cities of Valencia, Murcia, and Alicante, the onset of spring and summer is marked dramatically by bonfires and other pyrotechnics, suggesting the important role played by nature and agriculture in the region's livelihood. Together these fiestas pack more color and pageantry than any other part of Spain; only Andalusia comes close. In addition to bullfights, typical fiestas called Moros y Cristianos commemorate the medieval struggle for land between the Islamic Moors and the Christian Spaniards..

VALENCIA

Spain's third-largest city, Valencia is a vivacious and chaotic metropolis with some of the best nightlife in Europe. Though it lacks the coherence and charm of a Barcelona or Madrid, Valencia's vibrant

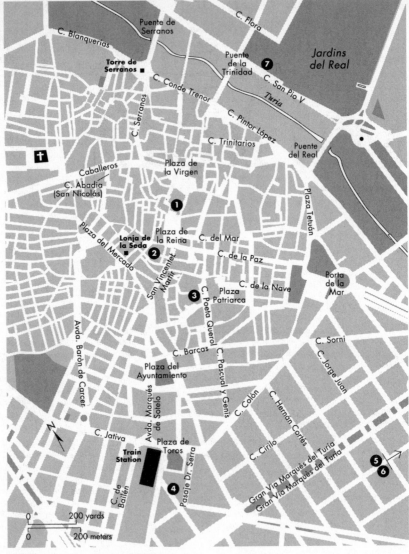

VALENCIA

C. Flora

Puente de Serranos

C. Blanquerias

Jardins del Real

Puente de la Trinidad

7

C. San Pio V

Torre de Serranos ■

C. Conde Trenor

Turia

C. Serranos

C. Pintor López

Puente del Real

C. Trinitarios

✝

Caballeros

Plaza de la Virgen

C. Abadía (San Nicolás)

1

Plaza Tetuán

Plaza del Mercado

Lonja de la Seda ■

Plaza de la Reina

C. del Mar

Porta de la Mar

2

C. de la Paz

San Vicente Mártir

C. de la Nave

3

C. Poeta Querol

Plaza Patriarca

Avda. Barón de Cárcer

C. Sorni

C. Barcas

C. Pascual y Genís

C. Jorge Juan

Plaza del Ayuntamiento

C. Hernán Cortés

C. Colón

Avda. Marqués de Sotelo

C. Cirilo

C. Jativa

Train Station

Plaza de Toros

Pasaje Dr. Serra

5

4

Gran Vía Marqués del Turia

Gran Vía Marqués del Turia

6

C. de Bailén

| 0 | 200 yards |
| 0 | 200 meters |

energy, handful of cultural sites, palm trees, and nearly daily dose of sunshine supply the area's 1.5 million residents with a livable, cosmopolitan air.

Five centuries ago Valencia was the most important city on the Mediterranean. Today locals are taking steps to reaffirm its importance to Europe, most obviously the construction of a massive, new art-and-science complex outside the city center.

Valencia was founded by the Romans in 138 BC but reached its zenith under the Moors. In 1238 King James I claimed it for the Christians, and by the 14th and 15th centuries Valencia ruled the Mediterranean as its cultural and financial capital.

Led by writer Vicente Blasco Nuñez, Valencia experienced a *renaixença,* or renaissance, of local language and culture in the early 20th century, and heeded its calls for political self-determination. (Valencià is technically a dialect of Catalan, but many of its speakers consider it a full-blown language.) For part of the Spanish Civil War, Valencia was the Republican capital, opposed to the Centralist forces of General Franco. Though the area still leans left, calls for independence aren't nearly as loud today as in neighboring Catalonia or in the Basque Country. Ironically, it was in Valencia in 1981 that neo-Francoist forces temporarily held the Spanish parliament hostage in an attempted military coup; in the end, the failed takeover proved a historical hiccup, affirming the strength of post-Franco democracy.

Present-day Valencia bustles with a lively university, a significant gay scene, and a good urban beach. The city's soccer team made a name for itself in 2000 with a superb showing in the European Champions League.

BASICS

VISITOR INFORMATION

Valencia has four **tourist offices.** The central office is in City Hall (Plaza del Ayuntamiento 1, tel. 963/510417; open weekdays 8:30–2:15 and 4:15–6:15, Sat. 8:30–12:45). The largest branch (C. La Paz 48, tel. 963/986422; open weekdays 10–6:30, Sat. 10–2) is the ultimate information source and has been known to set out a bowl full of palm-shape gummy treats. The only office open on Sunday is in the Teatro Principal (Poeta Querol s/n, tel. 963/514907; open weekdays 10–2:30 and 4:30–7, weekends 11–2); finally, there's an office in the train station, open weekdays 9–6:30.

The Valencia Bus Touristic departs from Plaza de la Reina, in front of the cathedral, five times a day for 90-minute city tours in English. The route covers all the major sights, including such out-of-the-way landmarks as the Music Palace and the City of the Arts and Sciences, so it's a good investment (1,000 ptas.) if you don't have much time to spend here.

CURRENCY EXCHANGE

American Express, in the travel agency Viajes Duna (Cirilo Amorós 88, near Plaza Cánovas, tel. 963/741562), open weekdays 10–2 and 5–8, changes traveler's checks. **MoneyGram** (Plaza Santa Catalina 2, tel. 963/155160), open daily 9–9, is another option.

CONSULATES

United States (C. Paz 6, tel. 963/516973).

CYBERSPACES

There's no topping free access. The **Centro Cultural Bancaja** (Plaza de Tetuán 23, tel. 963/875527; open weekdays 9–2 and 4–9, Sat. 9–2) lets you use any of 20 top-of-the line computers free for an hour when you present a driver's license or passport. There's no catch; it's very friendly. The center is one block from the tourist office—coming from Calle La Paz, pass the Bancaja bank and enter via the Plaza de Tetuán. Enter the edifice, turn right, and take the elevator to the fifth floor.

On Sunday, when Bancaja is closed, take a quick cab to **NetKombat** (Ernesto Ferrer 13, tel. 963/392804), where you'll pay 400 ptas. an hour. They're open Sunday 11–2 and 4:30–11, Tuesday–Thursday 5–11, Friday 5 PM–1 AM, Saturday 11–2 and 4:30 PM–1 AM.

EMERGENCIES

Hospital Clínico Universitario (Avda. Blasco Ibañez 17, tel. 963/862600) is just outside the old city. To get here by Metro, take the red 3 line to Facultats.

ENGLISH-LANGUAGE BOOKS

The **English Book Centre** (Pascual y Genis 16, tel. 963/519288), a five-minute walk from Plaza del Ayuntamiento, has a wide selection of classic and contemporary literature.

LAUNDRY

El Mercat (C. Plaza del Mercado 12, tel. 963/912010) has coin-operated machines, but the price is the same—1,100 ptas. total for wash and dry—if you leave your smellies for them to deal with.

MAIL

The main **post office** (Plaza del Ayuntamiento 24, tel. 963/915715; open weekdays 8:30–8:30, Sat. 9:30–2) is across from City Hall.

COMING AND GOING

From the fruity battlements of the train station, follow Avenida Marqués de Sotelo a few blocks to the center of town, Plaza del Ayuntamiento, where you'll see the monumental city hall and the attractive main post office. At the far end of the plaza, the road forks left along Calle María Cristina to the main market and the Lonja silk exchange; to the right, Calle San Vicente Martir goes to Plaza de la Reina and the cathedral. This central area was walled until the mid-19th century, when the city decided to integrate its neighboring towns; the River Túria is also gone, rerouted to prevent flooding. The empty riverbed is now a long stretch of attractive, sunken city park, punctuated by the twin pentagonal Serrano towers at the northern edge of the old town. Outside the riverbed there is little of monumental significance except near the university, where nightlife is lived.

BY BUS

The **bus station** (Avda. Menéndez Pidal 13, tel. 963/497222), in contrast to the train depot, is an ugly, unmarked metal hangar across from the river near El Corte Inglés. The bus line Ubesa (tel. 963/400855) goes to **Benidorm** (2 hrs, 1,510 ptas.) and **Alicante** (3 hrs, 1,980 ptas.). Auto Res (tel. 963/492230) goes to **Madrid** (4 hrs, 2,875 ptas.). Bacoma (963/48–7908) is the southern connection to **Seville** (11 hrs, 6,485 ptas.) and **Granada** (8 hrs, 4,995 ptas.). Should you suddenly feel a need for **Paris,** Eurolines (tel. 963/493822) will get you there (18 hrs, 16,950 ptas.).

To reach **Malvarrosa Beach,** take local Bus 19 from Plaza del Ayuntamiento, in front of Citibank. At night Bus N1 runs in both directions every 45 minutes. Call 963/528399 for info on city buses. **CVT** buses (tel. 962/110008) run to the airport and the town of **Manises.**

BY TRAIN

Estació del Nord (Xátiva 24, 963/520202) has every right to be called the most attractive train station in Spain. *Cercanías* (commuter) trains serve **Gandía** (1 hr, 505 ptas.), **Xátiva** (1 hr, 390 ptas.), and **Cullera** (25 mins, 325 ptas.). Bigger, faster trains head to **Alicante** (2 hrs, 1,400–3,200 ptas.), **Barcelona** (4 hrs, 5,000 ptas.), **Madrid** (6 hrs, 2,945 ptas., or 3½ hrs, 5,700 ptas.), and **Seville** (9 hrs, 5,500 ptas.).

BY PLANE

Valencia-Manises Airport (tel. 961/598500) is 8 km (5 mi) outside the city. *Cercanías* (commuter) trains connect it with Estació del Nord, and yellow CVT buses (tel. 962/110008) with the bus station; each takes 20 minutes. In addition to Iberia, several European airlines touch down here.

BY BOAT

Trasmediterránea (Estación Marítima, southeast corner of university district, tel. 902/454645) runs ferries to **Ibiza** (8 hrs, 2,850 ptas.) and **Palma de Mallorca** (8 hrs, 5,100 ptas.). Prices rise by as much as 20,000 ptas. during high season (July 25–Sept. 5).

GETTING AROUND

A **taxi** (963/70–3333) gets you from the city center to the nightspots in 5 minutes flat.

BY METRO

Valencia's subway system (tel. 900/461040) runs daily 5 AM–midnight. For sightseers' purposes, there are two convenient metro stops in the city center, one near the train station (Xátiva, red/3 line) and one outside the bus station (Túria, yellow/1 line). A free transfer at the Benimaclet stop to the tramway/4 line gets you to the beach. A single-ride ticket is 130 ptas.

WHERE TO SLEEP

Do yourself a favor and stay away from hotels in areas other than the Plaza del Ayuntamiento—the beach hotels are generally disgraceful, and the ones near the station are frightful. All lodgings listed below are quite near the plaza. There are two *hostales* near the Lonja silk exchange, but if you care for cleanliness, only one is worth a stay—**Hostal El Rincón** (Carda 11, tel. 963/917998)—and within El Rincón, only the eight renovated double rooms are acceptable. Ask for *una habitación con ducha,* which gets you a private bathroom with shower for a mere 3,600 ptas.

UNDER 6,000 PTAS. • Hostal Castelar. If you can score one of the six rooms with Plaza del Ayuntamiento views, you'll get good value, as doubles are but 4,500 ptas. here. Six other rooms have small balconies overlooking the pedestrian side street, which may distract you from the fluorescent lighting and the six scary hall bathrooms. The remaining rooms are not recommended. *Ribera 1, tel. 963/513199. 19 rooms, 12 with shower. Cash only.*

Hostal Moratín. Around the corner from the Plaza del Ayuntamiento, these lodgings are by far Valencia's best value for money, and owner Javier will take care of you. Rooms on the lower floor shine with new tile and furnishings but are a touch more costly. Each room has a sink and a shower, five have complete facilities, and the shared baths are very clean. The breakfast room doubles as a TV salon. Doubles run 4,500–6,000 ptas. according to season. *Moratín 15, tel. 963/521220. 19 rooms, 5 with bath.*

UNDER 8,000 PTAS. • Hostal Londres. The furnishings are old-fashioned, but rooms are spacious, clean, and attached to private bathrooms. The high-season rate is too much (8,100 ptas.); the 6,500 ptas. levied at certain times in the summer, when everyone disappears to the beach, is more like it. Weekends are usually 1,000 ptas. cheaper; as a trade-off, air-conditioning costs an extra 1,000 Spanish smackers. The breakfast corner, with wide glassed-in views of the Plaza del Ayuntamiento, gives a bright start to your day. *Barcelonina 1, tel. 963/512244, fax 963/521508. 60 rooms.*

Hotel Alkazar. Location is prime here: you're on a pedestrian street around the corner from Plaza del Ayuntamiento. The very few renovated rooms are the best—clean and sunny (ask for *una habitación renovada).* Doubles with bath cost 7,000–8,000 ptas. The attached restaurant, Taberna Alkazar, serves standard tavern fare in a lively yet elegant setting. *Mosén Femades 11, tel. 963/515551, fax 963/512568. 18 rooms.*

WHERE TO EAT

Paella, probably Spain's most famous dish, is the heart and soul of southeastern Spanish cuisine, which draws fruits and vegetables from the fertile coastal gardens and almost always features rice, grown in the region's inches-deep marshlands. In a proper paella *valenciana,* the rice is flavored with saffron and mixed with seafood, poultry, meat, peas, and peppers; popular jazzlike improvisations on this staple include *arroz a banda* (rice in fish stock) and *arroz negro* (rice black from squid ink). Any dish cooked *all i pebre* involves garlic and pepper.

Unfortunately, the authenticity of paella may suffer at some of Valencia's restaurants. Riuá is your best bet. Steer clear of patently touristy places, which often display pictures of food and try to arrange at least one meal in a smaller town elsewhere in the province. At bars a wonderful thing to ask for is *agua de valencia*—the "city water" is a refreshing combination of champagne, OJ, vodka, and Cointreau served in a cute pitcher.

UNDER 2,000 PTAS. • Al Pomodoro. La Pappardella's sister restaurant, this spot is five minutes from its sibling; the menu consists mainly of pizza. The decor is modern—each wall has its own color or texture scheme, and the balcony is small, so second-floor tables interact visually with those down below. *C. del Mar 22, tel. 963/914800.*

Clot Taberna. For good eating in this weird little square (*see* Worth Seeing, *below*), tuck into a *menú del día* that includes paella valenciana for 1,250 ptas., or 1,500 ptas. if you eat on the terrace. There's a tiny dining room upstairs, but the fun is being outside on the circular plaza, so it's worth the extra pesetas. It's easy to become disoriented around here, so look for Clot's spring-coil logo hanging outside. *Plaza Circular 1, tel.963/924665.*

EASY NUT TO SWALLOW

Horchata—ortxata *in Valenciá*—*is a light and refreshing cold, milky beverage made with ground nuts called* chufas *(tiger nuts). A bit like coconut milk, it's sporadically available throughout Spain in the summer, yet easy to find in Valencia year-round. Valor Chocolatería (Plaza de la Reina 20) makes good horchata, and the second floor has views of the plaza through billowing white drapes. If horchata doesn't provide your calcium fix, tuck into one of the sumptuous ice-cream desserts.*

If you end up swooning for the nutty concoction, consider a pilgrimage to its real hometown, neighboring Alboraya. Now swallowed up by Valencia, Alboraya is at the northern end of Malvarossa Beach; chufa nuts are grown in fields here. Take the red/3 Metro line to the Palmaret stop, and you'll exit onto none other than Avenida de la Orxata. Orxatería Daniel (No. 41) has tables outside. Don't neglect the delicious homemade pastries with which horchata is traditionally drunk—as churros are to chocolate, so fartóns (another fried, elongated creation) are to horchata.

La Lluna. The upstairs room of this vegetarian restaurant is uninviting, but the ground floor features the childlike art of "Pepo," aromas wafting from an open kitchen, and, of course, a company of the like-minded. Pasta salad and *tarta de chocolate* with coconut shavings and fresh cream are the highlights of the 900-pta. lunch menu; the entrées, which include vegetable risotto and vegetarian croquettes, are merely okay. There's live music on occasion. *San Ramón 23 (a narrow side street off C. Beneficia), tel. 963/922146. Closed Sun.*

La Pappardella. This fun, young Italian restaurant near the Miguelete Tower is run by—who else?—fun, young Italians, and it draws a like-minded Spanish crowd. The music is loud and the food delicious, with large servings. Try the tagliatelle bolognese or the spaghetti carbonara; the house wines, though, aren't up to snuff. *Bordadores 5, tel. 963/918915.*

Taj-Mahal. Why *not* choose Valencia, Spain, for your next authentic Indian meal at a reasonable price? Meat is served here, but even a simple vegetarian meal will leave you satisfied—try *channa masala* (chickpeas in a tomato sauce with onions) with basmati rice and *papad* (a big, crispy, fried chip) or *naan* (flat bread cooked in a tandoori oven). A thick mango *lassi* (yogurt drink) keeps things cool, and for dessert there's always *gulab jumun* (deep-fried balls of dough in sweet syrup). Service is excellent. *Dr. Manuel Candela 20, tel. 963/306264. No lunch Tues.*

Tijuana. Finding good nachos in Spain can be a problem, but you're guaranteed to get them here; this spot serves the most authentic Tex-Mex in Iberia. The margaritas are tasty, too, and the lively waitstaff speaks English. *Sancho Tello 19 (off Avda. de Aragón, near English-language movie theater Cines Babel), tel. 963/891111.*

UNDER 3,000 PTAS. • Riuá. This local secret serves delicious traditional Valencian fare in a colorful dining room splashed with ceramic tiles. To order any paella dish, you need to be at least two in number and will pay 1,000–1,500 ptas. per person. *Merluza albufera* is local freshwater hake; *pulpitos guisados* are stewed baby octopuses. Wash it all down with a bottle of Llanos de Titaguas, a dry yet snappy white Valencian wine. *C. del Mar 27 (just off Plaza de la Reina), tel. 963/914571. Closed Mon. No dinner Sun.*

WORTH SEEING

CATHEDRAL

Valencia's 13th- to 15th-century cathedral is the heart of the city and is definitely worth a stop. For one thing, the **Holy Grail** is here. Enter the cathedral from Plaza de la Reina and look for the vessel in the Capilla (Chapel) del Santo Cáliz, on the right: reputed to be the very one used by Jesus during the Last Supper, it's a purple-agate chalice with a heart-shape stem. If the Grail is not actually in a waterfall on some mountainside cave, à la Indiana Jones, then this old stone chapel, decorated with thick iron chains, serves it well. A (non-trap) door leads to the cathedral's museum (admission 200 ptas.), which contains a 1,300-kilogram gold, silver, and platinum *custodia* encrusted with diamonds, used to carry the Host through the city streets during Holy Week.

The first chapel to the right inside the entrance has two **paintings by Goya.** The one on the left shows St. Francis Borja, duke of Gandia, bidding his family farewell before joining Ignacio de Loyola's newly formed Society of Jesus. On the right is a famously misunderstood scene: St. Francis is on the right, fighting to save the soul of an impenitent, while ghouls linger about the man's body like vultures. The blood-red rays shooting from the Francis's cross have led to misreadings of the picture as an exorcism. Goya originally had the man naked; the body was painted over after the artist's death.

Spain lags behind some nations in the category of Tall Things to Climb, so the 207 steps up the **Miguelete Tower** (admission amounts to roughly 1 pta. per step) provide a refreshing international equalizer and, of course, great views of the city. The view from the top platform holds some surprises: first, you're near the ocean, something easy to forget in big, fat Valencia; the city is crowned many times over by bright blue cupolas (made of ceramic tiles from nearby Manises); and the roofs of the old town create a kaleidoscope of orange and brown terra-cotta. The tower was built in 1381, the final spire added in 1736.

Head back into the cathedral and walk behind the altar to see the **left arm of St. Vincent,** martyred in Valencia in 304. Seventeen centuries later, the arm is, naturally enough, brown and gross. In 1104 the bishop of Valencia took it with him on a trip to the Holy Land, but he died in Italy en route and there the arm stayed until the Italians returned it to Valencia in 1970. *Plaza de la Reina, tel. 963/918127. Cathedral open Mon.–Sat. 7:15–1 and 4:30–8:30, Sun. 7:30–1 and 5–8:30. Treasury Museum open Dec.– Feb., Mon.–Sat. 10–1; March–May and Oct.–Nov., Mon.–Sat. 10–1 and 4:30–6; June–Sept., Mon.–Sat. 10–1 and 4:30–7; closed Sun. Miguelete Tower open weekdays 10–12:30 and 4:30–6:30, weekends 10–1:30 and 5–6:30.*

CALLE DEL MAR

At the end of Plaza da la Reina opposite the cathedral is the Santa Catalina Tower. Across from here is an interesting side street, Calle del Mar, at No. 31 of which is a former bar/museum called **Johann Sebastian Bach.** No, Bach never slept here; the owner just likes him. The bar was shut down in 1998 and was slated to reopen by 2001, but the site was a curiosity even when it was closed, covered completely with signs and paintings protesting City Hall's role in its closing. The building's arches and balconies cascade vines and generally drip with greenery; and photos posted on the facade hinted at the lushness of the three-story gardened interior. Apparently, too, there were once live lions inside. It's clear from the exuberance and artistic vigor of the placards, dolls, and protest paraphernalia that the site was beloved. Check out the grounds and enjoy the cool, lounging atmosphere.

PLAZA DE LA VIRGEN

Behind the cathedral is Plaza de la Virgen, site of the colossal floral Virgin that goes up in flames during the festivities of Las Fallas. Here you'll find the **Basilica de la Virgen de los Desamparados** (Basilica of the Virgin of the Forsaken, open daily 7–2 and 4–9), where light religious music plays in the small yet ballroomlike marble interior, complete with chandeliers. A footbridge, designed for priests' use, connects it to the cathedral. Every Thursday at noon, the **Puerta de los Apóstoles** (Apostles' Door; the cathedral's ground-level Gothic entrance) is the gathering point for the **Tribunal de las Aguas** (Water Court), for which ritual a group of dignified elders emerges from the public library across the way, passes through a crowd of curious onlookers, and proceeds to discuss issues of water and irrigation affecting the city and the fertile farmlands nearby. After due debate, the council delivers oral judgments on farmers' complaints on the spot, in the Valencian tongue. Records prove these weekly meetings have transpired for more than 1,000 years. If you're in Valencia on a Thursday, do venture forth by noon to witness this sight.

THE SUN'S MIRROR

Eleven kilometers (7 miles) south of Valencia is a large freshwater lagoon protected as Parque Nacional de la Albufera. Named by Moorish poets ("the Sun's Mirror"), the Albufera is a marshland separated from the Mediterranean by a series of sand dunes and pine forests. A nesting site for 250 species of birds and home to an extraordinary variety of fish and marine species as well as rice paddies, the park (6 km/4 mi wide) has miles of beautiful walking trails.

The island town of El Palmar controls Albufera fishing regulations. The first fishing permit was issued here in 1250 by King Jaume the Conqueror, and to qualify, you must still be: a male native of El Palmar, over 22, son of a fisherman, married, and a lucky winner of the annual license raffle held the second Sunday in July.

Fishermen offer boat rides through the lagoon's innumerable canals. From Valencia, Herca buses depart on the hour (every half hour in summer) daily 7 AM–9 PM; present yourself at the corner of Sueca and Gran Vía de Germanías. There's a visitor center on the highway in El Palmar (tel. 961/627345).

The plaza's real treat may be the inconspicuous fenced-in garden, the **Jardín de la Generalitat.** To recover from sightseeing, spend an afternoon here surrounded by the fragrance of jasmine, and perhaps enjoy some bread and cheese on a bench in the shade of the single, large pine, which has very bad posture. The park is at the head of Calle Caballeros, the main nocturnal thoroughfare and site of medieval mansions once occupied by the cream of Valencian society.

PLAZA CIRCULAR

True, it's not on the typical list of things to see, but you shouldn't fail to inspect Valencia's Plaza Circular (sometimes called Plaza Redonda). It's tucked away to the left of Calle San Vicente Martir as you head to the cathedral from Plaza del Ayuntamiento—take the left turn before the Santa Catalina Tower. Some historians have called this square—which is actually round, like a miniature Plaza de Toros (bullring)—Europe's first trading center. Vendors sell birds, fabrics, clothes, and postcards beneath a large, circular metal pavilion, and the bustle nearly distracts you from noticing the surrounding apartments. Head to the pigeon-regaling central fountain to admire these old, weather-beaten, highly poetic abodes, which face each other intimately from balconies along the plaza's interior.

MUSEO DE BELLAS ARTES

Valencia's Museum of Fine Arts has a superb collection, one of the best in Spain, with works by El Greco, Goya, and Velázquez, among others. To find it, walk behind the cathedral and cross the Puente de la Trinidad (Trinity Bridge); the museum is at the edge of the Jardines del Real park. *San Pío V s/n, tel. 963/605793. Admission free. Open Tues.–Sat. 10–2:15 and 4–7:30, Sun. 10–7:30.*

PALACIO DEL MARQUÉS DE DOS AGUAS

This is in many ways the most fascinating Baroque building in Valencia, its stone facade richly embellished with Churrigueresque fruit and vegetable ornamentation. Inside is the **Museo Nacional de Cerámica,** with a magnificent collection of mostly local ceramics headlined by the Valencian kitchen on the second floor. *C. Poeta Querol 2 (off Plaza Patriarca), tel. 963/51–6392. Admission 400 ptas., free Sat. afternoon and Sun. Open Tues.–Sat. 10–2 and 4–8, Sun. 10–2.*

IVAM

Another impressive art museum, IVAM (Instituto Valenciano de Arte Moderno), is dedicated to contemporary works. Between September and June IVAM runs a second branch nearby, the **Centro del Carmen** (C. Museo 2, northwest of Plaza de la Virgen, tel. 963/863000; admission free; open Tues.–Sun. 11–2:30 and 4:30–7), dedicated to temporary exhibits of up-and-coming artists. *Guillem de Castro 118 (near riverbed), tel. 963/863000. Admission 350 ptas., free Sun. Open Tues.–Sun. 10–7.*

MUSEO TAURINO

The world's oldest taurine museum is behind the Plaza de Toros (bullring), next to the train station. *Pasaje Dr. Serra 10, tel. 963/511850. Admission free. Open Tues.–Sat. 10–1 and 4:30–8:30, Sun. 11–2.*

CIUDAD DE LAS ARTES Y LAS CIENCIAS

Touted as the "largest urban complex under development in Europe for cultural, educational, and leisure purposes," the City of Arts and Sciences should be half complete by the time you read this. The bulk of the complex was designed by local architect Santiago Calatrava, author of one of the city's exuberant bridges. The jury is still out on the futuristic look and feel of this "city," portions of which appear to have been lifted directly from *The Jetsons.*

The structure has four *barrios.* **L'Hemisféric,** the eyeball-shape IMAX theater, has been open for a few years while construction continues under its gaze. The interactive **Museo de las Ciencias Príncipe Felipe** (Prince Philip Science Museum) sits to the side of the eye like a busy crustacean, with its spindly disjointed beams. The **Palacio de las Artes** includes an 1,800-seat hall for music and theater, a 400-seat chamber-music hall, and a 2,500-seat amphitheater that looks like you could land aircraft on it. **L'Oceanográfic,** a massive aquarium, mixes killer whales with a restaurant. *Take Bus 13, 14, or 15 from front door of post office in Plaza del Ayuntamiento.*

PALAU DE LA MÚSICA

On one of the nicest stretches of the Turia riverbed, a pond is backed by a huge glass vault, Valencia's Palace of Music. Supported by 10 porticoed pillars, the glass dome gives the illusion of a greenhouse, both from the street and from within its sun-filled, tree-landscaped interior. Home of the Orquesta de Valencia, the main hall also hosts visiting performers of international stature. A good way to see the building without concert tickets is to pop into the art gallery, which hosts free changing exhibits. *Paseo de la Alameda 30, tel. 963/375020. Gallery open daily 10–1:30 and 5:30–8:30.*

PARKS

To feast your eyes on thousands of species of palms, ferns, cacti, and a cat or two, head into the **Jardín Botánico** (C. Beato Gaspar Bono 6, 1 block southeast of Puente Glorias Valencianas, across from bus station, tel. 963/911657; admission 50 ptas.; open Tues.–Sun. 10–7). Valencia's most bizarre green space is **Parque Gulliver** (Túria riverbed park, at Puente Angel Custodio, tel. 963/370204; open weekdays 10–7:30, weekends 10–8), with a huge, climbable sculpture of Swift's creation. The **Jardines del Real,** or Viveros Municipales (C. San Pío V s/n, tel. 963/623512; open daily 8 AM–sunset), has rose gardens, a duck pond, and a train for kids.

FIESTAS

Beware the Ides of March, and cover your ears. Every year beginning March 15, scores of towns across the province of Valencia celebrate Las Fallas, a wickedly loud five-day fiesta culminating, on the final night, with the burning of papier-mâché effigies to mark the arrival of spring. The effigies, known as *fallas* and generally imbued with timely satirical significance, are serious craftworks: some towns can only afford one or two. The apogee of Mediterranean fire rituals takes place in Valencia, with nearly 400 such monsters set alight and a series of highly traditional processions actively involving more than 100,000 people. In a word, Valencia *is* Las Fallas.

Be warned: if you don't like loud noises, this could become the most obnoxious experience of your life. Every day between March 1 and March 19, the Plaza del Ayuntamiento fills at noon with thousands of spectators for a six-minute bomb explosion called a *mascletá,* an aural bombardment of which Valencians are proud. The old city is closed to motor traffic the entire week of the 15th, enabling relaxed streams of people to stroll around, snacking and creating a general mood of holiday leisure (which you'll adore, until a huge firecracker explodes at your feet). *Falleros,* the 100,000 men and women who

PORTRAIT OF AN ARTISTA FALLERO

In Valencia, Las Fallas peak on March 19, Día de San José (St. Joseph's Day), when families throughout Spain celebrate Father's Day. The time-honored feast of Las Fallas derives from the fact that St. Joseph is the patron saint of carpenters, and in the Middle Ages carpenters' guilds honored his feast day by making huge bonfires with their wood shavings.

Today the fallas, or papier-mâché constructions, are designed and built by venerated artistas falleros, who earn a living from these yearly creations. Each falla is made up of about 10 smaller units called ninots, and the actions of each group of ninots are comically expressed in rhyming verse on cards staked before them—irreverent politics mixed with social satire, usually centering on local and national politicians and sports heroes. A different kind of ninot, and usually the most popular, depicts sentimental scenes of local traditional life. Oh, and some have to do with sex, but some things need no translation—one recent ninot featured a pregnant Snow White casting an evil eye in Dopey's direction.

But there is one Valencia falla that's different—the one designed by Alfredo Ruiz. You'll know his work when you see it. In past years Ruiz's monochrome totemic creations have dealt with social issues, such as children's rights, and abstract concepts, as in his 1998 treatment of classical music.

Ruiz, nicknamed by locals El Chispa (the Spark), says he's not an iconoclast; he's been practicing this open interpretation of falla design for more than 30 years. The tradition, however, still doesn't seem to know where to place him: each year he wins first place in a category created just for him, "Innovation"— a distancing he doesn't like. Yet his falla attracts intellectuals and artists who would otherwise eschew their city's fiesta, finding it all in poor taste.

It's hard to predict where you can see Ruiz's work, but he'll probably continue to be chosen as a falla maker; look in front of the 15th-century Quart towers (former entries to the medieval city walls) or enter any doorway marked CASAL and ask where to look for El Chispa's falla. Each group knows what the others are up to.

belong to a particular *comisión*, or *falla* group, gather in the streets around their home-base *casals* (clubhouses) for big paella cookouts.

On March 17 and 18 the falleros carry floral offerings from the train station to the Plaza de la Virgen—it takes two full days, from morning till after midnight, to get them all in—for the *ofrenda de flores*. The women have spent thousands of dollars on their elaborate, colorfully embroidered, mostly silk dresses typical of 18th-century Valencia, and each caps off her dress with a similarly anachronistic hairdo that required a full year's growth: a complex series of spiraled buns held in place with gold pins and ornaments. A shoulder-to-waist sash displays the red-and-yellow stripes of Valencia's ubiquitous flag. The general air of an epic beauty pageant is enhanced by the fact that each comisión has its own court led by the elected queen, the *fallera mayor.*

When they finally make it to the plaza, it's common for falleras to break into tears at the sight of the three-story Virgin and Child made up of red, pink, and white carnations. They hand their bouquets to men called *vestidores* (dressers), who climb up the wooden scaffold and plug the flowers into the Virgin's floral dress.

Las Fallas' final night, March 19, is called La Nit del Foc—the Night of Fire. Beginning with the children's fallas (located beside each grown-up falla and lighted at 11 PM rather than midnight), papier-mâché figures go up in flames on street corners throughout the city, and a year's worth of planning and design goes to ash. Incorporated into the fiesta-closing cremation is forgiveness for all the subjects satired—a restoration of clean slates until another year of human life calls for more gasoline and a match.

AFTER DARK

It's no coincidence a bat hovers over Valencia's coat of arms on the city seal. Sunset here brings the city to life, and in many ways the nightlife here is Spain's best. Valencia was the uncontested after-dark leader in the 1980s, when the *ruta del bacalao* (referring not to codfish but to the slang name of Spain's most popular dance music) required sleepless weekends—from Friday night to Monday morning—of techno-crazed frenzy along the beachfront discos. Things have calmed down a bit, but nighttime options are still fantastic in number.

Outside summer, Valencia—like Madrid and Barcelona—is too large for a centralized nightlife zone; there are pockets of bars and discos all over the city. And a voyage outside the city center, based on a local recommendation, can be very rewarding.

BARS AND DISCOS

For quiet after-dinner drinks near the cathedral, try the jazzy, lighthearted, almost silly bar **Café de la Seu** (Santo Cáliz 7, tel. 963/915715), whose colorful interior features pop art and animal-print chairs.

BARRIO DEL CARMEN • From the Plaza de la Virgen in front of the basilica, walk down Calle Caballeros, the old city's central nightlife artery. You'll pass big bouncer clubs (don't worry, you're in) including **Fox Congo, Johnny Maracas,** and **Babal.** The side streets off Caballeros are worth exploring, especially Calle Calatrava—turn left here and walk down a block to **Plaza del Negrito,** named after its black sculpture of a little boy. Pubs surround this plaza, starring **Negrito,** which has a lively drinking atmosphere. **La Comedia** (Calatrava 19) is a smaller place, best when playing jazz to match its vintage-pool-parlor aesthetic. Continue back down Caballeros to Carmen.

CARMEN AND PLAZA DEL TOSSAL • An 11th-century Arab wall is incorporated into the 18th-century palace that is **Carmen** (C. Caballeros 38, tel. 963/925273), a sleek bar-club of various floors connected by a series of ramps. Twelve permanent art installations are on display, and the music is always sharp. Wednesday night features a candlelighted literature series with poetry readings and film and theater presentations; Thursday night is dedicated to electronic music spun by guest DJs. Pick up a monthly program inside. Carmen may be, in the end, your most vivid memory of Valencia.

To the left of Carmen is Plaza del Tossal, where the city's nightlife peaks. Here are **Café Bolsería** and **Café Infante,** the latter an especially cool place to start your night. Back across the street from Carmen is an attractive two-story bar known simply as **El Café.** About 20 yards farther down this street—known as Plaza San Jaime, though there's no real square here—the road forks. To the left on Calle Alta is a run of trendy cafés and bars, including **Café Cola-Caos,** a hip place to get *agua de valencia,* and, farther on across the street, the looser **Circus.**

At 3:30 AM or 4 AM, the Carmen scene winds down. If you feel like dancing, take a cab to 69 Monkeys.

69 MONKEYS • The fully translated name of this discotheque is "69 Monkeys on a Steel Wire." It's a classy venue, and if you want to dance, you'll appreciate the good size and comfortable feel here. Admission is free until 3:30 AM on Thursday and 2:30 AM on Friday; Saturday there's a small fee of about 1,000 ptas., which entitles you to a drink at the bar. Look for flyers at bars across the city. *Eduardo Boscá 27–29, tel. 963/918567.*

AVENIDA BLASCO IBAÑEZ • Across the riverbed on the other side of town, head for Avenida Blasco Ibañez, near the university. Off the avenue, Plaza del Cedro has a wonderful cluster of alternative bars. **El Asesino,** with the Jimi Hendrix mural outside, has loud music and lot of tables; **Tasca Gat,** next door, has a decidedly rougher edge. Across from this pair, on Calle Campoamor, **El Tornillo** (with a screwdriver in the facade) has an artsy decor and serves teas but is in no way pretentious. Farther down the street is the huge, red **Café Sonora,** where you can hear recorded Pixies and often live music. Another block down Calle Campoamor is the real champion, **Velvet** (look for the Velvet Underground drawing). Why can't English-speaking countries produce hangouts of this caliber? The large, winding interior is packed with a young, alternative crowd sitting in various nooks, and the paintings around the bar have some artistic merit, as do the challenging sayings in English and Spanish. You're likely to hear Beck, and lighted album covers on the walls promote American independent bands such as Pavement and Yo La Tengo. Next door, **Matisse** is a dance hall for an older, yuppie set that parties even harder than the kids at Velvet. None of the above levies a cover charge.

Two more-popular discos are back across Avenida Blasco Ibañez at Plaza Honduras. **Warhol** plays dance alternative. **Acción,** next door, is darker, funkier, and plays more-commercial dance music. The cover for each is 1,000 ptas., which includes one drink. The plazas behind Honduras are creeping with bars and pubs; among them, **Café Comic** is a civilized retreat from the mayhem.

Avenida de Aragón, though it begins with some rather intimidating large buildings and flashing neon billboards, is another hot street. On the parallel back street, **Black Note** (Polo y Peyrolón 15, tel. 963/933663 for concert times) is a local mecca for jazz lovers, with live music nightly.

ENGLISH-LANGUAGE MOVIE THEATERS

Valencia has three excellent cinemas showing films in their original version (V.O.). The only one in the city center is **Filmoteca** (Plaza del Ayuntamiento 17, tel. 963/512336), with changing monthly programs and an artsy haunt of a café. A five-minute cab ride from the city center are **Albatros Multicines** (Plaza de Fray Luis Colomer 4, tel. 963/932677) and **Babel** (Vicente Sancho Tello 10, off Avda. Aragón, tel. 963/626795), both with special shows Friday and Saturday nights at 1 AM.

OUTDOOR ACTIVITIES

Club Valenciano de Piraguismo (tel. 963/617311) arranges boat rides on the Albufera Lagoon as well as kayaking and canoeing down the region's rivers.

NORTH OF VALENCIA

The provincial capital of Castellón de la Plana, on the coast north of Valencia, is a pleasant, relatively new town with some Modernist buildings in its center. Farther north along Castellón's Costa del Azahar (Orange-Blossom Coast), Benicàssim has some of the nicest beaches around. Peñíscola has an attractive old town topped by the Pope Pedro Luna Castle, which juts out to sea past a narrow isthmus. Benicarló and Vinarós are the last beach towns before reaching Catalonia. Inland, toward Aragón, is Morella, one of Spain's most impressive castle towns.

MORELLA

The most interesting and authentic town in the province of Castellón, Morella is still not necessarily worth the long haul from the beach. But if you happen to be driving to Zaragoza, stop here for a fierce visual thrill—Morella's medieval fortress towers straight up from the top of this hillside town, a bastion of vertical intimidation. The rest of the town gathers in the skirt of this castle, along with the powerful, octagonal double-tower San Miguel gate, built in 1360. The tourist office (Plaza de San Miguel 3, tel. 964/173032; open daily 10–2 and 4–7) is on your right inside this entrance. The town does feel pleasingly old, and its lamps charm after dark. If you're here at sunset, you may be lured to spend the night.

Roman aqueducts that once brought water are scattered outside town in a few good-looking chunks; the nearest is a short walk downhill from the San Miguel gate. Almost 5,000 ft of wonderful stone wall, complete with windows and loopholes, still surround much of Morella, as do 15 well-preserved towers (placards relate their names and dates). Climb one to survey the flat, dry countryside and dream of battle.

WHERE TO SLEEP

UNDER 5,000 PTAS. • Hostal La Muralla. The best, most affordable lodging in Morella provides clean and spacious rooms with colorful sheets and charges but 4,000–4,500 ptas. for a double with facilities. The friendly owner serves up breakfast (400 ptas.) in the modern salon area. *Muralla 12, tel. 964/160243. 19 rooms.*

BENICÁSSIM

Twenty minutes north of Castellón de la Plana, Benicássim is a lethargic summer resort with fine blueflag, white-sand beaches. However, camping here for a weekend during the **International Festival of Independent Music** will embed the name *Benicássim* in your mind forever. Music festivals in the United States are sullen, commercialized affairs compared to such bashes as this, drawing more than 30,000 fans and scores of the very top names in avant rock. Björk was the headline act in 1999. You can buy festival tickets at music outlets throughout Spain, but if you decide to attend on a whim, you can buy a tent and sleeping bag for about 4,000 ptas. in a good megastore supermarket.

Besides the indie-music fest, Benicássim is worthy of another musical note: Francisco Tárrega, whose guitar pieces are in every classical player's repertoire, was born here. The **Francisco Tárrega International Guitar Festival** is held every year at the end of August. Call the tourist office (Médico Segarra 4, tel. 964/300962, fax 964/300139) for details. Be aware that dates, prices, and performers for both the indie and the guitar festivals are firmed up only a few months in advance.

SOUTH OF VALENCIA

As you work your way south along the coast, you'll pass through the Albufera wetlands, other lonely marshlands, and deserted beaches. After Cullera and Gandía, you'll come to Denia and the start of the Costa Blanca (White Coast). Driving south to Alicante along an amazing 250 km (150 mi) of white coastline, you'll discover some of the cleanest, most unspoiled beaches on Spain's east coast.

CULLERA

Now that the threat of pirate attacks has diminished considerably, Cullera's 15 km (9 mi) of great beachfront have been stocked with apartments and hotels, making it the best place near Valencia for an easy sea retreat. The old quarter, Barrio del Pozo, still huddles behind a castle-topped mountain, safely away from the water, and the town does have a smattering of museums and some worthy nightlife in summer (Arlequín, on Agustín Olivert, is best). Cullera also has its own freshwater lagoon (*estany*), lined with some wonderful restaurants serving authentic paella.

From the town side of the mountain, make your way up to the **castle** past charming white houses. The market, which surrounds a gardened plaza nearby, is equally cute. The castle, next to the **Ermita de Nuestra Señora del Castillo** (Hermitage of Our Lady of the Castle), is the highest point for miles and gives ace perspectives of the rice paddies in the *huerta* (fertile, irrigated coastal plain). At press time, the castle was closed for renovation, and they're hedging their bets on a reopening date.

Back down at sea level, near the lighthouse at the northern edge of the town's winding coastline, is the **Cueva Dragut** (Dragut Cave), named for the pirate who laid siege to Cullera in 1550. Inside, the **Casa Museo del Dragut** (admission 500 ptas., open weekends 11–2 and 5–8) is a pirate museum. The town also has a combination archaeology museum/*fallas* museum (Cullera burns 14 *fallas* in March), the **Museo Aqueológico y Fallero** (admission free; open Tues.–Fri. 9–2, weekends 10–1 and 5–7).

Also worth a stop is the **Museo del Arroz** (admission free; open Tues.–Fri. 9–2, weekends 10–1 and 4–6)—yes, the Museum of Rice—set within the Sants de la Pedra hermitage. An old tower, **El Torre del Marenyet,** stands on the opposite side of the river, near the lagoon (the river once flowed closer to the tower); and there's a small museum inside (admission free; open Thurs.–Fri. 10–1, weekends 10–1 and 5–7).

BASICS

There are two **tourist offices,** one in a hut just off the main beach (Plaza Constitución, tel. 961/731586; open fall–spring, Tues.–Sun. 10–2 and 5–7:30; summer, daily 10–2 and 3–9) and another in town (Carrer del Riu 38, tel. 961/720974; open weekdays 10:30–4 and 5–8, Sat. 10:30–4).

WHERE TO SLEEP

The most affordable options are only slightly cheaper than El Chalet (*below*). **L'Escala** (Marqués de la Romana 4, tel. 961/746723) rents doubles with bath for 5,500–7,000 ptas. **Carabela II** (Diagonal País Valenciá 49, tel. 961/724070) offers the same for 5,800–8,400 ptas.

UNDER 9,000 PTAS. • El Chalet. On the sand of Cullera's last and perhaps finest beach, Bahía de los Naranjos (Bay of Oranges), this hotel offers a great deal of privacy. Rooms are clean and modern, with balconies overlooking the water. A double with bath will run you 7,000 ptas., 8,000 ptas. in July and August. The host family runs a restaurant downstairs. *Punta Negra 4, tel. 961/746535. 24 rooms.*

WHERE TO EAT

UNDER 3,000 PTAS. • Casa Picanterra. Even if you don't stay in Cullera, consider stopping here for some authentic paella. The setting is exceedingly tranquil: you dine on a terrace facing the calm lagoon, where flat fishing boats linger in the reeds. The soothing scene is vitalized by terrific smells from the kitchen, which offers 18 kinds of paella as well as homemade crepes for dessert. It's tricky to stay under 3,000 ptas. per person, but it can be done: a 400-pta. Valencian salad and a generous *sopa de marisco* (mixed seafood soup) for 700 ptas. will start you off well, followed by paella (which starts at 1,000 ptas. per person, assuming paella for two). If you're driving from Cullera, cross the stone bridge opposite the post office and stay left, following the signs for the *estany. Estany de Cullera, tel. 961/722627.*

GANDÍA

Gandía, the next big coastal town heading south, was a sleepy village until it won a European Commission award in 1992 for having the most pristine beach in Europe. That was the end of that . . . bathers have been arriving by the busload ever since. But the sand remains fine and clean.

Gandía does have a grand past. It was the birthplace of St. Francis Borja (1510–72), duke of Gandía, who appears in two remarkable Goya paintings in Valencia's cathedral. Francis did much to redeem his family's reputation, sullied by Borgia pope Alexander VI, the most notorious of all Renaissance prelates. **The Palacio de los Duques** (Ducal Palace), signposted from the city center, was founded by St. Francis in 1546 and still serves as a Jesuit college. Once you've seen this, you can enjoy the beach guilt-free.

BASICS

The town of Gandía and its beach are separated by a 3-km (2-mi) stretch of farmland traversed by a single bus, which departs from the **tourist office** (C. Marqués de Campo, across from train station, tel. 962/877788; open July–Sept., weekdays 10–2 and 4:30–7:30; shorter hrs off season). The **train station** (C. Marqués de Campo s/n, tel. 962/865471) sends trains to Valencia (1 hr, 470–535 ptas.) every half hour.

WHERE TO SLEEP

Gandía has only a handful of cheap lodgings, and they're often full. A good low-end bet is **Hostal Duque Carlos** (C. Duque Carlos de Borja 34–36, tel. 962/872844), with 19 fairly large doubles, each 3,745 ptas. a night. **Hotel Mavi** (Legazpi 18, tel. 962/840020, fax 962/840020), across from the train station, has 42 double rooms at 5,000 ptas. each.

OUTDOOR ACTIVITIES

Explore the beach and countryside on horseback by hitting up **Hípica Los Robles** (Segador de Morant s/n, tel. 962/840094), beneath the San Juan castle.

BENIDORM

Benidorm is the leading tourist destination on Spain's Mediterranean coast. Long viewed by culture mavens as a nightmarish resort spot—there are no "sights" here, no there there—the city garners predominantly sun-seeking, package-touring Britons. Over the years the town's commercial construction has grown completely disproportionate to the size of its two beaches (even with 5 km/3 mi of sand); one hotel is so large it's a skyscraper by American standards.

And the crowds will only get bigger. A new theme park, Terra Mítica, billed by the Valencian government as "the Route of Dreams" and "the Greatest Leisure Center in Europe," opened in August 2000. Because the park took many years to build, it was the subject, prior to its opening, of much *fallas* ridicule; Valencians were, however, overjoyed at the prospect of their own Disney-style amusement park.

The old town, behind the hill called El Canfali, has the energy of a busy city, with a chaos of signage and 24-hour video stores. A permanent group of mimes and clowns is supported by a never-ending stream of vacationers.

BASICS

Benidorm has three **tourist offices**: Avenida Martinez Alejos 6, tel. 965/851311; Calle Derramador, tel. 966/805914; and Avenida de Europa, tel. 965/860095. All are open daily 9:30–1:30 and 4:30–7:30.

The best Internet center, **Mundo Internet** (Escuelas 1, tel. 966/831266; open daily 4 PM–2 AM, daily 11 AM–2 PM in summer) charges only 300 ptas. an hour.

WHERE TO SLEEP

The town is blanketed by hotels, many of which are affordable but most of which are booked year-round through prepaid extended-stay package deals. Arriving in town without a reservation can be a real problem; hope for a cancellation.

Benidorm will seem far more pleasant if you're staying on the beach. The two affordable, professionally run spots listed below will put you near town without the feeling of being lost in a suburban tourist nightmare.

UNDER 10,000 PTAS. • Hotel Colón. The majority of the spacious rooms (28 of 37) at this friendly hotel look out from Canfali Hill to the palm trees and sands of Playa de Poniente. Rooms are well furnished and have new floor tiles, and the bathrooms are very clean. There's no air-conditioning, but each nest has a pleasant balcony with a little table. Prices for en-suite doubles vary but are low for Benidorm year-round, starting at 5,000 ptas. in the dead of winter and hitting 10,000 in the dead of summer. *Paseo Colon 3, tel. 965/854381. 37 rooms. Closed Nov.– Dec.*

UNDER 15,000 PTAS. • Hotel Canfali. This hotel is pricier than Colón, but it hangs out over the water with a complete view of the arch of sand at Levante Beach. If you're looking for a beach vacation, and can snag a balcony room, you'll have no complaints; this is one of the best locations on all the coast. May prices are half the August tally (7,500–16,400 ptas.; price includes three all-you-can eat buffet meals). *Plaza San Jaime 5, tel. 965/853040, fax 966/805652. Closed Nov.–Dec. Cash only.*

WHERE TO EAT

Like other such foreigners' haunts, Benidorm serves an international array of cuisines. Small English restaurants and pubs are everywhere, catering to Brits on holiday. A number of all-you-can-eat buffets offer to fill you up for 1,000 ptas. or less.

UNDER 2,000 PTAS. • Spice of Life. Given all the fast food around here, it's nice to be able to get excellent service and tasty food in a pleasant setting. Spice serves Indian cuisine in a dining room bedecked with chandeliers and wooden Art Nouveau mirrors. *Dr. Orts Llorca s/n, tel. 965/866881.*

UNDER 3,000 PTAS. • The Secret Garden. Down a little street on Canfali Hill in the nicest part of Benidorm, six tables are arranged around plastic trees and plants (they look true enough if you squint). The fixed menu price of 1,950 ptas. includes fillet of pork Stroganoff, chicken in brandy and pepper sauce, and French and English desserts. *Carrer del Condestable Zaragoza 21, tel. 966/806918.*

WORTH SEEING

TERRA MÍTICA • This amusement park is designed to replicate the Mediterranean Sea: five historically themed lands surround a central lake, representing the sea itself. The lands—Iberia, Egypt, Rome, Greece, and the Islands—feature roller coasters, stunt shows, performances, role-playing employees, and numerous water rides. If you're traveling in the summer, it will be hard indeed to resist cooling off here. *Carretera Benidorm Afinestrat Camino del Moralet, tel. 902/020220. Admission 4,600 ptas. Open daily 10 AM–midnight.*

THE BEACHES • Off the old town, **Playa de Levante** is the most popular beach, while **Playa de Poniente** is calmer and prettier. The two are separated by **Canfali Hill,** a pleasant balcony over the Mediterranean with a few attractive plazas.

To lose the crowds, hike along the roads or trails of the **Sierra Helada** (Frozen Range), which breaks the coastline in two between Benidorm and Altea. The mountains begin at Punta de Pinet, at the end of Playa de Levante, and cross to the Albir, where the next beach begins. Ask the tourist office for the English-language pamphlet "Routes across Sierra Helada."

ISLA DE BENIDORM • Not far offshore, this little rock island looks like a large waterski ramp. Glass-bottom boats run by **Excursions Marítimas** (tel. 965/850052) tool around it; the trip takes an hour each way and costs 1,200 ptas. round-trip. The same company offers coastal cruises (2,000 ptas.) from Benidorm to Calpe; boats leave the Benidorm port at 11:30 AM and return from Calpe at 4.

AFTER DARK

People come to Benidorm to let go, so the discotheques here are happening throughout the year. Summer is madness. On the beachfront Avenida D'Alcoi, **El Ku Beach, Penelope,** and **Racha** shake their respective things. The real deal is near the highway—**K.M.** and **Ku.**

A zone of **English pubs** runs for three blocks behind Avenida del Mediterraneo, essentially bounded on the east and west by Avenida de Cuenca and Avenida de Filipinas. Expatriate youngsters earn money as "public relations" workers, hustling and hassling you into certain bars and restaurants. They do often have money-saving two-for-one coupons.

INLAND: XÁTIVA AND ALCOY

Xátiva and Alcoy are among some of the most rustic villages in the Southeast, where people live far more traditional lives than most of their compatriots. Farther south are Elche, famous for its ancient palm trees, and Oriheula, with an ornate seaside exposition of Gothic, Renaissance, and Baroque architecture.

XÁTIVA

As long as you have air-conditioning, Xátiva (pronounced *cha*-tee-va) may be the finest place in Spain to retire. For younger folk passing through, it's an oasis of quietude, peace, and charm. Xátiva's medieval castle looks like a freshly minted movie set, and the old town packs street after narrow cobblestone street of picture-perfect balconies bursting with plant life over colorful facades. The stillness at siesta time is impressive.

Setabenses (as the locals are called, since the Romans named this place Saetabis) saw their heyday in the 15th and 16th centuries, when two of their own became pope—Calixtus III and his nephew Alexander VI. The latter issued the famous 1493 papal bull granting the Indies to Ferdinand and Isabella, though he's more often remembered for his scandalous private life, including fathering Caesar and Lucrezia. Don't feel bad if you don't recall all this from high school right away; such a winsome town will inspire you to learn more.

BASICS

To find the **tourist office** (Alameda 50, tel. 962/273346; open Tues.–Fri. 10–2:30 and 5–7, weekends 10–2:30) from the train station, walk a few blocks down Bajada de la Estación and turn left at Alameda de Jaume I. The tourist office is down the block, across from a park that separates City Hall from the post office.

Praise be to the **tourist tram** (400 ptas.) that hauls you all the way up the mountain from the tourist office to the castle. Most of the year the tram departs Tuesday–Sunday at 12:30 and 4:30; in summer, 12:30 only.

WHERE TO SLEEP
Hotel Vernisa. If you're making a stay of it, Vernisa is a good-looking, well-run hotel worth the extra money (7,000 ptas. for a double with bath). You're a block behind City Hall, and there's a decent restaurant on-site. *Académico Maravall 1, tel. 962/281365, fax 962/281365. 39 rooms.*

WHERE TO EAT
Across from Casa Abuela (*see below*) is another fine restaurant, **El Rincón** (C. Reina 20). Pizza solutions are available at **Il Padrino** (Plaza Bassa 10), behind C. Reina.

UNDER 3,000 PTAS. • Casa Abuela. Daintily decorated to resemble (as the name suggests) your Spanish grandma's house, Casa Abuela is *the* place to eat in Xátiva. If you skip the 2,000-pta. *menú del día* in favor of an à la carte meal, try *higado de pato al Pedro Ximenez* (duck liver in sweet sherry; 2,100 ptas.) or *alcochofas rellenas de gambas gratinadas* (artichokes stuffed with shrimp au gratin; 1,400 ptas.). The wine list is a winner. *C. Reina 17, tel. 962/270525. Closed Sun.*

WORTH SEEING
In Xátiva you must do at least two things: wander through the quiet old town and see the castle.

The **Basilica de la Seu** (Plaza de la Seu; open Mon.–Sat. 10:30–1) has a mighty tower that marks the historic center of the old town. In front are statues of the town's two Borgia popes, Calixtus III and Alexander VI. From the basilica square, a road leads back and up to the castle.

En route to the castle, the views of town get more fabulous the higher you climb—if you haven't already taken your old-town walk, this perspective will convince you to do so. One of the best lookouts is from the patio of the 18th-century church of Sant Josep, halfway up the hill. From here cross the road to find the 13th-century **Ermita de San Feliu Hermitage** (St. Felix Hermitage). Four central arches connect across the ceiling in this simple stone church, which has tomb markers across the floor and a beautiful group of faded frescos. During off hours knock at the attached house to be let in. It's a fascinating space. *Open Mon.–Sat. 10–1 and 3–6, Sun. 10–1.*

The handsome **Castillo de Xátiva** (Xátiva Castle) is the swanky local choice for wedding photos. You enter through a narrow gate under a flowered pergola, which leads to a lovely complex with upper, middle, and lower sections. The castle has been so well maintained the first two sections feel something like a country club. Just inside the main entrance (in the middle section), a small museum has a black-and-white drawing of Xátiva from 1563 showing the tight arc of the walled town as protected from above by the mighty castle. What a place. Looking down at the town and countryside from the battlements, you can still see Xátiva's 16th-century form, and your esteem for the town broadens.

Embroidered scarlet carpets hang and gargoyles peer in the castle's medieval rooms and towers. The lower section includes sections of Roman paving, and its old quarters and halls are in a more crumbled state. A dark prison reveals what a bummer of a place this was to be locked up, the fate of the count of Urgel (1378–1433), who eventually died and was buried here in the chapel of Santa Maria.

Look for the bathrooms at the Gate of Emergency Relief (Puerta del Socorro). *Open fall–spring, Tues.–Sun. 10–6; summer, Tues.–Sun. 10–7. Admission 300 ptas.*

If you're wondering about the upside-down man being sold on city souvenirs, the answer's in the **Museu de L'Almudí** (Almudin Art Museum). Look for a portrait of Felipe V, the man who burned the city and expelled its inhabitants in 1707 as payback for their opposition to the War of Spanish Secession—the king's likeness is now hung in this disrespectful position. Among the right-side-up works are paintings by Xátiva-born José Ribera, known as El Españoleto. *Open Tues.–Fri. 10–2 and 4–6, weekends 10–2.*

AFTER DARK
Nightlife happens in the **Plaza del Mercado.**

ALCOY

Locally spelled *Alcoi,* this place is interesting for its strange physical arrangement: the city is separated by deep gorges, crossed by a number of bridges and viaducts. Successful textile and paper industries account for Alcoy's surprising wealth and population (nearly 70,000), both evident in the string of fancy, themed discotheques around the Plaza Gonçal Cantó. Gaudí, for instance, pays homage to the Catalan architect.

But Alcoy is known above all for its **Moros y Cristianos** festival, held every April 22–24. It may well be that Alcoy takes more pride in its fiesta than any other town in Spain; surely in no other locality does the cult of historical lavishness reach such extremes. Though the fiesta lasts three days, its high point is the six-hour entrance procession the morning of April 22, complete with swaggering ranks of costumes that fall somewhere between medieval and post-apocalyptic.

The fiesta commemorates a St. George–inspired Christian defense of the city from the Moors in 1276. To participate in the main events, you must belong to one of 28 ranks, or *filás,* split between Christians and Moorish camps. There are two main avenues to joining a particular filá: birth and death—that is, membership is hereditary. This is serious stuff, and people drop a year's worth of savings into an outlandish costume representing their *filá's* designation. The difference between *vestido* and *disfraz* (clothing and costume) is a source of considerable irritation; don't use the latter word. Parade order rotates one turn per year so that each Moor and Christian rank gets the supreme honor of emerging first every 14 years.

On April 24, men spend the day discharging 7,000 kilograms of gunpowder through the streets of town, a loud ceremony that's best avoided, but the fiesta's culmination at 9 PM is not to be missed. A six-year-old boy, chosen yearly as the representation of Sant Jordi (St. George), appears over a faux castle wall, tossing silver arrows into the crowd of thousands.

ALICANTE

Alicante is a pure expression of Mediterranean life, with palm trees, buckets of sunshine, a packed beach, and nightlife galore. It's photo-famous Explanada de España, a long palm-lined walk of black, red, and white undulating tiles, was *made* for lazy warm-night strolls.

BASICS

CURRENCY EXCHANGE
A slew of exchanges and banks line the Esplanade and its side streets; rates are better at the banks. **MoneyGram** (tel. 901/201010) wire transfers are available at a few locations, including the exchange bureau at Calle Ingienero La Farga 2, tel. 965/206223.

CONSULATES
United Kingdom (C. Calvo Sotelo 1, tel. 965/216022).

CYBER SPACES
As in Valencia and Castellón, the Fundación Bancaja offers free Internet access. This branch is called **Centro Cultural Rambla.** Go upstairs and turn right, toward the *ciberoteca*; you'll be asked to show ID and give a local address. When you can't remember your hotel address, say, "Calle Mayor 1." *Rambla Méndez Núñez 4, tel. 965/140380. Open weekdays 9–2 and 4–9, Sat. 9–2.*

If the Centro Cultural Rambla is filled with foreign students who know a good thing when they find one, try **Boxes** (Alemania 2, tel. 965/982037; open Mon.–Sat. 10–8:30, Sun. 10–2), which charges only 400 ptas. an hour.

ENGLISH-LANGUAGE BOOKS
Librería Internacional (Altamira 6, tel. 965/217925) has two shelves of English publications.

LAUNDRY
La Rosa Blanca (Virgen de los Virtudes 6, tel. 965/172266), on Plaza Nueva, is the cheapest central laundry service, charging 1,100 ptas. to wash and dry.

MAIL
The main **post office** (Alemania 7, tel. 965/131887; open weekdays 8:30–8:30, Sat. 9:30–2) is a five-minute walk from the tourist office.

MEDICAL AID

A general **health line** (tel. 900/161161, toll-free in Spain) answers basic questions. For emergencies head to **Hospital de Alicante** (Avda. Pintor Baeza s/n, tel. 965/908300 or 965/908224).

VISITOR INFORMATION

The slick Alicante **tourist office** (Rambla Méndez Núñez 23, tel. 965/200000 or toll-free in Spain 900/ 211027; open weekdays 10–7, Sat. 10–2 and 3–7), with a wall of flipping photo panels, will give you the scoop. If you have time to explore the region, ask for hiking maps and/or the free book on rural accommodations. There's another helpful **kiosk** in the middle of a little park a few blocks down the road from the main office, toward the sea (Portal de Elx, tel. 965/149240; open weekdays 10–2 and 5–8), plus an office at the **airport** (tel. 966/919367; open Tues.–Sat. 10–9) and a little desk in the *ayuntamiento* (town hall; open weekdays 9–2:30).

COMING AND GOING

From the bus station take Calle Portugal three blocks to the water and turn left to reach the Esplanade.

BY PLANE

Aeropuerto Internacional de El Altet (tel. 966/919000) is 11 km (7 mi) west of town. For Iberia airlines call 902/400500. Frequent buses connect the airport with the bus station.

BY TRAIN

From the **RENFE station** (Avda. de la Estación, tel. 902/240202), trains go to **Xàtiva** (90 mins, 1,120 ptas.), **Valencia** (90 mins, 1,400–3,200 ptas.), **Murcia** (90 mins, 575 ptas.), **Madrid** (4 hrs, 4,000 ptas.), and **Barcelona** (5 hrs, 6,000 ptas.).

The station is a 15-minute walk from the city center. You can hail a **taxi** at the station or call 965/ 252511. If you decide to hoof it, walk straight down Avenida Estación to the round Plaza de los Luceros and turn right down Avenida Federico Soto, which becomes Avenida Doctor Gadea. At the water, turn left and take the Explanada de España to the end—down a block to your left is the Plaza del Ayuntamiento, center of the old city; to your right are the marina and the beach.

Valencia runs its own railway (Ferrocarriles de la Generalitat Valenciana, Avda. Villajoyosa 2, tel. 965/ 262731) along the **Costa Blanca,** from Alicante to Denia. The station is about half a mile down Playa del Postiguet. In July and August an all-night service called **Trensnochador** keeps partygoers from drinking and driving by stopping at the discotheques in Benidorm (650 ptas. round trip). The train also runs to Benidorm's Terra Mítica theme park (395 ptas. round trip; free if you buy a park admission ticket at train station).

BY BUS

Alicante's **bus station** (Portugal 18, tel. 965/130700) is about a 10-minute walk from town. Alcoyana (tel. 965/130104) heads to **Alcoy** (45 mins, 380 ptas.). ALSA (tel. 965/125868) heads to **Murcia** (600 ptas.) and **Valencia** (1,980 ptas.). ALSA's subsidiary Enatcar (24-hr reservation line tel. 902/422242), heads to **Málaga** (8 hrs, 4,565 ptas.), **Seville** (10 hrs, 6,255 ptas.), **Barcelona** (8 hrs, 4,650 ptas.), and **Madrid** (6½ hrs, 3,345 ptas.).

WHERE TO SLEEP

Alicante abounds with cheap, slightly grubby places to stay. A score of lodgings line Calle San Fernando and crowd the old town in general; most, however, are far from new. Try to reserve a room at Les Monges.

UNDER 6,000 PTAS. • Hostal Les Monges Palace. Spain's top 5,000-peseta *hostal* just got better. Renovations, scheduled to be finished in early 2001, will equip all rooms with private bath (one with whirlpool bath) and transform the reception area into a Moderniste-style wonder, complete with original Gaudí-era lamps. The rooms are tastefully decorated with antiques and original art—yes, that is a *real* Dalí. If you're here on a weekend and want to sleep, don't stay here; it's in the heart of the city, and nights in Alicante are loud. *Monjas 2, tel. 965/215046. 19 rooms.*

La Milagrosa. If you can't get into Les Monges, you can still be among the first to discover the revamped rooms at this *hostal* overlooking Plaza de Santa María. At press time, totally new double rooms—

redecked from furniture to bathrooms—were available for the same old price of 3,500–4,000 ptas. Half the rooms have balconies overlooking the plaza, and there's a nice plant-covered rooftop garden with views of the castle and the rooftops of town. *C. Villavieja 8, tel. 965/216918. 20 rooms, 10 with bath. Cash only.*

UNDER 8,000 PTAS. • Hotel Rialto. If it's high season and the hotels above are full, you can head to the Rialto for fine rooms with clean tiles and small but new private baths. It's comfortable, if nothing fancy, and you get your own alarm clock (a forgotten amenity in Spain) for your 6,000 ptas. (7,500 ptas. in summer). *Castaños 30, beside Teatro Principal, tel. 965/206433, fax 965/141367. 30 rooms.*

WHERE TO EAT

The Esplanade and Rambla present the usual cast of fast-food characters, from McDonald's to KFC. The marina offers stylish settings, while the town has cheap but worthwhile eateries, listed below.

UNDER 2,000 PTAS. • El Sultan. A young crowd is drawn to this brightly colored, theme-parkish Arabic setting. As is usually the case with Middle Eastern food, you can eat well for quite little. Salads, hummus, and falafel run 350 ptas., and you can get two kebabs for 975 ptas. *San Fernando 8, tel. 965/ 210247.*

La Taberna del Gourmet. You might find better values here than anywhere else in Alicante, especially at lunchtime, when the menú del día costs but 1,300 ptas. Options include fresh fish—*brocheta de salmón, calamares,* or *gambas* (skewered salmon, squid, or shrimp)—and *montaditos* (sandwich tapas) with *mojama* (a salmonlike fish) and caviar, the latter a mere 225 ptas. *San Fernando 10, tel. 965/ 204233.*

Taberna de Labradores. From the notepad menu check off sangria (served in large ceramic pitchers) and *chupi-chupi* (pork in a house sauce). Loud music from the bar next door makes the outdoor tables a lively choice in the evening. A few yards down the street, you're sure to spot the candles and large umbrellas of the **Red Lion,** a neighboring Irish pub that's also decent for dinner. *C. San Pascual 3, tel. 639/372876. Cash only.*

UNDER 3,000 PTAS. • Mirador. In keeping with the loftiness of the space, expect a fair measure of snootiness here, on the 26th floor of the narrow Hotel Gran Sol, where the menú del día costs 2,400 ptas. The fare is typically Spanish, augmented by seafood specialties. With a terrace wrapping around three sides of the dining room, however, the view is to dine for. *Rambla Méndez Núñez 3, tel. 965/203000.*

WORTH SEEING

If you hit the beach and spent a night out on the town, you'll probably like Alicante, and you will have seen its two most important sights in the bargain. But you may be left wondering about the third—that mountain rising across the street from the beach, shielding a row of apartments from any view except that of the waterfront. Take an elevator to the top of Monte de Benacantil (700 ft), and you'll find the remains of a very old castle.

CASTILLO DE SANTA BARBARA

St. Barbara's Castle was originally built as a Carthaginian fortress around 3 BC and took its current form in the 9th century. Most of what remains is from the 16th century. When you get off the elevator, you'll find models of the castle showing what it looked like at various points in time. Make no mistake, Alicante was quite a little paradise in its day, supported from this upper bastion.

Within the complex are three exhibits of art and city history, each with slightly different hours. The main reason to come, however, is the 360-degree view of the mountains linking the landscape to the sea.

The elevator (400 ptas.) is across the street from Playa del Postiguet (Postiquet Beach), on Calle Virgen del Socorro. If you walk up (a good 45 minutes), you can ride down for free. If you're driving, follow the beach highway to Alicante Norte; after a loop, signs will lead you up the hill. *Tel. 965/263131. Open daily 9–7.*

MUSEO DE LA ASEGURADA

The oldest civil edifice in Alicante, built as a town granary in 1685, now houses a contemporary-art museum. An expansion is creating more rooms to showcase the 20th-century works, including pieces by Bacon, Dalí, Picasso, Rauschenberg, and Chagall. *Vilavella 3, tel. 965/140768. Free. Open summer, Tues.–Sat. 10–2 and 5–9, Sun. 10–2; fall–spring, Tues.–Sat. 10–2 and 4–8, Sun. 10–2.*

CHURCH OF SANTA MARÍA

Across the street from the art museum, on quiet Plaza de Santa María, is the church of the same name, built over an older mosque. The church has two towers, a rich 18th-century Baroque facade, and an organ made in 1653. The only other thing on this square is a vegetarian restaurant, and aside from the cute house cat, everything about that place is astonishingly poor. *Open daily 10–1 and 5–9.*

AYUNTAMIENTO

City Hall is housed in an 18th-century Baroque palace. Just inside, at the foot of the main stairwell next to a tourist-info stand, is a simple plaque marking the COTA ZERO—sea level zero—for all of Spain. Elsewhere, each city has a large oval plaque comparing its height above sea level to that of Alicante; in Madrid, for instance, the Alicante sea marker stands prominently outside City Hall in Puerta del Sol. While you're here, have a peek inside the rococo chapel. *Open weekdays 9–2, Sat. 9–1.*

FIESTAS

If you're ready to redefine your notion of party and it happens to be June 20–24, make tracks for Alicante. The **Hogueras** (Bonfires) fiesta is easily the wildest street party in its province and one of the biggest in Spain, yet it retains much traditional appeal. And call the whole thing your own—you can count on one hand the number of English-speaking foreigners here (who, when asked to describe the fiesta, can only repeat the word *crazy* over and over).

As Valencia burns *fallas* (effigies) to mark the start of spring, Alicante begins summer with its own fallas torching. In fact, the fiesta is a copy of Valencia's ancient Fallas: Alicante, too, has large-scale processions of men and women in traditional dress, a flower offering, a daily *mascletá* (bomb explosion), and on the night of the 23rd, a determination to set the city ablaze. Perhaps the best place to be on this night is near the falla set up on the water in the marina—firemen douse the thousands of spectators with water after putting out the ashen figure.

Alicante's Hogueras may be the passing traveler's most effective dose of Spanish fiesta, given its manageable scale, seaside location, and manic exuberance. Although it can't match the colossal scale of Valencia's classic pageantry, the weather is better in June than in March, and the beach plays a starring role in the fun. Street dancing blankets the city for four glorious nights, and many head to the beach for early morning swims. The crowd gains momentum throughout the day until large-scale concerts begin on stages set up near the sand, and the whole thing starts all over again.

SHOPPING

Avenida Maisonnave, the main shopping street, is flanked at either end by El Corte Inglés (tel. 965/924001 for both).

AFTER DARK

Alicante's nightlife is sickeningly good. While Valencia's diversity makes it a great place to go out in different parts of town, Alicante's nightlife is perfect for out-of-towners, as the madness is concentrated in two areas. The marina hoards modern, spacious bars and dance clubs; the old town, sometimes called the Barrio de Santa Cruz, is, in the classic Spanish fashion, a never-ending sequence of door-to-door bars. You could dedicate one long night to each; for best results, sleep from dinner until 2 AM and then head out.

The old town is a romp. Addresses are nearly pointless, as the whole city seems to be a labyrinth of bars. It's fun to get lost, and stumble from bar to bar saying, "Hey, look where we are again." To help you remember last night: the **Cave** (C. Cienfuegos) was the punk rock place with wall drawings (one reads, "Welcome to my nightmares!"), **Cienfuegos** (C. Cienfuegos) was the one with two floors of house music, and **La Naya** (C. Labradores) had the Latin jazz. Lest you forget where you are in Spain, *cienfuegos* means "100 fires."

On Calle Santo Tomás alone you'll find **Iguana River, Velvet, Cherokee, Desdén, Nepal,** and **Laguardia.** If some of their breathless interiors leave you hungry for fresh air, **Astrónomo,** near street's end, has a large outdoor terrace (a plaza of its own, really), **Desafinado** has an outdoor alley with tables, and **Nazca** has a rooftop garden. Explore as far as the Plaza del Carmen.

El Forat (Plaza Santísima Faz) is on a quieter plaza and draws an older crowd. Its Wonderland-size furry couch, candles, hanging perfume bottles, disco ball, oversize Oscar, slide projectors, tango music, and general weirdness make it the most memorable place for a drink.

The **marina** would be memorable at half its actual size. You arrive to a front of five or so bars, among them **Ay Carmela,** the **Last Pirate,** and **Puerto di Roma.** The last of these is the star, for although it lacks the fanciful themes of the others, it has a lot of dance space occupied by enthusiastic salsa lovers. Outside, 100 tables face the water. Farther on are **Mascarón, Capitá Haddock,** and **Potato,** another dance hot spot. On the back side of the marina, **Cola de Gallo** has slick orange chairs beneath outdoor umbrellas, **Luxor** has an Egyptian theme, and **H₂O** dazzles with shiny stuff. The port continues with more of everything, including restaurants and arcades, in a collectively great position around the glittering marina.

The best Latin spot is **Santiago de Cuba,** at the end of the Esplanade (No. 26). With outdoor tables, this is also a good daytime stop for a relaxing drink or snack.

If you're some kind of party freak and none of this is enough, take the Trensnochador train (*see* Coming and Going, *above*) to Benidorm.

MURCIA

The driest and least-visited Autonomous Community in Spain, Murcia is not a compulsory stop if you're breezing through the country. It *is* of interest to archaeology buffs, however, as this region has a long history, beginning with the arrival of the Carthaginians in the 3rd century BC.

The provincial capital, a modern university city of 350,000, was first settled by the Romans; later, in the 8th century, the conquering Moors used Roman bricks to build the city proper. The whole was reconquered and annexed to the crown of Castile in 1243. The Murcian dialect contains many Arabic words, and the regional tongues of the Mediterranean cease as Valencià gives way to the Andalusian accent. Many Murcians clearly reveal Moorish ancestry.

BASICS

EMERGENCIES
Police (Plaza Ceballos 13, tel. 968/355414). **Ambulance** (tel. 968/222222). **Hospital Morales Meseguer** (Avda. Marqués de Vélez 22, tel. 968/360900).

ENGLISH-LANGUAGE BOOKS
Antaño (Puerta Nueva 8, tel. 968/232050), aimed at university students, has a fair selection of classic and contemporary English fiction.

MAIL
From Plaza Santo Domingo take the tree-lined Gran Vía Alfonso X El Sabio to the main **post office** (Plaza Circular 8, tel. 968/242044; open weekdays 8:30–8:30, Saturday 9:30–2).

VISITOR INFORMATION
The **regional tourist office** (C. San Cristóbal, off Trapería before Plaza Santo Domingo, tel. 968/366100), open weekdays 9–2 and 5–7, Saturday 10:30–1, gives out colorful maps that illustrate important city sights.

COMING AND GOING

The **Glorieta de España** is the area of pleasant gardens and fountains where the **ayuntamiento** (city hall) and Palacio Episcopal face the Segura River. Behind the Glorieta is Murcia's nerve center, Plaza Cardenal Belluga, centered on the intricate facade of the **cathedral.** The cathedral's attractive bell tower sits on Plaza Hernandez Andres, from which **Calle Trapería,** the narrow commercial thoroughfare (with banks for changing money) runs to the large Plaza Santo Domingo. To the right (east) a few blocks is the university complex. The bus and train stations are outside the city center; for a **taxi** *from* town, call 968/297700.

BY TRAIN

Major destinations from the **RENFE** station (Plaza Industria, tel. 902/240202; taxi into town) include **Alicante** (90 mins, 565 ptas.), **Valencia** (3½ hrs, 1,965 ptas.), **Madrid** (4 hrs, 5,300 ptas.), **Barcelona** (7 hrs, 6,500 ptas.), and **Seville** (10 hrs, 10,300 ptas.).

BY BUS

Murcia's **bus station** (San Andrés, tel. 968/292211) is a good place to store bags while you take a Gimenez Garcia **bus** (tel. 968/291911) to the beaches of **La Manga** (55 mins, 675 ptas.). Accessible at the same window and phone number, Lycar goes to **Cartagena** (90 mins, 430 ptas.). Trapemusa (tel. 968/292211) heads to **Lorca** (90 mins, 620 ptas.). ALSA (tel. 968/294126) heads to **Alicante** (90 mins, 600 ptas.), **Valencia** (3½ hrs, 1,850 ptas.), **Seville** (7 hrs, 4,900 ptas.), and **Madrid** (3,200 ptas.). The train line to Granada is poorly set up, but Alsina Graells (tel. 968/291612) drives you there in three-and-a-half hours for 2,480 ptas.

A **taxi** from the station to town costs less than 1,000 ptas.

WHERE TO SLEEP

UNDER 6,000 PTAS. • Hispano 1. Neglected older brother of the much fancier, much pricier Hispano 2, in back, this budget hotel has big, clean rooms but crummy beds and no air-conditioning. There is a TV salon, for what it's worth, and the location is as central as you can get. Most doubles have private bathrooms for 5,000 ptas.; a few, costing 1,000 ptas. less, have showers but share hall toilets. Ask for a view of Calle Trapería. *C. Trapería 8–10, tel. 968/216152, fax 968/216859. 46 rooms, 36 with bath or shower.*

Pensión El Perro Azul. Run by the same young guy who runs the bar downstairs (*see* After Dark, *below*), the Blue Dog is not luxury, but it is fun. You may just feel like part of the Murcia scene when you can swing downstairs and see the coolest people in town. Rooms are simple and cute, rather like cheerful dorm rooms with an occasional antique piece. Every room has a refrigerator and private sink and shower; three rooms (5,000 ptas. each, instead of 4,000) also have a little kitchen with a microwave; a desk; a big TV; and an interior toilet. For the shower-only rooms, tiny private toilets are humorously arranged side by side (with doors corresponding to your room number) out in the hall. *Simon García 19, tel. 968/221700. 11 rooms. Cash only.*

WHERE TO EAT

Ensalada murciana, a red salad of olives, tuna, and steamed onions in olive oil, is a local specialty. Harder to find outside fiesta season is a wonderful local dessert called *paparajote*—lemon-tree leaves covered with a sweet batter, fried, and sprinkled with sugar and cinnamon. (Pluck the leaves out.)

The best place for a real meal is **Plaza San Juan,** an attractive, nearly enclosed square filled with outdoor tables. Rimming the plaza are the following restaurants: **Fujiyama,** with sushi and other Japanese fare, a rarity in Spain; **La Tarentella Pizzeria Trattoria,** self-explanatory; **La Réunion,** serving French cuisine; and side by side with traditional Murcian dishes, **La Parranda, La Pequeña Taberna Típica,** and **La Alegría de la Huerta.** Not only does the latter have the best name, it's affordable (1,000 ptas. for the menú del día, 850 ptas. if you eat at the bar) and quite nice inside, with potted trees, ceramics displays, and baskets of the famed Murcian vegetables.

UNDER 1,500 PTAS. • Think of these joints, indeed most joints in Murcia, as bar-restaurants, better for tapas than for sit-down meals.

Itaca. This is where you'd go to read Octavio Paz over a eucalyptus tea. The atmosphere is not only friendly but exudes tolerance and open-mindedness, with books and South American products (jewelry, folk musical instruments) for sale at *comercio justo,* or "fair commerce," prices. The background music is usually ethnic—sitar, Swahili, folk. Readings and live performances are often staged here, and exhibits spotlight art and photography. If you're looking to make friends in Murcia, why not start here? Doors are open daily till 2 AM. *Mariano Vergara 6.*

La Caña de España. With just a few tables and a brick wall, this place looks like a typical Spanish eatery, and you should act accordingly by ordering tapas and a glass of wine. However, there's something more going on here; a fun, young, occasionally campy local crowd gathers nightly. Maybe it's the poster that spoofs Almodóvar, maybe its just a cheap, easy way to eat on this popular street. Practice your colloquial Spanish by ordering *tomate partio con boquerones*—split tomatoes with anchovies (partio is short for *partido,* which means "split"). *Cánovas del Castillo 29.*

La Rata Escarlata. Since it's managed by the same creative spirit that dreamed up Ahorcado Feliz (*see* After Dark, *below*), the decor at the Scarlet Rat is predictably winning. Opening its doors nightly at 8, this *mesón* (traditional tavern) is best for tapas and a great selection of foreign beers. *Cánovas del Castillo 26.*

WORTH SEEING

CATHEDRAL

A masterpiece of eclectic architecture, Murcia's 14th- to 18th-century cathedral is the city's gem. It was not until 1737 that the church received its trademark facade, which is very obviously (ahem) Churrigueresque—one of the best examples, in fact, of this particular Baroque style, complete with a decorative stone chain around the building's exterior. The miserable, modern office building across Plaza Belluga was actually designed as an abstract mirror to the cathedral, but the concept may have been inappropriate given the arrangement of so many styles. Nineteenth-century English traveler Richard Ford described this cathedral as "rising in compartments, like a drawn-out telescope." The 15th century brought the Gothic Door of the Apostles and, inside, the splendid Vélez Chapel, with a beautiful star-shape stone vault. Peek into the **museum,** off the north transept, to see carvings by famed local sculptor Francisco Salzillo, including a polychrome wood sculpture of the penitent St. Jerome.

The monumental **bell tower** has been closed for renovations the past few years, but it might be open by the time you read this. The view from 312 ft up, under the graceful octagonal dome, clarifies Murcia's position in the dry southeastern landscape. The tower was built section by section between 1519 and 1793—hence its own diversity of style. *Plaza de la Cruz, tel. 968/239346. Open daily 10–1 and 5–7.*

CASINO DE MURCIA

This traditional Murcian gentlemen's club, all billiards and newspapers, has the style and aura of its British counterparts. Visit the Alhambra-inspired Moorish courtyard, French ballroom, and ladies powder room, open to ladies *and* gentlemen for a peek at the painted ceiling. *Traperia 22, tel. 968/212255. Admission 100 ptas. Open daily 10–2 and 4:30–8:30.*

MUSEO SALZILLO

Sculptor Francisco Salzillo, born in Murcia in 1707, sculpted numerous disturbing, realistic figures still used in the region's Semana Santa *pasos* (Holy Week floats). These and other works are on view here in a former church on Plaza San Agustín, near the bus station. *Plaza San Agustín 3, tel. 968/291893. Open May–Sept., Sun.–Fri. 9:30–1 and 4–7, Sat. 9:30–1; Oct.–Apr., Tues.–Sat. 9:30–1 and 4–7, Sun. 11–1.*

AFTER DARK

Murcia is a university town, and in Spain that means you're guaranteed a good time. But this place has some extra-creative energy that many other cities lack, and its alternative and gay scenes are well above par. Bars, of course, tend to come and go, but the route—both sides of the university—stays the same. Head to this general area, and you'll do no wrong. **Calle Doctor Fleming** is on the south end of the university; off Fleming try the small **Pub Siddhartha** (C. Vitorio 23), or take the first left after that to **Rocky Raccoon** (C. Trinidad 12), which leads the alternate rock scene. **Maricoco** (C. Vitorio s/n,), open after 11 PM Thursday to Saturday, is Murcia's best-known gay bar. A well-dressed young set gathers on the streets in front of the Teatro Romea; **Los Claveles** (C. Alfaro 10; closed Sun.–Tues.) is the center of action in this zone. When these places close, there's always the main disco in the city center, **De Nai Clú** (Centrofama, C. Puerta Nueva s/n, tel. 968/245900).

For a bit of the old country, **Fitzpatrick's Irish Pub,** in Plaza Cetina, has an attractive, subdued interior.

El Ahorcado Feliz, or The Happy Hanged Man (Cánovas del Castillo 35), is a stunningly cool bar with a good sense of humor and style to match. There's no better decor in Murcia—or in Madrid or Barcelona, for that matter. Where to begin? Rajasthani sheets and hand-forged iron chandeliers hang from the ceiling; an intricate mosaic of dish tiles decorates the floor; a raised bar area with hundreds of liquor bottles lined up on planks is topped by alternating headboards and antique mirrors; and the decor is rounded out by mismatched chairs, old portraits, red-velvet sofas, and walls covered with newspapers painted over with a clear black varnish à la New York School. The floor is open to reveal the candle-lighted dungeon basement, though you can't go down. Do have a beer here. If you're wondering about the name, wonder on: the owner's last successful enterpricse (not a triumph of this magnitude, but Murcia's best bar in its time) was called La Taberna del Cordero Degollao—roughly, Tavern of the Slit-Throat Lamb.

The music at **El Perro Azul** (Simon García 19), generally reggae, tends to be as mellow as the soft floorboards that give with each step. The wooden ceiling, antique organ, and homegrown art make it a friendly, moody place to get a drink. The black back room—more like a little haunted house, lighted with blue and green lamps—gives your dark side a chance to luxuriate. It *is* called the Blue Dog, after all.

SHOPPING

Paparajote (C. Apósteles 14, behind cathedral, tel. 968/215825), named after the local dessert, is a tasteful souvenir shop selling local food products such as sacks of Calsparra rice, the only rice in Spain with its own *denominación de origen* (a guarantee of quality traditionally reserved for wines) and cute mementos such as colorful Fiesta de Primavera mugs.

There's an **El Corte Inglés** at Plaza Fuensanta (Avda. de la Libertad 1, tel. 968/299500).

FIESTAS

What other fiesta sees thousands of young kids walking around drunk at 10 AM? Not content to settle back down after Holy Week (*see* Box: Holy Week East), Murcia throws a **Fiesta de Primavera,** or Spring Festival, just hours after Easter.

There are two big days to this party. The first, **El Bando de la Huerta** (very roughly, the Farm Gang) takes place the Tuesday after Easter. Teens and college kids wake up, dress in traditional farmer outfits, and take to the streets after 9 AM to get blitzed. They succeed rapidly, and within an hour there are plenty of young initiates in traditional dress vomiting in the city plazas. It's like nothing you've ever seen, and the madness lasts until evening. Typical wooden *barracas* (cottages) are set up around the city, and there's no better time to savor traditional local fare.

Saturday brings the **Entierro de la Sardina** (Sardine Burial), traditionally a Carnival event but transposed in Murcia to the Spring Festival. A huge parade is staged, with folks throwing food and toys into the frenzied crowds from floats depicting Murcian country life. This may be the only chance you'll ever have to dive for a turnip. The fiesta ends with a papier-mâché sardine, the fiesta's symbol, going up in flames.

SOUTH OF MURCIA

Not far southeast of Murcia are the important naval town of Cartagena and the beaches of La Manga del Mar Menor.

CARTAGENA

To put it diplomatically, Cartagena is not the most attractive town in Spain, but it has plenty of history. Carthaginians founded the city in the 227 BC, only to see it overrun by the Romans 18 years later. In 734 Arabs took possession of the city, and managed to keep the ascendant Christian Spaniards at bay until 1245.

The **Museo Arqueológico Municipal** (Ramón y Cajal 45, tel. 968/128801; open summer, weekdays 9–2; fall–spring, Tues.–Fri. 10–2 and 5–8, weekends 11–2) is one of Spain's oldest, built over a 6th-century Roman necropolis. Home of Spain's largest naval base, Cartagena also has a **Museo Naval** (Menén-

HOLY WEEK EAST

Murcia, Cartagena, and Lorca hold three of the most expressive Semana Santa celebrations in Spain. If you're here in late March or April, a tri-town itinerary beginning Holy Thursday night will give you a pure, intense dose of this hallowed Spanish custom.

Cartagena's processions are split into cofradías (brotherhoods), who battle for superior form. On Holy Thursday everyone's up through the night, bouncing between bars and the pasos (floats). Processions are conducted in a holy hush, the deep silence broken only by a spontaneous burst of mournful song, called a saeta, by someone in the crowd. Eventually, at 6:15 AM, the santo reencuentro, or holy reunion, occurs when two pasos—one a statue of Jesus, the other a Virgin sculpted by Francisco Salzillo—converge in the Plaza de la Merced.

Immediately after this spectacle, zoom up to **Murcia**, whose big Holy Week moment begins at 7 AM on Good Friday, when the purple-clad Cofradía de Nuestro Padre Jesús Nazareno (Brotherhood of Our Father, Jesus of Nazareth) emerges with eight striking pasos designed for them by Salzillo in the mid-18th century.

Lorca's procession may be the most interesting in Spain. As in Cartagena, the two big cofradías are rivals; but here the Blues and the Whites break out in a virtual civil war. The Azules (Blues) venerate the Virgen de los Dolores, the Blancos (Whites) the Virgen de la Amargura—Pain and Bitterness, indeed. The groups divide families, take separate routes, and go as far as to shout insults at the other group's Virgin. In place of traditional solid-color garb, the groups don biblical costumes of theatrical richness, and eventually King Solomon, Roman troops, ranks of Ethiopians, carriage-drawn Egyptians, horseback soldiers of the Persian king Nebuchadnezzar, and the 12 tribes of Israel make their way across town.

These affairs are social as well as sacred, with tapas and drinks between each group's pasos. Needless to say, you have to pull an all-nighter to experience the passion and drama; and some locals spend a full day holding their viewing spots before the action.

dez Pelayo 8, tel. 968/127138; open Tues.–Sun. 10–1:30) and a **Museo Arqueológico Marítima** (Dique de Navidad s/n, tel. 968/121166; open Tues.–Sun. 10–3), with exhibits from salvaged shipwrecks.

The best time to come here is the last week of September, when Cartagena commemorates the Roman capture of the city with seven days of fiesta. In a style akin to that of Moros y Cristianos events, Cartagena's **Fiesta de Cartagineses y Romanos** alternates days between the two costumed contingents. Hannibal's wedding is reenacted on Friday, the peak (Roman Circus) day, when the troops march around the city. Of course, this festival isn't just for lovers of ancient history; it's a week of solid partying, guaranteed to top whatever you proudly experienced in the flush of your youth.

LA MANGA DEL MAR MENOR

Minutes northeast of Cartagena, mud-blackened bodies and neon-pink birds form a striking summer contrast on Murcia's playground, **La Manga** (the Sleeve). The descriptive name denotes the fortuitous 15-mi-long volcanic accumulation of narrow beach that helps enclose Europe's largest saltwater lake, the **Mar Menor** (Minor Sea; it's really a lagoon), just off the Mediterranean.

La Manga has 42 km (26 mi) of immense, sandy beaches on both sides, giving you a choice of exposed or protected perches and warmer or colder water according to season and weather. Since the Mar Menor is perpetually wave-free, it's great for sailing, jet skiing, paddleboating, and all the other aquatic pursuits for which you can rent equipment on the shore. There are five volcanic islands here, and shipwrecks on the seabed. The area around Islas Hormigas is a marine reserve. Isla del Ciervo (Deer Island) is linked to La Manga by a strip of landfill. Boats leave periodically for the island of Perdiguera, where clear water invites swimming.

The shallow water in the Mar Menor is higher in iodine than the Mediterranean and is thus known as a therapeutic health resort for rheumatism patients. A few hotels and spas (*see below*) offer health programs, but you can also do it yourself: you'll see generally older bathers covering themselves from head to toe with the black tar found along the shore, especially in an area called La Puntica de Lo Pagan.

The north end of La Manga has no bridge; you have to drive around the long way to see the Parque Natural de las Salinas y Arenales (Sands and Saltworks Natural Park) de San Pedro del Pinatar. In summer migrating flamingos stop in the square, shallow salt marshes found here and at La Manga's south end.

The Sleeve's expensive hotels, **Cavanna** (Gran Vía s/n, tel. 968/563600) and **Entremares** (Gran Vía s/n, tel. 968/563100), offer therapeutic programs, as do the mainland spas **Sol y Mar** (Avda. Francisco Franco 292, Santiago de la Ribera, tel. 968/187092) and **Aguas Salinas** (C. Crucero Baleares, San Pedro del Pinatar, tel. 968/563100).

Other than a **campground** on the Mar Menor, there are no budget accommodations near La Manga. The cheapest lodging, with doubles for about 10,000 ptas. in high season, is **Dos Mares** (Plaza Bohemia, tel. 968/140093), on the beach. In mainland Santiago de la Ribera, on the north end of Mar Menor, doubles at the beachside **Madrid** (Zarandona, tel. 968/570504) run about 6,000 ptas. in high season.

THE BALEARIC ISLANDS

BY SHANE CHRISTENSEN

etween May and September each year, sun worshipers and disco fanatics from across Europe descend on the Balearic Islands in droves of charter flights, a sort of mechanized pilgrimage. For the duration the islands' otherwise intimate seaside communities and ancient mountain villages are transformed into Europe's best-known summer party, with Germans edging out Brits in sheer numbers: 4 million to 3. The airport at Palma de Mallorca becomes the busiest in Europe.

For most Europeans, Los Baleares represent the height of hedonistic vacationing. The natives don't take much offense at this narrow perception of their islands, as the summer disruption provides many with their only livelihood. But after the mass exodus every September, prices go down, bars close, and the islanders take refuge once more in tranquillity. In fact, Menorca and Formentera are largely spared the summer invasion altogether, giving you a quick escape hatch, if necessary, from the throngs of party goers on Ibiza and Mallorca.

Folks have been fighting over these islands for a long time, first because of their strategic position between Europe and Africa, then because of their prime beachfront property. Had you tried to approach the Balearics in 800 BC, the Greeks, who had succeeded in ousting the Phoenicians a few hundred years earlier, would have pelted you into submission with stones, aided by slingshots (they even named the islands a variant of *ballein*—"to throw from a sling"). Somehow the Carthaginians got through, only to yield to the Romans, Vandals, and Byzantines in the centuries to follow. The Moors put an end to this nonsense in AD 902, making the islands an important maritime trading and staging post, and ruled until Jaume I of the House of Aragón kicked them out in 1229. The Balearics became part of a united Spain in 1469, when Isabella of Castile married Ferdinand of Aragón. The British and (and for a short time the French) wrested control from the Spanish during the 18th century, then gave the islands back in 1802.

Today Los Baleares form a political Autonomous Community, where Mallorquín, the islanders' version of the Catalan language (which dominated before Franco banned its use) is rapidly replacing Castilian Spanish as the lingo of choice. Don't arrive hoping to immerse yourself in Spanish, as locals speak primarily Mallorquín. All four islands share a near-perfect Mediterranean climate—warm with lovely sea breezes—and arguably the prettiest beaches in Spain. **Ibiza** is the wildest and most expensive isle, attracting cross-dressers, hippies, European models, the utterly normal, and everyone else to the streets of Ibiza Town every night. Off Ibiza's southern tip, **Formentera** is the smallest and most isolated island, with spectacular beaches and nature trails. Palma, the capital of the archipelago, is on **Mallorca,** the

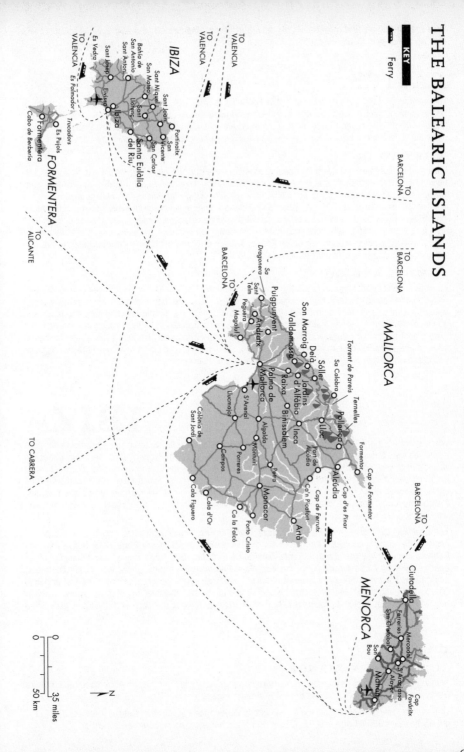

THE BALEARIC ISLANDS

KEY

Ferry

IBIZA

TO VALENCIA
TO VALENCIA
TO VALENCIA
TO VALENCIA
TO BARCELONA
TO BARCELONA

Es Vedra
Sant Josep
Bahía de San Antonio
San Antonio
Sant Mateu
Sant Miquel
Sant Joan
Eivissa
Ibiza
Sant Llorenç
San Vicente
Santa Eulalia
San Carlos
Santa Eulalia del Riu
Portinatx

Es Palmador
Es Pujols
Formentera
Cabo de Berbería

FORMENTERA

Trucadors

TO ALICANTE

MALLORCA

Sa Dragonera
Sant Telm
Peguera
Magaluf
Andratx
Puigpunyent
Son Marroig
Deià
Valldemossa
Jardins d'Alfàbia
Sóller
Sa Calobra
Torrent de Pareis
Ternelles
Raixa
Palma de Mallorca
Binissalem
Inca
Lluc
Pollença
Formentor
Cap de Formentor
Cap d'es Pinar
Port d'Alcúdia
Alcúdia
Ca'n Picafort
Cap de Ferrutx
Artà
Porto Cristo
Ca la Falcó
Cala d'Or
Cala Figuera
Colònia de Sant Jordi
Campos
Porreres
Montuïri
Petra
Manacor
Algaida
Llucmajor
S'Arenal

TO CABRERA

MENORCA

TO BARCELONA
Ciutadella
Ferreries
Mercadal
Santa Galdana
Son Bou
S'Arcaipessa
Alaior
Son Xoriguer
Maó
Cap Favàritx

N

0
0
35 miles
50 km

largest, best-known, and most heavily visited of the islands. **Menorca,** to the east, has the sedate charm of a place not yet fully discovered.

BASICS

Your greatest challenge as a traveler to the Balearics is finding a place to stay. Hotels are sometimes booked solid weeks in advance, and even when rooms are available, you may have to pay through the nose for them. The rugged rover will rent a moped and crash on a deserted beach (camping on unofficial sites is forbidden, but in practice few people ever get shooed away from obscure beaches).

WHEN TO GO

Ibiza and Mallorca explode with European holiday makers during Holy Week, and the dust doesn't settle until late September. This is the best time to come if you're into raging nightlife and beach landscapes of endless bodies; it's the worst time for anyone seeking island serenity. July and August are hot and, on the main beaches, almost unbearably crowded; finding accommodations is next to impossible. Menorca and Formentera are less crowded, but they offer correspondingly fewer lodging options. Fall and spring are considerably more peaceful than summer, and enough travelers remain to keep restaurants, hotels, and discos open. Except in Palma, tourism is dead from January through March, with the weather turning cool and many establishments closing.

COMING AND GOING

From mainland Spain you can reach the Balearics by ferry or plane. The small number of ferry companies conspires to keep prices high, so flying is not an extravagance in comparison. Flight prices change regularly—check with mainland travel agencies for the deal of the moment and take care to reserve in advance during the sizzling summer season. Flying from Barcelona takes a quick 40 minutes; the fastest boat takes four hours, and the traditional overnight ferry takes 11 hours. From Valencia the trip takes slightly longer. You can also fly from Madrid. Planes and ferries land on either Mallorca or Ibiza; you can then take an interisland service to Menorca and Formentera.

IBIZA

When most northern Europeans, stuck in the misery of Continental weather, dream of a raging, sun-drenched Mediterranean summer vacation, they're thinking of Ibiza. Everything you've heard about the island's decadent scene is probably true: Ibiza's bars are packed at sundown, and its discos—among the most plentiful and sophisticated in the world—rock right through sunrise. Look beyond the flashing lights, however, and you'll see an honest-to-gosh island. Picturesque hiking trails twist along hillsides, the chaotic tourist dens are watched over by peaceful villages, and the sea begs you to get your feet wet, whether you dive or sail or windsurf.

The best way to escape the madness of **Ibiza Town,** known locally as Eivissa, is to hop on a bus and explore the island's endless stretches of sand. The nearest beaches are **Playa d'En Bossa** and **Ses Salines;** farther away, the beach at **Santa Eulàlia** (northeast of Ibiza Town) is lined with hotels but is not nearly as frenetic or developed as the resort of **Sant Antoni de Portmany,** on the west coast. **Portinatx,** along the island's north coast, is a series of small coves with sandy beaches, of which the first and last, Cala Xarraca and Caló d'Es Porcs, are the best. If you tire of the crowds at any of these places, you can hop on a boat that circles the island and hop off at any beach along the way—some are only accessible by water.

BASICS

CURRENCY EXCHANGE

In Ibiza Town, **Banca March** (Juan de Austria 1) changes currency and has an ATM machine. **La Caixa** (Avda. Isadoro Macábich) also has decent exchange rates.

Unlike some private enterprises, the travel agency **Viajes Iberia** (C. Vicente Cuervo 9, tel. 971/311111, open weekdays 9:30–1 and 4:30–7:30, Sat. 9:30–1) changes currency commission-free.

CONSULATES
United Kingdom (Isidoro Macábich 25, tel. 971/301818).

CYBERSPACE
Eurocenter (C. Joan de Austria 22, tel. 971/310909) is open weekdays 9–noon and, in summer, 4–8:30. Web use costs 800 ptas. an hour.

EMERGENCIES
General emergencies: dial 112. **Police:** 091 or 971/315861. **Ambulance:** 061. **Fire department:** 080 or 971/313030. For urgent medical care, go to **Hospital Can Misses** (Barrio Can Misses, tel. 971/397000).

ENGLISH-LANGUAGE BOOKSTORE
Libromania (C. Ceramist Joan Daifa Ed. Transat B5, tel. 971/315985) has a limited selection of English books and magazines.

MAIL
The main **post office** (C. Madrid s/n, tel. 971/311380) is open weekdays 8:30–8:30 and Saturday 9:30–2.

VISITOR INFORMATION
The tourist office in **Ibiza Town** (Passeig Vara del Rey 13, tel. 971/301900) is open on summer weekdays 9:30–1:30 and 5–7, Saturday 10:30–1; in winter it's open weekdays 8:30–2:30 and Saturday 10:30–1. There's another information booth at the airport. In **Santa Eulàlia** the main office (Mariano Riquer Wallis s/n, tel. 971/330728) is open weekdays 9:30–1:30 and 5–7:30, Saturday 9:30–1:30; an additional office on Paseo Salamera, opposite the town hall, is open daily 10–2 and 4:30–8:30.

COMING AND GOING

Trasmediterránea (Estación Marítima, tel. 971/315050) ferries serve **Barcelona** (3–6/week, 8 hrs, 6,300 ptas.), **Valencia** (5/week, 8 hrs, 4,400 ptas.), and **Palma** (1/week, 5 hrs, 3,150 ptas.). **Trasmapi-Sercomisa-Flebasa** (Puerto Marítimo, tel. 971/314005) has about 15 daily ferries to Formentera (1 hr, 1,350 ptas.) and two weekly ferries to Denia, north of Alicante (8 hrs, 3,500 ptas. with 48 hours' advance purchase; otherwise 5,475 ptas.). **Inserco** (C. del Carmen, next to Estación Marítima, tel. 971/31–11–57) serves Formentera several times daily (1 hr, 1,100 ptas.).

The major carriers at Ibiza's **airport** (tel. 971/300300) are **Iberia/Aviaco** (tel. 971/300300) and, should you wish to follow the largest Balearic throng back home, **Lufthansa/Condor** (tel. 971/303390). An hourly bus connects the airport to Ibiza Town (15 min, 105 ptas.); in town; catch it a block east of the bus station on Avinguda Isidoro Macàbich.

GETTING AROUND

Buses and ferries can get expensive and overcrowded, so if you're planning to beach- or disco-hop, rent a **bike** (1,200 ptas.), **scooter** (3,000 ptas.), or **car** (6,500 ptas.) for the day at **Extra Rent** (Avda. Santa Eulàlia 27, tel. 971/191717). **Union Rent a Car** (airport, 971/308529 or 971/395830) is Ibiza's cheapest car-rental agency, but you'll still pay a minimum of 5,000 ptas. per day for the smallest car you've ever seen—and even more in summer. For a **taxi** call 971/ 307000.

BY BUS
If you opt for public transport, you'll find several bus companies at the small station on Avinguda Isidoro Macàbich. **H. F. Vilas** (tel. 971/311601) goes to local **beaches** such as Santa Eulàlia and Portinatx (300 ptas.). **Autobuses San Antonio** (tel. 971/340510) runs a 24-hour "Disco Bus" with hourly service to **Sant Antoni** and **Playa d'En Bossa** (300 ptas.).

BY BOAT
Boats leave the ferry port in Ibiza Town for nearby **beaches** at regular intervals, with most companies charging around 1,200 ptas. one way. Call Trasmediterránea (971/315100) for information.

IBIZA TOWN (EIVISSA)

It's doubtful that the Carthaginians, who settled this island in the 5th century BC, would now recognize their former home. Eivissa sits on the throne of Europe's summer nightlife—a wildly permissive city that attracts both high fashion and alternative lifestyles. A migration of hippies in the 1960s and the development of a large gay community have helped perpetuate the city's liberal atmosphere. Be warned that a lot of travelers not unlike yourself came here for a quick vacation and never quite left.

WHERE TO SLEEP

Reservations are a must in the summer—book a month in advance for July–September, two weeks for April–June. The streets parallel to Passeig de Vara de Rey hold a number of *casas de huéspedes,* identifiable by the standard blue CH sign. Your best bets for camping are **Es Canar** (Santa Eularia, tel. 971/342117), open May–September, and **Cala Nova** (Santa Eularia, tel. 971/331774), open April–October. Both charge 600 ptas. per site plus 500 ptas. per person.

UNDER 8,000 PTAS. • Hostal Residencia Las Nieves. Slightly more up to date than Hostal Juanito, its very basic sibling across the street, Las Nieves (whose name refers, oddly, to snow) is right in the heart of Ibiza's frenzied action. Doubles, some of which have private bathrooms, will set you back 5,000 ptas. in summer. *Juan de Austria 18, tel. 971/190319. 44 rooms.*

Hostal Residencia Ripoli. Centrally located, Ripoli offers the best value in its area. Bathrooms are shared, but the rooms have small twin beds, tile floors, sinks, and large windows or fans, and those on the third floor enjoy nice views of the old town. Doubles run 3,500 in winter, 6,000 in summer. The staff speaks English. *C. Vicente Cuervo 10–14, tel. 971/314275. 15 rooms.*

Hostal Sol y Brisa. At first glance the rooms may remind you of a bad dorm experience, but in summer this is about the cheapest place you'll find in Ibiza Town, and it's clean, relaxed, and family-run. The rooms are sparsely decorated, and there are zero amenities; even bathrooms are shared. You do have the luxury of knowing that you won't be here forever. Doubles are 6,000 ptas. in summer, 3,500 in winter. *Avda. Bartolomé Vte. Ramón 15, tel. 971/310818, fax 971/303032. 19 rooms. No credit cards.*

UNDER 10,000 PTAS. • Hostal Residencia Parque. Adjacent to the trendy Passeig Vara del Rey, this German-run *hostal* is the city's most popular. All the light-filled rooms (some of which are triples) have private bathrooms and air-conditioning; a few have terraces. There's a busy cafeteria on the first (that is, second) floor, and a TV lounge for rest and relaxation. Doubles start at 8,000 ptas. *C. Vicente Curevo 3, tel. 971/301358. 29 rooms.*

FOOD

Because most produce comes to Ibiza from the mainland via Palma, the cost of dining out here is comparatively high. Sa Penya, the old fishermen's quarter that grew famous as a hippie haven in the 1960s, is lined with restaurants of all kinds. A typical local specialty is *sofrit pagès,* a tomato-based dish spiked with onion and garlic that can include anything from potatoes and red peppers to lamb and chicken. Less refined palates can head for a fast-food joint in the old town, south of the marina.

UNDER 1,500 PTAS. • Forn Café. This corner café and bakery serves up cheap, decent food and prime people-watching on the Passeig Vara del Rey. Nibble on a sandwich or some pasta, or just enjoy an ice cream or coffee at one of the sidewalk tables. *Passeig Vara del Rey 18, tel. 971/190909.*

Il Giardinetto. Located right on the port, this is one of Ibiza Town's better pizzerias. The tables have water views, a variety of Italian dishes are served, and there's a good selection of reasonably priced wines to accompany both. *Puerto Deportivo, Marina Botafoch, tel. 971/314929.*

UNDER 3,000 PTAS. • Ca n'Alfredo. This family-run restaurant is the oldest, best-known, and most popular eatery in town. Authentic local dishes include seven styles of paella, *bacalla Ca n'Alfredo* (salt cod with baked potatoes), and *suquet de peix,* a seafood stew. Many entrées are sized for two people. Make a reservation because every table is filled by 10 PM. *Passeig Vara de Rey 16, tel. 971/311274. Closed Mon.*

Comidas San Juan. This small café at the beginning of Sa Penya has marble-top tables reminiscent of a Paris bistro. The gloss-painted decor is sterile, but the owners are cheerful and the fish dishes tasty. Try the grilled sole. *Carrer Montgri 8, tel. 971/310766. No credit cards.*

WORTH SEEING

Ibiza Town offers more than sunshine and all-night revelry, though these remain the principal attractions. The historic old town, **Dalt Vila,** stands in stark contrast to the town's modern parts: it's a walled city with a 14th-century cathedral, a castle dating from the time of the Moors, and a panoramic view of the bay from the Bastió de Sant Bernardo. Within the old town are Ibiza Town's main square, Plaça d'Espanya, and a statue of Guillem de Montgri, who captured the city from the Moors in 1235.

Straight down from Dalt Vila lies **La Marina,** with its fashionable seafront cafés, shops, and restaurants. The port is *the* spot for people-watching during the day, what with a passing mélange of fishermen, café folk, tourists, and entrepreneurs, and it's not a bad place to catch some rays. **Sa Penya,** running along the quay at the far end, was traditionally a fishermen's quarter and home to the island's poorest residents. Today fishing and poverty coexist with a booming tourist industry of hippie markets, bars, and trendy restaurants.

AFTER DARK

If you're easily turned off by wanton displays of wealth, sequins, and flesh, Ibiza may not be the place for you. If, on the other hand, you fancy yourself a disco king (or queen) and have been planning your trip around nonstop nightlife, you've arrived in heaven. The cycle is simple: beach, bar, disco, beach, bar, and so on, until your body (or wallet) can't take it anymore. From 10 PM to midnight, Ibiza's old town and port are jam-packed with people clinging to tables and checking each other out. The voice of Enrique Iglesias is everywhere.

Most bars see a very mixed crowd. In town the creative **Café Kumaras** (Plaza del Parque, tel. 670/870474) is a psychedelic temple to alternative tastes, filled with candles and kaleidoscope murals. Dwelling in the world of trance music, it's perfect for a pre-disco drink. There is occasional live music on the small stage. One of the coolest bars among those who live here year-round is **Km 5** (Sant Josep, tel. 971/ 396349), 5.6 km outside Ibiza Town. Calle de la Virgen has a cluster of gay bars, including **JJ Bar** (C. de la Virgen 79; open May–Oct.) and **Bar Teatro** (C. de la Virgen 83), the latter open May to September only.

At around 2 AM people head for the discos, which thump nonstop from late April through September and charge roughly 4,000–7,000 ptas. for entrance. You can save a few pesetas by picking up discount coupons in bars; any number of slick, young hawkers plant themselves outside the bars along the marina to dole out these cards, which usually throw in a free drink. Expect to pay at least 1,000 ptas. per drink after that.

Pachá (Paseo Marítimo, Ibiza, tel. 971/313600), considered the chicest club on Ibiza, caters to a slightly older, moneyed crowd. It's the only disco that stays open year-round (weekends only in winter). **Amnesia** (Carretera San Antonio, tel. 971/198064) is the most famous disco, known for its wild special events like foam parties on Wednesday and Sunday. **Es Paradis** (Sant Antoni, tel. 971/342893) holds a variety of special events, including *Clockwork Orange* theme nights. The biggest, craziest party, however, takes place at **Privilege** (Carretera San Antoni, tel. 971/314474), which has outdoor pools, bars, stages, gardens, and a variety of seedy shows. Just when you think the night is over, head to **Space** (Far end of Playa d'En Bossa, tel. 971/306990), which *opens* at 5 AM, and rock right through the morning. All these clubs are on the Disco Bus line—except Pachà, which is a 20-minute walk north of Estación Marítima—and all are replete with fly girls and guys, bizarre murals, and great sound and lights.

OUTDOOR ACTIVITIES

Ibizan beach resorts offer windsurfing, water-skiing, and sailing schools aplenty: try **Club Surf Ibiza** (Playa den Bossa, tel. 971/315343), **Club Surf Portmany** (Caló des Moro, Sant Antoni), or **Centro Deportivo Nautico Boca Rio** (Sta. Eulàlia, tel. 971/330004). There are several more windsurfing schools in Cala Talamanca (outside Ibiza Town) and Cala Vadella (west of Sant Josep), and waterskiing in Es Canar (north of Santa Eulàlia) and Portinatx.

Some of the best diving visibility in the Mediterranean, up to 130 ft, beckons off Ibiza and Formentera. For information on scuba diving, contact **La Sirena** (C. Balanzat, 29 bajos, Edif. bahia Sant Antoni Portmany, tel. 971/342966) in San Antoni, **Aquamatic** (tel. 971/340972) at Cala Vadella, or **Centro Poseidon Nemrod 1** (tel. 971/339457) at Cala Pada, in Santa Eulàlia. La Sirena has the island's only decompression chamber, open March to November.

SANTA EULÀLIA DEL RIU

The Balearics' only riverside town, Santa Eulàlia del Riu lies 15 km (9 mi) northeast of Ibiza Town. The *riu* (river) is little more than a stream, but the village is worth visiting for its Moorish-influenced church and its picturesque waterfront. A large international presence means the restaurants, cafés, and shops are first-rate.

FOOD

UNDER 3,000 PTAS. • C'as Pages. This old farmhouse, with bare stone walls, wood beams, and columns made of giant olive-press screws, is not for vegetarians. Try the leg of *cordero asado* (roast lamb with baked potato), *pimientos rellenos* (roast peppers), or the *sofrit pagès* (lamb and chicken stew), topped off with *graixonera* (a mixture of sugar, milk, eggs, and cinnamon). *Carretera de San Carlos, Km 10, no phone. No credit cards. Closed Tues. and Feb.–Mar.*

Sa Capella. Set in the resort of Sant Antoni, a 20-minute drive west of Santa Eulàlia, Sa Capella is a former chapel converted with style and flair. Try the roast suckling pig, perhaps the best on the island. *Puig d'en Basora, tel. 971/340057. Closed Nov.–Mar.*

BALAFI

Just 10 km (6 mi) northeast of Santa Eulàlia is Balafi, a fortified Moorish village with fewer than a dozen whitewashed houses and two towers that once protected them. To dodge hungry pirates, residents would climb a ladder to the tower's second floor and pull it up after them; their rate of success was not 100%. The contrast between modern Ibiza Town and ancient Balafi is remarkable.

FORMENTERA

Formentera is the smallest and quietest Balearic island, the one most people pass over and many have never even heard of. As such, it is the archipelago's best-kept secret, a peaceful land of beach and countryside perfect for a morning hike, a swim, and an afternoon picnic—in short, hangover relief after a rough night in Ibiza Town. There are only about 500 permanent residents, though a number of Europeans make Formentera their home away from home.

Measuring less than 20 km (12 mi) from east to west, Formentera makes a perfect day trip. Ferries pull into **La Sabina,** at the island's north end, where you can rent a bike or a moped and set off to explore. A mere 3 km (2 mi) south is Formentera's tiny capital, **Sant Francesc Xavier,** where there's an active hippie market in the small plaza before the church. The interior of the whitewashed church is quite simple, its rough, old wooden door encased in iron and studded with nails. Down a short street directly opposite the church, on the left, is a good antiques and junk shop, complete with a small art gallery featuring paintings and olive-wood carvings.

Back on the main road, turn right toward **Sant Ferran,** 2 km (1 mi) away. Beyond Sant Ferran the road travels for 7 km (4 ½ mi) along a narrow isthmus, keeping slightly closer to the rougher northern side, where waves come crashing over the rocks when the wind blows. Just beyond El Pilar you'll see a windmill on the right, still in good order, with all of its sails flying.

The plateau on the island's east side ends at the lighthouse **Faro de la Mola.** Nearby stands a monument to Jules Verne, who set part of his novel *Journey Through the Solar System* in Formentera. Despite being trampled by herds of tourists, the bare rock around the lighthouse is carpeted with flowers, purple thyme, and sea holly in spring and fall, while hundreds of swallows soar below. At the edge of the cliff you may see turquoise-viridian lizards.

Back on the main road, turn right at Sant Ferran toward Es Pujols. The few hotels here are the closest Formentera comes to beach resorts, but they're expensive, and the beach is not the best. Beyond Es Pujols the road skirts **Estany Pudent,** one of two lagoons that almost enclose La Sabina. Salt was once extracted from Pudent—hence its name, "Stinking Pond." On most days the pond smells fine, as does its neighbor, Estany de Peix (Fish Pond), which was once a fish farm.

At the northern tip of Pudent, a road to the right becomes a footpath that runs the length of **Trucadors,** the narrow sand spit that leads to Es Palmador. The beaches here are excellent.

BASICS

The island's one **tourist office** is in the port (La Sabina, tel. 971/322057). It's open weekdays 10–2 and 5–7, Saturday 10–2.

COMING AND GOING

You can only reach Formentera by ferry from Ibiza. Ferry, catamaran, and hydrofoil services are offered by **Transmapi** (tel. 971/314513 or 971/320703), **Marítima de Formentera** (tel. 971/320157), and **Flebasa** (tel. 971/310927).

GETTING AROUND

Formentera's small size and flat terrain make **cycling** ideal. La Sabina has numerous places to rent bikes and scooters, with bikes renting for 500–1,000 ptas. per day and scooters cashing in at about 2,500 ptas.; try **Moto Rent Mirada** (tel. 971/328329). A very limited **bus** service connects Formentera's villages, shrinking to one bus each way between San Francisco and Pilar on Saturday and disappearing altogether on Sunday and holidays. Ibizan newspapers publish the details.

MALLORCA

The grand island of Mallorca receives the bulk of Balearic-bound tourists—from the Germans, who rent homes in the north and west, to the British, who descend on the west-coast town of Peguera, to the French, who flood the port town of Alcúdia. Everyone who visits this horse head–shape island eventually winds up in the capital city of Palma, whose old town, despite the general hustle and bustle, maintains an air of antiquity. Palma's impressive Gothic cathedral is notable for its lack of a *coro,* the standard choir found in the center of most Spanish cathedrals, and for its striking detail work by Antoni Gaudí.

Outsiders may outnumber locals in Palma during the summer, but you can easily escape to a remote beach or trail when the crowds get old. Mallorca boasts more than 75 white-sand beaches; just avoid overcrowded package-tour resorts like Magaluf, which is recommended if you're not here exclusively to party. For hikers the mountains of the Serra de Tramuntana present a wealth of possibilities, including the difficult but breathtaking 10-km (6 mi) trek that once inspired Frédéric Chopin. The best excursions are on the island's north and west coasts.

Advice: include the ancient villages of Valldemosa and Deià—former haunts of writers and artists like Robert Graves, D. H. Lawrence, and George Sand—in your itinerary, as well as trips to the beautiful coastal towns of Port de Sóller, Port Pollença, and Alcúdia. If you rent a car, take the stunning drive to Cap Formentor; if not, take the traditional train ride from Palma to Sóller, which whisks you through mountain gorges and fruit orchards.

BASICS

VISITOR INFORMATION

Palma has two main **tourist offices,** one at Plaça de la Reina 2 (tel. 971/712216), the other at Carrer Sant Domingo 11 (tel. 971/724090). Both provide free maps, bus schedules, restaurant information, and accommodation lists and are open weekdays 9–7:30, Saturday 10–1. A **tourist booth** opens at the airport in summer (tel. 971/789556).

The **Asociación Agencias de Viajes de Mallorca** (Association of Mallorcan Travel Agents; Plaça del Rei Joan Carles I, tel. 971/722244) can organize individual and group tours around the island. A regional tourist office with information on all the Balearic Islands is the **Conselleria de Turisme de Balears** (Montenegro 5, tel. 971/176191), open weekdays 9–3.

Outside Palma you'll find local tourist offices in **Alcúdia** (Carretera Port d'Alcúdia Arta 68, tel. 971/892615), **Sóller** (Plaça de Sa Constitució 1, tel. 971/630200), and **Valldemossa** (Cartuja de Valldemossa, next to monastery, tel. 971/612106).

CURRENCY EXCHANGE
There are cash machines all around Palma. For in-person transactions, the **Banco Central Hispano** (Passeig del Born 17, tel. 971/725146) offers decent rates.

CONSULATES
United States (Avda. Jaume III 26, Palma, tel. 971/725051). **United Kingdom** (Plaça Major 3D, Palma, tel. 971/718501).

CYBERSPACE / PHONES
CyberCentral, near the Plaça de la Reina tourist office (C. Soledad 4 bajos, tel. 971/712927, open weekdays 10–8:30, Saturday 10–6), offers fast connections for 100 ptas./six minutes. You can also connect your laptop, send faxes, and make international calls.

EMERGENCIES
General emergencies: dial 112. **Police:** 091 or 092. **Ambulance:** 061. **Fire department:** 080. You can get drop-in medical care at **Clínica Juaneda** (C. Son Espanyolet, tel. 971/722222) or **Hospital Son Dureta** (Andrea Doria 55, tel. 971/175000). Pharmacies are open late by rotation; schedules are posted on the door of each pharmacy and in local newspapers.

ENGLISH-LANGUAGE BOOKSTORES
Two bookshops in Palma sell publications in English, as well as Spanish and (*claro*) German: **Dialog International Bookshop** (Carme 14 near C. Olms and La Rambla, tel. 971/228129) and **Book Inn** (C. Huertos 20, off La Rambla, tel. 971/713898). At either shop you can pick up copies of the *Reader,* an English weekly covering events across the Balearic Islands, and the *Mallorcan Daily Bulletin,* the island's best English-language newspaper.

LAUNDRY
You may be best off doing laundry in the sink of your hotel room, as laundry facilities here are slow and inconvenient. **Self Press** (Aníbal 14, tel. 971/730643) is one of the few places with automatic self-service machines. Hotel laundry service often amounts to staff members washing clothes by hand and can take forever.

MAIL
Palma's main **post office** (Constitució 5, tel. 971/721867) is open weekdays 8:30–8:30, Saturday 9:30–2.

TRAVEL AGENCIES
For cheap plane and ferry tickets try **Viajes Baixas, S.A.** (C. Soledad 4, tel. 971/725254).

COMING AND GOING
Most people fly to Mallorca, as plane fares are comparable to (or even cheaper than) ferry tickets. Prices change constantly, so ask local travel agencies about current deals. **Iberia** (tel. 971/262600) flies daily between Palma and **Barcelona, Madrid, Valencia, Ibiza,** and **Mahón.** Your other option is **Air Europa** (tel. 971/178100), with flights to **Barcelona, Madrid,** and **Valencia.** Interisland flights hover around 15,000 ptas. round-trip, slightly less if you book in advance. Bus 17 (½ hr, 300 ptas.) runs between Palma's airport and the bus station at Plaça Espanya. Expect to pay 2,000 ptas. for a taxi from the airport to downtown.

Trasmediterránea ferries (Estación Marítima 2, tel. 971/405014) connect Mallorca to **Barcelona** (7–10/week, 9 hrs, 6,300 ptas. one-way), **Valencia** (6/week, 8 hrs, 6,300 ptas.), **Ibiza** (2/week, 6 hrs, 3,400 ptas.; fast boat 3/week, 2½ hrs, 5,300 ptas.), and **Mahón** (1/week, 6 ½ hrs, 3,100 ptas.). From the ferry terminal take Bus 1 to Plaça Reina and cheap digs.

GETTING AROUND

BY BUS

Buses are the cheapest way to explore Mallorca. Transports a Palma (tel. 971/711393) runs city buses from **Plaça Espanya** (175 ptas.; 750 ptas. for a 10-ride Bonobus ticket); ask the tourist office about bus service around the island.

BY TRAIN

Mallorca has two rail lines, one a modern metropolitan train to the leather-industry town of **Inca** (40 min, 255 ptas.), the other an antique wooden train that winds through the mountains to **Sóller** (1½ hrs, 380 ptas; 735 ptas. for the 10:30 AM "tourist" train). Both depart from the train station at Plaça Espanya (tel. 971/752051). The ride to Sóller is particularly scenic.

BY CAR

Renting a car is the easiest, if not the cheapest, way to get around. Pursue the best rates at **Hasso** (Camí Ca'n Pastilla 100, tel. 971/261005), in Ca'n Pastilla, 15 minutes east of Palma on Bus 100. Prices start at 3,800 ptas. per day, but rates are lower if you rent for more than four days or pay in cash up front. Reserve a week ahead of time for the best selection. For a **radio taxi** in Palma, call 971/755440.

PALMA

A vibrant, picturesque city of 350,000, Palma is dominated by a breathtaking cathedral overlooking the waterfront—one of Spain's most impressive landmarks. Behind the cathedral lies Palma's old town, whose centuries-old buildings and wandering cobblestone streets lead to hidden restaurants and upscale shops. Remnants of the defensive walls erected by the Moors in the 12th century remain; you can see them at Ses Voltes along the seafront, west of the cathedral.

The city makes an excellent base of explorations: political capital of the Balearic Islands, it's fairly cosmopolitan and well prepared for tourists. City sights are well maintained, most restaurants offer English-language menus, and car-rental agents stand ready. Regardless of budget, you should also have little difficulty finding rooms in the city center—*if* you reserve ahead for summer stays.

WHERE TO SLEEP

The bulk of Palma's cheap *hostales* are just west of Plaça Reina, in the narrow lanes of the old town. Campers can take the Port Alcúdia bus from Plaça Espanya to the year-round campground **Sun Club Picafort** (Carretera Artá–Puerto Alcúdia, Km 23.4, tel. 971/860002; open year-round), where sites are 2,500 ptas. plus 550 ptas. per person; or drive to the cheaper **Club San Pedro** (Cala dels Camps, Colonia San Pedro, tel. 971/589023), open June–mid-September, where sites are 1,500 ptas. plus 550 ptas. per person.

UNDER 5,000 PTAS. • Hostal Monleon. Don't come here for luxury or charm, as this stark building offers neither. On the plus side, the Monleon is walking distance from the historic center, the staff is hospitable, and the dark rooms are the cheapest around. Doubles without bath go for 4,300; doubles with bath, 5,000. *La Rambla 3, tel. 971/715317. 38 rooms. No credit cards.*

Ritzi. The Ritz it ain't, but it's one of the most popular lodgings in town. The rooms in this well-preserved five-story house are spacious if spartan, and a full English breakfast is served. Doubles cost 5,000 ptas. with shared bathroom, 6,000 ptas. with private shower. *C. Apuntadores 6, tel. 971/714610. 17 rooms.*

UNDER 8,000 PTAS. • Hotel Cannes. Just off a popular pedestrian shopping street, this modern two-star offers a marble entry and a nice breakfast nook. The rooms are air-conditioned, and breakfast is on the house. Doubles cost 7,500 ptas. *C. Cardenal Pou 8, tel. 971/726943, fax 971/726943. 50 rooms.*

Hostal Brondo. The best *hostal* in town is also the most centrally located. Brondo's colorful rooms have matching linens, nightstands, and even desks. Number 6, perhaps designed for women travelers, is bathed in pink with a Tiffany-style lamp, handsome wooden furniture, and a charming balcony. The self-contained apartment on the top floor is perfect for threesomes, and the inn's charming sitting room is great for meeting like-minded globetrotters. Doubles without bath are 5,000 ptas.; with bath, 6,000. *C. Ca'n Brondo, tel./fax 971/719043. 10 rooms, 6 with bath.*

Hostal Apuntadores. This hostal is clean and comfortable, and you're never far from a lukewarm shower or Palma's most popular restaurants and bars. Balconied rooms on the top floor have inspiring views of the cathedral. Drawback: service is shoddy, no matter who's working the front desk. Doubles run 3,900–5,500 ptas., shared bath all. *C. Apuntadores 8, tel. 971/713491. 28 rooms.*

FOOD

Finding tasty food is no problem here; just remember that most restaurants close at midnight. West of Plaça Reina, Calles Apuntadores and Vallseca are rife with restaurants of all shapes and sizes. If you want a vegetarian meal, try **Bon Lloc** (Sant Feliu 7, tel. 971/718617) or **Green Garden** (Balanguera 25, tel. 971/458674). Buy supplies at **Supermercado SYP** (C. Bonaire 6, off Avda. Jaime III), open weekdays 9–2 and 5:30–8:30, Sat. 5:30–8:30.

UNDER 1,500 PTAS. • Restaurante La Zamorana. If you enjoy the reassurance of inspecting your ingredients before they're cooked, this typical Mallorcan eatery is for you. You're greeted by a display case of fresh fish and meats, including some surprising pigs' feet dangling from the spit. Back in the grottolike dining rooms, blond-wood tables are surrounded by Mallorquín speakers clinking glasses of sangria and nibbling on paella; less adventurous tourists were spotted deconstructing roast half chickens and succulent lamb chops. Omelets, steaks, and a number of with-the-head fish dishes round out the menu. *C. Apuntadores 14, tel. 971/726205. Closed Wed.*

Vecchio Giovanni. This popular Italian restaurant is loud, smoky, fun, and popular—make reservations if possible. The diverse menu offers seafood lasagna and stuffed red peppers as well as favorites like roast lamb, veal, salmon, pizzas, salads, and vegetarian entrées. The Andina salad, with lettuce, orange, nuts, and ground Roquefort cheese, is especially tasty. *C. San Juan 3, tel 971/722879.*

C'an Joan de S'Aigo. On a hot day in Mallorca this might be just what the doctor ordered: delicious ice-cream concoctions are served in a charming old house with marble tables and a small garden and fountain. *Ca'n Sanç. 10, tel. 971/710759. No credit cards.*

UNDER 3,000 PTAS. • Caballito de Mar. Beloved by locals, this is probably the best seafood restaurant in town. Across from the Llotja at the center of Palma's port, it specializes in *caldereta de pescado* (fish soup) and all kinds of fish concoctions. Service is good and ingredients fresh; just watch what you order, as prices can quickly add up. *Passeig de Sagrera 5, tel. 971/721074.*

WORTH SEEING

You can easily explore Palma on foot. A ring of wide boulevards, known as the Avingudas, zigzags around the old city. Two principal arteries are Passeig de la Rambla and Passeig d'Es Born, the latter hosting Palma's traditional evening *paseo* (promenade). Lined with towering plane trees and fashionable shops, the Born has a pedestrian promenade down its center. If you like to shop, you'll enjoy finding locally made shoes, handbags, and other leather goods here, all of excellent quality.

CATHEDRAL

Palma's breathtaking Gothic cathedral is one of the largest in the world. It was begun under Jaume I of Aragón after he expelled the Moors in 1229, though it must be said that it took another 400 years to complete. At the beginning of the 20th century, Antoni Gaudí restored the cathedral, and his distinctive style is evident in the asymmetrical canopy suspended above the Royal Chapel, in the shape of the altar, and in the addition of electric lighting. The bell tower above the Plaça Almonia door holds nine bells, the largest of which is known as N'Eloi, meaning "praise." Cast in 1389, N'Eloi weighs 4 tons, needs 12 men to ring it, and has been known to shatter stained-glass windows with its sound. There's a small museum on the bell tower's ground floor. *Plaça de l'Almonia, tel. 971/723133. Apr.–Oct., open weekdays 10–6, Sat. 10–2:30; Nov.–March, open weekdays 10–2. Admission free; museum 500 ptas.*

PALAU DE L'ALMUDAINA

Opposite the cathedral, this Gothic palace served as the residence of the royal house of Mallorca during the Middle Ages and was originally an Arab citadel. It is now a military headquarters and can be visited only on guided tours (every half hour). The palace has two courtyards: one for the king, one for the queen. *C. del Palau Reial, tel. 971/727145. Open April–Sept., weekdays 10–6:30, Sat. 10–2; Oct.–March, weekdays 10–2 and 4–6, Sat. 10–2. Admission 400 ptas.*

After you visit the cathedral and Palau de l'Almudaina, consider a walk to the **Llotja** (Exchange), on the seafront a little west of the Born. Built in the 15th century, this masterpiece of decorative turrets, battlements, and buttresses is the Mediterranean's finest example of civic Gothic architecture. Museum lovers may want to stop into the **Museu de Mallorca** (C. de la Portella 5, tel. 971/717540; open Tues.–Sat. 10–2 and 4–7, Sun. 10–2; admission 325 ptas.), just down from the Plaça Santa Eulàlia, a mixture of prehistoric, Moorish, and Gothic artwork. The **Museu Fondació Pilar y Joan Miró** (C. Joan de Saridakis 29, tel. 971/701420; open Mon.–Sat. 11–6, Sun. 10–3; admission 700 ptas.) displays numerous works by the famous Catalan artist, who spent his last years on Mallorca (1979–83).

Outside the city center, the **Castell de Bellver** (Bellver Castle) overlooks the city and bay from a hillside above the Terreno nightlife area. The **Poble Espanyol** (Spanish Village), in the western 'burbs, is a reproduction of various Spanish buildings and styles, complete with old-fashioned shops and craft studios.

AFTER DARK

Many of Palma's best bars are clustered around Plaça de la Lonja and Carrer Apuntadores. Don't bother showing up before midnight. Locals and foreigners meet at MacGowan's (C. Mar 18, tel. 971/719847) for Kilkenny Irish beer, billiards, and European sports games. Try the laid-back **Blues Ville** (C. Ma d'es Moro 3, off C. Apuntadores) for nightly live blues and soul; there's no cover, but drinks are about 400 ptas. during the shows. For a taste of the tropics head to **Jahfarai** (Sant Feliu 6), a popular reggae pub open after 10 PM. **The Royal Golden Door** (C. Apuntadores 3, tel. 971/720817) is a chic international bar and dance club with a thirtysomething crowd. Champagne and cocktails are served, and there's no cover. Poke your head into **Abaco** (C. Sant Joan 1, tel. 971/715911) to gawk at the opulence within: candelabras, marble columns, and rich, tanned people sipping pricey drinks.

The hottest discos are strung out along Paseo Marítimo, also known as Passeig Marítim. **Bolsa del Marítimo** (Paseo Marítimo 33) is perfect for a pre-club cocktail to the tunes of Latin or general pop. **Tito's** (Plaça Gomilia 1, tel. 971/737642; cover 1,500 ptas.) overlooks the Mediterranean from the glass elevator leading to its overflowing dance floor. **Pachá** and **IB's** are within easy walking distance on Avinguda Gabriel Roca. Among the best gay bars are **Sombrero** (Avda. Joan Miró, tel. 971/731600) and **Baccus** (C. Luis Fábregas 2).

OUTDOOR ACTIVITIES

Palma acts as a perfect base from which to explore the island's best **beaches** (there are more than 75 to choose from). Stay away from sprawling package-tour resorts like Magaluf, and head to one of the following instead, chosen for their natural beauty, swimming conditions, and relative serenity: in the southwest, **Palmanova, Cala Vinyas, Santa Ponça,** and **Camp de Mar;** in the northeast, **Cala Molins, Platja de Formentor** (accessed by a spectacular road), **Platjes de Pollença, Platja d'Alcudia,** and **Platja de Muro;** in the east, **Sa Coma** and **Cala d'Or;** and in the south, try **D'Es Caragol, Es Trenc,** or—the beach closest to Palma—**Platja de Palma.** Water sports are plentiful at most beach resorts, and you can easily rent windsurfing equipment.

Opportunities for **scuba diving** are abundant on Mallorca, and the clear, relatively warm waters (up to 75° F/24°C in summer) make diving a pleasure year-round. The tourist office has a map of the best dive sites, which include the areas around Soller, Alcúdia, and even the bay of Palma. **Escuba Palma** (C. Jaume I s/n, tel. 971/694968) is the city's primary scuba connection.

Mallorca is ace for **hiking.** Begin your expedition by picking up a copy of the free "20 Hiking Excursions on the Island of Majorca" leaflet, with detailed maps and itineraries, at the tourist office. The best hiking areas are near Deià and Valldemossa, where routes take you along the coast and through olive trees, woods, and mountains. To reach the trailhead, take the **Bus Nort Balear** (pick it up north of Plaça Espanya) to Valldemossa (40 minutes, 200 ptas.), walk 80 ft farther along the crazy, winding road, and look closely on your right for the marked trail to Deià. Excellent hiking trails also extend from Inca and Alcúdia in the north. For additional maps and drawings, track down *12 Classic Hikes Through Majorca,* by the German author Herbert Heinrich, available in bookstores at key sights. For more information contact the **Grup Excursionista de Mallorca** (Mallorcan Hiking Association; Can Cavalleria 17, tel. 971/711314).

JARDINS D'ALFÀBIA

Seven kilometers (4 miles) before Sóller on the road from Palma, you'll come to the lovely Alfàbia Gardens and their antiques-filled hacienda. Surrounded by mountains, these terraced gardens of palms, bamboo, ficus trees, orange groves, and bougainvillea are a great place for a stroll, especially if you're trying to romance your travel companion. A full-service bar in the central courtyard makes the experience that much more enchanting. *Open weekdays 9:30–5:30, Sat. 9:30–1. Admission 700 ptas.*

FOOD

Restaurante Ses Porxeres. Next to the garden stands a rustic country restaurant covered in ivy. Dishes are fresh from the hunt—among the more creative plates are duck with almonds and pears, roast milk-fed lamb, and cod with garlic cream. You should be able to get out for under 3,000 ptas. if you don't drink too much wine. Stay away from the black (read: blood) pudding. *Carretera de Sóller, Km 17, tel. 971/613762.*

SÓLLER

From Palma the 30-km (19-mi) drive to Sóller on the C710 is gorgeous, the road winding its way along the coast past olive and citrus groves, rugged mountains, and ancient villages. Sóller is actually divided into the Village of Sóller and the Port of Sóller. The **village** is a rough but intimate gray-stone town with a mountain feel; it's connected to the beautiful **port** by a small, red tram that runs along the beach (15 ptas.). The boardwalk is lined with hotels, restaurants, and shops. Sóller's small, occasionally pebbly beach is not ideal for swimming, as yachts pollute the harbor in summer; but all is crystal blue in winter.

From the port make the half-hour climb to the **Torre Picada.** Accessible via an easy tarmac road (follow signs from the jetties on the port, behind the tram terminus), the watchtower offers a great view of Sóller's coastline, best experienced at sunset.

WHERE TO SLEEP

Hotel Miramar. Overlooking Sóller's port, the four-story Miramar shows a rather stark white exterior but hides comfortable rooms inside. All rooms have private bathrooms, and some have seaside balconies. The sidewalk restaurant in front is popular for its rich paella. Doubles start at 5,000 ptas. *C. Marina 12–14, tel. 971/631350. 30 rooms.*

FOOD

Mar y Sol. The large outdoor patio of this touristy restaurant overlooks the water and bustles with pleasing activity. Perfect for an afternoon ice cream or beer, the Mar y Sol also serves sandwiches, pizzas, and pasta. If you're up before noon, the breakfast selection is fairly robust. *C. Marina 7, tel. 971/631031.*

DEIÀ

Nine kilometers (5½ miles) west of Sóller is breathtakingly beautiful Deià, an ancient mountain village in the Tramuntara Mountains adjacent the sea. Deià has long been an artists' haven—the English poet, novelist, and scholar Robert Graves lived here until his death in 1985, and D. H. Lawrence and Arthur Rackham hung their hats here as well. The village café, up some steps on the left as you enter the village, remains a favorite haunt of creative types. A walk through the town takes you past houses frozen in time to the **village church and cemetery,** where Graves is buried. From here you have a spectacular view of the surrounding mountains, terraced with olive trees, and the beach coves below.

La Residencia (Finca son Canals, tel. 971/639011), a 16th-century manor house that has hidden everyone from the late Princess Diana to Van Morrison, Pierce Brosnan, and Kate Moss, is a worthy splurge—we're talking 26,000–41,000 ptas. for two—if you're looking for a truly memorable hotel experience (you don't have any cheap lodging options here, anyway). A mile down from the village in a rocky cove lies Deià's **beach bar,** patronized by locals and jet-setters alike.

VALLDEMOSSA

Another eye-candy mountain village, Valldemossa (18 km/11 mi north of Palma) gets a lot of traffic thanks to its 14th-century **monastery,** which housed Frédéric Chopin and French novelist George Sand for the difficult winter of 1838–39 (both the weather and their affair have always been described as tempestuous). The tourist office, in the plaza next to the church, sells a 1,200-pta. ticket that admits you to all the monastery's various attractions, including Chopin's quarters and original piano, which he carried up the mountain in sections. Short recitals of the composer's music are performed every hour except Monday and Thursday mornings, when Mallorcan dancers perform. The monastery is open Monday through Saturday 9:30–1 and 3–5:30 in winter, 9:30–1 and 3–6:30 in summer.

ALCÚDIA

The ancient city of Alcúdia, 54 km (34 mi) northeast of Palma, wears its history with charm and elegance. Take an hour to explore the Moorish city walls, interspersed with gates, and the maze of narrow streets and charming 17th-century houses within.

The Phoenicians settled here around 700 BC and left a host of small archaeological wonders, now displayed at the **Museu Monogràfic de Pollentia.** Prehistoric religious objects and oil lamps are mixed with more newfangled Roman artifacts. *C. Sant Jaume 30, tel. 971/547004. Summer, open Tues.–Sat. 10–1:30 and 5–7, Sun. 10:30–1; winter, open Tues.–Sat. 10–1:30 and 4–6, Sun. 10:30–1. Admission 350 ptas.*

The **Port de Alcúdia** is nothing particularly special, though a number of restaurants, bars, and hotels line its crowded beach. Along the port road, however, a signposted lane leads to the small, 1st-century BC **Teatre Romá** (Roman Amphitheater), which is carved from the rock of a hillside—facing south, so audiences could enjoy the setting sun. Excavated in the 1950s, the haunting site is always open.

From the Teatre Romá, turn back to Alcúdia, but at the Inca junction keep to the right for **Port de Pollença.** This town is less hectic than Alcúdia, and its seafront is lined with relaxing cafés and bars. An international music festival is held here in August and early September, with some concerts performed in the cloisters of the former **monastery of Santo Domingo.**

OUTDOOR ACTIVITIES

One of Mallorca's best **hikes** starts just off the port road in Alcúdia, taking you to a spectacular panoramic view of the Bay of Pollença and the Formentor peninsula. Numerous inviting coves along the way beckon for a swim. **Scuba diving** is also excellent in these parts, with visibility of 100 ft or more in the Bay of Pollença: contact Oceano Sub (Avda. Del Mal Pas, Alcúdia, tel. 971/545517). **Bicycling** is perfect in the flatlands around Port de Pollença, Alcúdia, and C'an Picafort. The roads have special bike lanes, and there's a rental outlet on every corner in the towns.

POLLENÇA

This 13th-century village watches the mountains of the Sierra de Tramuntana tumble to the sea. If you're up to it, climb the **Calvari,** a stone staircase with 365 steps: at the top stands a tiny chapel with a wooden Gothic crucifix and a panoramic view of the bays, Alcúdia and Pollença, and the Formentor and Pinar peninsulas. Drink in more breathtaking views from the **Ermita de Nostra Senyora del Puig** (Hermitage of Our Lady of the Hill), at the town's southern end.

If you have a rental car, make the 20-km (13-mi) drive from Port de Pollença to **Cap de Formentor,** where the twisty, scenic road threads its way between huge teeth of rock before reaching a lighthouse at the extreme tip. The **Platja de Formentor** is a romantic spot for a picnic.

LLUC

The **Monastir de Nostra Senyora de Lluc,** in the remote mountain village of Lluc, 20 km (13 mi) west of Port de Pollença, has drawn pilgrims for centuries and is widely considered Mallorca's spiritual sanctuary, as the famous carved-wood statue of La Moreneta—also known as the Black Virgin of Lluc—is on display in the 17th-century church. A boy's choir sings psalms in the chapel every evening at 7:30 (except June and July), and the Christmas Eve performance of the pre-Christian Cant de la Siblia (Song of the Sybil) is an annual choral delight. A small **museum** (tel. 971/517025) has an eclectic collection of ceramics, paintings, clothing, folk costumes, and religious items; it's open daily 10–5:30 and charges 350 ptas.

WHERE TO STAY

Santuari de Lluc. You can join (other) religious pilgrims in staying right at the monastery in cells once occupied by priests. Although the vast building has three Mallorcan restaurants and a bar, nightlife is restricted, with guests asked to be silent after 11 PM. Your donation of 4,000 ptas. for a simple, clean, apartmentlike double helps keep the monastery operating. *Santuari de Lluc, tel. 971/517025, fax 971/ 517096. 113 rooms.*

MENORCA

Not long ago, word got out that Menorca was an isolated paradise, and every middle-class British family with a few pounds to spare got on the next plane south. Locals in Mahón and Ciutadella tend to be pretty fed up with English-speaking guests by August. If you know any Spanish at all, use it. Package holidays notwithstanding, however, Menorca is a relatively quiet haven of small, pretty beaches and quiet country roads, far less commercialized than Mallorca and Ibiza. The pristine beaches are relatively remote, the rugged landscape unspoiled, allowing a taste of how these islands must have appeared centuries ago.

As on all the Balearics, the best beaches are as far from the towns as possible: if you have a scooter, hit the beaches west of **Fornells,** on the north coast, or those east of **Cala Morell,** in the northwest. Rent a bike for access to **Punta Prima,** the largest of an attractive series of beaches south of Mahón.

BASICS

VISITOR INFORMATION

Mahón's tourist office (Plaça S'Esplanada 40, tel. 971/363790) is open weekdays 9–2 and 5–7, Saturday 9:30–1. In summer there's also a tourist booth at the airport (tel. 971/157115). The helpful tourist office in **Ciutadella** (Plaça Catedral 5, tel. 971/382693), which can point you to Menorca's best beaches, is open weekdays 9–1:30 and 5–7, Saturday 9–1.

CURRENCY EXCHANGE

In Mahón, change money at **La Caixa** (S'Arravaleta 30).

CYBERSPACE

Pickings are slim. The **Bar and Café Telegraph** (*see* Food, *below*) has a temperamental video-game-like Internet machine into which you drop 100 ptas. and pray that you get your six minutes' worth. It's open daily from 4 PM to midnight. Ciutadella has one cybercafé, **Accesso Directo** (Plaça de S'Explanada, also known as Plaç dels Pins, tel. 971/484026), open Monday through Saturday 9–9 (closed February) and charging 400 ptas. per hour.

EMERGENCIES

Police: 091 or, in Ciutadella, 971/381095. **Ambulance:** 061. **Fire department:** 080. You can get medical care in Mahón at **Hospital Verge del Toro** (C. Barcelona, tel. 971/157700) and in Ciutadella at **Canal Salat** (C. St. Antoni M. Claret s/n, tel. 971/480111). Pharmacies are open late by rotation; schedules are posted on the door of each pharmacy and in local newspapers.

MAIL

Mahón's main **post office** (C. Bonaire 11–13, tel. 971/363892) is open weekdays 8:30–8:30, Saturday 9:30–2. Ciutadella's beautiful marble-floor post office (Plaça des Born 9, tel. 971/380081) is open weekdays 8:30–2, Sat. 9:30–1.

COMING AND GOING

Iberia has multiple flights to and from **Palma** every day (14,880 ptas.). **Trasmediterránea** (tel. 971/366050) ferries connect Mahón to **Palma** (8 hrs, 3,150 ptas.), **Valencia** (15 hrs, 6,300 ptas.), and **Barcelona** (11 hrs, 6,300 ptas.). **Flebasa** (tel. 971/480012) shuttles between Ciutadella and **Alcúdia,** Mallorca (3½ hrs, 3,245 ptas.).

GETTING AROUND

You'll need your own wheels to seek out more remote areas, such as the north-coast beaches. The cheapest **scooter** rentals (about 2,500 ptas. per day) are at **Valls** (Plaça Espanya 13, tel. 971/362839, fax 971/354239); for the best selection call two days before you arrive. You can rent sturdy **mountain bikes** at **Just Bicicletas** (C. Infanta 19, at Hostal Orsi, tel. 971/364751) for 1,000 ptas. per day, or 2,500 ptas. for three days.

For the full motor works, try **Europcar** (Plaça S'Esplanada 8, Mahón, tel. 971/360620; Avda. Conquistador, Ciutadella, tel. 971/382998). For a **radio taxi** call 971/367111 in Mahón; 971/382896 in Ciutadella.

BY BUS

In general, buses stick to the main road connecting **Mahón** and **Ciutadella** (45 min, 500 ptas.), calling at the island's other principal towns (**Alayor, Mercadal,** and **Ferreries**) en route. In Mahón most depart from Plaça S'Esplanada; some leave from C. Josep M. Quadrado. For information contact **TMSA Transportes Minorca,** tel. 971/360361. From the smaller villages there are daily buses to Mahón and connections, though often indirect, to Ciutadella. A regular bus service from the west end of Ciutadella's Plaça S'Esplanada shuttles travelers between the city and resorts to the south and west.

MAHÓN

Menorca's capital (called Maó in Catalan), is less a tourist attraction than a base for other sojourns, though the harbor, where most restaurant and bar activity is centered, is an attractive place to while away an evening. In town there are two places moderately worth seeing, after which you should get out of the city and have some fun. The **Ateneo** (C. Compte de Cifuentes 25, off Plaça de S'Esplanada; open daily 10–2 and 3–10) is a cultural and literary society with displays of wildlife, seashells, seaweed, minerals, and stuffed birds. The church of **Santa María,** originally built in the 13th century but rebuilt during the British occupation, is proudest of its 3,200-pipe Baroque organ, imported from Austria in 1810. Shopwise, Mahón is known for its gin and shoes, both introduced by the British; you'll also spot good-quality leatherwear and costume jewelry.

WHERE TO SLEEP

Finding a place to stay in Mahón can be a challenge, especially if you arrive without a reservation. If you don't land a room in a hostal, try one of the two official campgrounds, **S'Atalaia** (Carretera Cala Galdana, Km 4, tel. 971/374232) and **Torre Soli Nou** (Carretera Sant Jaume, Km 3.5, tel. 971/372605), each of which charges around 1,500 ptas. per night, cash only, and is open year-round. The Mahón-Cala Galdana bus stops within a kilometer of S'Atalaia.

UNDER 6,000 PTAS. • Hostal La Isla. A father-son operation, La Isla begins with a casual restaurant/bar and moves upstairs to three floors of tidy rooms with private baths. You can arrange to have all meals included in your room rate; without meals, doubles are 5,200 ptas. *Santa Caterina 4, tel. 971/366492. 22 rooms.*

Jume. Despite an austere lobby with pale green chairs, this hostal has clean (if small) rooms with private baths and comfortable mattresses. It's popular with English and Spanish backpackers. Doubles run 5,300 ptas., breakfast included. *C. Conceptión 6, tel. 971/363266, fax 971/364878. 35 rooms. No credit cards.*

Hostal Residencia Orsi. Run by an incredibly helpful British couple, this is the most affordable place in town and throws in breakfast to boot. All rooms have private baths. Doubles run 4,400–5,000 ptas. *C. Infanta 19, tel. 971/364751. 17 rooms.*

UNDER 10,000 PTAS. • **Sheila.** This comfortable two-star hotel is a bit of a splurge, but you can usually negotiate your rate if it's not full. Within easy walking distance of Mahón's historic center and armed with more amenities than the hostales above (hotter water, better soap, nicer shampoo . . .). Come here if you're tired of roughing it. Prices drop as low as 5,000 ptas. for a double in winter but can jump to 12,000 ptas. in summer. *Santa Cecilia, tel. 971/364855. 19 rooms.*

FOOD

The best dining options are along the port, but these are also the priciest. To avoid big spending, stop in at **La Tropical** (C. Luna 36, tel. 971/360556), where a whopping plate of sautéed veggies goes for about 600 ptas. To buy your own local produce, visit the **mercado** (open Monday–Saturday 8–1:30) inside the cloister of the church of El Carmen, near Plaça de la Miranda. Expect omnipresent mayonnaise—*mahónesa* was invented here. Note that things are quiet in winter, with many restaurants closed during the week.

UNDER 1,500 PTAS. • **Bar & Café Telegraph.** This multipurpose lounge in the Hotel Capri serves as a café, cyberstop, and one of Mahón's few worthwhile bars. Decorated with old copies of the *Daily Telegraph* and popular with British tourists, it serves standard pub grub and a variety of whiskeys. *San Esteban 8, tel. 971/361400. No lunch.*

UNDER 3,000 PTAS. • **Gregal.** "You will eat very well at Gregal," the locals will tell you, and they're right. Fresh seafood selections include salmon with chicory; baked sea bass with potatoes, onions, and spiced tomatoes; steamed mussels; and seafood pasta. There are meat and poultry dishes to boot, and service is attentive and professional. *Moll de Llevant 306, tel. 971/366606.*

J'ágaro. Stash your backpack somewhere else and settle in for a romantic evening along the waterfront. This is among Mahon's best seafood spots, and a number of selections ring in at less than 2,000 ptas., including mixed paella, swordfish with a red-pepper sauce, and various steaks. Finish with *creme menorquina,* a delicious cream-filled pastry smothered in powdered sugar. *Moll de Llevant 334, tel. 971/362390.*

AFTER DARK

Mahón's nightlife is really quite dismal. On weekends and in summer the bars opposite the ferry terminal fill with locals after midnight. The best bar for the twenty- and thirtysomething crowd is **Akelarre** (tel. 971/368520), in the port; jazz and blues bands play downstairs, and there's a mixed straight and gay crowd at the disco upstairs. A quieter bar with occasional live music is **Bar Nou** (C. Nou, 2nd floor), in the city center. **Pachá,** a branch of Ibiza's famous disco, is on the left at the entrance to San Luis, and **Karai** is ensconced in a cave at the edge of Mahón.

OUTDOOR ACTIVITIES

Fornells Bay, on Menorca's north shore, is windsurfing heaven, a protected area several miles long and a mile wide—ample security for beginners. **Windsurfing Fornells** (tel. 971/376400) rents boards and gives quality lessons in English or Spanish. Mahón's **Es Fornás** (tel. 971/364422) organizes horseback-riding tours of Menorca for all levels of riders. If you've taken to bird-watching, head to **S'Albufera,** a wetland nature reserve north of Mahón that attracts many species of migratory birds.

CIUTADELLA

Ciutadella is a joy to wander, a historic port city that was the capital of Menorca before the British moved things to Mahón. Watch a slower, more traditional Menorca while away the hours in the **Plaça de la Catedral** and the **Plaça de S'Esplanada.** A walk along the **Mirador d'es Port,** which follows the length of the harbor, is another invitation to relax. There are no must-see attractions, but Ciutadella is surrounded by some of Menorca's most impressive prehistoric sites. The "Archaeological Guide to Minorca," available from the tourist office, can help you plan an attack.

Following the road from Ciutadella to Mahón, you can walk the 4 km (2½ mi) to **Naveta des Tudons,** the largest preserved Talayotic settlement in the Balearic Islands and some of the oldest ruins in Europe. Two other Talayotic settlements, **Torretrencada** and **Torrellafuda,** are accessible by a 7-km (4-mi) trek from Ciutadella toward Mahón on the old Camí Vell road, which runs parallel to the main road.

WHERE TO SLEEP

UNDER 8,000 PTAS. • Hotel Geminis. This two-star beauty is a five-minute walk from the historic center. Rooms are light-filled and Mediterranean in feel; some have small terraces over an outdoor garden. There are a pool resembling an oversize Jacuzzi and a rooftop solarium with a Ping-Pong table and sunbathing area. Doubles run 7,900 ptas. *C. Josefa Rossinyol s/n, tel. 971/384644, fax. 971/383683. 30 rooms.*

Hostal Residencia Ciutadella. Ciutadella's only year-round hostal is modern, friendly, and centrally located. A marble staircase leads to well-equipped rooms with refrigerators and private tile baths. The cafeteria serves inexpensive local specialties, and breakfast is included in the room rate (5,900 ptas. for a double). *C. San Eloy 10, tel. 971/383462. 17 rooms.*

Ses Persianes. Open only in summer, this small pension and café offers clean, startlingly inexpensive rooms: doubles go for 4,000 ptas. *Plaça d'Artrutx 2, tel. 971/381445.*

FOOD

UNDER 1,500 PTAS. • Es Palau. A popular student hangout with a small sidewalk patio and a rustic indoor room, Es Palau is all things to all people: a tapas restaurant, a *salón de té,* an afternoon bar, and a smoker's paradise. Ham sandwiches and Spanish coffee await you. *Plaça d'es Born, no phone. Cash only.*

Triton Bar. A watering hole for old sailors and local fishermen, this casual eatery serves cheap, delicious tapas. Favorites include Spanish tortillas, grilled shrimp, *albondigas* (meatballs), calamari, and fried fish. Don't count on quiet conversation: the espresso machine is deafening. *Port de Ciutadella 55, tel. 971/380002.*

UNDER 3,000 PTAS. • Café Balear. You'll feast on fish soup, grilled fish, and dessert at this busy waterfront restaurant. Excellent three-course meals are 1,900 ptas. on weekdays and 2,500 ptas. on weekends, a price hike attributed to better-quality fish (which are apparently caught only on weekends). *Port de Ciutadella, tel. 971/380005. Closed Mon. in winter, Sun. in summer.*

AFTER DARK

Weeknights are rather quiet here. On weekends a few bars and clubs open along the Porto de Ciutadella. The best bar/disco in town, **Esfera** (no phone), is in the port.

MONTE TORO

Almost in the center of the island, Monte Toro is Menorca's highest point, at 1,181 ft above sea level. From here you have a seriously panoramic view of the island, and on a clear day you can see across the sea to Mallorca. Monte Toro has been an important religious site for centuries: Christians built a monastery atop the hill in the 17th century. Today you can enjoy the church's small courtyard and outdoor café while taking in the view. Monte Toro is 24 km (14 mi) northwest of Mahón, easily found by following the signs to Es Mercadal.

TORRE D'EN GAUMÉS

Archaeology buffs will love this Talayotic village dating from 1500 BC. You will see three Talayots, including a *taula* sanctuary—that is to say, Torre d'en Gaumés is a complex set of prehistoric ruins with fortifications, monuments, deep pits of ruined dwellings, and huge vertical slabs. The truly discerning will notice remnants of a storage and filtration system for the hill's running water, revealed in the variegated cavities of the surrounding rock.

BARCELONA

BY ANNELISE SORENSEN

With the playfulness of a Moderniste building, the adroitness of a *camarero* (waiter) at a sidewalk café, and the aggressiveness of Barça, the city's idolized soccer team, Barcelona has a way of seducing all who pass through. Catalonia's capital inspired Pablo Picasso to paint, Ernest Hemingway to write, Antoni Gaudí to build, and, more recently, artist Keith Haring to say, "I've known many cities in my life, but Barcelona—there's a special magic here." In one afternoon you can lose yourself in the bewitching lanes and archways of the medieval Barri Gòtic, dip your toes into the Mediterranean Sea, and ease into the warm evening with a drink at a terrace café—and then it's almost time to hit the clubs.

Barcelona's centerpiece is La Rambla, the pedestrian street that poet and playwright Federico García Lorca called "the very spirit of the city." Cutting a wide swath through the old town, from Plaça Catalunya to the sea, the Rambla is at all hours of the day and night a teeming river of humanity. Street performers—jugglers tossing balls into the air, buskers strumming soulful tunes, spray-painted human statues striking poses—compete for attention from the passing crowds, yet at its core, the Rambla is a thriving commercial strip of the simplest kind. Street-side florists do a brisk trade wrapping up fragrant bouquets; bird vendors with cages of squawking parakeets ring up ongoing sales; newsstands sell everything from the *Herald-Tribune* to porno mags; caricaturists sketch their way through reams of paper; and barkers invite you to *tomar una copa* (have a drink) in their respective cafés and bars. The Rambla seems to revel in mixing the traditional Spanish *paseo* (stroll) with the very business acumen that has helped make Catalonia the wealthiest region in Spain. Indeed, the one Catalan adage that has spread through Spain intact is "La pela es la pela" (in Spanish it would be "La peseta es la peseta")—money is money.

Modernisme—the Catalan form of what is widely known as Art Nouveau—left an indelible mark on Barcelona, particularly along the broad, stately avenues of the Eixample neighborhood, where light-hearted Moderniste homes stand in quiet but delightful contrast to their stately neighbors. Barcelona's golden boy of architecture is Antoni Gaudí, whose mad and genius vision produced such unforgettable, unclassifiable monuments as the otherworldly Sagrada Familia church and the whimsical Parc Güell, both of which make fitting symbols for a city proud of its progressive outlook. With such an artistic heritage, it's only fitting that Barcelona has become one of Europe's leading centers for contemporary design, a talent that emerges vividly in the city's restaurants and nightclubs. Contemporary designer Javier Mariscal (creator of the 1992 Olympic mascot Codi) has stepped in where Gaudí left off, with a series of only-in-Barcelona creations such as the surreal Torres de Ávila nightclub in Montjüic.

Spanish writer Camilo José Cela once wrote that Barcelona was a city "de la mar alegre, la tierra jocunda, el aire claro"("of happy sea, jocund earth, and clear air"). For a long time it seemed as though Barcelona had lost sight of its "happy sea"—until the 1992 Olympics. As the rest of the world looked to Barcelona, residents looked to the water and readied their town for the international spotlight by tearing down and rebuilding whole sections of the waterfront. Results include the floating Port Vell walking pier and the Port Olímpic promenade.

Notwithstanding all this agglomeration, Barcelona's historical heft is impressive. The city was founded more than 2,000 years ago by (it is generally believed) Carthaginian general Hamilcar Barca, who in any case gave the city its first recorded name, Barcino (pronounced *Bark*-ino). In 133 BC, Barcino was taken as a colony by the Romans, who ruled it until the 5th century AD (you can still see parts of the Roman's defensive walls near the cathedral, in the Gothic quarter). After that the power struggle was ongoing. In the 5th century the Visigoths took over and made Barcelona their capital; later the Moors gained control and ruled Barcelona for most of the 8th century. In the 9th century the Franks moved in and made Barcelona part of their defensive border against the Muslims. In the late 10th century the autonomous counties of Catalonia gained independence from the Franks, and in the 12th century Barcelona and its environs were united with Aragón, to the west. During this time Barcelona grew into a successful maritime capital. Barcelona's portside power diminished considerably in the 15th century, when Catalonia became part of Castilian Spain, and even further when Catalonia was excluded from the rich trade rising up with the New World in the 16th century. During the War of the Spanish Succession in the early 16th century, Catalonia backed the wrong (Habsburg) side and was punished severely: victorious Felipe V dismantled much of Barcelona's power and made Castilian the official language for all of Spain, effectively banning Catalan. In the 19th century Barcelona anchored the Catalan Renaixença (Renaissance), during which the Catalan language was revived and creativity flourished, expressed largely through Moderniste design.

It was during the Spanish Civil War that Catalonia exerted itself most aggressively against Madrid's central government: fueled by anti-Franco sentiment, Catalonia became the most important Republican stronghold in Spain. After a fierce fight the Republicans lost to Franco's forces in 1939 and thus began the difficult, depressing *posguerra* (postwar) period, when Franco took revenge on Catalonia's wartime opposition by setting out to suppress—ideally, to abolish—Catalan culture. This was not possible, for although Catalans were forbidden to write, teach, or speak their language, underground efforts kept it vibrantly alive; and when Franco died in 1975, Catalonia was poised to become itself again. The Catalans' resilience and pride are responsible for today's bilingual Barcelona: street signs are in Catalan, and most news media broadcast or print in Catalan. True, everyone speaks Spanish as well, but most conversations are conducted in Catalan. Part of the success of this tongue is that Catalans are eager to make it accessible to everyone, rather than use it to talk behind people's backs; if you manage a phrase or two in Catalan, you'll prompt smiles and even hugs. Try *Bon día* (Hello; literally, "Good day,") or *Visca el Barça!* (Go, Barça!), and you'll have a grand old time in Barcelona.

BASICS

AMERICAN EXPRESS

Cardholders can withdraw cash, buy traveler's checks, cash personal checks, and pick up mail at AmEx's **main office** on Passeig de Gràcia, near the Diagonal (at C. Rossello, tel. 93/217–0070; Metro: Diagonal). Have snail mail addressed to: your name c/o American Express Barcelona, Passeig de Gràcia 101, 08008 Barcelona. Everyone can use the currency exchange, though cardholders get better rates. The office is open weekdays 9:30–6, Saturday 10–noon. There's a branch office for **currency exchange** at Rambla 74 (tel. 93/301–1166), open April–September, daily 9 AM–midnight; October–March, weekdays 9–8:30, Sat. 10–7.

CURRENCY EXCHANGE

Banks are everywhere, most with a main office on or near Plaça Catalunya. Most banks have 24-hour ATM machines, and a growing number have automatic cash-exchange machines, including the Caja de Madrid on Plaça Catalunya and the Banco Santander on Plaça Sant Jaume, though you need fairly new, crisp bills to use them.

The Rambla is dotted with *casas de cambio,* but their rates are considerably worse than those of banks, and the area is crawling with pickpockets. The only advantage to using cambios is their late hours: They stay open till 11 PM or midnight. **Exact Change** (Rambla 85 and 130, tel. 93/302–2351), open daily 9 AM–10 PM, has slightly better rates than the others. Banks with longer exchange hours include those in the **tourist office** complex (*see* Visitor Information, *below*) in Plaça Catalunya, open daily 9–9 (just beware the long lines on weekends) and in **Sants-Estació** train station, open daily 8 AM–10 PM.

CONSULATES

Australia (Gran Via Carles III 98, tel. 93/330–9496; open weekdays 10–noon). **Canada** (Passeig de Gràcia 77, tel. 93/215–0704; open weekdays 9–1). **Great Britain** (Avda. Diagonal 477, tel. 93/419–9044; open fall–spring, weekdays 9–2; winter, weekdays 9–1 and 4–5). **Ireland** (Gran Via Carles III 94, tel. 93/491–5021; open weekdays 10–1). **New Zealand** (Travesia de Gràcia 64, tel. 93/209–0399; open weekdays 9–2 and 4–6). **United States** (Passeig Reina Elisenda 23, tel. 93/280–2227; open weekdays 9–12:30 and 3–5).

CYBERSPACE

Barcelona has a slew of Internet centers, some with cafés or bars, where you can check your Web-based e-mail. Prices at **easyEverything the Internet shop** (Ronda Universidat 35, tel. 93/410–1397) fluctuate depending on crowds but are usually the best in town—usually 400 ptas. an hour. The shop is huge, comfortable, and just off Plaça Catalunya. **Cybermundo Internet Centre** (C. Bergara 3, tel. 93/317–7142; Metro: Universitat), between the university and Plaça Catalunya, is another biggie, with more than 40 computers and long hours (open daily 9 AM–midnight, Sat. 10 AM–midnight, Sun. 11 AM–midnight). Rates are 590 ptas. per hour and 400 ptas. per half hour, with discounts for students. **L@ F@ctor.i@** (in Restaurante Factoria, Plaça Universitat 1, tel. 93/451–0833; Metro: Universitat; open Mon.–Thurs. 8:30 AM–midnight, Fri. 8:30 AM–2 AM, Sat. 10:30 AM–2 AM, Sun. 12:30 PM–12:30 AM) normally asks 130 ptas. for 20 minutes, 390 ptas. an hour, but if you come before 11:30 AM or after 10 PM, it's 130 ptas. an *hour,* virtually free.

Net-Movil (Rambla 130, tel. 93/342–4204; Metro: Catalunya) is right on the Rambla, near Plaça Catalunya; the rate here is 300 ptas. for 15 minutes. **Inetcorner** has two locations, one in the Barri Gòtic (Plaça Ramon Berenguer 2, tel. 93/268–7355; Metro: Jaume I) and one in the Eixample (C. Sardenya 306, tel. 93/244–8080; Metro: Sagrada Familia). For 850 ptas. an hour you get free apples and coffee, decent consolations if you've got no mail.

In the Born district, **Local.Bar** (Plaça Fossar de les Moreres 7, tel. 93/319–1357; Metro: Jaume I) has only two computers (700 ptas. an hour), but you can order a beer while you wait. **Idea Llibreria-Cafè-Internet** (Plaça Comercial 2, tel. 93/268–8787), also in the Born, is a bright, comfortable café charging 500 ptas. for an hour of computer use and nothing for perusal of its many books and magazines. English-language publications include the *Economist,* the *International Herald-Tribune,* the *Independent,* and *USA Today* as well as some classic and contemporary fiction. Computer use is free if you drop more than 300 ptas. in the café.

DISCOUNT TRAVEL AGENCIES

USIT Unlimited (Ronda Universidad 16, tel. 93/412–0104; Metro: Plaça Catalunya or Universitat), open weekdays 10–7:30 and Saturday 10–2, is Barcelona's main youth travel agency. There's a definite hostel vibe: waiting their turn, backpackers lounge around smoking, drinking vending-machine coffee, and exchanging travel tips. The multilingual staff can help arrange budget digs in Barcelona, day trips nearby, and discount rail or plane tickets to anywhere in the world, sometimes even for those over 30. The branch office (C. Rocafort 115–122, tel. 93/483–8377; open weekdays 10–2 and 4–8) has similar services. Adjoining the USIT office on Carrer Rocafort is the **Catalunya Jove** complex (tel. 93/483–8363), open weekdays 9–2 and 4–6, where you can get general advice on budget and youth travel.

The Gothic quarter's **Centre d'Informacio i Assessorament per a Joves** (C. Ferran 32, at C. Avinyo, tel. 93/402–7800; Metro: Liceu or Jaume I), open weekdays 10–2 and 4–8, has loads of info on youth travel, including maps, guidebooks, and brochures. **Nouvelles Frontieres** (C. Balmes 8, northwest of Plaça Catalunya, 93/304–3233; Metro: Universitat), open weekdays 9:30–7:30 and Saturday 10–6, is another good source for discount travel information and tickets.

EMERGENCIES

Barcelona's main police office is at Via Laietana 43, but the 24-hour **police station** at Rambla 43 (across from Plaça Reial) offers visitor assistance and counseling services in English. During spring and summer travelers can call a special **tourist police** number (tel. 93/301–9060). The rest of the year, call the police at **092**, remembering that they may not understand English.

Barcelona has several large hospitals, including **Hospital de la Creu Roja de Barcelona** (C. Dos de Maig 301, tel. 93/433–1551), **Hospital Clinic** (C. Villaroel 170, 93/227–5400), and **Hospital de la Santa Creu i de Sant Pau** (C. Sant Antoni Maria Claret 167, tel. 93/291–9000). In a medical emergency call an ambulance at **061.**

ENGLISH-LANGUAGE PUBLICATIONS

Most of the newspaper kiosks on the **Rambla** sell the *International Herald-Tribune* and the international versions of *Time* and *Newsweek*. The kiosk in the department store **FNAC El Triangle** (Plaça Catalunya 4, tel. 93/344–1800), open daily 10–10, has one of the city's better selections of international magazines, including such glam publications as *Spin, George, Talk, Wallpaper*, the *Face*, and the *Spectator*, though the issues are sometimes a few weeks old. Inside, FNAC's bookstore has a great section of English titles.

Barcelona's own English-language magazine, the monthly *Metropolitan*, has extensive listings of current art exhibits, plays, concerts, and the like, along with such useful things as new Internet centers and cinemas showing movies in English. Pick it up at cafés and bars throughout Barcelona, including Café de la Opera, Schilling, and Bar del Pi, all in the Barri Gòtic.

The largest of the English-only bookstores is **Come In** (C. Provenca 203, tel. 93/453–1204; closed Aug.), with a sizable second-floor selection of English literature from Shakespeare to Martin Amis, with Ernest Hemingway, Graham Greene, Paul Theroux, and Iris Murdoch sure to be in stock. Coffee-table books are another option. If you're bitten by the Barcelona bug, this is a good place to investigate English-teaching opportunities and/or Spanish or Catalan classes. **BCN Books** (C. Roger de Lluria 118, tel. 93/476–3343) has the latest in contemporary fiction and some reference books for English teachers. Many of Barcelona's bigger bookstores have English-language sections; *see* Books *in* Shopping, *below*.

LAUNDRY

If your clothes are at the point where they can stand on their own, try the large, self-service **Wash 'n Dry Lavanderia** (C. Provenca 356, at Bailen, tel. 93/207–2946), open daily 7 AM–midnight, where you can wash a load for 700 ptas. and dry it for 400 ptas. Drop it off, and they'll do the washing and drying for 1,500 ptas.

LOST AND FOUND

There's an **Oficina de Objetos Perdidos** (C. Ciutat 9, 93/402–3161), open weekdays 9–2, in the *ajuntament* (city hall), on Plaça Sant Jaume.

MAIL

The main **post office** (Plaça Antoni Lopez s/n, tel. 93/318–3831) has telegram services, sells stamps, and holds mail. Have it sent to Your Name, Lista de Correos, 08002 Barcelona Central. You can buy stamps at all post offices and at most *estancs* (tobacco shops).

PHARMACIES

Each pharmacy is marked by large green or red flashing cross. Every Barcelona neighborhood has a pharmacy on duty 24 hours, but they take turns; call **010** to find out which pharmacy nearest you is open. Some pharmacies never close, including **Farmacia Clapes** (Rambla 98, tel. 93/301–2843) and **Farmacia Alvarez** (Passeig de Gràcia 26, tel. 93/302–1124).

SAFETY

Unfortunately, as Barcelona's popularity and level of illegal immigration have risen simultaneously, the Rambla has become Ground Zero for petty criminals preying on tourists. Muggings are depressingly common here and in the Barri Gòtic. Beware of pickpockets as you saunter; dress in subtle hues and leather footwear (rather than sneakers) if at all possible; and avoid conspicuous map reading and picture taking.

TELEPHONES

Most phone booths throughout the city accept coins, Telefónica phone cards, and other long-distance cards. Telefónica phone cards are sold in denominations of 1,000 and 2,000 ptas. at *estancs* (tobacco shops), post offices, Telefónica offices, and most newsstands. If you have several calls to make, a phone card is the way to go. The minimum charge for a local call is about 25 ptas.; you then pay about 15 ptas.

for every three minutes. The main **Telefónica office,** open daily 8 AM–10 PM, is inside Sants-Estació. The Telefónica office on Plaça Catalunya is more geared toward residents, but you can buy phone cards here and use the phone booth inside. Barcelona's **directory assistance** number, operative Monday–Saturday 8 AM–10 PM, is **010**—dial it for reliable, up-to-date addresses and phone numbers for about 200 ptas. If they don't have what you need, try national directory assistance at **1003** (72 ptas.).

International calls are charged at regular rates from 8 AM to 11 PM, reduced rates overnight. A private **phone center** can be handy if you don't feel like messing with phone cards; you call from a private booth, then pay the precise amount you incurred. Alas, these places sometimes charge as much as double the going rate, and you can't resort to your phone company's calling card. The **BCC Phone Center,** open weekdays 9–9, Saturday 10 AM–9 PM, and Sunday 2–8, is in the underground RENFE station at Plaça Catalunya. Dial **025** for international directory assistance, a most impressive service for 270 ptas.

VISITOR INFORMATION

No stranger to tourism, Barcelona has wholeheartedly stepped up to the challenge of accommodating the increasing hordes who descend on the city every summer. If you arrive by train, stop by the tourist office in **Sants-Estació** (tel. 906/301282; open July–Sept., daily 8:30–8:30; Oct.–June, weekdays 8–8, weekends 8–2) to pick up a map. There are two tourist offices in the **airport,** one in the international terminal (tel. 93/478–4704; open Mon.–Sat. 9:30–8, Sun. 9:30–3) and one in the EU arrivals terminal (tel. 93/478–0565; open Mon.–Sat. 9:30–3).

In town the **main tourist office** (Plaça Catalunya 17-S, tel. 906/301282 inside Spain, 93/304–3421 from outside Spain), open daily 9–9, is more of a tourist complex. Though it's actually underneath Plaça Catalunya, the office is clearly marked above ground by a big red-and-white *I*. The helpful maps and brochures are printed in various languages, and the staff speaks English. Next to the tourist counter and open the same hours are a Caixa Catalunya currency exchange and a bookstore/gift shop with a decent selection of glossy books on Barcelona and Catalonia. The tourist office has another **branch** on Plaça Sant Jaume in the Barri Gòtic (tel. 906/301282), open Monday–Saturday 10–8 and Sunday 10–2.

From late June to late September the tourist office unleashes *casacas rojas* (red jackets)—tourist-office personnel who walk up and down the Rambla and through the Barri Gòtic in said garb just to answer travelers' questions. Isn't that nice?

For information on the rest of Catalonia, head to the massive **regional tourist office** in Palau Robert (Passeig de Gràcia 105, tel. 93/238–4000), open Monday–Saturday 10–7 and Sunday 10–2. Brochures are accompanied by temporary exhibits on Catalan culture.

COMING AND GOING

BY BUS

Spain's bus system is complicated. Ask the nearest tourist office which of the many bus companies serves your destination and where to find its office (many companies are headquartered in or near the main station, Estació del Nord). Within Barcelona you can also dial **010** for information on most bus routes and bus-company headquarters. Trying to get through to the bus companies by phone is often next to impossible—you'll get a perpetual busy signal or no answer at all—so it's best to trek to the company office or to a travel agency in person. Note that fares change fairly often depending on season and demand.

Most buses arrive and depart from the central **bus station,** Estació del Nord (C. d'Ali Bei 80, tel. 93/265–6508; Metro: Arc de Triomf). The biggest company based here is Enatcar (tel. 93/245–2528), which serves **Madrid** (8 hrs, 3,300 ptas.), **Valencia** (4½ hrs, 3,100 ptas.), and other parts of Spain. Bacoma (tel. 93/231–3801) heads to **Granada** (14 hrs, 8,150 ptas.) and **Seville** (16 hrs, 9,000 ptas.); Irbarsa (tel. 93/265–6061) to **San Sebastián** (7 hrs, 3,350 ptas.) and **Pamplona** (6 hrs, 2,820 ptas.); Sarfa (tel. 93/265–1158) to the Costa Brava, including **Cadaqués** (2½ hrs, 2,100 ptas.); and Alsina-Graells (tel. 93/265–6866) to **Andorra** (4 hrs, 2,750 ptas.) and most of inland Catalonia, including **La Seu d'Urgell** (3½ hrs, 2,475 ptas.) and **Lleida** (2 hrs, 1,950 ptas.).

For international destinations, **Eurolines** is the biggie. Look for their office in Estació del Nord (tel. 93/232–1092) and at Ronda Universitat 5, near the university (tel. 93/317–6454). Eurolines covers much of Spain, ventures down to Morocco, and heads back up to Europe's major cities, including Marseille (7 hrs, 7,400 ptas.), Paris (14 hrs, 12,450 ptas.), Rome (21 hrs, 16,100 ptas.), London (25 hrs, 14,650 ptas.), Frankfurt (17 hrs, 14,300 ptas.), Prague (14½ hrs, 15,300 ptas.), and Tangier (24 hrs, 12,900 ptas.). **Linebus** (Avda. Paral.lel 116, tel. 93/265–0700) serves London (25 hrs, 14,650 ptas.) and Milan (17½ hrs, 12,700 ptas.), with some youth fares.

BY TRAIN

Most trains arrive and depart from the **Sants-Estació,** northwest of the city center. Some trains, especially those to and from France, use the **Estació França,** near the port and Barri Gòtic. There are also RENFE stations at the intersection of Passeig de Gràcia and Carrer Aragó, and at Plaça Catalunya. For train information call **RENFE** at 902/240202.

Sants-Estació (Plaça dels Països Catalans) serves most national and international destinations. Trains rumble daily to Madrid (9–10 hrs, 6,500–8,000 ptas.), Tarragona (1 hr, 670 ptas.), Valencia (7 hrs, 4,500 ptas.), Bilbao (8½ hrs, 5,200 ptas.), Pamplona (5½ hrs, 4,200 ptas.), Granada (12½ hrs, 6,500 ptas.), and the rest of Spain. The ticket office is open daily 7 AM—10 PM. To get from here to the Rambla, hop right on the Metro (Line 3, direction Montbau) and get off at Liceu or Drassanes. If you arrive late at night, Buses N2, N12, and N14 can whisk you to Plaça Catalunya.

Estació França (Avda. Marqués de l'Argentera) has trains to Paris (11 hrs, 16,900 ptas.), Geneva (9½ hours, 14,000 ptas.), and Milan (13 hrs, 14,000 ptas.). Tickets are sold daily 7 AM–10 PM. França is a short walk from the Barri Gòtic: from the train station head southwest (toward the Columbus monument) on Avingunda Marqués de l'Argentera and turn right onto Via Laietana or, farther down, the Rambla. The closest Metro stop, Barceloneta, is just behind the station, toward the port.

There are **luggage lockers** (open daily 6 AM–11 PM, 400–600 ptas. per day) in the Sants and França stations.

BY CAR

Barcelona is well linked to the rest of Spain and Europe by various *autopistas* (toll highways) and toll-free roads. The latter tend to be more crowded, including the N-II north to France and west into Catalonia.

If you want to rent a car, know that it's generally much cheaper to reserve one before you leave home. Increasingly, however, Spanish rental agencies are offering competitive prices; if you're flexible with travel dates and have the patience to hunt around, you might find some good deals. A handful of local firms can be cheaper than the big names: at **Ronicar** (C. Europa 34–36, tel. 93/405–0951) and **Vanguard Rent-A-Car** (C. Londres 31, tel. 93/439–3880), prices range from 18,000 ptas. to 28,000 ptas. per week for a small car with unlimited mileage. Many agencies have weekend specials.

The tourist office on Plaça Catalunya has a complete list of the city's car-rental outfits. **Avis** and **Hertz** have several offices here, including branches at the airport; Hertz also has an office at the Sants train station.

BY FERRY

Ferries for the Balearic Islands arrive and depart from the **Estació Maritima** (tel. 93/295–9100), at the port south of the Rambla, in front of the statue of Columbus (Metro: Drassanes). **Trasmediterránea** (tel. 902/454645) conveys most foot passengers; in summer (June 9–end of September), several boats leave daily for Palma de Mallorca (3½ hrs on faster boat, 8,990 ptas.; 6½ hrs on overnight boat, 6,450 ptas.) and once daily to Ibiza (7½ hrs on overnight boat, 6,450 ptas.) and Menorca (9½ hrs on overnight boat, about 7,000 ptas.). The rest of the year, boats leave once daily for Palma, six times weekly for Ibiza, and thrice weekly for Menorca. The car ferry **Buquebus** (tel. 902/414242) charges 9,100 ptas. per person and 19,800 ptas. per car on its three-hour trip to Palma.

BY PLANE

Barcelona's international **Aeroport del Prat** (93/298–3838) is 12 km (9 mi) south of the city, in the suburb of Prat de Llobregat. **Iberia** (C. Diputacio 258, tel. 902/400500) occasionally discounts tickets for the under-26 crowd. Tourist offices in the airport (*see* Visitor Information, *above*) can give you local addresses and phone numbers for the airlines touching down here. For airlines flying into Barcelona, see Air Travel in Chapter 1.

BETWEEN THE AIRPORT AND THE CITY • RENFE trains (tel. 902/240202) leave the airport every half hour for the Sants train station, then continue to Plaça Catalunya (335 ptas.), putting you smack in the middle of town near the budget lodgings of the Rambla and Barri Gòtic. Trains depart every half hour, 6:13 AM–10:43 PM on weekdays and 6:11 AM–10:41 PM on weekends and holidays. Trains *to* the airport leave the RENFE/Metro station beneath Plaça Catalunya (and, a few minutes later, Sants) every half hour daily from 6 AM to 10 PM.

The **Aerobus** (tel. 010 for information) is a bit more expensive (500 ptas.), but it leaves the airport every 15 minutes (weekdays 5:30 AM–midnight, weekends and holidays 6 AM–midnight) and stops at several useful points in the city, including Plaça d'Espanya, Plaça Universitat, Plaça Catalunya (in front of the department store El Corte Inglés), and Passeig de Gràcia. In the other direction, the last bus leaves Plaça Catalunya for the airport at 11:15 PM.

A **taxi** from the airport into town should cost around 2,500 ptas., give or take some, depending on traffic. Call 93/358–1111 if you can't seem to find one.

GETTING AROUND

For such a major metropolis, Barcelona is blessedly compact and eminently walkable: you can cover much of it on foot, particularly the Barri Gòtic (Gothic quarter). The city's nerve center and transportation hub is the sprawling, airy Plaça Catalunya. Upon arrival, this jam-packed *plaça* can be confusing; you may want to walk around it a few times to get your bearings, as Barcelona's main sightseeing neighborhoods fan out from here. The Rambla extends from the south side of Plaça Catalunya toward the Mediterranean Sea. Passeig de Gràcia, the city's most fashionable thoroughfare, heads north from the plaça, cutting through the Eixample into upper Barcelona. As you walk down the Rambla from Plaça Catalunya, the Barri Gòtic is to your left, the Raval neighborhood to your right. If you're looking for a place to stay, turn left into any busy street off the Rambla (Carrer Portaferrissa and Carrer Ferran are two good ones), and in seconds you'll be in the mazelike Barri Gòtic.

Beneath Plaça Catalunya are underground stations for the Metro, the Ferrocarril (FGC; commuter rail), and RENFE (national trains). Above ground, the Aerobus connects all these with the airport.

If you'll be in town more than a few days, buy a T-1 ticket (*see* By Metro, *below*) for 10 discounted rides on most of the city's transportation systems. Call Barcelona's **information line** (010) for general information on public transport, including schedules, fares, and locations of Metro and bus stops. The call costs slightly more than a regular local call.

BY BUS

Most routes on the city's extensive bus system are operative from 6 AM to 10 PM, with a few trucking on until midnight. Bus stops are clearly marked and easy to spot, and all buses bear the names of their destinations on the front. The tourist office has a wonderfully detailed bus map. Two buses traverse the entire city: **Bus 64** goes from Barceloneta, near Port Vell, to Avenida Paral.lel (in the Poble Sec neighborhood, near Montjüic) to Plaça Universitat to Pedralbes, a chichi residential quarter near the Camp Nou soccer stadium. **Bus 50** travels from near Parc de la Trinitat, in northeastern Barcelona, down to Calle Mallorca, passing the Sagrada Familia, then runs along Passeig Sant Joan to Gran Via, ending up in Plaça Espanya, near Montjüic. Dial **010** for more information on bus routes.

Buses are particularly handy late at the night after the Metro shuts down: there are about 15 night buses, most running from about 11 PM to 4 AM. Most start or finish in Plaça Catalunya. Note that you cannot use T-1 cards (*see* By Metro, *below*) on night buses— you must pay the single fare (160 ptas.).

Barcelona's splashy, open-top **Bus Turistic** is everywhere. If you're only in town for a day or two, you may want to hop sheepishly on, as it's a good way to see a lot in very little time. The big perk is that you can board and leave the vehicle wherever you like, as many times as you like; so if you're taken with a particular sight, no one herds you back onto the bus. There are two routes, northern and southern, and you can also switch between them at several main stops. A Bus Turistic ticket also gets you entrance-fee discounts at most major sights. A one-day ticket costs 2,000 ptas., a two-day ticket 2,500 ptas. Buy tickets on the bus, at the tourist office in Plaça Catalunya, or at the Sants train station.

BY METRO

The five-line **Metro** is fast, cheap, easy to figure out, and extensive—no matter where you lose yourself, you're never more than a 10-minute ride from the center of town. Moreover, you never have to wait more than five minutes for a train. The Liceu stop (named for the opera house above it) shoots you onto the dizzying center of the Rambla, on the edge of the Barri Gòtic. The Drassanes stop deposits you at the foot of the Rambla, near the Columbus statue and the waterfront; from here it's a short walk to the city's beaches. Metro stop Jaume I is in the center of the La Ribera (home to the Picasso Museum), near the hip Born neighborhood. Gaudí's Sagrada Familia church, in the Eixample, is accessed by a Metro stop of the same name.

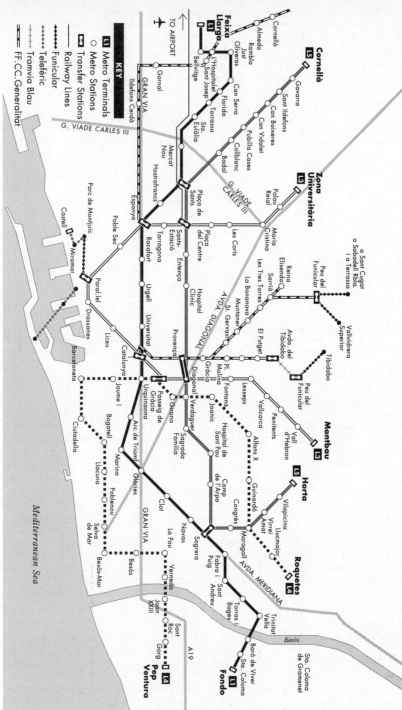

BARCELONA METRO

Single-ride Metro tickets cost 150 ptas. If you'll be here more than a few days, buy the multiride T-1 ticket (Tarjeta Multiviatge, 825 ptas.), good for 10 rides on the Metro, bus, or commuter train. The T-1 ticket is sold in most Metro stations. at the ticket counter and/or ticket machines.

The bad news is that during the week (Mon.–Thurs.), the Metro goes to bed at 11 PM, when most restaurants are still serving dinner and the nightclubs are unlocking their doors. Trains do keep running till 2 AM on Friday and Saturday nights and till midnight on Sunday. After all of these witching hours, the city's fleet of night buses takes over (*see above*), with buses to and from Plaça Catalunya all night long. The Metro revives each morning at 5 AM (6 AM on Sunday).

All Metro maps also show the **FGC** lines (Ferrocarrils de la Generalitat de Catalunya; C. Diputació 239, tel. 93/205–1515). Barcelona's commuter rail basically covers the city's northern- and easternmost neighborhoods, beyond the Metro's reach. The FGC shares several key stations with the Metro, including Plaça Catalunya and Plaça Espanya, and keeps roughly the same hours; during the week it runs slightly later, until about 11:30 PM. You'll want the FGC line to Avenida Tibidabo if you fancy catching the funicular up to Tibidabo itself. There are also two stops in the Eixample, Gràcia and Provença, and helpful stops in Sarrià and Reina Elisenda. Within the city each trip costs 150 ptas.; for longer excursions, such as the one-hour trip to Montserrat (605 ptas.), you'll pay a little more.

BY TAXI

You can hail yellow-and-black taxis from most obvious spots in the city; a green light on the roof indicates that a cab is free to pick up passengers. The fare is 300 ptas. plus a daytime rate of about 110 ptas. per kilometer. After 10 PM and on weekends, the rate is about 125 ptas. On weekends and holidays, particularly late at night, the wait for a free taxi can be long; call **Radio Movil** (tel. 93/358–1111) or **Barnataxi** (tel. 93/357–7755) if you can't seem to find one.

WHERE TO SLEEP

Happily, Barcelona's cheap sleeps are clustered around the Barri Gòtic and the Rambla, an easy stroll from—if not in the middle of—the city's star attractions. Unfortunately, most of these places fill to capacity during high season, from mid-July to mid-August, and during Semana Santa (Holy Week), usually in April. It is *imperative* to book in advance. Here's the catch-22: many *hostales* and pensions insist on a credit-card number to hold your room, and summer staffers at the cheapest places might be transient and less than perfectly organized. If it's summer and you don't have reservations, try to arrive in Barcelona in the morning, as most rooms open up between 10 and 1 (noon is the usual checkout time); after 2, rooms at most *hostales* and pensions are already booked.

Nearly all of Barcelona's *hostales* and pensions offer rooms with and without private bath. If you're counting pesetas and want only a place to crash, get a room without bath (*sin baño*). You'll still have a sink and mirror in your room (though in some dismal cases the "mirror" is just a reflective metal surface hung askew on the wall), and the shared bathroom is usually just down the hall and quite clean.

One of the delights of staying on the Rambla or in the Barri Gòtic is having your own balcony. Usually made of wrought iron, this little terrace overlooks whatever bustling street you're temporarily living on. In most budget lodgings half the rooms have exterior balconies (ask for *una habitación exterior con balcón*), while the other half have either a window or a balcony over the interior courtyard. The drawbacks to these popular districts are three: street noise from exterior rooms; rip-offs (do not be shy about inspecting a room before you take it, especially if the property is not reviewed here); and petty crime. *Never* leave valuables in your room; lock your bags and if possible chain them to something sturdy in the room.

LA RAMBLA

Depending on your taste, you can live, eat, bar-hop, *and* sightsee on a single street in Barcelona; you don't really have to leave. The Rambla is literally lined with hotels, *hostales*, and pensions. The priciest hotels have staked out spots at the top of the Rambla, but there are plenty of budget joints in-between. Rooms get cheaper and less luxurious as you walk south.

Note that rooms on the Rambla are slightly more expensive than their counterparts in the Barri Gòtic, and because they're so easy to find, they fill up far more quickly in summer. The payoff is that many have exterior balconies, putting the Rambla literally at your feet and inviting you to watch the greatest street theater in the world from the best seat in the house.

UNDER 4,000 PTAS. • Hostal Marítima. This longtime backpackers' favorite at the foot of the Rambla rents scruffy but well-kept rooms for an incredible 2,000 ptas. a person. There's a washing machine on site (800 ptas. for a load), and you can store your luggage for 300 ptas. *Rambla 4, next to Wax Museum, tel. 93/302–3152. Metro: Drassanes. 15 rooms, none with bath. Cash only.*

UNDER 6,000 PTAS. • Hostal Noya. If Pension Canaletes (*below*) is full, try this *hostal*—it's in the same building on a lower floor. Basic rooms with less impressive Rambla views go for slightly higher prices here than at the neighbor's; doubles with shared bath are 5,500 ptas. *Rambla 133, 1st floor, tel. 93/301–4831. Metro: Catalunya. 15 rooms, none with bath. Cash only.*

Hostal Parisien. Most rooms overlook the Rambla, and the owner and his wife both speak English. Basic doubles with full bath are 6,000 ptas.; with shower only, 5,500 ptas.; without bath, 5,000 ptas. *Rambla 114, tel. 93/301–6283. Metro: Liceu. 13 rooms, 2 with bath, 2 with shower only. Cash only.*

Pensión Canaletes. Rising high above La Rambla, this shabby but clean pension has doubles with shared bath for 5,000 ptas. It's a serious trek up the stairs, but the reward (from most rooms) is a phenomenal, sweeping vista encompassing Plaça Catalunya, the entire lower Rambla, and Columbus-by-the-port. *Rambla 133, 3°, tel. 93/301–5660. Metro: Catalunya. 10 rooms, none with bath. Closed Dec. 15–Jan. 15. Cash only.*

Pensión Marbella. If you can't find a room farther up the Rambla, give Marbella a shot. Occupying part of a tall, narrow house, it offers a mixture of tiny and large rooms; if you have a choice, have a look. Doubles with shared bath go for 5,000 ptas. *Rambla 25, tel. 93/302–3158. Metro: Liceu or Drassanes. 8 rooms, none with bath. Cash only.*

BARRI GÒTIC

If you've been pounding the pavement (that is, the cobblestones) of the Gothic quarter and finding all the cheapies full, don't despair: this 'hood overflows with tiny *hostales* and pensions that often go unnoticed by the masses. Walk down the less-traveled alleys and side streets for an hour, and you're bound to find a place that fits your budget. (Many of the smaller, less-publicized *hostales* that cater to locals don't have big signs; look instead for a bank of doorbells to one side of the front door, where many *hostales* and pensions list their name.) If you shop for a room in the morning and get a whole lot of "no," be persistent—ask if you can come back just before checkout (there are always unforeseen checkouts). If that doesn't work, always ask the proprietor to recommend another place in the area, as many innkeepers are buddies with each other.

If all the digs listed below are full, look into **Pensión Bahia** (C. Canuda 2, tel. 93/302–6153) and the **Hostal Campi,** next door (C. Canuda 4, tel. 93/301–4133; cash only)—both have basic, slightly tattered rooms for 5,000 ptas. a night. **Hostal-Residencia Colom** (C. de Colom 3, tel. 93/318–0631), just off Plaça Reial, often seems to have space when no one else does; dorm beds (in rooms that fit six or eight) go for 1,400 ptas., overpriced double rooms for 7,500 ptas., though most of the latter have balconies overlooking Plaça Reial.

UNDER 4,000 PTAS. • Hostal Malda. Run by a friendly family, this large *hostal* is more than meets the eye: it was once a palace, and the shopping gallery below was once the palace garden. Some of the rooms are correspondingly grand, and the small, cylindrical tower jutting out from the rooftop lends character, not to mention a 360-degree city view for the lucky inhabitant—the tower has a single room, which you can rent for a negligible 1,000 ptas. Room sizes differ, but many of the shared-bath doubles are quite roomy (3,000 ptas.); one double room has its own bath (3,500 ptas.). If you can get in here, it's an amazing deal. *C. del Pino 5, above shopping gallery, tel. 93/317–3002. Metro: Liceu. 25 rooms, 1 with bath.*

Hostal New-York. This place has a dark, gloomy air, but the prices are rock bottom, and the owners are friendly. There are 10 double rooms (3,800 ptas.) with shared bath; the rest of the beds are in dorm rooms sleeping four, six, or eight (1,900 ptas. per bed). Sheets cost a one-time fee of 200 ptas., and blankets are free. *C. Gignas 8, off C. Avinyó, tel. 93/315–0304. Metro: Jaume I or Liceu. 10 rooms, none with bath; 69 dorm beds. Cash only.*

UNDER 6,000 PTAS. • Hostal Fina. Welcoming budget travelers for 35 years now, this agreeable family-owned joint offers clean, basic doubles with bath for 5,950 ptas., without bath for 4,950 ptas. Most rooms have balconies overlooking the busy Carrer Portaferrissa, so noise can be a problem. *C. Portaferrissa 11, tel. 93/317–9787. Metro: Liceu. 24 rooms, 12 with bath. Cash only.*

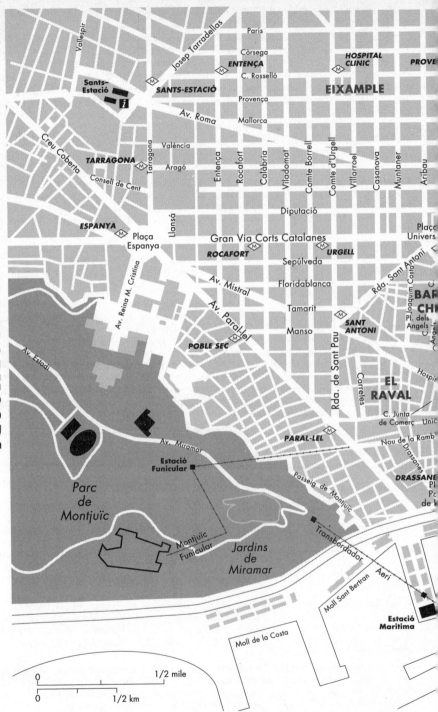

Vallespir

Josep Tarradellas

Paris

Còrsega

ENTENÇA

C. Rosselló

**HOSPITAL
CLINIC**

PROVE

Sants–
Estació

SANTS-ESTACIÓ

EIXAMPLE

Av. Roma

Provença

Creu Coberta

Mallorca

TARRAGONA

Tarragona

València

Entença

Rocafort

Calàbria

Viladomat

Comte Borrell

Comte d'Urgell

Villarroel

Casanova

Muntaner

Aribau

Consell de Cent

Aragó

Diputació

Plaça
Univers

ESPANYA

Plaça
Espanya

Llansà

Gran Via Corts Catalanes

ROCAFORT

URGELL

Rda. Sant Antoni

**BAR
CH**

Sepúlveda

Joaquim Costa

Pl. dels
Angels

Av. Mistral

Floridablanca

Av. Reina M. Cristina

Av. Paral-lel

Tamarit

**SANT
ANTONI**

Angels

Av. Estadi

Manso

Rda. de Sant Pau

**EL
RAVAL**

Hospit

POBLE SEC

C. Junta
de Comerç

Unić

Av. Miramar

Carretes

Nou de la Ramb

PARAL-LEL

Estació
Funicular

Drassanes

DRASSANE

**Parc
de
Montjuïc**

Passeig de Montjuic

Pl
Po
de

Montjuïc
Funicular

**Jardins
de
Miramar**

Transbordador

Aeri

Moll Sant Bertran

**Estació
Marítima**

Moll de la Costa

0

1/2 mile

0

1/2 km

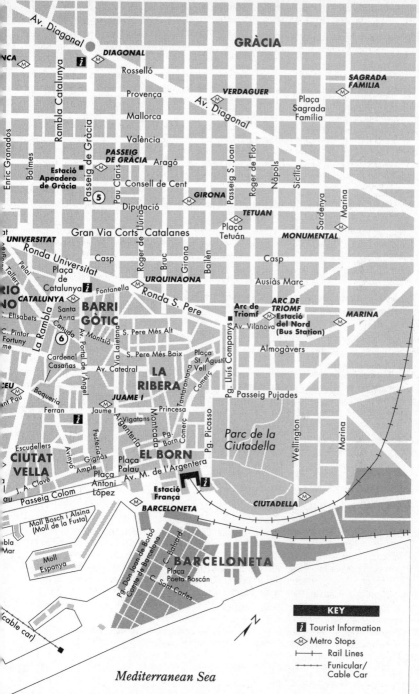

Hostal Fontanella. The comfy Fontanella has spic-and-span doubles for 5,500 ptas. with bath, 4,500 ptas. without bath. *Via Laietana 71, tel. 93/317–5943. Metro: Urquinaona. 10 rooms, 5 with bath.*

Hostal Levante. Spacious and centrally located—just off Carrer Avinyó—these clean, tidy doubles rent for 5,500 ptas. with bath, 4,000 ptas. without bath. The staff is notably friendly. *Baixada de Sant Miquel 2, tel. 93/317–9565. Metro: Liceu. 25 rooms, 10 with bath.*

Pensión-Residencia Lourdes. Right on Carrer Princesa, between Via Laietana and the Picasso Museum, this large pension has basic, clean doubles with shared bath for 3,500–4,500 ptas. The kicker is you have to pay 300 ptas. to take a shower. *C. Princesa 14, tel. 93/319–3372. Metro: Jaume I. 30 rooms, none with bath. Cash only.*

UNDER 8,000 PTAS. • Hostal-Albergue Fernando. Large and impersonal, this inn-cum-hostel is centrally located on Carrer Ferran, near Plaça Reial. Clean double rooms with bath cost 6,500 ptas.; without bath, 4,800 ptas. Most travelers come here for the dorm rooms, in which four or eight people sleep on 2,000-pta. beds. *C. Ferran 31, tel. 93/310–7993. Metro: Liceu. 25 rooms, 10 with bath; 25 dorm rooms.*

Hostal Lausanne. This appealing hostal off Plaça Catalunya offers well-maintained doubles with bath for 6,000 ptas., without bath for 5,000 ptas. *Avda. Portal de l'Angel 24, tel. 93/302–1139. Metro: Catalunya. 18 rooms, 8 with bath.*

Hostal Layetana. This well-kept facility is a real find: just off Via Laietana, it overlooks a small square behind the cathedral and some sections of the ancient Roman walls. The great antique elevator is in perfect working order, happy to haul you and your pack down to reception. Doubles are 6,400 ptas. with bath, 5,000 ptas. without. *Plaça Ramón Berenguer el Gran 2, tel. 93/319–2012. Metro: Jaume I. 20 rooms, 12 with bath.*

Hostal Residencia Rembrandt. Wonderfully clean and tidy doubles go for 6,500 (with bath) or 5,000 (without) ptas. at this friendly hostal. Room balconies overlook happening Carrer Portaferrissa. The wonderful balconied single goes for 3,500 ptas.; the other is interior. *C. Portaferrissa 23, tel. 93/318–1011. Metro: Liceu. 18 rooms, 5 with bath. Cash only.*

Hotel Jardi. It's hard to beat this location: you step out the front doors onto Plaça Sant Josep Oriol, one of the most popular little squares in the Barri Gòtic and home to the equally popular Bar del Pi. Well-maintained doubles in the old wing are 5,500–6,000 ptas.; prices go up to 7,000–8,000 ptas. if you want to stay in the remodeled wing, with balcony views of the Plaça below. Every room has a bathroom; just note that prices are expected to rise in mid-2001. Continental breakfast is served for 700 ptas., but it's hard to beat alfresco coffee at the Bar del Pi, even if you just stumbled home from this haunt last night. *Plaça Sant Josep Oriol 1, tel. 93/301–5900, fax 93/318–3664. Metro: Liceu. 42 rooms.*

Pensión Villanueva. This large pension on the large Plaça Reial, one of the Gothic quarter's most active old squares, has a wide range of basic rooms and prices to match: doubles with shared bath start as low as 3,000 ptas. (for small interior rooms) and go up to 6,000 ptas. (for large rooms with balcony). Bathrooms send costs up to 5,900–9,600 ptas., the latter for a room overlooking Plaça Reial. *Plaça Reial 2, tel. 93/301–5084. Metro: Liceu. 30 rooms, 15 with bath.*

EL RAVAL / BARRIO CHINO

This part of town—west of the Rambla—holds a slew of budget options, particularly on Carrer Tallers, Carrer de Sant Pau (the blocks nearest the Rambla), and Carrer de L'Hospital. Carrer Junta de Commerc, a small street connecting Carrer de L'Hospital and Carrer de Sant Pau, packs more than 200 rooms in its collection of budget digs. A note on the area: if you get the willies walking around here by day, then don't stay the night, as things only get worse after nightfall. Generally, the farther west you go, the more shady characters you'll see loitering on street corners. That said, most lodgings listed are at most a five-minute walk from the Rambla, so you're never far from civilization and, for better or worse, crowds.

UNDER 5,000 PTAS. • Hostal La Terrassa. Although the building is run-down and institutional and the basic rooms are nothing to get excited about, La Terrassa offers some of the cheapest beds in the area. Pluses are the bright white sheets, firm beds, and—in the best five-star tradition—individually wrapped soaps on your sink. The simple courtyard terrace can provide some respite from the Rambla crowds. Doubles cost 4,600 ptas. with bath, 3,800 without. *C. Junta de Commerc 11, tel. 93/302–5174, fax 93/301–2188. Metro: Liceu. 50 rooms, 25 with bath.*

Pension Dani. If your idea of lodging is to sleep and go, any of the simple, cheapo rooms here in the home of Señora González should do the trick. Doubles with bath are 4,000 ptas., without bath 3,500 ptas. Proximity to action? You can see the Rambla from the front door. *C. Tallers 9, tel. 93/302–1146. Metro: Catalunya or Liceu. 8 rooms, 4 with bath. Cash only.*

Pension Venecia. A large, ramshackle family house turned pension, Venecia offers clean doubles with bath for 5,000 ptas., without bath for 3,700 ptas. Note that some rooms have no windows. *C. Junta de Commerc, 13, tel. 93/302–6134. Metro: Liceu. 14 rooms, 7 with bath. Cash only.*

UNDER 8,000 PTAS. • Hosteria Grau. Tucked away on a pleasant side street, Grau is nonetheless mere paces from the Rambla. Rooms are well kept and comfortable, if a bit bland; doubles with bath will set you back 8,000 ptas., without bath 6,000 ptas. *C. Ramelleres 27, at C. Tallers, tel. 93/301–8135, fax 93/317–6825. Metro: Catalunya. 22 rooms, 12 with bath.*

Hotel Peninsular. Here the rooms are musty and cramped, but the vast interior courtyard is a verdant oasis, with a skylighted cathedral ceiling, hanging plants, and a sunbathed sitting area with rattan tables and chairs where you can chat with other travelers. Doubles with bath go for 8,000 ptas., without bath 6,000 ptas. Continental breakfast, included in the price, is served in the spacious downstairs restaurant where, if the mood strikes, you can tickle the upright piano. *C. Sant Pau, 34, tel. 93/302–3138, fax 93/412–3699. Metro: Liceu. 80 rooms, 40 with bath.*

UNDER 11,000 PTAS. • Hotel España. This aging landmark has seen better days, but if architecture is your bag, you'll get a kick out of staying here—the eye-catching interior was designed by Domenech i Montaner. Alas, the character-free rooms are not on a par with the lobby; they're clean but frayed and worn. Doubles with bath cost 10,800 ptas. *C. Sant Pau 9 and 11, tel. 93/318–1758, fax 93/317–1134. Metro: Liceu. 60 rooms.*

ESTACIÓ FRANÇA / EL BORN

The area around the Francia train station is near the Port Vell waterfront, Barcelona's beaches, and the Born part of the Barri Gòtic. It's a good place to stay if you'll be arriving late at this particular station and don't want to hoof it into town or, conversely, if you'll be leaving for France early in the morning. Prices are generally higher than those in the Barri Gòtic, however, as choices are fewer.

UNDER 7,000 PTAS. • Hostal Miramar. This place makes up for its musty rooms by being cheap and near the water (and supplying a refrigerator in each room). Doubles with shower—but shared toilet—are 6,000 ptas.; without any bath facilities 5,000 ptas. *C. Reina Cristina 2, tel. 93/319–9003. Metro: Barceloneta. 34 rooms, 10 with shower.*

Hostal Nuevo Colón. Right across the street from Estació França, the strangely named New Columbus Hostal has smallish but clean doubles for 6,500 ptas. with bath, 4,600 ptas. without bath. *Avda. Marqués de l'Argentera 19, tel. 93/319–5077. Metro: Barceloneta. 33 rooms, 8 with bath.*

UNDER 8,000 PTAS. • Hostal Orleans. Most rooms here have balconies, from which you can see the impressive França station. Doubles with bath are rather overpriced at 7,500 ptas.; the doubles with half bath (shower and sink) are better values at 6,500 ptas. *Avda. Marqués de l'Argentera 13, tel. 93/319–7382. Metro: Barceloneta. 26 rooms, 5 with bath. Cash only.*

EIXAMPLE

The broad, leafy boulevards of the residential Eixample are more the province of well-heeled apartment dwellers than peseta-pinching travelers, but there are some affordable lodgings scattered about. The payoff for slightly higher room rates is that you're removed from the riffraff and noisy crowds of the Rambla but only a ten-minute walk away.

UNDER 8,000 PTAS. • Hostal Eden. Occupying several floors of an upmarket apartment building (think how well that would fly in New York), Eden has tidy basic rooms for 7,500 ptas. with bath, 5,000 ptas. without. Some rooms are much nicer than others; ask for one with a bathtub (*una habitación con bañero*). The tub is large, and the shower head has a massage contraption on it, perfect after a long day of sight-schlepping. *C. Balmes, 55, 1° 2a, tel. 93/452–6620, fax 93/452–6620. Metro: Passeig de Gràcia. 17 rooms, 2 with bath.*

Hostal Goya. The large rooms in this Moderniste building have been well preserved, each with a different Moderniste tile floor and lots of character. Two rooms have balconies overlooking Pau Claris; and another four face an interior courtyard, less spectacular but much quieter. Clean, comfortable doubles with bath cost 7,200 ptas., without bath 6,000. *C. Pau Claris 74, tel. 93/302–2565, fax 93/412–0435. Metro: Urquinaona. 12 rooms, 6 with bath.*

LA CUINA CATALANA

Among savants, Catalan cooking has become a highly touted regional cuisine, characterized by the meeting of land and sea. Hearty signature meals include llagosta i pollastre *(lobster and chicken, usually served in a sweet tomato sauce)*, a delectable mix of sweet and savory. With strong roots in farm country, the food retains a down-home quality—botifarra amb mongetes *(grilled pork sausage with white beans)* is still a mainstay on menús del día. Sides feature veggies, as in samfaina—*a delicious mix of grilled peppers, tomatoes, eggplant, and onion doused with olive oil and garlic—and the simpler* escalivada, *with peppers, onions, and garlic.* Espinacas a la catalana *is spinach cooked with olive oil, garlic, pine nuts, raisins, and bits of bacon. The backbone of every Catalan meal is* pan amb tomaquet *(bread with tomato), hearty slices rubbed with ripe tomatoes, topped with olive oil, and sprinkled with salt. For dessert it's* crema catalana, *creamy custard coated with sugar that caramelizes when baked, traditionally in a ceramic dish.*

Hostal Oliva. Right on stylish Passeig de Gràcia, this cozy *hostal* has neat, clean doubles with bath for 6,500 ptas., 6,000 without. *Passeig de Gràcia 32, tel. 93/488–0163. Metro: Passeig de Gràcia. 8 rooms, 6 with bath.*

UNDER 10,000 PTAS. • Hostal Cisneros. Looming over the corner of Carrers Aribau and Aragó, west of the Plaça Catalunya, this large facility has cramped rooms for 8,560 ptas. with bath, 6,420 ptas. without. The price includes a Continental breakfast. The fifth-floor common room has a big-screen TV and an adjoining terrace overlooking the streets below. *C. Aribau 54, tel. 93/454–1800, fax 93/451–3908. Metro: Passeig de Gràcia. 101 rooms, 80 with bath.*

FOOD

If there's one motto by which Barcelonans live, it's "To live well, you need to eat well"—and they do. From swank dining halls to designer eateries to traditional dives, the choices are endless. The Barri Gòtic is jam-packed with restaurants, especially around Plaça Reial. The Born, around Passeig de Born and along Avenida Marqués de l'Argentera, is another thriving area full of excellent, reasonably priced restaurants. Seafood is best in Barceloneta, the old fishing quarter near the port.

The best way to eat well without going broke is to do as locals do: make a late lunch of the fixed-price menú del día (menu of the day), which usually includes two dishes (a starter and a main course), bread, wine, and dessert. Most restaurants serve a menú del día between 2 and 4, but increasingly—mostly to attract tourists—they repeat the offer in the evening, though it's often a little pricier. As in the rest of Spain, restaurants do not open for dinner until 8:30 or 9. Stave off hunger pangs by diving into the tapas ritual, which takes place when the rest of the world is eating dinner.

Tapas, those ubiquitous little nibbles, form such an integral part of Spanish culinary culture that nearly every café and bar serves them. Choices can range from *tortilla de patata* (the classic potato omelet) to *patatas bravas* (potatoes with a spicy sauce) to *anchoas* (anchovies) to *croquetas* (croquettes). Making a meal out of tapas can be surprisingly cost effective, especially if you eat at the bar; most restaurants charge extra if you sit at a table or, if applicable, outside on the plaza. If you're on a supertight budget,

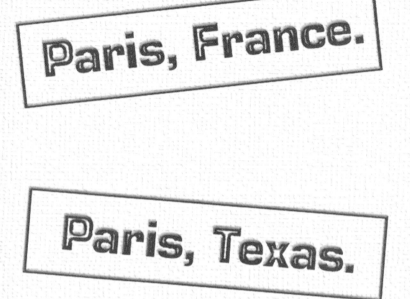

Paris, France.

Paris, Texas.

When it Comes to Getting Cash at an ATM,

Same Thing.

Whether you're in Yosemite or Yemen, using your Visa® card or ATM card with the PLUS symbol is the easiest and most convenient way to get cash. Even if your bank is in Minneapolis and you're in Miami, Visa/PLUS ATMs make getting cash so easy, you'll feel right at home. After all, Visa/PLUS ATMs are open 24 hours a day, 7 days a week, rain or shine. And if you need help finding one of Visa's 627,000 ATMs in 127 countries worldwide, visit **visa.com/pd/atm**. We'll make finding an ATM as easy as finding the Eiffel Tower, the Pyramids or even the Grand Canyon.

It's Everywhere You Want To Be.®

SEE THE WORLD
IN FULL COLOR

Fodor's Exploring Guides bring all the great sights vividly to life with hundreds of photographs, fascinating historical background, and colorful anecdotes. Detailed maps and practical information keep you headed in the right direction.

Pair a Fodor's Exploring Guide with your trusted Fodor's upCLOSE for a complete planning package.

you can always settle into a café-bar and order a simple and filling *bocadillo* (baguette sandwich) for 300–500 ptas., available day and night.

Of course, the cheapest way to eat is to stock up at the market and have a picnic. There are supermarkets all over the city (*see* Markets, *below*), and every neighborhood has a spate of small family-run grocery stores. For fresh bread and pastries, stop into any *forn del pa* (bakery; literally, "bread oven") and try an *ensaimada* (fluffy roll topped with powdered sugar) or empanada, a savory pastry stuffed with *atún* (tuna), *pollo* (chicken), or chorizo sausage.

BARRI GÒTIC

Restaurants and cafés abound in the Gothic quarter, so even if you can't get into your joint of choice (summer often means long lines at popular restaurants), you'll find another just around the corner. Indeed, exploring the streets until a cheery spot catches your eye can be the best way to go: of all Barcelona's neighborhoods, the Barri Gòtic has the highest concentration of little, decades-old family-run restaurants and cafés. Often limited to a bar and a few tables, these are places where you can eat simply and cheaply with a crusty old local who's been dining thus for years.

UNDER 1,000 PTAS. • La Fonda Escudellers. This bright, spacious two-tiered restaurant serves ample and appetizing Catalan fare at great prices, including fish paella (785 ptas.) and cod with the vegetable mixture samfaina (875 ptas.). Unfortunately, this is no secret; long lines often trail out the door. Management also runs Les Quinze Nits, in Plaça Reial (*see below*). *C. Escudellers 10, tel. 93/301–7515. Metro: Liceu.*

Les Quinze Nits. Overlooking Plaça Reial, the large, airy Quinze Nits offers home-style Catalan cuisine at affordable prices (800–1,000 ptas.), so—big surprise—there's a long line out the door most nights. Though you certainly can't tell by looking at it, this place is part of a chain of tremendously popular and excellent restaurants, each with its own look and menu (including La Fonda Escudellers, *above*), that have been popping up all over Barcelona. *Plaça Reial 6, tel. 93/317–3075. Metro: Liceu.*

Venus Delicatessen. Vegetarian alert: this playful, inviting café-restaurant serves up various vegetarian and choice Mediterranean-style meals. The slew of savory salads includes the Caribeña (750 ptas.), made with crab, shrimp, papaya, and corn. *C. Avinyó 25, tel. 93/301–1585. Metro: Liceu. Closed Sun.*

UNDER 2,000 PTAS. • Can Culleretes. The oldest restaurant in Barcelona, Can Culleretes has been dishing out hearty Catalan fare since 1786. The interior is fittingly old-fashioned, with wood-beamed ceilings and aging black-and-white photos of prior famous clients. Appetizers like spinach cannelloni are about 900 ptas., while entrées, including succulent duck with prunes, run 1,100–1,700 ptas. During the week there's a menú del día for 1,600 ptas. and a menú de la noche for 2,100. *C. Quintana 5, tel. 93/317–3022. Metro: Liceu. Closed Mon. and 3 wks in July.*

La Taberna Real. With an entirely white interior—the only breaks in the color scheme are flashes of chrome here and there—the sleek, minimalist Royal Tavern packs in the natty crowd, who enjoy the many salads, excellent cheeses from all over Spain, and good wine list. *C. Heures 6–10, off Plaça Reial, tel. 93/412–5279. Metro: Liceu. Closed Sun.*

La Veronica. Popular with a gay crowd, this sassy, stylish pizza place offers a zesty change of pace. The crunchy, innovative pizzas include one with smoked salmon, fresh peppermint, and mozzarella (1,200 ptas.) and the signature Veronica pizza, topped with apple, Gorgonzola, and mozzarella (also 1,200 ptas.). Vegetarians will much appreciate the array of meatless pizzas and hearty salads. *C. Avinyó 30, tel. 93/412–1222. Metro: Liceu. Closed Mon.*

Meson Jesus. Complete with stone fireplace and crocheted curtains, this rustic tavern offers a hearty, home-style Catalan menú del día for 1,400 ptas. and, even better, a similar menú de la noche for 1,400 ptas. The food is best described as *comida casera*—changing house specials depending on what's fresh at the market. You might start with *sopa de pescado* (fish soup), gazpacho, or *lentejas* (lentils), then move on to *pollo asado* (roast chicken) or *lomo a la plancha* (grilled pork loin). *C. Ciegos de la Boqueria 4, tel. 93/317–4698. Metro: Liceu. Closed Sun. No dinner Sat.*

Opaqo. Tucked behind Plaça Sant Jaume, the stylish, friendly Opaqo serves excellent Mediterranean food. Ordering the nighttime *menú de degustació* (taster's menu) brings forth a mass of mouthwatering samples, from fresh squid to oversize olives to pungent cheeses. If there's a wait, repair to the great little Bar L'Ascensor nearby. *C. Ciutat 10, tel. 93/318–4676. Metro: Liceu or Jaume I. Closed Sun.*

EAT AND WALK

Once you've mastered the Spanish art of the paseo, try it with a warm bocadillo (sandwich) in hand. Exploring the Barri Gòtic usually calls for a midafternoon energy boost (especially if you're not yet accustomed to dining at 10 PM), and a few hole-in-the-wall bocadillo joints do it better than anyone else. At **Can Conesa** (C. de la Llibreteria 1, tel. 93/310–1394), on Plaça Sant Jaume, you'll see the line before you see the front door—people have come here in droves since the place opened in 1951. One bite of their toasty bocadillos, oozing with cheese if you please, will make you a convert: try the one with fresh chicken breast (400 ptas.) or go for the crowd favorite, an extra-long frankfurter (300 ptas.). Across Plaça Sant Jaume is the tiny **Frankfurt Sant Jaume**—basically a counter and grill—where the finger-licking fare is equally good. Finally, the ubiquitous **Pans y Company**—a Barcelona bocadillo chain that has successfully adopted the American fast-food concept—has startlingly fresh and filling bocadillos and weekly specials that can be as cheap as 190 ptas.

Taxidermista. This gem embodies the best of old-meets-new Barcelona: a splendid relic (in this case, a 1926 taxidermist shop) that's been artfully updated to Barcelona chic with an eye to preserving all the trappings of the building's previous life. Glass doors let you peer into the original stone-wall hallways. The Catalan cuisine includes such concoctions as white tuna with pumpkin purée (1,450 ptas.) and duck with potato purée stuffed with truffles (1,550 ptas.). Alternatively, you could easily make a meal of the fab selection of tapas, including squid (420 ptas.) and chicken brochette with sesame seeds (450 ptas.). On Tuesday and Sunday evenings there's live music downstairs. *Plaça Reial 8, tel. 93/412–4556. Metro: Liceu.*

EL RAVAL/BARRIO CHINO

UNDER 1,500 PTAS. • Carles. Made pleasant and intimate with tasteful, vertical wooden grids between the tables, Carles serves hearty local cuisine, including grilled veal (900 ptas.) and roasted cod (1,400 ptas.). The menú del día costs a modest 1,200 ptas. *C. Tallers 29, tel. 93/302–2501. Metro: Catalunya.*

El Sol. This comfortable eatery is a perennial favorite because the hearty menú del día (1,000 ptas.) is guaranteed to fill you up. They also have a lengthy menu of tempting tapas, from fried calamares (squid) doused in olive oil to *gambas al ajillo*, fresh shrimp infused with potent garlic. *C. Tallers 75, tel. 93/318–1026. Metro: Catalunya.*

L'Antic Forn. You'll see this kind of simple neighborhood restaurant all over the Gothic quarter, mixing antique kitchen cabinets with Formica-top tables and a cigarette machine. L'Antic Forn sets itself apart with a particularly good menu of filling Catalan fare for 1,100 ptas. If you pass this way around 2 PM, join the crowd of neighborhood locals who take their daily midday meal here. *C. Pintor Fortuny 28, tel. 93/412–0286. Metro: Catalunya.*

UNDER 2,000 PTAS. • Egipte. There's nothing Egyptian about this place; the owner claims the former proprietor liked to sing along to Egyptian operas (ahem), hence the name. Mere paces but worlds away from the Rambla, this Barri Gòtic favorite occupies an 18th-century building with a lovely Moderniste interior: ornate ceilings and chandeliers, heavy, old mirrors, and walls painted with colorful wreaths of flowers. On weekdays, pull a chair up to a marble-top table and dive into a savory menú del día of Catalan and Mediterranean fare for 1,150 ptas.—you have more than 60 options, including *ensal-*

ada de boquerones y tomate (anchovy and tomato salad*), cogollos a la vinagreta* (lettuce hearts with a vinaigrette dressing), *muslo de pavo con ciruelas* (turkey drumstick with prunes), and *berenjenas rellenas de carne* (eggplant stuffed with meat). By night there's a menú de la noche. If the upstairs dining room looks full, don't turn away; there are several more in the cellar, their ancient stone walls and archways interspersed with large wooden tables. The crowd is predictably touristy, but Egipte is a long-running hit with locals, including opera greats hungry after a hard night at the Liceu. *Rambla 79, tel. 93/317–9545. Metro: Liceu.*

UNDER 3,000 PTAS. • Salsitas. By day this sumptuous all-white restaurant—with an over-the-top decor of white palm trees rising grandly to the high ceiling, illuminating the room with coconut light-bulbs—serves crisp Mediterranean salads and novel, flavorful pasta dishes. By night it turns into one of the liveliest bar-clubs this side of the Rambla, with a frolicsome crowd that often starts dancing on the tables. Dinner is served from 8 to midnight; doors stay open till 3. *C. Nou de la Rambla 22, tel. 93/318–0840. Metro: Liceu or Drassanes. No lunch.*

Silenus. Elegant yet comfortable, with changing art exhibits on the walls, Silenus has a range of innovative seafood and vegetarian dishes, including *bacalao al crocanti* (salt cod fried in almond batter) and rice tossed with vegetables and mint. *C. dels Àngels 8, tel. 93/302–2680. Metro: Catalunya.*

EL BORN

Occupying the far-eastern corner of the Barri Gòtic, flanked by the Parc Ciutadella to the north and the França train station to the east, the Born neighborhood has in the last few years become the most fashionable enclave in the old quarter. Antique apartments have been converted to stylish bars, and trendy contemporary restaurants share *plaça* space with dark holdovers from another era. Every weekend hip locals in search of a lively night out come here to graze on Basque tapas (the cuisine of the moment) and sip cocktails at fashionably stark bars with exposed brick walls. As so often happens, the same yuppies who once would not dream of venturing south of Diagonal (the fat avenue that traditionally bisected the city between rich and poor) are the very crowd now falling in love with this "authentic" Barcelona. Of course, it's easy to see why: the Born has all the medieval atmosphere of the Barri Gòtic without the tourist crowds and souvenir shops. It's reassuring to sit down in a restaurant and not see a menu printed in eight languages. The neighborhood is named after the Born market, a massive wrought-iron wholesale-food market that operated as such from 1870 until 1970. Thirty years later even this structure is being resurrected: sometime in the next few years it will become Barcelona's main public library.

Passeig del Born is the area's main drag, with a string of lively cocktail bars. Running alongside the França train station, Avenida Marqués de l'Argentera has several top-notch restaurants, and a handful of popular eateries have livened up Pla del Palau (Plaça de la Pau). Plaça de les Olles is the home of two longtime favorites, La Catalana II and the popular tapas bar Cal Pep (*see* Tapas Bars, *below*).

UNDER 1,500 PTAS. • La Catalana II. From its lovely interior of stone arches and pale yellow walls, this bustling traditional restaurant overlooks Plaça de les Olles, in the heart of the Born. It's packed full at lunchtime, when people come from all over the city for ace Catalan food at great prices: the weekday menú del día is 1,100 ptas. À la carte dishes like *pollo al ajillo* (garlic chicken) start at 800 ptas. You can dine outside on the square in nice weather. *Plaça de les Olles 5, tel. 93/319–0693. Metro: Jaume I.*

Salero. The name means "saltshaker," and you'll feel like you're walking into one—this place is all white, with some great funky touches like white candles sunk into a little pillow of salt crystals and a collection of arty books (an interpretation of Lou Reed's songs, for example) through which you can thumb while waiting at the bar. The food is Greek Mediterranean with an Asian twist, with dishes like *pollo teriyaky* (teriyaki chicken; 1,175 ptas.) and couscous *con cordero y verduras* (couscous with lamb and vegetables; 1,250 ptas.). Late at night the popular bar takes over. *C. Rec 60, tel. 93/319–8022. Metro: Jaume I. Closed Sun. No lunch Sat.*

UNDER 2,500 PTAS. • Coses de Menjar. With a distinctively whimsical decor of ceiling lights made from upside-down milk pails and wall designs in cutlery, Coses de Menjar—"Things to Eat"—is the newest, most innovative addition to the Pla del Palau. The food can be pricey, but it's delicious, well worth the splurge. *Brac d'un gitano moreno* ("dark gypsy's arm," the romantic name for Catalan black sausage) is 875 ptas., while foie gras, a house specialty, is 2,300 ptas. *Pla de Palau 7, tel. 93/310–6001. Metro: Jaume I.*

MY KINGDOM FOR SOME GREENS

After a few days of perusing Spain's menus, vegetarians can start to lose heart. Barcelona is a long way from catering to this taste, but a handful of good, cheap restaurants beckons those in search of meatless meals. **Carrer Pintor Fortuny,** *off the Rambla in cluttered El Raval, may seem an unlikely spot for salubrious restaurants, but it holds a cluster. Big, comfy* **Biocenter** *(C. Pintor Fortuny 25, tel. 93/301–4583; open Mon.–Sat. 1–5; cash only) has a hearty veg menú del día for 1,150 ptas. weekdays and 1,500 ptas. on Sat., an all-you-can-eat salad bar for only 650 ptas., several vegan options, and a friendly staff. The bulletin board is a good source of local information on yoga, spiritual dance, and such. Across the street, the store* **Biocenter** *(C. Pintor Fortuny 24, tel. 93/302–3567) has all sorts of veggie treats, including a tofu pâté and shelves of muesli and bran-related everything. Farther down the street is* **L'Hortet** *(C. Pintor Fortuny 3, tel. 93/317–6189; open Sun.–Thurs. 1:15–4, Fri.–Sat. 1:15–4 and 8:30–11; cash only), a cozy space with wood-beam ceilings, checkered tablecloths, and a diverse veg set menú for 1,100 ptas. Nearby, the stylish little* **Mama Café** *(C. Dr. Dou 10, tel. 93/301–2940; open Mon. 1–5, Tues.–Sat. 1–1; closed 3 wks in Aug.; cash only for bills under 3,000 ptas.) serves food until midnight. Though not 100% vegetarian, it has a veg-friendly menú del día for 1,000 ptas. and a changing selection of fresh, flavorful vegetarian dishes.*

In the Barri Gòtic, **Self Naturista** *(C. Santa Anna 11-17, tel. 93/318–2388; closed Sun.) is a bit spartan inside, but the vegetarian menú (1,250 ptas.) is top-notch.*

UNDER 3,000 PTAS. • Txakolin. Basque cuisine is presently all the rage in Barcelona, and this swank Basque restaurant has made quite a name for itself serving excellent Basque-inspired fish and meat dishes. The downstairs restaurant may be too expensive for your taste (entrées start at 2,500 ptas.), but you can feast on a fantastic array of Basque tapas upstairs, perched comfortably at the massive bar. After choosing from heaping plates of victuals and wolfing them gracefully down, you pay 150 ptas. for some items and 250 ptas. for others. *Avda. Marqués de L'Argentera 19, tel. 93/268–1781. Metro: Jaume I.*

EIXAMPLE

Most of the city's designer restaurants are in its designer neighborhood, often on the small streets branching off Passeig de Gràcia. Generally speaking, restaurants in the upper (northern) Eixample are classier and pricier, while those in the lower Eixample, closer to Plaça Catalunya and the university, are more casual and affordable.

UNDER 1,500 PTAS. • Heidelberg. It looks like nothing more than a beer bar, but this long-established German eatery serves cheap bratwurst, kielbasa, and other hefty sausages in portions that will stick to your ribs and fuel you for the better part of a day, especially when accompanied by sauerkraut (called *choucroute* in Spain) or fries. The crowd is a lively mix of students from the nearby university and office workers on lunch break. *Ronda Universitat 21, tel. 93/318–1032. Metro: Universitat.*

UNDER 2,500 PTAS. • Mordisco. This may still be the best-kept dining secret in the Eixample (word has been leaking out, so there may be a line on weekends). Mordisco's formula for success is simple: assemble one of the freshest salad and seafood bars in town and let people have at it. Prices are reasonable, the seafood comes right off the boat, and service is friendly whether you opt for the buffet or order à la carte. *C. Roselló 265, tel. 93/218–3314. Metro: Diagonal.*

Qu Qu. The front delicatessen-bar sells a tantalizing array of hams, cheeses, and fresh salads. To sit down, be served, and dig in, snag an outdoor table on the Passeig de Gràcia or repair to the back of the store. *Passeig de Gràcia 24, tel. 93/317–4512. Metro: Passeig de Gràcia.*

UNDER 3,000 PTAS. • El Japones. El Tragaluz (*see below*) used to operate a small Japanese eatery on its ground floor, but the annex became so popular that the owners moved it across the street and made it a full-fledged restaurant, beautifully designed with high ceilings, pearly gray walls (plus one in red granite), and long wooden tables for groups, as well as nooks for two. Every one of the excellent sushi, sashimi, and tempura meals comes with soy sauce (*salsa de soja*). *Passeig de la Concepció, tel. 93/487–2592. Metro: Diagonal.*

SPLURGE • El Tragaluz. During the day a skylight (*tragaluz*; literally, "light swallower") showers the tables with sun; at night you can look up at the stars. Designed by Javier Mariscal, creator of the 1992 Olympic mascot Cobi, and painted with colorful scenes of food and wine by local artist Isabel Esteva, this restaurant is a divine place to spend an evening. The Mediterranean cuisine is not cheap—a full dinner with drinks costs about 3,500 ptas.—but in these surroundings it's well worth the price. Sea-related pickings like *pasta con espárrago y langosta* (pasta with succulent asparagus and fresh lobster) are joined by vegetarian dishes that, unlike those at many other restaurants, are not just after-thoughts—we found a tangy salad of asparagus, artichokes, tomato, celery, and Parmesan cheese (*ensalada de espárrago, alchacha, tomate, apio, y parmesan*). *Passeig de la Concepció, tel. 93/487–0621. Metro: Diagonal.*

GRÀCIA

UNDER 1,500 PTAS. • El Glop Taverna. This buzzing pub-style hangout has been popular with Gràcia locals for years. Hearty meat dishes are complemented by a surprisingly wide-ranging vegetarian menu that includes *verduras a la brasa* (grilled vegetables; 770 ptas.) and an excellent cheese selection. *C. Montmany 40, tel. 93/213–7058. Metro: Joanic.*

No Me Quite Pá. Taken from a French song most famously sung by Jacques Brel ("Ne me quittes pas," or "Don't Leave Me"), the name morphs cleverly in Spanish and Catalan to "Don't take my bread." This lively place serves up tasty, simple fare—hamburgers, *torrades* (thick toasted bread with a variety of toppings), and salads—until 1 AM, making it popular with hungry bar-hoppers. *Marià Cubi 192, tel. 93/414–0376. FGC: Gràcia.*

UNDER 2,000 PTAS. • Flash Flash. Unlike its many imitators, this groovy restaurant, with leatherette seats and silhouettes of 1970s figures spray-painted onto the walls, is not just retro; it really *is* from the '70s. Most of the regulars, who include some of Barcelona's most influential architects and writers, first came here as flashy young things; they now show up with briefcase or child in hand. The house specialty is tortillas (omelets; *truitas,* in Catalan)—they serve more than 100 varieties, including tortilla with *pollo y bechamel* (chicken and béchamel sauce), with *pan, queso, y tomate frito* (bread, cheese, and fried tomatoes), or with *alcachofas* (artichokes) in season. For dessert? Sweet omelets, of course, perhaps with marmalade or *manzana* (sweetened apple). *La Granada del Penedés 25, tel. 93/237–0990. FGC: Gràcia.*

BARCELONETA / PORT OLÍMPIC

If you want seafood, head for the sea. Barcelona's former fishing quarter, Barceloneta, has its own Metro stop; from here a short walk toward the water brings you to Passeig Joan de Borbó, lined with restaurants that ladle out seafood paella and excellent fish dishes. Many are little mom-and-pop out-fits with far more authenticity (and lower prices) than you'd find in the any of the waterfront-mall restaurants nearby. If you encounter two menús del día in one restaurant, know that the cheaper one, usually around 1,100 ptas. and served only on weekdays, is geared toward locals on their lunch break. Though simpler than the higher-priced menu aimed at tourists, this workman's option is just as tasty and filling. Note that many of these restaurants are closed either Monday or Tuesday. In the

I PREFER THE ONE-PIECE

Edible bikinis? Well, sort of. In Barcelona and Catalunya a bikini is a grilled ham-and-cheese sandwich, traditionally made with sliced white bread (called pan Bimbo after the popular brand name.) In most of the rest of Spain, it's just called a mixto *or a* sandwich de jamón y queso.

Port Olímpic, Passeig Marítim de la Barceloneta has a string of decent waterfront restaurants, of which Agua is by far the best.

UNDER 1,000 PTAS. • El Palau del Pollastre. What this simple place lacks in aesthetics it makes up for in value: the specialty of the house is *pollastre* (chicken), and you can get half a chicken with french fries, a green salad, and a drink for 750 ptas. Fried eggs with potatoes make an even cheaper protein boost (375 ptas.). If you prefer, order everything to go (*para llevar*) and find atmosphere elsewhere. *Passeig Joan de Borbó, tel. 93/221–4989. Metro: Barceloneta.*

UNDER 2,000 PTAS. • Agua. This bright, airy restaurant stands out from the others on the water with its distinctive, arty ambience—every table sports a funky little sculpture of a spiked piece of (fake) fruit—and superb menu. Carpaccio *de atún con aceite de piñones y tomatoes* (tuna carpaccio with pine oil and tomatoes) costs a moderate 1,200 ptas., and a nourishing dish of *verduras a la brasa* (grilled vegetables) goes for 900 ptas. *Passeig Marítim de la Barceloneta 30, tel. 93/225–1272. Metro: Ciutadella-Port Olímpic.*

Cal Manel la Puda. Founded in 1870, this seriously longtime favorite serves first-rate Catalan cuisine at reasonable prices, including delicious *bacalao a la plancha* (grilled salt cod; 1,200 ptas.), *bistec* (steak; 975 ptas.), and fresh *salmón* (1,600 ptas.). Its claim to fame, however, is seafood paella, which you can scarf in this ideal environment for 1,400 ptas. a person. *Passeig Joan de Borbó 60–61, tel. 93/221–5013. Metro: Barceloneta.*

TAPAS BARS

There are tapas, and then there are tapas. Although virtually every bar and restaurant in Spain serves some version of these snacks, Barcelona has a host of establishments where tapas are the main foods served. And since tapas are traditionally taken with a cocktail in the early evening, preceding a possible night on the town, most tapas bars foster a jovial, boisterous TGIF ambience every day of the week.

Bar Tomàs. Every Barcelonan know there's only one place to go for the city's best *patatas bravas* and *patatas amb allioli,* and that's the lovably scruffy Bar Tomàs, in Sarrià (order the *doble mixta* to sample both sauces). Who knew spuds could be so savory? Neighborhood locals and a lively student crowd from the nearby university pack the place daily. *Major de Sarrià 49, tel. 93/203–1077. FGC: Sarrià. Closed Wed.*

Cal Marqués. With its glowing blue ceilings and brick walls, this whimsical, welcoming tapas joint near the beach in Barceloneta has a catchy new concept—traditional tapas in a contemporary setting. Options include *buñuelos de bacalao* (fried balls of cod; 300 ptas.) and *calamares* (fried squid; 450 ptas.); a *copa de vino* (glass of wine) is nicely priced at 200 ptas. *Passeig Joan de Borbó 66, tel. 93/221–6233. Closed Mon. No dinner Sun. or Oct.–Apr.*

Cal Pep. Dominated by a long bar and little else, this city institution invites you to pull up a stool and dig in. The tapas menu centers on *plats especials segons mercat*—whatever's best off the boat that day—which might be fresh *bacalao* (cod) or calamares. *Plaça de les Olles 8, tel. 93/310–7961. Metro: Jaume I.*

El Xampanyet. Near the Picasso Museum, this place is a full tapas *experience*, with colorfully tiled walls, low tables, free-flowing *cava* (Catalan sparkling wine, the house specialty), pitchers of hard cider, and boisterous crowds hitting plate after plate of toothsome tapas. Anchovies in a secret sauce are another specialty, so if you're going to try them in Spain, do it here. *C. Montcada 22, tel. 93/319–7003. Metro: Jaume I .*

Estrella de Plata. This snazzy, appealing restaurant has outdoor tables on Pla del Palau. The tapas are reasonably priced and refreshingly innovative—the combo of *corazones de alcachofa, caviar, y huevos de codorniz* (artichoke hearts, caviar, and quail eggs) is scrumptious, as is the house specialty, bacalao, heaped with fresh tomatoes and onions. When you've eaten your fill, you can hit the Born bars. *Pla del Palau 9, tel. 93/319–6007. Metro: Jaume I.*

Quimet i Quimet. For a taste of Barcelona's best *and* most authentic tapas, head to the working-class neighborhood of Poble Sec, just west of Montjüic. Specializing in mussels, this convivial place has been run by the same family for generations; Quimet is a nickname for Joaquim, moniker of several of the clan's men. *C. Poeta Cabanyes 25, tel. 93/442–3142. Metro: Poble Sec. Closed Wed.*

CAFÉS

Sipping a *café con leche* on the sun-dappled terrace of a Barcelona café while a vest-and-bowtie waiter attends to your whims has to rank up there with life's greatest pleasures. Here in Barcelona you can plop yourself down at such an establishment on just about any street or plaça on the map.

Bar Kasparo. This outdoor café-bar has staked out a wonderful corner on the refreshingly peaceful Plaça Vicenc Martorell. The fresh daily specials, all 850 ptas. or less, might include Thai chicken curry, hummus, Greek salad, or focaccia topped with mozzarella, pesto, and *salchicha* (sausage). By night the "bar" part of the name takes over, and the place hums to chatter fueled by hard cider (400 ptas.) and beer. *Plaça Vicenc Martorell 4 (off C. Elisabets), tel. 93/302–2072. Metro: Catalunya or Liceu. Cash only.*

Cafe de L'Opera. Perched on the Rambla across from the Liceu opera house, this 19th-century café is a Barcelona institution. Replete with lovely Moderniste touches and antique mirrors, it's one of the city's most pleasant spots to while away an afternoon. In the evening the vibe turns barlike, with a mixed crowd of gay folk, students, older couples, and tourists. Founded as a *chocolatería*, the café still serves phenomenal desserts, including tarts, ice-cream sundaes, and good old *churros con chocolate* (fried loops of dough served with thick, dark cocoa). Snag an outdoor table to best ogle the human parade. *Rambla 74, tel. 93/317–7585. Metro: Liceu. Cash only.*

Cafe Salambó. Literary and film types gather for coffee and nibbles in this stylish, high-ceiling venue, testifying to the ongoing vibrancy of the Gràcia neighborhood's intellectual aura. Specialties on the substantial menu include salmon carpaccio (half portion, 650 ptas.; full portion, 1,160 ptas.) and an array of Hungarian *melegs*, doughy pizzas topped with hearty mixtures like veal, bacon, and cheese (840 ptas.). *C. Torrijos 51, tel. 93/218–6966. Metro: Diagonal or FGC: Gràcia.*

Cafe Zurich. This large see-and-be-seen establishment presides over one of the busiest, most entertaining corners in town: Plaça Catalunya at the head of the Rambla. Join the crowd—there always is one—of trendy locals, university students, recent arrivals (with backpacks in tow), and lots and lots of German/Italian/you-name-it tourists. *Plaça Catalunya, 1, tel. 93/317–9153. Metro: Catalunya. Cash only.*

Escribà Confiteria i Fleca. Antoni Escribà and his award-winning pastries and cakes are a Barcelona tradition. Once an Escribà shop window—filled with luscious cakes and inventive chocolates—has caught your eye, it's hard to resist popping in. The store has several branches; the one on the Rambla is housed in the Antigua Casa Figueres, a beautiful old Moderniste pastry shop with beautiful tiled mosaics around the entrance. The Platja Bogatell store is a full-fledged, pricey restaurant called Escribà Xiringuito, named for Barcelona's onetime seaside fish shanties. *Rambla 83, tel. 93/301–6027. Metro: Liceu. Gran Via 546, tel. 93/454–7535. Metro: Urgell. Litoral Mar 42, Platja Bogatell, tel. 93/221–0729. Metro: Barceloneta.*

La Cerería. Tucked into a lovely balconied, arch-roof Barri Gòtic walkway, this casual café is the kind of place where you can spend whole afternoons—and many in the arty crowd do—sipping strong coffee or lunching on a light menu ranging from sweet rolls and croissants to more substantial items like samosas (550 ptas.) and lemon chicken (700 ptas.). *Baixada de Sant Miquel 3–5 (off C. Avinyó), tel. 93/301–8510. Metro: Liceu or Jaume I. Closed 1st Wed. of each month. Cash only.*

BE IT EVER
SO HUMBLE

Allioli (all i oli, *garlic and oil*) is savory garlic mayonnaise, most often seen heaped on fried potatoes but also served with meat and seafood. If you find yourself addicted to it, a common problem, here's how to make the stuff at home:

1 egg

4 cloves of garlic

6 oz. (¼ liter) olive oil

1 tbsp. lemon juice

½ tsp. salt

Place the egg and peeled garlic in a blender, and beat until smooth. Add oil in a slow stream until mixture is thick. Add lemon juice and salt.

La Valenciana. This old-fashioned ice-creamery next to the university can satisfy sweet teeth with a delectable array of sundaes, shakes, dessert crepes, and *horchata* (*orxata*, in Catalan), a sweet milky drink made with *chufas* (tiger nuts). Orxata is usually served only in summer, but here you can try it year-round. *C. Aribau 1, tel. 93/453–1138. Metro: Universitat.*

Tèxtil Cafè. Tuckered out after the Picasso Museum? Duck into this inviting café-restaurant in the sunny courtyard of the Museum of Clothing and Textiles. Nourishments include a delicious tomato, mozzarella, and basil salad (650 ptas.), *baba ganoush* (650 ptas.), and chili with chicken (975 ptas.). *C. Montcada 12, tel. 93/268–2598. Metro: Jaume I.*

MARKETS

The **Champion** supermarket is about as central as markets get (Rambla 113, near C. Pintor Fortuny). The department store **El Corte Inglés** (Plaça Catalunya 14), has a well-stocked supermarket with a particularly good wine section. The ground floor of **Marks & Spencer**, also on Plaça Catalunya, has a small supermarket with all kinds of imported goodies.

The massive, historic **Boqueria** produce market, just off the Rambla, is the only place to go for fresh fruit, vegetables, meats, and fish, not least because the sights and smells make the site an attraction in itself (*see* Exploring Barcelona: Barri Gòtic, *below*). On the other side of the Rambla, local merchants sell honey, cheese, *turrón* (nougat candy), pâté, and other country fare in the **Plaça a del Pi,** Friday–Sunday 11–2 and 5–9.

Barcelona supermarkets close on Sunday, so that's when you'll love **Nuria**, at the top of the Rambla (tel. 93/302–3847), open weekdays and Sunday until 1 AM, Saturday until 2 AM. The store up front sells hams, cheeses, bread, jam, beer, and wine; the restaurant in back serves decent bocadillos and *platos combinados* (basic combo platters of meats and vegetables). Another late-night and Sunday savior is **Vips** (Rambla Catalunya 7–9, tel. 93/317–4805; Metro: Catalunya; open weekdays until 1 AM, Fri.–Sun. until 3 AM), which has a small grocery, CD, and bookshop in front.

EXPLORING BARCELONA

The Catalan capital is ripe for the taking—all you need is a map and your own two feet. You'll probably want to start with a walk along the colorful Rambla or through the medieval streets of the Barri Gòtic. Adjoining the Gothic quarter, the Ribera neighborhood is home to the excellent Museu Picasso and the city's fabulous Moderniste concert hall, the Palau de la Música. Uptown, northwest of Plaça Catalunya, the Eixample packs most of the Moderniste buildings, including Gaudí's Sagrada Família church and Casa Milà. The hilly, airy parkland of Montjüic, off to the south, puts you high above the city amid some top-notch museums, including the beautiful Fundació Miró and the Museu Nacional d'Art de Catalunya, with a focus on medieval Romanesque art. Barcelona's main park, the Ciutadella, is a peaceful, verdant spot to pass an afternoon and contains the all-important city zoo. Note that most museums are closed one day each week, usually Monday.

If and when you finish sightseeing, head toward the water: slickly rebuilt for the 1992 Olympics, Barcelona's port is worth checking out, particularly with a paella lunch at one of the string of outdoor restaurants, or at night when the bars and clubs of the Port Olímpic become party central. The city's beaches are crowded, but they're clean and well maintained.

For those on whirlwind tours, the **Bus Turistic** (*see* Getting Around, *above*) is not a bad way to get around, as you can design your own itinerary and hop on and off at will. Art junkies may find the **Articket** worthwhile, as it buys you half-price entry to six major museums: the Museu Nacional d'Art de Catalunya, Fundació Joan Miró, Casa Milà, Fundació Antoni Tàpies, and Centre de Cultura Contemporània. Available at the Plaça Catalunya tourist office, any of the member museums, or Tel-Entrada (tel. 902/101212; from abroad, tel. 934/799920), the ticket costs 1,997 ptas. (12 euros). The tourist office also leads **walking tours** of the Barri Gòtic (1,000 ptas.) on weekends at 10 in English, noon in Spanish and Catalan. Stop into the Plaça Catalunya office or call 906/301282 to reserve a spot.

LA RAMBLA

It says something about a city when the number one tourist attraction is a street, yet said street is as well loved—and used—by locals as by travelers. Barcelona's vibrant, bustling pedestrian thoroughfare is both a practical route from Plaça Catalunya to the Mediterranean Sea and an ongoing spectacle of street theater. Thronged around the clock, the Rambla is lined with flower stalls, bird vendors, newsstands, performance artists, and buskers. The Rambla *is* Barcelona; it's hard to imagine either one without the other.

The Rambla is named after the river (*raml* in Arabic) that used to run this course; it's a mere and joyous coincidence that the name connotes "ramble" in English. Though everyone calls this drag La Rambla, it's actually a series of five streets (technically, Las Ramblas) laid end to end. Walking south from Plaça Catalunya, the Rambla de Canaletes is the first stretch: Here, on the right, you'll see the Font de Canaletes, a 19th-century wrought-iron fountain inscribed with the legend purporting that all who drink from it will fall in love with Barcelona and return perpetually. You may want to skip the drinking part.

Rambla dels Estudis, also called Rambla dels Ocells (of the birds) for the parakeets sold here, starts at Carrer de Santa Anna and runs south to Carrer Portaferrissa. Rambla de Sant Josep—also called Rambla de les Flors—is the third and most colorful stretch, with the famous flower stands, the busy Boqueria food market, and a large, eye-catching pavement mosaic by artist Joan Miró. Rambla dels Caputxins, running from the Boqueria to Carrer dels Escudellers, is home to the beautiful Gran Teatre Liceu (and the delightful Café de l'Opera) and leads off to the grand Plaça Reial. The home stretch, closest to the sea, is Rambla de Santa Mònica, where caricaturists and palm readers like to set up shop. Punctuating it all like a period is the Columbus monument, pointing out to sea.

When you tire of jostling for space on the Rambla proper, join the families and couples walking hand in hand on Rambla Catalunya, a genteel pedestrian street running north from Plaça Catalunya to Diagonal (parallel to Passeig de Gràcia). Lined with upscale boutiques and *pastelerías* (pastry shops), it's the perfect place for a peaceful, pricey coffee at a shaded café in the center of the walkway.

TREAT STREET

A Spanish proverb dictates, "Las cosas claras, y el chocolate espeso" (Make things clear, but chocolate thick). The thing about Spanish chocolate (xocolata in Catalan), Spain's decadent version of hot chocolate, is that it's not just rich— it's as thick as pudding. Popular dipping implements include melindros (finger-length sugar cookies), ensaimadas (light, fluffy rolls topped with powdered sugar), churros (beveled sticks of fried dough), and croissants.

The traditional chocolaterías on the narrow, balconied Carrer Petrixol, off Carrer Portaferrissa in the Barri Gòtic, have been sating sugar cravings for decades; in some cases even the waiters are original. On weekends nattering families, teenagers, young couples, and old ladies sit elbow to elbow over steaming cups. **La Pallaresa** *(C. Petritxol 13, tel. 93/302–2036), always abustle, has chocolate for 300 ptas., churros for 150 ptas., and fresones con nata (large strawberries with whipped cream) for 350 ptas. Next door,* **Xocoa** *(C. Petritxol 11, tel. 93/301–1197) serves similar goodies in a series of dim, intimate rooms with honey-color walls. At the end of the street, just before Plaça del Pi,* Granja Dulcinea *(C. Petrixol 2, tel. 93/302–6824) has low wood-beam ceilings and owners who could stand in for Santa and Mrs. Claus. Chocolate is traditionally a winter beverage, so in summer most of these places turn their talents to horchata (a sweet grain-based drink) and granizados (a crushed-ice drink, usually lemon-flavor).*

GRAN TEATRE DEL LICEU

Founded in 1847, Barcelona's grande dame opera house has long been one of the city's most beloved cultural icons, indeed one of the most beautiful such theaters in Europe. No mere provincial hall, the Liceu introduced the world to such Catalan musical lights as Montserrat Caballé, José Carreras, and Victoria de los Angeles. Sadly, the building has suffered chronic bad luck—it was gutted by fire twice, in 1861 and 1994—but its latest restoration gets rave reviews. If you're up bright and early, do take a tour, especially to see the ornate **Saló dels Miralls** (Hall of Mirrors), in which mirrors reflect the colorful neo-classical ceiling art, and the **Cercle del Liceu,** an old-time social club and exquisite Moderniste enclave. To reserve a visit, you must call between 11 and 2:30 one to three days in advance; for information on opera tickets, *see* After Dark, *below. C. de Sant Pau at Rambla, tel. 93/485–9900. Metro: Liceu. Open daily 9:45 AM–11 AM (last admission 10:15 AM). Closed July 26–Aug 31.*

MERCAT DE LA BOQUERIA

It happens to everyone: pulses quicken, noses flare, and eyes widen upon entering this cavernous, jam-packed food market just west of the Rambla. Stacks of glistening apples and oranges face whole pigs and enormous cuts of beef, which in turn share a coveted corner stall with towering mounds of cheese. Nearby, an aproned vendor hawks crabs, lobsters, and shrimp; close inspection reveals that said *mariscos* (shellfish) are still briskly waving their feelers and pincers, oblivious to their doom. Freshness is the name of the game here; no-nonsense housewives haggle hard for the meats and veggies that will go into that afternoon's *comida* (meal). Join right in if your language skills are up to snuff, as the Boqueria sells top-quality produce at the best prices in Barcelona. Stalls near the main entrance sell masses of dried fruits and nuts, making them a great place to stock up on late-night munchies for your room. *Rambla 91. Metro: Liceu or Catalunya. Open Mon.–Sat. 7 AM–8 PM.*

PALAU DE LA VIRREINA

Built in 1778 by the viceroy of Peru—the name literally means "Palace of the Viceroy's Wife—this neo-classical pile houses an array of temporary exhibits, ranging from photography to paintings to audiovisual installations. Next to the entrance is **the Institut de Cultural de Barcelona,** a handy information office with reams of glossy brochures on museums and current arts events. Their helpful guide to Barcelona's museums (200 ptas.), updated every six months, also has information on changing exhibits. *Rambla 99, tel. 93/301–7775. Metro: Liceu. Palace open Tues.–Sat. 11–8, Sun. 11–3; cultural office open weekdays 10–2 and 4–8.*

PALAU GÜELL

Like many fledgling artists, Antoni Gaudí initially made a living designing homes for wealthy patrons. This magnificent palace was commissioned in 1886 by one of Gaudí's most important supporters, Count Eusebi de Güell, who became the young architect's springboard to fame and also remained an ardent lifelong fan. As on many of Gaudí's creations, the facade is an amalgam of architectural styles (Moderniste, Gothic, Moorish), but the building is most impressive inside, with some gorgeous dark-wood ceiling work and spectacular stained glass. Palau Güell is the only Gaudí-designed house open fully to the public, as most of the others, notably Casa Milà, still have some private residents. *C. Nou de la Rambla 9, tel. 93/317–3974. Metro: Liceu. Admission: 400 ptas. Open Mon.–Sat. 10–2 and 4–8.*

MONUMENT A COLOM

You know you've reached the end of the Rambla when you see the Columbus monument towering above you, built for the 1888 Universal Exposition to commemorate Columbus's visit to Barcelona after his return from the Americas. You can take an elevator to the top for phenomenal views of the city, though you might face a long wait during the summer, as only four can go up at a time. *Metro: Drassanes. Elevator: 250 ptas. Open Apr.–May, weekdays 10–1:30 and 3:30–7:30, weekends 10–7:30; June–Sept., daily 9–8:30; Oct.–Mar., weekdays 10–1:30 and 3:30–6:30, weekends 10–6:30.*

MUSEU MARÍTIM

This impressive museum is housed in the 13th-century **Drassanes Reials** (Royal Shipyards), just west of the Columbus monument. Barcelona's grand Gothic shipyards are arranged in a series of large bays, with an enormous central courtyard where ships were once stored in the winter. Plunge inside for a voyage through Catalonia's nautical history, from the Middle Ages to the late 19th century. Exhibits include model ships, navigational instruments, maps, charts, and an interesting selection of figureheads. *Avda. de les Drassanes s/n, tel. 93/342–9920. Metro: Drassanes. Admission: 800 ptas. Open Oct.–June, daily 10–7; July–Sept., Mon.–Thurs. and weekends 10–7, Fri. 10 AM–11 PM.*

MUSEU DE L'ERÒTICA

Equal parts tawdry and titillating, the Museum of Erotic Art is appropriately located right on the Rambla, a few blocks from what was once (and still is, to a much lesser extent) the Barrio Chino's prostitute row. Though some of the exhibits verge on silly and/or tasteless, the museum somewhat redeems itself with an interesting series of historic Kama Sutra drawings and fascinating photos of the underground sex trade in the 1930s Barrio Chino. *Rambla 96, tel. 93/318–9865. Metro: Liceu. Admission: 975 ptas. Open daily 10 AM–midnight.*

BARRI GÒTIC

Barcelona's Gothic quarter is the most atmospheric *barrio* in town, a chaotic warren of dark, narrow treasure-filled streets that's best explored by wandering with no fixed itinerary in mind. Venture through a gloomy medieval portal and behold a light-filled courtyard with a fountain; climb some crumbling steps and rest on an antique stone bench. The official heart of the Barri Gòtic is Plaça Sant Jaume, halfway between the Rambla and the busy Via Laietana. For old-time social interaction, head to the Plaça Reial, a beautiful Moderniste square lined with bars and restaurants. Another appealing square is the little Plaça del Pi, where you can bask in the barrio's intimate ambience at an outdoor café.

The Barri Gòtic was once fully encircled by Roman walls, remnants of which you can see near the front of the cathedral. The Museu d'Història de la Ciutat (City History Museum), which you enter from the

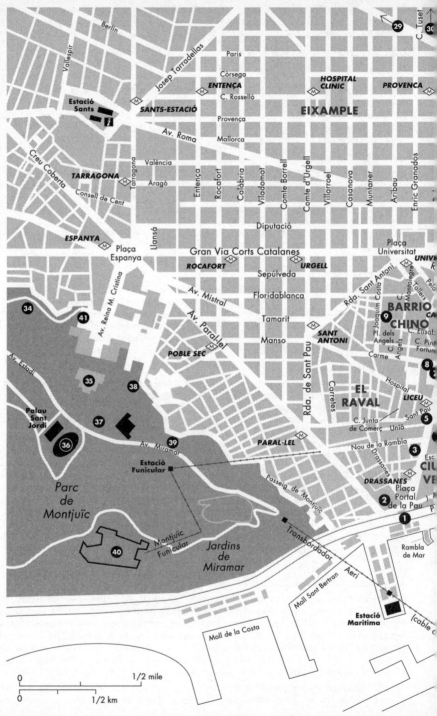

Berlin

Josep Tarradellas

Paris

Còrsega

ENTENÇA

C. Rosselló

HOSPITAL CLINIC

PROVENCA

Estació Sants

SANTS-ESTACIÓ

Provença

EIXAMPLE

Av. Roma

Mallorca

Creu Coberta

València

TARRAGONA

Aragó

Consell de Cent

Entença

Rocafort

Calàbria

Viladomat

Comte Borrell

Comte d'Urgell

Villarroel

Casanova

Muntaner

Aribau

Enric Granados

Diputació

Plaça Universitat

ESPANYA

Plaça Espanya

Llansá

Gran Via Corts Catalanes

UNIV

ROCAFORT

URGELL

Sepúlveda

Rda. Sant Antoni

BARRIO CHINO

Av. Mistral

Floridablanca

9

Pl. dels Angels

C. Elisab

Av. Paral·lel

Tamarit

SANT ANTONI

Carme

C. Pint Fortun

POBLE SEC

Manso

Rda. de Sant Pau

EL RAVAL

Hospital

8

34

41

35

Carretes

LICEU

C. Junta de Comerç

Sant Pau

5

38

Av. Estadi

37

Unió

3

Palau Sant Jordi

Av. Miramar

39

PARAL-LEL

Nou de la Rambla

36

Estació Funicular

DRASSANES

Esc

CIU VE

Passeig de Montjuïc

Plaça Portal de la Pau

2

Parc de Montjuïc

Montjuïc Funicular

40

Jardins de Miramar

Transbordador

1

Rambla de Mar

Moll Sant Bertran

Aeri

Estació Marítima

(cable c

Moll de la Costa

0   1/2 mile

0   1/2 km

Casa Milà, **27**
Castell de
Montjuïc, **40**
Castells des
Tres Dragons, **19**
Catedral
de la Seu, **11**
Estadi Olímpic, **36**
Fundació
Francisco Godia, **26**
Fundació Miró, **39**
Fundació Tàpies, **25**
Gran Teatre, **5**
Hospital de la
Santa Creu, **33**
La Cascada, **20**
Manzana de la
Discòrdia, **24**
Mercat de la
Boqueria, **7**
Mies van der Rohe
Pavilion, **41**
Monument a
Colom, **1**
Museu
Arqueològic, **38**
Museu
Barbier-Mueller, **16**
Museu d'Art
Contemporani
de Barcelona, **9**
Museu
d'Art Modern, **21**
Museu de
l'Eròtica, **6**
Museu
Etnològic, **37**
Museu Frederic
Marès, **12**
Museu Marítim, **2**
Museu Picasso, **18**
Museu Tèxtil i
d'Indùmentaria, **15**
Palau de la Música
Catalana, **14**
Palau de la Virreina, **8**
Palau Güell, **3**
Palau Nacional, **35**
Parc Güell, **32**
Parc Zoològic, **22**
Plaça del Rei, **13**
Plaça Reial, **4**
Plaça Sant Jaume, **10**
Poble Espanyol, **34**
Port Olímpic, **23**
Santa Maria
del Mar, **17**
Sarrià/Pedralbes, **29**
Temple Expiatori
de la Sagrada
Família, **28**
Tibidabo, **30**

KEY

i Tourist Information
Ⓜ Metro Stops
├─┼─ Rail Lines
▷◁▷◁ Funicular/
Cable Car

AVOID GOING NUTS

Cons and scams have been around since time immemorial, and many of the Rambla's con artists look like they have, too. In your peregrinations you may see a raucous group of people standing around a makeshift cardboard table and cheering on a guy who appear to be playing the ancient game of hiding a seed under one of three walnut shells. He goads passersby to pick a shell, any shell, and see if they can guess where the seed is; someone takes the bait, and the scam has begun. You'll choose correctly and "win" at the beginning, but the moment you start handing over betting money, it becomes noticeably more difficult—all but impossible—to guess the right shell. This is a scam, through and through, and the people standing around cheering the guy on are his friends or paid accomplices. The whole thing is actually quite entertaining to watch, so the key is to stand at a distance, observe for kicks, and move on. The latest trend (even scammers have to stay fresh) is to use hollowed-out carrot tops rather than walnut shells.

starkly medieval Plaça del Rei, sends you underground to walk through an extensive swath of the ancient Roman city itself.

CATEDRAL DE LA SEU

Soaring majestically above the Gothic quarter, Barcelona's Gothic cathedral still serves, with its adjoining square, as the barrio's religious and social center. Construction on the cathedral began in 1298, but the spire and neo-Gothic facade were added in 1892. At night, the cathedral is floodlighted in striking yellows; even the stained-glass windows are backlighted from inside. The original Gothic interior is appropriately mysterious and gloomy, mitigated by lights that help clarify such details as the lovely carved choir stalls. The **crypt** contains the tomb of one of Barcelona's patron saints, Santa Eulalia, surrounded by beautiful reliefs tracing the saint's suffering and martyrdom. The elegant alabaster sarcophagus was carved by Italian sculptor Lupo di Francesco in 1327. One of the cathedral's side chapels is a **Black Virgin**, similar to the famous one in Montserrat (*see* Near Barcelona, *below*).

In the center of the magnificent **cloister** is a verdant **tropical garden** populated by white geese. Absorbing the sweeping views from the cathedral's spire (elevator 200 ptas.) can be a religious experience in itself—on a clear day you can see all of Barcelona beneath you, from the Columbus statue to Gaudí's Sagrada Familia. The **museum** (admission: 200 ptas.) has an interesting collection of tapestries and religious artifacts. On Sunday at noon the Plaça de la Seu, out front, fills with people dancing the *sardana,* Catalonia's national dance (*see* Box: Shake That Thing). *Plaça de la Seu, tel. 93/315–2213. Metro: Liceu. Free. Open daily 8:30–1:30 and 4–7:30.*

PLAÇA SANT JAUME

This large, stately square in the heart of the Gothic quarter looks and feels powerful, and, of course, it is: the governments of both Barcelona and Catalonia are headquartered here. As far as city and regional politics go, the peseta stops here. If you enter the plaça from Carrer Ferran, the 15th-century Catalan Gothic **ajuntament** (city hall) is on your right. The fine, old interior includes a beautiful Josep Maria Sert mural (1928) chronicling important events in Catalonia's history and the famous Saló de Cent, lavishly draped in the reds and yellows of the Catalan flag, from which the Council of One Hundred ruled Barcelona between 1372 and 1714. You can visit only on weekends from 10 to 2, during which time a guide will take you around.

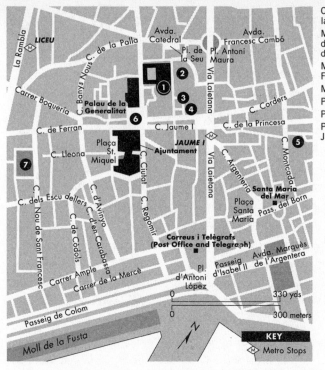

Catedral de
la Seu, **1**
Museu
d'Historia
de la Ciutat, **4**
Museu
Frederic Marès, **2**
Museu Picasso, **5**
Plaça del Rei, **3**
Plaça Reial, **7**
Plaça Sant
Jaume, **6**

Across from City Hall is the courtly **Palau de la Generalitat** (seat of the Catalan government), a building that pays homage to Catalonia's patron, Sant Jordi, in several ways: One side of the Palau bears an impressive carved relief of St. George, and there's a 15th-century chapel dedicated to Sant Jordi inside, not to mention a gilded ceiling in the room called Saló de Sant Jordi. Guided tours, including English, are available the second and fourth Sunday of each month from 11 to 1:30; you can also visit on April 23, St. George's Day, but the rest of Barcelona has the same idea, so you'll be in line for a long time. *Plaça Sant Jaume. Ajuntament: tel. 93/402–7000. Palau de la Generalitat: tel. 93/402–4600. Metro: Liceu or Jaume I. Free.*

PLAÇA REIAL

Just east of the Rambla, this 19th-century arcaded square is one of the liveliest crossroads in the Barri Gòtic. By day the sidewalk cafés swarm with folks out for sun and caffeine (don't you love Spain?), and by night the restaurants and bars fill to capacity. Most of the time Plaça Reial is a great place to soak in the local ambience, planted with lofty palm trees and ringed by elegant lemon-yellow houses. The wrought-iron **fountain** in the center depicts the Three Graces, and the iron Moderniste lampposts were designed by a young Gaudí in 1879. On Sunday morning there's a lively **coin and stamp market** here. The plaça can be sketchy at night, with too many shady characters lurking in corners, so if you come here to sample the nightlife, keep an eye, or hand, on your valuables. Fortunately, police presence in the area is high, and patrol cars prowl the square quite often.

PLAÇA DEL REI / MUSEU D'HISTORIA DE LA CIUTAT

Just southeast of the cathedral, Plaça del Rei is one of the best-preserved medieval squares in Barcelona, rimmed by such stark regal buildings as the 14th-century **Palau Reial Major** and the cavernous **Saló de Tinell**, an enormous, austere Catalan Gothic banquet hall (this is where Ferdinand and Isabella received Columbus on his happy return from the Americas). The adjoining chapel of **Santa Agueda** holds a superb 15th-century altarpiece. Flanking the western side of the square is the **Palau del Lloctinent** (Lieutenant's Palace), dominated by the **Torre del Rei Martí,** a watchtower with fetching views over the Barri Gòtic including close-ups of the cathedral spires. All these buildings form part of the

SHAKE THAT THING

In towns across Catalonia people gather on weekends to dance the traditional circular sardana, *described by Catalan poet Joan Maragall as "la movil, magnifica anilla" ("the magnificent, moving ring"). The circle can have as few as five or as many as 40 people, all of whom hold hands. A comparatively subdued form of boogie, the sardana looks simple, but watch the dancers' feet— you'll see tiny, mincing steps; broader, bolder jumps; and a surprising level of intricacy and skill. At various points you'll see everyone in the circle stop, raise their hands in perfect unison and then, after a minuscule pause, continue stepping to the music. Many dancers wear* espardenyas *(espadrilles), whose flat soles and soft uppers aid in their footwork.*

The sardana is thought to have originated in Sardinia, an early Catalan settlement. It was popularized in the mid-1800s, when Pep Ventura (after whom a Barcelona Metro stop is named) composed what is now the standard music. The band contains a flute, a small drum, and several woodwind and brass instruments.

In most towns the sardana is danced on Sunday, and often Saturday as well, in the Plaça Major or near the church. You're welcome to join in—as sedate as it looks, the sardana is a social event, with a festive, informal mood. Dancers throw their bags and jackets in the middle of the circle, and kids run all over the place. In Barcelona the sardana is danced on Sunday at noon (and sometimes early Saturday evening) in the Plaça de la Seu, and in Plaça Sant Jaume early Sunday evening.

Museu d'Història de la Ciutat (City History Museum), housed in the 15th-century medieval Casa Padellàs, just off the square itself. Inside the museum you can peruse Roman and Visigothic relics, then descend to the old Roman city of Barcino itself and amble through the stone ruins on special metal walkways. It's very cool. *Museum: Palau Padellàs, C. del Veguer 2, tel. 93/315–1111. Metro: Liceu. Admission: 500 ptas.; free 1st Sat. of month 4–8. Open June–Sept., Tues.–Sat. 10–8, Sun. 10–2; Oct.– May, Tues.–Sat. 10–2 and 4–8, Sun. 10–2.*

MUSEU FREDERIC MARÈS

The 20th-century Catalan sculptor Frederic Marès had a passion for collecting and the money to pursue it. The results are displayed in this remarkable museum, opened by the artist himself in 1948. Religion icons and sculptures form the bulk of the holdings, but the eccentric Marès also roamed the world and amassed a mind-boggling collection of *things*, from walking sticks to watches to perfume bottles, all of which are on display. *Plaça Sant Iu 5–6, tel. 93/310–5800. Metro: Jaume I. Admission: 500 ptas. Open Tues. and Thurs. 10–5, Wed. and Fri.–Sat. 10–7, Sun. 10–3.*

EL RAVAL / BARRIO CHINO

Spreading out west of La Rambla, El Raval is the Gothic quarter's seedier cousin, with a checkered past of prostitution and drugs—particularly in its southern sector, the Barrio Chino. The area has considerably cleaned up its act in the last several years, however, especially with the arrival of the very contemporary **Barcelona Museum of Contemporary Art.** The Raval also has a slew of budget hotels and restaurants, and some of the most atmospheric old bars in the city.

MUSEU D'ART CONTEMPORANI DE BARCELONA

The Barcelona Museum of Contemporary Art (MACBA) opened in 1995 to much fanfare and controversy, the latter owing to its brash (or so some felt) intrusion into the Raval, a working-class neighborhood of typical old buildings. Enormous, sleek, and white, designed by American architect Richard Meier, the MACBA stands in total contrast to the surrounding buildings. Of course, that's not necessarily a bad thing; many now agree the museum has benefited the rundown Raval by bringing in a new crowd, namely arty types, tourists, and the attendant pesetas. Lately the flap has taken a new turn: some say the collection is far less impressive than the building in which it's housed. Sound familiar, Bilbao fans?

Still and all, if you're into 20th-century art, the MACBA is definitely worth a trip. The permanent collection packs its share of big names, including Paul Klee, Alexander Calder, Jean Dubuffet, and Catalans Joan Miró and Antoni Tàpies. Most locals come here for the top-notch temporary exhibits, which can include photography and mixed media as well as painting and sculpture. The museum store has a great selection of books on Barcelona art and design as well as the usual gift items. *Plaça dels Àngels 1, tel. 93/412–0810. Metro: Catalunya. Admission: 750 ptas., 375 ptas. on Wed. Open Mon.* and *Wed.–Fri. 11–7:30, Sat. 10–8, Sun. and holidays 10–3.*

Just northwest of the MACBA, the **Centre de Cultura Contemporània de Barcelona** (CCCB) hosts contemporary-art exhibits, film screenings, and lectures. Check out the large interior courtyard—one side is formed by a gigantic, angled glass wall, cleverly designed to reflect Barcelona's skyline. *C. Montalegre 5, tel. 93/306–4100. Metro: Catalunya. Admission: 1 exhibit 600 ptas. (Wed. 400 ptas.), 2 exhibits 900 ptas.; courtyard free. Open mid-June–mid-Sept., Tues.–Sat. 11–8, Sun. and holidays 11–3; mid-Sept.–mid-June, Tues.* and *Thurs. 11–2 and 4–8, Wed. and weekends 11–8.*

LA RIBERA / EL BORN

Cross busy Via Laietana from the Barri Gòtic, and you're in La Ribera, another lovely section of the old town and home of the museum and stunning, Moderniste Palau de la Música Catalana. Like the Barri Gòtic, this is a maze of medieval streets and balconied houses, but La Ribera lacks the crowds and T-shirt shops that can plague parts of the Barri Gòtic. It feels more like a neighborhood proper, where residents still outnumber tourists.

Nearby, still part of the old town, is El Born, Barcelona's most up-and-coming barrio. Long dotted with outdoor restaurants and cafés on little plaças, the Born now also hides funky cocktail bars and hip nightclubs in converted antique lofts.

MUSEU PICASSO

Housed in a pair of medieval palaces, Barcelona's Picasso Museum is by far its most popular. Presented chronologically, this collection is strong on Pablo Picasso's early work, giving you a rare chance to observe the front end of the artist's creative development. You begin with doodles from the margins of Picasso's schoolbooks, sketches and studies from his days as an art student in Barcelona, paintings from his somber Blue Period (1901–1904) and lighter, more playful Rose Period (1904–1905), and a series of cubist works. Although the museum has few of Picasso's best-known works (*Guernica,* for example, is in Madrid's Reina Sofía Museum), the tradeoff is a feeling of having "discovered" Picasso before he became famous. It's interesting to see how Picasso painted the same subject at different times in his life: look for the subtle changes in the paintings of his sister Lola, with her trademark loose bun of hair. The collection also includes a fulsome series of lesser-known etchings and engravings, from erotic drawings of ex-lovers to mythical minotaurs to the Quatre Gats restaurant menus that Picasso designed in 1899 and 1900 (*see* Where to Eat, *above*). *C. Montcada 15–19, tel. 93/319–6310. Metro: Jaume I. Admission: permanent collection 725 ptas., temporary exhibit 800 ptas., both 1,250 ptas. Open Tues.–Sat. 10–8, Sun. 10–3.*

MUSEU TÈXTIL I D'INDÙMENTARIA CLOTHING

The closest most people get to this museum is the delightful restaurant-café in its intimate courtyard (*see* Cafés, *above*). But if you're intrigued by the ways in which textiles and fashions have evolved through the ages, duck inside. The surprisingly large collection includes some fine examples of early

FERTILE SOIL: MODERNISTE BARCELONA

If there's one artistic movement that has defined Barcelona physically, it's Modernisme, which in one form or another was en vogue throughout Europe in the late 19th century (in France it was called art nouveau; in Germany, Jugendstil.) The word modernisme essentially means "affinity for what is modern," and indeed the movement lasted longer, and was perhaps more enthusiastic, in Barcelona than anywhere else in the world. Economics and politics had a lot to do with this: in the early 19th century Catalonia was flush with prosperity from new industrial advances. Nationalist pride and the attendant eagerness to beautify the Catalan capital were at an all-time high. Add to this the creation of new neighborhoods, notably the Eixample, where the vibrant movement could take root, and Barcelona became the perfect breeding ground for Modernisme. Architectural design flourished all over the city, loosely defining the movement by natural, curved lines and fanciful ornamentation. The first major Catalan Moderniste architect, Lluís Domènech i Montaner, whose slew of structures includes the city's spectacular Palau de la Música, in La Ribera. Antoni Gaudí, was of course, another master, though his style was so distinct that he's almost in a class by himself. The third big Barcelona name was Josep Puig i Cadafalch, who left his mark on the Eixample with the Gothic-influenced Casa Amatller, on Passeig de Gràcia, and Casa Terrades, also known as Casa de les Punxes, on Avinguda Diagonal. (The punxes are wrought-iron, scepter-like rods that top the mansion's towers and hold up its balconies.)

The tourist office on Plaça Catalunya has a helpful map of the so-called Ruta del Modernisme (Modernist Route), which guides you to 50 of the city's noteworthy Moderniste sights. For 600 ptas. you can buy a Ruta del Modernisme ticket at the **Centre de Modernisme** in Casa Amatller (Passeig de Gràcia 41, tel. 93/488–0139; Metro: Passeig de Gràcia; open Mon.–Sat. 10–7, Sun. 10–2) and get 50% off admission to every Moderniste stop on the map, including the Museu d'Art Modern in Parc Ciutadella.

(16th-century) embroidery and needlepoint, as well as Egyptian and Islamic textiles. *C. Montcada 12, tel. 93/310–4516. Metro: Jaume I. Admission: 400 ptas. Open Tues.–Sat. 10–8, Sun. 10–3.*

MUSEU BARBIER-MUELLER D'ART PRECOLOMBI

Next door to the Museu Tèxtil, the Barbier-Mueller Museum specializes in pre-Colombian art, drawing from the Aztec, Mayan, Incan, and other indigenous Central and South American cultures. *C. Montcada 14, tel. 93/310–4516. Metro: Jaume I. Admission: 400 ptas. Open Tues.–Sat. 10–8, Sun. 10–3.*

SANTA MARIA DEL MAR

Just down the street from the Museu Picasso is the supremely elegant church of Santa Maria del Mar, Barcelona's best example of the measured, unornamented Catalan Gothic style. The simple, high, spacious interior is set off by a beautiful stained-glass rose window above the front entrance. Built between 1329 and 1383, the church is dedicated to St. Mary of the Sea, patron saint of sailors, and you can see vestiges of the church's maritime roots here and there, including an old model ship near one of the statues of the Virgin. *Plaça de Sant Maria. Metro: Jaume I. Open daily 9–1:30 and 5–8.*

PALAU DE LA MÚSICA CATALANA

Gaudí's buildings get more press, but a tour of Moderniste Barcelona just isn't complete until you've ventured inside the magnificent Palau de la Música Catalana, designed by Domènech i Montaner in 1908. The key word is *inside*—though the mosaic pillars and stone busts on the redbrick exterior are nothing if not eye-catching, it's the hall itself that will take your breath away. An inverted-dome stained-glass skylight ringed by ethereal angels' heads tops the opulent auditorium, flanked by glossy painted rosettes and arcs of giant peacock feathers. The backdrop of the massive stage is a curved wall of rust-color tile populated by the mosaic skirts and protruding busts of muses playing instruments, so bizarre as to be downright distracting in concert. To the right of the stage, immense Wagnerian horses charge forth in stone. The best way to bask in the Palau's utterly unique aesthetics is to attend a performance (*see* After Dark, *below*), but a guided tour will certainly do, and English is spoken. If all else fails, behold the wonderful Moderniste lobby-bar area, full of color-tile vaulting and stained-glass dividers. *C. Sant Francesc de Paula 2, tel. 93/268–1000. Metro: Urquinaona. Guided tours: 700 ptas. Open daily 10–3:30; tours every ½ hr.*

THE EIXAMPLE

North of Plaça Catalunya, the Eixample—a Catalan word meaning "extension" or "enlargement"—unfolds in a vast gridlike series of perfectly proportioned blocks intersected by a few broad, imposing avenues including Passeig de Gràcia, the Rambla Catalunya, and Avinguda Diagonal. Seen from the air (every Rambla newsstand has a postcard of the aerial view), the Eixample is amazing in its uniformity, but scratch its graph-paper surface, and you find a 'hood that means many things to many people. To its largely moneyed residents, the Eixample is home; to a vast number of Barcelona professionals, it's the office; to travelers, it's a handy cluster of celebrated Moderniste buildings; and to everyone, it's a fabulous place to shop.

The Eixample was designed by Ildefons Cerda in the 1850s, when the city of Barcelona started to grow by leaps and bounds and could no longer be contained in its medieval walls. People set up house almost as soon as construction began, and the neighborhood reached a saturation point in the 1970s; at one point the Eixample was so crowded it was found to have one of the lowest proportions of open space per inhabitant in urbanized Europe. This problem could have been avoided if some of Cerda's more innovative plans had been followed—one of his visions was to create a park in the center of each block, each park at least as wide as the tallest adjoining building. Some of these parks still exist, and the city government has spearheaded a project, ProEixample, to replant as many as possible.

TEMPLE EXPIATORI DE LA SAGRADA FAMILIA

Architect Antoni Gaudí's unfinished masterpiece of a cathedral is one of Barcelona's most symbolic and memorable sights. Massive, brazen, and somewhat surreal, the Sagrada Familia (Holy Family) is like no other church in the world, and its signature dripping spires, more than 300 ft high, have come to mark the Barcelona skyline. Gaudí's initial plan was to build a cathedral that would represent the entire Bible; he finally settled on just the New Testament. The building has three grand facades: Nativity, on the east side, with Jesus, Mary, and Joseph surrounded by singing angels; Passion, on the west side, detailing the Crucifixion of Jesus in contemporary sculpture; and the hypothetical Glory, on the south side facing the sea, which Gaudí envisioned as an iconographic representation of man and his place in the Creation. The facades are linked by a magnificent cloister that encircles the entire building.

Gaudí's habit of incorporating natural and animal forms into his designs is in marvelous evidence here, especially on the Nativity facade. Sculpted blossoming flowers represent birth and growth, and many of the carved animals—snails, lizards, turtles—represent Catalan fauna. The high windows are adorned with fruits from every season of the year, including oranges, persimmons, and figs; topping the windows are colorful, eye-catching baskets of said fruits, representing the joyful harvest that comes with maturation and the nourishment that humans draw from nature. Gargoyles feature snails and writhing snakes;

GAUDÍ AT A GLANCE

Antoni Gaudí (1852–1926) was born to a coppersmith and died the world-renowned architect of the church of the Sagrada Familia. Along the way he changed the face of Barcelona and rocked the entire architectural world with his inventive, outlandish creations. Throughout his career Gaudí had his fans and his critics: was he a genius or a lunatic? A visionary or an eccentric dabbler? Today folks concern themselves not so much with understanding Gaudí as with sitting back and appreciating him. Barcelona is an open-air Gaudí museum, with displays from his first commissions by the city of Barcelona (the street lamps on Plaça Reial) to the whimsical Parc Güell, named after the architect's wealthy longtime patron.

Organic forms appear in all of Gaudí's works, from the serpentine mosaic bench at Parc Güell to the rounded, almost fleshy protruding balconies on Casa Milà (La Pedrera). Gaudí often said that although he had been formally taught at the University of Barcelona, "My true master is the tree outside my workshop." To the end, he credited his working-class roots with his traditional values and clarity of vision. His death, then, seems to have brought him full circle: he was hit by a tram near the Sagrada Familia and, unrecognized for several days, died alone in a paupers' ward.

spire pinnacles look to be sprouting carrot tops. Inside the church, the nave and aisles were designed to look like a forest, with light filtering in at varying angles just as light shines through the leaves and branches of a forest canopy.

The construction cranes looming amid the Sagrada Familia's spires seem to have become an inextricable part of the structure itself—which, it seems, is exactly what Gaudí intended. At the outset, the young architect knew a cathedral of such magnitude would probably not be finished in his lifetime, yet he felt it was not the end that counted but rather the means: by inviting the Catalan people to help build the church, he aimed to create a true temple for the community. In his words, "The Church of the Holy Family is being built by the people and is a reflection of their way of being"—and to this day construction is funded entirely by private donations and admission fees. Gaudí worked on the Sagrada Familia for more than 40 years, from age 31 to age 74; in 1926 he was killed by a tram while crossing the street right near his beloved cathedral (*see* Box: Gaudí at a Glance).

These days the Sagrada Familia appears to have another dedicated genius at the helm, Catalan architect and sculptor Josep Maria Subirach, who has tirelessly devoted himself to the cathedral (like Gaudí, he has even taken to living in the building's nether regions). In 1987 Subirach began work on the Passion facade, depicting the last days of Jesus with a series of unmistakable angular figures, including, in homage to Gaudí, some space-age Roman knights in the style of the chimneys on Casa Milà. The elevator (200 ptas.) can take you to the top of one of the spires, but it's well worth walking up the spiral stairs if you can, as the views from each landing are phenomenal. *Plaça Sagrada Familia, tel. 93/207–3031. Metro: Sagrada Familia. Admission: 800 ptas. Open Apr.–Aug., daily 9–8, elevator 9:30–7:45; Mar. and Sept.–Oct., daily 9–7, elevator 9:30–6:45; Jan.–Feb. and Nov.–Dec., daily 9–6, elevator 9:30–5:45. Guided tours (500 ptas.) Apr.–Oct. 11:30, 1, 4, and 5:30; Nov.–Mar. 11:30 and 1.*

CASA MILÀ (LA PEDRERA)

With an undulating stone facade fluidly hugging an entire corner of a long Passeig de Gràcia block, Casa Milà, also called La Pedrera (the Stone Quarry), is a Gaudí tour de force. Still, nothing quite prepares you for what's upstairs: accessed by elevator from a graceful Moderniste lobby, the rooftop is another world, populated by an alien race of menacing, earth-tone mosaic chimneys. The **Espai Gaudí** (Gaudí Space), in the attic, has an impressive collection of Gaudí's drawings and architectural models, including an upside-down model of the Sagrada Familia made of hanging beads. Interestingly, La Pedrera is still a residential building, with families who have been living here for decades; and thanks to Barcelona's rent control, they don't even pay for the privilege. One **Pis de la Pedrera** (Pedrera Apartment) is open to the public as a "typical bourgeois Barcelona home" of the Moderniste era, with remarkably well conserved trimmings; the front door is ringed with sculpted flowers. *Passeig de Gràcia 92-C., Provença 261–265, tel. 93/484–5995. Metro: Diagonal. Admission: 600 ptas. for rooftop and museum, 600 ptas. for Pis de la Pedrera, 1,000 ptas. for both. Open daily 10–8.*

MANZANA DE LA DISCÒRDIA

The Manzana de la Discòrdia (Block of Discord; *manzana* means both "city block" and "apple" in Spanish) is so named because of the various forms of Moderniste architecture that somehow flourish on this one block of Passeig de Gràcia. At No. 35 is the elaborate **Casa Lleó Morera**, designed by the daddy of Catalan Modernisme, Domènech i Muntaner (who also designed the Palau de la Música). At No. 41 is the quasi-Gothic, Flemish-influenced **Casa Amatller**, designed by Puig i Cadalfach; this building holds the **Modernisme Center**, where you can buy tickets for the entire Ruta de Modernisme (*see* Box: Fertile Soil). Next door, at No. 43, is Gaudí's photogenic **Casa Batlló**, its multicolor tile facade interspersed with rounded balconies that look eerily like the tops of skulls keeping watch. Alas, you are generally not allowed to tour the interiors, but postcards of all three abound; look for interior pix of the stained-glass wall in Lleó Morera's dining room. *Passeig de Gràcia 35, 41, and 43, between Consell de Cent and Aragó. Metro: Passeig de Gràcia.*

> *As you stand in the endless line to get into the Sagrada Familia, Gaudí's belief that "people from all over the world will come to admire it" seems prophetic indeed.*

FUNDACIÓ TÀPIES

This excellent museum houses works by the experimental painter and sculptor Antoni Tàpies, one of Catalonia's best-known contemporary artists. For a taste of what's inside, look up: topping the building is a spectacular Tàpies sculpture made of wire. The museum also has excellent temporary exhibits and installations of contemporary art. *C. Aragó 255, tel. 93/487–0315. Metro: Passeig de Gràcia. Admission: 700 ptas. Open Tues.–Sun. 10–8.*

FUNDACIÒ FRANCISCO GODIA

A compelling new addition to Barcelona's museum scene, this foundation has an impressive collection of medieval paintings and sculptures, plus Spanish ceramics from the 14th to 19th centuries. *C. Valencia 284, tel. 93/272–3180. Metro: Passeig de Gràcia. Admission: 700 ptas. Open Wed.–Mon. 10–8.*

HOSPITAL DE LA SANTA CREU I DE SANT PAU

Designed by Domenech i Montaner in 1901, this working hospital looks like anything. A sprawling complex covering four city blocks, it's easily the city's most functional Moderniste building. Wrought-iron gates swing open onto well-tended gardens dappled with Moderniste sculptures and peaceful paths, where patients can stroll and relax. Several of the mansions with towering turrets, many decorated with colorful mosaics. You're welcome to wander the grounds; the most scenic approach is the Avinguda del Gaudí, which heads straight north from the Sagrada Familia. *C. Sant Antoni Maria Claret 167, tel. 93/291–9000.*

PARC DE LA CIUTADELLA

The Ciutadella is not your run-of-the-mill urban park: among the requisite park benches and rowboat-spotted lake are a collection of notable museums, the Catalan parliament's assembly hall, the ever-popular Barcelona Zoo, La Cascada, the park's enormous centerpiece of a fountain, and plenty of great places to simply lie on the grass amid chirping birds. The park was built in the late 1860s on the site of an old military fortress (*ciutadella*, or citadel).

THIS PLACE HAS POTENTIAL

While tourists gawk at La Pedrera, locals shop next door, at the design emporium **Vinçon** *(Passeig de Gràcia 96, tel. 215–6050) for creative home accoutrements. With everything from funky tool sets to swank sofas to unorthodox bathroom fixtures, Vinçon achieved national fame in the 1960s for its avant-garde furniture and accessories, but it has managed to keep up with the times and the fickle tastes of Barcelona's savvy customers. The wares are expensive, to be sure, but the inventive window displays alone are worth seeing. The store is open Monday to Saturday 10–2 and 4:30–8:30.*

You can walk here from the Barri Gòtic in 20 minutes; alternatively, three different Metro stops put you near the park entrances (Barceloneta, Ciutadella–Villa Olímpic, and Arc de Triomf). The most impressive way to approach the park is from the Arc de Triomf stop, named after the massive brick Arc de Triomf (built for the 1988 Universal Exposition) that towers near the park's western edge. If you're zoo-bound, get off at Ciutadella–Villa Olímpic.

LA CASCADA
One look at this massive, over-the-top Baroque fountain, replete with cascading waterfalls and sculptures of winged horses leaping into the air, and you can probably guess who had a hand in creating it: The fountain's chief architect was Josep Fontseré, designer of the park itself, and his young assistant was none other than Antoni Gaudí. Walk around the fountain's perimeter to discover all sorts of arched entryways and staircases that you can explore. *Near Passeig dels Àlbers entrance.*

MUSEU D'ART MODERN
Sharing a palatial building with the Catalan parliament, this well-organized museum has a large collection of Catalan art from the 19th and early 20th centuries ("modern" is a relative term here). The impressive section on Moderniste art features works by Santiago Rusinyol and Ramon Casas as well as furniture designed by Gaudí for Casa Batlló, in the Eixample. *Parc de la Ciutadella, tel. 93/319–5728. Metro: Arc de Triomf or Barceloneta. Admission: 500 ptas. Open Tues.–Sat. 10–7, Sun. 10–2:30.*

CASTELLS DES TRES DRAGONS / MUSEU DE ZOOLOGÍA
Dominating the western end of the Ciutadella, this chateau-style behemoth is popularly called the Castell des Tres Dragons (Castle of the Three Dragons). Designed by Domènech i Montaner as the café for the 1988 Universal Exposition, it now holds the **Museu de Zoología**, where exhibits ranging from minerals to medicinal plants to stuffed animals aim to educate and enlighten us humans about the rest of the natural world. *Passeig Picasso s/n (near Passeig Lluí Companys), tel. 93/196912. Metro: Arc de Triomf. Admission: 700 ptas. Open Tues., Wed., and Fri.–Sun. 10–2, Thurs. 10–4:30.*

PARC ZOOLÒGIC (ZOO)
The Ciutadella's most popular attraction is the zoo, home to the much-loved Snowflake ("Copito de Nieve"), the world's only captive albino gorilla. The bird sanctuary and reptile house are also worth investigation. *Parc de la Ciutadella, tel. 93/225–6780. Metro: Ciutadella–Port Olímpic. Admission: 1,550 ptas., children 975 ptas. Open summer, daily 9:30–8; fall–spring, daily 10–5.*

THE PORT
For many foreigners the 1992 Olympics put Barcelona on the map. To prepare for the games and the international scrutiny, city officials resolved to give the Barcelona coastline a makeover. The transformation was remarkable: the slick, new Port Olímpic was constructed, and the beaches, once forgotten,

littered with trash, and populated mainly by transients, were aggressively cleaned up. Tons of new sand were brought in, slick signposts erected, and, this being Barcelona, scads of young architects commissioned to create funky beachside sculptures. The result, of course, is that everyone goes to the beach—in the summer it can take some hunting to find an unoccupied patch of sand. But if the crowds become unbearable, it's a mere 10-minute walk into the cool, dark alleys of the Barri Gòtic.

PORT VELL

Near the Columbus monument, on Moll d'Espanya, are Port Vell and the colossal Maremàgnum mall (from Columbus follow the undulating, floating wooden gangway). The mall contains the usual array of mediocre fast-food joints, from Chicken in the Box to Pita Inn, and chain stores. Glass elevators head up to the mall's two discos, Nayandei and Star Winds (see After Dark, below), both jam-packed on weekends. Near the mall is Barcelona's vast, three-story aquarium, in which you can walk through a 260-ft-long underwater tunnel and amuse yourself or your kids with a slew of interactive exhibits (alas, admission is not kid-size: 1,450 ptas. for adults, 950 for the little ones). Next door is the giant IMAX theater, with flicks in Spanish and Catalan.

BARCELONETA

After the megamall commerciality of Maremàgnum, the working-class waterfront barrio of Barceloneta is a welcome change, one of the few port areas largely untouched by the Olympic frenzy. Once a maritime village on the outskirts of the city, this neighborhood is now classic Barcelona, its narrow streets crammed with old-time shops, apartment buildings, and, on each block, the requisite dark and narrow local bar. Most outsiders come here for the tapas and the seafood paellas dished out by the restaurants on Passeig Joan de Borbó (see Where to Eat, above; and note that on some maps, this street is still called Passeig Nacional). At the top end of Passeig Joan de Borbó,

On Friday and Saturday nights in the summer, La Pedrera's fabulously eerie rooftop is open for drinks and music from 9 to midnight. Admission is 1,500 ptas.; inquire at the front desk.

near the Barceloneta Metro station, is the **Palau de Mar,** an old port warehouse built in 1900 and now housing the large, glossy Museum of the History of Catalonia (Plaça Pau Vila 3, tel. 93/225–4700; admission 500 ptas.; open Tues.–Sat. 10–7, Wed. 10–8, Sun. 10–2:30), where five floors of interactive exhibits take you from Paleolithic times to the present. Be warned that it's popular with Catalan school groups. Near the Palau, along Plaça Pau Vila, is a handful of pricey but top-notch restaurants overlooking the water.

Saunter down Passeig Joan de Borbó toward the water, and you can walk right onto **Platja Sant Sebastiá,** the first major beach on this end of the urban coast. A little farther on is **Platja Barceloneta.** Here you'll see the beginning of a strip of café-bars with tables right on the beach, where you can sip a drink with your feet nestled in the sand. Most of these are open only in summer, at which time they're far cheaper options than their counterparts at the Port Olímpic.

PORT OLÍMPIC

On sunny days Frank Gehry's mammoth **fish sculpture** shimmers like a disco ball. It's all but impossible to miss, as is the Olympic Port stretching out beneath it. One of the landmarks here is the **Hotel Arts,** occupying one of a pair of behemoth skyscrapers (Barcelona's first) that have forever altered the cityscape. On the hotel's ground floor is the **Gran Casino** (Marina 12–21, tel. 93/225–7878), which carries an entrance fee of 750 ptas. and this brochure advisory: "It is not compulsory to wear a tie and suit, but you will certainly feel more comfortable this way, especially in the evenings."

The Gehry sculpture actually towers over **Marina Village,** a minimall of restaurants and shops with a surprisingly pleasant open-air terrace built over the water. The mall's most famous former occupant, Planet Hollywood, rather mysteriously closed in May 2000 due to "financial difficulties." Shucks . . .

Across the street from Marina Village, the Port Olímpic hits full stride with an string of cafés along the boardwalk and the beachfront walkway just below it. This is where you'll find the fantastic restaurant Aqua (see Where to Eat, above). At night the Port Olímpic is the party strip for young locals and out-of-towners, when the beachside bars (see After Dark, below) turn up the music, and the beer flows freely.

MONTJÜIC

Rising magnificently above the city, the 700-ft-high Montjüic contains almost 500 acres of idyllic parkland and holds a slew of top-notch museums, the giant Olympic Stadium, the Poble Espanyol (Spanish

Village), and stupendous views of Barcelona. You could easily spend a day (or two, or three) traipsing around this hill, named for the Jewish cemetery once set on its slopes.

There are several ways to approach steep Montjüic. From the Plaça Espanya Metro stop, you can walk or take Bus 61 or Bus 55, depending on the sights you want to see; if you decide to hoof it, escalators can help relieve your trek—and every time you look over your shoulder, vistas of Barcelona stretch out below you. Alternatively, take the Metro to Paral.lel and catch the **funicular** to Montjüic, or take it to Poble Sec and hike into the middle section of the park, near the Miró Foundation.

Plaça Espanya holds the **Fira de Barcelona** (Avda. Reina Maria Cristina s/n, tel. 93/233–2000), a massive convention hall that gets some interesting trade shows, including an annual autumn book fair.

CASTELL DE MONTJÜIC
Built in 1640, the fortresslike Castle of Montjüic is a somber reminder of Franco's bloody suppression of Catalan autonomy. Throughout the Civil War the castle was used as a prison for Catalan rebels; and here, in 1940, Franco's troops executed the president of the Catalan Generalitat. In 1960 the army turned the building over to the city, and it now houses a **military museum**, with an interesting section on Catalonia's military history. The real reason to make it up here, however, is to gaze out at fantastic **views** of Barcelona, with the castle's lush, well-tended **gardens** blooming all around you. *Carretera de Montjüic 66, tel. 93/329–8613. Metro: Espanya or Paral.lel. Admission: 250 ptas. Open Apr.–Sept., Tues.–Sat. 10–2 and 4–7, Sun. 10–8; Oct.–Mar., Tues.–Sat. 10–2 and 4–7, Sun. 10–2.*

POBLE ESPANYOL
Rounding out western Montjüic is the Poble Espanyol, or Spanish Village. Built in 1929 for the Universal Exposition, this little 'hood contains reproductions of architecture from all over Spain. It's overrated, overpriced, and terribly popular, particularly with Europe-in-a-week tour groups. A stroll through the *poble* takes you past a Zaragozan belfry and a Catalan Romanesque monastery on a Segovian Plaza Mayor, not to mention whitewashed Andalusian houses and crafts workshops. Small restaurants surround the plaza, most serving Catalan cuisine. If you can handle the steep entrance fee and the noisy schoolkids thronging the entrance, the Poble Espanyol is a good place to load up on souvenirs from all over Spain, including bottles of potent sangria (900 ptas.) that are produced and bottled in a store called **Museu del Vi** (Bajada de Cervantes 10, tel. 93/423–9765). There's also a handful of pricey but surprisingly innovative jewelry and metalwork **shops** tucked into some of the alleyways. Oddly, the Poble Espanyol has become a popular **nightspot**; the designer club Torres de Ávila (*see* After Dark, *below*) draws revelers from all over town. *Avda. Marquès de Commillas, tel. 93/325–7866. Metro: Espanya. Admission: 950 ptas. Open July–Aug., Mon.–Thurs. 9–2, Fri.–Sat. 9–4, Sun. 9–midnight; Sept.–June, Mon. 9–8, Tues.–Thurs. 9–2, Fri.–Sat. 9–4, Sun. 9–midnight.*

ESTADI OLÍMPIC / PALAU SANT JORDI
Originally built for the 1929 Universal Exposition, Barcelona's Olympic Stadium was enthusiastically rebuilt for the 1992 Olympics, with seating for 70,000 people. Today it's used primarily for concerts and soccer games. Next door is the **Palau Sant Jordi**, an sleek spaceship of a sports palace/concert hall designed by the Japanese architect Arata Isozaki and named for Catalonia's patron saint (George). A modern-day structural marvel, the Palau is entirely free-standing—no pillars or beams to obstruct the view. *Passeig Olympic, tel. 93/426–2089. Metro: Espanya or Paral.lel. Open weekdays 10–2 and 4–7, weekends 10–6.*

FUNDACIÓ MIRÓ
If you visit only one museum of contemporary art in Barcelona, make it the Miró Foundation. Flooded with light in this high spot, the impressively airy white galleries are ideal settings for the primary-color yet subtle paintings of Joan Miró, one of Catalonia's most celebrated 20th-century artists. The building was designed by Josep Lluís Sert, a friend of Miró's, and the collection (some 250 paintings and 150 sculptures) was donated by the artist himself. Particularly impressive is the gigantic **tapestry**—woven in 1979 in trademark Miró colors and shapes—that dominates an entire wall. One of Miró's better-known works is *Hombre y Mujer delante de un montón de excrementos* (*Man and Woman in Front of a Pile of Excrement*), a relatively small painting from 1935. Like most of Miró's works, it's abstract, so you might not guess what it was without the titillating title; once you read it, all is quite clear. Stridently anti-Franco, Miró lived for years in self-imposed exile in France, so most of the works in this museum have French titles. *Étoile Matinal* (*Morning Star*), from the early 1940s, is a colorful, energetic picture of stars floating amid abstract birds' heads, eyeballs, and arrows. In addition to Miró's works, there's a spectacular mer-

cury fountain by Alexander Calder, and the museum is known for excellent temporary exhibits, including **Espai 13**, a space dedicated to young contemporary artists. *Avda. Miramar 71, tel. 93/329–1908. Metro: Paral.lel. Admission: 800 ptas. Open July–Sept., Tues.–Wed. and Fri.–Sat. 10–8, Thurs. 10–9:30, Sun. 10–2:30; Oct.–June, Tues.–Wed. and Fri.–Sat. 10–7, Thurs. 10–9:30, Sun. 10–2:30.*

MUSEU ARQUEOLÒGIC

Housed in the 1929 **Palace of Graphic Arts**, Barcelona's Museum of Archaeology has a large collection of Greek and Roman artifacts from throughout Catalonia and the Balearic Islands, including an exquisite display of Carthaginian jewelry. One sizable section is devoted to artifacts from the Greek ruins of Empúries, on the Costa Brava—if you're planning a trip to that town, a look through this stuff will greatly enhance your time there. *Passeig Santa Madrona 39, tel. 93/423–2149. Metro: Espanya or Poble Sec. Admission: 400 ptas. Open Tues.–Sat. 9:30–1:30 and 3:30 –7, Sun. 9–2.*

MUSEU ETNOLÒGIC

Near the Museum of Archaeology, the ample Ethnological Museum houses cultural artifacts from Asia, Africa, South America, Australia, and the Middle East, plus solid temporary exhibits. *Passeig Santa Madrona s/n, tel. 93/424–6807. Metro: Espanya or Poble Sec. Admission: 400 ptas. Open Tues. and Thurs. 10–7; Wed. and Fri.–Sat. 10–2.*

MIES VAN DER ROHE PAVILION

To your right as you head up to the Palau Nacional from Plaça Espanya, this elegant, symmetrical structure was designed by German architect and sculptor Mies van der Rohe for the 1929 Universal Exposition. Reconstructed in 1986, the austere Bauhaus building is built of reflective and stone surfaces (glass, green onyx, white marble) and adjoined by a shallow, shimmering pool of water. You can get a good feel for the building simply by walking around it; the interior is much the same. A striking nude **statue** by Georg Kolbe, *Morning*, stands in solitary stillness, set off by the reflecting pool around it and by the building's stark lines. *Avda. Marquès de Comillas s/n, tel. 93/423–4016. Metro: Espanya or Poble Sec. Admission: 400 ptas. Open daily 10–8.*

PALAU NACIONAL / MUSEU NACIONAL D'ART DE CATALUNYA

Built in 1929 for the Universal Exposition (like so much on Montjüic), the imposing National Palace towers grandly over the broad Avinguda de la Reina Maria Cristina, leading up from Plaça Espanya. At the base of the Palau is **Plaça de les Cascades**, with a **Font Magica** (Magic Fountain) designed by Carles Buigas. On Thursday, Friday, and Saturday nights in the summer, the fountains are illuminated in various colors from 8 to midnight for a splashy sound-and-light show.

Inside the National Palace is the massive Catalan National Museum of Art, which has spent the last decade amassing art from throughout Catalonia, with the goal of displaying pieces from every period in Catalonia's history. The results so far are truly formidable, with major sections on Romanesque and Gothic art. The stunning **Romanesque collection** is the museum's crown jewel, indeed one of the most comprehensive and important such troves in the world. Most of the pieces were culled from village churches in the Pyrenees, an area renowned for its rich Romanesque heritage—if you have any notion of driving into the Pyrenees after Barcelona, do check out this museum before you go. In room after room, stunning medieval frescoes are displayed exactly as they once appeared in their tiny mountain homes, accompanied by in-depth explanations (including English translations) and maps of the church layouts. The centerpiece is a trove of Catalan Romanesque art at its most emblematic: in the 12th century, an anonymous artist known as the Master of Taüll painted his way through a handful of small Pyrenean churches, transforming their dusty interiors with a series of vibrant murals. His works depicted Jesus and his disciples in hauntingly simple fashion—their figures outlined in bold black lines, topped by primitive, elongated visages. The central apse of the church from Sant Climent de Taüll rises (literally and figuratively) above the collection, showcasing Christ in Majesty (with two fingers raised) flanked by angels, bearded apostles, and soaring beasts with bold eyes on their fluttering wings. Jesus, richly colored and outlined in black, sits suspended in a deep blue sky.

The Gothic section consists largely of Catalan works, supplemented by examples from other parts of Europe; of particular importance are the paintings by Catalan artist Bernat Martorell. Fine temporary exhibits round out the experience. *Mirador del Palau 6, tel. 93/423–7199. Metro: Espanya. Admission: 900 ptas., 500 ptas. for temporary exhibits only. Open Tues.–Sat. 10–7, Sun. 10–2:30.*

GO, BARÇA!

Whoever said it's not whether you win or lose—it's how you play the game—had never been to a match between FC Barcelona ("Barça") and Real Madrid. Sparks fly when the age-old rivalry between these two cities hits the playing field. Supporting Barça is not about being a soccer fan; it's about being Catalan and the Barça slogan, solemnly intoned by every fan is, "Més que un club" ("More than a club"). Barça plays between September and June at Camp Nou, a massive stadium that seats 130,000. The Camp Nou **Museu FC Barcelona** *(Arístides Maillol 7/9, tel. 93/496–3600; Metro: Collblanc) is one of the most popular in Barcelona, with a huge array of trophies, photographs, and audio-visual displays of the 100-year-old club. Admission is 500 ptas.; it's open Monday–Saturday 10–6:30, Sunday 10–2.*

UPPER BARCELONA

GRÀCIA

The proud, self-styled neighborhood of Gràcia, just north of the Eixample, was once a village of its own and sometimes behaves as though it still were. After being annexed to Barcelona in the late 19th century, Gràcia evolved into a community known for progressive politics, a reputation that drew artists, bohemians, and other leftists, particularly in the '60s and '70s. The neighborhood has mellowed considerably since then and lost much of its political edge, but Gràcia still seems to march to the beat of a different drum. Though it borders the Eixample, this neighborhood couldn't look more different: it has retained its village atmosphere, with narrow streets spilling onto little plaças. One of Gaudí's earlier works, the elaborately tiled **Casa Vicens**, is at Carrer Carolines 24, off Avenida Príncep d'Astúries.

The best time to come to Gràcia, particularly on weekends, is at night, when the whole neighborhood livens up, and people stream in from all over Barcelona to the bars around **Plaça del Sol** and **Plaça de la Virreina**.

PARC GÜELL

Gaudí's organic, nature-based architecture seems to flourish more freely here in the outdoors than in any of his indoor works. The architect's longtime patron, Eusebi Güell, commissioned this park as a residential garden with 60 houses, but most of the wealthy families slated to move in found the architecture too flamboyant and strange, and in the end only two house plots were sold. In the 1920s the land was turned over to the city and eventually opened to the public. With magnificent views of Barcelona opening around every bend, Parc Güell makes a splendid place to chill out after sightseeing overload, and anyway Gaudí's theatrical designs are best appreciated at a leisurely pace. Stroll through some of the stone archways, held up by angled pillars that seem to mushroom from the earth (Gaudí's secret lay in using stronger materials, such as brick, on the inside of each). As you walk through the pillared colonnade, inspect the majestic ceiling, made up of a series of circular mosaic designs. Each mosaic is distinct—some hold wine bottles, stuck in at playful angles, while others sport fragments of a teapot and teacups. These eye-catching ceilings and portions of the mosaic bench were actually the work of Gaudí's chief pupil and collaborator, José María Jujol. On the park's upper level, bask in the sun on the long, curved, multicolor mosaic bench, source of many an abstract postcard. *C. d'Olot 3. Metro: Lesseps, then walk 10 mins up the steep hill or catch Bus 24 to park entrance. Open May–Aug., daily 10–9; Apr. and Sept., daily 10–8; Mar. and Oct., daily 10–7; Nov.–Feb., daily 10–6.*

Within Parc Güell is the pink **Casa-Museu Güell,** designed by architect Francesc Berenguer, where Gaudí lived between 1906 and 1926. Most of the interior has been untouched since Gaudí called it home, including the architect's surprisingly simple bedroom, which contains just a bed and a few personal religious artifacts. The rest of the house is exactly how you would imagine it to be: ornate Moderniste rooms filled with outlandish oversize chairs, tables, and cupboards. *Parc Güell; from main entrance head uphill and to the right, tel. 93/284–6446. Admission: 400 ptas. Open May–Sept., daily 10–8; Mar.–Apr. and Oct., daily 10–7; Nov.–Feb., daily 10–6.*

SARRIÀ / PEDRALBES

Rounding out Barcelona's upper residential sectors, Sarrià and Pedralbes are lovely, peaceful neighborhoods with well-groomed houses and residents. The beautiful Pedralbes Monastery houses a superb Thyssen-Bornemisza collection of mainly Renaissance art. Most locals come to this part of town for one reason only: to cheer on Barça, their beloved football team, at the Camp Nou stadium (*see* Box: Go, Barça!).

MONESTIR DE PEDRALBES / COLLECCIÓ THYSSEN-BORNEMISZA • An oasis of tranquillity in quiet Pedralbes, this ancient monastery removes you completely—spiritually, at least—from the city's crowds and bluster. Founded for an order of Clarist nuns in 1326, the convent is still functioning, though now the nuns occupy a newer building next door. Highlights include a magnificent three-story **cloister** and a lovely chapel; you can also wander through the old living quarters, kitchen, and infirmary. All this alone would be worth a visit, but the amazing Thyssen-Bornemisza collection tops it off with mostly religious paintings by such headliners as Tiepolo, Tintoretto, Velázquez, and Rubens, displayed in a high-ceiling gallery with original 14th-century windows. *Baixada del Monestir 9, tel. 93/280–1434. Metro: María Cristina, FGC: Reina Elisenda. Admission: monastery 400 ptas., Thyssen-Bornemisza collection 400 ptas., both 700 ptas. Open Tues.–Sun. 10–2.*

MUSEU DE CERÀMICA • Set in the **Palau Reial de Pedralbes** (Royal Palace of Pedralbes), the Ceramics Museum has a beautiful array of Spanish ceramics from the 11th century to the present, including some pieces by Miró and Picasso. *Avda. Diagonal 686, tel. 93/280–1621. Metro: Palau Reial. Admission: 400 ptas. Open Tues.–Sat. 10–6, Sun. 10–3.*

TIBIDABO

The main draw on Mount Tibidabo, looming over northwest Barcelona, is its **Parc d'Attraccions** (Amusement Park; tel. 93/211–7942), a 100-year-old mixture of old-fashioned games and the latest/fastest/highest rides around. The park is open daily in July and August (Mon.–Thurs. noon–10, Fri.–Sat. noon–1 AM), weekends noon–8 the rest of the year. If fun fairs aren't your thing, come to Tibidabo for the spectacular views—on a clear day you can see as far as the Pyrenees. A choice vantage point is the popular bar Mirablau (*see* After Dark, *below*).

The gigantic communications tower **Torre de Collserola** (Collserola Tower) was designed by the British architect Norman Foster for the 1992 Olympics. Head up to the top in a glass elevator for more great views (500 ptas.); it's open Wednesday–Friday 11–2:30 and 3:30–7, weekends 11–7.

To get to Tibidabo, take the Ferrocarril (FCG) to Avinguda de Tibidabo, then hop on the tram (*tramvia blau*) to Plaça del Dr. Andreu, where you catch the Tibidabo funicular to the top. The tram runs daily in summer but only on weekends the rest of the year; a bus takes over on weekdays. Of course, you can also walk the tram route if you're feeling spry enough, a steep but pleasant 20-minute undertaking.

SHOPPING

Cosmo Barcelona is a fabulous place to shop. The city's legendary flair for design is particularly evident in jewelry, clothing, shoe, and interior-design stores. The Barri Gòtic hides numerous little jewelry and design shops selling innovative silver work and housewares; the Eixample is peppered with sleek, more expensive design stores that you can treat as museums if you're not ready to spring for a reproduction Dalí chair. Barcelona's eye for style comes through in its taste for clothes and shoes. Scattered around town are boutiques showcasing creative clothing by young local designers; Catalan designer Antonio Miró has his flagship store on Rambla Catalunya. Spain being known for its well-crafted shoes at reasonable prices, Barcelona is packed with footwear, particularly on Rambla Catalunya and Carrer Pelai.

A BOOK BY ANY OTHER NAME

On April 23 Catalans takes to the streets for El Día de Sant Jordi (St. George's Day) in honor of their patron saint. Traditionally, men give women roses and women give men books, so in Barcelona, the Rambla, Plaça Catalunya, and Passeig de Gràcia are transformed into open-air bookstores and flower marts, and happy couples mill about clutching their gifts. Roses honor St. George, while books pay tribute to Cervantes and, interestingly, Shakespeare, both of whom died on April 23, 1616.

DEPARTMENT STORES AND SHOPPING MALLS

For one-stop shopping, head to Spain's omnipresent El Corte Inglés, where clothing, electronics, home accessories, and food are sold under one roof at fairly competitive prices. If you're looking for cheap threads, including basic T-shirts, head to the top floor and hit the bargain bins. The well-stocked **supermarket** in the basement of the Plaça Catalunya store is popular with locals and travelers alike and includes an excellent selection of well-priced wine. At the very top of the same store is a cafeteria-style restaurant with mediocre food but primo views over the Plaça Catalunya. *Four locations: Plaça Catalunya 14, tel. 93/306–3800, Metro: Catalunya; Avda. Diagonal 617, tel. 93/419–2828, Metro: Maria Cristina; Plaça Francesc Macià, Avda. Diagonal 471, tel. 93/419–2020, Metro: Diagonal or Hospital Clinic; Portal L'Angel 19–21, tel. 93/306–3800, Metro: Catalunya or Urquinaona.*

Also on Plaça Catalunya, the British stalwart chain **Marks & Spencer** (Plaça Catalunya 32, tel. 93/363–8090) tries to give El Corte Inglés a run for its money with several floors of clothing, shoes, and household items. The downstairs supermarket is small, but it features fancy imports such as packaged Indian naan bread, heat-and-eat lime-and-cilantro chicken strips, and tubs of hummus.

Nearby, the slew of shops in **El Triangle mall** (C. Pelayo 39, at Plaça Catalunya, tel. 93/318–0108) includes the giant media-oriented French chain store FNAC, with books, CDs, computers, and software, and the massive, also French cosmetics and perfume store Sephora.

In the Eixample, **La Bulevard Rosa** (Passeig de Gràcia 53, tel. 93/215–8331; Metro: Passeig de Gràcia), one of the city's first shopping malls, has more than 100 clothing and shoe stores. Next door, **Bulevard dels Antiquaris** (Passeig de Gràcia 55, tel. 93/215–4499) is an antiques mall with more than 70 shops selling everything between porcelain dolls and Moderniste furniture. The latest addition to Barcelona's mall scene is the massive, high-end **L'illa Diagonal** (Avda. Diagonal 557, tel. 93/444–0000; Metro: Maria Cristina or Les Corts), with three floors of sleek clothing and jewelry stores plus branches of FNAC and Marks & Spencer. The enormous **Centre Barcelona Glòries** (Avda. Diagonal 208, tel. 93/486–0404; Metro: Glòries), with a mélange of jewelry, clothing, and gifts, is built around a central square and has a smattering of bars and cafés.

FLEA MARKETS

Barcelona has some fabulous flea markets, where time and patience can yield real finds. **Les Encants** (Plaça de les Glòries, tel. 93/246–3030; Metro: Glòries; open Mon., Wed., and Fri.–Sat. 10–8) is the granddaddy of them all, with antique cigarette cases, secondhand clothes, plastic toys, you name it. Go in the morning for the best selection, and do not be shy about haggling.

The longtime **Mercat de Sant Antoni** (Metro: Sant Antoni), open Sunday 9–1, is *the* place to go for old books, coins, postcards, and photographs. It can be uncomfortably crowded, so give yourself ample time to browse.

On Sunday morning the **Plaça Reial** hosts a long-running coin and stamp market, where you might see anything from a shabby stockpile hauled down from someone's attic to superb antique specimens.

SPECIALTY SHOPS

ANTIQUES

In the Barri Gòtic, near the Plaça del Pi and Plaça Sant Josep Oriol, **Carrer Banys Nous** has a string of excellent antiques shops, including **Germanes García** (C. Banys Nous 15, tel. 93/318–6646), founded in the early 1900s, with a spectacular selection of old-fashioned wicker furniture. Nearby, the shops on tiny **Carrer de la Palla** specialize in rare books and maps.

BOOKS

Bookstores abound here, particularly near the university (Metro: Universitat). **Altair** (C. Balmes 69–71, tel. 93/454–2966) is the largest travel bookstore, with plenty of guidebooks and coffee-table volumes in English. Check out or post a message on the bulletin board if you want to hook up with other travelers. **Laie Llibreria Cafè** (C. Pau Claris, tel. 93/318–1739; Metro: Urquinaona) stocks a great selection of art and architecture books, plus a wide range of fiction. The pleasant **Llibreria Pròleg** (C. Dagueria 13, tel. 93/319–2425) specializes in books by and for women.

A handful of stores are devoted to English-language material (*see* Basics, *above*), but some of the larger general bookshops have decent English *sections*, including **Crisol** (C. Consell de Cent 341, tel. 93/215–3121; Rambla Catalunya 81, tel. 93/215–2720), **Happy Books** (C. Pelai 20, tel. 93/317–0768; Passeig de Gràcia 77, 93/487–9571), and **The Bookstore** (C. La Granja 13, tel. 93/237–9519).

CLOTHING

The Eixample is filled with high-end boutiques, particularly on **Passeig de Gràcia, Avinguda Diagonal,** and **Rambla Catalunya.** South of Plaça Catalunya, heading east off the Rambla, **Carrer Portaferrissa,** packs trendy fashion shops and shoe stores. *See also* Shoes, *below*.

One forgets where Spain's young women shopped before **Zara** splashed onto the scene a few years ago (Avda. Diagonal 280, tel. 93/486–0134; Carrer Pelai 58, tel. 93/301–0978). Mixing elegant linen suits and fringed suede jackets with funky minis to basic black T-shirts, this Galician chain has made a name for itself with stylish threads at decent prices. **Mango** (Passeig de Gràcia 65, tel. 93/215–7530; Avda. Pau Casals 12, tel. 93/200–3709; Carrer Pelai 48, tel. 93/317–6985; Carrer Portaferrissa 16, tel. 93/301–8483) is where sassy young females pick up beaded halter tops and denim hip-huggers. **System Action** (Avda. Portal de l'Angel 1, tel. 93/302–2090; Passeig de Gràcia 44, tel. 93/488–0754; Rambla Catalunya 108, tel. 93/215–0956; Carrer Portaferrissa 12, tel. 93/301–2526) has all the latest styles, toned down a notch to be classy, comfortable, durable, and relatively affordable. Catalan couturier **Antonio Miró** (C. Consell de Cent 349, tel. 93/487–0670), who began his career as a tailor, has clients worldwide and a growing clientele here in Spain. He first made his mark in menswear—Miró suits are comfortable, sporty, and made of natural fibers—and has since expanded into accessories, particularly stylish watches, and women's clothes. Miró's original showcase, **Groc** (Rambla Catalunya 100, tel. 93/215–0180), is a high-end boutique for both men and women. **Miró Jeans** (C. Provença 249, tel. 93/272–0166) features the designer's newest line, sporty streetwear geared toward a younger set.

For snazzy bags and belts at unbeatable prices, make for **Misako** (Rambla Catalunya 110, tel. 93/487–7246; Carrer Calvet 38, tel. 93/201–3385; Plaça Joaquim Folguera 7, tel. 93/253–0372), whose name is a riff on *mi saco* ("my bag"). Made from leather, latex, and everything in between, the bags are about 2,500 ptas., belts about 500 ptas.

FC Barcelona fans can deck themselves out accordingly at **La Botiga del Barça** (Aristides Maillol s/n, tel. 93/330–9411; Maremagnum Mall, tel. 93/225–8045), a soccer shop with shelves upon shelves of FC-emblazoned T-shirts, caps, lighters, key rings, and so on.

FOOD AND WINE

A true Spanish specialty is *turrón* (*torròn,* in Catalan), a nougat candy usually eaten around Christmastime. Turrón comes in two main varieties: a soft, slightly oily bar made of ground almonds, and a hard bar with whole almonds. **Casa Colomina** (C. Portaferrissa 8, tel. 93/412–2511; C. Cucurulla 2, tel. 93/317–4681), one of the oldest sweet shops in Barcelona (established 1908), makes some of the best turrón in town, charging 1,300–1,700 ptas. for the biggest bars. Another Christmas tradition is sipping cava (Catalan sparkling wine) with turròn—for the bubbly, try **Xampany** (València 200, tel. 93/453–9338), the only store in Barcelona dedicated solely to cava, with more than 100 varieties.

GIFTS / DESIGN ITEMS

For ceramics and other crafts from all over Spain, stop by **Art Escudellers** (C. Escudellers 5, tel. 93/412–6801). The wine cellar has an excellent selection of fruits of the vine. **D Barcelona** (C. Diagonal 367, tel. 93/216–0346) has innovative Moderniste-style gifts such as refrigerator magnets featuring Park Güell dragons, and flowerpot holders shaped like the balconies on Casa Milà. Most of the trinkets at **Raima** (C. Comtal 27, tel. 93/317–4966)—letter openers, key rings—also have a Moderniste theme. The very hip **Aspectos** (C. Rec 28, tel. 93/319–5285) has an eye-catching mix of wares, from funky lamps to brash bedspreads, by established and up-and-coming artists from all over world. **Ici et Là** (Pl. Santa Maria 2, tel. 93/268–1167) sells eclectic contemporary furniture and home accessories. The experimental team at **Zeta** (C. Avinyó 22, near C. Ferran, tel. 93/412–5186) concocts such unique items as lamps fashioned out of watering cans or colanders. The designers at **Urbana** (C. Seneca 13, tel. 93/237–3644) specialize in what they call "industrial makeovers"—they hunt through old, defunct stores and factories, gather furniture and appliances, and restore and adapt them for new spaces. A hospital operating table becomes a dining-room table; a wooden door becomes the base of a child's bed. You need to be loaded to shop at the exclusive furniture and design store **Bd Ediciones de Diseño** (C. Mallorca 291, tel. 93/458–6909), but the browsing is free. Founded in 1972 by five architects, the store occupied a Moderniste building by Domènech i Montaner. Reproductions of furniture and accessories by Gaudí and Dalí are joined by home furnishings from Spain's hottest designers. **Popul-art** (C. Montcada 22, tel. 93/310–7849) and **Dos Bis** (C. Bisbe 2 bis, near Plaça Sant Jaume, tel. 93/315–0954) specialize in papier-mâché items, most handcrafted by Barcelona artisans. They also sell ceramics from all over Spain.

You can't miss Barcelona's *100 ptas. i mes* ("100 ptas. and more") stores, Spain's version of the Dollar Store, selling anything from bags of marbles to duct tape to oversized makeup brushes to Sagrada Familia ashtrays. **Muy Mucho** (Rambla Catalunya 35, tel. 93/488–3666) is a cut above the others, with candles from 100 ptas. and mini espresso makers—a steal at 800 ptas.

The city's **museum stores** are great places for classy souvenirs, particularly at the smaller museums. The Picasso Museum, Textile Museum, and City History Museum, all in the Gothic quarter, have excellent shops, as do the Museum of the History of Catalonia, in the Palau de Mar near Barceloneta, and the Miró Foundation on Montjüic. Another Barri Gòtic landmark is **Cereira Subirà** (Baixada Llibreteria 7, tel. 93/315–2606), the oldest shop in Barcelona: founded in 1761, it specializes in candles of every shape, size, and color.

Montfalcón (Rambla 111, tel. 93/302–5645) is packed to the rafters with antique and contemporary fans (*abánicos* in Spanish, *ventalls* in Catalan), many of them painted by hand.

SHOES

Spain leads the world in retail selection of shoes, most made of high-quality Spanish leather and sold at reasonable prices. As the nation's fashion capital, Barcelona has reams of phenomenal shoe stores; **Carrer Pelai,** cutting west off the Rambla near Plaça Catalunya, has a string of trendy stores. On the other side of Plaça Catalunya, heading down toward the Barri Gòtic, **Avinguda Portal de l'Angel** is chockablock with shoe, clothing, and jewelry stores. For higher-end footwear, head to Rambla Catalunya, where the long-established **Joan Sagrera** (Rambla Catalunya 102–104, tel. 93/215–4386) sells a wide-ranging collection of men's and women's shoes. One of Spain's most popular brands is **Camper** (C. València 249, tel. 215–6390; Rambla Catalunya 122, tel. 93/217–2384), which burst onto the scene in the early '80s with comfortable yet fashionable footwear.

Traditionally farmers' shoes, Spanish *espardenyas* (espadrilles) are comfortable, cheap, and available in every color of the rainbow. If you fancy a pair, stop into **La Manual Alpargatera** (C. Avinyó, tel. 93/301–0172), a combination workshop-shoestore in the heart of the Barri Gòtic. *Manual* means "made by hand," and *alpargata* is the Spanish word for espardenya—the store has been in business since 1841, but during the Franco regime, when Catalan was strictly forbidden, it had to translate its name (which means "espadrille craftsman") into Castilian.

VINTAGE AND RESALE CLOTHING

Les Encants flea market (*see* Flea Markets, *above*) is a good place to browse for secondhand clothes, though you may have to pick through a lot of dusty throwaways to find anything of worth. **Otra Vez** (C. Avinyò, tel. 93/472–0743), whose name means "Another Time," is a great little store with quality vintage clothes and accessories. **Carrer Rauric**, just off Carrer Ferran, is a tiny, atmospheric street with several small vintage-clothing stores, most open only in the afternoon.

AFTER DARK

The Spanish propensity for *la vida nocturna* (nightlife) is legendary, and Barcelona has a correspondingly staggering number of bars and clubs where you can sample it for yourself. Between the dark dives of the Barri Gòtic and the open-air beach bars of the Port Olímpic, the Barcelona night scene is hard to top. In the Barri Gòtic, Carrer Ferran and the Plaça Reial get lively at night. The Born area has become the trendiest place for a cocktail. Bar-hopping in Gràcia, particularly around Plaça del Sol and Plaça de la Virreina, has long been de rigueur. For an all-out party scene, head to the waterfront bars in the **Port Olímpic,** jam-packed on summer weekends.

Nightclubs usually open around 10:30 PM or 11 PM and stay open till 4 AM or 5 AM. If you're in Barcelona mainly for the nightlife, focus on Thursday, Friday, and Saturday nights. Many clubs close early on Sunday and Monday.

The weekly *Guia de Ocio*, sold at newsstands throughout the city (125 ptas.), lists all of the city's bars and clubs and all theater, film, and music events. Look also for *b-guided*, a free, very hip quarterly with sections like "b-seen" (the latest on the nightclub scene) and "b-served" (ditto on restaurants). *B-guided* is hard to track down, but if you keep your eyes peeled, you might come across it in a bar or restaurant.

The uniform worn by Catalonia's police force, the Mossos de Squadro, on official occasions includes a bowler-type hat, representing los ricos (the rich), and espardenyas, representing los pobres (the poor).

BARS

Bar del Pi. Thanks to its prime locale on the lovely Plaça Sant Josep Oriol, this is a small bar with a big following: it's packed most every night of the week with a friendly crowd of locals and travelers. Tables inside, crammed onto two itty-bitty floors, are as popular as those out on the square. The bar's business card says, among other things, "You should watch over your handbag." *Plaça Sant Josep Oriol 1, tel. 93/302–2123. Metro: Liceu.*

Bar L'Ascensor. This longtime favorite has an old-fashioned, dark-wood elevator (*ascensor*) for a front door. The crowd is a pleasant mix of lively young Barcelona dwellers, older, laid-back locals, and travelers. Among the mixed drinks are some inventive rum-based house specialties. *C. Bellafila 3 (near C. de la Ciutat), no phone. Metro: Liceu*

Boadas Cocktail Bar. Just off the Rambla, this tiny, triangular cocktail bar has been around since the early 1930s. It still pours the meanest martini in town; indeed, Maria Dolores Boadas, daughter of the bar's founder, tends bar most nights. *C. Tallers 1, tel. 93/318–9592. Metro: Catalunya.*

Cafe Royale. Tucked into an grimy, unlikely corner of Plaça Reial, Cafe Royale is a sleek, '70s-groovy spot with low leatherette couches and lots of orange. A mix of funksters, gay guys, and cha-cha chicks show up nightly to dig the eclectic tunes (Duke Ellington, Barry White, Nuyorican) spun by DJs. *Nou de Zurbano 3, tel. 93/317–6124. Metro: Liceu.*

Casa Quimet. Founded in 1939, Casa Quimet (a.k.a. the Guitar Bar) is a relaxed place where the guitars—lining the walls and ceiling—far outnumber the people. You're more than welcome to take one down and start strumming, but prepare to lead an unexpected sing-along if you do. *Rambla de Prat 9, tel. 93/217–5327. Metro: Fontana.*

Els Quatre Gats. In 1900, when he was just 18, Picasso had his first real exhibit in this 1897 Barri Gòtic establishment. For a time it was Barcelona's premier bohemian bar. The name (the Four Cats) comes from the founding quartet of bons vivants, including Moderniste artists Santiago Rusinyol and Ramon Casas. It's now a restaurant proper (with entrées starting at 1,300 ptas.) but is still a great spot for a drink, particularly on weekend evenings. *C. Montsió, tel. 93/302–4140. Metro: Jaume I.*

Bar Pastis. A shrine to Edith Piaf and *pastis* (the liquor), this tiny, dimly lighted bar positively drips with decadence and eccentricity. Founded in 1947, it lives up to its long reputation as a place where anything can happen, either within its doors or just outside them on Carrer Santa Monica—once the stomping ground of Barrio Chino prostitutes and still lined with purveyors of debauchery. *C. Santa Monica 4, tel. 93/318–7980. Metro: Drassanes.*

Barcelona has two raucous venues where you can dine while saucy drag queens strut their stuff, impersonating history's great divas. Done up in sumptuous '80s kitsch, **Miranda** *(C. Casanova, tel. 93/453–5249; Metro: Universitat) has a leopard-print motif, a sultry candlelight atmosphere, and big bouquets of flowers along the bar. The Mediterranean cuisine takes such forms as* ternera con garbanzos *(veal with garbanzo beans) or* calamares y esparragos *(squid and asparagus); dinner and a show total 3,500 ptas.* **La Diva** *(C. Diputació, tel. 93/454–6398; Metro: Universitat), designed as an opera hall, is more elegant, with dim lighting and round tables draped in velvet. The menu is billed as "Mediterranean fusion," with dishes like* terciopelo de tomate con almejas al vapor *(velvet tomato sauce with steamed clams) and* bacalao gratinado con brie *(cod with melted Brie). Dinner and a show total 4,500 ptas.*

Gimlet. This ultrapopular '50s-style joint was one of the first cocktail bars in the Born. Gimlet still has a spot on Rec Street there, but the bigger, more popular branch is on Carrer Santaló (known for its hopping nightlife), in the Sant Gervasi neighborhood north of Diagonal. *C. Rec 24, tel. 93/310–1027, Metro: Jaume I; Santaló 46, tel. 93/210–5306, FGC: Muntaner or Sant Gervasi.*

La Cafetera. Next door to Virreina (*see below*), this relaxed Gràcia site with comfortable wicker chairs makes a similarly prime spot to sip a drink amid the hum of the paseo on handsome Plaça Virreina. *Plaça de la Virreina 2, tel. 93/218–8564. Metro: Joanic.*

La Vinya del Senyor. Ambitiously named "the Lord's Vineyard," this snug, classy wine bar exudes a warm, golden glow onto its corner of the medieval Plaça de Santa Maria. Wine lovers crawl from all over town to sample the cosmopolitan wine list and connect with others while doing it. *Plaça Santa Maria 5, tel. 93/310–3379. Metro: Jaume I.*

London Bar. Since 1910 this dark, cluttered bar has been privy to the barstool commentary of every leftist to pass through Barcelona, including student radicals, anti-Francoists, grown-up intellectuals, and the likes of Gaudí, Miró, Picasso, and Hemingway. The friendly crowd now consists mainly of students and artist types. *C. Nou de la Rambla 34, tel. 93/318–5261. Metro: Liceu.*

Mirablau. Fronted by huge windows, the popular Mirablau commands phenomenal views of all of Barcelona from its prime perch at the top of Avenida Tibidabo. Downstairs, the dance floor throbs to '70s and '80s tunes until 5 AM. *Plaça Dr. Andreu s/n, tel. 93/418–5879. FCG: Avda. de Tibidabo.*

Padam. You can count on one thing: the eccentric bar madam and resident DJ will play Edith Piaf's "Padam" at least once before you leave. Cozy and dimly lighted, Padam is a beguiling little place to duck into for the night and a favorite with neighborhood locals, Piaf junkies, and the gay crowd. *C. Rauric 9, off C. Ferran, tel. 93/302–5062. Metro: Liceu.*

Schilling. Barcelona thirtysomethings out for a good chat mix with hip, young travelers in this new yet crucial addition to the Gothic quarter's bar scene. By Barcelona standards it's a big place, with high ceilings and some great stylistic touches: walls literally covered with wine bottles, and big windows onto Carrer Ferran. It's like watching *Barri Gòtic: The Movie. C. Ferran, tel. 93/317–6787. Metro: Liceu.*

Virreina. *Overlooking Gràcia's lovely Plaça Virreina, this casual bar with outdoor tables draws a lively crowd on weekends.* Plaça Virreina 1, tel. 93/237–9880. Metro: Joanic.

CLUBS

Abaixadors Deu. This hip, clubby lounge space sits above a beautiful, old interior courtyard in the middle of the Born. The changing roster of events includes DJ dance-music nights, poetry readings, and even classical music concerts, and food is served until 2 AM. There's no sign, but at Abaixadors 10 (the club's name), you'll see a small door to the right of a restaurant—go through here into the courtyard and look up. *Abaixadors 10, tel. 93/268–1019. Metro: Jaume I.*

Al Limón Negro. A combination restaurant-nightspot near Plaça Reial, the funky Black Lemon is Barcelona's best showcase for ethnic and world-music concerts, augmented by art exhibits and performance art. Meals feature excellent "world cuisine" at good prices. *C. Escudullers Blancs 9, tel. 93/318–9770. Metro: Liceu. Closed Sun.*

Arena VIP's. This long-established gay club is a great place to end up after you've scoured Barcelona's bars. The music is always good for dancing, the crowd is a friendly mix of gays and straights, and the cover is usually under 1,000 ptas., not the case everywhere else. *Gran Via de les Corts Catalanes 593, tel. 93/487–8342. Metro: Universitat.*

Baja Beach Club. When night falls, throngs of young partyers flock to the *bar-musical* scene on the Port Olímpic's Passeig Marítim, and the big-and-loud Baja Beach Club makes everyone's short list of the best places thereat. *Passeig Marítim 3, tel. 93/225–9100. Metro: Ciutadella–Vila Olímpica.*

Llantiol. Sip a drink and check out what's happening onstage at this tiny, eccentric theater-bar. Programs range from stand-up comedy to magic tricks to puppetry. *C. Riereta 7, no phone. Metro: Sant Antoni.*

Medusa. Newish on the scene, Medusa has become one of Barcelona's hottest gay clubs. Weekend crowds dance and flirt to DJ house tunes. *C. Casanova, tel. 93/454–5363. Metro: Urgell.*

Nayandei Boîte and Nayandei Disco. On the rooftop terrace of the vast, port-side Maremàgnum mall, the two Nayandei (as in "Night and Day") discos draw large crowds, particularly in summer. Nayandei Boîte plays a mélange of '60s, '70s, and '80s music, while the Nayandei Disco spins house and disco. There's usually no cover, but drinks are pricey; beers are about 800 ptas., and mixed drinks start at 1,000. *Terrassa Maremàgnum, tel. for both 93/225–8010. Metro: Drassanes or Barceloneta.*

Octopussy. A changing roster of DJs, each hipper than the next, circulates house and techno tunes all night long in this trendy nightspot, the busiest on the Port Vell waterfront. *Moll de la Fusta 4, tel. 93/221–4031. Metro: Drassanes.*

Otto Zutz. An ultramodern three-story nightclub with an impressive eight bars, Otto Zutz was once the coolest club in Barcelona. It's not quite the name it used to be, but it's still popular, particularly with Barcelona's well-groomed well-heeled crowd (think model types with their rich boyfriends). *C. Lincoln 15, tel. 93/238–0722. FGC: Gràcia.*

Satanassa. The reigning king (er, queen) of Barcelona's underground scene, this large gay club has erotic wall art, otherworldly sculptures, and a free-for-all atmosphere—all of which makes for a night you probably won't forget. *C. Aribau 27, tel. 93/451–3944. FGC: Provença.*

Sidecar. It used to be one of the hipper clubs on Plaça Reial, but that's all changed; some nights, Sidecar is one big teen dance factory. Still, the drinks are fairly cheap, the music (mostly pop, some hip-hop) is fun to dance to, and Plaça Reial is convenient if you're staying in the Barri Gòtic. The name is pronounced the Spanish way ("see-deh-car"), and yes, there actually is a sidecar enshrined inside. *C. Heures 4–6, off Plaça Reial, tel. 93/302–1586. Metro: Liceu.*

Star Winds. Sharing the Maremàgnum terrace with the Nayandei nightclubs (*see above*), this large disco also packs 'em in, with thumping house music and greatest hits from decades past. *Terrassa Maremàgnum, tel. 93/225–8221. Metro: Drassanes or Barceloneta.*

Torres de Ávila. True, the Poble Espanyol seems an unlikely place for a nightclub, but the Torres de Ávila is a magical spectacle, created by Barcelona artists Javier Mariscal and Alfred Arribas: it's housed in the two faux medieval towers (copies of those punctuating Ávila's city wall) at the entrance to the Poble Espanyol. Though the club once drew an exclusive crowd, it has loosened up (and the entrance fee has gone down to 1,500 ptas.), so the crowd is somewhat mixed. *Marqués de Comillas s/n, Poble Espanyol, tel. 93/424–9309. Metro: Espanya.*

Woman Caballero. This hip basement nightclub fills on weekends with a stylish crowd. Bop to house and techno in one of the three variously decorated spaces, or chill out to blues and jazz in another. *Avda. Marqués de l'Argentera 6, tel. 93/300–4017. Metro: Jaume I.*

HOW MUCH IS THIS? NO, THIS . . .

What do you get when you cross Barcelona's designer savvy with its fondness for a night on the town? A place where you can order a cocktail and then buy the glass you drank it in, or the chair you're sitting on, or the ashtray on the table. All these props are for sale at the chic little restaurant-bar **Pilé 43** *(C. N'Agla 4, tel. 93/317–3902; Metro: Liceu), just off Plaça Reial. The eclectic array of renovated furniture, lamps, and other accessories hails mainly from the 1960s and '70s By day, the tasty vegetarian menu centers on bocadillos on your choice of bread (garlic, olive, or walnut); by night, cocktails are served to a stylish crowd.*

Nearby, the snazzy café-bar **So_da** *(C. Avinyó 24, tel. 93/412–2776) practices a similar synergy with clothes rather than household items. The apparel, for men and women both, tends toward creative retro designs. Shop for clever threads in the front room while the sun shines, then settle down in back for coffee or drinks after 5. Come evening the lights are dimmed, the music is turned up, and So_da evolves into a cozy little bar to while away the night hours.*

LIVE MUSIC

Blues Café. In the heart of Gràcia, this casual bar has live blues and jazz every Saturday and Sunday from 8 to 10, and a sizable beer list including pints of Guinness. *C. La Perla 37, tel. 93/416–0965. Metro: Joanic.*

Jamboree. This smooth, underground (literally—it's below the Plaça Reial) club has live jazz nightly from 11 to 1, then morphs into a dance club and plays hip-hop, rap, and R&B till 5. The cover is steep (1,800 ptas.), but it includes one drink, and if you show up for the usually excellent jazz, you can pretty much spend the whole night here. At 1 AM Jamboree takes over the adjoining Tarantos flamenco club (*see* Opera, Classical Music, and Dance, *below*) and starts blaring *música espanyola* (Spanish pop music) and salsa. *Plaça Reial 17, tel. 93/301–7564. Metro: Liceu.*

Harlem Jazz Club. One of the best jazz haunts in Barcelona, this friendly, laid-back club in the heart of the Gothic quarter fills up on weekends, but no matter: when the seats run out, people sit down on the floor around the small stage and go right on grooving to the top-notch jazz and blues lineup. *Comtessa de Sobradiel 8, tel. 93/310–0755. Metro: Jaume I.*

Jazz Si Club. A cozy little gem in the Raval district, Jazz Si Club features a live lineup that has wandered from jazz to rock to soul and even flamenco now and again. *C. Requesens 2, tel. 93/329–0020. Metro: Urgell.*

La Boîte. This large, popular musical space on the Diagonal hosts some of the best concerts in town, from jazz to blues to hip-hop to soul. *Avda. Diagonal, tel. 93/419–5950. Metro: Diagonal.*

La Cova del Drac. Come to this long-standing Gràcia jazz club for some of the best weekend jam sessions in Barcelona. *C. Vallmajor 33, tel. 93/200–7032. Metro: Muntaner.*

Luz de Gas. In a converted antique music hall, this handsome club has live music nightly, including jazz and blues. Programs occasionally veer into other creative territory, with spoken-word and poetry sessions. The upper Diagonal location means a moneyed, well-dressed crowd. *C. Muntaner 246, tel. 93/209–7711. Metro: Diagonal.*

Pipiolo. Amiable and well priced, Pipiolo is the kind of place where by night's end someone has picked up a guitar and everyone is howling gustily along. *C. Balmes 113, at C. Provença, tel. 93/323–5972. FGC: Provença.*

THE GAY SCENE

Barcelona has a thriving gay and lesbian nightlife scene, and it's hardly exclusive. Some of the liveliest, most entertaining nightclubs in town are the gay venues, and with a few exceptions they welcome all sexual orientations. There's a handful of gay bars and clubs around the **Esquerra Eixample** (Left Eixample), near the university, and along **Carrer Diputació.** Two well-established bars where you can start your night and collect recommendations for late-night clubbing options are the amiable bar **Punto BCN** (C. Muntaner, tel. 93/453–6123; Metro: Drassanes) and the popular café-nightclub **Dietrich** (C. Consell de Cent 255, tel. 93/451–7707; Metro: Urgell). Stop into the store **Sestienda** (C. Rauric 11, tel. 93/318–8676; Metro: Liceu) for a free map and guide to gay events, bars, and clubs throughout Barcelona. The free *b-guided*, available at intermittent bars and restaurants, also has good listings on the newest gay bars and nightclubs.

Of course, some of the best gay nightlife in Spain is half an hour down the coast, in the beach town of **Sitges** (*see* Near Barcelona, *below*).

FILM

Studies have shown that the average denizen of Barcelona watches more movies per month than anyone else in Europe. Though most movies are dubbed into Spanish, an increasing number of films are shown in their original language with Spanish subtitles—look for the designation VO (*versión original*). The **Icària Yelmo Cineplex** (C. Salvador Espriu 61, tel. 93/221–7585; Metro: Ciutadella-Port Olímpic) shows lots of films in VO; other theaters showing recent releases in VO include **Boliche** (Avda. Diagonal 508, tel. 93/218–1788; Metro: Diagonal), **Alexis** (Rambla Catalunya 90, tel. 93/215–0506; Metro: Diagonal or Passeig de Gràcia), and **Verdi Park** (Torrijos 49, tel. 93/238–7990; Metro: Fontana). Just around the corner from Verdi Park, **Verdi** (Verdi 32, tel. 93/238–7990.) shows an excellent mix of independent films, classics, and new releases. **Casablanca** (Passeig de Gràcia 115, tel. 93/218–4345; Metro: Diagonal) also shows both mainstream and indie films in VO. Movie tickets start at 800 ptas., though most theaters lower prices to about 625 ptas. one day each week (usually Wednesday), listed as "*día del espectador.*" The *Guía del Ocio* has the latest information on what films are playing where, which ones are in VO, and which days are discounted.

For innovative retrospectives and international art films, look to the **Filmoteca de la Generalitat de Catalunya** (Avda. Sarrià 33, tel. 93/410–7590; Metro: Hospital Clinic). You might see anything from a Luis Buñuel retrospective to a short festival of horror films from the 1950s. All films are shown in VO. Tickets usually start at 400 ptas.

OPERA, CLASSICAL MUSIC, AND DANCE

If you manage to snag tickets, the premiere place to attend an opera is the Rambla's magnificent **Grand Teatre del Liceu** (Rambla 63, tel. 93/485–9913). Prices start at 2,800 ptas. (Zona 8), but for 1,000 ptas. you can opt for seats where you can hear but not see the performance. You do need to reserve tickets, sometimes as much as a month or two in advance; to do so with a credit card, call 902/332211 or, from outside Spain, 93/417–0060. If you're already here: the box office is *usually* open weekdays 10–1 and 3–7 in summer, weekdays 2–8:30 the rest of the year

Barcelona's premier concert hall is the spectacular **Palau de la Música Catalana** (*see* La Ribera / El Born *in* Exploring Barcelona, *above*), where ticket prices start at 1,000 ptas. and zoom up to 15,000 ptas. The new **Auditori de Barcelona** (C. Lepant 150, tel. 93/317–1096; Metro: Glòries) is another major site for concerts and operas. **Auditori Winterthur** (Avda. Diagonal 547, tel. 93/412–3640; Metro: Maria Cristina), is, oddly enough, in the L'illa shopping mall, but that doesn't detract from its fine lineup of music and opera.

Many of the city's old **churches**, including the cathedral, Santa Maria del Mar, and Santa Maria del Pi occasionally host concerts; the tourist office has details.

L'Espai de Dansa i Música de la Generalitat de Catalunya—a.k.a L'Espai (the Space)—is the city's primary dance venue, with a full program of contemporary dance productions and occasional concerts.

FLAMENCO

If you have any pretensions to doing as the Romans do, know that most Barcelonans would not be caught dead in a flamenco bar. Flamenco is an Andalusian art, bearing no relation to Catalonia, and is performed here mainly for foreign tourists. If you have pesetas to burn and are determined to see some castanets, head to the oldest flamenco club in town, **Tarantos** (Plaça Reial 17, tel. 93/318–3067; Metro: Liceu). Performances start at 10 PM Monday–Saturday; tickets are 4,000 ptas., including one drink. The other venue of choice is **El Tablao de Carmen** (C. dels Arcs, Poble Espanyol, tel. 93/325–6895), on Montjüic, with lively dancing every night at 9:30 and 11. Tickets are 4,325 ptas. for dancing only, 8,550 with dinner.

THEATER

Barcelona is a lively theater town. Several local companies, including **Els Comediants, La Cubana,** and **Els Joglars,** have garnered international attention for their unique schtick, which combines drama, music, dance, and wild visual effects. Most shows are in Catalan, but they're enough of a spectacle that you'll have a riot of a time even if you understand not a word. Ask the tourist office when and where these troupes have upcoming shows; Els Comediants often performs outdoors, in plaças and parks.

Barcelona's bulwark brick-and-mortar stage is the **Teatre Nacional de Catalunya** (Plaça de les Arts 1, tel. 93/306–5700; Metro: Glòries), a stupendous theater designed in the early 1990s by Barcelona architect Ricard Bofill. Here the Catalan productions are joined by works from all over Europe. The long-established **Teatre Lliure** (C. Montseny 47, tel. 93/218–9251; Metro: Fontana) has an excellent program of Catalan and Castilian Spanish productions. The **Mercat de les Flors** theater (C. Lleida 59, tel. 93/318–8590; Metro: Plaça Espanya), named after the enormous flower market that once flourished here, shows a wide range of classic and contemporary plays. Nearby is the **Teatre Grec** (Greek Theater), a key site for the summer Festival del Grec. **Teatre Poliorama** (C. Rambla Estudios 115, tel. 93/317–7599; Metro: Catalunya) also roves from traditional to avant-garde.

You can buy tickets at most theaters' box offices or over the phone—many theaters sell tickets through **Servi-Caixa** (902/332211) or **Tel-entrada** (902/101212). For shows at Mercat de les Flors, you can buy tickets in the **Palau de la Virreina** cultural office (Rambla 99, tel. 93/318–8599).

CABARET

Barcelona has a rich and raunchy history in cabaret, and some of the traditional music halls are still around, staging big, glitzy high-kicking shows as well as sultry piano-bar numbers. Most of these venues are right where you'd expect them to be: along Avenida Paral.lel in the old-time working-class neighborhood of **Poble Sec**, where the audience ranges from old guys taking a breather from the nearby bar to families out on the town. **Teatre Arnau** (Avda. Paral.lel 60, tel. 93/441–4881) and **Teatre Apolo** (Avda. Paral.lel 57, 93/441–4881) both put on entertaining shows. The longtime cabaret lounge **Bodeha Bohemia** (C. Lancaster 2, tel. 93/302–5061) is showing its age in both decor and performers, but that's part of the fun. Cabaret tickets generally start at 1,500 ptas.

NEAR BARCELONA

Venture outside Barcelona to get a sense of how varied is this part of Spain. One hour inland is the spiritual center of Catalonia, the monastery at **Montserrat**, perched amid surreal, spectacular rocky peaks; in the other direction—and at the other extreme—is **Sitges**, one of Spain's most popular gay beach resorts.

MONTSERRAT

Looking like giant, dribbled sandcastles, the voluptuous, seemingly sculpted rock formations of Montserrat rise magnificently above the Catalan countryside just northwest of Barcelona. Their other-worldly grandeur has drawn many in search of spiritual guidance, but it was the Benedictines who founded a **monastery** here in the 11th century. Rebuilt in the 19th century, it contains a magnificently ornate **basilica,** which in turn houses Montserrat's enduring symbol, the **Black Virgin.** Sadly, this beautiful Romanesque carving of St. Mary of Montserrat sits behind a protective Plexiglas shield, with one part exposed for pilgrims and visitors to touch. Montserrat is also known for its **boys' choir,** or *escolania*, the oldest such group in Europe—they've been around since the 13th century. Hearing them sing in the basilica is an experience not to be missed; it happens Monday–Saturday at 1 and 6:45, Sunday at noon and 6:45, and Christmas Day at noon. The lads break during July and December 26–January 8. The impressive collection in the monastery **museum** includes liturgical gold work from the 15th century and paintings by El Greco, Caravaggio, Picasso, Dalí, Monet, and Degas.

If anything can spoil a Montserrat trip, it's the massive tourist crowds, which can reach scary proportions in summer. Don't come hoping for a meditative stroll on the monastery grounds, at least during high season, unless you can arrive around 6 or 7 AM (before doors open), when no one's afoot but you and the mountain peaks, rising into the silent morning mist. *Tel. 93/877–7777. Basilica: admission free; open daily 8–10:30 and 12:15–6:30, plus 7:30–8:15 on weekends. Museum: admission 600 ptas.; open daily 10–6, weekends 9:30–6:30.*

Montserrat is more than a man-made spiritual center: Catalan poet Joan Maragall called it "la terra misteriosa," and one of the best ways to get close to the land is to go outside and bond with it. Beyond the monastery and tour-bus fleet, accessible by funicular, is a **nature park** crisscrossed by walking trails. One path leads through a verdant valley forest to the peak of Sant Jeroni (4,054 ft), with stunning views; on a clear day you can see as far as the Pyrenees and Mallorca. Another trail takes you to the **Santa Cova** (Holy Cave) and an 18th-century **chapel** where the Black Virgin was originally housed.

BASICS

The **information office** (Plaça de la Creu, tel. 93/877–7701; open July–Sept., daily 10–6; Mar.–June, daily 10–5; Nov.–Feb., daily 10–4) is a great source of just that, particularly if you want to stay overnight or make further inquiries about hiking.

WHERE TO SLEEP AND EAT

It's easiest and cheapest to make Montserrat a day trip from Barcelona, but there are several lodging options in case you want to spend a few days up here. Note that you should reserve rooms through the information office (*see above*), not the properties themselves. Prices fluctuate wildly by season at **Hotel Abat Cisneros** (Plaça Santa Maria s/n)—doubles rent for 11,650 ptas. in high season, 5,720 ptas. in the dead of winter. Much cheaper are the nearby apartments of **Cel.les Abat Oliba** (Plaça Santa Maria s/n), where two people can rent a pad for 4,000–4,800 ptas.; in July and August the catch is a required stay of at least seven days. Each apartment is fully furnished and has a kitchen, TV, and telephone.

The **monastery** also has single rooms for those who come to pursue spiritual and religious growth. If this is you, call Padre Martín at 93/877–7766.

Dining options are limited. Near the tourist office, a big self-service cafeteria serves basic snack food (bocadillos, burgers) and simple meals. The **Restaurant Abat Cisneros,** inside the hotel (*see above*), is chichi and pricey, with a menú del día for about 2,500 ptas.

COMING AND GOING

The best views of Montserrat open up as you ascend the mountain, with the bizarre peaks soaring magnificently above and around you. From Barcelona take the **FGC train** (Ferrocarril; tel. 93/205–1515) from Plaça Espanya to Montserrat Aeri—from here cable cars leave every 15 minutes for the spectacular seven-minute ride up to Plaça del Monestir, just below the monastery. The train ride costs 625 ptas. oneway, 950 ptas. round-trip; you can also buy a round-trip ticket including train and cable car for around 2,000 ptas. In July–August the cable car runs daily 10–1:45 and 2:20–6:35; in March–June and September–October, daily 10–1:45 and 3–6:35; and in November–February, daily 10–1:45 and 2:20–5:35.

Julià **buses** (tel. 93/490–4000) leave Barcelona's Sants-Estació for Montserrat daily at 9 AM, returning at 5 PM (6 PM in summer). On weekdays the round-trip ticket is 1,230 ptas.; on weekends, 1,400.

SITGES

The small, laid-back beach town of Sitges is also one of the hottest gay resorts on the Mediterranean, which means you can spend your days getting a tan and your nights showing it off. The streets in the center of town, particularly **Carrer Primer de Maig** (also called Calle del Pecado, or "Street of Sin"), are jam-packed with bars and clubs where you can cavort and carouse until morning. At the same time, Sitges is a popular weekend getaway for Barcelonans, who come to loll on the beaches and eat paella in waterfront restaurants.

The first beaches to fill up are those along **Passeig Marítim**, the main waterfront strip. If you can't find a suitable patch of sand here, head toward the **Aiguadolç Port** (Sweet Water Port)—the lovely beaches on the way are usually less crowded.

Sitges positively explodes in February and/or March for **Carnival**, which it celebrates in trademark flamboyant fashion: outrageous floats and drag-queen contests are cheered on by appreciative crowds fueled with free-flowing beer. Several times a year the illustrious *castells* (human castles, a Catalan tradition) arrive from nearby Vilafranca, known for fielding one of the best such teams; ask the tourist office for details.

BASICS

The **tourist office** is conveniently located near the train station (C. Sínia Morera, tel. 93/894–4251; open July–Sept., daily 9–9; Oct.–June, weekdays 9:30–2 and 4–6:30, Sat. 10–1). For the scoop on gay bars and clubs, pick up a free "Gay Map" at **Parrot's** (Plaça Industria 2, no phone), the most popular gay bar in Sitges and a great place to people-watch from outdoor tables.

COMING AND GOING

The **train station** is a 10-minute walk from the center of town (Plaça Eduard Maristany s/n, tel. 93/490–0202). Stop into the tourist office (*see above*) on your way toward civilization. Trains leave Barcelona's Sants-Estació for Sitges every half hour between 5:40 AM and 11:20 PM; from Sitges, trains head back to Barcelona every half hour from around 6:30 AM to 10 PM. The fare is 350 ptas., usually slightly higher on weekends.

WHERE TO SLEEP

Sitges is packed with places to stay, but many of them fill up quickly in the summer (and, of course, inflate their rates). Do reserve in advance. Many lodgings close between October and April or May, with the exception of Carnival, so if you plan to be here in winter, call the tourist office to confirm what's open for business.

Budget lodgings abound on **Carrer de Parellades**, which runs from near the center of town to Plaça Espanya. Another good bet is the waterfront **Passeig de la Ribera**, along with the small streets branching off it. **Hostal R. Parrellades** (C. Parellades 11, tel. 93/894–0801; cash only) has well-maintained doubles with bath for 5,400 ptas., without bath for 4,500 ptas.; nearby, the friendly **Hostal Mariangel** (C. Parellades 78, tel. 93/894–1357) has basic doubles with bath for 5,500 ptas., without bath starting at 3,500 ptas. The laid-back **Hostal Maricel** (C. d'en Tacó 11, tel. 93/894–3627; cash only) has clean doubles with bath, and some with sea-view balconies, for 7,000 ptas. Solo travelers looking to meet up with others enjoy the lively social atmosphere at **Hostal Lido** (C. Bonnaire 26, tel. 93/894–4848), where doubles with bath are a bit pricier at 7,500 ptas. Near the train station, **Hostal Residencia Internacional** (C. Sant Francesc 52, tel. 93/894–2690) has comfy doubles with bath for 6,000 ptas., without bath for 5,500 ptas.

WHERE TO EAT

Menu prices will remind you that Sitges is a serious resort town. The consolation is that many of the waterfront restaurants on **Passeig de Marítim** and **Passeig de la Ribera** serve excellent paellas topped with the seafood of the day. **Mare Nostrum** (Passeig de la Ribera 60, tel. 93/894–3393) is one of the longest-running seafood joints on the waterfront, and its prices reflect that; the top-notch fish dishes start at 1,600 ptas, and during the week there's often a menú del día for about the same price. **Carrer Primer de Maig,** the aforementioned "Street of Sin," has a slew of bar-cafés where you can eat and drink cheaply, with bocadillos and simple platos combinados. **Restaurant La Borda** (C. Sant Bonaventura 5, tel. 93/811–2002), hugely popular with the gay crowd, serves delicious Catalan cuisine for 1,500 ptas. and up; you must pay cash if your bill is less than 3,000 ptas.

WORTH SEEING

When you're satisfied with your tan and want a bit of culture, investigate some of Sitges's museums. Founded by Catalan artist Santiago Rusinyol (1861–1931), the **Museu Cau Ferrat** contains some of his own paintings, along with two El Grecos and a large collection of Catalan ceramics. Next door, the **Museu Maricel** (from *mar i cielo,* "sea and sky") has an unusual collection of Romanesque and Moderniste art and sculpture, and some lovely ceramics. *C. Fonollar s/n, Museu Cau Ferrat tel. 93/894–0364. All Sitges museums: Admission 500 ptas. Open Mon.–Sat. 9:30–2 and 4–9, Sun, 9:30–2.*

CATALONIA

BY ANNELISE SORENSEN

T he land of *mar i muntanya* (sea and mountains) is a spectacular study in contrasts, from the soaring peaks of the Pyrenees to the clear blue water of the Mediterranean's shallow coves. The showy swagger of the Costa Brava's megaresorts mixes deliciously with the stillness of ancient parish churches hidden deep in farm country. Despite being wildly diverse, however, Catalonia (Catalunya) is quite compact, so it's possible—as locals enjoy telling you—to ski on snow in the morning and sunbathe on the beach in the afternoon.

For all its rampant colonization, the Costa Brava, stretching north of Barcelona to the French border, stills lives up to its name: the Rugged Coast. Craggy cliffs plunge dramatically into the shimmering aquamarine sea, and remote little coves hide behind jutting rocks and untamed vegetation. Just north of Barcelona, package tourism drives at full throttle, leaving a strip of indistinguishable resort towns where concrete apartment blocks rise over tacky trinket shops and belching tour buses arrive daily with cargoes of sunbathers. Head north of here and the rugged coast is yours and in some places, yours alone.

Looming gracefully over all of northern Catalonia are the Pyrenees, where snowcapped peaks reach more than 9,000 ft and fierce rivers cleave the verdant valleys. You can ski and hike anywhere in these mountains, aided by a slew of ski centers and vast stretches of natural parkland. Nestled in the valleys and clinging to the mountains are centuries-old alpine villages, each with its own little Romanesque church—collectively forming an open-air rural museum of early medieval architecture. Going back farther in time, the Greeks and Romans left their marks in a big way here; tramp through their ruined cities at Empúries, on the Costa Brava, and the seaside city of Tarragona, where Roman columns stand amid modern high-rises. Still, Catalonia's heart and soul are inland, where Catalanisme (the catch-all term for regional pride) is more than a way of life—it's a way of being. Here, Catalan traditions such as the circular *sardana* dance are a part of everyday life, and most every town, no matter how small, celebrates its annual *festa major* (main festival) with religious fervor and madcap revelry.

Catalan pride and identity are deeply rooted in the long struggle to protect Catalan traditions, language, and economy. The first stirrings of Catalonia's independent spirit occurred back in the time of one Guifré el Pilós (Wilfred the Hairy), the self-proclaimed patriarch of Catalonia who broke away from Frankish control in 874 and began uniting the Catalan counties. Though he died battling the Moors in 897, Wilfred had laid the foundations for what would become one of Spain's wealthiest and most powerful Autonomous Communities. In the 12th century Catalonia was united with Aragón through marriage and became the illustrious capital of Aragón's Mediterranean empire. In the 15th century another marriage—that of Ferdinand and Isabella—made the result a part of Castile-León and, eventually, of Spain

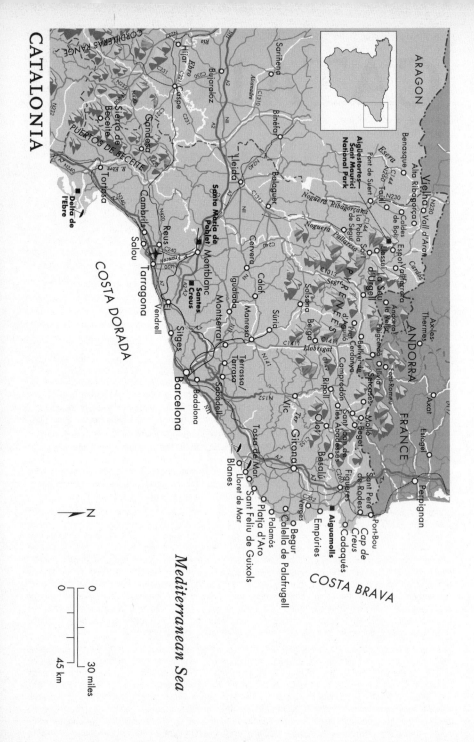

as we know it. Maritime attention turned westward, across the Atlantic. In 1562, when Madrid became the national capital, Catalonia continued to function somewhat independently. During the War of the Spanish Succession, Barcelona backed the Habsburgs and was punished postwar by a victorious Felipe V: the Catalan language was banned, as was any display of Catalan nationalism. The industrial revolution propelled Catalonia to prominence once more, and the region's newfound wealth sparked the Renaixença, a Catalan renaissance of art and culture. During the Spanish Civil War (1936–39), Catalonia again backed the unsafe side, vociferously maintaining the Republican cause; and when Barcelona was finally lost to Francisco Franco in 1939, the Catalans again reaped retaliation: Franco forbade them to read, write, speak, or teach the Catalan language and changed the official names of Catalonia's towns and streets to Castilian Spanish. Throughout Franco's long dictatorship, Catalan pride and spirit remained stubbornly intact, and when he died in 1975, Catalan culture bounced back without delay. Barcelona's Generalitat was reestablished as Catalonia's regional government in 1980, and thus began a modern-day Renaixença of Catalan culture and traditions that is still going strong. Spend a few days exploring Catalonia's coast, peaks, and heartland, and you'll begin to feel its fascination.

GETTING AROUND

You can cross Catalonia by car in less than six hours, and it takes less than two hours to changes climates—to go from, say, a scorching beach to a quiet, shady peach orchard. Exploring the Pyrenees, especially the more remote areas, is significantly easier with a car; otherwise, most of Catalonia is served by train and bus connections. **RENFE trains** (tel. 902/240202) stop at both coastal and inland towns, north to the French border and south toward Valencia. Several trains a day leave Barcelona for Pyrenean base camps, from which buses take you farther into the mountains. Alsina Graells, Sarfa, and Teisa are the three main **bus companies** in this region, taking over where the trains leave off. Alsina Graells covers much of the interior and the Pyrenees; Sarfa heads north along the Costa Brava and around Girona; and Teisa travels north along the coast, inland, and into parts of the Pyrenees. In Barcelona many buses leave from **Estació del Nord** (C. d'Ali Bei 80, tel. 93/265–6508, Metro: Arc de Triomf), but not all; call ahead or consult a tourist office when planning a bus trip.

THE COSTA BRAVA

As a natural phenomenon, the Costa Brava is stunning. Craggy bluffs jut over secluded coves and expanses of silky sand; woodland pine, almond and citrus trees, and rosemary and thyme cling to the looming rock faces. But it's the water that gets most people gushing. The Mediterranean here is vibrantly blue yet utterly transparent, opening an ethereal window onto the swaying tendrils of sea plants and darting schools of fish on the seafloor.

As a tourist phenomenon, the Costa Brava is also, unfortunately, stunning. Package tourism—with all the concrete high-rises, quadrilingual menus, and tacky bars that go with it—has effectively conquered much of the northern Catalan coast, to the point where it's sometimes hard to see the sand and water for the throngs (and the thongs). The oily bodies commence just north of Barcelona, but it's in **Blanes,** the first big resort town, that you start seeing tour buses, restaurants proffering EGGS AND CHIPS, and bars advertising OKTOBERFEST NIGHT in neon. If you're here for late-night drinking and predawn dancing, hunker down. Each resort has its own "nationality," complete with bars and restaurants in that vein. Blanes could well be Little Germany—get used to prices listed in deutsche marks—while **Lloret de Mar,** just north of Blanes, is largely British territory. (That said, the distinctions seem to change places every few years or so.) **Platja d'Aro,** farther north, is the Costa Brava's party center, particularly for young foreigners, who carouse and then crash on the beach. Lloret de Mar also has lively nightlife.

Tossa de Mar and nearby **Sant Feliu de Guixols,** while still packed with people, are pleasant places to chill for a few days. Continue north from here and the coast seems to become itself again, or at least remember who it used to be. In some sleepy beach towns, the ratio of tourists to residents is still one to one; the lovely coastal hamlet of **Tamariu,** for instance (near Palafrugell), retains its village character even in the face of visiting crowds.

Noh of Palafrugell, the coast starts to get interesting historically and culturally, and your tan starts to matter less than the artistic significance of melting watches. The Museu-Teatre Salvador Dalí, in the friendly town of **Figueres,** is a shrine to the surreal, and nearby **Cadaqués,** still an artists' haunt, is one of the loveliest villages on the coast. Just south of Cadaqués is ancient **Empúries,** with the ruins of one of the most important Greco-Roman cities on the Iberian Peninsula.

There are more hotel rooms on the Costa Brava than there are bars (and that's saying something), but they fill up fast in the summer. Generally, the closer to the beach the building is, the more you'll pay—there's always a smattering of inexpensive digs inland. **Palafrugell** has a handful of budget lodgings from which you can day-trip to the beaches nearby. All pensions and *hostales* spike their prices in summer, particularly in August, when Barcelona empties out. Remember that you'll always pay considerably more on the Rugged Coast than you will inland; and if you're traveling in the colder months, note that restaurants and lodgings often close for part of the winter.

COMING AND GOING

The easiest way to cover the coast is with your own **car.** That's not to say it's the fastest option, as the scenic coastal road becomes a parking lot on summer weekends; you're lucky if you move an inch every half hour. Take the inland A7 *autopista.* **RENFE trains** (tel. 902/240202) travel from Barcelona to Port Bou, on the French border; the line stops in Blanes and then goes inland, calling at Girona, Figueres, and a few more coastal towns en route to Port Bou. **Sarfa buses** (tel. 93/265–1158) travel daily up and down the coast and inland, an efficient and sometimes necessary accompaniment to the train if you want to move beyond the larger towns. **Barcelona Bus** (tel. 93/232–0459) travels to Girona and Figueres several times daily. Sarfa and Barcelona Bus both depart from Barcelona's Estació del Nord.

TOSSA DE MAR

Medieval walls and a well-preserved old city—the **Vila Vella**—founded by the Romans set Tossa de Mar apart. The beaches *are* overrun with crowds, but look beyond them and the view from your beach towel is spectacular: Before you is the sparkling Mediterranean, with little fishing boats bobbing on the waves; turn your head just slightly and you'll see the old town's fortified walls and towers outlined against the bright blue sky. Tossa's past-meets-present allure has drawn artists from afar since the early 1900s, including Marc Chagall, who left a little gift: The **Municipal Museum** (Plaça Roig i Soler 1, tel. 972/340709; admission: 500 ptas.; open mid-June–mid-Sept., daily 10–10; mid-Sept.–mid-June, Tues.–Sun. 10–1:30 and 4–7) has a Chagall painting of the view from his room here in Tossa. The museum also has archaeological finds from the Vila Vella and a strong collection of works by contemporary Catalan artists.

BASICS

The **tourist office** (Avda. del Pelegri 25, tel. 972/340108; open June–Sept., Mon.–Sat. 10–8, Sun. 10–1; Oct. and May, Mon.–Sat. 10–1 and 4–8; Nov.–Apr., weekdays 10–1 and 4–7, Sat. 10–1) has a list of all the lodgings in town, helpful if you have no luck on your own.

Tossa de Mar is well connected by **bus** to the other coastal resorts; buses head every half hour to **Lloret.** Sarfa runs seven or eight buses daily between Tossa and **Barcelona;** the last one leaves Tossa at 7:10 PM, possibly later in summer.

WHERE TO SLEEP AND EAT

There are plenty of budget digs here, especially in the old quarter. **Can Tort** (C. Pescadors 1, tel. 972/341185, cash only), in the heart of the Vila Vella, has basic doubles for 5,500 ptas. including breakfast, though in August the price can shoot up to 7,500 ptas. Nearby, **Fonda Lluna** (C. Roqueta 20, tel. 972/340365, cash only) has doubles for 5,000 ptas. in August, 4,000 ptas. June–July, and 3,500 ptas. in spring and fall (it's closed Dec.–Feb.). Breakfast is included. **Pensió Codolar** (C. Codolar 12, tel. 972/340468, cash only) has simple doubles for 4,400 ptas., also including breakfast.

Touristy restaurants, and correspondingly touristy prices, abound in Tossa, but they frequently offer specials and "deals of the week," so sniff around streets like Carrer La Guardia for an appealing *menú del día.* **Restaurant Veramar** (C. Enrique Granados, tel. 972/342889) serves a tasty set menu, with lots of seafood options, for 1,600 ptas. Beer and *bocadillos* (sandwiches) are popular at the bustling corner **Cafeteria Rem-Vell** (Avda. Sant Ramon de Penyafort, tel. 972/340597), overlooking the beach; just note that it's closed weekdays in winter. From a high perch in the old town, **Bar Vila Vella** (inside medieval walls, tel. 972/340288) commands gorgeous views of Tossa's beach and rooftops and serves simple but tasty fare, such as bocadillos and crunchy pizzas. At night it morphs into more of a bar—a great vantage point for gazing down, drink in hand, at Tossa's glittering lights. It's open from Easter to October, usually until 8 PM, but until 3 AM or later during June–September if there's a crowd hanging out. Folks dance till the wee hours at **Discoteca Ely** (between C. Pola and Avda. Costa Brava); it opens at 10 PM and closes around 5 AM. The bowling alley next door is surprisingly popular, and good for grins.

PALAFRUGELL

The amiable inland town of Palafrugell is popular with budget travelers, as you can sleep and eat here cheaply yet still be within a day trip's reach of the prettiest beaches, including Calella de Palafrugell, Llafranc, and Tamariu. The town's bustling Sunday market draws vendors and browsers from all over the area. If one day you decide to forgo the beaches, check out the **Museu del Suro**, or Museo del Corcho (Cork Museum; C. Tarongeta 31, tel. 972/303998), the only one of its kind—it's dedicated to the history and multiple uses of cork, once an important industry in the surrounding Empordà, La Selva, and Gironès regions. The museum is open fall–spring, Tuesday–Saturday 10–1 and 5–8, Sunday 11–2; winter, Monday–Saturday 5–8.

Just southeast of Palafrugell, the fishing village of **Calella de Palafrugell** comprises lovely coves and small beaches tucked into craggy hillsides. Many of the fishermen's cottages are well preserved, and the town still feels refreshingly rooted in its humble beginnings. Calella also has the distinction of hosting (usually on the first Saturday in July) the popular *cantada d'havaneres* festival, which involves performances of traditional Spanish-Cuban sailor songs. The drink of choice is *cremat*, coffee with rum flambé. The **Costa Brava Jazz Festival,** held in July and August, takes place at the Jardí Botànic de Cap Roig (Botanical Gardens of Cap Roig), just above Calella.

Llafranc is another pretty coastal town, but because it has one very long beach (as opposed to Calella's collection of small ones), it feels less intimate. The layout does aid in people-watching, however, and Llafranc hosts its own *havaneres* festival on the first Saturday in August.

Tamariu, a few kilometers north of Llafranc, is the smallest and most sheltered (in all senses of the word) beach on this part of the coast. Catalan writer Josep Pla, born in Palafrugell, compared the beautiful simplicity of Tamariu's coastline to that of a Chinese painting. Imagine the beach emptied of bodies and beach towels and you'll see what he means: a lovely, if faint, reminder of the untouched Costa Brava.

BASICS

VISITOR INFORMATION • Palafrugell's tourist office (C. del Carrilet, tel. 972/300228; open July–Aug., Mon.–Sat. 10–8, Sun. 10–1; Apr.–June and Sept., Mon.–Sat. 10–1 and 5–8, Sun. 10–1; Oct.–Mar., Mon.–Sat. 10–1 and 4–7) is a good place to pick up info and bus schedules. **Tamariu's** office (C. de la Riera s/n, tel. 972/620193), which can point you toward water-sports outfitters, is open mid-June to mid-September, Mon.–Sat. 10–1 and 5–8, Sunday 10–2.

CYBERSPACE • There aren't too many Internet joints on the coast, so you might want to check your e-mail at the pleasant **Cybercafé** (C. dels Valls s/n, no phone; closed Mon.), near the center of Palafrugell. Access costs 600 ptas. an hour. Grab a bocadillo and a drink while you're here.

COMING AND GOING

In the summer, **shuttle buses** (150 ptas.) travel between Palafrugell, Calella, and Llafranc throughout the day (7:40 AM–8:45 PM). In winter they slow to two or three times a day. If you want to do some walking, get off at Calella, relax on the beach for awhile, then hit the coastal Camino de Ronda for the 25-minute walk to Llafranc. **Sarfa buses** (tel. 972/300623) travel to and from **Barcelona** (2 hrs, 1,690 ptas.), **Tamariu** (15 min, 155 ptas.), and **Girona** (1 hr, 575 ptas.) several times daily.

WHERE TO SLEEP

PALAFRUGELL • Palafrugell has few cheap beds, and they fill up very quickly in the summer. Reserve in advance if at all possible, and note that many *hostales* and pensions close for part of the winter. **Residencia Familiar** (C. Sant Sebastià 29, tel. 689/269538, cash only) has comfortable doubles without bath for 5,000 ptas. and single rooms for a song (2,000 ptas.), but only in the summer—they're closed from September 15 to Easter. Across the street, **Hostal Plaja** (C. Sant Sebastià 34, tel. 972/300526) has a beautiful domed lobby and rooms that overlook a leafy interior courtyard. Clean, well-maintained doubles cost 6,000 ptas. **Fonda La Estrella** (C. de les Quatre Cases 13–17, tel. 972/300005, cash only) has basic doubles without bath for 4,500 ptas., and is closed from November to March.

TAMARIU • The cheapest place to stay in Tamariu is the **Tamariu Platja** (C. de Foraió, tel. 972/620437), which rents double rooms for 8,500 ptas. in July and August, 7,000 ptas. the rest of the year, barring winter, when it often closes altogether. If you can spend a bit more, consider the newly renovated

Hotel Tamariu (Paseo del Mar, tel. 972/620031), overlooking the beach—doubles with hotel amenities go for 13,000 ptas. in summer, 10,000–11,000 ptas. the rest of the year.

Most hotels in Calella and Llafranc are on the pricey side, but a handful of places are in the budget range. In Calella, **Hosteria del Plancton** (C. de Codina 16, tel. 972/615081, cash only) has doubles without bath for 4,500 ptas. In Llafranc, **Pensión La Barraca** (C. de Santa Rosa 9, tel. 972/300408, cash only) has basic doubles with bath for 5,000 ptas.

WHERE TO EAT

In general, you'll have cheaper, more authentic meals in Palafrugell than at the touristy waterfront joints. **La Taverna** (C. de Firalt i Subirós, tel. 972/300430), near the center of town, cooks up simple but excellent Mediterranean dishes, including *pebrots del piquillo farcits de rap i gambes* (red peppers stuffed with fish and prawns, 900 ptas.). If you're counting your pesetas, feast on grilled chicken with fries for 550 ptas. It doesn't look like much from the outside, but **R. Pizzeria Can Moragas** (Plaça Nova 16, tel. 972/301044) has been around for more than 100 years. Pizza (700 ptas.) is a newcomer to the menu, but you can still opt for entrées the restaurant has been preparing for a whole century, including *escalivada con tostada y anchoas* (a typical Catalan dish of grilled peppers, onion, and eggplant, served here with toasted bread and anchovies; 975 ptas.), and *revuelto de setas con jamón* (scrambled eggs with mushrooms and ham, 915 ptas.).

Many small Spanish towns used to have a central social hall that served, in addition to the church, as a gathering place. A few have survived the years: For a step into Palafrugell's past, drop into the cavernous **Centre Fraternal–Societat Cultural i Recreativa** (Plaça Nova 4, tel. 972/300003), a recreation hall founded in the late 19th century. You're welcome to have a drink here, watching some old men play chess and listening to other old men discuss the issues of the day at a high decibel level. The club is open 365 days a year.

OUTDOOR ACTIVITIES

The clear waters of the Costa Brava offer great snorkeling and scuba diving. Most towns have dive shops that rent equipment and lead diving excursions; ask the local tourist office for a list. The waters around the **Tamariu** coves are particularly beautiful for diving. Run by a long-resident German, **Stolli's Tauchbasis,** on the Tamariu waterfront (Paseo del Mar 26, tel. 972/620245), can meet all your diving needs, including night dives; a half-day dive costs about 4,500 ptas.

INLAND FROM PALAFRUGELL

PERATALLADA

Northwest of Palafrugell, tiny, medieval Peratallada (population 400), is an enchanting little town that seems quite happily stuck in the Middle Ages. Its medieval buildings are better preserved than most in this region, and the narrow, cobbled streets and arched walkways between them invite you to lose yourself in another century for an afternoon. The town is encircled by an astonishing moat carved entirely out of rock—hence its name, which means "carved rock."

Peratallada has its share of little festivals, including a **Festa Medieval** on the first weekend in October, for which everyone dresses up in medieval costume and parades through the streets. The **Fira Peratallada,** the last Sunday in April, involves a bustling cheese market and arts-and-crafts stands in the main square. The town's *festa major* (main festival) is held August 6 and 7.

WHERE TO SLEEP AND EAT • Bask in Peratallada's rustic ambience at **Ca L'Aliu** (C. Roca 6, tel. 972/634061), a renovated *casa rural* (country house) where lovely rooms with antique furniture cost 7,000 ptas. a night, including breakfast. The friendly management will fill you in on what's going on around the village and lend you a free bicycle if you want.

The only other hotel in town is a real splurge: the classy **Castell de Peratallada** (Plaça del Castell 1, tel. 972/634021, fax 972/634011), set in the town's medieval castle. Each of these eight individually, sumptuously decorated rooms goes for 25,000 ptas., including a small banquet of a breakfast. Most people come here for the restaurant, where you can dine beneath soaring stone arches or, on warm summer nights, on the cobbled terrace. There's an expensive (8,000 ptas.) *menú gastronómica* for every season; fresh fish abounds in summer. On winter weekdays, only lunch is served.

Elsewhere in Peratallada, the food is still good and the prices are lower. The inventive fare at **Can Nau** (Plaça Esuiladors 2, tel. 972/634035) has included *conejo a la cazuela con salsa de almendras* (rabbit in casserole with almond sauce, 1,300 ptas.) and *butifarra dulce a la cazuela con compota de manzana* (sweet country sausage with stewed apples, 1,300 ptas.). **PssstCafé** (Plaça de les Voltes 11, tel. 972/634001, cash only) has outdoor tables with funky tabletop art; tuck into tostadas made with *pa de coca* (thin bread that's crunchy in the middle and doughy on the edges), crepes with spinach and béchamel, or *sobrasada con miel* (a typical Mallorcan sausage, served with honey). **L'Arc Vell** (Plaça Castell 2, tel. 972/634000) serves a variety of regional fare, such as *codornices a la brasa* (grilled quail; 750 ptas.) to *bocadillos de anchoas de l'Escala* (sandwiches with anchovies from l'Escala; 700 ptas.).

PÚBOL—CASA-MUSEU CASTELL GALA DALÍ

North of Palafrugell, near La Bisbal, stands **Castell Púbol,** the Renaissance castle that Salvador Dalí bought for his wife, Gala, in the late 1960s. She lived here until her death in 1982, and Dalí moved here shortly thereafter (the pair had unusual living arrangements). When fire struck parts of the castle, the artist had his own brush with death, and later went to live in the tower adjoining his home in Figueres (*see below*). The castle is decorated in vintage Dalí style: Stuffed animal heads protrude from walls, domed ceilings are painted in quasi-religious and mythological motifs, and the gardens are home to Dalí's signature cement elephants, with giraffe legs and trunks that spurt water every few hours.

Castell Púbol is one of three Dalí sights in this region; the other two are the museum in Figueres and the house in Port Lligat near Cadaqués (*see below*). Sarfa buses en route from Girona to Palafrugell stop at Púbol. *Rte. 255 toward La Bisbal (15 km/9 mi east of A7), tel. 972/488655. Admission 600 ptas. Open mid-June–mid-Sept., daily 10:30–8; mid-Sept.–Oct. and mid-March–mid-June, daily 10:30–6.*

FIGUERES

The pleasant midsize town of Figueres is the capital of the Alt Empordà region and home to one the most popular galleries in Spain, the Teatre Museu Salvador Dalí. Native son Dalí returned to Figueres specifically to create this homage to surrealism, and what an homage it is: Bizarre, magical, and mischievously interactive, the museum is all you'd expect from the world's most celebrated surrealist.

Indeed, the museum's whimsy seems to have rubbed off on the whole neighborhood. Carrer de la Jonquera, near Plaça Gala i Salvador Dalí, is lined with lively toy stores and kid-friendly restaurants, and venues throughout town incorporate the Dalí aesthetic into their decor—matter-of-factly, which of course makes it all the more surreal. (*See* Hostal Isabel II *and* Dalícatessen, *below.*) And there's plenty in the way of shopping, from quasi-dripping clocks to oddball stationery.

And yet there's more to Figueres than Dalí. Cutting a wide swath through the center of town is La Rambla de Figueres, a graceful, leafy pedestrian street lined with modern houses and pleasant outdoor cafés. The Museu Empordà, with local archaeological finds, and the nearby Castell de Sant Ferran, a massive fortification with sprawling grounds, are also worth checking out.

BASICS

The **tourist office** (Plaça del Sol, tel. 972/503155), open Monday–Saturday 9–8, is west of the museum.

COMING AND GOING • The train and bus stations are both in eastern Figueres, an easy walk from the town center and Museu Dalí. Several **RENFE trains** (tel. 902/240202) leave Barcelona for Figueres daily (2 hrs), as do vehicles run by **Barcelona Bus** (93/232–0459) from Barcelona's Estació del Nord (2½ hrs). By **car,** the fastest route is the A7 *autopista* toward Girona.

WHERE TO SLEEP • Budget lodgings are scattered about town. There's a handful of good places just north of the museum, on Carrer Isabel II and Carrer Barceloneta. Each room in the friendly, slightly eccentric **Hostal Isabel II** (C. Isabel II, tel. 972/504735, cash only) is done up as pink or blue child's bedroom—most overlook a playground as well—and each sports a Daliesque painting by a local artist. A double costs 4,800 ptas. a night. Nearby, **Hotel Los Angeles** (C. Barceloneta, tel. 972/510661) offers hotel amenities—helpful staff, comfy lobby/TV lounge—at nonhotel prices: Doubles range from 6,700 ptas. to 7,200 ptas., including breakfast. A few blocks from the museum, Señora Navarro rents out simple rooms in **Pensió Alay** (C. de la Jonquera 15, tel. 972/506442, cash only) above her small store, called "Tot a 100—i Una Mica Mès" ("Everything under 100 ptas.—and a Little More"). **Hostal Galicia** (Avda. Perpinyá 34, tel. 972/501566, cash only), a little farther from the city center, has dank but large doubles nicely priced at 4,900 ptas. In the local bar-restaurant downstairs, old barflies sit around and talk politics over the blaring TV in the corner. Check out the pen collection surrounding the bar—anyone can add to it, so here's a chance to leave your mark on Figueres. To get here, walk northwest from the museum on Carrer de la Jonquera, which turns into Avda. Per-

FAR FROM THE
BUSTLING SWARM

"There is a very little thing in a very high place. I'm happy, I'm happy, I'm happy, I'm happy. The needles pierce the little tender sweet nickels. My friend has a cork hand and it is covered with Paris lace. One of my friend's breasts is a placid sea urchin, the other a bustling swarm."

— Salvador Dalí, 1928

pinyá. **La Barretina** (C. Lasauca 13, tel. 972/673425), just off La Rambla near the tourist office, has basic rooms for 6,000 ptas.

WHERE TO EAT

Locals descend on homey **Mesón Asador** (Pujada del Castell 4, tel. 972/510104) in droves to feast on the house specialty, excellent grilled meats. Prices start at 1,500 ptas. If there's a line at the asador and you just want *eat,* head to the nearby restaurant-bar **La Venta del Toro** (C. Pep Ventura 5, tel. 972/510510). It's much simpler, but the hearty menú del día will do the trick, usually for less than 1,400 ptas.

Bustling Carrer de la Jonquera, near the museum, has a slew of restaurants with outdoor tables. True, it's often crawling with tourists, but in summertime Figueres you just can't escape them. The specialty at **Restaurante Tutti Frutti** (C. de la Jonquera 20, tel. 972/511291) is standing skewers (*pinchos*) of meat or seafood (1,500 ptas.) that kids and their adults have a silly old time eating. The weekday menú del día (lunchtime only in winter), which includes a tasty paella, costs a mere 1,000 ptas. On a small street just off Carrer de la Jonquera, the family-run **Restaurant La Paella** (C. dels Tins 9, tel. 972/501837) presents an excellent 1,000-ptas. set menu with paella and a dish of succulent fresh mussels. The tapas menu is also tops. Adventurous palates should try the kidneys in sherry sauce (450 ptas.), snails (600 ptas.), or octopus (1,000 ptas.).

You'll recognize café-bar **Dalícatessen** (C. Sant Pere 19, tel. 972/511193) by its catchy logo depicting an egg sporting a mustache. Designed by young artist-owner Martin Dacosta, the logo became so popular (people were forever walking off with plates and glasses) that Dacosta procured a trademark on it and started selling egg-embossed T-shirts and cups in a little shop next door. The café serves tasty bocadillos, ice cream, and other simple snacks and is a perfect distraction from the monotony of standing in the museum line. The Dacosta family has owned this place for generations (it used to be a shoe store), and though Martin has long been inspired by—and earned a living off—the local deity, he says with a big smile that he has "never much liked his art."

WORTH SEEING

MUSEU TEATRE SALVADOR DALÍ • You can't miss the museum—the tower rising beside it has a roof topped with giant eggs and a red facade bulging with protruding loaves. Dalí spent the last years of his life here, until he died in 1989. Housed in a former theater, the museum is designed around a huge courtyard that's ringed by white ceramic sinks and gold mannequins inspired by Academy Award statues. Light streams in through a transparent, geodesic dome ceiling (designed by Emilio Pérez Piñero) that resembles the eye of a fly, in a nod to Dalí's obsession with insects. The artist liked flies but was repulsed by ants, which he often depicted crawling out of eyeballs in his paintings.

Dalí created the museum to be an all-around sensory and surreal experience. Stick 100 ptas. in special binoculars to see *Gala Nude Looking at the Sea, Which at a Distance of Eighteen Meters Is Transformed into a Portrait of Abraham Lincoln,* or revive a dead body lying in a coffin made of circuit boards. Everyone's favorite is *The Face of Mae West That Can Be Used as a Drawing Room,* in which Mae's giant nose has a fireplace (complete with logs) built into each nostril, and her fleshy red lips are a couch. Look through the distance-enhancing viewfinder and voilà, it's the one and only Mae West. The **Sala del Tresor** (Treasure Room) houses many of Dalí's better-known works, including *The Specter of Sex Appeal,* which explores his famous sex phobia. Other emblematic works are *Soft Self-Portrait with Fried Bacon*, in which Dalí's dripping visage is propped up by little sticks, and *Venus de Milo with Drawers*. In the summer, usually late July to early September, the museum often stays open into the evening, at which time the price of admission includes a glass of cava. *Plaça Gala i Salvador Dalí 5, tel. 972/511800. Admission: 1,000 ptas. Open July–Sept., daily 9–7:45; Oct.–June, daily 10:30–7:45.*

CASTELL DE SANT FERRAN • This imposing 18th-century fortified castle—one of the largest in Europe—stands just northwest of Figueres. Only by exploring the castle grounds and walking its 4-km (2½-mi) perimeter can you really appreciate how immense it is, with parade grounds that extend for acres and arched stables that can house more than 500 horses. If you have 2½ hours to spare, take the new guided "adventure tour" on which you tool the grounds in a Land Rover, explore some of the castle's underground tunnels, have an aperitif, and ride a small boat through the cisterns. The castle is still used by the army, and there may be times during the year when visits are not allowed; contact Figueres's tourist office for an update. Sant Ferran was the site of the last official meeting of Spain's Republican parliament (on February 1, 1939) before it surrendered to Franco's forces. *1 km (½ mi) northwest of Figueres, tel. 972/506094. Admission 350 ptas.; adventure tour 1,800 ptas. Open June–Sept., daily 10:30–7; Oct.–May, daily 10:30–2. Adventure tours daily 11 and 5; call for reservations several days in advance for weekday tours, 1–2 weeks in advance for weekend tours.*

MUSEU EMPORDÀ • This museum displays archaeological finds from the surrounding Alt Empordà region and a large collection of works by Catalan artists from the 18th century to the present. One floor is devoted to artists from the Empordà region, many of whom painted the Empordá countryside and villages; another floor features Catalan painters and sculptors generally, including the well-known painter Ramón Casas. The archaeological items include columns and capitals from the Monestir de Sant Pere de Rodes. *Rambla 2, tel. 972/502305. Admission 300 ptas. Open mid-June–mid-Sept., Tues.–Sat. 11–7, Sun. 10–2; mid-Sept.–mid-June, Tues.–Sat. 11–1:30 and 3:30–5, Sun. 11–1:30.*

MUSEU DEL JOGUET DE CATALUNYA • From bronze Roman rattles to antique toy circuses and 20th-century optical-illusion games, the Toy Museum of Catalonia takes a playful romp through the history of having fun. Particularly curious are the religious items, which include altar boys' clothes from 1905 and miniature churches with tiny movable figures of priests. More than 4,000 objects are crammed into three rooms, so the museum actually feels pretty small—something to consider before you fork over the admission fee. *C. Sant Pere 1/Rambla 10, tel. 972/504585. Admission 750 ptas. Open July–Sept., weekdays 10–1 and 4–7, Sun. 11–1:30 and 5–7:30; Oct.–June, Mon. and Wed.–Sat. 10–1 and 4–7, Sun. 11–1:30. Closed Jan. 15–Mar. 1.*

CADAQUÉS

Perched around a craggy cove, Cadaqués is a gorgeous little fishing village of whitewashed houses and waterfront cafés. Salvador Dalí vacationed here as a child, and eventually returned permanently to neighboring Port Lligat (*see below*). If the rocky, otherworldly coastline looks familiar, it's because Dalí often depicted it in his works; and when you see the views from his Port Lligat home, you'll know why.

Exuding an air of free thinking, Cadaqués has long been an artists' haunt, owing partly to Dalí's presence. (His favorite bar has long drawn creative luminaries from from far and wide.) The town is still very much a village, where everyone knows everyone else's business, opening hours are determined by the owner's whim, and directions are given by landmarks rather than street names. The town has worked hard at this timelessness, imposing strict height limitations on new buildings and little tolerance for outside development. The result: a vintage gem, and a very cool little place to hang out for a while.

Centre d'Art Perrot (C. Vigilant 1, tel. 972/258231) displays paintings by Picasso and Dalí. Call ahead or ask the tourist office for hours, as recent renovations have shut the museum down for months at a time.

BASICS
The **tourist office** (C. Cotxe 2, tel. 972/258315; open July–Sept., Mon.–Sat. 10–1 and 4–8, Sun. 10–1; Oct.–June, Mon.–Sat. 10–1; hrs may vary, so call ahead) has lots of info on the town and the surrounding area, including Port Lligat and Cap de Creus. If banks are closed, seek the best exchange rates at the currency exchange adjoining **Paperia Rahola** (tel. 972/258349), a small bookshop on Avda. Caritat Serinyana just off the main square. The hours for both are Monday–Saturday 8–2 and 4–8:30, and Sunday 8–2.

SALVADOR +
GALA 4EVA

Dalí had many obsessions, but none quite like his love for Gala, his beloved wife and lifelong muse, whom he met when she was visiting Cadaqués in 1929 with her French poet husband, Paul Eluard. It was love—or something—at first sight, and the pair took off to Port Lligat, near Cadaqués, in 1930, leaving home and husband in the dust. After he went off and grew famous, Dalí returned to Cadaqués and he and Gala repaired once more to Port Lligat, where they lived until Gala's death in 1982. In 1970 Dalí bought Castell de Púbol, near Girona (see Inland from Palafrugell, above), as a gift for Gala, and it was truly her castle—and she the queen. Rumor has it that Gala had many a tryst here with many a young man, and that she imposed strict rules on Dalí, such as a moratorium on visiting unless he checked with her first. After Gala died, Dalí left Port Lligat and moved into the Púbol Castle himself, retiring a few years later to the tower alongside the Museu Dalí in Figueres—you know, the one topped with giant eggs.

COMING AND GOING

The **bus station** (tel. 972/258713) is on Carrer Vicens, west of the town center just off Avenida Caritat Serinyana. **Sarfa** (tel. 972/258713) runs three buses daily to and from **Figueres** (1 hr), one to and from **Girona** (1¼ hrs), and one to and from **Barcelona** (1¾ hrs).

WHERE TO SLEEP

Cadaqués's budget lodgings, all an easy walk from the town center, fill up quickly in high season. The friendly local couple in charge of **La Fonda** (C. Sa Tórtora 64, tel. 972/258019) will happily give you the scoop on Cadaqués and its history; their comfortable, spic-and-span double rooms cost 7,000 ptas. in July and August, 5,500 ptas. the rest of the year. The amiable **Pensión Cala d'Or** (C. Sa Fitora 1, tel. 972/258149) rents clean doubles with shared bath for 4,000 ptas., and the homey restaurant downstairs has an inexpensive menú del día. **Hostal El Ranxo** (Avda. Caritat Serinyana 93, tel. 972/25-80-05) has simple doubles without bath for 3,500 ptas.

In the center of town, prices go up: **Fonda Marina** (C. Riera 3, tel. 972/258199) has basic, clean doubles for 7,000 ptas., or 4,800 ptas. without bath; solo travelers will like the single rooms at 3,500 or 2,000 ptas. respectively. Next door, **Hostal Christina** (C. Riera s/n, tel. 972/258138) is a step up in price but not much else, with basic doubles for 8,000 ptas.

WHERE TO EAT

The bustling, atmospheric **Restaurante Casa Anita** (C. Miguel Roset, tel. 972/258471), just north of Avda. Caritat Serinyana, has beamed ceilings, stone arches, and shelves of wine barrels. The excellent seafood and Catalan fare ranges widely in price; among the cheaper dishes are *anchoas de Cadaqués* (local anchovies, 900 ptas.) and basic but delicious *pollo con patates* (chicken with potatoes, 800 ptas.). The walls are plastered with signed pics of celebrities who have passed through, including Elton John. Adjoining the restaurant is an inviting old bar where you can retire for a *digestif* after your meal.

Just off the main square overlooking the water, you'll find the bustling, outdoor **Marítim Bar** (tel. 972/258004), where you can watch fishermen haul in their nets. Tucked into a small courtyard at the end of an alleyway off Passeig Marítim (at No. 7), the pleasant little **El Jardí** serves a fresh, vegetarian-friendly menu of tabouli (500 ptas.), Indian daal (475 ptas.), and chicken saté (850 ptas.). It's usually open only in summer. The cozy, bric-a-brac-filled **Restaurante Cala d'Or** (C. Sa Fitora 1, tel. 972/258149) serves an excellent menú del día for 1,000 ptas. and a good array of fresh seafood, including *musclos* (mussels, 800 ptas.) prepared a variety of ways.

AFTER DARK

Some of Cadaqués's best bars have been around forever. The cavernous **L'Hostal** is an institution, and a must for Dalí fans: The great man used to hang out here (indeed, he supposedly called it "the most beautiful place on earth"), and lent a hand in redesigning it in 1975. At some point in the evening—every evening, as L'Hostal is open 365 days a year—everyone passes through. As you walk in, look down: Dalí designed the "eye"-tiled floor. German-born owner Marci is a real character, and a fixture at the bar; he's played host to everyone from Mick Jagger to Gabriel García Marquez, the latter of whom left a pen-and-ink sailboat drawing inscribed "Para Marci, Con Un Barco—Gabriel," which is good surrealist nonsense ("To Marci, With a Boat—Gabriel"). The García Marquez quote is inscribed on the house matches, as is a color picture of Marci's wife. It seems she may be his Gala.

Next to the Restaurante Casa Anita is the dark, wood-paneled **Bar Anita Nit,** which the owner calls his *whiskeria* because of the phenomenal selection of old whiskeys on offer. A glass of whiskey that's 8–10 years old costs 900 ptas.; for stuff more than 20 years old, the price (and the taste?) catapults to 3,500 ptas. Either way, this is a great little place to spend the evening. On a warm summer night, head for the leafy patio at **Tropical Café** (C. Miguel Roset 19, tel. 972/258801), where owners François and Julie serve margaritas and *mojitos* (both 900 ptas.), the latter a Cuban drink very popular in Spain, made with rum, sugarcane, limes, and fresh mint.

OUTDOOR ACTIVITIES

The clear water around Cadaqués makes for excellent snorkeling and scuba diving, particularly near Cap de Creus (*see below*). The **Sotamar Diving Center** (Avda. Caritat Serinyana 17, tel. 972/258876) arranges dive trips starting at 2,800 ptas., equipment included.

To see Dalí's vision on the big screen, check art-house listings for Le Chien Andalou, *a short film he co-directed with Spanish director Luis Buñuel. One famous scene shows an eyeball being cut by a razor.*

NEAR CADAQUÉS

PORT LLIGAT

Port Lligat is a tiny fishing village about 1 km (½ mi) north of Cadaqués. Salvador Dalí and his wife, Gala, made their home here, and you can now snoop around it through the **Casa-Museu Salvador Dalí.** The house is a whitewashed marvel overlooking the water; the large windows frame wonderful views of the small harbor, with fishing boats bobbing on the waves and craggy cliffs rising in the distance. A visit to Port Lligat, more than any other Dalí locale, lets you see how the couple really lived and worked. In Dalí's studio you'll see his huge Mogul harem–style couches and the 3-D glasses he wore to work on his optical-illusion pieces. After moving into the house in the 1930s, the couple spent considerable time decorating and expanding it, so the home was not in fact completed until 1971.

In Gala's "album room" the walls are plastered with magazine covers, press clippings, and photographs documenting Dalí's extraordinary career—and Gala's indispensable role in it. Through a small doorway you enter Gala's sanctuary, a sumptuous domed room with echoing acoustics and all sorts of strange little objects, like a stool with legs made of animal hooves and a mounted rhinoceros head with eagle wings.

Salvador and Gala were very particular about whom they let into their inner sanctum, and so they usually entertained outdoors. The patio is shaded by trees planted in giant whitewashed teacups, and the phallus-shape pool is surrounded by found objects, including a roly-poly Michelin tire man stuck into a wall and a giant pink couch shaped like lips, reminiscent of Mae West's lips in the Figueres museum. Installed at the head of the pool are two thrones (for Dalí and Gala to hold court), behind which looms part of an old lighthouse from nearby Cap de Creus. *1 km (½ mi) north of Cadaqués along beach, tel. 972/251015. Admission 1,300 ptas. Visits scheduled every half hour; call to reserve day and time, ideally two or three days in advance. Usually open mid-June–mid-Sept., Tues.–Sat. 10:30–9, mid-March–mid-June 14 and mid-Sept.–Jan. 6, Tues.–Sat. 10:30–6.*

A CATALAN CHRISTMAS

The most popular figure in the Catalan pessebre *(nativity scene) is "El Caganer," a little guy going to the bathroom (caca or caga means "poop"). He's usually hidden in back, behind the cows or horses, but a Catalan crèche wouldn't be complete without him. Dating to the 12th century, the caganer has traditionally been a farmer, who, of course, fertilizes the earth. Over the years his names have included* home que caga *("the pooping man") and* home que fa les seves feines *(roughly, "the man who does his own thing"). If you're in Barcelona just before Christmas, check out the rows upon rows of* caganers *for sale in the cathedral square,* Plaça de la Seu.

The Toy Museum in Figueres hosts Catalonia's only caganer *exhibit, from mid-December to mid-January every odd-numbered year, with displays of hundreds of little defecators, from antiques to the very latest. In the same cheerful yuletide vein is the Catalan Christmas tradition of the* tio, *a magical log that when smacked with sticks by household youth, "poops" gifts for everyone.*

CAP DE CREUS

Land meets sea in a powerful crashing of waves upon rocks at stunning Cap de Creus, the easternmost point of Spain. A lighthouse sits high above the craggy coast, and sheer cliffs give way to rocky coves. The waters around Cap de Creus are home to a diverse marine life, and in 1998 this area became the **Parc Natural Cap de Creus,** which has the distinction of being the first "marine-terrestrial" natural park in Catalonia. Hiking trails crisscross the surrounding countryside, and two visitor centers provide maps and guides to get started. The park's **Cadaqués office** is just outside town on the way to Port Lligat (tel. 972/159111; open June–Sept., daily 10–4; Oct.–May, weekends 10–4). The headquarters and **main visitor center** (tel. 972/193191; open June–Sept., weekdays 10–2 and 4–7, weekends 10–1 and 4–8; Oct.–May, weekends 10–2 and 3–6) is just downhill from the Monestir de Sant Pere de Rodes (*see below*).

Cap de Creus is about 9 km (6 mi) northeast of Cadaqués, a 10-minute drive by car through wild, rocky fields. You can also walk from Cadaqués along the Camí de Creus; the Cadaqués tourist office has info on this trail.

WHERE TO SLEEP AND EAT • The homey **Bar Restaurant Cap de Creus** (Carretera Cap de Creus s/n, tel. 972/199005, closed Fri. in winter) sits on a hill just above the cliffs; kick back on the terrace and bask in the jaw-dropping views of the craggy coast and pounding waves. The menu is quite a mix, including Catalan and Indian fare. Upstairs, there are three furnished, fully equipped **apartments,** a good deal if you split the cost: nightly prices range from 8,000 ptas. in low season to 12,000 ptas. in summer.

PARC NATURAL AIGUAMOLLS DE L'EMPORDÀ

Stretching between the Rivers Mua and Fluvià, just south of Cap de Creus, these marshy wetlands are home to more than 300 aquatic bird species, including purple herons, kingfishers, and white storks. The best time to visit is in the spring, when migrating water birds, unable to cross the Pyrenees because of powerful northern winds (*tramuntana*), arrive in droves. Walking trails invite leisurely strolls among salt marshes, lagoons (*aiguamolls* translates roughly as "swamps"), and enclosed meadows (*closes* in Catalan), spacious fields encircled by poplars, elms, and willows.

The park's **visitor center** (tel. 972/454222; open Apr.–Sept., daily 9:30–2 and 4:30–7; Oct.–Mar., daily 9:30–2 and 3:30–6:30) is near El Cortalet, between Castelló d'Empúries and Sant Pere Pescador, and is well signposted from the road. The park itself is open during daylight hours.

Sarfa buses stop at **Sant Pere Pescador** (7 km/4 mi south of the park) and **Castelló d'Empúries** (5 km/3 mi north). It's fairly easy to walk from either place, but you might want to call the park office for tips and details. The **train** from Barcelona to Port Bou stops at Figueres and several other towns in the vicinity, including Camallera and Sant Miquel de Fluvià.

MONESTIR DE SANT PERE DE RODES

St. Peter's Monastery is a short drive or a long, scenic hike off a small road just west of the fishing village of El Port de la Selva. Massive and beautifully preserved, the building sits high on a hill, surrounded by rocky plains. The views from up here are spectacular, with rugged hillsides swooping grandly below, and Cap de Creus in the distance. The monastery was built between the 10th and 12th centuries, and various sections were added through the 18th century, resulting in a giant amalgam of soaring arches, carved stone pillars, and dizzying spiral staircases. A highlight is the **Romanesque church,** built in the late 10th and early 11th centuries, with a massive basilica and crypt and a lovely cloister. Above the monastery are the ruins of the **Castell de Sant Salvador,** to which you can walk for more great views. Sarfa buses go to El Port de la Selva, and you can walk from there; the road is quite safe, and as you ascend into the hills, there are great views 'round every bend. *7 km (4 mi) west of El Port de la Selva, then 10-minute walk from parking lot. Tel. 972/387559. Admission 300 ptas.; parking 200 ptas. Open June–Sept., Tues.–Sun. 10–7:40, Oct.–May, Tues.–Sun. 10–5:10.*

Ask the El Port de la Selva **tourist office** (C. Mar 1, tel. 972/387025; open May 15–Sept, Mon.–Sat. 10–1 and 4–8, Sun. 10–1) for the hiking guide detailing five itineraries through the surrounding area. If the office is closed, head upstairs to the friendly **ajuntament** (town hall; open Mon.–Wed. and Fri. 8–3, Thurs. 8–3 and 5–7; Sat. 9–1).

L'ESCALA

L'Escala is a small beach resort with waterfront cafés and a crowded but attractive little beach. As Costa Brava resorts go, it's much less frenetic and more pleasant than its counterparts farther south. Just as important to anquity buffs, however, L'Escala is only 1½ km (1 mi) from the Greco-Roman ruins of Empúries (*see below*), and has some good affordable lodgings.

BASICS • The **tourist office** (Plaça de les Escoles 1, tel. 972/770603; open June–Oct., Mon.–Sat. 9–8:30, Sun. 10–1; Nov.–May, weekdays 9–1 and 4–7, Sat. 10–1 and 4–7, Sun. 10–1) doubles as the visitor center for the ruins and is a good place to stock up on maps. **El Carrilet** (Barcelona office: tel. 93/7654784), a little tourist train, goes to the ruins from various points in L'Escala. It runs from May to October: daily 10–8 in May–June and September–October, 10 AM–midnight in July and August. The tourist office has copies of the schedule.

Sarfa buses run four to five times daily from **Figueres** and L'Escala (1 hr; en route to Sant Feliu de Guixols). Two daily buses connect L'Escala with **Girona** (1 hr) and **Barcelona** (2 hrs). Call the tourist office for details.

WHERE TO SLEEP AND EAT • **Pensió Torrent** (C. Riera 28, tel. 972/770278, cash only), just behind the town hall, has tidy doubles for 4,500 ptas. **Hostal Poch** (C. Grácia 10, tel. 972/770092), near the water, has basic, clean doubles for 5,000 ptas., breakfast included.

Anchoas (anchovies) are the much-heralded local food specialty; the Greeks of nearby Empúries actually introduced the practice of salting them. To eat on the cheap, hunt around any street branching off the main waterfront, and you'll find some amiable spots with set menus for less than 1,200 ptas. **Restaurant-Pizzeria Capri** (Avda. Montgó 4, no phone, closed Oct.–Feb.) serves a weekday menú for 1,000 ptas., but only between 1 and 2:30; after that, it's 2,300 ptas. **El Llagut** (C. de la Torre 71, tel. 972/771016) serves a simple but filling menú for 975 ptas., though the price often goes up in July and August. It includes *torrada de anchoas de L'Escala* (toasted bread with L'Escala anchovies). **Phenicia** (Passeig Marítim 16, tel. 972/772223), near the water, usually offers a good daytime menu for 1,000 ptas. **Pub Byblos** (C. Torre 58, tel. 972/772043) is a cozy spot for a drink, and it's open until 3 AM.

EMPÚRIES

Empúries was one of the first settlements on the Iberian Peninsula. The Greeks set up a trading colony here in 600 BC, hoping to tap the wealthy Iberian market. They named the peninsula for its dwellers along

NOT JUST A BORDER TOWN

Port Bou's fate seems to have been sealed back in 1898, when the train station was built. Since then, every international train rumbling through has had to make a pit stop here—just 3 km/2 mi from France—to change to Spain's wider-gauge railway system. Although it does have all the usual trappings of a port town (cafeteria waiting rooms, souvenir shops), the scene changes if you venture beyond them. Fishing boats nose onto its small beach, and you can laze away the afternoon at one of the inviting outdoor cafés and restaurants overlooking the water.

Stopping in Port Bou also gives you the chance to see an unusual and affecting monument, a memorial to German philosopher Walter Benjamin. Born in Berlin in 1892, Benjamin, a longtime anti-Nazi, fled when Hitler came into power and went into exile in Paris. In 1940, when France fell to Hitler, he escaped again, this time into Spain, with the eventual goal of reaching the United States. Crossing the border at Port Bou, he was captured, and he committed suicide rather than surrender to the Germans. Benjamin is buried in the Port Bou cemetery, which shares a hilltop on the outskirts of town with a memorial dedicated solely to him: Titled "Passages," it was built in 1995 to commemorate Benjamin and other European exiles from 1933 to 1945. Jointly financed by the German government and the Generalitat of Catalonia and designed by architect Dani Karavan, this is an astounding work of art. A heavy iron staircase burrows tunnel-like through the hillside toward the sea, and at the bottom a plate-glass window angled directly over the rocks and waves makes you feel, as you descend, that you could walk right into the depths. Engraved on the glass is a passage from Benjamin's philosophical writings: "It is more arduous to honor the nameless than the renowned. Historical construction is devoted to the memory of the nameless." As you're heading into Port Bou from the south, the memorial is just off the main road to the right; watch for the sign.

the Iberus (Ebro), and Empúries for its commercial value (*emporion* = "market"). Later, in 218 BC, at the beginning of the Second Punic War, the Romans arrived at Empúries to begin *their* Iberian conquest. The vast **ruins** extend from an area near the shore, where most of the Greek city once stood, to the even larger Roman site farther inland. Only 25% of the remains have been excavated, but there's more than enough to see, and multilingual signs are posted throughout. The Greek ruins range from massive fortified walls to the crumbling remains of a small market built around a cistern. The spectacular Hellenistic mosaic dating from 200 BC was once the floor of someone's living room. The Roman city also has beautiful mosaics and the remains of a huge forum, the political and economic heart of the city.

On display at the **museum,** at the upper edge of the Greek city, are excavated objects, including some well-preserved drinking vessels. Video monitors show the ongoing excavation activities live; you can even reposition the cameras and zoom in and out for a better good look at the site and its layout. *Admission 400 ptas. Open June–Sept., daily 10–8; Oct.–May, daily 10–6.*

GIRONA

The lively provincial capital of Girona, 35 km (22 mi) inland from the Costa Brava, boasts a spectacular walled medieval quarter perched on a hill above the city—prime exploring territory, with narrow cobbled alleyways, ancient balconied houses, old stairways, and shady little *plaças*. Clinging to the banks of the River Onyar, as it meanders through the center of town, is a long row of picturesque pastel-color houses, the Cases de l'Onyar, once attached to the medieval city walls.

Historically, Girona has seen it all, at least by Spanish standards. The Romans settled here, and called the town Gerunda; later, the Moors loitered; and a vibrant Jewish community flourished for more than six centuries. Girona's Call, the medieval Jewish quarter, remains one of the best-preserved ghettos in Spain. Rambla de la Llibertat, running along the river, is the city's grand promenade, where locals take their daily paseo down a bustling strip of shops and restaurants.

BASICS

VISITOR INFORMATION
The **tourist office** (Rambla de la Llibertat 1, tel. 972/226575; open July–Aug., Mon.–Sat. 8–8, Sun. 9–2; Sept.–June, weekdays 8–8, Sat. 8–2 and 4–8, Sun. 9–2) has loads of city info and a useful map.

CURRENCY EXCHANGE
Most of Girona's **banks** are on Gran Vía de Jaume I and Carrer Nou. If you need cash after hours in the summer, head to the **train station,** where a bank is open weekdays 8:30–2 and 3–8:30. Another bank in the **bus station** is open every day but Sunday in July and August only, 8–11 and 4–8. Otherwise, head to the department store **Hypercor** (Carretera Barcelona 100–110), where a bank stays open Monday–Saturday 10–10.

CYBERSPACE
Frangipane Internet Café (C. Bastiments 7, tel. 972/239538) charges 600 ptas. an hour. Smaller but more centrally located is **La Teranyena** (C. Peralta 2, tel. 972/416151), with similar prices.

EMERGENCIES
Hospital Trueta (Avda. de Francia 60, tel. 972/202700) has a 24-hour ER. **Police:** 092.

ENGLISH-LANGUAGE BOOKS
Girona Books (C. Rutlla 22, tel. 972/224612) has a small but varied selection.

LAUNDRY
Despite the name, you can drop your clothes at **Laso Self-Service** (C. Balmes 6, tel. 972/205125) and pay by the piece: 200 ptas. to have a shirt or blouse washed and dried, 300 ptas. for a pair of pants.

MAIL
The main **post office** (Avda. Ramón Folch 1, tel. 972/222111) seems to handle a lot more mail in the winter. From June to September it's open weekdays 8:30–2, Saturday 9–2; from October to May, weekdays 8–8:30 and Saturday 9–2.

COMING AND GOING

Girona is a transportation hub—trains and buses head to Barcelona, the Costa Brava, and inland Catalonia. The **train station** (tel. 872/207093) is near Plaça Espanya, just south of the new part of town. There are hourly trains to **Barcelona** (1¼ hrs, 900 ptas.) and **Figueres** (½ hr, 330 ptas). The **bus station** (tel. 972/212319) is behind the train station; buses leave often for **Barcelona, Olot,** and various towns on the Costa Brava. Girona's **airport** (tel. 972/186600), 12 km (9 mi) south of town, handles mostly tours and charter flights to the Costa Brava.

WHERE TO SLEEP

Girona has lots of budget lodgings, many in the old town, particularly on and around Carrer Ciutadans. The friendly **Pensión Viladomat** (C. Ciutadans 5, tel. 972/203176, cash only) has ample, clean doubles for 3,400 ptas. **Pensión Barnet** (C. Santa Clara 16, tel. 972/200033, cash only), across the river from the old town, has basic, musty rooms without bath for 3,400 ptas. **Pensión Coll** (C. Hortes 24, tel. 972/203086), just north of Pensión Barnet, has simple doubles for 4,000 ptas. South of Plaça Catalunya on the west side of the river, the **Hotel Condal** (C. Joan Maragall 10, tel. 972/204461) is a step up in price, but if you're tired of roughing it, a spic-and-span double with a clean bathroom is well worth the 6,500 (shower) or 7,000 ptas. (bathtub). North of here, at **Hotel Peninsular** (C. Nou 3, tel. 972/203800), sleep cheap by opting for one of the bland but clean doubles with shared bath for 4,000 ptas. (with bath 7,000 ptas.). Near the cathedral, **Apartaments Històric Barri Vell** (C. Bell Mirall 4, tel. 972/223583) rents furnished apartments, with one or two bedrooms, bathroom, kitchen, and living room, for 7,000 ptas. a night.

WHERE TO EAT

Girona abounds with atmospheric restaurants and hip cafés and bars—especially outdoors on the **Rambla de la Llibertat,** which everyone cruises at least once daily. Just east of the Rambla is the bustling **Plaça del Vi,** where you can sip a glass of *vi* (wine) and soak up the old-town ambience. The popular **La Crêperie Bretonne** (Cort Reial 14, tel. 972/218120) serves decadent sweet and savory crepes for 500–700 ptas. The always-packed **Restaurante Boira** (Plaça. de la Independencia, tel. 972/203096) has several excellent Catalan set menus priced between 1,200 and 1,900 ptas. **La Polenta** (Cort Reial 6, tel. 972/209374) serves top-notch vegetarian fare at nice prices: 600–1,200 ptas.

WORTH SEEING

Most of Girona's sights and museums are in and around the old quarter, an easy walk from the city center and Rambla de la Llibertat. Note that, aside from the cathedral, most sights are closed on Monday.

JEWISH QUARTER

The warren of narrow streets and alleyways around Carrer de la Força was Girona's Jewish community, the Call, for more than 600 years. In the 10th century Jews were a prosperous and influential sector of Girona society, but this changed over the 11th and 12th centuries, when the area became the target of racist attacks and eventually a ghetto, where the Jews were virtually imprisoned—confined within neighborhood limits, banned from the rest of the city. This continued until 1492, when all Jews were expelled from Spain. Before or after you explore the cramped quarter, stop into the **Centre Bonastruc ça Porta** (just off Carrer de la Força, tel. 972/216761; admission 200 ptas.; open July–Aug., Tues.–Sat. 10–8, Sun. 10–3; Sept.–June, Tues.–Sat. 10–6, Sun. 10–3), which mounts changing exhibitions on the history of Jews in Girona and Spain, and has a pleasant little café.

CATHEDRAL

Looming majestically over the old quarter, Girona's cathedral is a true amalgam of architectural styles. The Romanesque cloister and tower are the only parts remaining from the original 11th-century building, and the cathedral was continually rebuilt and expanded through the 18th century. The Gothic nave, from the 15th and 16th centuries, is the largest in the world; also impressive are the 14th-century silver altarpiece and the Gothic tombs. The adjoining **Museu Capitular** (admission 500 ptas.; open July–Aug., Tues.–Sat. 10–2 and 4–7, Sun. 10–2; Sept.—June, Tues.–Sat. 10–2 and 4–6, Sun. 10–2) is a trove of religious artifacts, including medieval gold pieces, a 10th-century Mozarabic manuscript of a commentary by the monk Beatus, and an 11th-century tapestry depicting the Creation. Admission to the museum also gets you into the lovely cloister.

ESGLESIA DE SANT FELIU

This large city church gives an interesting visual overview of the transition between the Romanesque and Gothic styles. The 13th-century Romanesque interior is topped by a grand Gothic nave, and a Baroque tower looms over the western facade. The highlight is the Catalan Gothic statue of Crist Jacent

(Recumbent Christ). Hours vary, but the church generally follows the cathedral's hours, and is always open for mass: Monday to Saturday at 11 AM and 7:30 PM, Sunday at 10 AM and noon.

BANYS ARABS

The Arab baths were built in the 12th century, taking their inspiration from the Romans' public bathhouses. The Romanesque building (with Moorish elements) contains three graceful rooms, each with its own pool; most notable is the *frigidarium* (cold-water room), whose elegant columns support a central dome. *C. Ferran el Catòlic s/n, two blocks from Esglesia de Sant Feliu. Admission 200 ptas. Open July–Aug., Tues.–Sat. 10–7, Sun. 10–2; Sept.–June, Tues.–Sat. 10–2, Sun. 10–2.*

MONESTIR DE SANT PERE DE GALLIGANTS

This impressive Romanesque Benedictine monastery near the baths now houses a **Museu Arqueològic** with a large collection of finds from Girona excavations, including beautiful Hebrew tombstones. *Plaça de Santa Llúcia s/n, tel. 972/202632. Admission 300 ptas. Open July–Aug., Tues.–Sat. 10:30–1:30 and 4–7, Sun. 10–2; Sept.–June, Tues.–Sat. 10–2 and 4–6, Sun. 10–2.*

MUSEU D'ART

Housed in the Palau Episcopal (Bishop's Palace) near the cathedral, Girona's art museum has a wide-ranging collection of Romanesque, Gothic, and modern art. *Pujada de la Catedral 12, tel. 972/203834. Admission 300 ptas. Open July–Aug., Tues.–Sat. 10–7, Sun. 10–2; Sept.–June, Tues.–Sat. 10–6, Sun. 10–2.*

AFTER DARK

When you're ready to hit the bars, try **La Terra** (C. Ballesteries 23, no phone), overlooking the river, where local twentysomethings converge on weekends. **Café Bistrot** (Pujada Sant Domènec 4, tel. 972/218803) serves a range of crepes and salads and is a great place to spend the evening, either at an outside table or in the dark and classy interior.

In July and August, outdoor bars called *carpas* ("awnings") set up outdoor terraces with tent roofs in the **Parc La Devesa.** The popular **Bar Platea** (C. Real de Font Clara s/n, tel. 972/227288) offers live music on Wednesday night and what they call *café teatro* (short plays, mime, and live music) on Thursday night. Another area with happening nightlife is **Pedret,** on the *carretera* heading out of town toward Palamós: just as you leave Girona, look for a clump of happening bars to your right.

NEAR GIRONA

BESALÚ

About 50 km (31 mi) north of Girona lies the medieval hamlet of Besalú, a captivating sight: a spectacular fortified bridge spans the River Fluvia at the town entrance, beyond which church towers rise up amid beautifully preserved stone houses. A series of counts, starting with Wilfred the Hairy's nephew in 927, made Besalú their base, and it served as the capital of the region until power was transferred to Barcelona at the beginning of the 12th century. Besalú's highlights are its 12th-century **Jewish baths** (*migwe*) and its two Romanesque churches, **Sant Pere** and **Sant Vincenç.** The gracefully arcaded **Plaça Major** is strewn with outdoor cafés and restaurants.

BASICS

The **tourist office** (Plaça de la Llibertat 1, tel. 972/591240; open daily 10–2 and 4–7) conducts guided English-language tours of the church of Sant Pere at 11, 1, 5, and 6:30. They can also arrange tours of the whole town, including the Jewish baths and Sant Vincenç, but for this you need to phone 2–3 days in advance.

WHERE TO SLEEP AND EAT

Hostal Marià (Plaça Llibertat 15, tel. 972/590106, cash only), housed in an old convent, has a lovely courtyard with vines crawling up the walls. Fully modernized double rooms go for 4,500 ptas. a night. **Habitacions Venéncia** (C. Major 8, tel. 972/591257) has basic, clean doubles for 4,500 ptas.

TREE-HOUSE MAZE

Roughly 3 km (2 mi) outside Besalú, visible off the main road to Olot, is a massive tree house—a tree manse, really—that looks like a realization of every kid's fantasy. Meticulously built of planks and boards held together by rope and nails, it occupies a series of towering trees. Up close, you'll see that it's actually a giant labyrinth, a series of tunnels snaking up, around, and through the trees. A hand-painted sign at the entrance warns: "Una persona normal entra en una casa por la puerta. Aquí para subir arriba del arbol, hay que pasar por el laberinto. Es bonito saber jugar" *("A person normally enters a house through its front door. Here, to get to the top, you need to go through the labyrinth. It's good to know how to play"). Join the other bewildered explorers and try to reach the top: it's much harder than it looks. Devilish signs goad and coax you at every dead end; in one such infuriating spot, a rocking chair is accompanied by the invitation,* "Si no sabeu sortir, podeu seure aqui" *("If you don't know how to get out, you can sit here"); in another,* "Pasiencia. No desperar. Ay que bolber a empezar" *("Patience. Don't despair. You need to start again").*

The structure was built by a local eccentric, who adds on to it every few months, so the maze changes—and gets harder. It is said he lives up here, staying out of sight by day and returning when his visitors have gone. Entrance is free, though you're welcome to make a donation in the box by the entrance.

Bar Manolo is a simple café-bar with outdoor tables on Plaça Sant Pere and cheap but filling *platos combinados* (combo platters) for 600 ptas. **Restaurant Oliveras** (C. Pau Claris 13, tel. 972/590392), on the outskirts of town, serves tasty Catalan cuisine including *fideuàda,* a Catalan noodle-based paella. A full meal here will set you back 2,000–2,500 ptas.

OLOT AND THE GARROTXA

The amiable, midsize city of Olot is a provincial capital with a popular *rambla* (Passeig d'en Blay), busy shopping streets, and a pleasant Plaça Major dotted with outdoor cafés. Olot's other name is La Ville des Volcans (the City of Volcanoes), as it sits in the middle of the Garrotxa Volcanic Zone (*see below*), a nature park with more than 30 extinct volcanic cones and craters. The park's stunning and varied landscapes, from sheer cliffs to lush valleys, inspired the highly respected Olot School of landscape painters, founded in the 1800s by Joaquim Vayreda. Many of the resulting works are now on display at Olot's excellent **Museu Comarcal de la Garrotxa** (C. de l'Hospici 8, tel. 972/279130; admission 300 ptas.; open Tues.–Sat. 11–2 and 4–7).

Catalonia has few *plaças de toros* (bullrings), as many Catalans feel bullfighting is best left to other, less civilized, parts of Spain. Of them, Olot has the oldest **bullring** in Catalonia, where you can see a bullfight for as little as 3,500 ptas. for a seat *sol* (in the sun) or 4,000 ptas. for a seat *sombra* (in the shade). Ask the tourist office for a schedule.

With buses to Camprodon, in the Pyrenees, Olot is one of several possible jumping-off points to the mountains.

BASICS

The **tourist office** (C. del Bisbe Lorenzana 15, tel. 972/260141; open July–Sept., Mon.–Sat. 9–2 and 4–7, Sun. 11–2; Oct.–June, weekdays 9–2 and 4–7, Sat. 9–2, Sun. 11–2) has loads of info on the town and the Garrotxa region. There's also a well-stocked **Volcanic Zone park office** here, called the Casal dels Volcans (Avda. de Santa Coloma, tel. 972/266202); for details *see* Around Olot, *below.*

The **bus station** (tel. 972/260141) is across the street from the tourist office. **Teisa buses** (tel. 972/260196) travel daily to **Barcelona** (2 hrs, 1,855 ptas.), **Besalú** (½ hr, 295 ptas.), **Girona** (1 hr 20 min, 685 ptas.), **Sant Joan de les Abadesses** (½ hr, 340 ptas.) and on to **Ripoll** (50 min, 500 ptas.) and **Camprodon** (1½ hrs, 780 ptas.).

WHERE TO SLEEP AND EAT

Hostal La Garrotxa (Plaça Mora 3, tel. 972/261612, cash only) has clean, if slightly musty, doubles for 3,500 ptas. a night. **Hostal Stop** (C. San Pedro Mártir 29, tel. 972/261048, cash only) is a dingy hostel adjoining an equally dingy bar, but if you're counting your pesetas and plan to spend most of your time outside, the price is right at 3,000 ptas. for a double with a shower in the room. The friendly **Hostal Residencia Sant Bernat,** on a hill above town (Carretera de les Feixes, tel. 972/261919), has clean doubles with shower for 3,500 ptas. The restaurant serves a menú del día for 950 ptas.

Olot has a good selection of affordable restaurants and lively bars, none of which take credit cards. For a cheap meal, there's no place quite like the local favorite **Can Guix** (C. Mulleras 3, tel. 972/261040), where you can get *ous ferrats* (fried eggs) for 125 ptas., *pollastre* (chicken) for 250 ptas., *ensalada verde* (green salad) for 130 ptas., and *helado de crocanti* (ice cream topped with sweet, crunchy nuts) for 300 ptas. Cozy **El Cornet** (Serra Ginesta 17, tel. 972/269758, closed Tues., no dinner Mon.) serves interesting pastas, including *espagetti a la carbonara* (775 ptas.) or *espagettis negres amb calamares* (black spaghetti with squid, 950 ptas.). **Restaurant Ramon** (Plaça Clarà 10, tel. 972/261001), overlooking the lovely Plaça Clarà, serves an excellent set Catalan menu for 1,075 ptas. during the week, slightly more on weekends. The two-story **Cafeteria 1900** (C. Sant Rafel 18, tel. 972/270969) is a snazzy café with old-fashioned stone walls and wood beams but a contemporary air. The simple, tasty menu includes a *bikini danés* (Danish bikini, a toasted bread sandwich with ham and brie) and *pa de pages torrat amb tomaquet* (toasted country bread with tomato, 450 ptas.); top it off with a *carajillo* (coffee with whiskey, 225 ptas.), a beloved Spanish way to end a meal. **El Farrolet** (C. Major, no phone), just off the Plaça Major, has a line out the door every night. Why? It sells the biggest, juiciest frankfurters in town, for 400–600 ptas. (Go figure.) **Cafe Europa** (Plaça Major s/n, tel. 972/273113) has outdoor tables on the square, perfect for watching the world go by. A few doors down is Olot's most happening nightspot, **Bar Cocodrilo** (C. Sant Roc 5, tel. 972/263124), hung with works by local artists and furnished with small, marble café tables. The bar starts filling up around 9 PM and stays that way until closing time, 2 AM Thursday–Saturday and midnight the rest of the week.

AROUND OLOT

PARQUE NATURAL DE LA ZONA VOLCÁNICA DE LA GARROTXA

The Garrotxa Volcanic Zone Nature Park lies along the Serralada Transversal, a mountain range extending from the Pyrenees to the peaks of Montseny, north of Barcelona. Within the park, 30 volcanic cones and craters are surrounded by remarkably lush vegetation: evergreen forests, oak groves, and shaded slopes of beech trees. Badgers, shrews, otters, and even wild boar roam the woods, while lizards and vipers hide out in the crevices of volcanic rocks. Numerous trails crisscross the park, including one leading up to the rim of **Volcá Santa Margarida,** one of the park's largest. More than a dozen small

Romanesque churches lie within park boundaries as well, including Sant Miquel del Mont, in the eastern reaches, and the Benedictine monastery of Sant Joan les Fonts, in the north. The lovely, well-preserved medieval village of **Santa Pau,** near the center of the park, is also worth a visit as you're trekking around. The village centers on an arcaded Plaça Major, where, of course, you can linger outdoors at one of several restaurants.

Before exploring the park, stop by the **Casal dels Volcans** in Olot (Volcanic Park information office; Avda. de Santa Coloma, tel. 972/266202; open July–Sept., weekdays 9–2 and 5–7, Sat. 10–2 and 5–7, Sun. 10–2; Oct.–June, weekdays 9–2 and 4–6, Sat. 10–2 and 4–6, Sun. 10–2) to stock up on trail maps and guides. Downstairs from the office is a **museum** (admission 300 ptas.; open same hrs) with exhibits on park history.

CASTELLFOLLIT DE LA ROCA

From a distance, this village is a stunning sight—it sits atop a basalt cliff, with sheer drops to the water from the very edges of houses. Thanks to the topography, a stroll through town is better than a roller-coaster ride. Make your way to the **church** at the tip of the precipice for a heady view of the River Fluvià, far below. Castellfollit is one of the main northern gateways to the Volcanic Zone, so several excellent **trails** start here.

VIC

Many consider Vic one of the most quintessentially Catalan towns, partly because the locals have a particularly strong Catalan pride, and partly because it's near the Ripoll area, cradle of Catalan history. It's worth a stop for its enormous, spectacular **Plaça Major,** where you can sit outdoors and feast *al aire libre* (al fresco) on traditional Catalan sausages: *butifarra* and *fuet* are the town specialties.

THE PYRENEES

"Oh Pirineo! En tus profundas simas, hijo de la llanura, preso me sentí. Con la mirada al alto cielo pido achura y viento."

"O Pyrenees! In your deep chasms, as a son of the plain, I feel captured. I look at the sky above, and ask for space and wind."

—Joan Maragall (1860–1911), Catalan poet

Hovering majestically over northern Spain, the spectacular Pyrenees have long been a formidable barrier between the Iberian Peninsula and the rest of Europe. Soaring peaks, verdant valleys, and wild rivers make the range paradise for outdoorsmen—trekking and skiing trails are everywhere. Baqueira Beret, in the spectacular Vall d'Aran (Aran Valley), is one of the premiere ski resorts in Spain; south of here is the Parc Nacional d'Aiguestortes i Estany de Sant Maurici, Catalonia's only national park, where you can hike to glacier lakes through untouched wilderness and meet not another soul along the way. The Pyrenees' Romanesque churches, sitting quietly in villages and occasionally out in the countryside, are some of the finest in Catalonia. Head off the main roads, and you'll stumble upon ancient villages that have lived in semi-isolation for years, such as the medieval hamlet of Beget, near Camprodon, with cobbled streets and centuries-old stone houses. Push open the heavy doors of Beget's parish church and you're in the dark quiet of another era.

THE ORIENTAL PYRENEES

If you have just a day or two to see the Pyrenees from Barcelona, aim toward the Oriental Pyrenees. The Vall de Camprodon is the easternmost valley, with the lively mountain town of Camprodon and numerous villages. Northwest of here is the Vallter ski resort, popular with Barcelonans.

CAMPRODON AND THE VALL DE CAMPRODON

This is where you really start to feel you're in the mountains: The air is crisp, the peaks rise up in all directions, and the streets are dotted with ski and mountaineering shops. Camprodon also has a wealthy, alpine-holiday air about it, particularly along the broad promenade of **Passeig Maristany,** where many well-to-do Catalans keep elegant mountain villas. Camprodon's handsome centerpiece is the 12th-century bridge **Pont Nou,** which spans the River Ter in the middle of town.

A number of fetching mountain villages dot the peaks and valleys north of Camprodon. Llanars sits on the River Ter, just a few kilometers north of Camprodon; its pretty 12th-century Romanesque church has a wood relief depicting the martyrdom of St. Stephen. Farther along the same road, 11 km (7 mi) north of Camprodon, is Setcases, popular with skiers heading to the nearby Vallter ski resort (tel. 972/136075), with 12 alpine trails built into a glacier mountain bowl. Setcases has a 12th-century church that has been rebuilt several times and holds an impressive Baroque altar. Molló, on the River Ritort 8 km (5 mi) northeast of Camprodon, has a lovely Romanesque church with an eye-catching bell tower and a notable arched portal. It's easiest to explore these sites by car, but a few buses crawl around the area, including a regular bus between Ripoll, Sant Joan de les Abadesses, and Camprodon. Buses also run (usually once a day, sometimes more often in summer) between Camprodon and Llanars, Setcases, and Molló. There are dozens of places to hike, either between the towns or on special mountain trails—ask the Camprodon tourist office about trail lengths, levels of difficulty, and conditions

BASICS

Camprodon's **tourist office** (Plaça Espanya 1, tel. 972/740010; open June–Sept., Mon.–Sat. 10–2 and 4–8, Sun. 10–2; in Aug. often open Sun. 4–7 as well; Oct.–May, weekdays 10–2 and 4–7, Sat. 10–2 and 4–8, Sun. 10–2) has loads of maps and information on all nearby towns, and listings of places to stay. There's a second **tourist office** (Carretera Comarcal 151, tel. 972/740936; open Mon. 10–2, Thurs.–Fri. 10–2 and 4–7, Sat. 10–2 and 4–8, Sun. 10–2) off the road leading into town.

Teisa buses (tel. 972/204868) arrive once a day from **Barcelona** (2 hrs, 1,100 ptas.), departing from Carrer Pau Claris 116, at the corner of Carrer Consell de Cent. Teisa also runs several daily buses from the train station in **Ripoll** (40 min, 645 ptas.).

WHERE TO SLEEP

Camprodon has but a few cheap lodgings. **Hostal Can Ganansi** (C. Josep Morer 9, tel. 972/740134) has varying prices throughout the year: Doubles with bath are 6,000 ptas. from September to June; they're only open on weekends from November to June. In July and August they require *medio pensión* (half board; dinner and one other meal) for 5,500–6,000 ptas. *per person.* **Hostal Els Avets** (Carretera de Molló 3, tel. 972/740071), on the outskirts of town on the way to Molló, has doubles for 7,000 ptas.

BEGET

Beget is nestled so deeply in a valley that you don't see it until you're almost there. When you do catch a glimpse, it's an enchanting sight: Tiny Beget looks just as it did centuries ago, with narrow cobbled streets, stone houses, and sturdy little bridges. An ancient stillness permeates the interior of the lovely 12th-century **Romanesque church,** where Beget's 30 people still gather for Sunday mass. The church's masterpiece is its 6½-ft Majestat, a carved-wood figure of Christ in a full-length tunic, arms outstretched. If the church is locked, stop by the nearby house at no. 15, where a villager keeps the key and sells an eccentric little collection of Beget souvenirs. The **Plaça Major** is a small, sandy square with a stone house at one end, in which the town hall and post office conduct their business.

Beget lies 17 km (11 mi) east of Camprodon on a very narrow paved road of hairpin turns and spectacular mountain terrain. The drive may be slow going, because the road really only fits one car, so you and passing cars have to tiptoe past each other. On the way here, you'll pass **Rocabruna,** another fetching little town, but not nearly as intact as Beget due to Civil War damage.

WHERE TO SLEEP AND EAT

El Forn (C. Josep Duñach En Felicia 9, tel. 972/741230) has a wooden terrace overlooking the lush valley, bridges and all. Feast on *cuina catalana* (Catalan cuisine) to the sounds of the gurgling stream—try the succulent chicken with plums and pine nuts (1,100 ptas.). Upstairs, you can rent a double room for

QUICK THINKING

Every Catalan schoolkid is taught the legend behind the Catalan flag: as Wilfred the Hairy lay mortally wounded after a valiant 9th-century battle to defend Catalan soil against Norman invasion, it occurred to him that it would be highly undesirable—lame, in present-day parlance—to die for a land that didn't even have a flag. He asked his uncle to help him dip his fingers into his blood, then ran his fingers along his golden shield, and thus the four bands of red on a yellow background.

5,000 ptas. *per person* per night, including breakfast. **Hostal-Restaurante Can Joanic** (C. Vell Aire 1, tel. 972/741241, closed Tues.), near the main town entrance, has rooms for 2,500 ptas. *per person,* including breakfast.

SANT JOAN DE LES ABADESSES

Eight kilometers (5 mi) south of Camprodon is Sant Joan de les Abadesses, named after the daughter of the 9th-century Guifré el Pilós (Wilfred the Hairy). One of the original counts of Barcelona, Wilfred was also one of the first, and most colorful, founders of Catalonia. Sant Joan is a pleasant place for a stroll, particularly through the elegant Plaça Major to the Gothic bridge over the River Ter. The beautiful 12th-century **monastery** holds a famed 13th-century wood sculpture called the *Santíssim Misteri,* depicting Christ's descent from the cross. The monastery is built on the site of the 9th-century convent in which Wilfred's daughter was abbess. The monastery **museum** displays religious statues and artifacts. *8 km (5 mi) south of Camprodon, or take bus from Ripoll to Sant Joan de les Abadesses. Admission 200 ptas. Hours vary; generally open June–Sept., daily 11–2 and 4–7; Oct.–May, daily 11–2.*

RIPOLL

The midsize working-class town of Ripoll is known as the Cradle of Catalonia, as it was here that Wilfred the Hairy staked his claim to what eventually became the Autonomous Community of Catalonia. Ripoll's highlight is the 9th-century **Monestir de Santa Maria**—the stupendous facade of the church portal, considered one of Spain's greatest works of Romanesque art, bears a series of sculptures depicting the Creation and other Biblical scenes in glorious detail. You can also visit the beautiful **cloister** and adjoining **museum.** *Admission to museum and cloister 300 ptas. Open June–Sept., daily 10–1 and 3–7; Oct.–May, Tues.–Sun. 10–1 and occasionally 3–7.*

BASICS

The **tourist office** (Plaça del Abat Oliba, tel. 972/702351) is open Monday–Saturday 10–1 and 5–7.

Ripoll's bus station and train station are near each other, a short walk from the center of town. Daily **RENFE trains** (tel. 902/240202) serve **Barcelona** (2 hrs, 790 ptas.), **Ribes de Freser** (¼ hr, 175 ptas.), and **Puigcerdà** (1 hr, 410 ptas.). Daily **Tiesa buses** (tel. 972/740295; offices in Girona and Camprodon only) serve **Camprodon, Olot, Sant Joan des Abedesses,** and **Ribes de Freser.**

WHERE TO SLEEP AND EAT

You can see all of Ripoll in less than a day. If you decide to stay, try **Ca la Paula** (C. Berenguer 8, tel. 972/700011), where basic doubles with shared bath go for 5,000 ptas. **Hostal del Ripollès** (Plaça Nova 11, tel. 972/700215) has comfortable doubles for 7,000 ptas. and a popular restaurant, La Piazzeta, serving excellent regional specialties and Italian fare. *Xai del Ripollès al forn* is grilled lamb from the Ripollès region. The menú del día is 1,200 ptas.

RIBES DE FRESER AND NÚRIA

The village of Ribes de Freser, north of Ripoll, is where you can catch the *cremallera* (literally, "zipper"), a local train that heads into the mountains toward the sanctuary of Núria and the neighboring ski center and hotel. The journey is spectacular: The little train follows the rushing Freser River and then, quite suddenly, begins to scale steep mountainsides along stomach-churning switchbacks, from which you get beautiful views of the river and valley far below. The trip takes a little less than an hour and costs 2,200 ptas. round trip. The *cremallera* runs from 7:45 AM to 8:05 PM, though in the winter the last train is at 6:25 PM.

The **Vall de Núria** (Núria Valley) has long been visited by pilgrims. The **Santuari de la Mare de Deu de Núria** (Sanctuary of the Mother of God of Núria) had its beginnings in a visit by Sant Gil of Nîmes, who came here on retreat in the 7th century. Gil left behind a wooden statue of the Virgin Mary, which became an object of veneration, and eventually the patron saint, among local shepherds. The sanctuary, as it's called, basically consists of a parochial church (built in 1911), a hermitage (a small, ancient-looking mountain church, built in 1615 and refurbished over the years), and some exhibits on the life of Sant Gil. Frankly, the entire complex, which includes the sanctuary, a hotel, and a café, is drab and unattractive, a blocky, greyish structure. Pilgrims still come to visit the hermitage and exhibits, and the church holds daily mass for locals, but the devout are usually outnumbered by skiiers in winter, hikers in summer, and those people who just want to try the cremallera year-round. The festival of Sant Gil, on September 1, draws clergymen from all over the region; the festival of the Virgen de Núria, on September 8, draws pilgrims and others from the surrounding area to pay their respects to the Virgin. The small Núria **ski center** (tel. 972/730713) is geared toward beginners, with about 10 alpine trails; in summer there's great trekking, from light to strenuous, in the surrounding mountains and valleys. Get more information at the tourist office in **Ribes de Freser** (Plaça de l'Ajuntament 3, tel. 972/727728; open Tues.–Sat. 10–2 and 5–8, Sun. 11–1) or **Núria** (inside *cremallera* train station, tel. 972/732020; open June–Sept., daily 8:15–8; Oct.–May, daily 8:15–6).

Several daily **trains** connect Ribes de Freser with **Barcelona** (via Ripoll), and several daily **buses** connect Ribes de Freser with **Ripoll.** For details *see* Ripoll, *above.*

LA CERDANYA

The lush Cerdanya Valley, hemmed in by towering peaks on the north and south, has long shared a geo-cultural affinity with France. The border snakes its way through the middle of the valley, but you can hardly tell where Spain ends and France begins; the Cerdanya has always been an independent entity with customs of its own. Catalan is spoken on both sides of the border. As the locals say, it's not quite Spain, and it's not quite France; it's simply La Cerdanya. The only Pyrenean valley running east–west, the Cerdanya enjoys more sunlight than any other part of the range, and is thus a popular summer spot for hikers and mountain bikers. In winter, skiers flock to La Molina and Masella, the two big ski resorts.

PUIGCERDÀ

The hilltop hamlet of Puigcerdà may well be one of the prettiest border towns you'll ever come across, not surprising in light of its physical situation: the town perches above the lush union of the Rivers Segre and Querol (*puig* is Catalan for "hill"; *cerdà* comes from Cerdanya), with the Pyrenees looming over it like expectant parents and France just a few kilometers north. With its cluster of budget lodgings and proximity to ski resorts, the town is a busy stopover for skiers, hikers, and mountain bikers.

Founded in 1177, Puigcerdà has a rich history, but, sadly, most of its old buildings were destroyed in the Civil War. Left standing, fortunately, was the 115-ft **campanaria** (bell tower) in graceful Plaça Santa Maria. Nearby, on Passeig 10 d'Abril, is the church of **Sant Domènic,** built in 1291 and restored after the Civil War; inside is a series of Gothic paintings from 1362. Next door is the **convent** of Sant Domènic, which now houses a library and archive.

As in many small towns ravaged by the Civil War, Puigcerdà's aged roots are best reflected in the layout and design of its narrow streets and plaças. The well preserved **Plaça Cabrinetty** (near Plaça de l'Ajuntament) has beautiful balconies and porticoes.

BASICS

The **tourist office** (C. Querol, at Plaça de l'Ajuntament, tel. 972/880542; open June–Sept., daily 9–2 and 3:30–8:30; Oct.–May, weekdays 10–1 and 4–7, Sat. 10–1:30 and 4–7:30) can arm you with a colorful array of brochures and maps.

COMING AND GOING

Puigcerdà sits on a steep hill, at the bottom of which is the **train station** (tel. 972/880165). Gear up for some huffing and puffing if you decide to walk into town: Follow the long flights of stairs to the central Plaça de l'Ajuntament, steps from the tourist office. Several daily trains connect Puigcerdà with **Barcelona** (3 hrs), passing through **Vic** and **Ripoll** on the way; several others head 10 minutes across the border to La Tour de Querol, **France,** where you can catch trains to Toulouse and Paris.

Alsina-Graells buses (tel. 973/350020), based near Puigcerdà's train station, serve **Barcelona** (3 hrs, 1,835 ptas.) twice a day during the week and once a day on weekends. Sister Cerdanya town **La Seu d'Urgell** (1 hr, 625 ptas.) gets several daily vehicles. One bus departs for—and two buses arrive from—**Lleida** (4 hrs, 2,325 ptas.) each day.

WHERE TO SLEEP

Affordable lodging hovers in the center of town, northeast of Plaça de l'Ajuntament. **Pensió Campaner** (C. Major 39, tel. 972/881427, cash only), down the street from the bell tower, is one of the best deals around, with clean doubles (shared bath) for 4,000 ptas. Ask for a room with a balcony and you'll wake up to views of the Pyrenees. **Fonda Cerdanya** (C. Ramon Cosp 7, tel. 972/880010, cash only) has large, musty doubles for 5,500 ptas., though the lively *dueña* (owner) might cut you a better deal if you're a student. The large **Hostal Muntanya** (C. Coronel Molera 1, tel. 972/880202, cash only), just off Plaça Barcelona, has clean but spartan doubles for 6,000 ptas., including breakfast. **Hostal Alfonso** (C. de Espanya 5, tel. 972/880246, cash only) has tidy doubles for 6,000 ptas., and each room has a TV, which could make up for the garish yellow wallpaper. **Camping Stel** (Carretera de Llívia s/n, tel. 972/882361), 1 km (½ mi) outside town on the road toward Llívia, charges 3,750 ptas. for two adults, payable in cash only.

WHERE TO EAT

When hunger pangs hit, look no farther than the family-run **El Caliu** (C. Alfons I 1, tel. 972/140825), a lovely corner restaurant whose front doors open onto the Plaça de l'Ajuntament and, just beyond, the Pyrenees themselves. The 1,500-pta. menú del día features delicious grilled meats. Another good bet is **Bar Refugi** (C. Major 52, tel. 972/881601), en route to the lake in the north part of town, where locals converge for yummy tapas and a cheap, hearty menú (1,200 ptas.). On weekends satisfy your sweet tooth (or fast-food tooth) with *churros* from one of the *churrerias* on Plaça dels Herois—a quarter kilo of these fried loops costs 450 ptas.

AFTER DARK

To wind down at the end of the day, duck into **Cervesería Claude** (Plaça Cabrinetty 22, tel. 972/881615), a cozy bar housed in a former dry-goods store overlooking the lovely square. Downstairs, Claude pours drinks for a crowd of town regulars and vacationing Barcelonans; upstairs, there's an intimate nook for quieter moments.

OUTDOOR ACTIVITIES

La Molina ski center (tel. 972/892031), one of the largest in Catalonia with 27 alpine trails, is 15 km (9 mi) south of Puigcerdà. If you're new to skiing, the ski school can get you started. There's also a slew of hiking and biking options; ask the tourist office for a guide to local trails. La Molina is the penultimate stop on the train from Barcelona to Puigcerdà, and in winter several buses connect La Molina with Puigcerdà.

LLÍVIA

In 1659 the town of Llívia officially became a tiny Spanish enclave in France, a geographical oddity that has garnered a mention mainly in guidebooks ever since, Though the Spanish ceded 33 villages to France that year, Llívia, deemed a town, remained Spanish, and still sits just across the border, 6 km (4 mi) from Puigcerdà. If you fancy a hike, you can walk there; otherwise, hop on one of the buses in front of Puigcerdà's train station (twice daily on weekdays, once daily on weekends). Either way, Llívia makes a delightful day trip, if only to lose yourself in the town's medieval aura, which becomes increasingly more apparent and impressive the higher you go.

From the main road leading into town, walk up to Llívia's 15th-century **fortified church** (open daily 10–1 and 3–7 but often closed in winter) and adjoining Bernat de So Tower. The latter contains Llívia's **tourist office,** usually open weekday mornings in summer but prone to caprice; if it's closed, make your inquiries at the nearby **Municipal Museum** (C. dels Forns 12, tel. 972/896011; admission 150 ptas.; open Mon.–Sat. 10–1 and 3–6). This facility occupies what is thought to be the oldest pharmacy in Europe, founded in the early 15th century, so its impressive collection of Renaissance coffers, with portraits of saints, is joined by some ancient pharmaceutical implements. If you're in town in August or December, ask about Llívia's annual **music festival** (tel. 972/896313), which draws orchestras, choirs, and stars (including Catalan opera great Montserrat Caballé, in 1985) from all Europe to perform in the acoustically extraordinary church.

WHERE TO SLEEP AND EAT

There are few affordable beds here, but if you find yourself charmed—or stuck—try **Fonda Can Marcelli** (C. Frederic Bernades 9, tel. 972/146096, cash only), where a basic double costs 6,000 ptas.

If you suddenly feel compelled to splurge, do it at the excellent **Can Ventura** (C. Plaça Major 1, tel. 972/896178; closed Mon.–Tues.), a 17th-century farmhouse-turned-rustic-restaurant serving choice Catalan cuisine. Entrées are simple but exquisite, like *bacalao con ajo* (cod seasoned with garlic, 1,850 ptas.). To finish with a flourish, ask for the *carta de puros* (cigar menu); a Cuban Montecristo will set you back 1,000 ptas. Back down in the budget range, **Can Francesc** (C. dels Forns 9, tel. 972/896364) has a savory 1,300-ptas. menú del día that includes a delicious *trinxat de Cerdanya,* a local specialty of mushrooms, potatoes, and bacon.

BELLVER DE CERDANYA

Overlooking the River Segre, the lovely village of Bellver de Cerdanya (*bell* meaning beautiful, *ver* meaning "to see" or "to view") is aptly named: The Pyrenean patina is unusually evident here, with rustic chalets lining the cobblestone streets and an elegant Plaça Major with impressive porticoes. Near the Plaça stands the Gothic church of **Sant Jaume,** and just south of town is the 12th-century Romanesque church of **Santa Maria de Talló,** presided over by a wooden statue of the Virgin. Bellver de Cerdanya's lifeblood is the River Segre, and trout fishing its chief industry (*see* Outdoor Activities, *below*).

BASICS

The **tourist office** (Plaça de Sant Roc 9, tel. 973/510229) is open June 15–September 15, Monday–Saturday 11–1 and 6–8, and Sunday 11–1.

Bellver de Cerdanya, about 25 km (15 mi) west of Puigcerdà, is one of the first stops on the **bus** route between Puigcerdà and La Seu d'Urgell.

WHERE TO SLEEP

It takes less than a day—if that—to explore this town, but the delightful **Fonda Biayna** (C. de Sant Roc 11, tel. 973/510475) may entice you to stay. This inviting guest house is one of the oldest in the Pyrenees, and the price for one of the beautifully renovated rooms, with hardwood floors and period furniture (7,500 ptas.) includes a sizable breakfast.

OUTDOOR ACTIVITIES

Ferretería Bellver (C. de San Roc 4, tel. 973/511248) sells fishing rods and equipment. For all the information you'll ever need on fishing in this area, ask for David Jordán at the nearby **Bar Blanch** (C. de San Roc 5, tel. 973/510208), where he works with his father—David issues fishing permits and can guide you toward choice fishing spots and equipment outfitters. To apply for the permit, however, you first need to visit the **Club de Pesca Riu de l'Ingla** (Paseo Pere Elías 1, tel. 973/510318, open weekdays 11–noon, plus weekends 11–noon during fishing season, usually March–Sept.). Finally, a few retired folks sell fishing equipment out of their homes; the tourist office can send you their way.

LA SEU D'URGELL

Known affectionately as Seu, the friendly town of La Seu d'Urgell sits amid looming peaks, with Andorra just 10 km (6 mi) to the north and the valleys of the rocky Sierra del Cadí nearby. As the seat of the regional archbishopric since the 6th century and of an outdoor market held continuously since 1029 (on Tuesday and Saturday), Seu has a formidable history and makes a good base for outdoor day trips.

BASICS

Seu's **tourist office** (Avda. Valls d'Andorra 44, tel. 973/351511; open July–Aug., weekdays 9–8, weekends 10–2 and 4–7, Sun. 10–2) is particularly well stocked, and the staff friendly; ask for their useful series of pamphlets and maps on hiking in the Cadí valleys. Plenty of **banks** line Avenida de Pau Claris, on the western edge of the old quarter.

COMING AND GOING

The **bus station** (tel. 973/350020), just north of the old quarter, is an easy walk from the tourist office. Several daily **Alsina Graells** (tel. 973/350020) buses serve **Barcelona** (3½ hrs, 2,545 ptas.), **Lleida** (2½ hrs, 1,735 ptas.), and **Puigcerdà** (1½ hrs, 625 ptas.). Buses run by **La Hispano-Andorrana** make the 10-km (6-mi) trip to Andorra.

WHERE TO SLEEP

There are plenty of cheap sleeps here, albeit often drab and character-free. The cheapest in town are at the run-down **Pensió Palomares** (C. Canonges 38, tel. 973/352178) and the equally run-down **Pensió Jove** (C. Canonges 42, tel. 973/350260). Both rent doubles for 3,000 ptas. a night (cash only) if locals haven't nabbed the rooms already, which they may well have. From here it's a step up in price, though not necessarily in quality, to the hotels on Carrer de Josep de Zulueta in the western part of town. **Hotel Cadí** (C. Josep de Zulueta 6, tel. 973/350150, cash only) has simple, musty doubles for 4,500–6,500 ptas. depending on season. **Hotel Empordanesa,** a little farther west (C. Llorenç Tomàs i Costa 43, tel. 973/351028), has motel-style rooms for 6,500 ptas. **Residencia Duc d'Urgell** (C. Josep de Zulueta 43, tel. 973/352195) has large, cheaply decorated rooms for 4,500–6,500 ptas. depending on season, and the cavernous **restaurant** next door serves a decent set menu for as little as 1,100 ptas.

If you have a car, try one of the many country farmhouses (called *cases de pages* or *cases de poble*) in this area, as most are reasonably priced (1,700–3,200 ptas. *per person*) and have a nice, homespun ambience that's a far cry from the dingy digs in town. The tourist office has a complete list of these lodgings; closest to Seu is the rustic **Residencia La Vall del Cadí** (tel. 973/350390), roughly 3 km (2 mi) south of town. Cross the River Segre, then head east toward Ortedò/Tuixent, and signs will point the rest of the way. Comfy doubles are 5,000 ptas., payable in cash.

WHERE TO EAT

For hearty Catalan fare, try the country-style **Restaurant Cal Pacho** (C. de la Font 11, tel. 973/352719) for innovative combinations like *pollo al cava* (chicken cooked with sparkling white wine, 1,000 ptas.). The *trucha del Segre* (trout from the River Segre, 900 ptas.) is also delicious. **Braseria Casa Nostra** (Passeig Joan Brudieu 20, tel. 973/353102) has a cozy dark-wood interior and a wide range of Catalan dishes for 850–1,000 ptas., including a delicious entrée of *cordonices* (quail). **Pizzeria Canigó** (C. de Sant Ot 3, tel. 973/351043) has cheap and filling pastas and pizzas for 600–800 ptas. The tiny, dark, divey café-bar **La Tasca** (C. Canonges 64, no phone), where old local men take their nightly vermouth, gives away a *caña* (glass of beer) for 150 ptas.

WORTH SEEING

The pleasantly mysterious medieval quarter is a small warren of narrow, arcaded streets that opens onto broader vistas. **Carrer dels Canonges,** the oldest street, cuts through the heart of the old quarter, littered with centuries-old buildings like Cal Roger, a pilgrim's hostel with wooden ceiling beams and some 14th-century Gothic carvings.

Seu's 12th-century cathedral of **Santa Maria**, off Plaça dels Oms, is a wonderfully preserved example of Romanesque architecture. The columns in its 13th-century cloister are topped with fabulous sculpted figures from medieval mythology, and the adjoining 11th-century Romanesque chapel of **Sant Miquel** is haunting and lovely. The **Museu Diocesano** has a striking collection of murals from various Pyrenean churches and a fabulous 10th-century illuminated Mozarabic manuscript of the monk Beatus's commentary on the Apocalypse, along with a film explaining this masterpiece in Spanish (it's still cool). *Admission to cathedral and cloister: 125 ptas.; museum, church, and cloister: 375 ptas. Open June–Sept., Mon.–Sat. 10–1 and 4–6; Sun. cathedral open for mass only, cloister open 10–1, museum closed; Oct.–May, cathedral, cloister and museum open Mon.–Sat. 10–1; Sun., cathedral open for mass only, cloister open noon–1.*

OUTDOOR ACTIVITIES

Canoe-slalom events in the 1992 Barcelona Olympics were actually held in La Seu d'Urgell, at the **Parc Olímpic del Segre** (tel. 973/360092), southeast of town along the river. The park still offers rafting, canoeing, and other water sports. In winter **cross-country skiing** is the sport of choice, with ski centers such as Sant Joan l'Erm and Lles (the oldest in the Pyrenees) totaling more than 120 (78 mi) of trails. Lots of great **hiking** trails connect the surrounding villages, too; the tourist office has maps and details.

VALL DE LA NOGUERA PALLARESA

The Noguera Pallaresa Valley is dominated by the powerful river of the same name, whose churning waters are an important source of hydroelectric power. Massive power plants sit along the banks. The *raiers* (logger-raftsmen) of La Pobla de Segur (*see below*) used to ride rafts of logs from the Pallars Forest all the way south to the lowlands; watch for the **Festa dels Raiers** (Raftsmen's Festival) if you're here the first Sunday in July, when locals race down the river on rafts.

The river's mighty flow has made this *the* place in Catalonia to go white-water rafting. The season lasts from April to the beginning of September, and plenty of outfitters stand ready to lead trips. The town of **Sort**, 30 km (18 mi) north of La Pobla de Segur, has become the region's white-water rafting hub, with a slew of aquatic-adventure shops. **Alta Ruta** (Avda. Condes del Pallars 15, tel. 973/620809) offers rafting, canoeing, and waterskiing trips, and has a second store in Esterri d'Àneu (C. Major 2, tel. 973/626513), northwest of Espot.

LA POBLA DE SEGUR

The amiable town of La Pobla de Segur is one of the largest in the Vall de la Noguera Pallaresa, and a good base for river rafting or just hanging around for a few days.

BASICS

The friendly staff in the **ajuntament** (town hall; Avda. Verdaguer 35; open Apr.–Sept., Mon.–Sat. 10–2 and 6–8; Oct.–Mar., Mon.–Sat. 10–2) has maps and brochures aplenty.

La Pobla de Segur is something of a transport hub for the surrounding region. **Alsina Graells buses** leave here for **El Pont de Suert, Boí,** and **Vielha,** in the Vall d'Aran. The bus from **Barcelona** to Esterri d'Àneu and Vielha (via Espot) also passes through here. The **bus station** (tel. 973/680336) is on Avenida Verdaguer; buses also stop at Plaça del Pou, off Carrer la Font.

La Pobla de Segur is the last stop on the train from **Lleida** (2½ hrs, 660 ptas.). The **train station** (Avda. del Estació s/n, tel. 973/680480) is at the south end of town.

WHERE TO SLEEP AND EAT

Pensió Can Frasersia (C. Major 4, tel. 973/680227, cash only) has comfortable doubles for 4,000 ptas. From the train station, cross the bridge into town, and you'll see the old town to your left: Make a sharp left onto a ramplike street, and you're on Carrer Major. **Hostal-Residencia Torrentet** (Plaça. Pedrera 5, tel. 973/680352, cash only) has simple, clean doubles for 5,000 ptas.

Bar-Restaurant Paradis (Avda. Estació 66, tel. 973/660000, closed Mon., no dinner Thurs.) has a simple yet savory menú del día for 1,200 ptas. **Restaurant La Riba** (Avda. Catalonia 7, tel. 973/660065) serves a hearty set menu for 1,300 ptas.

GERRI DE LA SAL

Heading north from La Pobla de Segur toward Sort, you come to the ramshackle village of Gerri de la Sal, named after the nearby salt mines. Next to the village, an old stone bridge leads to a beautiful 12th-century **monastery.** Though the building is closed to the public, this is a lovely place to walk. Just beyond Gerri de la Sal is a tunnel; the old road runs alongside the tunnel, hugging the rocky side of the mountain, and is open to hikers and bikers.

FEELING LIGHT-HEADED

If you're up for a challenge, try the Carros de Foc (Sky Runners) route through the park. The itinerary is simple—you trek past all nine of the park's refuges—but here's the hard part: you must return to the the first refuge within 24 hours. The challenge was born in the summer of 1987, when a bunch of park guards decided to touch all nine bases in one day, and a few succeeded. Most of the route is on high mountain terrain, at an average altitude of 7,870 ft. There are some rules to follow: The trek must be made between June 15 and September 20. To enter officially, you need to buy a Carros de Foc pass (2,500 ptas.), which will be stamped at every refuge you pass. If you want to spend the night at the refuge where you begin, remember to call ahead (tel. 973/642407). The current record is 11 hours and 10 minutes—a hard time to beat, but always worth a try.

PARC NACIONAL D'AIGÜESTORTES I ESTANY DE SANT MAURICI

Catalonia's only national park (one of nine in Spain) encompasses soaring peaks rising 9,000 ft and lush meadows irrigated by more than 150 lakes, streams, and waterfalls. Pine and fir forests blanket the valleys, and wild animals like the *isard* (also known as the chamois, a small antelope) roam the terrain. You might even spot a golden eagle or black woodpecker, both common to the park.

Hiking and trekking opportunities abound, from easy walks around Lake Sant Maurici to serious treks up the mountains. In winter you can also cross-country ski through the park, albeit not on marked trails. The park's western sector is best reached from the Vall de Boí (*see below*); the eastern portion, including Lake Sant Maurici, via Espot. You can pick up trail guides and park maps at the **visitor centers** in Boi and Espot. Park entrance is free, but private vehicles are not allowed and camping is prohibited, though there are refuges. Taxis can take you from Boí, Espot, or El Pont de Suert to certain parts of the park.

If you're planning only day treks, stay at one of the small towns on the park's perimeter, such as Espot or Boí. If you'll be hiking for several days at a time between June and September, you can stay at any of the nine refuges, each equipped with bunks topped with foam-rubber mattresses. Either visitor center can give you a list; call 973/642407 to reserve your bunk ahead of time. You reach the **Ernest Mallafré shelter,** near Lake Sant Maurici at the foot of the Els Encantats range, by taking the paved road from Espot to the lake, and then a half-hour hike. The **L'Estany Llong shelter,** in the Sant Nicolau Valley near Estany Llong (Long Lake), is accessed via 1½- to 2-hour hike from Boí. In case of emergency, there are also some shepherds' huts lying about.

ESPOT

Espot is a cozy mountain town hemmed in by a lovely green valley and towering peaks. In the winter, skiers pass through on their way to **Espot Esquí,** just north of town, with 27 alpine trails. The town is a gateway to the eastern section of the park, so you'll see one of the main park **visitor centers** on the right as you enter town (C. Prat del Guarda 3–4, tel. 973/624036; open Apr.–Oct., Mon.–Sat. 9–1 and 3:30–

7, Sun. 9–1; Nov.–Mar., Mon.–Sat. 9–2 and 3:30–6, Sun. 9–2). You can hire a guide here at 850 ptas. for a half day, 1,500 ptas. for a full day. A **taxi** (tel. 973/624105) can takes you to Lake Sant Maurici for 600 ptas. one way.

Espot is small—all lodging is but a few minutes' walk from the center of town. **Casa Felip** (C. Felip s/n, tel. 973/624093, cash only) is run by a friendly older couple; simple rooms with an old-fashioned decor are 5,000 ptas. in summer, less the rest of the year. **Casa Colom,** up the hill on the road to the ski center (C. Unica s/n, tel. 973/624010), has small but comfortable rooms ranging from 4,500 ptas. to 6,000 ptas. **Pensión Palmira** (C. Unica s/n, tel.973/624072) has institutional but clean doubles for 6,000 ptas., and its small restaurant serves a tasty menú del día for 1,350 ptas. **Restaurant Juquim** (Plaça Sant Martí, tel. 973/624009), in the center of town, has a hearty menú for 1,750 ptas.

The Alsina Graells **bus** from **Barcelona** to **Vielha,** in the Vall d'Aran, stops in Espot much of the year (4 hrs, 3380 ptas.), but the bus stop is down the hill 8 km (5 mi) from town. There are usually a few taxis waiting at the bus stop to take you into town. In the winter, this bus goes only as far as Esterri d'Àneu (north of Espot), not all the way to Vielha; the leg from Espot to Vielha normally takes 2 hours and costs 640 ptas.

ALTA RIBAGORÇA

Northwest of La Pobla de Segur and south of the Vall d'Aran, the Alta Ribagorça region is real mountain country, with peaks reaching 9,750 ft, imposing rocky terrain, and vast gorges gaping far beneath the road. The Noguera Ribagorça River cuts grandly through the rugged landscape, its banks lined with occasinal rows of abandoned houses: This is where laborers from all over the region lived while they built the river's hydroelectric dams.

BASICS

The small, busy town of **El Pont de Suert** is the regional capital. The **tourist office** (Plaça Mercadal 7, tel. 973/690640) is generally open only in July and August, Monday–Saturday 10–2 and 5–8; the rest of the year the staff at the **ajuntament** (town hall) can help out (Plaça Major 9, tel. 973/690005). A new **regional tourist office** (Avda. Victoriana Muñoz 48, tel. 973/690402; open weekdays 8–3), has information on the entire *comarca* (region).

Most **buses** to the Vall d'Aran (via Boí) pass through here on their way north. Because El Pont de Suert is an entrance to the national park, you can hire a **taxi** at the *parada de taxis* (taxi stand; Avda. Victoriano Muñoz 2, tel. 973/690445) to take you in for 600 ptas. one way.

WHERE TO SLEEP AND EAT

Hostal Cotori (Plaça Mercadal 8, tel. 973/690096, cash only) has basic double rooms for 5,000 ptas. a night. **Restaurant-Braseria Las Cumbres** (Avda. Victoriano Muñoz 29, tel. 973/691166) serves a filling menú del día for 1,500 ptas.

OUTDOOR ACTIVITIES

El Pont de Suert is a miniature sports center, with a bunch of rafting and aquatic-equipment stores. **Yeti Sports** (Avda. Victoriano Muñoz 12, tel. 973/691019) rents equipment and leads a whole range of trips, including river rafting (4,500 ptas. for one *bajada,* or descent), mountain biking, and climbing. **Rafting Noguera Aventura** (C. Ciutat de Lleida, tel. 973/690055) also runs a host of trips including rafting (4,200 ptas. for one descent) and kayaking (8,400 ptas.).

VALL DE BOÍ

Just west of the national park is the Boí Valley, anchored by the lovely mountain village of **Boí.**

BASICS

Here you'll find the other main park **visitor center** (Plaça Treio 3, tel. 973/696189; open Apr.–Oct., Mon.–Sat. 9–1 and 3:30–7, Sun. 9–1; Nov.–Mar., Mon.–Sat. 9–2 and 3:30–6, Sun. 9–2), where you can pick up trail maps and the latest weather forecast.

The main Vall de Boí **tourist office** is in Barruera, 5 km (3 mi) south of Boí (Passeig de Sant Feliu 43, tel. 973/694000; open Mon.–Sat. 9–2 and 5–7). Stop in for literature, including guides to the Romanesque churches.

A Boí **taxi** (tel. 973/696036 and 973/696037) can take you into the park for 600 ptas. one way.

WHERE TO SLEEP AND EAT

Hotel Pey (Plaça Treio 3, tel. 973/696036), next to the tourist office, has clean double rooms for 6,000 ptas. The adjoining restaurant-café serves a menú del día for 1,400 ptas. If you just want to sit back and contemplate the spectacular mountains above you, nab an outdoor table at **Ca la Pepa,** on the main road: delicious sweet and savory crepes can be yours for 400–600 ptas. each, as *can torrades* (toasted bread sandwiches).

WORTH SEEING

The Vall de Boí is renowned for its magnificent Romanesque churches. The 12th-century church of **Sant Climent,** in Taüll (admission 100 ptas.; open Tues.–Sat. 10:30–2 and 4–7, Sun. 10:30–2), 3 km (2 mi) above Boí, has an exquisite six-story belfry that rises gracefully above the town. The church's extraordinary, emblematic Romanesque murals, created by the so-called Master of Taüll, were transferred to Barcelona's Museu Nacional d'Art de Catalonia in 1922, so the ones in the church are copies. Near the village center is another Romanesque beauty, the church of **Santa Maria,** with a four-story belfry (open daily 10–7). Other Romanesque churches sit peacefully in Barruera, Boí, Cardet, Coll, and Erill-la-vall.

WHERE TO SLEEP AND EAT

The Vall de Boí is dotted with rustic *casas de payés* (country houses; also called *casas de pagès*), where the atmosphere is far above that of your typical *hostal* or pension, and rates are often in the same range. In Taüll, head to homey **Ca de Corral** (tel. 973/696028), just uphill from the church of Sant Climent. Here you can grill your dinner over the old-fashioned fireplace in the country kitchen, and overlook the small garden and farmyard, where chickens cluck and a peacock struts about, from the living-room balcony. Comfortable double rooms cost 4,000 ptas. For a list of other local *casas de pagès,* stop into the tourist office in Boí or El Pont de Suert, or call the **Associación de Alta Ribagorça Casas de Pagès** at 973/694000.

Near Ca de Corral, the bar-restaurant **La Bordeta** (Avda. les Feixes 4, tel. 973/696163) rents clean doubles for 6,000 ptas. and serves a good menú del día for 1,500 ptas.. The patio has fetching views of the mountains. The bar-restaurant **Sant Climent** (Avda. les Feixes 8, tel. 973/696052) also rents rooms (tidy doubles 5,000 ptas.) and furnished apartments with kitchens (9,000 ptas.). Downstairs, the menú del día is 1,600 ptas., and *platos combinados* run 800–1,000 ptas.

OUTDOOR ACTIVITIES

In the mountains above Taüll, the ski resort **Boí Taüll** is a big draw in snow season. **Caldes de Boí** (tel. 973/696210, open June 24–Sept. 30), at the top of the valley, is a hot-spring spa resort offering massage, thermal bath soaks, and other rejuvenating services.

VALL D'ARAN

Nudging the French border in the far northwest of the Catalan Pyrenees, the magnificent Vall d'Aran has long been geographically and culturally distinct from the rest of the Pyrenees. You can see the disparity in its architecture—French-style chalets dot the hillsides— and you can hear it on the streets: the language here is Aranés, a mix of Gascon French and Catalan. The valley drains toward the Atlantic and spills into the Garonne River, whose waters eventually feed the vineyards of Bordeaux.

The Vall d'Aran joined Catalonia-Aragón in the 12th century and was fully given over to Catalonia in 1389. Completely ringed by high peaks, however—some reaching almost 10,000 ft—it has always been difficult to access. For most of the valley's history, the only routes in from the Spanish side crossed the tricky Bonaigua or Bossòst passes, both accessible only in summer. This changed only in 1948, when the Vielha Tunnel opened on the N230 highway.

The valley's capital and commercial center is Vielha, a beautiful alpine town with one foot in its past as a quiet mountain village and the other in its present (and, presumably, future) as a resort. In winter the Vall d'Aran becomes ski country, drawing folks from all over Spain and France; King Juan Carlos skis at Baqueira Beret, one of Spain's premier ski resorts with 47 alpine trails.

The Vall d'Aran is divided into three sectors: Vielha e Mijaran (Middle Aran), Baish Aran (Lower Aran; northwest of Vielha near the French border), and Naut Aran (Upper Aran; east of Vielha). Both Upper and Lower Aran are ripe for exploration, each of their mountain villages more enchanting than the last. Hiking and trekking opportunities abound—trails wind all over the valley. You could easily spend a day or two trekking from one tiny village to the next, stopping for a hearty regional lunch in one and sleeping in a rustic farmhouse in the next. Salardú, Arties, and Unha make pleasant stopovers in Naut Aran; Bossòst, in Mijaran, has a beautiful Romanesque church.

One popular, clearly marked trail starts in the tiny village of Betren (next to Vielha), follows the River Garonne, and heads up to the village of Casarilh, granting fetching views over the entire valley. Another spectacular trek starts high in Beret (north of the ski resort), at 5,944 ft, and continues through the mountains to the Santuari de Montgarri, a lovely abandoned sanctuary.

VIELHA

The valley centers on the bustling town of Vielha, sometimes called the Aspen of Spain: On winter weekends, slickly outfitted skiers crowd the slopes and gear shops. **Baqueira Beret** (14 km/9 mi east of Vielha) draws discriminating skiers with serious funds, including His Royal Highness, a regular. After the snow melts, Vielha slips quietly back into its small-town self, when the hilly streets are empty and you can hear the church bell pealing in the mountainy stillness. The church of **Sant Miquel,** in the center of town, has a beautiful 15th-century altar.

BASICS

In summer, when hikers and bikers arrive, Vielha gets busy again. If you want to trek, pop into the well-stocked **tourist office** (C. Sarriulèra 5, tel. 973/640110; open Mon.–Sat. 10–1 and 4:30–7:30) for its excellent series of trail brochures. Another good source of books and guides is **Llibreria Ruda** (C. Castièro 5, tel. 973/640050), which carries an excellent brochure listing the Vall d'Aran's numerous refuges. Ski and sports gear is sold along **Pas d'Arro.** Vielha also has agencies that can arrange guided treks and other adventures; try **Camins del Pirineu** (Avda. Castièro 15, tel. 973/642444).

COMING AND GOING

Alsina Graells **buses** travel twice daily from **Barcelona** (7 hrs, 4,015 ptas.) to Vielha via **El Pont de Suert,** with a stop in **Lleida** (from Vielha, 3 hrs, 1,510 ptas.) lasting up to an hour. In summer, when the Bonaigua pass is open, buses to Vielha run once daily via La Pobla de Segur and **Espot** (2 hrs, 640 ptas.). You can also connect from Vielha to even smaller towns, such as Salardú, Arties, Bossòst, and Les.

For those traveling by **car,** highway N230 heads north from Lleida past El Pont de Suert and through the 6-km (4-mi) Túnel de Vielha to the Vall d'Aran. You can also drive north on C147 through La Pobla de Segur and Espot, then cross the Bonaigua Pass (6,796 ft)—just note that the pass is usually closed in winter, depending on snowfall and weather.

WHERE TO SLEEP

In addition to premium ski lodges, Vielha has a good selection of budget lodgings, so a few days here won't break the bank. **Hostal El Ciervo** (Plaça Sant Orenç 3, tel. 973/640165) has clean, well-maintained double rooms for 6,000 ptas., including breakfast. On the same square, **Hotel Irissa** (Plaça Sant Orenç 1, tel. 973/640709) has simple but comfortable doubles for 6,000 ptas., including breakfast. **Casa Vicenta** (Camin Reiau 3, tel. 973/640819), off the large Plaça Generalitat, has tidy doubles with rustic furniture for 6,000 ptas., also including a buffet breakfast. A few doors down, **Hostal Turrull** (Camin Reiau 7, tel. 973/640058, cash only) rents doubles for 5,500 ptas., many with hardwood floors. **Hotel Delavall,** on Avenida Pas D'Arro, the main drag (tel. 973/640013), has comfy spic-and-span doubles for 7,000 ptas., including a buffet breakfast. There's also has a swimming pool in summer, and a lounge bar where you can thaw with a hot drink after skiing. The price leaps to 8,500 during August, Christmas week, and Semana Santa (Holy Week). **Petit Hotel des Arts** (C. dera Palha 15, tel. 973/641848) is a big step up in price, but you get all the attendant comforts: a big, comfortable bed, TV, and a sparkling bathroom. From late July to the end of August, double rooms cost 10,150 ptas.; in spring and fall, rooms are a bargain, at 6,050 ptas.. The hotel is closed from November to March.

WHERE TO EAT

As you might expect in a resort town, Vielha packs many a stylized alpine restaurant with high prices and mediocre food. Beyond these, rustic eateries serve excellent regional dishes, and simple bar-cafés serve filling grub for less than 800 ptas. A hearty meal at the popular **Restaurante Basteret** (C. Major 6, tel. 973/640714) will cost you 1,800 ptas. For a splurge, try country-style **Restaurante Nicolas** (C. Deth Casteth 10, tel. 973/641820), where you can feast on *olla Aranesa* (Aranés stew), *zarzuela* (typical Spanish seafood casserole), or *escargots*; a full meal will set you back 2,500–3,000 ptas. **Bar-Restaurant Era Plaça** (tel. 973/642253), on Plaça dera Glèsia, next to the church, has simple *bocadillos de chorizo* (sausage sandwiches; 525 ptas.) and *platos combinados* (chicken, steak, or lamb) for 900 ptas., and you can eat outdoors in nice weather. Nearby, **Bar-Restaurant Dues Portes** (Plaça dera Glèsia s/n, tel. 973/640284) has a wide range of inexpensive combination menus at both lunch and dinner. One mixes a hamburger, french fries, dessert, and a Coke for 675 ptas.; another provides pasta bolognese, grilled chicken with potatoes, bread, dessert, and a Coke for 1,200 ptas. Locals converge at the cozy **Cafetería Aneto** (Avda. Pas d'Arro, tel. 973/642135), where the *menú del día* is 1,200 ptas. and yummy *bocadillos* go for 400–600 ptas. Locals love **Café Express** (Paseo de la Libertad 3, tel. 973/640119), which looks like a hole in the wall but is actually a store. Have a beer and check out the Aran specialties lining the wall, such as *mel de la muntanya* (alpine honey; ¼ kilogram for 400 ptas.), *cassis d'Aran* (cassis from Aran), and *llonganisa de pagès* (cured country sausage).

SALARDÚ

Politically, the ancient Vall d'Aran comprises thirty-three hillside villages. Most every one has a Romanesque church. Rustic Salardú, in Naut Aran, is one of the biggest, with a population of 372, but despite that rowdy crowd it remains a peaceful place to flee civilization without going broke. The church of **Sant Andreu** stands tall in its center, and the town is the trailhead for several excellent hikes, including one through the **Circ de Colomèrs**, a steep mountain range with forested peaks.

BASICS

The **tourist office** (C. Trauèssa de Balmes 2, tel. 973/645726; usually open Mon.–Sat. 10:30–1:30 and 5–8:30, but hrs vary) has details on local hiking trails. If the office is closed, try the **ajuntament** (town hall; C. Balmes 2, tel. 973/364–40–30; open weekdays 10–2). Near the town hall is a little **supermarket,** convenient for picnic supplies.

Alsina Graells buses connect Salarú with Vielha.

WHERE TO SLEEP AND EAT

Bar-Pensión Muntanya (C. Major 8, tel. 973/644108, cash only) has basic double roomss for 4,400 ptas. a night, and the bar serves decent tapas and bocadillos for 400–600 pta. The town's two large refuges are popular among hikers: **Refugi Juli Soler i Santaló** (Carretera del Port, tel. 973/645016) has comfy doubles with shared bath for 2,400 ptas. *per person,* but most people come for the dorm rooms, in which each bed costs 1,500 ptas. One of the oldest refuges in the Vall d'Aran, **Refugi Rosta** (Plaça Major 1, tel. 973/645308, cash only) is something of a Salardú institution, as its well-known bar, Delicatessen, is a homey hangout with wood stove, board games, and boisterous après-ski crowds. In the afternoon, it bar serves tasty crepes (500–600 ptas.) and pastries. In summer the bar is open until 1:30 AM; in winter, hours vary. Many of the guest rooms have hardwood floors and rustic furniture, such as old-fashioned school desks. Comfortable doubles are 6,000 ptas.; a dorm bed is 1,975 ptas., including breakfast. Another popular nightspot is **Toto's** (C. Era Molà 4).

NEAR SALARDÚ

Cross Salardú's small bridge and you're in the hamlet of **Unha,** whose church contains some Gothic paintings depicting Biblical scenes. The home-style country meals at **Casa Maria** (C. Santa Eulàlia, tel. 973/644169) include ample *truitas* (omelets; *tortillas* in Castilian) and grilled meats, with a full meal costing about 2,000 ptas.

The town of **Arties,** just east of Vielha, also has a lovely church but is known for having some of the valley's liveliest bars. Try **La Luna** (C. Major 10, tel. 973/641115) or **Divino** (C. Era Hònt 5, no phone).

Just northwest of Vielha, the tiny village of **Arros,** with narrow streets of old houses, is an idyllic place to explore as you trek through the valley. From here you can hike or mountain-bike to France on a mixture of mountain trails and paved roads; ask the tourist office about the **Camin Reiau** (Camino Real), a trail that traverses most of the Vall d'Aran, including the villages of Es Bordès and Era Bòrdeta. Farther north, the village church in **Bossost** is one of the finest examples of Aranés Romanesque architecture, with three naves and a spectacular bell tower. As you pass through Bossost (just 10 km/6 mi from France) and **Les** (the last town before you hit the border), the French influence becomes much more apparent in the buildings; it's still startling, though, to cross the border and see that most symbolic of French images: an old guy scurrying down the street with a baguette under his arm.

Alsina Graells **buses** connect most of the villages around Vielha, including Salardú, Arties, Bossòst, and Les.

THE COSTA DAURADA

From ancient Roman ruins to burgeoning beach resorts, southern Catalonia has more to offer than most travelers think, and it's all an easy day trip from Barcelona. The seaside city of Tarragona, once the most important Roman city on the Iberian Peninsula, lies an hour south of Barcelona. The Costa Daurada (Golden Coast) extends south from here, with long, sandy beaches, the trademark blue Mediterranean, and, alas, hordes of visitors in summer.

If you want a few days of mindless sun and sand, a string of built-up resorts provide just that: Salou has several large beaches, a palm-lined beachfront promenade, and streets filled with modern high-rise apartments, pubs, trinket shops, and cafeteria-style restaurants. Nearby Cambrils is a more authentic prospect; there are local vibes in the town and fishing marina, though the beach gets just as crowded as its counterparts. Trains and buses heading down the coast from Tarragona stop in both Salou and Cambrils. Near Salou, at Port Aventura, Spain's biggest theme park invites you on "an exciting voyage around the world," if you consider the cowboys-and-Indians "Far West" and "the spice of México" the world—all it takes is 4,600 ptas. (3,400 ptas. for kids) per person. The park is open from mid-March to November. Farther down the coast—and worlds away—is the Ebro Delta National Park (*see below*), a vast wetland park swarming with aquatic birds. Just north of the park is the historic little town of Tortosa.

TARRAGONA

Set on a rocky hill overlooking the sea, the ancient Roman stronghold of Tarragona is a splendid architectural mix of past and present. Roman pillars rise amid modern apartment buildings, and a Roman amphitheater shares the city coastline with trawlers and tugboats. Though contemporary Tarragona is very much an industrial town, with a large port and a thriving fishing industry, it has preserved its Roman heritage fantastically well. (Indeed, at press time Roman Tarragona was under consideration as a UNESCO World Heritage site.) Stroll along the town's cliff-side perimeter and you'll see why the Romans set up shop here: Tarragona is strategically positioned at land's edge, its lookout points commanding far-reaching, unobstructed sea views. The Romans arrived in Tarragona in 218 BC, named the site Tarraco, and established a military headquarters for the conquest of the Iberian Peninsula. By the 1st century AD, Tarragona was one of the most important urban and commercial centers in the empire, and it continued to flourish until the Moors deserted it in the 8th century.

Tarragona's main thoroughfare and walking street is the pleasant, shop-lined **Rambla Nova** (New Ramble), which cuts east through the center of town from the Plaça Imperial Tarraco to the sea. The Rambla ends with sweeping views of the coast from the Balcó del Mediterràni (Mediterranean Balcony). The **Rambla Vella** (Old Ramble), running parallel to the Rambla Nova just a few blocks north, divides Tarragona's old and new sections—the old walled city sits above (and north of) Rambla Vella, while the bustling new town stretches out below. Stop by the lively **indoor market** on Plaça Corsini, just below Rambla Nova, to see an orgy of fresh meats and produce, from hanging slabs of beef to towering piles of oranges. The market is as much a social scene as a shopping center; several small café-bars rest in the middle of the pandemonium, so if you don't mind sitting between legs of lamb and gutted fish, you can revive yourself with a *tallat* (coffee with a little bit of milk; *cortado* in Castilian) or a glass of house red.

Tarragona's main beach, called **Platja del Miracle,** is ample and clean, but in summer it's a miracle if you can find a patch of sand to call your own. To escape the crowds, travel a few kilometers up the coast to **Platja Arrabassada,** equally wide but less crowded with oil-slicked bodies.

BASICS

The **city tourist office** (C. Major 39, tel. 977/245203; open June–Sept., weekdays 9:30–8:30, Sat. 9:30–2 and 4–8:30, Sun. 10–2; Oct.–May, weekdays 10–2 and 4:30–7, weekends 10–2) has a useful map of the Roman sights. Just off Rambla Nova, there's a **regional tourist office** (C. Fortuny 4, tel. 977/233415; open June–Sept., weekdays 9–2 and 4–6:30, Sat. 9–2; Oct.–May, weekdays 9–2 and 4–7, Sat. 9–2) with city information plus literature on the rest of Spain.

CURRENCY EXCHANGE

Tarragona's **banks** line Rambla Nova. After hours, head to the Parque Central (Carretera de Valencia), a shopping mall on the outskirts of town, where the small bank La Caixa stays open Monday–Saturday 10–10.

CYBERSPACE

The restaurant **Hollywood** (Avda. Marquès de Montuliu 4, tel. 977/231404) has a few computers, on which you can access the Internet for 500 ptas. an hour.

EMERGENCIES

Hospital Juan XXIII (C. Doctor Mallfré, tel. 977/295-844) has 24-hour medical service. **Police:** tel. 092.

ENGLISH-LANGUAGE BOOKS

Several kiosks on the **Rambla Nova** sell English-language newspapers. **Librería Adsera** (Rambla Nova 94, tel. 977/235815) has a small selection of books.

LAUNDRY

Lavandería del Mar (C. Apodaca 38, tel. 977/234651) will wash and dry a load for 2,000 ptas.

MAIL

The main **post office** (tel. 977/240149, open weekdays 8–8, Sat. 8–1) is on Plaça Corsini.

COMING AND GOING

The **train station** (RENFE tel. 902/240202) is south of town, near the sea, roughly a 10-minute walk from Rambla Nova. From **Barcelona,** trains leave for Tarragona every hour from about 6:15 AM until 8:30 PM, and it's a lovely 80-minute ride along the coast (1,150 ptas.). From Tarragona, several trains leave daily for **Valencia** (2½ hrs, 3,700–4,200 ptas.), **Lleida** (1 hr, 1,300 ptas.), and **Madrid** (8 hrs, 6,000 ptas.).

The **bus station** (tel. 977/229126) is near Plaça Imperial Tarraco at the north end of Rambla Nova. Several **Hispania** buses (tel. 977/226818) come and go daily from **Barcelona** (1½ hrs, 1,150 ptas.), **Valencia** (3 hrs, 2,270 ptas.), **Lleida** (1½ hrs, 575 ptas.), and **Madrid** (6 hrs, 5,300 ptas.).

WHERE TO SLEEP

Tarragona has several concentrations of affordable lodging. Many of the cheapest, dingiest places are near the train station. **Via Augusta,** running parallel to Rambla Nova in the center of town, has another, slightly nicer group of budget spots; another good bet is **Plaça de la Font,** in the old quarter. If you don't mind paying a bit more, Rambla Nova has a few good places, one of which is a true find: **Hotel España** (Rambla Nova 9, tel. 977/232707), a simple but cared-for hotel with spic-and-span rooms. Doubles with sparkling bathrooms are 6,000 ptas. Ask for a room with a balcony overlooking the Rambla. **Hostal Noria** (Plaça de la Font 53, tel. 977/238717, cash only) has basic, clean doubles for 4,800 ptas. Near the train station, **Habitacions Mariflo** (C. General Contreras 29, tel. 977/238231, cash only) has basic, musty doubles for 4,000 ptas. without bath but, interestingly, with bidet. **Casa Carmen** (C. Cartagena 10, tel. 977/223387) has simple doubles for 4,000 ptas. **Pensión Pilarica** (C. Smith 20, tel. 977/240960, cash only) is a ramshackle house with dank rooms and tacky decor, but it's worth a try if the other places are full; it's just a few blocks from the station, and charges a modest 4,280 ptas. for a double. **Hotel Lauria** (Rambla Nova 20, tel. 977/236712), is a first-rate hotel with all the trimmings (pool, satellite TV, bar), so if you're here in the low season, it's well worth the 8,500 ptas. for a double room (10,700 ptas. in high season).

WHERE TO EAT

Tarragona has several top-notch restaurants, and the small streets branching off C. Unió yield a handful of excellent cheaper options. For fresh seafood, head to the Moll de Pescadors, the area near the fishermen's pier, southwest of town; for optimal people-watching, sidle over to a sidewalk café on Rambla Nova. If you like ice cream, you'll love this town—for some reason, every other block has an ice-cream emporium.

Every Catalan town should have a place like rustic **El Tiberi** (Martí d'Ardenya 5, tel. 977/235403), off Carrer Unió, where the specialty is an all-you-can-eat buffet of typical Catalan cuisine. For 1,450 ptas. you can heap and reheap your plate with anything from *butifarra negra* (black country sausage) and *escalivada* (grilled peppers, onions, and eggplant) to decadent cannelloni with loads of grated cheese. If nothing else, it's a chance to see all of Catalonia's classic dishes in one place, a study that can aid in deciphering menus later on. Nearby, **Piscolabis** (C. Martí d'Ardenya 6, tel. 977/234851) serves first-class Catalan cuisine, including *pimientos rellenos con bacalao* (peppers filled with cod) and *conejo* (rabbit), in an elegant dark-wood interior. Prices range widely, from 800 ptas. to 2,100 ptas., so choose carefully. The house specialty at busy **Pa amb tomaca** (C. Lleida 8, tel. 977/240045) is just as the name suggests, "bread with tomato"—topped with everything you can think of, including *anchoas* (anchovies), *salmón* (salmon), *jamón* (ham), and the ubiquitous *escalivada*.

In Moll de Pescadores, the seafood goes straight from the net to the frying pan and is accordingly delicious. **El Varadero** (C. Trafalgar 13, tel. 608/890615) is small, atmospheric, and packed at mealtime. Dishes include *calamares* (squid; 875 ptas.), fresh fish (800–1,600 ptas.), and a great array of seafood salads such as *ensalada de pulpo* (octopus salad; 750 ptas.). The room-length fish tank adds visual interest. A few doors down, sister restaurant **L'Ancora** has a similar menú and fish tank.

For Tarragona's best tapas, graze in the boisterous, bric-a-brac-filled **Bar Coimbra** (C. Gobernador González 6, tel. 977/232302), off Carrer Unió, where the array is delectable: *pops planxa* (grilled octopus; 500 ptas.), *musclos amb allioli* (mussels with garlic mayonnaise; 350 ptas.), *carxofes* (artichokes; 350 ptas.). If you're up for a challenge, go for *potes de porc* (pig trotters; 550 ptas.); if all else fails, there are the omnipresent *patates braves*, potatoes served with spicy sauce.

WORTH SEEING

Though the Roman ruins are scattered all over town, you can walk to most of them. You may want to start at the Museu d'Historia de Tarragona for an overview of the city's history. Note that most Roman sights and museums, except for the cathedral and Museu Diocesà, are closed on Monday; note, too, that if you have a ticket to Port Aventura, the nearby amusement park, you can enter most of Tarragona's sights free or at a substantially discounted price.

AMPHITHEATER

Just east of the city is the well-preserved Roman amphitheater, where gladiators fought wild animals in front of roaring crowds. Underneath the arena is a shrine for the gladiators, with a painting of the goddess Nemesis. *Parc del Miracle, tel. 977/242579. Admission 300 ptas. Open June–Sept., Tues.–Sat. 9–8, Sun. 9–3; Oct.–Mar., Tues.–Sat. 10–1:30 and 3:30–5:30, Sun. 10–2; Apr.–May, Tues.–Sat. 10–1:30 and 3:30–6:30, Sun. 10–2.*

CIRCUS MAXIMUS

Near the amphitheater are the remains of the Roman circus (built between AD 81 and AD 96), where chariot races were held. Only about a quarter of the structure has been excavated; the vaults you see were used to hold up the massive structure. *Plaça del Rei, tel. 977/241952. Admission 300 ptas. Open June–Sept., Tues.–Sat. 9–8, Sun. 9–3; Oct.–May, Tues.–Sat. 10–1:30 and 4–6:30, Sun. 10–2.*

PASSEIG ARQUEOLÒGIC

Starting at the Portal de Roser, in the old town, this circular, 1½-km (1-mi) path runs between two sets of walls spanning much of the old town's perimeter—on the inside, the spectacular 3rd-century Roman walls; on the outside, the fortified walls built by the British in 1707 during the War of the Spanish Succession. This easy amble is a great way to immerse yourself in Tarragona's history. *Tel. 977/245796. Admission 300 ptas. Open June–Sept., Tues.–Sat. 9–8, Sun. 9–3; Oct.–Mar., Tues.–Sat. 10–1:30 and 3:30–5:30, Sun. 10–2; Apr.–May, Tues.–Sat. 10–1:30 and 3:30–6:30, Sun. 10–2.*

LEGGO MY CAVA

If you've taken a liking to cava, Catalonia's answer to champagne, head due west from Barcelona to the Alt Penedès region, source of all of Catalonia's cava and many of its premiere wines. **Vilafranca del Penedès** *(55 km/34 mi west of Barcelona), the region's capital, is home to several wineries; nearby* **Sant Sadurní d'Anoia** *is the capital of cava. The two cava majors are Codorniu and Freixenet, the latter identifiable by its unique black bottle.* **Caves Codorniu** *(Avda. Codorniu, tel. 93/818–3232) has cellar tours and cava tastings weekdays 9–5 and weekends 9–1.* **Caves Freixenet** *(C. Joan Sala 2, tel. 93/891–7000) invites you in weekdays 10–11:30 and 3:30–5. For hours and locations of other Penedès wineries, call the tourist office in Villafranca del Penedès (C. Cort 14, tel. 93/892–0358; open weekdays 9–2 and 4–7, Sat. 9–2) or in Sant Sadurní d'Anoia (Plaça de l'Ajuntament 1, tel. 93/891–0325; open weekdays 8–3, weekends 10–2). Trains run several times a day from Barcelona to both towns.*

MUSEU I NECROPOLIS PALEOCRISTIANS

The Paleochristian Museum sits in the middle of the ruins of the ancient Roman necropolis—the best-preserved in the empire—where thousands upon thousands of Christian and pagan tombs have been excavated. Through a "Best of" synthesis, displays explore the ancient Roman rituals and ceremonies surrounding death. You'll see marble sarcophagi, some well-preserved craniums and skeletons, an ivory doll (once the plaything of a young girl), and lots of Roman-era drawings and plans for the giant corpse cabinet. *Avda. de Ramón y Cajal 80 (west of town center, off Passeig de la Independencia), tel. 977/ 251515. Admission 400 ptas.; joint ticket with Museu Nacional Arqueològic. Open June–Sept., Tues.–Sat. 10–8, Sun. 10–2; Oct.–May, Tues.–Sat. 10–1:30 and 4–7.*

CATHEDRAL

Rising impressively above the old town, Tarragona's cathedral is an amalgam of Romanesque and Gothic styles, and happens to be one of Spain's best illustrations of the transition between the two. Built on the site of a Roman temple, the building has Romanesque side doors and a richly Gothic portal; inside, the mix of styles is even more apparent. Unless mass is in progress, you can enter through the Gothic cloister. The **Museu Diocesà**, adjoining the cloister, has an eclectic collection of religious arti-facts, including ancient wooden sculptures of the Virgin. *Plaça de la Seu, tel. 977/238685. Admission 300 ptas. Open July–mid-Oct., daily 10–7; mid-Oct.–mid-Nov., daily 10–12:30 and 3–6; mid-Nov.–mid-Mar., daily 10–2; mid-Mar.–June, daily 10–1 and 4–7.*

CASA CASTELLARNAU / MUSEU D'HISTORIA DE TARRAGONA

From the cathedral, head toward Rambla Vella and you'll come upon this lovely Gothic mansion, filled with the opulent 18th-century furniture and decorations of the wealthy Castellarnau family. The building actually dates from the Roman era, but was done up in Gothic style to impress the Catalan nobility of the time. Now the Museum of the History of Tarragona, it presents an excellent rundown of the city's past in the same sumptuous chambers where the upper crust lived and played. The living and sitting rooms hold beautiful furniture (tables, couches, beds) and decorative pieces (ornate lamps) from the 16th to the 19th centuries; one rooms holds a series of Baroque murals. *C. Cavallers 14, tel. 977/*

242220. Admission 300 ptas. Open June–Sept., Tues.–Sat. 9–8, Sun. 9–3; Oct.–May, Tues.–Sat. 10–1:30 and 4–6:30, Sun. 10–2.

MUSEU NACIONAL ARQUEOLÒIC

Next door to the History Museum, the National Archaeological Museum has an impressive collection of sculpture and mosaics excavated from the Roman city. *Plaça del Rei 5, tel. 977/236209. Admission 400 ptas., free on Tues. Open June–Sept., Tues.–Sat. 10–8, Sun. 10–2; Oct.–May, Tues.–Sat. 10–1:30 and 4–7, Sun. 10–2.*

ACUEDUCTO ROMANO

Four kilometers (2½ mi) outside Tarragona on the road to Lleida is the wonderful Roman aqeuduct, popularly known as Puente del Diablo (Devil's Bridge). Spanning 712 ft and boasting 25 arches, the aqueduct brought water into town from the River Gayo, more than 30 km (18 mi) away. *Take Bus 5 (marked SANT SALVADOR) from Plaça Imperial Tarraco.*

TORTOSA

From its coveted position at the mouth of the Ebro River, the small, slow-paced town of Tortosa has seen all the conquerors come and go: the Greeks, Romans, Visigoths, and Moors were all here. This was also the site of some bloody fighting between the Republican and Nationalist forces during the Civil War. Tortosa's highlight is **La Suda,** an ancient fortified Arab castle perched on a hill with great views of the surrounding valley. It's been converted to a luxury parador, but you're welcome to visit and walk around the area. The 14th-century Gothic **cathedral** rises grandly over the old quarter, its impressive polychrome altarpiece dating from the 14th century.

BASICS

Tortosa's **tourist office** (Plaça Bimil.lenari, tel. 977/510822; open weekdays 10–1 and 4–7, Sat. 10–1) has town maps can fill you in on the Ebro Delta National Park (*see below*). **Trains** arrive several times daily from Tarragona, and **buses** fan out from Tortosa to several small villages in and around the Ebro Delta. One of the town's few cheap lodgings is **Pensión Virginia** (Avda. de la Generalitat 133, tel. 977/444186), where basic doubles cost 4,500 ptas.

DELTA DE L'EBRE

The magnificent Ebro Delta National Park is the largest wetland park in Catalonia, covering almost 20,000 acres. The endless salt marshes, sand dunes, reed beds, and rice paddies stick right out into the Mediterranean Sea on land deposited over the years by the Ebre (Ebro) River. The delta's waters teem with fish (large-mouth bass, pike, black bullheads), while frogs, toads, and spiny-footed lizards populate the marshlands and beaches. A vast variety of water birds (shoveler ducks, mallards, coots) descends by the thousand in October and November, when the rice has been harvested but the fields are still full of water. Morning and early evening in autumn and winter yield the best bird-watching. Unfortunately, the delta's most widespread critter is the mosquito, so you need a strong repellent to explore the wetlands.

Small towns dot the park's perimeter, and in the very center is the village of Deltebre. For more information on which parts of the park are currently accessible—and how best to get there—stop into the tourist **office in Deltebre** (C. Martí Buera 22, tel. 977/489679), **Amposta** (Avda. San Jaume 1, tel. 977/703453), west of the park, or **Sant Carles de la Ràpita** (Plaça Carles III 13, tel. 977/740100), south of the park. The office in **Tortosa** is another good source.

FESTIVAL FRENZY

Catalans take their festivals seriously (so to speak), and if you plan your trip around one, you can jump right in. Surely the most raucous affair is May's **Festa de la Patum,** *celebrated on Corpus Christi in the small town of Berga, west of Vic. For this occasion Berga's otherwise staid streets fill with parade floats of pagan and fantasy creatures—devils, dwarfs, dragons, dragon slayers—while revelers dance and shimmy, Rio de Janeiro style, behind the floats and on the sidelines. (The festival is named for the sound of a drum, and the crowd still chants "pa-tum" once they get energized.) To add to the hysteria, the creatures belch fireworks onto the crowds. Call Berga's tourist office (tel. 93/821–1384) for dates. Cervera's* **l'Aquilarre festival** *(100 km/62 mi west of Barcelona), usually the last Saturday in August, brings live music, dancing in the streets, and general merriment; the epicenter is Carrer de les Bruixes (Witches' Street), a medieval tunneled street running through the old town. Cervera's tourist office (tel. 973/530025) has details. From Barcelona, several daily buses pass through Berga and Cervera.*

SOUTHERN CATALONIA— INLAND

The oft-overlooked interior is Southern Catalonia's true heartland, full of towns where young and old gather every Sunday in the Plaça Major to dance the *sardana* to a *cobla* (the traditional sardana band), and the lead flutist might just be the *alcalde* (mayor). This is where you'll see first-hand the Catalan passion for festivals, especially each town's annual *festa major,* during which the streets overflow with revelers until the wee hours. The Patum festival in Berga is Catalonia's wildest, followed closely by l'Aquilarre, in Cervera (*see* Box: Festival Frenzy).

This is also farm and orchard country, where fields of wheat and rows of apple, peach, and pear trees stretch endlessly toward the horizon. A good harvest means a good year for this part of Spain. In some of the smaller farm villages, you'll come across older villagers who, despite all of Franco's efforts to force-feed them Spanish, still speak only Catalan. Whether you have one day or several, exploring the interior brings you face to face with what it means to be Catalan. The provincial capital of Lleida, Catalonia's second-largest city, is the social and commercial center and a major transportation hub.

Montblanc, 112 km (69 mi) west of Barcelona, is a lovely medieval village with an atmospheric Plaça Major and an impressive Gothic church. The **Monestir de Poblet,** west of Montblanc, is a massive monastery founded in the 12th century by Ramón Berenguer IV. Since 1940 Cistercian monks have lived and prayed here, working on its restoration; highlights include beautiful cloisters and a chapel containing tombs of the 12th- and 13th-century kings of Aragón. Guided tours of the monastery are given daily 10–12:30 and 3–6; admission is 500 ptas. Trains and buses from Barcelona arrive several times a day in Montblanc; some buses continue on to the monastery.

South of Montblanc lies the small town of **Valls,** capital of the Alt Camp region and best known as the birthplace of *castells,* Catalonia's famous human castles. Daring men and women called *castellers* climb onto each other's shoulders to form an incredible human tower, which is deemed complete when a child makes it to the top and waves to the crowd. The Casteller festival is held in June here; call the Valls tourist office (tel. 977/601050) for details. All daily Barcelona–Lleida trains stop in Valls.

LLEIDA

The pleasant provincial capital of Lleida (Lérida in Castilian) sits on the banks of the River Segre in the heart of Catalonia's agricultural and farm country. The Romans settled here around 200 BC, and the Arabs took control of the city in the 8th century. Later, in 1149, it became the seat of the regional bishopric.

The **Old Cathedral** (Seu Vella; admission 400 ptas.; open June–Sept., Mon.–Sat. 10–1:30 and 4–7:30, Sun. 10–1:30; Oct.–May, Mon.–Sat. 10–1:30 and 4–5:30, Sun. 10–1:30) looms grandly over the city, surrounded by fortified walls. Wander through the beautiful Gothic cloisters for stupendous views over Lleida and the countryside far below. The 18th-century **New Cathedral** (Seu Nova) rises over one end of Carrer Major, a principal street. The nearby **Museu Arqueològic** (open Tues.–Sat. noon–2 and 6–9), housed in the Gothic Hospital de Santa Maria, displays Roman artifacts discovered in this area.

BASICS
The **tourist office** (Avda. Madrid 36, tel. 973/270997; open June–Sept., weekdays 9–7, Sat. 9–2; Oct.–May, weekends 10–2 and 3:30–6) has the latest on bus and train schedules. Lleida abounds in bus and train connections north into the Pyrenees. **Buses** connect Lleida with **Barcelona** 8–10 times daily (2 hrs, 2,045 ptas.), and depart Lleida for **Vielha** (in the Vall d'Aran; 3 hrs, 1,510 ptas.) and **La Seu d'Urgell** (in the Cerdanya; 3 hrs, 1,735 ptas.) once or twice a day. **Trains** are hourly to and from Barcelona, and almost as frequent to **Tarragona** (1½ hrs, 1,700 ptas.), **Zaragoza** (2 hrs, 2,500 ptas.), and **Madrid** (4 hrs, 5,800 ptas.).

WHERE TO SLEEP AND EAT
The centrally located **Hostal Mundial** (Plaça Sant Joan 4, tel. 973/242700) offers basic, clean doubles for 3,400 ptas. Lleida's culinary specialty is *caragols* (snails), but they're served mainly (and best) at high-end restaurants. One of these, **Restaurante La Dolceta** (Camino de Montcada 28, tel. 973/231364), on the outskirts of town, serves an excellent snail salad and top-notch grilled meats; a full meal runs 2,000–2,500 ptas.

SOLSONA

The unspoiled medieval town of Solsona, northeast of Lleida, is capital of El Solsonès, the "region of 1,000 farms." Dating from the 10th century, Solsona has maintained its ancient infrastructure particularly well, with impressive medieval walls and gates and a dark, mazelike *casc antic* (old city). The **cathedral,** in true Catalan Gothic style, is dark and imposing, with a notable Baroque altarpiece and one of the oldest organs in Catalonia. Its star attraction is its 12th-century miniature Virgin carved of black stone—the Mare de Déu del Claustre, the patron of Solsona. Originally attached to a column, the statue inclines forward at an angle; the sculptor signed it in Latin on its back: GILABERTUS ME FECIT (Gilabertus made me). Adjoining the cathedral is the **Museu Diocesà** (admission 300 ptas.; open May–Sept., Mon.–Sat. 10–1 and 4:30–7, Sun. 10–2; Oct.–Apr., Mon.–Sat. 10–1 and 4–6, Sun. 10–1), whose splendid collection includes 15th-century processional crosses and Gothic stone statues. Because the diocesan museum is one of Catalonia's oldest—it was founded in 1896—Solsona is rare among small towns in having held on to its religious and artistic treasures. The annual *festa major* is held September 7–11, when the streets fill with dancing giants, dragons, eagles, and *trabucaires* (armed men), all traditional folklore figures dating from the 17th century.

BASICS
The helpful **tourist office** is at Carretera de Bassella 1 (tel. 973/482310; open mid-Apr.–Sept., Mon.–Thurs. 10–1, Fri.–Sun. 10–1 and 4–6; Oct.–mid-Apr., Mon.–Thurs. 10–1, Fri.–Sun. 10–2). Alsina-Graells **buses** run from **Barcelona** through Solsona and nearby Cardona on the way to **La Seu d'Urgell.**

ELS CASTELLS DE CATALUNYA

Catalonia's interior is dotted with old castles and fortified towers that rise grandly—and often unexpectedly—out of the wilderness. One of these wonders is the magnificent 100-ft **Torre de Vallferosa**, *the highest defense tower in Catalonia. Dating from around the 10th century, it looms in solitary grandeur over the countryside. In times of peril, the townspeople would gather here to be safe from marauding armies. Tunnels led from underneath the tower to far-off fields so the villagers could get food and water. It is said that, to mock the invaders, the villagers would throw fresh fish from the top, proving they were able to come and go as they pleased. The tower lies just off the road south from Solsona toward Torá; at the 19½-km (12-mi) mark there is a sign. It's then a 20-minute walk along a trail. The owners of the* casa de pagès *(country house) nearby will happily fill you in on the history of the area, and then you can just kick back amid peaceful surroundings.* **La Collita** *(Masia Cal Cristòfal, tel. 973/473399, cash only), just off the Solsona–Torá road after the tower, charges 5,300 ptas. per person, including all meals and use of the pool and. Tennis courts are available for 500 ptas. an hour.*

The neighboring province of La Segarra contains more castles than anywhere else in Catalonia. The **Ruta dels Castells de la Segarra** *takes off from Cervera, the lovely old provincial capital and meanders to all the splendid castles and fortified towers of the area. For a guide of the route, stop by the Cervera* **tourist office** *(Passeig Jaume Balmes 12, tel. 973/531303; open weekdays 8–3, Sat. 10–2 and 4–8, Sun. 10–2). Cervera is 100 km (62 mi) west of Barcelona, off the Highway N-II. Trains arrive several times daily from Barcelona.*

WHERE TO SLEEP AND EAT

Fonda Pilar (C. Dominics 4, tel. 973/480156, cash only) has clean, airy double rooms for a remarkable 2,400 ptas. a night. **Hostal Crisami** (Carretera de Manresa, tel. 973/480413) has simple, well-maintained doubles for 6,000 ptas. The homey, family-run **Restaurant Mare de la Font** (Carretera de Bassella, tel. 973/480152) is 1½ km (1 mi) outside town, in a small park where locals go to picnic on the weekends. The hearty Catalan menú del día runs 1,200–1,800 ptas.

ARAGÓN

BY ANNELISE SORENSEN

14

ragón was one of the most powerful ancient kingdoms in ancient Iberia. Now the fourth-largest Autonomous Community in Spain, it comprises three provinces (Huesca, Teruel, and Zaragoza) extending south from the Pyrenees over hot, dry central plains to a bold landscape of desolate rugged peaks and deep fertile gorges. And although Spain is now one of the world's top travel destinations (behind only its neighbor to the north), Aragón exists beyond the tourist radar—few people have caught on, leaving the region awash in unspoiled natural terrain. In the Ansó and Hecho valleys of the eastern Aragonese Pyrenees, you can trek the wild hills and not see another soul. For more of this kind of solitude, head for the hauntingly barren Maestrazgo, in Aragón's deep south, where the only signs of human life show up in dusty old villages that seem to grow right out of the earth.

Aragón's nerve center is the thriving, culturally rich city of Zaragoza, an urbane provincial capital of lively shopping streets, wide plazas, and happening nightlife. Zaragoza's Basilica del Pilar, dedicated to the Virgin of the Pillar—patron saint of the entire Hispanic world—draws pilgrims from around the globe; the city also has a strong Moorish legacy and a slew of striking Mudéjar buildings. Indeed, the Moors of Aragón left a vivid mark throughout the region: Teruel, provincial capital of southern Aragón, is famous for its Mudéjar towers, with their ornate, typically Moorish brick-and-tile designs. The chief cities in the north, Huesca and Jaca, are key jumping-off points for the formidable Pyrenean peaks, which pack boundless opportunities for both trekking and skiing. Astún and Candanchu, just north of Jaca, are popular ski resorts; farther east, near the small mountain town of Benasque, are the Cerler resort and Pico Aneto, the highest peak in the Pyrenees, whose 3,400 m (11,150 ft) of sheer cliffs and glaciers draw mountain climbers from all over Europe.

It is in the ancient villages sprinkled across the mountains and valleys that you'll feel the beating of Aragón's ancient heart. Perched on a green hill or tucked along a back road, each village is more bewitching than the last, its narrow cobbled streets lined with stone houses topped by conical chimneys and slate roofs. Aragón's most celebrated native son, the painter Francisco Goya, was born in one such modest community just south of Zaragoza; and you'll find his works, from frescoes to etchings, in museums and churches across the region. Last but not least, the region hides some wonderful alpine monasteries, including San Juan de la Peña (just south of Jaca), carved out of a massive rock mountain.

OKAY, YOU CAN STAY

The Moors occupied much of Spain for almost 800 years. After the Christian Reconquest and Inquisition, many were allowed to stay, even though they did not convert to Christianity. Muslims living under Christian kings were called Mudéjars, from an Arabic word meaning "allowed to remain;" today the word mudéjar *is applied to Spanish architecture and decorations crafted by this group or designed with a Moorish influence.*

BASICS

COMING AND GOING

Zaragoza, in the center of Aragón, is connected by bus and train to the rest of the region and to many major cities in Spain, including Logroño, Pamplona, San Sebastián, Barcelona, and Madrid. With plenty of time and patience you can slowly make your way on regional buses through some isolated mountain terrain and southern backcountry; but be prepared for erratic schedules and long waits. Huesca and Jaca, in the north, and Teruel, in the south, are key transportation hubs. To explore the Pyrenees and remote southern Aragón fully, having your own wheels is much easier.

ZARAGOZA

Lively Zaragoza is the capital and crossroads of Aragón: a confident and cosmopolitan city that's grounded in its deeply felt—and much celebrated—religious and cultural traditions. And as home to more than half the region's residents, Zaragoza is Aragón's melting pot. Chic professionals sip espressos at glossy cafés, while just around the corner an old farmer sits with his cronies in a dark turn-of-the-20th-century bar. Wide avenues lined with department stores and elegant boutiques run alongside the gloomy, narrow alleyways of the old quarter. Country and city folk share the sidewalks and the streets and, fervently, the grand Basilica del Pilar. It would be hard to find another city as devoted to a patron saint as the Zaragozanos are to Nuestra Señora del Pilar (Our Lady of the Pilar). She is believed to have descended from heaven and alighted on a marble pillar before Santiago (St. James) in the 9th century. The cathedral built to house and honor her is a massive Baroque display of adoration and the true emotional heart of the city. At all hours of the day the faithful pass through—even if only for a moment during their lunch break—to say a prayer to the Virgen del Pilar.

Head toward the middle of it all—the huge Plaza del Pilar, where everyone ends up at some time or other, for morning coffee, daily prayer, or the evening *paseo*. And locals might remind you that Zaragoza is a city of two cathedrals, the other one being the Gothic marvel La Seo, on the eastern end of Plaza del Pilar. The streets around the plaza are lined with little shops bursting with Pilar doodads: key chains and lighters and icebox magnets, all sporting the Virgin's image. The week to be here is around October 12, when Zaragoza celebrates the Fiestas del Pilar, with processions, concerts, bullfights, and traditional offerings of flowers. The city fills to capacity, of course, so expect to pay twice the usual price for lodging.

The Romans put the city on the map when they settled here in the 1st century BC and called it Caesaraugusta, a name that gradually evolved into Zaragoza. Roman ruins, including the underground remains of a market, are scattered throughout the city. The Arabs also left their mark, and elements of the Mudéjar style are particularly noticeable in the lavish Aljafería Palace and many of the smaller churches.

North of the old quarter, the mighty Río Ebro forges through Zaragoza, spanned by several bridges, including the Puente de Piedra (Stone Bridge), near Plaza del Pilar. Zaragoza's commercial zone spreads around the stately Plaza España and the wide avenues that branch off it.

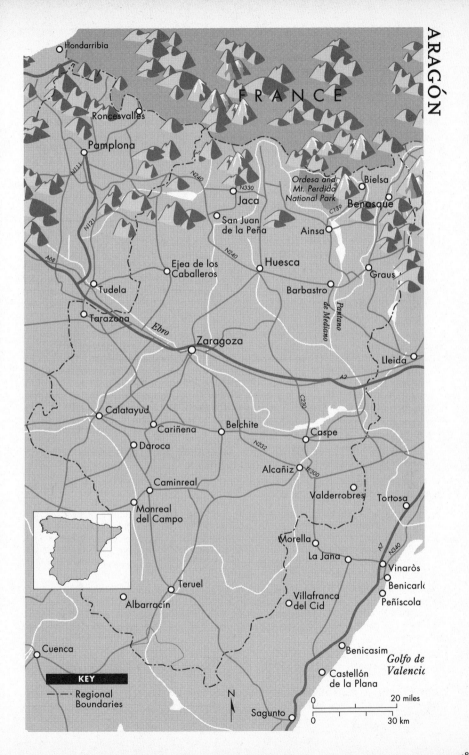

FRANCE

Hondarribia

Roncesvalles

Pamplona

N240

N330

Jaca

Ordesa and
Mt. Perdido
National Park

Bielsa

N121

San Juan
de la Peña

Benasque

Ainsa

Ejea de los
Caballeros

N240

Huesca

Graus

A68

Tudela

Barbastro

Tarazona

Ebro

Pantano
de Mediano

Zaragoza

Lleida

A2

C230

Calatayud

Cariñena

Belchite

Caspe

Daroca

N232

Alcañiz

N300

Caminreal

Valderrobres

Tortosa

Monreal
del Campo

Morella

A7

N340

La Jana

Vinaròs

Teruel

Villafranca
del Cid

Benicarló

Albarracín

Peñíscola

Cuenca

Benicasim

Golfo de
Valencia

KEY

— · — Regional
Boundaries

N

Castellón
de la Plana

Sagunto

0   20 miles

0   30 km

BASICS

VISITOR INFORMATION

Zaragoza has a slew of **tourist offices.** The main branch (976/201200; open daily 10–8) is on Plaza Pilar, opposite the basilica. The friendly multilingual staff can answer any and all questions and give you a useful city map; they also conduct guided city tours (at 9:30, 2, 4, and 7) and tours of the *casco histórico,* or historic quarter (at 11, noon, 5, and 6). During Semana Santa (Holy Week), tourist-office people in yellow shirts roam the streets near the main sights to answer questions.

There's a branch tourist office in the train station (open Mon–Sat. 11–2:30 and 4:30–8) and another small branch at Plaza Sas 7, just off Calle Alfonso I (tel. 976/998438), open weekdays 10–1 and 5–7, Saturday 10–1. The branch in Plaza César Augosto is often closed due to the ongoing excavation of Roman remains.

COMING AND GOING

BY TRAIN

The **train station** (Avda. Anselmo Clave, tel. 902/240202) sits southwest of town. To reach the old quarter on foot, you'll trek 20 minutes on busy streets. Much easier: hop on Bus 22, which takes you from Avenida Anselmo Clave, in front of the station, to Plaza España, from which it's an easy 10-minute walk through the old quarter to Plaza Pilar. Several trains daily serve **Madrid** (4½ hrs, 4,000 ptas.) and **Barcelona** (5 hrs, 4,000 ptas.) as well as smaller towns such as **Teruel** (3 hrs, 1,405 ptas.) and **Huesca** (1 hr, 660 ptas.)

BY BUS

Buses fan out in all directions from Zaragoza. There is no main bus station—each company has its own—so when you call, be sure to ask precisely where to pick up your bus. The tourist office has a useful list of all the bus companies and their destinations. **Ágreda Automóvil/La Oscense** (Passeig. Maria Agustín, tel. 976/229343) sends frequent long-distance vehicles to **Madrid, Barcelona, Galicia,** and **Extremadura;** regional buses serve **Huesca** and **Jaca** daily. **Jimenez** (C. Juan Pablo Bonet 13, tel. 976/276179) runs frequent daily buses to **Logroño, Burgos, Teruel, Valencia, Benidorm,** and **Alicante,** among others. The Basque Country is served by **Autobuses Conda** (Avda. de Navarra 81, tel. 976/333371), which heads several times daily to **Pamplona** and **San Sebastián.**

BY PLANE

Zaragoza's **airport** (5 km/3 mi outside the city, tel. 976/712300) mainly serves domestic destinations like Madrid and Barcelona, with occasional international flights.

WHERE TO SLEEP

There's plenty of cheap lodging on Calle Alfonso I, so you might want to head up this street and keep your eyes peeled. Plaza Pilar, in the bustling center of town, also has its share of budget beds. Many hostels and pensions are dingy and threadbare, but their low prices mean you can hang out for a few days without breaking the bank. Note, however, that there will be no room at the inn during the Fiestas del Pilar (the week of October 12) or Semana Santa (Holy Week, before Easter) unless you reserve in advance and prepare to pay double the usual rate.

UNDER 4,000 PTAS. • Fonda Satue. This hostel in the heart of the old quarter is housed in a gloomy old building with nicely priced but rundown doubles with shared bath for 3,600 ptas., plus a few with private bath for 4,000. It caters mostly to older, permanent residents and is often filled up, but it's worth trying for one of the few available rooms. *C. Espoz y Mina 4, tel. 976/225595. 8 rooms, 2 with bath. Cash only.*

Pensión Sándalo. This agreeable pension near Plaza España is one of the better deals in town, with cozy, clean doubles with shared bath for 3,800 ptas. (5,000 ptas. the weeks of October 12 and Semana Santa). *C. Coso 95, tel. 976/398933. 10 rooms, none with bath. Cash only.*

UNDER 6,000 PTAS. • Hostal Ambos Mundos. You can't get more central than this large, ramshackle hostel right on Plaza del Pilar. Musty basic doubles, most with a shower in the room, are 4,500 ptas. The hostel has recently set its sights on becoming a sort of old folks' home, so be prepared for lots of the geriatric set dozing in the downstairs lounge. *Plaza del Pilar 16, tel. 976/299704. 58 rooms, 12 with full bath. Cash only.*

Hostal Santiago. This basic hostel, which sits just off the main thoroughfare of Calle Alfonso I, has simple, clean rooms, most with bath, for 5,000 ptas. *C. Santiago, tel. 976/394550. 25 rooms, 20 with bath. Cash only.*

Pensión Huéspedes. Look for the sign FONDA, CAMAS (*camas* means "beds") on this street near Plaza Pilar, off Calle Alfonso I, to find this simple pension, which has clean doubles with shared bath for 4,000 ptas. *C. Manifestación 36, tel. 976/295821. 8 rooms, none with bath. Cash only.*

UNDER 8,000 PTAS. • Hotel Catalunya. Set on the southern edge of the old quarter, this friendly hotel has comfortable doubles with private bath for 6,500 ptas. *C. Coso 94–96, tel. 976/216938, fax 976/210803. 51 rooms.*

Hostal Plaza. Just a few doors down from the Hostal Ambos Mundos there's a friendly, newly renovated hostel where clean doubles with spic-and-span bathrooms cost 6,900 ptas. during Semana Santa, the Pilar festivals, and July–August. The price dips to 5,900 ptas. at other times. *Plaza del Pilar 14, tel. 976/ 294830. 14 rooms, 10 with bath.*

Hotel San Jorge. If you're looking for a step up in comfort from the hostel scene, try this pleasant hotel, whose well-maintained doubles go for 6,000 ptas. Triples are a also a good deal at 8,000 ptas. *C. Mayor, tel. 976/397462, fax 976/ 398577. 29 rooms.*

UNDER 10,000 PTAS. • Hotel Principe. A few blocks from Plaza del Pilar, off Calle Alfonso I, stands a rather institutional hotel that has ample doubles that go for 8,800 ptas. in summer (through early October) and 7,400 the rest of the year. *C. Santiago 12, tel. 976/294101, fax 976/299047. 45 rooms.*

UNDER 12,000 PTAS. • Hotel Sauce. This centrally located hotel has comfortable, clean doubles for 11,900 ptas. in July and August and during the Pilar festivals in early October. The rest of the year doubles cost 8,400 ptas. *C. Espoz y Mina 33, tel. 976/390100, fax 976/398597. 40 rooms.*

WHERE TO EAT

Zaragoza abounds with places to eat, from lively tapas bars to rustic *asadores*. Calles Don Jaime I and San Vicente de Paul in the old quarter are known for these brasserie-style restaurants, which specialize in the hearty grilled meats typical of Aragonese cuisine. A delicious regional specialty featured everywhere is *ternasco de Aragón* (spring lamb).

RESTAURANTS

UNDER 2,000 PTAS. • Cafeteria Principal. This simple yet classy restaurant is on graceful Plaza Sinue, near the Teatro Principal, and has a restful dark-wood and forest-green interior. The tasty *menú del día* (1,200 ptas.) suggests dishes like *ensalada de garbanzos con setas y ajos* (chickpea salad with mushrooms and garlic) and *ternasco a la brasa* (grilled spring lamb). *Plaza Sinue (off Don Jaime I, near C. Coso), no phone.*

El Fuelle. Its walls sporting farm implements and old bicycles, this lively, cavernous restaurant has a rustic look and a hearty menu. Comfort-food options include *solomillo de ternera* (veal; 1,700 ptas.), *conejo a la brasa* (grilled rabbit; 800 ptas.), and *esparragos blancos con jamón* (white asparagus with ham; 900 ptas.). *C. Mayor 59, tel. 976/398033.*

Ensanche La Yedra. Given an owner as friendly as José Maria, and the fact that everyone walks out with a smile, you know this cozy place is a favorite. The excellent tapas, starting at 500 ptas., will probably include *ancas de rama* (frogs' legs) and *setas con gambas* (mushrooms with shrimp); for something more substantial, try bonito tuna with capers, cornichons, and *cebolla de fuentes de Ebro,* a special local onion with a mild, sweet flavor. *C. Mayor 28–30, tel. 976/393705.*

Mesón-Asador. When it comes time to splurge, make sure you're at this elegant stone-walled restaurant, where the house specialties are hearty meats cooked in an *horno de leña* (wood-fired brick oven). Try the succulent *ternasco de Aragón*. *C. Santiago 14, tel. 976/390594. Closed Mon. No dinner Sun.*

TAPAS BARS

Zaragozanos take their tapas seriously, and the streets and plazas of the old town are lined with tapas bars, many with their own house specialty. Locals throng on the weekends to Plaza Santa Marta to enjoy their tapas al fresco at popular outdoor restaurants. If you're into olive oil, head to **Taberna El Lince** (tel. 976/290934), which has an excellent array of *tostadas* (open-face toasted sandwiches) liberally doused with it. Try the tostada *con salmón ahumado* (with smoked salmon; 350 ptas). Top it off with a glass of vino Cariñena for a mere 100 ptas. Next door, **Tasca Vitorinos II** serves a slew of tasty tapas, including *caracoles* (snails), *anchoas en vinagre* (anchovies in vinegar), and *bonito en escabeche* (bonito tuna in a mixture of peppers, *boquerones* (fresh anchovies), and olive oil.

El Ancla. Zaragozanos pack this simple, no-nonsense place to graze on seafood specialties, including *mejillones a la cerveza* (mussels cooked in beer; 350 ptas.) and *salmón* (1,100 ptas.). For more filling fare try the *paella de mariscos* (seafood paella; 1,500 ptas). *C. Don Jaime I 38, tel. 976/291300.*

La Olla. This bustling and amiable spot—with a mounted bull's head watching over the packed tables and old bullfight posters on the walls— serves a long list of savory tapas, including *caracoles* (snails) and *ternera* (veal), prepared a variety of ways. *C. Mayor 1, tel. 976/398257.*

Marisqueria Tony. Join the crowds sitting at the long bar and tear into a big old plate of shrimp (800 ptas.) washed down with a beer. It's messy and informal, with shrimp shells on the floor and regulars who shout out their orders as they walk in. *C. Don Jaime I 40, tel. 976/390414. Cash only.*

CAFÉS

Zaragoza has heaps of stylish cafés where you can kick back amid elegant surroundings. **Gran Café Zaragoza** (C. Alfonso I 25, tel. 976/290882) is sumptuously done up with gilded ceilings, heavy burgundy curtains, dark wood, and round marble tables. Try a *granizado* (a summertime Slurpee-style drink) with or without alcohol, or pick from a long list of inventive coffee drinks—maybe the Cleopatra: iced coffee, condensed milk, and cream.

WORTH SEEING

Most of Zaragoza's sights are in the old town, near Plaza Pilar. One of the best ways to soak up the ambience is to spend a day wandering the old quarter's maze of streets, which extend south of the Río Ebro. Along the way, stop by the modern Central Market (Mercado Central, open weekdays 9–2 and 5–8, Sat. 9–2), where you can fill your arms with fresh produce at low prices. In addition to the city's two grand cathedrals, Zaragoza is dotted with lots of smaller churches, many with Moorish elements: **San Pablo** (C. San Pablo 42), just west of the old quarter, and **Santa Maria Magdalena,** at the east end of Calle Major, both have magnificent Mudéjar towers, as does **San Miguel,** southeast of the old quarter.

BASILICA DE NUESTRA SEÑORA DEL PILAR

This massive cathedral, whose main dome is surrounded by 10 smaller domes decorated in multicolor tiles, is a fitting symbol for the Virgen del Pilar, the patron saint of all *hispanidad* (the Hispanic world). Construction began on the cathedral in the 16th century, but it has been continually expanded and upgraded over the years. The immense towers that rise at the four corners weren't completed until the end of the 19th century. The famed El Pilar statue (called *La Pilarica*) is a small Gothic woodcarving just 15 inches high, though her appearance is much embellished by the sumptuous embroidered mantle (changed every day) on her large pedestal. Enshrined in a wall behind the Virgin is a small piece of rose-color marble believed to have come from the pillar upon which the Virgin first appeared to Santiago. The devout come from all over to kiss and touch the well-worn piece, and pilgrims touch their souvenirs to the marble to bless them. The cathedral's organ, one of the largest in Spain, rears its 6,000 pipes over a spectacular choir, with three tiers of dark, ornately carved stalls for a total of 124 singers (imagine the sound). Look closely and you'll see that each seat is unique and that many sport fantastical beings—like the headless wood nymphs carved in the legs of one seat. The splendid 16th-century alabaster high altar, with detailed carvings of the Virgin surrounded by saints, is one of oldest parts of the church. The paintings in the cupola above the sanctuary were done by Velázquez, and those in the surrounding cupolas by Goya, including a small one completed when he was 28 and a larger, more mature work done six years later. If you visit during the October 12 Fiesta del Pilar, you can join the thousands who come to put flowers on the Virgin's mantle. The adjoining **Museo Pilarista** displays Goya's and Velazquez's sketches for the cupola paintings and a collection of jewelry used to adorn the Virgin. *Open daily 5:45 AM–8:30 PM (until 9:30 in summer). Museum admission: 150 ptas.; open daily 9–2 and 4–6.*

LA SEO

Zaragoza's other cathedral, built on the site of a mosque, is the grand La Seo, which looms over the eastern end of Plaza Pilar. In 1998 the cathedral reopened its doors after years of renovations. The beautifully tiled floors, whose patterns mirror the ceiling decorations, have been redone, and the carved alabaster high altar has been cleaned and shined. The cathedral is a spectacular fusion of different architectural styles. It began life as a Romanesque church in 1119, though only an apse still exists from that period; in the 14th to 15th centuries it was rebuilt as a Gothic cathedral; in the 16th century the dome was completed in a Mudéjar style of brick and colored tiles; and in the 18th century the neoclassical main facade was built. Be sure to notice its beautiful Moorish paneled ceiling and the exterior Mudéjar walls of the chapel of La Parroquieta. Among the ring of lovely chapels around the high altar are that of Santo Cristo de la Seo, topped by a lavish dome of *pan de oro* (gold leaf; literally, "gold bread"); the wonderful Gothic chapel of Santo Bernardo; and that of Sant Miguel, with its lovely portal. If the doors on Plaza Pilar are closed, head around to Plaza de San Bruno (filled with young skateboarders on weekends) and enter there. Near this entrance is a spectacular 16th-century archway with porticoes. **The Museo de Tapices** (Tapestry Museum) houses a rich collection of Belgian tapestries from the 15th and 16th centuries, including one depicting the Crucifixion and the Resurrection. *Open spring–fall, weekdays 10–2 and 5–7, Sat. 10–1 and 5–7, Sun. 10–noon and 5–7; in winter, weekdays 10–2 and 4–6, Sat. 10–1 and 4–6, Sun. 10–noon and 4–6. Museum admission 200 ptas.; open Mon.–Sat. 10–2 and 5–7 (in winter 4–6), Sun. 10–2.*

MUSEU ARQUEOLÓGICO DEL FORO DE CAESARAUGUSTA

Zaragoza takes great care of its Roman remains, and this is evident in the underground archeological museum below the Plaza de la Seo. The well-lit ancient ruins have diagrams and explanations of where they once fit into the Roman city structure. There are still-standing walls of market shops and the remains of an immense sewer system that used to carry the city's wastes to the Río Ebro. A 20-minute film "narrated" by the Río Ebro describes all that transpired along its banks during the Roman era. Near the forum museum are the remains of walls that once formed the northeastern section of the forum complex (enter from the adjoining Plaza de San Bruno). And just south, at Calle San Juan y San Pedro, Nos. 3–7, are the remains of Roman latrines and what was once a grand swimming pool surrounded by pillars. *Plaza de la Seo 2, tel. 976/399752. Admission 300 ptas. for museum; 600 ptas. for all sites. Open Tues.–Sat. 10–2 and 5–8, Sun. 10–2.*

LA LONJA (THE EXCHANGE)

Holding its own amid the two massive basilicas stands the elegant Renaissance exchange building, once the trade and business center of Zaragoza's thriving grain industry. It was built in the 16th century, and its immense pillars rise up to Gothic vaulted ceilings. The Exchange is often the scene of temporary art exhibits.

TORREÓN DE LA ZUDA (ZUDA TOWER)

West of Plaza Pilar on Plaza César Augosto rises the last standing remnant of the 10th-century Muslim Zuda Palace. Nearby are the Murallas Romanas, remains of the Roman walls.

MUSEO DE ZARAGOZA

Housed in a stately brick building constructed for the 1908 Universal Exhibition, this museum has an excellent collection of paintings by Goya and other Aragonese painters, Roman mosaics, and prehistoric objects discovered around Aragón. *Plaza de los Sitios 6, tel. 976/222181. Admission 200 ptas.; free for EU citizens. Open Tues.–Sat. 9–2, Sun. 10–2.*

The museum's ethnological branch, the **Museo Etnológico,** lies south of the city in the Parque Primo Rivera. The collection includes regional costumes and furniture and an entire section devoted to Aragonese ceramics. The Parque Primo de Rivera (also called Parque de Zaragoza) is awash in fountains and lush greenery and makes for a pleasant getaway from the hustle and bustle of the city. *Parque Primo de Rivera, tel. 976/553726. Open Tues.–Sat. 9–2, Sun. 10–2.*

MUSEU DE CAMÓN AZNAR

Set in a Renaissance palace, this extensive museum holds paintings from the 15th to the 20th centuries and a series of etchings by Goya. *C. Espoz y Mina 23, tel. 976/397328. Admission 100 ptas. Open Tues.–Fri. 9–2:15 and 6–9, Sat. 10–2, Sun. 11–2.*

MUSEO PABLO GARGALLO

Here you'll find the collected works of the renowned Aragonese sculptor Pablo Gargallo, including a series of his bronzes and many sketches and engravings. *Plaza San Felipe 3, tel. 976/392058. Open Tues.–Sat. 10–2 and 5–9, Sun. 10–2.*

A TALE OF TWO CITIES

Of all the painful reminders of the Spanish Civil War (1936–1939), few are as haunting as Belchite, where a war-torn old town stands silent and deserted next to its younger sibling. The new town, a series of bland 1950s houses on grass, goes about its business seemingly immune to the ruins next door. Buses shuttle daily from Zaragoza (Autobuses del Bajo Aragón, tel. 976/229886).

The sign at the crumbling village gate reads simply BELCHITE, PUEBLO VIEJO (old town), and what awaits is eerie and affecting. Dusty, rock-strewn streets are lined with empty shells of houses, their ravaged wrought-iron balconies twisting off and dangling askew. Rusty-hinged shutters open and close creakily with each passing wind. Walls and doors bear bullet scars. The churches of San Martín and San Agustín, naked husks of their former selves, are unsettlingly beautiful: jagged holes in the ceilings gape at the sky, and rocks litter the ground where pews used to be. Shepherds and their flocks, the only inhabitants, slowly pick their way to the fields beyond.

EL PALACIO DE LA ALJAFERÍA

The Moorish kings built this sumptuous pleasure palace from the 9th to the 11th centuries, and it's one of the most marvelous Mudéjar creations in Aragón. In the 15th and 16th centuries the kings of Aragón lived here; Ferdinand and Isabella added a palatial Gothic section. The result is an idiosyncratic mix of styles and sentimentalities, with elegant Gothic staircases that climb to royal sitting rooms topped by splendid Mudéjar ceilings. Highlights include the mihrab (Muslim prayer room), and the lovely courtyard of Santa Isabella. Currently, the parliament of Aragón meets here. The palace lies west of the city center, near Plaza Emilio Alfaro. *Admission 300 ptas.; free Sun. Open April–Oct., Sat.–Wed. 10–2 and 4:30–8, Fri. 4:30–8; Nov.–Mar., Mon.–Wed. and Sat. 10–2 and 4–6:30, Fri. 4–6:30, Sun. 10–2.*

PALACIO DE SÁSTAGO

Zaragoza was once a two-casino town, with one for the upper classes and another for everybody else. The two casinos sit right across from each other on Calle Coso, which runs along the southern border of the old quarter, but only the wealthy could try their luck at the 16th-century Sástago Palace. The high wood-beamed ceilings supported by elegant columns now look down on temporary art exhibits of all kinds, from Yoko Ono's paintings to modern sculpture. The working class gambled across the street in the Casino Mercantil, now closed to the public. *C. Coso 44, tel. 976/288880. Open Tues–Sat. 11–2 and 6–9, Sun. 11–2.*

SHOPPING

Zaragoza has a range of outdoor markets where you can hunt for bargains. On Sunday morning **El Rastro** (the Flea Market) gets lively, with vendors selling antiques and bric-a-brac. The market takes place around the *plaza de toros* (bullring) that lies southwest of the old quarter. Also on Sunday morning, a **coin and stamp market** is held in Plaza San Francisco, south of town near the university. For contemporary clothes and household items, try the **Mercadillo** (market) held Wednesday and Sunday mornings at La Romareda Estadio de Fútbol (the soccer stadium), south of town near the Parque Primo de Rivera.

AFTER DARK

Zaragozans enthusiastically do their part in upholding Spain's reputation for nonstop nightlife. From stylish jazz clubs to thumping disco bars, it's a city that knows how to party—you can leave your hostel when the sun sets and not return until it rises again. On the narrow streets of the old quarter you'll hear lively tunes coming from whole strings of little bars with flashing neon signs. Head to the maze of streets west of Calle Alfonso I for most of the action. Also jumping is the part of the old quarter called El Tubo (the Tube), for all the tubelike bar-lined streets that snake their way through the area.

The bars that ring the shaded Plaza Santa Cruz, off Calle Don Jaime I, fill up early and stay that way till late. In the twilight hours families and couples tip back aperitifs at the pleasant outdoor tables, and later, at around 10, a fresh crop of revelers comes through on their nocturnal jaunts. **Café Praga** (Plaza Santa Cruz 13, tel. 976/200251) has an outside scene early in the evening and then it starts getting lively inside at the bar and in the downstairs dance lounge. In the nearby Plaza Ariño you'll find **Chaston Jazz Club** (as in "Charleston"; tel. 976/397456), a smooth nightspot with intimate nooks of circular pillowed benches and low tables. The friendly owner is a longtime jazz aficionado who occasionally brings together some great improvisational groups. Around the corner, **La Bodeguilla de Santa Cruz** (C. Santa Cruz 3, no phone), a tiny, dark, seductive bar with rich red walls and lots of bric-a-brac, serves wine and tapas *"con todos los recuerdos del ayer"* ("with all the memories of yesterday"). To continue in a nostalgic mood, move on to **Paris Gallerie** (Plaza San Pedro Nolasco 2, tel. 976/291689), where you can recline on low sofas in the dimly lit back room and imagine you're in 1920s Paris. The amiable and cozy **La Migueria** (C. Contamina 17, tel. 976/200736) has pale yellow walls, a small bar, and a few tables where a friendly, boisterous crowd comes *para charlar* (to chat) over drinks and tapas. **Versus Disco Bar** (C. Mendez Nuñez 36, no phone) cranks the dance music up and keeps it that way until the wee hours.

NEAR ZARAGOZA

Venture south of Zaragoza, and you enter the land of Goya and of wine. The quiet town of **Muel** has a small church with paintings by Goya, who was born nearby in the village of Fuendetodos (*see below*). And around the small town of **Cariñena,** the center of Aragon's wine production, the countryside is lush with green vineyards and red soil. There are a few bodegas in town, as well as bars where you can sample the region's offerings. As you head farther south, alternating fields of grain, vines, and almond trees stretch toward the horizon in an undulating plateau.

Just 8 km (5 mi) north of Zaragoza there's a Carthusian monastery, the **Cartuja de Aula Dei,** which has early Goya frescoes of Christ and the Virgin Mary. It's a working monastery, so visiting hours are limited to the last Saturday of the month. You need to make a reservation (tel. 976/714934), preferably a month or two in advance. Bus 28, departing from several places in Zaragoza (including Paseo de la Independencia) several times a day will take you to a stop near the monastery. Make sure you tell the driver you want to get off there.

FUENDETODOS

This simple village of silent cobbled streets lined with stone and whitewashed houses produced one of Spain's greatest artists, Francisco Goya y Lucientes, who was born here in 1746. At **Casa Natal de Goya** (just off the Plaza de Goya, tel. 976/143830; open Tues.–Sun. 11–2 and 4–7) you can wander through the restored cottage, decorated with period crockery and furniture, where the kitchen and other rooms look just as they did in the days of Goya's childhood. Just down the road, the **Museo del Grabado de Goya** has a broad collection of Goya's etchings and sells beautiful reproductions of them (C. Zuloaga 3, tel. 976/143857; admission 300 ptas. for museum and Casa Goya; same hrs as Casa Goya). For food and a bed head to the **Hospedería El Capricho de Goya** (Paseo Vista Alegre 2, tel. 976/143810), where a basic double with bath costs 5,000 ptas., including breakfast. Its *menú del día* (1,200 ptas), offers dishes like *merluza a la romana* (fried hake) and *ternasco* (veal). Two buses depart daily from Zaragoza for Fuendetodos.

NORTHERN ARAGÓN AND THE PYRENEES

With soaring peaks, lushly forested slopes, and thundering rivers, the Aragón Pyrenees are one of Spain's national treasures. If you're looking for the great outdoors, this is a land of verdant gorges, waterfalls, and trout-filled streams. Lace up your ski or hiking boots, and take to the wild valleys and snow-capped mountaintops in any season. Ski stations dot the range, including the busy resorts of Astún and Candanchu, north of Jaca, and Cerler, near Benasque. Miles of hiking trails traverse the gorgeous Ansó and Hecho valleys and the magnificent Parque Nacional de Ordesa y Monte Perdido. Huesca and Jaca are the two biggest cities in the north, with lots of bus connections into the Pyrenees.

HUESCA

As capital of one of the three provinces that make up Aragón, Huesca is a pleasant mix of urban and rural, with modern apartment buildings lining its perimeter, and a dark, atmospheric old quarter with bars and outdoor cafés. Huesca's history is formidable. The Romans first settled here, calling it Osca. The Moors arrived in the south of Spain in 711 and by 718 had made their way north, where they took over Huesca and ruled it for almost 400 years. In 1096 it became the capital of the Aragón kingdom until power was transferred to Zaragoza in the early 12th century. Huesca was hit particularly hard during the Spanish Civil War and saw several years of fierce battles between the Republicans and Franco's forces.

BASICS

The wonderfully helpful **tourist office** (Plaza de la Catedral 3, tel. 902/240202; open daily 9–2 and 4–8) has lots of useful info on Huesca and on the province, including worthwhile day trips and transportation.

COMING AND GOING

Huesca is a hub, with buses to all parts of northern Aragón and the Pyrenees. Several buses daily serve Zaragoza, Lérida, and Barcelona; two buses daily serve Benasque. Buses to Jaca (8–10 daily) pass by Sabiñanigo, where you can make connections to Ainsa and Torla, near the Parque Nacional de Ordesa y Monte Perdido. The **bus station** (C. del Parque 3, tel. 974/210700) is south of the Plaza de la Catedral.

Trains leave the **train station,** also south of the Plaza de la Catedral (974/242159), for Zaragoza and Madrid 3–5 times daily and for Sabiñanigo, Jaca, and Canfranc 1–3 times daily.

WHERE TO SLEEP

Huesca has a host of cheap accommodations, many clustered in the old quarter. If it's the high season and you're finding most places full, head east of the train station, near Calle San Lorenzo and Calle Padre Huesca, for some more budget options. This area is also packed with bars that fill up (and get loud) on the weekends, so if you're a light sleeper, beware.

Hostal Lizana (Plaza Lizana 6, tel. 974/220776), just east of the Plaza de la Catedral, has basic rooms (some are quite cramped) with shower for 5,800 ptas. Nearby is the newer **Hostal Lizana 2** (Plaza Lizana 8, tel. 974/220776), offering spiffed-up doubles with bath for 6,800 ptas.; owner Antonio is friendly and chatty and can fill you in on what to see and do in Huesca. Across the street, Paco rents simple rooms above his restaurant, **Casa Paco** (C. Ricafort 2, tel. 974/221470), for 3,000 ptas. without bath. Staying at the **Hostal Rugaca** (Porches de Galicia 1, tel. 974/226449) puts you right near the heart of the old town: the building sits above an arcaded walkway, overlooking lively outdoor cafés that fill with locals in the evenings. Clean doubles with bath are 6,000 ptas., going up to 7,500 ptas. in August. **Hostal Joaquín Costa** (C. Joaquín Costa 20, tel. 974/241738), just north of Plaza de la Catedral, has simple doubles with bath for 6,000 ptas.; if it's full, inquire about rooms at the **Bar Los Molinos,** down the street.

Hotel Sancho Abarca (Plaza Lizana 13, tel. 974/225169), across from Hostal Lizana, is one of Huesca's higher-end lodgings, with comfortable, spic-and-span double rooms for 13,300 ptas.

WHERE TO EAT

Clustered on and around Plaza Lizana, in the old quarter, Huesca's restaurants range from old, cheap, family-run eateries to swanky places with the best in Aragonese cuisine. **Bar-Restaurante La Campana** (C. Coso Alto 78, tel. 974/229500) is a town favorite, with a tasty menú del día for 1,500 ptas. and such innovative plates as *conejo en salsa de almendras* (rabbit in almond sauce), *trucha a la mostaza* (trout in a mustard sauce), and *berenejenas rellenas de jamón y gambas* (eggplant stuffed with ham and shrimp). With an entrance spanned by brick arches, **Restaurante El Bodegón** (C. Pedro IV 4, on Plaza Lizana, tel. 974/231681) serves an excellent menú del día for 1,500 ptas. during the week (closed Wed.) and 2,500 ptas. on weekends. Tasty starters include *ensalada Aragonesa* (salad of tomato, asparagus, tuna, and boiled egg) and *gambas a la plancha* (grilled shrimp). Wood-walled **Casa Paco** (C. Ricafort 2, tel. 974/221470, menú del día 1,200 ptas.), on Plaza Lizana, is a combination dining room–bar with a long, rectangular window between the two so that diners can watch the tube. The *trabajadores* (workers) arrive around 9 PM; the second shift begins around 10:30, when other locals come to dine before hitting the bars. **Mesón La Vicaría** (C. San Orencio 9, tel. 974/225195), amid a slew of bars in the old quarter, has a cozy brick-and-stone interior with wooden booths. The menú del día costs 1,200 ptas. (1,500 ptas. on weekends), but *raciones* (large portions of tapas) are also served, including *albóndigas* (meatballs, 100 ptas.), *bacalao* (salt cod, 300 ptas), and *bocadillos calientes* (hot sandwiches of ham, pork, or grilled peppers, 500 ptas).

If it's your birthday, or you're just feeling flush, splurge on **Las Torres** (C. María Auxiliadora 3, tel. 974/228213). Though in the least attractive part of town, it's one of Huesca's most respected restaurants, with a beautifully decorated two-tier dining area and a 6,000-pta. *menú gastronomique* of regional cuisine with a French twist.

WORTH SEEING

Huesca's highlight is the Gothic **cathedral,** which towers over the shady Plaza de la Catedral. Sightseeing over, you can gaze at the beautiful front portal from a comfortable plaza café. Inside, the crown jewel is the alabaster altarpiece by Italian artist Damián Forment; the **Museo Diocesano** also displays a collection of religious art from churches throughout the region (tel. 974/231099; admission 200 ptas; open in summer, Mon.–Sat. 10:30–1:30 and 4–7:30; fall–spring, 10:30–1:30 and 4–7, Sat. 10:30–1:30). Across from the cathedral stands the 16th-century **ayuntamiento** (town hall), which has a beautiful Baroque staircase and a painting, called *The Bell of Huesca,* depicting one of the more macabre moments in Huesca's history. In the 12th century, King Ramiro II ordered the beheading of a group of his noblemen (essentially for treason, but they'd been getting on his nerves for a while), and after the grisly deed had been done, he had their heads laid out in a circle—like the base of a bell—and suspended one of the heads on a rope over the circle, like the *badajo* (clapper) of the bell. This lovable monarch is buried in the 12th-century church of **San Pedro del Viejo** (Plaza San Pedro, tel. 974/222387; open Mon.–Sat. 10–2 and 6–8, Sun. 10–2); do take a stroll through its graceful cloister. The **Museo Arqueológico Provincial** (tel. 974/220586; open Tues–Sat. 10–2 and 5–8, Sun. 10–2), just north of the Plaza de la Catedral, is housed in the 12th-century Palacio Real (Royal Palace) of the Aragón kings. The collection includes Roman artifacts discovered in the region, medieval paintings, and several lithographs by Goya.

AFTER DARK

Huescans know how to have a good time. On warm summer weekends, the outdoor bars and cafés of the old quarter overflow with revelers. Head to the **Porches de Galicia,** the arched gallery just off Calle Coso Alto, to start the night. Folks flock to the terrace of **Bar Puerto Rico** (underneath Hostal Rugaca), and then head to the nearby bar-lined streets of the old quarter. Calle Berenguer, Calle Padre Huesca, and Calle San Lorenzo all get lively when it gets dark. **Da Vinci** (C. Padre Huesca 13, tel. 974/225353) has popular outdoor tables and a comfortable indoor bar.

LEAVING HUESCA

Thirty-two kilometers (20 miles) northwest of Huesca, the **Castillo de Loarre,** a massive 11th-century castle and fortress, rises mightily above the rocky terrain. The mazelike interior makes for great exploring: tunnels lead down to dark cellars, and narrow stairs wind up to lookout towers that command wonderful views over far-reaching fields. The castle is open daily 10–2 and 4–7 or 4–8, depending on when the sun sets (there's no electric light). A few buses run daily from Huesca to Loarre, but from there it's a tiring 6-km (4-mi) walk to the castle.

As you continue west toward Pamplona, just north of Ayerbe you'll start seeing otherworldly towering rock formations off in the distance. They're called **Los Mallos** (the Mallets), and a good place to snap pictures of them is in Riglos, near the Río Gallego.

PARQUE NACIONAL DE ORDESA Y MONTE PERDIDO

All of Aragón's landscapes seem to meet here with a crash of cymbals. Looming over this national park is the **Monte Perdido** (Lost Mountain) range, the largest limestone mountain chain in Western Europe. Luxuriant valleys blanketed in beech, fir, and pine cut through the terrain, and clear blue streams and gushing waterfalls keep the fields moist and fertile. After the snow melts, honeysuckle, primroses, and irises blossom in rock crevices and on shaded slopes. Vultures and eagles soar overhead, chamois scamper up the mountainsides, and the ice-cold streams teem with trout. Small alpine villages, their stone houses topped by sandstone-tile roofs and conical chimneys, dot the hillsides and make for pleasant stops along the routes meandering throughout the park. The semi-abandoned villages of **Fragen,** at the western edge of the park, and **Vió,** near the southern perimeter, are particularly good examples of ancient Aragonese architecture.

The park is divided into four sections: **Ordesa** (to the east), **Añisclo** (to the south), and **Escuaín** and **Pineta** (to the west). The Park Information Center and the tourist offices in Torla and Ainsa (*see below*) have useful guides and maps of the *senderos* (trails) crisscrossing the park, and you can pick up trail maps and supplies in small gateway towns at the perimeter.

The tourist office in **Torla,** near the entrance of the Valle de Ordesa, is open weekdays 8–3, weekends 9–2 and 3:30–6. Between July 1 and October 15, cars are not allowed into the Ordesa section, and Torla sets up a parking lot in town (75 ptas. per hour 9–8; free 8 PM–9 AM), from which a bus runs every 20 minutes into the park (375 ptas. round-trip; last departure back to Torla 8:30 PM). The bus drops you off at the **Park Information Center** (Centro de Visitantes El Parador; tel. 974/486421; open daily 9–2 and 3:30–6), at the park entrance, 8 km (5 mi) northeast of Torla.

Hikers can take easy strolls along flat terrain or go in for serious mountain treks. One popular route is the 4½-hour **Circo de Soaso,** which heads east through the Valle de Ordesa past wild vegetation and waterfalls to the **Refugio de Góriz,** at 7,085 ft. This is the only refuge in the park (tel. 974/341201), and it has 100 *literas* (bunk beds) and a kitchen. It's open year-round but fills up in summer, so call ahead— and bring cash.

There are strict restrictions on camping in this park. You can only camp in the Ordesa sector at above 6,890 ft, in the Pineta sector above 8,200 ft, and in the Añisclo and Escuaín sectors above 5,900 ft.; and you must set up your tent at sunset and dismantle it at sunrise. There are, however, campgrounds just outside the park, particularly around Torla.

Torla has a handful of budget lodgings, including the friendly **Hostal Altoaragón** (tel. 974/486172), which has clean double rooms with bath for 5,500 ptas. The same owner has the **Hotel Ballarín** (tel. 974/486155), which is a step up in quality and in price, with comfortable double rooms for 6,800 ptas. **Restaurante El Taillón** (tel. 974/486304), just up the hill from the tourist office, has a good menú del día for 1,500 ptas., and a tasty à la carte dish of *salmón en salsa de casa* (salmón in a house sauce).

Cars are allowed into the other sections of the park throughout the year, and a popular drive goes to the **Cañon de Añisclo** via the town of Escalona. The lovely village of **Ainsa,** just south of here, is a pleasant spot to spend a night or two if you plan to make day trips into the park. The tourist office (tel. 974/500767) is open daily July–August, 9–2 and 4:30–9; September–June, 10–2 and 4:30–8. Ainsa's old quarter, perched above town, has a 12th-century Romanesque church and an elegant central plaza. You can stay at the **Casa el Hospital** (tel. 974/500750, cash only), in an old pilgrim's hospital, which has double rooms for 5,000 ptas. It also has a triple with a kitchen for 6,500 ptas.

Hudebus buses (tel. 974/213277) travel daily between Sabiñanigo (east of Jaca) and Ainsa, stopping at several towns on the way, including Biescas, Torla, Broto, and Boltaña. Leaving Sabiñanigo at 11 AM, the bus passes through Torla at noon and arrives in Ainsa at 1:10; in July and August an additional bus leaves Sabiñanigo at 6:30 PM on the same route.

BENASQUE

The pleasant alpine town of Benasque, in the far eastern reaches of Aragón, is full of a hardy mix of skiers and mountain trekkers, drawn by the phenomenal Pyrenean peaks that rise up over town. **Pico de Aneto,** at 11,165 ft the highest mountain in the Pyrenees, is right in Benasque's backyard, so to speak. Aneto is for serious mountain climbers with crampons and ice axes; everyone else goes hiking in the surrounding countryside. Skiers make for the resort at nearby **Cerler** (tel. 974/551012), one of the highest points in the Pyrenees, with 38 trails.

BASICS

Benasque's **tourist office** (C. San Pedro, tel. 974/551289, open June–Aug., daily 9–2 and 4–9; Sept.–May, daily 10–2 and 5–9) has trail maps and other info on trekking throughout the area.

COMING AND GOING

Several **buses** travel daily between Benasque and Huesca. The bus "station" is Calle Mayor at the entrance to town.

WHERE TO SLEEP AND EAT

Twelve kilometers (8 miles) north of Cerler is the large **Hospital de Benasque** (tel. 974/552012), a popular hostel, inn, and refuge rolled into one. It sits in the middle of the natural parkland surrounding the peaks of **Posets** (11,057 ft) and **Maladeta** (10,850 ft) and makes for a pleasant base as you're hiking the area. The comfortable hostel rooms cost 4,900 ptas. per person, in a room for six the price is 3,000 ptas, and a bunk in a dormitory is 2,250 ptas—all including breakfast. You'll need your own sleeping bag in the six-bed rooms or the dormitory.

Among the budget lodgings in Benasque, you might try the four-room **Casa Rural,** above the Regalos Molsa store (tel. 974/551073, cash only), where simple double rooms with shared bath go for 3,500 ptas. Because many skiers and hikers like to sleep and eat in the same place, lots of the hostels and hotels offer only room-and-board deals. **Hostal Valero** (Carretera Anciles, tel. 974/551061) charges 3,800 ptas. per person, including breakfast, and also offers *media pensión* (half-board), which is breakfast and your choice of lunch or dinner, for 5,300 ptas. The same owners run the **Hotel Aneto,** where *media pensión* is 6,350 ptas. per person. **Hostal Solana** (Plaza Mayor, tel. 974/551439), in the center of town, has comfortable doubles for 7,500 ptas. (including breakfast) in July–August, Christmas, and Easter; for 5,500 ptas. the rest of the year.

WORTH SEEING

Exploring Benasque yields some ancient treasures, including the lovely Romanesque **church of Santa María Mayor** and the clusters of typical Aragón stone houses with tile roofs.

JACA

The busy industrial town of Jaca is one of the main commercial crossroads and transportation hubs of northern Aragón. It's also home to a bevy of ancient sights that powerfully evoke the town's long and impressive history. Jaca was founded by the Romans and then conquered by the Moors in the early 8th century. In 760 it was won back by *los Cristianos* in a victory still celebrated annually on the first Friday in May, when townspeople re-create the battle and all end up singing regional hymns in the center of town. In the 11th century Jaca became the first capital of the Aragón kingdom, though by the end of the century the power had shifted to Huesca.

In the last few years Jaca has become quite the ski resort; on winter weekends the town's hostels and bars fill up with skiers on their way to and from the Pyrenees. The popular ski centers at **Astún** (tel. 974/373088) and **Candanchu** (tel. 974/373192) are just over 30 km (19 mi) away. In the first week of August every odd-numbered year, Jaca hosts the **Festival Folclórico de los Pirineos.** People stream in from all over the Pyrenees to show off their cultural traditions with regional dances, performances, and food. The **Festival Internacional en el Camino de Santiago** (International Festival of the Way of St. James) also takes place in August (exact dates vary yearly), with classical- and religious-music concerts. Jaca gets an intellectual boost in summer from students who arrive for summer sessions of the University of Zaragoza.

BASICS

The **tourist office** has a useful map of Jaca and lots of general info on the Pyrenees, including guides with trail maps (Avda. Regimiento Galicia 2, tel. 974/360098; open July–mid-Sept., weekdays 9–2 and 4:30–8, Sat. 10–1:30 and 5–8, Sun. 10–1:30; mid-Sept.–June, weekdays 9–1:30 and 4:30–7, Sat. 10–1 and 5–7).

COMING AND GOING

Jaca is a transportation hub, with bus and train connections to towns throughout Aragón and the surrounding regions. The **train station** (tel. 974/361332) is a 25-minute walk north of the town center, but the city bus can take you there in no time; it pulls up 10 minutes before each hour, 8:50 AM–9:50 PM. Trains go several times a day to Canfranc, Huesca, and Zaragoza; long-distance trains hit Barcelona, Madrid, and Valencia. The **bus station** (Avda. Jacetania, tel. 974/355060) is right in the center of town near the cathedral. Buses run several times weekly (and once or twice weekends) to Huesca, Zaragoza, Hecho, Canfranc, Pamplona, and Barcelona.

WHERE TO SLEEP

Jaca has a handful of budget lodgings, many of which fill up quickly in July and August and during ski season. One of the cheapest is **Hostal Paris** (Plaza San Pedro 5, tel. 974/361020, cash only), near the cathedral, where comfortable double rooms with firm beds and hardwood floors are 4,000 ptas. The friendly manager will gladly fill you in on where to eat and drink well. **Hostal El Abeto** (C. Bellido 15, tel. 974/361642, cash only), in the center of the old quarter, has basic doubles with bath for 5,500 ptas. and a few without bath for 4,400 ptas. **Hostal Ciudad de Jaca** (C. Sancho Ramirez, tel. 974/364311), near Jaca's ancient Torre del Reloj (Clock Tower) in the town center, offers clean double rooms with bath for 6,000 ptas. **Hostal Somport** (C. Echegaray 11, tel. 974/363410) has well-maintained double rooms for 5,500 ptas., triples for 7,000 ptas., and rooms for four at 9,000 ptas.

WHERE TO EAT

Restaurante La Cadiera (C. Domingo Miral 19, tel. 974/355559) fills up with locals in the know who come for the satisfying menú del día at 1,200 ptas. **El Viejo Aragón** (Avda. Primer de Rivera 8—on many maps called C. Primer Viernes de Mayo—tel. 974/361214) has a large downstairs bar where you can go for a drink in the evening, and an ample, rustic *comedor* (dining room) upstairs with a hearty menú del día for 1,300 ptas. The à la carte menu includes innovative regional dishes, such as *berenjenas rellenas de bacalaos y verduritas* (eggplant stuffed with cod and vegetables), *pollo guisado con frutos de Aragón y trufas* (chicken stewed with Aragón fruit and truffles), and *conejo con caracoles* (rabbit with snails). At the top end (think 3,000 ptas. for a full dinner with wine), **La Cocina Aragonesa** (Aragón Kitchen; Paseo de la Constitución 3, tel. 974/361050), part of the upmarket Hotel Conde Aznar, serves superb Aragonese cuisine. Also well worth a splurge is the rustic **Restaurante El Portón** (Plaza Lacadena 1, tel. 974/355854), where a delicious regional meal comes to 2,500 ptas.

WORTH SEEING

Jaca's jewel is its beautiful 11th-century Romanesque **cathedral,** one of the oldest in Spain. Adjoining the cathedral cloister, the **Museo Diocesano** (tel. 974/361330; admission 300 ptas.; open summer, Tues.–Sun., 10–2 and 4–8; winter, 11–1:30 and 4–6:30) displays an extensive collection of religious art and artifacts from mountain churches throughout the area. It's hard to miss Jaca's immense 16th-century **Ciutadella** (citadel; admission 300 ptas; open Apr.–June, daily 11–noon and 4–6; July–Aug., daily 11–noon and 6–7; Sept.–Oct., daily 11–noon and 5–6; Nov.–Mar., daily 11–noon and 4–5), which looms just east of the center of town, as though keeping a vigilant eye on the town's activities. Wander along the citadel's fortified walls for lovely views of the lush countryside. Jaca has long been an important stop for pilgrims journeying on the section of the Camino de Santiago that crosses from France into Spain at Somport in the Pyrenees. The main pilgrim entrance into town is the splendid medieval **Puente de San**

Miguel (San Miguel Bridge), which spans the Río Aragón. From Jaca the Camino continues westward into Navarre and eventually converges with the other major branch of the Camino in the town of Puente la Reina. As befits its pilgrim past, Jaca has an interesting collection of churches, including the lovely 11th-century church of **Santiago.**

MONASTERIO DE SAN JUAN DE LA PEÑA

The Monastery of San Juan de la Peña, south of Jaca, is one of the most stunning sacred buildings in all of Spain. Tucked protectively under the overhang of a giant boulder, it's built right into a rocky mountain. The melding of a natural rock formation and a man-made structure amid the echoing silence of the surrounding parkland makes a beautiful image. Dating from the 9th century, the monastery is named for a saintly hermit who lived in solitude atop the towering cliff (*peña*). The elegant 12th-century cloister, shaded by the bulging rock face that looms over it, boasts magnificent ornate capitals, some fully ringed by saints and apostles, depicting different scenes from the Bible. The monastery (tel. 974/348099; admission 400 ptas.) is open mid-March–May, daily 10–2 and 4–7; June–mid-Oct., 10–2:30 and 3:30–8; mid-Oct.–mid-Mar., 11–2 and 4–5:30. If you can't make it during those hours, pay a visit anyway, because the exterior is the most worth seeing, and if you climb the stairs to the right of the monastery you can peek into the cloister, which is the other highlight.

As one Jaca local put it, "When you want good food at good prices, look for the favorite restaurants of los trabajadores, los camioneros, y los curos"—laborers, truck drivers, and priests—and follow suit.

The monastery sits amid protected natural parkland, and a series of well-marked trails fan out through the forest, including one popular path to the village of **Santa Cruz de los Serós,** which has a Romanesque church. The trek takes a little more than an hour. A little more than 2 km (1 mi) up the main road is another, newer (Baroque) monastery, also called San Juan de la Peña; it's generally not open to the public, though the surrounding area gets busy on weekends with families who come to picnic and hike. Alas, no buses travel this route; you need a car to visit either of the San Juan de la Peñas.

VALLE DE ANSÓ AND VALLE DE HECHO

The stunning **Ansó and Hecho valleys,** northwest of Jaca, burrow deep into the Pyrenees and offer unparalleled opportunities to explore the wild terrain virtually on your own. Many parts of the Pyrenees, particularly in Catalunya, were discovered long ago by trekkers, skiers, and, let's face it, lots of tourists. The western reaches of the Aragón Pyrenees have long been virgin territory, though visitors are starting to trickle in during July and August. Nevertheless, if you're looking for peace and solitude, this is where to find it, particularly in the Valle de Hecho. The forested mountain slopes and the valley are home to wildlife including bear, deer, squirrels, and raptors. Tucked into the folds of the valleys and perched atop verdant slopes are tiny villages of stone houses and cobbled streets.

A helpful stop before you plunge into the mountains is the village of **Hecho,** where you can pick up area maps and lodging listings at the **tourist office** (tel. 974/375002; open July–Sept., Mon.–Sat. 10–2 and 5–8, Sun. 10–2). At other times you can pick up maps and info from the **ayuntamiento** (town hall, tel. 974/375329; open weekdays 8–3). The *hostal* half of **Lo Foraton Hotel-Hostal** (974/375247) has cozy double rooms for 5,000 ptas.; in the hotel, rooms are 7,000 ptas. The large restaurant has views of the valley and an excellent 1,600-pta. set menu; you can also select from a range of local dishes à la carte, including *costillas de cordero con guarnición* (grilled lamb chops with garnish, 1,200 ptas.) or if you're feeling brave, the *cabeza de cordero al horno* (baked lamb's head, 750 ptas.).

A little farther north of Hecho is the tiny ancient village of **Siresa,** flanked on all sides by lush green valleys and forested mountains. Pay a visit to the lovely 12th-century **church of San Pedro,** once part of a large monastery. It's usually open 10–1 and 4–7:30; but if it's closed, ask for the key at the Bar Pirineos. Serene and unspoiled—and blessed with phenomenal vistas of the surrounding valleys—Siresa makes for an ideal overnight stay, particularly because there's affordable lodging. **Hotel Castillo d'Acher** (tel.

974/375313) has comfortable double rooms for 6,000 ptas. The large adjoining restaurant serves a tasty menú del día for 1,250 ptas. and draws locals from all over the valley. **Bar Pirineos,** owned by the same family, is a dark, old watering hole where you can join the town regulars for an evening drink.

SOUTHERN ARAGÓN

From the resplendent sierras of Albarracín to the deserted, wild Maestrazgo, southern Aragón is a region rich in natural beauty and age-old customs. It's the least populated, least visited province in Aragón, and sprinkled across its unspoiled landscape are ancient villages that have existed in semi-isolation for centuries. The lovely town of **Albarracín** itself, with narrow cobbled alleyways and sturdy stone houses, is one of the region's medieval gems. Southern Aragón's main city is **Teruel,** which is closer to the Castilian town of Cuenca than to Zaragoza—so it's here that you start seeing architectual elements of central and southern Spain. Teruel is famous for its well-preserved Mudéjar architecture, and the town's restaurants serve gazpacho, a typically southern dish.

TERUEL

Which draws bigger crowds: Teruel's spectacular Mudéjar buildings or its prized *jamón* (ham) Teruel? Never mind; you'll have plenty of chances to sample both. As the provincial capital, Teruel is an important administrative and transportation hub with the corresponding number of large plazas, most with pleasant terraces whence you can watch the world go by. **Plaza del Torico** sits in the very center of the *casco antiguo* (antique quarter). Just southeast of there, **Plaza Bretón,** lined with shops, is home to the tourist office. **Plaza San Juan,** a little farther south is a large space ringed by government buildings, including the **Palacio de Justicia.** When it's time to try *jamón* Teruel, you'll find *carnicerías* (butcher shops) all over town where you can buy this top-notch thinly sliced, melt-in-your-mouth ham. **Vicente Maicas Aboy** (C. San Juan 6, tel. 978/602057) is a small, well-stocked store with heaps of ham products. If you're carrying enough in your pack already, then make for Teruel's lively string of bars and restaurants to get your fill. At Teruel's raucous Fiestas del Angel, starting on the second Sunday in July, you can go to dances and concerts and get chased by bulls running through the streets.

BASICS

The **tourist office,** just off Plaza Bretón (C. Tomás Nogues 1, tel. 978/602279; open July–Sept., daily 9–2 and 5–9, Sun. 9–2; Oct.–June, Mon.–Sat. 9–2 and 5–7:30), has loads of info on Teruel the town and Teruel the province, including maps and transport schedules.

COMING AND GOING

Teruel is a key junction for regional transport. The train station is west of town, an easy walk from the old quarter. Trains leave several times daily for Zaragoza and Valencia; call **RENFE** for information (tel. 902/240202). From the bus station, just east of the center of town, **Tezasa** (tel. 978/601014) sends four buses to Zaragoza daily; **Autotransportes** (tel. 978/601680) goes to points all over the region, including Albarracín; and **Abasa** (tel. 978/830871) goes to Alcañiz each weekday. Daily long-distance buses serve Valencia, Cuenca, and Madrid.

WHERE TO SLEEP

There is no shortage of budget lodging in Teruel, and most hostels and pensions are clustered in the old quarter, just north of Plaza Torico. **Hostal Aragon** (C. Santa María 4, tel. 978/601387) is a large, comfortable house with musty rooms. Doubles with big, clean bathrooms are 5,300 ptas.; without bath the price drops to 3,000 ptas. **Hostal Continental** (C. Juan Pérez 5, tel. 978/602317, cash only) has dank double rooms with big, comfy beds and bath for 5,000 ptas. Ask for a room with a balcony so you can get a breeze going through. **Hostal Alcazaba** (C. Tozal 34, tel. 978/610761, cash only) has clean double rooms for 6,000 ptas. July–September, 5,000 ptas. at other times. Its large downstairs restaurant gets packed at lunchtime with locals who come for the 1,200-pta. set menu. Just outside town, on the road to Alcañiz, stands **El Busto** (tel. 978/610781), a hostel and restaurant that's also popular as a bar among the young crowd, perhaps because it's open until 3 AM on weekends. Basic doubles with bath are 4,500 ptas. (cash only), but prices go up during the Fiesta del Angel in July. The restaurant's 1,200-pta. menú del día draws workers on their lunch break.

WHERE TO EAT

As you might expect, ham figures prominently on most restaurant menus, and you'll pay a lot less for it here than you would elsewhere. **La Parrilla** (C. San Esteban 2, tel. 978/605917), with its beamed ceiling, plaid tablecloths, and open grill, is a good place to tuck into some rustic dishes starting at 1,500 ptas. Try the *costillas de cerdo a la brasa al perfume de finas hierbas* (grilled ribs perfumed with herbs) or the *conejo a la brasa* (grilled rabbit). **Restaurante Ambeles** (Ronda Ambles 6, tel. 978/ 610806), near the bus station, is a local institution and its large, bustling back dining room fills up quickly at lunchtime. The menú del día is 1,300 ptas., and they also serve a wide array of such dishes as *esparragos blancos templados con salmón* (white asparagus with salmon; 1,200 ptas.). You can also fill up on excellent tapas at the bar. Their *jamón de Teruel* (950 ptas.) is served in a variety of ways, including with fried eggs. **Cafeteria Restaurante Centro** (C. Tozal 8, tel. 978/606449), at the end of a small mall of shops, is nothing special to look at, but it serves a nicely priced and filling menú del día for 1,200 ptas. that includes such items as *gazpacho Andalúz* and *pechugas a la plancha* (grilled chicken breasts).

Massive pig haunches hang over the bar, and wine bottles line the intimate back nook at the cozy **Taberna Rokelin** (C. El Rincón 2, tel. 978/604642). Delectable Teruel ham is sliced right there at the bar and served, in whatever size you like, on heavy hand-painted ceramic plates. A tapas-size plate is 600 ptas., a *ración* 1,000 ptas., and a *bocadillo* (sandwich) with Teruel ham is 350 ptas. It also serves a wide selection of Aragonese wines, including some from the Cariñena area and some from La Rioja.

WORTH SEEING

Teruel's abundance of Mudéjar holdings stems from its once large and flourishing Moorish population. Though the city was reconquered by Alfonso II in the 12th century, many of the town's Moorish residents were allowed to stay on, and their legacy gives Teruel an exotic, international flavor. The **Torre del Salvador** (tel. 978/602061), rising over the southern part of town, is one of the Mudéjar highlights, with an ornately patterned brick-and-tile design. The tower is open daily 11–2 and 5–8, and admission is 250 ptas. Near the tower, look for the **Escalanita** (a beautiful Mudéjar brick-and-tile staircase (*escalera*). A number of other Mudéjar towers are scattered around town, including the **Torre de San Martín,** just west of the center, but only the Torre del Salvador is open to the public.

Teruel's **cathedral** (admission 300 ptas.; open 11–2 and 4–8), presided over by a Mudéjar tower, was built in the 12th century and rebuilt in the 16th. It has a stunning *techumbre mudéjar* (coffered ceiling), which combines Arabic geometric designs with painted depictions of hunting scenes and of *la vida cotidiana* (daily life) of the 13th century. The nearby **Museo Diocesano** (admission 150 ptas.; open Mon.–Sat. 10–2) has an eclectic collection of religious art.

Just north of Plaza Bretón is the **church of San Pedro** (also with a Mudéjar tower), famous for its adjoining **Mausoleo de los Amantes** (Lovers' Mausoleum). Herein lie the tombs of Diego and Isabel, two Teruel lovers who died, it is said, of broken hearts. Diego left Teruel to seek his fortune and on his return found that his beloved Isabel was engaged to another man. He asked for a last kiss, but Isabel refused, and he died on the spot. At his funeral Isabel did grant him his last kiss, but as their lips touched, she died in his arms. The mausoleum (admission 50 ptas.) is open Mon.–Sat. 10–2 and 5–7:30, Sunday 10:30–2 and 5–7:30.

ALBARRACÍN

West of Teruel are the grand **Sierras de Albarracín,** a vast massif carved into spectacular ravines by the powerful Guadalaviar and Curvo rivers. Rocky mountain plateaus loom above fertile valleys rich with wild vegetation, hulking pine and fir trees, and a population of deer and wild boar—which often end up as succulent dishes on the menus of mountain restaurants. Trekking trails cross the region, much of which remains refreshingly untamed, and there are 30-odd delightful villages, with ancient stone and wood houses and cobbled streets.

The area's natural and cultural riches all seem to come together in the small town of Albarracín, and if you have a limited time in southern Aragón, put it at the top of your list. Perched at 3,840 ft above a luxuriant gorge with the Guadalaviar rushing below, the village makes a spectacular picture of ancient stone houses and crenellated walls, against a gorgeous backdrop of evergreen hills and craggy cliffs. Climb the steep cobbled streets past tiny old-fashioned *carnicerías* (butcher shops) and groups of old men leaning on their canes, and you really start feeling like you're in ancient Aragón.

Near Albarracín, on the road to Bezas, a series of prehistoric **pinturas rupestres** (cave paintings) has been discovered in small caves and on rocky outcrops. Some are just a few minutes' walk from the main road; others require longer hikes into the woods. From Albarracín, a marked 4-km (3-mi) walking trail leads to the general area, then numerous signs point through the woods to the caves themselves. If you're driving, head toward Bezas and follow signs to the cave paintings.

BASICS

The **tourist office** is near Plaza Mayor (C. Diputación 4, tel. 978/710251; open Tues.–Sat. 10–2 and 4–7, Sun. 10–2). If it's closed, go to the ayuntamiento (town hall, tel. 978/700400; open weekdays 8:30–3, Sat. 8:30–1).

COMING AND GOING

One **bus** leaves Albarracín (from a parking lot near the town entrance) for **Teruel** every day but Sunday—at 8:45 AM. The bus from Teruel to Albarracín continues on to the villages of Torres de Albarracín and Noguera.

WHERE TO SLEEP

You can do no better in Albarracín than to bed down at **Casa Santiago** (Subida a las Torres 11, tel. 978/700316), a delightful rustic hostel tucked at the top of an ancient staircase near Plaza Mayor. The beautifully restored country house has comfortable sitting areas on every floor. A cozy common room is outfitted with oversize brown-leather sofas that you can sink into, a rope-woven rocking chair, and big baskets of magazines. One flight up brings you to a sunlit attic suite with a wrought-iron writing desk and stupendous views of the valley and the red-tile roofs of town. The individually decorated double rooms are 8,500 ptas. in high season and 7,500 ptas. in low. **Los Palacios** (C. Los Palacios 21, tel. 978/700327) is a large, comfortable hostel whose double rooms with bath go for 4,500 ptas. Ask for a room with a balcony, and bask in the valley and river views. The lovely **Posada del Adarve** (C. Portal de Molina 23, tel. 978/700304) has a range of comfortable rooms on several floors of a restored country house with beamed ceilings and solid furniture. A downstairs dining room opens onto a small garden terrace. Doubles with bath start at 5,500 ptas.

WHERE TO EAT

Restaurant El Portal (C. Portal de Molina 14) serves a savory menú del día for 1,500 and quite an array of *platos combinados* (combination dishes), including a hefty serving of *tostadas con tomate, lomo, huevo, chorizo, longaniza, y patatas* (toasted bread with tomato, pork loin, egg, sausages, and potatoes; 1,100 ptas.), and *alcachofas con mahonesa* (artichokes with mayonnaise; 800 ptas.). On Plaza Mayor, the **Cafeteria La Taberna** is a favorite local hangout, fine for a drink or a meal; dishes include that favorite Aragonese country dish *migas a la pastora con huevo* (bread crumbs all fried up with sausage and egg; 500 ptas.) and *pinchos morunos caseros con patatas fritas y pimientos* (spicy meat kebabs with fried potatoes and peppers; 750 ptas.) Just across the way from Los Palacios hostel is its **Restaurante Los Palacios,** which has a tasty set menu for 1,300 ptas. and a large terrace overlooking the Albarracín countryside.

If it's cheap local wine you want, stop by **Bodegas Muñoz** (C. Portal de Molina 7, tel. 978/710328) and stand in line with all the farmers and workers who are refilling their jugs with wine from big barrels along the back. Strapping their dripping jugs to big baskets in the back of their bicycles, they slowly pedal their way back to the fields. The wine comes from nearby Calatayud, and it costs 185 ptas. a liter. You can also buy all kinds of meats, especially sausages, such as *fuet* (thin, cured), *salchichon* (fat, salami-style), and *sobrasada* (soft, spicy, spreadable).

WORTH SEEING

Albarracín's center is its Plaza Mayor, with the ayuntamiento and the tourist office. Above the plaza is the **cathedral,** with a beautiful 16th-century *retablo* (altarpiece) featuring St. Peter. **The Museu Dioce-**

sano (tel, 978/710093; open 10:30–2 and 4–6), in the 13th-century Palacio Episcopal, has an eclectic collection of religious art and sculptures.

THE MAESTRAZGO

From desolate rocky mountains to plunging fertile gorges, the Maestrazgo is a region of wild and varied terrain that extends northeast of Teruel. This is Aragón's outback country, with tiny medieval villages that seem quite happily stuck in a time warp amid a rugged landscape that stretches endlessly toward the horizon. Tourists are far and few between, which is, of course, part of its appeal. To explore the region fully, you'll need a car, but you can venture into sections of it by bus. Most Maestrazgo towns have at least one hostel. In the smaller villages there's usually someone who rents out rooms. Ask around when you arrive, and you'll be pointed in the direction of whoever is currently taking in travelers.

Spain's famous soldier—indeed, epic hero—El Cid galloped through this barren backwater on his route across Spain, and along the way you'll find towns named after him, including **La Iglesuela del Cid** (113 km/70 mi northeast of Teruel), a dusty little village with a church, stone houses, and little else. Just north is **Cantavieja,** with a Gothic church and a lovely Plaza Mayor surrounded with arched galleries and wrought-iron balconies. Among the handful of lodgings in town there's **Hotel Balfagon** (C. Maestrazgo 20, tel. 964/185076), which has well-maintained double rooms for 6,500 ptas. Farther north there's a simple little town called **Alcañiz,** with a Baroque church (Santa María) and a small hilltop castle that now serves as a comfortable parador and restaurant.

BASICS

One or two buses travel daily from Teruel to La Iglesuela del Cid and Cantavieja. The latter town's **tourist office** (Plaza Cresto Reig 33, tel. 964/185243) is open July–September, Tuesday–Sunday 10:30–2 and 4–7, October–June, weekdays 10–2. If it's closed, head to the ayuntamiento (town hall; tel. 964/185001), open weekdays 9–2.

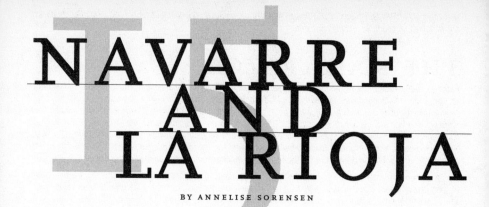

NAVARRE AND LA RIOJA

BY ANNELISE SORENSEN

F rom lush mountain valleys south to wide, dry plains, Navarre (Navarra) is a resplendent blend of landscapes. Sprinkled across the region are atmospheric clusters of stone houses, their balconies bursting with poppies and geraniums. Navarre's centerpiece is its capital, Pamplona, famous the world over for its July Fiesta de San Fermín—the region's biggest, wildest party, centered on the running of the bulls.

Sandwiched by the Navarre and the Basque Country to the north, Aragón to the east, and Castile-León to the west and the south, La Rioja is one of the smallest Autonomous Communities in Spain, but its name has one of the biggest reputations. Rioja's famous wines have found their way to more dining-room tables around the world than any other Spanish product.

NAVARRE

The main branch of the Camino de Santiago (Way of St. James), the ancient pilgrims' trail to Santiago de Compostela, enters Spain from France at Roncesvalles, a lovely alpine village in the Navarran Pyrenees. Over the centuries the passage of pilgrims westward has engendered artistic riches along the Way, with the result that Navarre is packed with centuries-old monasteries and churches including the wonderful Monasterio del Leyre, near Aragón, and a superb collection of Romanesque and Gothic churches in Puente la Reina, where the main Camino route merges with another.

Navarre is one of the oldest kingdoms in Spain and, along with the neighboring Basque Country, one of the most individualistic. Navarre and the Basque region actually share more than just a border; for centuries they have had strong cultural bonds, from politics down to dress and cuisine. Throughout the region, especially in Pamplona, you'll see signs and menus in Euskera (the Basque language) and often hear it spoken in the streets. Proud and strong-willed, the Navarrese have managed to conserve their institutions, laws, and cultural identity against a series of invaders, from the French Visigoths to the Spanish central government; and in 1841 Madrid agreed to the Fueros de Navarra (Navarran Rights), effectively allowing the province to make its own laws.

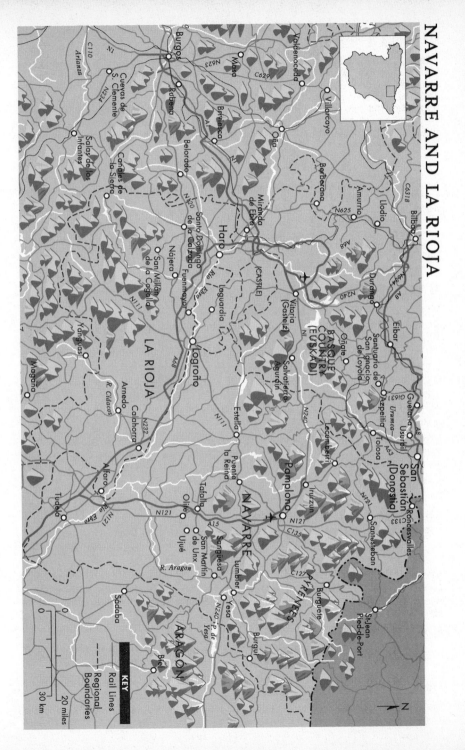

499

PAMPLONA

"Then we crossed a wide plain, and there was a big river off on the right shining in the sun from between the line of trees, and away off you could see the plateau of Pamplona rising out of the plain, and the walls of the city, and the great brown cathedral . . .." Thus Hemingway immortalized Pamplona in his 1926 novel *The Sun Also Rises* as a quintessential Spanish town, with its airy central square, explosive bullfights, riotous bars, and fiesta to end all fiestas, the bull run of San Fermín, which takes place annually July 6–14. Revelers pour in from all over the world for San Fermín, and for one week Pamplona becomes a giant party that starts every morning at 8 sharp, when the bulls are let out of their corral to race through the streets of town—along with lots of foolhardy souls—to the bullring, where one unlucky bull is selected for that evening's bullfight. Pamplona's population triples during this time, as do room prices. It's nigh impossible to snag a bed on arrival, so reserve months in advance if you want to witness this spectacle.

All of Pamplona's activity seems to emanate from the central **Plaza del Castillo.** Cafés and bars line the square's perimeter, including Hemingway's hangout—the lovely turn-of-the-20th-century Café Iruña, a restful place to take in the breezes and goings-on. The surrounding warren of narrow, bustling streets makes up Pamplona's atmospheric **old quarter;** packed with bars, restaurants, and budget digs, this is the liveliest part of town and prime exploring territory. Stretching west and south of the old quarter are several city parks and the **Ciudadela,** an immense old fortress that now rests in lush parkland and inviting gardens.

BASICS

VISITOR INFORMATION

The **tourist office** (C. Eslava 1, tel. 948/206540; open July 6–14, daily 10–5; July 15–Sept., Mon.–Sat. 10–2 and 4–7, Sun. 10–2; Sept.–July 5, weekdays 10–2 and 4–7, Sat. 10–2) has maps, brochures, and detailed listings of all the beds in town.

CURRENCY EXCHANGE

Most of Pamplona's **banks** are on and around Plaza del Castillo. Once they close, you can change currency at some of the bigger hotels, but they charge a high commission. **Hotel Tres Reyes** (C. Jardines de la Taconera s/n, tel. 948/226600) changes money 24 hours a day.

CYBER SPACES

Libreria Auzolan (C. Tudela 16, tel. 948/153867), near the bus station, charges 500 ptas. per hour; **Iturnet** (C. Iturrama 1, tel. 948/270400), southwest of the city near the university, charges 450 ptas. an hour.

EMERGENCIES

General emergency: 112. **Municipal police:** 092. **Hospital de Navarra:** C. Irunlarrea 3, tel. 948/422100.

ENGLISH-LANGUAGE BOOKS

If you forgot your Hemingway, head to the small but well stocked **Librería Gómez** (Plaza del Castillo 28, tel. 948/226702). There's another branch at Avenida Pio XII and Calle Rioja, southwest of town (tel. 948/257561).

LAUNDRY

Lavandería Lavanor (C. Castillo de Maya 48, tel. 948/241523) charges 1,200 ptas. for a small load of your smellies. There are several branches; another handy one is at Calle Monasterio de Urdax 21 (tel. 948/175048).

MAIL

The main **post office** is at Paseo de Sarasate 9 (tel. 948/221263), open weekdays 8:30–8:30 and Saturday 8:30–2.

COMING AND GOING

The **train station** (C. Muelle s/n, tel. 902/240202) is at the north end of town, a long hike from the old quarter. Bus 9 travels throughout the day between the station and the center of town. Trains leave several times daily for major cities in the surrounding regions, including San Sebastián and Zaragoza. The **bus station** (Avda. Conde Oliveto 6, tel. 948/220997) is a 10-minute walk south of the Plaza del Castillo. Buses depart several times daily for towns all over Navarre, including Estella and Olite, and also for major cities in the surrounding regions, including Logroño, San Sebastián, and Zaragoza.

WHERE TO SLEEP

Many of Pamplona's lodgings take bookings for San Fermín as much as six months in advance, so it's highly unlikely that a Johnny-come-lately will find a bed. Rates double and triple anyway, though you can always join the crowds and sleep on a patch of grass or a bench in one of the city's parks. If that's your plan, store your pack elsewhere (say, in one of the lockers at the bus station) or arrange to keep a hypervigilant eye on your belongings, as robberies are extremely common. Strap your valuables to your body, beneath your clothes, and forget about watches and jewelry. Thieves come to Pamplona from elsewhere just to prey on foreigners during San Fermín. In late July and August, traditional tourist months, it's still a wise to reserve, but the rest of the year it's fairly easy to find a room in one of the many budget lodgings.

Many of Pamplona's cheap rooms are clustered on the small streets around Plaza del Castillo, particularly Calles San Nicolás and San Gregorio, west of the square. If you find everything full, keep an eye out for bars and restaurants advertising rooms (signs will say CAMAS, meaning "beds," or HABITACIONES, meaning "guest rooms"). **Casa García** (C. San Gregorio 12, tel. 948/223893) has a few double rooms for a cheap 4,000 ptas., though many are often taken by *fijos* (permanent residents). The Casa also serves a basic *menú del día* for 1,100 ptas. **Bar-Restaurante San Nicolás** *(see* Where to

"At noon of Sunday, the 6th of July, the festival exploded. There is no other way to describe it." — Ernest Hemingway on the San Fermín phenomenon, in The Sun Also Rises.

Eat, *below),* on Calle San Nicolás, has a few simple doubles with shared bath for 1,500 ptas. per person, a few with balconies. If you exhaust the options in the old quarter, make for the streets near the bus station, where you'll find a bunch of clearly marked hostels and pensions. If worse comes to worst, or if you *prefer* to camp, there's always the **Ezcaba campground** (tel. 948/330315), 5 km (3 mi) outside Pamplona, with sites for 1,200 ptas. per person (twice that during San Fermín). Four buses go to the campground daily from Pamplona's Avenida de la Baja Navarra, the first at 9:10 AM and the last at 7:35 PM; a one-way ticket is 100 ptas.

Traditionally, *toreros* (bullfighters) stay either at the **Hotel Yoldi** (*see below*), the **Trip Sancho Ramírez** (C. Sancho Ramírez 11–13, tel. 948/212045), where doubles run 9,000–14,000 ptas. (25,000 ptas. during San Fermín), or the other longtime torero headquarters, **La Perla** (Plaza del Castillo 1, tel. 948/227706), with en-suite doubles for 11,500 ptas., doubles with shared bath for 7,900 ptas. (31,000 and 16,750 ptas. during the bash). La Perla's owner, well known in bullfighting circles, has the distinction of being a *pastor*, one of the professionals who smack the bulls with sticks to get them off to a running start each San Fermín morning.

UNDER 4,000 PTAS. • Fonda-Bar La Montañesa. Rooms in this run-down *hostal* are musty and spartan, but if you just want a place to crash on the cheap, you'll like the price: 1,600 ptas. per person in a single, double, or triple all year long. *C. San Gregorio 2, tel. 948/224380. 6 rooms, none with bath. Cash only.*

UNDER 5,000 PTAS. • Camas. In the heart of the old quarter, several blocks from Plaza de San Francisco, this small family-run hostel—creatively named "Beds"—has hardwood floors and basic double rooms with a clean shared baths for 4,000 ptas. *C. Nueva 24, tel. 948/227825. 10 rooms, none with bath. Cash only.*

Hostal Aragonesa. You can't get more central than this large, institutional *hostal* just paces from Plaza del Castillo. Basic, ample doubles with shared bath are 4,500 ptas. July–September (9,000 ptas. during San Fermín), 3,400 the rest of the year. To overlook the lively Calle San Nicolás, ask for a room *con balcón,* with balcony. Reception is across the street at the Hostal Bearán (*see below*). *C. San Nicolás 34–36, tel. 948/223428. 10 rooms, none with bath.*

Pensión Santa Cecilia. Set in a Baroque mansion, this rambling pension has comfortable rooms with hardwood floors and lots of light. Double rooms with shared bath are 4,000 ptas. The shared bathrooms are small but clean, and—bonus—you can have a load of clothes washed and dried for 1,000 ptas. *C. Navarrería 17, tel. 948/222230. 10 rooms, none with bath.*

BEST SUPPORTING ACTOR

After Lady Brett Ashley, the **Café Iruña,** *on Plaza del Castillo, gets top billing in* The Sun Also Rises: *this is where Hemingway's cast of expats sit around drinking wine with bullfighters and crusty Pamplonans. With a terrace on the plaza and a sumptuous interior featuring marble tables and tile floors, this Parisian-style café remains the city's prime hangout and looks just as it did in the '20s, when the gang spent their days "looking out from the cool of the arcade at the big square."*

UNDER 6,000 PTAS. • **Pensión Sarasate.** Set in a beautifully restored house built in 1845, this place is a real find. All rooms have hardwood floors, period furniture, and firm beds dressed up in organic cotton sheets, with wool blankets woven at a nearby artisans' colony. Double rooms with sparkling bathrooms are 5,000 ptas., zooming to 14,000 ptas. during San Fermín. *Paseo Sarasate 30, tel. 948/223084. 7 rooms. Cash only.*

UNDER 7,000 PTAS. • **Hostal Bearán.** Owned by the same folks who run Hostal Aragonesa, this higher-end *hostal* has comfortable doubles for 6,500 ptas. July–September (15,000 ptas. during San Fermín) and 5,500 ptas. the rest of the year. Rooms with balconies open onto the old-quarter bustle. *C. San Nicolás 25, tel. 948/223428. 17 rooms.*

Pensión Arrieta. This cozy pension near the bus station has clean, fresh-smelling rooms, each with an alarm clock to get you up for the running of the bulls. Doubles cost 6,000 ptas. in summer (14,000 ptas. during San Fermín), 5,000 ptas. the rest of the year. *C. Arrieta 27, tel. 948/228459. 6 rooms, 1 with bath. Cash only.*

UNDER 8,000 PTAS. • **Hostal Navarra.** Across the street from the bus station, this airy hostel has spic-and-span doubles for 7,000 ptas., most with balconies and insulated windows. During San Fermín the price shoots up to 14,500 ptas. *C. Tudela 9, tel. 948/225164. 14 rooms.*

Hotel Eslava. Just off beautiful Plaza Virgen de la O, this sizable ramshackle hotel has institutional double rooms for 7,000 ptas., a price that jumps during San Fermín to 16,000. *Plaza Virgen de la O 7, tel. 948/222270. 28 rooms bath.*

Pensión Leyre. This homey pension a few blocks from the bus station has comfy, though overpriced, double rooms with shared bath for 5,500 ptas (the bonus room with private bath is 7,000 ptas.). Many rooms overlook the street but have double-paned windows to minimize nighttime cacophony. *C. Bergamín 5, tel. 948/211647. 8 rooms, 1 with bath. Cash only.*

UNDER 10,000 PTAS. • **Hotel Yoldi.** This classic, well-maintained hotel sits on the main street running south from Plaza de Castillo toward the bus station. Rooms are clean and comfortable, and the staff is courteous and professional. Small doubles are 8,500 ptas., larger rooms 10,600 ptas. (during San Fermín, 22,000 ptas. and 28,500 ptas.). *Avda. San Ignacio 11, tel. 948/212045. 52 rooms.*

WHERE TO EAT

The old quarter abounds with restaurants and cafés serving everything from tapas to hearty Navarran meals.

UNDER 2,000 PTAS. • **Bar-Restaurante San Nicolás.** This large, amiable joint has a basic bar (with the requisite video slot machines and blaring TV) and a pleasant dining room where you can tuck into regional dishes like *toro estofado* (stewed bull), *chipirones en su tinta* (squid in their own ink), and *bacalao a la Ajoarriero* (cod cooked in a Navarrese-style sauce of garlic and peppers). *C. San Nicolás, tel. 948/221319.*

Bodegón Sarria. Set on the main bull-running street, this tavern centers, naturally enough, on meat. Immense hams hang over the bar, the beer tap is shaped like a fleshy hindquarter, and you can get your protein fix a variety of ways: *rabo de buey* (oxtail), say, or *filete de ternera con pimientos* (veal with peppers). You can also make a meal out of tasty tapas, such as the cheap and savory *tostadas de jamón* (toasted ham sandwiches). Black-and-white photos of old Pamplona, including Hemingway in various poses, adorn the walls. *C. Estafeta 52, tel. 948/227713. Cash only.*

Hosteria del Temple. Named for its proximity to the cathedral, this restaurant is pleasantly decorated with ceramic tiles. The regional *menú del día* (1,500 ptas. weekdays, 2,000 ptas. weekends) is delicious. *C. Curia 3, tel. 948/225171.*

Ostatu Asador. Next door to Bodegón Sarria, this cozy restaurant has brick walls, beamed ceilings, and a bustling open kitchen. Try the *trucha a la Navarra* (trout in the style of Navarre; 1,000 ptas.), *pimientos rellenos de merluza* (peppers stuffed with hake; 1,600 ptas.), or *costillas de cordero a la brasa* (grilled lamb chops; 2,000 ptas.). *C. Estafeta 53, tel. 948/225613.*

Restaurante Sarasate. When it's time for a break from pig haunches and grilled bull, try this centrally located vegetarian restaurant, decorated with pale yellow walls and colorful paintings of fruit. Its excellent, fresh menú del día is 1,300 ptas. and includes *ensalada de tomate* (tomato salad), *puré de zanahoria* (carrot purée), potato and pesto dishes, and a desert of flan, fruit, or yogurt. *C. San Nicolás 19–21, tel. 948/225727. Closed Sun. No dinner Mon.–Thurs. Cash only.*

UNDER 3,000 PTAS. • The rustic **Asador La Chisteria** (C. San Nicolás 40–42, tel. 948/210512) is on the pricey side, but it's worth the splurge if you want an excellent regional meal. It offers two menús del día (2,000 or 3,000 ptas.) along with many interesting dishes like *alcachofas rellenas de marisco* (seafood-stuffed artichokes; 1,600 ptas.) and *revuelto de ajo fresco y anchoas* (a mix of fresh garlic and anchovies).

> *During San Fermín, poor souls straggle into the tourist office daily to complain that they were robbed while sleeping on a park bench. They've heard every story in the book—feel free to ask them for tips.*

WORTH SEEING

CATEDRAL DE SANTA MARÍA

Pamplona's graceful 15th-century cathedral towers over the eastern end of the old quarter. The elegant cloister has high Gothic arches, and the **Museu Diocesano** displays centuries-old sacred art and artifacts, including woodcarvings and imposing altarpieces. *C. Dormitalería (near Plaza San José), tel. 948/210827. Admission 500 ptas. Cathedral and museum open July–Sept., Mon.–Sat. 10–7; Oct.–June, weekdays 10–1:30 and 4–7, Sat. 10–1:30. In summer, guided 1-hr tours begin at 10:30, 11:30, 12:30, 1:30, 4, 5, and 6.*

MUSEO DE NAVARRA

Housed in an old pilgrims' hospital, the Museum of Navarre has a large collection of archaeological finds—including some interesting Roman mosaics—and some fine paintings, including one by Goya. Some Romanesque capitals from the cathedral are also displayed. *C. Santo Domingo, tel. 948/426492. Admission 300 ptas.; free Sat. afternoon and Sun. Open mid-July–mid-Sept., Tues.–Fri. 10–7, Sat. 10–2; mid-Sept.–mid-July, Tues.–Sat. 10–2 and 5–7, Sun. 11–2.*

MONUMENTO A LOS FUEROS DE NAVARRA

In 1893, 85,000 Navarrans met in Pamplona to protest the Spanish government's attempt to apply the same taxes to Navarre as to the rest of Spain (Navarre had been granted special *fueros*, or rights, in 1841). The government backed off, and this monument, looming over the east end of Paseo Sarasate just off Plaza del Castillo, commemorates that victory. The plaque reads, in Spanish, that the monument was erected to symbolize "the union of the Navarran people in defense of their liberties, which are even more worthy of love than life itself"—a sentiment otherwise known as "Give me liberty or give me death."

AFTER DARK

Pamplona's lively nightlife centers on the **old quarter,** particularly Calles San Nicolás and San Gregorio. Calles Calderería and San Agustín, east of Plaza del Castillo, are also full of bars. North of the plaza,

YES, WE RECYCLE

The tradition of carrying a rolled-up newspaper to the encierro (ostensibly to swat the bulls) started because the first thing everyone does on festival mornings is buy one of Navarre's two main dailies, the Diario de Navarra *or* Diario de Noticias, *to look for a photo of himself running with the bulls—both papers have extensive coverage and plenty of pictures of each day's event. After looking for a memorial to his glory, the runner rolls up the paper for use in his next death-defying dash.*

Calles Jarauta and San Lorenzo fill up with crowds of teen- and college-age locals on weekends. Folks patronize the large **Museo Bar** (C. San Gregorio 48, tel. 948/222050) to drink, flirt, and graze on tapas. **Ulzama Bar** (C. San Nicolás 12, tel. 948/222095) is a friendly beer-and-tapas joint near Plaza del Castillo. The snug, low-ceiling **Café Roch** (C. Comedias 6, tel. 948/222390), founded in 1898, is one of the oldest in town, an atmospheric little place to start the evening (it closes at 10:30 PM). Locals gather here to drink, *charlar* (chat), and eat their fill of delectable Basque-style tapas. Plaza del Castillo is lined with cafés and bars, including **Casino Eslava** (Plaza del Castillo 16), where you can munch outdoors on *pincho moruna* (a spicy meat kebab; 450 ptas.) and *tortilla de gambas* (shrimp omelet; 600 ptas.) with a drink, or hang at the bar inside. The casino upstairs is for members only.

FIESTA DE SAN FERMÍN: RUNNING WITH THE BULLS

On the morning of a bull running (called an *encierro*, or "enclosing"), the air is charged with fear and excitement. Throngs of onlookers gather along the enclosed streets as early as 6 AM, while those brave enough to make the run don the traditional Navarran outfit, a white shirt and white pants with a red kerchief around the neck—traditionally capped off with a rolled-up newspaper to hit the bulls with. At 8 AM, guns go off, and the bulls are released from the holding pens (*corrales*) to race along the streets through the center of Pamplona to the bullring, south of the old quarter. The entire process usually takes between 2½ and five minutes. The danger of injury, and even death, is real—if you plan to run, be sure to get advice from people who have done so before, and walk the route in advance. Beginning near the Parque de Santo Domingo, just north of the old quarter, the route heads southeast on Calle Santo Domingo through Plaza Constitutional and then onto Calle Estafeta, a straight shot to the **Plaza de Toros.** There are escape hatches along the route, but these are for emergencies only, which means that once you're on the course, it's nearly impossible to get off it.

Each festival day finishes with a *corrida (*bullfight) at 6:30 PM. All the festival's rituals and traditions (including the encierro, whose original main purpose was to get the bulls to the ring) have been leading up to this moment, and there's a palpable excitement as the crowds fill the bullring. The bad news for travelers is that 80% of the tickets have already been sold long before the festival; the trick is to try and get your hands on one of the remaining 20%. These go on sale at the bullring the night before the fight in question, just after that day's corrida ends (usually at 8 PM, but sometimes as early as 7). Join the long lines and try your luck; alas, most of these tickets are snapped up by scalpers long before innocents like you get to the ticket booth, and are then sold for three to four times the actual price. If you're eager to watch the action, buying from a scalper may be your only way in. The cheapest tickets are in the *sol* (sun) section, which is also where the crowd is most entertaining: a boisterous young group dominates, singing along as *charrangas* (traditional Spanish brass bands) perform. *Sombra* (shade) tickets are decidedly more expensive and genteel.

If you can't score bullfight tickets, there are other ways—one of them free—to get near the bulls and be a part of the excitement. The bulls are brought to Pamplona at the end of June and kept in small holding pens called *coralillos del gas,* just north of the old quarter. On weekdays, local aficionados come here to check out the bulls and see if they're in good fighting form. The coralillos are open to all (admission usually 300 ptas., open 10–2 and 5–8), but hours vary, so inquire at the tourist office. The night before the encierro, the bulls are trotted from their holding pens to a larger corral nearby via the Puente de la Rochapea (Rochapea Bridge), which usually happens between 10:30 and 11 PM. You're welcome to watch, though to do so from an area called the *zona* (the best vantage point), you need—sigh—one of the tickets that the town hall gives out free at the beginning of July; ask the tourist office for the date as summer approaches. If this, too, fails, join the rest of the crowd and watch the bulls from a little farther off. Another chance to see the beasts is the *apartado* (selection), a lottery held daily at noon in the bull-ring to match each bull with a *torero* (bullfighter). This generally costs 500 ptas.; again, inquire at the tourist office, as times and prices may vary.

Unfortunately, in recent years San Fermín has begun to resemble a prolonged frat party, to the point where it's impossible to avoid the beer-guzzling crowds thronging the streets, bars, and restaurants. If this isn't your scene, you may want to attend an encierro in a smaller Navarran town instead, such as Estella or Tafalla (*see below*)—here the bulls, not the beer kegs, are still the stars of the show.

THE NAVARRAN PYRENEES

Across upper Navarre stretch the lofty mountain peaks and evergreen gorges of the western Pyrenees. A series of spectacular valleys cleave the range, including the northern Valle de Baztán, where lush forested hills give way to wide stretches of farmland. To the east, the Salazar and Roncal valleys are prime hiking territory, with shaded ravines and rocky slopes blanketed in pine trees. *Casas rurales* (country guest houses), sprinkled throughout the mountains, make for pleasant overnight stops; for locations and prices call the **Casas Rurales** association (tel. 948/229328) or stop into Pamplona's tourist office.

Navarre's vineyards share the fertile soil of neighboring Rioja. Pamplona's **Vinoteca Murillo** *(C. San Miguel 16–18, tel. 948/ 221015) sells* pacharán, *a liquor made from mountain berries, and a range of local wines.*

The main branch of the Camino de Santiago enters Spain in Roncesvalles, imbuing it with great historic and religious significance. South of Roncesvalles, Hemingway fans can stop by the trout-fishing town of Burguete and spend a night in the very same hostal—even the same bed—where Hemingway stayed when he escaped to the mountains to fish and write.

Renting a car will make Pyrenean life much easier, but a few buses do travel to some of the larger mountain towns, including Roncesvalles.

RONCESVALLES

Roncesvalles (population 30) sits 3,477 ft above sea level near the Ibañeta pass, an important medieval crossing point on the Camino de Santiago. This area figured prominently in the "Song of Roland," a 12th-century French epic ballad commemorating the battle—and untimely death—of Roland and a small band of Charlemagne's forces against the Moors.

BASICS
The tourist office (tel. 948/760301; open daily 10–2 and 3–6) is in an 18th-century *molino* (windmill). Look below it for the wind-powered fountain that gushes water all day long. The friendly staff has lots of info on the Camino de Santiago and on the surrounding valleys. Ask about the guided visits around Roncesvalles that usually leave hourly (if there are enough people) every day from 10 to 7 (the last one starts at 5:45). Two buses a day (one on weekends) travel between Pamplona and Roncesvalles.

WHERE TO SLEEP AND EAT
There are but a few places to stay: the **Hostal La Posada** (Carretera Francia/N135, Km 48, tel. 948/ 760225), set in a 17th-century pilgrims' rest station, where basic double rooms are 6,500 ptas. and the one quad room goes for 8,800. The menú del día is 1,600 ptas. (for pilgrims, 1,000 ptas.). Just up the hill is **Casa Sabina** (tel. 948/760012), which has clean double rooms for 6,200 ptas. The restaurant gets packed with locals who come for the delicious well-priced menú del día: 1,300 ptas. on weekdays, 1,500 ptas. on weekens. You can also try dishes like *trucha con jamón* (trout with ham, 750 ptas.) and *lomo con pimientos* (pork loin with grilled peppers, 750 ptas.). The comfortable **pilgrims' hostel** (tel. 948/760000) has 57 beds for declared *peregrinos* (pilgrims), and in summer they sometimes expand into the nearby youth hostel.

WORTH SEEING

Most towns along the Camino built a church or monument to Santiago; here it's a lovely 12th-century **Romanesque chapel,** with an ancient bell that was used to guide pilgrims over the pass. Nearby, the 13th-century **Colegiata de Santa María** has a peaceful cloister with elegant Gothic arches and stunning stained glass windows. The adjoining chapel houses the remains of King Sancho VII el Fuerte (the Strong), whose tomb is more than 7 ft long, supposedly his real height. The church museum has a collection of religious paintings, sculptures, and books dating from the Middle Ages. The cloister, *sala capitular* (chapter house), and museum are open daily 10–1:40 and 4–6:40. and admission is 300 ptas. The nearby old pilgrims' hospital now houses an Albergue de Juventud (Youth Hostel).

The Centro de Visitantes Itzandegia (C. Unica s/n, tel. 948/790442), named with a Basque word meaning "place of rest," has a small **museum** (admission 200 ptas.; open Apr.–Oct., daily 10–6) that recounts the history of Navarre using old photos, maps, and annotation, including English. The accompanying store is well stocked with regional goodies, including canned *asparrago* (asparagus) and Navarran pimientos.

A stone menhir serves as a monument to **Roland** 2 km (1 mi) north of Roncesvalles. You can drive on the Carretera a Francia or, even better, walk along the well-signposted Camino de Santiago, which leads right to the menhir.

BURGUETE

South of Roncesvalles lies the cozy mountain hamlet of Burguete, where bright flowers spill over balcony rails on the usual string of Navarran stone houses. Hemingway fished for trout in the icy streams nearby, a process tantalizingly described in *The Sun Also Rises*. Tiny and untrampled, Burguete is a great place to kick back and spend a lazy afternoon in some crisp mountain air. Hemingway aficionados will delight in staying at the family-run **Hostal Burguete** (C. Unica 59, tel. 948/760005), where Don Ernesto came to relax and write in the early '20s; comfortable double rooms with private bath are 5,800 ptas. You can even stay in Papa's old room, which still has all the same furniture. For the full groupie experience, round out your evening by ordering the *menú de Hemingway* (1,700 ptas.) in the hostal's rustic dining room, and scarf the author's favorite dishes: *sopa de verdura* (vegetable soup), *trucha con jamón,* and *pastel de fresas* (strawberry cake). For less cash and no flash, stay at the **Hostal Juandeaburre** (tel. 948/760078, cash only), just down the street, where basic doubles with shared bath are 3,800 ptas.

SOUTHERN AND EASTERN NAVARRE

A string of monasteries and villages was born along the Camino and flourished as pilgrims trod through them. It's in southern and eastern Navarre—less traveled than the rest—that you'll stumble onto tiny medieval villages that really evoke the region's ancient past.

MONASTERIO DE LEYRE

The massive Monasterio de Leyre dates from the 9th century, when it was founded by religious hermits who had been living in nearby caves. In the 10th and 11th centuries it rose to prominence as one of Navarre's main spiritual, political, and cultural centers and became a key stop on the Camino de Santiago. The monastery was abandoned in 1836 after the *ley de desamortización,* which empowered the government to sell monasteries and disband religious orders that were deemed too rich and powerful; the Benedictine order regained possession in 1954 and has been restoring the monastery ever since. Many of the monastic buildings date from the 17th and 18th centuries, but the church is Romanesque, with a magnificent 12th-century portal. The Benedictine monks are famous for their singing (think *Chant,* recorded near Burgos)—not only can you buy recordings of their Gregorian chants here, but the monks sing during mass, usually held daily at 9 AM and 7 PM and always open to the public.

By car take the N240 from Pamplona toward Jaca and follow the signs that appear just before Yesa. Oscense buses (tel. 948/222079) leave Pamplona for Sanguesa/Jaca Monday–Thursday at 8:30 AM,

Friday and Sunday at 3:30 PM; strangely, there is no bus on Saturday. When you board, you *must* tell the driver you want to be dropped off at Yesa; and ask if you can be picked up on the bus's way back (buses pass back through Yesa around 6:30 PM Monday–Thursday, 9 PM Friday and Sunday). From Yesa follow the signs and pilgrims on foot or pop into a restaurant and indicate that you want a taxi, which won't cost more than 1,000 ptas. *50 km (31 mi) southeast of Pamplona; 4 km (2½ mi) from Yesa, which is served by bus from Pamplona and Jaca. Tel. 948/884150. Admission 250 ptas. Open weekdays 10:15–2 and 3:30–7 (3:30–6:30 Dec.–Jan.), weekends 10:15–2 and 4–7 (4–6:30 Dec.–Jan.).*

WHERE TO SLEEP

Next door to the monastery is the stylish **Hotel Hospedería de Leyre** (tel. 948/884100), open March 2–December 9. Double rooms with bath are 9,240 ptas.; a menú del día in the restaurant is 1,550.

SANGÜESA

The spirited little town of **Sangüesa,** southeast of Pamplona near Aragón, has long been—indeed, remains—an important resting point for pilgrims who enter Spain via Somport (rather than Roncesvalles) and continue south toward Canfranc and Jaca, in Aragón. The town's major sight is the mesmerizing Romanesque doorway to the 13th-century church of **Santa María,** so loaded with sculptures that you need to stand back to take them all in. Christ in Majesty—that is, seated on a throne with his right-hand second and third fingers pointing up toward the heavens—rises in the center, surrounded by the apostles and a tumultuous mix of attendants, soldiers, winged beasts, angels, and musicians.

The **tourist office** (tel. 948/871411; open Easter–Oct., weekdays 10–2 and 4–7, weekends 10–2, Nov.–Easter, weekdays 10–4, weekends 10–2) leads tours of the church for 300 ptas. every day but Sunday at 11, noon, 1, 4 , 5, and 6 in summer, less often in winter. You can also explore the church on your own half an hour before mass, which in summer is usually held Monday–Saturday 8 PM and Sunday 10 AM and 1 PM. The tourist office also leads guided 500-pta. tours of Sangüesa every day but Sunday at noon, with sights including the lovely early Gothic church of **Santiago.** A few daily buses link Sangüesa with Zaragoza and Pamplona.

UJUÉ

Secluded and unspoiled, the medieval village of Ujué is an exquisite reminder of the Navarre of long ago. Perched high on the plains 22 km (14 mi) from Olite (south of the NA-132 between Sanguesa and Tafalla), it's ravishing at first sight, with ancient stone houses, steep cobbled alleys, and the enchanting 13th-century church of **Santa María** soaring over the little slate rooftops. Founded by Charles II el Malo (the Bad; named for his fiery temper), the church is believed to house his heart; in any case, it houses a beautiful silver Romanesque sculpture of the Virgin and Child, venerated as the Reina de Ujué y Navarra Central (Queen of Ujué and Central Navarre.) The church dominates the highest point in Ujué, and from its windswept terrace you can gaze down at the undulating Navarran landscape—from the dry Olite plains to the fertile Ribera, a vast Río Ebro valley that extends to Navarre's southern reaches. On a clear day you can see the towering peaks of the Pyrenees to the north and east.

COMING AND GOING

Alas, Ujué is not served by public transport. If you're carless, ask in San Martín (*see below*) if anyone's headed that way—you may be able to catch a ride.

WHERE TO EAT

UNDER 2,000 PTAS. • Mesón Las Migas. Ujué doesn't seem big enough to support two substantial restaurants, yet there's another one just down the hill from Las Torres (*see below*) with a similar bill of fare, albeit slightly lower quality and prices. *Migas* (bread crumbs soaked in olive oil and garlic, sometimes with chorizo and pepper) go for 750 ptas. If you want to join the local *trabajadores* (workers), come here mid-morning (10–noon) and have your migas with fried eggs and sausage, plus wine and coffee, for 1,100 ptas. You may want to call ahead, as the *mesón's* hours change throughout the year. C. Villeta 19, tel. 948/739044.

UNDER 3,000 PTAS. • Mesón Las Torres. Navarrans have come to Ujué for years just to have a first-class country lunch at this rustic restaurant. The house specialty is *migas de pastor* (shepherd's crumbs), a peasant dish of migas, *sebo* (lard), and chorizo. Though heavy and filling by most standards, it tastes better than it sounds, and a heaping plate of this classic Navarran dish costs 950 ptas. The *mesón* also serves a wide range of local meat and fowl, including *codornices en salsas de casa* (quail in a house sauce; 1,700 ptas.), and *lomo de cerdo* (pork loin; 900 ptas.). *C. Santa María 9, tel. 948/ 739052. No dinner.*

OLITE

Five kilometers (3 miles) south of Tafalla sits the fetching little town of Olite, whose centerpiece is its magnificent Palacio Real, a fortified palace built by Carlos III el Noble (the Noble) at the beginning of the 15th century. The palace was constructed over city walls built by the Romans. In its heyday, it was one of the grandest in Europe, and you'll get a good idea of its former splendor if you venture into the parador that occupies one massive wing (*see below*). Olite's Gothic church of **Santa María** boasts a handsome portal, graceful stained-glass windows, and a couple of storks who have made their home at the tip-top of the church. East of the town's center is the 11th-century church of **San Pedro**, designed in an evocative mix of Gothic and Baroque, with an impressive Romanesque cloister. The **tourist office** (tel. 948/741703; open in summer, weekdays 10–2 and 4–7, weekends 10–2; fall–spring, Tues.–Fri. 10–4, weekends 10–2) is near Plaza de Carlos III. Ask there about the **Museo de Vino** (Wine Museum), due to open in or around 2001.

WHERE TO SLEEP

There aren't a whole lot of budget lodgings in Olite, so you may want to press on. If you've been contemplating a stay in one of Spain's paradors, consider the 13th-century **Parador de Olite** (tel. 948/ 740000), as it's one of the cheapest and most impressive in the system. The interior has been beautifully restored, with stained-glass windows of the royal coat of arms, sumptuous *salas* (sitting rooms), stone-wall dining halls, and spacious bedrooms with dark-wood period furniture and wrought-iron fixtures. Doubles cost 16,500 ptas. March–October, 14,500 ptas. November–February.

Otherwise, head into town to Plaza Carlos III, where an eccentric local couple rents out musty rooms at No. 22 (tel. 948/740597). In summer they sometimes hang out a small CAMAS sign. Prices fluctuate according to demand, sometimes dipping as low as 1,500 ptas. per person.

WHERE TO EAT

A number of homey restaurants dot Olite's back streets, including **Casa del Preboste** (Rua de Mirapies 8, tel. 948/712250), which has alternating stone and gold-painted walls and an open grill. The filling menú del día (1,600 ptas.; on Sun., 1,800 ptas.) is a rich array of Navarran cuisine; fresh pizzas are another option.

SHOPPING

The well-stocked **Vinoteca Algarra** (Rúa San Francisco 21, tel. 948/712279) has a great selection of various regional products, including asparagus, bright-red *pimientos del piquillo* (piquilla peppers), and *pacharán*, the local liquor made of wild *endrinas* (mountain berries). The friendly owner is a font of information on Navarre and its culinary specialties.

WESTERN NAVARRE

After passing through Pamplona, the Camino de Santiago cuts southwest across Navarre. Many of the towns on this stretch sprang up as pilgrims' way stations, including the bustling town of Estella and the charming village of Puente La Reina.

PUENTE LA REINA

It is in Puente la Reina, 21 km (13 mi) southwest of Pamplona, that the two pilgrimage routes from France—one entering Spain at Roncesvalles, the other at Somport—come together and join forces toward Santiago de Compostela. A pilgrims' monument stands at the entrance to town, and the namesake bridge (*puente*), named after an unknown queen, spans the Río Arga with six graceful arches.

The nave in the **Iglesia del Crucifijo** (Church of the Crucifix) is half late-Romanesque and half early Gothic. The sculpture of Christ on the cross is shaped like a tree; it was a gift from German pilgrims in the late Middle Ages. The church of **Santiago** was built in the 12th century and successively rebuilt in the 15th and 16th; the Romanesque facade remains from its early years. A lively **market** fills the Plaza Mena on Saturday morning.

One of the few budget accommodations in town is **Hotel Bidean** (C. Mayor 11, tel. 948/341156), with double rooms for 7,500 ptas. and a few smaller doubles for 5,000 ptas. The **pilgrims' hostel** (tel. 948/340050), near the Iglesia del Crucifijo, has 33 beds for accredited pilgrims only.

ESTELLA

Twenty kilometers (12 miles) west of Puente la Reina is the attractive town of Estella, its balconied stone houses strung along the banks of the meandering Río Ega. The 12th-century Palacio de los Reyes de Navarra (Palace of the Navarran Kings), in the center of town, is the only example of a civic Romanesque structure in Navarre. Inside, the **Museo de Gustavo de Maeztu y Whitney** (tel. 948/546037; open Tues.–Sat. 11–1 and 5–7, Sun. 11–1) displays the works, mostly portraits, of the Basque-born Romantic artist Gustavo de Maeztu y Whitney. The 12th-century church of **San Pedro de la Rúa** has a splendid Romanesque cloister with capitals depicting historic scenes. The church is generally only open to the public half an hour before mass, which is held at 7 PM Monday–Saturday and noon on Sunday. The 12th- to 14th-century church of **San Miguel**, north of the river, has an impressive late-Romanesque facade.

BASICS

Estella's **tourist office** (C. San Nicolás 1, tel. 948/556301; open June–Sept., Mon.–Sat. 9–8, Sun. 10–2; Oct.–May, 10–2 and 4–7, Sun. 10–2) has maps and literature. For 350 ptas. a head, with a minimum of 6–8 people, the office leads guided tours in English of the San Pedro de la Rúa; another tour, 600 ptas., covers all the churches in town.

Buses travel several times daily to Pamplona and Logroño.

If you missed the bull run in Pamplona, test your mettle against the mighty black beasts in the town of Estella, in western Navarre (first week of August), or in Tafalla, just north of Olite (mid-August).

WHERE TO SLEEP

There's a handful of budget stays in town, among them the **Hostal Cristina** (C. Baja Navarra 1, tel. 948/550450, cash only), where double rooms with firm beds, balconies, and bath go for 6,000–7,000 ptas.

LA RIOJA

For a while, the borders are blurry—you can't tell one Autonomous Community from the next on their perimeters—but there's no doubt when you're *deep* in La Rioja. Verdant vineyards stretch endlessly toward the horizon, and in late September and early October, warm winds carry the pungent aroma of ripe grapes everywhere. Blessed with a fertile soil, a mild climate, and plenty of sun, Rioja is prime territory for grape growing. The Romans planted the first grapevines here, and the region has been exporting wine since the 12th century; now the production of wine and the attendant rituals define Rioja, from the celebrations of the *cosecha* (harvest) to the careful selection of premium oak casks for the aging process. Rioja's wine culture is boisterous and welcoming—locals offer wine as freely as they shake hands, and every town has bars and bodegas where you can relax with a glass of red, then buy a few bottles to take home. Wine has also brought considerable wealth, and over the years the region has drawn a sizable immigrant population for the consistent work and good pay.

Lively Logroño is Rioja's capital, and an excellent place to base yourself: budget lodgings abound, and most of the region's buses start and end here. Moreover, you must spend an evening (or two) feasting on *pinchos* (tapas) along Logroño's Calle Laurel, a bustling strip that draws folks from all over Rioja. Extending west of Logroño, La Rioja Alta (the Upper Rioja), is home to major vineyards; the city of Haro, where many of the largest *bodegas* (wineries) are headquartered; and a handful of wonderful monasteries.

Of course, long before wine made Rioja famous, pilgrims moved determinedly toward Santiago through the center of the region, and pilgrims' hostels still line the way. Among the important monasteries that sprang up along the Camino are the Monasterio de Yuso, near the village of San Millán de la Cogolla—where the first written record of the Castilian language was discovered. Rioja also has a ski resort, Valdezcara, 15 km (9 mi) south of the village of Ezcaray.

WHERE WINE FLOWS FREELY

Just south of Estella, the sprawling **Monasterio de Irache** *(open Tues.–Sat.) is an amalgam of styles from Romanesque to Baroque. Next to the splendid 12th-century* **church** *are two faucets, installed in 1991 to make the pilgrimage a touch less tedious: one dispenses water, the other red wine. The tasteful iron plaque says, "Pilgrim, if you want to reach Santiago with strength and vitality, have a drink of this great wine and toast to happiness. To drink without abuse we invite you readily."*

LOGROÑO

Strung along the Río Ebro and surrounded by lush vineyards, the lovely city of Logroño exudes a warmth and openness that's hard to resist, especially after a glass or two of prime Rioja red. The wine is plentiful, top-notch, nicely priced, and served absolutely everywhere, from tiny underground bodegas to shaded outdoor cafés. Logroño's central square, the large, leafy Espolón, is ringed with pleasant cafés and park benches, where older locals while away the afternoon; the old quarter, with lively bars, rustic restaurants, and most of the budget lodgings, extends north of the Espolón toward the river. Calle Laurel, branching off Calle Capitan Gallarza, is Logroño's most happening street, with heaps of pinchos bars, each serving its own specialty. On September 21 the city celebrates La Vendimia, the wine festival, with parades, grape stomping, and lots of wine-tasting opps.

The city began life as a Roman settlement but first gained prominence in the Middle Ages as an important stop along the Camino de Santiago. In the 11th century San Juan de Ortega built the **Puente de Piedra** (Stone Bridge) to aid pilgrims in crossing the Ebro en route to Santiago de Compostela, and Logroño slowly grew around the bridge. A newer bridge, built in 1884, still marks the pilgrims' entrance to Logroño. A great way to savor the city's history is to walk the pilgrimage route through town; you might fall into step with some present-day pilgrims as well. The entire Camino de Santiago, across France as well as Spain, is marked by yellow arrows and scallop shells.

BASICS

CURRENCY EXCHANGE
Most of Logroño's **banks** are on Calle Miguel Villanueva, along the southern border of the Espolón.

MAIL
The main **post office,** open weekdays 9–2 and Saturday 9–1, is at Plaza San Agustín 1 (tel. 941/220066).

EMERGENCIES
General emergency: 112. Police: 092. Hospital San Millán: Avda. Autonomía de la Rioja 3, tel. 941/294500.

CYBERSPACE
Videoclub Fenix (C. Chile s/n, off Plaza Primero de Mayo, tel. 941/203522) charges 350 ptas. an hour.

LAUNDRY
Lavandería Lavomatique (C. Gonzalo de Berceo 11, tel. 941/225491) charges 1,000 ptas. to wash and dry a small load of laundry. The nearby **Lavandería Valunera** (C. Gonzalo de Berceo 48, tel. 941/209476) has similar prices.

VISITOR INFORMATION

The centrally located **tourist office** sits at the east end of the Espolón (Paseo Espolón 1, tel. 941/260665; open April–Oct., Mon.–Sat. 10–2 and 4:30–7, Sun. 10–2; Nov.–May, hrs vary, and it closes earlier in the afternoon). For a cool Rioja memento, ask for a wine poster.

COMING AND GOING

BY BUS

The **bus station** (Avda. de España, tel. 941/235983) is an easy 10-minute walk from town on Calle del General Vara de Rey. National bus lines head to anchor cities in the neighboring regions: **La Estellesa** (tel. 941/237168) goes to Pamplona and San Sebastián, **Jimenez** (tel. 941/231234) to Burgos and Zaragoza, and **Continental** (tel. 941/237168) to Madrid and Soria. Local buses serve much of the region, including Calahorra and Nájera, several times daily.

BY TRAIN

The **train station** (Plaza de Europa, tel. 902/240202) is just south of the bus station. Trains head to Zaragoza (2,000 ptas.), Burgos (1,900 ptas.), Bilbao (2,000 ptas.), Haro (1,200 ptas.), and other main towns in nearby regions several times daily.

WHERE TO SLEEP

Hostal Sebastian (C. Juan 21, tel. 941/242800, cash only) has clean, simple double rooms with shared bath for 3,600 ptas. Upstairs in the same building, and run by the same family, **Residencia Daniel** (tel. 941/252948, cash only) has similar doubles at the same prices. Many rooms in both joints have balconies; ask for an *habitación con balcón* when you check in. The innkeepers also own the unfussy Bar García, across the street, where you can fill up on the cheap with *paté de cerdo con queso* (pork pâté with cheese; 150 ptas.) or a *bocadillo de jamón y queso* (ham and cheese sandwich; 300 ptas.).

UNDER 6,000 PTAS. • Fonda La Bilbaina. One of the best deals in town is this spic-and-span inn, where the hardwood floors gleam and double rooms—many with wrought-iron balconies—cost 3,500 ptas. with shared bath, 4,000 with private loo. *C. del Capitán Gallarza 10, tel. 941/254226. 9 rooms, 1 with bath. Cash only.*

UNDER 8,000 PTAS. • Hostal-Residencia Numantina. This comfortable, centrally located hostal is just off the leafy Espolón. Basic, clean doubles, most with balconies and all with bath, go for 6,250 ptas. If you get cabin fever, sprawl out on a leatherette couch in the small lounge. *C. Sagasta 4, tel. 941/251411. 17 rooms.*

UNDER 10,000 PTAS. • Hostal Niza. If you're not having any luck with the places above, head across the street from Fonda La Bilbaina and rent one of these overpriced, institutional doubles with bath for 7,700 ptas. *C. Capitan Gallarza 13, tel. 941/206044. 18 rooms.*

Hotel Marqués de Vallejó. Half these comfortable, fresh-smelling, air-conditioned rooms have balconies, and all have firm beds and sparkling bathrooms. Doubles are overpriced at 9,900 ptas., and there's laundry service for an additional hefty fee. The large, comfortable bar/lounge is open from 8 PM to midnight. *C. Marqués de Vallejo 8, tel. 941/248333, fax 941/240288. 30 rooms.*

WHERE TO EAT

Logroño's old quarter is bursting with atmospheric *asadores* (restaurants specializing in grilled meat) and homey eateries. Many streets were named after their medieval trade guilds, and you still need look no further than the tiny Calle Carnicerías (Butcher Shops' Street) for top-notch animal flesh.

UNDER 2,000 PTAS. • The cozy **La Taberna de Cachi** (C. San Agustin 10, tel. 941/213544, cash only), its walls bedecked with leather bullfighting paintings, is the place to go for *cocina típica Riojana*, a range of dishes featuring Riojan produce and meats. Try the *alcachofas con jamón* (artichokes with ham; 800 ptas.) or *pimiento relleno de morcilla* (pepper stuffed with blood sausage). For ample *platos* (dishes), join the locals at **Las Cubanas** (C. San Agustín 17, tel. 941/220050), where *pollo a la plancha* (grilled chicken) starts at 1,400 ptas., and *callos a la Riojana* (Rioja-style tripe), cooked in a tasty tomato sauce, goes for a mere 1,000 ptas.

I'LL HAVE THE
BLACK-SHEEP BLEND

La Rioja's wine gets all the attention, but its coffee is also top-notch. Much local java is supplied by Cafés El Pato (C. Hermanos Moroy 26, tel. 941/251946; C. Calvo Sotelo 41, tel. 9041/253392), where they've been roasting and toasting since 1923. If you want to go right to the source, stop into one of their two comfortable Logroño cafés and kick back with a warm cup in hand to breathe in the rich aromas.

Among the beans packaged for travel, Café Colombia beans (1,900 ptas. per kilogram) are the most popular; they yield a rich, smooth brew guaranteed to get you out of bed in the morning. Slightly sweeter and nuttier are Café Costa Rica beans (1,800 ptas.). If you like your potion strong, go for the Café Kenya beans (1,800 ptas.). The house brew served in the cafés is a bold blend of all the above, but you can request a cup specially made from your chosen variety.

Café Moderno. "Modern" is a relative term here. This is Logroño's oldest café, with turn-of-the-20th-century marble-and-wrought-iron tables and black-and-white photos of old Logroño. Older locals gather to feast on the menú del día (1,200–1,500 ptas.) and filling tapas like *albondigas* (meatballs) and *pimientos rellenos* (stuffed peppers). *Plaza Martinez Zaporta, tel. 941/220042.*

Las Escallerias. Near the steps leading to Plaza del Mercado, this small pop-and-son operation has specialized in *cabrito asado* (grilled kid) for generations; the young goats, milk-fed from birth, are usually 30–40 days old. The narrow, comfortably cluttered restaurant looks much as it did a few decades ago—the menu and ambience are refreshingly homespun. Gathering around wooden tables in picnic style, you start off with hunks of bread and Rioja wine. The kid is grilled in a rickety, old-fashioned oven in back, then brought to the table sizzling and carved right in front of you. Each person gets a quarter cabrito; a hearty meal is 1,800 ptas. *C. Carnicerías 2, tel. 941/249372.*

UNDER 3,000 PTAS. • La Chata. They've been grilling meat and fish since 1821 in this rustic restaurant of hardwood floors, checkered tablecloths, and an *horno de leña* (wood oven). Try the cabrito asado or any of the tasty fish dishes and appetizers, including *tortilla de bacalao* (cod tortilla; 850 ptas.), *pimientos rellenos de carne* (peppers stuffed with meat; 1,100 ptas.), and *bandeja Riojana*, a Riojan dish of chorizo sausage, *morcilla* (blood sausage), and *pimientos del Piquillo* (grilled red peppers). A full meal can cost upwards of 1,800 ptas., especially if you go for grilled meat. *C. Carnicerías 3, tel. 941/251296.*

PINCHOS BARS

When it's time for tapas, look no further than Calle Laurel, Logroño's famous street of pinchos bars, where you can sample your way from one end to the other through the best little eats in Rioja. The vibe is informal and lively. Join the crowd at each bar and point to what you want; chew, swallow, and savor; then move on to the next bustling spot. Hit **Bar Sebas** (tel. 941/220196, cash only) for its tasty pimientos rellenos and *tortilla de patata* (thick potato omelet); they also, interestingly, prepare tapas *para llevar* (to go). Head for **Casa Pali** (tel. 941/256795, cash only) to feast on various preparations of *berbenjena* (eggplant). The popular **Bar El Muro** has a large circular bar and plenty of tables; eat your fill of *setas con jamón* (wild mushrooms with ham) or *caracoles* (snails) here, or go for the hearty 1,500-pta. menú del día. Locals flock also to **Bar Lorenzo** (Travesía Laurel, at end of C. Laurel, tel. 941/200929, cash only), a small, simple bar with sawdust scattered on the floor to catch the mess. House specialty: excellent *pinchos morunos* (spicy meat kebabs). Nearby, **Bar Soriano** (tel. 941/228807, cash only) serves big, juicy *champiñones* (mushrooms), grilled at the bar in full view of the salivating crowds.

WORTH SEEING

Starting at the stone bridge, follow the scallop shells onto cobbled Calle Ruavieja, Logroño's oldest street. To your left you'll see Logroño's oldest house of worship, the 11th-century church of **Santa María del Palacio,** dominated by an impressive Gothic tower. Cross Calle de Sastago and continue on Calle Barriocepo, and you'll soon come across the 16th-century church of **Santiago,** with a magnificent equestrian statue of Santiago Matamoros (St. James the Moorslayer) looming over its front entrance. As you approach the church, you'll cross **Plaza de Santiago**—check out its nifty floor-tile version of a popular Spanish board game called Juego de la Oca (Goose's Game), which depicts the stops along the Camino de Santiago. In one corner of the plaza is the pilgrims' fountain, supplied with potable refreshment. Just beyond the church you'll pass the **Muralla del Revellín,** Logroño's last bit of medieval wall. From here the route continues out of town, but if you turn left onto Calle del Once de Junio you can circle back into the old quarter along Calle de Bretón de los Heroes, a lively street of bars and cafés.

Looming over the center of the old town is the 15th-century **Catedral de Santa María de la Redonda,** known for its Baroque twin towers and its *calvario,* a Crucifixion scene on wood by Michelangelo (no one seems to know how it got here). East of the cathedral, on Calle de San Bartolomé, stands the 12th-century church of **San Bartolomé,** with an elegant brick Mudéjar tower.

The **Museo de la Rioja** is housed in a Baroque palace on Plaza San Agustín, east of the cathedral. The collection includes religious works from churches around La Rioja and Romanesque, Gothic, and Renaissance paintings. *Plaza San Agustín s/n, tel. 941/291259. Free. Open Tues.–Sat. 10–2 and 4–9, Sun. 11:30–2.*

After entering the restaurant trade, the ancient Bodegas Reja Dorada moved its wines to a nearby cellar because "wines—like humans— need their peace and quiet, especially during the aging process."

AFTER DARK

Logroño's swinging night scene revolves around the outdoor bars and cafés on **Calle de Bretón de los Herreros.** Party Central for the teen and early-twenties set is southwest of the old quarter on **Calle Ciudad de Vitoria** and the streets that branch off it, including Calles Guevara, Labradores, and Chile.

Logroño's literary offerings may pale by comparison with its viticultural riches, but the written word is enthusiastically celebrated at **Café Bretón** (C. Bretón de los Herreros 32, tel. 941/286038), a Parisian-style café-bar that's been around since the late 1800s. In the 1920s it flourished as a cabaret bar, and in the 1990s it joined forces with a local publishing house to award an annual prize to a new Spanish-language writer. The winner's works are proudly displayed in the back salon. The house specialties are coffee and a wide range of libations, including the Mediterraneo—coffee with cream and a liqueur of *crema catalana* (the traditional Catalan version of crème brûlée)—and the Bretón, coffee with cream and mandarin liqueur. Check out the nifty sugar packets with original poems and drawings by local artists, all celebrating the joys of coffee, with such thought-provoking sentiments as "El café es el tinte que usa el corazón para teñirse el pelo" ("The heart uses coffee to color the hair").

SHOPPING

The shelves in Logroño's many wine stores groan with Riojas, from *gran reserva* (premiere wines that have been aged the longest) to *vinos jovenes* (young wines, also called *cosecha*), just a year or two old. Most wine-shop owners are a font of information, so pick their brains before buying and ask for a *tarjeta* (card) or *folleto* (brochure) listing the best years of Riojan wines (*see* Wine Wise, *above*). **La Catedral del Vino** (C. Portales 25, tel. 941/254144), facing the other cathedral, has a wide selection of wines and other Riojan specialties, including *Riojanitos* (marzipan covered with chocolate) and an array of Riojan hams; and there's a small tasters' bar in the back where you can sample the wines you're interested in. A bottle of Marqués de Caceres, one of La Rioja's better-known labels, is 1,400 ptas. **Licores Espinosa** (C. San Agustin 13, tel. 941/228009) also has a good selection. The tourist office is a good source of information on any new wine shops or wholesalers that might have opened up; ask for directions to the **Palacio del Vino,** a large wine warehouse on the outskirts of Logroño, as they have a huge selection of good-quality wines at great prices.

If your budget wasn't supposed to include bottled alcohol, try one of Logroño's well-stocked **supermarkets,** where young (cheap) wines go for as little as 600 ptas. a bottle.

WINE WISE

Ready to stash some in your pack? Riojan wines are divided into four categories. Vino Joven (Young Wine), labeled simply cosecha *(harvest), is a year or two old and has a light, fruity flavor. Crianza refers to wines less than three years old that have spent at least one year aging in an oak barrel. The more select Reserva wines have been aged at least three years, with a minimum of one year in the barrel, and the Gran Reserva have been aged at least two years in the barrel and three years in the bottle. A Gran Reserva can cost 5–10 (or more) times as much as a young wine. Excellent years in the last decade were 1995 and 1994;* muy buena *(very good) years were 1996 and 1991. Different parts of Rioja yield their own species of grapes; the mainstay of the region is the Tempranillo, from Upper Rioja, known for its bold flavor. Graciano grapes lead to bright red wine with a full, fragrant bouquet. Among white varieties, Viura grapes produce a fresh, fruity wine, and the Malvasia make a fruity wine that ages well.*

LA RIOJA ALTA

Most of Rioja's riches—the endless vineyards, gorgeous monasteries, and Camino de Santiago—are in the Upper Rioja, stretching west of Logroño. Wine lovers should make a pilgrimage to Haro, center of wine production and home to many of the biggest bodegas. Literary types will like the Monasterio del Yuso, near the village of San Millán de Cogolla, as this is where the first written record of the Spanish language was discovered.

NÁJERA

The tidy town of Nájera lies on the Camino de Santiago just 27 km (17 mi) from Logroño, and is worth a short stop to see the Gothic **Monasterio de Santa María la Real** (admission 200 ptas.; open Tues.–Sat. 9:30–1:30 and 4–7:30, Sun. 10–1 and 4–7), originally built in the 9th century and rebuilt in the 15th and 16th. Wander through the elegant cloisters and go inside to see the striking Romanesque altar. The portal of the nearby Parroquia de Santa Cruz displays the Spanish coat of arms, with a pomegranate at its center representing Granada in commemoration of that city's recapture from the Moors. The **Albergue de Peregrinos** (Pilgrims' Hostel), with 60 beds, adjoins the monastery.

The **tourist office** (C. Constantio Garrán 8, tel. 941/360041; open Tues.–Sat. 10–2 and 4:30–7, Sun. 10:30–2:30) has general info on Nájera and environs. The several daily **buses** to and from Logroño and Burgos use a bus stop on Paseo San Julián, near Hotel San Fernando.

MONASTERIOS DE YUSO Y SUSO

Southwest of Nájera, near the small village of **San Millán de la Cogolla,** lie two of Rioja's most important monasteries. The Monasterio de Suso (*suso* means "upper" in old Castilian) is at the top of a hill, with the **Monasterio de Yuso** ("lower" in old Castilian) just below it in the valley. The first written record of the Castilian language was discovered in the library at the Monasterio de Yuso: 12 lines in a manuscript called the San Millán Glosses were translated from Latin into Castilian by an anonymous monk in the 10th century. The monastery, dating from the 11th century and successively rebuilt between the 16th and 18th centuries, still houses an impressive library and archives containing texts from the 11th to

15th centuries. Lots of tour buses make a pit stop here, but only a few head up to the hill to the smaller, 10th-century Mozarabic **Monasterio de Suso**, which—having been built to guard the cave where hermit San Millán lived—sits in beautiful solitude high above the sweeping green hills. Much of the monastery is being restored, but it's well worth a visit just to soak up the medieval aura in the restorative peace and quiet of the hilltop. Suso also has a Castilian-language legacy, this one from the 12th century; it was here that Gonzalo de Berceo, the first poet to write in Castilian, penned many of his works. *Admission 400 ptas. Both monasteries open summer, Tues.–Sun. 10–1 and 4–6:30; winter, Tues.–Sun. 10:30–12:30 and 4–6. Hrs may vary.*

From Logroño, two buses daily (one daily on weekends) pass through San Millán de la Cogolla. San Millán's **tourist office** (tel. 941/373259; open Tues.–Fri. 10:30–2, Sat. 10:30–2 and 5–7) is near the Monasterio de Yuso. If you're driving, take the N120 from Logroño toward Burgos; just before you hit Nájera, turn left for Tricio, then follow signs another 18 km (11 mi) to the monasteries.

SANTO DOMINGO DE LA CALZADA

Another important pilgrim stop on the Camino de Santiago, this small town 20 km (12 mi) west of Nájera is named for an 11th-century saint who dedicated his life to building bridges, roads, and lodgings expressly for pilgrims. Santo Domingo's most impressive structure is its 12th-century **cathedral,** a fluid blend of the Romanesque and Gothic. Check out the beautiful chapel of San Pedro, the building's only remaining Romanesque chapel. Most people come here to see the live cock and hen that live in a stone Gothic henhouse inside the cathedral and to contemplate the legend surrounding them, which involves a young pilgrim who stopped in Santo Domingo long enough for a local girl to fall in love with him. Alas, the feeling was not mutual, and in revenge, the girl hid a silver goblet in the young man's suitcase and accused him of theft. He was sentenced to death and hanged. When the young man's parents came to bid a final goodbye to their son, they found him miraculously alive and believed that Santo Domingo had saved his life. They took their tale to the town judge, but he laughed them off, saying their son was no more alive than the roast chicken he was about to eat—and at that moment the chicken fluttered its wings and flew off the table. In honor of Santo Domingo the cathedral has been home to a cock and hen ever since; a new pair of birds moves in every month. *Plaza del Santo s/n, no phone. Admission 250 ptas. Open Mon.–Sat. 10–6:30.*

The cathedral's freestanding **tower**, across the plaza, dates from the 18th century. The first tower was destroyed by lightning; its replacement, built a few centuries later, was soon deemed unsafe. It was finally decided to build this third tower apart from the cathedral. For 125 ptas. in season you can climb to the top of the 230-ft structure for dizzying views of the town's rooftops and the surrounding countryside. *Open June–mid-Sept. 10:30–2 and 3:30–7:30.*

BASICS
The **tourist office** (C. Mayor 70, tel. 941/341230; open Mon.–Sat. 10–2 and 4:30–7:30, Sun. 10–2) has loads of info on the town and surrounding area. One or two **buses** from Logroño pass through Santo Domingo each day.

HARO

La Rioja's amiable wine hub sits on the Cerro (Hill) de La Mota, which rises above the junction of the rivers Ebro and Tirón surrounded by acre upon acre of verdant vineyards. Though Haro grew steadily between the 11th and 15th centuries, it wasn't until the 19th century that the big bodegas made it into Rioja's busiest wine-trading center. Most production began after 1863, the year the phylloxera plague ravaged many French vineyards: the catastrophe brought Bordeaux winemakers across the border to Rioja, and simultaneously increased demand for Riojan wines.

The Plaza de la Paz, in the center of town, is a prime spot to sip Riojan wine while lounging, Spanish-style, at an outdoor café. Most of Haro saunters through here on a daily *paseo* (stroll).

BASICS

CURRENCY EXCHANGE
Most of Haro's **banks** are on Calle La Vega. After hours you can sometimes change money at Hotel Los Agustinos (C. San Agustín 2, tel. 941/311308).

EMERGENCIES

General emergency: 112. **Municipal police:** tel. 941/310125. **Centro de Salud de Haro** (Medical Center of Haro): C. Bartolomeo de Cossio 10, tel. 941/310539.

MAIL

The main **post office** (tel. 941/311869, open weekdays 8:30–2:30, Sat. 9–1) is at Avenida de la Rioja 10, at the corner of Calle Alemania.

VISITOR INFORMATION

Ask the **tourist office** (Plaza Monseñor Florentino Rodriguez, tel. 941/303366; open Tues.–Fri. and Sun. 10–2, Sat. 10–2 and 4–7) about the latest hours and extra summer tours at the bodegas.

COMING AND GOING

Haro is equally well served by bus and train. The **bus station** (tel. 941/311543) is just south of the town center; buses fan throughout La Rioja and on to Navarre and the Basque Country. Haro's **train station** (tel. 941/311597), northwest of town, is a 25-minute trek from the center. Several trains daily serve Logroño and other major towns.

WORTH SEEING

Most of Haro's bodegas are clustered around the train station, across the river from the rest of town. It's quite possible to hop off the train, tour a winery, buy a few bottles, and board the next train without seeing the town proper, but Haro makes for a pleasant one-night stop, mainly because the best way to enjoy the local vino is in the restaurants and bars. Most commercial bodegas don't open their doors to the curious public; the only two that offer tours and wine tastings are **Bodegas Bilbaínas,** just south of the train station (tel. 941/310147; free weekend tours at 10 and noon), and the nearby **Bodegas Muga** (tel. 941/310498; admission 500 ptas.; daily tours at 11 and 4:30).

Haro's **Museo del Vino** (Avda. Bretón de los Herreros, tel. 941/310547; admission 300 ptas.; open Mon.–Sat. 10–2 and 4–8, Sun. 10–2) is a three-floor affair with glossy exhibits and color photos detailing the wine-making process, tools of the trade, and a whole wall plastered with all the region's wine labels. Whether Haro is your first or last stop in Rioja, the museum will round out your stay and your knowledge of wine even if you can't read the Spanish-only annotation.

WHERE TO SLEEP

Haro has a host of cheap lodgings, many on the main drag, Calle La Vega. **Hostal La Peña** (C. La Vega 1, tel. 941/310022, cash only) has basic doubles with bath for 5,000 ptas., without bath 4,000 ptas. Each room has a balcony overlooking the bustling strip below, and the adjoining restaurant serves a decent set menu for 1,200 ptas., including wine. **Hostal Aragón** (C. La Vega 9, tel. 941/310004, cash only) has clean doubles with shower for 4,500 ptas., many with balconies or pretty white-washed *miradores* (windowed alcoves). For a little more cash, **Hostal Higinia** (Plaza Monseñor Florentino Rodríguez, tel. 941/304344), near the tourist office, has comfortable double rooms for 8,000 ptas.

WHERE TO EAT

You'll find a slew of nicely priced restaurants on and around Plaza de la Paz.

UNDER 2,000 PTAS. • Bar-Restaurante Vega. In addition to a filling menú del día for 1,300 ptas., Vega proffers a whole range of tasty dishes like *gambas a la plancha* (grilled shrimp; 1,650 ptas.), *bacalao a la Riojana* (cod in a Riojan sauce), and *pimientos rellenos con merluza, bacalao, o carne* (peppers stuffed with your choice of hake, cod, or meat; 1,100 ptas.) An array of tapas and rich little *bocadillos* (sandwiches) rounds things out. Upstairs, a few double rooms with shared bath are rented for 4,000 ptas., though most are occupied by *fijos,* or permanent residents. *Plaza Juan García Gato 1, tel. 941/303280.*

Mesón Atamauri. Amid stone walls, a beamed ceiling, and festoons of garlic, this place serves a wide range of regional dishes, including *alcachofas salteados* (salted artichokes; 900 ptas.), *cocido Riojano* (a Riojan stew of chorizo and beans; 650 ptas.), and a lineup of what they call *platos fuertes* (literally "strong plates"), including *bistec de ternera* (veal steak; 1,200 ptas.). *Plaza Juan García Gato, tel. 941/303220.*

UNDER 3,000 PTAS. • Las Cigueñas. Overlooking the plaza from the second floor, this cavernous restaurant serves hearty Riojan cuisine, including *chuletón de ternera* (veal cutlet) by weight: 500 grams for 1,600 ptas., 750 grams for 2,400ptas., and if you're really hungry, a kilogram for 3,200 ptas. Also tasty are the *perdiz escabechada* (pickled quail; 2,100 ptas.) and *cordero asado* (roast lamb; 1,500 ptas.). *Plaza de la Paz 11, tel. 941/310122.*

AFTER DARK

Haro's nightlife centers on the *casco viejo* (old town), in an area called La Heradura—near Plaza de la Paz, along Calles **Santo Tomás** and **San Martín.** Many bars in this area serve regional tapas and a range of local Riojan wines, usually *jovenes* and *crianzas*.

SHOPPING

Many of Haro's excellent wine shops are on and around the Plaza de la Paz, including the **Catedral de los Vinos** (C. de Santo Tomás 4, tel. 941/312143) and **Mi Bodega** (C. Santo Tomás 13, tel. 941/304003). **Bar Oñate** (Plaza de la Paz 11, tel. 941/310010), right on the plaza, sells wine and a range of Riojan tapas, including chorizo *Riojano* (spicy Riojan sausage), *asparrago*, and various pâtés.

FIESTA

If you're around at the end of June, come to Haro on June 29 for **La Batalla del Vino,** the famous Wine Battle, in which everyone sprays and douses everyone else with all the fruit-of-the-vine they can get their hands on.

INDEX